Annual Abstract of Statistics

2004 edition

United Kingdom

No 140

Editor: David Penny

London: TSO

Contact points
For enquiries about this publication,
contact the Editor, David Penny:
Tel: **020 7533 5086**

To order this publication, call TSO on
0870 600 5522. See also back cover.

For general enquiries, contact the
National Statistics Customer Contact
Centre on **0845 601 3034**
(minicom: 01633 812399)
E-mail: **info@statistics.gov.uk**
Fax: 01633 652747
Letters: Room D115,
          Government Buildings,
          Cardiff Road,
          Newport NP10 8XG

You can also find National Statistics on the
internet – go to **www.statistics.gov.uk**.

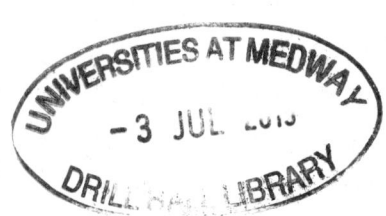

A National Statistics publication
National Statistics are produced to high
professional standards set out in the
National Statistics Code of Practice.
They undergo regular quality assurance
reviews to ensure that they meet
customer needs. They are produced
free from any political interference.

About the Office for National Statistics
The Office for National Statistics (ONS) is
the government agency responsible for
compiling, analysing and disseminating
many of the United Kingdom's economic,
social and demographic statistics, including
the retail prices index, trade figures and
labour market data, as well as the periodic
census of the population and health
statistics. The Director of ONS is also the
National Statistician and the Registrar
General for England and Wales, and the
agency administers the registration of
births, marriages and deaths there.

CONTENTS

CONTENTS

CONTENTS

9 Health

10 Social protection

11 Crime and justice

CONTENTS

12 Lifestyles

13 Environment

CONTENTS

CONTENTS

16 National accounts

17 Prices

CONTENTS

18
Government finance

19
External trade and investment

CONTENTS

CONTENTS

UNITS OF MEASUREMENT

Length
1 millimetre (mm)		= 0.03937 inch
1 centimetre (cm)	= 10 millimetres	= 0.3937 inch
1 metre (m)	= 1,000 millimetres	= 1.094 yards
1 kilometre (km)	= 1,000 metres	= 0.6214 mile

1 inch (in.)		= 25.40 millimetres or 2.540 centimetres
1 foot (ft.)	= 12 inches	= 0.3048 metre
1 yard (yd.)	= 3 feet	= 0.9144 metre
1 mile	= 1,760 yards	= 1.609 kilometres

Area
1 square millimetre (mm²)		= 0.001550 square inch
1 square metre (m²)	= one million square millimetres	= 1.196 square yards
1 hectare (ha)	= 10,000 square metres	= 2.471 acres
1 square kilometre (km²)	= one million square metres	= 247.1 acres

1 square inch (sq. in.)		= 645.2 square millimetres or 6.452 square centimetres
1 square foot (sq. ft.)	= 144 square inches	= 0.09290 square metre or 929.0 square centimetres
1 square yard (sq. yd.)	= 9 square feet	= 0.8361 square metres
1 acre	= 4,840 square yards	= 4,046 square metres or 0.4047 hectare
1 square mile (sq. mile)	= 640 acres	= 2.590 square kilometres or 259.0 hectares

Volume
1 cubic centimetre (cm³)		= 0.06102 cubic inch
1 cubic decimetre (dm³)	= 1,000 cubic centimetres	= 0.03531 cubic foot
1 cubic metre (m³)	= one million cubic centimetres	= 1.308 cubic yards

1 cubic inch (cu.in.)		= 16.39 cubic centimetres
1 cubic foot (cu. ft.)	= 1,728 cubic inches	= 0.02832 cubic metre or 28.32 cubic decimetres
1 cubic yard (cu. yd.)	= 27 cubic feet	= 0.7646 cubic metre

Capacity
1 litre (l)	= 1 cubic decimetre	= 0.2200 gallon
1 hectolitre (hl)	= 100 litres	= 22.00 gallons

1 pint		= 0.5682 litre
2 pints	= 1 quart	= 1.137 litres
8 pints	= 1 gallon	= 4.546 litres
36 gallons (gal.)	= 1 bulk barrel	= 1.637 hectolitres

Weight
1 gram (g)		= 0.03527 ounce
1 hectogram (hg)	= 100 grams	= 3.527 ounces or 0.2205 pound
1 kilogram (kg)	= 1,000 grams or 10 hectograms	= 2.205 pounds
1 tonne (t)	= 1,000 kilograms	= 1.102 short tons or 0.9842 long ton

1 ounce avoirdupois (oz.)		= 28.35 grams
1 pound avoirdupois (lb.)	= 16 ounces	= 0.4536 kilogram
1 hundredweight (cwt.)	= 112 pounds	= 50.80 kilograms
1 short ton	= 2,000 pounds	= 907.2 kilograms or 0.9072 tonne
1 long ton (referred to as ton)	= 2,240 pounds	= 1,016 kilograms or 1.016 tonnes

1 ounce troy	= 480 grains	= 31.10 grams

Energy
British thermal unit (Btu)	= 0.2520 kilocalorie (kcal) = 1.055 kilojoule (kj)
Therm	= 10^5 British thermal units = 25,200 kcal = 105,506 kj
Megawatt hour (MWh)	= 10^6 watt hours (Wh)
Gigawatt hour (GWh)	= 10^6 kilowatt hours = 34,121 therms

Food and drink
Butter	23,310 litres milk	= 1 tonne butter (average)
Cheese	10,070 litres milk	= 1 tonne cheese
Condensed milk	2,550 litres milk	= 1 tonne full cream condensed milk
	2,953 litres skimmed milk	= 1 tonne skimmed condensed milk
Milk	1 million litres	= 1,030 tonnes
Milk powder	8,054 litres milk	= 1 tonne full cream milk powder
	10,740 litres skimmed milk	= 1 tonne skimmed milk powder
Eggs	17,126 eggs	= 1 tonne (approximate)
Sugar	100 tonnes sugar beet	= 92 tonnes refined sugar
	100 tonnes cane sugar	= 96 tonnes refined sugar

Shipping
Gross tonnage	= The total volume of all the enclosed spaces of a vessel, the unit of measurement being a 'ton' of 100 cubic feet.
Deadweight tonnage	= Deadweight tonnage is the total weight in tons of 2,240 lb. that a ship can legally carry, that is the total weight of cargo, bunkers, stores and crew.

ACKNOWLEDGEMENTS

The Editor would like to thank the following people for their help in producing this book:

Production team:	Sharon Adhikari
	Mario Alemanno
	Nicola Amaranayake
	Andrew Corris
	Michael Crawley
	Jonathan Elphick
	Usuf Islam
	Dharma Mahesan
	Mark Nevill
	Steve Whyman
	Brian Yin

Contributors

The Editor also wishes to thank all his colleagues in the ONS, the rest of the Government Statistical Service and all contributors in other organisations for their generous support and helpful comments, without whose help this publication would not be possible.

INTRODUCTION

Welcome to the 2004 edition of the *Annual Abstract of Statistics*. This compendium draws together statistics from a wide range of official and other authoritative sources. Their help is gratefully acknowledged.

Regional information, supplementary to the national figures in this *Annual Abstract*, appears in *Regional Trends*. The next edition will be published on the 26 February 2004 and will also be available electronically on the National Statistics Website free of charge. The previous edition is already available on the website. This can be accessed from the *Regional Trends* entry under the Compendia and Reference theme, or directly at:www.statistics.gov.uk/statbase product.asp?vlnk= 836. Earlier editions are available via The Stationery Office (TSO).

The five Parts of the *Annual Abstract*, illustrated in the contents, align with their equivalents in *UK 2004: The Official Yearbook of the United Kingdom of Great Britain and Northern Ireland*, so that the two books can be consulted as complementary volumes, painting a picture of the UK in words and figures.

Current data for many of the series appearing in this *Annual Abstract* are contained in other ONS publications, such as *Economic Trends, Monthly Digest of Statistics, Population Trends, Health Statistics Quarterly* and *Financial Statistics*. All are published by TSO.

The name and telephone number of the organisation providing the statistics are shown under each table. In addition, a list of Sources is given at the back of the book, which sets out the official publications or other sources to which further reference can be made.

Changes from the 2003 edition

In addition to the usual small changes of table numbers resulting from the annual addition or deletion of tables, this year the opportunity has been taken to increase the number of Housing tables in *Annual Abstract*. In consequence a new Housing chapter, numbered 14, has been created. This means that all the following chapter numbers have increased by 1. For example, Transport and communications is now numbered 15. As a result of this change chapter 13 is now called "Environment".

Identification codes

The four-letter identification code at the top of each data column, or at the side of each row is the ONS reference for this series of data on our database. Please quote the relevant code if you contact us requiring any futher information about the data. On some tables it is not possible to include these codes, so please quote the table number in these cases.

Definitions and Classification

Time Series
So far as possible annual totals are given throughout, but quarterly or monthly figures are given where these are more suitable to the type of series.

Explanatory notes
Most sections are preceded by explanatory notes which should be read in conjunction with the tables. Definitions and explanatory notes for many of the terms occurring in the *Annual Abstract* are also given in the *Annual Supplement* to the *Monthly Digest of Statistics*, published annually in the January editions. Detailed notes on items which appear in both the *Abstract* and *Financial Statistics* are given in an annual supplement to the latter entitled *Financial Statistics: Explanatory Handbook*. The original sources listed in the Sources may also be consulted.

Standard Industrial Classification
A Standard Industrial Classification (SIC) was first introduced into the United Kingdom in 1948 for use in classifying business establishments and other statistical units by the type of economic activity in which they are engaged. The classification provides a framework for the collection, tabulation, presentation and analysis of data about economic activities. Its use promotes uniformity of data collected by various government departments and agencies.

Since 1948 the classification has been revised in 1958, 1968, 1980 and 1992. One of the principal objectives of the 1980 revision was to eliminate differences from the activity classification issued by the Statistical Office of the European Communities (Eurostat) and entitled 'Nomenclature générale des activités économiques dans les Communautés Européennes', usually abbreviated to NACE. In 1990, the European Communities introduced a new statistical classification of economic activities (NACE Rev 1) by regulation. The regulation made it obligatory for the UK to introduce a new Standard Industrial Classification SIC(92), based on NACE Rev 1.

UK SIC(92) is based exactly on NACE Rev 1 but, where it is thought necessary or helpful, a fifth digit has been added to form subclasses of the NACE 1 four digit system. There are 17 sections, 16 subsections, 60 divisions, 222 groups, 503 classes and 253 subclasses. Full details are available from *UK Standard Industrial Classification of Economic Activities 1992* (TSO 1997, price £25.00) and *Indexes to the UK Standard Industrial Classification of Economic Activities 1992* (TSO 1997, price £22.50).

Introduction

Revisions to contents

Some of the figures, particularly for the latest year, are provisional and may be revised in a subsequent issue of the *Annual Abstract*.

Symbols and conventions used

Change of basis
Where consecutive figures have been compiled on different bases and are not strictly comparable, a footnote is added indicating the nature of the difference.

Geographic coverage
Statistics relate mainly to the United Kingdom. Where figures relate to other areas this is indicated on the table.

Units of measurement
The various units of measurement used are listed opposite the inside back cover.

Rounding of figures
In tables where figures have been rounded to the nearest final digit, the constituent items may not add up exactly to the total.

Symbols
The following symbols have been used throughout:

.. = not available or not applicable (also information suppressed to avoid disclosure).

- = nil or less than half the final digit shown.

National Statistics Online: www.statistics.gov.uk

Web-based access to time series, cross sectional data and metadata from across the Government Statistical Service (GSS), is available using the site search and index functions from the homepage. Download many datasets, in whole or in part, or consult directory information for all GSS statistical resources, including censuses, surveys, periodicals and enquiry services. Information is posted as PDF electronic documents or in XLS and CSV formats, compatible with most spreadsheet packages.

Complete copies of this publication are available to download free of charge on the following web page: www.statistics.gov.uk/statbase/product.asp?vlnk=94.

Contact point

The Editor welcomes any feedback on the content of the *Annual Abstract*, including comments on the format of the data and the selection of topics. Comments and requests for general information should be addressed to:

David Penny
Social Analysis and Reporting Division
Room B5/04
Office for National Statistics
1, Drummond Gate
London SW1V 2QQ

or

Email: info@statistics.gov.uk

January 2004

1 Area

Area

The United Kingdom comprises Great Britain and Northern Ireland. Great Britain comprises England, Wales and Scotland only.

Physical Features

The United Kingdom (UK) constitutes the greater part of the British Isles. The largest of the islands is Great Britain. The next largest comprises Northern Ireland and the Irish Republic. Western Scotland is fringed by the large island chain known as the Hebrides, and to the north east of the Scottish mainland are the Orkney and Shetland Islands. All these, along with the Isle of Wight, Anglesey and the Isles of Scilly, have administrative ties with the mainland, but the Isle of Man in the Irish Sea and the Channel Islands between Great Britain and France are largely self-governing, and are not part of the United Kingdom. The UK is one of the 15 member states of the European Union (EU).

With an area of about 243 000 sq km (94 000 sq miles), the United Kingdom is just under 1 000 km (about 600 miles) from the south coast to the extreme north of Scotland and just under 500 km (around 300 miles) across at the widest point.

- Highest mountain: Ben Nevis, in the highlands of Scotland, at 1 343 m (4 406 ft)

- Longest river: the Severn, 354 km (220 miles) long, which rises in central Wales and flows through Shrewsbury, Worcester and Gloucester in England to the Bristol Channel

- Largest lake: Lough Neagh, Northern Ireland, at 396 sq km (153 sq miles)

- Deepest lake: Loch Morar in the Highlands of Scotland, 310 m (1 017 ft) deep

- Highest waterfall: Eas a'Chual Aluinn, from Glas Bheinn, in the highlands of Scotland, with a drop of 200 m (660 ft)

- Deepest cave: Ogof Ffynnon Ddu, Wales, at 308 m (1 010 ft) deep

- Most northerly point on the British mainland: Dunnet Head, north-east Scotland

- Most southerly point on the British mainland: Lizard Point, Cornwall

- Closest point to mainland continental Europe: Dover, Kent. The Channel Tunnel, which links England and France, is a little over 50 km (31 miles) long, of which nearly 38 km (24 miles) are actually under the Channel.

1.1 Area of the United Kingdom, 2002

	sq km		sq km
		Worcestershire County	1 741
UNITED KINGDOM	242 514		
		Herefordshire and Worcestershire	*3 920*
GREAT BRITAIN	228 937	*Former county of Shropshire*	*3 488*
		Former county of Staffordshire	*2 714*
ENGLAND AND WALES	151 013		
		EAST	19 110
ENGLAND	130 281		
		Luton UA	43
NORTH EAST	8 573	Peterborough UA	343
		Southend-on-Sea UA	42
Darlington UA	197	Thurrock UA	163
Hartlepool UA	94		
Middlesbrough UA	54	Bedfordshire County	1 192
Redcar and Cleveland UA	245	Cambridgeshire County	3 046
Stockton-on-Tees UA	204	Essex County	3 465
		Hertfordshire	1 643
Durham County	2 226	Norfolk	5 371
Northumberland	5 013	Suffolk	3 801
Tyne and Wear (Met County)	540		
		Former county of Bedfordshire	*1 235*
Tees Valley	*794*	*Former county of Cambridgeshire*	*3 390*
Tees Valley less Darlington	*597*	*Former county of Essex*	*3 670*
Former county of Durham	*2 424*		
		LONDON	1 572
NORTH WEST	14 106		
		Inner London	319
Blackburn with Darwen UA	137	Outer London	1 253
Blackpool UA	35		
Halton UA	79	**SOUTH EAST**	19 069
Warrington UA	181		
		Bracknell Forest UA	109
Cheshire County	2 083	Brighton and Hove UA	83
Cumbria	6 768	Isle of Wight UA	380
Greater Manchester (Met County)	1 276	Medway UA	192
Lancashire County	2 903	Milton Keynes UA	309
Merseyside (Met County)	645	Portsmouth UA	40
		Reading UA	40
Former county of Cheshire	*2 343*	Slough UA	33
Former county of Lancashire	*3 075*	Southampton UA	50
		West Berkshire UA	704
YORKSHIRE AND THE HUMBER	15 408	Windsor and Maidenhead UA	197
		Wokingham UA	179
East Riding of Yorkshire UA	2 408		
Kingston upon Hull, City of UA	71	Buckinghamshire County	1 565
North East Lincolnshire UA	192	East Sussex County	1 709
North Lincolnshire UA	846	Hampshire County	3 679
York UA	272	Kent County	3 544
		Oxfordshire	2 605
North Yorkshire County	8 038	Surrey	1 663
South Yorkshire (Met County)	1 552	West Sussex	1 991
West Yorkshire (Met County)	2 029		
		Former county of Berkshire	*1 262*
The Humber	*3 517*	*Former county of Buckinghamshire*	*1 874*
Former county of North Yorkshire	*8 310*	*Former county of East Sussex*	*1 791*
		Former county of Hampshire	*3 769*
EAST MIDLANDS	15 607	*Former county of Kent*	*3 736*
Derby UA	78	**SOUTH WEST**	23 837
Leicester UA	73		
Nottingham UA	75	Bath and North East Somerset UA	346
Rutland UA	382	Bournemouth UA	46
		Bristol, City of UA	110
Derbyshire County	2 547	North Somerset UA	374
Leicestershire County	2 083	Plymouth UA	80
Lincolnshire	5 921	Poole UA	65
Northamptonshire	2 364	South Gloucestershire UA	497
Nottinghamshire County	2 085	Swindon UA	230
		Torbay UA	63
Former county of Derbyshire	*2 625*		
Former county of Leicestershire	*2 538*	Cornwall and the Isles of Scilly	3 563
Former county of Nottinghamshire	*2 159*	Devon County	6 564
		Dorset County	2 542
WEST MIDLANDS	12 998	Gloucestershire	2 653
		Somerset	3 451
Herefordshire, County of UA	2 180	Wiltshire County	3 255
Stoke-on-Trent UA	93		
Telford and Wrekin UA	290	*Bristol/Bath area*	*1 326*
		Former county of Devon	*6 707*
Shropshire County	3 197	*Former county of Dorset*	*2 653*
Staffordshire County	2 620	*Former county of Wiltshire*	*3 485*
Warwickshire	1 975		
West Midlands (Met County)	902		

1.1 Area of the United Kingdom, 2002
continued

	sq km		sq km
WALES	20 732	Dumfries and Galloway	6 426
Blaenau Gwent	109	Dundee City	60
Bridgend	251	East Ayrshire	1 262
Caerphilly	278	East Dunbartonshire	175
Cardiff	139	East Lothian	679
Carmarthenshire	2 394		
		East Renfrewshire	174
Ceredigion	1 792	Edinburgh, City of	264
Conwy	1 126	Eilean Siar (Western Isles)	3 071
Denbighshire	837	Falkirk	297
Flintshire	438	Fife	1 325
Gwynedd	2 535		
		Glasgow City	175
Isle of Anglesey	711	Highland	25 659
Merthyr Tydfil	111	Inverclyde	160
Monmouthshire	849	Midlothian	354
Neath Port Talbot	441	Moray	2 238
Newport	190		
Pembrokeshire	1 589	North Ayrshire	885
		North Lanarkshire	470
Powys	5 181	Orkney Islands	990
Rhondda, Cynon, Taff	424	Perth and Kinross	5 286
Swansea	378	Renfrewshire	261
Torfaen	126	Scottish Borders	4 732
The Vale of Glamorgan	331		
Wrexham	504	Shetland Islands	1 466
		South Ayrshire	1 222
		South Lanarkshire	1 772
SCOTLAND	77 925	Stirling	2 187
		West Dunbartonshire	159
Aberdeen City	186	West Lothian	427
Aberdeenshire	6 313		
Angus	2 182		
Argyll and Bute	6 909	**NORTHERN IRELAND**	13 576
Clackmannanshire	159		

Source: Office for National Statistics

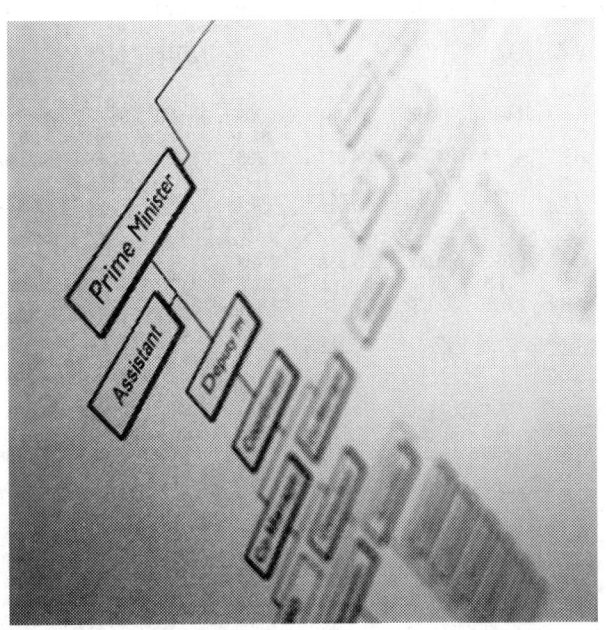

2 Parliamentary elections

2.1 Parliamentary elections[1]

Thousands and percentages

	26 May 1955	8 Oct 1959	15 Oct 1964	31 Mar 1966	18 June 1970[1]	28 Feb 1974	10 Oct 1974	3 May 1979	9 June 1983	11 June 1987	9 April 1992	1 May 1997	7 June 2001
United Kingdom													
Electorate	34 852	35 397	35 894	35 957	39 615	40 256	40 256	41 573	42 704	43 666	43 719	43 846	44 403
Average-electors per seat	55.3	56.2	57.0	57.1	62.9	63.4	63.4	65.5	66.7	67.2	67.2	66.5	67.4
Valid votes counted	26 760	27 863	27 657	27 265	28 345	31 340	29 189	31 221	30 671	32 530	33 614	31 286	26 367
As percentage of electorate	76.8	78.7	77.1	75.8	71.5	77.9	72.5	75.1	71.8	74.5	76.7	71.4	59.4
England and Wales													
Electorate	30 591	31 109	31 610	31 695	34 931	35 509	35 509	36 695	37 708	38 568	38 648	38 719	39 228
Average-electors per seat	55.9	56.9	57.8	57.9	63.9	64.3	64.3	66.5	67.2	68.8	68.8	68.0	68.9
Valid votes counted	23 570	24 619	24 384	24 116	24 877	27 735	25 729	27 609	27 082	28 832	29 897	27 679	23 243
As percentage of electorate	77.0	79.1	77.1	76.1	71.2	78.1	72.5	75.2	71.8	74.8	77.5	71.5	59.3
Scotland													
Electorate	3 388	3 414	3 393	3 360	3 659	3 705	3 705	3 837	3 934	3 995	3 929	3 949	3 984
Average-electors per seat	47.7	48.1	47.8	47.3	51.5	52.2	52.2	54.0	54.6	55.5	54.6	54.8	55.3
Valid votes counted	2 543	2 668	2 635	2 553	2 688	2 887	2 758	2 917	2 825	2 968	2 931	2 817	2 313
As percentage of electorate	75.1	78.1	77.6	76.0	73.5	77.9	74.5	76.0	71.8	74.3	74.2	71.3	58.1
Northern Ireland													
Electorate	873	875	891	902	1 025	1 027	1 037	1 028	1 050	1 090	1 141	1 178	1 191
Average-electors per seat	72.8	72.9	74.2	75.2	85.4	85.6	86.4	85.6	61.8	64.1	67.1	65.4	66.2
Valid votes counted	647	576	638	596	779	718	702	696	765	730	785	791	810
As percentage of electorate	74.1	65.8	71.7	66.1	76.0	69.9	67.7	67.7	72.9	67.0	68.8	67.1	68.0
Members of Parliament elected: (Numbers)	630	630	630	630	630	635	635	635	650	650	651	659	659
Conservative	344	364	303	253	330	296	276	339	396	375	336	165	166
Labour	277	258	317	363	287	301	319	268	209	229	271	418	412
Liberal Democrat	6	6	9	12	6	14	13	11	17	17	20	46	52
Social Democratic Party	-	-	-	-	-	-	-	-	6	5	-	-	-
Scottish National Party	-	-	-	-	1	7	11	2	2	3	3	6	5
Plaid Cymru	-	-	-	-	-	2	3	2	2	3	4	4	4
Other[2]	3	2	1	2	6	15	13	13	18	18	17	20	20

1 The Representation of the People Act 1969 lowered the minimum voting age from 21 to 18 years with effect from 16 February 1970.
2 Including the Speaker.

Source: University of Plymouth for the Electoral Commission: 01752 233205

2.2 Parliamentary by-elections

	April 1992 - April 1997	General[1] Election April 1992	May 1997 - June 2001	General[1,2] Election May 1997	June 2001 - November 2003	General[1] Election June 2001
Numbers of by-elections	18		17		3	
Votes recorded						
By party (percentages)						
Conservative	21.4	40.1	27.0	25.1	18.8	20.9
Labour	39.5	36.2	29.7	40.1	42.8	58.1
Liberal Democrat	24.6	16.4	22.1	14.4	23.9	13.1
Scottish National Party	5.2	3.1	6.0	4.1	-	-
Plaid Cymru	0.5	0.2	2.5	2.3	5.7	4.3
Other	8.8	4.1	12.7	14.1	8.8	3.5
Total votes recorded						
(percentages)	100.0	100.0	100.0	100.0	100.0	100.0
(thousands)	625	808	435	723	67	98

1 Votes recorded in the same seats in the previous General Election.
2 Proportions of 'other' votes inflated by the fact that votes were cast for the retiring Speaker as 'The Speaker seeking re-election' and not as a party candidate.

Source: University of Plymouth for the Electoral Commission: 01752 233205

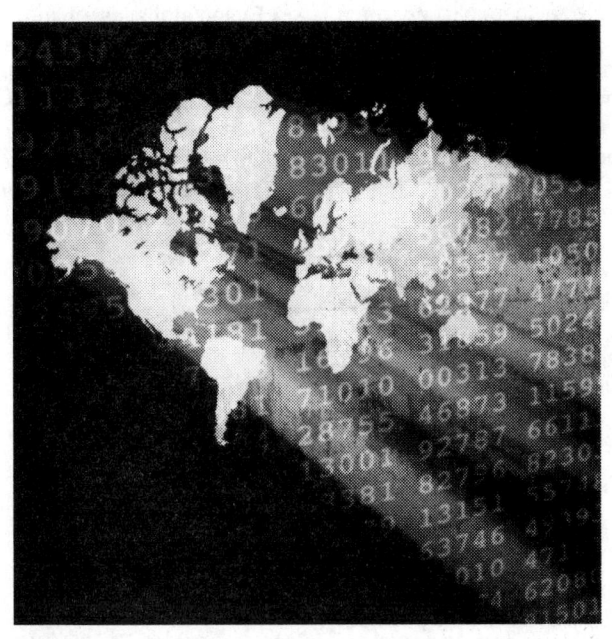

3 International development

International development

Overseas development assistance
(Tables 3.1 and 3.2)

The UK development assistance programme is administered by the Department for International Development (DFID) to promote the economic development and welfare of recipient countries. It is managed within financial years, the money being voted annually by Parliament. Since 1992 the statistics relating to the programme are also published on a financial year basis and on a calendar year basis for both international aid comparisons and for national purposes such as the balance of payments.

Aid flows can be measured before (gross) or after (net) deduction of repayments of principal on past loans. These tables show only the gross figures.

Assistance is provided in two main ways: *bilateral*, that is directly to recipient countries or to institutions in the United Kingdom for work on behalf of such countries, or *multilateral*, that is to international institutions for their development assistance programmes. Table 3.1 shows the main groups of multilateral agencies, the International Development Association being the largest in the World Bank Group.

Bilateral assistance takes various forms:

Project or sector aid is finance for investment schemes primarily designed to increase the physical capital of the recipient country, including contributions for local and recurrent costs.

Sector-wide programmes (typically in education, health or agriculture) comprise a combination of assistance including direct budget support, financial assistance in the form of projects and technical co-operation.

Programme aid is financial assistance to fund imports, sector support programmes or budgetary expenditure, usually as part of or in conjunction with a World Bank/IMF co-ordinated structural adjustment programme.

Technical co-operation is the provision of know-how in the form of personnel, training, research and associated costs.

Grants and other aid in kind are used to provide equipment and supplies, and support to the development work of UK and international voluntary organisations.

Humanitarian assistance comprises food aid and other disaster relief.

Aid and Trade Provision is a special allocation to soften the terms of credit to developing countries by mixing aid funds with private export credits. The ATP scheme lacked poverty elimination as its central focus and was closed in November 1997.

CDC Capital Partners (formerly The Commonwealth Development Corporation) invests in productive public or private sector projects in developing countries.

Other Government Departments' expenditure covers debt relief, drug-related assistance and support to the British Council or voluntary organisations.

Most of the expenditure not allocable by region in Table 3.2 is for assistance provided through organisations in the United Kingdom.

Fuller statistics of the UK's development assistance effort are published annually in *Statistics on International Development* (obtainable from Statistics Department, Abercrombie House, East Kilbride, Glasgow G75 8EA). International comparisons are available in the OECD Development Assistance Committee's annual report. The latest is *2001 Report: Development Co-operation* (available from The Stationery Office).

3.1 UK Gross public expenditure on aid (GPEX)[1]

£ Thousands

		1994 /95	1995 /96	1996 /97	1997 /98	1998 /99	1999 /00	2000 /01	2001 /02	2002 /03
Bilateral Assistance										
Department for International Development										
Project or Sector Aid	LUJS	121 812	121 456	106 361	96 448	127 634	174 951	186 210	254 246	288 367
Programme Aid	LUJW	113 510	83 494	96 299	84 784	133 574	140 372	254 995	253 519	216 208
Technical Co-operation Projects	LUOS	430 447	446 788	457 060	487 003	479 621	515 257	541 269	590 510	705 803
Grants & Other Aid in Kind	LUOT	149 556	184 315	191 152	172 665	189 311	170 124	178 811	200 159	270 620
Humanitarian Assistance	LUOU	205 368	141 410	121 886	94 680	113 159	227 157	210 363	189 749	292 272
Debt Relief	LUOV	28 144	27 337	23 529	23 161	25 659	23 140	21 188	18 322	22 353
Aid and Trade Provision	LUOW	59 987	71 988	61 978	60 711	56 898	37 790	27 645	23 094	17 733
CDC Investments	LUOX	215 295	279 986	189 082	249 062	166 716	268 518	206 239	159 438	199 196
Other Government Departments	LUOY	33 034	61 606	34 224	170 171	87 147	100 721	149 128	314 794	464 330
Total Bilateral Assistance	LUOZ	1 357 153	1 418 381	1 281 571	1 438 684	1 379 719	1 658 030	1 775 848	2 003 831	2 476 882
Multilateral Assistance										
European Community	LUPA	612 080	693 690	636 418	557 287	754 549	757 863	719 315	750 635	881 751
World Bank Group	LUPB	227 728	206 877	174 398	189 851	175 254	170 277	276 653	246 672	247 617
International Monetary Fund	LUPC	90 000	30 000	20 000	20 000	18 000	17 000	–	11 147	11 434
UN Agencies	LUPD	127 880	116 772	130 775	141 300	133 983	175 730	245 124	226 505	188 387
Regional Development Banks	LUPE	71 212	69 513	58 833	60 411	66 295	67 178	54 803	75 382	90 587
Other	LUPF	27 904	27 036	30 665	30 846	30 357	32 581	36 647	42 070	43 838
Total Multilateral Assistance	LUPG	1 156 804	1 143 887	1 051 089	999 695	1 178 438	1 220 629	1 332 542	1 352 411	1 463 614
Administrative Costs	LUPH	70 314	72 198	82 133	91 436	98 645	104 601	120 262	112 222	129 074
Total Gross Public Expenditure on Aid	LUPI	2 584 270	2 634 465	2 414 793	2 529 815	2 656 802	2 983 260	3 228 652	3 468 464	4 069 570

1 See chapter text.

Source: Department for International Development: 01355 843612

3.2 Total bilateral gross public expenditure on aid (GPEX): by main recipient countries and regions[1]

£ Thousands

		1994 /95	1995 /96	1996 /97	1997 /98	1998 /99	1999 /00	2000 /01	2001 /02	2002 /03
Main recipients										
India	LUPJ	98 622	154 730	111 789	114 022	110 374	107 283	128 800	204 528	187 250
States of Former Yugoslavia[2]	ZBXN	43 511	38 905	42 639	20 669	3 954	65 609	21 190	3 112	879
Uganda	LUPN	46 615	40 590	49 207	59 325	64 261	90 286	97 572	68 724	54 868
Tanzania	LUPK	31 633	29 900	56 414	51 437	78 085	75 099	112 034	205 812	98 892
Bangladesh	LUPM	57 441	54 282	44 329	39 078	67 361	71 794	79 347	62 983	77 419
Mozambique	LUPV	25 068	22 026	26 610	48 311	28 902	70 630	43 304	134 671	39 617
Indonesia	LUPZ	51 404	57 265	38 472	48 689	25 420	58 714	28 324	18 350	42 674
Ghana	LUPL	23 530	26 305	28 474	30 428	62 912	52 032	75 215	54 619	87 761
Malawi	LUPP	41 174	35 720	44 876	30 651	52 629	49 337	57 499	49 067	52 535
South Africa	LUPT	15 706	17 666	23 214	28 372	35 110	47 838	36 755	44 178	38 422
Zambia	LUPO	56 629	58 915	40 529	46 742	33 567	46 779	93 488	59 288	45 705
Rwanda	LUQA	45 284	11 958	9 704	6 198	13 568	14 294	32 708	27 027	32 344
Nepal	LUQC	15 475	16 485	15 271	16 953	16 041	14 847	17 695	23 414	27 887
Kenya	LUPR	30 691	29 378	26 438	30 025	42 163	32 927	62 806	35 007	55 773
Sierra Leone	ZBXQ	8 345	8 963	10 841	3 293	9 153	30 044	35 148	37 177	32 761
Russian Federation	LUPW	32 753	30 884	32 205	33 617	30 887	27 728	26 114	25 405	27 011
China	LUPS	28 344	32 803	30 956	38 616	39 190	26 260	56 766	50 418	44 625
Pakistan	LUPY	63 487	60 234	59 365	32 654	26 904	23 471	16 345	44 911	47 062
Montserrat	LUPU	5 815	6 568	14 441	37 867	31 096	22 640	20 811	24 417	23 800
Zimbabwe	LUPX	35 394	20 191	21 007	13 715	29 394	17 363	14 716	15 726	30 145
Total Main Recipients	LUQD	756 921	753 768	726 781	730 662	800 971	944 975	1 056 637	1 188 834	1 047 430
Total Other Countries	LUQE	600 232	664 613	554 790	708 021	578 748	713 055	719 211	814 997	1 429 452
Regional Totals										
Africa	LUQF	475 626	437 146	445 153	450 076	574 289	631 475	783 332	879 084	871 018
America	LUQG	132 407	192 769	107 291	271 336	170 125	239 831	183 828	170 274	216 550
Asia	LUQH	415 812	465 945	401 402	391 763	349 939	381 890	422 557	545 264	619 917
Europe	LUQI	137 995	129 941	137 934	114 537	83 171	191 891	114 155	98 214	384 745
Pacific	LUQJ	16 291	14 053	12 458	26 890	20 251	7 248	5 134	7 042	5 578
World Unallocated[3]	LUQK	179 023	178 527	177 333	184 081	181 943	205 694	266 842	303 953	379 074
Total Bilateral GPEX	LUQL	1 357 153	1 418 381	1 281 571	1 438 683	1 379 719	1 658 030	1 775 848	2 003 831	2 476 882

1 See chapter text.
2 The totals for the period prior to 1998/99 include amounts for the successor states of the former Yugoslavia. The figures for 1999/00 and 2000/01 include humanitarian assistance to Kosovo.

3 World Unallocated comprises block grants to the British Council, VSO, CSOs, Research Institutions and Commonwealth Organisations based in the UK, and some ATP Technical Co-operation.

Source: Department for International Development: 01355 843612

4 Defence

Defence

This section includes figures on Defence expenditure, on the size and role of the Armed Forces and on related support activities.

Much of the material in this section can be found in *UK Defence Statistics 2003 (The Stationery Office)*.

Defence expenditure *(Table 4.1)*
UK Defence Expenditure - the move from cash to resource accounting
Up until financial Year 1998/99, Government expenditure was accounted for on a Cash basis. For the years 1999/00 and 2000/01 there was a transitional period from Cash to Resource Accounting & Budgeting (RAB), whereby Government Departments continued to be controlled on a cash basis, but were required to produce consolidated resource accounts. Since 2001/02 Government expenditure has been accounted for on a resource basis only. The main difference arising from the adoption of RAB is that costs are accounted for as they are incurred, rather than when payment is made (the principle of accruals). This gives rise to timing differences in accounting between the Cash and RAB systems and also to the recognition of depreciation. Additionally, under RAB, departments are required to account for a cost of capital charge, equivalent to an interest charge on the capital (in the form of net assets) held on the Balance Sheet.

The change from cash based accounting to resource (accruals) based accounting, and the two stage introduction of RAB (outlined below) has affected the time series comparability of the data.

Please refer to UK Defence Statistics 2002 Chapter 1 – Resource Accounting & Budgeting section for a summary of the key events leading to the introduction of RAB. Back copies of this publication are available at *www.dasa.mod.uk/national statistics*.

Managing Resources
Under Resource Accounting, Government Departments are accountable for their spending against Resource and Capital Departmental Expenditure Limits (DELs). Spending against the Resource DEL covers current items such as in year personnel costs, equipment/ stock consumption, maintenance of land and buildings etc. The Capital budget, whilst part of the overall DEL, reflects investment spending that will appear on the Department's balance sheet and be consumed over a number of years. Departments are also responsible for Annually Managed Expenditure (AME). This spending is demand led (for example, payment of War Pensions) and therefore cannot be controlled by Departments in the same way.

Stage 1 of RAB covered the financial years 2001/02 and 2002/03. Unlike cash, costs were accrued as they were incurred, rather than when payment was made. For 2001/02 and 2002/03 the Resource DEL did not include the non-cash costs associated with Resource Accounting, such as depreciation and the cost of capital charge. During the stage 1 period these non-cash costs fell within Annually Managed Expenditure (AME) and were not controlled to the same degree as DELs. This arrangement was applied in Stage 1 only and allowed departments an interim period to gain experience of managing the new non-cash costs, to reconsider their holdings of stocks and fixed assets, which impact the non-cash costs, prior to the charge impacting on the more tightly controlled DELs.

Stage 2 of RAB began at the start of the financial year 2003/04. This involved the movement of the primary non-cash costs (depreciation and the cost of capital charge) from AME into the Resource DEL.

The change in definition of the DELs combined with volatile non-cash costs over the Stage 1 period make time series comparisons over the period 2001/02 - 2003/04 complex. Additionally, the mix of cash and non-cash costs may be subject to change in future years.

Factors affecting Cash to RAB data consistency
i) There are timing differences as to when payments are seen to be made.

ii) The movement of Non-Cash items of expenditure from AME into the Resource DEL from 2003/04 onwards has the 'apparent' effect of inflating the Resource DEL.

iii) In financial year 2003/04 the Cost of Capital Charge is reduced from 6 per cent to 3.5 per cent. This non-cash cost may change in future years.

Under Resource Accounting the individual headings consist of the following:-

Equipment support: Internal and contracted out costs for equipment repair and maintenance.

Stock consumption: Consumption of armament, medical, dental, veterinary, oil, strategic weapon systems, clothing, and general stores.

Property management: Estate and facilities management services and costs for building's maintenance.

Movements: Cost of transportation of freight and personnel.

Accommodation and utilities: Charges include rent, rates, gas, electricity, water and sewerage costs.

Professional fees: Includes legal and consultancy fees.

Fuel: Relates to fuel consumption by military vehicles, ships and aircraft.

Expenditure on fixed asset categories: Includes disposal receipts but include in particular:-

Intangible assets: comprise the development costs of major equipment projects and Intellectual Property Rights.

Assets in the course of construction: largely consist of major weapons platforms under construction in the Defence Procurement

Agency (there is a smaller element of buildings under construction). Once construction is complete, those platforms will transfer to the relevant top level budget holder as Fighting Equipment.

Capital spares: are items of repairable material used to replace parts of assets undergoing repair, refurbishment, and maintenance, servicing, modification, enhancement or conversion. Examples include aircraft engines and ships.

Departmental Annually Managed Expenditure (AME) is spending that is outside the Departmental Expenditure Limit (DEL), but included in departmental budgets. This includes the provision for Armed Forces Pensions and non-cash items such as depreciation, cost of capital charges, and provision. At present, these non-cash items are not subject to the same controls and are included in Annually Managed Expenditure but from 2003/04 they will be included as part of the DEL.

For 2001/02 through to 2003/04, the "other" category contains the sum of movements, cash release and cost of capital credit on nuclear provisions and also QinetiQ loan repayments. In addition, for 2001/02 and 2002/03 this category includes depreciation and the cost of capital charge. The 2002/03 figure includes a supplementary estimate for additional funding to cover the asset write off in this year.

Service personnel (*Tables 4.2, 4.4, 4.5, 4.8 and 4.10*)
The Regular Forces consist entirely of volunteer members serving on a whole-time basis, figures for which include both Trained and Untrained personnel and exclude Gurkhas, Full Time Reserve Service personnel, the Home Service battalions of the Royal Irish Regiment, mobilised reservists and Naval Activated Reservists.

Locally Entered Personnel are recruited outside the United Kingdom for whole-time service in special formations with special conditions of service and normally restricted locations. The Brigade of Gurkhas is an example.

The Regular Forces are supported by Reserves and Auxiliary Forces. There are both regular and volunteer Reserves. Regular Reserves consist of former Service personnel with a Reserve liability. Volunteer Reserves are open to both former Service personnel and civilians. The call out liabilities of the various reserve forces differ in accordance with their roles.

All three Services run cadet forces for young people and the Combined Cadet Force, which is found in certain schools where education is continued to the age of 17 or above, may operate sections for any or all of the Services.

Full-Time Reserve Service personnel represent reserves serving full-time in regular posts. This was made possible by the Reserve Forces Act 1996. None existed before 1998. FTRS figures include Full Commitment (FC), Home Commitment (HC) and Limited Commitment (LC) individuals.

Home Service battalions of the Royal Irish Regiment. Up until 1 July 1992, this was the Ulster Defence Regiment. The figures for the Territorial Army include Officer Training Corps and non-regular permanent staff.

The figures for cadet forces for each service include the Combined Cadet Force. Naval Service figures include officers and civilian instructors. The Army and Royal Air Force figures exclude officers and civilian instructors.

Intake of UK regular forces from civilian life: by service (*Table 4.2*)
This table shows all intakes to UK Regular Forces including re-enlistments and rejoined reservists.

Formation of the armed forces (*Table 4.3*)
This table shows the number of units which comprise the "teeth" elements of the Armed Forces and excludes supporting units.

Outflow of UK regular forces: by service (*Table 4.4*)
This table does not include promotions to officer from other ranks and miscellaneous outflow.

Civilian personnel (*Table 4.6*)
This table gives an analysis of the number of civilians employed in the various management areas. The attribution of civilian staff can change according to circumstances so that figures for successive years may not always be comparable. The figures include UK based civilians serving overseas. Other civilian staff are engaged overseas to work locally as circumstances demand.

Prior to April 1995 all part-timers were counted as half of full time. From that date they are counted as the number of hours worked as a proportion of normal conditioned hours. The average part timer works about 60% of full time.

The Centre includes all MOD Police. From 1991 it includes staff in the Meteorological Office (transferred from RAF), staff in the Chemical Defence Establishment (transferred from Procurement Executive), and all personnel serving overseas in support of the services (other than in British Army on the Rhine (BAOR) or RAF Germany). Communications staff are excluded after 1993 and the Meteorological staff after 1995. From 1996, those staff in the procurement executive are included in the Centre.

Prior to becoming Trading Funds the Defence Evaluation Agency and the Hydrographic Office were included in Procurement Executive.

As from 1 April 2000 a new top level budget was formed in the Centre called Defence Logistics Organisation, replacing the top level budgets CinC Fleet Support, Quarter Master General and RAF Logistics Command.

The Devonport and Rosyth Dockyards were contractorised with effect from 6 April 1987. The Atomic Weapons Establishment was contractorised with effect from 1 April 1992.

Defence

Family accommodation and defence land holdings (Table 4.7)

In November 1996 most of the MOD's housing stock in England and Wales was sold to a private company, Annington Homes. The homes retained for use by Service families were leased back, with the condition that the MOD release a certain number of houses each year for disposal by Annington. The proceeds of the sale are being used to upgrade the housing stock.

The table also presents statistics of land and foreshore in the United Kingdom owned or leased by the Ministry of Defence or over which it has limited rights under grants or licences. Land declared as surplus to Defence requirements is also included.

Deployment of Service personnel (Table 4.8)

The figures for Service personnel in England, Wales, Scotland and Northern Ireland are obtained from a different source from that used to compile the United Kingdom total. Consequently the sum of the national figures can differ from the United Kingdom total. The figures for Northern Ireland include all personnel who are serving on emergency tours of duty but exclude the former Ulster Defence Regiment, now the Home Services element of the Royal Irish Regiment. The figures for overseas countries include service personnel who are on loan to countries in the areas shown. Royal Navy and Royal Marines personnel on board ship are included in the United Kingdom figure if the ship was in home waters on the situation date or otherwise against the appropriate overseas area. All Defence Attaches and Advisers and their staffs are included under "Other Locations" and not identified within specific areas. From 2001 the grouping of overseas locations has been changed to give a more relevant overview.

UK regular forces - deaths (Table 4.9)

Rates have been standardised to 2002 Tri-Service age and sex structure.

Health (Table 4.10)

The Services operate a number of hospitals in this country and in areas abroad where there is a significant British military presence. These hospitals take as patients, members of all three Services and their dependants; in addition, the hospitals in the United Kingdom take civilian patients under arrangements agreed with the National Health Service. Medical support is also supplied by Service medical staff at individual units, ships and stations.

Defence services and the civilian community (Table 4.11)

This table covers incidents in which Rescue Coordinating Centres (RCCs) in the United Kingdom coordinated search and rescue (SAR) action in which elements of the Armed Forces were involved. The table also includes urgent medical incidents in which the Forces SAR facilities gave assistance (eg inter-hospital transfers). More than one element of the SAR services are called to the same incident. Consequently, the number of callouts is likely to be greater than the number of incidents.

Persons rescued refers to civilian or military personnel who were removed from a hazardous environment or were transported from the scene by SAR Units in order to receive urgent medical attention. People assisted by Mountain Rescue Teams, but subsequently transported from the scene by helicopter, are credited as having been rescued by the helicopter unit concerned. The total incidents figure also includes any HM Coastguard incidents under the control of ARCC Kinloss.

The Ministry of Defence helps the civil community in a variety of ways, for example by providing assistance in time of natural disasters or other emergencies and by undertaking community projects which are of training value to the Services. In some cases facilities established primarily for defence purposes also provide benefits to the general public.

Service assistance may be provided during an industrial dispute at the request of the civil ministries in order to maintain services essential to the life of the community (eg maintenance of emergency fire services). Figures for the number of man weeks spent by service personnel are no longer collected, so this has been removed from the table.

The Royal Navy Fishery Protection squadron operates within the British fishery limits under contract to the Department for Environment, Food and Rural Affairs. Boardings carried out by vessels of the Executive Environment and Rural Affairs Department and the Department of Agriculture for Northern Ireland are not included.

4.1 UK Defence expenditure[1]

£ millions

		1998 /99	1999 /00	2000 /01			2001 /02	2002[2] /03	2003[3] /04
Total expenditure at outturn prices[4]	KDAA	22 482	22 572	23 552	**Departmental Expenditure Limits (DEL)**	SNKJ	24 439	26 460	36 880
					Resource DEL				
					Expenditure on personnel	SNKK	9 422	10 171	10 370
					Armed forces	SNKL	7 102	7 806	7 827
					Civilians	SNKM	2 320	2 365	2 543
Expenditure on personnel	KDAB	8 556	8 530	8 768	Depreciation/impairments	SNKN	..	..	7 638
of the Armed Forces	KDAC	6 286	6 257	6 500	Cost of capital	SNKO	..	..	2 969
of civilian staff	KDAE	2 270	2 273	2 268	Equipment support	SNKP	2 419	3 218	3 658
					Stock consumption	SNKQ	1 294	1 032	1 236
					Property management	SNKR	1 222	1 506	1 192
					Movements	SNKS	718	551	542
					Accommodation and utilities	SNKT	572	619	697
Expenditure on equipment[5]	KDAF	9 889	9 715	10 008	Professional fees	SNKU	559	552	456
Sea systems	KDAG	2 319	..	..	Fuel	SNKV	160	195	155
Land systems	KDAH	1 665	..	..	Other	SNKW	2 155	2 405	1 839
Air systems	KDAI	4 572	..	..					
Other	KDAJ	1 333	..	..	**Capital DEL**				
					Expenditure on fixed asset categories				
					Intangible assets	SNKX	1 031	1 557	1 609
					Land and buildings	SNKY	-163	-224	344
					Fighting equipment[6]	SNKZ	34	274	-6
Other expenditure	KDAK	4 037	4 327	4 776	Plant, machinery and vehicles	SNLA	99	134	158
Works, buildings and land	KDAL	1 761	1 800	1 919	IT and communications equipment	SNLB	84	110	132
Miscellaneous stores and services	KDAM	2 276	2 527	2 857	Assets in the course of construction	SNLC	4 479	4 045	3 439
					Capital spares	SNLD	353	314	452
					Annually Managed Expenditure (AME)	SNLF	14 962	21 085	1 151
Adjusted defence budget[7]					War pensions	SNLG	1 238	1 166	1 158
at 2001/02 prices	GPWI	24 065	23 591	24 082	Other	SNLH	13 724	19 919	-7

1 See chapter text.
2 Estimated outturn.
3 Planned.
4 Calculated using cash accounting basis.

5 The split between sea, land and air is no longer available, due to a change in accounting practice.
6 In 2003/04 there is a forecasted drop in fighting equipment spend due to a large disposal receipt.
7 Adjusted to 2001/02 prices using the GDP deflator.

Source: Ministry of Defence/DASA (Procurement): 0117 913 4585

4.2 Intake of UK regular forces from civilian life: by service[1]

Numbers

		1992 /93	1993 /94	1994 /95	1995 /96	1996 /97	1997[2] /98	1998 /99	1999 /00	2000 /01	2001 /02	2002 /03
All services:												
Male	KCJB	13 070	10 620	11 150	15 500	19 230	20 190	22 560	22 390	20 410	20 950	23 040
Female	KCJC	1 750	1 330	1 850	2 180	2 940	3 340	3 440	3 160	2 610	2 700	3 240
Total	KCJA	14 820	11 950	13 010	17 670	22 160	23 520	26 000	25 550	23 020	23 650	26 280
Naval service:												
Male	KCJE	1 890	1 280	960	2 010	3 400	3 970	4 110	4 250	3 990	4 270	4 420
Female	KCJF	380	260	340	350	560	630	660	700	630	740	800
Total	KCJD	2 270	1 540	1 300	2 360	3 960	4 600	4 770	4 950	4 620	5 010	5 220
Army:												
Male	KCJJ	10 290	8 760	9 490	11 510	13 580	13 390	15 010	14 750	13 450	13 620	15 060
Female	KCJK	1 100	810	1 190	1 380	1 940	2 010	1 980	1 750	1 320	1 240	1 550
Total	KCJI	11 390	9 580	10 680	12 890	15 520	15 400	16 990	16 500	14 770	14 850	16 610
Royal Air Force:												
Male	KCJM	890	580	700	1 980	2 250	2 830	3 450	3 380	2 980	3 070	3 550
Female	KCJN	270	260	320	450	430	700	800	710	660	720	890
Total	KCJL	1 160	840	1 020	2 420	2 680	3 530	4 250	4 100	3 630	3 780	4 450

1 See chapter text.
2 The definitions of intake used have been standardised from 1997/98 to give a more consistent picture across the three services.

Source: Ministry of Defence/DASA (Tri-Service): 020 7218 0390

4.3 Formation of the UK armed forces[1]
As at 1 April

Numbers

		Front Line Units	1993	1994	1995	1996	1997	1998	1999	2000	2001	2002	2003
Royal Navy[2]													
Submarines	KCGA	Vessels	23	23	16	15	15	15	15	16	16	16	16
Carriers and assault ships	KCGB	Vessels	5	5	5	5	5	5	6	6	6	4	4
Cruisers, Destroyers and Frigates	KCGC	Vessels	40	37	35	36	35	35	35	32	32	32	31
Mine counter-measure	KCGE	Vessels	35	18	18	18	18	19	20	21	23	22	22
Patrol ships and craft	KCGF	Vessels	25	34	32	32	34	28	24	24	23	23	22
Fixed wing aircraft[3]	KCGG	Squadrons	3	3	3	3	3	3	3	1	1	1	1
Helicopters[4]	KCGH	Squadrons	17	17	15	15	15	12	12	9	9	8	8
Royal Marines	KCGI	Commandos	3	3	3	3	3	3	3	3	3	3	3
Regular Army													
Royal Armoured Corps[5,6]	KCGJ	Regiments	14	12	11	11	11	11	11	11	10	10	10
Royal Artillery[5]	KCGK	Regiments	18	16	16	16	16	15	15	15	15	15	15
Royal Engineers[7]	KCGL	Regiments	13	12	10	10	10	10	10	11	11	11	11
Infantry	KCGM	Battalions	48	45	41	41	40	40	40	40	40	40	40
Special Air Service	KCGN	Regiments	1	1	1	1	1	1	1	1	1	1	1
Army Air Corps[4]	KCGO	Regiments	6	6	5	5	5	5	5	–	–	–	–
Royal Air Force													
Strike/attack	KCGP	Squadrons	8	6	6	6	6	6	5	5	5	5	5
Offensive support[3]	KCGQ	Squadrons	5	5	5	5	5	5	5	2	2	2	2
Air defence	KCGR	Squadrons	7	6	6	6	6	6	5	5	5	5	4
Maritime patrol	KCGS	Squadrons	3	3	3	3	3	3	3	3	3	3	3
Reconnaissance	KCGT	Squadrons	5	5	5	5	5	5	5	5	5	5	5
Airborne early warning[8]	KCGU	Squadrons	1	1	1	2	2	2	2	2	2	2	2
Air transport and tankers and helicopters[3]	KCGV	Squadrons	16	15	14	14	13	14	14	8	9	9	9
Search and rescue	KCGX	Squadrons	2	2	2	2	2	2	2	2	2	2	2
Ground based air defence	KCGY	Squadrons	5	5	5	6	6	6	4	4	4	4	4
Field	KCGZ	Squadrons	5	5	5	5	5	5	5	5	6	6	6
Joint Helicopter Command													
Royal Navy Helicopter	JUAT	Squadrons	..	..	..	..	..	..	..	4	4	4	4
Army Aviation	JUAU	Squadrons	..	..	..	..	..	..	..	5	5	5	5
Royal Air Force Helicopter	JUAV	Squadrons	..	..	..	..	..	..	..	6	6	6	6
Joint Force Harrier													
Royal Navy	JUAW	Squadrons	..	..	..	..	..	..	..	3	3	3	3
Royal Air Force	JUAX	Squadrons	..	..	..	..	..	..	..	3	3	3	3

1 See chapter text.
2 Only active vessels are shown from 1995 onwards. All vessels are included before then.
3 From 2000 excludes aircraft transferred to the Joint Force Harrier squadron.
4 From 2000 excludes helicopters transferred to the Joint Helicopter command.
5 Figure for 1994 includes one training regiment.

6 From 2000 includes one Armoured Regiment which is committed to the new Joint Nuclear Biological and Chemical Regiment.
7 Figure for 2000 includes an additional Close Support Regiment formed as a result of the Stategic Defence Review.
8 Figure for 2001 includes an embedded Operational Conversion Unit at the Sentry Operation Establishments.

Source: Ministry of Defence/DASA (Tri-Service): 020 7218 0390

4.4 Outflow of UK regular forces: by service[1]

Numbers

		1992 /93	1993 /94	1994 /95	1995 /96	1996 /97	1997[2] /98	1998 /99	1999 /00	2000 /01	2001 /02	2002 /03
All Services:												
Male	KDNA	31 140	29 700	31 050	25 750	29 320	21 860	24 490	23 840	22 500	22 340	21 760
Female	KDNB	2 520	2 430	2 990	3 120	3 680	2 490	2 970	2 740	2 430	2 350	2 330
Total	KDNC	33 660	32 130	34 040	28 860	33 000	24 340	27 460	26 580	24 930	24 690	24 090
Naval Service:												
Male	KDND	4 660	4 610	5 500	4 310	6 190	4 650	4 920	5 160	4 480	5 110	4 680
Female	KDNE	460	490	680	630	940	620	610	630	550	690	620
Total	KDNF	5 110	5 110	6 180	4 940	7 130	5 270	5 530	5 800	5 040	5 800	5 300
Army:												
Male	KDNI	20 990	19 630	20 230	13 940	13 760	13 180	15 310	14 600	13 880	13 270	13 410
Female	KDNJ	1 340	1 290	1 650	1 510	1 600	1 280	1 730	1 570	1 330	1 090	1 130
Total	KDNK	22 330	20 920	21 880	15 440	15 350	14 460	17 040	16 170	15 210	14 360	14 550
Royal Air Force:												
Male	KDNL	5 490	5 450	5 310	7 500	9 380	4 020	4 250	4 080	4 140	3 960	3 670
Female	KDNM	730	650	660	980	1 140	590	640	540	540	570	580
Total	KDNN	6 220	6 100	5 970	8 480	10 520	4 610	4 890	4 620	4 680	4 530	4 250

1 See chapter text. Comprises all those who left the Regular Forces and includes deaths.
2 The definitions of outflow used have been standardised from 1997/98 to give a more consistent picture across the three services.

Source: Ministry of Defence/DASA (Tri-Service): 020 7218 0390

4.5 UK Defence: service manpower strengths[1]
As at 1 April

Thousands

		1993	1994	1995	1996	1997	1998	1999	2000	2001	2002	2003
UK service personnel												
Full-time trained strength	ZBTR	267.1	248.4	226.3	211.6	197.4	194.0	191.1	190.5	188.8	187.1	188.6
Trained Naval Service	ZBTS	55.3	52.4	48.2	45.6	41.7	40.5	39.3	38.9	38.5	37.5	37.6
UK regulars	ZBTT	55.3	52.4	48.2	45.6	41.7	40.4	39.1	38.3	38.0	36.8	36.6
Full-time reserve service	ZBTU	..	..	..	..	..	0.1	0.3	0.3	0.5	0.7	1.0
Trained Army	ZBTV	132.9	121.8	108.7	103.6	101.5	100.9	99.9	100.4	100.2	100.4	102.1
UK regulars	ZBTW	126.5	116.1	104.5	99.5	97.8	97.5	96.3	96.5	96.3	96.0	97.6
Full-time reserve service	ZBTX	..	..	..	..	..	..	0.2	0.5	0.6	0.9	1.1
Gurkhas	ZBTY	6.5	5.6	4.2	4.0	3.8	3.4	3.4	3.4	3.4	3.4	3.4
Trained Royal Air Force	ZBTZ	78.9	74.2	69.4	62.5	54.2	52.7	51.9	51.2	50.1	49.2	48.9
UK regulars	ZBUA	78.9	74.2	69.4	62.5	54.2	52.7	51.8	51.0	49.8	48.9	48.5
Full-time reserve service	ZBUB	..	..	..	..	..	..	0.1	0.2	0.3	0.3	0.4
Untrained UK regulars	ZBUC	14.2	11.8	11.2	14.3	17.2	19.7	21.5	21.9	21.5	23.4	24.5
Naval Service	ZBUD	4.1	3.4	2.7	2.8	3.5	4.1	4.6	4.6	4.4	4.9	5.0
Army	ZBUE	8.1	6.9	7.2	9.3	11.1	12.4	13.4	13.6	13.2	14.4	14.9
Royal Air Force	ZBUF	2.0	1.5	1.3	2.2	2.7	3.2	3.5	3.7	3.9	4.1	4.7
Locally Entered Personnel (excluding Gurkhas)	ZBUG	1.3	1.2	0.6	0.6	0.4	0.4	0.4	0.4	0.3	0.4	0.4
Royal Irish Regiment Home Service batallions	ZBUH	5.6	5.4	5.3	5.0	4.8	4.6	4.4	4.2	3.8	3.6	3.5
Reserve personnel	ZBUI	334.2	334.1	329.6	327.3	323.6	319.4	307.0	294.8	283.6	272.6	259.3
Regular Reserves	ZBUJ	258.3	262.2	264.1	264.6	259.5	254.9	247.6	241.6	234.7	224.6	212.6
Naval Services	ZBUK	22.0	23.3	23.3	23.9	24.1	24.8	24.7	24.2	23.5	23.5	23.2
Army	ZBUL	190.1	192.5	195.3	195.5	190.1	186.2	180.5	175.5	169.8	161.1	151.5
of which mobilised:	SNEO	..	..	..	..	..	0.2	0.1	0.3	0.2	0.3	0.4
Royal Air Force	ZBUM	46.1	46.4	45.5	45.2	45.4	43.9	42.4	41.9	41.6	40.3	37.9
of which mobilised:	SNEP	..	..	..	..	..	..	..	..	..	..	–
Volunteer Reserves	ZBUN	75.9	71.9	65.5	62.7	64.1	64.5	59.4	53.2	48.9	47.9	46.7
Royal Naval Reserve and Royal Marine Reserve[2]	ZBUO	5.6	4.6	3.7	3.5	4.3	4.4	4.5	4.8	4.8	5.0	4.9
of which mobilised:	SNEQ	..	..	..	..	..	..	..	..	..	..	0.4
Territorial Army	ZBUP	68.5	65.0	59.7	57.3	57.6	57.6	52.3	45.6	41.9	40.9	39.2
of which mobilised:	SNER	..	..	..	..	..	0.6	0.5	0.8	0.4	0.5	4.1
Royal Auxilliary Air Force	ZBUQ	1.8	2.3	2.1	1.9	2.2	2.5	2.6	2.7	2.6	2.6	2.6
of which mobilised:	SNES	..	..	..	..	..	–	0.1	–	0.1	0.8
Cadet Forces	ZBUR	135.9	135.7	133.9	134.7	133.1	132.0	132.9	136.4	142.1	143.3	155.6
Naval Service	ZBUS	27.1	26.7	26.5	26.9	26.3	25.9	24.5	24.1	23.8	23.8	23.2
Army	ZBUT	65.1	65.2	63.7	65.4	65.1	64.9	65.7	68.5	66.4	66.8	78.7
Royal Air Force	ZBUU	43.7	43.8	43.7	42.4	41.8	41.2	42.7	43.7	51.9	52.7	53.7

1 See chapter text.
2 Figures before 1997 do not include University Royal Navy Units.

Source: Ministry of Defence/DASA (Tri-Service): 020 7218 1546

4.6 UK Defence: civilian manpower strengths[1]
As at 1 April

Thousands: Full-time Equivalent

		1993	1994	1995	1996	1997	1998	1999	2000	2001	2002	2003
Ministry of Defence civilians												
Centre												
Non-industrial	KDQE	23.7	18.9	17.3	20.0	21.2	20.6	20.0	18.1	17.7	18.5	19.3
Industrial	KDQF	0.8	0.8	0.7	0.9	1.1	1.1	1.0	0.9	0.9	0.8	0.7
Defence Logistics Organisation												
Non-industrial	ZBTJ	..	..	..	..	..	..	..	19.0	17.0	16.5	16.2
Industrial	ZBTK	..	..	..	..	..	..	..	11.3	8.2	6.1	4.2
Naval Service												
Non-industrial	KYCW	15.5	15.8	15.2	13.7	12.6	12.2	11.6	3.6	3.5	3.6	3.6
Industrial	KYCX	14.1	13.0	12.0	9.7	9.0	8.0	6.8	2.7	2.6	2.3	2.2
Army												
Non-industrial	KDQK	22.0	22.5	22.1	21.4	20.7	20.5	20.3	15.4	15.5	14.9	15.7
Industrial	KDQL	15.1	14.9	14.5	13.7	13.2	11.8	10.3	5.7	5.6	5.4	5.3
Royal Air Force												
Non-industrial	KDQM	10.3	10.3	10.1	9.9	10.0	10.1	10.6	5.6	5.6	5.6	5.8
Industrial	KDQN	7.2	7.0	6.7	6.5	6.4	6.1	7.1	3.4	3.3	3.3	3.3
Procurement Executive												
Non-industrial	KDQO	16.4	15.3	15.1	–	–	–	–	–	–	–	–
Industrial	KDQP	4.1	3.1	2.5	–	–	–	–	–	–	–	–
Total UK based[2]	KDQB	129.2	121.6	116.1	109.9	109.2	104.0	100.9	100.3	80.0	77.1	76.7
Non-industrial	KDQC	87.9	82.8	79.8	77.1	77.9	75.7	74.5	75.2	59.4	59.1	60.9
Industrial	KDQD	41.3	38.8	36.3	32.7	31.3	28.3	26.4	25.1	20.6	18.0	15.8
Locally engaged overseas	KDQA	26.6	20.7	16.9	16.9	15.7	15.0	14.8	14.7	13.3	14.1	13.8
Non-industrial	KDQT	9.6	7.3	6.4	7.1	7.0	6.7	6.7	6.7	6.3	6.5	6.5
Industrial	KDQU	17.0	13.4	10.5	9.8	8.7	8.2	8.0	8.0	7.0	7.6	7.4
Total	KFHT	155.8	142.3	133.0	126.8	124.9	119.0	115.7	114.7	93.3	91.2	90.5
Trading funds	GQHI	..	..	..	14.0	15.1	13.6	13.0	14.2	18.4	12.2	12.0

1 See chapter text. Individuals on temporary and geographic (T&G) promotion are classed as non-industrial. The figures refer to personnel above the line.
2 From 2001 does not include trading funds.

Source: Ministry of Defence/DASA (Civilian): 020 7218 6019

4.7 Family accommodation and defence land holdings[1]
As at 1 April

			1993	1994	1995	1996	1997	1998	1999	2000	2001	2002	2003
Family accommodation													
United Kingdom: total	KDPA	Thousands	71.8	71.1	69.7	72.1	68.6	67.3	65.5	64.8	59.2	55.8	53.8
Land holdings		Thousand											
United Kingdom		hectares											
Land[2]	KDPF	"	224.1	223.5	221.0	222.6	221.0	220.0	220.2	219.9	224.3	222.4	221.4
Foreshore[2]	KDPH	"	18.4	18.5	18.4	18.5	18.6	18.6	18.6	18.6	18.6	18.6	18.6
Rights held	KDPJ	"	100.2	100.4	122.3	124.3	124.5	124.5	124.8	124.8	124.8	124.9	131.1
Defence land													
Used for agricultural purposes	KDPL	"	107.1	107.6	107.9	107.4	96.2	103.5	114.5	92.2	98.6	91.8	103.0
Used for grazing only	KDPM	"	62.4	61.3	61.8	60.7	51.9	59.6	65.5	50.3	66.6	60.0	70.2
Full agricultural use	KDPN	"	44.6	46.3	46.1	46.7	44.3	43.9	49.0	41.9	32.0	31.8	32.8

1 See chapter text.
2 Freehold and leasehold.

Sources: Ministry of Defence/Defence Housing Executive: 020 7305 3051;
Ministry of Defence/Defence Estates: 0121 311 3818

4.8 Deployment of UK service personnel[1]
As at 1 July

Thousands

		1993	1994	1995	1996	1997	1998	1999	2000	2001	2002	2003
UK Service personnel, Regular Forces:												
UK distribution[2]												
In United Kingdom[3,4]	KDOB	204.3	192.1	182.2	177.4	171.6	173.4	171.7	170.3	172.0	..	..
England	KDOC	167.1	156.5	149.4	146.6	142.6	144.6	144.3	143.0	144.1	..	..
Wales	KDOD	5.1	4.8	5.2	4.3	3.3	3.2	3.3	3.2	2.6	..	..
Scotland	KDOE	19.4	18.4	16.9	15.5	13.9	14.2	14.9	15.1	14.5	..	..
Northern Ireland	KDOF	12.5	12.3	9.9	10.5	11.5	11.0	9.0	8.4	9.4	..	..
Global deployment[2]												
United Kingdom[3]	MKCN	205.4	193.6	180.7	172.0	167.5	165.0	161.0	163.1	162.8	..	..
Overseas	KDOG	65.5	56.2	50.0	48.5	42.6	43.1	47.1	43.0	40.9	..	..
Mainland European States[5]	KDOI	–	–	–	11.7	6.2	6.9	15.2	8.2	8.6	..	..
Germany[6,7]	KDOH	45.6	37.2	33.4	20.8	21.2	20.3	18.0	19.5	17.3	..	..
Balkans	MKCO	..	..	..	..	..	..	..	..		..	..
Mediterranean[8]	KDOM	2.8	2.4	0.6	0.5	0.3	1.2	1.3	1.1	2.3	..	..
Gibraltar	KDOJ	1.3	1.5	0.6	0.6	0.5	0.5	0.6	0.6	0.5	..	..
Cyprus	KDOL	4.7	4.1	4.4	4.0	3.9	3.6	3.6	3.5	3.5	..	..
Far East/Asia[9]	MKCT	2.2	2.0	1.2	1.2	1.5	0.3	0.3	1.0	0.3	..	..
Africa	MKCP	..	..	..	..	..	..	..	..	–	..	..
North America	MKCQ	..	..	..	..	..	..	..	..	2.5	..	..
Central/South America	MKCR	..	..	..	..	..	..	..	..	–	..	..
Falkland Islands	MKCS	..	..	..	..	..	..	..	..	0.8	..	..
Other locations, including unallocated	KDOQ	8.8	8.9	9.4	9.8	9.0	10.4	8.2	9.1	5.1	..	..
Locally entered service personnel:[10]												
United Kingdom	KDOS	1.4	1.5	1.8	1.7	2.1	2.1	2.0	2.1	2.3	2.6	2.6
Gibraltar	KDOT	0.2	0.2	0.2	0.2	0.2	0.4	0.4	0.3	0.4	0.4	0.4
Hong Kong	KDOV	4.4	3.7	1.8	1.6	0.7	..	..	..	..	..	..
Brunei	KDOW	0.8	0.7	0.9	0.7	1.0	0.9	0.8	0.8	0.8	0.8	0.8
India/Nepal	KDOX	1.2	0.2	0.5	0.7	0.9	0.5	0.5	0.5	0.4	0.3	0.4
Total	KDOK	7.9	7.1	5.1	4.9	4.7	4.0	3.7	3.7	3.9	4.2	4.1

1 See chapter text.
2 Data not available from 2002, because of concerns over the quality of source data. A review of data sources is being undertaken.
3 Figures for global deployment of service personnel are compiled using different methodologies to those for UK distribution. Comparison is therefore not possible between the two sets of UK personnel figures.
4 Includes personnel within the UK whose location is unknown on the 1st July.
5 Includes the Balkans until 2001.

6 Prior to 1994, personnel serving in Northern Ireland on emergency tours of duty but remaining under the command of the Commander-in-Chief, British Army of the Rhine, are included in these numbers. Personnel serving on emergency tours of duty in other overseas areas are included in the numbers for that area.
7 Prior to 1996, figures for the Federal Republic of Germany and Mainland European States were combined.
8 Includes Med Near East and Middle East
9 Prior to 1997 figures include personnel serving in Hong Kong.
10 Including Gurkhas.

Source: Ministry of Defence/DASA (Tri-Service): 020 7218 0390

4.9 UK regular forces - deaths[1]

		1993	1994	1995	1996	1997	1998	1999	2000	2001	2002
Deaths											
Total Number	SNIA	238	216	201	142	160	162	139	148	140	144
Male	SNIB	227	209	192	140	151	154	136	144	137	135
Female	SNIC	11	7	9	2	9	8	3	4	3	9
Rates per thousand											
Tri-service	SNIH	0.90	0.89	0.93	0.64	0.79	0.77	0.67	0.72	0.68	0.70
Navy	SNII	0.83	0.70	0.56	0.63	0.86	0.62	0.61	0.62	0.79	0.66
Army[2]	SNIJ	0.95	0.11	0.98	0.73	0.90	0.85	0.72	0.81	0.71	0.86
RAF	SNIK	0.91	0.61	0.82	0.44	0.49	0.64	0.49	0.62	0.48	0.44

1 See chapter text.
2 Excludes Gurkhas.

Source: Ministry of Defence/DASA (Health Statistics): 01225 468008

4.10 Strength of uniformed UK medical staff[1]
As at 1 April

Numbers

		1993	1994	1995	1996	1997	1998	1999	2000	2001	2002	2003
Qualified doctors:												
Naval Service	KDMA	270	270	260	240	210	210	210	210	220	220	230
Army	KDMB	520	490	470	430	430	440	450	460	470	480	550
Royal Air Force	KDMC	370	360	330	270	220	210	200	180	180	180	180
All Services	KDMD	1 160	1 120	1 070	940	870	850	860	860	870	890	970
Qualified dentists:												
Naval Service	KDME	80	80	70	60	60	60	60	60	60	60	60
Army	KDMF	180	170	150	140	140	140	140	140	150	140	150
Royal Air Force	KDMG	120	120	110	100	90	80	80	80	80	80	80
All Services	KDMH	370	360	340	310	290	280	290	280	290	280	280
Support staff:[2]												
Naval Service	KDMI	1 360	1 400	1 410	1 290	1 020	950	1 060	1 080	1 030	1 110	1 170
Nursing services	ZBTL	..	..	..	..	..	..	220	190	200	240	280
Support	ZBTM	..	..	..	..	..	..	850	880	830	860	890
Army	KDMJ	4 290	3 760	3 460	3 280	3 020	3 090	3 100	3 150	3 170	3 320	3 410
Nursing services	ZBTN	..	..	..	..	..	..	510	510	520	650	710
Support	ZBTO	..	..	..	..	..	..	2 600	2 640	2 650	2 670	2 700
Royal Air Force	KDMK	2 040	1 840	1 800	1 400	1 210	1 190	1 360	1 460	1 480	1 500	1 590
Nursing services	ZBTP	..	..	..	..	..	..	330	400	420	450	470
Support	ZBTQ	..	..	..	..	..	..	1 030	1 060	1 070	1 050	1 130
All Services	KDML	7 690	7 000	6 660	5 980	5 260	5 230	5 520	5 680	5 680	5 930	6 180

1 See chapter text. Includes staff employed at units (including ships) and in hospitals.
2 Includes all members of the Nursing Services/Nursing Corps. From 1999, figures for support staff have been split so that nurses are separate from other support staff.

Source: Ministry of Defence/DASA (Tri- Service): 020 7218 0390

4.11 UK Defence services and the civilian community[1]

Numbers

		1992	1993	1994	1995	1996	1997	1998	1999	2000	2001	2002
Search and rescue operations at home												
Call outs	GPYC	2 305	2 145	2 017	2 297	2 164	1 941	1 898	1 914	1 941	1 763	1 685
of Royal Navy helicopters	GPXO	544	606	560	665	512	495	463	499	499	502	436
of Royal Air Force helicopters	GPXP	1 475	1 260	1 215	1 392	1 392	1 258	1 257	1 237	1 278	1 115	1 123
of Contractorised and other helicopters	GPXQ	91	47	26	24	27	16	20	–	–	–	–
of Royal Air Force Nimrod aircraft	GPXR	64	73	74	78	69	79	71	65	71	54	46
of other fixed wing aircraft[2]	GPXS	1	2	3	6	1	2	2	–	1	1	1
of HM ships and auxilliary vessels[2]	KCMG	5	8	6	7	1	3	3	–	–	–	–
of Royal Air Force mountain rescue teams	KCMH	125	149	133	125	162	88	82	113	92	91	79
Persons rescued: total	KCMI	1 431	1 508	1 391	1 445	1 598	1 258	1 245	1 163	1 297	1 181	1 213
By rescue service												
Royal Navy helicopters	GPXT	318	406	369	424	371	358	285	343	348	390	311
Royal Air Force helicopters	GPXU	1 015	952	893	957	1 116	878	937	800	925	776	892
Royal Air Force mountain rescue teams	GPXV	23	97	49	44	101	16	12	20	24	15	10
Other	GPXW	75	53	80	20	10	6	11	–	–	–	–
By type of rescue												
Rescue	GPXX	365	479	464	275	307	219	317	302	272	281	342
Medrescue	GPXY	793	764	766	825	919	710	667	621	703	621	648
Medivac	GPXZ	193	194	123	220	275	224	209	201	236	226	199
Recovery	GPYA	29	32	25	44	38	54	43	31	29	36	20
Other	GPYB	51	39	13	81	59	51	9	8	57	17	4
Search and rescue incidents: Total	KCMM	2 035	1 892	1 791	2 036	1 919	1 750	1 697	1 715	1 781	1 608	1 543
Fishery protection												
Vessels boarded	KCMO	2 465	2 540	2 080	1 878	2 224	1 758	1 829	1 777	1 658	1 531	1 274

1 See chapter text.
2 Not permanently on stand-by.

Source: Ministry of Defence/DASA (Logistics): 01225 468769/467249

5 Population and vital statistics

Population and vital statistics

This section begins with a summary of population figures for the United Kingdom and constituent countries for 1851 to 2026 and for Great Britain from 1801 (Table 5.1). Table 5.2 analyses the components of population change. Table 5.3 gives details of the national sex and age structures for years up to the present date, with projected figures up to the year 2026. Legal marital condition of the population is shown in Table 5.4. The distribution of population at regional and local levels is summarised in Table 5.5.

In the main, historical series relate to census information, while mid-year estimates, which make allowance for under-enumeration in the census, are given for the recent past and the present (from 1961 onwards).

Population (Tables 5.1 - 5.3)

Figures shown in these tables relate to the population enumerated at successive censuses, (up to 1951), mid-year estimates (from 1961 to 2002) and population projections (up to 2026). The population estimates for 2001 and 2002 are based on the 2001 Census and include provisional results from the Manchester matching exercise, released on 4 November 2003. Population estimates for 1992 to 2000, at a national level (for the UK, Great Britain, England and Wales), are interim revised population estimates. They are subject to revision in Spring 2004. Further information can be found on the National Statistics website (*www.statistics.gov.uk/popest*)

Definition of resident population
The estimated population of an area includes all those usually resident in the area, whatever their nationality. HM Forces serving abroad are excluded from, but non-UK Armed Forces stationed here are included within the estimates of resident population. Students are taken to be resident at their term-time addresses.

The projections of the resident population of the United Kingdom and constituent countries are prepared by the Government Actuary, in consultation with the Registrars General, as a common framework for use in national planning in a number of different fields. New projections are made every second year on assumptions regarding future fertility, mortality and migration which seem most appropriate on the basis of the statistical evidence available at the time. The population projections in Tables 5.1 - 5.3 are based on the estimates of the population of the United Kingdom at mid-2001 made by the Registrars General.

Marital condition (de jure): estimated population (Table 5.4)

This table shows population estimates by marital status. The mid-1991 marital status estimates for England and Wales have not been revised in light of results of the 2001 census; the final revised series 1982 to 2000 will be available in Spring 2004. The 2001 marital status estimates for England and Wales are based on the 2001 Census and include provisional results from the Manchester matching exercise.

Geographical distribution of the population (Table 5.5)

The population enumerated in the censuses for 1911-1951, and the mid-year population estimates for later years, are provided for standard regions of the United Kingdom, for metropolitan areas, for broad groupings of local authority districts by type within England and Wales, and for some of the larger cities. Projections of future sub-national population levels are prepared from time to time by the Registrar General, but are not shown in this publication.

Migration into and out of the United Kingdom (Tables 5.7 - 5.9)

A migrant is defined as a person who changes his or her country of usual residence for a period of at least a year, so that the country of destination effectively becomes the country of usual residence.

The main source of international migration data is the International Passenger Survey (IPS). This is a continuous voluntary sample survey that provides information on passengers entering and leaving the UK by the principal air, sea and tunnel routes. Being a sample survey, the IPS is subject to some uncertainty; therefore it should be noted that international migration estimates, in particular the difference between inflow and outflow, may be subject to large sampling errors. The IPS excludes routes between the Channel Islands and Isle of Man and the rest of the world.

The IPS data are supplemented with three types of additional information in order to provide a full picture of total international migration:

1. The IPS is based on intentions to migrate and intentions are liable to change. Adjustments are made for visitor switchers (those who intend to stay in the UK or abroad for less than one year but subsequently stay for longer and become migrants) and for migrant switchers (those who intend to stay in the UK or abroad for one year or more but then return earlier so are no longer migrants). These adjustments are primarily based on IPS data but for years prior to 2001, Home Office data on short-term visitors who were subsequently granted an extension of stay for a year or longer for other reasons have been incorporated.

2. Home Office data on applications for asylum and dependants of asylum seekers entering the UK are used to estimate inflows of asylum seekers and dependants not already captured by the IPS. In addition, Home Office data on removals and refusals are used to estimate outflows of failed asylum seekers not identified by the IPS.

3. Migration flows between the UK and the Irish Republic are added to these data, as the IPS did not cover this route until recently and the quality of these data are still being assessed. Migration flows are obtained mainly from the Quarterly National Household Survey and are agreed between the Irish Central Statistics Office and ONS.

The international migration estimates in Table 5.7 are derived from all these sources and represent total international migration. The estimates in Tables 5.8 and 5.9 are based on the International Passenger Survey only (without the three adjustments outlined above).

Acceptances for settlement in the United Kingdom (Table 5.10)
This table presents in geographic regions, the statistics of individual nationalities, arranged alphabetically within each region. The figures are on a different basis from those derived from IPS (Tables 5.8 and 5.9) and relate only to people subject to immigration control. Persons accepted for settlement are allowed to stay indefinitely in the United Kingdom. They exclude temporary migrants such as students and generally relate only to non-EEA nationals. Settlement can occur several years after entry to the country.

Applications received for asylum in the United Kingdom, excluding dependants (Table 5.11)
This table shows statistics of applications for asylum in the United Kingdom. Figures are shown for the main applicant nationalities by geographic region. The basis of assessing asylum applications, and hence of deciding whether to grant asylum in the United Kingdom, is the 1951 United Nations Convention on Refugees.

Marriages (Table 5.12)
The figures in this table relate to marriages solemnised in the constituent countries of the UK. They take no account of the growing trend towards marrying abroad.

Divorces (Tables 5.13 and 5.14)
A marriage may be either *dissolved* following a petition for divorce and the granting of a decree absolute, or *annulled*, following a petition for nullity and the awarding of a decree of nullity. The first group of decrees are known as dissolutions of marriage and the second as annulments of marriage. In Table 5.13 the term 'divorce' includes *both* types of decrees, although strictly speaking, it should refer only to dissolutions.

Births (Tables 5.15 –5.17)
For Scotland and Northern Ireland the number of births relate to those registered during the year. For England and Wales the figures up to and including 1930-32 are for those **registered,** while later figures relate to births **occurring** in each year.

All data for England and Wales and for Scotland include births occurring in those countries to mothers not usually resident in them. Data for Northern Ireland, and hence UK, prior to 1981 include births occurring in Northern Ireland to non-resident mothers; from 1981, such births are excluded.

Deaths (Tables 5.19 and 5.21)
The figures relate to the number of deaths registered during each calendar year. However, from 1993 onwards, the figures for England and Wales represent occurrences. This change has little effect on annual totals.

Infant and maternal mortality (Table 5.20)
On 1 October 1992 the legal definition of a stillbirth was altered from baby born dead after 28 completed weeks gestation or more, to one born after 24 completed weeks of gestation or more. The 258 stillbirths of 24 to 27 weeks gestation which occurred between 1 October and 31 December 1992 are excluded from this table.

Life tables (Table 5.22)
The interim life tables are constructed from the estimated populations in 2000-2002 and the births and deaths occurring in those years for England and Wales and registered in those years for Scotland and Northern Ireland.

The population estimates used in these interim life tables are the estimates, or revised estimates, following the 2001 Census issued on the following dates:

Mid-year population estimates

	2000	2001	2002
England	October 2003	November 2003	November 2003
Wales	October 2003	September 2003	September 2003
Scotland	February 2003	September 2002	June 2003
Northern Ireland	October 2002	September 2002	August 2003

Adoptions (Table 5.23)
The figures shown within this table relate to the date the adoption was entered in the Adopted Children Register. Figures based on the date of court order are available for England and Wales from the volume *Marriage, divorce and adoption statistics 2000* (no. 28 in the FM2 series) available on the National Statistics website *www.statistics.gov.uk* or from the enquiry point in the ONS shown at the foot of the table.

5.1 Population summary

Thousands

	United Kingdom[1]			England and Wales[1]			Wales[1]	Scotland			Northern Ireland		
	Persons	Males	Females	Persons	Males	Females	Persons	Persons	Males	Females	Persons	Males	Females
Enumerated population: Census figures													
1801	..	..	..	8 893	4 255	4 638	587	1 608	739	869	..	..	..
1851	22 259	10 855	11 404	17 928	8 781	9 146	1 163	2 889	1 376	1 513	1 442	698	745
1901	38 237	18 492	19 745	32 528	15 729	16 799	2 013	4 472	2 174	2 298	1 237	590	647
1911	42 082	20 357	21 725	36 070	17 446	18 625	2 421	4 761	2 309	2 452	1 251	603	648
1921[2]	44 027	21 033	22 994	37 887	18 075	19 811	2 656	4 882	2 348	2 535	1 258	610	648
1931[2]	46 038	22 060	23 978	39 952	19 133	20 819	2 593	4 843	2 326	2 517	1 243	601	642
1951	50 225	24 118	26 107	43 758	21 016	22 742	2 599	5 096	2 434	2 662	1 371	668	703
1961	52 709	25 481	27 228	46 105	22 304	23 801	2 644	5 179	2 483	2 697	1 425	694	731
Resident population: mid-year estimates													
	DYAY	BBAB	BBAC	BBAD	BBAE	BBAF	KGJM	BBAG	BBAH	BBAI	BBAJ	BBAK	BBAL
1967	54 959	26 673	28 286	48 272	23 451	24 821	2 710	5 198	2 496	2 702	1 489	726	763
1968	55 214	26 784	28 429	48 511	23 554	24 957	2 715	5 200	2 498	2 702	1 503	733	770
1969	55 461	26 908	28 553	48 738	23 666	25 072	2 722	5 209	2 503	2 706	1 514	739	776
1970	55 632	26 992	28 641	48 891	23 738	25 153	2 729	5 214	2 507	2 707	1 527	747	781
1971	55 928	27 167	28 761	49 152	23 897	25 255	2 740	5 236	2 516	2 720	1 540	755	786
1972	56 097	27 259	28 837	49 327	23 989	25 339	2 755	5 231	2 513	2 717	1 539	758	782
1973	56 223	27 332	28 891	49 459	24 061	25 399	2 773	5 234	2 515	2 719	1 530	756	774
1974	56 236	27 349	28 887	49 468	24 075	25 393	2 785	5 241	2 519	2 722	1 527	755	772
1975	56 226	27 361	28 865	49 470	24 091	25 378	2 795	5 232	2 516	2 716	1 524	753	770
1976	56 216	27 360	28 856	49 459	24 089	25 370	2 799	5 233	2 517	2 716	1 524	754	770
1977	56 190	27 345	28 845	49 440	24 076	25 364	2 801	5 226	2 515	2 711	1 523	754	769
1978	56 178	27 330	28 849	49 443	24 067	25 375	2 804	5 212	2 509	2 704	1 523	754	770
1979	56 240	27 373	28 867	49 508	24 113	25 395	2 810	5 204	2 505	2 699	1 528	755	773
1980	56 330	27 411	28 919	49 603	24 156	25 448	2 816	5 194	2 501	2 693	1 533	755	778
1981	56 357	27 412	28 946	49 634	24 160	25 474	2 813	5 180	2 495	2 685	1 543	757	786
1982	56 291	27 364	28 927	49 582	24 119	25 462	2 804	5 165	2 487	2 677	1 545	757	788
1983	56 316	27 371	28 944	49 617	24 133	25 484	2 803	5 148	2 479	2 669	1 551	759	792
1984	56 409	27 421	28 989	49 713	24 185	25 528	2 801	5 139	2 475	2 664	1 557	761	796
1985	56 554	27 489	29 065	49 861	24 254	25 606	2 803	5 128	2 470	2 658	1 565	765	800
1986	56 684	27 542	29 142	49 999	24 311	25 687	2 811	5 112	2 462	2 649	1 574	768	805
1987	56 804	27 599	29 205	50 123	24 371	25 752	2 823	5 099	2 455	2 644	1 582	773	809
1988	56 916	27 652	29 265	50 254	24 434	25 820	2 841	5 077	2 444	2 633	1 585	774	812
1989	57 076	27 729	29 348	50 408	24 510	25 898	2 855	5 078	2 443	2 635	1 590	776	814
1990	57 237	27 819	29 419	50 561	24 597	25 964	2 862	5 081	2 444	2 637	1 596	778	818
1991	57 439	27 909	29 530	50 748	24 681	26 067	2 873	5 083	2 445	2 639	1 607	783	824
1992	57 582	27 979	29 604	50 873	24 741	26 132	2 877	5 086	2 445	2 640	1 623	792	831
1993	57 711	28 043	29 668	50 983	24 797	26 186	2 882	5 092	2 448	2 644	1 636	798	837
1994	57 855	28 112	29 743	51 109	24 857	26 253	2 886	5 102	2 453	2 649	1 644	802	842
1995	58 005	28 197	29 808	51 252	24 940	26 312	2 887	5 104	2 453	2 650	1 649	804	845
1996	58 139	28 275	29 864	51 385	25 018	26 367	2 889	5 092	2 447	2 645	1 662	810	851
1997	58 283	28 356	29 927	51 528	25 098	26 430	2 892	5 083	2 442	2 641	1 671	816	856
1998	58 440	28 441	29 999	51 685	25 184	26 502	2 896	5 077	2 439	2 638	1 678	819	859
1999	58 635	28 556	30 079	51 884	25 301	26 583	2 897	5 072	2 437	2 635	1 679	818	861
2000	58 817	28 659	30 157	52 071	25 407	26 664	2 904	5 063	2 432	2 631	1 683	820	862
2001[3]	59 051	28 810	30 241	52 297	25 551	26 746	2 908	5 064	2 434	2 630	1 689	824	865
2002[3]	59 229	28 911	30 318	52 478	25 651	26 827	2 919	5 055	2 432	2 623	1 697	829	868
Resident population: projections (mid-year)[4]													
2006	59 995	29 329	30 666	53 252	26 071	27 181	2 942	5 022	2 417	2 605	1 720	841	880
2011	61 022	29 853	31 169	54 287	26 600	27 687	2 971	4 984	2 398	2 586	1 751	855	896
2021	63 239	30 897	32 342	56 517	27 661	28 856	3 038	4 911	2 354	2 557	1 811	882	929
2026	64 178	31 297	32 880	57 492	28 088	29 404	3 060	4 854	2 319	2 535	1 831	890	941

1 Mid-1992 to mid-2000 population estimates for the UK, England and Wales are interim revised population estimates. They are subject to revision in Spring 2004.
2 Figures for Northern Ireland are estimated. The population at the Census of 1926 was 1 257 thousand (608 thousand males and 649 thousand females).
3 Mid-2001 and mid-2002 estimates for the UK and England include provisional results from the Manchester matching exercise.
4 These projections are 2002-based. See chapter text for more detail.

Sources: Office for National Statistics: 01329 813233;
General Register Office for Scotland;
Northern Ireland Statistics and Research Agency;
Government Actuary's Department: 020 7211 2622

5.2 Population changes

Thousands

	Population[1] at start of period	Average annual change				
		Overall annual change	Births	Deaths[2]	Natural change	Net migration and other changes
United Kingdom						
1901 - 1911	38 237	385	1 091	624	467	-82
1911 - 1921	42 082	195	975	689	286	-92
1921 - 1931	44 027	201	824	555	268	-67
1931 - 1951	46 038	213	793	603	190	22
1951 - 1961	50 225	258	839	593	246	12
1961 - 1971	52 807	312	962	638	324	-12
1971 - 1981	55 928	42	736	666	69	-27
1981 - 1991	56 357	108	757	655	103	5
1991 - 2001	57 439	161	731	631	100	61
2001 - 2002[3]	59 051	178	663	601	62	116
2011 - 2021	61 022	222	703	584	119	103
England and Wales						
1901 - 1911	32 528	354	929	525	404	-50
1911 - 1921	36 070	182	828	584	244	-62
1921 - 1931	37 887	207	693	469	224	-17
1931 - 1951	39 952	193	673	518	155	38
1951 - 1961	43 758	244	714	516	197	47
1961 - 1971	46 196	296	832	560	272	23
1971 - 1981	49 152	48	638	585	53	-5
1981 - 1991	49 634	111	664	576	89	23
1991 - 2001	50 748	155	647	556	92	63
2001 - 2002[3]	52 297	180	591	530	61	119
2011 - 2021	54 287	223	633	515	118	105
Scotland						
1901 - 1911	4 472	29	131	76	54	-25
1911 - 1921	4 761	12	118	82	36	-24
1921 - 1931	4 882	-4	100	65	35	-39
1931 - 1951	4 843	13	92	67	25	-12
1951 - 1961	5 096	9	95	62	34	-25
1961 - 1971	5 184	5	97	63	34	-30
1971 - 1981	5 236	-6	70	64	6	-11
1981 - 1991	5 180	-7	66	63	3	-10
1991 - 2001	5 083	-2	60	60	-1	-1
2001 - 2002	5 064	-9	51	57	-6	-3
2011 - 2021	4 984	-7	49	54	-6	-2
Northern Ireland						
1901 - 1911	1 237	1	31	23	8	-6
1911 - 1921	1 251	1	29	22	7	-6
1921 - 1931	1 258	-2	30	21	9	-11
1931 - 1951	1 243	6	28	18	10	-4
1951 - 1961	1 371	6	30	15	15	-9
1961 - 1971	1 427	11	33	16	17	-6
1971 - 1981	1 540	-	28	17	11	-11
1981 - 1991	1 543	6	27	16	12	-5
1991 - 2001	1 607	8	24	15	9	-
2001 - 2002	1 689	7	21	14	7	-
2011 - 2021	1 751	6	22	15	7	-1

1 Census enumerated population up to 1951; mid-year estimates of resident population from 1961 to 2001 and mid-2002-based projections of resident population thereafter.

2 Including deaths of non-civilians and merchant seamen who died outside the country. These numbered 577 000 in 1911-1921 and 240 000 in 1931-1951 for England and Wales; 74 000 in 1911-1921 and 34 000 in 1931-1951 for Scotland; and 10 000 in 1911-1926 for Northern Ireland.

3 Mid-2001 and mid-2002 population estimates for the UK and England & Wales include provisional results from the Manchester matching exercise.

Sources: Government Actuary's Department: 020 7211 2622;
Office for National Statistics: 01329 813233;
General Register Office for Scotland;
Northern Ireland Statistics and Research Agency

5.3 Age distribution of the resident population

Thousands

		Population enumerated in Census			Estimated mid-year resident population						Projected mid-year resident population[1]				
		1901	1931	1951	1961	1971	1981	1991	2001[2]	2002[2]	2006	2011	2016	2021	2026
Persons: All ages	KGUA	38 237	46 038	50 225	52 807	55 928	56 357	57 439	59 051	59 229	59 995	61 022	62 134	63 239	64 178
Under 1[3]	KGUK	938	712	773	4 274	899	730	790	662	660	679	686	702	708	696
1 - 4	KABA	3 443	2 818	3 553		3 654	2 726	3 077	2 816	2 747	2 698	2 720	2 773	2 826	2 811
5 - 9	KGUN	4 106	3 897	3 689	3 819	4 684	3 677	3 657	3 731	3 680	3 479	3 377	3 407	3 476	3 535
10 - 14	KGUO	3 934	3 746	3 310	4 267	4 232	4 470	3 485	3 886	3 906	3 727	3 474	3 372	3 402	3 471
15 - 19	KGUP	3 826	3 989	3 175	3 748	3 862	4 735	3 719	3 673	3 752	3 932	3 769	3 517	3 415	3 445
20 - 29	KABB	6 982	7 865	7 154	6 570	7 968	8 113	9 138	7 486	7 388	7 588	8 123	8 213	7 801	7 451
30 - 44	KABC	7 493	9 717	11 125	10 529	9 797	10 956	12 125	13 396	13 476	13 192	12 377	11 927	12 282	12 657
45 - 59	KABD	4 639	7 979	9 558	10 605	10 202	9 540	9 500	11 157	11 301	11 736	12 219	12 943	12 738	11 965
60 - 64	KGUY	1 067	1 897	2 422	2 788	3 222	2 935	2 888	2 881	2 888	3 258	3 768	3 474	3 854	4 257
65 - 74	KBCP	1 278	2 461	3 689	3 977	4 764	5 195	5 067	4 942	4 965	5 063	5 578	6 435	6 634	6 773
75 - 84	KBCU	470	844	1 555	1 885	2 159	2 677	3 119	3 291	3 341	3 415	3 521	3 786	4 300	5 032
85 and over	KGVD	61	113	224	346	485	603	873	1 129	1 124	1 229	1 409	1 585	1 803	2 087
School ages (5-15)	KBWU	..	..	7 649	..	9 704	9 086	7 818	8 372	8 352	8 001	7 575	7 442	7 557	7 693
Under 18	KGUD	–	..	13 248	..	15 798	14 472	13 120	13 343	13 285	12 938	12 459	12 300	12 458	12 570
Pensionable ages[4]	KFIA	2 387	4 421	6 828	7 747	9 123	10 035	10 557	10 833	10 905	11 372	12 205	12 450	12 737	13 892
Males: All ages	KGWA	18 492	22 060	24 118	25 528	27 167	27 412	27 909	28 810	28 911	29 329	29 853	30 392	30 897	31 297
Under 1[3]	KGWK	471	361	397	2 194	461	374	403	338	338	347	351	359	362	356
1 - 4	KBCV	1 719	1 423	1 818		1 874	1 400	1 572	1 443	1 406	1 380	1 392	1 419	1 446	1 438
5 - 9	KGWN	2 052	1 967	1 885	1 956	2 401	1 889	1 871	1 911	1 885	1 777	1 723	1 739	1 774	1 804
10 - 14	KGWO	1 972	1 892	1 681	2 185	2 175	2 295	1 784	1 991	2 002	1 908	1 772	1 719	1 734	1 770
15 - 19	KGWP	1 898	1 987	1 564	1 897	1 976	2 424	1 905	1 877	1 926	2 016	1 929	1 794	1 741	1 756
20 - 29	KBCW	3 293	3 818	3 509	3 288	4 024	4 103	4 578	3 739	3 685	3 787	4 079	4 123	3 903	3 717
30 - 44	KBCX	3 597	4 495	5 461	5 237	4 938	5 513	6 045	6 646	6 681	6 527	6 093	5 855	6 026	6 233
45 - 59	KBUU	2 215	3 753	4 493	5 137	4 970	4 711	4 732	5 530	5 597	5 803	6 018	6 363	6 244	5 835
60 - 64	KGWY	490	894	1 061	1 250	1 507	1 376	1 390	1 410	1 413	1 592	1 838	1 693	1 881	2 059
65 - 74	KBWL	565	1 099	1 560	1 605	1 999	2 264	2 272	2 305	2 325	2 405	2 667	3 078	3 171	3 247
75 - 84	KBWM	196	335	617	675	716	922	1 146	1 307	1 337	1 413	1 523	1 685	1 935	2 273
85 and over	KGXD	23	36	70	105	126	141	212	312	315	374	468	566	680	809
School ages (5-15)	KBWV	–	..	3 895	..	4 982	4 666	4 001	4 290	4 280	4 093	3 866	3 795	3 855	3 925
Under 18	KGWD	–	..	6 753	..	8 108	7 430	6 711	6 838	6 809	6 622	6 367	6 281	6 361	6 419
Pensionable ages[4]	KFIB	785	1 471	2 247	2 385	2 841	3 327	3 630	3 924	3 977	4 192	4 658	5 329	5 785	6 329
Females: All ages	KGYA	19 745	23 978	26 107	27 279	28 761	28 946	29 530	30 241	30 318	30 666	31 169	31 742	32 342	32 880
Under 1[3]	KGYK	466	351	376	2 079	437	356	387	324	322	331	335	342	345	339
1 - 4	KBWN	1 724	1 397	1 735		1 779	1 327	1 505	1 373	1 341	1 317	1 328	1 354	1 380	1 372
5 - 9	KGYN	2 054	1 930	1 804	1 863	2 283	1 788	1 786	1 819	1 795	1 703	1 654	1 668	1 702	1 730
10 - 14	KGYO	1 962	1 854	1 629	2 083	2 057	2 175	1 701	1 895	1 903	1 819	1 702	1 653	1 668	1 701
15 - 19	KGYP	1 928	2 002	1 611	1 851	1 887	2 311	1 815	1 796	1 826	1 917	1 840	1 723	1 675	1 689
20 - 29	KBWO	3 690	4 047	3 644	3 282	3 945	4 009	4 560	3 746	3 703	3 801	4 044	4 090	3 898	3 733
30 - 44	KBWP	3 895	5 222	5 663	5 292	4 859	5 442	6 080	6 751	6 795	6 665	6 285	6 072	6 257	6 424
45 - 59	KBWR	2 424	4 226	5 065	5 467	5 231	4 829	4 769	5 627	5 704	5 932	6 201	6 580	6 494	6 130
60 - 64	KGYY	577	1 003	1 361	1 539	1 715	1 559	1 498	1 471	1 475	1 665	1 931	1 782	1 973	2 198
65 - 74	KBWS	713	1 361	2 127	2 372	2 765	2 931	2 795	2 637	2 640	2 658	2 911	3 356	3 463	3 526
75 - 84	KBWT	274	509	937	1 210	1 443	1 756	1 972	1 985	2 004	2 002	1 998	2 101	2 365	2 759
85 and over	KGZD	38	77	154	241	359	462	661	816	810	855	941	1 019	1 123	1 278
School ages (5-15)	KBWW	–	..	3 753	..	4 722	4 421	3 817	4 083	4 072	3 908	3 709	3 647	3 702	3 768
Under 18	KGYD	–	..	6 495	..	7 690	7 042	6 409	6 505	6 475	.6 316	6 093	6 020	6 097	6 151
Pensionable ages[4]	KFIC	1 601	2 950	4 580	5 362	6 282	6 708	6 927	6 909	6 928	7 181	7 548	7 122	6 951	7 563

5.3 Age distribution of the resident population
continued

Thousands

		England							Wales					
		Estimated mid-year resident population				Projected population[1]			Estimated mid-year resident population				Projected population[1]	
		1981	1991	2001[2]	2002[2]	2011	2026		1981	1991	2001	2002	2011	2026
Persons: All ages	KCCI	46 821	47 875	49 390	49 559	51 315	54 432	KERY	2 813	2 873	2 908	2 919	2 971	3 060
Under 1	KCCJ	598	660	557	558	585	598	KFAC	36	38	32	30	32	31
1 - 4	KCCK	2 235	2 560	2 363	2 307	2 313	2 409	KFBX	136	153	136	132	128	128
5 - 9	KCCL	3 011	3 019	3 117	3 076	2 855	3 014	KFCA	185	186	185	183	161	168
10 - 14	KCCM	3 666	2 865	3 235	3 255	2 906	2 950	KFCB	222	177	196	197	176	171
15 - 19	KCCN	3 897	3 067	3 040	3 110	3 148	2 925	KFCC	233	187	185	190	191	170
20 - 29	KCEG	6 734	7 651	6 294	6 214	6 850	6 365	KFCD	381	415	336	333	377	336
30 - 44	KCEH	9 175	10 147	11 249	11 331	10 526	10 834	KFCE	536	583	608	610	535	557
45 - 59	KCEQ	7 948	7 920	9 316	9 433	10 197	10 158	KFCF	485	486	571	578	600	545
60 - 64	KCEW	2 449	2 399	2 393	2 395	3 145	3 560	KFCG	158	154	153	156	205	214
65 - 74	KCGD	4 347	4 222	4 108	4 127	4 651	5 635	KFCH	272	284	264	265	304	357
75 - 84	KCJG	2 249	2 626	2 760	2 800	2 946	4 227	KFCI	139	164	183	185	186	273
85 and over	KCKJ	511	739	958	954	1 192	1 757	KFCK	29	45	59	59	77	109
School ages (5-15)	KCWX	7 451	6 439	6 977	6 965	6 367	6 546	KFCL	453	397	419	419	374	373
Under 18	KCWY	11 871	10 840	11 133	11 093	10 501	10 719	KFCM	721	662	662	659	608	600
Pensionable ages [4]	KEAA	8 403	8 827	9 043	9 101	10 206	11 619	KFEB	525	573	584	588	659	739
Males: All ages	KEAB	22 795	23 291	24 144	24 240	25 165	26 621	KFEI	1 365	1 391	1 408	1 411	1 436	1 467
Under 1	KEAC	306	336	285	286	299	306	KFEJ	18	20	16	16	16	16
1 - 4	KEAD	1 147	1 307	1 211	1 180	1 184	1 233	KFEK	70	78	70	68	65	66
5 - 9	KEAE	1 547	1 545	1 597	1 575	1 457	1 539	KFEL	95	95	95	94	83	86
10 - 14	KEAF	1 883	1 467	1 656	1 668	1 482	1 504	KFFA	113	91	101	101	90	87
15 - 19	KECA	1 996	1 572	1 556	1 598	1 613	1 492	KFFN	119	95	94	97	98	87
20 - 29	KECB	3 404	3 835	3 150	3 104	3 437	3 171	KFHA	193	207	166	163	190	170
30 - 44	KECC	4 623	5 064	5 601	5 640	5 208	5 345	KFHB	270	289	297	296	250	266
45 - 59	KECD	3 938	3 957	4 620	4 676	5 039	4 988	KFHW	240	242	282	285	291	251
60 - 64	KECE	1 154	1 159	1 175	1 175	1 535	1 731	KFQO	73	74	75	77	100	102
65 - 74	KECF	1 902	1 900	1 925	1 942	2 230	2 712	KFQV	118	128	124	125	146	170
75 - 84	KECG	777	970	1 101	1 127	1 281	1 914	KFUK	48	60	73	74	81	124
85 and over	KECH	119	181	267	269	398	685	KFUL	7	11	16	16	25	43
School ages (5-15)	KECI	3 827	3 295	3 574	3 569	3 249	3 341	KFUV	232	204	215	215	192	191
Under 18	KECJ	6 096	5 545	5 705	5 686	5 367	5 476	KFVE	370	339	340	338	312	307
Pensionable ages[4]	KECK	2 798	3 050	3 293	3 337	3 910	5 310	KFVF	173	198	212	215	252	336
Females: All ages	KEJV	24 026	24 584	25 246	25 319	26 151	27 811	KFVL	1 448	1 482	1 500	1 508	1 536	1 593
Under 1	KEJW	292	324	273	272	285	292	KFYW	18	19	15	15	16	15
1 - 4	KEJX	1 088	1 253	1 153	1 126	1 129	1 176	KFZJ	66	75	66	65	63	63
5 - 9	KEKP	1 464	1 474	1 520	1 500	1 398	1 475	KGCK	90	91	90	89	79	82
10 - 14	KEKQ	1 783	1 399	1 578	1 586	1 424	1 445	KGCM	109	86	95	96	86	83
15 - 19	KEKR	1 901	1 495	1 484	1 512	1 536	1 433	KGCN	114	91	92	93	93	83
20 - 29	KEKS	3 330	3 816	3 145	3 110	3 414	3 194	KGCO	189	208	170	170	187	166
30 - 44	KENR	4 553	5 083	5 648	5 690	5 318	5 488	KGCP	265	294	311	314	285	290
45 - 59	KEOQ	4 009	3 964	4 696	4 758	5 158	5 170	KGGZ	246	244	289	293	309	295
60 - 64	KEOZ	1 295	1 239	1 218	1 220	1 610	1 829	KGIY	85	80	78	80	105	112
65 - 74	KEQJ	2 445	2 323	2 183	2 185	2 421	2 923	KGKR	154	156	141	140	158	187
75 - 84	KEQK	1 472	1 656	1 658	1 673	1 664	2 314	KGTQ	91	104	110	111	105	149
85 and over	KEQL	392	558	691	685	794	1 073	KGTZ	22	34	43	43	51	67
School ages (5-15)	KEQM	3 625	3 143	3 403	3 396	3 118	3 205	KGVG	221	194	204	204	182	182
Under 18	KEQN	5 775	5 295	5 428	5 407	5 134	5 243	KGVH	351	323	322	321	297	293
Pensionable ages[4]	KEQO	5 605	5 777	5 750	5 763	6 296	6 309	KGVK	352	375	372	374	406	403

5.3 Age distribution of the resident population

continued

Thousands

		Scotland							Northern Ireland					
		Estimated mid-year resident population				Projected population[1]			Estimated mid-year resident population				Projected population[1]	
		1981	1991	2001	2002	2011	2026		1981	1991	2001	2002	2011	2026
Persons: All ages	KGVP	5 180	5 083	5 064	5 055	4 984	4 854	KIOY	1 543	1 607	1 689	1 697	1 751	1 831
Under 1	KHAQ	69	66	52	51	48	46	KIOZ	27	26	22	22	21	20
1 - 4	KHCT	249	258	224	217	193	189	KIPA	106	106	93	91	85	84
5 - 9	KHDN	348	320	306	299	253	244	KIPN	133	131	123	122	108	109
10 - 14	KHDQ	433	313	323	323	276	242	KIPP	148	129	132	131	116	109
15 - 19	KHDT	459	337	318	319	307	244	KIPQ	146	128	130	132	123	106
20 - 29	KHDU	771	820	630	619	645	537	KIPR	227	253	225	222	251	212
30 - 44	KHDV	971	1 080	1 163	1 158	967	899	KIPS	273	315	376	378	349	367
45 - 59	KHFK	880	853	979	993	1 082	923	KIPT	227	241	290	296	342	338
60 - 64	KHOZ	260	265	262	262	325	363	KIPU	68	70	74	75	93	120
65 - 74	KHTU	460	441	447	449	477	592	KIPV	116	120	123	125	145	189
75 - 84	KHUO	232	259	272	276	302	406	KIPW	57	69	77	79	87	126
85 and over	KHUQ	49	70	89	88	109	170	KIPX	14	19	23	24	31	50
School ages (5-15)	KHVV	871	697	694	687	586	534	KIPY	311	285	282	281	248	240
Under 18	KIMT	1 377	1 150	1 098	1 086	947	864	KIQL	504	467	451	447	403	387
Pensionable ages [4]	KIMU	882	912	944	950	1 036	1 168	KIQM	224	246	262	266	305	365
Males: All ages	KIMV	2 495	2 445	2 434	2 432	2 398	2 319	KIQN	757	783	824	829	855	890
Under 1	KIMW	35	34	26	26	25	23	KIQO	14	13	11	11	11	10
1 - 4	KIMX	128	132	115	111	99	96	KIQP	54	54	48	47	43	43
5 - 9	KIMY	178	164	156	153	129	124	KIQQ	69	67	63	63	55	55
10 - 14	KIMZ	222	161	166	165	140	123	KIQR	76	66	68	67	59	55
15 - 19	KINA	234	171	161	163	156	123	KIQS	75	66	66	68	63	54
20 - 29	KINB	390	410	311	308	324	268	KIQT	117	127	113	111	128	108
30 - 44	KINC	483	535	563	560	465	440	KIQU	137	156	185	186	169	181
45 - 59	KIND	424	415	483	490	521	435	KIQV	109	118	144	147	167	160
60 - 64	KINE	118	124	125	125	157	169	KIQW	32	32	35	36	45	57
65 - 74	KINR	194	192	200	202	222	276	KIRJ	50	53	56	56	69	90
75 - 84	KINS	77	91	103	106	125	179	KIRK	21	26	30	31	36	56
85 and over	KINT	11	16	23	23	35	63	KIRL	4	5	6	6	10	19
School ages (5-15)	KINU	446	357	356	352	299	271	KIRM	160	146	145	144	127	122
Under 18	KINV	706	588	562	556	483	440	KIRN	259	239	231	229	206	197
Pensionable ages[4]	KINW	282	299	327	331	381	518	KIRO	75	83	92	94	115	165
Females: All ages	KINX	2 685	2 639	2 630	2 623	2 586	2 535	KIRP	786	824	865	868	896	941
Under 1	KINY	33	32	26	25	23	22	KIRQ	13	13	10	11	10	10
1 - 4	KINZ	121	126	109	106	94	92	KIRR	52	52	45	44	41	41
5 - 9	KIOA	170	157	149	146	124	120	KIRS	65	64	60	59	53	54
10 - 14	KIOB	211	153	157	157	135	119	KIRT	72	63	65	64	57	54
15 - 19	KIOC	225	166	156	156	151	121	KIRU	70	62	64	65	60	52
20 - 29	KIOO	381	411	319	311	320	270	KISH	110	126	113	111	123	104
30 - 44	KIOP	488	545	600	598	502	459	KISI	137	159	191	192	180	186
45 - 59	KIOQ	456	437	496	504	560	487	KISJ	118	123	146	149	174	178
60 - 64	KIOR	142	141	137	137	168	194	KISK	37	38	38	39	48	63
65 - 74	KIOS	265	249	246	247	255	317	KISL	66	67	68	68	77	99
75 - 84	KIOT	155	168	169	171	178	227	KISM	37	44	47	48	51	70
85 and over	KIOU	38	54	66	65	75	107	KISN	10	14	17	17	21	31
School ages (5-15)	KIOV	424	340	339	335	288	262	KISO	151	139	138	137	122	118
Under 18	KIOW	671	562	536	530	464	424	KISP	245	228	220	218	197	190
Pensionable ages[4]	KIOX	600	612	617	619	655	651	KISQ	150	163	170	173	191	200

1 2002-based projections are made as described in the chapter text.
2 Mid-2001 and mid-2002 population estimates for the UK and England include provisional results from the Manchester matching exercise.
3 1961 estimates are for ages 0 - 4.
4 The pensionable age population is that over state retirement age. The 2011 figures take account of planned changes in retirement age from 65 for men and 60 for women at present to 65 for both sexes. This change will be phased in between April 2010 and March 2020.

Sources: Office for National Statistics: 01329 813233; General Register Office for Scotland; Northern Ireland Statistics and Research Agency; Government Actuary's Department: 020 7211 2622

5.4 Marital condition (de jure): estimated population
England and Wales

Thousands

			Males					Females			
			1971	1981	1991[1]	2001		1971	1981	1991[1]	2001
All ages:											
	Single	KRPL	10 507	10 614	11 320	12 245	KUBS	9 584	9 424	9 829	10 897
	Married	KRPM	12 522	12 238	11 745	11 099	KVCC	12 566	12 284	11 838	11 138
	Widowed	KRPN	682	698	731	732	KVCD	2 810	2 939	2 978	2 741
	Divorced	KRPO	187	611	1 200	1 475	KVCE	296	828	1 459	1 970
Age groups:											
0 - 14:	Single	KRPP	5 984	5 181	4 991	5 030	KVCF	5 672	4 910	4 720	4 791
15 - 19:	Single	KRPQ	1 677	2 095	1 677	1 642	KVCG	1 491	1 923	1 554	1 558
	Married	KRPR	34	20	8	6	KVCH	142	93	32	16
	Widowed	KRPS	–	–	–	1	KVCI	–	–	–	1
	Divorced	KRPT	–	–	–	1	KVCJ	–	–	–	1
20 - 24:	Single	KRPU	1 211	1 420	1 764	1 483	KVCK	745	1 007	1 421	1 386
	Married	KRPV	689	466	249	74	KVCL	1 113	811	490	178
	Widowed	KRPW	–	1	–	1	KVCM	2	2	1	1
	Divorced	KRPX	3	10	12	3	KVCN	9	27	29	8
25 - 34:	Single	KRPY	637	906	1 718	2 239	KVCO	326	496	1 135	1 765
	Married	KRPZ	2 450	2 508	2 100	1 408	KVCP	2 635	2 791	2 488	1 765
	Widowed	KRQA	4	4	2	3	KVCQ	12	13	8	10
	Divorced	KRQB	38	151	245	136	KVCR	63	218	312	230
35 - 44:	Single	KRQC	317	316	482	955	KVEH	201	170	280	690
	Married	KRQD	2 513	2 519	2 658	2 492	KVEI	2 529	2 540	2 760	2 647
	Widowed	KRQE	13	12	12	12	KVEJ	48	41	34	36
	Divorced	KRQF	48	178	388	408	KVEK	66	222	444	557
45 - 54:	Single	KRQG	279	254	251	418	KVEL	248	169	144	255
	Married	KUAR	2 605	2 338	2 347	2 512	KVEM	2 570	2 292	2 322	2 545
	Widowed	KUBA	47	38	31	37	KVEN	187	150	118	110
	Divorced	KUBB	46	134	290	446	KVEO	69	158	332	556
55 - 59:	Single	KUBC	118	128	101	128	KVEP	148	108	69	73
	Married	KUBD	1 250	1 192	1 050	1 155	KVEQ	1 154	1 130	982	1 124
	Widowed	KUBE	49	46	34	34	KVER	213	186	136	112
	Divorced	KUBF	20	49	95	174	KVES	31	63	107	209
60 - 64:	Single	KUBG	105	98	104	96	KVET	174	109	80	62
	Married	KUBH	1 140	1 029	997	979	KVEU	985	936	908	905
	Widowed	KUBI	77	64	63	50	KVEV	332	284	250	178
	Divorced	KUBJ	16	35	70	125	KVEW	25	51	82	151
65 - 74:	Single	KUBK	132	149	150	155	KMGN	332	263	176	130
	Married	KUBL	1 407	1 594	1 574	1 567	KMGO	1 133	1 291	1 317	1 321
	Widowed	KUBM	226	234	229	188	KMGP	959	978	879	696
	Divorced	KUBN	14	43	74	139	KMGQ	26	68	107	177
75 and over:	Single	KUBO	47	67	81	98	KMGR	249	270	250	187
	Married	KUBP	434	573	763	908	KMGS	304	401	541	638
	Widowed	KUBQ	266	300	360	406	KMGT	1 056	1 285	1 554	1 596
	Divorced	KUBR	3	11	25	44	KMGU	6	23	46	81

1 Mid-1991 population estimates by marital status are subject to revision.
These revisions will be available in Spring 2004.

Source: Office for National Statistics: 01329 813233

5.5 Geographical distribution of the population

Thousands

		Population enumerated in Census			Mid-year population estimates					
		1911	1931	1951	1961	1971	1981	1991	2001[1]	2002[1]
United Kingdom	KIUR	42 082	46 074	50 225	52 807	55 928	56 357	57 439	59 051	59 229
Great Britain	KISR	40 831	44 795	48 854	51 380	54 388	54 815	55 831	57 362	57 532
England	KKOJ	33 650	37 359	41 159	43 561	46 412	46 821	47 875	49 390	49 559
Standard Regions										
North	KKNA	2 729	2 938	3 009	3 246	3 152	3 117	3 073	3 007	3 002
Yorkshire and Humberside	KKNB	3 896	4 319	4 567	4 630	4 902	4 918	4 936	4 971	4 983
East Midlands	KKNC	2 467	2 732	3 118	3 108	3 652	3 853	4 011	4 183	4 215
East Anglia	KKND	1 191	1 231	1 381	1 489	1 688	1 894	2 068	2 181	2 191
South East	KKNE	11 613	13 349	14 877	16 346	17 125	17 011	17 511	18 549	18 622
South West	KKNF	2 818	2 984	3 479	3 436	4 112	4 381	4 688	4 937	4 960
West Midlands	KKNG	3 277	3 743	4 423	4 762	5 146	5 187	5 230	5 283	5 304
North West	KKNH	5 659	6 062	6 305	6 545	6 634	6 459	6 357	6 279	6 282
Government Office Regions										
North East	JZBU	..	..	..	..	2 679	2 636	2 587	2 519	2 513
North West (including Merseyside)	JZBV	..	..	..	..	7 108	6 940	6 843	6 767	6 771
Yorkshire and The Humber	JZBX	..	..	..	..	4 902	4 918	4 936	4 971	4 983
East Midlands	JZBY	..	..	..	..	3 652	3 853	4 011	4 183	4 215
West Midlands	JZBZ	..	..	..	..	5 146	5 187	5 230	5 283	5 304
South West	JZCA	..	..	..	..	4 112	4 381	4 688	4 937	4 960
East	JZCB	..	..	..	..	4 454	4 854	5 121	5 401	5 420
London	JZCC	..	..	..	..	7 529	6 806	6 829	7 308	7 355
South East	JZCD	..	..	..	..	6 830	7 245	7 629	8 021	8 037
Wales	KKNI	2 421	2 593	2 599	2 635	2 740	2 813	2 873	2 908	2 919
Scotland	KGJB	4 761	4 843	5 096	5 184	5 236	5 180	5 083	5 064	5 055
Northern Ireland	KGJC	1 251	1 280[4]	1 371	1 427	1 540	1 543	1 607	1 689	1 697
Greater London	KKNJ	7 161	8 110	8 197	7 977	7 529	6 806	6 829	7 308	7 355
Inner London[2]	KISS	4 998	4 893	3 679	3 481	3 060	2 550	2 599	2 838	2 867
Outer London[2]	KITF	2 162	3 217	4 518	4 496	4 470	4 255	4 230	4 470	4 488
Metropolitan areas of England & Wales	KITG	9 716	10 770	11 365	11 686	11 862	11 353	11 085	10 876	10 880
Tyne and Wear	KGJN	1 105	1 201	1 201	1 241	1 218	1 155	1 124	1 078	1 074
West Yorkshire	KGJP	1 852	1 939	1 985	2 002	2 090	2 067	2 062	2 084	2 089
South Yorkshire	KGJO	963	1 173	1 253	1 298	1 331	1 317	1 289	1 266	1 267
West Midlands	KGJQ	1 780	2 143	2 547	2 724	2 811	2 673	2 619	2 570	2 576
Greater Manchester	KGJR	2 638	2 727	2 716	2 710	2 750	2 619	2 554	2 512	2 513
Merseyside	KGJS	1 378	1 587	1 663	1 711	1 662	1 522	1 438	1 366	1 361
Principal Metropolitan Cities[2]	KITH	3 154	3 906	3 915	4 204	3 910	3 550	3 415	3 337	3 343
Newcastle	KGJT	267	286	292	336	312	284	275	261	260
Leeds	KGJX	446	483	505	710	749	718	707	716	717
Sheffield	KGJV	455	512	513	581	579	548	520	513	512
Birmingham	KGKF	526	1 003	1 113	1 179	1 107	1 021	1 005	986	990
Manchester	KGKJ	714	766	703	657	554	463	433	419	422
Liverpool	KGKM	746	856	789	741	610	517	476	442	441
Other metropolitan districts[2]	KITI	6 562	6 864	7 450	7 482	7 952	7 803	7 670	7 539	7 538
Non-metropolitan districts of England & Wales	KITJ	19 194	21 072	24 196	26 533	29 761	31 475	32 834	34 113	34 242
Non-metropolitan cities[2,3]	KITK	..	..	..	4 670	4 715	4 617	..	..	..
Incl. Kingston-upon-Hull	KKNZ	278	314	299	302	288	274	263	243	241
Leicester	KKOA	227	239	285	286	285	283	281	283	284
Nottingham	KKNX	260	269	308	311	302	278	279	269	270
Bristol	KKNV	357	397	443	436	433	401	392	384	382
Plymouth	KITL	207	215	225	240	249	253	251	241	239
Stoke-on-Trent	KKOD	235	277	275	276	265	252	249	240	239
Cardiff	KKOB	182	224	244	289	291	281	297	307	309
Industrial districts[2,3]	KITM	..	..	..	6 004	6 486	6 713	..	..	..
New Towns[2,3]	KITN	..	..	..	1 552	1 895	2 194	..	..	..
Resort, port and retirement districts[2,3]	KITO	..	..	..	2 828	3 184	3 368	..	..	..
Urban and mixed urban/rural districts[2,3]	KITP	..	..	..	7 240	8 821	9 446	..	..	..
Remoter, mainly rural districts[2,3]	KITQ	..	..	..	4 239	4 661	5 137	..	..	..
City of Edinburgh local government district	KGKU	320	439	467	..	478	446	436	449	448
City of Glasgow local government district	KGKT	784	1 088	1 090	..	983	774	629	579	577
Belfast	KGKV	387	438[4]	444	..	..	315	293	277	274

1 Mid-2001 and mid-2002 population estimates for the UK, England and Manchester include provisional results from the Manchester matching exercise.

2 Details of the classification by broad area type are given in recent issues of the ONS annual reference volume *Key Population and Vital Statistics; local and health authority areas* (Series VS). The ten broad area types include all local authorities in England and Wales.

3 The breakdown of non-metropolitan districts by area type has not been provided from mid-2001 onwards. This is because the effect of boundary changes due to the major local government reorganisation on 1 April 1995 and 1 April 1996 (particularly in Wales) make the comparison of 2001 data with data for earlier years invalid.

4 Figures for Northern Ireland and the City of Belfast relate to the 1937 Census.

Sources: Office for National Statistics: 01329 813233; General Register Office for Scotland; Northern Ireland Statistics and Research Agency

5.6 Population by age and ethnic group
United Kingdom
Average over the period Spring 2002 to Winter 2002/03

Percentages and thousands

	Age-group											All ages (=100%) (thousands)
	0 to 4	5 to 9	10 to 14	15 to 19	20 to 24	25 to 29	30 to 34	35 to 44	45 to 59	60 to 74	75 and over	
White												
British[2]	5	6	7	6	6	6	7	16	20	14	7	51 010
Other[2]	4	4	4	4	8	12	11	18	18	11	6	1 946
Mixed												
White and Black Caribbean	19	21	16	12	8	5	4	9	-	-	-	234
White and Black African	19	19	12	10	-	11	-	11	-	-	-	72
White and Asian	19	15	14	11	7	7	8	10	4	-	-	129
Other Mixed	14	19	14	9	-	7	-	13	-	-	-	74
Asian												
Indian	7	7	7	8	9	9	10	17	18	8	1	1 016
Pakistani	11	11	11	10	11	9	8	12	11	5	1	718
Bangladeshi	14	12	10	10	10	12	9	11	6	5	-	273
Other Asian	8	7	7	6	8	13	12	17	14	6	-	302
Black												
Black Caribbean	8	7	7	8	6	5	8	25	12	11	3	584
Black African	12	11	8	8	8	8	11	20	10	3	-	541
Black Other	14	-	10	10	11	-	-	16	10	-	-	59
Chinese	4	5	5	9	15	12	9	19	15	6	-	199
Other	8	8	6	6	8	11	10	21	14	5	2	458
All[1]	6	6	7	6	6	6	8	16	19	13	7	59 330

1 Includes ethnic group not stated.

2 These data are presented for Great Britain only and exclude Northern Ireland. Detailed level ethnicity questions are not asked of the White group in Northern Ireland.

Source: Office for National Statistics, Labour Force Survey

5.7 Total international migration estimates[1]: citizenship
United Kingdom

Thousands

	All citizenships	British	Non-British	European Union[2]	Commonwealth		Other foreign[4]
					Old[3]	New	
Inflow							
1994	314.4	108.3	206.2	50.4	21.3	58.7	75.7
1995	311.9	83.9	228.0	61.2	26.7	58.3	81.7
1996	317.8	93.6	224.2	72.5	29.0	49.2	73.5
1997	326.1	88.9	237.2	71.5	31.2	58.7	75.7
1998	390.3	103.1	287.3	81.8	53.9	51.0	100.5
1999	453.8	116.4	337.4	66.6	54.4	66.5	149.9
2000	483.4	104.1	379.3	63.1	57.2	90.9	168.1
2001	479.6	106.3	373.3	60.4	67.4	83.9	161.6
2002	512.8	94.6	418.2	62.8	65.6	92.9	196.8
Outflow							
1994	237.6	125.1	112.6	41.7	14.2	16.8	39.9
1995	236.5	135.5	101.0	38.0	17.6	11.9	33.5
1996	263.7	155.7	108.0	44.0	17.3	14.3	32.4
1997	279.2	148.7	130.6	53.2	20.1	19.8	37.5
1998	251.5	125.8	125.7	48.9	19.7	13.2	44.0
1999	290.8	139.2	151.6	58.6	28.8	12.3	51.9
2000	320.7	161.1	159.6	57.0	32.2	14.9	55.5
2001	307.7	159.2	148.5	49.1	32.1	18.6	48.6
2002	359.4	185.7	173.7	51.7	42.3	15.8	63.9
Balance							
1994	76.8	-16.8	93.6	8.7	7.1	41.9	35.9
1995	75.4	-51.6	127.0	23.3	9.2	46.5	48.2
1996	54.1	-62.1	116.2	28.5	11.7	34.9	41.1
1997	46.8	-59.8	106.6	18.3	11.2	38.9	38.2
1998	138.8	-22.7	161.6	33.0	34.2	37.9	56.6
1999	163.0	-22.8	185.8	8.0	25.6	54.2	98.0
2000	162.8	-57.0	219.7	6.1	25.0	76.0	112.6
2001	171.8	-53.0	224.8	11.2	35.2	65.4	113.0
2002	153.4	-91.1	244.5	11.1	23.4	77.1	132.9

1 Based mainly on data from the International Passenger Survey. Includes adjustments for (1) those whose intended length of stay changes so that their migrant status changes; (2) asylum seekers and their dependants not identified by the IPS; and (3) flows between the UK and the Republic of Ireland.

2 Figures for all years show EU as it was constituted on 1 January 1995.

3 Includes estimates for South African citizenship for all years.

4 Figures for all years include Hong Kong.

Source: Office for National Statistics: 01329 813255

33

5.8 Estimates of migration into and out of the United Kingdom[1]
Analysis by usual occupation[2] and sex

Thousands

	Total			Professional and managerial			Manual and clerical			Not gainfully employed[3]		
	Persons	Males	Females	Persons	Males	Females	Persons	Males	Females	Persons	Males	Females
Inflow												
	KGOA	KGOB	KGOC	KGOD	KGOE	KGOF	KGOG	KGOH	KGOI	KGOJ	KGOK	KGOL
1991	255	117	138	76	47	28	53	22	31	127	48	79
1992	207	95	112	59	37	22	42	16	26	106	42	65
1993	204	97	108	63	40	23	41	20	21	100	37	63
1994	243	121	121	79	47	32	54	30	24	110	44	65
1995	235	125	111	83	55	28	44	19	25	108	51	57
1996	261	124	137	86	51	35	55	24	31	120	50	71
1997	273	137	136	89	57	33	42	23	19	141	57	84
1998	318	160	158	112	65	47	71	35	35	136	60	76
1999	354	181	173	131	77	54	77	41	36	146	63	83
2000	364	191	173	163	98	65	64	34	30	137	60	77
2001	372	187	185	142	78	63	77	38	39	154	71	82
2002	386	200	186	142	78	64	83	44	39	161	77	83
Outflow												
	KGPA	KGPB	KGPC	KGPD	KGPE	KGPF	KGPG	KGPH	KGPI	KGPJ	KGPK	KGPL
1991	247	124	123	87	50	37	51	29	21	110	46	64
1992	235	117	118	85	51	33	49	24	25	101	41	60
1993	223	117	106	73	39	33	46	25	21	105	53	52
1994	197	96	102	57	33	24	50	24	26	90	38	52
1995	198	105	93	64	43	21	43	23	20	91	39	52
1996	223	109	114	87	54	32	48	23	24	89	31	58
1997	232	125	107	88	59	29	50	23	26	94	43	51
1998	206	103	103	82	48	34	42	22	21	82	33	48
1999	245	132	114	97	60	38	69	32	37	79	41	39
2000	278	154	124	128	80	48	59	36	23	90	37	53
2001	251	136	115	104	67	37	60	30	30	88	39	49
2002	306	162	144	124	79	45	80	41	40	102	42	59
Balance												
	KGRA	KGRB	KGRC	KGRD	KGRE	KGRF	KGRG	KGRH	KGRI	KGRJ	KGRK	KGRL
1991	8	−7	16	−11	−3	−8	2	−8	10	17	3	14
1992	−28	−22	−6	−26	−14	−12	−7	−8	1	5	−	5
1993	−19	−20	2	−9	−	−10	−5	−5	−	−4	−15	11
1994	45	26	20	22	14	8	4	6	−2	20	6	13
1995	37	19	18	18	11	7	1	−4	6	17	12	5
1996	37	15	22	−1	−3	2	7	−	7	31	18	13
1997	40	12	29	1	−2	3	−7	−1	−7	47	14	33
1998	113	57	55	30	17	13	28	13	15	54	27	27
1999	109	49	60	33	17	16	8	9	−2	67	22	45
2000	87	38	49	35	18	17	5	−2	8	47	22	24
2001	121	51	69	38	11	26	17	8	10	66	33	34
2002	80	38	42	18	−1	19	3	4	−1	59	35	24

1 See chapter text. A small weighting adjustment has been applied to IPS data
for 1991 to 1998. This reflects the estimated effect of applying the weighting
improvements made to IPS data for 1999 onwards.
2 Refers to regular occupation before migration.
3 Includes housewives, students, children and retired persons.

Source: Office for National Statistics: 01329 813255

5.9

Estimates of migration into and out of the United Kingdom[1]
Analysis by citizenship and country of last or next residence

Thousands

| | All migrants | British citizens | | | | | | European Union citizens[2] (excluding British) | | | |
| | | | Country of last/next residence | | | | | | Country of last/next residence | | |
	Total	Total	European[2] Union	Old[3] Common- wealth	New Common- wealth	United States of America	Other countries	Total	European[2] Union	Other Europe	Other countries
Inflow											
	KEZR	KGLA	KGLB	KGLC	KGLD	KGLE	KGLF	KGLG	KGLH	KGLI	KGLJ
1991	255	110	39	27	19	9	16	33	28	–	4
1992	207	94	47	19	10	7	11	25	23	–	2
1993	204	86	31	21	13	9	12	26	22	1	3
1994	243	111	45	19	14	15	18	31	27	1	3
1995	235	86	32	14	12	12	16	42	36	–	6
1996	261	97	33	18	16	13	17	55	49	1	5
1997	273	90	36	20	10	7	17	62	56	–	6
1998	318	104	29	29	14	16	16	70	62	–	7
1999	354	117	32	38	16	11	20	60	55	–	5
2000	364	104	34	29	14	8	19	59	53	–	6
2001	372	106	26	31	17	10	22	57	54	–	3
2002	386	94	29	22	10	9	24	59	53	3	3
Outflow											
	KEZS	KGMA	KGMB	KGMC	KGMD	KGME	KGMF	KGMG	KGMH	KGMI	KGMJ
1991	247	141	46	43	16	13	22	32	24	2	6
1992	235	137	45	35	13	17	27	17	14	–	3
1993	223	130	45	35	12	17	21	24	21	–	3
1994	197	111	34	29	11	15	21	23	19	–	4
1995	198	122	38	35	10	18	21	20	16	–	4
1996	223	143	53	38	16	16	21	24	19	–	5
1997	232	135	41	38	13	16	27	32	27	1	4
1998	206	114	37	36	8	15	19	26	21	1	4
1999	245	115	37	41	8	14	14	47	41	–	6
2000	278	141	41	48	9	19	24	46	39	1	6
2001	251	134	43	47	7	15	22	40	34	1	5
2002	306	165	69	44	10	18	24	42	38	–	4
Balance											
	KEZT	KGNA	KGNB	KGNC	KGND	KGNE	KGNF	KGNG	KGNH	KGNI	KGNJ
1991	8	–30	–7	–17	3	–4	–6	–	5	–2	–2
1992	–28	–43	2	–16	–3	–9	–16	8	9	–	–
1993	–19	–44	–14	–14	1	–8	–9	2	1	–	1
1994	45	–	11	–10	2	–	–3	8	9	1	–1
1995	37	–36	–6	–21	2	–6	–5	22	21	–	2
1996	37	–46	–20	–20	–	–3	–3	31	31	1	–
1997	40	–45	–5	–18	–2	–9	–10	30	29	–1	2
1998	113	–10	–8	–7	7	1	–3	44	41	–1	4
1999	109	2	–6	–3	7	–3	6	13	14	–	–2
2000	87	–37	–8	–19	6	–12	–4	13	14	–1	–
2001	121	–28	–17	–15	10	–6	–	17	20	–1	–1
2002	80	–70	–40	–21	–	–9	–1	17	15	3	–1

Population and vital statistics

5.9 Estimates of migration into and out of the United Kingdom[1]
Analysis by citizenship and country of last or next residence
continued

Thousands

| | Commonwealth citizens — Country of last/next residence | | | | | | | | | | Other foreign citizens — Country of last/next residence | | | | |
	Total	Australia	Canada	New Zealand	South Africa	Bangladesh, India, Sri Lanka	Pakistan	Other African Common-wealth	Caribbean Common-wealth	Other countries	Total	European[2] Union	Other Europe	United States of America	Other countries
Inflow															
	KGLK	KGLL	KGLM	KGLN	KTDK	KGLO	KGLP	KGLQ	KGLR	KGLT	KGLU	KGLV	KGLW	KGLX	KGLY
1991	61	11	4	6	1	9	7	8	2	13	51	6	7	14	25
1992	47	9	2	6	–	6	5	6	2	11	41	2	7	9	23
1993	48	10	3	5	2	9	4	5	–	10	44	2	11	11	19
1994	48	9	2	6	1	6	3	8	–	12	52	6	14	11	22
1995	56	12	5	6	2	8	3	4	–	16	52	2	10	11	29
1996	59	14	3	7	4	8	7	6	1	10	49	–	7	15	27
1997	75	14	5	7	5	15	5	6	1	18	45	–	7	11	27
1998	88	24	5	13	11	10	4	10	1	11	56	4	7	18	27
1999	98	26	2	12	12	14	6	14	3	9	79	3	19	15	42
2000	114	23	6	11	14	21	9	13	1	16	87	2	11	13	61
2001	123	32	4	10	12	21	9	18	2	14	87	1	12	12	61
2002	124	22	5	9	20	27	6	23	2	9	109	2	11	16	81
Outflow															
	KGMK	KGML	KGMM	KGMN	KTDL	KGMO	KGMP	KGMQ	KGMR	KGMT	KGMU	KGMV	KGMW	KGMX	KGMY
1991	33	7	4	5	–	2	2	3	–	10	41	2	3	17	20
1992	28	6	2	5	1	2	1	3	1	7	53	1	12	20	21
1993	32	8	2	4	1	3	1	4	1	8	38	2	3	17	16
1994	28	6	2	4	1	2	3	2	1	8	35	1	10	8	16
1995	27	6	1	4	2	1	1	2	1	9	30	–	5	9	16
1996	29	8	2	3	2	2	–	2	–	9	27	1	7	5	14
1997	36	7	1	5	5	2	2	2	1	12	29	2	5	9	13
1998	30	9	1	3	4	2	1	2	–	6	35	2	7	9	18
1999	38	11	2	6	4	1	–	1	–	11	45	–	9	14	21
2000	43	12	3	8	5	2	2	2	1	8	48	3	11	9	24
2001	44	15	3	6	5	3	1	2	1	7	33	1	9	7	16
2002	52	18	6	9	5	3	2	2	–	7	47	2	12	16	18
Balance															
	KGNK	KGNL	KGNM	KGNN	KTDM	KGNO	KGNP	KGNQ	KGNR	KGNT	KGNU	KGNV	KGNW	KGNX	KGNY
1991	28	5	–	2	1	7	5	5	2	3	10	4	4	–3	5
1992	19	3	–	1	–1	5	4	3	1	3	–13	1	–5	–11	2
1993	16	2	1	1	1	6	2	1	–	2	7	–	8	–5	3
1994	20	3	1	2	–	5	1	6	–1	4	17	4	4	3	7
1995	29	5	4	2	–	6	3	2	–1	7	22	2	5	2	13
1996	30	7	1	4	2	5	7	4	1	–	22	–1	–	10	13
1997	39	7	4	2	1	13	3	4	–	7	16	–2	2	3	14
1998	59	15	3	10	7	7	3	8	1	5	21	2	–	9	9
1999	60	15	–	6	8	13	6	12	3	–2	34	3	10	2	20
2000	71	11	3	3	9	19	8	10	–	7	40	–1	–	4	36
2001	79	17	–	4	7	18	9	16	1	7	53	–	3	5	45
2002	72	4	–1	–	15	24	4	21	2	2	61	–	–2	–	63

1 A small weighting adjustment has been applied to IPS data for 1991 to 1998. This reflects the estimated effect of applying the weighting improvements made to IPS data from 1999 onwards.
2 Figures for all years show EU as it was constituted on 1 January 1995.
3 Figures for all years include South Africa in the Old Commonwealth.

Source: Office for National Statistics: 01329 813255

5.10 Acceptances for settlement by nationality[1]
United Kingdom

Number of persons

Geographical region and nationality		All acceptances for settlement			Geographical region and nationality		All acceptances for settlement		
		2000	2001	2002			2000	2001	2002
All nationalities	KGFA	125 945	108 410	115 965	**Africa(continued)**				
					Somalia	KGHG	12 495	8 405	10 000
Europe[1]					South Africa	KGHH	4 300	4 755	6 135
					Sudan	KGHI	1 555	655	560
Bulgaria	KGFW	295	310	365	Tanzania	KGHJ	430	310	290
Cyprus	KGFN	515	260	270	Tunisia	KGHK	125	190	160
Former Czechoslovakia	KGFX	760	920	875	Uganda	KGHL	3 435	755	745
Of which,					Zambia	KGHM	440	345	330
Czech Republic[2]	LQLS	415	490	495	Zimbabwe	KGHN	955	1 040	3 530
Slovakia	LQLT	345	430	380	Other Africa	KOSU	2 090	2 015	2 550
Hungary	KGFZ	250	215	270					
Malta	KGFP	75	95	80	Africa	KGHO	44 845	31 925	39 165
Poland	KGGA	830	945	875					
Romania	KGGB	310	360	390	**Asia**				
Switzerland	KGFS	220	220	145					
Turkey	KGFT	5 220	3 310	2 920	**Indian sub-continent**				
Former USSR	KGGC	2 095	2 025	2 535	Bangladesh	KGHP	3 685	4 050	4 725
Of which,					India	KGHQ	8 050	7 320	8 005
Estonia	LQLU	25	40	50	Pakistan	KGHR	11 105	11 645	11 935
Latvia	LQLV	60	70	75					
Lithuania	LQLW	150	135	170	Indian sub-continent	KGHS	22 840	23 020	24 665
Russia[3]	LQLX	1 185	1 025	1 365					
Ukraine	LQLY	385	405	460	**Middle East**				
Other former USSR	LQLZ	300	340	415	Iran	KGHT	1 985	1 560	1 715
Former Yugoslavia	KGFU	4 450	5 080	2 830	Iraq	KGHU	2 780	1 715	1 955
Of which,					Israel	KGHV	365	320	375
Croatia	LQMA	660	710	310	Jordan	KGHW	255	175	170
Slovenia	LQMB	20	10	25	Kuwait	KGHX	60	30	65
Serbia & Montenegro[4]	LQMC	2 640	2 785	1 540	Lebanon	KGHY	990	265	365
Other former Yugoslavia	LQMD	1 130	1 575	955	Saudi Arabia	KGHZ	50	45	40
Other Europe	KOSO	135	255	190	Syria	KGIA	245	195	170
					Yemen	KOSV	295	380	300
Europe[1]	KOSP	15 155	13 990	11 740	Other Middle East	KOSW	205	140	190
Americas					Middle East	KGIB	7 230	4 830	5 345
Argentina	KGGF	80	120	120					
Barbados	KGGG	95	115	100	**Remainder of Asia**				
Brazil	KGGH	460	575	510	China	KGIC	1 710	1 515	1 705
Canada	KGGI	1 325	1 320	1 300	Hong Kong[6]	KOSX	795	605	460
Chile	KGGJ	80	75	100	Indonesia	KGID	210	205	225
Colombia	KGGK	820	785	805	Japan	KGIE	1 720	1 695	1 785
Guyana	KGGM	200	210	190	Malaysia	KGIF	780	710	745
Jamaica	KGGN	2 095	2 855	2 675	Philippines	KGIG	1 915	1 355	1 505
Mexico	KGGO	125	130	160	Singapore	KGIH	230	225	220
Peru	KGGP	160	150	155	South Korea	KOTE	485	480	485
Trinidad and Tobago	KGGQ	490	365	410	Sri Lanka	KGII	7 615	4 240	2 935
USA	KGGR	4 585	4 385	4 355	Taiwan	KOSY	175	165	200
Venezuela	KGGT	80	85	80	Thailand	KGIJ	955	1 260	1 335
Other Americas	KOSR	945	810	720	Other Asia	KOSZ	1 265	3 840	4 980
Americas	KGGU	11 550	11 975	11 680	Remainder of Asia	KGIL	17 850	16 305	16 575
Africa					Asia	KGIM	47 920	44 155	46 585
Algeria	KGGV	1 015	775	855					
Angola	KOSS	320	280	660	**Oceania**				
Congo (Dem. Rep.)[5]	KOST	935	800	1 260	Australia	KGIN	2 925	3 205	3 500
Egypt	KGGW	485	420	500	New Zealand	KGIO	1 925	2 185	2 645
Ethiopia	KGGX	2 745	475	345	Other Oceania	KOTA	55	60	100
Ghana	KGGY	3 140	2 440	2 585					
Kenya	KGHA	1 135	1 025	1 055	Oceania	KGIP	4 905	5 455	6 250
Libya	KGHB	375	370	445					
Mauritius	KGHC	675	375	455	British Overseas citizens	KGIQ	635	520	330
Morocco	KGHD	590	575	520	Stateless	KGIS	930	390	215
Nigeria	KGHE	6 525	5 045	5 325					
Sierra Leone	KGHF	1 075	875	855	**All nationalities**	KGFA	125 945	108 410	115 965

1 Excluding European Economic Area nationals
2 Includes Czechoslovakian passport holders.
3 Includes Soviet Union passport holders.

4 Includes holders of passports of the former Yugoslavia.
5 Formerly known as Zaire.
6 Includes Hong Kong stateless persons.

Source: Home Office: 020 8760 8289

5.11 Applications[1] received for asylum in the United Kingdom, excluding dependants, by nationality, 1994 to 2002

Number of principal applicants

Nationality		1994	1995	1996	1997	1998	1999[2]	2000[2]	2001[3]	2002[4]
Europe										
Albania	LQME	75	110	105	445	560	1 310	1 490	1 065	1 150
Czech Republic	LQMF	5	15	55	240	515	1 790	1 200	825	1 365
FRY	ZAFA	..	..	400	1 865	7 395	11 465	6 070	3 230	2 265
Macedonia	PTDW	..	..	15	20	50	90	65	755	310
Moldova	VQHP	5	10	..[5]	20	25	180	235	425	820
Poland	DMLX	360	1 210	900	565	1 585	1 860	1 015	615	990
Romania	KEAV	355	770	455	605	1 015	1 985	2 160	1 400	1 210
Russia	ZAEQ	..	..	205	180	185	685	1 000	450	295
Turkey	KEAW	2 045	1 820	1 495	1 445	2 015	2 850	3 990	3 695	2 835
Ukraine	ZAER	..	..	235	490	370	775	770	445	365
Other Former USSR	ZAES	590	785	960	1 325	2 235	2 460	2 275	895	1 245
Other Former Yugoslavia	ZAET	1 385	1 565	620	375	535	2 625	2 200	85	90
Europe Other	ZAEU	535	770	1 035	1 575	1 260	200	415	335	300
Europe Total	KEAZ	5 360	7 050	6 475	9 145	17 745	28 280	22 880	14 215	13 235
Americas										
Colombia	KEBZ	405	525	1 005	1 330	425	1 000	505	365	420
Ecuador	KYDB	105	250	435	1 205	280	610	445	255	315
Jamaica	PTDX	110	150	125	130	105	180	310	525	1 310
Americas Other	PTDY	265	415	205	165	165	240	155	170	240
Americas Total	KECT	890	1 340	1 765	2 825	975	2 025	1 420	1 315	2 290
Africa										
Algeria	KOTB	995	1 865	715	715	1 260	1 385	1 635	1 140	1 060
Angola	KECU	605	555	385	195	150	545	800	1 015	1 420
Burundi	PTDZ	50	95	60	85	215	780	620	610	700
Cameroon	VQHU	75	85	105	175	95	245	355	380	615
Congo	PTEA	40	80	75	90	150	450	485	540	600
Congo (Dem. Rep.)	KEEH	775	935	680	690	660	1 240	1 030	1 370	2 215
Eritrea	PTEC	110	245	135	125	345	565	505	620	1 180
Ethiopia	KECW	730	585	205	145	345	455	415	610	700
Gambia	DMMA	140	1 170	245	125	45	30	50	65	130
Ghana	KECX	2 035	1 915	780	350	225	195	285	190	275
Ivory Coast	DMLZ	705	245	125	70	95	190	445	275	315
Kenya	KOTC	1 130	1 395	1 170	605	885	485	455	305	350
Nigeria	KECY	4 340	5 825	2 900	1 480	1 380	945	835	810	1 125
Rwanda	ZAEV	100	135	80	90	280	820	760	530	655
Sierra Leone	KOTD	1 810	855	395	815	565	1 125	1 330	1 940	1 155
Somalia	KECZ	1 840	3 465	1 780	2 730	4 685	7 495	5 020	6 420	6 540
Sudan	KEEE	330	345	280	230	250	280	415	390	655
Tanzania	DMMC	205	1 535	225	90	80	80	60	80	40
Uganda	KEEG	360	365	215	220	210	420	740	480	715
Zimbabwe	GRFS	55	105	130	60	80	230	1 010	2 140	7 655
Africa Other	PTEB	530	750	600	425	375	465	670	670	1 295
Africa Total	KEEJ	16 960	22 545	11 290	9 515	12 380	18 435	17 920	20 590	29 390
Middle East										
Iran	KEEK	520	615	585	585	745	1 320	5 610	3 420	2 630
Iraq	KEEL	550	930	965	1 075	1 295	1 800	7 475	6 680	14 570
Middle East Other	ZAEX	910	755	600	675	745	1 045	1 330	1 165	1 115
Middle East Total	KEGY	1 985	2 295	2 150	2 335	2 785	4 165	14 415	11 265	18 315
Asia										
Afghanistan	DMLY	325	580	675	1 085	2 395	3 975	5 555	8 920	7 205
Bangladesh	ZAEY	310	685	645	545	460	530	795	510	720
China	KEGZ	425	790	820	1 945	1 925	2 625	4 000	2 390	3 675
India	KEIL	2 030	3 255	2 220	1 285	1 030	1 365	2 120	1 850	1 865
Pakistan	KEIM	1 810	2 915	1 915	1 615	1 975	2 615	3 165	2 860	2 405
Sri Lanka	KEIN	2 350	2 070	1 340	1 830	3 505	5 130	6 395	5 510	3 130
Vietnam	VQIB	5	5	10	10	35	105	180	400	840
Asia Other	PTEE	260	385	270	255	615	1 120	1 025	1 040	915
Asia Total	KEJO	7 515	10 685	7 885	8 570	11 940	17 465	23 230	23 480	20 755
Nationality not known	KEJP	125	50	80	105	190	785	450	160	145
Grand Total	KEJQ	32 830	43 965	29 640	32 500	46 015	71 160	80 315	71 025	84 130

1 Figures rounded to the nearest 5.
2 May exclude some cases lodged at Local Enforcement Offices between January 1999 and March 2000.
3 Revised figures.
4 Provisional figures.
5 Figure = 1 or 2.

Source: Home Office: 020 8760 8280

5.12 Marriages

Numbers

		1991	1992	1993	1994	1995	1996	1997	1998	1999	2000	2001
United Kingdom												
Marriages	KKAA	349 739	356 013	341 608	331 232	322 251	317 514	310 218	304 797	301 083	305 912	286 129
Persons marrying per 1,000 resident population[1]	KKAB	*12.2*	*12.4*	*11.8*	*11.5*	*11.1*	*10.9*	*10.6*	*10.4*	*10.3*	*10.4*	*9.7*
Previous marital status												
Bachelors	KKAC	256 538	258 567	245 996	236 619	227 717	221 826	216 237	214 005	211 820	213 777	202 690
Divorced men	KKAD	83 069	87 419	85 824	85 261	85 743	87 113	85 625	82 977	81 750	84 771	76 852
Widowers	KKAE	10 132	10 027	9 788	9 352	8 791	8 575	8 356	7 815	7 513	7 364	6 587
Spinsters	KKAF	259 084	260 252	248 063	237 241	228 462	221 697	216 776	215 399	213 246	215 865	205 048
Divorced women	KKAG	81 224	86 361	84 268	85 220	85 396	87 618	85 648	82 016	80 816	83 166	74 807
Widows	KKAH	9 431	9 400	9 277	8 771	8 393	8 199	7 794	7 382	7 021	6 881	6 274
First marriage for both partners	KMGH	222 369	222 142	210 567	200 910	192 078	185 293	181 135	180 404	178 759	180 020	171 912
First marriage for one partner	KMGI	70 884	74 535	72 925	72 040	72 023	72 937	70 743	68 596	67 548	69 602	63 914
Remarriage for both partners	KMGJ	56 486	59 336	58 116	58 282	58 150	59 284	58 340	55 797	54 776	56 290	50 303
Males												
Under 21 years	KKAI	13 271	11 031	8 767	7 091	6 302	5 497	5 126	5 173	5 234	5 019	4 625
21-24	KKAJ	79 877	74 458	65 129	56 877	49 432	42 488	36 875	32 723	29 390	28 467	25 840
25-29	KKAK	115 637	118 255	114 101	111 108	105 218	101 647	97 345	94 696	90 412	85 870	78 687
30-34	KKAL	56 970	62 470	63 848	65 490	68 245	69 867	70 904	71 096	72 129	73 809	70 657
35-44	KKAM	48 147	51 125	50 553	51 310	53 350	56 513	58 292	59 838	62 114	68 019	65 242
45-54	KKAN	20 915	23 290	23 841	24 136	24 786	26 252	26 472	26 118	26 581	28 791	26 122
55 and over	KKAO	14 922	15 384	15 369	15 220	14 918	15 250	15 204	15 153	15 223	15 937	14 956
Females												
Under 21 years	KKAP	38 305	32 618	26 839	22 903	20 643	18 485	17 254	16 793	16 082	15 938	13 874
21-24	KKAQ	105 505	102 494	93 125	84 171	75 071	66 191	59 549	54 645	50 350	48 578	45 687
25-29	KKAR	99 851	105 223	104 517	102 803	100 644	99 651	97 932	97 181	94 703	92 753	85 647
30-34	KKAS	43 617	48 514	49 546	52 359	54 819	57 752	58 589	59 349	60 446	62 478	59 859
35-44	KKAT	37 582	40 075	40 090	41 213	43 115	45 969	47 267	47 721	50 136	54 697	52 209
45-54	KKAU	16 473	18 504	18 800	19 280	19 720	21 025	21 038	20 708	20 822	22 621	20 459
55 and over	KKAV	8 406	8 585	8 691	8 503	8 239	8 441	8 589	8 400	8 544	8 847	8 394
England and Wales												
Marriages	KKBA	306 756	311 564	299 197	291 069	283 012	278 975	272 536	267 303	263 515	267 961	249 227
Persons marrying per 1,000 resident population[1]	KKBB	*12.1*	*12.2*	*11.7*	*11.4*	*11.0*	*10.9*	*10.6*	*10.3*	*10.2*	*10.3*	*9.5*
Previous marital status												
Bachelors	KKBC	222 823	224 152	213 476	206 077	198 208	193 306	188 268	186 329	184 266	186 113	175 721
Divorced men	KKBD	74 860	78 473	76 986	76 633	76 967	78 003	76 839	74 029	72 617	75 378	67 678
Widowers	KKBE	9 073	8 939	8 735	8 359	7 837	7 666	7 429	6 945	6 632	6 470	5 828
Spinsters	KKBF	224 812	225 608	214 987	206 332	198 603	192 707	188 457	187 391	185 328	187 717	177 506
Divorced women	KKBG	73 408	77 542	75 904	76 857	76 869	78 939	77 098	73 330	71 971	74 092	66 120
Widows	KKBH	8 536	8 414	8 306	7 880	7 540	7 329	6 981	6 582	6 216	6 152	5 601
First marriage for both partners	KMGK	192 238	191 732	181 956	174 200	166 418	160 680	156 907	156 539	155 027	156 140	148 642
First marriage for one partner	KMGL	63 159	66 296	64 551	64 009	63 975	64 653	62 911	60 642	59 540	61 550	55 943
Remarriage for both partners	KMGM	51 359	53 536	52 690	52 860	52 619	53 642	52 718	50 122	48 948	50 271	44 642
Males												
Under 21 years	KKBI	11 416	9 471	7 540	6 175	5 520	4 877	4 574	4 608	4 629	4 536	4 160
21-24	KKBJ	68 547	63 932	55 963	49 073	42 711	36 713	31 907	28 389	25 424	24 764	22 436
25-29	KKBK	100 891	102 942	99 314	96 862	91 607	88 338	84 644	82 135	78 364	74 367	67 934
30-34	KKBL	50 403	55 012	56 129	57 848	60 014	61 582	62 265	62 323	63 212	64 611	61 409
35-44	KKBM	43 013	45 364	44 863	45 514	47 330	50 038	51 654	52 812	54 528	59 834	56 872
45-54	KKBN	18 929	20 925	21 440	21 794	22 349	23 661	23 688	23 385	23 676	25 470	22 949
55 and over	KKBO	13 557	13 918	13 948	13 803	13 481	13 766	13 804	13 651	13 682	14 379	13 467
Females												
Under 21 years	KKBP	33 428	28 541	23 469	20 250	18 343	16 510	15 439	15 065	14 379	14 421	12 467
21-24	KKBQ	91 338	88 553	80 470	72 937	65 126	57 296	51 766	47 446	43 691	42 265	39 746
25-29	KKBR	87 244	91 735	91 134	89 941	87 680	86 838	85 352	84 399	82 250	80 312	73 799
30-34	KKBS	38 425	42 675	43 559	46 119	48 216	50 799	51 405	51 982	52 721	54 649	51 865
35-44	KKBT	33 755	35 660	35 662	36 651	38 367	40 889	41 838	42 245	44 199	48 245	45 672
45-54	KKBU	14 891	16 619	16 969	17 409	17 791	18 992	18 938	18 575	18 572	20 083	18 071
55 and over	KKBV	7 675	7 781	7 934	7 762	7 489	7 651	7 798	7 591	7 703	7 986	7 607

5.12 Marriages
continued

Numbers

		1992	1993	1994	1995	1996	1997	1998	1999	2000	2001	2002
Scotland												
Marriages	KKCA	35 057	33 366	31 480	30 663	30 242	29 611	29 668	29 940	30 367	29 621	29 826
Persons marrying per 1,000 resident population	KKCB	*13.8*	*13.1*	*12.3*	*12.0*	*11.9*	*11.7*	*11.7*	*11.8*	*12.0*	*11.7*	*11.8*
Previous marital status												
Bachelors	KKCC	26 106	24 609	23 004	22 126	21 454	20 994	20 987	21 052	21 201	20 737	20 671
Divorced men	KKCD	8 027	7 879	7 654	7 741	8 048	7 845	7 934	8 142	8 427	8 238	8 475
Widowers	KKCE	924	878	822	796	740	772	747	746	739	646	680
Spinsters	KKCF	26 274	25 103	23 248	22 410	21 799	21 303	21 241	21 308	21 608	21 223	21 180
Divorced women	KKCG	7 935	7 469	7 487	7 542	7 718	7 621	7 754	7 949	8 141	7 825	8 008
Widows	KKCH	848	794	745	711	725	687	673	683	618	573	638
First marriage for both partners	KEZV	22 588	21 214	19 644	18 822	18 071	17 751	17 677	17 680	17 864	17 468	17 426
First marriage for one partner	KEZW	7 204	7 284	6 964	6 892	7 111	6 795	6 874	7 000	7 081	7 024	6 999
Remarriage for both partners	KEZX	5 265	4 868	4 872	4 949	5 060	5 065	5 117	5 260	5 422	5 129	5 401
Males												
Under 21 years	KKCI	1 172	902	680	577	452	406	421	490	364	371	367
21-24	KKCJ	7 958	6 870	5 693	4 915	4 191	3 494	3 147	2 853	2 720	2 489	2 395
25-29	KKCK	11 587	11 266	10 812	10 209	10 056	9 495	9 439	9 031	8 536	7 949	7 468
30-34	KKCL	6 022	6 214	6 176	6 574	6 574	6 911	6 988	7 179	7 419	7 464	7 692
35-44	KKCM	4 950	4 803	4 864	5 021	5 412	5 649	5 945	6 470	7 018	7 215	7 328
45-54	KKCN	2 083	2 093	2 050	2 124	2 288	2 459	2 412	2 575	2 960	2 816	3 033
55 and over	KKCO	1 285	1 218	1 205	1 243	1 269	1 197	1 316	1 342	1 350	1 317	1 543
Females												
Under 21 years	KKCP	3 060	2 461	1 959	1 728	1 423	1 302	1 289	1 322	1 171	1 111	996
21-24	KKCQ	10 503	9 506	8 291	7 264	6 474	5 568	5 248	4 778	4 581	4 343	4 171
25-29	KKCR	10 457	10 368	9 895	9 904	9 818	9 574	9 764	9 539	9 495	8 994	8 520
30-34	KKCS	4 822	5 002	5 145	5 401	5 675	5 927	6 036	6 433	6 463	6 618	6 832
35-44	KKCT	3 847	3 774	3 917	4 025	4 378	4 722	4 726	5 150	5 633	5 712	6 115
45-54	KKCU	1 673	1 606	1 648	1 689	1 794	1 844	1 900	1 994	2 279	2 147	2 322
55 and over	KKCV	695	649	625	652	680	674	705	724	745	696	870
Northern Ireland												
Marriages	KKDA	9 392	9 045	8 683	8 576	8 297	8 071	7 826	7 628	7 584	7 281	7 599
Persons marrying per 1,000 resident population	KKDB	*11.6*	*11.1*	*10.6*	*10.4*	*10.0*	*9.7*	*9.3*	*9.1*	*9.0*	*8.6*	*9.0*
Previous marital status												
Bachelors	KKDC	8 309	7 911	7 538	7 383	7 066	6 975	6 689	6 502	6 463	6 232	6 404
Divorced men	KKDD	919	959	974	1 035	1 062	941	1 014	991	966	936	1 059
Widowers	KKDE	164	175	171	158	169	155	123	135	155	113	136
Spinsters	KKDF	8 370	7 973	7 661	7 449	7 191	7 016	6 767	6 610	6 540	6 319	6 530
Divorced women	KKDG	884	895	876	985	961	929	932	896	933	862	940
Widows	KKDH	138	177	146	142	145	126	127	122	111	100	129
First marriage for both partners	KEZY	7 822	7 397	7 066	6 838	6 542	6 477	6 188	6 052	6 016	5 802	5 934
First marriage for one partner	KEZZ	1 035	1 090	1 067	1 156	1 173	1 037	1 080	1 008	971	947	1 066
Remarriage for both partners	KFBI	535	558	550	582	582	557	558	568	597	532	599
Males												
Under 21 years	KKDI	388	325	236	205	168	146	144	115	119	94	77
21-24	KKDJ	2 568	2 296	2 111	1 806	1 584	1 474	1 187	1 113	983	915	937
25-29	KKDK	3 726	3 521	3 434	3 402	3 253	3 206	3 122	3 017	2 967	2 804	2 771
30-34	KKDL	1 436	1 505	1 466	1 657	1 711	1 728	1 785	1 738	1 779	1 784	1 902
35-44	KKDM	811	887	932	999	1 063	989	1 081	1 116	1 167	1 155	1 223
45-54	KKDN	282	308	292	313	303	325	321	330	361	357	432
55 and over	KKDO	181	203	212	194	215	203	186	199	208	172	257
Females												
Under 21 years	KKDP	1 017	909	694	572	552	513	439	381	346	296	282
21-24	KKDQ	3 438	3 149	2 943	2 681	2 421	2 215	1 951	1 881	1 732	1 598	1 650
25-29	KKDR	3 031	3 015	2 967	3 060	2 995	3 006	3 018	2 914	2 946	2 854	2 832
30-34	KKDS	1 017	985	1 095	1 202	1 278	1 257	1 331	1 292	1 366	1 376	1 477
35-44	KKDT	568	654	645	723	702	707	750	787	819	825	898
45-54	KKDU	212	225	223	240	239	256	233	256	259	241	330
55 and over	KKDV	109	108	116	98	110	117	104	117	116	91	130

1 Rates are based on interim population estimates for the UK, and England and Wales which were released on 23 October 2003. The interim revised estimates are subject to revision. Revised estimates for 1992-2000 for the UK and England and Wales will be published in Spring 2004.

Sources: Office for National Statistics: 01329 813339;
General Register Office for Scotland;
Northern Ireland Statistics and Research Agency

5.13 Divorce

		1992	1993	1994	1995	1996	1997	1998	1999	2000	2001	2002
United Kingdom												
Decrees absolute granted[1,2]:												
Number	ZBRL	175 144	180 018	173 611	170 050	171 729	161 087	160 057	158 746	154 628	156 814	160 726
Duration of marriage:												
0-4 years	ZBRM	39 191	39 530	37 978	36 594	37 016	33 719	33 087	31 047	28 933	28 306	28 591
5-9 years	ZBRN	47 990	50 883	49 215	48 309	48 670	45 040	44 243	43 357	41 621	42 360	42 924
10-14 years	ZBRO	32 261	33 221	31 177	30 257	30 159	29 085	29 706	30 270	30 166	30 849	31 257
15-19 years	ZBRP	22 179	22 324	21 336	21 040	21 379	20 211	20 078	20 147	19 902	20 568	21 881
20 years and over	ZBRQ	33 516	34 055	33 898	33 840	34 487	33 020	32 935	33 916	34 000	34 729	36 073
Not stated	ZBRR	7	5	7	10	18	12	8	9	6	2	–
Age of wife at marriage:												
16-19 years	ZBRS	44 347	43 368	38 464	35 145	33 590	28 987	27 627	25 440	23 505	22 558	22 107
20-24 years	ZBRT	81 574	83 806	80 594	78 341	78 075	72 971	71 416	69 509	66 215	66 282	66 264
25-29 years	ZBRU	27 109	29 213	30 576	31 611	33 634	33 452	34 195	35 585	36 009	37 418	39 116
30-34 years	ZBRV	10 582	11 272	11 716	12 322	13 122	12 968	13 719	14 420	14 892	15 842	17 374
35-39 years	ZBRW	5 531	6 018	5 979	6 172	6 470	6 155	6 571	6 848	6 993	7 417	8 070
40-44 years	ZBRX	3 017	3 260	3 247	3 335	3 507	3 375	3 360	3 557	3 568	3 778	4 104
45 years and over	ZBRY	2 933	3 004	2 952	3 052	3 239	3 094	3 086	3 291	3 352	3 429	3 572
Not stated	ZBRZ	51	77	83	72	92	85	83	96	94	90	119
Age of wife at divorce:												
16-24 years	ZBSA	14 604	13 895	11 845	10 517	9 298	7 371	6 758	5 671	5 115	4 874	4 998
25-29 years	ZBSB	38 186	38 632	35 824	33 354	32 808	28 814	26 968	24 120	21 280	19 635	18 340
30-34 years	ZBSC	38 220	39 879	39 456	38 839	39 497	37 257	36 795	36 052	34 356	34 194	33 555
35-39 years	ZBSD	29 044	30 746	30 000	30 280	31 497	30 641	31 688	32 605	32 588	33 997	35 050
40-44 years	ZBSE	23 756	23 943	22 847	22 791	22 843	22 246	22 810	23 614	23 879	25 579	27 564
45 years and over	ZBSF	31 276	32 841	33 549	34 187	35 684	34 662	34 947	36 578	37 311	38 442	41 102
Not stated	ZBSG	58	82	90	82	102	96	91	106	99	93	117
Divorces in which there were:												
No children aged under 16[4]	ZBSH	77 709	78 803	78 913	78 844	..	..	..	..	..	..	..
One or more children aged under 16[4]	ZBSI	97 435	101 215	94 698	91 206	..	..	..	..	..	..	..
England and Wales												
Decrees absolute granted[1,2]:												
Number	KKEA	160 385	165 018	158 175	155 499	157 107	146 689	145 214	144 556	141 135	143 818	147 735
Rate per 1,000 married couples	KKEB	*13.8*	*14.3*	*13.8*	*13.7*	*14.0*	*13.2*	*13.1*	*13.2*	*12.9*	*12.9*	*13.3*
Duration of marriage:												
0-4 years	KKEC	36 898	37 252	35 695	34 507	34 924	31 767	31 136	29 307	27 474	26 987	27 344
5-9 years	KKED	43 745	46 536	44 769	44 304	44 609	41 260	40 239	39 676	38 206	39 079	39 730
10-14 years	KKEE	29 285	30 156	28 073	27 365	27 332	26 215	26 698	27 384	27 459	28 176	28 592
15-19 years	KKEF	20 160	20 233	19 200	18 943	19 321	18 027	17 934	18 072	17 870	18 603	19 784
20 years and over	KKEG	30 290	30 836	30 431	30 370	30 912	29 408	29 199	30 108	30 120	30 971	32 285
Not stated	KKEH	7	5	7	10	9	12	8	9	6	2	–
Age of wife at marriage:												
16-19 years	KKEI	39 734	38 811	34 069	31 322	29 927	25 579	24 276	22 486	20 930	20 218	19 828
20-24 years	KKEJ	74 701	76 853	73 291	71 360	71 123	66 167	64 453	62 853	59 874	60 211	60 353
25-29 years	KKEK	25 173	27 178	28 360	29 441	31 396	31 022	31 533	32 867	33 282	34 759	36 387
30-34 years	KKEL	9 939	10 593	11 007	11 585	12 335	12 094	12 788	13 507	13 972	14 890	16 339
35-39 years	KKEM	5 200	5 673	5 615	5 800	6 051	5 767	6 153	6 432	6 562	6 956	7 623
40-44 years	KKEN	2 872	3 091	3 064	3 121	3 254	3 156	3 135	3 331	3 378	3 559	3 841
45 years and over	KKEO	2 766	2 819	2 769	2 870	3 021	2 904	2 876	3 080	3 137	3 225	3 364
Age of wife at divorce:												
16-24 years	KKEP	13 482	12 924	10 956	9 783	8 615	6 871	6 298	5 318	4 839	4 643	4 808
25-29 years	KKEQ	34 853	35 362	32 608	30 563	30 075	26 435	24 586	22 173	19 650	18 231	17 227
30-34 years	KKER	34 901	36 300	35 848	35 538	36 274	33 967	33 446	32 837	31 420	31 489	30 982
35-39 years	KKES	26 577	28 162	27 195	27 550	28 727	27 715	28 605	29 663	29 820	31 164	32 282
40-44 years	KKET	21 783	21 891	20 765	20 739	20 774	20 125	20 521	21 325	21 469	23 190	25 017
45 years and over	KKEU	28 782	30 374	30 796	31 316	32 633	31 564	31 750	33 231	33 931	35 099	37 419
Not stated	KKEV	7	5	7	10	9	12	8	9	6	2	–
Divorces in which there were:												
No children aged under 16[4]	ZBSJ	68 960	70 103	69 684	69 632	70 174	66 019	64 738	65 258	64 359	64 541	66 738
One or more children aged under 16[4]	ZBSK	91 425	94 915	88 491	85 867	86 933	80 670	80 476	79 298	76 776	79 277	80 997

5.13 Divorce
continued

Numbers

		1992	1993	1994	1995	1996	1997	1998	1999	2000	2001	2002
Scotland												
Decrees absolute granted[1,2]												
Number	KKFA	12 479	12 787	13 133	12 249	12 308	12 222	12 384	11 864	11 143	10 631	10 826
Rate per 1,000 married couples	KKFB	*10.8*	*11.1*	*11.5*	*10.8*	*10.9*	*11.0*	*11.2*	*10.8*	*10.3*	*9.7*	*9.8*
Duration of marriage:												
0-4 years	KKFC	2 085	2 092	2 095	1 908	1 914	1 793	1 766	1 588	1 304	1 159	1 128
5-9 years	KKFD	3 610	3 722	3 790	3 399	3 432	3 224	3 360	3 095	2 890	2 721	2 689
10-14 years	KKFE	2 454	2 539	2 592	2 407	2 310	2 385	2 456	2 368	2 168	2 163	2 183
15-19 years	KKFF	1 675	1 745	1 786	1 698	1 709	1 804	1 729	1 686	1 622	1 562	1 705
20 years and over	KKFG	2 655	2 689	2 870	2 837	2 934	3 016	3 073	3 127	3 159	3 026	3 121
Not stated	ZBSL	–	–	–	–	9	–	–	–	–	–	–
Age of wife at marriage:												
16-19 years	ZBSM	3 755	3 768	3 641	3 091	2 939	2 749	2 654	2 374	2 043	1 839	1 845
20-24 years	ZBSN	5 821	5 890	6 197	5 845	5 822	5 714	5 744	5 453	5 142	4 873	4 823
25-29 years	KKFJ	1 685	1 812	1 926	1 887	1 933	2 151	2 314	2 333	2 318	2 233	2 316
30-34 years	KKFK	575	612	628	654	697	791	824	829	805	827	895
35-39 years	KKFL	301	312	329	338	393	360	382	379	378	401	407
40-44 years	KKFM	138	152	163	196	234	199	198	208	170	193	235
45 years and over	KKFN	153	164	166	166	198	173	185	192	193	175	186
Not stated	KKFO	51	77	83	72	92	85	83	96	94	90	119
Age of wife at divorce:												
16-24 years	KKFP	963	844	767	622	583	426	377	301	232	182	180
25-29 years	KKFQ	2 807	2 775	2 750	2 353	2 269	2 021	1 957	1 597	1 330	1 109	974
30-34 years	KKFR	2 785	3 037	3 045	2 747	2 708	2 736	2 767	2 642	2 381	2 215	2 174
35-39 years	KKFS	2 092	2 212	2 390	2 290	2 307	2 469	2 562	2 450	2 298	2 311	2 281
40-44 years	KKFT	1 685	1 771	1 788	1 734	1 761	1 819	1 951	1 929	1 999	1 963	2 110
45 years and over	KKFU	2 096	2 071	2 310	2 431	2 587	2 667	2 687	2 848	2 810	2 760	2 990
Not stated	KKFV	51	77	83	72	93	84	83	97	93	91	117
Divorces in which there were:												
No children aged under 16[4]	KKFW	6 927	6 951	7 390	7 515	..	..	..	..	..	..	..
One or more children under 16[4]	KKFX	5 552	5 836	5 743	4 734	..	..	..	..	..	..	..
Northern Ireland												
Decrees absolute granted[1,3]:												
Number	ZBSO	2 280	2 213	2 303	2 302	2 314	2 176	2 459	2 326	2 350	2 365	2 165
Duration of marriage:												
0-4 years	ZBSP	208	186	188	179	178	159	185	152	155	160	119
5-9 years	ZBSQ	635	625	656	606	629	556	644	586	525	560	505
10-14 years	ZBSR	522	526	512	485	517	485	552	518	539	510	482
15-19 years	ZBSS	344	346	350	399	349	380	415	389	410	403	392
20 years and over	ZBST	571	530	597	633	641	596	663	681	721	732	667
Age of wife at marriage:												
16-19 years	ZBSU	858	789	754	732	724	659	697	580	532	501	434
20-24 years	ZBSV	1 052	1 063	1 106	1 136	1 130	1 090	1 219	1 203	1 199	1 198	1 088
25-29 years	ZBSW	251	223	290	283	305	279	348	385	409	426	413
30-34 years	ZBSX	68	67	81	83	90	83	107	84	115	125	140
35-39 years	ZBSY	30	33	35	34	26	28	36	37	53	60	40
40-44 years	ZBSZ	7	17	20	18	19	20	27	18	20	26	28
45 years and over	ZBTA	14	21	17	16	20	17	25	19	22	29	22
Age of wife at divorce:												
16-24 years	ZBTB	159	127	122	112	100	74	83	52	44	49	10
25-29 years	ZBTC	526	495	466	438	464	358	425	350	300	295	139
30-34 years	ZBTD	534	542	563	554	515	554	582	573	555	490	399
35-39 years	ZBTE	375	372	415	440	463	457	521	492	470	522	487
40-44 years	ZBTF	288	281	294	318	308	302	338	360	411	426	437
45 years and over	ZBTG	398	396	443	440	464	431	510	499	570	583	693
Divorces in which there were:												
No children aged under 16[4]	ZBTH	1 822	1 749	1 839	1 697	1 676	1 573	1 807	1 649	1 051	1 054	972
One or more children aged under 16[4]	ZBTI	458	464	464	605	638	603	652	677	1 299	1 311	1 193

1 Includes decrees of nullities.
2 Marriage and divorce rates in England and Wales for 1986-2000 have been calculated using the interim revised marital status estimates (based on the original mid-2001 estimates) and are subject to further revision; revised estimates will be published in Spring 2004. Marital estimates for Scotland 1986-2000 will be revised in Spring 2004. Rates for 2002 are based on 2001 marital status estimates.
3 Marital estimates are not available for Northern Ireland - no divorce rate for UK/Northern Ireland
4 Children of the family as defined by the Matrimonial Causes Act 1973.

Sources: Office for National Statistics: 01329 813339; General Register Office for Scotland; Northern Ireland Statistics and Research Agency

5.14 Divorce proceedings

Numbers

		1992	1993	1994	1995	1996	1997	1998	1999	2000	2001	2002
United Kingdom												
Dissolution of marriage[1]												
Decree absolute/decree granted	ZBXR	174 718	179 539	173 178	169 621	171 309	160 733	159 688	158 418	154 273	156 562	160 529
On grounds of:												
Adultery	ZBXS	45 458	45 759	42 743	41 313	41 127	38 652	37 302	35 545	34 082	33 452	33 389
Behaviour	ZBXT	77 648	78 686	75 029	71 733	72 581	68 546	68 685	67 851	65 687	66 818	68 499
Desertion	ZBXU	1 096	1 193	1 185	1 196	1 101	956	828	748	722	718	727
Separation (2 years and consent)	ZBXV	37 955	41 002	41 144	41 969	42 265	39 398	39 627	40 368	39 763	40 699	42 579
Separation(5 years)	ZBXW	11 806	12 183	12 317	12 699	13 547	12 552	12 697	13 389	13 653	14 575	15 076
Combination of more than one ground and other	ZBXX	755	716	760	711	688	629	549	517	366	300	259
Decree absolute/decree granted to[2]:												
the wife	ZBXY	125 833	128 797	123 256	118 869	119 570	111 912	111 556	109 828	106 958	107 345	108 106
the husband	ZBXZ	48 509	50 407	49 507	50 268	51 247	48 393	47 764	48 236	47 069	49 015	52 251
both	ZBYA	379	345	423	490	493	430	369	358	247	202	173
Nullity of marriage												
Decree absolute/decree granted	ZBYB	426	479	433	429	420	354	369	328	355	252	198
England and Wales												
Dissolution of marriage												
Petitions filed	KKGA	189 329	184 471	175 510	173 966	177 970	163 769	165 870	162 137	157 809	161 580	171 054
Decree nisi granted	KKGM	149 126	160 625	154 241	155 739	157 588	148 310	144 231	143 106	143 729	146 932	160 943
Decree absolute granted	KKGN	159 967	164 556	157 756	155 076	156 692	146 339	144 851	144 233	140 783	143 568	147 538
On grounds of:												
Adultery	KKGB	44 128	44 466	41 449	40 178	40 012	37 592	36 319	34 584	33 310	32 839	32 829
Behaviour	KKGC	73 906	74 583	70 932	68 168	68 986	65 047	65 257	64 816	63 182	64 768	66 480
Desertion	KKGD	1 021	1 118	1 062	1 108	1 030	912	790	713	680	689	681
Separation (2 years and consent)	KKGE	30 995	34 144	33 996	35 030	35 422	32 638	32 394	33 482	32 820	33 703	35 476
Separation(5 years)	KKGF	9 181	9 556	9 589	9 930	10 626	9 592	9 616	10 193	10 498	11 355	11 896
Combination of more than one ground and other	ZBYC	736	689	728	662	616	558	475	445	293	214	176
Decree absolute granted to:												
the wife	ZBYD	115 393	118 127	112 415	108 764	109 489	102 173	101 583	100 469	98 227	98 992	102 676
the husband	ZBYE	44 195	46 084	44 918	45 823	46 712	43 739	42 902	43 413	42 311	44 378	44 694
both	ZBYF	379	345	423	489	491	427	366	351	245	198	168
Nullity of marriage												
Petitions filed	KKGO	535	634	822	881	702	485	505	549	452	657	758
Decree nisi granted	KKGR	369	365	705	425	332	248	281	495	274	297	158
Decree absolute granted	KKGS	418	462	419	423	415	350	363	323	352	250	197
Judicial separation												
Petitions filed	KKGT	2 434	2 251	4 358	3 349	2 795	1 078	916	882	650	535	499
Decrees granted	KKGW	1 452	1 413	1 350	1 543	1 199	589	519	696	540	925	331

5.14 Divorce proceedings
continued

Numbers

		Scotland										
		1992	1993	1994	1995	1996	1997	1998	1999	2000	2001	2002
Scotland												
Dissolution of marriage[1]												
Decree granted	ZBYG	12 476	12 777	13 125	12 243	12 307	12 220	12 383	11 860	11 142	10 631	10 826
On grounds of:												
Adultery	ZBYH	1 136	1 092	1 099	956	943	909	832	770	610	473	428
Behaviour	ZBYI	3 407	3 757	3 711	3 203	3 184	3 081	3 005	2 611	2 099	1 639	1 656
Desertion	ZBYJ	58	56	103	72	61	33	28	18	34	24	43
Separation (2 years and consent)	ZBYK	5 823	5 800	6 078	5 846	5 835	5 773	6 121	5 908	5 878	5 943	6 101
Separation(5 years)	ZBYL	2 052	2 072	2 134	2 166	2 284	2 424	2 397	2 553	2 521	2 552	2 598
Decree granted to[2]												
the wife	ZBYM	8 865	9 190	9 278	8 545	8 559	8 266	8 329	7 774	7 191	6 775	4 025
the husband	ZBYN	3 614	3 597	3 855	3 704	3 749	3 956	4 055	4 090	3 952	3 856	6 802
Nullity of marriage												
Decree granted	ZBYO	3	10	8	6	1	2	1	4	1	–	1
Northern Ireland												
Dissolution of marriage												
Petitions filed	ZBYP	2 597	2 610	2 875	2 875	2 695	2 808	2 760	2 414	3 005	2 869	2 929
Decree nisi granted	ZBYQ	2 386	2 384	2 535	2 535	2 419	2 532	2 904	2 393	2 456	2 615	2 454
Decree absolute granted	ZBYR	2 274	2 206	2 296	2 302	2 310	2 174	2 454	2 325	2 348	2 363	2 165
On grounds of:												
Adultery	ZBYS	194	201	195	179	172	151	151	191	162	140	132
Behaviour	ZBYT	335	346	386	362	411	418	423	424	406	411	363
Desertion	ZBYU	17	19	20	16	10	11	10	17	8	5	3
Separation (2 years and consent)	ZBYV	1 137	1 059	1 072	1 093	1 010	991	1 112	978	1 065	1 053	1 002
Separation(5 years)	ZBYW	573	555	594	603	637	536	684	643	634	668	582
Combination of more than one ground and other	ZBYX	18	26	29	49	70	67	74	72	73	86	83
Decree absolute granted to:												
the wife	ZBYY	1 574	1 480	1 562	1 560	1 522	1 473	1 644	1 585	1 540	1 578	1 405
the husband	ZBYZ	700	726	734	741	786	698	807	733	806	781	755
both	ZBZA	–	–	–	1	2	3	3	7	2	4	5
Nullity of marriage												
Petitions filed	ZBZB	1	2	5	5	5	7	5	1	2	1	5
Decree nisi granted	ZBZC	3	2	3	5	5	2	6	2	5	2	2
Decree absolute granted	ZBZD	6	7	7	–	4	2	5	1	2	2	–
Judicial separation												
Petitions filed	ZBZE	17	44	57	84	63	70	64	50	54	40	27
Decrees granted	ZBZF	22	6	15	30	22	34	40	31	23	25	15

1 The terms Petition filed, Decree nisi granted, Decree absolute and Judicial separation are not used in Scotland. Decree absolute granted to 'both' and 'Combination of more than one ground and other' are not procedures used in Scotland.
2 Information on Decree granted for the wife or husband for Scotland includes nullities (these are identified separately under 'Nullity of marriage'); figures excluding nullities are not available.

Sources: Office for National Statistics: 01329 813339;
General Register Office for Scotland;
Northern Ireland Statistics and Research Agency;
The Court Service (E&W and NI);
Scottish Courts Administration

5.15

Births[1]
Annual averages or calendar years

Thousands

| | Live births | | | | Rates | | | | |
	Total	Male	Female	Sex ratio[2]	Crude birth rate[3]	General fertility rate[4]	TFR[5]	Still-births[6]	Still-birth rate[6]
United Kingdom[7,8]									
1900 - 02	1 095	558	537	1 037	28.6	115.1	..	..	..
1910 - 12	1 037	528	508	1 039	24.6	99.4	..	..	..
1920 - 22	1 018	522	496	1 052	23.1	93.0	..	..	..
1930 - 32	750	383	367	1 046	16.3	66.5	..	..	..
1940 - 42	723	372	351	1 062	15.0	..	1.89	..	..
1950 - 52	803	413	390	1 061	16.0	73.7	2.21	..	..
1960 - 62	946	487	459	1 063	17.9	90.3	2.80	18.6	19.2
1970 - 72	880	453	427	1 064	15.8	82.5	2.36	11.3	12.7
1980 - 82	735	377	358	1 053	13.0	62.5	1.83	5.0	6.8
1990 - 92	790	405	385	1 051	13.8	63.7	1.81	3.6	4.6
2000 - 02	672	345	328	1 052	11.4	54.7	1.64	3.6	5.4
	BBCA	KBCZ	KBCY	KMFW	KBCT	KBCS	KBCR	KBCQ	KMFX
1991	792	406	386	1 052	13.8	63.6	1.82	3.7	4.7
1992	781	400	381	1 052	13.6	63.4	1.79	3.4	4.4
1993	762	391	371	1 054	13.2	62.4	1.76	4.4	5.7
1994	750	385	365	1 054	13.0	61.6	1.74	4.3	5.8
1995	732	375	357	1 052	12.6	60.1	1.71	4.1	5.6
1996	733	376	357	1 055	12.6	60.2	1.73	4.1	5.5
1997	727	372	354	1 051	12.5	59.7	1.72	3.9	5.3
1998	717	367	350	1 052	12.3	58.9	1.72	3.9	5.4
1999	700	359	341	1 056	11.9	57.4	1.69	3.7	5.3
2000	679	348	331	1 051	11.5	55.5	1.64	3.6	5.3
2001	669	343	326	1 050	11.3	54.5	1.63	3.6	5.3
2002	669	343	327	1 054	11.3	54.3	1.64	3.8	5.6
England and Wales[8]									
1900 - 02	932	475	458	1 037	28.6	114.7	..	..	..
1910 - 12	884	450	433	1 040	24.5	98.6	..	..	..
1920 - 22	862	442	420	1 051	22.8	91.1	..	..	..
1930 - 32	632	323	309	1 047	15.8	64.4	..	27.0	..
1940 - 42	607	312	295	1 057	15.6	61.3	1.81	22.0	..
1950 - 52	683	351	332	1 058	15.6	72.1	2.16	16.0	..
1960 - 62	812	418	394	1 061	17.6	88.9	2.77	15.6	18.9
1970 - 72	764	394	371	1 061	15.6	81.4	2.31	9.7	12.5
1980 - 82	639	328	311	1 053	12.9	61.8	1.81	4.3	6.7
1990 - 92	698	358	340	1 051	13.8	63.8	1.82	3.2	4.5
2000 - 02	598	307	292	1 052	11.4	55.2	1.65	3.2	5.4
	BBCB	KMFY	KMFZ	KMGA	KMGB	KMGC	KMGD	KMGE	KMGF
1991	699	358	341	1 052	13.8	63.6	1.82	3.3	4.6
1992	690	354	336	1 053	13.6	63.6	1.80	3.0	4.3
1993	673	346	328	1 056	13.2	62.7	1.76	3.9	5.7
1994	665	341	323	1 055	13.0	62.0	1.75	3.8	5.7
1995	648	332	316	1 051	12.6	60.5	1.72	3.6	5.5
1996	649	333	316	1 055	12.6	60.6	1.74	3.5	5.4
1997	643	330	314	1 051	12.5	60.0	1.73	3.4	5.3
1998	636	326	310	1 051	12.3	59.3	1.73	3.4	5.3
1999	622	319	303	1 055	12.0	57.9	1.70	3.3	5.3
2000	604	310	295	1 050	11.6	56.0	1.66	3.2	5.3
2001	595	305	290	1 050	11.4	54.8	1.64	3.2	5.3
2002	596	306	290	1 055	11.4	54.8	1.65	3.2	5.4

5.15
Births[1]
Annual averages or calendar years
continued

Thousands

	Live births				Rates				
	Total	Male	Female	Sex ratio[2]	Crude birth rate[3]	General fertility rate[4]	TFR[5]	Still-births[6]	Still-birth rate[6]
Scotland									
1900 - 02	132	67	65	1 046	29.5	120.6	..	..	..
1910 - 12	123	63	60	1 044	25.9	107.4	..	..	..
1920 - 22	125	64	61	1 046	25.6	105.9	..	..	..
1930 - 32	93	47	45	1 040	19.1	78.8	..	..	..
1940 - 42	89	46	43	1 051	18.5	73.7	..	4.0	..
1950 - 52	91	47	44	1 060	17.9	81.4	2.41	2.0	..
1960 - 62	102	53	50	1 060	19.7	97.8	2.98	2.2	20.8
1970 - 72	84	43	41	1 057	16.1	83.3	2.46	1.1	13.5
1980 - 82	68	35	33	1 051	13.1	62.2	1.80	0.4	6.3
1990 - 92	66	34	32	1 052	13.0	59.2	1.68	0.4	5.7
2000 - 02	52	27	26	1 046	10.3	48.6	1.48	0.3	5.6
	BBCD	KMEU	KMEV	KMEW	KMEX	KMEY	KMEZ	KMFM	KMFN
1991	67	34	33	1 056	13.1	59.8	1.69	0.4	5.5
1992	66	34	32	1 044	12.9	59.3	1.68	0.4	5.4
1993	63	32	31	1 046	12.4	57.4	1.61	0.4	6.4
1994	62	31	30	1 038	12.0	56.0	1.58	0.4	6.1
1995	60	31	29	1 043	11.7	54.5	1.55	0.4	6.6
1996	59	31	29	1 061	11.6	54.0	1.56	0.4	6.4
1997	59	31	29	1 055	11.6	54.3	1.58	0.3	5.3
1998	57	29	28	1 060	11.3	52.6	1.55	0.4	6.1
1999	55	28	27	1 050	10.9	50.8	1.51	0.3	5.2
2000	53	27	26	1 051	10.5	49.1	1.48	0.3	5.6
2001	53	27	26	1 041	10.4	48.8	1.49	0.3	5.7
2002	51	26	25	1 047	10.1	49.4	1.48	0.3	5.4
Northern Ireland[7]									
1900 - 02	..	..	..	..	..	..	..	..	..
1910 - 12	..	..	..	..	..	..	..	..	..
1920 - 22	31	16	15	1 048	24.2	105.9	..	..	..
1930 - 32	26	13	12	1 047	20.5	78.8	..	..	..
1940 - 42	27	14	13	1 078	20.8	73.7	..	..	..
1950 - 52	29	15	14	1 066	20.9	81.4	..	..	..
1960 - 62	31	16	15	1 068	22.5	111.5	3.47	0.7	22.0
1970 - 72	31	16	15	1 074	20.4	105.7	3.13	0.5	14.3
1980 - 82	28	14	13	1 048	18.0	87.5	2.59	0.2	8.4
1990 - 92	26	13	13	1 051	16.1	74.8	2.15	0.1	4.6
2000 - 02	22	11	11	1 054	12.8	58.8	1.78	0.1	5.0
	BBCE	KMFO	KMFP	KMFQ	KMFR	KMFS	KMFT	KMFU	KMFV
1991	26	13	13	1 066	16.2	75.1	2.16	0.1	4.7
1992	25	13	12	1 040	15.6	72.7	2.09	0.1	4.9
1993	25	13	12	1 025	15.1	70.3	2.01	0.1	5.2
1994	24	12	12	1 053	14.7	68.0	1.95	0.2	6.3
1995	24	12	11	1 078	14.4	66.6	1.91	0.1	6.1
1996	24	12	12	1 032	14.7	67.8	1.96	0.2	6.2
1997	24	12	12	1 048	14.4	66.4	1.93	0.1	5.4
1998	24	12	12	1 039	14.1	65.0	1.90	0.1	5.1
1999	23	12	11	1 084	13.7	62.9	1.86	0.1	5.7
2000	22	11	10	1 070	12.8	58.7	1.75	0.1	4.3
2001	22	11	11	1 058	13.0	59.7	1.80	0.1	5.1
2002	21	11	11	1 035	12.6	58.1	1.77	0.1	5.7

1 See chapter text.
2 Males per 1,000 females (calculated using whole numbers).
3 Rate per 1,000 population and produced using whole numbers.
4 Rate per 1,000 women aged 15 - 44.
5 Total period fertility rate is the average number of children which would be born to a woman if she experienced the age-specific fertility rates of the period in question throughout her child-bearing life span. UK figures for the years 1970-72 and earlier are estimates.
6 On 1 October 1992 the legal definition of a stillbirth was changed from a baby born dead after 28 completed weeks gestation or more to one born dead after 24 completed weeks gestation or more. Between 1 October and 31 December 1992 in the UK there were 258 babies born dead between 24 and 27 completed weeks gestation (216 in England and Wales, 35 in

Scotland and 7 in Northern Ireland). If these babies were included in the still-birth figures given, the stillbirth rate would be 4.7 for the UK and England and Wales, while Scotland and Northern Ireland stillbirth rate would remain as stated.
7 From 1981, data for the United Kingdom and Northern Ireland have been revised to exclude births in Northern Ireland to non-residents of Northern Ireland.
8 From 1992-2000 the population estimates for UK and England and Wales have been revised and were released on 23 October 2003. These interim revised estimates are subject to revision. Revised estimates for 1992-2000 for the UK, England and Wales will be published in the Spring 2004.

Sources: Office for National Statistics: 020 7533 5113;
General Register Office for Scotland;
Northern Ireland Statistics and Research Agency

5.16 Birth occurrence inside and outside marriage by age of mother

Thousands

	Inside marriage						Outside marriage					
	All ages	Under 20	20 - 24	25 - 29	Over 30	Mean[1] age (Years)	All ages	Under 20	20 - 24	25 - 29	Over 30	Mean[1] age (Years)
United Kingdom[2]												
	KKEY	KKEZ	KKFY	KKFZ	KKGX	KKGY	KKGZ	KKIC	KKID	KKIE	KKIF	KKIG
1961	890	55	273	280	282	27.7	54	13	17	10	13	25.5
1971	828	70	301	271	185	26.4	74	24	25	13	12	23.8
1981	640	36	193	231	180	27.3	91	30	33	16	13	23.4
1986	596	21	159	231	185	27.9	158	45	60	31	22	23.7
1987	598	18	153	235	192	28.1	178	48	68	37	26	23.9
1988	589	16	144	234	195	28.2	198	51	76	42	29	24.1
1989	570	14	130	228	198	28.4	207	49	79	46	32	24.3
1990	576	13	121	233	209	28.6	223	51	83	53	37	24.5
1991	556	10	109	224	213	28.9	236	50	87	58	41	24.8
1992	540	9	98	216	218	29.1	241	46	86	62	46	25.1
1993	520	8	87	204	221	29.3	242	44	84	64	50	25.4
1994	510	7	78	194	231	29.6	240	41	80	65	55	25.7
1995	486	6	69	180	232	29.8	246	42	79	66	60	25.9
1996	473	6	61	170	237	30.1	260	45	80	69	66	26.0
1997	460	6	55	159	240	30.3	267	47	79	71	71	26.1
1998	447	6	51	149	243	30.5	270	49	77	70	74	26.2
1999	428	6	47	136	239	30.7	272	49	77	68	77	26.3
2000	411	5	44	126	237	30.9	268	47	77	66	78	26.4
2001	401	5	44	116	236	30.9	268	45	77	64	82	26.7
2002	397	5	44	109	239	31.1	272	44	80	62	85	26.7
Great Britain												
	KKIH	KKII	KKIJ	KKIK	KKIL	KKIM	KKIN	KKIO	KKIP	KKIQ	KKIR	KKIS
1961	859	53	264	270	272	27.7	53	13	17	10	13	25.5
1971	797	68	293	261	176	26.4	73	24	25	13	12	23.8
1981	614	34	186	223	171	27.2	89	29	32	16	13	23.3
1986	572	20	153	222	177	27.9	155	44	59	30	22	22.9
1987	574	17	147	227	184	28.0	174	46	66	36	25	23.4
1988	566	16	138	226	186	28.2	194	49	74	42	29	23.6
1989	549	13	125	220	190	28.4	202	48	77	45	32	24.2
1990	554	12	116	225	201	28.6	218	49	81	52	36	24.6
1991	535	10	105	216	205	28.9	231	48	85	57	41	24.8
1992	520	9	94	208	210	29.1	235	45	84	61	46	25.1
1993	500	7	84	196	213	29.3	236	42	82	62	49	25.4
1994	492	7	75	188	222	29.6	235	41	78	63	53	25.7
1995	468	6	66	173	223	29.8	240	40	77	65	59	25.9
1996	455	6	59	163	227	30.1	254	44	78	68	65	26.0
1997	442	6	53	152	231	30.3	261	46	76	69	69	26.2
1998	430	6	49	143	233	30.5	263	48	74	68	73	26.3
1999	412	6	46	131	230	30.7	265	48	74	67	76	26.4
2000	396	5	43	121	228	30.9	261	46	74	65	77	26.5
2001	386	5	43	112	227	30.9	261	44	75	62	80	26.6
2002	383	5	43	105	230	31.1	265	43	77	61	84	26.7

1 The mean ages presented in this table do not take into account the changing population distribution of women.
2 From 1981, data for the United Kingdom exclude births in Northern Ireland to non-residents of Northern Ireland.

Sources: Office for National Statistics: 01329 813339;
General Register Office for Scotland;
Northern Ireland Statistics and Research Agency

5.17 Live births by age of mother

Numbers

All live births - United Kingdom[1,3]

Age-group:	Under 20	20 - 24	25 - 29	30 - 34	35 - 39	40 - 44	45 and over	All ages
	KMDV	KMDW	KMDX	KMDY	KMDZ	KMES	KMET	KMBZ
1992	54 922	184 359	277 315	189 020	63 768	10 802	553	780 799
1993	51 463	171 096	267 413	193 565	66 235	11 123	582	761 526
1994	47 874	157 468	259 367	202 880	70 871	11 432	536	750 480
1995	47 646	147 056	246 017	204 601	73 945	12 008	585	731 882
1996	50 793	141 090	238 857	210 490	78 335	12 832	638	733 163
1997	52 851	133 257	229 429	212 162	84 508	13 731	618	726 622
1998	54 822	127 230	218 072	212 876	88 729	14 453	640	716 888
1999	54 921	124 036	204 808	208 986	91 272	15 210	695	699 976
2000	52 060	120 304	191 583	202 893	95 400	16 032	708	679 029
2001	50 157	121 664	179 776	202 017	97 379	17 271	831	669 123
2002	49 164	123 845	171 852	203 260	101 379	18 274	968	668 777

Age-specific fertility rates - United Kingdom[2]

Age-group:	Under 20	20 - 24	25 - 29	30 - 34	35 - 39	40 - 44	45 and over	All ages
	KMBR	KMBS	KMBT	KMBU	KMBV	KMBW	KMBX	KMBY
1992	31.8	85.5	117.8	87.2	33.2	5.5	0.3	63.4
1993	30.8	81.6	114.6	87.1	33.8	5.8	0.3	62.4
1994	28.7	78.0	112.4	89.0	35.4	6.0	0.3	61.6
1995	28.3	75.4	108.6	87.9	36.1	6.4	0.3	60.2
1996	29.6	75.7	106.7	89.5	37.1	6.8	0.3	60.2
1997	30.3	74.8	104.4	89.8	39.0	7.1	0.3	59.7
1998	31.1	73.6	101.4	90.5	40.4	7.4	0.3	58.9
1999	30.9	71.9	98.1	89.5	40.2	7.6	0.4	57.4
2000	29.3	68.9	94.1	87.9	41.0	7.8	0.4	55.5
2001	27.9	68.2	91.7	88.2	41.4	8.2	0.4	54.5
2002	26.9	68.2	91.2	89.8	42.8	8.5	0.5	54.3

All live births - England and Wales

Age-group:	Under 20	20 - 24	25 - 29	30 - 34	35 - 39	40 - 44	45 and over	All ages
	KGSA	KGSB	KGSC	KGSD	KGSE	KGSF	KGSG	KGSH
1992	47 861	163 311	244 798	166 839	56 650	9 696	501	689 656
1993	45 121	151 975	235 961	171 061	58 824	9 986	539	673 467
1994	42 026	140 240	229 102	179 568	63 061	10 241	488	664 726
1995	41 938	130 744	217 418	181 202	65 517	10 779	540	648 138
1996	44 667	125 732	211 103	186 377	69 503	11 516	587	649 485
1997	46 372	118 589	202 792	187 528	74 900	12 332	582	643 095
1998	48 285	113 537	193 144	188 499	78 881	12 980	575	635 901
1999	48 375	110 722	181 931	185 311	81 281	13 617	635	621 872
2000	45 846	107 741	170 701	180 113	84 974	14 403	663	604 441
2001	44 189	108 844	159 926	178 920	86 495	15 499	761	594 634
2002	43 468	110 958	153 379	180 532	90 449	16 441	895	596 122

Age-specific fertility rates - England and Wales[2]

Age-group:	Under 20	20 - 24	25 - 29	30 - 34	35 - 39	40 - 44	45 and over	All ages
	KGSI	KGSJ	KGSK	KGSL	KGSM	KGSN	KGSO	KGSP
1992	31.7	86.2	117.5	87.3	33.4	5.5	0.3	63.6
1993	30.9	82.6	114.4	87.3	34.1	5.9	0.3	62.7
1994	28.9	79.1	112.4	89.3	35.8	6.1	0.3	62.0
1995	28.5	76.4	108.7	88.2	36.4	6.5	0.3	60.5
1996	29.7	77.0	106.8	89.7	37.5	6.9	0.3	60.6
1997	30.3	75.9	104.5	89.8	39.3	7.3	0.3	60.0
1998	31.3	74.8	101.5	90.7	40.4	7.5	0.3	59.3
1999	31.1	73.1	98.4	89.7	40.6	7.7	0.4	57.9
2000	29.5	70.1	94.5	88.1	41.4	8.0	0.4	56.0
2001	28.1	69.2	91.9	88.2	41.6	8.4	0.5	54.8
2002	27.1	69.2	91.6	89.9	43.2	8.7	0.5	54.8

5.17 Live births by age of mother

continued

Numbers

All live births - Scotland[1]

Age-group:	Under 20	20 - 24	25 - 29	30 - 34	35 - 39	40 - 44	45 and over	All ages
	KGTA	KGTB	KGTC	KGTD	KGTE	KGTF	KGTG	KGTH
1992	5 206	15 405	23 571	15 973	4 877	674	23	65 789
1993	4 750	13 923	22 758	16 088	5 049	697	23	63 337
1994	4 303	12 637	21 851	16 705	5 346	736	26	61 656
1995	4 280	11 913	20 395	16 803	5 799	811	26	60 051
1996	4 544	11 026	19 511	17 038	6 126	891	32	59 296
1997	4 835	10 607	18 782	17 455	6 740	936	19	59 440
1998	4 802	9 804	17 477	17 207	6 893	1 027	43	57 319
1999	4 755	9 440	16 011	16 722	7 034	1 096	41	55 147
2000	4 599	8 962	14 676	16 233	7 395	1 133	29	53 076
2001	4 444	9 121	13 763	16 206	7 701	1 224	40	52 527
2002	4 195	9 267	12 694	16 038	7 727	1 267	47	51 270

Age-specific fertility rates - Scotland

Age-group:	Under 20	20 - 24	25 - 29	30 - 34	35 - 39	40 - 44	45 and over	All ages
	KGTI	KGTJ	KGTK	KGTL	KGTM	KGTN	KGTO	KGTP
1992	33.1	77.7	113.6	80.7	27.8	3.9	0.1	59.3
1993	31.2	72.5	110.0	79.8	28.0	4.1	0.1	57.4
1994	28.5	68.2	106.5	81.3	28.8	4.4	0.2	56.0
1995	28.2	66.6	101.3	80.6	30.4	4.8	0.1	54.6
1996	29.7	64.5	98.5	81.9	31.4	5.2	0.2	54.1
1997	31.0	65.5	97.4	83.9	34.0	5.3	0.1	54.4
1998	30.6	62.8	94.3	83.2	34.1	5.7	0.3	52.7
1999	30.3	61.0	90.4	82.0	34.3	5.9	0.2	50.9
2000	29.3	57.6	86.5	81.3	35.6	6.0	0.2	49.2
2001	28.4	57.8	85.1	82.2	36.9	6.3	0.2	48.8
2002	26.7	59.2	80.5	99.1	39.2	6.1	0.3	49.4

All live births - Northern Ireland[3]

Age-group:	Under 20	20 - 24	25 - 29	30 - 34	35 - 39	40 - 44	45 and over	All ages
	KMDF	KMDG	KMDH	KMDI	KMDJ	KMDK	KMDL	KMDM
1992	1 855	5 643	8 946	6 208	2 241	432	29	25 354
1993	1 592	5 198	8 694	6 416	2 362	440	20	24 722
1994	1 545	4 591	8 414	6 607	2 464	455	22	24 098
1995	1 428	4 399	8 204	6 596	2 629	418	19	23 693
1996	1 582	4 332	8 243	7 075	2 706	425	19	24 382
1997	1 644	4 061	7 855	7 179	2 868	463	17	24 087
1998	1 735	3 889	7 451	7 170	2 955	446	22	23 668
1999	1 791	3 874	6 866	6 953	2 957	497	19	22 957
2000	1 615	3 601	6 206	6 547	3 031	496	16	21 512
2001	1 524	3 699	6 087	6 891	3 183	548	30	21 962
2002	1 502	3 619	5 779	6 690	3 203	566	26	21 385

Age-specific fertility rates - Northern Ireland

Age - group:	Under 20	20 - 24	25 - 29	30 - 34	35 - 39	40 - 44	45 and over	All ages
	KMDN	KMDO	KMDP	KMDQ	KMDR	KMDS	KMDT	KMDU
1992	30.2	90.2	141.3	103.2	43.0	8.8	0.6	72.7
1993	26.1	83.3	136.1	104.3	43.9	8.9	0.4	70.3
1994	25.4	75.0	131.2	104.9	44.3	9.2	0.4	68.0
1995	23.4	73.5	129.1	102.7	45.5	8.4	0.4	66.6
1996	25.7	73.8	129.4	108.3	45.4	8.4	0.4	67.8
1997	26.4	71.1	124.2	109.2	46.6	8.8	0.3	66.4
1998	27.8	69.6	119.0	108.4	47.2	8.2	0.4	65.0
1999	28.6	70.6	112.3	105.6	46.1	8.9	0.4	62.9
2000	25.6	66.0	103.9	100.4	46.2	8.5	0.3	58.7
2001	23.9	67.5	105.1	106.0	48.0	9.1	0.6	59.7
2002	23.3	66.0	102.9	104.2	48.2	9.2	0.5	58.1

1 The 'All ages' figure for Scotland includes births to mothers whose age was not known. There were 65 such births in 1990, 103 in 1991, 60 in 1992, 49 in 1993, 52 in 1994, 24 in 1995, 128 in 1996, 66 in 1997, 66 in 1998, 48 in 1999, 49 in 2000, 28 in 2001 and 35 in 2002. In 2002 there was 1 not stated for Northern Ireland.

2 Rates are based on interim population estimates for the UK, and England and Wales which were released on 23 October 2003. The interim revised estimates are subject to revision. Revised estimates for 1992-2000 for the UK and England and Wales will be published in Spring 2004.

3 From 1981, data for the United Kingdom and Northern Ireland have been revised to exclude births in Northern Ireland to non-residents in Northern Ireland.

Sources: Office for National Statistics: 01329 813339;
General Register Office for Scotland;
Northern Ireland Statistics and Research Agency

5.18 Legal abortions
Total by age for residents

Numbers

England and Wales

	All ages	Under 15	15	16 - 19	20 - 24	25 - 29	30 - 34	35 - 39	40 - 44	45 and over	Not stated [1]
1986	147 619	924	2 970	33 819	45 316	28 656	18 005	12 977	4 521	409	22
1987	156 191	907	2 858	35 167	49 256	31 243	18 960	12 639	4 757	390	14
1988	168 298	859	2 709	37 928	54 067	34 584	20 000	12 681	5 047	412	11
1989	170 463	803	2 580	36 182	54 880	36 604	21 284	12 713	5 020	388	9
1990	173 900	873	2 549	35 520	55 281	38 770	22 431	12 956	5 104	404	12
1991	167 376	886	2 272	31 130	52 678	38 611	23 445	13 035	4 901	408	10
1992	160 501	905	2 095	27 589	49 052	38 430	23 870	13 252	4 844	452	12
1993	157 846	964	2 119	25 806	46 846	38 139	24 690	13 885	4 889	494	14
1994	156 539	1 080	2 166	25 223	44 871	38 081	25 507	14 156	5 008	440	7
1995	154 315	946	2 324	24 945	43 394	37 254	25 759	14 352	4 868	457	16
1996	167 916	1 098	2 547	28 790	46 356	39 311	28 228	16 118	5 027	428	13
1997	170 145	1 020	2 414	29 947	44 960	40 159	28 892	16 858	5 413	482	-
1998	177 871	1 103	2 656	33 236	45 766	40 366	30 449	18 174	5 576	511	34
1999	173 701	1 066	2 537	32 807	45 004	38 492	29 139	18 341	5 755	502	58
2000	175 542	1 048	2 700	33 218	47 099	37 852	28 735	18 589	5 794	459	48
2001	176 364	1 066	2 592	33 431	48 267	36 506	28 782	19 146	6 094	456	24
2002	175 569	957	2 557	32 244	48 387	35 790	28 495	19 548	6 638	479	474

Scotland [2]

	All ages	Under 15	15	16 - 19	20 - 24	25 - 29	30 - 34	35 - 39	40 - 44	45 and over
1986	9 628	74	236	2 529	2 985	1 744	1 081	708	249	22
1987	9 460	70	210	2 417	2 996	1 729	1 082	697	242	17
1988	10 128	65	218	2 529	3 304	1 970	1 107	663	257	15
1989	10 209	53	209	2 561	3 202	1 968	1 229	706	266	15
1990	10 219	54	186	2 539	3 242	2 063	1 161	700	253	21
1991	11 068	77	203	2 571	3 486	2 253	1 445	743	262	28
1992	10 818	73	174	2 377	3 389	2 291	1 444	799	254	17
1993	11 076	92	193	2 300	3 368	2 447	1 492	891	264	29
1994	11 392	78	215	2 312	3 486	2 431	1 648	877	315	30
1995	11 143	79	233	2 169	3 399	2 438	1 609	887	296	33
1996	11 978	87	236	2 362	3 571	2 603	1 801	960	331	27
1997	12 109	85	204	2 431	3 444	2 651	1 854	1 093	322	25
1998	12 485	73	213	2 707	3 426	2 749	1 807	1 149	339	22
1999	12 167	69	182	2 635	3 354	2 553	1 810	1 180	361	23
2000	11 995	93	181	2 610	3 355	2 403	1 768	1 176	381	28
2001[3]	12 126	66	210	2 722	3 460	2 322	1 818	1 127	378	23
2002[4]	11 594	77	190	2 607	3 354	2 117	1 703	1 143	375	28

1 The information collected on the abortion notification form and the design of the form changed in 2002. Early problems with the completion of the new form by practitioners and with the processing system have resulted in the late return to practitioners of incomplete and incorrectly completed forms. As a result there is a larger than usual number of cases where age is not known.
2 Refers to therapeutic abortions notified in accordance with the Abortion Act 1967.
3 Revised.
4 Provisional.

Sources: Office for National Statistics; Scottish Executive

5.19 Deaths: analysis by age and sex[1]
Annual averages or calendar years

Numbers

	All ages[2]	Under 1 year	1-4	5-9	10-14	15-19	20-24	25-34	35-44	45-54	55-64	65-74	75-84	85 and over
United Kingdom														
Males														
1900 - 02	340 664	87 242	37 834	8 429	4 696	7 047	8 766	19 154	24 739	30 488	37 610	39 765	28 320	6 563
1910 - 12	303 703	63 885	29 452	7 091	4 095	5 873	6 817	16 141	21 813	28 981	37 721	45 140	29 397	7 283
1920 - 22	284 876	48 044	19 008	6 052	3 953	5 906	6 572	13 663	19 702	29 256	40 583	49 398	34 937	7 801
1930 - 32	284 249	28 840	11 276	4 580	2 890	5 076	6 495	12 327	16 326	29 376	47 989	63 804	45 247	10 022
1940 - 42	314 643	24 624	6 949	3 400	2 474	4 653	4 246	11 506	17 296	30 082	57 076	79 652	59 733	12 900
1950 - 52	307 312	14 105	2 585	1 317	919	1 498	2 289	5 862	11 074	27 637	53 691	86 435	79 768	20 131
1960 - 62	318 850	12 234	1 733	971	871	1 718	1 857	3 842	8 753	26 422	63 009	87 542	83 291	26 605
1970 - 72	335 166	9 158	1 485	1 019	802	1 778	2 104	3 590	7 733	24 608	64 898	105 058	82 905	30 027
1980 - 82	330 495	4 829	774	527	652	1 999	1 943	3 736	6 568	19 728	54 159	105 155	98 488	31 936
1990 - 92	312 521	3 315	623	372	396	1 349	2 059	4 334	6 979	15 412	40 424	87 849	106 376	43 032
2000 - 02	288 261	2 065	365	233	326	1 032	1 502	4 270	7 181	15 370	32 328	66 808	98 363	58 419
	KHUA	KHUB	KHUC	KHUD	KHUE	KHUF	KHUG	KHUH	KHUI	KHUJ	KHUK	KHUL	KHUM	KHUN
1982	329 971	4 555	760	456	632	1 966	1 971	3 661	6 462	18 867	53 531	103 426	101 281	32 403
1983	328 824	4 230	695	469	609	1 834	1 899	3 601	6 537	18 238	54 493	100 469	103 038	32 712
1984	321 095	3 995	725	423	580	1 708	1 999	3 595	6 425	17 647	53 715	95 420	102 513	32 350
1985	331 562	4 003	728	393	583	1 612	2 031	3 452	6 728	17 316	52 502	97 458	109 241	35 515
1986	327 160	4 219	653	384	444	1 676	2 067	3 668	6 712	16 814	50 352	95 987	108 123	36 061
1987	318 282	4 105	657	377	470	1 612	2 125	3 776	6 793	15 950	47 675	93 348	105 773	35 621
1988	319 119	4 110	680	433	460	1 525	2 160	3 983	6 860	16 016	46 001	91 893	107 082	37 916
1989	320 193	3 799	699	414	398	1 537	2 118	3 968	6 832	15 560	43 693	90 304	109 450	41 421
1990	314 601	3 614	674	376	406	1 487	2 197	4 354	6 991	15 507	41 983	88 458	107 451	41 103
1991	314 427	3 377	636	395	404	1 417	2 049	4 270	7 102	15 493	40 256	88 014	107 416	43 598
1992	308 535	2 954	559	346	377	1 144	1 932	4 379	6 845	15 236	39 033	87 075	104 261	44 394
1993[1]	317 796	2 746	582	325	401	1 072	1 907	4 442	6 672	15 631	38 734	90 160	105 693	49 431
1994	303 333	2 660	497	319	400	1 041	1 829	4 741	6 661	14 983	36 469	86 896	98 982	47 855
1995	310 722	2 595	447	314	388	1 115	1 810	4 748	6 754	15 644	36 068	85 459	103 324	52 056
1996	305 323	2 562	489	267	352	1 104	1 693	4 746	6 789	15 796	35 033	81 333	102 090	53 069
1997	300 414	2 391	456	300	364	1 111	1 712	4 583	6 667	15 689	33 707	77 870	101 365	54 199
1998	300 160	2 327	463	283	343	1 058	1 539	4 684	6 902	15 825	33 778	75 718	101 468	55 772
1999	300 368	2 318	456	257	319	1 085	1 553	4 516	6 946	15 849	33 338	73 736	101 795	58 200
2000	290 186	2 120	380	253	326	1 042	1 491	4 397	7 081	15 470	32 556	69 499	98 075	57 496
2001	286 760	2 042	347	223	330	1 061	1 508	4 262	7 156	15 515	32 005	66 111	97 816	58 384
2002	287 837	2 032	368	223	321	992	1 508	4 150	7 305	15 126	32 423	64 814	99 198	59 377
Females														
1900 - 02	322 058	68 770	36 164	8 757	5 034	6 818	8 264	18 702	21 887	25 679	34 521	42 456	34 907	10 099
1910 - 12	289 608	49 865	27 817	7 113	4 355	5 683	6 531	15 676	19 647	24 481	32 813	46 453	37 353	11 828
1920 - 22	274 772	35 356	17 323	5 808	4 133	5 729	6 753	14 878	18 121	24 347	34 026	48 573	45 521	14 203
1930 - 32	275 336	21 072	9 995	3 990	2 734	4 721	5 931	12 699	15 373	24 695	39 471	59 520	56 250	18 886
1940 - 42	296 646	17 936	5 952	2 743	2 068	4 180	5 028	11 261	14 255	23 629	42 651	70 907	71 377	24 658
1950 - 52	291 597	10 293	2 098	880	625	1 115	1 717	5 018	8 989	18 875	37 075	75 220	92 848	36 844
1960 - 62	304 871	8 887	1 334	627	522	684	811	2 504	6 513	16 720	36 078	73 118	105 956	51 117
1970 - 72	322 968	6 666	1 183	654	459	718	900	2 110	5 345	15 594	36 177	75 599	109 539	68 024
1980 - 82	330 269	3 561	585	355	425	733	772	2 099	4 360	12 206	32 052	72 618	117 760	82 743
1990 - 92	328 218	2 431	485	259	255	520	714	1 989	4 340	9 707	25 105	61 951	115 467	104 994
2000 - 02	317 356	1 586	283	188	208	446	536	1 877	4 426	10 270	20 549	47 324	101 650	128 012
	KIUA	KIUB	KIUC	KIUD	KIUE	KIUF	KIUG	KIUH	KIUI	KIUJ	KIUK	KIUL	KIUM	KIUN
1982	332 830	3 342	561	304	410	689	767	2 057	4 312	11 759	32 183	71 705	119 362	85 379
1983	330 277	3 126	568	318	374	719	698	1 914	4 318	11 384	32 197	69 266	118 940	86 455
1984	323 823	3 005	537	304	344	665	722	1 932	4 269	10 947	32 262	66 432	116 649	85 756
1985	339 094	3 027	574	314	355	626	729	1 852	4 397	10 581	32 010	68 505	122 445	93 679
1986	333 575	2 961	561	275	307	635	769	1 882	4 387	10 211	29 954	67 313	120 663	93 657
1987	326 060	2 972	550	265	288	614	733	1 974	4 454	10 177	29 037	65 570	117 266	92 160
1988	330 059	2 951	552	264	251	612	745	1 915	4 615	9 887	28 154	65 020	117 731	97 362
1989	337 540	2 743	551	271	268	598	773	1 955	4 506	9 834	27 324	64 575	120 975	103 167
1990	327 198	2 658	489	249	273	534	700	1 967	4 463	9 718	26 350	62 019	116 357	101 421
1991	331 754	2 448	512	280	264	538	738	2 005	4 295	9 699	24 952	62 200	116 924	106 899
1992	325 703	2 187	455	249	228	489	704	1 994	4 262	9 705	24 013	61 635	113 119	106 663
1993[1]	340 685	2 084	436	239	283	465	659	2 121	4 204	9 973	23 900	63 767	114 905	117 649
1994	324 303	1 989	410	205	232	406	626	2 053	4 285	10 081	22 401	62 069	106 816	112 730
1995	334 771	1 931	370	224	250	449	592	2 140	4 203	10 389	22 093	60 988	110 247	120 895
1996	330 701	1 904	355	214	224	493	589	2 140	4 215	10 301	21 406	57 889	109 578	121 393
1997	329 332	1 862	333	215	239	487	574	1 960	4 323	10 412	20 999	55 687	108 276	123 965
1998	329 012	1 752	347	213	215	486	568	1 971	4 289	10 430	20 874	54 200	107 135	126 532
1999	331 694	1 727	338	195	240	473	553	1 924	4 372	10 430	21 045	52 240	106 841	131 316
2000	318 180	1 671	277	177	203	449	535	1 961	4 509	10 459	20 533	48 994	101 711	126 701
2001	315 508	1 622	297	208	207	439	552	1 821	4 385	10 287	20 481	46 964	100 907	127 338
2002	318 379	1 465	276	180	214	449	521	1 849	4 385	10 063	20 633	46 013	102 333	129 998

5.19

Deaths: analysis by age and sex[1]
Annual averages or calendar years

continued

Numbers

	All ages[2]	Under 1 year	1-4	5-9	10-14	15-19	20-24	25-34	35-44	45-54	55-64	65-74	75-84	85 and over
England and Wales														
Males														
1900 - 02	288 886	76 095	32 051	7 066	3 818	5 611	7 028	15 869	21 135	26 065	31 600	33 568	23 835	5 144
1910 - 12	257 253	54 678	24 676	5 907	3 348	4 765	5 596	13 603	18 665	24 820	32 217	38 016	24 928	6 036
1920 - 22	240 605	39 796	15 565	5 151	3 314	4 901	5 447	11 551	17 004	25 073	34 639	42 025	29 685	6 455
1930 - 32	243 147	23 331	9 099	3 844	2 435	4 354	5 580	10 600	14 041	25 657	41 581	54 910	39 091	8 624
1940 - 42	268 876	19 393	5 616	2 834	2 051	3 832	3 156	9 484	14 744	25 983	50 058	68 791	51 779	11 158
1950 - 52	266 879	11 498	2 131	1 087	778	1 248	1 947	4 990	9 489	23 815	46 948	75 774	69 496	17 677
1960 - 62	278 369	10 157	1 444	812	742	1 523	1 624	3 278	7 524	22 813	54 908	77 000	73 180	23 364
1970 - 72	293 934	7 818	1 259	860	677	1 524	1 788	3 079	6 637	21 348	56 667	92 389	73 365	26 522
1980 - 82	290 352	4 168	657	452	555	1 716	1 619	3 169	5 590	16 909	47 144	92 485	87 338	28 551
1990 - 92	275 550	2 926	545	325	338	1 157	1 757	3 717	6 057	13 258	34 977	77 063	94 672	38 757
2000 - 02	253 706	1 836	323	200	282	862	1 244	3 619	6 104	13 184	27 696	58 114	87 481	52 761
	KHVA	KHVB	KHVC	KHVD	KHVE	KHVF	KHVG	KHVH	KHVI	KHVJ	KHVK	KHVL	KHVM	KHVN
1982	290 166	3 914	652	391	546	1 669	1 668	3 122	5 526	16 144	46 521	91 079	89 940	28 994
1983	289 419	3 654	604	391	514	1 580	1 635	3 071	5 581	15 632	47 315	88 622	91 531	29 289
1984	282 357	3 443	610	348	501	1 484	1 728	3 033	5 512	15 113	46 904	83 728	90 983	28 970
1985	292 327	3 510	638	328	503	1 374	1 738	2 953	5 776	14 838	45 704	85 695	97 362	31 908
1986	287 894	3 724	573	325	380	1 429	1 746	3 104	5 767	14 370	43 637	84 437	96 201	32 201
1987	280 177	3 637	578	309	404	1 389	1 811	3 218	5 823	13 678	41 367	82 021	94 060	31 882
1988	280 931	3 649	587	374	402	1 279	1 802	3 367	5 855	13 701	39 791	80 870	95 306	33 948
1989	281 290	3 368	606	371	337	1 325	1 782	3 380	5 947	13 407	37 680	79 012	97 027	37 048
1990	277 336	3 207	593	333	338	1 295	1 889	3 714	6 060	13 342	36 405	77 604	95 539	37 017
1991	277 582	2 966	554	341	354	1 208	1 760	3 687	6 160	13 316	34 853	77 227	95 815	39 341
1992	271 732	2 606	487	302	322	969	1 621	3 751	5 952	13 117	33 674	76 357	92 662	39 912
1993[1]	279 561	2 407	510	276	340	912	1 596	3 813	5 784	13 416	33 347	78 881	93 754	44 525
1994	267 555	2 367	432	278	331	843	1 550	4 065	5 769	12 923	31 320	76 270	88 230	43 177
1995	274 449	2 305	391	269	340	910	1 533	4 043	5 880	13 487	30 973	74 970	92 291	47 057
1996	268 682	2 272	441	236	291	925	1 409	4 064	5 843	13 565	30 066	71 046	90 708	47 816
1997	264 865	2 137	412	267	325	947	1 442	3 940	5 707	13 484	28 907	68 024	90 207	49 066
1998	264 707	2 070	413	240	291	875	1 292	4 013	5 895	13 595	29 052	66 099	90 450	50 422
1999	264 299	2 075	405	218	275	902	1 270	3 847	5 934	13 620	28 689	64 296	90 431	52 337
2000	255 547	1 886	335	217	284	872	1 224	3 755	6 048	13 367	27 898	60 593	87 126	51 942
2001	252 426	1 808	318	185	281	882	1 266	3 633	6 065	13 271	27 469	57 492	87 013	52 743
2002	253 144	1 813	315	197	280	833	1 243	3 470	6 198	12 915	27 721	56 258	88 304	53 597
Females														
1900 - 02	269 432	60 090	30 674	7 278	4 010	5 265	6 497	15 065	18 253	21 474	28 424	35 307	29 118	7 977
1910 - 12	242 079	42 642	23 335	5 883	3 519	4 522	5 256	12 742	16 363	20 611	27 571	38 489	31 363	9 782
1920 - 22	229 908	29 178	14 174	4 928	3 456	4 719	5 533	12 244	15 142	20 580	28 633	41 010	38 439	11 871
1930 - 32	233 915	16 929	8 013	3 338	2 293	3 969	5 039	10 716	13 022	21 190	33 798	50 844	48 531	16 234
1940 - 42	253 702	14 174	4 726	2 265	1 695	3 426	4 198	9 470	12 093	20 413	36 814	60 987	61 891	21 550
1950 - 52	252 176	8 367	1 727	732	520	893	1 365	4 131	7 586	16 161	31 875	65 087	81 154	32 579
1960 - 62	266 849	7 409	1 103	527	444	591	700	2 147	5 576	14 389	31 083	63 543	93 548	45 789
1970 - 72	284 181	5 677	1 020	562	396	620	806	1 814	4 585	13 417	31 222	65 817	96 952	61 293
1980 - 82	290 026	3 064	511	301	365	635	670	1 821	3 740	10 420	27 606	63 023	103 676	74 194
1990 - 92	288 851	2 161	420	227	217	455	625	1 718	3 765	8 347	21 446	53 783	101 752	93 914
2000 - 02	279 482	1 412	251	168	182	382	455	1 629	3 805	8 893	17 659	40 734	89 387	114 525
	KIVA	KIVB	KIVC	KIVD	KIVE	KIVF	KIVG	KIVH	KIVI	KIVJ	KIVK	KIVL	KIVM	KIVN
1982	291 695	2 861	485	253	353	588	672	1 781	3 708	9 990	27 751	62 221	104 745	76 287
1983	290 189	2 727	489	269	332	629	597	1 655	3 708	9 786	27 792	59 913	104 844	77 448
1984	284 524	2 594	454	260	302	575	621	1 676	3 658	9 343	27 764	57 813	102 744	76 720
1985	298 407	2 631	497	260	308	544	630	1 583	3 803	9 111	27 664	59 285	108 099	83 992
1986	293 309	2 589	491	248	272	562	674	1 646	3 834	8 761	25 785	58 360	106 463	83 624
1987	286 817	2 635	489	237	246	525	639	1 708	3 897	8 774	25 000	56 858	103 354	82 455
1988	290 477	2 621	498	232	218	542	650	1 670	4 025	8 448	24 104	56 567	103 666	87 236
1989	295 582	2 440	472	241	226	531	650	1 678	3 925	8 406	23 336	55 932	106 000	91 745
1990	287 510	2 357	434	220	230	472	616	1 702	3 875	8 337	22 511	53 770	102 440	90 546
1991	292 462	2 192	439	248	222	462	644	1 729	3 703	8 369	21 303	54 156	103 268	95 727
1992	286 581	1 933	387	214	199	432	615	1 722	3 717	8 336	20 585	53 423	99 548	95 470
1993[1]	299 238	1 835	374	194	246	394	575	1 802	3 625	8 614	20 423	55 245	100 947	104 964
1994	285 639	1 753	364	187	204	357	535	1 771	3 669	8 688	19 039	53 921	94 197	100 954
1995	295 234	1 677	333	196	210	382	502	1 859	3 644	9 001	18 891	52 987	97 162	108 390
1996	291 453	1 687	320	175	196	430	507	1 852	3 658	8 852	18 244	50 195	96 679	108 658
1997	290 416	1 663	297	177	209	426	490	1 718	3 737	9 016	17 949	48 293	95 508	110 933
1998	290 308	1 555	309	177	189	407	480	1 724	3 678	9 066	17 927	46 894	94 713	113 189
1999	291 819	1 546	300	168	215	385	470	1 668	3 786	9 029	18 031	45 100	93 878	117 243
2000	280 117	1 491	246	156	179	384	466	1 688	3 874	9 090	17 635	42 174	89 310	113 424
2001	277 947	1 432	270	188	178	378	467	1 591	3 768	8 917	17 610	40 465	88 808	113 875
2002	280 383	1 314	236	159	189	384	432	1 608	3 772	8 672	17 733	39 564	90 043	116 277

5.19 Deaths: analysis by age and sex[1]
Annual averages or calendar years
continued

Numbers

	All ages[2]	Under 1 year	1-4	5-9	10-14	15-19	20-24	25-34	35-44	45-54	55-64	65-74	75-84	85 and over
Scotland														
Males														
1900 - 02	40 224	9 189	4 798	1 083	672	1 069	1 292	2 506	2 935	3 591	4 597	4 531	3 117	834
1910 - 12	35 981	7 510	3 935	962	595	826	910	1 969	2 469	3 325	4 356	5 113	3 182	813
1920 - 22	34 649	6 757	2 847	710	489	747	791	1 616	2 128	3 314	4 785	5 624	3 928	911
1930 - 32	32 476	4 426	1 771	610	365	568	706	1 352	1 848	2 979	5 095	6 906	4 839	1 010
1940 - 42	36 384	3 973	1 011	449	321	668	888	1 643	2 090	3 348	5 728	8 556	6 317	1 337
1950 - 52	32 236	1 949	349	175	105	200	265	693	1 267	3 151	5 574	8 544	8 094	1 871
1960 - 62	32 401	1 578	222	121	102	146	185	456	1 013	2 986	6 682	8 505	7 980	2 425
1970 - 72	32 446	944	168	119	93	178	233	396	875	2 617	6 641	10 176	7 383	2 624
1980 - 82	31 723	451	80	56	71	206	233	423	776	2 280	5 601	10 152	8 804	2 591
1990 - 92	29 421	287	57	34	40	137	230	485	744	1 730	4 402	8 611	9 311	3 353
2000 - 02	27 526	165	30	23	30	119	196	523	882	1 775	3 781	7 038	8 535	4 430
	KHWA	KHWB	KHWC	KHWD	KHWE	KHWF	KHWG	KHWH	KHWI	KHWJ	KHWK	KHWL	KHWM	KHWN
1982	31 801	436	77	53	69	220	225	410	733	2 195	5 669	10 015	9 052	2 647
1983	31 196	380	67	53	65	185	178	406	764	2 131	5 769	9 414	9 204	2 580
1984	30 731	389	87	53	65	172	202	429	696	2 017	5 493	9 337	9 222	2 569
1985	31 147	342	57	49	58	174	208	390	759	1 959	5 486	9 339	9 569	2 757
1986	31 111	334	66	44	49	177	238	436	757	1 967	5 354	9 169	9 574	2 946
1987	30 384	331	54	46	47	163	212	415	779	1 870	5 131	9 058	9 383	2 895
1988	30 195	324	64	39	42	181	246	475	808	1 915	4 997	8 763	9 314	3 027
1989	31 025	331	62	24	45	150	246	445	719	1 721	4 889	9 028	9 922	3 443
1990	29 617	297	62	31	50	138	240	502	745	1 734	4 512	8 635	9 499	3 172
1991	29 312	299	59	42	34	150	211	441	757	1 741	4 382	8 657	9 209	3 330
1992	29 334	265	51	28	36	123	238	511	731	1 716	4 313	8 541	9 225	3 556
1993[1]	30 504	240	50	39	37	107	225	490	725	1 817	4 375	9 031	9 470	3 898
1994	28 416	212	42	27	48	133	212	538	715	1 684	4 114	8 575	8 446	3 670
1995	28 791	197	37	30	30	152	195	563	698	1 746	4 144	8 449	8 604	3 946
1996	29 223	206	41	23	46	139	212	556	755	1 845	4 087	8 259	8 926	4 128
1997	28 305	186	32	22	27	114	208	521	788	1 794	3 876	7 909	8 791	4 037
1998	28 132	183	37	34	39	134	200	524	843	1 796	3 828	7 746	8 585	4 183
1999	28 605	161	31	23	33	138	215	545	818	1 820	3 773	7 569	8 908	4 571
2000	27 511	173	33	24	28	115	198	512	842	1 716	3 789	7 224	8 523	4 334
2001	27 324	155	22	27	35	131	179	510	902	1 820	3 751	6 950	8 433	4 409
2002	27 743	167	34	17	27	111	211	546	901	1 789	3 804	6 940	8 648	4 548
Females														
1900 - 02	39 891	7 143	4 477	1 162	747	1 058	1 246	2 625	2 732	3 130	4 485	5 273	4 305	1 508
1910 - 12	36 132	5 854	3 674	981	618	836	910	2 149	2 473	2 909	3 960	5 636	4 588	1 552
1920 - 22	34 449	5 029	2 602	687	489	711	889	1 947	2 266	2 828	4 157	5 587	5 443	1 814
1930 - 32	32 377	3 319	1 602	527	339	568	666	1 508	1 812	2 731	4 380	6 630	6 178	2 117
1940 - 42	33 715	2 852	921	373	283	595	656	1 382	1 672	2 528	4 630	7 674	7 613	2 536
1950 - 52	31 525	1 432	284	115	84	185	293	714	1 127	2 188	4 204	8 157	9 310	3 431
1960 - 62	30 559	1 107	170	80	63	72	87	287	762	1 897	4 115	7 752	9 991	4 177
1970 - 72	30 978	694	118	69	46	73	74	231	608	1 769	4 036	7 823	10 112	5 324
1980 - 82	32 326	337	49	37	44	74	73	213	493	1 456	3 565	7 781	11 333	6 871
1990 - 92	31 747	190	45	20	29	49	72	218	458	1 093	2 966	6 630	11 079	8 898
2000 - 02	30 235	123	24	14	21	50	64	199	493	1 110	2 341	5 326	9 785	10 685
	KIWA	KIWB	KIWC	KIWD	KIWE	KIWF	KIWG	KIWH	KIWI	KIWJ	KIWK	KIWL	KIWM	KIWN
1982	33 221	317	50	35	45	78	60	203	479	1 444	3 552	7 735	11 867	7 356
1983	32 258	266	51	33	33	67	76	201	504	1 317	3 568	7 558	11 340	7 244
1984	31 614	283	62	32	37	72	78	205	475	1 320	3 703	6 979	11 134	7 234
1985	32 820	282	55	37	34	63	76	207	481	1 179	3 563	7 449	11 604	7 790
1986	32 356	247	50	16	24	50	77	188	441	1 181	3 372	7 251	11 476	7 983
1987	31 630	232	44	21	34	60	70	195	429	1 160	3 301	7 032	11 262	7 790
1988	31 762	219	33	22	21	54	63	197	470	1 115	3 250	6 879	11 361	8 078
1989	33 992	223	56	23	27	54	104	224	470	1 156	3 279	7 052	12 100	9 224
1990	31 910	213	32	16	34	46	68	204	468	1 099	3 109	6 685	11 233	8 703
1991	31 729	174	54	22	31	57	74	225	463	1 070	2 974	6 542	11 059	8 984
1992	31 603	184	50	23	21	45	73	225	442	1 109	2 816	6 663	10 944	9 008
1993[1]	33 545	172	45	34	27	55	60	258	460	1 089	2 793	6 918	11 330	10 304
1994	30 912	170	29	11	19	33	74	229	495	1 102	2 723	6 617	10 008	9 402
1995	31 709	178	26	16	26	50	70	231	435	1 100	2 601	6 449	10 452	10 075
1996	31 448	159	24	31	21	49	67	218	453	1 172	2 573	6 206	10 256	10 219
1997	31 189	130	23	28	21	43	71	199	496	1 128	2 480	5 985	10 164	10 421
1998	31 032	137	26	28	19	55	68	198	485	1 106	2 416	5 955	9 913	10 626
1999	31 676	115	26	20	17	65	58	201	467	1 128	2 431	5 837	10 198	11 113
2000	30 288	132	20	10	21	46	56	222	510	1 086	2 324	5 512	9 875	10 474
2001	30 058	135	20	16	21	47	71	189	480	1 111	2 361	5 235	9 695	10 677
2002	30 360	103	32	15	20	58	65	185	489	1 134	2 339	5 232	9 784	10 904

5.19
Deaths: analysis by age and sex[1]
Annual averages or calendar years
continued

Numbers

	All ages[2]	Under 1 year	1-4	5-9	10-14	15-19	20-24	25-34	35-44	45-54	55-64	65-74	75-84	85 and over
Northern Ireland														
Males														
1900 - 02	11 554	1 958	985	280	206	367	446	779	669	832	1 413	1 666	1 368	585
1910 - 12	10 469	1 697	841	222	152	282	311	569	679	836	1 148	2 011	1 287	434
1920 - 22	9 622	1 491	596	191	150	258	334	496	570	869	1 159	1 749	1 324	435
1930 - 32	8 626	1 083	406	126	90	154	209	375	437	740	1 313	1 988	1 317	388
1940 - 42	9 383	1 258	322	117	102	153	202	379	462	751	1 290	2 305	1 637	405
1950 - 52	8 197	658	105	55	36	50	77	179	318	671	1 169	2 117	2 178	583
1960 - 62	8 080	499	67	38	27	49	48	108	216	623	1 419	2 037	2 131	816
1970 - 72	8 786	396	58	40	32	76	83	115	221	643	1 590	2 493	2 157	881
1980 - 82	8 420	211	37	20	26	77	92	144	202	539	1 414	2 518	2 346	795
1990 - 92	7 550	102	21	13	18	55	73	132	178	423	1 044	2 175	2 393	922
2000 - 02	7 029	64	13	11	14	50	62	128	195	411	851	1 656	2 347	1228
	KHXA	KHXB	KHXC	KHXD	KHXE	KHXF	KHXG	KHXH	KHXI	KHXJ	KHXK	KHXL	KHXM	KHXN
1982	8 004	205	31	12	17	77	78	129	203	528	1 341	2 332	2 289	762
1983	8 209	196	24	25	30	69	86	124	192	475	1 409	2 433	2 303	843
1984	8 007	163	28	22	14	52	69	133	217	517	1 318	2 355	2 308	811
1985	8 088	151	33	16	22	64	85	109	193	519	1 312	2 424	2 310	850
1986	8 155	161	14	15	15	70	83	128	188	477	1 361	2 381	2 348	914
1987	7 721	137	25	22	19	60	102	143	191	402	1 177	2 269	2 330	844
1988	7 993	137	29	20	16	65	112	141	197	400	1 213	2 260	2 462	941
1989	7 878	100	31	19	16	62	90	143	166	432	1 124	2 264	2 501	930
1990	7 648	110	19	12	18	54	68	138	186	431	1 066	2 219	2 413	914
1991	7 533	112	23	12	16	59	78	142	185	436	1 021	2 130	2 392	927
1992	7 469	83	21	16	19	52	73	117	162	403	1 046	2 177	2 374	926
1993[1]	7 731	99	22	10	24	53	86	139	163	398	1 012	2 248	2 469	1 008
1994	7 362	81	23	14	21	65	67	138	177	376	1 035	2 051	2 306	1 008
1995	7 482	93	19	15	18	53	82	142	176	411	951	2 040	2 429	1 053
1996	7 418	84	7	8	15	40	72	126	191	386	880	2 028	2 456	1 125
1997	7 244	68	12	11	12	50	62	122	172	411	924	1 937	2 367	1 096
1998	7 321	74	13	9	13	49	47	147	164	434	898	1 873	2 433	1 167
1999	7 464	82	20	16	11	45	68	124	194	409	876	1 871	2 456	1 292
2000	7 128	61	12	12	14	55	69	130	191	387	869	1 682	2 426	1 220
2001	7 010	79	7	11	14	48	63	119	189	424	785	1 669	2 370	1 232
2002	6 950	52	19	9	14	48	54	134	206	422	898	1 616	2 246	1 232
Females														
1900 - 02	12 735	1 537	1 013	317	277	495	521	1 012	902	1 075	1 612	1 876	1 484	614
1910 - 12	11 397	1 369	808	249	218	325	365	785	811	961	1 282	2 328	1 402	494
1920 - 22	10 415	1 149	547	193	188	299	331	687	713	939	1 236	1 976	1 639	518
1930 - 32	9 044	824	380	125	102	184	226	475	539	774	1 293	2 046	1 541	535
1940 - 42	9 229	910	305	105	90	159	174	409	490	688	1 207	2 246	1 873	572
1950 - 52	7 896	494	87	33	21	37	59	173	276	526	996	1 976	2 384	834
1960 - 62	7 463	371	61	20	15	21	24	70	175	434	880	1 823	2 417	1 151
1970 - 72	7 809	295	45	23	17	25	20	65	152	408	919	1 959	2 475	1 407
1980 - 82	7 917	160	26	17	17	23	29	65	127	329	881	1 813	2 752	1 678
1990 - 92	7 620	80	20	12	9	16	17	53	117	267	672	1 538	2 636	2 182
2000 - 02	7 638	50	9	7	5	13	17	49	129	266	548	1 263	2 479	2 802
	KIXA	KIXB	KIXC	KIXD	KIXE	KIXF	KIXG	KIXH	KIXI	KIXJ	KIXK	KIXL	KIXM	KIXN
1982	7 914	164	26	16	12	23	35	73	125	325	880	1 749	2 750	1 736
1983	7 830	133	28	16	9	23	25	58	106	281	837	1 795	2 756	1 763
1984	7 685	128	21	12	5	18	23	51	136	284	795	1 640	2 770	1 802
1985	7 867	114	22	17	13	19	23	62	113	291	783	1 771	2 742	1 897
1986	7 910	125	20	11	11	23	18	48	112	269	797	1 702	2 724	2 050
1987	7 613	105	17	7	8	29	24	71	128	243	736	1 680	2 650	1 915
1988	7 820	111	21	10	12	16	32	48	120	324	800	1 574	2 704	2 048
1989	7 966	80	23	7	15	13	19	53	111	272	709	1 591	2 875	2 198
1990	7 778	88	23	13	9	16	16	61	120	282	730	1 564	2 684	2 172
1991	7 563	82	19	10	11	19	20	51	129	260	675	1 502	2 597	2 188
1992	7 519	70	18	12	8	12	16	47	103	260	612	1 549	2 627	2 185
1993[1]	7 902	77	17	11	10	16	24	61	119	270	684	1 604	2 628	2 381
1994	7 752	66	17	7	9	16	17	53	121	291	639	1 531	2 611	2 374
1995	7 828	76	11	12	14	17	20	50	124	288	601	1 552	2 633	2 430
1996	7 800	58	11	8	7	14	15	70	104	277	589	1 488	2 643	2 516
1997	7 727	69	13	10	9	18	13	43	90	268	570	1 409	2 604	2 611
1998	7 672	60	12	8	7	24	20	49	126	258	531	1 351	2 509	2 717
1999	8 199	66	12	7	8	23	25	55	119	273	583	1 303	2 765	2 960
2000	7 775	48	11	11	3	19	13	51	125	283	574	1 308	2 526	2 803
2001	7 503	55	7	4	8	14	14	41	137	259	510	1 264	2 404	2 786
2002	7 636	48	8	6	5	7	24	56	124	257	561	1 217	2 506	2 817

1 See chapter text.
2 In some years the totals include a small number of persons whose age was not stated.

Sources: Office for National Statistics: 01329 813223;
General Register Office for Scotland;
Northern Ireland Statistics and Research Agency

5.20 Infant and maternal mortality[1]

| | Deaths of Infants under 1 year of age per thousand live births | | | | | | | | | | | | Maternal deaths per thousand live births[3] | | | |
| | United Kingdom | | | England and Wales[2] | | | Scotland | | | Northern Ireland | | | United Kingdom | England and Wales | Scotland | Northern Ireland |
	Total	Males	Females	Total	Males	Females	Total	Males	Females	Total	Males	Females				
1900 - 02	142	156	128	146	160	131	124	136	111	113	123	103	4.71	4.67	4.74	6.03
1910 - 12	110	121	98	110	121	98	109	120	97	101	110	92	3.95	3.67	5.65	5.28
1920 - 22	82	92	71	80	90	69	94	106	82	86	95	77	4.37	4.03	6.36	5.62
1930 - 32	67	75	58	64	72	55	84	94	73	75	83	66	4.54	4.24	6.40	5.24
1940 - 42	59	66	51	55	62	48	77	87	66	80	89	70	3.29	2.74	4.50	3.79
1950 - 52	30	34	26	29	33	25	37	42	32	40	45	36	0.88	0.79	1.09	1.09
1960 - 62	22	25	19	22	24	19	26	30	22	27	30	24	0.36	0.36	0.37	0.43
1970 - 72	18	20	16	18	20	15	19	22	17	22	24	20	0.17	0.17	0.17	0.12
1980 - 82	12	13	10	11	13	10	12	13	10	13	15	12	0.09	0.09	0.14	0.06
1990 - 92	7	8	6	7	8	6	7	8	6	7	8	6	0.07	0.07	0.10	-
2000 - 02	5	6	5	5	6	5	5	6	5	5	6	5	0.07	0.06	0.12	0.05
	KKAW	KKAX	KKAY	KKAZ	KKBW	KKBX	KKBY	KKBZ	KKCW	KKCX	KKCY	KKCZ	KKDW	KKDX	KKDY	KKDZ
1980	12.2	13.4	10.6	12.0	13.3	10.7	12.1	13.6	10.4	13.4	15.1	11.5	0.11	0.11	0.15	0.07
1981	11.2	12.7	9.5	11.1	12.6	9.4	11.3	12.3	10.2	13.2	14.7	11.6	0.09	0.09	0.19	0.04
1982	11.0	12.3	9.5	10.8	12.2	9.4	11.4	12.9	9.8	13.6	14.8	12.4	0.07	0.07	0.09	0.07
1983	10.1	11.3	8.9	10.1	11.3	8.9	9.9	11.3	8.5	12.1	13.9	10.1	0.09	0.09	0.12	0.15
1984	9.6	10.7	8.4	9.5	10.6	8.3	10.3	11.7	8.9	10.5	11.4	9.6	0.09	0.08	0.12	0.11
1985	9.4	10.4	8.3	9.4	10.4	8.2	9.4	10.0	8.7	9.6	10.6	8.5	0.07	0.07	0.13	0.07
1986	9.5	10.9	8.1	9.6	11.0	8.0	8.8	9.9	7.7	10.2	11.0	9.2	0.07	0.07	0.11	-
1987	9.1	10.3	7.9	9.2	10.4	7.9	8.5	9.7	7.2	8.7	9.6	7.7	0.06	0.07	0.03	0.04
1988	9.0	10.2	7.7	9.0	10.3	7.7	8.2	9.5	6.8	8.9	9.6	8.2	0.06	0.06	0.12	0.07
1989	8.4	9.5	7.2	8.4	9.6	7.3	8.7	10.2	7.2	6.9	7.4	6.3	0.08	0.08	0.06	-
1990	7.9	8.8	6.8	7.9	8.9	6.8	7.7	8.8	6.6	7.5	8.1	6.8	0.08	0.08	0.06	-
1991	7.4	8.3	6.3	7.4	8.3	6.4	7.1	8.7	5.3	7.4	8.3	6.4	0.07	0.06	0.13	0.04
1992	6.6	7.4	5.7	6.6	7.4	5.8	6.8	7.9	5.7	6.0	6.4	5.6	0.07	0.07	0.11	-
1993	6.3	7.0	5.6	6.3	7.0	5.6	6.5	7.4	5.6	7.1	7.8	6.3	0.06	0.05	0.11	-
1994	6.2	6.9	5.4	6.2	6.9	5.4	6.2	6.8	5.6	6.1	6.5	5.6	0.08	0.08	0.15	-
1995	6.2	6.9	5.4	6.1	6.9	5.3	6.2	6.4	6.1	7.1	7.5	6.6	0.07	0.07	0.10	-
1996	6.1	6.8	5.4	6.1	6.9	5.4	6.2	6.7	5.5	5.8	6.7	4.8	0.07	0.07	0.10	0.04
1997	5.8	6.4	5.3	5.9	6.5	5.3	5.3	6.1	4.5	5.6	5.5	5.8	0.06	0.06	0.07	-
1998	5.7	6.3	5.0	5.7	6.4	5.0	5.6	6.2	4.9	5.6	6.1	5.1	0.07	0.07	0.09	0.04
1999	5.8	6.4	5.1	5.8	6.5	5.1	5.0	5.7	4.3	6.4	6.8	5.9	0.05	0.05	0.13	-
2000	5.6	6.1	5.0	5.6	6.1	5.1	5.7	6.4	5.1	5.1	5.5	4.6	0.07	0.06	0.15	-
2001	5.5	6.0	5.0	5.4	5.9	4.9	5.5	5.8	5.2	6.1	7.0	5.2	0.07	0.07	0.11	0.09
2002	5.2	5.9	4.5	5.2	5.9	4.5	5.3	6.4	4.1	4.7	4.8	4.6	0.06	0.06	0.10	0.05

5.20 Infant and maternal mortality[1]
continued

Deaths per thousand live births

		1989	1990	1991	1992	1993	1994	1995	1996	1997	1998	1999	2000	2001	2002
								Analysis by sex of infant							

Total

United Kingdom:

		1989	1990	1991	1992	1993	1994	1995	1996	1997	1998	1999	2000	2001	2002
Stillbirths[4]	KHNQ	4.7	4.6	4.7	4.3	5.7	5.8	5.6	5.5	5.3	5.4	5.3	5.3	5.3	5.6
Perinatal[4]	KHNR	8.3	8.1	8.1	7.7	9.0	8.9	8.9	8.7	8.3	8.3	8.2	8.1	8.0	8.3
Neonatal	KHNS	4.7	4.5	4.4	4.3	4.2	4.1	4.2	4.1	3.9	3.8	3.9	3.9	3.6	3.5
Post neonatal	KHNT	3.7	3.3	3.0	2.3	2.2	2.1	2.0	2.0	2.0	1.9	1.9	1.7	1.8	1.7
England and Wales:															
Stillbirths[4]	KHNU	4.7	4.6	4.6	4.3	5.7	5.7	5.5	5.4	5.3	5.3	5.3	5.3	5.3	5.6
Perinatal[4]	KHNV	8.3	8.1	8.0	7.6	8.9	8.9	8.7	8.6	8.3	8.2	8.2	8.2	8.0	8.3
Neonatal	KHNW	4.8	4.6	4.4	4.3	4.2	4.1	4.1	4.1	3.9	3.8	3.9	3.9	3.6	3.6
Post neonatal	KHNX	3.7	3.3	3.0	2.3	2.1	2.1	2.0	2.0	2.0	1.9	1.9	1.7	1.9	1.7
Scotland:															
Stillbirths[4]	KHNY	5.0	5.3	5.5	4.9	6.4	6.1	6.6	6.4	5.3	6.1	5.2	5.6	5.7	5.4
Perinatal[4]	KHNZ	8.7	8.7	8.6	8.5	9.6	9.0	9.6	9.2	7.8	8.7	7.6	8.4	8.5	7.6
Neonatal	KHOA	4.7	4.4	4.4	4.6	4.0	4.0	4.0	3.9	3.2	3.6	3.3	4.0	3.8	3.2
Post neonatal	KHOB	4.0	3.3	2.7	2.2	2.5	2.2	2.2	2.2	2.1	2.0	1.7	1.8	1.7	2.1
Northern Ireland:															
Stillbirths[4]	KHOC	5.1	4.4	4.7	4.9	5.2	6.3	6.1	6.3	5.4	5.1	5.7	4.3	5.1	5.7
Perinatal[4]	KHOD	8.2	7.6	8.4	8.2	8.8	9.7	10.4	9.4	8.2	8.1	10.0	7.3	8.5	8.9
Neonatal	KHOE	4.0	4.0	4.6	4.1	4.9	4.2	5.5	3.7	4.2	3.9	4.8	3.8	4.5	3.5
Post neonatal	KHOF	2.9	3.5	2.8	1.9	2.1	1.9	1.6	2.0	1.4	1.7	1.6	1.3	1.6	1.2

Males

		1989	1990	1991	1992	1993	1994	1995	1996	1997	1998	1999	2000	2001	2002
United Kingdom:															
Perinatal[4]	KHOG	9.3	8.8	8.7	8.3	9.7	9.6	9.4	9.1	8.7	8.8	8.7	8.7	8.6	8.9
Neonatal	KHOH	5.4	5.0	4.9	4.8	4.7	4.6	4.6	4.6	4.2	4.2	4.3	4.2	4.0	4.0
Infant mortality	KHOI	9.5	8.8	8.3	7.4	7.0	6.9	6.9	6.8	6.4	6.3	6.4	6.1	6.0	5.9
England and Wales:															
Perinatal[4]	KHOK	9.2	8.8	8.6	8.1	9.5	9.6	9.3	9.0	8.7	8.8	8.6	8.7	8.5	8.9
Neonatal	KHOL	5.4	5.1	4.8	4.7	4.6	4.6	4.6	4.6	4.2	4.3	4.3	4.2	3.9	4.0
Infant mortality	KHOM	9.6	8.9	8.3	7.4	7.0	6.9	6.9	6.9	6.5	6.4	6.5	6.1	5.9	5.9
Scotland:															
Perinatal[4]	KHOO	10.0	9.1	9.8	9.8	10.8	9.6	10.1	10.0	8.1	9.6	8.4	9.5	9.2	7.9
Neonatal	KHOP	5.3	4.7	5.5	5.5	4.5	4.4	4.1	4.3	3.4	4.0	3.8	4.5	4.0	3.7
Infant mortality	KHOQ	10.2	8.8	8.7	7.9	7.4	6.8	6.4	6.7	6.1	6.2	5.7	6.4	5.8	6.4
Northern Ireland:															
Perinatal[4]	KHOS	8.7	8.7	7.9	8.6	10.3	10.4	10.4	10.1	8.5	8.9	10.5	8.0	9.8	10.0
Neonatal	KHOT	4.5	4.8	5.5	4.5	5.9	4.3	5.7	4.3	4.3	4.4	5.5	4.2	5.3	3.8
Infant mortality	KHOU	7.4	8.1	8.3	6.4	7.8	6.5	7.5	6.7	5.5	6.1	6.8	5.5	7.0	4.8

Females

		1989	1990	1991	1992	1993	1994	1995	1996	1997	1998	1999	2000	2001	2002
United Kingdom:															
Perinatal[4]	KHOW	7.4	7.4	7.5	7.0	8.2	8.2	8.3	8.2	7.9	7.7	7.8	7.5	7.4	7.7
Neonatal	KHOX	4.0	4.0	3.8	3.8	3.6	3.6	3.7	3.6	3.5	3.3	3.4	3.5	3.3	3.1
Infant mortality	KHOY	7.2	6.8	6.3	5.7	5.6	5.4	5.4	5.4	5.3	5.0	5.1	5.0	5.0	4.5
England and Wales:															
Perinatal[4]	KHPA	7.4	7.4	7.5	7.0	8.3	8.1	8.1	8.2	7.9	7.7	7.8	7.6	7.3	7.7
Neonatal	KHPB	4.0	4.0	3.9	3.9	3.6	3.6	3.6	3.6	3.6	3.3	3.5	3.5	3.2	3.1
Infant mortality	KHPC	7.3	6.8	6.4	5.8	5.6	5.4	5.3	5.4	5.3	5.0	5.1	5.1	4.9	4.5
Scotland:															
Perinatal[4]	KHPE	7.3	8.2	7.4	7.1	8.3	8.4	9.2	8.4	7.5	7.9	6.7	7.2	7.8	7.2
Neonatal	KHPF	4.1	4.1	3.2	3.7	3.5	3.6	3.9	3.5	2.9	3.2	2.8	3.5	3.5	2.6
Infant mortality	KHPG	7.2	6.6	5.3	5.7	5.6	5.6	6.1	5.5	4.5	4.9	4.3	5.1	5.2	4.1
Northern Ireland:															
Perinatal[4]	KHPI	7.6	6.4	9.0	7.9	7.2	8.9	10.5	8.6	8.0	7.3	9.5	6.5	7.0	7.8
Neonatal	KHPJ	3.5	3.2	3.7	3.6	3.9	4.1	5.2	3.1	4.0	3.4	4.1	3.4	3.6	3.1
Infant mortality	KHPK	6.3	6.8	6.4	5.6	6.3	5.6	6.6	4.8	5.8	5.1	5.9	4.6	5.2	4.6

1 See chapter text.
2 From 1937 to 1956 death rates are based on the births to which they relate in the current and preceding years.
3 Deaths in pregnancy and childbirth.
4 Deaths per 1,000 live and stillbirths.

Sources: Office for National Statistics: 01329 813758;
General Register Office for Scotland;
Northern Ireland Statistics and Research Agency

5.21 Death rates per 1,000 population[1]
United Kingdom
Analysis by age and sex

	All ages	0-4	5-9	10-14	15-19	20-24	25-34	35-44	45-54	55-64	65-74	75-84	85 and over
Males													
1900 - 02	18.4	57.0	4.1	2.4	3.7	5.0	6.6	11.0	18.6	35.0	69.9	143.6	289.6
1910 - 12	14.9	40.5	3.3	2.0	3.0	3.9	5.0	8.0	14.9	29.8	62.1	133.8	261.5
1920 - 22	13.5	33.4	2.9	1.8	2.9	3.9	4.5	6.9	11.9	25.3	57.8	131.8	259.1
1930 - 32	12.9	22.3	2.3	1.5	2.6	3.3	3.5	5.7	11.3	23.7	57.9	134.2	277.0
1940 - 42	..	..	..	..	..	..	..	..	..	..	..	..	..
1950 - 52	12.6	7.7	0.7	0.5	0.9	1.4	1.6	3.0	8.5	23.2	55.2	127.6	272.0
1960 - 62	12.5	6.4	0.5	0.4	0.9	1.1	1.1	2.5	7.4	22.2	54.4	123.4	251.0
1970 - 72	12.4	4.6	0.4	0.4	0.9	1.0	1.0	2.4	7.3	20.9	52.9	116.3	246.1
1980 - 82	12.1	3.2	0.3	0.3	0.8	0.9	0.9	1.9	6.3	18.2	46.7	107.1	224.9
1990 - 92	11.2	2.0	0.2	0.2	0.7	0.9	1.0	1.8	4.6	14.2	38.6	93.0	201.4
2000 - 02	10.0	1.4	0.1	0.2	0.5	0.9	1.0	1.6	4.0	10.4	29.0	75.3	188.0
	KHZA	KHZB	KHZC	KHZD	KHZE	KHZF	KHZG	KHZH	KHZJ	KHZK	KHZL	KHZM	KHZN
1981	12.3	3.2	0.3	0.3	0.9	0.9	1.0	2.0	6.4	18.4	47.5	110.6	239.5
1982	12.1	2.9	0.3	0.3	0.8	0.9	0.9	1.8	6.1	17.9	46.4	106.4	226.1
1983	12.0	2.7	0.3	0.3	0.8	0.8	0.9	1.8	5.9	18.0	46.3	104.7	223.4
1984	11.7	2.6	0.2	0.3	0.7	0.9	0.9	1.7	5.7	17.5	45.0	100.9	214.3
1985	12.1	2.6	0.2	0.3	0.7	0.9	0.9	1.8	5.6	17.5	44.9	104.9	224.1
1986	11.9	2.6	0.2	0.2	0.7	0.9	0.9	1.7	5.5	17.0	43.5	102.0	217.0
1987	11.5	2.5	0.2	0.3	0.7	0.9	0.9	1.7	5.2	16.3	41.9	97.6	202.5
1988	11.5	2.5	0.2	0.3	0.7	0.9	1.0	1.7	5.1	15.9	41.1	96.9	204.2
1989	11.5	2.3	0.2	0.2	0.7	0.9	0.9	1.7	4.9	15.3	40.2	97.1	211.5
1990	11.3	2.2	0.2	0.2	0.7	1.0	1.0	1.8	4.8	14.7	39.3	94.2	202.0
1991	11.3	2.0	0.2	0.2	0.7	0.9	1.0	1.8	4.7	14.2	38.7	93.4	203.4
1992	11.0	1.8	0.2	0.2	0.6	0.9	1.0	1.8	4.4	13.8	37.9	91.5	198.8
1993	11.3	1.7	0.2	0.2	0.6	0.9	1.0	1.7	4.4	13.6	38.6	94.8	208.6
1994	10.8	1.6	0.2	0.2	0.6	0.9	1.0	1.7	4.1	12.8	36.8	90.3	194.8
1995	11.0	1.6	0.2	0.2	0.6	0.9	1.0	1.7	4.2	12.6	36.7	90.1	202.2
1996	10.8	1.6	0.1	0.2	0.6	0.9	1.0	1.7	4.2	12.3	35.2	86.0	199.7
1997	10.6	1.5	0.2	0.2	0.6	1.0	1.0	1.7	4.1	11.8	33.9	83.3	196.9
1998	10.6	1.5	0.1	0.2	0.6	0.9	1.0	1.7	4.1	11.6	33.0	81.9	193.9
1999	10.5	1.5	0.1	0.2	0.6	0.9	1.0	1.7	4.1	11.2	32.3	80.9	195.9
2000	10.1	1.4	0.1	0.2	0.6	0.9	1.0	1.6	4.0	10.8	30.3	76.8	188.2
2001	10.0	1.3	0.1	0.2	0.6	0.9	1.0	1.6	4.0	10.4	28.7	74.9	187.1
2002	10.0	1.4	0.1	0.2	0.5	0.8	1.0	1.6	4.0	10.1	27.9	74.2	188.7
Females													
1900 - 02	16.3	47.9	4.3	2.6	3.5	4.3	5.8	9.0	14.4	27.9	59.3	127.0	262.6
1910 - 12	13.3	34.0	3.3	2.1	2.9	3.4	4.4	6.7	11.5	23.1	50.7	113.7	234.0
1920 - 22	11.9	26.9	2.8	1.9	2.8	3.4	4.1	5.6	9.3	19.2	45.6	111.5	232.4
1930 - 32	11.5	17.7	2.1	1.5	2.4	2.9	3.3	4.6	8.3	17.6	43.7	110.1	246.3
1940 - 42	..	..	..	..	..	..	..	..	..	..	..	..	..
1950 - 52	11.2	6.0	0.5	0.4	0.7	1.0	1.4	2.3	5.3	12.9	35.5	98.4	228.8
1960 - 62	11.2	4.9	0.3	0.3	0.4	0.5	0.8	1.8	4.5	11.0	30.8	87.3	218.5
1970 - 72	11.3	3.6	0.3	0.2	0.4	0.4	0.6	1.6	4.5	10.5	27.5	76.7	196.1
1980 - 82	11.4	2.3	0.2	0.2	0.3	0.4	0.5	1.3	3.9	9.9	24.8	67.2	179.5
1990 - 92	11.1	1.5	0.1	0.2	0.3	0.3	0.4	1.1	2.9	8.4	22.1	58.7	157.2
2000 - 02	10.5	1.1	0.1	0.1	0.2	0.3	0.4	1.0	2.6	6.4	17.9	51.2	157.5
	KHZO	KHZP	KHZQ	KHZR	KHZS	KHZT	KHZU	KHZV	KHZW	KHZX	KHZY	KHZZ	KHZI
1981	11.6	2.5	0.2	0.2	0.3	0.4	0.5	1.3	3.9	10.0	25.5	70.4	190.6
1982	11.5	2.3	0.2	0.2	0.3	0.4	0.5	1.2	3.8	9.9	24.9	66.7	179.2
1983	11.4	2.1	0.2	0.2	0.3	0.3	0.5	1.2	3.6	9.8	24.7	65.0	176.2
1984	11.2	2.0	0.2	0.2	0.3	0.3	0.5	1.2	3.5	9.7	24.3	62.4	168.7
1985	11.7	2.0	0.2	0.2	0.3	0.3	0.5	1.2	3.4	9.9	24.6	64.7	176.5
1986	11.4	2.0	0.2	0.2	0.3	0.3	0.5	1.1	3.3	9.5	23.9	63.1	170.3
1987	11.2	2.0	0.2	0.2	0.3	0.3	0.5	1.1	3.3	9.3	23.2	60.8	160.9
1988	11.3	1.9	0.2	0.2	0.3	0.3	0.5	1.2	3.2	9.2	23.1	60.5	163.6
1989	11.5	1.8	0.2	0.2	0.3	0.3	0.5	1.1	3.1	9.0	23.0	61.4	166.3
1990	11.1	1.7	0.1	0.2	0.3	0.3	0.4	1.1	3.0	8.8	22.2	58.8	158.7
1991	11.2	1.6	0.2	0.2	0.3	0.3	0.4	1.1	2.9	8.4	22.3	59.1	157.1
1992	11.0	1.4	0.1	0.1	0.3	0.3	0.4	1.1	2.8	8.1	21.9	58.1	155.7
1993	11.5	1.3	0.1	0.2	0.3	0.3	0.5	1.1	2.8	8.1	22.5	60.6	165.2
1994	10.9	1.3	0.1	0.1	0.2	0.3	0.4	1.1	2.8	7.6	21.7	57.6	154.8
1995	11.2	1.2	0.1	0.1	0.3	0.3	0.5	1.1	2.8	7.5	21.8	57.9	161.5
1996	11.1	1.2	0.1	0.1	0.3	0.3	0.5	1.1	2.7	7.3	21.0	56.5	159.5
1997	11.0	1.2	0.1	0.1	0.3	0.3	0.4	1.1	2.7	7.1	20.5	55.2	160.4
1998	11.0	1.2	0.1	0.1	0.3	0.3	0.4	1.0	2.7	7.0	20.2	54.4	160.0
1999	11.0	1.2	0.1	0.1	0.3	0.3	0.4	1.0	2.7	6.9	19.7	54.3	163.9
2000	10.6	1.1	0.1	0.1	0.3	0.3	0.5	1.0	2.7	6.6	18.5	51.7	156.0
2001	10.4	1.1	0.1	0.1	0.2	0.3	0.4	1.0	2.6	6.4	17.8	50.9	156.0
2002	10.5	1.0	0.1	0.1	0.2	0.3	0.4	1.0	2.6	6.2	17.4	51.1	160.6

1 The figures for 1992 to 2000 have been revised using the latest population estimates.

Sources: Office for National Statistics: 01329 813223; General Register Office for Scotland; Northern Ireland Statistics and Research Agency

5.22 Life tables[1]

	Interim life tables, 2000-02							
	United Kingdom				England and Wales			
	Males		Females		Males		Females	
Age(x)	l_x	e^0_x	l_x	e^0_x	l_x	e^0_x	l_x	e^0_x
0 years	100 000	75.7	100 000	80.4	100 000	75.9	100 000	80.6
5 years	99 300	71.2	99 434	75.9	99 301	71.5	99 434	76.0
10 years	99 239	66.3	99 382	70.9	99 242	66.5	99 382	71.1
15 years	99 158	61.3	99 328	65.9	99 163	61.6	99 328	66.1
20 years	98 883	56.5	99 204	61.0	98 902	56.7	99 207	61.2
25 years	98 464	51.7	99 055	56.1	98 506	51.9	99 064	56.3
30 years	98 011	46.9	98 879	51.2	98 079	47.2	98 892	51.4
35 years	97 482	42.2	98 625	46.3	97 574	42.4	98 643	46.5
40 years	96 815	37.4	98 246	41.5	96 932	37.7	98 271	41.7
45 years	95 875	32.8	97 634	36.7	96 027	33.0	97 676	36.9
50 years	94 383	28.3	96 639	32.1	94 576	28.4	96 705	32.2
55 years	92 129	23.9	95 110	27.5	92 394	24.1	95 208	27.7
60 years	88 514	19.8	92 757	23.2	88 890	19.9	92 913	23.3
65 years	82 778	15.9	89 073	19.0	83 324	16.0	89 323	19.1
70 years	74 145	12.5	83 371	15.1	74 845	12.6	83 755	15.2
75 years	61 420	9.5	74 281	11.7	62 231	9.6	74 809	11.7
80 years	44 817	7.1	60 830	8.7	45 578	7.1	61 444	8.7
85 years	27 025	5.1	43 030	6.2	27 620	5.1	43 670	6.2
90 years	11 677	3.7	23 308	4.3	11 983	3.7	23 743	4.3

	Interim life tables, 2000-02							
	Scotland				Northern Ireland			
	Males		Females		Males		Females	
Age(x)	l_x	e^0_x	l_x	e^0_x	l_x	e^0_x	l_x	e^0_x
0 years	100 000	73.3	100 000	78.8	100 000	75.2	100 000	80.1
5 years	99 277	68.8	99 427	74.2	99 318	70.7	99 444	75.6
10 years	99 205	63.9	99 381	69.3	99 235	65.8	99 386	70.6
15 years	99 115	59.0	99 315	64.3	99 133	60.8	99 345	65.7
20 years	98 748	54.2	99 155	59.4	98 752	56.1	99 242	60.7
25 years	98 133	49.5	98 954	54.5	98 203	51.4	99 089	55.8
30 years	97 406	44.8	98 729	49.6	97 684	46.6	98 908	50.9
35 years	96 628	40.2	98 415	44.8	97 160	41.9	98 694	46.0
40 years	95 690	35.5	97 957	40.0	96 507	37.1	98 361	41.2
45 years	94 395	31.0	97 202	35.3	95 594	32.5	97 674	36.4
50 years	92 514	26.6	95 978	30.7	94 094	27.9	96 652	31.8
55 years	89 580	22.3	94 129	26.2	91 713	23.6	95 108	27.3
60 years	84 859	18.4	91 205	22.0	88 088	19.4	92 723	22.9
65 years	77 590	14.9	86 681	18.0	82 116	15.7	88 958	18.7
70 years	67 648	11.7	79 855	14.3	73 177	12.3	83 061	14.9
75 years	53 963	9.0	69 540	11.1	60 350	9.3	73 654	11.4
80 years	37 878	6.8	55 235	8.2	43 595	6.9	60 326	8.4
85 years	21 715	5.0	37 320	6.0	25 533	5.0	41 898	5.9
90 years	9 024	3.8	19 553	4.2	10 595	3.6	22 033	4.1

Note Column l_x shows the number who would survive to exact **age(x)**, out of 100,000 born, who were subject throughout their lives to the death rates experienced in the three-year period indicated. Column e^0_x is 'the expectation of life', that is, the average future lifetime which would be lived by a person aged exactly x if likewise subject to the death rates experienced in the three-year period indicated.

1 See chapter text.

Source: Government Actuary's Department: 020 7211 2622

5.23 Adoptions by date of entry in Adopted Children Register: by age and sex

	All ages		Under 1		1-4		5-9		10-14		15-17	
	Numbers	Percentages	Numbers	Percentages	Numbers	Percentages	Numbers	Percentages	Numbers	Percentages	Numbers	Percentages
United Kingdom **Persons**												
	VOXI	VOXJ	VOXK	VOXL	VOXM	VOXN	VOXO	VOXP	VOXQ	VOXR	VOXS	VOXT
1997	5 928	100	259	4	1 789	30	2 170	37	1 380	23	330	6
1998	4 996	100	213	4	1 647	33	1 793	36	1 098	22	245	5
1999	4 951	100	234	5	1 795	36	1 714	35	957	19	251	5
2000	5 503	100	283	5	2 203	40	1 745	32	1 025	19	247	4
2001[1]	6 588	100	272	4	2 874	44	2 047	31	1 103	17	290	4
2002	6 239	100	313	5	2 737	44	1 937	31	999	16	253	4
Males												
	VOXU	VOXV	VOXW	VOXX	VOXY	VOXZ	VOYA	VOYB	VOYC	VOYD	VOYE	VOYF
1997	2 918	100	145	5	911	31	1 050	36	669	23	143	5
1998	2 514	100	110	4	854	34	880	35	562	22	108	4
1999	2 428	100	115	5	903	37	833	34	459	19	118	5
2000	2 740	100	144	5	1 115	41	867	32	491	18	123	4
2001[2]	3 314	100	138	4	1 483	45	1 006	30	547	17	139	4
2002	3 140	100	176	6	1 425	45	935	30	488	16	116	4
Females												
	VOYG	VOYH	VOYI	VOYJ	VOYK	VOYL	VOYM	VOYN	VOYO	VOYP	VOYQ	VOYR
1997	3 010	100	114	4	878	29	1 120	37	711	24	187	6
1998	2 482	100	103	4	793	32	913	37	536	22	137	6
1999	2 523	100	119	5	892	35	881	35	498	20	133	5
2000	2 763	100	139	5	1 088	39	878	32	534	19	124	4
2001[2]	3 274	100	134	4	1 391	42	1 041	32	556	17	151	5
2002	3 099	100	137	4	1 312	42	1 002	32	511	16	137	4
England and Wales **Persons**												
	GQTP	GQTQ	GQTR	GQTS	GQTT	GQTU	GQTV	GQTW	GQTX	GQTY	GQTZ	GQUA
1997	5 307	100	225	4	1 606	30	1 914	36	1 265	24	297	6
1998	4 386	100	195	4	1 489	34	1 545	35	937	21	220	5
1999	4 317	100	196	5	1 627	38	1 477	34	803	19	214	5
2000	4 940	100	251	5	2 019	41	1 549	31	906	18	215	4
2001[1]	5 981	100	246	4	2 648	44	1 845	31	983	16	257	4
2002	5 680	100	287	5	2 532	45	1 748	31	900	16	213	4
Males												
	GQUB	GQUC	GQUD	GQUE	GQUF	GQUG	GQUH	GQUI	GQUJ	GQUK	GQUL	GQUM
1997	2 610	100	122	5	824	32	917	35	619	24	128	5
1998	2 214	100	100	5	775	35	755	34	489	22	95	4
1999	2 115	100	96	5	816	39	712	34	390	18	101	5
2000	2 452	100	127	5	1 022	42	759	31	434	18	110	4
2001[2]	3 011	100	124	4	1 370	45	904	30	494	16	118	4
2002	2 871	100	160	6	1 324	46	846	29	443	15	98	3
Females												
	GQUN	GQUO	GQUP	GQUQ	GQUR	GQUS	GQUT	GQUU	GQUV	GQUW	GQUX	GQUY
1997	2 697	100	103	4	782	29	997	37	646	24	169	6
1998	2 172	100	95	4	714	33	790	36	448	21	125	6
1999	2 202	100	100	5	811	37	765	35	413	19	113	5
2000	2 488	100	124	5	997	40	790	32	472	19	105	4
2001[2]	2 970	100	122	4	1 278	43	941	32	489	16	139	5
2002	2 809	100	127	5	1 208	43	902	32	457	16	115	4

5.23 Adoptions by date of entry in Adopted Children Register: by age and sex
continued

	All ages		Under 1		1-4		5-9		10-14		15-17	
	Numbers	Percentages	Numbers	Percentages	Numbers	Percentages	Numbers	Percentages	Numbers	Percentages	Numbers	Percentages
Scotland **Persons**												
	GQUZ	GQVA	GQVB	GQVC	GQVD	GQVE	GQVF	GQVG	GQVH	GQVI	GQVJ	GQVK
1997	471	100	26	6	137	29	192	41	88	19	28	6
1998	490	100	16	3	126	26	198	40	128	26	22	4
1999	489	100	34	7	135	28	176	36	117	24	27	6
2000	391	100	24	6	140	36	123	31	85	22	19	5
2001	468	100	18	4	176	38	161	34	92	20	21	4
2002[3]	385	100	13	3	143	37	130	34	73	19	26	7
Males												
	GQVL	GQVM	GQVN	GQVO	GQVP	GQVQ	GQVR	GQVS	GQVT	GQVU	GQVV	GQVW
1997	230	100	17	7	64	28	100	43	37	16	12	5
1998	235	100	8	3	63	27	94	40	60	26	10	4
1999	247	100	17	7	71	29	91	37	54	22	14	6
2000	210	100	13	6	75	36	71	34	43	20	8	4
2001	241	100	11	5	93	39	83	34	40	17	14	6
2002[4]	193	100	8	4	75	39	60	31	37	19	13	7
Females												
	GQVX	GQVY	GQVZ	GQWA	GRFK	GRFL	GRFM	GRFN	GRFO	GRFP	GRFQ	GRFR
1997	241	100	9	4	73	30	92	38	51	21	16	7
1998	255	100	8	3	63	25	104	41	68	27	12	5
1999	242	100	17	7	64	26	85	35	63	26	13	5
2000	181	100	11	6	65	36	52	29	42	23	11	6
2001	227	100	7	3	83	37	78	34	52	23	7	3
2002[5]	192	100	5	3	68	35	70	36	36	19	13	7
Northern Ireland **Persons**												
	VOYS	VOYT	VOYU	VOYV	VOYW	VOYX	VOYY	VOYZ	VOZA	VOZB	VOZC	VOZD
1997	150	100	8	5	46	31	64	43	27	18	5	3
1998	120	100	2	2	32	27	50	42	33	28	3	3
1999	145	100	4	3	33	23	61	42	37	26	10	7
2000	172	100	8	5	44	26	73	42	34	20	13	8
2001	139	100	8	6	50	36	41	29	28	20	12	9
2002	174	100	13	7	62	36	59	34	26	15	14	8
Males												
	VOZE	VOZF	VOZG	VOZH	VOZI	VOZJ	VOZK	VOZL	VOZM	VOZN	VOZO	VOZP
1997	78	100	6	8	23	29	33	42	13	17	3	4
1998	65	100	2	3	16	25	31	48	13	20	3	5
1999	66	100	2	3	16	24	30	45	15	23	3	5
2000	78	100	4	5	18	23	37	47	14	18	5	6
2001	62	100	3	5	20	32	19	31	13	21	7	11
2002	76	100	8	11	26	34	29	38	8	11	5	7
Females												
	VOZQ	VOZR	VOZS	VOZT	VOZU	VOZV	VOZW	VOZX	VOZY	VOZZ	VPAA	VPVD
1997	72	100	2	3	23	32	31	43	14	19	2	3
1998	55	100	–	–	16	29	19	35	20	36	–	–
1999	79	100	2	3	17	22	31	39	22	28	7	9
2000	94	100	4	4	26	28	36	38	20	21	8	9
2001	77	100	5	6	30	39	22	29	15	19	5	6
2002	98	100	5	5	36	37	30	31	18	18	9	9

1 Includes two cases where age was greater than 17.
2 Includes one case where age was greater than 17.
3 Includes four adoptions where age was greater than 17 - these have been
  included in the '15-17' age group.
4 Includes one adoption where age was greater than 17 - this has been included in the '15-17' age group.
5 Includes three adoptions where age was greater than 17 - these have been
  included in the '15-17' age group.

Sources: Office for National Statistics: 01329 813339;
General Register Office for Scotland

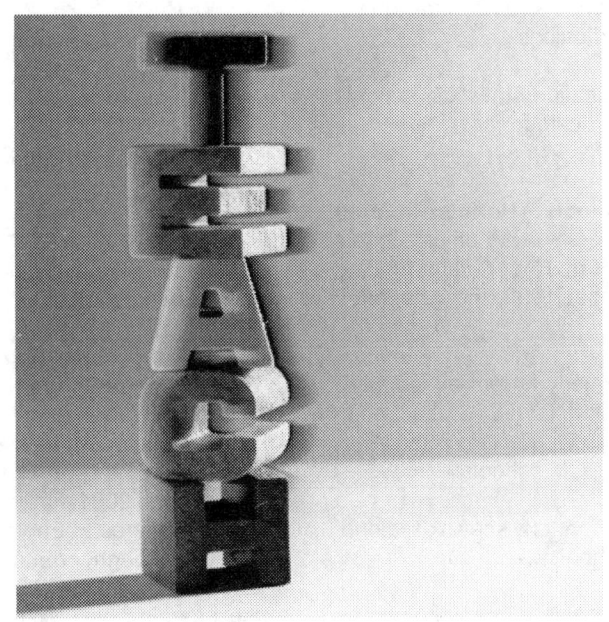

6 Education

Education

Educational establishments in the United Kingdom are administered and financed in several ways. Most schools are controlled by local education authorities (LEAs), which are part of the structure of local government, but some are 'assisted', receiving grants direct from central government sources and being controlled by governing bodies which have a substantial degree of autonomy. Completely outside the public sector are non-maintained schools run by individuals, companies or charitable institutions.

For the purposes of UK education statistics, schools fall under the following broad categories:

Mainstream state schools
(Grant-aided mainstream schools in Northern Ireland)
These schools work in partnership with other schools and local education authorities and they receive funding from LEAs. Since 1 September 1999, the categories (typically in England) are:

Community - schools formerly known as 'county' plus some former Grant-maintained (GM) schools;

Foundation - most former GM schools;

Voluntary Aided - schools formerly known as 'aided' and some former GM schools;

Voluntary Controlled - schools formerly known as 'controlled'.

Non-maintained mainstream schools consisting of

(a) Independent schools
Schools which charge fees and may also be financed by individuals, companies or charitable institutions. These include Direct Grant schools, where the governing bodies are assisted by Departmental grants and a proportion of the pupils attending them do so free or under an arrangement by which local education authorities meet tuition fees. City technology colleges and Academies (applicable in England only) are also included as independent schools.

(b) Non-maintained schools
Run by voluntary bodies who may receive some grant from central government for capital work and for equipment, but their current expenditure is met primarily from the fees charged to the LEAs for pupils placed in schools.

Special schools
Provide education for children with special educational needs (SEN) (Record of Needs, in Scotland) who cannot be educated satisfactorily in an ordinary school. Maintained special schools are run by LEAs, while non-maintained special schools are financed as shown at (b) above.

Pupil Referral Units
Pupil Referral Units (PRUs) operate in England and Wales and provide education outside of a mainstream or special school setting, to meet the needs of difficult or disruptive children.

Schools in Scotland are categorised as Education Authority, Grant-Aided, Opted-out/Self-governing (these three being grouped together as 'Publicly funded' schools), Independent schools and Partnership schools.

The home Government Departments dealing with education statistics are:

Department for Education and Skills (DfES);

National Assembly for Wales (NAfW);

Scottish Executive (SE);

Northern Ireland Department of Education (DENI);

Northern Ireland Department for Employment and Learning (DELNI).

Each of the home Education Departments in Great Britain, along with the Northern Ireland Department of Education, have overall responsibility for funding the schools sectors in their own country.

Up to March 2001, further education (FE) courses in FE sector colleges in England and in Wales were largely funded through grants from the respective Further Education Funding Councils. In April 2001, however, the Learning and Skills Council (LSC) took over the responsibility for funding the FE sector in England, and the National Council for Education and Training for Wales (part of Education and Learning Wales – ELWa) did so for Wales. The LSC in England is also responsible for funding provision for FE and some non-prescribed higher education in FE sector colleges; it also funds some FE provided by LEA maintained and other institutions referred to as 'external institutions'. In Wales, the National Council – ELWa, funds FE provision made by FE institutions via a third party or sponsored arrangements. The Scottish Further Education Funding Council (SFEFC) funds FE colleges in Scotland, while the Department for Employment and Learning funds FE colleges in Northern Ireland.

Higher education courses in higher education establishments are largely publicly funded through block grants from the HE funding councils in England and Scotland, the Higher Education Council – ELWa in Wales, and the Department of Employment and Learning in Northern Ireland. In addition, some designated HE (mainly HND/HNC Diplomas and Certificates of HE) is also funded by these sources. The FE sources mentioned above fund the remainder.

Statistics for the separate systems obtained in England, Wales, Scotland and Northern Ireland are collected and processed separately in accordance with the particular needs of the responsible Departments. Since 1994/95 the Higher Education Statistics Agency (HESA) has undertaken the data collection for all higher education institutions (HEIs) in the UK. This includes the former Universities Funding Council (UFC) funded UK universities previously collected by the Universities Statistical Record. There are some structural differences in the information collected for schools, further and higher education in each of the four home countries and in some tables the GB/UK data presented are amalgamations from sources that are not entirely comparable.

Stages of education

There are five stages of education: foundation, primary, secondary, further and higher education, and education is compulsory for all children between the ages of five (four in Northern Ireland) and sixteen. The non-compulsory fourth stage, further education, covers non-advanced education, which can be taken at both further (including tertiary) education colleges, higher education institutions and increasingly in secondary schools. The fifth stage, higher education, is study beyond A levels and their equivalent which, for most full-time students, takes place in higher education institutions.

Foundation education

In recent years there has been a major expansion of pre-school education, and in England, the National Curriculum has been extended to include the Foundation stage and covers children's education from the age of three to the end of reception year, when most are just five and some almost six years old. Children under five attend a variety of settings including state nursery schools, nursery classes within primary schools and, in England and Wales, reception classes within primary schools, as well as settings outside the state sector such as voluntary pre-schools or privately run nurseries.

Primary education

The primary stage covers three age ranges: nursery (under 5), infant (5 to 7 or 8) and junior (up to 11 or 12) but in Scotland and Northern Ireland there is generally no distinction between infant and junior schools. Most public sector primary schools take both boys and girls in mixed classes. It is usual to transfer straight to secondary school at age 11 (in England, Wales and Northern Ireland) or 12 (in Scotland), but in England some children make the transition via middle schools catering for various age ranges between 8 and 14. Depending on their individual age ranges middle schools are classified as either primary or secondary.

Secondary education

Public provision of secondary education in an area may consist of a combination of different types of school, the pattern reflecting historical circumstance and the policy adopted by the local education authority. Comprehensive schools largely admit pupils without reference to ability or aptitude and cater for all the children in a neighbourhood, but in some areas they co-exist with grammar, secondary modern or technical schools. In 2002/03, 88 per cent of secondary pupils in England attended comprehensive schools while all secondary schools in Wales are comprehensive schools. The majority of education authority secondary schools in Scotland are comprehensive in character and offer six years of secondary education; however in remote areas there are several two-year and four-year secondary schools. In Northern Ireland, post primary education is provided by secondary intermediate and grammar schools.

Special schools

Special schools (day or boarding) provide education for children who require specialist support to complete their education, for example because they have physical or other difficulties. Many pupils with special educational needs are educated in mainstream schools. All children attending special schools are offered a curriculum designed to overcome their learning difficulties and to enable them to become self-reliant.

Further education

The term further education may be used in a general sense to cover all non-advanced courses taken after the period of compulsory education, but more commonly it excludes those staying on at secondary school and those in higher education, i.e. courses in universities and colleges leading to qualifications above GCE A Level, SCE H Grade, GNVQ/NVQ level 3, and their equivalents. Since 1 April 1993 sixth form colleges in England and Wales have been included in the further education sector.

Higher education

Higher education is defined as courses that are of a standard that is higher than GCE A level, the Higher Grade of the Scottish Certificate of Education, GNVQ/NVQ level 3 or the Edexcel (formerly BTEC) or SQA National Certificate/Diploma. There are three main levels of HE course: (i) postgraduate courses are those leading to higher degrees, diplomas and certificates (including postgraduate certificates of education and professional qualifications) which usually require a first degree as entry qualification; (ii) first degrees which includes first degrees, first degrees with qualified teacher status, enhanced first degrees, first degrees obtained concurrently with a diploma, and intercalated first degrees; (iii) other undergraduate courses which includes all other higher education courses, for example HND's and Diplomas in HE. As a result of the 1992 Further and Higher Education Act, former polytechnics and some other higher education institutions were designated as universities in 1992/93. Students normally attend HE courses at higher education institutions, but some attend at further education colleges. Some also attend institutions which do not receive public grant (such as the University of Buckingham) and these numbers are excluded from the tables.

6.1 Number of schools[1] by type and establishments of further and higher education

Academic years

		1990 /91	1995 /96	1997 /98	1998 /99	1999 /00	2000[2] /01	2001[2] /02	2002[3] /03
United Kingdom:									
Public sector mainstream									
Nursery[4,5]	KBFK	1 364	1 486	1 681	2 369	2 864	3 228	3 227	3 394
Primary[6]	KBFA	24 135	23 441	23 230	23 125	23 036	22 902	22 800	22 638
Secondary[7]	KBFF	4 790	4 463	4 434	4 418	4 405	4 337	4 306	4 284
of which 6th form colleges	KPGM	116	..	..	..	..	..	..	..
Non-maintained mainstream[1]	KBFU	2 508	2 436	2 499	2 482	2 457	2 414	2 409	2 380
Special - all	KBFP	1 830	1 565	1 517	1 522	1 523	1 498	1 483	1 471
maintained	KPVX	..	1 456	1 419	1 428	1 426	1 401	1 387	1 367
non maintained	KPGO	..	109	98	94	97	97	96	104
Pupil referral units	KXEP	..	315	332	325	325	338	340	389
Universities (including Open University)[8]	KAHG	48	89	88	88	88	89	89	89
All other further and higher education institutions	KJPQ	588	609	596	581	574	551	543	527
Higher education institutions	KPVY	..	66	63	58	58	60	60	60
Further education institutions	KSNY	..	543	533	523	516	491	483	467
of which 6th form colleges	KPGP	..	110	108	107	105	103	101	103
England:									
Public sector mainstream									
Nursery	KBAK	566	547	533	520	514	506	494	475
Primary	KBAA	19 047	18 480	18 312	18 234	18 158	18 069	17 985	17 861
Secondary[7]	KBAF	3 897	3 594	3 567	3 560	3 550	3 481	3 457	3 436
of which 6th form colleges	KPGS	114	..	–	..	..	..	..	..
Non-maintained	KBAU	2 289	2 266	2 244	2 231	2 204	2 205	2 206	2 180
Special - all	KBAP	1 380	1 263	1 229	1 209	1 197	1 175	1 161	1 160
maintained	KPGT	..	1 191	1 164	1 148	1 134	1 113	1 098	1 088
non maintained	KPGU	..	72	65	61	63	62	63	72
Pupil referral units	KXEQ	..	291	309	298	295	308	312	360
Universities (including Open University)[8]	KAHM	37	72	71	70	70	72	72	72
All other further and higher education institutions	KJPR	460	503	491	482	458	449	442	427
Higher education institutions	KPXA	..	50	48	47	47	46	46	46
Further education institutions	KPWC	..	453	443	435	411	403	396	381
of which 6th form colleges	KPGV	..	110	108	107	105	103	101	103
Wales:									
Public sector mainstream									
Nursery	KBBK	54	52	47	46	42	41	40	37
Primary	KBBA	1 717	1 681	1 673	1 660	1 644	1 631	1 624	1 602
Secondary[7]	KBBF	230	228	228	229	228	229	227	227
of which 6th form colleges	KPGY	2	..	..	..	..	..	..	..
Non-maintained	KBBU	71	62	57	54	55	54	56	59
Special (Maintained)	KBBP	61	54	50	48	47	45	44	43
Pupil referral units	KZBF	..	24	23	27	30	30	28	29
Universities[8]	KAHS	1	2	2	2	2	2	2	2
All other further and higher education institutions	KJQP	38	31	30	28	28	29	29	29
Higher education institutions	KSNZ	..	5	4	4	4	5	5	5
Further education institutions	KPGZ	..	26	26	24	24	24	24	24
Scotland:									
Public sector mainstream									
Nursery[5]	KBDK	659	796	1 010	1 712	2 213	2 586	2 597	2 782
Primary	KBDA	2 372	2 332	2 300	2 291	2 293	2 278	2 271	2 258
Secondary	KBDF	424	405	401	392	389	389	387	386
Non-maintained[1]	KBDU	131	87	176	175	176	129	122	119
Special - all	KBDP	343	201	191	218	229	230	230	221
maintained	KYCZ	343	164	158	185	195	195	197	189
non-maintained	KYDA	..	37	33	33	34	35	33	32
Universities[8]	KAHX	8	13	13	14	14	13	13	13
All other further and higher education institutions	KJRA	64	56	56	52	52	54	53	53
Higher education institutions	KPWE	..	9	9	5	5	7	7	7
Further education institutions	KPHB	..	47	47	47	47	47	46	46
Northern Ireland:									
Grant aided mainstream									
Nursery[4]	KBEK	85	91	91	91	95	95	96	100
Primary[6]	KBEA	999	948	945	940	941	924	920	917
Secondary	KBEF	239	236	238	237	238	238	235	235
Non-maintained	KBEU	17	21	22	22	22	26	25	22
Special (Maintained)	KBEP	46	47	47	47	50	48	48	47
Universities	KIAD	2	2	2	2	2	2	2	2
Colleges of education	KIAE	2	2	2	2	2	2	2	2
Further education colleges	KIAG	24	17	17	17	17	17	17	16

1 See chapter text. From 1997/98 to 1999/00, non-maintained schools in Scotland with more than one department have been counted once for each department e.g. a school with nursery, primary and secondary departments has been counted 3 times. Subsequent figures show primary and secondary only.

2 Includes revised data.

3 Provisional. Includes 2001/02 UK higher education institution data and further education institution data for Wales.

4 Excludes voluntary and private pre-school education centres in Northern Ireland (363 in total in 2002/03).

5 Nursery schools figures for Scotland prior to 1998/99 only include data for Local Authority pre-schools. Data thereafter include partnership pre-schools.

6 From 1995/96, includes Preparatory Departments in Northern Ireland Grammar Schools (20 in total in 2002/03).

7 From 1993/94 excludes sixth form colleges in England and Wales which were reclassified as further education colleges on 1 April 1993.

8 From 1993/94 includes former polytechnics and colleges which became universities as a result of the Further and Higher Education Act 1992.

Source: Education Departments: 01325 392754

6.2 Full-time and part-time pupils in school[1] by age[2,3] and sex
United Kingdom
All schools at January[4]

		1993	1994	1995	1996	1997	1998	1999	2000	2001	2002[5]	2003[6]
Age at previous 31 August[7]												
Number (thousands)												
England[8]	KBIA	7 842	7 883	8 013	8 110	8 195	8 261	8 310	8 346	8 374	8 369	8 367
Wales	KBIB	493	498	504	508	510	513	513	512	512	511	509
Scotland[2]	KBIC	832	841	845	846	848	850	844	874	882	876	874
Northern Ireland[3]	KBID	346	349	351	353	354	352	352	349	348	346	345
United Kingdom	KBIE	9 513	9 571	9 714	9 816	9 907	9 975	10 020	10 081	10 116	10 102	10 095
Boys and girls												
2 - 4[9]	KBIF	1 082	1 103	1 135	1 146	1 148	1 149	1 154	1 184	1 187	1 180	1 189
5 - 10	KBIG	4 392	4 462	4 517	4 583	4 628	4 668	4 661	4 629	4 597	4 537	4 489
11	KBIH	727	713	718	717	744	746	762	783	771	783	791
12 - 14	KBII	2 112	2 179	2 179	2 157	2 151	2 182	2 211	2 256	2 297	2 320	2 343
15	KBIK	638	651	700	722	716	701	706	705	732	737	751
16	KBIL	313	259	259	279	289	288	283	285	287	298	290
17	KBIM	215	180	181	191	206	217	218	213	219	223	217
18 and over	KBIN	35	23	24	22	22	24	25	27	27	23	24
Boys												
14	KBIO	338	367	376	370	365	368	367	381	384	391	401
15	KBIP	327	333	358	368	365	358	361	359	374	377	384
16	KBIQ	154	128	127	137	141	140	137	138	139	145	140
17	KBIR	104	88	88	92	100	104	104	101	105	107	104
18 and over	KBIS	18	12	13	12	12	13	13	14	15	13	13
Girls												
14	KBIT	322	347	358	355	349	350	352	364	365	373	384
15	KBIU	311	318	342	354	351	343	345	346	358	360	368
16	KBIV	159	131	132	143	148	149	146	147	148	153	150
17	KBIW	111	92	93	99	107	113	114	111	114	116	113
18 and over	KBIX	16	11	11	10	10	11	11	13	12	11	11

1 From 1 April 1993 excludes 6th form colleges in England and Wales which were reclassified as further education colleges.
2 Figures for Scotland are estimates using the stage rolls.
3 In Northern Ireland, a split is not collected by age but is available by year group and so this is used as a proxy.
4 In Wales and Scotland, as at the previous September.
5 Includes revised data.

6 Provisional.
7 1 July for Northern Ireland and 31 December for Scotland.
8 From 1992, figures for independent schools in England include pupils aged less than 2.
9 Includes the so-called "rising 5s" (i.e. those pupils who become 5 during the autumn term).

Source: Education Departments: 01325 392754

6.3 Number of pupils and teachers, and pupil:teacher ratios[1] by school type
United Kingdom
At January[2]

		1998	1999	2000[3]	2001[3,4]	2002[3,4]	2003[3,5]
All schools or departments							
Total							
Pupils (thousands)							
Full-time and full-time							
equivalent of part-time	KBCA	9 741.3	9 782.6	9 828.3	9 856.3	9 858.1	9 853.7
Teachers[6] (thousands)	KBCB	533.6	540.4	545.6	553.1	558.3	561.6
Pupils per teacher[6]:							
United Kingdom	KBCC	18.2	18.2	18.1	17.9	17.7	17.6
England	KBCD	18.5	18.4	18.3	18.1	18.0	17.9
Wales	KBCE	19.1	18.8	18.7	18.4	18.1	18.1
Scotland	KBCF	15.8	15.4	15.4	15.4	15.4	14.9
Northern Ireland	KBCG	17.1	17.1	16.9	16.6	16.4	16.3
Public sector mainstream schools or departments							
Nursery							
Pupils (thousands)							
Full-time and full-time							
equivalent of part-time	KBFM	61.7	61.1	75.3	77.5	85.6	84.8
Teachers[6] (thousands)	KBFN	3.0	3.0	3.1	3.4	3.6	3.6
Pupils per teacher[6]	KBFO	20.7	20.6	24.2	23.1	23.6	23.6
Primary[7]							
Pupils (thousands)							
Full-time and full-time							
equivalent of part-time	KBFB	5 213.8	5 202.5	5 167.9	5 130.5	5 083.4	5 025.7
Teachers[6] (thousands)	KBFD	225.4	226.7	228.0	229.6	231.5	228.8
Pupils per teacher[6]	KBFE	23.1	22.9	22.7	22.3	22.0	22.0
Secondary[8]							
Pupils (thousands)							
Full-time and full-time							
equivalent of part-time	KBFG	3 741.1	3 793.3	3 859.0	3 915.5	3 948.0	3 991.7
Teachers[6] (thousands)	KBFH	228.7	230.4	232.9	237.0	241.2	243.3
Pupils per teacher[6]	KBFI	16.4	16.5	16.6	16.5	16.4	16.4
Special schools							
Pupils (thousands)							
Full-time and full-time							
equivalent of part-time							
all	KBFQ	114.5	..	..	..	..	..
maintained	KPGE	108.4	108.5	107.4	106.5	105.4	104.5
non-maintained[9]	KPGF	6.0	..	..	..	..	..
Teachers[6] (thousands)							
all	KBFS	18.1	..	..	..	..	..
maintained	KPGG	16.7	16.9	17.0	17.0	17.0	17.0
non-maintained[9]	KPGH	1.4	..	..	..	..	..
Pupils per teacher[9]							
all	KBFT	6.3	..	..	..	..	..
maintained	KPGI	6.5	6.4	6.3	6.3	6.2	6.1
non-maintained[9]	KPGJ	4.4	..	..	..	..	..

1 'All schools' pupil:teacher ratios exclude Pupil Referral Units and non-maintained special schools.
2 In Scotland and Wales the school census date is September whereas that for the rest of the United Kingdom remains at January.
3 Nursery schools for Scotland refer to pre-school education centres and are not therefore directly comparable with earlier years.
4 Includes revised data.

5 Provisional.
6 Figures of teachers and of pupil:teacher ratios take account of the full-time equivalent of part-time teachers.
7 Includes preparatory departments attached to grammar schools in Northern Ireland.
8 Includes voluntary grammar schools in Northern Ireland.
9 England and Scotland only.

Source: Education Departments: 01325 392754

6.4 Full-time and part-time pupils with special educational needs (SEN)[1], 2002/03[2]
United Kingdom
By type of school

Thousands and percentages

	United Kingdom	England[3]	Wales	Scotland	Northern Ireland
All schools					
Total pupils	10 100.4	8 366.8	509.2	874.0	350.4
SEN pupils with statements	296.9	250.5	16.0	20.0	10.3
Incidence (Percentages)[4]	*2.9*	*3.0*	*3.1*	*2.3*	*3.0*
Maintained schools[5]					
Nursery[6]					
Total pupils	159.7	40.5	2.1	105.1	12.1
SEN pupils with statements	2.6	0.6	-	2.0	0.1
Incidence (Percentages)[4]	*1.6*	*1.4*	*0.6*	*1.9*	*0.5*
Placement (Percentages)[7]	*0.9*	*0.2*	*0.1*	*10.0*	*0.6*
Primary[9]					
Total pupils	5 178.2	4 309.0	278.7	413.7	176.8
SEN pupils without statements	710.0	685.1	..	..	24.9
SEN pupils with statements	84.2	71.0	5.8	4.2	3.2
Pupils with statements - incidence (Percentages)[4]	*1.6*	*1.6*	*2.1*	*1.0*	*1.8*
Pupils with statements - placement (Percentages)[7]	*28.4*	*28.4*	*36.1*	*20.8*	*30.8*
Secondary					
Total pupils	3 995.0	3 308.0	214.3	316.9	155.7
SEN pupils without statements	440.0	430.1	..	..	10.0
SEN pupils with statements	92.9	79.3	6.1	4.9	2.6
Pupils with statements - incidents (Percentages)[4]	*2.3*	*2.4*	*2.8*	*1.5*	*1.7*
Pupils with statements - placement (Percentages)[7]	*31.3*	*31.7*	*38.0*	*24.3*	*25.3*
Special[9,10]					
Total pupils	105.6	88.9	3.8	8.0	4.9
SEN pupils with statements	101.7	85.8	3.7	7.7	4.5
Incidence (Percentages)[4]	*96.3*	*96.5*	*98.5*	*96.6*	*91.8*
Placement (Percentages)[7]	*34.3*	*34.2*	*23.3*	*38.6*	*43.3*
Pupil referral units[9,11]					
Total pupils	12.4	12.0	0.4	..	..
SEN pupils with statements	2.1	2.0	0.1	..	..
Incidence (Percentages)[4]	*17.0*	*16.8*	*25.5*	*..*	*..*
Placement (Percentages)[7]	*0.7*	*0.8*	*0.7*	*..*	*..*
Other schools					
Independent					
Total pupils	643.5	603.3	9.8	29.4	0.9
SEN pupils with statements	7.6	7.0	0.3	0.3	..
Incidence (Percentages)[4]	*1.2*	*1.2*	*3.0*	*1.0*	*..*
Placement (Percentages)[7]	*2.6*	*2.8*	*1.9*	*1.4*	*..*
Non-maintained special[9]					
Total pupils	5.9	4.9	..	1.0	..
SEN pupils with statements	5.8	4.8	..	1.0	..
Incidents (Percentages)[4]	*97.9*	*97.8*	*..*	*98.7*	*..*
Placement (Percentages)[8]	*2.0*	*1.9*	*..*	*4.9*	*..*

1 See chapter text. For Scotland, pupils with a Record of Needs including some who had an Individualised Educational Programme.

2 Provisional.

3 Includes new codes for recording SEN status following the introduction of a new SEN Code of Practice from January 2002. Data are therefore not directly comparable prior to 2001/02.

4 Incidence of pupils - the number of pupils with statements within each school type expressed as a proportion of the total number of pupils on roll in each school type.

5 Grant-Aided schools in Northern Ireland.

6 Includes pupils in Voluntary and Private Pre-School Centres in Northern Ireland funded under the Pre-School Expansion Programme which began in 1998/99.

7 Placement of pupils - the number of pupils with statements within each school type expressed as a proportion of the number of pupils with statements in all schools.

8 Includes nursery classes (except for Scotland, where they are included with Nursery Schools) and reception classes in primary schools.

9 England and Wales figures exclude dually registered pupils.

10 Including general and hospital special schools.

11 England and Wales only.

Source: Education Departments: 01325 392754

6.5 GCE, GCSE and SCE[1] and vocational qualifications obtained at a typical age[2,3], and by students of any age

United Kingdom

Percentages and thousands

| | Pupils in their last year of compulsory education[2] | | | | | Pupils/students in education[3] | | | |
| | | | | | | % achieving GCE A Levels and equivalent | | | |
	5 or more grades A*-C[4]	1-4 grades A*-C[4]	Grades D-G[5] only	No graded results	Total (=100%) (Thousands)	2 or more passes[6,7]	1 pass[8]	1 or more passes	Population aged 17 (thousands)
Students at a typical age (percentages and thousands)									
1997/98									
All	47.5	25.2	21.1	6.5	698.4	33.5	6.5	40.1	751.0
Males	42.3	25.4	24.9	7.5	356.1	29.9	6.0	35.9	384.9
Females	52.8	25.0	17.1	5.3	342.3	37.4	7.2	44.5	366.1
1998/99									
All	49.1	24.8	20.3	5.9	703.6	33.7	6.7	40.3	744.2
Males	43.8	25.2	24.1	6.9	359.6	30.1	6.1	36.2	381.4
Females	54.6	24.3	16.3	4.8	344.0	37.4	7.3	44.7	362.8
1999/00[1]									
All	50.4	24.5	19.7	5.5	703.7	34.5	6.5	41.0	732.2
Males	45.0	25.0	23.6	6.4	357.7	30.5	6.0	36.6	376.0
Females	55.9	23.9	15.7	4.5	346.0	38.6	7.1	45.6	356.3
2000/01[1]									
All	51.0	24.1	19.4	5.5	729.7	37.2	4.7	41.9	735.4
Males	45.7	24.6	23.1	6.5	372.1	32.9	4.5	37.4	378.5
Females	56.5	23.6	15.5	4.4	357.6	41.7	4.9	46.6	356.9
2001/02[1]									
All	52.5	23.7	18.4	5.4	732.5	38.5	4.6	43.1	735.2
Males	47.2	24.4	22.0	6.4	374.0	34.1	4.4	38.5	377.0
Females	58.0	23.1	14.6	4.3	358.5	43.2	4.8	48.0	358.2

| | GCSE and SCE S Grade/Standard Grade (SG) | | | | GCE A Level and SCE/NQ Higher Grade | | |
	5 or more grades A*-C[4,9]	1-4 grades A*-C[4,9]	Grades D-G[5,10] only	No graded results[11]	2 or more passes[6,7]	1 pass[8]	Total 1 or more passes
Students of all ages (thousands)							
1997/98							
All	335.3	336.4	233.9	37.4	260.4	70.3	330.6
Males	152.8	162.3	129.5	18.3	119.2	30.5	149.7
Females	182.5	174.1	104.5	19.2	141.2	39.8	181.0
1998/99							
All	341.0	323.7	229.8	31.2	257.9	69.9	327.8
Males	162.3	150.6	128.1	15.6	118.4	30.6	149.0
Females	178.7	173.2	101.7	15.6	139.5	39.3	178.8
1999/00							
All	357.7	311.6	224.4	30.3	258.8	65.6	324.4
Males	162.8	150.9	125.3	15.2	118.0	28.7	146.6
Females	194.9	160.7	99.1	15.1	140.9	36.9	177.7
2000/01							
All	375.1	335.0	227.3	31.8	280.8	64.2	345.1
Males	171.8	164.1	127.3	16.0	128.4	29.1	157.5
Females	203.3	170.9	100.1	15.8	152.4	35.2	187.6
2001/02							
All	394.9	381.1	234.2	50.6	286.7	67.8	354.5
Males	182.4	188.7	131.1	27.9	130.0	31.6	161.6
Females	212.4	192.3	103.1	22.7	156.7	36.2	192.9

1 From 1999/00 National Qualifications (NQ) were introduced in Scotland but not all are shown until 2000/01. NQs include Standard Grades, Intermediate 1 & 2 and Higher Grades. The figures for Higher Grades combine the new NQ Higher and the old SCE Higher and include Advanced Highers.

2 Pupils aged 15 at the start of the academic year, pupils in year S4 in Scotland.

3 Up to 1999/00, pupils in schools and students in further education institutions aged 16-18 at the start of the academic year in England, Wales and Northern Ireland as a percentage of the 17 year old population. From 2000/01, pupils in schools and students in further education institutions aged 17-18 at the start of the academic year in England, aged 17 in Wales, and aged 16-18 in Northern Ireland, as a percentage of the 17 year old population. Pupils in Scotland generally sit Highers one year earlier and the figures relate to the results of pupils in year S5/S6.

4 Standard Grades 1-3/Intermediate 2 A-C/Intermediate 1 A-B in Scotland.

5 Grades D-G at GCSE and Scottish Standard Grades 4-6/Intermediate 1 (C)/ Access 3 (pass).

6 3 or more SCE/NQ Higher Grades/ 2 or more Advanced Highers/ 1 Advanced Higher with more than 2 Higher passes in Scotland.

7 Includes Vocational Certificates of Education (VCE) and, previously, Advanced level GNVQ/GSVQ which is equivalent to 2 GCE A levels or AS equivalents/3 SCE/NQ Higher grades. Includes VCE Single awards in Northern Ireland.

8 2 AS levels or 2 Highers/ 1 Advanced Higher or 1 each in Scotland, count as 1 A Level pass. Includes those with 1.5 A level passes.

9 Includes GNVQ/GSVQ Intermediate Part 1, Full and Language unit which are equivalent to 2, 4 and 0.5 GCSE grades A*-C/SCE Standard grades 1-3 respectively. Figures include those with 4.5 GCSEs.

10 Includes GNVQ/GSVQ Foundation Part 1, Full and Language unit which are equivalent to 2, 4 and 0.5 GCSE grades D-G/SCE Standard grades 4-7 respectively.

11 Figures for Scotland include students in Year S4 only.

Source: Education Departments: 01325 392754

6.6 Students in further education[1] by country, mode of study[2], sex and age,[3] during 2001/02

United Kingdom - Home and overseas students

Thousands

	United Kingdom		England[4]		Wales		Scotland[5]		Northern Ireland	
	Full-time	Part-time	Full-time	Part-time	Full-time	Part-time	Full-time	Part-time	Full-time	Part-time
All persons										
Age under 16	15.7	95.0	12.8	52.8	1.1	5.2	1.8	33.3	0.1	3.7
16	272.7	91.8	240.7	66.6	14.5	4.0	9.8	16.2	7.7	5.0
17	221.3	100.1	194.6	76.3	11.2	4.5	8.6	15.4	6.9	4.0
18	110.7	103.5	95.4	85.5	5.4	4.9	6.0	10.4	3.9	2.6
19	53.4	90.9	47.1	75.8	2.2	4.7	2.9	8.6	1.2	1.8
20	34.5	84.6	31.0	71.7	1.3	4.3	1.8	7.1	0.4	1.5
21	27.5	86.8	25.1	74.5	0.8	4.4	1.3	6.5	0.2	1.4
22	22.3	84.7	20.5	72.9	0.6	4.2	1.0	6.3	0.1	1.3
23	18.8	80.0	17.3	69.2	0.5	3.9	0.9	5.6	0.1	1.3
24	16.8	78.0	15.6	67.8	0.4	3.7	0.7	5.3	0.1	1.2
25	15.9	81.7	14.8	71.2	0.4	3.9	0.6	5.5	0.1	1.2
26	15.3	83.5	14.4	73.0	0.3	3.8	0.6	5.6	-	1.1
27	15.0	85.5	14.0	74.8	0.4	4.1	0.6	5.6	-	1.1
28	14.6	88.6	13.7	77.4	0.4	4.1	0.5	5.9	-	1.1
29	14.4	92.2	13.6	80.7	0.3	4.4	0.5	5.9	-	1.2
30+	255.6	2 852.9	242.5	2 479.8	5.1	142.8	7.6	201.9	0.4	28.3
Unknown	3.7	47.5	3.6	43.6	0.1	3.1	-	-	-	0.7
All ages	1 128.2	4 227.1	1 016.7	3 613.6	45.0	210.0	45.1	345.0	21.4	58.4
Males										
Age under 16	8.7	50.5	6.9	28.7	0.7	3.1	1.1	16.4	0.1	2.4
16	135.3	47.3	118.1	35.9	7.3	1.9	5.5	7.2	4.4	2.3
17	108.4	53.0	94.8	41.2	5.3	2.5	4.4	7.5	3.9	1.8
18	58.3	55.4	50.2	45.1	2.8	2.8	3.0	6.2	2.4	1.4
19	29.7	45.6	26.4	37.3	1.2	2.6	1.5	4.8	0.7	0.9
20	18.9	39.7	17.0	33.1	0.7	2.2	1.0	3.8	0.2	0.6
21	14.5	37.9	13.3	32.2	0.4	2.0	0.7	3.2	0.1	0.5
22	11.5	35.2	10.6	30.1	0.3	1.8	0.5	2.8	0.1	0.4
23	9.5	32.1	8.8	27.7	0.2	1.6	0.4	2.4	0.1	0.4
24	8.5	31.2	7.9	27.2	0.2	1.6	0.3	2.1	-	0.4
25	7.9	32.8	7.4	28.6	0.2	1.7	0.3	2.2	-	0.4
26	7.7	33.6	7.3	29.4	0.1	1.5	0.2	2.3	-	0.4
27	7.5	34.1	7.1	29.9	0.1	1.6	0.3	2.2	-	0.3
28	7.3	34.9	6.9	30.5	0.1	1.6	0.2	2.4	-	0.3
29	7.1	36.2	6.8	31.7	0.1	1.7	0.2	2.4	-	0.4
30+	125.9	1 047.5	121.5	910.1	1.7	53.9	2.6	75.1	0.1	8.4
Unknown	2.2	18.4	2.2	16.7	-	1.4	-	-	-	0.3
All ages	569.0	1 665.5	513.2	1 415.6	21.6	85.5	22.1	143.1	12.1	21.4
Females										
Age under 16	7.1	44.4	5.9	24.1	0.4	2.1	0.7	16.9	0.1	1.3
16	137.4	44.5	122.6	30.7	7.2	2.1	4.3	9.0	3.3	2.7
17	112.9	47.1	99.8	35.0	5.8	2.0	4.2	7.9	3.1	2.2
18	52.3	48.0	45.2	40.4	2.7	2.1	2.9	4.3	1.5	1.3
19	23.6	45.3	20.8	38.5	1.0	2.1	1.4	3.8	0.5	0.9
20	15.6	44.9	14.0	38.6	0.6	2.1	0.8	3.3	0.2	0.9
21	13.0	48.9	11.8	42.3	0.4	2.4	0.6	3.3	0.1	0.9
22	10.8	49.6	9.9	42.9	0.3	2.4	0.5	3.4	0.1	0.9
23	9.4	47.9	8.5	41.6	0.3	2.3	0.5	3.2	0.1	0.8
24	8.4	46.8	7.7	40.6	0.2	2.1	0.4	3.2	-	0.8
25	8.0	48.8	7.4	42.6	0.2	2.2	0.3	3.2	-	0.8
26	7.6	49.9	7.0	43.6	0.2	2.3	0.3	3.3	-	0.8
27	7.4	51.4	6.9	44.8	0.2	2.5	0.3	3.3	-	0.8
28	7.3	53.7	6.7	46.9	0.2	2.5	0.3	3.5	-	0.8
29	7.3	56.0	6.8	49.0	0.2	2.7	0.3	3.5	-	0.8
30+	129.7	1 805.4	121.1	1 569.7	3.4	88.9	4.9	126.9	0.3	19.9
Unknown	1.5	29.1	1.4	26.9	-	1.7	-	-	-	0.4
All ages	559.2	2 561.6	503.5	2 198.1	23.4	124.5	22.9	202.0	9.3	37.0

1 Further education (FE) institution figures are whole year counts except for Northern Ireland, which are on a snapshot basis. Higher education (HE) institution figures are based on the HESA July 'standard registration' count and are not directly comparable with previous years.
2 Full-time includes sandwich. Part-time comprises both day and evening, including block release and open/distance learning.
3 Ages as at 31 August 2001 (1 July in Northern Ireland and 31 December in Scotland).

4 Further education institution figures for England include colleges and LSC funded external institutions, but exclude Specialist designated colleges. Figures for 2001/02 are not therefore directly comparable with those shown for 2000/01.
5 Figures for Scotland further education colleges are enrolments rather than headcounts.

Source: Education Departments: 01325 392754

6.7 Students in further education[1] by country, mode of study[2], sex and subject group, during 2001/02[3]

United Kingdom - Home and overseas students

Thousands

	United Kingdom		England[3]		Wales		Scotland[4]		Northern Ireland	
	Full-time	Part-time	Full-time	Part-time	Full-time	Part-time	Full-time	Part-time	Full-time	Part-time
All persons										
Subject group										
Medicine & Dentistry	-	-	-	-	-	-	-	-	-	-
Allied Medicine	144.0	325.9	141.0	309.7	-	-	1.5	14.3	1.6	1.9
Biological Sciences	9.3	11.5	9.2	6.8	-	-	0.2	4.7	-	-
Agriculture	22.5	64.2	21.0	51.4	-	-	1.4	12.4	0.1	0.4
Physical Sciences	9.3	5.1	9.3	3.6	-	-	-	1.3	-	0.2
Mathematical and Computing Sciences	23.3	132.5	18.0	27.0	-	-	3.4	90.0	1.8	15.5
Engineering & Technology	72.9	175.8	64.4	152.3	-	0.1	6.1	19.6	2.5	3.8
Architecture	43.6	128.0	36.3	115.5	-	-	3.5	10.2	3.8	2.2
Social Sciences	66.7	389.8	59.3	356.4	-	-	6.6	30.7	0.8	2.7
Business & Financial	100.9	457.1	90.4	404.1	-	-	6.8	42.4	3.8	10.6
Documentation	99.3	699.6	98.0	690.3	-	-	0.6	9.0	0.7	0.3
Languages	49.9	168.0	49.1	144.4	-	0.2	0.9	21.4	-	2.1
Humanities	25.8	109.2	25.4	108.3	-	-	0.3	0.9	-	-
Creative arts	117.8	265.4	108.7	237.1	0.1	-	6.5	25.0	2.5	3.3
Education[5]	3.5	26.2	-	1.9	-	0.2	2.8	20.2	0.6	3.9
Other subjects[6]	206.5	816.3	198.2	755.4	0.4	6.3	4.5	43.0	3.4	11.5
Unknown	132.9	452.5	88.5	249.3	44.4	203.2	-	-	-	-
All subjects	1 128.2	4 227.1	1 016.7	3 613.6	45.0	210.0	45.1	345.0	21.4	58.4
Males										
Subject group										
Medicine and Dentistry	-	-	-	-	-	-	-	-	-	-
Allied Medicine	56.1	102.2	55.8	95.5	-	-	0.2	6.5	0.1	0.2
Biological Sciences	3.5	4.4	3.4	1.6	-	-	0.1	2.8	-	-
Agriculture	11.1	30.2	10.3	24.1	-	-	0.8	5.9	-	0.2
Physical Sciences	5.8	2.4	5.8	1.7	-	-	-	0.6	-	0.1
Mathematical and Computing Sciences	14.1	48.2	10.1	9.8	-	-	2.5	33.4	1.4	5.1
Engineering & Technology	65.9	153.2	58.0	134.0	-	0.1	5.6	15.7	2.4	3.5
Architecture	41.6	116.0	34.5	105.3	-	-	3.4	8.5	3.7	2.2
Social Sciences	27.4	114.6	26.3	108.2	-	-	1.0	6.2	0.1	0.3
Business & Financial	46.9	161.7	43.6	142.0	-	-	2.2	16.9	1.2	2.8
Documentation	63.5	274.9	62.7	271.3	-	-	0.3	3.5	0.4	0.1
Languages	19.9	60.3	19.5	50.6	-	0.1	0.4	8.8	-	0.8
Humanities	10.3	34.2	10.2	33.8	-	-	0.1	0.4	-	-
Creative arts	50.5	72.0	48.0	65.3	-	-	1.9	6.4	0.6	0.4
Education[5]	2.1	10.9	-	0.5	-	0.1	1.6	8.9	0.4	1.3
Other subjects[6]	84.3	306.1	80.4	280.7	0.2	2.3	2.0	18.7	1.8	4.5
Unknown	65.9	174.1	44.5	91.1	21.3	83.0	-	-	-	-
All subjects	569.0	1 665.5	513.2	1 415.6	21.6	85.5	22.1	143.1	12.1	21.4
Females										
Subject group										
Medicine & Dentistry	-	-	-	-	-	-	-	-	-	-
Allied Medicine	87.9	223.7	85.2	214.2	-	-	1.2	7.7	1.5	1.7
Biological Sciences	5.8	7.1	5.8	5.2	-	-	0.1	1.9	-	-
Agriculture	11.3	34.0	10.7	27.2	-	-	0.6	6.6	0.1	0.2
Physical Sciences	3.5	2.7	3.5	1.9	-	-	-	0.7	-	0.1
Mathematical and Computing Sciences	9.2	84.3	7.9	17.3	-	-	0.9	56.6	0.4	10.4
Engineering & Technology	7.0	22.6	6.4	18.3	-	-	0.5	4.0	0.1	0.4
Architecture	2.0	12.0	1.8	10.2	-	-	0.1	1.7	0.1	0.1
Social Sciences	39.3	275.2	33.0	248.3	-	-	5.6	24.6	0.7	2.4
Business & Financial	54.0	295.3	46.8	262.1	-	-	4.6	25.4	2.6	7.8
Documentation	35.8	424.7	35.3	419.0	-	-	0.3	5.5	0.3	0.2
Languages	30.0	107.7	29.6	93.8	-	0.1	0.5	12.6	-	1.3
Humanities	15.4	75.0	15.2	74.5	-	-	0.2	0.5	-	-
Creative arts	67.3	193.4	60.7	171.8	-	-	4.6	18.6	1.9	2.9
Education[5]	1.4	15.3	-	1.4	-	0.2	1.2	11.3	0.2	2.5
Other subjects[6]	122.1	510.2	117.8	474.7	0.2	4.1	2.5	24.3	1.6	7.0
Unknown	67.1	278.4	44.0	158.3	23.1	120.2	-	-	-	-
All subjects	559.2	2 561.6	503.5	2 198.1	23.4	124.5	22.9	202.0	9.3	37.0

1 Further education (FE) institution figures are whole year counts except for Northern Ireland, which are collected on a snapshot basis. Higher education (HE) institution figures are based on the HESA July 'standard registration' count and are not directly comparable with previous years.

2 Full-time includes sandwich. Part-time comprises both day and evening including block release and open/distance learning.

3 Provisional. Further education institution figures for England include colleges and LSC funded external institutions, but exclude Specialist designated colleges. Figures for 2001/02 are not therefore directly comparable with those shown for 2000/01.

4 Figures for Scotland further education colleges are enrolments rather than headcounts. Due to a reclassification of subject groupings, subject categories for Scotland cannot be directly compared with previous years prior to 1999/00.

5 Includes ITT and INSET.

6 Includes Combined and general categories, plus, for England further education institutions, Hotel and Catering and Basic Education.

Source: Education Departments: 01325 392754

6.8 Students in higher education[1] by level, mode of study[2], sex and age[3], 2001/02[4,5]
United Kingdom
Home and overseas students

Thousands

	Postgraduate level						First degree		Other undergraduate		Total higher education[6]	
	PhD and equivalent		Masters and others		Total postgraduate							
	Full-time	Part-time	Full-time	Part-time	Full-time	Part-time	Full-time	Part-time	Full-time	Part-time	Full-time	Part-time
All persons												
Age under 16	-	-	-	-	-	-	-	-	-	0.4	-	0.4
16	-	-	-	-	-	-	0.4	-	0.8	1.0	1.2	1.1
17	-	-	-	-	-	-	10.1	0.1	5.0	1.8	15.1	1.9
18	-	-	-	-	-	-	152.9	1.0	23.8	7.2	176.9	8.2
19	-	-	0.1	0.1	0.1	0.1	205.4	2.9	30.2	11.7	235.9	14.7
20	0.1	-	1.2	0.2	1.3	0.2	213.3	4.6	24.0	13.9	238.6	18.8
21	0.9	-	14.5	1.6	15.4	1.7	145.0	6.3	15.9	14.6	176.3	22.6
22	3.1	0.2	21.6	5.2	24.8	5.3	66.2	6.2	10.8	14.4	101.8	26.1
23	4.8	0.3	18.5	7.6	23.4	7.9	32.0	5.0	7.8	14.1	63.1	27.1
24	5.2	1.2	14.3	8.3	19.5	9.5	18.5	4.4	6.1	14.1	44.2	28.0
25	4.1	2.4	10.9	8.9	15.0	11.2	12.8	4.0	5.4	14.5	33.1	29.8
26	3.4	2.4	8.6	9.0	12.0	11.4	9.8	3.9	4.8	14.6	26.6	29.9
27	2.9	2.2	7.2	9.5	10.0	11.7	8.0	3.7	4.3	14.7	22.3	30.1
28	2.4	2.2	5.9	9.7	8.3	11.9	7.0	3.8	3.8	15.7	19.1	31.3
29	2.1	2.1	5.2	10.0	7.2	12.1	6.2	3.7	3.8	15.9	17.2	31.8
30+	13.6	29.4	35.8	171.3	49.4	200.7	60.9	67.1	43.5	375.2	153.9	643.6
Unknown	-	0.1	0.2	2.1	0.2	2.2	0.3	0.3	0.2	13.8	0.6	16.2
All ages	42.6	42.4	144.0	243.4	186.6	285.8	948.7	117.0	190.2	557.6	1 326.2	961.7
Males												
Age under 16	-	-	-	-	-	-	-	-	-	0.1	-	0.1
16	-	-	-	-	-	-	0.2	-	0.3	0.5	0.4	0.5
17	-	-	-	-	-	-	4.5	0.1	2.0	0.8	6.5	0.9
18	-	-	-	-	-	-	68.9	0.5	11.0	4.0	80.0	4.6
19	-	-	-	-	-	-	94.5	1.6	14.1	6.7	108.7	8.4
20	-	-	0.5	0.1	0.6	0.1	98.5	2.6	10.9	7.5	110.1	10.2
21	0.5	-	6.0	0.6	6.4	0.6	71.1	3.4	7.2	7.2	84.8	11.1
22	1.9	0.1	9.8	2.1	11.7	2.2	34.9	3.3	4.7	6.2	51.3	11.7
23	2.8	0.2	8.6	3.1	11.4	3.2	17.1	2.6	3.2	5.6	31.6	11.4
24	3.0	0.7	6.8	3.3	9.8	3.9	9.9	2.0	2.4	5.5	22.1	11.5
25	2.2	1.4	5.4	3.7	7.6	5.1	6.6	1.7	2.0	5.6	16.2	12.3
26	1.8	1.4	4.1	3.7	6.0	5.0	4.8	1.5	1.7	5.6	12.5	12.2
27	1.5	1.2	3.5	3.9	5.1	5.1	3.9	1.4	1.5	5.8	10.4	12.4
28	1.4	1.2	3.0	4.3	4.4	5.5	3.2	1.5	1.3	6.1	8.9	13.1
29	1.2	1.2	2.7	4.6	3.9	5.7	2.9	1.5	1.3	6.3	8.1	13.5
30+	8.0	16.8	18.9	78.7	26.9	95.5	21.7	21.4	11.9	139.3	60.6	256.5
Unknown	-	-	0.1	0.9	0.1	1.0	0.1	0.1	0.1	4.7	0.4	5.8
All ages	24.4	24.1	69.4	108.9	93.8	133.0	442.8	45.1	75.7	217.4	612.7	396.2
Females												
Age under 16	-	-	-	-	-	-	-	-	-	0.2	-	0.2
16	-	-	-	-	-	-	0.2	-	0.5	0.5	0.7	0.6
17	-	-	-	-	-	-	5.6	0.1	3.0	1.0	8.6	1.0
18	-	-	-	-	-	-	84.0	0.5	12.8	3.1	96.9	3.6
19	-	-	0.1	-	0.1	-	111.0	1.2	16.1	5.0	127.2	6.3
20	-	-	0.7	0.1	0.7	0.1	114.7	2.0	13.0	6.4	128.5	8.6
21	0.4	-	8.5	1.1	8.9	1.1	73.9	2.9	8.7	7.5	91.5	11.5
22	1.2	0.1	11.9	3.1	13.1	3.2	31.3	3.0	6.1	8.2	50.5	14.4
23	2.1	0.2	9.9	4.5	12.0	4.7	14.9	2.5	4.6	8.5	31.4	15.7
24	2.2	0.5	7.5	5.0	9.7	5.5	8.6	2.4	3.8	8.6	22.1	16.6
25	1.8	1.0	5.5	5.2	7.4	6.2	6.2	2.4	3.3	8.9	16.9	17.5
26	1.6	1.1	4.5	5.3	6.1	6.4	5.0	2.3	3.1	9.0	14.1	17.8
27	1.3	1.0	3.6	5.6	5.0	6.6	4.1	2.2	2.8	8.9	11.9	17.8
28	1.0	1.0	2.9	5.4	3.9	6.4	3.8	2.3	2.5	9.6	10.2	18.3
29	0.9	0.9	2.5	5.5	3.4	6.4	3.3	2.2	2.5	9.6	9.2	18.2
30+	5.5	12.5	16.9	92.6	22.5	105.1	39.2	45.7	31.6	235.9	93.3	387.1
Unknown	-	-	0.1	1.1	0.1	1.2	0.1	0.1	0.1	9.1	0.3	10.4
All ages	18.2	18.3	74.6	134.5	92.8	152.9	505.9	71.8	114.5	340.2	713.5	565.5

1 Includes Open University students. Part-time figures include dormant modes, those writing up at home and on sabbaticals.
2 Full-time includes sandwich. Part-time comprises both day and evening, including block release and open/distance learning.
3 Ages as at 31 August 2001 (1 July in Northern Ireland and 31 December in Scotland).
4 Figures for higher education (HE) institutions are based on the HESA July 'standard registration' count and are not directly comparable with previous years. Figures for further education (FE) institutions (other than in Scotland FE colleges) are snapshots counted at a particular point in the year [November for FE institutions in England and Northern Ireland, and December for FE institutions in Wales].

5 Provisional. Revised to include HESA July 'standard registration' count data, and 2001/02 figures for HE students in FE institutions in Wales and Northern Ireland, and FE colleges in Scotland.
6 Includes data for higher education students in further education institutions in Wales which cannot be split by level.

Source: Education Departments: 01325 392754

6.9 Students in higher education[1] by level, mode of study[2], sex and subject group, 2001/02[3,4]

United Kingdom - Home and overseas students

Thousands

| | Postgraduate level | | | | | | First degree | | Other undergraduate | | Total higher education[5] | |
| | PhD and equivalent | | Masters and others | | Total postgraduate | | | | | | | |
	Full-time	Part-time	Full-time	Part-time	Full-time	Part-time	Full-time	Part-time	Full-time	Part-time	Full-time[5]	Part-time[5]
All persons												
Subject group												
Medicine & Dentistry	2.8	3.9	2.9	6.2	5.7	10.2	31.3	0.1	0.2	0.1	37.3	10.4
Allied Medicine	2.0	2.4	3.9	22.7	5.9	25.0	58.3	32.0	67.8	66.8	132.0	123.9
Biological Sciences	6.6	4.4	4.5	5.5	11.1	9.9	66.3	3.5	1.9	2.6	79.3	16.0
Agriculture	1.0	0.8	1.2	1.1	2.2	1.9	10.5	0.4	4.5	3.2	17.3	5.5
Physical Sciences	6.8	3.2	4.6	3.2	11.4	6.3	43.1	1.8	1.0	3.5	55.6	11.6
Mathematical and Computing Sciences	2.9	1.9	13.1	10.0	15.9	12.0	79.2	6.6	15.1	20.7	110.2	39.2
Engineering & Technology	6.4	4.5	10.9	12.8	17.3	17.2	73.4	7.9	12.1	28.0	102.9	53.1
Architecture	0.6	0.7	4.2	7.1	4.7	7.9	19.8	6.5	3.1	11.6	27.6	25.9
Social Sciences	4.4	5.3	24.6	24.5	29.0	29.8	114.1	12.6	10.5	34.3	153.6	76.8
Business & Financial	1.6	2.7	24.5	53.6	26.0	56.3	112.0	15.0	29.4	78.6	167.5	149.9
Documentation	0.2	0.3	3.8	4.0	4.0	4.3	21.0	1.0	4.8	6.5	29.8	11.8
Languages	2.5	2.8	5.0	4.9	7.4	7.8	55.6	3.2	2.9	24.7	66.0	35.6
Humanities	2.5	3.2	4.0	7.4	6.4	10.6	33.1	3.9	0.9	22.2	40.5	36.7
Creative arts	0.8	1.1	6.4	4.3	7.2	5.4	86.9	4.5	22.0	13.3	116.1	23.3
Education[6]	0.9	4.4	27.5	54.5	28.5	58.9	44.7	6.3	2.8	22.9	76.0	88.1
Other subjects[7]	0.7	0.7	3.0	21.4	3.7	22.2	98.7	11.1	10.5	216.5	112.9	249.7
Unknown[5]	-	-	-	0.1	-	0.1	0.6	0.4	0.3	2.2	1.6	4.0
All subjects	42.6	42.4	144.0	243.4	186.6	285.8	948.7	117.0	190.2	557.6	1 326.2	961.7
Males												
Subject group												
Medicine and Dentistry	1.2	2.2	1.2	3.0	2.4	5.1	13.8	0.1	0.1	-	16.3	5.2
Allied Medicine	0.9	1.0	1.2	5.9	2.1	6.8	13.2	3.8	9.4	6.8	24.7	17.5
Biological Sciences	2.7	2.0	1.7	1.8	4.4	3.7	24.3	1.3	1.0	1.1	29.7	6.1
Agriculture	0.5	0.4	0.6	0.5	1.1	0.9	3.9	0.2	1.9	1.5	6.9	2.6
Physical Sciences	4.5	2.1	2.6	1.8	7.2	4.0	26.2	1.0	0.7	2.0	34.0	7.0
Mathematical and Computing Sciences	2.2	1.5	9.4	6.6	11.6	8.1	60.5	5.0	12.1	11.1	84.2	24.1
Engineering & Technology	5.0	3.8	8.7	10.9	13.7	14.6	61.9	7.3	10.6	25.8	86.2	47.7
Architecture	0.4	0.5	2.5	4.7	2.9	5.2	14.2	5.1	2.5	9.3	19.6	19.7
Social Sciences	2.4	2.8	10.7	9.5	13.1	12.3	45.1	4.7	2.6	8.8	60.8	25.8
Business & Financial	1.0	1.8	13.5	28.9	14.4	30.7	53.0	6.6	12.9	29.6	80.3	66.9
Documentation	0.1	0.2	1.3	1.5	1.4	1.6	8.1	0.4	3.3	3.9	12.9	5.9
Languages	1.0	1.2	1.5	1.6	2.6	2.8	15.5	0.9	1.3	9.2	19.3	12.9
Humanities	1.4	1.9	1.9	3.4	3.3	5.3	15.4	1.5	0.3	7.5	19.1	14.3
Creative arts	0.4	0.6	2.7	1.8	3.1	2.4	34.8	1.6	10.5	4.7	48.4	8.7
Education[6]	0.4	2.0	8.3	15.3	8.6	17.3	10.5	1.5	1.4	5.9	20.6	24.6
Other subjects[7]	0.4	0.4	1.5	11.8	1.9	12.2	42.2	4.0	5.0	89.6	49.1	105.8
Unknown[5]	-	-	-	0.1	-	0.1	0.2	0.2	0.1	0.6	0.7	1.5
All subjects	24.4	24.1	69.4	108.9	93.8	133.0	442.8	45.1	75.7	217.4	612.7	396.2
Females												
Subject group												
Medicine & Dentistry	1.6	1.8	1.7	3.3	3.3	5.1	17.5	0.1	0.2	-	21.0	5.2
Allied Medicine	1.1	1.4	2.7	16.8	3.8	18.2	45.1	28.2	58.4	60.0	107.3	106.4
Biological Sciences	3.9	2.4	2.8	3.7	6.6	6.2	42.1	2.1	0.9	1.6	49.6	9.9
Agriculture	0.5	0.3	0.6	0.7	1.1	1.0	6.7	0.3	2.6	1.6	10.4	2.9
Physical Sciences	2.3	1.1	2.0	1.3	4.3	2.4	16.9	0.7	0.4	1.4	21.6	4.6
Mathematical and Computing Sciences	0.7	0.5	3.7	3.4	4.3	3.9	18.7	1.7	3.0	9.6	26.0	15.2
Engineering & Technology	1.4	0.7	2.2	1.9	3.6	2.6	11.5	0.6	1.5	2.2	16.6	5.4
Architecture	0.2	0.2	1.7	2.4	1.9	2.7	5.6	1.4	0.5	2.2	8.0	6.3
Social Sciences	2.0	2.5	13.9	15.0	15.9	17.5	69.0	7.9	7.9	25.5	92.8	51.0
Business & Financial	0.6	1.0	11.0	24.7	11.6	25.6	59.0	8.5	16.5	49.0	87.2	83.1
Documentation	0.1	0.2	2.4	2.5	2.6	2.7	12.9	0.6	1.5	2.6	16.9	5.9
Languages	1.4	1.6	3.4	3.4	4.9	5.0	40.2	2.3	1.6	15.5	46.7	22.8
Humanities	1.1	1.3	2.1	4.0	3.2	5.3	17.7	2.4	0.6	14.7	21.5	22.4
Creative arts	0.4	0.6	3.7	2.5	4.1	3.1	52.0	2.9	11.6	8.6	67.7	14.6
Education[6]	0.6	2.4	19.3	39.2	19.8	41.6	34.2	4.8	1.4	17.0	55.4	63.5
Other subjects[7]	0.3	0.4	1.5	9.6	1.8	10.0	56.5	7.1	5.5	126.9	63.8	144.0
Unknown[5]	-	-	-	0.1	-	0.1	0.4	0.2	0.2	1.6	1.0	2.5
All subjects	18.2	18.3	74.6	134.5	92.8	152.9	505.9	71.8	114.5	340.2	713.5	565.5

1 Higher Education Statistics Agency (HESA) higher education institutions include Open University students. Part-time figures include dormant modes, those writing up at home and on sabbaticals.

2 Full-time includes sandwich. Part-time comprises both day and evening, including block release and open/distance learning.

3 Revised to include HESA July 'standard registration' count data, and 2001/02 figures for HE students in FE institutions in Wales and Northern Ireland, and FE colleges in Scotland. FE institution figures for England also now exclude Specialist designated colleges.

4 Figures for higher education (HE) institutions are based on the HESA July 'standard registration' count and are not directly comparable with previous years. Figures for further education (FE) institutions (other than in Scotland FE colleges) are snapshots counted at a particular point in the year [November for FE institutions in England and Northern Ireland, and December for FE institutions in Wales]. Students starting courses after these dates will not therefore be counted. Figures for Scotland, however, are whole year (not snapshot) enrolments (rather than headcounts).

5 Includes data for higher education students in further education institutions in Wales which cannot be split by level. Figures for home, part-time UK higher education institution dormant modes, those writing up at home, and on sabbaticals, which cannot be identified by subject are also included in the 'Unknown' row, throughout the levels.

6 Including ITT and INSET.

7 Includes Combined and general categories, plus, for England further education institutions, Hotel and Catering and Basic Education.

Source: Education Departments: 01325 392754

6.10 Students[1] obtaining higher education qualifications[2] by level, sex and subject group, 2001/02

United Kingdom

Thousands

| | Sub-degree[3] | First degree | Postgraduate | | | Total higher education |
			PhD and equivalent	Other	Total	
All persons						
Subject group						
Medicine & Dentistry	0.1	6.1	1.0	2.4	3.5	9.6
Subjects Allied to Medicine	25.1	20.9	0.7	5.5	6.2	52.2
Biological Sciences	1.1	18.2	1.8	3.1	4.9	24.2
Vet. Science, Agriculture & related	1.3	2.9	0.3	0.9	1.2	5.4
Physical Sciences	0.8	12.2	1.6	2.4	4.0	17.0
Mathematical & Computer Sciences	6.2	17.9	0.6	7.1	7.8	31.9
Engineering & Technology	4.8	19.8	1.5	6.3	7.9	32.4
Architecture, Building & Planning	1.8	6.2	0.1	3.3	3.4	11.4
Social Sciences[4]	5.8	31.6	1.1	19.0	20.1	57.5
Business & Financial Studies	9.5	32.6	0.4	24.5	24.9	67.0
Librarianship & Info Science	0.6	5.2	0.1	2.9	2.9	8.8
Languages	1.9	15.5	0.6	3.1	3.7	21.1
Humanities	1.0	9.8	0.7	2.8	3.5	14.3
Creative Arts & Design	3.4	23.0	0.2	4.6	4.8	31.2
Education[5]	6.0	12.5	0.5	30.5	31.0	49.5
Combined, gen.	13.8	32.6	0.2	6.4	6.6	52.9
All subjects	83.1	267.1	11.4	124.8	136.2	486.4
Males						
Subject group						
Medicine and Dentistry	-	2.8	0.5	1.0	1.5	4.3
Subjects Allied to Medicine	3.0	4.1	0.3	1.4	1.7	8.8
Biological Sciences	0.6	6.6	0.8	1.0	1.8	8.9
Vet. Science, Agriculture & related	0.6	1.1	0.2	0.4	0.6	2.3
Physical Sciences	0.6	7.3	1.1	1.3	2.4	10.3
Mathematical & Computer Sciences	4.4	13.3	0.5	4.8	5.3	23.0
Engineering & Technology	4.3	16.8	1.3	5.1	6.4	27.4
Architecture, Building & Planning	1.3	4.5	0.1	2.0	2.1	7.8
Social Sciences[4]	1.7	12.2	0.6	8.0	8.6	22.5
Business & Financial Studies	4.0	14.6	0.3	12.8	13.1	31.8
Librarianship & Info Science	0.3	2.0	-	1.0	1.0	3.3
Languages	0.7	4.0	0.3	0.9	1.2	5.9
Humanities	0.4	4.4	0.4	1.3	1.7	6.5
Creative Arts & Design	1.5	8.9	0.1	1.8	1.9	12.4
Education[5]	1.8	2.9	0.2	8.4	8.7	13.4
Combined, gen.	5.0	13.4	0.1	3.7	3.8	22.2
All subjects	30.2	118.8	6.7	55.1	61.8	210.8
Females						
Subject group						
Medicine & Dentistry	0.1	3.3	0.5	1.4	1.9	5.3
Subjects Allied to Medicine	22.1	16.8	0.4	4.1	4.5	43.4
Biological Sciences	0.5	11.6	1.0	2.1	3.1	15.3
Vet. Science, Agriculture & related	0.7	1.8	0.1	0.5	0.6	3.1
Physical Sciences	0.3	4.9	0.5	1.1	1.6	6.8
Mathematical & Computer Sciences	1.8	4.7	0.1	2.3	2.4	8.9
Engineering & Technology	0.5	3.0	0.3	1.2	1.5	5.0
Architecture, Building & Planning	0.6	1.7	-	1.3	1.4	3.6
Social Sciences[4]	4.1	19.4	0.5	11.0	11.5	35.0
Business & Financial Studies	5.4	18.0	0.1	11.6	11.8	35.2
Librarianship & Info Science	0.3	3.3	-	1.9	1.9	5.5
Languages	1.2	11.5	0.4	2.1	2.5	15.1
Humanities	0.6	5.4	0.3	1.5	1.8	7.8
Creative Arts & Design	1.9	14.1	0.1	2.8	2.8	18.8
Education[5]	4.2	9.6	0.3	22.1	22.4	36.1
Combined, gen.	8.8	19.2	0.1	2.7	2.8	30.7
All subjects	53.0	148.2	4.7	69.7	74.4	275.6

1 Includes students on Open University courses.
2 Includes higher education in higher education institutions in the UK only. Excludes qualifications from the private sector and higher education qualifications in further education institutions (approximately 6% of the total number of students).

3 Excludes students who successfully completed courses for which formal qualifications are not awarded.
4 Includes Law.
5 Includes ITT and INSET.

Source: Education Departments: 01325 392754

6.11 Qualified teachers: by type of school and sex

Thousands

	Public sector mainstream schools		Non-maintained mainstream schools	All special schools	Total
	Nursery and primary	Secondary[1]			
All full-time teachers					
Great Britain					
1990/91	200.3	223.2	44.9	18.2	486.6
1996/97	202.8	211.4	48.2	16.3	478.7
1997/98	201.3	209.8	49.1	16.0	476.2
United Kingdom					
1998/99	210.8	221.7	50.5	16.7	499.7
1999/00[2]	211.1	223.0	51.2	16.6	502.0
2000/01[3,4,5]	211.5	225.3	52.3	16.6	505.7
2001/02[6]	211.6	226.6	52.8	16.3	507.3
of which:					
England and Wales[7]	181.5	194.2	50.2	13.5	439.4
Scotland	21.5	22.7	2.5	2.1	48.8
Northern Ireland	8.6	9.7	0.1	0.8	19.1
Full-time male teachers					
Great Britain					
1990/91	35.8	116.0	20.6	5.8	178.2
1996/97	33.0	101.7	20.6	5.1	160.4
1997/98	31.9	99.4	20.7	5.0	157.1
United Kingdom					
1998/99	33.0	103.4	20.8	5.1	162.4
1999/00[2]	32.6	102.9	21.1	5.0	161.6
2000/01[3,4,5]	32.1	102.8	21.3	5.0	161.2
2001/02[6]	31.9	102.4	21.5	4.9	160.7
of which:					
England and Wales[7]	28.9	87.8	20.5	4.3	141.5
Scotland	1.5	10.7	1.0	0.5	13.6
Northern Ireland	1.5	3.9	-	0.1	5.6
Full-time female teachers					
Great Britain					
1990/91	164.5	107.1	24.3	12.4	308.4
1996/97	169.8	109.7	27.6	11.2	318.3
1997/98	169.3	110.3	28.5	11.0	319.1
United Kingdom					
1998/99	177.8	118.3	29.6	11.6	337.8
1999/00[2]	178.5	120.1	30.2	11.6	340.4
2000/01[3,4,5]	179.4	122.5	30.9	11.6	344.5
2001/02[6]	179.7	124.2	31.2	11.5	346.6
of which:					
England and Wales[7]	152.6	106.4	29.7	9.2	297.9
Scotland	20.0	12.0	1.5	1.7	35.2
Northern Ireland	7.1	5.8	0.1	0.6	13.6
All full time equivalents (FTE) of part-time teachers					
Great Britain					
1990/91	..	..	..	..	30.0
1996/97	17.8	15.7	9.4	1.4	44.3
1997/98	18.0	16.2	10.7	1.4	46.4
United Kingdom					
1998/99	19.7	16.8	9.8	1.5	47.8
1999/00[2,3]	20.0	17.3	10.3	1.6	49.2
2000/01[3,4,5]	21.9	16.7	10.3	1.6	50.4
2001/02[6]	23.3	17.4	10.5	1.8	53.0

1 From 1993/94 excludes sixth form colleges in England and Wales which were reclassified as further education colleges on 1 April 1993.
2 Includes 1998/99 data for Northern Ireland.
3 Includes revised data.
4 Includes 1999/00 nursery data for Scotland.
5 Includes 2001/02 data for Northern Ireland.
6 Provisional.

7 A gender breakdown of public sector teachers in England and Wales is only available from the Database of Teachers Records (DTR) where some in service teachers may be shown as not in service because their service details are not recorded. A complete coverage of teachers in England and Wales is available from the Form 618G survey, and published in *Statistics of Education: School workforce in England (including teachers pay for England and Wales)*.

Source: Education Departments: 01325 392754

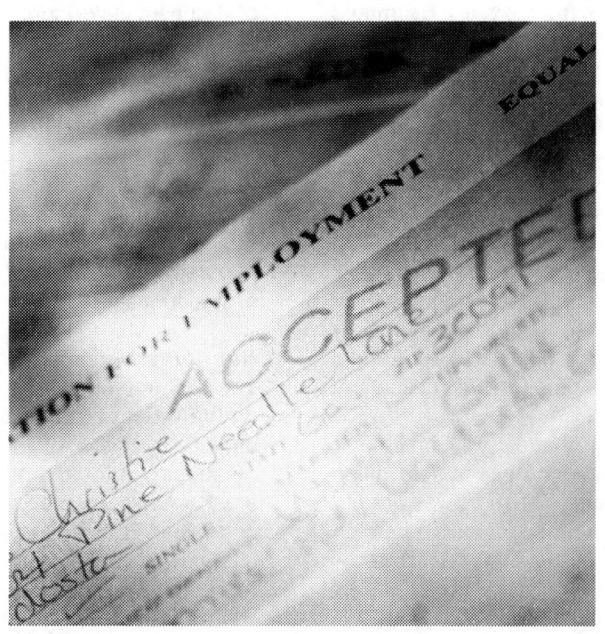

7 Labour market

Labour market

Labour Force Survey
(Tables 7.1 to 7.3, 7.6, 7.9, 7.10, 7.12 and 7.15 to 7.17)

The impact of Census 2001 on LFS data
(Tables 7.1 to 7.3, 7.6, 7.9 to 7.10, 7.15 to 7.17)
The first results of the 2001 Census, published on 30 September 2002, showed that previous estimates of the total UK population were about 1 million too high. Please see the introduction for more details. Estimates of employment and unemployment levels from the LFS released before 30 October 2002 are therefore too high, with rates also affected. This has led to the Labour Force Survey (LFS) needing to reweight their estimates to the new population figures.

ONS has published interim reweighted LFS estimates for the UK, which have been used in this chapter. The interim reweighted figures only cover top-level seasonally adjusted series published in the Labour Market Statistics First Release. The non-seasonally adjusted series, used in previous editions of the Annual Abstract, were not available in time for this publication.

Future editions of the Annual Abstract will continue to show seasonally adjusted data for these tables, in line with other headline publications. These figures are not directly comparable to the non-seasonally adjusted figures previously published in the Annual Abstract.

(Tables 7.12 and 5.6)
Interim reweighted figures for table 7.12, and table 5.6 in the population chapter, are not yet available and have been produced from unrevised not seasonally adjusted data. They are based on the old population estimates and are not in line with the results of the 2001 Census. Future editions of the Annual Abstract will show seasonally adjusted data for table 7.12, in line with the rest of the chapter.

Background
The LFS is the largest regular household survey in the United Kingdom. LFS interviews are conducted continuously throughout the year. In any 3-month period, a nationally representative sample of approximately 102,000 people aged 16 or over in around 57,000 households are interviewed. Each household is interviewed five times, at 3 monthly intervals. The initial interview is done face-to-face by an interviewer visiting the address. The other interviews are done by telephone wherever possible. The survey asks a series of questions about respondents' personal circumstances and their labour market activity. Most questions refer to activity in the week before the interview.

The concepts and definitions used in the LFS are agreed by the International Labour Organisation (ILO) - an agency of the United Nations. The definitions are used by European Union member countries and members of the Organisation for Economic Co-operation and Development (OECD).

The Labour Force Survey was carried out every two years from 1973 to 1983. The ILO definition was first used in 1984. This was also the first year in which the survey was conducted on an annual basis with results available for every spring quarter (representing an average of the period from March to May). The survey moved to a continuous basis in spring 1992 in Great Britain and in winter 1994/5 in Northern Ireland, with average quarterly results published 4 times a year for seasonal quarters: spring (March to May), summer (June to August), autumn (September to November) and winter (December to February). From April 1998, results are published 12 times a year for the average of 3 consecutive months.

The LFS collects information on a sample of the population. To convert this information to give estimates for the population the data must be grossed. This is achieved by calculating weighting factors (often referred to simply as weights) which can be applied to each sampled individual in such a way that the weighted-up results match estimates or projections of the total population in terms of age distribution, sex, and region of residence.

Strengths and limitations of the LFS
The LFS produces coherent labour market information on the basis of internationally standard concepts and definitions. It is a rich source of data on a wide variety of labour market and personal characteristics. It is the most suitable source for making comparisons between countries. The LFS is designed so that households interviewed in each three month period constitute a representative sample of UK households. The survey covers those living in private households and nurses in National Health Service accommodation. Students living in halls of residence have been included since 1992 as information about them is collected at their parents' address.

However the LFS has its limitations. It is a sample survey and is therefore subject to sampling variability. The survey does not include people living in institutions such as hostels or residential homes. 'Proxy' reporting (when members of the household are not present at the interview, another member of the household answers the questions on their behalf) can affect the quality of information on topics such as earnings, hours worked, benefit receipt and qualifications. Around one third of interviews are conducted 'by proxy', usually by a spouse or partner but sometimes by a parent or other near relation.

Sampling Variability
Survey estimates are prone to *sampling variability*. The easiest way to explain this concept is by example. In the September to November 1997 period, ILO unemployment in Great Britain (seasonally adjusted) stood at 1,847,000. If we drew another sample for the same period we could get a different result, perhaps 1,900,000 or 1,820,000.

In theory, we could draw many samples, and each would give a different result. This is because each sample would be made up of different people who would give different answers to the questions. The spread of these results is the sampling variability. Sampling variability is determined by a number of factors including the sample size, the variability of the population from which the sample is drawn and the sample design. Once we know the sampling variability we can calculate a range of values about the sample estimate that represents the expected variation with a given level of assurance. This is called a confidence interval. For a 95% confidence interval we expect that in 95% of the samples (19 times out of 20) the confidence interval will contain the true value that would be obtained by surveying the entire population. For the example given above, we can be 95% confident that the true value was in the range 1,791,000 to 1,903,000.

Unreliable estimates

Very small estimates have relatively wide confidence intervals making them unreliable. For this reason, the ONS does not publish LFS estimates below 10,000.

Non-Response

Non-response can introduce bias to a survey, particularly if the people not responding have characteristics that are different from those who do respond. The LFS has a response rate of around 80 per cent to the first interview, and over 90 per cent of those who are interviewed once go on to complete all five interviews. These are relatively high levels for a household survey. Any bias from non-response is minimised by *weighting* the results.

Weighting (or grossing) converts sample data to represent the full population. In the LFS, the data are weighted separately by age, sex and area of residence to population estimates based on the Census. Weighting also adjusts for people not in the survey and thus minimises non-response bias.

Labour Force Survey Concepts and Definitions

Discouraged workers - a sub-group of the economically inactive population, defined as those neither in employment nor unemployed (on the ILO measure) who said they would like a job and whose main reason for not seeking work was because they believed there were no jobs available.

Economically active - people aged 16 and over who are either in employment or ILO unemployed.

Economic activity rate - the percentage of people aged 16 and over who are economically active.

Economically inactive - people who are neither in employment nor unemployed. This group includes, for example, all those who were looking after a home or retired.

Employment - people aged 16 or over who did at least one hour of paid work in the reference week (whether as an employee or self-employed); those who had a job that they were temporarily away from (on holiday, for example); those on Government-supported training and employment programmes (from spring 1983); and those doing unpaid family work (from spring 1992).

Employees - the division between employees and self-employed is based on survey respondents' own assessment of their employment status.

Full Time - the classification of employees, self-employed and unpaid family workers in their main job as full-time or part-time is on the basis of self-assessment. Up until autumn 1995, people who were on government work-related training programmes are classified as full-time or part-time according to whether their usual hours of work per week were over 30 or 30 and under; from winter 1995/96 onwards, the full-time/part-time classification for this group has been changed to self-assessment, in line with the other groups outlined above. People on Government-supported training and employment programmes who are at college in the survey reference week are classified, by convention, as part-time.

Government-supported training and employment programmes - comprise all people aged 16 and over participating in one of the Government's employment and training programmes (Youth Training, Training for Work and Community Action), together with those on similar programmes administered by Training and Enterprise Councils in England and Wales, or Local Enterprise Companies in Scotland.

Hours worked - respondents to the LFS are asked a series of questions enabling the identification of both their usual hours and their actual hours. Total hours include overtime (paid and unpaid) and exclude lunchbreaks.

Unemployment – Unemployment figures from the Labour Force Survey (LFS), which are based upon the International Labour Organisation (ILO) definition, were re-labelled 'unemployment' rather than 'ILO unemployment' in January 2003. This emphasises that the LFS figures provide the official and only internationally comparable measure of unemployment in the UK. For more details see the National Statistics website at www.statistics.gov.uk/cci/nugget.asp?id=251

The International Labour Office (ILO) measure of unemployment used throughout this supplement refers to people without a job who were available to start work in the two weeks following their LFS interview and who had either looked for work in the four weeks prior to interview or were waiting to start a job they had already obtained. This definition of unemployment is in accordance with that adopted by the 13th International Conference of Labour Statisticians, further clarified at the 14th ICLS, and promulgated by the ILO in its publications.

Unemployment (rate) - the percentage of economically active people who are unemployed on the ILO measure.

Unemployment (duration) - defined as the shorter of the following two periods: (a) duration of active search for work; and (b) length of time since employment.

Part-Time - see full-time

Labour market

Second jobs - jobs which LFS respondents hold in addition to a main full-time or part -time job.

Self-employment - See Employees

Temporary employees - in the LFS these are defined as those employees who say that their main job is non permanent in one of the following ways: fixed period contract; agency temping; casual work; seasonal work; other temporary work.

Unpaid Family Workers - the separate identification from spring 1992 of this group in the LFS is in accordance with international recommendations. The group comprises persons doing unpaid work for a business they own or for a business that a relative owns.

Distribution of workforce *(Table 7.4)*

Claimant unemployed - those people who were claiming unemployment-related benefits (Unemployment Benefit, Income Support or National Insurance credits) at Employment service local offices on the day of the monthly count. The seasonally adjusted claimant unemployment series allows for all relevant changes which, unless adjusted for, would distort comparisons over time.

Workforce jobs (formerly workforce in employment) - comprises employee jobs, self-employment jobs (from the Labour Force Survey), HM Forces and government supported trainees.

HM Forces (provided by Ministry of Defence) - represent the total number of UK service personnel, male and female, in HM Regular Forces, wherever serving and including those on leave.

Self-employed jobs - estimates are based on the results of the Labour Force Survey. The Northern Ireland estimates are not seasonally adjusted.

Government-supported trainees - include all participants on government training and employment programmes who are receiving some work experience on their placement but who do not have a contract of employment (those with a contract are included in the employee jobs series). The numbers are not subject to seasonal adjustment.

Persons employed in local authorities *(Table 7.8)*
The full-time equivalents for local authorities are derived by applying factors to the numbers of part-time workers in three groups based on average hours worked in each group nationally.

Jobseekers allowance claimant count
(Tables 7.13 and 7.14)
This is a count of all those people who are claiming Jobseeker's Allowance (JSA) at Jobcentre Plus local offices. People claiming JSA must declare that they are out of work capable of, available for and actively seeking work during the week in which the claim is made. All people claiming Jobseeker's Allowance (JSA) on the day of the monthly count are included in the claimant count, irrespective of whether they are actually receiving benefits.

Labour disputes *(Table 7.18)*
These figures exclude details of stoppages involving fewer than ten workers or lasting less than one day except any in which the aggregate number of working days lost is 100 or more. There may be some under-recording of small or short stoppages; this would have much more effect on the total of stoppages than of working days lost. Some stoppages which affected more than one industry group have been counted under each of the industries but only once in the totals. Stoppages have been classified using *Standard Industrial Classification (SIC) 1992.*

The figures for working days lost and workers involved have been rounded and consequently the sum of the constituent items may not agree with the totals. Classifications by size are based on the full duration of stoppages where these continue into the following year. Working days lost per thousand employees are based on the latest available mid-year (June) estimates of employee jobs.

Earnings *(Tables 7.19 to 7.23, 7.25)*
The total gross remuneration employees receive before any statutory deductions (tax, national insurance). Income in kind and pension funds are excluded.

Average earnings index *(Tables 7.21 and 7.22)*
The Average Earnings Index (AEI) is designed to measure changes in the level of earnings, i.e. wage inflation in Great Britain. Average earnings are calculated as the total wages and salaries paid by firms, divided by the number of employees paid. Like all indices, changes are measured against a base year, whose index value is set to 100. The current base year is 2000 for Tables 7.21 and 7.22.

Users should note that the data contained in table 7.22 are not comparable with those previously published in Annual Abstract. The ONS has withdrawn the old set of 26 industry sectors and has a new set of 20 industries that better reflect the current state of the economy. The new series are available in the format of excluding bonus index, including bonus index, and an annual percentage change for including and excluding bonuses. An article covering the reasons for the change can be found on our website *www.statistics.gov.uk/ labour.*

The AEI is published monthly in the Labour Market Statistics First Release. The main indicator of growth, the headline rate, is based on the annual change in the seasonally adjusted index values for the latest 3 months compared with the same period a year ago. The use of a 3-month average reduces the level of volatility seen in the data on a month-on-month basis.

Strengths of the AEI
The AEI, based on monthly survey data, is a timely indicator of changes in the level of earnings.

Limitations of the AEI
The index is not adjusted for any changes in the composition of the workforce such as changes in the share of full-time and part-time workers, or in the share of skilled and unskilled workers. Similarly, the index does not account for changes in the number of hours worked, or any temporary factors that affect earnings.

The sample of the Monthly Wages and Salaries Survey on which the AEI is based is not designed to provide information on the level of earnings. The sample is not completely representative of the economy as firms with fewer than 20 employees are excluded, as are the earnings of self employed persons.

The AEI only covers earnings in Great Britain as earnings information is not collected for Northern Ireland and regional data are not available.

Earnings *(Table 7.24)*
Those whose pay in the survey period was not affected by absence. Weekly earnings figures refer to April in each year and are gross before deductions, generally excluding the value of incomes in kind but including bonus, overtime and commission payments for the pay period.

Trade unions *(Table 7.26)*
The statistics relate to all organisations of employees known to Certification Officer with head offices in the United Kingdom that fall within the appropriate definition of a trade union in the 1992 Trade Union and Labour Relations Act. Included in the data are home and overseas membership figures of contributory and non-contributory members. Employment status of members is not provided and the figures may therefore include some people who are self-employed, unemployed or retired.

The membership part of this table was revised in 2001, so that statistics presented here are on a consistent basis with the GB table produced by the Certification Officer in his Annual Report and with tables produced in the annual Labour Market Trends Trade Union article. There is a break in the time series for the figures in this table between the years 1988 (contained within previous publications) and 1989. GB data for 1989-95 are DTI analyses of annual returns, with 1996-1999 as published in the Certification Officer's Annual Report. Data for Northern Ireland for 1989-1991 are DTI analyses of annual returns, with 1992-1999 from the Certification Officer's Annual Report.

Vacancies at jobcentres *(Table 7.27)*
Publication of the jobcentre vacancy statistics has been deferred. This publication contains vacancy data only up to April 2001 because the figures from May 2001 are affected by the introduction of Employer Direct. This major change involves transferring the vacancy taking process from local Jobcentres to regional Customer Service Centres, as part of modernising the Employment Service. ONS and the Employment Service will continue to monitor and review the data with the aim

of publishing the series as soon as it is possible to produce a consistent measure. Vacancies notified to and placings made by jobcentres do not represent the total number of vacancies/engagements in the economy. Latest estimates suggest that about a third of all vacancies are notified to jobcentres: and about a quarter of all engagements are made through jobcentres. Inflow, outflow and placings figures are collected for four or five-week periods between count dates; the figures in this table are converted to a standard 4 1 / 3 week month. Table excludes vacancies on government programmes except vacancies on Enterprise Ulster and Action for Community Employment (ACE) which are included in the seasonally adjusted figures for Northern Ireland. The latest national seasonally adjusted vacancy figures are provisional and subject to revision in the following month.

Vacancy - This is a job opportunity notified by an employer to a Jobcentre.

Unfilled vacancy - (also known as "Stock of vacancies")
This is the number of vacancies which have not been filled or cancelled on the count date.

Inflow of vacancy - (also known as "Notified vacancies")
This is the number of job opportunities notified by employers to Jobcentres in the period between two successive count dates.

Outflow of vacancy - This is a derived statistic which represents the total of vacancies filled plus cancelled between count dates. This concept can also be expressed as "vacancy stock" at the beginning of the period plus notified vacancies (inflows) minus "vacancy stock" at the end of the period.

Placings - This is the number of Jobseekers placed into employment by individual Jobcentres.

7.1 Summary for United Kingdom labour force[1,2]
Spring each year. Seasonally adjusted.

Thousands

| | All aged 16+[3] | All aged 16 and over | | | | Economic activity rate 16-59/64 (%)[4] | Employment rate - all aged 16+ (%)[5] | Employment rate 16-59/64 (%)[6] | Unemployment rate (%)[7] |
		Total economically active	Total in employment	Total unemployed	Economically inactive				
All									
	MGSL	MGSF	MGRZ	MGSC	MGSI	MGSO	MGSR	MGSU	MGSX
1993	45 041	28 258	25 304	2 954	16 783	78.7	56.2	70.3	10.5
1994	45 089	28 227	25 475	2 753	16 861	78.5	56.5	70.7	9.8
1995	45 200	28 221	25 749	2 472	16 979	78.2	57.0	71.2	8.8
1996	45 345	28 357	26 012	2 345	16 988	78.4	57.4	71.8	8.3
1997	45 494	28 504	26 461	2 043	16 990	78.5	58.2	72.7	7.2
1998	45 643	28 492	26 713	1 779	17 150	78.3	58.5	73.3	6.2
1999	45 825	28,799	27 037	1 762	17 026	78.7	59.0	73.8	6.1
2000	46 054	29 056	27 416	1 641	16 998	79.0	59.5	74.4	5.6
2001	46 351	29 110	27 675	1 435	17 241	78.6	59.7	74.7	4.9
2002	46 628	29 368	27 835	1 533	17 260	78.6	59.7	74.5	5.2
2003	46 903	29 595	28 110	1 484	17 309	78.8	59.9	74.7	5.0
Men									
	MGSM	MGSG	MGSA	MGSD	MGSJ	MGSP	MGSS	MGSV	MGSY
1993	21 651	15 799	13 828	1 972	5 852	85.9	63.9	75.1	12.5
1994	21 670	15 737	13 928	1 809	5 933	85.5	64.3	75.6	11.5
1995	21 728	15 706	14 112	1 594	6 022	85.1	64.9	76.3	10.1
1996	21 805	15 705	14 179	1 526	6 101	85.0	65.0	76.6	9.7
1997	21 881	15 705	14 422	1 283	6 176	84.7	65.9	77.7	8.2
1998	21 957	15 653	14 580	1 072	6 304	84.2	66.4	78.4	6.9
1999	22 057	15 781	14 707	1 075	6 276	84.5	66.7	78.7	6.8
2000	22 181	15 885	14 906	979	6 296	84.6	67.2	79.4	6.2
2001	22 354	15 868	15 015	853	6 486	84.1	67.2	79.5	5.4
2002	22 511	15 956	15 039	917	6 555	83.9	66.8	79.0	5.7
2003	22 661	16 122	15 221	900	6 539	84.1	67.2	79.4	5.6
Women									
	MGSN	MGSH	MGSB	MGSE	MGSK	MGSQ	MGST	MGSW	MGSZ
1993	23 390	12 459	11 476	982	10 931	70.9	49.1	65.2	7.9
1994	23 419	12 490	11 546	943	10 929	70.9	49.3	65.4	7.6
1995	23 471	12 515	11 636	878	10 956	70.9	49.6	65.8	7.0
1996	23 540	12 652	11 833	819	10 887	71.4	50.3	66.7	6.5
1997	23 613	12 799	12 039	760	10 814	71.8	51.0	67.4	5.9
1998	23 685	12 839	12 133	707	10 846	71.9	51.2	67.9	5.5
1999	23 768	13 017	12 330	687	10 750	72.5	51.9	68.6	5.3
2000	23 873	13 171	12 510	662	10 702	72.9	52.4	69.1	5.0
2001	23 996	13 242	12 659	582	10 755	72.8	52.8	69.5	4.4
2002	24 117	13 412	12 796	616	10 704	73.0	53.1	69.6	4.6
2003	24 242	13 473	12 889	584	10 770	73.0	53.2	69.8	4.3

1 See chapter text.
2 The data in this table have been adjusted to reflect the latest 2001 Census population data.
3 Population in private households, and from 1992, student halls of residence.
4 Economically active of working age as a percentage of all persons of working age.

5 Total employed as a percentage of all persons 16 and over.
6 Total employed of working age as a percentage of all persons of working age (men 16-64, women 16-59).
7 Total unemployed as a percentage of all economically active.

Source: Labour Force Survey, Office for National Statistics

7.2 Employment status, full-time/part-time, second jobs, temporary employees[1,2]
United Kingdom
Spring each year. Seasonally adjusted.

Thousands

	All in employment[3]					Total employment[3]		Employees[3]		Self-employed[3]			
	Total	Employees	Self employed	Unpaid family workers	Government supported training and employment programmes[4]	Full-time	Part-time	Full-time	Part-time	Full-time	Part-time	Workers with second jobs[5]	Temporary employees
All													
	MGRZ	MGRN	MGRQ	MGRT	MGRW	YCBE	YCBH	YCBK	YCBN	YCBQ	YCBT	YCBW	YCBZ
1993	25 304	21 662	3 142	149	351	19 231	6 073	16 467	5 195	2 564	579	1 033	1 343
1994	25 475	21 750	3 250	144	330	19 247	6 227	16 419	5 331	2 644	606	1 138	1 473
1995	25 749	22 027	3 303	138	280	19 475	6 274	16 620	5 407	2 679	624	1 279	1 607
1996	26 012	22 402	3 238	126	246	19 506	6 506	16 745	5 658	2 596	642	1 281	1 644
1997	26 461	22 843	3 284	117	217	19 812	6 649	17 054	5 790	2 602	682	1 241	1 757
1998	26 713	23 228	3 210	101	174	20 014	6 699	17 387	5 841	2 501	709	1 171	1 710
1999	27 037	23 637	3 144	100	155	20 251	6 786	17 683	5 954	2 461	683	1 260	1 673
2000	27 416	24 081	3 086	108	140	20 517	6 899	18 016	6 065	2 397	688	1 169	1 686
2001	27 675	24 334	3 097	96	147	20 711	6 964	18 164	6 169	2 446	651	1 163	1 684
2002	27 835	24 489	3 149	95	102	20 802	7 033	18 279	6 209	2 451	698	1 130	1 546
2003	28 110	24 598	3 338	86	89	20 859	7 252	18 268	6 330	2 532	806	1 131	1 499
Men													
	MGSA	MGRO	MGRR	MGRU	MGRX	YCBF	YCBI	YCBL	YCBO	YCBR	YCBU	YCBX	YCCA
1993	13 828	11 213	2 345	42	228	12 821	1 007	10 547	666	2 145	200	463	594
1994	13 928	11 232	2 434	48	214	12 851	1 077	10 513	719	2 223	211	500	647
1995	14 112	11 397	2 494	42	179	12 984	1 128	10 615	782	2 266	228	534	739
1996	14 179	11 573	2 412	42	153	12 977	1 202	10 706	867	2 180	231	537	728
1997	14 422	11 830	2 421	38	133	13 144	1 278	10 873	957	2 176	245	542	799
1998	14 580	12 099	2 341	29	112	13 293	1 287	11 138	961	2 079	262	509	756
1999	14 707	12 254	2 316	35	102	13 377	1 330	11 243	1 011	2 066	250	527	786
2000	14 906	12 555	2 232	36	84	13 553	1 354	11 524	1 031	1 968	264	487	767
2001	15 015	12 615	2 269	35	96	13 654	1 361	11 558	1 057	2 028	241	470	768
2002	15 039	12 636	2 316	28	59	13 624	1 414	11 545	1 091	2 035	281	460	711
2003	15 221	12 711	2 427	30	53	13 661	1 561	11 526	1 185	2 096	332	459	678
Women													
	MGSB	MGRP	MGRS	MGRV	MGRY	YCBG	YCBJ	YCBM	YCBP	YCBS	YCBV	YCBY	YCCB
1993	11 476	10 450	797	107	123	6 410	5 066	5 920	4 530	418	379	570	749
1994	11 546	10 518	817	96	116	6 396	5 150	5 906	4 612	421	396	638	826
1995	11 636	10 630	809	96	101	6 491	5 146	6 006	4 625	413	396	745	868
1996	11 833	10 830	827	84	93	6 529	5 304	6 039	4 791	416	411	744	916
1997	12 039	11 013	863	79	84	6 667	5 372	6 180	4 833	426	436	699	959
1998	12 133	11 129	869	72	62	6 721	5 412	6 249	4 880	422	447	662	954
1999	12 330	11 383	828	66	53	6 874	5 456	6 440	4 944	395	433	734	887
2000	12 510	11 527	854	72	57	6 964	5 545	6 492	5 035	429	425	682	919
2001	12 659	11 718	828	62	51	7 056	5 603	6 606	5 112	418	410	693	916
2002	12 796	11 853	833	67	43	7 177	5 619	6 734	5 119	415	417	670	835
2003	12 889	11 887	911	56	36	7 198	5 691	6 743	5 144	437	474	672	821

1 See chapter text.
2 The data in this table have been adjusted to reflect the latest 2001 Census population data.
3 People whose main job is full or part-time.
4 Those on employment and training programmes are classified as in employment. Some of those on programmes may consider themselves to be employees or self employed so appear in other categories.

5 Second jobs reported in LFS in addition to person's main full or part-time job.

Source: Labour Force Survey, Office for National Statistics

7.3 Employment[1,2]
United Kingdom
By age and sex. At Spring each year. Seasonally adjusted.

Thousands and percentages.

	All aged 16 and over	16-59/64	16-17	18-24	16-24	25-34	35-49	50-64 (m) 50-59 (f)	65+ (m) 60+ (f)
Thousands									
All									
	MGRZ	YBSE	YBTO	YBTR	PXLA	YBTU	YBTX	MGUW	MGUZ
1995	25 749	24 956	600	3 315	3 915	6 863	9 371	4 807	793
1996	26 012	25 244	649	3 268	3 917	6 889	9 521	4 917	768
1997	26 461	25 662	691	3 213	3 904	7 032	9 569	5 157	800
1998	26 713	25 940	682	3 165	3 847	7 009	9 684	5 400	773
1999	27 037	26 219	659	3 178	3 837	6 973	9 825	5 584	818
2000	27 416	26 583	662	3 236	3 898	6 916	10 034	5 734	833
2001	27 675	26 852	665	3 271	3 936	6 784	10 198	5 934	822
2002	27 835	26 940	650	3 363	4 013	6 577	10 349	6 001	895
2003	28 110	27 172	658	3 362	4 020	6 394	10 527	6 231	938
Men									
	MGSA	YBSF	YBTP	YBTS	PXLB	YBTV	YBTY	MGUX	MGVA
1995	14 112	13 824	298	1 729	2 027	3 832	5 064	2 900	288
1996	14 179	13 913	325	1 685	2 010	3 828	5 099	2 976	266
1997	14 422	14 154	334	1 672	2 006	3 887	5 134	3 127	268
1998	14 580	14 308	334	1 645	1 979	3 885	5 199	3 245	273
1999	14 707	14 419	322	1 652	1 974	3 833	5 262	3 350	288
2000	14 906	14 618	328	1 688	2 016	3 803	5 385	3 414	288
2001	15 015	14 748	332	1 709	2 041	3 732	5 442	3 534	267
2002	15 039	14 745	322	1 754	2 076	3 606	5 513	3 551	294
2003	15 221	14 881	322	1 760	2 082	3 496	5 616	3 688	341
Women									
	MGSB	YBSG	YBTQ	YBTT	PXLC	YBTW	YBTZ	MGUY	MGVB
1995	11 636	11 132	302	1 585	1 887	3 031	4 307	1 907	504
1996	11 833	11 331	324	1 584	1 908	3 061	4 422	1 941	502
1997	12 039	11 508	357	1 541	1 898	3 145	4 435	2 030	531
1998	12 133	11 633	348	1 520	1 868	3 124	4 485	2 156	500
1999	12 330	11 800	337	1 526	1 863	3 141	4 563	2 234	530
2000	12 510	11 964	333	1 548	1 881	3 113	4 650	2 320	545
2001	12 659	12 104	333	1 562	1 895	3 053	4 756	2 401	555
2002	12 796	12 195	329	1 610	1 939	2 971	4 836	2 449	601
2003	12 889	12 291	337	1 602	1 939	2 898	4 911	2 543	598
Rates[3]									
All									
	MGSR	MGSU	YBUA	YBUD	PXLD	YBUG	YBUJ	YBUM	YBUP
1995	57.0	71.2	45.1	64.1	60.2	75.5	79.3	63.0	7.8
1996	57.4	71.8	46.4	65.8	61.5	75.8	79.7	63.5	7.5
1997	58.2	72.7	48.0	66.5	62.2	77.8	79.9	64.5	7.8
1998	58.5	73.3	47.8	66.4	62.1	78.4	80.6	65.5	7.5
1999	59.0	73.8	46.9	66.5	62.1	79.4	81.0	66.2	7.9
2000	59.5	74.4	46.7	67.5	62.8	80.2	81.6	66.7	8.1
2001	59.7	74.7	45.4	67.4	62.3	80.3	81.8	68.0	7.9
2002	59.7	74.5	43.2	68.0	62.2	79.8	81.8	67.9	8.6
2003	59.9	74.7	43.3	66.3	61.0	79.5	82.1	69.9	8.9
Men									
	MGSS	MGSV	YBUB	YBUE	PXLE	YBUH	YBUK	YBUN	YBUQ
1995	64.9	76.3	44.4	67.1	62.4	84.6	86.3	65.0	8.0
1996	65.0	76.6	46.0	68.2	63.3	84.6	85.9	65.9	7.3
1997	65.9	77.7	46.0	69.9	64.3	86.4	86.4	67.3	7.3
1998	66.4	78.4	46.4	69.8	64.3	87.5	87.3	67.9	7.4
1999	66.7	78.7	45.2	70.0	64.3	87.8	87.5	68.6	7.7
2000	67.2	79.4	45.5	71.2	65.2	88.8	88.5	68.8	7.7
2001	67.2	79.5	44.3	70.9	64.6	88.8	88.3	70.3	7.0
2002	66.8	79.0	41.7	71.2	64.1	88.1	88.2	69.9	7.6
2003	67.2	79.4	41.3	69.5	62.9	87.8	88.7	72.0	8.7
Women									
	MGST	MGSW	YBUC	YBUF	PXLF	YBUI	YBUL	YBUO	YBUR
1995	49.6	65.8	45.9	61.2	58.1	66.4	72.4	60.3	7.7
1996	50.3	66.7	46.7	63.3	59.7	67.0	73.5	60.2	7.7
1997	51.0	67.4	50.0	63.2	60.2	69.2	73.6	60.6	8.1
1998	51.2	67.9	49.1	63.1	60.0	69.5	74.1	62.1	7.6
1999	51.9	68.6	48.5	63.2	59.9	71.1	74.6	62.8	8.1
2000	52.4	69.1	47.9	63.9	60.4	71.7	74.9	63.9	8.3
2001	52.8	69.5	46.6	63.9	60.0	71.8	75.4	64.8	8.4
2002	53.1	69.6	44.8	64.8	60.3	71.6	75.6	65.1	9.1
2003	53.2	69.8	45.5	63.2	59.2	71.4	75.7	67.1	9.0

1 See chapter text.
2 The data in this table have been adjusted to reflect the latest 2001 Census
  population data.
3 Total in employment as a percentage of all persons in the relevant group.

Source: Labour Force Survey, Office for National Statistics

7.4 Distribution of the workforce[1]
At mid-June each year

Thousands, seasonally adjusted

		1993	1994	1995	1996	1997	1998	1999	2000	2001	2002	2003
United Kingdom												
Claimant count	KAMO	2 902	2 625	2 294	2 135	1 572	1 344	1 263	1 094	963	952	948
Males	KAMP	2 235	2 016	1 756	1 625	1 208	1 028	969	836	734	721	713
Females	KAMQ	667	609	538	509	364	317	294	258	229	231	235
Workforce jobs	DYDC	26 814	26 955	27 277	27 694	28 179	28 389	28 860	29 271	29 495	29 492	29 695
Males	KAMS	14 290	14 337	14 506	14 577	14 951	15 101	15 405	15 599	15 664	15 661	15 791
Females	KAMT	12 524	12 618	12 771	13 117	13 228	13 288	13 456	13 672	13 831	13 831	13 904
HM Forces	KAMU	271	250	230	222	210	210	209	207	204	204	207
Males	KAMV	252	232	214	206	195	194	192	190	188	187	189
Females	KAMW	19	18	16	16	15	16	16	17	17	17	18
Self-employment jobs	DYZN	3 395	3 489	3 543	3 540	3 527	3 399	3 407	3 319	3 307	3 363	3 563
Males	KAMZ	2 486	2 571	2 614	2 599	2 541	2 437	2 449	2 375	2 380	2 416	2 559
Females	KANA	909	917	929	942	986	962	959	944	927	947	1 004
Employees jobs	BCAJ	22 821	22 900	23 264	23 738	24 270	24 649	25 114	25 626	25 882	25 829	25 825
Males	KANC	11 348	11 334	11 523	11 654	12 109	12 394	12 684	12 961	13 034	13 000	12 984
Females	KAND	11 473	11 566	11 741	12 085	12 161	12 255	12 430	12 665	12 848	12 829	12 842
of whom												
Total, production and construction industries	KANF	5 211	5 194	5 245	5 292	5 398	5 525	5 382	5 348	5 192	4 966	4 854
Total, all manufacturing industries	KANG	3 955	3 970	4 073	4 138	4 191	4 209	4 060	3 960	3 808	3 628	3 502
Government-supported trainees	KANH	326	317	240	194	171	131	131	118	101	96	101
Males	KANI	203	199	156	119	105	76	81	73	63	58	60
Females	KANJ	124	118	84	75	66	55	50	46	38	38	40
Great Britain												
Claimant count	KANN	2 798	2 527	2 207	2 048	1 510	1 287	1 212	1 052	923	915	913
Males	KANO	2 155	1 940	1 687	1 559	1 159	983	929	804	704	693	686
Females	KANP	643	587	519	489	351	304	283	248	220	222	227
Workforce jobs	KANQ	26 167	26 296	26 595	27 014	27 476	27 673	28 137	28 526	28 741	28 732	28 931
Males	KANR	13 932	13 974	14 134	14 210	14 571	14 713	15 017	15 197	15 259	15 258	15 388
Females	KANS	12 236	12 322	12 461	12 803	12 904	12 960	13 120	13 329	13 482	13 475	13 542
HM Forces	BCAH	271	250	230	222	210	210	209	207	204	204	207
Males	KANU	252	232	214	206	195	194	192	190	188	187	189
Females	KANV	19	18	16	16	15	16	16	17	17	17	18
Self-employment jobs	KANW	3 311	3 403	3 451	3 455	3 436	3 311	3 322	3 226	3 212	3 274	3 474
Males	KANX	2 414	2 497	2 538	2 527	2 468	2 363	2 379	2 297	2 300	2 342	2 485
Females	KANY	898	906	914	928	968	948	942	929	911	932	989
Employee jobs	KANZ	22 275	22 342	22 689	23 159	23 672	24 036	24 487	24 984	25 231	25 165	25 156
Males	KAOA	11 074	11 055	11 237	11 368	11 812	12 089	12 372	12 643	12 713	12 676	12 659
Females	KAOB	11 201	11 286	11 452	11 791	11 860	11 946	12 115	12 341	12 517	12 489	12 497
of whom												
Total, production and construction industries	KAOC	5 091	5 069	5 115	5 158	5 256	5 383	5 240	5 205	5 049	4 827	4 721
Total, all manufacturing industries	KAOD	3 853	3 868	3 968	4 034	4 083	4 102	3 954	3 856	3 706	3 531	3 410
Government-supported trainees	KAOE	310	301	224	178	157	117	119	109	94	89	94
Males	KAOF	192	189	145	109	96	67	73	66	58	53	56
Females	KAOG	118	112	79	69	61	50	47	43	36	36	38

Note: Because the figures have been rounded independently totals may differ from the sum of the components. Also the totals may include some employees whose industrial classification could not be ascertained.

1 The data in this table have not been adjusted to reflect the 2001 Census population data. See chapter text.

Source: Earnings and Employment Division, Office for National Statistics:
01633 812318

7.5 Employee jobs[1]
Analysis by industry based on the Standard Industrial Classification 1992
At June in each year

Thousands, not seasonally adjusted

			United Kingdom						Great Britain						
		SIC 1992	1998	1999	2000	2001	2002	2003		1998	1999	2000	2001	2002	2003
All sections	KAOH	A - Q	24 569	25 045	25 572	25 846	25 796	25 794	LMAB	23 957	24 421	24 932	25 196	25 134	25 127
Index of production and construction industries	KAOI	C - F	5 504	5 366	5 336	5 184	4 960	4 849	LMAH	5 362	5 224	5 193	5 041	4 822	4 716
Index of production industries	KAOJ	C - E	4 406	4 256	4 153	4 013	3 834	3 704	LMAF	4 294	4 145	4 044	3 907	3 731	3 607
of which, manufacturing industries	KAOK	D	4 197	4 051	3 954	3 805	3 627	3 501	KAPQ	4 090	3 946	3 850	3 703	3 529	3 408
Service industries	KAOL	G - Q	18 743	19 362	19 915	20 383	20 578	20 712	LMAJ	18 289	18 895	19 434	19 890	20 069	20 192
Agriculture, hunting and forestry and fishing	KAOM	A/B	322	318	321	279	258	233	KAPS	306	302	305	264	244	219
Agriculture hunting and forestry	KPHI	A	311	305	310	270	248	223	KOVW	295	290	295	256	234	209
Agriculture hunting & related activities	KPHJ	01	303	297	304	260	235	210	KOVX	287	282	288	246	221	196
Fishing	KPHK	B	12	13	11	9	10	10	KOVY	11	12	11	9	10	10
Mining and quarrying	KPHL	C	75	74	73	73	73	70	KOVZ	73	72	71	72	71	68
Mining and quarrying of energy producing materials	KPHM	CA	46	46	44	44	44	43	KOWA	46	45	43	44	44	43
Mining	KAPG	10/12	..	..	..	..	..	..	KOWB	13	14	13	13	12	11
Extraction of crude petroleum	KPHN	11	..	..	..	..	..	..	KOWC	33	31	31	31	32	32
Mining and quarrying except of energy producing materials	KPHO	CB(13/14)	29	28	29	29	28	28	KOWD	27	27	28	28	27	26
Energy and water supply industries	KAOO	C/E	209	205	200	208	207	203	LMAM	204	199	194	203	202	198
Manufacturing	KPHP	D	4 197	4 051	3 954	3 805	3 627	3 501	LMAD	4 090	3 946	3 850	3 703	3 529	3 408
Manufacture of food products Beverages and tobacco	KPHQ	DA	502	499	493	479	469	467	LMAN	482	480	474	460	450	448
Of food	KPHR	151 to 158	..	..	..	..	..	..	KOWH	428	425	421	406	396	394
Of beverages and tobacco	KPHS	159/16	..	..	..	..	..	..	KOWI	54	54	53	53	54	54
Manufacture of textiles and textile products	KPHT	DB	336	294	258	223	199	180	KOWJ	314	275	242	210	187	170
Of textiles	KPHU	17	178	162	149	135	120	112	KOWK	167	152	141	127	114	106
Of made-up textile articles except apparel	KPHV	174	..	..	..	..	..	..	KOWL	36	34	34	34	32	31
Of textiles excluding made-up textile	KPHW	Rest of 17	..	..	..	..	..	..	KOWM	132	118	106	93	81	75
Of wearing apparel,dressing and dyeing of fur	KPHX	18	159	133	109	88	78	68	KOWN	147	123	101	83	73	65
Manufacture of leather and leather products including footwear	KPHY	DC	35	30	26	21	18	15	KOWO	34	30	25	20	18	14
Of leather and leather goods	KPHZ	191/192	..	..	..	..	..	..	KOWP	12	11	10	9	8	7
Of footwear	KPIA	193	..	..	..	..	..	..	KOWQ	22	19	15	11	10	8
Manufacture of wood and wood products	KPIB	DD(20)	87	84	83	82	83	82	LMAP	84	81	80	78	80	79
Manufacture of pulp paper and paper products,publishing and printing	KPIC	DE	473	469	464	450	443	437	LMAQ	466	463	458	444	437	430
Of pulp paper and paper products	KPID	21	110	104	100	95	89	90	KOWT	107	102	98	93	88	88
Publishing printing and reproduction of recorded media	KPIE	22	363	365	364	356	354	347	KOWU	359	361	360	351	349	342
Manufacture of coke refined petroleum products and nuclear fuel	KPIF	DF(23)	24	26	26	28	26	25	KOWV	24	26	26	27	26	25
Manufacture of chemicals,chemical products and man-made fibres	KPIG	DG(24)	258	249	238	235	231	224	LMAR	254	246	235	232	228	221
Manufacture of rubber and plastics	KPIH	DH(25)	253	244	237	227	222	216	LMAS	246	237	230	220	215	209
Manufacture of other non-metallic mineral products	KPII	DI(26)	146	140	140	134	129	127	KOWZ	141	135	135	129	124	121
Manufacture of basic metals and fabricated metal products	KPIJ	DJ	553	534	521	490	461	450	KOXA	548	528	515	484	455	444
Of basic metals	KPIK	27	133	124	117	107	97	94	KOXB	133	124	116	107	96	94
except machinery	KPIL	28	420	410	404	383	365	356	KOXC	415	405	398	377	359	351

7.5
Employee jobs[1]
Analysis by industry based on the Standard Industrial Classification 1992
continued At June in each year

Thousands, not seasonally adjusted

			United Kingdom							Great Britain					
			1998	1999	2000	2001	2002	2003		1998	1999	2000	2001	2002	2003
		SIC 1992													
Manufacture of Machinery and Equipment not elsewhere classified	KPIM	DK(29)	389	368	356	351	338	327	LMAU	382	361	349	344	331	321
Manufacture of electrical and optical equipment	KPIN	DL	519	497	494	480	425	389	LMAV	508	486	481	467	414	379
Of office machinery and computers	KPIO	30	49	51	53	50	42	38	KOXF	47	49	51	48	39	36
Of electrical machinery and apparatus	KPIP	31	191	181	178	169	151	138	KOXG	188	179	175	166	148	135
Of electric motors etc control apparatus and insulated cable	KPIQ	311 to 313	..	..	..	..	..	..	KOXH	104	103	101	96	85	76
Of accumulators, primary cells, batteries, lamps and electrical equipment	KPIR	314 to 316	..	..	..	..	..	..	KOXI	85	76	74	70	63	59
Radio television and communication equipment	KPIS	32	133	125	129	126	102	90	KOXJ	127	120	123	120	98	87
Of electronic components	KPIT	321	..	..	..	..	..	..	KOXK	52	50	45	40	35	32
Of radio TV and telephone apparatus, sound and video recorders	KPIU	322/323	..	..	..	..	..	..	KOXL	75	70	78	80	64	55
Of medical precision and optical equipment, watches	KPIV	33	146	140	134	135	130	123	KOXM	145	138	132	134	128	121
Manufacture of transport equipment	KPIW	DM	411	403	402	390	376	361	LMAW	399	390	389	377	363	350
Of motor vehicles and trailers	KPIX	34	245	232	226	212	207	199	KOXO	241	228	222	207	202	194
Of other transport equipment	KPIY	35	166	171	176	178	169	162	KOXP	158	163	168	169	161	155
Manufacturing not elsewhere classified	KPIZ	DN(36/37)	211	211	216	215	206	200	KOXQ	208	207	212	211	202	196
Electricity gas and water supply	KPJA	E	134	131	127	135	134	133	KOXR	127	127	123	132	131	130
Electricity gas steam and hot		·							KOXS	98	97	92	97	98	97
water supply	KPJB	40	..	..	..	..	..	..	KOXT	66	67	61	63	64	64
Collection purification and distribution of water	KPJC	41	..	..	..	..	..	..	KOXU	32	30	31	35	33	33
Construction	KPJD	F(45)	1 098	1 110	1 183	1 170	1 126	1 145	LMAY	1 069	1 079	1 148	1 135	1 090	1 109
Services	KPJE	G - Q	18 743	19 362	19 915	20 383	20 578	20 712	KOXX	18 289	18 895	19 434	19 890	20 069	20 192
Wholesale and retail trade; Repair of motor vehicles, motorcycles and personal household goods	KPJF	G (50 - 52)	4 301	4 325	4 369	4 469	4 503	4 451	LMAZ	4 202	4 223	4 264	4 362	4 390	4 337
Sale maintenance and repair of motor vehicles, retail of automotive fuel	KPJG	50	577	576	567	565	580	584	KOXZ	563	562	553	550	565	568
Sale of motor vehicles, motorcycles and parts, motorcycle repair and sale of automotive fuel	KPJH	501/503 - 505	..	..	..	..	..	..	KOYA	412	404	387	386	392	388
Maintenance and repair of motor vehicles	KPJI	502	..	..	..	..	..	..	KOYB	151	158	166	164	173	180
Wholesale trade and commission trade except motor vehicles	KPJJ	51	1 141	1 167	1 175	1 163	1 132	1 108	KOYC	1 119	1 144	1 153	1 140	1 109	1 085
Wholesale on a fee of contract basis	KPJK	511	..	..	..	..	..	..	KOYD	49	58	62	60	53	49
Wholesale agricultural raw materials and live animals	KPJL	512	..	..	..	..	..	..	KPLD	24	24	23	24	23	25
Wholesale food beverages & tobacco	KPJM	513	..	..	..	..	..	..	KPLE	208	206	199	193	190	188
Wholesale household goods	KPJN	514	..	..	..	..	..	..	KPLF	243	254	266	271	265	259
Wholesale of non-agricultural intermediate products waste & scrap	KPJO	515	..	..	..	..	..	..	KPLG	230	239	243	234	235	222
Wholesale machinery eqpt. & supplies	KPJP	516	..	..	..	..	..	..	KPLH	258	256	252	251	242	240
Other wholesale	KPJQ	517	..	..	..	..	..	..	KPLI	106	107	107	107	102	102
Retail trade except of motor vehicles and motorcycles; repair of personal and household goods	KPJR	52	2 583	2 582	2 627	2 741	2 791	2 759	KPLJ	2 519	2 517	2 558	2 672	2 717	2 683
Non-specialised stores selling mainly food beverages & tobacco	KPJS	5211/5221-4,5227	..	..	..	..	..	..	KPLK	956	968	999	1 069	1 098	1 098
Other non-specialised stores second hand shops & sales not in stores	KPJT	5212/525-526	..	..	..	..	..	..	KPLL	367	381	381	379	375	377

7.5 Employee jobs[1]
Analysis by industry based on the Standard Industrial Classification 1992
continued   At June in each year

Thousands, not seasonally adjusted

		SIC 1992	United Kingdom							Great Britain					
			1998	1999	2000	2001	2002	2003		1998	1999	2000	2001	2002	2003
Alcoholic & other beverages, tobacco	KPJU	5225 to 5226	..	..	..	..	..	..	KPLM	87	70	68	68	64	57
Pharmaceutical & medical goods cosmetics & toilet articles	KPJV	523	..	..	..	..	..	..	KPLN	98	88	89	92	98	95
Clothing footwear & leather goods	KPJW	5242/5243	..	..	..	..	..	..	KPLO	337	339	343	350	345	339
Textile furniture lighting equipment electrical household appliances radio and TV paints glass hardware and household goods not elsewhere classified	KPJX	5241/5244-46	..	..	..	..	..	..	KPLP	279	266	278	288	299	289
Books newspapers and stationery, other retail in specialised stores	KPJY	5247/5248	..	..	..	..	..	..	KPLQ	378	384	378	402	412	405
Repair of personal and household goods	KPJZ	527	..	..	..	..	..	-	KPLR	17	20	23	24	25	24
Hotels and restaurants	KPKA	H	1 571	1 649	1 685	1 701	1 737	1 818	LMBA	1 537	1 613	1 647	1 662	1 697	1 779
Hotels camp sites short-stay accom.	KPKB	551/552	..	..	..	..	..	..	KPLT	342	371	375	371	365	364
Restaurants	KPKC	553	..	..	..	..	..	..	KPLU	465	478	493	509	531	538
Bars	KPKD	554	..	..	..	..	..	..	KPLV	517	534	543	527	540	545
Canteens and catering	KPKE	555	..	..	..	..	..	..	KPLW	213	229	237	255	261	333
Transport, storage and communication	KPKF	I	1 416	1 459	1 523	1 585	1 569	1 549	KPLX	1 392	1 434	1 497	1 558	1 541	1 522
Land transport, transport via pipelines	KPKG	60	515	519	514	522	537	547	KPLY	504	508	503	510	525	535
Transport via railways	KPKH	601	..	..	..	..	..	..	KPLZ	50	49	49	50	51	52
Other land transport and via pipelines	KPKI	602/603	..	..	..	..	..	..	KPMA	455	460	453	461	474	483
Water transport	KPKJ	61	20	20	19	17	17	15	KPMB	20	20	18	17	17	15
Air transport	KPKK	62	82	89	94	93	88	87	KPMC	81	88	93	92	87	86
Supporting and auxiliary transport activities, activities of travel agents	KPKL	63	335	354	381	403	391	377	KPMD	331	349	376	398	386	372
Travel agencies and tour operators	KPKM	633	..	..	..	..	..	..	KPME	105	115	125	132	125	108
Post and telecommunications	KPKN	64	464	477	515	550	536	523	LMBC	456	469	506	541	526	514
National post and courier activities	KPKO	641	..	..	..	..	..	..	KPMG	277	276	283	300	288	279
National post activities	KPKP	6411	..	..	..	..	..	..	KPMH	221	216	216	229	219	208
Courier activities	KPKQ	6412	..	..	..	..	..	..	KPMI	56	60	66	71	69	71
Telecommunications	KPKR	6420	..	..	..	..	..	..	KPMJ	180	193	223	241	239	235
Financial intermediation	KPKS	J	1 046	1 074	1 068	1 065	1 043	1 050	LMBD	1 032	1 059	1 053	1 049	1 027	1 033
Financial intermediation except insurance and pension funding	KPKT	65	596	618	605	596	576	595	KPML	587	609	595	586	565	583
Insurance and pension funding except compulsory social security	KPKU	66	232	232	227	225	220	218	KPMM	230	230	225	223	218	216
Activities auxiliary to financial intermediation	KPKV	67	218	223	236	243	247	237	KPMN	216	220	233	240	244	234
Except insurance and pension funding	KPKW	671	..	..	..	..	..	..	KPMO	71	79	95	107	108	102
Auxiliary to insurance and pension funding	KPKX	672	..	..	..	..	..	..	KPMP	145	141	138	133	136	132
Real estate renting & business activities	KPKY	K	3 423	3 572	3 752	3 951	3 973	3 965	KPMQ	3 383	3 526	3 703	3 899	3 919	3 909
Real estate activities	KPKZ	70	292	313	350	364	366	362	LMBE	289	310	347	360	362	358
Activities with own property, letting of own property	KPLA	701/702	..	..	..	..	..	..	KPMS	174	187	213	219	219	217
Activities on a fee or contract basis	KPLB	703	..	..	..	..	..	..	KPMT	115	122	133	141	143	141

7.5

Employee jobs[1]
Analysis by industry based on the Standard Industrial Classification 1992

continued · At June in each year

Thousands, not seasonally adjusted

		SIC 1992	United Kingdom							Great Britain					
			1998	1999	2000	2001	2002	2003		1998	1999	2000	2001	2002	2003
Renting of machinery and equipment without operator & of personal & household goods	KPLC	71	133	148	154	157	164	167	KPMU	131	146	152	155	162	165
Construction and civil engineering machinery	KOUU	7132	..	..	..	..	..	..	KPMV	39	39	42	45	46	45
All other goods and equipment	KOUV	Rest of 71	..	..	..	..	..	..	KPMW	92	108	109	110	116	120
Computer and related equipment	KOUW	72	354	418	463	508	503	508	KPMX	351	415	458	503	497	503
Research and development	KOUX	73	96	97	100	104	106	110	KPMY	95	96	98	102	105	109
Other business activities	KOUY	74	2 548	2 595	2 686	2 818	2 835	2 818	KPMZ	2 516	2 560	2 649	2 779	2 793	2 774
Legal, accounting,book-keeping & auditing activities	KOUZ	741	..	..	..	..	..	..	KPNA	620	663	698	732	744	720
Legal activities	KOVA	7411	..	..	..	..	..	..	KPNB	232	233	240	242	252	249
Accounting, book-keeping auditing, tax consultancy	KOVB	7412	..	..	..	..	..	..	KPNC	164	190	206	208	198	187
Market research business and consultancy activities	KOVC	7413/7414	..	..	..	..	..	..	KPND	190	202	219	249	263	254
Management activities of holding companies	KOVD	7415	..	..	..	..	..	..	KPNE	34	38	33	31	30	30
Architectural engineering activities and related technical consultancy, technical testing	KOVE	742/743	..	..	..	..	..	..	KPNF	319	324	324	334	334	322
Advertising	KOVF	744	..	..	..	..	..	..	KPNG	77	83	86	93	90	89
Industrial cleaning	KOVG	747	..	..	..	..	..	..	KPNH	478	445	430	421	400	380
Public administration and defence, compulsory social security	KOVH	L(75)	1 399	1 400	1 408	1 409	1 443	1 477	LMBG	1 341	1 342	1 349	1 349	1 382	1 414
Education	KOVI	M(80)	1 852	2 044	2 125	2 140	2 180	2 234	LMBH	1 788	1 979	2 059	2 074	2 112	2 165
Health and social work	KOVJ	N	2 582	2 600	2 694	2 744	2 782	2 850	LOJV	2 489	2 506	2 599	2 646	2 682	2 746
Human health, veterinary activities	KOVK	851/852	..	..	..	..	..	..	KPNL	1 584	1 600	1 693	1 738	1 770	1 826
Social work activities	KOVL	853	..	..	..	..	..	..	KPNM	906	906	906	909	912	920
Other community social and personal service activities,private households with employed persons, extra-territorial organisations and bodies	KOVM	O - Q	1 152	1 240	1 290	1 320	1 348	1 318	LMBK	1 126	1 213	1 262	1 291	1 318	1 287
Sewage and refuse disposal; sanitation	KOVN	90	106	110	99	102	103	98	KPNO	103	107	97	100	100	94
Activities of membership organisations	KOVO	91	210	212	219	215	221	215	KPNP	203	205	212	207	213	207
Recreational cultural and sporting activities	KOVP	92	568	625	660	686	701	689	KPNQ	555	612	646	672	686	674
Motion picture video radio TV news agencies and entertainment activities	KOVQ	921 to 924	..	..	..	..	..	..	KPNR	175	203	211	216	227	214
Library archives museums and other cultural activities	KOVR	925	..	..	..	..	..	..	KPNS	73	74	80	79	80	84
Sporting activities and other recreational activities	KOVS	926/927	..	..	..	..	..	..	KPNT	307	335	355	377	379	376
Other service activities,private households with employed persons, extra territorial organisations	KOVT	93/95/99	269	293	312	316	323	317	KPNU	265	289	308	312	319	312
Washing, dry cleaning of textile and fur products	KOVU	9301	..	..	..	..	..	..	KPNV	44	46	45	48	47	48
Hairdressing, other beauty treatment, physical and well-being activities	KOVV	9302/9304	..	..	..	..	..	..	KPNW	92	97	100	100	101	96

1 The data in this table have not been adjusted to reflect the 2001 Census population data. See chapter text.

Sources: Department of Manpower Services (Northern Ireland); Earnings and Employment Division, ONS: 01633 812318

7.6 Weekly hours worked[1,2,3]
United Kingdom
At Spring each year. Seasonally adjusted.

Hours

	All workers' weekly hours[4]		Average actual weekly hours of work		
	Total (millions)	Average	Full-time employment[4,5]	Part-time employment[5]	Second jobs[6]
All					
	YBUS	YBUV	YBUY	YBVB	YBVE
1993	828.8	32.9	38.1	14.7	9.7
1994	841.4	33.2	38.5	15.0	8.9
1995	857.2	33.4	38.7	15.1	9.1
1996	861.6	33.2	38.7	15.1	8.8
1997	878.7	33.3	38.7	15.2	9.4
1998	885.5	33.2	38.6	15.2	9.1
1999	887.3	32.9	38.2	15.3	9.0
2000	893.2	32.6	37.9	15.4	8.9
2001	906.2	32.8	38.0	15.7	9.4
2002	906.6	32.6	37.8	15.6	9.4
2003	902.4	32.1	37.4	15.6	9.3
Men					
	YBUT	YBUW	YBUZ	YBVC	YBVF
1993	530.7	38.6	40.0	14.3	10.7
1994	539.0	38.9	40.4	14.8	9.5
1995	550.2	39.2	40.8	14.6	9.9
1996	550.5	39.0	40.7	14.8	9.6
1997	559.6	38.9	40.7	14.8	10.7
1998	564.5	38.8	40.7	15.0	9.7
1999	560.9	38.2	40.1	15.1	9.7
2000	564.4	37.9	39.8	15.1	9.3
2001	570.0	38.0	39.9	15.7	10.2
2002	565.9	37.7	39.6	15.1	10.3
2003	562.3	37.0	39.1	15.5	10.2
Women					
	YBUU	YBUX	YBVA	YBVD	YBVG
1993	298.0	26.1	34.2	14.7	8.9
1994	302.5	26.3	34.5	15.0	8.5
1995	306.9	26.4	34.4	15.2	8.5
1996	311.1	26.4	34.6	15.1	8.2
1997	319.1	26.6	34.7	15.3	8.4
1998	320.9	26.5	34.6	15.3	8.7
1999	326.3	26.5	34.5	15.3	8.5
2000	328.8	26.3	34.1	15.5	8.6
2001	336.2	26.6	34.4	15.7	8.9
2002	340.7	26.7	34.4	15.8	8.8
2003	340.1	26.4	34.1	15.7	8.7

1 See chapter text.
2 The data in this table have been adjusted to reflect the latest 2001 Census population data.
3 Average hours actually worked in the reference week which includes hours worked in second jobs.
4 Main and second job.

5 People whose main job is full-time or part-time.
6 Second jobs reported in the LFS in addition to persons' main full time job.

Source: Labour Force Survey, Office for National Statistics

7.7 Civil Service staff
Analysis by ministerial responsibility[1,2]
At 1 April each year

Full-time equivalents (thousands)[3]

		1992	1993	1994	1995	1996	1997	1998	1999	2000	2001	2002
Agriculture, Fisheries and Food	BCDA	11.0	11.0	11.0	10.6	10.8	10.1	10.8	11.7	10.8	11.4	–
Cabinet Office	BBGD	2.0	6.0	12.0	11.7	12.3	7.8	7.7	7.6	6.9	6.9	6.9
Chancellor of the Exchequer's Departments:												
Customs and Excise	BCDC	27.0	25.0	25.0	24.1	23.2	23.1	23.4	22.5	21.9	21.7	21.8
Inland Revenue	BCDD	70.0	68.0	64.0	59.1	56.5	54.4	53.4	61.3	66.3	66.9	68.2
Department for National Savings	BCDE	6.0	6.0	6.0	5.4	4.7	4.3	4.1	0.1	0.1	0.1	0.1
Treasury and others	BCDF	10.0	5.0	5.0	4.3	6.0	5.1	5.1	5.0	5.5	5.5	5.6
Total	BCDB	113.0	105.0	99.0	92.9	90.3	86.8	86.0	89.0	93.8	94.2	95.7
Culture, Media and Sport	DMTC	–	–	–	–	–	–	0.6	0.6	0.6	0.6	0.7
Education	BCDG	3.0	3.0	2.0	2.5	–	–	–	–	–	–	–
Education and Employment	BBFT	–	–	–	–	40.8	34.1	33.6	34.6	36.5	38.3	–
Education and Skills	LNFW	–	–	–	–	–	–	–	–	–	–	7.2
Environment	BCDJ	23.0	18.0	10.0	9.4	10.9	9.6	–	–	–	–	–
Environment, Food and Rural Affairs	LNFX	–	–	–	–	–	–	–	–	–	–	14.6
Environment, Transport and the Regions	CKUZ	–	–	–	–	–	–	21.2	21.8	23.2	25.4	–
Foreign and Commonwealth	BCDK	10.0	10.0	8.0	7.5	7.1	6.6	5.4	5.5	5.5	5.5	5.7
Health	BAKR	7.0	7.0	7.0	6.2	4.8	4.7	4.6	4.8	7.0	7.2	5.1
Home	BCDL	50.0	52.0	51.0	51.4	50.8	50.4	50.7	50.0	53.6	60.1	61.0
International Development	DMUA	–	–	–	–	–	–	1.1	1.2	1.2	1.3	1.5
Legal Departments	BBGE	29.0	30.0	29.0	28.7	27.8	26.3	25.4	25.5	24.9	25.0	26.9
National Heritage	BBGF	1.0	1.0	1.0	1.0	1.0	1.0	–	–	–	–	–
Northern Ireland	BBGG	–	–	–	0.2	0.2	0.2	0.2	0.2	0.2	0.2	0.2
Scotland	BCDN	13.0	14.0	13.0	12.1	11.7	11.8	12.0	12.5	13.6	13.7	14.3
Social Security	BAKS	81.0	86.0	90.0	89.2	91.5	93.1	87.2	81.6	83.5	81.9	–
Trade and Industry	BCDQ	13.0	13.0	12.0	11.1	11.2	10.3	10.4	10.5	11.0	11.4	12.0
Transport	BCDR	15.0	15.0	14.0	12.9	11.3	11.4	–	–	–	–	–
Transport, Local Government and the Regions	LNFZ	–	–	–	–	–	–	–	–	–	–	23.9
Welsh Office	BCDS	2.0	3.0	2.0	2.2	2.1	2.2	2.1	2.3	2.7	3.2	3.5
Work and Pensions	LNGA	–	–	–	–	–	–	–	–	–	–	122
Total civil departments	BCDU	431.0	431.0	418.0	400.8	384.6	366.3	359.1	359.1	375.1	384.4	401.2
Defence	BCDW	140.0	130.0	122.0	116.1	109.9	109.2	104.2	100.9	100.3	98.3	89.0
Total all departments	BCDX	571.0	560.0	540.0	516.9	494.5	475.6	463.3	460.0	475.4	482.7	490.2
of which												
Non-industrial staff	BCDY	509.0	509.0	494.0	474.1	458.7	439.6	430.5	429.2	446.0	453.8	462.9
Industrial staff	BCDZ	61.0	52.0	46.0	42.0	35.9	36.0	32.8	30.8	29.4	28.9	27.3

1 The figures include non-industrial and industrial staff but exclude casual or seasonal staff and employees of the Northern Ireland Civil Service.
2 A comprehensive list of Machinery of Government changes is listed on the Cabinet Office's web site at: www.civil-service.gov.uk/statistics

3 Figures included are measured as 'full-time equivalent' staff. Part-time staff are recorded as a proportion of full-time employees according to the proportion of a full week that they work.

Source: Cabinet Office: 020 7276 1532

7.8 Persons employed in local authorities[1]

Thousands (Full-time equivalents)[2]

		1993	1994	1995	1996	1997	1998	1999	2000	2001	2002	2003
England												
Education	ATAM	712.1	692.8	698.4	691.8	691.8	693.9	707.3	731.5	768.2	775.8	818.1
Construction	BCHC	70.9	67.4	63.5	58.8	55.0	51.9	52.3	51.2	48.7	40.6	37.2
Transport	BCHD	1.4	1.4	1.4	1.4	1.4	1.4	1.4	–	–	–	–
Social services	BCHE	225.8	233.3	234.3	230.6	227.3	221.3	215.9	213.0	213.3	205.1	190.8
Public libraries and museums	BCHF	31.9	31.8	32.7	31.5	31.4	31.1	31.5	31.1	32.3	31.8	32.1
Recreation, parks and baths	BCHG	68.6	67.2	65.2	63.6	60.7	59.8	58.1	57.2	59.8	58.7	61.6
Environmental health	BCHH	19.0	18.5	17.4	17.2	17.4	16.9	17.2	17.7	17.9	18.5	18.6
Refuse collection and disposal	BCHS	21.8	20.5	25.1	24.5	24.6	24.0	23.7	21.8	21.8	21.1	18.6
Housing	BCHT	65.5	65.7	68.0	66.8	65.5	64.7	65.4	65.0	66.5	67.9	69.7
Town and country planning	BCHU	22.5	22.2	25.9	27.1	27.3	26.8	27.7	27.7	28.4	28.8	29.3
Fire service												
regulars	BAIV	34.2	33.9	33.8	33.6	33.3	33.1	34.0	33.8	34.5	35.1	35.9
others	BAIW	5.7	5.7	5.8	5.7	5.6	5.6	6.3	6.2	6.4	6.5	6.6
Other services[3]	BCHM	226.7	217.0	191.3	183.8	177.9	173.1	178.1	177.8	182.2	189.2	191.0
Total of above	BCHN	1 506.1	1 477.4	1 462.8	1 436.4	1 419.2	1 403.6	1 417.5	1 434.0	1 480.0	1 479.1	1 509.5
Police Service												
police: all ranks	BCHO	121.4	121.0	118.8	118.4	118.5	119.2	119.2	117.0	118.6	120.1	122.4
cadets	BAIX	0.2	0.1	0.1	0.3	0.3	0.1	–	–	–	–	–
traffic wardens	BAIY	4.9	4.7	4.5	4.3	4.1	3.5	3.3	2.8	2.6	2.2	2.2
civilians	BAIZ	46.7	46.9	48.1	49.8	50.0	50.3	50.5	50.8	51.1	53.0	55.8
Magistrates courts	BAJA	10.0	9.9	10.0	9.9	9.2	8.9	9.0	8.9	9.1	9.3	9.5
Probation staff												
officers	BAJB	7.1	7.2	7.2	6.9	6.9	6.2	6.8	7.1	7.2	7.2	7.2
others	BAJC	7.9	8.0	8.5	7.2	7.1	5.4	7.1	7.5	8.0	8.0	8.0
Total law and order	BAJD	198.2	197.8	197.2	196.8	196.1	193.6	195.9	194.1	196.6	199.8	205.1
Agency staff	BAJE	1.4	1.6	0.9	0.8	0.8	0.8	–	–	–	–	–
Total	BCHR	1 705.7	1 676.8	1 660.9	1 634.0	1 616.1	1 598.0	1 613.4	1 628.1	1 676.6	1 678.9	1 714.6
(excluding special employment and training measures)												
Wales												
Education	ATAN	48.2	47.9	48.7	50.6	49.5	49.9	51.6	51.7	52.8	54.4	56.9
Construction	BCGC	5.9	5.8	5.9	6.0	5.5	5.5	5.7	5.6	5.1	5.2	4.1
Transport	BCGD	–	–	–	–	–	–	–	–	–	–	–
Social services	BCGE	16.0	17.0	18.3	18.5	19.0	18.8	19.2	19.3	18.9	19.2	18.4
Public libraries and museums	BCGF	1.7	1.7	1.7	1.5	1.6	1.5	1.6	1.6	1.8	1.8	1.6
Recreation, parks and baths	BCGG	6.0	6.0	6.3	5.8	6.4	6.1	6.1	6.2	6.5	6.5	6.0
Environmental health	BCGH	1.5	1.5	1.5	1.6	1.5	1.3	1.4	1.5	1.6	1.5	1.8
Refuse collection and disposal	BCGI	1.6	1.5	2.2	2.9	2.9	2.9	2.8	2.6	2.6	2.7	2.4
Housing	BCGJ	3.1	3.1	3.4	3.3	3.6	3.6	3.8	3.7	3.6	3.4	–
Town and country planning	BCGK	1.8	1.8	2.2	1.9	2.0	2.0	2.1	2.1	2.0	2.0	2.2
Fire service												
regulars	BAKT	1.8	1.8	1.8	1.9	1.9	1.9	1.9	1.9	1.9	1.8	2.0
others	BAKU	0.4	0.4	0.3	0.3	0.3	0.3	0.4	0.4	0.4	0.4	–
Other services	BCGM	23.5	19.8	15.6	14.2	14.6	14.0	15.1	15.2	15.6	14.6	14.8
Total of above	BCGN	111.5	108.1	107.9	108.5	108.8	107.8	111.7	111.9	112.9	113.5	114.8
Police Service												
police: all ranks	BCGO	6.6	6.5	6.4	6.4	6.6	6.6	6.6	6.6	6.9	7.1	7.2
cadets	BAKV	–	–	–	–	–	–	–	–	–	–	–
traffic wardens	BAKW	0.2	0.2	0.2	0.2	0.2	0.2	0.2	0.2	0.1	0.2	0.2
civilians	BAKX	2.1	2.2	2.2	2.5	2.4	2.4	2.8	2.7	2.9	3.1	3.4
Magistrates courts	BAKY	0.7	0.7	0.7	0.6	0.6	0.6	0.7	0.7	0.6	0.6	0.7
Probation staff												
officers	BAKZ	0.4	0.4	0.4	0.4	0.4	0.3	0.4	0.4	0.4	0.4	0.4
others	BALA	0.4	0.4	0.4	0.4	0.4	0.3	0.4	0.4	0.5	0.5	0.5
Total law and order	BALB	10.4	10.4	10.3	10.5	10.6	10.4	10.3	10.2	10.5	11.0	11.5
Agency staff	BALC	–	–	–	–	–	–	–	–	–	–	–
Total	BCGR	121.9	118.5	118.2	119.0	119.4	118.2	122.0	122.1	123.4	124.5	126.3
(excluding special employment and training measures)												

7.8 Persons employed in local authorities[1]
continued

Thousands (Full-time equivalents)[4]

		1992	1993	1994	1995	1996	1997	1998	1999	2000	2001	2002
Scotland												
Education	ATAO	87.5	80.0	77.1	77.6	74.7	73.6	75.5	76.7	79.2	80.5	82.7
Construction	BCMC	23.1	22.9	22.0	21.7	20.7	20.6	20.5	20.4	20.6	20.6	21.0
Transport	BCMD	0.8	0.8	0.9	0.9	0.9	0.9	0.9	0.9	0.9	0.9	0.9
Social Services	BCME	36.8	37.3	38.3	39.1	38.4	37.9	37.0	34.6	36.4	37.0	38.2
Public libraries and museums	BCMF	4.5	4.6	4.7	4.7	4.2	4.2	4.2	4.1	4.0	4.1	4.2
Recreation, leisure and tourism	BCMG	13.3	13.7	13.9	13.9	11.4	11.4	11.3	11.3	11.4	11.4	11.6
Environmental health	BCMH	2.5	2.7	2.7	2.6	3.4	3.4	3.3	3.1	3.0	3.9	4.0
Cleansing	BCMI	8.1	8.2	8.1	8.0	7.3	7.2	7.2	7.2	7.2	7.3	7.4
Housing	BCMJ	7.2	7.4	7.8	7.9	7.9	8.4	8.5	8.5	8.6	8.9	9.5
Physical planning	BCMK	2.1	2.2	2.2	2.2	3.7	3.4	3.3	3.3	3.4	3.4	3.5
Fire service	BCML	5.2	5.3	5.3	5.2	5.8	5.6	5.7	5.7	5.7	5.5	5.4
Other services[3]	BCMM	48.1	48.0	52.1	51.5	40.7	40.7	38.5	39.0	37.2	33.8	33.3
Total of above	BCMN	239.2	233.1	235.1	235.3	219.1	217.3	215.9	214.8	217.6	217.3	221.7
Police service												
police (all ranks)	BCMO	13.9	14.2	14.2	14.4	13.7	14.2	14.3	14.4	14.2	14.6	14.8
others[5]	BCMP	4.8	5.1	5.2	5.2	5.2	5.3	5.4	5.4	5.3	5.5	5.6
Administration of district courts	BCMQ	0.1	0.2	0.2	0.2	0.2	0.2	0.2	0.2	0.2	0.2	0.2
Total (excluding special employment and training measures)	BCMR	258.0	252.6	254.7	255.1	238.2	237.0	235.8	234.8	237.3	237.6	242.3

1 Figures are based on surveys undertaken on behalf of central and local government by the ONS and the Scottish Executive and the Convention of Scottish Local Authorities (COSLA).
2 Based on the following factors to convert part-time employees to approximate full-time equivalents: for teachers and lecturers in further education, 0.295; teachers in primary and secondary education and all other non-manual employees, 0.53; manual employees, 0.41.
3 Including civil/central services departments (eg engineers and finance) and all services not shown separately.
4 Based on the following factors to convert part-time employees to approximate full-time equivalents: for lecturers and teachers, 0.40; non-manual staff (excluding teachers), 0.58; manual employees, 0.46.
5 Includes civilian employees of police forces and traffic wardens.

Sources: Office for National Statistics: 0117 987 8675;
Home Office;
Scottish Executive;
Scottish Joint Staffing Watch.

7.9 Duration of unemployment[1,2]
United Kingdom

At Spring each year. Seasonally adjusted.

Thousands

		1993	1994	1995	1996	1997	1998	1999	2000	2001	2002	2003
All												
All unemployed	MGSC	2 954	2 753	2 472	2 345	2 043	1 779	1 762	1 641	1 435	1 533	1 484
Duration of unemployment												
Less than 6 months	YBWF	1 139	1 064	1 021	1 040	972	964	997	962	851	975	965
6 months & less than 1 year	YBWG	569	459	396	395	304	247	263	239	214	225	201
1 year or more	YBWH	1 246	1 229	1 056	910	767	568	502	439	370	334	318
1 year or more as % of total	YBWI	*42.2*	*44.7*	*42.7*	*38.8*	*37.5*	*31.9*	*28.5*	*26.8*	*25.8*	*21.8*	*21.4*
Men												
All unemployed	MGSD	1 972	1 809	1 594	1 526	1 283	1 072	1 075	979	853	917	900
Duration of unemployment												
Less than 6 months	MGYK	684	599	562	585	533	510	551	521	457	532	549
6 months & less than 1 year	MGYM	367	294	250	251	184	160	162	139	130	150	125
1 year or more	MGYO	922	916	782	690	567	402	361	319	266	235	226
1 year or more as % of total	YBWJ	*46.7*	*50.6*	*49.0*	*45.2*	*44.2*	*37.5*	*33.6*	*32.6*	*31.1*	*25.6*	*25.1*
Women												
All unemployed	MGSE	982	943	878	819	760	707	687	662	582	616	584
Duration of unemployment												
Less than 6 months	MGYL	455	465	458	455	440	454	446	442	393	442	416
6 months & less than 1 year	MGYN	202	165	146	144	120	87	101	100	84	75	76
1 year or more	MGYP	325	313	274	220	200	165	141	120	105	99	92
1 year or more as % of total	YBWK	*33.1*	*33.2*	*31.2*	*26.9*	*26.4*	*23.4*	*20.5*	*18.1*	*18.0*	*16.0*	*15.7*

1 See chapter text.
2 The data in this table have been adjusted to reflect the latest 2001 Census population data.

Source: Labour Force Survey, Office for National Statistics

7.10 Unemployment[1,2]
United Kingdom
By age group and sex. At Spring each year. Seasonally adjusted.

Thousands and percentages

	All aged 16 and over	16-59/64	16-17	18-24	16-24	25-34	35-49	50-64 (m) 50-59 (w)	65+ (m) 60+ (w)
All	**Thousands**								
	MGSC	YBSH	YBVH	YBVN	PXLG	PXLJ	PXLM	PXLP	PXLS
1994	2 753	2 726	144	665	809	748	707	460	27
1995	2 472	2 453	144	602	746	674	648	385	19
1996	2 345	2 324	164	553	717	641	610	357	21
1997	2 043	2 019	167	483	650	518	533	318	24
1998	1 779	1 759	156	431	587	468	435	268	21
1999	1 762	1 742	166	422	588	425	459	269	20
2000	1 641	1 623	175	400	575	372	414	261	17
2001	1 435	1 420	147	372	519	328	382	191	15
2002	1 533	1 511	164	392	556	349	388	218	22
2003	1 484	1 466	177	404	581	312	363	211	18
Men									
	MGSD	YBSI	YBVI	YBVO	PXLH	PXLK	PXLN	PXLQ	PXLT
1994	1 809	1 798	76	429	505	494	451	349	11
1995	1 594	1 585	79	379	458	434	403	291	..
1996	1 526	1 514	96	356	452	400	393	270	12
1997	1 283	1 271	89	299	388	325	331	227	12
1998	1 072	1 063	83	256	339	278	253	194	..
1999	1 075	1 066	98	249	347	246	278	195	..
2000	979	972	94	238	332	216	238	186	..
2001	853	846	85	220	305	190	212	139	..
2002	917	907	90	243	333	202	227	144	10
2003	900	893	101	244	345	188	211	149	..
Women									
	MGSE	YBSJ	YBVJ	YBVP	PXLI	PXLL	PXLO	PXLR	PXLU
1994	943	927	68	236	304	255	257	112	16
1995	878	868	65	223	288	241	245	94	10
1996	819	810	68	198	266	241	216	87	..
1997	760	747	78	183	261	194	202	90	12
1998	707	696	73	175	248	191	183	74	11
1999	687	676	68	174	242	179	181	75	11
2000	662	651	81	162	243	157	176	75	10
2001	582	574	63	151	214	138	171	51	..
2002	616	604	73	148	221	148	161	73	12
2003	584	573	76	160	236	123	152	62	10
All	**Rates[3]**								
	MGSX	YBTI	YBVK	YBVQ	PXLV	PXLY	PXMB	PXME	PXMH
1994	9.8	9.9	19.9	16.3	16.8	10.0	7.1	8.9	3.3
1995	8.8	9.0	19.3	15.4	16.0	8.9	6.5	7.4	2.3
1996	8.3	8.4	20.1	14.5	15.5	8.5	6.0	6.8	2.6
1997	7.2	7.3	19.5	13.1	14.3	6.9	5.3	5.8	2.9
1998	6.2	6.3	18.6	12.0	13.2	6.3	4.3	4.7	2.6
1999	6.1	6.2	20.2	11.7	13.3	5.7	4.5	4.6	2.4
2000	5.6	5.8	20.9	11.0	12.9	5.1	4.0	4.4	2.0
2001	4.9	5.0	18.1	10.2	11.6	4.6	3.6	3.1	1.8
2002	5.2	5.3	20.1	10.4	12.2	5.0	3.6	3.5	2.4
2003	5.0	5.1	21.2	10.7	12.6	4.7	3.3	3.3	1.9
Men									
	MGSY	YBTJ	YBVL	YBVR	PXLW	PXLZ	PXMC	PXMF	PXMI
1994	11.5	11.6	20.7	19.4	19.6	11.6	8.3	10.9	4.0
1995	10.1	10.3	20.9	18.0	18.4	10.2	7.4	9.1	..
1996	9.7	9.8	22.7	17.4	18.3	9.5	7.2	8.3	4.3
1997	8.2	8.2	21.0	15.2	16.2	7.7	6.1	6.8	4.3
1998	6.9	6.9	19.9	13.5	14.6	6.7	4.6	5.6	..
1999	6.8	6.9	23.4	13.1	14.9	6.0	5.0	5.5	..
2000	6.2	6.2	22.3	12.3	14.1	5.4	4.2	5.2	..
2001	5.4	5.4	20.3	11.4	13.0	4.8	3.7	3.8	..
2002	5.7	5.8	22.0	12.2	13.9	5.3	4.0	3.9	3.3
2003	5.6	5.7	23.9	12.2	14.2	5.1	3.6	3.9	..
Women									
	MGSZ	YBTK	YBVM	YBVS	PXLX	PXMA	PXMD	PXMG	PXMJ
1994	7.6	7.8	19.1	12.6	13.6	7.9	5.7	5.7	3.0
1995	7.0	7.2	17.7	12.4	13.2	7.4	5.4	4.7	2.0
1996	6.5	6.7	17.3	11.1	12.2	7.3	4.7	4.3	..
1997	5.9	6.1	17.9	10.6	12.1	5.8	4.4	4.3	2.2
1998	5.5	5.6	17.4	10.3	11.7	5.8	3.9	3.3	2.2
1999	5.3	5.4	16.8	10.2	11.5	5.4	3.8	3.2	2.0
2000	5.0	5.2	19.5	9.5	11.4	4.8	3.7	3.1	1.8
2001	4.4	4.5	15.8	8.8	10.1	4.3	3.5	2.1	..
2002	4.6	4.7	18.3	8.4	10.3	4.7	3.2	2.9	1.9
2003	4.3	4.5	18.4	9.1	10.8	4.1	3.0	2.4	1.7

1 See chapter text.
2 The data in this table have been adjusted to reflect the latest 2001 Census population data.

3 Total unemployment as a percentage of all economically active persons in the relevant age group.

Source: Labour Force Survey, Office for National Statistics

7.11 Claimant count[1] by age and duration
Computerised claims
United Kingdom

Thousands, not seasonally adjusted

		1996	1997	1998	1999	2000	2001	2002
Annual averages								
Males								
All ages								
All durations	GEZG	1 601.0	1 216.3	1 031.0	954.6	834.0	740.6	714.8
Up to 6 months	GEZH	667.1	569.4	541.1	530.6	488.8	455.9	463.5
Over 6 and up to 12 months	GEZI	300.6	200.6	188.5	166.8	143.2	125.9	124.5
All over 12 months	GEZJ	633.4	446.3	301.4	257.1	202.0	158.8	126.8
All over 24 months	GEZK	372.7	269.7	169.8	128.9	102.4	77.5	50.6
Aged 18 to 24								
All durations	GEZL	378.1	284.6	237.5	205.2	182.2	167.8	168.0
Up to 6 months	GEZM	203.8	172.5	159.8	160.9	149.6	141.3	140.9
Over 6 and up to 12 months	GEZN	81.0	53.2	44.2	34.3	28.3	23.4	23.8
All over 12 months	GEZO	93.5	58.9	33.5	10.0	4.4	3.1	3.3
All over 24 months	GEZP	35.3	22.1	10.7	2.3	0.5	0.3	0.3
Aged 25 to 49								
All durations	IACI	957.7	729.1	619.4	582.9	506.2	446.0	421.9
Up to 6 months	IACK	363.5	313.7	303.2	291.3	266.9	248.2	254.9
Over 6 and up to 12 months	IACN	173.7	118.2	117.3	107.4	92.8	83.1	80.9
All over 12 months	IACQ	420.6	297.2	198.9	184.3	146.5	114.7	86.1
All over 24 months	IACT	257.5	185.6	112.4	88.0	70.5	52.4	29.2
Aged 50 and over								
All durations	IACW	255.6	193.0	165.8	158.0	137.7	119.8	118.4
Up to 6 months	IACZ	91.2	74.3	70.3	70.6	65.0	59.8	61.6
Over 6 and up to 12 months	IADC	45.1	28.6	26.6	24.6	21.6	18.9	19.5
All over 12 months	IADF	119.2	90.1	69.0	62.8	51.1	41.0	37.3
All over 24 months	IADI	80.0	62.0	46.7	38.6	31.5	24.8	21.1
Females								
All ages								
All durations	GEZR	506.9	373.5	321.8	296.3	260.6	233.7	232.1
Up to 6 months	GEZS	267.4	216.3	203.0	195.5	177.9	165.8	168.5
Over 6 and up to 12 months	GEZT	102.1	62.1	54.5	48.1	41.3	35.4	35.9
All over 12 months	GEZU	137.4	95.2	64.2	52.7	41.4	32.5	27.7
All over 24 months	GEZV	67.0	48.9	30.9	22.9	18.2	13.9	9.7
Aged 18 to 24								
All durations	GEZW	164.9	121.8	101.5	88.9	79.2	73.4	74.9
Up to 6 months	GEZX	100.1	80.1	72.4	71.1	65.6	62.1	62.8
Over 6 and up to 12 months	GEZY	33.6	21.6	17.3	14.0	11.7	9.8	10.4
All over 12 months	GEZZ	31.1	20.1	11.8	3.8	1.9	1.4	1.7
All over 24 months	GEYU	9.9	6.6	3.3	0.8	0.2	0.2	0.2
Aged 25 to 49								
All durations	IACJ	253.3	181.7	157.4	147.1	127.9	113.4	111.3
Up to 6 months	IACL	127.8	100.8	96.1	90.3	80.7	74.4	76.5
Over 6 and up to 12 months	IACO	52.3	29.9	27.0	24.7	21.3	18.6	18.5
All over 12 months	IACR	73.3	51.1	34.3	32.1	25.9	20.4	16.2
All over 24 months	IACU	37.2	27.5	16.9	13.4	10.9	8.2	4.7
Aged 50 and over								
All durations	IACX	81.5	62.8	56.7	54.0	47.5	41.3	40.4
Up to 6 months	IADA	33.0	28.6	28.6	28.2	26.0	23.9	24.0
Over 6 and up to 12 months	IADD	15.6	10.2	9.9	9.1	7.9	6.7	6.6
All over 12 months	IADG	32.9	23.9	18.1	16.7	13.6	10.7	9.7
All over 24 months	IADJ	20.0	14.9	10.7	8.7	7.1	5.5	4.8

1 Count of claimants of unemployment-related benefits; computerised claims only.

Sources: Jobcentre Plus administrative system; Office for National Statistics: 020 7533 6094

7.12 Unemployment rates[1,2]
At Spring each year. Not seasonally adjusted.

Percentages

		1993	1994	1995	1996	1997	1998	1999	2000	2001	2002	2003
North East	BENU	12.0	12.5	11.4	10.8	9.7	8.0	9.9	8.9	7.3	6.8	6.5
North West	BENV	10.8	10.3	9.0	8.4	6.9	6.7	6.4	5.6	5.4	5.6	5.0
Yorkshire and Humber	BENY	10.0	9.9	8.7	8.1	8.0	7.0	6.6	6.1	5.1	5.4	5.4
East Midlands	BENZ	9.1	8.3	7.4	7.4	6.4	4.9	5.2	5.1	4.9	4.3	4.2
West Midlands	BEOA	11.8	10.0	8.9	9.2	6.7	6.2	6.8	6.3	5.1	5.6	5.8
East	BEOB	9.2	8.2	7.5	6.1	6.0	5.1	4.3	3.7	3.7	3.6	4.1
London	BEOC	13.2	13.1	11.5	11.3	9.4	8.3	7.7	7.2	6.1	6.8	7.0
South East	BEOD	8.0	7.1	6.4	6.0	5.4	4.4	3.7	3.5	3.1	3.9	3.8
South West	BEOE	9.2	7.5	7.8	6.3	5.3	4.6	4.9	4.2	3.6	3.6	3.8
Wales	BEOG	9.6	9.4	8.8	8.3	8.4	7.0	7.3	6.4	6.0	6.0	4.4
Scotland	BEOH	10.2	10.0	8.4	8.7	8.5	7.4	7.4	7.6	5.8	6.9	5.6
Northern Ireland	BEOI	12.5	11.6	11.0	9.5	7.9	7.5	7.3	7.0	6.2	5.4	5.3

1 See chapter text.
2 The data in this table have been adjusted to reflect the latest 2001 Census
  population data.
  - Data not available on a consistent basis.

Source: Labour Force Survey, Office for National Statistics

7.13 Claimant count rates[1]
Seasonally adjusted annual averages

Percentages

		1992	1993	1994	1995	1996	1997	1998	1999	2000	2001	2002
United Kingdom	BCJE	9.2	9.7	8.8	7.6	7.0	5.4	4.6	4.2	3.6	3.2	3.1
North East	DPDM	11.3	12.1	11.7	10.8	9.5	7.7	7.1	7.1	6.3	5.7	5.2
North West	IBWC	9.8	10.0	9.3	8.1	7.5	5.9	5.1	4.6	4.1	3.7	3.6
Yorkshire and the Humber	DPBI	9.4	9.7	9.1	8.1	7.5	6.1	5.4	5.0	4.4	4.0	3.7
East Midlands	DPBJ	8.6	9.0	8.3	7.1	6.5	4.7	4.0	3.7	3.4	3.1	2.9
West Midlands	DPBN	9.8	10.3	9.4	7.7	6.9	5.3	4.5	4.5	4.0	3.7	3.5
East	DPDP	8.1	8.8	7.6	6.2	6.2	4.4	3.3	2.9	2.4	2.1	2.1
London	DPDQ	9.9	10.9	10.1	8.9	8.4	6.3	5.2	4.5	3.7	3.3	3.6
South East	DPDR	7.4	8.1	6.9	5.6	4.7	3.2	2.6	2.3	1.9	1.6	1.7
South West	DPBM	8.7	9.0	7.7	6.5	5.9	4.2	3.4	3.1	2.5	2.1	2.0
England	VASQ	9.1	9.7	8.7	7.5	6.9	5.1	4.3	3.9	3.4	3.0	3.0
Wales	DPBP	9.5	9.8	8.9	8.1	7.7	6.2	5.5	5.0	4.4	4.0	3.6
Scotland	DPBQ	8.9	9.2	8.7	7.5	7.3	6.1	5.4	5.1	4.6	4.0	3.9
Northern Ireland	DPBR	13.7	13.6	12.6	11.2	10.8	8.1	7.3	6.4	5.3	4.9	4.5
Great Britain	DPAJ	9.1	9.6	8.7	7.5	6.9	5.3	4.5	4.1	3.5	3.1	3.1

1 The number of unemployment-related benefit claimants as a percentage of
  the estimated total workforce (the sum of claimants, employee jobs, self-employed, participants on work-related government training programmes and
  HM Forces) at mid-year. Excluded are claimants under 18, consistent with
  current coverage. See chapter text.

Sources: Jobcentre Plus administrative system;
Office for National Statistics: 020 7533 6094

7.14 Claimant count[1]
Analysis by Government Office Regions
Seasonally adjusted

Thousands

	North East	North West	Yorkshire and the Humber	East Midlands	West Midlands	East	London	South East	South West	England	Wales	Scotland	Great Britain	Northern Ireland	United Kingdom
	DPDG	IBWA	DPAX	DPAY	DPBC	DPDJ	DPDK	DPDL	DPBB	IBWK	DPBE	DPBF	DPAG	DPBG	BCJD
1989 Jan	140.3	301.4	192.6	116.8	190.9	89.5	242.3	114.6	109.2	1 495.9	108.1	254.2	1 859.9	107.4	1 967.3
Apr	132.3	283.0	178.6	106.6	171.9	80.2	221.3	103.4	99.9	1 375.7	99.4	238.9	1 715.5	105.1	1 820.6
Jul	124.4	269.7	171.3	101.7	163.0	78.4	216.1	100.6	95.5	1 322.0	93.2	226.3	1 640.2	102.8	1 743.0
Oct	118.0	256.5	164.5	97.8	155.9	76.8	204.8	99.7	91.5	1 265.2	88.5	217.7	1 571.7	100.0	1 671.7
1990 Jan	112.5	243.7	159.5	93.8	151.1	74.3	199.4	95.5	86.5	1 215.7	84.4	207.9	1 508.6	97.3	1 605.9
Apr	109.3	238.0	154.0	92.7	145.0	75.3	194.7	95.1	86.5	1 189.9	82.8	200.8	1 474.2	96.0	1 570.2
Jul	109.1	237.7	156.1	96.1	147.1	83.8	203.9	107.2	94.1	1 234.7	83.2	194.3	1 512.6	94.4	1 607.0
Oct	112.3	248.0	165.0	104.8	157.3	98.2	226.6	127.5	106.4	1 345.5	88.7	197.3	1 632.1	93.8	1 725.9
1991 Jan	116.7	261.8	176.4	113.1	171.0	112.5	255.8	149.7	122.2	1 478.8	95.0	200.9	1 775.1	96.0	1 871.1
Apr	126.2	285.9	197.5	132.0	203.5	138.5	303.2	190.5	146.9	1 723.9	108.8	212.7	2 045.7	97.9	2 143.6
Jul	130.5	305.4	211.9	145.5	225.4	158.9	342.3	221.3	165.7	1 906.8	115.5	220.1	2 242.5	98.8	2 341.3
Oct	133.2	318.2	219.6	154.5	240.0	172.4	368.9	240.9	178.6	2 025.9	119.3	224.0	2 369.6	100.5	2 470.1
1992 Jan	133.9	325.4	222.7	160.4	250.6	183.3	389.8	258.4	188.4	2 112.6	121.3	228.0	2 462.2	102.2	2 564.4
Apr	135.7	332.8	227.6	168.0	260.0	196.0	409.6	277.7	199.0	2 205.5	123.4	231.8	2 561.6	103.4	2 665.0
Jul	136.7	335.2	232.4	172.1	266.1	205.1	426.2	288.9	206.6	2 268.9	124.1	235.2	2 628.6	104.6	2 733.2
Oct	141.4	343.6	240.2	178.8	277.4	218.6	448.0	308.4	215.3	2 371.1	129.2	242.4	2 743.3	105.1	2 848.4
1993 Jan	146.2	348.3	247.5	185.2	286.2	229.5	464.6	325.2	222.6	2 454.4	131.4	245.3	2 832.0	105.5	2 937.5
Apr	148.0	345.2	246.5	183.6	285.1	228.2	469.5	321.4	220.0	2 446.6	130.3	243.2	2 821.0	104.5	2 925.5
Jul	148.5	338.0	240.9	180.8	278.7	223.5	466.3	314.0	214.4	2 404.4	129.3	241.2	2 775.6	102.5	2 878.1
Oct	147.5	331.1	237.8	177.8	271.5	216.6	460.4	306.6	208.4	2 356.8	127.8	236.6	2 722.1	101.8	2 823.9
1994 Jan	145.6	325.1	233.7	174.7	262.3	210.0	451.4	296.7	203.6	2 302.3	126.7	236.0	2 665.8	100.2	2 766.0
Apr	141.6	314.5	227.4	170.7	252.0	200.4	440.4	280.9	194.5	2 221.7	123.3	231.7	2 577.4	98.9	2 676.3
Jul	139.1	304.2	222.7	166.3	242.3	191.0	428.1	268.1	188.1	2 148.8	119.0	227.4	2 496.3	97.2	2 593.5
Oct	136.0	291.7	215.9	160.1	230.5	180.5	415.4	251.1	178.9	2 059.0	112.9	218.1	2 391.1	93.8	2 484.9
1995 Jan	133.0	280.1	210.6	153.2	218.5	172.3	401.4	237.9	171.4	1 977.5	108.3	209.3	2 296.0	91.3	2 387.3
Apr	130.0	270.8	206.8	148.1	211.0	167.1	395.0	229.7	166.0	1 923.8	106.2	200.3	2 231.0	88.6	2 319.6
Jul	128.2	266.1	204.6	145.3	206.9	165.0	390.2	225.1	162.5	1 892.8	106.7	195.3	2 195.9	87.6	2 283.5
Oct	126.4	260.9	200.7	142.3	201.3	160.7	383.2	219.1	159.4	1 852.7	105.4	193.5	2 152.9	85.8	2 238.7
1996 Jan	123.1	255.8	197.0	140.0	196.5	157.2	376.8	213.3	155.6	1 814.6	104.0	193.2	2 112.5	85.9	2 198.4
Apr	121.7	254.9	195.7	137.7	194.2	153.5	367.9	207.6	152.3	1 785.1	104.6	194.9	2 085.0	86.1	2 171.1
Jul	116.9	248.2	188.8	131.8	187.6	146.8	357.5	198.9	146.8	1 722.5	101.8	191.9	2 017.0	86.4	2 103.4
Oct	110.5	238.4	181.1	124.9	177.8	138.5	341.6	185.5	137.9	1 635.0	98.2	186.3	1 920.7	81.7	2 002.4
1997 Jan	101.0	218.5	166.4	111.8	160.1	123.5	312.6	163.3	126.0	1 483.2	90.3	173.8	1 747.3	71.1	1 818.4
Apr	95.2	201.3	154.7	102.4	147.3	110.6	284.9	144.4	112.1	1 352.9	82.5	162.2	1 597.6	65.0	1 662.6
Jul	92.4	188.9	148.2	95.0	138.0	102.5	264.3	131.0	100.7	1 261.0	78.1	153.6	1 492.7	61.4	1 554.1
Oct	90.4	177.6	142.0	87.6	131.7	94.3	246.4	120.4	93.0	1 183.4	73.6	146.5	1 403.5	60.6	1 464.1
1998 Jan	87.6	170.6	137.2	82.8	126.1	88.5	234.3	112.3	88.7	1 128.1	70.9	141.6	1 340.6	59.9	1 400.5
Apr	84.1	165.4	134.1	79.9	122.3	85.2	229.4	108.0	85.1	1 093.5	69.3	138.7	1 301.5	57.9	1 359.4
Jul	81.8	163.7	133.3	80.0	121.4	83.7	225.2	105.5	84.1	1 078.7	68.6	139.4	1 286.7	57.3	1 344.0
Oct	82.1	160.9	130.9	79.9	121.4	82.0	219.3	102.5	81.8	1 060.8	68.1	136.9	1 265.8	56.1	1 321.9
1999 Jan	82.6	159.5	129.5	79.0	122.6	80.3	214.5	101.2	81.2	1 050.4	67.8	135.6	1 253.8	55.9	1 309.7
Apr	82.5	157.2	127.0	78.2	123.1	79.1	207.8	98.8	78.4	1 032.1	67.1	133.9	1 233.1	55.0	1 288.1
Jul	80.3	153.8	122.4	75.9	120.2	76.6	202.2	94.4	74.9	1 000.7	63.8	130.2	1 194.7	50.0	1 244.7
Oct	76.7	150.0	118.3	73.6	115.9	73.6	196.5	91.1	71.4	967.1	61.0	126.1	1 154.2	46.5	1 200.7
2000 Jan	75.7	145.7	114.6	73.2	112.1	70.3	189.4	87.2	68.0	936.2	59.3	123.2	1 118.7	44.2	1 162.9
Apr	73.6	139.9	108.9	70.0	108.1	66.9	181.6	81.3	63.8	894.1	57.8	119.0	1 070.9	42.4	1 113.3
Jul	72.0	135.4	104.9	68.7	107.2	62.5	172.0	77.5	61.1	861.3	57.1	115.1	1 033.5	41.2	1 074.7
Oct	69.5	131.0	102.5	67.7	106.5	60.7	165.0	74.3	58.1	835.3	56.4	111.7	1 003.4	41.3	1 044.7
2001 Jan	66.2	127.2	99.7	66.5	104.1	57.1	158.1	69.6	54.8	803.3	54.8	108.8	966.9	40.8	1 007.7
Apr	63.0	124.8	97.5	64.9	100.7	54.7	152.1	66.4	53.5	777.6	52.3	104.9	934.8	39.8	974.6
Jul	61.3	121.6	95.1	63.1	97.3	53.8	150.9	65.1	52.2	760.4	50.0	102.4	912.8	39.2	952.0
Oct	61.7	121.1	93.4	61.9	95.8	54.2	156.2	65.9	51.3	762.2	49.2	104.6	916.0	38.7	954.7
2002 Jan	60.8	120.9	91.1	60.1	95.5	55.1	162.7	68.4	50.8	765.4	47.8	104.0	917.2	38.0	955.2
Apr	59.1	119.2	89.4	59.2	93.7	56.4	166.6	71.0	50.9	765.5	47.5	104.1	917.1	37.6	954.7
Jul	58.3	118.1	89.0	58.5	93.1	57.4	167.2	72.0	50.3	763.9	46.9	101.5	912.3	36.2	948.5
Oct	56.1	116.9	88.0	58.4	93.7	57.2	167.5	72.2	49.5	759.5	46.7	100.8	907.0	35.2	942.2
2003 Jan	54.5	114.7	86.2	57.2	94.0	56.8	168.0	72.4	48.2	752.0	45.8	99.6	897.4	35.0	932.4
Apr	53.7	113.0	84.7	58.8	95.5	58.7	172.3	75.9	48.9	761.6	45.5	99.7	906.7	34.3	941.1
Jul	52.4	112.2	84.0	59.7	94.9	58.7	171.8	76.3	49.2	759.2	45.0	99.6	903.8	33.9	937.7
Oct	51.4	109.9	82.2	59.5	94.3	57.5	170.4	76.1	47.7	749.1	43.3	99.7	891.9	34.8	926.9

1 The figures are based on the number of claimants receiving unemployment related benefits and are adjusted for seasonality and discontinuities to be consistent with current coverage. See chapter text. The latest national and regional seasonally adjusted claimant count figures are provisional and subject to revision in the following month.

Sources: Jobcentre Plus administrative system;
Office for National Statistics: 020 7533 6094

7.15 Economic activity: by age and sex[1,2]
United Kingdom
At Spring each year. Seasonally adjusted.

Thousands and percentages

	All aged 16 and over	16-59/64	16-17	18-24	16-24	25-34	35-49	50-64 (m) 50-59 (w)	65+ (m) 60+ (w)
All	**Thousands**								
	MGSF	YBSK	YBZL	YBZO	PXMK	YBZR	YBZU	YBZX	YCAD
1995	28 221	27 409	744	3 917	4 661	7 537	10 019	5 192	812
1996	28 357	27 568	813	3 821	4 634	7 529	10 131	5 274	789
1997	28 504	27 681	858	3 695	4 553	7 550	10 103	5 475	824
1998	28 492	27 699	838	3 596	4 434	7 477	10 119	5 669	793
1999	28 799	27 961	825	3 600	4 425	7 398	10 285	5 853	838
2000	29 056	28 206	837	3 637	4 474	7 288	10 449	5 995	850
2001	29 110	28 272	812	3 643	4 455	7 112	10 580	6 125	837
2002	29 368	28 451	814	3 755	4 569	6 926	10 737	6 218	917
2003	29 595	28 638	835	3 766	4 601	6 706	10 890	6 442	956
Men									
	MGSG	YBSL	YBZM	YBZP	PXML	YBZS	YBZV	YBZY	YCAE
1995	15 706	15 409	377	2 108	2 485	4 266	5 467	3 191	297
1996	15 705	15 427	421	2 040	2 461	4 228	5 493	3 246	277
1997	15 705	15 425	423	1 971	2 394	4 211	5 466	3 355	280
1998	15 653	15 371	417	1 901	2 318	4 163	5 452	3 439	282
1999	15 781	15 485	420	1 901	2 321	4 078	5 541	3 545	297
2000	15 885	15 590	423	1 926	2 349	4 019	5 622	3 600	295
2001	15 868	15 594	416	1 929	2 345	3 921	5 654	3 673	274
2002	15 956	15 652	412	1 997	2 409	3 807	5 740	3 696	304
2003	16 122	15 774	422	2 003	2 425	3 685	5 827	3 837	348
Women									
	MGSH	YBSM	YBZN	YBZQ	PXMM	YBZT	YBZW	YBZZ	YCAF
1995	12 515	12 000	367	1 809	2 176	3 272	4 552	2 001	515
1996	12 652	12 141	392	1 781	2 173	3 302	4 638	2 028	511
1997	12 799	12 255	436	1 724	2 160	3 339	4 637	2 120	543
1998	12 839	12 328	421	1 695	2 116	3 314	4 668	2 230	511
1999	13 017	12 477	405	1 700	2 105	3 320	4 744	2 308	541
2000	13 171	12 616	414	1 710	2 124	3 269	4 826	2 396	555
2001	13 242	12 679	396	1 713	2 109	3 191	4 926	2 452	563
2002	13 412	12 800	402	1 758	2 160	3 119	4 998	2 523	612
2003	13 473	12 864	413	1 762	2 175	3 021	5 063	2 605	608
All	**Rates[3]**								
	MGWG	MGSO	YCAG	YCAJ	PXMN	YCAM	YCAP	MGWP	MGWS
1995	62.4	78.2	55.9	75.8	71.7	82.9	84.8	68.1	8.0
1996	62.5	78.4	58.0	76.9	72.8	82.8	84.8	68.1	7.7
1997	62.7	78.5	59.5	76.5	72.6	83.5	84.4	68.5	8.1
1998	62.4	78.3	58.7	75.5	71.6	83.7	84.2	68.7	7.7
1999	62.8	78.7	58.7	75.4	71.6	84.2	84.8	69.3	8.1
2000	63.1	79.0	59.1	75.9	72.0	84.5	85.0	69.7	8.2
2001	62.8	78.6	55.4	75.1	70.5	84.1	84.9	70.2	8.1
2002	63.0	78.6	54.1	75.9	70.8	84.0	84.9	70.4	8.8
2003	63.1	78.8	54.9	74.3	69.8	83.4	85.0	72.2	9.1
Men									
	MGWH	MGSP	YCAH	YCAK	PXMO	YCAN	YCAQ	MGWQ	MGWT
1995	72.3	85.1	56.2	81.8	76.5	94.2	93.1	71.5	8.2
1996	72.0	85.0	59.5	82.6	77.5	93.4	92.5	71.8	7.6
1997	71.8	84.7	58.2	82.4	76.7	93.6	92.0	72.2	7.6
1998	71.3	84.2	57.9	80.7	75.4	93.7	91.5	72.0	7.6
1999	71.5	84.5	59.1	80.5	75.6	93.5	92.2	72.6	8.0
2000	71.6	84.6	58.6	81.2	76.0	93.9	92.4	72.5	7.8
2001	71.0	84.1	55.6	80.1	74.3	93.3	91.8	73.1	7.2
2002	70.9	83.9	53.4	81.0	74.5	93.0	91.8	72.8	7.9
2003	71.1	84.1	54.2	79.1	73.3	92.5	92.0	74.9	8.9
Women									
	MGWI	MGSQ	YCAI	YCAL	PXMP	YCAO	YCAR	MGWR	MGWU
1995	53.3	70.9	55.7	69.8	66.9	71.6	76.6	63.2	7.9
1996	53.7	71.4	56.5	71.2	68.0	72.3	77.1	62.9	7.8
1997	54.2	71.8	60.9	70.7	68.5	73.5	76.9	63.3	8.3
1998	54.2	71.9	59.4	70.4	67.9	73.8	77.1	64.3	7.8
1999	54.8	72.5	58.3	70.3	67.7	75.1	77.5	64.9	8.2
2000	55.2	72.9	59.5	70.6	68.2	75.3	77.7	65.9	8.5
2001	55.2	72.8	55.3	70.1	66.8	75.1	78.2	66.2	8.6
2002	55.6	73.0	54.8	70.8	67.2	75.1	78.1	67.1	9.3
2003	55.6	73.0	55.7	69.5	66.4	74.4	78.1	68.7	9.2

1 See chapter text.
2 The data in this table have been adjusted to reflect the latest 2001 Census population data.
3 Total economically active as a percentage of all persons in the relevant age group.

Source: Labour Force Survey, Office for National Statistics

7.16 Economically inactive: by age and sex[1,2]
United Kingdom
At Spring each year. Seasonally adjusted.

Thousands and percentages

	All aged 16 and over	16-59/64	16-17	18-24	16-24	25-34	35-49	50-64 (m) 50-59 (w)	65+ (m) 60+ (w)
Thousands									
All									
	MGSI	YBSN	YCAS	YCAV	PXMQ	YCAY	YCBB	MGWA	MGWD
1995	16 979	7 627	586	1 252	1 838	1 558	1 796	2 436	9 352
1996	16 988	7 589	588	1 148	1 736	1 563	1 822	2 469	9 399
1997	16 990	7 599	583	1 136	1 719	1 491	1 868	2 520	9 391
1998	17 150	7 688	590	1 168	1 758	1 458	1 893	2 579	9 462
1999	17 026	7 575	581	1 176	1 757	1 384	1 846	2 587	9 451
2000	16 998	7 518	580	1 156	1 736	1 334	1 846	2 603	9 479
2001	17 241	7 695	653	1 211	1 864	1 341	1 885	2 606	9 546
2002	17 260	7 730	690	1 192	1 882	1 317	1 912	2 619	9 530
2003	17 309	7 728	685	1 303	1 988	1 337	1 928	2 475	9 581
Men									
	MGSJ	YBSO	YCAT	YCAW	PXMR	YCAZ	YCBC	MGWB	MGWE
1995	6 022	2 701	294	469	763	263	403	1 272	3 321
1996	6 101	2 731	286	429	715	298	444	1 273	3 370
1997	6 176	2 781	304	422	726	287	476	1 292	3 396
1998	6 304	2 882	303	455	758	279	505	1 339	3 422
1999	6 276	2 843	291	460	751	285	470	1 337	3 433
2000	6 296	2 831	299	445	744	262	461	1 365	3 465
2001	6 486	2 955	333	480	813	281	508	1 354	3 531
2002	6 555	3 004	359	467	826	285	511	1 382	3 551
2003	6 539	2 977	357	529	886	299	505	1 288	3 562
Women									
	MGSK	YBSP	YCAU	YCAX	PXMS	YCBA	YCBD	MGWC	MGWF
1995	10 956	4 926	291	783	1 074	1 295	1 393	1 163	6 030
1996	10 887	4 858	301	719	1 020	1 264	1 377	1 196	6 029
1997	10 814	4 819	279	714	993	1 204	1 392	1 229	5 995
1998	10 846	4 806	288	713	1 001	1 179	1 388	1 240	6 040
1999	10 750	4 732	290	717	1 007	1 099	1 376	1 250	6 019
2000	10 702	4 687	281	711	992	1 072	1 385	1 238	6 015
2001	10 755	4 740	320	731	1 051	1 060	1 377	1 252	6 015
2002	10 704	4 726	331	725	1 056	1 032	1 401	1 237	5 979
2003	10 770	4 750	328	774	1 102	1 038	1 424	1 187	6 019
Rates[3]									
All									
	YBTC	YBTL	LWEX	LWFA	PXNF	LWFD	LWFG	LWFJ	LWFM
1995	37.6	21.8	44.1	24.2	28.3	17.1	15.2	31.9	92.0
1996	37.5	21.6	42.0	23.1	27.2	17.2	15.2	31.9	92.3
1997	37.3	21.5	40.5	23.5	27.4	16.5	15.6	31.5	91.9
1998	37.6	21.7	41.3	24.5	28.4	16.3	15.8	31.3	92.3
1999	37.2	21.3	41.3	24.6	28.4	15.8	15.2	30.7	91.9
2000	36.9	21.0	40.9	24.1	28.0	15.5	15.0	30.3	91.8
2001	37.2	21.4	44.6	24.9	29.5	15.9	15.1	29.8	91.9
2002	37.0	21.4	45.9	24.1	29.2	16.0	15.1	29.6	91.2
2003	36.9	21.2	45.1	25.7	30.2	16.6	15.0	27.8	90.9
Men									
	YBTD	YBTM	LWEY	LWFB	PXNG	LWFE	LWFH	LWFK	LWFN
1995	27.7	14.9	43.8	18.2	23.5	5.8	6.9	28.5	91.8
1996	28.0	15.0	40.5	17.4	22.5	6.6	7.5	28.2	92.4
1997	28.2	15.3	41.8	17.6	23.3	6.4	8.0	27.8	92.4
1998	28.7	15.8	42.1	19.3	24.6	6.3	8.5	28.0	92.4
1999	28.5	15.5	40.9	19.5	24.4	6.5	7.8	27.4	92.0
2000	28.4	15.4	41.4	18.8	24.0	6.1	7.6	27.5	92.2
2001	29.0	15.9	44.4	19.9	25.7	6.7	8.2	26.9	92.8
2002	29.1	16.1	46.6	19.0	25.5	7.0	8.2	27.2	92.1
2003	28.9	15.9	45.8	20.9	26.7	7.5	8.0	25.1	91.1
Women									
	YBTE	YBTN	LWEZ	LWFC	PXNH	LWFF	LWFI	LWFL	LWFO
1995	46.7	29.1	44.3	30.2	33.1	28.4	23.4	36.8	92.1
1996	46.3	28.6	43.5	28.8	32.0	27.7	22.9	37.1	92.2
1997	45.8	28.2	39.1	29.3	31.5	26.5	23.1	36.7	91.7
1998	45.8	28.1	40.6	29.6	32.1	26.2	22.9	35.7	92.2
1999	45.2	27.5	41.7	29.7	32.3	24.9	22.5	35.1	91.8
2000	44.8	27.1	40.5	29.4	31.8	24.7	22.3	34.1	91.5
2001	44.8	27.2	44.7	29.9	33.2	24.9	21.8	33.8	91.4
2002	44.4	27.0	45.2	29.2	32.8	24.9	21.9	32.9	90.7
2003	44.4	27.0	44.3	30.5	33.6	25.6	21.9	31.3	90.8

1 See chapter text.
2 The data in this table have been adjusted to reflect the latest 2001 Census population data.
3 Total economically inactive as a percentage of all persons in the relevant age group.

Source: Labour Force Survey, Office for National Statistics

7.17 Economically inactive: by reason[1,2]
United Kingdom
At Spring each year. Seasonally adjusted.

Thousands

| | Total economically inactive | Does not want job[3] | Wants job[3] but not seeking in last 4 weeks | | | | | | | | Wants job[3] and seeking work but not available to start[4] | | |
| | | | Total | Availability to start work in next 2 weeks | | Discouraged workers[5] | Long term sick/ disabled | Looking after family/ home | Students | Other | All | Students | Other |
				Available	Not available[4]								
All[6]													
	YBSN	YBVZ	YCFF	YCFI	YCFL	YCFO	YCFR	YCFU	YCFX	YCGA	YCGD	YCGG	YCGJ
1996	7 589	5 290	2 116	890	1 227	103	573	774	259	407	183	85	98
1997	7 599	5 225	2 169	776	1 393	88	683	744	265	390	205	91	114
1998	7 688	5 314	2 157	727	1 430	70	739	740	245	363	217	92	125
1999	7 575	5 271	2 092	680	1 411	67	739	676	238	371	212	91	121
2000	7 518	5 217	2 113	664	1 449	62	757	652	238	404	189	78	110
2001	7 695	5 511	1 990	616	1 374	34	720	633	249	355	194	72	122
2002	7 730	5 479	2 068	631	1 436	33	753	634	256	391	183	74	109
2003	7 728	5 597	1 934	584	1 350	35	696	578	247	379	197	81	116
Men													
	YBSO	YBWA	YCFG	YCFJ	YCFM	YCFP	YCFS	YCFV	YCFY	YCGB	YCGE	YCGH	YCGK
1996	2 731	1 847	799	334	466	59	355	68	138	179	84	40	44
1997	2 781	1 859	828	267	561	50	411	68	134	165	94	52	42
1998	2 882	1 917	859	272	587	43	461	73	127	155	105	54	52
1999	2 843	1 919	834	266	568	39	450	70	120	155	90	43	47
2000	2 831	1 906	846	257	589	33	457	63	113	180	79	40	38
2001	2 955	2 045	819	251	568	22	437	66	124	170	92	41	51
2002	3 004	2 055	866	268	599	20	459	65	133	189	82	36	46
2003	2 977	2 085	800	238	563	20	421	65	122	171	92	41	51
Women													
	YBSP	YBWB	YCFH	YCFK	YCFN	YCFQ	YCFT	YCFW	YCFZ	YCGC	YCGF	YCGI	YCGL
1996	4 858	3 443	1 317	556	761	44	218	706	121	228	99	45	54
1997	4 819	3 366	1 341	510	831	38	272	675	131	225	111	39	72
1998	4 806	3 397	1 298	455	843	27	278	667	118	208	112	39	73
1999	4 732	3 352	1 258	414	844	28	289	606	119	216	122	47	75
2000	4 687	3 311	1 267	407	860	29	301	589	124	224	110	38	72
2001	4 740	3 466	1 171	366	806	12	282	568	124	185	102	31	71
2002	4 726	3 424	1 201	364	838	13	294	569	123	202	101	38	63
2003	4 750	3 512	1 133	346	788	14	274	513	124	207	105	40	65

1 See chapter text.
2 The data in this table have been adjusted to reflect the latest 2001 Census population data.
3 According to responses to LFS question.
4 Not available to start work in next two weeks, including a few people who could not state whether or not they were available.

5 People whose reason for not seeking work was that they believed no jobs were available.
6 All persons of working age (men 16-64, women 16-59).

Source: Labour Force Survey, Office for National Statistics

7.18 Labour disputes[1]
United Kingdom

Thousands and numbers

		1996	1997	1998	1999	2000	2001	2002
SIC 1992								
Working days lost through all stoppages in progress: total	KBBZ	1 303	235	282	242	499	525	1 323
Analysis by industry								
Mining, quarrying, electricity, gas and water	DMME	2	2	..	..	3	25	..
Manufacturing	BBFX	97	86	34	57	52	43	21
Construction	DMMG	8	17	13	49	49	10	17
Transport, storage and communication	BBFY	884	36	139	50	97	107	96
Public administration and defence	BBFZ	158	29	28	35	50	216	488
Education	BBGA	129	28	6	25	50	43	376
Health and social work	BBGB	8	7	16	5	122	73	148
Other community, social and personal services	DMML	3	5	30	7	36	4	107
All other industries and services	DMMM	15	25	15	12	40	4	70
Analysis by number of working days lost in each stoppage								
Under 250 days	KBFC	14	12	8	11	12	9	7
250 and under 500 days	KBFJ	13	6	11	13	9	11	8
500 and under 1,000 days	KBFL	13	17	11	16	21	15	15
1,000 and under 5,000 days	KBFY	61	72	48	69	71	59	47
5,000 and under 25,000 days	KBFZ	123	101	118	133	85	140	104
25,000 and under 50,000 days	KBGS	54	26	..	..	..	72	122
50,000 days and over	KBGT	1 025	..	86	..	301	220	1 021
Working days lost per 1 000 employees all industries and services	KBHA	55	10	11	10	20	20	51
Workers directly and indirectly involved: total	KBHB	364	130	93	141	183	180	943
Analysis by industry								
Mining, quarrying, electricity, gas and water	DMMN	1	..	1	..	1	3	..
Manufacturing	DMMO	34	28	14	31	28	17	10
Construction	DMMP	3	13	2	18	16	3	17
Transport, storage and communications	DMMQ	146	24	39	42	39	69	33
Public administration and defence	DMMR	32	20	4	17	29	46	171
Education	DMMS	122	15	4	28	17	34	388
Health and social work	DMMT	5	5	2	..	28	6	144
Other community, social and personal services	DMMU	2	1	22	2	13	1	103
All other industries and services	DMMV	21	23	4	2	12	1	76
Analysis by duration of stoppage								
Not more than 5 days	KBHM	208	108	57	129	82	98	828
Over 5 but not more than 10 days	KBHN	133	7	32	8	9	43	57
Over 10 but not more than 20 days	KBJQ	4	14	1	3	8	4	3
Over 20 but not more than 30 days	KBJR	3	..	..	..	..	..	1
Over 30 but not more than 50 days	KBJS	16	1	1	..	83	6	1
Over 50 days	KBJT	1	..	1	..	1	30	55
Numbers of stoppages in progress: total	KBLG	244	216	166	205	212	194	146
Analysis by industry								
Mining, quarrying, electricity, gas and water	DMMW	6	1	1	..	3	3	2
Manufacturing	DMMX	67	53	36	37	38	32	33
Construction	DMMY	11	11	13	20	16	9	3
Transport, storage and communications	DMMZ	72	68	57	91	116	94	51
Public administration and defence	DMNA	22	23	10	17	7	22	20
Education	DMNB	35	35	19	21	18	16	16
Health and social work	DMNC	9	7	6	4	10	12	14
Other community, social and personal services	DMND	12	8	17	8	13	10	11
All other industries and services	DMNE	11	12	7	8	5	9	12
Analysis of number of stoppages by duration								
Not more than 5 days	KBNH	196	184	130	179	187	162	118
Over 5 but not more than 10 days	KBNI	20	15	21	8	14	15	16
Over 10 but not more than 20 days	KBNJ	7	8	3	9	5	7	3
Over 20 but not more than 30 days	KBNK	6	2	4	4	1	1	3
Over 30 but not more than 50 days	KBNL	10	6	3	3	3	4	1
Over 50 days	KBNM	5	1	5	2	2	5	5

1 See chapter text.

Source: Labour Market Statistics, Office for National Statistics: 01633 819205

7.19 Average earnings[1] and hours of manual employees by industry division
Full time employees on adult rates: pay unaffected by absence: Great Britain
At April

	Agriculture, Hunting and Forestry	Fishing	Mining and Quarrying	Manufacturing	Electricity, Gas and Water Supply	Construction	Wholesale and Retail Trade; repair of motor vehicles, cycles, personal and household goods

Standard Industrial Classification: Revised 1992

Full-time manual men

Weekly earnings

	KOTK	KOTL	KOTM	KOTN	KOTO	KOTP	KOTQ
1998	260.3	..	408.3	352.6	418.6	342.3	292.2
1999	272.4	..	396.0	354.6	440.5	351.3	299.4
2000	273.2	..	398.4	365.4	453.8	371.5	305.7
2001	284.8	..	416.1	378.5	464.1	393.9	318.8
2002	310.0	..	427.1	388.0	489.1	411.1	335.5

Hours worked

	KOTZ	KPFV	KOUA	KOUB	KOUC	KOUD	KOUE
1998	47.0	..	50.1	44.3	42.5	46.9	44.3
1999	47.5	..	51.7	43.5	42.8	46.4	43.9
2000	45.8	..	49.5	43.6	41.4	46.6	43.8
2001	45.6	..	49.4	43.5	42.3	46.6	43.7
2002	47.4	..	47.4	43.1	42.6	45.7	43.9

Hourly earnings

	KOUN	KPFW	KOUO	KOUP	KOUQ	KOUR	KOUS
1998	5.54	..	8.14	7.96	9.85	7.29	6.59
1999	5.75	..	7.66	8.15	10.30	7.56	6.84
2000	5.91	..	8.08	8.35	10.93	7.92	7.03
2001	6.25	..	8.61	8.69	11.02	8.50	7.25
2002	6.56	..	9.04	9.01	11.49	8.97	7.63

Full-time manual women

Weekly earnings

	KOYL	KPFX	KOYM	KOYN	KOYO	KOYP	KOYQ
1998	185.7	..	..	224.2	..	..	203.6
1999	199.0	..	..	231.7	..	..	215.3
2000	224.7	..	..	241.0	..	..	216.2
2001	227.3	..	..	251.4	..	..	230.3
2002	..	..	..	260.5	..	..	238.2

Hours worked

	KOYZ	KPFY	KOZA	KOZB	KOZC	KOZD	KOZE
1998	42.0	..	..	40.7	..	..	40.3
1999	41.8	..	..	40.4	..	..	39.9
2000	41.9	..	..	40.5	..	..	39.2
2001	41.1	..	..	40.4	..	..	39.5
2002	..	..	..	40.2	..	..	39.7

Hourly earnings

	KOZN	KOZO	KOZP	KOZQ	KOZR	KOZS	KOZT
1998	4.43	..	..	5.52	..	..	5.06
1999	4.74	..	..	5.74	..	..	5.44
2000	5.37	..	..	5.94	..	..	5.45
2001	5.67	..	..	6.22	..	..	5.81
2002	..	..	..	6.48	..	..	5.99

Full-time manual adults

Weekly earnings

	KPBO	KPFZ	KPBP	KPBQ	KPBR	KPBS	KPBT
1998	251.7	..	403.8	329.9	416.2	340.9	280.3
1999	264.1	..	392.5	333.7	439.5	350.9	287.7
2000	265.6	..	392.3	343.5	452.8	368.6	295.2
2001	280.1	..	..	357.8	..	393.8	305.4
2002	305.6	..	..	368.7	..	410.3	322.2

Hours worked

	KPCT	KPGA	KPCU	KPCV	KPCW	KPCX	KPCY
1998	46.4	..	49.9	43.7	42.4	46.9	43.8
1999	46.8	..	51.6	43.0	42.7	46.4	43.4
2000	45.4	..	48.7	43.1	41.4	46.5	43.2
2001	45.2	..	49.0	43.0	42.4	46.4	43.2
2002	46.8	..	..	42.6	..	45.7	43.3

Hourly earnings

	KPDV	KPGB	KPDW	KPDX	KPDY	KPDZ	KPFA
1998	5.42	..	8.07	7.56	9.81	7.27	6.40
1999	5.65	..	7.61	7.77	10.29	7.56	6.66
2000	5.86	..	8.06	7.98	10.93	7.92	6.84
2001	6.20	..	8.56	8.32	11.01	8.49	7.07
2002	6.55	..	..	8.64	..	8.97	7.42

7.19 continued

Average earnings[1] and hours of manual employees by industry division
Full time employees on adult rates: pay unaffected by absence: Great Britain
At April

	Hotels and restaurants	Transport, Storage and Communication	Financial Inter-mediation	Real Estate, Renting and Business	Public Administration and Defence; compulsory social security	Educa-tion	Health and Social work	Other community, social and personal service activities

Standard Industrial Classification: Revised 1992

Full-time manual men

Weekly earnings

	KOTR	KOTS	KOTT	KOTU	KOTV	KOTW	KOTX	KOTY
1998	227.0	344.0	394.8	302.7	289.0	277.9	264.4	289.0
1999	230.5	359.6	377.9	312.3	307.5	285.2	267.7	300.8
2000	242.2	368.8	394.3	322.0	310.7	293.5	284.9	301.9
2001	249.3	386.7	417.1	340.8	329.8	305.1	295.3	315.9
2002	262.1	381.5	420.1	346.6	333.5	324.4	308.2	340.8

Hours worked

	KOUF	KOUG	KOUH	KOUI	KOUJ	KOUK	KOUL	KOUM
1998	42.5	48.0	42.5	46.4	41.9	41.7	42.1	44.8
1999	42.1	47.5	39.9	45.5	42.2	40.8	41.8	44.8
2000	41.8	47.4	39.5	45.1	41.3	40.2	42.0	43.5
2001	42.0	46.9	41.2	45.6	41.2	40.3	42.4	43.4
2002	42.3	45.8	41.6	45.5	40.8	40.3	42.2	43.7

Hourly earnings

	KOUT	KOYE	KOYF	KOYG	KOYH	KOYI	KOYJ	KOYK
1998	5.34	7.17	9.28	6.53	6.90	6.67	6.26	6.47
1999	5.48	7.56	9.46	6.86	7.30	7.00	6.41	6.72
2000	5.74	7.75	9.72	7.20	7.56	7.22	6.91	6.95
2001	5.99	8.28	9.93	7.51	7.83	7.68	7.01	7.26
2002	6.25	8.34	10.10	7.63	8.18	8.06	7.31	7.81

Full-time manual women

Weekly earnings

	KOYR	KOYS	KOYT	KOYU	KOYV	KOYW	KOYX	KOYY
1998	170.8	292.7	..	211.9	232.2	203.7	187.2	178.1
1999	180.5	311.5	..	221.5	232.3	223.0	199.5	197.4
2000	187.5	323.9	..	234.5	240.1	228.4	204.5	207.8
2001	196.5	336.9	..	250.7	246.9	235.5	221.5	215.5
2002	209.1	340.0	..	252.7	275.3	250.7	230.1	228.4

Hours worked

	KOZF	KOZG	KOZH	KOZI	KOZJ	KOZK	KOZL	KOZM
1998	39.4	42.0	..	41.4	39.6	38.3	39.3	39.6
1999	39.3	41.5	..	40.4	38.6	38.0	39.1	39.8
2000	39.4	41.8	..	40.6	38.5	38.0	39.3	39.4
2001	39.4	41.5	..	40.9	38.6	37.6	39.6	39.3
2002	39.7	40.5	..	40.5	38.2	37.8	39.3	39.2

Hourly earnings

	KOZU	KOZV	KOZW	KOZX	KOZY	KOZZ	KPBN	KTDJ
1998	4.30	6.98	..	5.08	5.89	5.32	4.75	4.50
1999	4.55	7.52	..	5.48	6.09	5.86	5.10	4.94
2000	4.72	7.69	..	5.82	6.38	6.00	5.24	5.25
2001	4.99	8.10	..	6.16	6.79	6.27	5.52	5.41
2002	5.29	..	..	6.27	..	6.64	5.84	5.83

Full-time manual adults

Weekly earnings

	KPBU	KPBV	KPBW	KPBX	KPBY	KPBZ	KPCR	KPCS
1998	203.6	340.0	367.3	289.1	280.7	254.8	218.9	258.3
1999	210.3	355.7	353.6	298.2	296.9	266.0	227.8	273.8
2000	217.1	363.3	359.6	308.7	301.3	270.3	237.2	274.1
2001	227.4	381.0	..	326.3	312.7	287.1	252.2	285.1
2002	240.5	377.6	..	331.9	325.4	303.2	262.2	309.1

Hours worked

	KPCZ	KPDO	KPDP	KPDQ	KPDR	KPDS	KPDT	KPDU
1998	41.2	47.6	41.6	45.6	41.6	40.7	40.5	43.3
1999	41.0	47.0	39.7	44.7	41.7	40.0	40.2	43.5
2000	40.7	46.9	39.5	44.1	40.8	39.5	40.0	42.2
2001	40.9	46.2	40.9	44.8	40.7	39.6	40.9	42.4
2002	41.2	45.3	..	44.7	40.4	39.6	40.5	42.4

Hourly earnings

	KPFB	KPFC	KPFD	KPFE	KPFF	KPFG	KPFT	KPFU
1998	4.93	7.16	8.84	6.33	6.76	6.27	5.40	5.97
1999	5.12	7.56	8.92	6.67	7.15	6.66	5.66	6.29
2000	5.33	7.74	9.11	7.00	7.41	6.86	5.95	6.51
2001	5.58	8.26	9.86	7.31	7.69	7.27	6.15	6.74
2002	5.87	8.35	..	7.44	8.05	7.67	6.46	..

1 See chapter text.

Source: New Earnings Survey, Office for National Statistics: 01633 819024

7.20 Average weekly and hourly earnings[1] and hours of full-time employees on adult rates: Great Britain

At April

	All Industries				Manufacturing industries			
			Average hourly earnings				Average hourly earnings	
	Average weekly earnings[2]	Average hours	including overtime	excluding overtime	Average weekly earnings	Average hours	including overtime	excluding overtime
	£		£	£	£		£	£
All adults								
	BAPY	BAQM	BAPZ	BAQA	BAPM	BAQJ	BAPN	BAPO
1999	400.1	40.0	10.01	10.03	395.3	41.4	9.55	9.49
2000	419.7	39.8	10.53	10.51	412.5	41.4	9.96	9.86
2001	444.3	39.8	11.15	11.18	435.5	41.3	10.53	10.49
2002	464.6	39.6	11.69	11.74	455.8	41.0	11.02	11.08
2003	475.8	39.6	12.00	12.03	469.3	41.0	11.43	11.40
All men								
	BAQC	BAQN	BAQD	BAQE	BAPQ	BAQK	BAPR	BAPS
1999	442.4	41.4	10.68	10.75	424.6	42.0	10.10	10.06
2000	464.1	41.2	11.24	11.26	441.7	42.0	10.49	10.40
2001	490.5	41.2	11.90	11.97	463.9	42.0	11.04	11.02
2002	513.8	40.9	12.50	12.60	484.1	41.6	11.53	11.61
2003	525.0	40.9	12.80	12.88	496.4	41.6	11.91	11.91
Manual men								
	KFHX	KFHY	KIWU	KIWV	KFJT	KFJU	KIWW	KIWX
1998	328.5	45.0	7.30	7.10	352.6	44.3	7.96	7.71
1999	335.0	44.4	7.54	7.36	354.6	43.5	8.15	7.92
2000	344.8	44.3	7.79	7.54	365.4	43.6	8.35	8.07
2001	359.9	44.3	8.14	7.92	378.5	43.5	8.69	8.44
2002	368.2	43.9	8.39	8.21	388.0	43.1	9.01	8.76
Non-manual men								
	KFJX	KFJY	KIWY	KIWZ	KFMU	KFMV	KIXO	KIXP
1998	506.1	39.1	12.90	12.94	525.9	39.8	13.17	13.23
1999	525.5	39.0	13.49	13.52	541.6	39.6	13.68	13.73
2000	550.9	38.9	14.14	14.14	562.1	39.6	13.92	14.18
2001	582.4	39.0	14.95	14.99	592.4	39.7	14.97	14.99
2002	610.4	38.9	15.62	15.68	615.5	39.5	15.54	15.61
All women								
	BAQG	BAQO	BAQH	BAQI	BAPU	BAQL	BAPV	BAPW
1999	326.5	37.5	8.71	8.70	292.1	39.0	7.49	7.46
2000	343.7	37.4	9.17	9.13	307.9	38.9	7.91	7.86
2001	366.8	37.5	9.77	9.76	333.4	38.9	8.56	8.54
2002	383.2	37.5	10.21	10.21	351.8	38.7	8.94	9.06
2003	396.0	37.4	10.57	10.56	365.2	38.8	9.41	9.40
Manual women								
	KFMY	KFMZ	KIXU	KIXV	KFPS	KFPT	KIXW	KIXX
1998	210.8	40.2	5.23	5.14	224.2	40.7	5.52	5.39
1999	221.9	39.9	5.56	5.48	231.7	40.4	5.74	5.62
2000	229.1	39.9	5.76	5.65	241.0	40.5	5.94	5.81
2001	241.8	39.9	6.06	5.97	251.4	40.4	6.22	6.07
2002	251.0	39.7	6.33	6.26	260.5	40.2	6.48	6.37
Non-manual women								
	KFRY	KFRZ	KIXY	KIYA	KFUY	KFUZ	KIYB	KIYC
1998	330.1	37.0	8.90	8.89	317.2	37.9	8.38	8.36
1999	346.9	37.0	9.37	9.36	341.5	37.9	9.02	9.01
2000	364.5	37.0	9.85	9.80	358.4	37.8	9.34	9.46
2001	388.8	37.1	10.48	10.47	389.5	37.9	10.14	10.27
2002	405.2	37.1	10.91	10.91	408.1	37.8	10.78	10.78

1 See chapter text.
2 Excluding those whose pay was affected by absence.

Source: New Earnings Survey, Office for National Statistics: 01633 819024

7.21 Average earnings index[1]: all employees: main industrial sectors
Great Britain
Analyses by industry based on Standard Industrial Classification 1992

2000 = 100

	Annual averages	Jan-uary	Feb-ruary	March	April	May	June	July	August	Sept-ember	Oct-ober	Nov-ember	Dec-ember
Unadjusted													
Whole economy (Divisions 01 - 93)													
LNMM													
2001	104.4	103.4	107.7	108.4	103.3	102.7	104.0	103.7	102.8	102.6	103.0	103.4	107.8
2002	108.1	106.4	110.8	111.6	107.2	106.5	107.8	107.6	106.3	106.3	107.3	108.1	111.3
2003	..	109.9	113.8	116.8	110.0	110.0	111.2	111.8	110.2	110.4	110.9	..	..
Manufacturing industries (Divisions 15 - 37)													
LNMN													
2001	104.2	102.0	103.7	107.2	104.2	103.7	103.5	104.4	102.9	103.4	104.1	104.5	107.3
2002	107.9	105.1	106.3	110.5	107.8	107.2	107.3	108.4	106.8	106.8	108.1	108.8	112.0
2003	..	109.1	111.0	117.9	110.5	110.5	110.4	111.8	109.8	110.6	111.6	..	..
Production industries (Divisions 10 - 41)													
LNMO													
2001	104.2	102.0	104.0	107.2	104.2	103.6	103.7	104.2	102.8	103.2	103.8	104.2	107.1
2002	107.8	105.0	106.2	110.9	107.7	107.1	107.6	108.2	106.7	106.8	107.8	108.6	111.7
2003	..	108.9	110.7	118.2	110.7	110.4	110.9	111.6	109.7	110.4	111.3	..	..
Service industries (Divisions 50 - 93)													
LNMP													
2001	104.4	104.0	109.2	108.8	103.0	102.2	103.8	103.3	102.6	102.2	102.6	102.9	107.9
2002	108.1	106.9	112.3	111.5	107.0	106.3	107.7	107.3	106.0	105.9	107.0	107.8	111.0
2003	..	110.1	114.9	116.3	109.9	110.0	111.3	111.9	110.4	110.1	110.5	..	..
Private sector services (unadjusted) (Divisions 50-99)													
JJGF													
2001	104.1	104.8	111.6	111.0	102.2	101.2	103.0	102.2	101.1	100.8	101.5	101.9	107.9
2002	107.6	107.2	114.5	113.3	106.3	105.4	107.0	106.3	104.8	104.5	105.3	106.0	110.2
2003	..	109.6	115.9	117.5	108.2	108.5	109.8	110.3	108.1	108.1	108.8	..	..
Seasonally adjusted													
Whole economy (Divisions 01 - 93)													
LNMQ													
2001	104.4	103.2	103.6	103.7	103.9	104.0	104.3	104.4	104.8	105.0	105.1	105.2	105.8
2002	108.2	106.3	106.9	106.7	108.0	107.9	108.2	108.4	108.6	108.8	109.1	109.5	109.4
2003	..	109.8	109.9	111.4	110.8	111.3	111.6	112.3	112.4	112.8	113.2	..	..
Manufacturing industries (Divisions 15 - 37)													
LNMR													
2001	104.3	102.7	103.4	103.5	103.9	104.1	104.3	104.4	104.8	105.2	105.2	105.2	105.4
2002	108.0	105.9	106.0	106.4	107.4	107.7	108.1	108.3	108.8	108.8	109.3	109.5	109.9
2003	..	109.9	110.7	113.3	110.2	111.1	111.3	111.8	111.9	112.5	112.8	..	..
Production industries (Divisions 10 - 41)													
LNMS													
2001	104.2	102.7	103.7	103.3	103.7	104.0	104.1	104.3	104.6	105.0	105.1	105.0	105.2
2002	107.9	105.8	106.0	106.5	107.2	107.6	108.0	108.2	108.7	108.7	109.2	109.4	109.8
2003	..	109.8	110.6	113.1	110.2	111.0	111.3	111.6	111.8	112.3	112.6	..	..
Service industries (Divisions 50 - 93)													
LNMT													
2001	104.4	103.3	103.8	103.8	103.9	103.9	104.2	104.3	104.8	104.9	105.0	105.1	105.7
2002	108.1	106.3	107.1	106.6	108.0	107.9	108.2	108.3	108.5	108.7	109.0	109.5	108.9
2003	..	109.6	109.8	110.9	110.9	111.5	111.8	112.5	112.6	113.0	113.2	..	..
Private sector services (seasonally adjusted) (Divisions 50-93)													
JJGH													
2001	104.2	103.6	104.0	103.8	103.8	103.6	103.9	103.9	104.4	104.5	104.7	104.7	
2002	107.7	106.0	107.0	105.9	108.1	107.7	108.0	108.0	108.2	108.3	108.4	108.8	
2003	..	108.6	108.7	109.8	110.0	110.7	110.8	111.6	111.5	111.9	112.1	..	

1 See chapter text.

Source: Office for National Statistics: 01633 819002

7.22 Average earnings index[1] : all employee jobs: by industry (not seasonally adjusted)
Great Britain

2000 = 100

	Agriculture, forestry and fishing	Mining and quarrying	Food products, beverages and tobacco	Textiles, leather and clothing	Chemicals and man-made fibres	Basic metals and metal products	Engineering and allied industries	Other manufacturing	Electricity, gas and water supply	Construction
SIC 1992	(A,B)	(C)	(DA)	(DB,DC)	(DG)	(DJ)	(DK, DL,DM)	(DD,DE,DF, DH,DI,DN)	(E)	(F)

Excluding bonuses

	JVUZ	JVVA	JVVB	JVVC	JVVD	JVVE	JVVF	JVVG	JVVH	JVVI
2001	106.0	102.9	104.1	104.2	104.5	104.2	104.9	104.9	102.5	106.3
2002	112.7	106.8	108.5	108.2	108.3	106.6	109.1	109.4	103.3	110.5
2001 Mar	103.0	102.2	102.8	103.4	104.7	102.5	103.9	102.8	100.1	105.1
Apr	103.7	102.2	104.4	102.9	103.6	104.3	104.9	104.5	101.7	105.0
May	107.8	103.0	105.0	104.3	103.4	105.1	104.8	104.8	101.8	105.8
Jun	102.9	103.0	105.1	103.9	105.3	105.8	105.2	105.1	102.2	107.4
Jul	104.1	104.0	103.9	104.3	105.5	105.6	105.6	105.2	103.0	107.8
Aug	109.6	102.2	104.6	103.9	104.6	104.7	104.8	105.0	105.3	105.1
Sep	114.3	102.5	104.3	104.9	104.9	104.6	105.3	106.2	102.3	107.2
Oct	110.3	105.2	104.3	106.4	104.9	105.8	105.3	106.7	102.6	108.2
Nov	109.8	103.6	105.4	105.7	105.6	104.8	105.8	107.3	103.1	108.7
Dec	109.6	104.6	106.8	104.6	105.8	103.5	106.7	106.8	105.5	107.8
2002 Jan	107.7	104.2	105.8	104.9	105.8	104.6	106.5	106.7	101.8	107.9
Feb	108.0	104.3	105.3	105.2	105.5	104.7	107.1	107.1	103.4	109.7
Mar	113.3	103.6	107.2	106.1	106.0	104.8	107.8	107.3	102.1	109.8
Apr	110.5	106.3	107.7	108.0	108.3	107.6	108.5	109.1	103.0	110.3
May	109.4	106.4	108.3	106.8	108.6	106.5	109.0	110.2	101.5	110.5
Jun	110.6	107.8	109.3	108.0	108.7	106.7	109.9	109.6	103.3	111.4
Jul	110.2	106.9	107.8	111.0	109.6	107.7	110.3	109.8	104.0	111.8
Aug	114.8	107.7	109.1	107.8	108.3	105.8	109.4	109.3	103.7	109.4
Sep	119.5	108.2	109.0	109.3	109.6	107.1	109.1	110.3	104.9	110.9
Oct	113.9	106.8	109.6	110.7	109.2	108.0	110.1	111.1	104.3	111.2
Nov	115.9	107.2	110.4	109.6	108.5	108.0	110.5	111.5	104.5	111.9
Dec	118.8	111.9	112.2	110.6	111.0	108.0	111.2	111.2	103.6	111.7
2003 Jan	114.9	111.0	110.2	110.2	108.9	108.1	110.6	110.3	103.3	111.3
Feb	118.2	108.6	110.3	109.3	109.4	109.8	111.0	111.1	103.7	112.3
Mar	119.9	112.1	110.6	111.2	110.7	109.0	112.2	111.0	106.2	113.4
Apr	116.3	110.5	113.8	111.4	111.3	109.3	112.7	110.9	104.9	112.3
May	115.7	112.3	113.5	111.2	111.3	111.2	113.1	111.6	107.0	111.9
Jun	116.7	111.5	112.1	112.7	112.8	110.8	113.2	112.3	105.4	114.0
Jul	117.1	114.3	112.0	116.0	112.5	111.4	113.3	112.5	107.3	113.6
Aug	118.1	114.8	112.5	113.6	113.1	109.7	112.3	112.3	108.5	111.0
Sep	120.4	114.4	112.6	114.8	113.5	111.4	112.8	113.1	106.9	114.9
Oct	118.5	112.8	112.8	114.2	113.1	112.3	113.6	113.6	107.6	115.3

Percentage change on the year

	JVVT	JVVU	JVVV	JVVW	JVVX	JVVY	JVVZ	JVWA	JVWB	JVWC
2002 Mar	10.0	1.4	4.3	2.6	1.2	2.2	3.7	4.4	2.0	4.5
Apr	6.5	4.0	3.2	4.9	4.6	3.2	3.4	4.4	1.2	5.0
May	1.5	3.4	3.1	2.4	5.0	1.3	4.0	5.2	−0.3	4.4
Jun	7.5	4.7	4.0	3.9	3.2	0.8	4.4	4.3	1.0	3.7
Jul	5.9	2.7	3.8	6.4	3.9	1.9	4.5	4.3	0.9	3.7
Aug	4.7	5.4	4.3	3.8	3.6	1.1	4.4	4.1	−1.5	4.0
Sep	4.6	5.6	4.5	4.2	4.4	2.3	3.6	3.9	2.6	3.5
Oct	3.3	1.5	5.1	4.0	4.1	2.1	4.5	4.1	1.7	2.8
Nov	5.6	3.5	4.7	3.7	2.7	3.1	4.5	4.0	1.3	3.0
Dec	8.4	7.0	5.1	5.7	4.9	4.3	4.2	4.1	−1.7	3.6
2003 Jan	6.7	6.5	4.2	5.0	2.9	3.4	3.8	3.5	1.5	3.2
Feb	9.4	4.1	4.8	3.9	3.7	4.9	3.6	3.8	0.3	2.4
Mar	5.8	8.2	3.2	4.7	4.4	4.0	4.1	3.4	4.0	3.3
Apr	5.2	3.9	5.7	3.2	2.7	1.6	3.9	1.6	1.8	1.8
May	5.8	5.5	4.8	4.2	2.4	4.4	3.8	1.2	5.4	1.3
Jun	5.5	3.4	2.5	4.3	3.8	3.8	3.0	2.5	2.1	2.3
Jul	6.3	6.9	3.8	4.5	2.6	3.5	2.7	2.5	3.2	1.6
Aug	2.9	6.5	3.1	5.3	4.3	3.7	2.6	2.7	4.5	1.5
Sep	0.8	5.7	3.3	5.0	3.6	4.0	3.4	2.6	1.9	3.5
Oct	4.1	5.6	2.9	3.2	3.6	4.0	3.2	2.2	3.2	3.7

7.22 continued Average earnings index[1] : all employee jobs: by industry (not seasonally adjusted)
Great Britain

2000 = 100

	Wholesale trade	Retail trade and repairs	Hotels and restaurants	Transport, storage and communication	Financial interm-ediation	Real estate renting and business activities	Public admini-stration	Education	Health and social work	Other services
Excluding bonuses										
SIC 1992	(G:51)	(G:50,52)	(H)	(I)	(J)	(K)	(L)	(M)	(N)	(O)
	JVVJ	JVVK	JVVL	JVVM	JVVN	JVVO	JVVP	JVVQ	JVVR	JVVS
2001	103.1	102.9	104.5	104.7	105.5	106.0	104.7	105.3	106.2	102.3
2002	105.4	106.7	111.2	108.2	108.4	110.7	109.0	109.5	112.9	105.4
2001 Mar	102.2	100.7	101.5	104.7	105.3	104.6	102.6	101.4	102.9	100.5
Apr	103.0	102.9	103.8	104.7	105.7	105.5	103.8	105.0	106.1	99.6
May	102.6	103.7	103.7	105.4	106.3	105.7	103.8	104.3	107.3	101.4
Jun	103.3	104.2	104.8	104.8	105.7	106.3	104.5	105.7	107.1	102.2
Jul	103.3	103.2	105.7	105.0	106.1	105.8	104.8	108.7	106.8	102.8
Aug	103.7	104.6	106.5	104.1	106.6	106.0	105.1	109.0	107.1	104.5
Sep	103.8	104.7	106.9	104.6	105.2	106.1	106.4	108.1	107.1	103.2
Oct	103.9	103.6	105.8	105.5	105.4	107.3	106.4	106.8	107.7	103.5
Nov	104.3	102.9	105.8	106.3	106.2	107.4	106.6	106.0	108.1	103.6
Dec	104.5	103.1	109.1	106.4	106.5	108.0	107.6	106.7	108.4	104.0
2002 Jan	103.8	104.5	106.3	106.3	107.0	109.0	106.9	105.6	109.7	104.9
Feb	104.8	103.4	107.2	105.9	108.1	109.5	107.1	105.8	108.6	104.5
Mar	105.7	105.3	110.4	107.6	106.9	109.9	107.1	106.0	109.2	105.0
Apr	105.8	106.6	109.7	107.1	108.2	110.6	108.4	108.1	112.7	104.3
May	105.9	106.7	111.1	107.5	108.2	111.1	107.8	108.3	112.9	105.0
Jun	105.5	109.3	112.2	108.6	108.1	111.2	108.2	109.0	114.0	106.0
Jul	105.5	107.7	112.8	108.4	108.3	111.1	108.3	109.5	115.1	106.3
Aug	105.5	108.4	113.6	107.4	108.1	110.1	107.7	111.2	113.5	106.3
Sep	105.3	108.1	111.3	109.5	108.3	110.5	108.2	111.4	113.8	103.7
Oct	105.2	107.1	112.1	109.5	109.1	111.7	112.0	113.5	114.8	104.8
Nov	105.7	106.9	111.7	109.8	110.0	112.0	115.3	113.3	114.8	106.3
Dec	106.3	106.5	116.4	110.3	110.2	111.5	110.6	112.7	116.2	107.0
2003 Jan	107.5	109.2	113.2	110.5	110.3	112.3	110.2	111.6	116.6	106.5
Feb	107.8	108.1	112.9	108.5	111.5	112.6	111.4	112.0	115.0	104.9
Mar	108.5	108.8	113.2	110.9	111.4	112.9	112.1	112.1	115.9	104.2
Apr	108.5	110.3	116.3	111.6	111.6	112.1	113.0	115.5	117.7	106.2
May	108.8	113.0	116.2	112.0	112.8	113.0	113.1	114.7	118.0	106.2
Jun	109.4	111.7	116.0	112.9	112.5	113.1	112.9	115.7	119.1	106.2
Jul	109.2	112.2	116.8	113.0	112.2	113.4	114.0	116.9	121.8	106.6
Aug	109.3	112.9	117.7	113.2	111.0	113.3	114.0	117.7	122.3	107.2
Sep	109.1	113.0	116.5	114.0	111.1	113.4	114.4	118.2	120.6	105.9
Oct	109.6	111.0	116.5	114.2	111.6	114.2	114.3	116.8	121.0	106.6
Percentage change on the year										
	JVWD	JVWE	JVWF	JVYJ	JVYK	JVYL	JVYM	JVYN	JVYO	JVYP
2002 Mar	3.4	4.6	8.7	2.8	1.6	5.1	4.4	4.5	6.2	4.5
Apr	2.7	3.6	5.6	2.3	2.4	4.9	4.4	3.0	6.2	4.8
May	3.3	2.9	7.1	2.0	1.8	5.1	3.8	3.9	5.2	3.6
Jun	2.2	4.9	7.1	3.6	2.2	4.6	3.5	3.1	6.4	3.7
Jul	2.1	4.3	6.6	3.3	2.0	5.0	3.3	0.7	7.8	3.4
Aug	1.7	3.6	6.6	3.2	1.5	3.9	2.5	2.0	6.0	1.7
Sep	1.5	3.3	4.2	4.7	2.9	4.1	1.6	3.1	6.3	0.5
Oct	1.2	3.4	5.9	3.8	3.4	4.0	5.2	6.2	6.6	1.3
Nov	1.3	3.8	5.6	3.3	3.6	4.3	8.2	6.8	6.2	2.6
Dec	1.8	3.3	6.7	3.7	3.5	3.2	2.7	5.6	7.2	2.9
2003 Jan	3.5	4.6	6.5	3.9	3.1	3.0	3.1	5.7	6.3	1.5
Feb	2.9	4.5	5.4	2.5	3.1	2.9	4.0	5.9	5.9	0.4
Mar	2.7	3.3	2.5	3.0	4.2	2.7	4.7	5.8	6.1	−0.7
Apr	2.6	3.5	6.0	4.2	3.1	1.3	4.3	6.8	4.5	1.7
May	2.7	5.9	4.6	4.2	4.3	1.7	4.9	5.9	4.6	1.1
Jun	3.7	2.2	3.4	4.0	4.1	1.7	4.3	6.2	4.5	0.2
Jul	3.5	4.2	3.6	4.2	3.7	2.1	5.3	6.8	5.8	0.3
Aug	3.6	4.1	3.6	5.4	2.7	2.9	5.9	5.9	7.7	0.9
Sep	3.6	4.5	4.7	4.1	2.5	2.6	5.8	6.0	6.0	2.1
Oct	4.2	3.7	4.0	4.3	2.3	2.3	2.0	3.0	5.4	1.8

7.22 continued

Average earnings index[1] : all employee jobs: by industry (not seasonally adjusted)
Great Britain

2000 = 100

	Agriculture, forestry and fishing	Mining and quarrying	Food products, beverages and tobacco	Textiles, leather and clothing	Chemicals and man-made fibres	Basic metals and metal products	Engineering and allied industries	Other manufacturing	Electricity, gas and water supply	Construction

Including bonuses

SIC 1992	(A,B)	(C)	(DA)	(DB,DC)	(DG)	(DJ)	(DK, DL,DM)	(DD,DE,DF, DH,DI,DN)	(E)	(F)
	JVUF	JVUG	JVUH	JVUI	JVUJ	JVUK	JVUL	JVUM	JVUN	JVUO
2001	105.9	105.9	102.9	103.2	104.7	104.7	104.4	104.4	101.0	105.8
2002	112.0	112.6	106.2	106.1	108.7	106.7	108.7	108.2	103.1	109.4
2001 Mar	103.5	113.0	105.6	104.9	115.7	105.8	107.1	106.1	104.8	106.7
Apr	104.0	108.8	102.8	101.4	106.2	105.6	103.9	104.4	100.0	104.3
May	107.2	103.6	104.7	102.1	102.4	104.6	103.8	103.5	100.1	105.1
Jun	102.2	102.2	102.1	101.9	102.1	105.3	103.5	104.1	108.1	108.6
Jul	103.4	103.3	102.4	103.0	101.3	107.0	105.1	104.4	99.4	107.4
Aug	109.8	100.1	102.3	102.1	101.3	103.9	103.3	102.9	100.8	104.8
Sep	113.2	104.9	101.9	103.3	100.4	103.8	103.5	104.5	97.9	106.3
Oct	109.3	103.7	100.2	104.4	100.7	106.9	104.0	105.4	98.3	105.9
Nov	109.3	102.7	101.7	104.4	102.1	105.3	104.9	105.5	98.5	107.4
Dec	112.6	106.4	108.1	106.6	111.5	104.9	106.8	107.5	101.8	109.2
2002 Jan	108.0	106.1	103.4	103.6	103.9	105.3	106.0	105.2	102.5	104.7
Feb	107.1	106.6	104.9	104.4	111.0	104.4	106.7	106.0	102.2	107.4
Mar	113.4	127.1	112.6	108.5	120.7	105.8	109.4	109.9	111.1	114.3
Apr	110.2	112.6	103.9	105.3	110.6	108.5	108.4	107.7	102.0	109.5
May	109.1	112.0	105.1	104.2	106.1	104.9	108.4	108.5	100.5	108.2
Jun	109.1	112.2	105.7	105.9	105.0	105.7	108.7	108.0	110.9	109.7
Jul	108.2	109.3	105.0	107.2	107.8	108.9	109.5	108.5	102.4	110.2
Aug	112.9	110.3	105.4	104.6	109.0	104.0	108.0	106.6	101.8	107.4
Sep	118.1	114.4	105.2	105.5	105.3	105.6	107.5	107.9	101.5	109.3
Oct	112.4	110.1	105.7	106.9	104.9	109.3	108.9	108.6	101.0	108.7
Nov	114.4	111.1	107.1	106.6	104.9	108.2	110.2	109.6	101.0	109.8
Dec	121.6	119.0	110.4	111.1	114.8	109.2	113.1	111.8	100.4	113.1
2003 Jan	114.0	113.3	108.1	107.6	107.5	109.2	110.4	108.5	102.4	109.5
Feb	116.9	113.7	109.8	106.4	115.9	109.5	112.2	109.7	101.6	109.8
Mar	121.4	138.7	119.9	110.7	138.2	111.5	118.6	113.6	113.1	119.3
Apr	114.8	132.0	110.0	106.6	115.0	110.0	112.4	107.8	101.8	109.8
May	113.8	114.8	108.2	107.1	109.8	109.8	113.5	108.9	104.1	108.5
Jun	115.0	113.9	107.7	107.2	110.6	109.4	112.8	109.5	118.7	111.3
Jul	115.8	115.4	109.8	111.1	110.9	114.1	113.4	110.1	104.8	111.7
Aug	115.5	116.4	108.9	108.7	112.4	108.2	111.2	108.6	103.9	108.0
Sep	118.0	117.1	110.8	109.6	111.3	108.7	111.8	109.7	102.8	112.9
Oct	116.9	114.6	108.1	109.6	110.6	113.8	113.0	110.7	104.1	113.7

Percentage change on the year

	JVYQ	JVYR	JVYS	JVYT	JVYU	JVYV	JVYW	JVYX	JVYY	JVYZ
2002 Mar	9.5	12.4	6.6	3.4	4.3	–	2.2	3.6	6.0	7.2
Apr	6.0	3.4	1.0	3.8	4.2	2.8	4.3	3.2	2.0	5.0
May	1.8	8.0	0.4	2.0	3.6	0.3	4.4	4.8	0.3	2.9
Jun	6.7	9.8	3.5	3.9	2.8	0.4	5.0	3.8	2.6	1.0
Jul	4.7	5.8	2.5	4.1	6.4	1.8	4.2	3.9	3.0	2.6
Aug	2.9	10.2	3.0	2.4	7.6	0.1	4.6	3.6	0.9	2.5
Sep	4.4	9.0	3.3	2.2	4.9	1.8	3.9	3.2	3.7	2.8
Oct	2.8	6.1	5.5	2.4	4.1	2.3	4.7	3.0	2.7	2.6
Nov	4.7	8.2	5.4	2.1	2.8	2.8	5.0	3.9	2.6	2.3
Dec	8.0	11.8	2.2	4.3	2.9	4.2	5.8	3.9	−1.3	3.6
2003 Jan	5.5	6.8	4.5	3.9	3.4	3.6	4.2	3.1	−0.1	4.5
Feb	9.2	6.6	4.7	2.0	4.4	4.9	5.1	3.4	−0.5	2.2
Mar	7.1	9.1	6.5	2.1	14.5	5.4	8.4	3.4	1.7	4.4
Apr	4.2	17.2	5.9	1.3	4.0	1.3	3.7	0.1	−0.2	0.2
May	4.3	2.5	3.0	2.8	3.5	4.7	4.7	0.3	3.6	0.3
Jun	5.4	1.4	1.9	1.2	5.4	3.5	3.8	1.4	7.1	1.5
Jul	7.0	5.6	4.6	3.6	2.8	4.7	3.6	1.5	2.3	1.4
Aug	2.3	5.5	3.3	3.9	3.2	4.0	3.0	1.8	2.1	0.6
Sep	−0.1	2.4	5.3	3.8	5.7	2.9	4.0	1.7	1.3	3.3
Oct	4.0	4.1	2.3	2.5	5.5	4.1	3.8	2.0	3.0	4.6

7.22
continued

Average earnings index[1] : all employee jobs: by industry (not seasonally adjusted)
Great Britain

2000 = 100

	Wholesale trade	Retail trade and repairs	Hotels and restaurants	Transport, storage and communication	Financial interm-ediation	Real estate renting and business activities	Public admini-stration	Education	Health and social work	Other services
Including bonuses										
SIC 1992	(G:51)	(G:50,52)	(H)	(I)	(J)	(K)	(L)	(M)	(N)	(O)
	JVUP	JVUQ	JVUR	JVUS	JVUT	JVUU	JVUV	JVUW	JVUX	JVUY
2001	103.6	102.9	106.4	104.2	105.1	104.4	104.4	105.1	106.1	102.7
2002	105.8	107.0	114.1	107.6	104.7	107.8	108.4	109.4	113.0	105.9
2001 Mar	115.0	102.5	104.1	104.9	136.3	110.2	102.3	101.3	102.8	102.0
Apr	102.2	103.4	105.6	103.4	98.2	103.4	103.4	104.7	106.2	99.7
May	101.6	104.3	105.8	105.7	89.0	103.2	103.3	104.1	107.2	101.1
Jun	101.2	104.7	108.0	107.7	93.8	105.3	104.2	105.4	107.1	102.0
Jul	101.3	102.6	108.1	103.7	92.2	104.4	104.3	108.5	106.7	102.6
Aug	101.2	103.1	108.3	102.4	89.1	102.3	104.8	108.9	106.9	103.7
Sep	100.9	103.3	108.0	102.0	87.8	101.8	105.9	108.0	106.9	102.2
Oct	100.8	103.1	106.8	103.5	87.0	103.8	105.9	106.6	107.5	104.8
Nov	103.0	102.9	108.5	104.2	87.5	104.0	106.0	105.9	108.0	103.8
Dec	109.3	102.8	112.3	107.4	114.4	108.2	107.2	106.6	108.4	105.9
2002 Jan	104.3	104.1	107.9	103.8	117.6	106.1	106.3	105.6	109.6	105.8
Feb	105.6	105.3	110.3	106.9	158.0	108.4	106.6	105.9	108.5	107.1
Mar	117.3	107.4	112.7	107.7	132.8	110.3	106.8	105.8	109.3	107.1
Apr	103.9	108.0	112.1	106.6	101.2	107.1	107.8	108.0	112.9	103.3
May	105.6	107.1	114.7	108.0	90.8	107.7	107.1	108.2	112.8	103.6
Jun	104.0	111.6	114.3	112.5	90.7	109.3	107.9	108.9	114.0	104.9
Jul	104.1	107.3	115.6	106.7	94.8	108.5	107.7	109.4	115.1	106.4
Aug	103.1	107.8	116.2	105.6	89.6	106.0	107.1	111.0	113.5	105.2
Sep	101.6	108.1	113.1	106.9	88.7	106.3	107.5	111.3	113.8	102.5
Oct	105.0	106.4	114.6	107.1	89.3	106.9	111.3	113.3	114.7	105.6
Nov	105.2	105.6	117.5	107.9	91.3	107.4	114.6	113.2	115.0	107.9
Dec	110.0	105.1	120.1	111.1	112.3	109.3	109.9	112.7	116.3	111.1
2003 Jan	107.6	106.8	116.1	107.6	112.6	108.3	109.5	111.7	116.7	110.2
Feb	108.3	109.0	117.4	106.5	155.2	111.3	110.8	111.8	115.2	107.0
Mar	122.2	111.7	117.2	112.2	143.3	112.9	111.6	112.0	116.2	108.7
Apr	108.7	109.8	118.3	108.5	101.5	106.9	112.3	115.3	117.9	107.5
May	109.1	111.6	120.0	110.6	93.7	109.1	112.5	114.4	118.1	107.8
Jun	111.6	112.1	118.1	117.8	92.0	110.5	112.2	115.6	119.1	108.2
Jul	110.1	112.1	119.4	111.8	97.6	110.7	113.3	116.8	121.9	109.8
Aug	107.8	111.7	119.3	110.4	90.4	108.5	114.4	117.4	122.3	108.2
Sep	108.3	112.6	118.5	110.8	90.3	108.1	113.7	117.9	120.6	106.2
Oct	110.2	110.1	118.7	111.1	92.0	109.4	113.7	116.5	120.9	108.8
Percentage change on the year										
	JVZA	JVZB	JVZC	JVZD	JVZE	JVZF	JVZG	JVZH	JVZI	JVZJ
2002 Mar	2.0	4.8	8.3	2.7	−2.5	0.1	4.3	4.4	6.3	5.0
Apr	1.7	4.4	6.2	3.1	3.1	3.5	4.3	3.1	6.3	3.5
May	4.0	2.8	8.4	2.2	2.0	4.4	3.7	3.9	5.3	2.5
Jun	2.8	6.6	5.8	4.5	−3.4	3.8	3.5	3.3	6.4	2.9
Jul	2.7	4.5	7.0	2.9	2.8	3.9	3.3	0.8	8.0	3.6
Aug	1.9	4.6	7.3	3.1	0.5	3.6	2.3	2.0	6.2	1.4
Sep	0.7	4.6	4.7	4.9	1.1	4.4	1.6	3.0	6.5	0.2
Oct	4.2	3.2	7.3	3.5	2.7	3.0	5.1	6.2	6.7	0.7
Nov	2.1	2.7	8.3	3.6	4.4	3.3	8.1	6.9	6.5	3.9
Dec	0.7	2.2	7.0	3.4	−1.8	1.0	2.5	5.7	7.3	4.9
2003 Jan	3.2	2.6	7.6	3.6	−4.2	2.1	3.0	5.7	6.4	4.2
Feb	2.6	3.5	6.4	−0.4	−1.7	2.7	3.9	5.6	6.2	−0.1
Mar	4.2	4.0	4.0	4.2	7.8	2.3	4.5	5.9	6.3	1.4
Apr	4.6	1.7	5.5	1.8	0.3	−0.2	4.2	6.8	4.5	4.2
May	3.3	4.2	4.6	2.5	3.2	1.3	5.0	5.8	4.7	4.1
Jun	7.2	0.4	3.4	4.7	1.5	1.1	4.0	6.1	4.5	3.1
Jul	5.8	4.5	3.2	4.7	3.0	2.1	5.2	6.7	5.8	3.3
Aug	4.5	3.6	2.7	4.5	0.9	2.4	6.8	5.8	7.8	2.9
Sep	6.5	4.2	4.8	3.6	1.8	1.7	5.7	6.0	5.9	3.7
Oct	4.9	3.5	3.6	3.8	2.9	2.4	2.2	2.9	5.4	3.1

1 See chapter text.

Source: Office for National Statistics: 01633 819024

7.23 Gross weekly and hourly earnings[1] of full-time adult employees
Great Britain
At April

	Gross weekly earnings					Gross hourly earnings				
	Lowest decile	Lower quartile	Median	Upper quartile	Highest decile	Lowest decile	Lower quartile	Median	Upper quartile	Highest decile
	£	£	£	£	£	£	£	£	£	£
All men										
	KBYD	KBYE	KBYF	KBYG	KBYH	KIYD	KIYE	KIYF	KIYG	KIYH
1995	181.6	237.0	323.7	444.2	604.3	4.33	5.55	7.62	10.94	15.68
1996	188.9	245.1	334.8	460.7	632.1	4.50	5.75	7.91	11.40	16.31
1997	198.6	256.4	349.7	480.0	656.9	4.71	6.00	8.24	11.89	17.00
1998	203.9	265.6	363.7	500.8	689.2	4.90	6.25	8.61	12.40	17.85
1999	211.1	274.9	374.8	518.2	715.3	5.10	6.50	8.94	12.99	18.71
2000	220.0	284.7	389.7	537.7	745.2	5.30	6.74	9.31	13.55	19.51
2001	229.1	296.3	407.3	567.2	798.4	5.53	7.05	9.74	14.33	20.94
2002	237.9	306.1	421.2	587.7	839.6	5.77	7.31	10.13	14.89	22.01
2003	243.8	314.1	431.9	604.6	854.9	5.96	7.51	10.39	15.36	22.37
Manual men										
	KFZY	KFZZ	KGAK	KGAL	KGAM	KIYN	KIYO	KIYP	KIYQ	KIYR
1995	166.9	211.1	271.8	347.1	437.5	3.97	4.86	6.09	7.66	9.43
1996	173.8	218.4	280.0	358.9	452.5	4.11	5.01	6.32	7.99	9.83
1997	182.4	228.8	292.5	373.9	472.8	4.32	5.25	6.60	8.28	10.17
1998	190.0	238.0	305.0	392.7	494.2	4.50	5.48	6.87	8.67	10.72
1999	194.9	244.8	312.8	399.0	500.6	4.68	5.69	7.11	8.95	11.04
2000	200.2	251.8	321.2	413.0	512.7	4.86	5.88	7.30	9.23	11.42
2001	209.7	262.0	336.1	431.3	536.1	5.05	6.11	7.66	9.63	11.90
2002	219.6	271.1	342.4	437.2	543.8	5.27	6.34	7.88	9.89	12.22
2003	..	..	..	..	..	..	..	..	..	..
Non-manual men										
	KGAS	KGAT	KGAU	KGAV	KGAW	KIYX	KIYY	KIYZ	KIZA	KIZB
1995	204.1	280.1	384.6	519.5	712.7	5.11	7.06	9.93	13.83	19.07
1996	211.1	287.9	399.4	544.0	752.4	5.28	7.28	10.28	14.38	19.87
1997	220.7	301.0	415.9	565.8	780.8	5.49	7.60	10.72	14.94	20.81
1998	225.5	309.1	430.7	586.1	823.4	5.62	7.79	11.09	15.54	21.74
1999	233.5	321.1	449.1	612.2	862.6	5.90	8.14	11.59	16.24	22.90
2000	243.8	334.3	463.9	634.6	902.1	6.14	8.42	12.03	16.86	23.88
2001	252.1	345.5	485.7	671.8	962.4	6.35	8.72	12.61	17.85	25.78
2002	259.8	355.4	500.4	695.6	1 011.3	6.54	8.97	12.99	18.44	26.95
2003	..	..	..	..	..	..	..	..	..	..

As percentages of the corresponding median

	Lowest decile	Lower quartile	Median	Upper quartile	Highest decile	Lowest decile	Lower quartile	Median	Upper quartile	Highest decile
All men										
	KBZH	KBZI	KBZJ	KBZK	KBZL	KBZM	KBZN	KBZO	KBZP	KBZQ
1995	56.1	73.2	100.0	137.2	186.7	56.9	72.9	100.0	143.6	205.8
1996	56.4	73.2	100.0	137.6	188.8	56.9	72.7	100.0	144.2	206.4
1997	56.8	73.3	100.0	137.2	187.8	57.2	72.8	100.0	144.3	206.3
1998	56.1	73.0	100.0	137.7	189.5	56.8	72.6	100.0	144.0	207.3
1999	56.3	73.3	100.0	138.3	190.8	57.1	72.8	100.0	145.4	209.4
2000	56.5	73.1	100.0	138.0	191.2	57.0	72.4	100.0	145.5	209.5
2001	56.2	72.7	100.0	139.2	196.0	56.8	72.4	100.0	147.2	215.1
2002	56.5	72.7	100.0	139.5	199.3	57.0	72.1	100.0	147.0	217.3
2003	56.4	72.7	100.0	140.0	197.9	57.4	72.3	100.0	147.8	215.2
Manual men										
	KGBS	KGBT	KGBU	KGBV	KGBW	KGBX	KGBY	KGBZ	KGCH	KGCI
1995	61.4	77.7	100.0	127.7	161.0	65.2	79.8	100.0	125.8	154.8
1996	62.1	78.0	100.0	128.2	161.6	65.0	79.3	100.0	126.4	155.6
1997	62.4	78.2	100.0	127.8	161.6	65.5	79.5	100.0	125.5	154.1
1998	62.3	78.0	100.0	128.8	162.0	65.5	79.8	100.0	126.2	156.1
1999	62.3	78.3	100.0	127.6	160.0	65.9	80.0	100.0	125.8	155.2
2000	62.3	78.4	100.0	128.6	159.6	66.6	80.6	100.0	126.4	156.5
2001	62.4	77.9	100.0	128.3	159.5	66.0	79.7	100.0	125.7	155.6
2002	64.1	79.2	100.0	127.7	158.8	66.9	80.5	100.0	125.5	155.1
2003	..	..	..	..	..	..	..	..	..	..
Non-manual men										
	KGCJ	KGCQ	KGCR	KGCS	KGCT	KGCU	KGCV	KGCW	KGCX	KGCY
1995	53.1	72.8	100.0	135.1	185.3	51.5	71.1	100.0	139.3	192.0
1996	52.9	72.1	100.0	136.2	188.4	51.3	70.8	100.0	139.9	193.2
1997	53.1	72.4	100.0	136.0	187.7	51.2	70.9	100.0	139.4	194.1
1998	52.4	71.8	100.0	136.1	191.2	50.7	70.2	100.0	140.1	196.0
1999	52.0	71.5	100.0	136.3	192.1	50.9	70.2	100.0	140.0	197.5
2000	52.6	72.1	100.0	136.8	194.5	51.0	69.9	100.0	140.1	198.4
2001	51.9	71.1	100.0	138.3	198.1	50.3	69.2	100.0	141.4	204.1
2002	51.9	71.0	100.0	139.0	202.1	50.4	69.0	100.0	141.9	207.4
2003	..	..	..	..	..	..	..	..	..	..

7.23
continued

Gross weekly and hourly earnings[1] of full-time adult employees
Great Britain
At April

	Gross weekly earnings					Gross hourly earnings				
	Lowest decile	Lower quartile	Median	Upper quartile	Highest decile	Lowest decile	Lower quartile	Median	Upper quartile	Highest decile
	£	£	£	£	£	£	£	£	£	£
All women										
	KCBK	KCBL	KCBM	KCBN	KCBO	KIZC	KIZD	KIZE	KIZF	KIZG
1995	140.8	179.5	238.0	334.1	432.9	3.69	4.69	6.26	8.92	12.39
1996	146.7	186.8	248.1	347.3	449.4	3.83	4.87	6.55	9.31	12.97
1997	154.5	196.1	260.5	364.7	472.1	4.03	5.11	6.84	9.79	13.54
1998	160.9	203.8	270.4	379.6	495.2	4.23	5.34	7.11	10.23	14.21
1999	170.0	214.2	285.4	400.4	522.6	4.47	5.60	7.49	10.80	15.06
2000	177.3	223.6	296.7	417.6	546.1	4.66	5.85	7.79	11.24	15.65
2001	185.7	233.9	313.2	446.4	584.4	4.90	6.14	8.23	12.01	16.72
2002	195.0	243.8	327.1	465.1	614.2	5.12	6.41	8.61	12.53	17.40
2003	202.0	252.7	338.6	480.0	634.2	5.34	6.66	8.97	12.97	17.91
Manual women										
	KGCZ	KGDA	KGDB	KGDC	KGDD	KIZM	KIZN	KIZO	KIZP	KIZQ
1995	114.8	137.4	171.0	222.1	282.6	3.02	3.56	4.32	5.37	6.61
1996	119.0	142.8	178.7	230.8	291.4	3.15	3.68	4.49	5.61	6.85
1997	122.4	148.7	185.4	237.3	300.0	3.25	3.83	4.66	5.81	7.16
1998	128.9	156.3	193.9	248.6	312.5	3.43	4.02	4.87	6.08	7.44
1999	140.4	164.7	201.4	260.9	327.8	3.73	4.27	5.08	6.37	7.93
2000	144.9	171.2	210.1	268.1	335.7	3.86	4.44	5.27	6.58	8.14
2001	151.0	179.3	220.0	280.0	360.1	4.01	4.65	5.55	6.94	8.64
2002	161.3	186.3	229.2	290.0	365.0	4.30	4.86	5.76	7.21	8.93
2003	..	..	..	..	..	..	..	..	..	..
Non-manual women										
	KGDJ	KGDK	KGDL	KGDM	KGDN	KIZW	KIZX	KIZY	KIZZ	KJAN
1995	155.6	194.7	256.2	355.6	445.3	4.13	5.22	6.83	9.61	13.09
1996	161.7	203.0	268.7	372.2	471.1	4.31	5.44	7.16	10.08	13.75
1997	171.4	212.8	283.3	390.7	495.1	4.53	5.68	7.53	10.61	14.38
1998	176.2	219.3	291.5	405.6	513.5	4.68	5.86	7.77	11.01	14.88
1999	184.0	230.3	305.0	422.3	540.9	4.92	6.14	8.16	11.52	15.78
2000	192.0	239.2	317.9	442.5	567.8	5.10	6.40	8.47	12.08	16.41
2001	200.9	249.8	335.9	472.6	613.3	5.35	6.67	8.94	12.86	17.57
2002	209.5	259.1	349.2	492.6	639.0	5.56	6.93	9.31	13.33	18.27
2003	..	..	..	..	..	..	..	..	..	..

As percentages of the corresponding median

	Gross weekly earnings					Gross hourly earnings				
All women										
	KGEO	KGEP	KGEQ	KGER	KGES	KGET	KGEU	KGEV	KGEW	KGEX
1995	59.2	75.4	100.0	140.4	181.9	59.0	74.9	100.0	142.5	198.0
1996	59.1	75.3	100.0	139.9	181.2	58.6	74.4	100.0	142.2	198.1
1997	59.3	75.3	100.0	140.0	181.3	58.8	74.7	100.0	143.0	197.9
1998	59.5	75.4	100.0	140.4	183.1	59.5	75.1	100.0	143.8	199.8
1999	59.6	75.1	100.0	140.3	183.1	59.8	74.8	100.0	144.3	201.2
2000	59.8	75.4	100.0	140.7	184.1	59.8	75.0	100.0	144.3	200.8
2001	59.3	74.7	100.0	142.6	186.6	59.5	74.5	100.0	145.8	203.1
2002	59.6	74.5	100.0	142.2	187.8	59.5	74.4	100.0	145.4	201.9
2003	59.7	74.6	100.0	141.8	187.3	59.6	74.2	100.0	144.6	199.8
Manual women										
	KGDT	KGDU	KGDV	KGDW	KGDX	KGDY	KGDZ	KGEA	KGEB	KGEC
1995	67.1	80.3	100.0	129.9	165.2	69.9	82.4	100.0	124.3	153.0
1996	66.5	79.9	100.0	129.1	163.0	70.2	82.0	100.0	125.1	152.6
1997	66.0	80.2	100.0	128.0	161.8	69.7	82.2	100.0	124.7	153.6
1998	66.5	80.6	100.0	128.2	161.2	70.4	82.6	100.0	124.9	152.7
1999	69.7	81.8	100.0	129.5	162.8	73.4	84.0	100.0	125.4	156.1
2000	69.0	81.5	100.0	127.6	159.8	73.3	84.2	100.0	124.8	154.4
2001	68.6	81.5	100.0	127.3	163.7	72.2	83.7	100.0	125.1	155.7
2002	70.3	81.3	100.0	126.5	159.2	74.6	84.3	100.0	125.1	155.0
2003	..	..	..	..	..	..	..	..	..	..
Non-manual women										
	KGED	KGEE	KGEF	KGEG	KGEH	KGEI	KGEJ	KGEK	KGEL	KGEM
1995	60.7	76.0	100.0	138.8	173.8	60.5	76.4	100.0	140.7	191.7
1996	60.2	75.6	100.0	138.5	175.3	60.2	76.0	100.0	140.7	192.1
1997	60.5	75.1	100.0	137.9	174.8	60.2	75.4	100.0	140.9	191.0
1998	60.4	75.2	100.0	139.1	176.2	60.2	75.5	100.0	141.7	191.5
1999	60.3	75.5	100.0	138.4	177.3	60.3	75.3	100.0	141.2	193.4
2000	60.4	75.2	100.0	139.2	178.6	60.2	75.5	100.0	142.5	193.7
2001	59.8	74.4	100.0	140.7	182.6	59.8	74.5	100.0	143.9	196.2
2002	60.0	74.2	100.0	141.1	183.0	59.7	74.4	100.0	143.1	196.1
2003	..	..	..	..	..	..	..	..	..	..

1 See chapter text.

Source: New Earnings Survey, Office for National Statistics: 01633 819024

7.24 Gross weekly and hourly earnings[1,2] of full-time adults
Northern Ireland
April of each year

	Gross weekly earnings					Gross hourly earnings				
	Lowest decile	Lower quartile	Median	Upper quartile	Highest decile	Lowest decile	Lower quartile	Median	Upper quartile	Highest decile
	£	£	£	£	£	p	p	p	p	p
All men										
	KCIF	KCIG	KCIH	KCII	KCIJ	KCIK	KCIL	KCIM	KCIN	KCIO
1996	163.0	213.7	296.9	424.0	549.8	399.4	512.3	695.7	1 073.9	1 402.8
1997	171.1	222.2	307.1	449.6	575.8	414.8	522.1	724.4	1 106.2	1 452.0
1998	175.4	227.4	322.1	455.1	596.1	435.8	548.8	763.0	1 137.2	1 497.5
1999	183.9	237.0	328.9	467.7	607.6	457.0	572.3	778.4	1 167.1	1 545.9
2000	190.1	247.3	342.4	491.3	636.3	476.3	601.0	799.8	1 204.6	1 596.9
2001	194.2	250.0	352.6	500.2	668.6	491.0	614.8	828.5	1 257.3	1 678.4
2002	208.7	261.2	360.5	516.4	701.4	522.4	644.1	854.4	1 282.2	1 752.7
2003	214.1	272.9	366.6	539.8	727.3	541.5	662.1	877.3	1 370.1	1 790.6
Manual men										
	KCIP	KCIQ	KCIR	KCIS	KCIT	KCIU	KCIV	KCIW	KCIX	KCIY
1996	150.6	187.2	240.7	310.1	389.9	369.9	448.0	563.7	684.6	860.6
1997	158.4	192.9	249.4	321.4	402.7	385.0	460.0	570.5	709.5	882.0
1998	165.0	200.9	262.9	340.5	422.8	408.3	487.3	595.3	767.3	940.7
1999	175.6	216.4	270.4	355.0	454.6	435.5	515.0	624.5	786.0	994.7
2000	180.0	225.5	279.8	363.9	457.0	445.0	535.7	650.0	814.5	987.3
2001	182.5	229.0	292.8	380.7	475.7	463.6	550.0	677.3	842.0	1 059.9
2002	196.0	237.0	296.3	380.1	471.0	494.0	576.7	700.0	862.0	1 062.0
2003	..	..	..	..	..	..	..	..	..	..
Non-manual men										
	KCIZ	KCJO	KCJP	KCJQ	KCJR	KCJS	KCJT	KCJU	KCJV	KCJW
1996	192.5	268.4	387.1	506.4	617.2	482.4	682.5	1 013.0	1 322.7	1 612.2
1997	198.3	277.4	403.0	533.1	666.6	491.4	690.9	1 048.2	1 363.0	1 638.2
1998	200.5	284.2	418.4	543.8	685.9	500.0	715.7	1 074.7	1 404.5	1 739.5
1999	200.0	296.8	424.0	546.8	680.6	502.8	740.4	1 103.6	1 461.9	1 779.4
2000	209.1	306.0	456.6	580.0	730.8	543.3	767.7	1 165.1	1 519.9	1 917.3
2001	220.6	317.9	459.8	609.5	788.4	555.6	800.3	1 188.9	1 583.6	2 017.6
2002	245.7	340.7	486.4	646.2	863.6	647.5	892.0	1 270.4	1 656.6	2 195.1
2003	..	..	..	..	..	..	..	..	..	..

As percentages of the corresponding median

	Gross weekly earnings					Gross hourly earnings				
	Lowest decile	Lower quartile	Median	Upper quartile	Highest decile	Lowest decile	Lower quartile	Median	Upper quartile	Highest decile
All men										
	KCJX	KCJY	KCJZ	KCKA	KCKB	KCKC	KCKD	KCKE	KCKF	KCKG
1996	54.9	72.0	100.0	142.8	185.2	57.4	73.6	100.0	154.4	201.6
1997	55.7	72.4	100.0	146.4	187.5	57.3	72.1	100.0	152.7	200.4
1998	54.5	70.6	100.0	141.3	185.1	57.1	71.9	100.0	149.0	196.3
1999	55.9	72.0	100.0	142.2	184.7	58.7	73.5	100.0	149.9	198.6
2000	55.5	72.2	100.0	143.5	185.9	59.5	75.1	100.0	150.6	199.6
2001	55.1	70.9	100.0	141.9	189.6	59.3	74.2	100.0	151.7	202.6
2002	57.9	72.4	100.0	143.2	194.6	61.1	75.4	100.0	150.1	205.1
2003	58.4	74.4	100.0	147.2	198.4	61.7	75.5	100.0	156.2	204.1
Manual men										
	KCKH	KCKI	KCKT	KCKK	KCKL	KCKM	KCKN	KCKO	KCKP	KCKR
1996	62.6	77.8	100.0	128.8	162.0	65.6	79.5	100.0	121.4	152.7
1997	63.5	77.3	100.0	128.9	161.5	67.5	80.6	100.0	124.4	154.6
1998	62.8	76.4	100.0	129.5	160.8	68.6	81.9	100.0	128.9	158.0
1999	64.9	80.0	100.0	131.3	168.1	69.7	82.5	100.0	125.9	159.3
2000	64.3	80.6	100.0	130.1	163.4	68.5	82.4	100.0	125.3	151.9
2001	62.4	78.2	100.0	130.0	162.5	68.5	81.2	100.0	124.3	156.5
2002	66.2	80.0	100.0	128.3	159.0	70.6	82.4	100.0	123.1	151.7
2003	..	..	..	..	..	..	..	..	..	..
Non-manual men										
	KCKQ	KCKS	KFZW	KCKU	KCKV	KCKW	KCKX	KCKY	KCKZ	KCLA
1996	49.7	69.3	100.0	130.8	159.4	47.6	67.4	100.0	130.6	159.2
1997	49.2	68.8	100.0	132.3	165.4	46.9	65.9	100.0	130.0	156.3
1998	47.9	67.9	100.0	130.0	163.9	46.5	66.6	100.0	130.7	161.9
1999	47.2	70.0	100.0	129.0	160.5	45.6	67.1	100.0	132.5	161.2
2000	45.8	67.0	100.0	127.0	160.1	46.6	65.9	100.0	130.4	164.6
2001	48.0	69.1	100.0	132.6	171.5	46.7	67.3	100.0	133.2	169.7
2002	50.5	70.1	100.0	132.9	177.6	51.0	70.2	100.0	130.4	172.8
2003	..	..	..	..	..	..	..	..	..	..

7.24
continued

Gross weekly and hourly earnings[1,2] of full-time adults
Northern Ireland
April of each year

	Gross weekly earnings					Gross hourly earnings				
	Lowest decile	Lower quartile	Median	Upper quartile	Highest decile	Lowest decile	Lower quartile	Median	Upper quartile	Highest decile
	£	£	£	£	£	p	p	p	p	p
All women										
	KCDS	KCDT	KCDU	KCDV	KCDW	KCDX	KCDY	KCDZ	KCFF	KCFG
1996	133.3	165.5	226.2	331.9	434.8	354.5	431.0	595.8	893.6	1 256.9
1997	137.5	170.0	231.3	334.4	450.9	360.0	441.6	602.6	906.2	1 285.5
1998	148.1	181.4	243.9	348.0	465.2	390.2	471.5	652.5	950.9	1 304.5
1999	151.3	191.9	257.8	374.3	485.9	404.3	494.7	683.3	1 026.6	1 410.6
2000	162.9	203.9	271.8	400.4	512.5	435.3	536.5	713.4	1 091.7	1 440.2
2001	173.2	211.8	287.9	412.7	517.4	456.6	560.4	748.4	1 106.1	1 462.8
2002	180.5	221.3	297.1	438.2	561.6	475.0	580.0	792.2	1 185.3	1 650.4
2003	189.7	231.2	307.3	455.1	574.0	500.0	609.9	816.7	1 215.2	1 650.4
Manual women										
	KCFH	KCFI	KCFJ	KCFK	KCFL	KCFM	KCFN	KCFO	KCFP	KCFQ
1996	110.9	132.5	161.1	197.1	248.7	293.9	345.7	408.0	496.2	599.7
1997	113.4	138.3	160.0	201.8	250.8	308.3	354.4	413.7	500.0	593.0
1998	120.0	146.5	172.9	213.6	258.4	309.0	385.7	440.0	549.0	631.2
1999	136.1	151.3	175.1	219.0	275.8	360.0	397.2	451.3	546.8	633.8
2000	144.0	163.7	195.0	240.1	282.3	395.1	435.5	509.7	592.9	713.9
2001	152.2	176.2	209.2	254.6	309.8	396.2	457.6	536.4	635.4	750.3
2002	155.0	179.4	212.5	258.4	325.6	423.8	471.6	553.5	663.7	775.9
2003	..	..	..	..	..	..	..	..	..	..
Non-manual women										
	KCFR	KCFS	KCFT	KCFU	KCFV	KCFW	KCFX	KCFY	KCFZ	KCHA
1996	145.3	182.5	253.0	364.7	437.0	385.0	490.2	675.6	997.3	1 302.6
1997	149.7	188.6	254.0	364.3	451.3	389.0	501.6	679.4	996.7	1 342.9
1998	156.6	200.2	270.9	383.8	475.5	412.8	530.7	725.0	1 028.2	1 373.9
1999	167.4	211.5	289.3	409.2	500.9	442.1	569.7	773.3	1 137.8	1 459.0
2000	174.3	219.9	299.1	426.8	517.4	458.7	590.2	793.3	1 170.2	1 507.1
2001	183.4	231.2	311.6	448.6	521.2	487.7	620.6	838.7	1 212.8	1 507.1
2002	192.7	244.6	331.4	469.0	574.3	516.9	655.0	886.1	1 272.1	1 700.2
2003	..	..	..	..	..	..	..	..	..	..

As percentages of the corresponding median

	Gross weekly earnings					Gross hourly earnings				
All women										
	KCHB	KCHC	KCHD	KCHE	KCHF	KCHG	KCHH	KCHI	KCHJ	KCHK
1996	58.9	73.2	100.0	146.7	192.2	59.5	72.3	100.0	150.0	211.0
1997	59.4	73.5	100.0	144.6	194.9	59.7	73.3	100.0	150.4	213.3
1998	60.7	74.4	100.0	142.7	190.7	59.8	72.3	100.0	145.7	199.9
1999	58.7	74.5	100.0	145.2	188.5	59.2	72.4	100.0	150.2	206.5
2000	59.9	75.0	100.0	147.3	188.6	61.0	75.2	100.0	153.0	201.9
2001	60.2	73.6	100.0	143.4	179.7	61.0	74.9	100.0	147.8	195.4
2002	60.8	74.5	100.0	147.5	189.0	60.0	73.2	100.0	149.6	208.3
2003	61.7	75.2	100.0	148.1	186.8	61.2	74.7	100.0	148.8	202.1
Manual women										
	KCHL	KCHM	KCHN	KCHO	KCHP	KCHQ	KCHR	KCHS	KCHT	KCHU
1996	68.8	82.2	100.0	122.3	154.4	72.0	84.7	100.0	121.6	147.0
1997	70.9	86.4	100.0	126.1	156.8	74.5	85.7	100.0	120.9	143.3
1998	69.4	84.7	100.0	123.5	149.4	70.2	87.7	100.0	124.8	143.5
1999	77.7	86.4	100.0	125.1	157.5	79.8	88.0	100.0	121.2	140.4
2000	73.9	84.0	100.0	123.1	144.8	77.5	85.4	100.0	116.3	140.1
2001	72.8	84.2	100.0	121.7	148.1	73.9	85.3	100.0	118.5	139.9
2002	73.0	84.4	100.0	121.6	153.2	76.6	85.2	100.0	119.9	140.2
2003	..	..	..	..	..	..	..	..	..	..
Non-manual women										
	KCHV	KCHW	KCHX	KCHY	KCHZ	KCIA	KCIB	KCIC	KCID	KCIE
1996	57.4	72.1	100.0	144.2	172.7	57.0	72.6	100.0	147.6	192.8
1997	58.9	74.3	100.0	143.4	177.7	57.3	73.8	100.0	146.7	197.7
1998	57.8	73.9	100.0	141.7	175.5	56.9	73.2	100.0	141.8	189.5
1999	57.9	73.1	100.0	141.5	173.2	57.2	73.7	100.0	147.1	188.7
2000	58.3	73.5	100.0	142.7	173.0	57.8	74.4	100.0	147.5	190.0
2001	58.9	74.2	100.0	143.9	167.3	58.1	74.0	100.0	144.6	179.7
2002	58.1	73.8	100.0	141.5	173.3	58.3	73.9	100.0	143.6	191.9
2003	..	..	..	..	..	..	..	..	..	..

1 See chapter text.
2 Data for 2003 has been coded using the Standard Occupational Classification 2000 which does not differentiate between manual and non-manual employees.

Sources: Department of Enterprise, Trade and Investment (Northern Ireland); 028 9052 9897

7.25 Average earnings by age group of full-time employees whose pay for the survey pay period was not affected by absence[1]: Great Britain

At April 2002

	Gross weekly earnings								Average weekly hours		Average hourly earnings excluding overtime pay
	Average		As a percentage of the median			As a percentage of the median		Percentage earning under £250			
	Total	Overtime pay	Lowest decile	Lower quartile	Median	Upper quartile	Highest decile		Total	Overtime	
	£	£	per cent	per cent	£	per cent	per cent				£
All males											
Under 18	169.5	8.8	56.0	77.4	159.7	125.3	156.5	90.2	40.8	1.4	4.1
18 to 20	251.3	17.5	68.8	82.6	228.0	124.5	159.2	61.5	41.0	2.1	6.0
21 to 24	341.4	19.6	66.1	79.2	302.8	130.2	165.6	29.4	40.7	1.9	8.2
25 to 29	448.9	21.8	60.3	75.5	391.8	132.7	172.8	13.4	40.5	2.0	11.0
30 to 39	544.1	26.9	58.2	74.0	455.0	136.7	192.5	7.5	41.0	2.2	13.3
40 to 49	589.6	27.9	56.2	72.0	483.8	138.9	198.4	6.8	40.9	2.3	14.5
50 to 59	551.3	26.0	56.0	71.4	453.2	141.0	201.1	9.3	41.0	2.2	13.5
60 to 64	438.3	26.6	61.2	77.1	358.1	137.7	191.6	17.7	41.9	2.6	10.4
All ages	520.6	25.6	55.9	72.3	427.9	140.4	198.7	12.0	40.9	2.2	12.8
Manual males											
Under 18	159.8	4.68	47.2	70.9	153.6	131.0	157.0	91.5	39.2	0.6	4.0
18 to 20	225.8	6.2	72.3	85.3	211.1	118.8	143.0	74.5	38.3	0.7	5.9
21 to 24	301.7	731	68.4	81.3	276.1	128.6	156.8	38.2	38.0	0.8	7.9
25 to 29	392.2	6.9	61.9	77.2	356.7	131.0	163.3	17.6	37.5	0.6	10.4
30 to 39	438.8	7.9	57.8	74.0	376.7	139.5	183.4	16.9	37.5	0.7	11.7
40 to 49	416.3	7.7	59.0	73.5	350.6	146.7	193.3	22.5	37.3	0.7	11.1
50 to 59	391.8	6.8	60.1	75.1	332.2	149.8	190.9	25.4	37.0	0.6	10.5
60 to 64	334.6	6.4	63.9	77.0	286.8	137.3	189.9	36.2	37.3	0.5	8.9
All ages	394.1	7.3	59.5	74.5	336.1	142.8	188.7	24.8	37.5	0.7	10.5
Non-manual males											
Under 18	..	..	..	..	..	..	..	..	..	..	..
18 to 20	243.7	10.7	71.9	83.4	226.8	121.5	149.7	64.4	39.3	1.4	6.12
21 to 24	353.8	11.6	66.4	79.4	302.1	130.1	171.8	29.8	39.1	1.2	8.81
25 to 29	493.4	15.1	58.3	75.0	423.2	133.9	185.0	10.8	39.0	1.2	12.63
30 to 39	626.9	15.5	55.7	73.6	517.0	137.3	198.6	5.6	39.0	1.1	16.07
40 to 49	688.5	14.7	54.0	74.3	569.5	135.1	200.9	4.5	38.8	1.0	17.83
50 to 59	666.6	11.8	51.4	71.8	550.0	138.1	199.5	6.4	38.8	0.9	17.21
60 to 64	564.4	11.1	55.4	73.1	430.1	141.7	223.1	11.9	39.4	1.0	14.11
All ages	606.8	14.0	51.3	70.5	499.0	138.7	201.9	9.2	38.9	1.1	15.59
All females											
Under 18	171.3	3.7	64.6	82.2	162.5	116.9	139.5	75.3	37.9	0.6	4.49
18 to 20	216.5	5.3	74.0	85.0	206.3	117.7	139.7	34.6	38.3	0.7	5.62
21 to 24	293.8	7.0	66.5	79.7	274.1	126.1	153.1	12.5	38.0	0.8	7.68
25 to 29	379.9	7.3	61.5	76.5	344.6	129.5	167.1	5.5	37.6	0.7	10.10
30 to 39	428.1	7.9	57.9	73.6	365.0	140.3	186.6	5.6	37.5	0.7	11.41
40 to 49	402.8	7.4	58.0	72.8	341.7	146.8	188.2	7.9	37.3	0.8	10.80
50 to 59	374.6	6.7	60.0	74.8	318.7	148.9	188.9	9.7	37.1	0.7	10.04
60 to 64	324.8	6.0	66.2	80.2	269.0	135.6	200.3	14.8	37.5	0.7	8.60
All ages	381.1	7.2	59	74.2	325.7	142.0	188.2	9.2	37.5	0.7	10.15
Manual females											
Under 18	162.7	5.5	69.8	85.6	154.4	126.2	156.4	73.7	39.2	1.0	4.12
18 to 20	196.4	5.5	74.6	84.8	187.7	117.4	142.0	52.7	39.3	0.9	4.99
21 to 24	236.0	11.2	72.7	81.2	217.5	127.9	150.3	33.9	39.8	1.4	5.87
25 to 29	267.4	14.8	65.7	77.1	249.2	127.1	161.9	23.5	39.8	1.8	6.67
30 to 39	268.9	13.8	68.0	80.5	247.8	127.2	156.6	20.4	39.7	1.7	6.72
40 to 49	253.0	16.3	70.5	81.4	231.3	126.6	159.8	26.0	39.9	2.0	6.26
50 to 59	243.5	13.7	71.8	82.9	223.7	126.1	156.4	28.3	39.5	1.7	6.08
60 to 64	231.3	9.7	75.7	85.7	213.0	121.8	148.8	32.0	39.0	1.4	5.90
All ages	249.8	13.6	70.0	81.2	193.6	126.7	159.3	27.8	39.7	1.7	6.23
Non-manual females											
Under 18	174.2	3.1	62.4	83.4	163.2	115.9	136.4	75.9	37.5	0.5	4.63
18 to 20	221.8	5.2	74.2	86.2	211.5	117.7	139.2	29.8	38.0	0.7	5.79
21 to 24	301.9	6.4	67.9	80.4	282.2	125.8	151.4	9.5	37.7	0.7	7.96
25 to 29	391.9	6.5	62.8	77.3	355.1	129.4	166.1	3.6	37.3	0.6	10.48
30 to 39	451.2	7.1	59.0	74.3	387.4	138.1	183.0	3.4	37.2	0.6	12.12
40 to 49	428.7	5.8	57.8	72.3	369.4	142.3	182.2	4.7	36.8	0.5	11.64
50 to 59	401.6	5.2	60.1	74.6	347.5	146.1	181.6	5.8	36.6	0.5	10.91
60 to 64	357.6	4.7	65.8	80.4	297.2	136.8	191.6	8.8	36.9	0.5	9.61
All ages	402.8	6.2	59.6	74.3	261.7	141.4	183.5	6.1	37.1	0.6	10.84

1 See chapter text.

Source: New Earnings Survey, Office for National Statistics: 01633 819024

7.26 Trade unions[1]
United Kingdom
At end of year

Percentages

		1991	1992	1993	1994	1995	1996	1997	1998	1999	2000	2001
Number of trade unions	KCLB	306	315	302	281	271	261	257	243	241	230	220
Analysis by number of members:												
Under 100 members	KCLC	15.7	14.3	15.9	16.4	15.5	13.0	16.0	16.9	18.7	22.2	19.1
100 and under 500	KCLD	23.2	22.9	24.8	23.1	23.2	27.2	22.2	21.4	20.3	17.8	18.6
500 and under 1,000	KCLE	6.9	9.8	7.6	8.9	10.0	8.0	12.1	10.7	9.5	9.6	11.4
1,000 and under 2,500	KCLF	17.0	17.1	15.2	15.3	15.1	17.2	14.8	13.2	14.1	12.2	10.0
2,500 and under 5,000	KCLG	9.5	8.9	8.9	9.3	8.9	7.7	7.8	9.5	9.5	9.1	11.4
5,000 and under 10,000	KCLH	5.9	6.0	6.3	6.4	5.9	5.7	5.8	6.2	5.4	5.7	4.5
10,000 and under 15,000	KCLI	1.6	1.6	2.0	2.1	3.0	2.7	2.7	2.1	1.7	1.7	2.7
15,000 and under 25,000	KCLJ	3.3	3.8	3.0	2.8	2.6	2.3	2.3	2.9	4.1	5.2	5.9
25,000 and under 50,000	KCLK	7.2	6.3	7.0	7.1	7.4	7.7	7.4	8.2	7.9	7.0	6.8
50,000 and under 100,000	KCLL	2.3	2.9	3.0	2.5	2.6	1.9	2.3	2.5	2.1	2.6	2.3
100,000 and under 250,000	KCLM	4.6	3.5	3.3	3.6	3.0	3.1	3.1	2.5	2.1	2.2	2.3
250,000 and over	KCLN	2.9	2.9	3.0	2.5	3.0	3.4	3.5	4.1	4.6	4.8	5.0
All sizes	KCLP	100	100	100	100	100	100	100	100	100	100	100
Membership												
Analysis by size of union:												
Under 100 members	KCLQ	–	–	–	–	–	–	–	–	–	–	–
100 and under 500	KCLR	0.2	0.2	0.2	0.2	0.2	0.3	0.2	0.2	0.2	0.2	0.2
500 and under 1,000	KCLS	0.2	0.2	0.2	0.2	0.2	0.2	0.3	0.2	0.2	0.2	0.2
1,000 and under 2,500	KCLT	0.9	1.0	0.9	0.9	0.9	0.9	0.8	0.7	0.7	0.6	0.5
2,500 and under 5,000	KCLU	1.1	1.1	1.1	1.1	1.1	0.9	0.9	1.1	1.1	0.9	1.2
5,000 and under 10,000	KCLV	1.3	1.5	1.5	1.6	1.4	1.3	1.3	1.4	1.2	1.2	0.9
10,000 and under 15,000	KCLW	0.6	0.6	0.8	0.9	1.3	1.2	1.1	0.9	0.7	0.6	0.9
15,000 and under 25,000	KCLX	1.8	2.3	1.8	1.7	1.5	1.3	1.3	1.6	2.3	2.8	3.3
25,000 and under 50,000	KCLY	8.3	8.0	8.6	8.9	9.1	8.8	8.1	8.4	8.2	7.1	6.8
50,000 and under 100,000	KCLZ	4.9	7.0	7.3	5.9	5.9	3.9	4.5	4.5	3.8	4.6	4.0
100,000 and under 250,000	KCMA	22.9	18.6	18.2	19.3	16.3	15.2	15.3	11.9	9.9	9.8	9.5
250,000 and over	KCMB	57.8	59.4	59.2	59.3	62.0	66.0	66.1	69.1	71.7	72.0	72.5
All sizes	KCMC	100	100	100	100	100	100	100	100	100	100	100
Total membership (thousands)	KCMD	9 555	9 171	8 848	8 297	8 111	7 982	7 841	7 894	7 940	7 823	7 796

1 See chapter text.

Source: Department of Trade and Industry: 020 7215 5780

7.27 Vacancies at jobcentres in the United Kingdom[1]
Seasonally adjusted

Thousands

	January	February	March	April	May	June	July	August	September	October	November	December
Numbers of vacancies remaining unfilled DPCB												
1991	140.0	138.9	133.9	119.8	110.2	105.6	106.0	109.2	112.5	109.6	111.8	117.4
1992	117.0	118.2	118.2	117.1	118.8	119.8	120.2	118.6	113.1	112.9	114.4	117.0
1993	119.0	120.3	124.3	123.6	125.9	124.8	129.2	129.8	129.5	133.2	136.3	138.2
1994	140.4	142.7	143.4	146.2	149.1	154.9	158.8	165.0	165.4	175.3	176.9	177.6
1995	175.2	174.3	177.5	186.0	185.4	182.9	181.8	181.7	184.5	181.7	185.2	186.7
1996	190.4	189.3	196.9	201.2	209.2	220.7	233.0	238.8	247.4	248.7	257.5	265.5
1997	272.6	279.2	279.6	279.4	277.3	283.9	288.0	295.2	297.2	293.7	275.2	278.2
1998	275.0	285.0	286.3	288.2	298.1	300.1	302.8	302.7	301.5	302.9	304.4	303.2
1999	305.3	300.8	298.5	295.7	304.6	305.6	307.8	315.8	314.7	336.5	338.5	347.4
2000	340.3	341.7	344.6	355.7	354.3	357.2	362.9	361.6	365.6	364.5	374.3	376.5
2001	395.7	391.6	394.9	387.8	..	..	..	..	..	..	..	..
Inflow of vacancies DRYW												
1991	185.4	167.8	168.0	182.8	182.2	163.9	165.6	168.7	170.7	168.3	164.9	167.1
1992	166.4	166.9	171.7	166.0	166.2	176.4	173.3	164.0	167.1	171.3	164.7	173.8
1993	180.2	175.9	181.5	179.3	180.2	183.5	190.5	183.4	191.5	189.6	193.9	197.2
1994	199.2	199.5	199.1	203.7	205.2	212.2	208.3	223.6	216.6	219.1	223.1	226.8
1995	218.2	219.5	215.2	205.4	227.7	223.1	225.6	230.9	226.5	231.9	232.9	222.1
1996	228.9	222.2	219.8	231.7	221.4	219.5	224.4	223.1	221.7	203.4	230.2	232.8
1997	202.9	239.3	242.9	239.1	236.2	226.2	226.4	220.8	227.6	222.6	217.9	216.2
1998	184.2	218.5	219.2	216.3	218.2	225.0	222.0	221.4	221.8	229.9	223.1	219.4
1999	237.7	222.8	221.8	229.6	224.4	226.2	231.2	234.0	230.2	235.0	235.3	236.7
2000	227.9	226.1	228.8	225.3	213.2	222.3	220.6	219.0	225.6	221.3	220.2	222.8
2001	224.9	233.2	232.8	237.6	..	..	..	..	..	..	..	..
Outflow of vacancies DRZL												
1991	176.4	168.7	172.4	197.5	197.1	168.3	165.0	164.9	168.7	170.2	159.9	160.8
1992	169.7	165.6	170.5	168.4	168.6	174.1	172.5	164.1	170.5	169.8	160.8	170.6
1993	178.8	173.6	176.6	180.1	181.0	184.0	185.6	182.0	189.8	186.4	191.0	195.3
1994	196.8	196.7	198.3	202.3	203.4	205.8	202.8	217.1	214.8	210.8	221.6	227.0
1995	219.0	220.6	214.1	195.1	229.0	225.0	224.6	230.4	225.5	237.1	229.7	219.2
1996	225.6	222.1	213.8	222.7	212.9	211.1	214.3	218.4	213.9	200.9	220.9	229.8
1997	208.5	232.1	238.0	236.8	234.1	220.9	225.0	215.0	216.8	224.2	232.5	219.9
1998	207.2	208.7	213.1	214.0	209.0	222.3	219.3	221.2	218.5	228.7	220.4	223.5
1999	236.9	224.4	220.9	232.3	219.4	225.2	227.6	226.5	229.0	219.6	233.6	231.1
2000	240.6	223.6	224.1	218.9	213.9	218.6	214.6	219.2	221.8	217.1	211.8	220.4
2001	212.1	237.6	226.1	241.1	..	..	..	..	..	..	..	..
Number of placings DTQR												
1991	129.4	122.5	127.6	148.4	148.4	123.9	123.2	120.9	122.1	122.7	114.8	115.9
1992	124.6	119.7	123.6	122.6	123.0	126.5	126.5	119.6	125.9	127.6	120.6	130.2
1993	134.3	132.1	131.7	134.0	134.9	136.3	139.0	136.1	144.1	140.6	146.4	148.2
1994	149.5	150.6	151.5	156.6	157.7	161.9	157.7	169.6	166.4	162.3	170.3	173.2
1995	166.2	169.1	164.6	145.8	179.8	173.6	174.4	178.5	172.5	183.5	179.7	167.4
1996	176.1	164.6	151.5	152.8	151.6	148.2	149.7	153.6	148.9	135.4	150.4	159.3
1997	147.9	157.7	163.6	164.0	151.8	143.1	138.6	127.1	126.4	123.1	120.2	116.9
1998	109.0	113.9	115.5	114.1	110.5	115.9	115.8	116.4	117.8	121.4	118.0	117.2
1999	119.8	120.3	116.7	126.5	118.1	121.0	123.0	121.8	122.7	120.3	123.1	122.6
2000	121.1	116.4	115.7	111.4	108.1	109.5	107.3	109.9	111.3	109.9	107.1	108.4
2001	110.2	108.6	109.1	117.5	..	..	..	..	..	..	..	..

1 See chapter text.

Sources: Jobcentre Plus administrative system;
Office for National Statistics: 020 7533 6094

8 Personal income, expenditure and wealth

Personal income, expenditure and wealth

Distribution of total incomes *(Table 8.1)*

The information shown in Table 8.2 comes from the Survey of Personal Incomes for the financial years 1997/98, 1998/99 & 2000/01. This is an annual survey that covers approximately 200,000 individuals across the whole of the UK. It is based on administrative data held by Inland Revenue offices on individuals who could be liable to tax.

The table relates only to those individuals who are taxpayers. The distributions cover only incomes as computed for tax purposes and above a level which for each year corresponds approximately to the single person's allowance. Incomes below these levels are not shown because the information about them is incomplete.

Investment income from which tax has been deducted at source is not always known to local tax offices. Estimates of missing bank and building society interest and dividends from United Kingdom companies are included in these tables. The missing investment income is distributed, in a manner consistent with information from the Expenditure and Food Survey and the National Accounts, to individuals for whom there is no investment income already reported by the tax office.

Superannuation contributions are estimated and included in total income. They have been distributed among earners in the Survey of Personal Incomes sample by a method consistent with information about the number of employees who are contracted in or out of the State Earnings Related Pension Scheme and the proportion of their earnings contributed.

When comparing results of these surveys across years, it should be noted that the Survey of Personal Incomes is not a longitudinal survey. However, sample sizes have increased in recent years to increase precision.

Estimates of self employment income in the annual surveys for 1996/97 to 1998/99 are incomplete due to the absence of data from a limited number of sole trader sources. The deficiency is estimated to be worth about ½ per cent of total income.

Withdrawal of the 1999/00 data from the Survey of Personal Incomes *(Table 8.1)*

Estimates based on the 1999-2000 Survey of Personal Incomes (SPI) have been withdrawn temporarily. The extraction of information for that survey from the Self Assessment (SA) business system was incomplete leading to some components of income being missed. Revised estimates will be issued as soon as possible after the publication of results based on the 2001-02 SPI due in the first quarter of 2004. Published estimates for 2000-01 and later years are based on the 2000-01 SPI and are not affected.

Average incomes of households *(Table 8.2)*

Original income is the total income in cash of all the members of the household before the deduction of taxes or the addition of state benefits. It includes income from employment, self-employment, investment income, etc. The addition of cash benefits (retirement pensions, child benefit, etc) and the deduction of income

tax, council tax, water charges, domestic rates and employees' national insurance contributions give disposable income. By further allowing for taxes paid on goods and services purchased, such as VAT, an estimate of "post-tax" income is derived. These income figures are derived from estimates made by the Office for National Statistics, based largely on information from the Expenditure and Food Survey (EFS), and published each year in *Economic Trends,* and, from 2002, available on the National Statistics website.

A retired household is defined as one where the combined income of retired members amounts to at least half the total gross income of the household, where a retired person is defined as anyone who describes themselves as "retired" or anyone over the minimum NI pension age describing themselves as "unoccupied" or "sick or injured but not intending to seek work."

Children are defined as persons aged under 16 or aged between 16 and 18, unmarried and receiving full-time non-advanced further education.

Expenditure and Food Survey
(Tables 8.3 - 8.5)

The Expenditure and Food Survey (formerly the Family Expenditure Survey), introduced in 1957, covers all types of private households in the United Kingdom. It is a continuous survey with fieldwork carried out in every month of the year. In 2002-03 around 6,900 households in the UK provided information. The main purpose of the survey is to provide a source for the weighting pattern for the Index of Retail Prices, so it is primarily concerned with household expenditure on goods and services. However, it does have several other important uses.

Although the survey is primarily concerned with the expenditure of private households, much additional information is collected about income and the characteristics of co-operating households. Consequently, the survey provides a unique fund of important economic and social data.

Like all surveys based on a sample of the population, its results are subject to sampling error, and to some bias due to non-response.

The results of the survey are published in an annual report, the latest being *'Family Spending 2002-2003'*. The report includes a list of definitions used in the survey, items on which information is collected and a brief account of the fieldwork procedure.

8.1 Distribution of total incomes before and after tax
United Kingdom
Years ended 5 April

| | 1997/98 Annual Survey | | | | | 1998/99 Annual Survey | | | |
| | Number of individuals (000s) | £ million | | | | Number of individuals (000s) | £ million | | |
		Total income before tax	Total tax	Total income after tax			Total income before tax	Total tax	Total income after tax
Lower limit of range of income					**Lower limit of range of income**				
All incomes[1]	26 200	461 000	79 500	381 100	All incomes[1]	26 900	498 000	88 000	409 000
Income before tax £					**Income before tax £**				
4 045	509	2 170	21	2 150	4 195	322	1 400	9	1 390
4 500	560	2 660	74	2 580	4 500	552	2 620	57	2 560
5 000	678	3 580	127	3 450	5 000	580	3 050	112	2 930
5 500	841	4 840	190	4 650	5 500	873	5 030	183	4 850
6 000	1 640	10 700	600	10 100	6 000	1 640	10 600	561	10 100
7 000	1 540	11 600	820	10 800	7 000	1 560	11 700	821	10 900
8 000	3 050	27 400	2 440	25 000	8 000	3 120	28 000	2 400	25 600
10 000	2 850	31 200	3 520	27 700	10 000	2 730	30 000	3 290	26 700
12 000	3 530	47 500	6 270	41 200	12 000	3 650	49 100	6 290	42 800
15 000	4 260	73 800	11 100	62 700	15 000	4 460	77 200	11 400	65 800
20 000	4 260	102 700	17 200	85 500	20 000	4 460	107 600	17 900	89 700
30 000	1 730	63 700	13 100	50 600	30 000	2 060	75 900	15 300	60 600
50 000	582	38 400	10 600	27 700	50 000	702	46 400	12 800	33 600
100 000	135	18 000	5 850	12 100	100 000	160	21 300	6 940	14 300
200 000 and over	51	22 400	7 560	14 900	200 000 and over	62	27 600	9 980	17 700
Income after tax £					**Income after tax £**				
4 045	629	2 710	33	2 680	4 195	394	1 730	14	1 710
4 500	683	3 350	112	3 240	4 500	701	3 420	91	3 330
5 000	812	4 470	186	4 280	5 000	725	3 990	175	3 810
5 500	1 000	6 050	281	5 770	5 500	1 010	6 060	260	5 800
6 000	1 960	13 600	885	12 700	6 000	1 990	13 700	839	12 900
7 000	1 900	15 600	1 270	14 300	7 000	1 840	15 000	1 210	13 800
8 000	3 750	37 600	3 840	33 800	8 000	3 740	37 100	3 630	33 500
10 000	3 230	40 500	5 100	35 400	10 000	3 280	41 000	5 010	36 000
12 000	3 760	58 800	8 390	50 400	12 000	3 940	61 600	8 610	53 000
15 000	4 030	82 800	13 300	69 500	15 000	4 220	86 400	13 600	72 800
20 000	3 070	89 100	15 900	73 200	20 000	3 390	98 800	17 500	81 300
30 000	1 030	50 100	12 300	37 900	30 000	1 250	60 400	14 500	45 900
50 000	291	27 700	8 460	19 200	50 000	352	33 400	10 200	23 200
100 000	63	12 800	4 350	8 420	100 000	76	15 400	5 290	10 100
200 000 and over	23	15 500	5 150	10 400	200 000 and over	28	19 300	7 060	12 300

8.1 continued
Distribution of total incomes before and after tax
United Kingdom
Years ended 5 April

	2000/01 Annual Survey			
	Number of individuals (000s)	£ million		
		Total income before tax	Total tax	Total income after tax
Lower limit of range of income				
All incomes[1]	29 300	594 700	105 600	489 100
Income before tax £				
4 385	786	3 690	23	3 660
5 000	1 360	7 470	139	7 330
6 000	3 270	22 800	986	21 800
8 000	2 960	26 700	2 070	24 600
10 000	2 740	30 200	3 030	27 100
12 000	2 590	33 600	3 950	29 700
14 000	2 340	35 100	4 540	30 500
16 000	2 040	34 600	4 730	29 900
18 000	1 750	33 300	4 850	28 400
20 000	5 400	131 000	20 800	110 200
30 000	2 780	103 500	19 700	83 800
50 000	961	65 500	16 900	46 600
100 000	216	28 800	9 150	19 600
200 000 and over	88	40 600	14 700	25 900
Income after tax £				
4 385	891	4 220	30	4 190
5 000	1 490	8 390	175	8 210
6 000	3 980	29 300	1 540	27 800
8 000	3 560	35 200	3 160	32 000
10 000	3 370	41 700	4 730	37 000
12 000	2 940	43 800	5 650	38 100
14 000	2 490	43 300	6 020	37 300
16 000	2 060	41 100	6 080	35 000
18 000	1 630	36 500	5 640	30 800
20 000	4 410	127 500	21 300	106 200
30 000	1 820	86 400	19 500	66 900
50 000	502	46 500	13 800	32 800
100 000	105	21 200	7 100	14 100
200 000 and over	43	29 700	10 900	18 900

1 See chapter text. All figures have been independently rounded.

Source: Board of Inland Revenue: 020 7438 4335

8.2 Average incomes of households before and after taxes and benefits[1], 2001/02
United Kingdom

	Retired households		Non-retired households								
	1 adult	2 or more adults	1 adult	2 adults	3 or more adults	1 adult with children	2 adults with 1 child	2 adults with 2 children	2 adults with 3 or more children	3 or more adults with children	All house-holds
Number of households in the population (thousands)	3 373	3 025	3 649	5 343	2 226	1 322	1 891	2 254	847	956	24 888
Average per household (£ per year)											
Original income	4 854	10 166	17 708	35 223	41 970	8 687	36 448	40 179	31 342	37 284	25 176
Disposable income	9 288	15 592	15 203	28 476	35 413	13 286	29 766	33 251	28 475	34 158	22 925
Post-tax income	7 754	12 297	12 412	23 280	28 236	10 354	24 412	27 469	22 562	27 205	18 595

1 See chapter text. Redistribution of Income, included in the Effects of taxes and benefits on household income, 2001/02, analysis published on the National Statistics website.

Source: Office for National Statistics: 020 7533 5772

8.3 Sources of gross household income[1]
United Kingdom

		1992	1993	1994 /95	1995 /96	1996 /97	1997 /98	1998[2] /99	1999[2] /00	2000[2] /01	2001[2] /02	2002[2] /03
Number of households supplying data	KPDA	7 418	6 979	6 853	6 797	6 415	6 409	6 630	7 097	6 637	7 473	6 927
Average weekly household income by source (£)												
Wages and salaries	KPCB	222.70	228.30	237.90	245.00	256.30	280.20	309.20	315.40	336.70	376.80	373.90
Self-employment	KPCC	29.60	29.20	35.30	32.90	37.50	32.90	37.20	46.00	44.50	43.80	44.50
Investments	KPCD	20.80	18.00	16.20	18.10	17.80	18.70	18.80	21.80	20.00	19.60	18.80
Annuities and pensions (other than social security benefits)	KPCE	19.60	21.90	23.50	26.00	26.00	28.90	30.30	32.80	35.00	36.10	39.90
Social security benefits	KPCF	45.00	48.90	49.90	52.40	54.10	55.00	55.80	58.00	60.10	63.50	68.50
Other sources	KPCH	5.20	6.70	6.50	6.60	5.30	5.20	5.70	5.90	6.20	6.70	6.70
Total	KPCI	342.90	353.00	369.30	380.90	396.90	420.80	457.00	479.90	502.50	546.50	552.30
Sources of household income as a percentage of total household income												
Wages and salaries	KPCJ	65	65	64	64	65	67	68	66	67	69	68
Self-employment	KPCK	9	8	10	9	9	8	8	10	9	8	8
Investments	KPCL	6	5	4	5	5	4	4	5	4	4	3
Annuities and pensions (other than social security benefits)	KPCM	6	6	6	7	7	7	7	7	7	7	7
Social security benefits	KPCN	13	14	14	14	14	13	12	12	12	12	12
Other sources	KPCP	2	2	2	2	1	1	1	1	1	1	1
Total	KPCQ	100	100	100	100	100	100	100	100	100	100	100

1 See chapter text.
2 Income based on weighted data.

Source: Expenditure and Food Survey, Office for National Statistics: 020 7533 5755

8.4 Households and their expenditure at current prices[1]
United Kingdom

		1992	1993	1994 /95	1995 /96	1996 /97	1997 /98	1998[2] /99	1999[2] /00	2000[2] /01	2001[2] /02	2002[2] /03
Number of households supplying data	KPDA	7 418	6 979	6 853	6 797	6 415	6 409	6 630	7 097	6 637	7 473	6 927

Average weekly household expenditure on commodities and services (£)

		1992	1993	1994 /95	1995 /96	1996 /97	1997 /98	1998[2] /99	1999[2] /00	2000[2] /01	2001[2] /02	2002[2] /03
Housing	KPEV	47.40	44.90	46.40	48.30	49.10	51.50	57.20	57.00	63.90	66.60	66.70
Fuel and power	KPEW	13.00	13.20	13.00	12.90	13.40	12.70	11.70	11.30	11.90	11.70	11.70
Food	KPEX	47.70	50.00	50.40	52.90	55.20	55.90	58.90	59.60	61.90	62.30	64.30
Alcoholic drink	KPEY	11.10	12.00	12.30	11.40	12.40	13.30	14.00	15.30	15.00	14.60	14.80
Tobacco	KPEZ	5.40	5.60	5.60	5.80	6.10	6.10	5.80	6.00	6.10	5.60	5.40
Clothing and footwear	KCWC	16.40	17.40	17.10	17.20	18.30	20.00	21.70	21.00	22.00	22.50	22.00
Household goods	KCWH	21.90	23.10	22.70	23.50	26.70	26.90	29.60	30.70	32.60	33.10	33.80
Household services	KCWI	13.40	15.40	15.10	15.10	16.40	17.90	18.90	18.90	22.00	23.80	23.30
Personal goods and services	KCWJ	10.20	11.00	10.80	11.60	11.60	12.50	13.30	13.90	14.70	14.90	15.20
Motoring expenditure	KCWK	35.70	36.30	36.20	37.00	41.20	46.60	51.70	52.60	55.10	58.50	61.70
Fares and other travel costs	KCWL	7.20	7.00	6.60	6.20	7.50	8.10	8.30	9.20	9.50	9.50	9.70
Leisure goods	KCWM	13.30	13.30	13.40	13.20	15.20	16.40	17.80	18.50	19.70	19.90	20.50
Leisure services	KCWN	27.60	25.60	31.20	32.10	34.00	38.80	41.90	43.90	50.60	52.30	53.60
Miscellaneous	KCWO	1.80	2.10	2.30	2.40	2.20	2.00	1.20	1.40	0.70	1.90	2.00
Total	KCWP	271.80	276.70	283.60	289.90	309.10	328.80	352.20	359.40	385.70	397.20	404.70

Expenditure on commodity or service as a percentage of total expenditure

		1992	1993	1994 /95	1995 /96	1996 /97	1997 /98	1998[2] /99	1999[2] /00	2000[2] /01	2001[2] /02	2002[2] /03
Housing	KPFH	17	16	16	17	16	16	16	16	17	17	16
Fuel and power	KPFI	5	5	5	5	4	4	3	3	3	3	3
Food	KPFJ	18	18	18	18	18	17	17	17	16	16	16
Alcoholic drink	KPFK	4	4	4	4	4	4	4	4	4	4	4
Tobacco	KPFL	2	2	2	2	2	2	2	2	2	1	1
Clothing and footwear	KPFM	6	6	6	6	6	6	6	6	6	6	5
Household goods	KCWQ	8	8	8	8	9	8	8	9	8	8	8
Household services	KCWR	5	6	5	5	5	5	5	5	6	6	6
Personal goods and services	KCWS	4	4	4	4	4	4	4	4	4	4	4
Motoring expenditure	KCWT	13	13	13	13	13	14	15	15	14	15	15
Fares and other travel costs	KCWU	3	3	2	2	2	3	2	3	2	2	2
Leisure goods	KCWV	5	5	5	5	5	5	5	5	5	5	5
Leisure services	KCWW	10	9	11	11	11	12	12	12	13	13	13
Miscellaneous	KPFR	1	1	1	1	1	1	–	–	–	–	–
Total	KPFS	100	100	100	100	100	100	100	100	100	100	100

1 See chapter text.
2 Averages based on grossed number of households. Expenditure based on weighted data and including children's expenditure.

Source: Expenditure and Food Survey, Office for National Statistics: 020 7533 5755

8.5 Availability in households of certain durable goods[1]
United Kingdom

Percentage

		1992	1993	1994 /95	1995 /96	1996 /97	1997 /98	1998[2] /99	1999[2] /00	2000[2] /01	2001[2] /02	2002[2] /03
Number of households supplying data	KPDA	7 418	6 979	6 853	6 797	6 415	6 409	6 630	7 097	6 637	7 473	6 927
Car	KPDB	68	69	69	70	69	70	72	71	72	74	74
One	KPDC	45	46	45	47	43	44	44	43	44	44	44
Two	KPDD	19	19	20	19	22	21	23	21	22	24	25
Three or more	KPDE	4	4	4	4	5	5	5	6	6	6	6
Central heating, full or partial	KPDF	82	83	84	85	87	89	89	90	91	92	93
Washing machine	KPDG	88	89	89	91	91	91	92	91	92	93	94
Refrigerator or fridge/freezer	KPDH	99	99	99	99	..	..	..	..	..	..	..
Fridge/freezer or deep freezer	KPDI	84	87	86	87	91	90	92	91	94	95	96
Refrigerator	KPDJ	..	..	..	..	49	51	52	53	..	..	..
Dishwasher	GPTL	..	..	18	20	20	22	23	23	25	27	29
Television	KPDK	98	..	..	..	..	..	..	..	..	..	..
Telephone	KPDL	88	90	91	92	93	94	95	95	93	94	94
Home computer	KPDM	19	..	..	..	27	29	33	38	44	50	55
Video recorder	KPDN	69	73	76	79	82	84	85	86	87	90	90
Internet access	ZBUZ	..	..	..	..	..	..	10	19	32	40	45

1 See chapter text.
2 Percentages based on grossed number of households.

Source: Expenditure and Food Survey, Office for National Statistics: 020 7533 5755

9 Health

Health

Hospital and family health services *(Table 9.1)*
The courses of treatment are for the General Dental Services (GDS). A course of treatment is complete when the treatment that is required – or such of it that the patient is willing to undergo – has been carried out. A dentist in accepting a patient for continuing care (adults) or capitation (children), undertakes to provide the care and treatment necessary to secure and maintain oral health.

Deaths: analysed by cause *(Table 9.5)*
All figures in this table for England and Wales represent the number of deaths **occurring** in each calendar year. All data for Scotland and Northern Ireland relate to the number of deaths **registered** during each calendar year. From 2001, all three constituent countries of the United Kingdom are coding their causes of death using the latest, tenth, revision of the International Statistical Classification of Diseases and Related Health Problems (ICD-10). All cause of death information from 2001 (also for 2000 for Scotland) presented in this table is based on the revised classification.

To assist users in assessing any discontinuities arising from the introduction of the revised classification, bridge-coding exercises were carried out on all deaths registered in 1999 in England and Wales and also in Scotland. For further information about ICD-10 and the bridge-coding carried out by The Office for National Statistics, see the ONS Report: Results of the ICD-10 bridge-coding study, England and Wales, 1999. *Health Statistics Quarterly* 14 (2002), pages 75-83 or log on to the National Statistics website at: *www.statistics.gov.uk*. For information on the Scottish bridge-coding exercise, consult the Annual Report of the General Register Office for Scotland or log on to their website at: *www.gro-scotland.gov.uk*. No bridge-coding exercise was conducted for Northern Ireland.

Neonatal deaths and homicide and assault
For England and Wales, neonatal deaths (those at age under 28 days) are included in the number of total deaths but excluded from the cause figures. This has particular impact on the totals shown for the chapters covered by the ranges P and Q, 'Conditions originating in the perinatal period' and 'Congenital malformations, deformations and chromosomal abnormalities'. These are considerably lower than the actual number of deaths because it is not possible to assign an underlying cause of death from the neonatal death certificate used in England and Wales.

Also, for England and Wales only, the total number shown for Homicide and assault, X85-Y09, will not be a true representation because the registration of these deaths is often delayed by adjourned inquests.

Occupational ill health *(Tables 9.7 and 9.8)*
There are a number of sources of data on the extent of occupational or work-related ill health in Great Britain. For some potentially severe lung diseases caused by exposures which are highly unlikely to be found in a non-occupational setting, it is useful to count the number of death certificates issued each year. This is also true for mesothelioma, a cancer affecting the lining of the lungs and stomach, for which the number of cases with non-occupational causes is likely to be larger (although still a minority). **Table 9.8** shows the number of deaths for *mesothelioma* and *asbestosis* (linked to exposure to asbestos), *pneumoconiosis* (linked to coal dust or silica), *byssinosis* (linked to cotton dust) and some forms of *allergic alveolitis* (including farmer's lung). For asbestos-related diseases the figures are derived from a special register maintained by HSE.

Most conditions which can be caused or made worse by work can also arise from other factors. The remaining sources of data on work-related ill health rely on *attribution* of individual cases of illness to work causes. In The Health and Occupation Reporting Network (THOR, formerly known as ODIN), this is done by specialist doctors - either occupational physicians or those working in particular disease specialisms (covering musculoskeletal, psychological, respiratory, skin, audiological and infectious disease). **Table 9.6** presents data from THOR for the last three years. It should be noted that not all cases of occupational disease will be seen by participating specialists; for example, the number of deaths due to mesothelioma (shown in Table 9.8) is known to be greater than the number of cases reported to ODIN.

Injuries at work *(Table 9.9)*
The appropriate 'responsible person' is required to report injuries arising from workplace activities to HSE or the local authority under the Reporting of Injuries, Diseases and Dangerous Occurrences Regulations 1995 (RIDDOR 95). This includes fatal injuries, non-fatal major injuries, as defined by the Regulations, and other injuries causing incapacity for work for more than 3 days. As of 1 April 2001, reports are to be made to an Incident Centre (ICC), based at Caerphilly.

HSE gets to know about virtually all workplace fatalities. However, it is known that employers and others do not report all non-fatal reportable injuries. To estimate the level of under-reporting by employers, HSE place questions each year with the Labour Force Survey (LFS), asking respondents if they have suffered a workplace injury in the past year.

The results from the LFS show that in Great Britain employers now report 42 per cent of reportable injuries. LFS results are indicating that the rate of improvement in non-fatal injury rates is slowing more recently. The self-employed report fewer that 1 in 20 reportable injuries.

9.1 Hospital and family health services
England and Wales

	Code	Units	England 1998	1999	2000	2001	2002	Code	Wales 1998	1999	2000	2001	2002
Hospital services[1]													
Average daily number of available beds	KNMY	Thousands	190	186	186	185	184	KNHY	14.9	14.7	14.6	14.4	14.3
Average daily occupation of beds:													
All departments	KNMX	"	157	154	156	157	157	KNHX	11.8	11.8	11.7	11.7	11.8
Psychiatric departments	KNMW	"	37	34	34	..	..	KNGZ	2.7	2.6	2.5	2.5	2.4
Persons waiting for admission at 31 March[2]	KNMV	"	1 298	1 037	1 007	1 035	992	KNGY	61.8	75.5	61.1	65.6	74.6
Finished consultant episodes													
Day case admissions	KNLY	"	3 421	3 593	3 629	3 592	..	KNBZ	126.2	121.9	133.4	130.0	109.4
Ordinary admissions	KIBS	"	8 563	8 604	8 636	8 761	..	KNEO	522.7	515.1	513.8	509.4	493.0
Out-patients													
New cases	KNLX	"	11 778	12 136	12 466	12 714	13 032	KNBY	691.4	694.1	698.9	697.1	737.3
Total attendances	KNLW	"	42 154	43 041	43 569	44 008	44 598	KNBX	2 678.4	2 706.2	2 736.8	2 761.9	2 842.5
Accident and Emergency:													
New cases	KOTH	"	12 811	13 167	12 953	12 853	12 945	KTCO	831.0	868.0	853.7	877.7	888.7
Total attendances	KOTI	"	14 280	14 629	14 293	14 044	14 046	KTCP	982.0	1 026.4	986.2	1 009.8	1 004.7
Ward attendances	KOTJ	"	1 068	1 073	1 078	1 089	1 179	KTCQ	..	..	..	..	..
Family health services[3]													
Medical services:													
Doctors on the list[4]	KNKX	Numbers	..	..	..	..	..	KNBR	1 749	1 761	1 775	1 785	1 782
Number of UPEs[5]	LQZZ		27 392	27 591	27 704	27 843	28 031	ZCMA	1 751	1 767	1 880	1 796	1 793
Number of patients per doctor	KNKW	"	1 866	1 845	1,853	1 841	1 838	KNBQ	1 713	1 694	1 695	1 685	1 704
Paid to doctors[6]	KNKV	£ millions	3 242	3 348	..	..	..	KNBP	186	201	213	222	..
Pharmaceutical services:[7,8]													
Number of prescription forms	KWUK	Millions	291	294	300	315	326	VQEU	..	..	..	..	23
Number of prescription items	KWUL	"	513	530	552	587	617	KNBO	41	42	44	47	49
Total cost	KWUM	£ millions	5 231	5 620	5 967	6 488	7 162	KNBN	373	404	434	472	..
Average total cost per prescription	KWUN	£	10.2	10.6	10.8	11.1	11.6	KNBK	9.0	10.0	10.0	10.0	..
Income from patients	KWUO	£ millions	341	367	387	408	423	KNBM	20	22	23	23	..
Dental services[9]:													
Principals on an FHSA/HA list at 30 September[10]	KIAZ	Numbers	15 820	16 089	16 276	16 451	16 445	KIBG	879	913	928	931	927
Number of adult courses of treatments[11]	KIBA	Thousands	26 171	25 915	26 353	26 318	26 284	KIBH	1 514	1 525	1 557	1 564	..
Number of adult patients accepted into continuing care provision at 30 September[12]	KIBB	"	16 721	16 649	16 813	16 793	16 739	KIBI	1 043	1 055	1 074	1 063	1 065
Number of children accepted into capitation at 30 September[12]	KIBC	"	6 775	6 821	6 845	6 784	6 733	KIBJ	405.0	408.0	411.5	403.3	399.9
Gross expenditure[13]	KIBD	£ Millions	1 439	1 479	1 556	1 629	1 709	KIBK	82 262	86 093	91 498	95 222	..
Paid by patients[13]	KIBE	"	421	433	455	470	487	KIBL	22 293	23 456	24 634	24 374	..
Paid out of public funds[13]	KIBF	"	1 018	1 046	1 102	1 159	1 222	KIBM	59 969	62 637	66 864	70 848	..
General ophthalmic services:													
Sight tests[11,14]	KNJL	Thousands	6 992	9 399	9 567	9 807	9 662	KNBD	477	631	659	668	647
Pairs of spectacles for which NHS vouchers redeemed[11]	KNJK	"	3 777	3 662	3 575	3 607	3 472	KNBC	288	275	273	273	252
Cost of services (gross)	KNJJ	£ millions	265	307	306	311	304	KNBA	18	20	21	22	..
Paid out of public funds:													
For sight testing	KNJH	"	114	160	163	167	166	KMZZ	7	10	10	11	..
For cost of vouchers[11]	WMPC		150	147	142	143	137	KMZX	10	9	10	10	..

1 Data shown reflect data for the financial year commencing the year in the heading (for example, the figures under 1999 represent 1999/2000 data). Out-patient figures do not include accident and emergency figures or ward attenders which are given separately. Information on general practitioner maternity clinics is not collected separately in England but is included for Wales.

2 People awaiting elective admission at NHS Trusts in England and Wales, as an inpatient or a day case.

3 Welsh FHS expenditure and income is based upon cash payments and receipts in each financial year, as accrued gross expenditure is not available in a common format for all years shown in this series.

4 For Wales, Principals providing unrestricted services as at 1 October

5 UPE's include Unrestricted Principals, PMS Contracted GP's and PMS salaried GP's.UPE data are at 1 October 1998 & 1999 and 30 September for other years

6 For Wales, includes PFMA but excludes GPFH drugs and payments to providers.

7 Welsh data are based on pricing bureau totals of prescriptions dispensed in a calendar year and paid during the financial year. Data shown reflect data for the financial year commencing the year in the heading (for example, the figures under 1999 represent 1999/2000 data).

8 The data cover all prescription items dispensed by community pharmacists and appliance contractors, dispensing doctors and prescriptions submitted by prescribing doctors for items personally administered. Total cost refers to the cost of the drug less discounts and includes on cost allowance, dispensing fees, container allowance, oxygen payments and VAT. The figures for income from patients are for financial years. Figures include charges retained by pharmacists, received by dispensing doctors, income from pre-payment certificates, and recoveries from patients.

9 See chapter text. Welsh Dental Service data excludes refunds of dental charges

10 Principals only. Assistants and vocational trainees are not included. Some dentists may have a contract with more than one Family Health Service /Health Authority. These dentists have been counted once only.

11 Data shown reflect data for the financial year commencing the year in the heading (for example, the figures under 1999 represent 1999/2000 data).

12 Figures for 1998 onwards are affected by the shortening of the registration period to 15 months.

13 Figures for England are for the financial year and are based on provisional outturn figures.

14 Number of NHS sight tests paid for by FHSAs/HAs in the period.

Sources: Department of Health;
National Assembly for Wales: 029 2082 5080

9.2 Hospital and primary care services
Scotland

			1992	1993	1994	1995	1996	1997	1998	1999	2000	2001	2002
Hospital and community services													
In-patients[1,2]:													
Average available staffed beds	KDEA	Thousands	48.7	46.7	44.2	42.4	40.6	38.4	36.8	35.2	33.5	32.1	30.9
Average occupied beds:													
All departments	KDEB	"	39.5	38.1	35.9	34.3	32.8	30.9	29.5	28.2	26.9	25.8	25.1
Psychiatric and learning disability	KDEC	"	15.5	14.6	13.2	12.6	11.7	10.8	10.0	9.1	8.3	7.6	7.0
Discharges or deaths[3]	KDED	"	920	942	952	960	973	965	978	977	965	957	952
Outpatients:[2,4]													
New cases	KDEE	"	2 426	2 457	2 503	2 577	2 666	2 675	2 715	2 734	2 766	2 744	2 743
Total attendances	KDEF	"	6 005	6 086	6 145	6 241	6 338	6 272	6 331	6 424	6 451	6 382	6 291
Medical and dental staff:[5]	JYXO	Numbers	8 069	8 078	8 317	8 524	8 774	9 098	9 157	9 367	9 325	9 646	10 256
Whole-time	KDEG	"	5 625	5 767	5 937	6 102	6 433	6 707	7 052	7 202	6 896	7 218	7 759
Part-time	KDEH	"	1 883	1 730	1 827	1 854	1 819	1 886	1 613	1 685	1 966	1 989	2 063
Honorary	JYXN	"	561	582	563	579	534	522	506	495	495	468	468
Professional and technical staff[6]:													
Whole-time	KDEI	"	9 759	9 953	10 062	10 452	10 584	10 740	10 884	11 261	11 261	11 705	12 265
Part-time	KDEJ	"	3 127	3 434	3 753	4 075	4 370	4 738	4 928	5 218	5 483	5 852	6 273
Nursing and midwifery staff[7]:													
Whole-time	KDEK	"	34 053	33 284	32 956	32 693	32 560	32 218	32 156	32 356	32 401	33 334	34 294
Part-time	KDEL	"	30 709	30 459	30 532	30 580	29 917	29 736	29 178	29 242	29 131	29 004	29 015
Administrative and clerical staff[8]:													
Whole-time	KDEM	"	14 447	15 125	15 723	15 815	15 155	14 707	14 564	14 541	14 710	15 361	16 200
Part-time	KDEN	"	5 815	6 113	6 624	7 005	6 986	7 174	7 265	7 456	7 677	8 075	8 630
Domestic, transport, etc, staff[9]:													
Whole-time	KDEO		10 805	10 205	9 574	9 037	8 596	8 187	8 090	7 972	7 848	7 625	7 768
Part-time	KDEP		15 753	15 403	14 464	14 105	13 554	13 082	12 716	12 424	12 272	11 522	11 915
Cost of services (gross)[10]	KDEQ	£ millions	2 768.0	2 940.5	3 050.5	3 269.5	3 430.6	3 610.3	3 856.0	4 309.7	4 862.6	..	..
Payments by patients[10]	KDER	"	2.00	2.30	0.40	0.02	0.01	0.01	0.01	0.01	0.01	..	..
Payments out of public funds[10]	KDES	"	2 766.0	2 938.2	3 050.1	3 269.5	3 430.6	3 610.3	3 855.9	4 309.7	4 862.6	..	..
Primary care services													
Medical services													
Doctors on the list[11]:													
Principals[12]	KDET	Numbers	3 421	3 456	3 490	3 524	3 573	3 625	3 660	3 698	3 707	3 756	3 765
Assistants	KDEU	"	31	22	25	28	22	22	27	19	25	39	37
Average number of patients per principal doctor[13]	KDEV	"	1 556	1 542	1 524	1 506	1 488	1 468	1 450	1 441	1 425	1 409	1 392
Payments to doctor[14]	KDEW	£ millions	263.8	275.3	291.7	311.9	333.2	356.4	365.9	377.5	404.7	429.6	467.5
Pharmaceutical services[15]													
Prescriptions dispensed	KDEX	Millions	46.10	48.18	49.27	51.08	54.62	56.64	58.52	60.36	62.34	65.56	68.81
Payments to pharmacists (gross)	KDEY	£ millions	370.2	406.1	434.9	474.2	543.4	588.4	627.2	693.7	731.0	788.6	868.9
Average gross cost per prescription	KDEZ	£	8.0	8.4	8.8	9.3	9.9	10.4	10.7	11.5	11.7	12.0	12.6
Dental services[16]													
Dentists on list[17]	KDFA	Numbers	1 702	1 772	1 763	1 764	1 772	1 798	1 854	1 833	1 831	1 866	1 891
Number of courses of treatment completed	KDFB	Thousands	2 569	2 647	2 723	2 711	2 825	3 406	3 349	3 406	3 395	3 390	3 148
Payments to dentists (gross)[18]	KDFC	£ millions	133.6	128.4	136.1	137.3	139.2	154.9	157.5	160.6	162.9	165.1	172.3
Payments by patients	KDFD	"	40.5	40.0	42.2	41.7	41.4	45.9	47.4	48.8	50.6	52.3	54.7
Payments out of public funds[18]	KDFE	"	93.2	88.4	93.9	95.6	97.8	109.0	110.1	111.8	112.3	112.9	117.6
Average gross cost per course	KDFF	£	39.0	37.0	38.0	38.0	40.1	36.5	38.0	38.0	37.0	38.0	42.0
General ophthalmic services													
Number of sight tests given[19]	KDFG	Thousands	537	568	..	614	618	635	656	657	850	861	877
Number of pairs of glasses supplied[20]	KDFH	"	404	463	..	473	461	474	488	485	494	439	463
Payments out of public funds for sight testing and dispensing	KDFK	£ millions	19.7	22.2	24.4	25.8	27.7	29.1	29.8	32.0	33.1	..	42.9

1 Excludes joint user and contractual hospitals.
2 In year to 31 March.
3 Includes transfers out and emergency inpatients treated in day bed units.
4 Including attendances at accident and emergency consultant clinics.
5 At 30 September. Figures exclude officers holding honorary locum appointments. There is an element of double counting of "heads" in this table as doctors can hold more than one contract. For example, they may hold contracts of different type, eg part time and honorary. Doctors holding two or more contracts of the same type, eg part time, are not double counted. Doctors, whose sum of contracts amounts to whole time, are classed as such.
6 At 30 September. Comprises Scientific and Professional, Professions Allied to Medicine and Technical staff
7 At 30 September. Excludes nurse teachers, nurses in training and students on '1992' courses. Between 1992 and 1993 the criterion for excluding nursing staff on low hours was changed from 0.25 hours to 2 hours. This partially accounts for any decrease in staff numbers between these two years.
8 At 30 September. Comprises Senior Management and Administrative and Clerical staff.
9 At 30 September. Comprises Ambulance, Works, Ancillary, Trades and Health Care Assistant staff.

10 These figures are for Health Boards only and do not include the 2 NHS Trusts in 1992/93, 17 in 1993/94, 39 in 1994/95 and 47 in 1995/96. Estimated from financial years
11 At 1 October.
12 Unrestricted principals in post.
13 Unrestricted principals: establishment.
14 Data relate to financial year, eg 1997 data are for year ending 31 March 1998. As 1994/95 data are unavailable for Dumfries & Galloway Health Board, 1993/94 data have been substituted for that board only.
15 For prescriptions dispensed in calendar year by all community pharmacists (including stock orders), dispensing doctors and appliance suppliers.
16 Data refer to financial year (eg 1991 data are for year ending 31 March 1992).
17 Comprises principals only.
18 Before 1991 excludes capitation payments , continuing care, weighted entry and item of service fees.
19 This figure represents sight tests paid for by health boards and GOS(s) ST(v) claimants. From 1994, data refer to financial years (eg 1994 data are for year ending 31 March 1995).
20 Does not include hospital eye service

Source: Common Services Agency and The Scottish Executive: 0131 551 8899

9.3 Hospital and general health services
Northern Ireland

			1993	1994	1995	1996	1997	1998	1999	2000	2001	2002
Hospital services[1]												
In-patients:												
Beds available[2]	KDGA	Numbers	10 878	10 356	10 054	9 464	9 006	8 818	8 639	8 571	8 419	8 301
Average daily occupation of beds	KDGB	*Per cent*	*77.9*	*78.1*	*77.7*	*78.9*	*80.8*	*81.9*	*81.0*	*82.0*	*83.0*	*84.0*
Discharges or deaths[3]	KDGC	Thousands	290	298	304	300	305	335	332	333	328	327
Out-patients[4]:												
New cases	KDGD	"	836	873	940	933	952	962	984	994	997	992
Total attendances	KDGE	"	1 967	2 051	2 087	2 070	2 084	2 091	2 111	2 114	2 131	2 122
General health services												
Medical services[1]												
Doctors (principals) on the list[5,6]	KDGF	Numbers	953	991	1 005	1 028	1 039	1 042	1 054	1 066	1 073	1 091
Number of patients per doctor	KDGG	"	1 731	1 738	1 725	1 698	1 690	1 693	1 678	1 661	1 651	1 632
GrossPayments to doctors[7]	KDGH	£ thousand	60 975	62 849	65 130	67 872	69 889	71 385	78 604	82 471	84 664	88 194
Pharmaceutical services[8]												
Prescription forms dispensed	KDGI	Thousands	11 291	11 152	12 017	12 802	13 246	13 489	13 454	13 666	14 277	14 622
Number of prescriptions	KDGJ	"	18 660	18 560	19 893	21 203	22 047	22 754	23 249	23 985	24 705	25 495
Gross cost	KDGK	£ thousand	165 638	173 064	197 579	219 978	236 746	248 845	266 535	278 405	303 489	327 045
Charges	KDGL	"	6 040	6 507	6 455	6 224	6 784	7 007	8 183	8 499	9 074	9 597
Net Cost	KDGM	"	159 463	166 764	191 324	213 950	229 962	241 837	258 353	269 906	294 415	317 448
Average gross cost per prescription	KDGN	£	8.88	9.32	9.93	10.38	10.74	10.94	11.46	11.61	12.28	12.80
Dental services[8,9]												
Dentists on the list[5]	KDGO	Numbers	541	568	581	596	609	634	660	674	689	689
Number of courses of paid treatment	KDGP	Thousands	801	825	832	928	1 053	1 088	1 097	1 120	1 129	1 126
Gross cost[10]	KDGQ	£ thousand	43 904	46 318	48 780	51 512	53 733	56 835	58 712	61 561	64 454	66 201
Patients[10]	KDGR	"	10 378	11 231	11 530	11 870	12 433	13 686	14 358	15 302	16 041	16 824
Contributions (Net cost)[10]	KDGS	"	33 525	35 086	37 250	39 642	41 300	43 149	44 354	46 260	48 413	49 376
Average gross cost per paid treatment	KDGT	£	55	56	59	56	51	52	54	55	57	58
Ophthalmic services[8]												
Number of sight tests given[11]	KDGU	Thousands	169	182	196	212	227	237	298	305	314	322
Number of optical appliances supplied[12]	KDGV	"	133	139	146	153	159	161	157	160	166	168
Cost of service (gross)[13]	KDGW	£ thousand	7 363	7 127	8 568	9 555	10 271	10 452	11 365	11 975	12 490	13 473
Health and social services[14]												
Medical and dental staff:												
Whole-time	KDGZ	Numbers	2 209	2 358	2 053	2 107	2 156	2 196	2 231	2 224	2 281	2 411
Part-time	KDHA	"	554	694	1 154	1 094	1 041	1 009	1 014	580	597	626
Nursing and midwifery staff:												
Whole-time	KDHB	"	11 445	11 047	10 896	10 578	10 114	10 117	10 135	9 926	9 828	10 248
Part-time	KDHC	"	7 952	8 662	9 169	8 943	9 015	8 287	8 813	7 591	7 814	8 395
Administrative and clerical staff:												
Whole-time	KDHD	"	6 696	7 006	7 078	7 055	6 915	7 019	7 230	7 373	7 536	7 966
Part-time	KDHE	"	2 050	2 186	2 306	2 518	2 708	2 776	2 910	2 972	3 136	3 372
Professional and technical staff:												
Whole-time	KDHF	"	2 695	2 786	2 862	2 939	2 933	3 014	3 177	3 642	3 762	3 975
Part-time	KDHG	"	710	804	921	985	1 060	1 146	1 226	1 283	1 369	1 499
Social services staff(excluding casual home helps):												
Whole-time	KDHH	"	3 550	3 480	3 470	3 441	3 349	3 262	3 319	3 017	3 127	3 284
Part-time	KDHI	"	1 766	1 933	2 110	2 250	2 394	2 241	2 358	868	911	986
Ancillary and other staff:												
Whole-time	KDHJ	"	4 679	4 364	3 982	3 812	3 569	3 423	3 426	3 506	3 472	3 426
Part-time	KDHK	"	4 767	4 609	3 685	3 482	3 558	3 913	4 508	4 925	5 125
Cost of services (gross)[15]	KDHL	£ thousand	1 002 326	1 043 745	1 111 507	1 120 563	1 153 741	1 292 348	1 422 920	1 576 657	1 639 283	1 868 538
Payments by recipients	KDHM	"	13 189	20 629	32 685	40 725	49 498	59 484	65 533	71 411	78 478	88 860
Payments out of public funds	KDHN	"	989 137	1 023 116	1 078 822	1 079 838	1 104 243	1 232 864	1 357 387	1 505 246	1 560 805	1 779 678

1 Financial Year.
2 Average available beds in wards open overnight during the year.
3 Includes transfers to other hospitals.
4 Includes consultant outpatient clinics and Accident and Emergency departments.
5 At beginning of period.
6 Doctors include assistants.
7 These costs refer to the majority of non-cash limited services: further expenditure under GMS is allocated through HSS Boards on a cash limited basis.
8 From 1995 onwards figures are taken from financial year.
9 Due to changes in the Dental Contract which came into force in October 1990 dentists are paid under a combination of headings relating to Capitation and Continuing Care patients.
10 Prior to 1992, headings read 'Payments to Dentists (Gross)', 'Payments by Patients', 'Payments out of Public Funds'.
11 Excluding sight tests given in hospitals and under the school health service and in the home.

12 Relates to the number of vouchers supplied and excludes repair/replace spectacles.
13 Gross cost is defined as net ingredient costs plus on-cost, fees and other payments.
14 Workforce figures until 1999 refer to 31st December and are taken from the Trust and Board payroll system. Figures from 2000 onwards are at 30th September and are taken from the Trust and Board Human Resource Management Systems. Figures for 2000 onwards exclude all home helps and all agency/bank staff but include Ambulance and Works staff in the Ancillary & Other Staff category. As a result, backward comparison of the workforce is not advisable as definitions differ. Some figures for 2000 have been revised.
15 Figures relate to the costs of the hospital, community health and personal social services, and have been estimated from financial year data.

Sources: Dept of Health, Social Services & Public Safety Northern Ireland: 028 9052 2509;
(Figures on Hospital Services: 028 9052 2800)

9.4 Health and personal social services: workforce summary
Great Britain

Numbers or whole-time equivalent

		1993	1994	1995	1996	1997	1998	1999	2000	2001	2002
Health service staff and practitioners at 30 September:											
Medical staff: total	KDBC	55 632	56 736	60 172	62 176	64 316	67 408	69 089	70 939	73 206	78 024
Hospital medical staff: total[3]	KDBD	52 476	53 787	57 299	59 592	61 937	65 088	66 812	68 767	71 107	76 122
Consultant	KDBE	18 251	18 808	20 246	21 066	21 699	23 139	24 250	25 067	26 106	27 951
Staff grade[1]	KADJ	1 230	1 536	2 037	2 440	2 785	3 458	3 868	4 423	4 720	5 409
Associate specialist	KDBF	1 032	1 013	1 128	1 223	1 340	1 439	1 527	1 572	1 609	1 780
Registrar group[2]	KWUG	..	..	..	11 898	12 435	12 863	13 299	13 372	13 826	14 530
Senior registrar	KDBG	4 130	4 281	4 540	..	..	..	..	..	..	..
Registrar	KDBH	7 103	7 273	7 294	..	..	..	..	..	..	..
Senior house officer	KDBI	14 586	14 942	15 661	16 616	17 353	17 760	17 518	17 945	18 377	19 850
House officer	KADK	3 792	3 781	4 003	4 025	4 163	4 287	4 364	4 518	4 560	4 944
Hospital practitioner	KDBL	183	178	197	212	198	220	230	231	223	248
Clinical assistant	KDBM	2 162	1 964	2 182	2 094	1 924	1 907	1 744	1 638	1 684	1 407
Other staff[3]	KDBK	8	11	11	18	38	16	11	1	1	3
Community health medical staff	KDBN	3 156	2 948	2 873	2 584	2 379	2 320	2 278	2 172	2 100	1 902
Dental staff: total[3]	KDBO	2 973	2 947	3 070	3 127	3 078	3 193	3 147	3 107	3 152	3 357
Hospital dental staff: total	KDBP	1 573	1 597	1 687	1 737	1 696	1 807	1 816	1 781	1 816	1 944
Consultant	KDBQ	521	537	549	556	524	570	581	580	578	610
Staff grade[1]	KADL	24	39	54	67	86	99	113	118	135	154
Associate specialist	KDBR	69	62	69	65	62	68	70	73	74	75
Registrar group[2]	LQMZ	..	..	..	..	..	309	314	295	311	339
Senior registrar	KDBS	135	124	123	138	169	..	..	..	..	..
Registrar	KDBT	184	178	186	183	125	..	..	..	..	..
Senior house officer	KDBU	353	394	446	490	491	531	496	497	513	572
Dental house officer	KDBV	126	101	86	68	58	59	68	60	61	60
Hospital practitioner	KDBX	17	20	17	23	22	21	23	21	18	20
Clinical assistant	KDBY	142	141	158	145	152	144	146	136	126	112
Other staff[3]	KDBW	2	2	..	3	6	5	6	..	..	1
Community health dental staff [3]	KDBZ	1 400	1 350	1 383	1 390	1 382	1 386	1 331	1 326	1 336	1 413
Non-medical staff[4]**: total**	KWUH	..	..	804 148	856 732	849 426	855 305	870 921	890 282	927 831	974 390
Nursing and midwifery staff:[5,6] (excluding agency): total *of which:*	KDCA	..	..	387 436	410 693	407 760	409 045	415 786	423 737	437 417	455 361
qualified	KSBR	..	..	282 200	300 371	298 483	299 654	303 644	309 682	320 685	335 313
unqualified	KSBS	..	..	99 946	106 181	106 313	106 773	109 687	111 931	114 532	117 582
learners	KSBT	..	..	4 580	2 804	2 356	2 178	1 961	2 054	2 201	2 387
All Professional and Technical staff (excluding works)	KSBM	..	..	106 544	118 403	120 439	123 902	128 116	131 943	138 348	146 804
Health care assistants	KWUI	..	..	13 090	18 025	19 268	22 026	22 746	24 919	30 047	33 301
Support staff	KWUJ	..	..	74 540	75 836	72 608	71 043	69 883	68 449	69 245	69 628
Ancillary, Works & Maintainance	KSBN	..	..	29 466	27 603	26 037	25 131	24 468	23 962	23 013	23 430
Administrative and Clerical staff	KSBO	..	..	172 948	183 049	183 112	184 711	190 421	197 327	209 004	224 490
Ambulance staff	KSBP	..	..	16 744	18 655	18 751	18 382	18 552	19 209	19 888	20 864
Others	KSBQ	..	..	3 180	4 159	1 079	906	780	746	711	512

9.4 Health and personal social services: workforce summary
Great Britain
continued

Numbers or whole-time equivalent

		1993	1994	1995	1996	1997	1998	1999	2000	2001	2002
Family Health services:[7]											
General medical practitioners at 1 October:											
All practitioners: total	GPYL	..	..	..	..	..	..	37 125	37 572	38 162	38 649
All practitioners (excluding GP Retainers)	LQZN	34 134	34 421	34 594	34 825	35 205	35 611	35 952	36 225	36 754	37 278
Unrestricted Principals & equivalents (UPE's)	LQZO	31 447	31 767	31 945	32 164	32 477	32 801	33 050	33 186	33 384	33 578
of which GMS UP's	LQZP	31 447	31 767	31 945	32 164	32 477	32 414	32 140	31 869	29 475	26 785
PMS contracted/salaried	PTKJ	..	..	..	..	..	387	908	1 317	3 909	6 793
Restricted principals	LQZS	161	156	137	126	111	106	97	94	102	92
Assistants	LQZT	539	626	684	890	891	750	690	671	533	496
GP Registrars[8]	LQZU	1 956	1 841	1 790	1 605	1 678	1 830	1 903	2 028	2 278	2 386
of which GMS[7]	LQZV	1 956	1 841	1 790	1 605	1 678	1 796	1 825	1 920	1 956	1 738
Salaried Doctors	LQZW	..	..	..	..	..	60	118	159	160	127
PMS Other[9]	LQZX	..	..	..	..	..	12	46	37	251	557
Associates	LQZY	31	31	38	40	48	52	50	51	49	44
GP Retainers	GPYM	..	..	..	..	..	..	1 181	1 347	1 408	1 371
General dental practitioners: total[10]	KDCQ	18 467	18 600	18 736	19 139	19 598	20 216	20 840	21 316	21 929	22 194
General Dental Service	GPYN	18 467	18 600	18 736	19 139	19 598	20 216	20 750	21 124	21 462	21 538
Personal Dental Service	GPYO	..	..	..	..	..	..	90	192	467	656
Ophthalmic medical practitioners [11]	KDCT	842	775	789	799	833	863	827	819	754	686
Ophthalmic opticians [11]	KDCU	7 080	7 185	7 333	7 582	7 790	8 024	8 423	8 742	8 650	8 761
Personal Social Services staff: total [12]:	KDDE	232 911	237 752	233 861	233 655	229 439	223 500	221 700	217 200	212 000	208 300
of which:											
Home help service	KSBU	57 593	59 391	56 961	55 430	53 573	50 417	47 227	42 583	40 200	37 300
Field Social Workers	KSBX	28 850	29 820	31 926	32 140	32 990	33 400	33 900	34 700	35 200	35 800
Day care establishments staff	KADV	30 221	31 270	31 109	31 605	30 839	30 300	30 800	30 800	29 500	29 300
Residential care staff	KADW	74 038	72 155	68 651	67 975	65 422	62 100	59 200	56 600	53 800	51 400

1 Figures include Senior Hospital Medical/Dental Officers (SHMO) without an allowance and other ungraded staff

2 Includes Specialist Registrar (SpR), senior Registrar and Registrar. The SpR grade was introduced formally on 1 April 1996

3 Whole-time equivalent. Figures exclude locums and occasional seasonal staff.

4 1995 data do not include Wales. A new system for classifying NHS non-medical staff was used for the first time in September 1995 non-medical workforce census classifying staff according to what they do (known as new occupation codes). Data for years prior to 1995 for all classes of non-medical staff are incomparable.

5 Excludes bank nurses for Wales.

6 Nursing total includes qualified, unqualified and others only.

7 GP Registrars in GMS Partnerships.

8 GP Registrars were formerly referred to as Trainees.

9 PMS other includes 2 Salaried Restricted Principals who are working in salaried GP's in Scotland.

10 Includes principals, assistants and Vocational Dental Practioners and PDS dentists not working in the GDS. Some dentists may have a contract with more than one Health Authority. These dentists have been counted only once. PDS pilots are only in operation in England and not the whole of Great Britian.

11 Figures for England and Wales relate to 31 December. Figures for Scotland relate to 31 March of the following year. OMPs and OOs holding contracts with FHSAs/HAs and/or Scottish Health Boards to carry out NHS sight tests. OOs with contracts with more than one Health Board and/or a Health Board and a FHSA/HA will be counted more than once.

12 Figures are for England only.

13 Breakdown for England not available in this form from 1993.

14 Includes care managers from 1993.

Sources: Scottish Health Service Common Services Agency;
Department of Health;
National Assembly for Wales

9.5 Deaths: analysed by cause
International Statistical Classification of Diseases, Injuries and Causes of Death
Ninth Revision 1979 and Tenth Revision 1999.

Numbers

	ICD-9 code	England and Wales			
		1997	1998	1999	2000
Total deaths		555 281	555 015	556 118	535 664
Deaths from natural causes	001-799	536 453	536 396	537 166	516 803
Certain infectious and parasitic diseases	001-139	3 496	3 410	3 613	3 767
Intestinal infectious diseases	001-009	384	418	476	547
Respiratory and other tuberculosis including late effects	010-018,137	437	453	437	427
Meningococcal infection	036	242	210	217	199
Viral hepatitis	070	165	173	179	200
AIDS (HIV - disease)	042-044	259	163	155	182
Neoplasms	140-239	137 618	138 306	136 181	134 793
Malignant neoplasms	140-208	135 647	136 329	134 135	132 686
Malignant neoplasm of oesophagus	150	5 855	5 952	6 040	6 061
Malignant neoplasm of stomach	151	6 613	6 442	6 139	5 779
Malignant neoplasm of colon	153	10 448	10 170	9 911	9 554
Malignant neoplasm of rectum and anus	154.1-154.8	4 177	4 182	4 059	4 024
Malignant neoplasm of pancreas	157	5 782	5 801	5 956	6 105
Malignant neoplasm of trachea, bronchus and lung	162	29 976	30 199	29 493	29 029
Malignant neoplasm of skin	172	1 378	1 468	1 476	1 536
Malignant neoplasm of breast	174-175	12 047	11 835	11 670	11 433
Malignant neoplasm of cervix uteri	180	1 225	1 158	1 107	1 106
Malignant neoplasm of prostate	185	8 523	8 573	8 533	8 293
Leukaemia	204-208	3 587	3 551	3 680	3 570
Diseases of the blood and blood-forming organs and certain disorders involving the immune mechanism	279-289	2 056	1 978	1 907	1 829
Endocrine, nutritional and metabolic diseases	240-278	7 335	7 501	7 508	7 209
Diabetes mellitus	250	5 890	5 938	5 963	5 773
Mental and behavioural disorders	290-319	9 725	10 430	11 173	10 865
Vascular and unspecified dementia	290	6 731	7 124	7 654	7 173
Alcohol abuse (inc. alcoholic psychosis)	291,303	344	350	347	331
Drug dependence and non-dependent abuse of drugs	292,304-305	736	895	935	1 049
Diseases of the nervous system and sense organs	320-389	9 772	10 035	10 192	9 632
Meningitis (including meningococcal)	320-322	224	216	182	206
Alzheimer's disease	331.0	2 185	2 374	2 406	2 182
Diseases of the circulatory system	390-459	228 446	226 677	219 087	207 228
Ischaemic heart diseases	410-414	122 432	121 037	115 119	108 418
Cerebrovascular diseases	430-438	57 747	57 516	56 051	52 516
Diseases of the respiratory system	460-519	92 517	90 192	97 755	92 461
Influenza	487	347	129	585	509
Pneumonia	480-486	56 719	54 631	59 273	56 329
Bronchitis, emphysema and other chronic obstructive pulmonary diseases	490-492,496	25 097	24 878	26 114	23 538
Asthma	493	1 439	1 366	1 364	1 272
Diseases of the digestive system	520-579	20 406	21 025	21 698	22 134
Gastric and duodenal ulcer	531-533	3 959	3 935	4 011	4 007
Chronic liver disease	571	4 107	4 494	4 718	4 770
Diseases of the skin and subcutaneous tissue	680-709	1 025	1 070	1 152	1 266
Diseases of the musculo-skeletal system and connective tissue	710-739	3 559	3 566	3 554	3 407
Rheumatoid arthritis and juvenile arthritis	714	797	778	697	675
Osteoporosis	733.0-733.1	1 282	1 273	1 335	1 268
Diseases of the genito-urinary system	580-629	6 757	6 946	7 299	7 270
Diseases of the kidney and ureter	580-594	3 767	3 803	3 844	3 799
Complications of pregnancy, childbirth and the puerperium	630-676	35	43	30	38
Certain conditions originating in the perinatal period (excluding neonatals)[1]	760-779	131	124	116	83
Congenital malformations, deformations and chromasomal abnormalities (excluding neonatals)[1]	740-759	1 283	1 247	1 194	1 165
Congenital malformations of the nervous system	740-742	121	124	104	116
Congenital malformations of the circulatory system	745-747	689	643	621	617
Symptoms, signs and abnormal clinical and laboratory findings not elsewhere classified	780-799	12 292	13 846	14 707	13 656
Senility without mention of psychosis (old age)	797	11 028	12 615	13 473	12 458
Sudden infant death syndrome	798.0	327	236	222	180
Deaths from external causes	E800-E999	16 311	16 201	16 517	16 526
All accidents	E800-E929	10 661	10 351	10 625	10 771
Land transport accidents	E800-E829	3 291	3 023	3 098	2 985
Accidental falls	E880-E888	3 885	3 865	3 993	4 281
Accidental poisonings	E850-E869	1 058	1 045	1 030	1 064
Suicide and intentional self-harm	E950-E959	3 424	3 614	3 690	3 480
Homicide and assault[1]	E960-E969	290	285	293	380
Event of undetermined intent	E980-E989	1 914	1 931	1 886	1 872

9.5

Deaths: analysed by cause
International Statistical Classification of Diseases, Injuries and Causes of Death

continued   Ninth Revision 1979 and Tenth Revision 1999.

Numbers

		England and Wales		
	ICD-9 code	ICD-10 code	2001	2002
Total deaths			530 373	533 527
Deaths from natural causes	001-799	A00-R99	511 667	515 262
Certain infectious and parasitic diseases	001-139	A00-B99	4 253	4 330
Intestinal infectious diseases	001-009	A00-A09	777	847
Respiratory and other tuberculosis including late effects	010-018,137	A15-A19,B90	446	443
Meningococcal infection	036	A39	201	115
Viral hepatitis	070	B15-B19	196	170
AIDS (HIV - disease)	042-044	B20-B24	180	198
Neoplasms	140-239	C00-D48	139 135	140 174
Malignant neoplasms	140-208	C00-97	135 839	136 777
Malignant neoplasm of oesophagus	150	C15	6 107	6 330
Malignant neoplasm of stomach	151	C16	5 606	5 588
Malignant neoplasm of colon	153	C18	9 436	9 504
Malignant neoplasm of rectum and anus	154.1-154.8	C20-C21	3 927	3 907
Malignant neoplasm of pancreas	157	C25	6 011	6 142
Malignant neoplasm of trachea, bronchus and lung	162	C33-C34	28 728	28 806
Malignant neoplasm of skin	172	C43	1 470	1 480
Malignant neoplasm of breast	174-175	C50	11 638	11 557
Malignant neoplasm of cervix uteri	180	C53	1 039	1 001
Malignant neoplasm of prostate	185	C61	8 912	8 973
Leukaemia	204-208	C91-C95	3 781	3 911
Diseases of the blood and blood-forming organs and certain disorders involving the immune mechanism	279-289	D50-D89	1 000	1 086
Endocrine, nutritional and metabolic diseases	240-278	E00-E90	7 711	7 897
Diabetes mellitus	250	E10-E14	6 119	6 192
Mental and behavioural disorders	290-319	F00-F99	14 143	14 444
Vascular and unspecified dementia	290	F01,F03	12 572	12 753
Alcohol abuse (inc. alcoholic psychosis)	291,303	F10	477	435
Drug dependence and non-dependent abuse of drugs	292,304-305	F11-F16,F18-F19	798	882
Diseases of the nervous system and sense organs	320-389	G00-H95	14 372	14 796
Meningitis (including meningococcal)	320-322	G00-G03	189	173
Alzheimer's disease	331.0	G30	4 579	4 771
Diseases of the circulatory system	390-459	I00-I99	211 842	209 433
Ischaemic heart diseases	410-414	I20-I25	105 895	102 833
Cerebrovascular diseases	430-438	I60-I69	58 517	59 068
Diseases of the respiratory system	460-519	J00-J99	67 391	69 900
Influenza	487	J10-J11	38	38
Pneumonia	480-486	J12-J18	31 636	32 631
Bronchitis, emphysema and other chronic obstructive pulmonary diseases	490-492,496	J40-J44	23 700	24 159
Asthma	493	J45-J46	1 268	1 264
Diseases of the digestive system	520-579	K00-K93	23 386	24 124
Gastric and duodenal ulcer	531-533	K25-K27	3 802	3 746
Chronic liver disease	571	K70,K73-K74	5 234	5 376
Diseases of the skin and subcutaneous tissue	680-709	L00-L99	1 291	1 470
Diseases of the musculo-skeletal system and connective tissue	710-739	M00-M99	4 588	4 647
Rheumatoid arthritis and juvenile arthritis	714	M05-M06,M08	970	966
Osteoporosis	733.0-733.1	M80-M81	1 542	1 605
Diseases of the genito-urinary system	580-629	N00-N99	7 682	8 452
Diseases of the kidney and ureter	580-594	N00-N29	3 848	4 072
Complications of pregnancy, childbirth and the puerperium	630-676	O00-O99	42	34
Certain conditions originating in the perinatal period (excluding neonatals)[1]	760-779	P00-P96	200	208
Congenital malformations, deformations and chromasomal abnormalities (excluding neonatals)[1]	740-759	Q00-Q99	1 280	1 233
Congenital malformations of the nervous system	740-742	Q00-Q07	119	127
Congenital malformations of the circulatory system	745-747	Q20-Q28	592	541
Symptoms, signs and abnormal clinical and laboratory findings not elsewhere classified	780-799	R00-R99	13 351	13 034
Senility without mention of psychosis (old age)	797	R54	11 900	11 645
Sudden infant death syndrome	798.0	R95	195	137
Deaths from external causes	E800-E999	V01-Y89	16 569	16 139
All accidents	E800-E929	V01-X59,Y85,Y86	10 733	10 382
Land transport accidents	E800-E829	V01-V89	2 949	2 929
Accidental falls	E880-E888	W00-W19	2 617	2 509
Accidental poisonings	E850-E869	X40-X49	1 037	814
Suicide and intentional self-harm	E950-E959	X60-X84,Y87.0	3 264	3 269
Homicide and assault[1]	E960-E969	X85-Y09,Y87.1	386	373
Event of undetermined intent	E980-E989	Y10-Y34, Y87.2	1 803	1 754

9.5
continued

Deaths: analysed by cause
International Statistical Classification of Diseases, Injuries and Causes of Death
Ninth Revision 1979 and Tenth Revision 1999.

Numbers

	ICD-9 code	ICD-10 code	Scotland					
			1997	1998	1999	2000	2001	2002
					ICD-9	ICD-10		
Total deaths			59 494	59 164	60 281	57 799	57 382	58 103
Deaths from natural causes	001-799	A00-R99	57 121	56 785	57 831	55 415	54 961	55 689
Certain infectious and parasitic diseases	001-139	A00-B99	431	486	498	476	558	651
Intestinal infectious diseases	001-009	A00-A09	19	34	31	51	65	96
Respiratory and other tuberculosis including late effects	010-018,137	A15-A19,B90	71	58	65	66	54	52
Meningococcal infection	036	A39	12	20	14	18	12	13
Viral hepatitis	070	B15-B19	15	22	17	14	6	13
AIDS (HIV - disease)	042-044	B20-B24	41	32	23	23	33	33
Neoplasms	140-239	C00-D48	15 054	14 907	14 966	15 255	15 475	15 391
Malignant neoplasms	140-208	C00-C97	14 889	14 752	14 789	14 958	15 196	15 051
Malignant neoplasm of oesophagus	150	C15	734	730	776	708	752	763
Malignant neoplasm of stomach	151	C16	710	680	650	649	678	621
Malignant neoplasm of colon	153	C18	1 065	996	1 018	1 052	1 062	975
Malignant neoplasm of rectum and anus	154.1-154.8	C20-21	477	448	474	400	405	384
Malignant neoplasm of pancreas	157	C25	556	607	574	633	595	562
Malignant neoplasm of trachea, bronchus and lung	162	C33-34	4 106	3 984	3 961	3 948	3 915	4 039
Malignant neoplasm of skin	172	C43	118	144	131	115	145	132
Malignant neoplasm of breast	174-175	C50	1 161	1 147	1 136	1 122	1 150	1 110
Malignant neoplasm of cervix uteri	180	C53	144	145	122	117	113	100
Malignant neoplasm of prostate	185	C61	708	677	769	773	777	775
Leukaemia	204-208	C91-C95	291	329	313	325	350	330
Diseases of the blood and blood-forming organs and certain disorders involving the immune mechanism	279-289	D50-D89	200	222	204	114	124	122
Endocrine, nutritional and metabolic diseases	240-278	E00-E90	727	797	870	828	891	902
Diabetes mellitus	250	E10-E14	510	574	670	616	695	676
Mental and behavioural disorders	290-319	F00-F99	1 611	1 725	1 901	2 309	2 425	2 446
Vascular and unspecified dementia	290	F01,F03	700	690	783	1 684	1 809	1 763
Alcohol abuse (inc. alcoholic psychosis)	291,303	F10	292	329	358	330	341	339
Drug dependence and non-dependent abuse of drugs	292,304-305	F11-F16,F18-F19	143	182	230	245	238	294
Diseases of the nervous system and sense organs	320-389	G00-H95	900	894	971	1 315	1 243	1 317
Meningitis (including meningococcal)	320-322	G00-G03	17	6	19	15	16	6
Alzheimer's disease	331.0	G30	121	142	140	329	324	388
Diseases of the circulatory system	390-459	I00-I99	25 911	25 153	24 787	23 657	22 666	22 688
Ischaemic heart diseases	410-414	I20-I25	14 013	13 419	13 337	12 412	11 914	11 692
Cerebrovascular diseases	430-438	I60-I69	6 959	6 900	6 785	6 803	6 621	6 722
Diseases of the respiratory system	460-519	J00-J99	7 891	8 011	8 870	6 547	6 435	6 806
Influenza	487	J10-J11	83	12	62	131	5	6
Pneumonia	480-486	J12-J18	4 028	4 064	4 526	2 312	2 370	2 466
Bronchitis, emphysema and other chronic obstructive pulmonary diseases	490-492,496	J40-J44	2 596	2 662	2 941	2 825	2 836	2 840
Asthma	493	J45-J46	113	120	119	131	101	131
Diseases of the digestive system	520-579	K00-K93	2 428	2 578	2 787	2 922	3 063	3 153
Gastric and duodenal ulcer	531-533	K25-K27	306	314	337	321	348	308
Chronic liver disease	571	K70,K73-K74	767	806	896	956	1 061	1 128
Diseases of the skin and subcutaneous tissue	680-709	L00-L99	87	94	90	89	90	118
Diseases of the musculo-skeletal system and connective tissue	710-739	M00-M99	268	284	295	405	357	384
Rheumatoid arthritis and juvenile arthritis	714	M05-M06,M08	89	86	87	126	125	133
Osteoporosis	733.0-733.1	M80-M81	40	46	53	58	56	59
Diseases of the genito-urinary system	580-629	N00-N99	904	890	936	844	969	1 013
Diseases of the kidney and ureter	580-594	N00-N29	652	644	619	563	638	627
Complications of pregnancy, childbirth and the puerperium	630-676	O00-O99	4	5	7	8	6	5
Certain conditions originating in the perinatal period	760-779	P00-P96	140	165	137	170	167	155
Congenital malformations, deformations and chromasomal abnormalities	740-759	Q00-Q99	182	176	157	154	172	168
Congenital malformations of the nervous system	740-742	Q00-Q07	24	23	13	25	16	31
Congenital malformations of the circulatory system	745-747	Q20-Q28	84	81	59	56	65	60
Symptoms, signs and abnormal clinical and laboratory findings not elsewhere classified	780-799	R00-R99	383	398	355	322	320	370
Senility without mention of psychosis (old age)	797	R54	95	111	185	161	172	191
Sudden infant death syndrome	798.0	R95	52	37	41	33	32	32
Deaths from external causes	E800-E999	V01-Y89	2 373	2 379	2 450	2 384	2 421	2 414
All accidents	E800-E929	V01-X59,Y85,Y86	1 299	1 303	1 359	1 341	1 350	1 315
Land transport accidents	E800-E829	V01-V89	387	394	326	338	367	321
Accidental falls	E880-E888	W00-W19	620	613	713	675	626	668
Accidental poisonings	E850-E869	X40-X49	30	38	30	34	50	37
Suicide and intentional self-harm	E950-E959	X60-X84,Y87.0	599	649	637	648	609	636
Homicide and assault	E960-E969	X85-Y09,Y87.1	86	94	121	93	92	118
Event of undetermined intent	E980-E989	Y10-Y34, Y87.2	275	229	237	230	278	263

9.5

Deaths: analysed by cause

continued

International Statistical Classification of Diseases, Injuries and Causes of Death

Ninth Revision 1979 and Tenth Revision 1999.

Numbers

	ICD-9 code	ICD-10 code	Northern Ireland					
			1997	1998	1999	2000 ICD-9	2001 ICD-10	2002
Total deaths			14 971	14 993	15 663	14 903	14 513	14 586
Deaths from natural causes	001-799	A00-R99	14 378	14 424	15 054	14 296	13 968	13 949
Certain infectious and parasitic diseases	001-139	A00-B99	61	53	47	73	117	134
Intestinal infectious diseases	001-009	A00-A09	-	-	1	4	7	11
Respiratory and other tuberculosis including late effects	010-018,137	A15-A19,B90	11	6	7	7	6	10
Meningococcal infection	036	A39	4	6	4	9	4	7
Viral hepatitis	070	B15-B19	2	1	2	6	-	0
AIDS (HIV - disease)	042-044	B20-B24	1	1	2	1	-	3
Neoplasms	140-239	C00-D48	3 672	3 769	3 654	3 647	3 802	3 766
Malignant neoplasms	140-208	C00-C97	3 589	3 648	3 552	3 541	3 696	3 652
Malignant neoplasm of oesophagus	150	C15	144	154	161	150	155	163
Malignant neoplasm of stomach	151	C16	172	215	187	180	174	164
Malignant neoplasm of colon	153	C18	308	329	303	301	271	270
Malignant neoplasm of rectum and anus	154.1-154.8	C20-C21	94	98	95	84	100	90
Malignant neoplasm of pancreas	157	C25	161	154	142	159	176	194
Malignant neoplasm of trachea, bronchus and lung	162	C33-C34	773	775	781	792	782	802
Malignant neoplasm of skin	172	C43	26	28	33	31	37	38
Malignant neoplasm of breast	174-175	C50	267	299	286	289	316	278
Malignant neoplasm of cervix uteri	180	C53	26	33	36	30	24	25
Malignant neoplasm of prostate	185	C61	208	220	195	213	214	193
Leukaemia	204-208	C91-C95	107	93	104	91	87	93
Diseases of the blood and blood-forming organs and certain disorders involving the immune mechanism	279-289	D50-D89	21	24	24	24	32	24
Endocrine, nutritional and metabolic diseases	240-278	E00-E90	105	85	118	122	200	238
Diabetes mellitus	250	E10-E14	77	55	93	89	145	187
Mental and behavioural disorders	290-319	F00-F99	137	145	190	207	381	411
Vascular and unspecified dementia	290	F01,F03	41	58	75	66	298	329
Alcohol abuse (inc. alcoholic psychosis)	291,303	F10	55	35	46	46	75	74
Drug dependence and non-dependent abuse of drugs	292,304-305	F11-F16,F18-F19	20	11	25	38	2	6
Diseases of the nervous system and sense organs	320-389	G00-H95	236	240	285	245	467	531
Meningitis (including meningococcal)	320-322	G00-G03	8	4	3	6	9	5
Alzheimer's disease	331.0	G30	65	80	98	81	211	246
Diseases of the circulatory system	390-459	I00-I99	6 506	6 367	6 422	5 776	5 829	5 729
Ischaemic heart diseases	410-414	I20-I25	3 764	3 654	3 568	3 234	3 148	2 948
Cerebrovascular diseases	430-438	I60-I69	1 646	1 602	1 679	1 469	1 531	1 573
Diseases of the respiratory system	460-519	J00-J99	2 665	2 627	3 161	3 019	1 975	1 883
Influenza	487	J10-J11	8	2	5	39	-	1
Pneumonia	480-486	J12-J18	1 775	1 727	2 130	2 027	1 028	951
Bronchitis, emphysema and other chronic obstructive pulmonary diseases	490-492,496	J40-J44	637	627	704	610	584	553
Asthma	493	J45-J46	32	44	38	33	38	36
Diseases of the digestive system	520-579	K00-K93	446	499	507	531	556	581
Gastric and duodenal ulcer	531-533	K25-K27	95	80	80	89	76	62
Chronic liver disease	571	K70,K73-K74	68	104	92	101	133	166
Diseases of the skin and subcutaneous tissue	680-709	L00-L99	25	36	27	21	24	21
Diseases of the musculo-skeletal system and connective tissue	710-739	M00-M99	44	30	54	40	94	90
Rheumatoid arthritis and juvenile arthritis	714	M05-M06,M08	14	6	13	26	31	21
Osteoporosis	733.0-733.1	M80-M81	5	4	11	5	12	19
Diseases of the genito-urinary system	580-629	N00-N99	242	265	242	292	278	333
Diseases of the kidney and ureter	580-594	N00-N29	187	184	173	201	192	246
Complications of pregnancy, childbirth and the puerperium	630-676	O00-O99	-	1	-	-	2	1
Certain conditions originating in the perinatal period	760-779	P00-P96	67	64	69	62	63	62
Congenital malformations, deformations and chromasomal abnormalities	740-759	Q00-Q99	59	70	93	57	83	53
Congenital malformations of the nervous system	740-742	Q00-Q07	5	9	9	14	16	7
Congenital malformations of the circulatory system	745-747	Q20-Q28	20	17	32	19	24	17
Symptoms, signs and abnormal clinical and laboratory findings not elsewhere classified	780-799	R00-R99	92	149	161	180	65	92
Senility without mention of psychosis (old age)	797	R54	36	105	122	146	37	63
Sudden infant death syndrome	798.0	R95	8	4	3	-	2	0
Deaths from external causes	E800-E999	V01-Y89	593	569	609	607	545	637
All accidents	E800-E929	V01-X59,Y85,Y86	428	381	430	364	361	424
Land transport accidents	E800-E829	V01-V89	157	131	134	142	148	144
Accidental falls	E880-E888	W00-W19	137	127	161	131	52	60
Accidental poisonings	E850-E869	X40-X49	38	36	38	25	13	30
Suicide and intentional self-harm	E950-E959	X60-X84,Y87.0	120	126	121	163	141	162
Homicide and assault	E960-E969	X85-Y09,Y87.1	24	36	24	56	20	27
Event of undetermined intent	E980-E989	Y10-Y34, Y87.2	18	24	33	22	17	21

1 See chapter text

Sources: Office for National Statistics;
General Register Office, Scotland;
Northern Ireland Statistics and Research Agency

9.6 Notifications of infectious diseases

		1992	1993	1994	1995	1996	1997	1998	1999	2000	2001	2002
United Kingdom												
Measles	KHQD	12 318	12 018	23 517	9 017	6 866	4 844	4 540	2 951	2 865	2 661	3 675
Mumps	KWNN	3 169	2 726	3 143	2 400	2 182	2 264	1 917	2 000	3 367	3 433	2 333
Rubella	KWNO	9 150	12 300	9 650	7 674	11 720	4 205	4 064	2 575	2 064	1 782	2 002
Whooping cough	KHQE	2 750	4 718	4 837	2 399	2 721	3 669	1 902	1 461	866	1 059	1 051
Scarlet fever	KHQC	5 978	7 341	8 031	6 863	6 101	4 639	4 708	2 956	2 544	2 320	2 749
Dysentery	KHQG	20 620	7 577	7 538	5 498	2 643	2 427	1 934	1 630	1 613	1 495	1 167
Food poisoning	KHQH	72 139	76 711	91 128	92 604	94 923	105 579	105 060	96 866	98 076	95 752	81 562
Typhoid and Paratyphoid fevers	KHQB	298	277	390	386	291	249	252	278	205	254	183
Hepatitis	KWNP	9 616	6 142	4 285	3 823	2 876	3 601	3 781	4 365	4 530	4 419	5 035
Tuberculosis	KHQI	6 442	6 565	6 230	6 176	6 238	6 367	6 605	6 701	7 100	7 204	7 239
Malaria	KWNQ	1 253	1 281	1 219	1 363	1 743	1 549	1 163	1 038	1 166	1 118	866
England and Wales[1]												
Measles	KHRD	10 268	9 612	16 375	7 447	5 614	3 962	3 728	2 438	2 378	2 250	3 187
Mumps	KWNR	2 412	2 153	2 494	1 936	1 747	1 914	1 587	1 691	2 162	2 741	1 997
Rubella	KWNS	6 212	9 724	6 326	6 196	9 081	3 260	3 208	1 954	1 653	1 483	1 660
Whooping cough	KHRE	2 309	4 091	3 964	1 869	2 387	2 989	1 577	1 139	712	888	883
Scarlet fever	KHRC	4 645	5 855	6 193	5 296	4 873	3 569	3 339	2 086	1 933	1 756	2 159
Dysentery	KHRG	16 960	6 841	6 956	4 651	2 312	2 274	1 813	1 538	1 494	1 388	1 167
Food poisoning	KHRH	63 347	68 587	81 833	82 041	83 233	93 901	93 932	86 316	86 528	85 468	72 649
Typhoid and Paratyphoid fevers	KHRB	282	268	370	370	276	241	243	276	204	250	175
Viral hepatitis	KWNT	8 993	5 557	3 722	3 296	2 437	3 186	3 183	3 424	3 541	3 388	3 859
Tuberculosis[2]	KHRJ	5 799	5 921	5 591	5 608	5 654	5 859	6 087	6 144	6 572	6 714	6 753
Malaria	KWNU	1 189	1 198	1 139	1 300	1 659	1 476	1 110	1 005	1 128	1 081	847
Total meningitis	KHRO	2 571	2 082	1 800	2 285	2 686	2 345	2 072	2 094	2 432	2 623	1 545
Meningococcal meningitis	KHRP	1 067	1 053	938	1 146	1 164	1 220	1 152	1 145	1 164	1 020	706
Meningococcal septicaemia	KWNV	277	398	430	707	1 129	1 440	1 509	1 822	1 614	1 238	842
Ophthalmia neonatorum	KHRI	424	340	268	245	246	224	198	163	176	115	91
Scotland												
Measles	KHSE	1 747	1 911	6 192	1 307	1 055	762	700	434	395	315	399
Mumps	KWNW	601	458	546	371	368	282	251	216	199	155	259
Rubella	KWNX	2 645	2 048	2 916	1 258	2 449	818	745	548	349	234	292
Whooping cough	KHSF	236	493	639	399	186	545	225	214	93	106	99
Scarlet fever	KHSD	808	911	1 319	1 065	750	645	883	438	301	281	376
Dysentery	KHSH	3 486	607	446	575	176	124	103	82	95	85	73
Food poisoning[3]	KHSI	7 877	7 170	8 291	9 297	10 234	10 144	9 186	8 517	9 263	8 640	7 693
Typhoid and Paratyphoid fevers	KHSB	15	7	18	16	14	6	6	2	1	3	4
Viral hepatitis	KWNY	319	290	296	405	360	359	490	863	943	1 008	1 165
Tuberculosis[4]	KHSL	559	554	546	478	509	433	457	496	469	442	418
Malaria	KWUC	50	75	74	58	70	57	30	20	27	24	17
Meningococcal infection	KWUD	207	207	201	190	201	271	313	329	301	256	175
Erysipelas	KHSC	128	130	118	125	84	95	66	64	41	39	41
Northern Ireland												
Measles	KHTD	303	495	950	263	197	120	112	79	92	96	89
Mumps	KHTR	156	115	103	93	67	68	79	93	1 006	537	77
Rubella	KHTQ	293	528	408	220	190	127	111	73	62	65	50
Whooping cough	KHTE	205	134	234	131	148	135	100	108	61	65	69
Scarlet fever	KHTC	525	575	519	502	478	425	486	432	310	283	214
Dysentery	KHTG	174	129	136	272	155	29	18	10	24	22	7
Food poisoning	KHTH	915	954	1 004	1 266	1 456	1 534	1 942	2 033	2 285	1 644	1 220
Typhoid and Paratyphoid fevers	KHTB	1	2	2	–	1	2	3	–	–	1	4
Infective hepatitis	KHTO	304	295	267	122	79	56	108	78	46	23	11
Tuberculosis	KHTI	84	90	93	90	75	75	61	61	59	48	68
Malaria	KWUE	14	8	6	5	14	16	23	13	11	13	2
Acute encephalitis/meningitis	KHTM	118	122	144	116	105	91	64	99	130	97	98
Meningococcal septicaemia	KWUF	27	34	39	42	67	56	87	145	123	90	98
Gastro-enteritis (children under 2 years)	KHTP	1 070	1 379	888	1 072	745	896	1 371	1 121	1 205	1 106	882

1 The figures show the corrected number of notifications, incorporating revisions of diagnosis, either by the notifying medical practitioner or by the medical superintendent of the infectious diseases hospital. Cases notified in Port Health Authorities are included.

2 Formal notifications of new cases only. The figures exclude chemoprophylaxis.

3 Scotland's food poisoning includes 'otherwise ascertained' for the first time in 1995.

4 Figures include cases of tuberculosis not notified before death.

Sources: Information and Statistics Division, NHS in Scotland;
General Register Office (Northern Ireland);
HPA Communicable Diseases Surveillance Centre: 020 8200 6868

9.7 Estimated number of cases of work-related disease reported by specialist physicians to THOR[1]

Great Britain

	All physicians			Disease specialist			Occupational physicians		
	2000	2001	2002	2000	2001	2002	2000	2001	2002
Musculoskeletal disorders									
					MOSS			OPRA	
Upper limb	5 055	4 930	5 254	1 752	1 824	1 708	3 303	3 106	3 546
Spine/ back	2 305	2 294	2 084	636	432	436	1 669	1 862	1 648
Lower limb	372	528	489	144	84	81	228	444	408
Other	216	360	303	48	84	51	168	276	252
Total number of diagnoses	8 092	8 292	8 206	2 628	2 484	2 328	5 464	5 808	5 878
Total number of individuals[2]	7 816	7 781	7 970	2 568	2 328	2 260	5 248	5 543	5 710
Mental ill health									
					SOSMI			OPRA	
Stress/ anxiety/ depression	6 327	6 903	6 591	2 820	2 316	1 851	3 507	4 587	4 740
Other	912	1 212	954	756	888	666	156	324	288
Total number of diagnoses	7 239	8 155	7 475	3 576	3 204	2 517	3 663	4 911	5 028
Total number of individuals[2]	6 555	7 575	6 946	3 420	3 096	2 410	3 135	4 479	4 536
Respiratory disease									
					SWORD			OPRA	
Asthma	785	649	670	482	414	398	303	235	272
Malignant mesothelioma	923	973	882	868	966	870	55	7	12
Benign pleural disease	1 064	865	935	1 040	853	899	24	12	36
Other	1 021	938	706	730	708	458	291	230	248
Total number of diagnoses	3 793	3 425	3 193	3 120	2 941	2 625	673	484	568
Total number of individuals[2]	3 711	3 353	3 118	3 038	2 869	2 562	673	484	556
Skin disease									
					EPIDERM			OPRA	
Contact dermatitis	3 377	2 724	2 878	2 040	1 702	1 922	1 337	1 022	956
Skin neoplasia	503	545	392	491	545	380	12	-	12
Other	507	389	389	230	245	163	277	158	226
Total number of diagnoses	4 387	3 658	3 659	2 761	2 492	2 465	1 626	1 180	1 194
Total number of individuals[2]	4 322	3 647	3 600	2 696	2 467	2 431	1 626	1 180	1 169
Audiological disease									
					OSSA			OPRA	
Sensorineural hearing loss	627	341	219	279	149	27	348	192	192
Other	170	126	16	170	78	16	-	48	-
Total number of diagnoses	797	467	235	449	227	43	348	240	192
Total number of individuals[2]	648	395	222	300	155	30	348	240	192
Infections									
					SIDAW				
Diarrhoeal diseases	..	..	..	374	539	2051	..	..	
Other	..	..	..	187	155	182	..	..	
Total number of diagnoses	..	..	..	561	694	2233	..	..	
Total number of individuals[2]	..	..	..	561	294	2233	..	..	..

1 See chapter text. THOR the Health and Occupation Reporting Network (formerly know as ODIN) comprises of the following schemes: OPRA: Occupational Physicians Reporting Activity; MOSS: Musculoskeletal Occupational Surveillance Scheme; SOSMI: Surveillance of Occupational Stress and Mental Illness; SWORD: Surveillance of Work-related and Occupational Respiratory Disease; EPIDERM: Occupational Skin Disease Surveillance by Dermatologists; OSSA: Occupational Surveillance Scheme for Audiologists; SIDAW: Surveillance of Infectious Disease at Work.

2 Individuals may have more than one diagnosis.

Source: Health and Safety Executive: 0151 951 4556

9.8 Deaths due to occupationally related lung disease[1]
Great Britain

		1991	1992	1993	1994	1995	1996	1997	1998	1999	2000	2001
Asbestosis (without mesothelioma)[2]	KADY	163	150	173	174	166	196	191	165	171	186	208
Mesothelioma [2]	KADZ	1 023	1 097	1 152	1 246	1 317	1 322	1 367	1 541	1 615	1 631	1 848
Pneumoconiosis (other than asbestosis)	KAEA	287	274	281	276	287	223	230	268	321	279	240
Byssinosis	KAEB	16	21	11	7	6	3	5	5	6	4	2
Farmer's lung and other occupational allergic alveolitis	KAEC	8	4	12	10	10	1	5	8	9	7	7
Total	KAED	1 497	1 546	1 629	1 713	1 786	1 745	1 798	1 987	2 122	2 107	2 305

1 See chapter text.
2 By definition every case of asbestosis is due to asbestos; the association with mesothelioma is also very strong, though there is thought to be a low natural background incidence.

Sources: Office for National Statistics; Health and Safety Executive: 0151 951 4540

9.9 Injuries to workers by industry and severity of injury[1]
Great Britain
As reported to all enforcing authorities

	Section	SIC (92)	Fatal 1999/00	2000/01	2001/02		Major 1999/00	2000/01	2001/02		Over 3 Days[2] 1999/00	2000/01	2001/02
Agriculture, hunting, forestry and fishing[3] KSYS	A,B	01,02,05	36	46	39 KSZN		726	655	695 KTAZ		1 456	1 398	1 597
Energy and water supply industries KSYT	C,E	10-14,40/41	7	8	14 KSZO		506	472	459 KTBH		2 511	2 375	2 261
Mining and quarrying KSYU	C	10-14	5	8	9 KSZP		313	296	282 KTBI		..	..	..
Mining and quarrying of energy producing materials KSON	CA	10-12	3	3	7 KSZQ		189	174	174 KTBJ		1 029	1 040	979
Mining and quarrying except energy producing materials KSOO	CB	13/14	2	5	2 KSZR		124	122	108 KTBK		474	441	438
Electricity, gas and water supply KSOP	E	40/41	2	–	5 KSZS		193	176	177 KTBL		1 008	894	844
Manufacturing KSOQ	D	15-37	41	50	48 KSZT		8 038	7 459	7 180 KTBM		39 460	38 187	35 034
of food products; beverages and tobacco KSOR	DA	15/16	1	4	7 KSZU		..	..	.. KTBN		9 796	9 417	8 779
of textile and textile products KSOS	DB	17/18	1	4	– KSZV		262	252	215 KTBO		1 341	1 131	973
of leather and leather products KSOT	DC	19	1	–	1 KSZW		38	22	19 KTBP		132	161	120
of wood and wood products KSOU	DD	20	1	4	2 KSZX		361	349	411 KTBQ		1 064	1 060	1 107
of pulp, paper and paper products; publishing and printing KSOV	DE	21/22	3	–	3 KSZY		493	466	473 KTBR		2 547	2 544	2 365
of coke, refined petroleum products and nuclear fuel KSOW	DF	23	–	–	2 KSZZ		48	42	19 KTBS		..	..	..
of chemicals, chemical products and man-made fibres KSOX	DG	24	2	–	2 KTAE		428	395	406 KTBT		1 936	1 846	1 708
of rubber and plastic products KSOY	DH	25	2	5	4 KTAF		653	619	608 KTBU		..	..	..
of other non-metallic mineral products KSOZ	DI	26	1	5	2 KTAG		428	417	404 KTBV		2 095	2 052	1 929
of basic metals and fabricated metal products KSYV	DJ	27/28	17	19	12 KTAH		1 556	1 534	1 333 KTBW		6 119	6 070	5 133
of machinery and equipment not elsewhere classified KSYW	DK	29	4	4	3 KTAI		638	629	541 KTBX		2 859	2 876	2 731
of electrical and optical equipment KSYX	DL	30-33	–	2	– KTAJ		473	428	371 KTBY		2 284	2 321	2 053
of transport equipment KSYY	DM	34/35	2	1	2 KTAK		721	654	586 KTBZ		4 100	3 799	3 351
Manufacturing not elsewhere classified KSYZ	DN	36/37	6	2	8 KTAL		403	308	376 KTCA		1 531	1 489	1 582
Construction KSZA	F	45	81	105	80 KTAM		4 749	4 708	4 595 KTCB		10 504	9 796	9 695
Total service industries KSZB	G-Q	50-99	55	83	70 KTAN		15 296	14 860	16 011 KTCC		82 182	83 064	81 985
Wholesale and retail trade, and repairs KSZC	G	50-52	11	15	13 KTAO		3 221	3 045	3 445 KTCD		15 568	15 154	14 376
Hotel and restaurants KSZD	H	55	1	4	1 KTAP		874	754	936 KTCE		3 439	3 358	3 215
Transport, storage and communication[4] KSZE	I	60-64	19	40	23 KTAQ		2 978	3 061	3 068 KTCF		20 603	22 596	22 531
Financial intermediation KSZF	J	65-67	–	1	1 KTAR		159	152	228 KTCG		579	586	857
Real estate, renting and business activities KSZG	K	70-74	10	7	13 KTAS		1 134	1 031	1 623 KTCH		3 879	3 474	4 882
Public administration and defence KSZH	L	75	3	2	4 KTAT		2 227	2 165	2 183 KTCI		14 908	15 067	14 296
Education KSZI	M	80	–	2	2 KTAU		1 475	1 462	1 447 KTCJ		4 767	4 682	4 373
Health and social work KSZJ	N	85	–	2	2 KTAV		1 863	1 857	1 800 KTCK		13 825	13 400	13 061
Other community, social and personal services activities KSZK	O-Q	90-99	11	10	11 KTAW		1 365	1 333	1 281 KTCL		4 614	4 747	4 394
Unclassified KSZL			–	–	– KTAX		–	–	– KTCM		–	–	–
All industries KSZM			220	292	251 KTAY		29 315	28 154	28 940 KTCN		136 113	134 820	130 572

1 See chapter text.
2 Injuries causing incapacity for normal work for more than 3 days.
3 Excludes sea fishing.

4 Injuries arising from shore based services only. Excludes incidents reported under merchant shipping legislation.

Source: Health and Safety Executive (HSE): 0151 951 4842

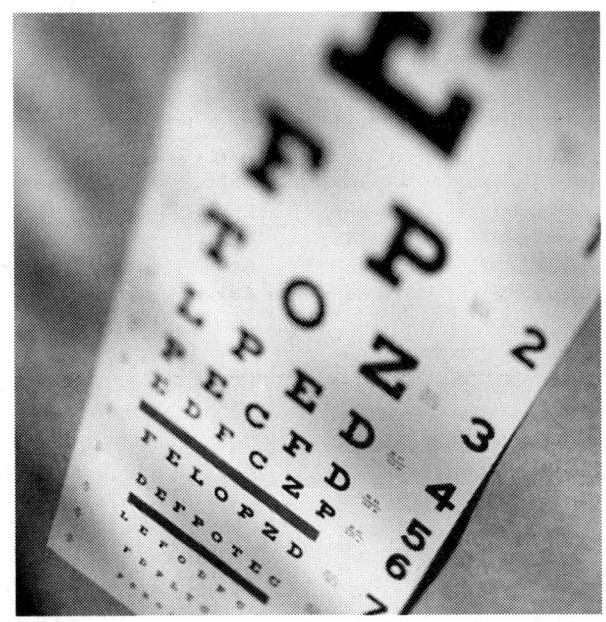

10 Social protection

Social protection

Social security
(Tables 10.2 - 10.8, 10.10, 10.11 and 10.13 to 10.16)
Tables 10.2 to 10.6 and 10.10 to 10.16 give details of contributors and beneficiaries under the National Insurance and Industrial Injury Acts, supplementary benefits and war pensions.

There are three types of contributor:

Class 1 Employed people, that is, people working for employers. Their contributions are paid partly by themselves and partly by their employers. They are covered for all benefits.

Class 2 Self-employed people, that is, people working on their own account. They are covered for all benefits other than unemployment and industrial injuries.

Class 3 Non-employed people, that is, people who do not work for gain. These people pay contributions on a voluntary basis. They are covered for benefits other than unemployment, sickness, industrial injuries and maternity allowances.

Class 4 Payable, in addition to Class 2 by self-employed people, and the amount payable is proportionate to profits or gains between a lower and upper limit in any one year.

An employer must pay a contribution for every employee whose earnings exceed a base level. Most employed people pay the full employee's contribution, but retirement pensioners working for an employer do not, and some married women and some widows who are working need not, unless they so wish, contribute except for industrial injuries benefit. Thus the total numbers in the analysis by benefit for which the contributions were payable are less than the total numbers in the analysis by class of contributor.

Jobseeker's Allowance *(Table 10.6)*
Jobseeker's Allowance (JSA) replaced Unemployment Benefit and Income Support for unemployed claimants on 7 October 1996. It is a unified benefit with two routes of entry: contribution-based which depends mainly upon national insurance contributions and income-based which depends mainly upon a means test. Some claimants can qualify by either route. In practice they receive income-based JSA but have an underlying entitlement to the contribution-based element.

Sickness Benefit, Invalidity Benefit and Incapacity Benefit *(Tables 10.7 and 10.8)*
Incapacity Benefit replaced Sickness Benefit and Invalidity Benefit from 13 April 1995. The first condition for entitlement to these contributory benefits is that the claimants are incapable of work because of illness or disablement. Secondly, that they satisfy the contribution conditions which depend on contributions paid as an employed (Class 1) or self-employed person (Class 2). Under Sickness and Invalidity Benefits the contribution conditions were automatically treated as satisfied if a person was incapable of work because of

an industrial accident or prescribed disease. Under Incapacity Benefit those who do not satisfy the contribution conditions in this case do not have them treated as satisfied. Class 1A contributions paid by employers are in respect of the benefit of cars provided for the private use of employees, and the free fuel provided for private use. These contributions do not provide any type of benefit cover.

Since 6 April 1983, most people working for an employer and paying National Insurance contributions as employed persons, receive Statutory Sick Pay (SSP) from their employer when they are off work sick. SSP was payable for a maximum of 8 weeks until 5 April 1986, and 28 weeks thereafter. People who do not work for an employer, and employees who are excluded from the SSP scheme, or those who have run out of SSP before reaching the maximum of 28 weeks and are still sick can claim benefit. Any period of SSP is excluded from the tables.

Spells of incapacity of 3 days or less do not count as periods of interruption of employment, and are excluded from the tables. Exceptions are where people are receiving regular weekly treatment by dialysis, or treatment by radiotherapy, chemotherapy or plasmapheresis where 2 days in any 6 consecutive days make up a period of interruption of employment, and those whose incapacity for work ends within 3 days of the end of SSP entitlement.

At the beginning of a period of incapacity, benefit is subject to 3 waiting days, except where there was an earlier spell of incapacity of more than 3 days in the previous 8 weeks. Employees entitled to SSP for less than 28 weeks and who are still sick can get Sickness Benefit or Incapacity Benefit Short Term (Low) until they reach a total of 28 weeks provided they satisfy the conditions. After 28 weeks SSP and/or Sickness Benefit (SB), Invalidity Benefit (IVB) was payable up to pension age for as long as the incapacity lasts. From pension age Invalidity Benefit was paid at the person's State Pension rate, until entitlement ceases when SP is paid or at deemed pension age (70 for a man, 65 for a woman). For people on Incapacity Benefit under State pension age there are two short-term rates: the lower rate is paid for the first 28 weeks of sickness and the higher rate for weeks 29 to 52. From week 53 the Long Term rate Incapacity Benefit is payable. The Short Term rate Incapacity Benefit is based on State Pension entitlement for people over State Pension age and is paid for up to a year if incapacity began before pension age.

The long-term rate of Incapacity Benefit applies to people under State Pension age who have been sick for more than a year. People with a terminal illness or who are receiving the higher rate care component of Disability Living Allowance will get the Long Term rate. The Long Term rate is not paid for people over pension age.

Under Incapacity Benefit, for the first 28 weeks of incapacity, people previously in work will be assessed on the 'own occupation' test - the claimant's ability to do their own job. Otherwise, incapacity will be based on a personal capability assessment, which will assess ability to carry out a range of work-related activities. The test will apply after 28 weeks of incapacity or from the start of the claim for people who did not previously have a job. Certain people will be exempted from this test.

The tables exclude all men aged over 65 and women aged over 60 who are in receipt of State Pension, and all people over deemed pension age (70 for a man and 65 for a woman), members of the Armed Forces, mariners while at sea, and married women and certain widows who have chosen not to be insured for sickness benefit. The tables include a number of individuals who were unemployed prior to incapacity.

The Short Term (Higher) and Long Term rates of Incapacity Benefit are treated as taxable income.

There were transitional provisions for people who were on Sickness or Invalidity Benefit on 12 April 1995. They were automatically transferred to Incapacity Benefit, payable on the same basis as before. Former IVB recipients continue to get Additional Pension entitlement, but frozen at 1994 levels. Also their IVB is not subject to tax. If they were over State Pension age on 12 April 1995 they may get Incapacity Benefit for up to 5 years beyond pension age.

Widow's Benefit and Bereavement Benefit
(Table 10.9 and 10.10)
Widow's Benefit is payable to women widowed on or after 11 April 1988 and up to and including 8 April 2001. There are three types of widow's benefits: Widow's Payment, Widowed Mother's Allowance and Widow's Pension. Women widowed before 11 April 1988 continue to receive Widow's Benefit based on the rules that existed before that date. Bereavement Benefit was introduced on 9 April 2001 as a replacement of Widows Benefit, payable to both men and women widowed on or after 9 April 2001. There are three types of Bereavement Benefits available: Bereavement Payment, Widowed Parent's Allowance and Bereavement Allowance.

Family Credit/ Working Families' Tax Credit
(Table 10.13)
Working Families' Tax Credit (WFTC) replaced Family Credit from 5 October 1999.

Family Credit was, and Working Families' Tax Credit is, available to families with at least one adult in remunerative work for at least 16 hours per week and who is responsible for at least one child under 16 (under 19 if in full time education up to A-level or equivalent standard). The rate of payment of WFTC depends on the number of such children and expenditure incurred on eligible childcare. It is also higher if the worker works for at least 30 hours per week, or if there are disabled children or severely disabled adults in the family. It is tapered away above an income threshold. Further details can be obtained from the Inland Revenue.

Government expenditure on social services and housing (Table 10.18 - 10.23)
The tables of general government expenditure on social services and housing in the United Kingdom comprise a summary table followed by separate tables for each

of the social services and housing. The definition of government expenditure used in these tables follows that in Table 9.4 of the *Blue Book 2002 Edition*, and covers both current and capital expenditure of the central government (including the National Insurance Fund) and local authorities. The housing table also includes the capital expenditure of public corporations concerned with housing. As in the *Blue Book*, government expenditure is measured after deducting fees and charges for services. Expenditure on administration includes the cost of common services (accommodation, stationery and printing, super-annuation, etc) some of which is not directly borne by the departments administering each service. Transfers from one part of government to another have been eliminated to avoid double counting. The figures relate to years ended 31 March.

It should be noted that the figures no longer include imputed rents for the use of fixed assets owned and used by general government. In the *Blue Book*, imputed rents have been replaced by capital consumption. Capital consumption, however, cannot be allocated to individual services and is therefore not included in these tables.

The following notes give brief descriptions of each of the main services shown in the tables.

Education (Table 10.19)
This covers expenditure by the Education Departments, local education authorities and the University Grants Committee on education in schools, training colleges, technical institutions and universities. It includes expenditure on school meals.

National Health Service (Table 10.20)
This covers expenditure by central government on hospital and community health, family practitioner and other health services. The expenditure by local authorities on the provision of health centres, health visiting, home nursing, ambulance services, vaccination and immunisation, etc, was transferred to central government on 1 April 1974. Only the net costs of providing these services are included in total government expenditure, receipts from patients being shown separately.

Personal social services (Table 10.21)
This covers local authority expenditure on the aged, handicapped and homeless, child care, care of mothers and young children, mental health, domestic help, etc. Also included are central government grants to voluntary approved schools.

Welfare foods (Table 10.21)
This covers the cost of providing welfare foods at reduced prices to children and expectant mothers. Only the net costs of providing these services are included in the total government expenditure, payments by the recipients of the services being shown separately.

Social security (Table 10.22)
This comprises both benefits under the Social Security schemes and non-contributory benefits and allowances, administered by the Department for Work and Pensions. The analysis by type of Income Support is

Social protection

not exact; the estimates are derived from average numbers in receipt of benefit and average amounts paid. Unified housing benefit (rent rebates and allowances) is also included as social security expenditure and not as housing expenditure. This is now mainly administered by local authorities who receive grants from central government.

Housing *(Table 10.23)*

The table shows, in addition to government expenditure on housing, the capital expenditure of public corporations and the total expenditure of the public sector on housing. The government expenditure figures cover subsidies paid by the housing departments towards the provision of housing by local authorities, new town development corporations and housing associations; subsidies by local authorities to their housing revenue accounts; rent rebates for tenants of housing owned by local authorities and new towns; rent allowances for tenants of privately-owned housing; grants to persons for the reduction of mortgage interest payments; capital expenditure on the provision of houses for letting; capital grants to housing associations; grants by local authorities towards the cost of conversion and improvement of privately-owned houses; net lending by the central government and local authorities for private house purchase; and improvement and loans for first time purchasers. The public corporations' figures cover capital expenditure on the provision of houses for letting and lending by the Housing Corporation to housing associations.

10.1 National Insurance Fund
United Kingdom
Years ended 31 March

£ millions

		1993 /94	1994 /95	1995 /96	1996 /97	1997 /98	1998 /99	1999 /00	2000 /01	2001 /02
Receipts										
Opening balance	KJFB	3 578	4 672	7 042	8 045	7 869	9 763	12 625	14 909	19 868
Contributions	JXVM	35 090	38 712	40 875	42 806	46 755	50 023	51 852	55 627	58 050
Grant from Consolidated Fund	KOTF	7 785	6 445	3 680	1 952	966	3	2	..	
Compensation for SSP/SMP	KJQM	1 158	563	475	542	601	576	625	688	710
Transfers from GB	KOTG	40	145	125	75	150	315	230	200	110
Income from investments	KJFE	488	365	459	489	474	667	724	884	1 146
Other receipts	KJFF	42	61	76	85	97	92	127	112	67
Redundancy receipts[1]	KIBQ	26	25	24	26	25	21	21	23	22
Total	JYJO	48 207	50 989	52 756	54 020	56 937	61 462	66 206	72 442	79 972
Expenditure										
Total benefits	JYJP	42 367	42 271	43 198	44 518	45 321	46 822	50 026	50 960	54 550
Unemployment	KJFH	1 690	1 331	1 131	605	–	..	..	..	..
Sickness[2]	KJFI	378	351	15	..	..	..	..	..	..
Invalidity[2]	KJFJ	7 341	8 009	600	..	..	..	..	..	..
Incapacity[2]	JYXL	..	..	7 623	7 993	7 739	7 574	7 206	6 982	7 074
Maternity	KETY	34	28	30	34	37	39	40	46	57
Widows' pensions	KEWU	1 076	1 057	1 051	1 017	1 021	1 008	1 020	1 008	1 132
Guardians' allowances and Child's special allowance[3]	KJFK	1	1	2	2	2	2	2	2	2
Retirement pensions[3]	JYJV	31 721	31 367	32 620	34 736	36 396	38 072	41 157	42 350	45 677
Pensioners' lump sum payments	KAAW	125	126	127	132	126	128	126	123	131
Other payments	KAAZ	35	9	14	17	19	18	19	21	29
Administration	KABE	1 605	1 324	1 219	1 065	1 073	1 053	847	1 197	873
Transfers to Northern Ireland	KABF	40	145	125	75	150	315	230	200	110
Redundancy payments	KIBR	272	199	155	134	120	140	174	195	232
Jobseeker's allowance (Contributory)[5]	LUQW	..	..	..	341	489	489	475	449	478
Total	JYJU	44 318	43 947	44 711	46 151	47 173	48 837	51 297	52 574	55 795
Accumulated funds	KABH	4 672	7 042	8 045	7 869	9 763	12 625	14 909	19 868	24 177

1 The Assets of the Redundancy Fund became those of the National Insurance Fund on 31 January 1991
2 Incapacity Benefit replaced Sickness Benefit and Invalidity Benefit from April 1995
3 Includes figures of Child's special allowance for Northern Ireland
4 Includes Figures for personal pensions
5 Jobseekers Allowance (Contributory) was introduced in October 1996 and replaced Unemployment Benefits

Sources: Board of Inland Revenue: 020 7438 7370;
Department for Work and Pensions: 01253 856123 Ext 62436;
Department of Health, Social Services and Public Safety (Northern Ireland);
028 9052 2062

10.2 Persons who paid National Insurance contributions in a tax year[1]
United Kingdom

Millions

		Total				Men				Women		
		1999 /00	2000 /01	2001 /02		1999 /00	2000 /01	2001 /02		1999 /00	2000 /01	2001 /02
Total[2]	KABI	27.51	28.11	28.35	KEYF	15.42	15.69	15.76	KEYP	12.10	12.42	12.59
Class 1	KABJ	24.94	25.46	25.62	KEYG	13.46	13.68	13.71	KEYQ	11.47	11.77	11.91
Not contracted out[3]	KABK	15.58	16.06	16.27	KEYH	8.61	8.90	9.05	KEYR	6.97	7.16	7.22
Contracted out	KABL	7.63	7.60	7.57	KEYI	4.11	4.00	3.89	KEYS	3.52	3.59	3.68
Mixed contracted in/out[4]	KABM	1.55	1.66	1.67	KEYJ	0.74	0.78	0.77	KEYT	0.81	0.88	0.89
Class 1 Reduced rate (including standard rate)	KABO	0.17	0.14	0.11	KEYL	..	..	..	KEYV	0.17	0.14	0.11
Class 2 exclusively	KABP	2.00	2.05	2.10	KEYM	1.58	1.60	1.62	KEYW	0.43	0.45	0.47
Mixed Class 1 and Class 2	KABQ	0.42	0.48	0.53	KEYN	0.30	0.33	0.36	KEYX	0.12	0.14	0.17
Class 3 exclusively[5]	KABR	0.15	0.13	0.11	KEYO	0.08	0.07	0.06	KEYY	0.07	0.06	0.05

1 See chapter text. The tax year commences on 6 April and ends on 5 April of the following year.
2 Not all figures agree because of rounding.
3 Includes those persons with an Appropriate Personal Pension (such persons pay contributions at the not contracted out rate but then receive a rebate).

4 Not included in the above rows
5 Persons who paid a mixture of Class 3 contributions and others are not included in this category.

Source: Board of Inland Revenue 020 7438 7370

10.3 Weekly rates of principal social security benefits[1]
Great Britain
At April

£

		1993	1994	1995	1996	1997	1998	1999	2000	2001	2002	2003
Unemployment benefit:[2,3]												
Men and women	KJNA	44.65	45.45	46.45	48.25	..	..	..	..	..	..	..
Jobseeker's allowance:[3]												
Personal allowances												
Single												
Aged under 18(Depending	KXDH	..	..	..	..	29.60	30.30	30.95	31.45	31.95	32.50	32.90
on their circumstances)	KXDI	..	..	..	..	38.90	39.85	40.70	41.35	42.00	42.70	43.25
Aged 18 - 24	KXDJ	..	..	..	..	38.90	39.85	40.70	41.35	42.00	42.70	43.25
Aged 25 or over	KXDK	..	..	..	..	49.15	50.35	51.40	52.20	53.05	53.95	54.65
Couple												
Both aged under 18[4]	KXDL	..	..	..	..	58.70	30.30	30.95	31.45	31.95	32.50	32.90
One or both aged												
18 or over	KXDM	..	..	..	..	77.15	79.00	80.65	81.95	83.25	84.65	85.75
Dependant children and												
young people												
Aged under 11	KXDN	..	..	..	..	16.90	17.30	20.20	26.60	31.45	33.50	38.50
Aged 11 - 16	KXDO	..	..	..	..	24.75	25.35	25.90	26.60	31.45	33.50	38.50
Aged 16 - 18	KXDP	..	..	..	..	29.60	30.30	30.95	31.75	32.25	34.30	38.50
Sickness benefit:[2,5]												
Men and women	KJNB	42.70	43.45	..	..	..	..	..	..	..	..	..
Invalidity benefit:[5]												
Invalidity pension	KJNC	56.10	57.60	..	..	..	..	..	..	..	..	..
Invalidity allowance:[5]												
High rate	KJND	11.95	12.15	12.40	12.90	13.15	13.60	14.05	14.20	14.65	14.90	15.15
Middle rate	KJNE	7.50	7.60	7.80	8.10	8.30	8.60	8.90	9.00	9.30	9.50	9.70
Low rate	KJNF	3.75	3.80	3.90	4.05	4.15	4.30	4.45	4.50	4.65	4.75	4.85
Increase for dependants:[5]												
Adult	KJNG	33.70	34.50	35.25	36.60	37.35	38.70	39.95	40.40	41.75	42.45	43.15
Each child[6]	KJNH	10.95	11.00	11.05	11.15	11.20	11.30	11.35	11.35	11.35	11.35	11.35
Incapacity benefit:												
Short term (Lower) Under pension age	KOSB	..	..	44.40	46.15	47.10	48.80	50.35	50.90	52.60	53.50	54.40
Increase for adult dependant	KOSC	..	..	27.50	28.55	29.15	30.20	31.15	31.50	32.55	33.10	33.65
Short term (Lower) Over pension age	KOSD	..	..	56.45	58.65	59.90	62.05	64.05	64.75	66.90	68.05	69.20
Increase for adult dependant	KOSE	..	..	33.85	35.15	35.90	37.20	38.40	38.80	40.10	42.45	41.50
Short term (Higher)	KOSF	..	..	52.50	54.55	55.70	57.70	59.55	60.20	62.20	63.25	64.35
Increase for dependants:												
Adult	KOSG	..	..	27.50	28.55	29.15	30.20	31.15	31.50	32.55	33.10	33.65
Child[6]	KOSH	..	..	11.05	11.15	11.20	11.30	11.35	11.35	11.35	11.35	11.35
Long term	KOSI	..	..	58.85	61.15	62.45	64.70	66.75	67.50	69.75	70.95	72.15
Increase for dependants:												
Adult	KOSJ	..	..	35.25	36.60	37.35	38.70	39.95	40.40	41.75	42.45	43.15
Child[6]	KOSK	..	..	11.05	11.15	11.20	11.30	11.35	11.35	11.35	11.35	11.35
Incapacity age addition:[7]												
Higher rate	KOSL	..	..	12.40	12.90	13.15	13.60	14.05	14.20	14.65	14.90	15.15
Lower rate	KOSM	..	..	6.20	6.45	6.60	6.80	7.05	7.10	7.35	7.45	7.60
Attendance allowance:												
Higher rate	KJNI	44.90	45.70	46.70	48.50	49.50	51.30	52.95	53.55	55.30	56.25	57.20
Lower rate	KJNJ	30.00	30.55	31.20	32.40	33.10	34.30	35.40	35.80	37.00	37.65	38.30
Mobility allowance[8]	KJNK	..	..	..	..	..	..	..	..	..	..	..
Disability living allowance:												
care component												
Higher rate	KXDC	44.90	45.70	46.70	48.50	49.50	51.30	52.95	53.55	55.30	56.25	57.20
Middle rate	KXDD	30.00	30.55	31.20	32.40	33.10	34.30	35.40	35.80	37.00	37.65	38.30
Lower rate	KXDE	11.95	12.15	12.40	12.90	13.15	13.60	14.05	14.20	14.65	14.90	15.15
mobility component												
Higher rate	KXDF	31.40	31.95	32.65	33.90	34.60	35.85	37.00	37.40	38.65	39.30	39.95
Lower rate	KXDG	11.95	12.15	12.40	12.90	13.15	13.60	14.05	14.20	14.65	14.90	15.15

10.3

Weekly rates of principal social security benefits[1]
Great Britain
At April

£

		1993	1994	1995	1996	1997	1998	1999	2000	2001	2002	2003
Maternity benefit:												
Maternity allowances for insured women[9]												
Higher rate	KOSN	..	..	52.50	54.55	55.70	57.70	59.55	60.20	..	..	..
Lower rate[10]	KJNL	43.75	44.55	45.55	47.35	48.35	50.10	51.70	52.25	..	..	..
Standard rate[11]	GPTJ	..	..	..	..	..	..	..	..	62.20	75.00	100.00
Threshold[12]	GPTK	..	..	..	..	..	..	..	..	30.00	30.00	30.00
Guardian's allowance	KJNN	10.95	11.00	11.05	11.15	11.20	11.30	11.35	11.35	11.35	11.35	11.55
Widow's benefit:												
Widow's pension	KJNO	56.10	57.60	58.85	61.15	62.45	64.70	66.75	67.50	72.50	75.50	77.45
Widowed mother's allowance	KJNP	56.10	57.60	58.85	61.15	62.45	64.70	66.75	67.50	72.50	75.50	77.45
Addition for each child	KJNQ	10.95	11.00	11.05	11.15	11.20	11.30	11.35	11.35	11.35	11.35	11.35
Bereavement benefit:												
Bereavement allowance	WMPF	..	..	..	..	..	..	..	..	72.50	75.50	77.45
Widowed parent's allowance	WMOZ	..	..	..	..	..	..	..	..	72.50	72.50	77.45
Addition for each child	WMPA	..	..	..	..	..	..	..	..	11.35	11.35	11.35
State Pension contributory:[13]												
Single person	KJNR	56.10	57.60	58.85	61.15	62.45	64.70	66.75	67.50	72.50	75.50	77.45
Married couple	KJNS	89.80	92.10	94.10	97.75	99.80	103.40	106.70	107.90	115.90	120.70	122.80
State Pension non contributory:												
Man or woman	KJNT	33.70	34.50	35.25	36.60	37.35	38.70	39.95	40.40	43.40	45.20	45.45
Married woman	KJNU	20.15	20.65	21.10	21.90	22.35	23.15	23.90	24.15	24.95	27.00	27.70
Industrial injuries benefit												
Disablement pension at 100 per cent rate	KJNW	91.60	93.20	95.30	99.00	101.10	104.70	108.10	109.30	112.90	114.80	116.80
Widow's or widower's pension	KJNX	56.10	57.60	58.85	61.15	62.45	..	..	..	..	..	..
Increase for dependants:[14]												
Adult	KJNY	27.55	28.05	28.65	29.75	..	..	..	..	..	..	..
Child benefit:[15]												
First child	KJOA	10.00	10.20	10.40	10.80	11.05	11.45	14.40	15.00	15.50	15.75	16.05
Subsequent children	KETZ	8.10	8.25	8.45	8.80	9.00	9.30	9.60	10.00	10.35	10.55	10.75
Family Credit[16]												
(maximum awards payable):[17]												
Families with 1 child												
Birth to September following 11th birthday	KJOB	53.25	55.15	56.50	58.20	59.70	61.15	64.95	..	..	..	..
From September following 11th birthday to September following 16th birthday	KJOC	60.35	62.45	64.00	65.90	67.60	69.25	70.70	..	..	..	..
From September following 16th birthday to day before 19th birthday	KJOD	64.70	67.00	68.55	70.60	72.45	74.20	75.95	..	..	..	..
Increase for each additional child												
Birth to September following 11th birthday	KJOF	10.75	11.15	11.40	11.75	12.05	12.35	15.15	..	..	..	..
From September following 11th birthday to September following 16th birthday	KJOG	17.85	18.45	18.90	19.45	19.95	20.45	20.90	..	..	..	..
From September following 16th birthday to day before 19th birthday	KJOH	22.20	23.00	23.45	24.15	24.80	25.40	25.95	..	..	..	..
War pension:												
Ex-private (100 per cent assessment)	KJOJ	97.20	98.90	101.10	105.00	107.20	111.10	114.70	116.00	119.80	121.80	..
War widow	KJOK	72.90	74.70	76.35	79.35	81.00	83.90	86.60	87.55	90.45	92.00	..

10.3
continued

Weekly rates of principal social security benefits[1]
Great Britain
At April

£

		1993	1994	1995	1996	1997	1998	1999	2000	2001	2002	2003
Income Support:												
Personal allowances[18]												
Single												
aged 16-17 either	KJOW	26.45	27.50	28.00	28.85	29.60	30.30	30.95	31.45	31.95	32.50	32.90
or depending on their												
circumstances	KABS	34.80	36.15	36.80	37.90	38.90	39.85	40.70	41.35	42.00	42.70	43.25
aged 18-24	KJOX	34.80	36.15	36.80	37.90	38.90	39.85	40.70	41.35	42.00	42.70	43.25
aged 25 or over	KJOY	44.00	45.70	46.50	47.90	49.15	50.35	51.40	52.20	53.05	53.95	54.65
Couple												
both aged under 18[4]	KJOZ	52.40	54.55	55.55	57.20	58.70	60.10	61.90	..	..	..	..
one or both 18 or over	KJPA	69.00	71.70	73.00	75.20	77.15	79.00	80.65	81.95	83.25	84.65	85.75
Lone parent												
aged 16-17 either	KJPB	26.45	27.50	28.00	28.85	29.60	30.30	30.95	31.45	31.95	32.50	32.90
or depending on their												
circumstances	KABT	34.80	36.15	36.80	37.90	38.90	39.85	40.70	41.35	42.00	42.70	43.25
aged 18 or over	KJPC	44.00	45.70	46.50	47.90	49.15	50.35	51.40	52.20	53.05	53.95	54.65
Dependant children and young												
people[16]												
1991-1996												
aged under 11	KJPD	15.05	15.65	15.95	16.45	..	..	..	..	..	..	..
aged 11-15	KJPE	22.15	23.00	23.40	24.10	..	..	..	..	..	..	..
aged 16-17	KJPF	26.45	27.50	28.00	28.85	..	..	..	..	..	..	..
aged 18	KABU	34.80	36.15	36.80	37.90	..	..	..	..	..	..	..
From 1997-1999												
Birth to September following												
11th birthday	KXDQ	..	..	..	..	16.90	17.30	20.20	..	..	..	..
From September following												
11th birthday to September												
following 16th birthday	KXDR	..	..	..	..	24.75	..	25.90	..	..	..	..
From September following												
16th birthday to day												
before 19th birthday	KXDS	..	..	..	..	29.60	30.30	30.95	..	..	..	..
From 2000												
Birth to September following												
16th birthday	WMOD	..	..	..	..	..	..	..	26.60	31.45	33.50	38.50
From September following												
16th birthday to day												
before 19th birthday	WMOP	..	..	..	..	..	..	..	31.75	32.25	34.30	38.50

1 See chapter text

2 Persons under the age of 18 are entitled to the appropriate adult rate.

3 Jobseeker's allowance, introduced 7 October 1996, replaced unemployment benefit and income support for the unemployed.

4 From 12 April 1999 the personal allowance for couples where both members are not yet 18 or one of the couples is aged 18 or over depends on the couple's circumstances. They may be entitled to a couple allowance or a single person's allowance dependant on certain criteria.

5 Incapacity benefit introduced from 13 April 1995, has replaced sickness benefit and invalidity benefit.

6 For the first child only the Child Dependency increase is from 1994, reduced by £1.30 to £9.90 because of child benefit.

7 The rate of age addition depends on age at date of onset of incapacity: higher rate for under age 35 and lower rate for age 35-44.

8 Disability living allowance replaced Mobility allowance from April 1992.

9 Following a EU Directive, employee's maternity benefit is aligned with the state benefit they would receive if off work sick.

10 Women who were either not employed or self-employed received the lower rate.

11 New Standard rate introduced from April 2000.

12 MA Earnings Threshold introduced April 2000.

13 Retirement pensioners over 80 receive 25p addition.

14 An allowance for one adult dependent was payable, where appropriate, with unemployment benefit, sickness benefit, retirement pension, injury benefit and maternity allowance.

15 From October 1991 the first child receives £9.25 and each subsequent child £7.50

16 Age bandings for children's personal allowances were revised on 7 April 1997. Some children have protected rights. Further information is available from the Department for Work and Pensions.

17 Maximum award does not include the 30 hour credit.

18 In addition to personal allowances, a claimant may also be entitled to premiums. The types of premiums are family, lone parent, pensioner, higher pensioner, disability, severe disability and disabled child.

Sources: Department for Work and Pensions;
Information and Analysis Directorate : 0191 225 7373;
Board of Inland Revenue: 020 7438 7370;
Ministry of Defence/DASA (Pay & Pensions) 020 7218 4271

10.4 National Insurance contributions

	Employee's standard contributions[1]		Employer's standard contributions[1]	
	not contracted-out rate	contracted-out rate[2]	not contracted-out rate	contracted-out rate[3]
Class 1				
Weekly earnings				
1997/98				
Below 62.00 (LEL)	-	-	-	-
62.00-109.99	2% on first £62.00;	2% on first £62.00;	3.0	-
110.00-154.99	10% on balance	8.4% on balance	5.0	2.0
155.00-209.99			7.0%	4.0%
210.00-465.00			10.0%	7.0%
Above 465.00 (LEL)	£41.54	£35.09	10.0%	10.0%
1998/99				
Below 64.00 (LEL)	-	-	-	-
64.00-109.99	2% on first £64.00;	2% on first £64.00;	3.0%	-
110.00-154.99	10% on balance	8.4% on balance	5.0%	2.0%
155.00-209.99			7.0%	4.0%
210.00-485.00			10.0%	7.0%
Above 485.00 (UEL)	£43.38	£36.64	10.0%	10.0%
1999/00				
Below 66.00 (LEL)	-	-	-	-
66.00-83.00	10.0%	8.4%		-
83.00-500.00	10.0%	8.4%	12.2%	9.2%
Above 500.00 (UEL)	£43.40	£36.46	12.2%	12.2%
2000/01				
Below 67.00 (LEL)	-	-	-	-
67.00-76.00 (PT)	-	See note 4	-	See note 5
76.00-84.00 (ST)	10.0%	-	-	
84.00-535.00 (UEL)	10.0%	8.4%	12.2%	9.2%
Above 535.00 (UEL)	£45.90	£38.41	12.2%	12.2%
2001/02				
Below 72.00 (LEL)	-	-	-	-
72.00-87.00 (PT/ST)	-	See note 4	-	See note 5
87.00-575.00 (UEL)	10.0%	8.4%	11.9%	8.9%
Above 575.00 (UEL)	£48.80	£40.75	11.9%	11.9%
2002/03				
Below 75.00 (LEL)	-	-	-	-
75.00-89.00 (PT/ST)	-	See note 4	-	See note 6
89.00-585.00 (UEL)	10.0%	8.4%	11.8%	8.3%
Above 585.00 (UEL)	£49.60	£41.44	11.8%	11.8%
2003/04				
Below 77.00 (LEL)	-	-	-	-
77.00-89.00 (PT/ST)	-	See note 4	-	See note 6
89.00-595.00 (UEL)	11.0%	9.4%	12.8%	9.3%
Above 595.00 (UEL)	1%	1%	12.8%	12.8%

	1997/98	1998/99	1999/00	2000/01	2001/02	2002/03	2003/04
Class 2							
Flat rate weekly	£6.15	£6.35	£6.55	£2.00	£2.00	£2.00	£2.00
Small earnings exception[7] (per annum)	£3,480	£3,590	£3,770	£3,825	£3, 955	£4,025	£4, 095
Class 3							
Flat-rate voluntary weekly contributions	£6.05	£6.25	£6.45	£6.55	£6.75	£6.85	£6.95
Class 4 (Self-employed; profit-related)							
Rate on profits between LPL and UPL	6.0%	6.0%	6.0%	7.0%	7.0%	7.0%	8.0%
Rate on profits above UPL	..	..	..	..	..	..	1%
Lower profits limit (LPL)	£7,010	£7,310	£7,530	£4,385	£4,535	£4.615	£4,615
Upper profits limit (UPL)	£24,180	£25,220	£26,000	£27,820	£29,900	£30,420	£30,940

Note: LEL: Lower Earnings Limit; UEL: Upper Earnings Limit. PT: Primary Threshold; ST: Secondary Threshold.

1 Married women opting to pay contributions at the reduced rate at 3.85% before 2003-04 and 4.95% in 2003-04 earn no entitlement to contributory National Insurance benefits as a result of these contributions. No women have been allowed to exercise this option since 1977, but around 200,000 women who have been continually married or widowed and in the labour market since that time have retained their right to pay the reduced rate.

2 The contracted-out rebate for employees' contributions is applied only between LEL and UEL. Earnings below LEL are charged at the appropriate not contracted-out rate (which depends on total earnings). Earnings above the UEL are not subject to employee NICs before 2003-04

3 The rates shown only apply to Contracted-Out Salary Related schemes. (COSR). Earnings below the LEL and above the UEL are charged at the appropriate not-contracted out rate. The employers' contracted-out rate applies only between the LEL and the UEL.

4 The contracted-out rebate for primary contributions is 1.6 per cent of earnings between the LEL and the UEL for all forms of contracting-out.

5 The contracted-out rebate for secondary contributions is 3 per cent of earnings between the LEL and the UEL.

6 The contracted out rebate for secondary contributions is 3.5 per cent of earnings between the LEL and the UEL.

7 If earnings from self-employment are below this annual limit and the contributor applies for and is granted a small earnings exception Class 2 contributions need not be paid. Class 2 or 3 contributions may be paid voluntarily.

Source: Board of Inland Revenue: 020 7438 7370

10.5 Social Security Acts: number of persons receiving benefit[1]
Great Britain
At any one time

Thousands

Persons receiving:		1993	1994	1995	1996	1997	1998	1999	2000	2001	2002	2003
Unemployment benefit[2]	KJHA	659.2	540.8	414.6	397.8	..	..	..	..	..	..	..
Jobseeker's allowance[2,3]	JYXM	..	..	..	..	1 406.3	1 181.2	1 105.8	972.7	848.3	827.5	832.3
Sickness and Invalidity benefit[4,5]	KJHB	1 727.0	1 808.6	1 894.1	..	..	..	..	..	..	..	..
Incapacity benefit[6]	KXDT	..	..	..	1 812.8	1 749.2	1 671.2	1 557.1	1 504.3	1 515.2	1 496.9	1 506.5
Attendance allowance[7]	KXDU	890.3	962.4	1 046.5	1 120.6	1 183.2	1 225.6	1 243.8	1 249.6	1 290.0	1 288.2	1 340.7
Disability living allowance[8]	KXDW	1 200.6	1 329.1	1 534.2	1 729.2	1 886.5	1 995.9	2 061.3	2 130.5	2 240.5	2 353.5	2 497.6
Widows' benefits[10]	KJHF	336.9	329.8	323.2	308.9	296.4	278.8	267.6	261.0	255.5	226.4	196.1
Bereavement Benefits>[10]	VQAA	..	..	..	..	..	..	..	..	..	36.8	44.4
National Insurance State pension contributory[5]:												
Males[10]	KJHH	3 533.4	3 555.9	3 590.1	3 688.2	3 786.5	3 880.4	3 956.3	4 039.4	4 083.9	4 141.5	4 205.5
Females[10]	KJHL	6 663.0	6 668.1	6 686.4	6 733.5	6 783.2	6 850.7	6 886.3	6 928.0	6 959.7	6 982.5	7 037.0
Total[10]	KJHG	10 196.4	10 224.0	10 276.5	10 421.7	10 569.7	10 731.1	10 842.6	10 967.4	11 043.6	11 124.0	11 242.5
State pension non contributory[5]:												
Males[10]	KJHI	5.4	5.5	5.4	5.7	5.6	5.5	5.1	5.2	5.1	5.0	5.4
Females[10]	KJHJ	23.1	22.2	21.8	22.3	20.9	19.8	18.8	18.0	18.2	18.2	18.1
Total[10]	KJHK	28.6	27.7	27.2	28.0	26.5	25.2	23.9	23.2	23.3	23.3	23.5
Industrial Injuries disablement pensions assessments[11]	KJHN	212.4	225.6	235.2	249.2	257.8	269.1	278.2	280.8	280.4	278.2	200.3
Reduced earnings allowance/ Retirement allowance assessments[11]	KEYC	156.0	154.3	152.1	154.9	155.6	152.8	153.5	153.5	152.3	148.7	143.0
Family Credit[12]	ZCGF	488	551	608	693	748	767	791	–	..	..	..
Income Support[13]	KABV	5 642.5	5 674.6	5 670.2	5 548.9	3 858.0	3 853.1	3 814.4	3 810.5	3 927.9	3 929.8	3 982.2
Housing Benefit and Council Tax Benefit												
Rent rebate	KABY	3 052.5	3 016.1	2 964.3	2 898.3	2 792.3	2 664.1	2 518.5	2 287.8	2 133.5	2 037.6	1 838.1
Rent allowance[14]	KABZ	1 480.6	1 633.9	1 770.1	1 877.6	1 847.1	1 810.6	1 794.6	1 745.5	1 740.9	1 775.0	1 958.3
Council tax benefit[15]	KJPO	5 251.8	5 496.5	5 623.9	5 611.2	5 498.3	5 325.7	5 166.1	4 830.1	4 673.4	4 601.7	4 627.8
War pensions[5]	KJHR	292.9	309.2	315.4	327.5	320.7	302.0	306.0	295.7	284.3	272.7	260.7

1 See chapter text. Caseload counts at a specific date in the year which varies from benefit to benefit.
2 Figures are given at May each year.
3 Jobseeker's Allowance introduced 7 October 1996, replacing unemployment benefit and Income Support for the unemployed.
4 A relatively small number of claims do not result in the payment of benefit but are included here because they indicate notified incapacity for work.
5 Includes overseas cases. As at end of March
6 Incapacity Benefit replaced Sickness Benefit and Invalidity Benefit from 13 April 1995. Figures are taken at the last day in February.
7 Attendance Allowance figures are based at 31 March until 1995 then at the end of May.
8 Figures are given as at May of each year.

9 Figures for 1999 as at November. Figure for 2000 as at August. Figure for 2001 and 2002 as at May
10 Includes overseas cases. As at March
11 Industrial injuries disablement pension, reduced earnings allowance, retirement allowance assessments starting first Monday in April. Includes an allowance for late returns. From 2003 data is person based as at March.
12 Family Credit was replaced by Working Families' Tax Credit from October 1999. See table 10.12 for latest figures.
13 From 9 October 1996 Income Support for the unemployed was replaced by Income-based Jobseeker's Allowance. Figures in this table up to and including 1996 include unemployed Income Support claimants. Figures from 1997 exclude unemployed who will be counted in the Jobseeker's Allowance claims.
14 Rent Allowance figures include registered social landlord tenants.
15 Figure excludes Second Adult Rebate Claims.
16 Includes overseas cases. As at March.

Sources: Department for Work and Pensions;
Information and Analysis Directorate : 0191 225 7373;
Board of Inland Revenue: 020 7438 7370;
Ministry of Defence/DASA (Pay & Pensions): 020 7218 4271

10.6 Jobseeker's allowance[1] claimants analysed by benefit entitlement

Great Britain as at May

Thousands

		1997	1998	1999	2000	2001	2002	2003
All Persons								
All with benefit - total	KXDX	1 406.3	1 181.2	1 105.8	972.7	848.3	827.5	832.3
Contribution-based JSA only	KXDY	181.1	154.2	158.2	148.2	147.0	162.6	167.3
Contribution based JSA & income-based JSA	KXDZ	28.3	23.5	27.1	19.0	18.3	19.4	18.9
Income-based JSA only payment	KXEA	1 196.8	1 003.6	920.4	805.5	683.1	645.5	646.1
No benefit in payment	KXEB	156.2	114.5	118.7	94.6	93.7	91.1	91.7
Total	KXEC	1 562.4	1 295.8	1 224.5	1 067.3	942.0	918.5	924.0
Males								
All with benefit - total	KXED	1 096.9	918.2	862.3	755.0	659.4	634.6	631.7
Contribution-based JSA only	KXEE	119.5	101.6	109.0	104.2	104.5	116.0	119.0
Contribution based JSA & income-based JSA	KXEF	25.4	20.7	24.4	17.2	16.7	17.5	16.6
Income-based JSA only payment	KXEG	952.0	795.9	728.9	633.6	538.2	501.1	496.1
No benefit in payment	KXEH	106.8	75.5	79.2	63.4	61.9	62.3	62.9
Total	KXEI	1 203.7	993.6	941.5	818.4	721.3	696.9	694.6
Females								
All with benefit - total	KXEJ	309.4	263.0	243.4	217.7	188.9	192.9	200.6
Contribution-based JSA only	KXEK	61.6	52.6	49.2	44.0	42.5	46.6	48.3
Contribution based JSA & income-based JSA	KXEL	3.0	2.8	2.7	1.8	1.5	1.9	2.3
Income-based JSA only payment	KXEM	244.8	207.7	191.5	171.9	144.9	144.4	150.0
No benefit in payment	KXEN	49.4	39.1	39.5	31.2	31.8	28.8	28.7
Total	KXEO	358.8	302.1	283.0	248.9	220.8	221.7	229.3

1 See chapter text. Jobseeker's Allowance has two routes of entry: contribution-based which depends mainly upon national insurance contributions and income-based which depends mainly on a means test. Some claimants can qualify by either route. In practice they receive income-based JSA but have an underlying entitlement to the contribution-based element.

Sources: Department for Work and Pensions; Information and Analysis Directorate : 0191 225 7373

10.7 Sickness benefit, invalidity benefit and incapacity benefit[1] claimants, by age and duration of spell

Great Britain at end of statistical year[2]

Thousands

		1993	1994	1995[3]	1996	1997	1998	1999	2000	2001	2002	2003
Age at 31 March[4]												
Males												
All durations: All ages	KJJA	1 468.0	1 544.4	1 629.9	1 627.0	1 577.9	1 530.1	1 458.4	1 432.0	1 458.5	1 454.7	1 467.3
Under 20	KJJB	7.1	6.8	7.8	8.7	8.8	10.7	10.7	11.2	10.2	12.7	21.2
20-29	KJJC	86.2	97.2	106.0	119.3	118.8	119.1	115.0	114.2	119.1	123.1	130.7
30-39	KJJD	145.7	160.4	189.7	202.6	208.5	216.6	217.6	222.5	234.8	236.4	239.6
40-49	KJJE	228.1	245.2	260.4	274.3	272.4	271.4	271.0	277.0	285.2	291.7	297.0
50-59	KJJF	426.1	441.7	468.7	475.4	473.4	474.1	467.3	469.8	473.5	468.9	465.5
60-64	KJJG	344.7	356.6	362.5	352.1	349.7	344.2	336.0	334.2	334.3	321.9	313.3
65 and over	KJJH	230.1	236.5	234.8	194.6	146.2	94.0	40.7	3.1	1.4	–	–
Over six months: All ages	KJJI	1 273.8	1 361.5	1 442.1	1 440.9	1 385.7	1 349.2	1 287.0	1 344.8	1 293.4	1 299.6	1 311.6
Under 20	KJJJ	2.8	2.9	3.0	3.9	3.6	4.7	4.9	7.4	4.7	5.6	13.8
20-29	KJJK	59.6	65.7	74.3	86.4	83.1	84.5	81.4	97.8	87.8	91.9	99.8
30-39	KJJL	112.9	126.5	152.1	165.1	166.8	177.2	181.2	203.9	197.6	201.6	205.4
40-49	KJJM	184.8	208.6	219.7	235.9	232.3	234.0	237.6	260.0	253.6	261.8	267.1
50-59	KJJN	367.2	389.2	418.2	426.5	423.8	428.2	423.8	446.8	431.6	431.7	428.1
60-64	KJJO	317.1	332.6	340.2	329.7	330.4	326.8	317.6	325.8	316.7	307.0	297.5
65 and over	KJJP	229.4	236.0	234.6	193.3	145.6	93.7	40.6	3.1	1.4	–	–
Females												
All durations: All ages	KJJQ	646.1	704.7	776.5	779.1	795.1	810.8	815.5	827.5	865.9	883.0	920.6
Under 20	KJJR	9.5	11.0	12.0	12.5	12.3	13.0	14.1	13.7	13.7	13.7	20.5
20-29	KJJS	75.9	74.9	79.4	88.6	89.0	87.8	85.3	84.6	85.1	87.3	96.1
30-39	KJJT	95.5	108.5	122.4	134.6	137.6	144.7	149.4	153.5	159.1	163.3	166.2
40-49	KJJU	162.6	176.0	200.7	201.9	206.5	209.7	217.2	221.0	232.0	237.1	246.3
50-59	KJJV	244.6	266.6	290.7	285.1	303.3	323.1	333.2	349.9	371.5	381.3	391.2
60 and over	KJJW	58.0	67.7	71.3	56.3	46.4	32.5	16.3	4.8	4.6	0.3	0.3
Over six months: All ages	KJJX	552.9	611.4	673.1	672.9	686.6	701.7	707.9	776.2	768.2	790.0	820.4
Under 20	KJJY	3.6	4.7	4.2	6.2	4.8	5.7	6.1	9.9	6.8	6.0	11.3
20-29	KJJZ	54.0	55.9	60.3	66.3	66.1	65.8	64.2	73.9	66.7	68.9	76.6
30-39	KJKA	79.3	92.3	103.2	113.2	117.5	120.9	126.3	142.4	139.4	143.6	146.3
40-49	KJKB	138.4	151.8	170.8	176.4	179.6	183.3	190.1	208.8	207.2	215.1	222.0
50-59	KJKC	220.8	239.9	263.7	256.6	273.1	294.1	305.2	336.5	343.5	356.4	364.1
60 and over	KJKD	56.8	66.8	70.9	54.3	45.4	31.9	16.0	4.6	4.5	0.1	0.2

1 See chapter text. Figures are based on a 1 per cent sample up to 1995 and 5% sample thereafter.
2 The end of the statistical year up to 1993/94 was the Saturday before the first Monday in April.
3 The statistical year for 1994/95 was extended to 12 April 1995, the day before the introduction of the new Incapacity Benefit which replaced Sickness and Invalidity Benefit from 13 April 1995.
4 Until 1995/96 then at 1 March. From 1995/96 the duration is taken on the the last day of February.

Sources: Department for Work and Pensions;
Information and Analysis Directorate : 0191 225 7373

10.8 Sickness, invalidity and incapacity benefit: days of certified incapacity

Great Britain analysis by age at end of period[1]

Years starting on first Monday in April[2]

Millions

		1991/92	1992/93	1993/94	1994[3]/95	1995/96	1996/97	1997/98	1998/99	1999/00	2000/01	2001/02
Age at 31 March[4]												
Males: All ages	KJKH	402.7	445.5	468.8	507.9	596.2	576.3	563.5	538.6	526.7	531.7	536.1
Under 20	KJKI	1.7	1.5	1.6	1.8	3.4	3.1	3.5	3.7	3.3	2.6	3.5
20 - 29	KJKJ	21.6	24.5	27.0	30.4	43.7	42.4	43.2	41.7	38.3	38.9	40.4
30 - 39	KJKK	36.1	41.4	46.6	56.0	72.3	73.9	77.7	78.2	75.8	81.3	84.0
40 - 49	KJKL	57.1	64.6	72.7	78.9	98.5	98.5	97.7	97.6	98.0	103.9	106.0
50 - 59	KJKM	112.8	121.7	129.8	141.4	172.0	170.7	172.2	170.0	161.9	165.9	168.5
60 - 64	KJKN	96.1	102.4	107.3	112.6	127.9	127.8	126.7	124.3	126.0	125.8	120.2
65 and over	KJKO	77.4	80.4	83.9	86.8	78.4	59.9	41.7	23.0	23.4	13.3	13.4
Females: All ages	KJKP	170.8	190.7	211.4	237.5	279.5	285.8	292.8	294.8	315.0	325.1	338.7
Under 20	KJKQ	2.2	2.1	2.4	2.6	4.8	4.1	4.4	4.5	4.0	3.5	3.9
20 - 29	KJKR	19.7	22.1	22.1	23.9	31.9	32.0	32.1	31.3	30.7	30.3	32.3
30 - 39	KJKS	25.6	28.5	32.7	37.6	48.0	49.8	51.4	53.4	54.9	58.9	59.9
40 - 49	KJKT	41.2	46.6	51.5	58.9	72.1	74.0	75.8	77.1	79.1	82.8	88.9
50 - 59	KJKU	63.8	71.3	79.1	88.4	101.0	107.5	115.3	120.0	134.3	142.2	145.9
60 and over	KJKV	18.2	20.1	23.6	26.1	21.7	18.4	13.8	8.4	12.0	7.3	7.9

1 See chapter text. The end of the statistical year up to 1993/94 was the Saturday before the first Monday in April.
2 Up to and including 1994/95 years start first Monday in April. The 1995/96 year started 13 April and ended 31 March. From 1996/97 years start 1 April
3 The statistical year for 1994/95 was extended to 12 April 1995, the day before the introduction of the new Incapacity Benefit which replaced Sickness and Invalidity Benefit from 13 April 1995.
4 Until 1995/96 then at 1 March.

Sources: Department for Work and Pensions;
Information and Analysis Directorate : 0191 225 7373

10.9 Widows' benefit (excluding widows' payment[1])
Great Britain
Number in payment analysed at March

Thousands

		1996	1997	1998	1999	2000	2001	2002	2003
All widows' benefit (excluding widows' allowance)									
All ages	KJGA	308.9	296.4	278.8	267.6	261.0	255.5	226.4	196.1
Under 30	KJGB	1.5	1.3	1.2	1.1	1.0	0.9	0.7	0.4
30 - 39	KJGC	13.0	12.5	12.5	11.2	11.4	10.6	9.0	7.2
40 - 49	KJGD	51.0	46.7	41.7	39.5	38.1	37.2	31.0	24.7
50 - 59	KJGE	199.1	194.3	189.8	183.1	182.2	179.1	158.4	136.5
60 and over	KJGF	44.3	41.7	33.5	32.6	28.4	27.7	27.3	27.3
Widowed mothers' allowance - with dependant children									
All ages	KJGG	51.6	50.4	48.5	46.7	47.0	46.6	40.4	33.1
Under 30	KJGH	1.4	1.3	1.1	1.1	1.0	0.9	0.6	0.4
30 - 39	KJGI	12.4	11.8	12.1	10.8	11.0	10.2	8.6	6.9
40 - 49	KJGJ	27.2	26.2	23.9	23.5	23.3	23.7	20.1	16.2
50 - 59	KJGK	10.1	10.7	11.2	11.2	11.6	11.5	10.8	9.2
60 and over	KJGL	0.4	0.4	0.2	0.2	0.2	0.4	0.3	0.4
Widowed mothers' allowance - without dependant children									
All ages	KJGM	5.6	4.9	3.8	3.1	2.9	2.5	2.2	1.9
Under 30	KJGN	0.1	–	–	–	0.1	–	–	–
30 - 39	KJGO	0.6	0.6	0.4	0.4	0.4	0.4	0.4	0.4
40 - 49	KJGP	3.0	2.4	1.8	1.6	1.2	1.1	1.0	0.9
50 - 59	KJGQ	1.9	1.8	1.4	1.1	1.1	1.0	0.8	0.6
60 and over	KJGR	0.1	0.1	0.1	–	0.1	–	–	0.1
Widows' pension									
All ages	KJGS	86.7	76.5	65.3	59.3	54.5	53.0	42.2	32.5
40 - 49	KJGT	–	–	–	–	–	–	–	–
50 - 59	KJGU	49.8	43.5	39.7	36.0	35.6	34.8	25.5	17.2
60 and over	KJGV	36.9	33.0	25.6	23.3	18.9	18.2	16.7	15.3
Age-related widows' pension[3]									
All ages	KJGW	165.0	164.6	161.1	158.4	156.6	153.4	141.6	128.6
40 - 49	KJGX	20.8	18.2	16.1	14.4	13.5	12.4	9.9	7.5
50 - 59	KJGY	137.3	138.2	137.5	134.8	133.8	131.9	121.3	109.5
60 and over	KJGZ	7.0	8.2	7.5	9.1	9.3	9.2	10.3	11.5

1 This is an especially high rate of benefit which is payable for the first 26 weeks of widowhood, provided that the widow is under pensionable age (age 60) or, if she is over that age, provided that her husband was not entitled to retirement pension.

2 Figures as at March.

3 Figures for widows' basic pension are included in age-related widows' pension.

Sources: Department for Work and Pensions; Information and Analysis Directorate : 0191 225 7373

10.10 Bereavement benefit (excluding bereavement payment[1,2])
Great Britain

Number in payment as at March by type of benefit and age of widow/er

Thousands

		Males				Females	
		2002	2003			2002	2003
All bereavement benefit (excluding bereavement allowance)							
All ages	WLSX	14.2	15.6	WLTC		22.6	28.8
Under 30	WLTD	–	–	WLTE		0.1	0.3
30 - 39	WLTQ	1.4	1.5	WLTR		1.5	3.2
40 - 49	WLTV	4.2	4.9	WLTW		4.8	7.3
50 - 59	WLTY	5.7	6.6	WLTZ		16.1	17.9
60 and over	WLUB	2.9	2.6	WLUC		–	–
Widowed parents' allowance - with dependant children							
All ages	WLUD	7.7	8.9	WLUH		5.7	11.3
Under 30	WLUI	–	–	WLUJ		0.1	0.3
30 - 39	WLUV	1.4	1.5	WLUW		1.5	3.1
40 - 49	WLUY	3.6	4.4	WLUZ		2.8	5.4
50 - 59	WLVD	2.4	2.8	WLVE		1.3	2.5
60 and over	WLVI	0.3	0.3	WLVJ		–	–
Widowed parents' allowance - without dependant children							
All ages	WLVK	–	0.1	WMMR		0.1	0.2
Under 30	WMMU	–	–	WMNI		–	–
30 - 39	WMNZ	–	–	WMOA		–	0.1
40 - 49	WMNQ	–	0.1	WMNR		–	0.1
50 - 59	WMNT	–	–	WMNW		–	–
60 and over	WMNX	–	–	WMNY		–	–
Age-related bereavement allowance							
All ages	WMOB	2.0	2.2	WMOC		8.0	8.3
40 - 49	WMOQ	0.5	0.5	WMOR		1.9	1.8
50 - 59	WMOS	1.5	1.7	WMOU		6.1	6.4
60 and over	WMOV	–	–	WMOW		–	–
Bereavement allowance (Not age related)							
All ages	WMOX	4.5	4.4	WMOY		8.8	9.1
40 - 49	WMPG	–	–	WMPH		–	–
50 - 59	WMPI	1.9	2.0	WMPJ		8.8	9.0
60 and over	WMPK	2.6	2.4	WMPM		–	–

1 Figures include overseas cases.
2 Bereavement Benefit replaced Widow's Benefit and is payable to both men and women widowed on or after 9 April 2001.

Source: Department for Work and Pensions: 0191 225 7874

10.11 Child benefits[1]

Thousands

		Great Britain As at 31 December								United Kingdom As at 31 August				
		1993	1994	1995	1996	1997[2]	1998[2]	1999[3]		1999	2000	2001	2002	2003
Families receiving allowances:														
Total	KJMU	6 913	6 955	6 996	7 024	6 956	6 976	7 102	VOWX	7 335	7 340	7 335	7 336	7 342
With 1 child	KJMV	2 920	2 941	2 970	2 983	..	..	3 015	VOWY	3 105	3 128	3 143	3 162	3 189
2 children	KJMW	2 772	2 781	2 783	2 794	..	..	2 822	VOWZ	2 905	2 898	2 891	2 894	2 890
3 children	KJMX	908	920	928	929	..	..	943	VOXA	983	977	970	954	942
4 children	KJMY	231	228	231	236	..	..	241	VOXB	255	251	247	242	239
5 or more children	KJMZ	81	84	84	82	..	..	82	VOXC	88	86	84	83	82
Families receiving Guardians Allowance	VOXG	2.0	2.1	2.1	2.2	2.3	2.3	2.3	VOXH	2.3	2.5	2.3	2.5	2.6

1 See chapter text.
2 Figures provided by Child Benefit Centre Management Information Statistics as a new scan was being developed.
3 As at 31 August.

Source: Board of Inland Revenue: 020 7438 7370

10.12 Contributory and non-contributory retirement pensions[1]
Great Britain

Numbers in payment analysed at end of March

Thousands (percentages in italics)

		1996	1997	1998	1999	2000	2001	2002	2003
Men:									
Age-groups:									
65-69	KJSB	1 084.5	1 142.8	1 199.3	1 243.2	1 288.8	1 287.5	1 296.1	1 319.4
Percentage	KJSC	*29.4*	*30.1*	*30.9*	*31.4*	*31.9*	*31.5*	*31.3*	*31.3*
70-74	KJSD	1 124.6	1 113.9	1 107.0	1 109.3	1 117.5	1 125.9	1 133.9	1 142.4
Percentage	KJSE	*30.4*	*29.4*	*28.5*	*28.0*	*27.6*	*27.5*	*27.3*	*27.1*
75-79	KJSF	752.4	790.3	838.3	872.3	867.4	860.5	862.0	861.7
Percentage	KJSG	*20.4*	*20.8*	*21.6*	*22.0*	*21.4*	*21.0*	*20.8*	*20.5*
80-84	KJSH	466.9	467.9	449.1	433.6	457.7	493.6	524.3	560.2
Percentage	KJSI	*12.6*	*12.3*	*11.6*	*10.9*	*11.3*	*12.1*	*12.6*	*13.3*
85-89	KJSJ	201.4	206.7	216.0	224.6	231.1	237.0	239.9	232.0
Percentage	KJSK	*5.5*	*5.5*	*5.6*	*5.7*	*5.7*	*5.8*	*5.8*	*5.5*
90 and over	KJSL	64.0	70.4	76.1	78.3	82.1	84.6	90.4	95.1
Percentage	KJSM	*1.7*	*1.9*	*2.0*	*2.0*	*2.0*	*2.1*	*2.2*	*2.3*
Total all ages	KJSA	3 693.9	3 792.1	3 885.9	3 961.4	4 044.6	4 089.0	4 146.5	4 210.9
Women:									
Age-groups:									
60-64	KJSO	1 150.4	1 185.4	1 245.2	1 284.9	1 332.2	1 339.4	1 346.2	1 376.0
Percentage	KJSP	*17.0*	*17.4*	*18.1*	*18.6*	*19.2*	*19.2*	*19.2*	*19.5*
65-69	KJSQ	1 432.0	1 422.1	1 415.9	1 406.7	1 396.5	1 392.4	1 396.5	1 416.5
Percentage	KJSR	*21.2*	*20.9*	*20.6*	*20.4*	*20.1*	*20.0*	*19.9*	*20.1*
70-74	KJSS	1 405.7	1 379.0	1 358.6	1 344.7	1 339.8	1 341.9	1 333.1	1 328.0
Percentage	KJST	*20.8*	*20.3*	*19.8*	*19.5*	*19.3*	*19.2*	*19.0*	*18.8*
75-79	KJSU	1 101.1	1 144.5	1 201.8	1 246.9	1 227.9	1 196.0	1 179.1	1 164.7
Percentage	KJSV	*16.3*	*16.8*	*17.5*	*18.1*	*17.7*	*17.1*	*16.8*	*16.5*
80-84	KJSW	871.6	858.5	815.4	775.9	793.2	843.3	878.3	925.3
Percentage	KJSX	*12.9*	*12.6*	*11.9*	*11.2*	*11.4*	*12.1*	*12.5*	*13.1*
85-89	KJSY	524.6	530.0	536.2	540.8	546.0	543.5	537.8	510.2
Percentage	KJSZ	*7.8*	*7.8*	*7.8*	*7.8*	*7.9*	*7.8*	*7.7*	*7.2*
90 and over	KJTA	270.5	284.9	297.7	305.1	310.7	321.6	329.9	334.5
Percentage	KJTB	*4.0*	*4.2*	*4.3*	*4.4*	*4.5*	*4.6*	*4.7*	*4.7*
Total all ages	KJSN	6 755.8	6 804.5	6 870.8	6 905.1	6 946.3	6 978.0	7 000.8	7 055.2

1 See chapter text. Including pensions payable to persons residing overseas.

Sources: Department for Work and Pensions;
Information and Analysis Directorate : 0191 225 7373

10.13 Family Credit/ Working Families' Tax Credit[1]

Thousands

		Great Britain As at 31 December							United Kingdom As at 30 November			
		1993	1994	1995	1996	1997	1998		1999	2000	2001	2002
Families in receipt:												
Total	KJTO	518.3	578.0	646.5	716.7	751.4	779.7	ZCMK	965.3	1 167.8	1 293.7	1 377.3
Two-parent families: total	KJTP	291.0	324.6	356.9	390.2	388.0	383.4	ZCML	467.6	565.9	617.2	639.8
With 1 child	KJTQ	73.3	80.1	89.7	98.6	96.6	95.4	ZCMM	116.8	144.8	151.6	159.0
2 children	KJTR	110.1	122.4	135.1	146.1	144.4	141.7	ZCMN	178.4	220.1	243.5	252.7
3 children	KJTS	66.9	76.4	83.4	91.1	91.4	89.1	ZCMO	107.8	129.2	142.9	147.3
4 children or more children	ZIYM	40.7	45.8	48.6	54.4	55.6	57.3	ZCMP	64.6	71.8	79.2	80.8
One-parent families: total	KJTW	227.3	253.4	289.6	326.5	363.4	396.3	ZIYI	497.8	601.8	676.5	737.6
With 1 child	KJTX	117.8	133.8	152.2	170.4	189.3	203.4	ZIYJ	259.6	313.7	349.5	381.2
2 children	KJTY	79.2	86.0	99.1	111.2	121.8	136.1	ZIYK	169.6	207.6	238.7	261.6
3 or more children	KJTZ	30.4	33.5	38.3	45.0	52.3	56.9	ZIYL	68.6	80.5	88.3	94.8

1 See chapter text. Family Credit was replaced by Working Families Tax Credit in October 1999. The WFTC figures for December 1999 include Family Credit awards made before October 1999 and still current (both FC and WFTC awards last for 26 weeks).

Sources: Board of Inland Revenue: 020 7438 7370;
Department for Work and Pensions;
Information and Analysis Directorate : 0191 225 7373

10.14 War pensions: Estimated number of pensioners[1]
Great Britain

At 31 March in each year

Thousands

		1993	1994	1995	1996	1997	1998	1999	2000	2001	2002	2003
Total	KADG	266.92	296.30	309.84	323.74	324.64	317.65	306.06	295.67	284.33	272.72	260.73
Disablement	KADH	214.53	245.44	260.30	265.37	264.59	259.16	248.93	240.76	231.62	222.25	212.59
Widows and dependants	KADI	52.39	50.86	49.54	58.37	60.05	58.49	55.85	54.92	52.71	50.48	48.13

1 See chapter text. From 1914 war; 1939 war and later service.

Source: Ministry of Defence/DASA (Pay & Pensions) 020 7218 4271

10.15 Income support: number of claimants receiving weekly payment[1]
Great Britain

On a day in May

Thousands

		1997	1998	1999	2000	2001	2002	2003
All income support	KACC	3 958	3 853	3 814	3 811	3 928	3 930	3 982
All aged 60 and over	KACD	1 720	1 659	1 624	1 615	1 717	1 746	1 778
State pensioners	KACE	1 383	1 338	1 308	1 305	1 406	1 428	1 450
In receipt of other NI benefit[2]	KACF	81	74	67	64	69	75	78
Others	KACG	256	248	249	246	242	244	250
All under 60	KACH	2 238	2 194	2 190	2 196	2 211	2 184	2 204
Disabled with contributory benefit[2]	KACK	180	195	196	207	220	229	232
Disabled without contributory benefit[2]	KFBJ	646	685	718	755	797	838	868
Lone parent premium not in other groups[3]	KACL	1 013	961	936	910	888	856	847
Others	KACM	398	353	341	324	306	261	257

1 See chapter text. Data are extracted from the Quarterly Statistical Enquiries undertaken each May from 1997-2003
2 Contributory/NI benefits other than State Pension are : (i) Incapacity Benefit and Widows Benefit from 1997 until 2000; (ii) Incapacity Benefit, Widow's Benefit and Bereavement Benefit from 2001;

3 Figures relate to one-parent families headed by a man or a woman, where the claimant is not receiving a pensioner or disability premium.

Sources: Department for Work and Pensions;
Information and Analysis Directorate : 0191 225 7373

10.16 Income support[1]
Great Britain

On a day in May

Thousands

		1995	1996	1997	1998	1999	2000	2001	2002	2003
Number of regular weekly payments	KACN	..	..	3 958	3 853	3 814	3 811	3 928	3 930	3 982
Total number of persons provided for	KACO	..	..	6 976	6 770	6 689	6 666	6 782	6 749	6 809
Number of dependants	KACP	..	..	2 464	2 379	2 344	2 317	2 289	2 242	2 230
Partners	KACQ	..	..	551	537	531	539	565	577	596
Total children under 16 years	KACR	..	..	2 306	2 224	2 188	2 158	2 123	2 074	2 054
Under 11	KACS	..	..	1 685	1 605	1 557	1 524	1 489	1 441	1 421
11 - 15 years	KACT	..	..	619	618	631	634	634	633	633
16 - 17 years	KACU	..	..	134	129	128	131	138	138	144
Other dependants										
18 years and over	KACV	..	..	28	26	28	28	28	30	32

1 See chapter text. Data are extracted from the the Quarterly Statistical Enquires. Figures exclude unemployed claimants in receipt of Income Support prior to the introduction of Jobseeker's Allowance in October 1996.

Sources: Department for Work and Pensions;
Information and Analysis Directorate : 0191 225 7373

10.17 Income support: average weekly amounts of benefit[1]
Great Britain
May

Thousands

		1995	1996	1997	1998	1999	2000	2001	2002	2003
All income support	KACW	..	..	58.03	58.72	61.42	65.72	70.21	69.64	73.40
All aged 60 and over	KJUB	..	..	42.24	42.29	45.30	48.18	50.73	49.69	50.76
Retirement pensioners	KACX	..	..	34.90	34.50	36.99	39.50	41.20	40.35	40.66
In receipt of other NI benefit[2]	KJUD	..	..	30.73	32.42	35.58	40.76	47.18	47.06	49.72
Others	KACY	..	..	85.56	87.30	91.70	96.20	107.13	105.22	109.71
All under 60	KACZ	..	..	70.17	71.14	73.36	78.61	85.34	85.60	91.65
Disabled with contributory benefit[2]	KADC	..	..	33.87	33.56	34.40	36.85	41.81	41.33	44.59
Disabled without contributory benefit[2]	KADD	..	..	70.38	72.86	75.88	79.25	84.81	86.63	90.74
Lone parent premium not in other groups[3]	KADE	..	..	79.21	79.67	82.01	91.21	101.44	105.39	115.72
Others	KADF	..	..	63.26	65.38	66.71	68.37	71.26	56.16	57.87

1 See chapter text. Data are extracted from the Quarterly Statistical Enquiries. From 1997 figures exclude unemployed claimants who transferred to Job-seeker's Allowance from 7 October 1996.
2 Contributory/NI benefits other than Retirement pension are Incapacity Benefit (previously IVB & Sickness Benefit), Widows Pension and Widowed Mothers Allowance.

3 Figures relate to one-parent families headed by a man or a woman, where the claimant is not receiving a pensioner or disability premium.

Sources: Department for Work and Pensions;
Information and Analysis Directorate : 0191 225 7373

10.18 Summary of government expenditure on social services and housing[1]
Years ended 31 March

£ millions

		1992 /93	1993 /94	1994 /95	1995 /96	1996 /97	1997 /98	1998 /99	1999 /00	2000 /01	2001 /02
Education[2]	KJAA	31 576	33 544	35 367	36 810	37 953	39 078	38 981	40 895	44 176	49 354
National health service	KJAB	35 413	37 259	39 879	40 691	42 383	43 878	47 194	48 362	53 039	59 852
Welfare services	CSWL	6 683	7 700	9 016	10 312	11 521	11 713	11 984	12 168	12 995	13 910
Social security benefits	KJAE	78 846	85 805	87 941	90 534	92 217	92 146	93 929	95 586	98 899	105 992
Housing	KJAF	6 984	5 919	5 634	5 445	4 593	3 415	3 605	2 825	2 947	2 973
Total government expenditure	KJAG	159 502	170 227	177 837	183 792	188 667	190 230	195 413	200 051	211 988	232 081
Current expenditure	KJAH	151 010	163 289	171 277	177 667	183 842	186 640	191 603	196 240	206 380	226 309
Capital expenditure	KJAI	8 492	6 938	6 560	6 125	4 825	3 590	4 090	3 596	5 676	5 772
Total government expenditure	KJAG	159 502	170 227	177 837	183 792	188 667	190 230	195 413	200 051	211 988	232 081
Central government	KJAK	116 304	126 371	130 819	134 954	137 487	142 132	155 510	159 791	169 168	185 167
Local authorities	KJAL	43 198	43 856	47 018	48 838	51 180	48 100	40 183	40 045	42 888	46 914
Total government expenditure	KJAG	159 502	170 227	177 837	183 792	188 667	190 230	195 413	200 051	211 988	232 081
Total government expenditure on social services and housing as a percentage of GDP[3]		25.86	26.11	25.72	25.22	24.41	23.08	22.47	21.92	22.16	23.12

1 See chapter text.
2 Includes school meals.
3 GDP adjusted to take account of change from rates to community charge.

Source: Office for National Statistics: 020 7533 5990

10.19 Government expenditure on education[1]
Years ended 31 March

£ millions

		1991/92	1992/93	1993/94	1994/95	1995/96	1996/97	1997/98	1998/99	1999/00	2000/01	2001/02
Current expenditure												
Nursery and primary schools	KEZN	7 247	8 262	8 712	9 094	9 352	9 697	10 405	23 069	24 441	26 926	29 867
Secondary schools	KJBC	7 787	8 347	8 615	8 875	8 844	9 194	9 322	..	..	..	..
Special schools	KJBD	1 245	1 354	1 420	1 451	1 493	1 578	1 655	..	..	..	..
Universities[2]	KJBG	2 437	3 361	..	..	..	..	..	..	..	..	..
Other Higher, Further and adult education[3]	KJBE	4 454	4 136	..	..	..	..	..	..	..	..	..
Higher Education Funding Council[3,4]	CSWM	..	..	4 908	5 192	5 472	5 729	5 693	4 726	5 166	5 813	5 628
Further Education Funding Council[5]	CSWO	..	..	3 072	3 200	3 392	3 694	3 718	5 064	5 216	5 167	6 810
Continuing Education	CSWP	..	..	380	294	1 801	1 891	1 960	..	..	..	..
Other education expenditure	KJBH	1 361	1 009	905	963	948	1 277	1 355	4 611	4 278	3 861	3 989
Related current expenditure:												
School welfare[6]	KJBJ	214	270	346	359	328	336	372	..	..	..	..
School meals[7]	KJBK	556	161	149	147	148	147	138	..	..	..	..
Youth service and physical training	KJBL	360	393	392	401	396	389	389	..	..	..	..
Maintenance grants and allowances to pupils and students[8]	KJBM	1 379	1 705	1 972	2 204	1 660	1 440	1 289	..	..	..	..
Transport of pupils	KJBN	442	417	444	486	507	526	584	..	..	..	..
Miscellaneous expenditure	KJBO	3	8	10	31	31	49	45	..	..	..	..
Total current expenditure[9]	KJBQ	27 485	29 424	31 325	32 697	34 372	35 947	36 925	37 470	39 101	41 767	46 294
Capital expenditure												
Nursery and primary schools	KEZP	376	384	414	517	497	482	546	1 357	1 472	1 762	2 031
Secondary schools	KJBT	493	518	485	565	482	515	601	..	..	..	..
Special schools	KJBU	35	32	31	37	51	52	44	..	..	..	..
Universities[2]	KJBX	231	236	..	..	..	..	..	..	..	..	..
Other Higher, Further and adult education[3]	KJBV	293	285	..	..	..	..	..	..	..	..	..
Higher Education Funding Council[3,4]	CSWQ	..	..	406	412	424	74	61	31	113	212	340
Further Education Funding Council[5]	CSWR	..	..	194	201	187	33	29	44	97	258	456
Continuing Education	CSWS	..	..	6	8	8	5	–	–	–	–	–
Other education expenditure	KJBY	33	25	12	45	25	24	30	57	111	177	232
Related capital expenditure	KJBZ	20	17	23	25	17	20	24	..	..	..	..
Total capital expenditure[9]	KJCA	1 481	1 496	1 571	1 810	1 691	1 205	1 335	1 511	1 793	2 409	3 058
VAT refunds to local authorities	KJBP	584	656	648	860	747	801	818	816	906	..	..
Total expenditure												
Central government	KJCB	4 288	4 722	8 186	9 490	10 853	11 388	12 167	11 422	13 177	14 369	16 404
Local authorities	KJCC	25 261	26 853	25 354	25 900	25 954	26 562	26 910	27 559	27 718	29 807	32 950
Total government expenditure on education[10]	KJAA	29 550	31 576	33 544	35 367	36 810	37 953	39 078	38 981	40 895	44 176	49 354
Total government education expenditure as a percentage of GDP[11]		4.98	5.12	5.15	5.11	5.05	4.91	4.74	4.48	4.48	4.62	4.92

1 See chapter text. From 1998/99 figures have been taken from HM Treasury Public Expenditure Statistical Analyses. They are not comparable with earlier years which used different sources. Schools expenditure no longer separately identifiable
2 Includes expenditure on University departments of Education for England and Wales
3 Includes tuition fees.
4 Includes expenditure on Higher Education Institutions in Northern Ireland.
5 Includes expenditure on Further Education Institutions in Northern Ireland.
6 Expenditure on the school health service is included in the National Health Service.
7 Expenditure on school meals in England has been recharged across other expenditure headings.

8 Excludes the secondment of teachers on further training. Includes student loans expenditure.
9 Due to rounding constituent figures may not sum to totals.
10 Excludes additional adjustment to allow for Capital consumption made for National Accounts purposes. From 1995/96, figures include expenditure on training programmes in England (such as Work Based Training for Young People) reclassified as education. Therefore the figures are not comparable with earlier years.
11 GDP includes adjustments to remove the distortion caused by the abolition of domestic rates.

Sources: Department for Education and Skills;
Office for National Statistics: 020 7533 5990

10.20 Government expenditure on the National Health Service[1]
Years ended 31 March

£ millions

		1991 /92	1992 /93	1993 /94	1994 /95	1995 /96	1996 /97	1997 /98	1998 /99	1999 /00	2000 /01	2001 /02
Current expenditure												
Central government:												
Hospitals and Community Health Services[2] and Family Health Services[3]	KJQA	29 061	32 195	35 567	37 698	38 514	39 425	40 993	43 600	48 275	52 599	59 355
Administration[4]	KJQB	1 119	1 258	–	–	–	–	–	–	–	–	–
less Payments by patients:												
Hospital services	KJQC	–540	–505	–368	–111	–42	–42	–48	–84	–138	–138	–156
Pharmaceutical services	KJQD	–270	–297	–324	–342	–383	–376	–396	–391	–405	–425	–480
Dental services	KJQE	–477	–470	–440	–464	–494	–447	–475	–470	–483	–506	–571
Total	KJQG	–1 287	–1 272	–1 132	–917	–919	–865	–919	–945	–1 026	–1 068	–1 205
Departmental administration	KJQH	293	319	270	256	242	265	245	227	231	324	366
Other central services	KJQI	865	1 301	1 651	2 304	2 538	3 124	3 242	4 980	1 601	1 931	2 900
Total current expenditure	KJQJ	30 051	33 801	36 356	39 341	40 375	41 949	43 561	46 910	48 055	52 707	59 477
Capital expenditure												
Central government	KJQK	1 791	1 612	903	538	316	434	317	284	307	332	375
Total government NHS Expenditure												
Central government	KJAB	31 842	35 413	37 259	39 879	40 691	42 383	43 878	47 194	48 362	53 039	59 852
Total NHS expenditure as a percentage of GDP[5]		5.37	5.74	5.72	5.77	5.58	5.48	5.32	5.43	5.30	5.54	5.96

1 See chapter text.
2 Including the school health service.
3 General Medical Services have been included in the expenditure of the Health Authorities. Therefore, Hospitals and Community Health Services and Family Practitioner Services (now Family Health Services) are not identifiable separately.

4 Administration costs are not separately identifiable from 1993/94.
5 GDP adjusted to take account of change from rates to community charge.

Source: Office for National Statistics: 020 7533 5990

10.21 Government expenditure on welfare services[1]
Years ended 31 March

£ millions

		1991 /92	1992 /93	1993 /94	1994 /95	1995 /96	1996 /97	1997 /98	1998 /99	1999 /00	2000 /01	2001 /02
Personal social services												
Central government current expenditure	KJCG	190	202	216	197	140	101	73	53	50	49	52
Local authorities current expenditure:												
Running expenses	CTKQ	5 725	6 122	7 113	8 400	9 716	10 947	11 131	11 378	11 563	12 405	13 279
Capital expenditure	KJCI	200	189	190	235	229	210	204	199	145	128	137
Total	KJAC	4 732	6 513	7 519	8 832	10 085	11 258	11 408	11 630	11 758	12 586	13 472
Welfare foods service												
Central government current expenditure on welfare foods (including administration)	KJCK	142	171	182	185	228	264	306	355	411	411	440
less Receipts from the public	KJCL	–1	–1	–1	–1	–1	–1	–1	–1	–1	–2	–2
Total	KJAD	141	170	181	184	227	263	305	354	410	409	438
Total government expenditure	CSWL	4 873	6 683	7 700	9 016	10 312	11 521	11 713	11 984	12 168	12 995	13 910
Total government expenditure as a percentage of GDP[2]		0.82	1.08	1.18	1.30	1.42	1.49	1.42	1.38	1.33	1.36	1.39

1 See chapter text.
2 GDP adjusted to take account of change from rates to community charge.

Source: Office for National Statistics: 020 7533 5990

10.22 Government expenditure on social security benefits[1]
Years ended 31 March

£ millions

		1991 /92	1992 /93	1993 /94	1994 /95	1995 /96	1996 /97	1997 /98	1998 /99	1999 /00	2000 /01	2001 /02
Government current expenditure												
National insurance fund:												
Retirement pensions	EKXK	25 691	27 076	28 481	28 925	30 162	32 146	33 643	35 782	37 918	39 361	43 222
Lump sums to pensioners	KJDB	114	115	122	123	124	129	118	120	123	128	134
Widows and guardians allowances	CSDH	884	1 014	1 041	1 034	1 018	974	992	973	990	982	1 113
Unemployment benefit	CSDI	1 627	1 761	1 623	1 277	1 099	588	1	–	–1	–1	–
Jobseeker's allowance[2]	CJTJ	–	–	–	–	–	379	590	474	462	435	441
Sickness benefit	CSDJ	278	365	294	426	12	–	–	–	–	–	–
Invalidity benefit	CSDK	5 461	6 198	7 146	8 042	271	–	–	–	–	–	–
Incapacity benefit[3]	CUNL	–	–	–	–	7 615	7 668	7 471	7 295	6 897	6 677	6 836
Maternity benefit	CSDL	40	42	32	17	28	32	36	39	40	52	56
Statutory sick pay	CSDQ	725	688	688	24	24	24	28	28	28	36	32
Statutory maternity pay	GTKZ	396	416	440	498	476	500	516	552	585	611	652
Total	ACHH	35 216	37 675	39 867	40 366	40 829	42 440	43 395	45 263	47 043	48 281	52 486
Redundancy Fund	GTKN	276	321	110	208	128	108	88	116	148	196	194
Social Fund	GTLQ	130	175	189	183	216	203	200	360	920	1 957	1 859
Non-contributory benefits:												
War pensions	KJDP	844	976	913	1 083	1 247	1 352	1 284	1 262	1 254	1 201	1 182
Family benefits:												
Child benefit	KJDQ	5 433	5 950	6 347	6 294	6 332	6 645	7 095	7 327	8 212	8 528	8 685
One parent benefit	KJDR	249	275	282	289	310	317	9	–	–	–	–
Family credit	KAAA	626	929	1 208	1 441	1 739	2 084	2 338	2 430	1 927	–788	–
Income support/Supplementary benefits:												
Income support	KAAB	12 325	15 578	16 997	16 387	16 650	14 438	11 998	11 793	12 227	13 076	14 222
Other non-contributory benefits:												
Old persons' pensions	KJDX	36	36	36	35	36	30	29	29	28	28	27
Lump sums to pensioners	KJDY	11	13	14	13	15	15	17	17	17	17	17
Attendance allowance	KJDZ	1 706	1 553	1 795	1 963	2 194	2 393	2 640	2 682	2 834	2 957	3 121
Invalid care allowance	KJEA	285	345	442	526	617	736	745	783	814	849	924
Mobility allowance	KJEB	1 063	68	–	–	–	–	–	–	–	–	–
Disability living allowance	EKXL	–	1 973	2 772	3 125	3 802	4 498	5 018	5 367	5 653	6 021	6 567
Disability working allowance	EKYE	–	3	7	11	19	34	44	49	40	–	–
Severe disablement allowance	KJEC	596	640	703	776	820	906	1 007	984	1 016	1 024	1 034
Industrial injury benefits	EKXM	655	668	687	706	731	744	754	–	–	–	–
Housing benefit	KJED	6 053	7 670	9 163	10 345	10 773	11 276	11 315	11 311	11 247	11 616	11 688
Administration	KJEE	3 617	3 998	4 273	4 190	4 076	3 998	4 170	4 349	3 737	3 936	3 986
Total government benefit expenditure	KJAE	69 121	78 846	85 805	87 941	90 534	92 217	92 146	93 929	95 586	98 899	105 992
Total government benefit expenditure as a percentage of GDP[4]		11.65	12.78	13.16	12.72	12.42	11.93	11.18	10.80	10.48	10.34	10.56

1 See chapter text.
2 Jobseeker's allowance was introduced in October 1996 to replace Unemployment benefit and Income Support for the unemployed.

3 Sickness benefit and Invalidity benefit were replaced by a single incapacity benefit in 1995.
4 GDP adjusted to take account of change from rates to community charge.

Source: Office for National Statistics: 020 7533 5990

10.23 Government and other public sector expenditure on housing[1]
Years ended 31 March

£ millions

		1991 /92	1992 /93	1993 /94	1994 /95	1995 /96	1996 /97	1997 /98	1998 /99	1999 /00	2000 /01	2001 /02
Government expenditure												
Current expenditure												
Central government												
housing subsidies:												
to local authorities	CTMN	1 144	992	874	814	687	717	711	737	466	438	976
to public corporations	ADVA	260	208	214	228	228	236	244	218	132	152	156
to housing associations	KJRC	40	135	180	207	235	215	216	−22	−111	252	−302
grants to housing associations	KJRD	117	59	13	3	1	1	–	–	–	–	–
Local authorities												
housing subsidies	KJVK	–	1	–	–	3	1	1	1	3	3	–
Administration, etc	KGVL	373	394	364	405	402	447	509	575	590	573	576
Total current expenditure	KJRH	1 934	1 789	1 645	1 657	1 556	1 617	1 681	1 509	1 178	1 398	1 406
Capital expenditure												
Investment in housing by local												
authorities	KGVM	822	913	780	842	1 009	937	−52	59	−729	−368	−280
Capital grants to housing												
associations	KJRJ	2 045	2 583	2 136	1 774	1 329	1 393	1 102	1 021	975	1 900	925
Improvement grants	ADCE	1 152	1 240	1 287	1 105	846	980	1 157	779	766	920	1 181
Net lending for house purchase	KJRL	−782	−211	−402	−141	−136	−719	−816	−168	−82	−84	−80
Capital grants to public corporations	KJRM	482	631	439	387	837	386	400	415	431	450	467
Net lending to public corporations	KJRN	−104	39	34	10	7	−1	−57	−10	−10	−11	−11
Total capital expenditure	KJRO	3 613	5 195	4 274	3 977	3 889	2 976	1 734	2 096	1 351	2 807	2 202
Total expenditure												
Central government	KJRP	3 697	4 595	3 839	3 409	3 313	2 362	1 962	2 359	2 276	2 287	2 292
Local authorities	KJRQ	1 850	2 389	2 080	2 225	2 132	2 231	1 453	1 246	549	660	681
Total government expenditure	KJAF	5 547	6 984	5 919	5 634	5 445	4 593	3 415	3 605	2 825	2 947	2 973
Public corporations' capital												
expenditure												
Investment in housing	KGVN	673	549	568	560	580	574	452	424	420	400	400
Net lending to private sector	AAFR	−4	3	1	−1	−5	−1	−1	–	–	–	–
Total	KJRU	669	552	569	559	575	569	451	424	420	400	400
Total public sector housing expenditure[2]	KJRV	5 838	6 866	6 015	5 796	5 176	4 777	3 523	3 624	2 824	3 116	2 917
Total public sector housing expenditure as a percentage of GDP[3]		0.98	1.11	0.92	0.84	0.71	0.62	0.43	0.42	0.31	0.33	0.29

1 See chapter text.
2 Total government expenditure *less* grants and loans to public corporations
  plus public corporations' capital expenditure.
3 GDP adjusted to take account of change from rates to community charge.

Source: Office for National Statistics: 020 7533 5990

11 Crime and justice

Crime and justice

There are differences in the legal and judicial systems of England and Wales, Scotland and Northern Ireland which make it impossible to provide tables covering the United Kingdom as a whole in this section. These differences concern the classification of offences, the meaning of certain terms used in the statistics, the effects of the several Criminal Justice Acts, and recording practices.

Recorded crime statistics *(Table 11.2)*

Crimes recorded by the police provide a measure of the amount of crime committed. The statistics are based on counting rules, revised with effect from 1 April 1998, which are standard for all the police forces in England and Wales and now include all indictable and triable-either-way offences together with a few summary offences which are closely linked to these offences. The new rules have changed the emphasis of measurement more towards one crime per victim, and have also increased the coverage of offences. These changes have particularly impacted on the offence groups of violence against the person, fraud and forgery, drugs offences and other offences.

For a variety of reasons many offences are either not reported to the police or not recorded by them. The changes in the number of offences recorded do not necessarily provide an accurate reflection of changes in the amount of crime committed.

In order to further improve the consistency of recorded crime statistics, and to take a more victim oriented approach to crime recording, the National Crime Recording Standard (NCRS) was introduced in England and Wales from 1 April 2002. Some police forces implemented the principles of NCRS in advance of its implementation across all forces in April 2002. It has been estimated that, without the inflationary effect of the NCRS, the total number of recorded crimes in 2001/02 and 2002/03 would have been up 2% and down 3% respectively compared to the previous year. Also, without the inflationary effect of the NCRS, it is estimated that the underlying trend in numbers of some crime types in 2002/03 as compared to the previous year were as follows:- theft and handling - down 4%; criminal damage - down 4%; burglary in a dwelling - down 2%; violence against the person - up 5%; robbery - down 14%. The NCRS will also have affected trends for offence groups in the previous year.

Further information is available from the Home Office: *Crime in England and Wales 2002/2003*, ed: Jon Simmons and Tricia Dodd.

Court proceedings and police cautions
(Tables 11.3 - 11.7, 11.13 - 11.17, 11.20 - 11.22)

The statistical basis of the tables of court proceedings is broadly similar in England and Wales, Scotland and Northern Ireland; the tables show the number of persons found guilty, recording a person under the heading of the principal offence of which he is found guilty, excluding additional findings of guilt at the same proceedings. A person found guilty at a number of separate court proceedings is included more than once.

The statistics on offenders cautioned in England and Wales cover only those who, on admission of guilt, were given a formal caution by, or on the instructions of, a senior police officer as an alternative to prosecution. Written warnings by the police for motor offences and persons paying fixed penalties for certain motoring offences are excluded. Formal cautions are not issued in Scotland. There are no statistics on cautioning available for Northern Ireland.

The Crime and Disorder Act 1998 created provisions in relation to reprimands and final warnings, new offences and orders which have been implemented nationally since 1 June 2000. They replace the system of cautioning for offenders aged under 18. Reprimands can be given to first-time offenders for minor offences. Any further offending results in either a final warning or a charge.

For persons proceeded against in Scotland, the statistics relate to the High Court of Justiciary, the Sheriff Court and the District Court. The High Court deals with serious solemn (ie Jury) cases and has unlimited sentencing power. The Sheriff Court is limited to imprisonment of 3 years for solemn cases, or 3 months (6 months when specified in legislation for second or subsequent offences and 12 months for certain statutory offences) for summary (ie non-Jury) cases. The District Court deals only with summary cases and is limited to 60 days imprisonment and level 4 fines. Stipendiary Magistrates sit in Glasgow District Court and have the summary sentencing powers of a Sheriff.

In England and Wales, indictable offences are offences which are:

(a) *Triable only on indictment*. These offences are the most serious breaches of the criminal law and must be tried at the Crown Court. 'Indictable-only' offences include murder, manslaughter, rape and robbery.

(b) *Triable either way*. These offences may be tried at the Crown Court or Magistrates' Court.

The Criminal Justice Act 1991 led to the following main changes in the sentences available to the courts in England and Wales:

(a) introduction of combination orders,

(b) introduction of the "unit fine scheme" at Magistrates' courts,

(c) abolishing the sentence of detention in a young offender institution for 14 year old boys and changing the minimum and maximum sentence lengths for 15 to 17 year olds to 10 and 12 months respectively, and

(d) abolishing partly suspended sentences of imprisonment and restricting the use of a fully suspended sentence.

The Criminal Justice Act 1993 abolished the "Unit Fine Scheme" in Magistrates' courts which had been introduced under the Criminal Justice Act 1991.

A *charging standard for assault* was introduced in England and Wales on 31 August 1994 with the aim to promote consistency between the police and prosecution on the appropriate level of charge to be brought.

The Criminal Justice and Public Order Act 1994 created several new offences in England and Wales, mainly in the area of Public Order, but also including male rape (there is no statutory offence of 'male rape' in Scotland, although such a crime may be charged as serious assault). The Act also:

(a)   extended the provisions of section 53 of the Children and Young Persons Act 1993 for 10 to 13 year olds,

(b)   increased the maximum sentence length for 15 to 17 year olds to 2 years,

(c)   increased the upper limit from £2,000 to £5,000 for offences of criminal damage proceeded against as if triable only summarily,

(d)   introduced provisions for the reduction of sentences for early guilty pleas, and

(e)   increased the maximum sentence length for certain firearm offences.

Provisions within the Crime (Sentences) Act 1997 (as amended by the Powers of Criminal Courts Sentencing Act 2000), in England and Wales, and the Crime and Punishment (Scotland) Act 1997, in Scotland, included:

a)   an automatic life sentence for a second serious violent or sexual offence unless there are exceptional circumstances (this provision has not been enacted in Scotland);

b)   a minimum sentence of seven years for an offender convicted for a third time of a class A drug trafficking offence unless the court considers this to be unjust in all the circumstances, and, in England and Wales.

c)   the new section 38A of the Magistrates' Courts' Act 1980 extending the circumstances in which a magistrates' court may commit a person convicted of an offence triable either way to the Crown Court for sentence - it was implemented in conjunction with section 49 of the Criminal Procedure and Investigations Act 1996, which involves the magistrates' courts in asking defendants to indicate plea before the mode of trial decision is taken and compels the court to sentence or commit for sentence any defendant who indicates a guilty plea.

Under the Criminal Justice and Court Service Act 2000 new terms were introduced for certain orders. Community rehabilitation order is the new name for a probation order. A community service order is now known as a community punishment order. Finally, the new term for a combination order is community punishment and rehabilitation order. In April 2000 the secure training order was replaced by the detention and training order. Section 53 of the Children and Young Persons Act 1993 was repealed on 25 August 2000 and its provisions were transferred to Sections 90-92 of the Powers of Criminal Courts (Sentencing) Act 2000. Reparation and Action plan order were implemented nationally from 1 June 2000. Drug

treatment and testing order was implemented nationally from October 2000. And Referral order was implemented nationally from April 2000. These changes are now reflected in Table 11.7.

The system of Magistrates' courts and Crown Courts in Northern Ireland operates in a similar way to that in England and Wales. A particularly significant statutory development, however, has been the Criminal Justice (NI) Order 1996 which introduces a new sentencing regime into Northern Ireland, largely replicating that which was introduced into England and Wales by the Criminal Justice Acts of 1991 and 1993. The order makes many changes to both community and custodial sentences, while introducing new orders such as the combination order, the custody probation order and orders for release on licence of sexual offenders.

Previous convictions of prisoners
(Tables 11.8 and 11.9)
Standard list offences consist of all the indictable offences plus some of the more serious summary offences. From 1 January 1996 a number of summary motoring offences became standard list offences. Excluding the new standard lists from the analysis presented in the table would slightly alter the percentages with previous convictions.

Information on previous convictions of prisoners published prior to 1995 was based upon Prison Service records. However, details of a prisoner's previous conviction were often not recorded (eg. this information was missing for 44 per cent of the 1990 male receptions under sentence). To overcome this problem the Home Office Offenders Index (a computerised database containing details of convictions for standard list offences) is now being used to provide information on prisoners' previous convictions. Unfortunately, this means that the most up-to-date information on previous convictions is not directly comparable with that previously published. Standard list offences include indictable offences and some of the more serious summary offences so the coverage is not as complete. The published information also does not relate to 'prison receptions' but to those sentenced to immediate custody for standard list offences (which accounted for 82 per cent of those sentenced to custody in 1993).

The problems with non-availability of previous history information are much less acute using the Offenders Index data source. Previous convictions were found for 95 per cent of the 1993 prison population sample. Some of the cases where information is missing would be accounted for by prisoners who are not sentenced for a standard list offence and have no previous record for such offences.

Previous convictions of prisoners
(Table 11.19)
The results shown in this table are reported on a cash basis for financial years 1991-92 to 2000-01 in line with funding arrangements. Financial year 2001-02 is reported on a resource accounting basis in line with the introduction of Resource Budgeting. Capital Charges were introduced with Resource Accounting and Budgeting.

11.1 Police forces: strength
End of year

Numbers

		1992	1993	1994	1995[1]	1996[1]	1997[1]	1998[1]	1999[1]	2000[1]	2001[1]	2002[1]
England and Wales												
Regular police												
Strength:												
Men	KERB	111 027	108 967	108 030	107 022	106 549	105 691	104 606	103 083	101 683	103 156	104 483
Women	KERC	15 841	16 571	17 263	17 688	18 501	19 124	19 659	19 967	20 519	21 794	22 784
Seconded:[2]												
Men	KERD	1 766	1 938	1 881	1 896	1 864	1 814	2 007	2 158	2 077	1 967	2 031
Women	KERE	167	182	184	202	209	233	232	256	307	294	305
Additional officers:[3]												
Men	KERF	68	63	97	105	111	200	267	324	361	493	567
Women	KERG	3	12	17	22	57	158	514	582	519	509	564
Special constables												
Enrolled strength:												
Men	KERH	12 251	13 240	12 772	12 751	12 594	12 483	11 331	10 667	9 120	8 238	8 014
Women	KERI	6 992	7 326	7 060	6 904	6 857	6 680	5 965	5 060	4 367	3 816	3 584
Scotland												
Regular police												
Strength[4]:												
Men	KERK	12 629	12 580	12 634	12 341	12 347	12 495	12 479	12 258	12 058	12 033	12 017
Women	KERL	1 465	1 559	1 679	1 665	1 856	2 019	2 202	2 098	2 115	2 363	2 440
Central service:[4,5]												
Men	KERM	70	73	79	96	94	85	85	88	95	131	118
Women	KERN	5	5	4	7	8	4	6	9	13	14	15
Seconded:[4,6]												
Men	KERO	120	109	110	108	105	101	101	85	130	49	20
Women	KERP	10	16	16	16	16	13	10	12	18	5	4
Additional regular police:												
Strength	KERR	90	58	91	90	72	72	97	91	84	88	91
Special constables												
Strength:												
Men	KERS	1 454	1 466	1 518	1 411	1 336	1 286	1 289	1 229	981	827	782
Women	KERT	393	431	474	467	450	437	444	422	355	309	309
Northern Ireland												
Regular police[7]												
Strength:												
Men	KERU	7 687	7 646	7 640	7 528	7 531	7 562	7 527	7 406	6 916	6 058	5 908
Women	KERV	791	818	853	887	897	923	933	987	978	918	1 032
Reserve[8]												
Strength:												
Men	KERW	4 060	4 027	4 052	3 976	3 727	3 587	3 469	3 199	2 959	2 620	2 223
Women	KERX	533	545	638	709	675	719	705	641	606	554	510

1 The 2002 figures for England and Wales are for 31 March, with the previous years' figures being for 30 September. Figures for Scotland are as at 31 December. From 1999, figures for Northern Ireland reflect the position at the end of the financial year, i.e. 1999 and 2000 figures are as at 31 March 2000 and 31 March 2001 respectively. Prior to this, the figures were as at 31 December.
2 NCS, NCIS, other inter-force units and officers in central service.
3 Includes Police Officers on loan to organisations outside the British Police Service such as the Royal Hong Kong police, those on career breaks, and those on maternity leave.

4 'Strength' includes central service and seconded police.
5 Instructors at Training Establishments, etc, formerly shown as secondments.
6 Scottish Crime Squad, officers on courses, etc.
7 Does not include officers on secondment.
8 Includes Part-Time Reserve, 929 at 31 March 2003 (592 males and 337 females).

Sources: Home Office: 020 7273 2583;
The Scottish Executive Justice Department: 0131 244 2225;
The Police Service of Northern Ireland: 028 9065 0222 ext 24135

11.2 Recorded crime statistics[1]
England and Wales

Thousands

		1992	1993	1994	1995	1996	1997	1998[2,3] /99		1998[3] /99	1999 /00	2000 /01	2001[4] /02	2002[4] /03
Violence against the person	BEAB	201.8	205.1	218.4	212.6	239.3	250.8	230.8	LQMP	502.8	581.0	600.9	650.2	835.1
Sexual offences	BEAC	29.5	31.3	32.0	30.3	31.4	33.2	34.9	LQMQ	36.2	37.8	37.3	41.4	48.7
Burglary	BEAD	1 355.3	1 369.6	1 256.7	1 239.5	1 164.6	1 015.1	951.9	LQMR	953.2	906.5	836.0	878.5	889.0
Robbery	BEAE	52.9	57.8	60.0	68.1	74.0	63.1	66.2	LQMS	66.8	84.3	95.2	121.4	108.0
Theft and handling stolen goods	BEAF	2 851.6	2 751.9	2 564.6	2 452.1	2 383.9	2 165.0	2 126.7	LQMT	2 191.4	2 223.6	2 145.4	2 267.1	2 365.5
Fraud and forgery	BEAG	168.6	162.8	145.3	133.0	136.2	134.4	173.7	LQMU	279.5	334.8	319.3	317.4	330.1
Criminal damage	BEAH	892.6	906.7	928.3	914.0	951.3	877.0	834.4	LQMV	879.6	945.7	960.1	1 064.5	1 109.4
Drug offences[5]	LQMO	..	..	..	..	..	..	21.3	LQYT	135.9	121.9	113.5	121.3	141.1
Other offences[5]	BEAI	39.4	41.0	47.7	50.7	55.8	59.8	42.0	LQYU	63.6	65.7	63.2	65.3	72.6
Total	BEAA	5 591.7	5 526.3	5 253.0	5 100.2	5 036.6	4 598.3	4 481.8	LQYV	5 109.1	5 301.2	5 170.8	5 527.1	5 899.5

1 See chapter text.
2 Estimates.
3 The counting rules were revised on 1 April 1998
4 The National Crime Recording Standard (NCRS) was introduced in England and Wales from 1 April 2002. For more details about the inflationary effects of the NCRS on the 2001/02 and 2002/03 figures see chapter text.

5 Prior to 1 April 1998 the offence of drug trafficking was included in the "Other offences" group. From 1 April 1999, under the new counting rules, drug trafficking became part of a new "Drug offences" group which, with the expanded coverage, now includes possession and other drug offences. For 1998/99, under the old counting rules, drug trafficking - the only drugs offence counted - has been listed under drugs offences.

Source: Home Office: 020 7273 2583

11.3 Offenders found guilty[1]: by offence group
Magistrates' courts and the Crown Court

England and Wales

Thousands

		1992	1993	1994	1995	1996	1997	1998	1999	2000	2001	2002
All ages[2]												
Indictable offences												
Violence against the person:	KJEJ	43.6	38.9	37.6	29.1	30.0	34.6	35.7	34.4	34.0	35.3	37.7
Murder	KESB	0.2	0.2	0.2	0.2	0.3	0.3	0.3	0.3	0.3	0.3	0.3
Manslaughter	KESC	0.3	0.2	0.2	0.2	0.3	0.3	0.3	0.3	0.3	0.3	0.3
Wounding	KESD	42.0	37.4	36.1	27.4	28.3	32.7	35.2	33.9	33.5	33.5	35.7
Other offences of violence against the person	KESE	1.1	1.0	1.0	1.2	1.2	1.3	1.3	1.3	1.3	1.2	1.4
Sexual offences	KESF	5.0	4.3	4.5	4.7	4.4	4.5	4.6	4.3	3.9	3.8	4.4
Burglary	KESG	44.3	40.3	38.0	35.3	32.2	31.7	30.8	29.3	26.2	24.8	26.7
Robbery	KESH	5.1	5.1	4.9	5.2	5.9	5.6	5.5	5.6	6.0	6.8	7.7
Theft and handling stolen goods	KESI	127.9	121.6	121.6	116.1	114.5	118.4	125.7	131.2	128.0	127.0	127.3
Fraud and forgery	KESJ	20.0	17.5	18.4	17.2	16.3	17.0	19.8	20.3	19.2	18.3	18.1
Criminal damage	KESK	9.8	9.4	10.0	9.6	9.8	10.5	10.9	10.9	10.2	10.7	11.0
Drugs	KBWX	22.7	21.9	27.8	31.6	34.1	40.7	48.8	48.7	44.6	45.6	49.0
Other offences (excluding motoring)	KESL	36.0	37.8	39.4	42.2	43.5	47.6	49.6	47.9	44.5	44.2	48.0
Motoring offences	KESM	10.7	10.8	12.0	11.2	9.9	9.5	9.0	8.1	7.6	7.7	8.2
Total	KESA	324.9	307.6	314.1	302.2	300.6	320.1	341.7	342.0	325.5	324.2	338.3
Summary offences[3]												
Assaults[4]	KESO	18.0	19.0	21.9	29.3	30.0	32.0	35.3	37.5	37.4	37.7	40.7
Betting and gaming	KESP	–	–	–	–	–	–	–	–	–	–	–
Offences with pedal cycles	KBWY	1.4	1.2	1.0	1.1	1.3	1.5	2.1	1.3	0.8	0.6	0.5
Other Highways Acts offences	KBWZ	4.5	3.6	3.4	2.6	2.8	3.2	3.1	2.9	2.7	2.4	2.2
Breach of local or other regulations	KESQ	8.2	10.5	9.4	6.7	5.9	6.4	5.8	6.5	5.0	4.3	3.9
Intoxicating Liquor Laws: Drunkenness	KESR	23.8	18.8	20.2	19.8	24.2	28.8	30.8	28.7	27.2	26.2	26.9
Other offences	KESS	1.2	0.8	0.7	0.7	0.5	0.6	0.6	0.5	0.4	0.3	0.4
Education Acts	KEST	2.0	2.3	2.8	3.1	3.5	3.7	5.0	5.1	5.1	5.6	5.8
Game Laws	KESU	0.8	0.6	0.6	0.4	0.4	0.3	0.4	0.3	0.2	0.2	0.3
Labour Laws	KESV	0.1	0.1	0.1	0.1	–	0.1	0.1	0.1	0.1	–	–
Summary offences of criminal damage and malicious damage	KESW	24.6	21.6	22.7	22.6	23.4	24.7	26.5	27.9	28.0	26.9	28.3
Offences by prostitutes	KESX	9.8	8.2	7.7	6.8	6.6	6.6	6.0	4.0	4.1	3.7	4.2
Railway offences	KESY	4.7	4.0	5.6	6.2	9.1	11.4	12.6	15.2	17.4	22.6	29.4
Revenue Laws[3]	KESZ	121.6	123.0	126.2	123.8	139.1	143.5	174.7	165.8	175.0	146.9	167.8
Vagrancy Acts	KETB	1.8	1.7	1.9	1.6	2.0	2.0	2.2	2.7	3.3	3.2	3.8
Wireless Telegraphy Acts[3]	KETC	170.3	168.7	162.9	113.8	164.9	77.0	76.6	55.8	105.7	83.8	96.6
Other summary offences	KETD	78.9	69.0	67.8	71.5	74.7	74.7	80.9	79.3	78.1	77.8	76.4
Motoring offences (summary)[3]	KETA	723.1	664.7	638.7	642.4	649.0	649.3	665.2	632.9	607.5	583.3	595.8
Total	KESN	1 194.8	1 117.7	1 093.5	1 052.4	1 137.4	1 065.8	1 128.0	1 066.5	1 098.2	1 025.5	1 083.0
Persons aged 10 to under 18[3,5]												
Indictable offences												
Violence against the person:	KETF	5.2	5.1	5.8	4.7	5.3	5.9	5.9	6.2	6.4	6.9	6.9
Murder	KBXA	–	–	–	–	–	–	–	–	–	–	–
Manslaughter	KBXB	–	–	–	–	–	–	–	0.2	–	–	–
Wounding	KBXC	5.2	5.1	5.7	4.7	5.3	5.8	5.9	5.9	6.3	6.8	6.8
Other offences of violence against the person	KCAA	–	–	–	–	–	0.1	0.1	–	0.1	0.1	0.1
Sexual offences	KETG	0.4	0.4	0.4	0.4	0.4	0.5	0.5	0.5	0.5	0.5	0.6
Burglary	KETH	9.5	8.7	8.9	9.1	8.6	8.6	8.5	7.8	6.8	6.3	6.4
Robbery	KETI	1.4	1.5	1.7	2.0	2.4	2.3	2.2	2.0	2.2	2.8	2.8
Theft and handling stolen goods	KETJ	15.2	14.1	14.4	18.2	19.0	19.6	21.9	22.7	21.0	20.6	18.4
Fraud and forgery	KETK	0.6	0.4	0.5	0.6	0.7	0.8	1.0	1.1	1.0	1.0	1.2
Criminal damage	KETL	1.6	1.7	2.0	2.1	2.2	2.3	2.3	2.7	2.6	2.9	2.9
Drugs	KCAB	1.0	0.8	1.1	1.3	1.6	1.8	2.7	3.1	3.7	4.3	5.0
Other offences (excluding motoring)	KETM	2.7	2.4	2.8	3.3	3.8	4.2	4.2	4.3	4.4	4.4	4.4
Motoring	KETN	0.5	0.3	0.3	0.4	0.4	0.4	0.4	0.4	0.6	0.7	0.8
Total	KETE	38.1	35.4	37.9	42.2	44.4	46.4	49.7	50.6	49.2	50.3	49.1
Summary offences[3]												
Offences with pedal cycles	KETP	0.2	0.1	0.1	0.2	0.2	0.2	0.3	0.3	0.2	0.2	0.2
Breach of local or other regulations	KETR	0.2	0.1	0.1	0.2	0.3	0.2	0.2	0.2	0.2	0.2	0.1
Summary offences of criminal damage and malicious damage	KETS	2.5	2.2	2.9	3.4	3.9	4.4	5.2	6.1	6.7	6.9	7.0
Railway offences	KETT	0.2	0.2	0.3	0.4	0.4	0.5	0.5	0.5	0.4	0.4	0.4
Other summary offences	KETU	11.3	8.3	9.7	7.2	8.8	10.1	12.1	11.7	11.3	11.6	11.7
Motoring offences (summary)[3]	KCAC	10.8	8.9	8.6	9.3	10.8	10.8	11.3	12.6	14.5	16.7	17.1
Total	KETO	25.2	19.9	21.7	25.6	30.3	22.0	36.8	39.6	42.2	45.2	45.4

1 See chapter text.
2 Includes 'Companies', etc.
3 It is estimated that in 1995 there was a shortfall of 75,100 offenders found guilty for certain summary offences.
4 A new charging standard was introduced for assault in 1994.
5 Figures for persons aged 10 to under 18 are included in the totals above.

Source: Home Office: 020 8760 8270

11.4 Offenders cautioned for indictable offences: by type of offence[1]
England and Wales

Thousands

		1992	1993	1994	1995	1996	1997	1998	1999	2000	2001	2002
All ages[2]												
Violence against the person	KELB	23.5	24.1	23.6	20.4	21.8	23.6	23.5	21.2	19.9	19.5	23.6
Murder	KCAD	–	–	–	–	–	–	–	–	–	–	–
Manslaughter	KCAE	–	–	–	–	–	–	–	–	–	–	–
Wounding	KCAF	23.2	23.8	23.2	20.1	21.4	23.3	22.9	20.6	19.3	18.9	22.9
Other violence against the person	KCAG	0.3	0.3	0.3	0.3	0.4	0.4	0.6	0.6	0.6	0.6	0.7
Sexual offences	KELC	3.4	3.3	3.0	2.3	2.0	1.9	1.7	1.5	1.3	1.2	1.1
Burglary	KELD	14.4	12.8	11.5	10.5	10.2	9.4	8.4	7.7	6.6	6.4	5.8
Robbery	KELE	0.6	0.7	0.6	0.6	0.6	0.7	0.6	0.6	0.6	0.5	0.4
Theft and handling stolen goods	KELF	130.3	117.2	104.8	104.9	93.6	82.8	83.6	75.4	67.6	63.5	54.2
Fraud and forgery	KELG	7.5	8.1	7.6	7.9	7.5	7.2	7.4	7.2	6.2	5.8	5.3
Criminal damage	KELH	4.0	4.1	4.3	3.8	3.1	2.8	2.7	3.0	3.2	3.4	3.1
Drug offences	KCAI	27.6	35.1	44.4	48.2	47.5	56.0	58.7	49.4	41.1	39.4	44.9
Other offences (excluding motoring)	KELI	4.8	4.2	4.0	4.0	4.4	5.0	5.0	4.6	4.4	4.2	4.4
Motoring offences	KCAJ	..	..	..	..	..	..	..	..	..	..	..
All offenders cautioned	KELA	216.2	209.6	209.8	202.6	190.8	189.4	191.7	170.6	150.9	143.9	142.9
Persons aged 10 to under 18[3]												
Violence against the person	KEMB	10.8	10.8	11.1	9.4	9.4	9.6	9.5	8.5	8.3	8.7	9.3
Murder	KCAN	–	–	–	–	–	–	–	–	–	–	–
Manslaughter	KCAO	–	–	–	–	–	–	–	–	–	–	–
Wounding	KCAP	10.7	10.8	11.1	9.4	9.4	9.6	9.4	8.4	8.2	8.6	9.2
Other violence against the person	KCCE	–	–	–	–	–	–	–	–	0.1	0.1	0.1
Sexual offences	KEMC	1.3	1.1	1.1	0.8	0.7	0.7	0.6	0.6	0.5	0.5	0.4
Burglary	KEMD	12.0	10.3	9.6	8.5	8.2	7.5	6.7	6.1	5.4	5.3	4.6
Robbery	KEME	0.6	0.6	0.6	0.5	0.6	0.6	0.5	0.5	0.5	0.5	0.4
Theft and handling stolen goods	KEMF	69.8	58.9	58.6	57.4	48.2	40.9	44.0	39.6	36.9	35.2	28.1
Fraud and forgery	KEMG	1.7	1.5	1.4	1.6	1.5	1.4	1.6	1.7	1.5	1.3	1.1
Criminal damage	KEMH	2.6	2.6	2.8	2.4	2.0	1.8	1.7	1.9	2.1	2.3	1.9
Drug offences	KCCF	5.4	6.7	8.5	8.7	7.9	9.7	11.0	9.6	7.9	8.5	9.5
Other offences (excluding motoring)	KEMI	1.4	1.4	1.4	1.3	1.3	1.5	1.5	1.4	1.3	1.3	1.3
Motoring offences	KCCG	..	..	..	..	..	..	..	..	..	..	..
All offenders cautioned	KEMA	105.6	94.1	95.1	90.6	79.9	73.7	77.2	69.8	64.3	63.5	56.6

1 See chapter text.
2 Includes 'Companies', etc.
3 Figures for persons aged 10 to under 18 are included in the totals above.

Source: Home Office: 020 8760 8270

11.5 Offenders found guilty of offences[1]: by age and sex
England and Wales
Magistrates' courts and the Crown Court

Thousands

		1992	1993	1994	1995	1996	1997	1998	1999	2000	2001	2002
Males												
Indictable offences												
All ages	KEFA	282.8	268.2	273.2	263.2	261.1	276.5	292.9	291.7	276.5	275.5	287.1
10 and under 15 years	KEFB	4.9	5.5	6.9	7.1	6.6	7.1	8.1	8.9	8.7	9.0	8.8
15 and under 18 years	KEFC	28.9	26.2	28.7	30.2	32.5	33.6	35.2	35.1	33.8	34.4	33.7
18 and under 21 years	KEFD	58.9	53.0	50.3	47.4	46.3	48.4	51.8	52.6	49.9	48.2	46.6
21 years and over	KEFE	190.1	183.4	187.4	178.6	175.6	187.3	197.9	195.0	184.0	183.9	198.0
Summary offences[2]												
All ages	KEFF	959.6	892.0	871.0	862.0	903.6	880.9	929.0	886.6	881.0	826.6	866.4
10 and under 15 years	KEFG	1.8	1.8	2.3	2.9	2.8	3.0	3.9	5.1	5.8	6.2	6.1
15 and under 18 years	KEFH	21.7	16.8	17.7	20.5	24.6	25.9	28.5	30.3	32.2	34.5	34.6
18 and under 21 years	KEFI	97.6	85.7	82.9	84.0	88.4	91.0	96.3	94.8	93.0	92.2	94.7
21 years and over	KEFJ	838.5	787.7	768.2	754.6	787.9	761.0	800.3	756.5	750.0	693.6	731.0
Females												
Indictable offences												
All ages	KEFK	40.0	37.8	39.5	37.5	38.0	42.2	47.3	49.0	47.7	47.4	50.0
10 and under 15 years	KEFL	0.6	0.7	1.0	1.0	1.0	1.0	1.4	1.4	1.5	1.6	1.6
15 and under 18 years	KEFM	3.6	3.1	3.8	4.0	4.2	4.6	5.1	5.2	5.2	5.3	5.1
18 and under 21 years	KEFN	7.3	6.3	6.2	5.7	5.7	6.3	7.1	7.6	7.5	7.0	6.9
21 years and over	KEFO	28.5	27.7	28.6	26.8	27.2	30.4	33.7	34.7	33.5	33.5	36.5
Summary offences[2]												
All ages	KEFP	219.0	213.3	211.5	180.5	222.9	174.9	188.3	171.0	208.3	190.2	208.7
10 and under 15 years	KEFQ	0.1	0.2	0.2	0.4	0.4	0.5	0.6	0.8	0.9	0.9	1.1
15 and under 18 years	KEFR	1.7	1.2	1.5	1.8	2.6	3.4	3.8	3.4	3.3	3.6	3.6
18 and under 21 years	KEFS	11.2	10.0	9.6	10.4	12.1	11.1	12.1	10.8	11.8	11.1	11.6
21 years and over	KEFT	206.0	201.9	200.2	167.9	207.9	160.0	171.7	155.4	192.3	174.7	192.4
Companies, etc												
Indictable offences	KEFU	2.1	1.7	1.4	1.5	1.5	1.3	1.5	1.3	1.3	1.3	1.2
Summary offences[2]	KEFV	16.2	12.5	10.9	9.9	10.9	10.0	10.7	8.9	8.8	8.6	7.9

1 See chapter text.
2 It is estimated that in 1995 there was a shortfall of 75,100 offenders found
  guilty for certain summary offences.

Source: Home Office: 020 8760 8270

11.6 Persons cautioned by the police[1]: by age and sex
England and Wales

Thousands

		1992	1993	1994	1995	1996	1997	1998	1999	2000	2001	2002
Males												
Indictable offences												
All ages	KEGA	155.0	153.6	153.6	149.3	142.6	143.3	142.9	126.1	109.7	103.8	104.4
10 and under 15 years	KEGB	35.0	31.4	32.3	29.2	25.1	22.9	23.7	22.0	20.3	19.7	16.7
15 and under 18 years	KEGC	41.1	37.1	35.5	35.3	33.0	32.0	32.0	28.7	25.0	24.5	23.3
18 and under 21 years	KEGD	23.8	24.5	25.0	24.8	24.3	25.2	25.7	22.7	20.1	18.5	18.9
21 years and over	KEGE	55.1	60.6	60.7	60.0	60.2	63.2	61.5	52.7	44.3	41.2	45.6
Summary offences												
All ages	KEGF	90.0	86.3	83.6	73.8	79.2	75.7	76.9	76.1	69.6	68.0	63.8
10 and under 15 years	KEGG	9.3	9.4	10.5	10.1	10.3	9.9	10.6	11.7	12.0	12.7	10.3
15 and under 18 years	KEGH	15.1	14.4	14.7	15.4	18.0	16.1	16.1	16.1	14.9	15.2	13.3
18 and under 21 years	KEGI	11.3	11.4	11.3	11.1	13.0	12.9	13.2	13.0	11.9	11.0	11.0
21 years and over	KEGJ	54.3	51.0	47.0	37.1	37.9	36.9	37.0	35.3	30.9	29.0	29.2
Females												
Indictable offences												
All ages	KEGK	61.1	55.9	56.2	53.3	48.2	46.0	48.8	44.5	41.2	40.1	38.5
10 and under 15 years	KEGL	14.3	12.8	15.2	14.0	10.8	9.2	11.1	9.8	10.0	10.1	8.4
15 and under 18 years	KEGM	15.2	12.8	12.4	12.2	10.9	9.5	10.3	9.3	9.0	9.3	8.3
18 and under 21 years	KEGN	7.3	6.7	6.1	6.0	5.6	5.7	5.9	5.7	5.2	4.9	4.8
21 years and over	KEGO	24.4	23.6	22.4	21.1	20.9	21.5	21.4	19.6	17.0	15.9	17.0
Summary offences												
All ages	KEGP	15.1	18.5	15.1	14.8	16.2	17.0	19.2	9.4	18.5	18.0	18.6
10 and under 15 years	KEGQ	1.2	1.3	1.5	1.7	1.8	1.7	2.1	2.5	2.8	2.9	2.7
15 and under 18 years	KEGR	2.5	2.3	2.5	2.7	3.2	3.2	3.7	3.9	3.7	3.8	3.6
18 and under 21 years	KEGS	2.0	2.1	1.9	1.9	2.1	2.3	2.6	2.7	2.5	2.3	2.4
21 years and over	KEGT	9.5	9.8	9.2	8.6	9.1	9.9	10.8	10.3	9.6	9.0	9.8

1 See chapter text.

Source: Home Office: 020 8760 8270

11.7 Sentence or order passed on offenders sentenced for indictable offences[1]: by sex
England and Wales

Magistrates' courts and the Crown Court

Percentages

		1992	1993	1994	1995	1996	1997	1998	1999	2000	2001	2002
Males												
Sentence or order												
Absolute discharge	KEJB	0.8	0.9	0.8	0.8	0.8	0.7	0.7	0.6	0.6	0.6	0.8
Conditional discharge	KEJC	18.0	18.6	17.4	16.2	15.6	15.5	15.3	15.0	14.1	13.4	12.4
Fine	KEJF	34.2	33.8	31.8	30.0	28.6	28.2	28.4	27.7	25.7	24.5	23.9
Community rehabilitation order	KEJD	9.1	9.3	10.2	10.0	9.9	10.0	10.0	10.1	10.1	10.7	10.6
Supervision order	KEJE	1.4	2.0	2.4	2.7	2.9	2.7	2.7	2.7	2.4	2.3	2.1
Community punishment order	KEJG	10.3	11.4	11.1	10.6	9.9	9.5	9.3	9.3	9.5	9.0	8.6
Attendance centre order	KEJH	1.8	1.9	2.0	2.0	1.9	1.8	1.7	1.8	1.5	1.2	0.7
Community punishment and rehabilitation order	KIJW	0.3	2.1	2.7	3.0	3.5	3.7	3.8	3.7	3.6	2.6	2.6
Curfew order	LUJP	..	..	..	..	0.1	0.1	0.2	0.3	0.5	0.7	1.1
Reparation order	SNFI	..	..	..	..	..	..	..	..	0.7	1.3	0.8
Action plan order	SNFJ	..	..	..	..	..	..	..	..	0.9	1.7	1.1
Drug treatment and testing order	SNFK	..	..	..	..	..	..	..	..	0.1	1.2	1.4
Referral order	SNFL	..	..	..	..	..	..	..	..	..	..	3.0
Fully suspended Imprisonment	KEJL	5.4	0.9	0.7	0.7	0.8	0.8	0.7	0.6	0.7	0.6	0.5
Sec 90-92	LUJQ	–	0.1	0.1	0.1	0.2	0.3	0.2	0.2	0.2	0.2	0.2
Detention and training order	LUJR	..	..	..	..	..	..	..	..	1.4	1.9	1.8
Young offender institution	KEJK	4.3	0.8	4.9	5.6	6.1	6.1	6.0	6.2	5.2	4.5	4.2
Unsuspended	KEJM	11.6	12.0	13.6	16.0	17.2	17.9	18.2	18.7	19.9	20.0	20.9
Other sentence or order	KEJN	2.5	2.5	2.3	2.2	2.4	3.0	2.6	3.1	3.1	3.4	3.3
Total number of offenders (thousands) = 100 per cent	KEJA	282.5	267.5	272.6	262.9	260.8	275.4	292.4	291.3	277.1	274.6	285.6
Females												
Sentence or order												
Absolute discharge	KEKB	1.0	0.9	0.9	0.8	0.9	0.8	0.7	0.7	0.6	0.6	0.9
Conditional discharge	KEKC	37.5	35.4	34.4	32.4	30.6	29.4	28.7	26.9	24.9	23.9	22.0
Fine	KEKF	26.2	29.2	25.6	24.1	22.5	21.8	21.3	20.8	20.1	18.6	17.9
Community rehabilitation order	KEKD	15.9	15.4	17.5	18.0	19.0	19.1	19.1	19.4	19.6	19.1	19.2
Supervision order	KEKE	1.3	1.8	2.4	2.7	2.9	2.9	3.1	2.9	2.8	2.7	2.1
Community punishment order	KEKG	5.3	6.1	6.4	6.6	6.5	6.5	6.5	7.1	7.5	7.3	6.8
Attendance centre order	KEKH	0.4	0.5	0.8	1.0	1.0	1.0	0.9	0.9	0.8	0.6	0.4
Community punishment and rehabilitation order	KIJX	0.2	1.4	2.1	2.4	3.0	3.2	3.4	3.3	3.0	2.1	2.1
Curfew order	LUJT	..	..	..	..	–	0.1	0.1	0.3	0.4	0.6	0.8
Reparation order	SNFX	..	..	..	..	..	..	..	..	0.8	1.6	0.8
Action plan order	SNFZ	..	..	..	..	..	..	..	..	1.0	2.0	1.2
Drug treatment and testing order	SNGA	..	..	..	..	..	..	..	..	0.1	1.4	1.7
Referral order	SNGB	..	..	..	..	..	..	..	..	..	..	3.9
Fully suspended Imprisonment	KEKL	4.8	1.2	1.1	1.4	1.5	1.6	1.5	1.3	1.3	1.2	1.1
Sec 90-92	LUJU	–	–	–	0.1	0.1	0.1	–	0.1	0.1	0.1	0.1
Detention and training order	LUJV	..	..	..	..	..	..	..	..	0.6	0.8	0.8
Young offender institution	KEKK	0.8	1.1	1.1	1.5	1.8	1.9	2.2	2.4	2.2	2.0	1.9
Unsuspended	KEKM	4.4	5.0	5.9	7.4	8.4	9.4	10.0	11.0	11.5	12.1	12.7
Other sentence or order	KEKN	2.2	1.9	1.7	1.8	2.0	2.2	2.5	3.0	2.9	3.5	3.4
Total number of offenders (thousands) = 100 per cent	KEKA	40.0	37.7	39.5	37.5	38.0	42.1	47.2	49.0	47.8	47.3	49.9

1 See chapter text.

Source: Home Office: 020 8760 8270

11.8 Offenders sentenced to immediate custody for standard list offences[1]
England and Wales
By sex and number of previous convictions

Percentages and numbers[2]

	Nil	1 - 2	3 - 6	7 - 10	11 and over	Total sentenced for standard list offences	Total sentenced to custody for all offences
				Number of previous convictions[3]			
Year and sex							
1998							
Males	20	14	20	15	30	91 800	94 000
Females	37	16	18	10	18	6 400	6 600
Total	22	14	20	15	29	98 200	100 600
1999							
Males	32	22	19	10	17	95 500	97 800
Females	49	23	15	6	7	7 300	7 500
Total	34	22	19	9	16	102 800	105 300
2000							
Males	30	17	14	11	28	95 700	98 300
Females	40	17	15	10	17	7 700	7 900
Total	31	17	14	11	27	103 400	106 200
2001							
Males	22	15	17	13	33	95 905	98 200
Females	33	15	18	14	20	7 903	8 100
Total	23	15	17	13	32	103 808	106 300

1 See chapter text.
2 The percentages are based on samples of 7 562, 6 096, 17 771 and 6 863 males and 459, 426, 1 361 and 603 females in the years 1998, 1999, 2000 and 2001 respectively. Percentages are rounded and therefore may not add to 100.

3 Counting one conviction per court appearance.

Source: Home Office: 020 7217 8786

11.9 Population in Prison Service establishments under sentence[1]
England and Wales
On 30 June each year: by sex and number of previous convictions

Percentages and numbers[2]

	Previous convictions not found[3]	Nil	1 - 2	3 - 6	7 - 10	11 and over	Number of prisoners
				Number of previous convictions[3]			
Year and sex							
1998							
Males	5	16	14	19	15	31	49 793
Females	11	35	17	17	8	13	2 366
Total	5	17	14	19	14	30	52 159
1999							
Males	8	12	15	21	15	28	47 989
Females	16	27	18	17	9	13	2 486
Total	9	13	15	21	15	27	50 475
2000							
Males	9	14	15	19	14	29	50 437
Females	10	32	15	17	10	14	2 633
Total	9	15	15	19	14	28	53 070
2001							
Males	9	15	13	19	14	29	51 623
Females	13	33	15	16	10	13	2 909
Total	9	16	14	19	13	28	54 532

1 Excludes fine defaulters.
2 The percentages are based on samples of 12 303, 12 341, 12 833 and 13225 males and 2 291, 2 472, 2 633 and 2909 females in the years 1998, 1999, 2000 and 2001 respectively. Percentages are rounded and therefore may not add to 100.

3 In some cases it was not possible to find details on previous convictions. This can happen when a prisoner is not sentenced for a standard list offence and has no previous record for such offences. See chapter text.

Source: Home Office: 020 7217 8786

11.10 Receptions and average population in custody
England and Wales

Numbers

		1992	1993	1994	1995	1996	1997	1998	1999	2000	2001	2002
Receptions												
Type of inmate:												
Untried	KEDA	49 869	53 565	57 079	55 287	58 888	62 066	64 697	64 572	54 892	53 467	58 699
Convicted, unsentenced	KEDB	21 250	30 098	34 563	32 039	34 987	36 424	43 387	45 893	43 889	46 851	53 301
Sentenced	KEDE	69 832	72 966	83 657	89 173	82 861	87 168	91 282	93 965	93 671	91 978	94 807
Immediate custodial sentence	KEDF	50 006	50 563	61 188	69 016	74 306	80 832	85 908	90 238	91 195	90 523	93 615
Young offenders	KEDG	13 174	13 205	14 956	16 244	17 593	18 743	19 599	21 020	21 333	20 969	20 236
Up to 12 months	KEDH	8 055	8 867	10 520	11 308	11 285	11 867	12 942	14 330	14 639	14 234	12 891
12 months up to 4 years	KEDJ	4 610	3 815	3 921	4 393	5 497	5 949	5 921	5 904	5 877	5 856	6 355
4 years up to and including life	KEDL	509	523	515	543	811	927	736	786	817	879	990
Adults	KFBO	36 832	37 358	46 232	52 772	56 713	62 089	66 309	69 218	69 862	69 554	73 379
Up to 12 months	KEDV	18 571	21 050	28 197	33 053	34 864	38 702	42 513	45 662	46 759	46 146	47 870
12 months up to 4 years	KEDW	14 225	12 540	14 146	15 328	16 560	17 546	18 100	17 751	17 290	17 116	18 313
4 years up to and including life	KEDX	4 036	3 768	3 889	4 391	5 289	5 841	5 696	5 805	5 813	6 292	7 196
Committed in default of payment of a fine	KEDY	19 826	22 403	22 469	20 157	8 555	6 336	5 374	3 727	2 476	1 455	1 192
Young offenders	KEEA	4 282	3 353	3 268	2 846	885	555	568	366	216	138	110
Adults	KAFQ	15 544	19 050	19 201	17 311	7 670	5 781	4 806	3 361	2 260	1 317	1 082
Non-criminal prisoners	KEDM	3 109	5 073	4 507	3 789	3 128	3 204	3 290	3 271	3 153	4 630	2 674
Immigration Act 1971	KEDN	1 272	1 837	1 641	1 825	1 857	2 122	2 348	2 443	2 455	4 035	2 093
Others	KEDO	1 837	3 236	2 866	1 964	1 271	1 082	942	828	698	595	581
Average population												
Total in custody	KEDP	45 817	44 565	48 794	51 047	55 281	61 114	65 298	64 771	64 602	66 301	70 861
Total in prison service establishments	KFBQ	44 718	44 551	48 621	50 962	55 281	61 114	65 298	64 771	64 602	66 301	70 778
Police cells[1]	KFBN	1 098	14	173	85	–	–	–	–	–	–	83
Untried	KEDQ	7 387	7 960	9 047	8 352	8 374	8 453	8 157	7 947	7 098	6 924	7 727
Convicted, unsentenced	KEDR	1 987	2 700	3 181	2 954	3 238	3 678	4 411	4 571	4 177	4 314	5 064
Remanded for medical examination	KEDS	14	12	15	9	6	8	9	8	..	40	..
Others	KEDT	1 973	2 688	3 166	2 945	3 232	3 670	4 402	4 563	..	4 274	..
Sentenced	KEDU	35 037	33 317	35 753	39 040	43 043	48 413	52 176	51 691	52 685	54 051	57 222
Immediate custodial sentence	KFBR	34 707	32 825	35 308	38 636	42 863	48 272	52 045	51 596	52 620	54 006	57 184
Young offenders	KFBS	5 382	5 054	5 258	5 752	6 700	7 821	8 490	8 335	8 435	8 559	8 777
Up to 12 months[2]	KFBU	2 808	2 671	2 736	1 721	1 788	1 820	1 964	1 997	2 414	2 330	2 051
12 months up to 4 years[3]	KFBV	1 999	1 800	1 902	2 987	3 748	4 466	4 795	4 674	4 517	4 562	4 867
4 years up to and including life	KFBW	575	583	620	1 042	1 164	1 534	1 730	1 665	1 504	1 667	1 860
Adults	KFCO	29 326	27 771	30 050	32 902	36 162	40 451	43 555	43 261	44 186	45 447	48 408
Up to 12 months[2]	KFCP	7 170	7 054	8 051	4 930	5 136	5 428	5 898	5 635	6 053	5 904	5 755
12 months up to 4 years[3]	KFCQ	9 416	8 445	9 164	11 976	13 383	15 073	16 079	15 048	15 161	15 525	16 845
4 years up to and including life	KFCR	12 740	12 272	12 835	15 998	17 644	19 950	21 580	22 578	22 971	24 021	25 808
Committed in default of payment of a fine	KFCS	330	492	446	403	180	141	131	95	64	45	37
Young offenders	KFEW	65	77	62	54	22	13	15	9	4	6	2
Adults	KFEX	265	415	384	349	158	128	116	86	60	39	35
Non-criminal prisoners	KEEB	308	574	640	615	626	571	554	558	641	1 012	847
Immigration Act 1971	KEEC	227	431	487	483	516	485	476	485	576	955	777
Others	KEED	81	143	153	132	111	87	78	73	63	57	70

1 Mostly untried prisoners.
2 Figures before 1995 relate to sentence length defined as "up to 18 months".
3 Figures before 1995 relate to sentence length defined as "18 months up to 4 years".

Source: Home Office: 020 7217 5567

11.11 Prison population serving sentences: analysis by age and offence[1]
England and Wales

Numbers

	Total	Age in years							
		15 - 17	18 - 20	21 - 24	25 - 29	30 - 39	40 - 49	50 - 59	60 and over
At 30 June 1997									
Offences									
Males									
Total	46 739	1 620	6 078	8 472	9 939	12 503	5 046	2 299	782
Violence against the person	10 045	216	1 039	1 631	2 181	3 014	1 234	549	181
Sexual offences	4 069	39	121	232	465	1 169	934	726	383
Burglary	7 983	448	1 574	2 184	1 938	1 515	245	71	8
Robbery	6 278	437	1 227	1 352	1 370	1 471	337	73	11
Theft, handling, fraud and forgery	5 052	167	605	865	1 020	1 417	638	272	68
Drugs offences	6 486	29	356	892	1 494	2 242	1 027	371	75
Other offences	1 746	142	437	296	324	321	141	64	21
Offence not known	5 080	142	719	1 020	1 147	1 354	490	173	35
Females									
Total	2 066	53	198	372	449	615	271	91	17
Violence against the person	391	18	43	72	61	105	62	22	8
Sexual offences	8	-	1	1	1	3	2	-	-
Burglary	101	4	13	29	31	17	6	1	-
Robbery	161	18	50	29	29	28	5	2	-
Theft, handling, fraud and forgery	455	3	25	78	100	148	71	25	5
Drugs offences	691	4	43	111	173	237	88	31	4
Other offences	68	-	8	12	15	25	4	4	-
Offence not known	191	6	15	40	39	52	33	6	-
At 30 June 1998									
Offences									
Males									
Total	49 902	1 627	5 807	8 780	10 590	14 109	5 485	2 608	896
Violence against the person	10 530	235	1 028	1 670	2 215	3 239	1 345	594	204
Sexual offences	4 781	51	140	224	560	1 366	1 113	872	455
Burglary	8 541	432	1 502	2 256	2 179	1 799	298	65	10
Robbery	6 452	449	1 244	1 319	1 427	1 587	350	61	15
Theft, handling, fraud & forgery	5 193	190	556	906	1 071	1 535	587	300	48
Drugs offences	7 103	38	308	944	1 616	2 569	1 092	441	95
Other offences	5 277	137	690	1 087	1 132	1 461	509	215	46
Offence not known	2 025	95	339	374	390	553	191	60	23
Females									
Total	2 367	62	210	425	501	709	332	116	12
Violence against the person	420	11	44	68	80	116	68	27	6
Sexual offences	16	1	1	1	2	5	5	1	-
Burglary	118	6	17	27	32	28	6	2	-
Robbery	177	24	45	33	36	28	8	3	-
Theft, handling, fraud & forgery	514	6	36	97	107	169	72	26	1
Drugs offences	794	3	32	134	181	267	131	44	2
Other offences	218	8	22	42	41	65	30	8	2
Offences not known	110	3	13	23	22	31	12	5	1
At 30 June 1999									
Offences									
Males									
Total	48 956	1 643	5 633	8 245	10 080	14 072	5 552	2 678	1 053
Violence against the person	10 435	250	1 070	1 548	2 033	3 260	1 428	608	238
Sexual offences	4 930	48	99	236	485	1 448	1 133	935	546
Burglary	8 626	447	1 441	2 207	2 230	1 899	322	73	7
Robbery	6 175	410	1 126	1 384	1 272	1 556	353	58	16
Theft, handling, fraud and forgery	5 027	208	585	886	1 065	1 418	529	279	57
Drugs offences	7 303	36	338	866	1 614	2 720	1 132	476	121
Other offences	5 224	185	742	968	1 120	1 422	541	197	49
Offence not known	1 236	59	232	150	261	349	114	52	19
Females									
Total	2 436	67	224	427	491	798	301	108	20
Violence against the person	429	17	65	50	77	125	63	25	7
Sexual offences	17	-	2	1	-	5	7	1	1
Burglary	158	7	27	37	38	41	6	2	-
Robbery	158	15	24	36	33	41	6	3	-
Theft, handling, fraud and forgery	502	11	33	113	99	159	58	24	5
Drugs offences	875	2	50	131	184	340	129	35	4
Other offences	220	13	9	45	43	68	26	16	-
Offence not known	77	2	14	14	17	19	6	2	3

11.11

continued

Prison population serving sentences: analysis by age and offence[1]
England and Wales

Numbers

	Total	15 - 17	18 - 20	21 - 24	25 - 29	30 - 39	40 - 49	50 - 59	60 and over
					Age in years				
At 30 June 2000									
Offences									
Males									
Total	50 514	1 788	5 911	8 691	10 060	14 454	5 720	2 749	1 140
Violence against the person	10 807	256	1 092	1 658	1 964	3 440	1 480	690	226
Sexual offences	5 070	58	139	261	460	1 424	1 157	937	635
Burglary	8 824	453	1 426	2 165	2 291	2 040	359	77	13
Robbery	6 158	399	1 087	1 343	1 315	1 556	387	57	14
Theft, handling, fraud & forgery	5 422	312	798	1 006	1 118	1 419	483	233	53
Drugs offences	7 526	43	405	949	1 591	2 765	1 188	480	106
Other offences	5 909	225	818	1 180	1 161	1 616	598	236	76
Offence not known	797	43	148	131	160	194	67	38	16
Females									
Total	2 666	65	266	457	563	863	335	102	15
Violence against the person	410	22	46	56	71	122	62	26	6
Sexual offences	20	-	1	1	1	7	5	2	2
Burglary	158	10	24	33	45	40	5	1	-
Robbery	195	13	43	39	39	50	10	1	-
Theft, handling, fraud & forgery	638	7	61	117	154	196	74	24	4
Drugs offences	947	6	58	151	200	354	141	34	2
Other offences	229	5	26	47	40	70	31	9	1
Offence not known	69	2	7	13	12	23	7	5	-
At 30 June 2001									
Offences									
Males									
Total	51 313	1 918	5 864	9 051	9 964	14 538	6 044	2 723	1 211
Violence against the person	11 347	343	1 180	1 810	1 997	3 432	1 631	702	252
Sexual offences	5 048	53	145	265	406	1 368	1 172	953	686
Burglary	8 410	383	1 176	2 039	2 190	2 158	389	61	15
Robbery	6 449	429	1 191	1 436	1 309	1 652	360	60	12
Theft, handling, fraud & forgery	5 370	318	742	1 086	1 080	1 362	510	217	55
Drugs offences	7 980	47	423	1 126	1 686	2 828	1 278	479	113
Other offences	5 868	285	840	1 146	1 163	1 541	616	213	66
Offence not known	841	61	165	143	133	196	90	40	13
Females									
Total	2 899	63	305	493	589	906	406	119	18
Violence against the person	441	18	63	55	72	123	81	24	6
Sexual offences	25	-	2	1	1	7	10	2	2
Burglary	153	9	29	44	29	36	5	2	-
Robbery	248	10	53	63	54	55	13	1	-
Theft, handling, fraud & forgery	594	12	53	100	155	178	64	29	4
Drugs offences	1 130	3	72	183	215	411	193	49	4
Other offences	249	8	27	40	50	82	32	9	2
Offence not known	59	3	7	8	14	14	9	4	-
At 30 June 2002									
Offences									
Males									
Total	53 967	1 979	5 799	9 789	10 198	15 400	6 623	2 821	1 359
Violence against the person	11 671	331	1 178	1 944	1 931	3 501	1 773	748	265
Sexual offences	5 283	62	169	289	409	1 340	1 234	990	790
Burglary	8 922	397	1 129	2 165	2 331	2 375	451	59	15
Robbery	7 197	502	1 269	1 649	1 387	1 857	447	70	17
Theft, handling, fraud and forgery	5 202	296	568	1 067	1 112	1 419	475	209	56
Drugs offences	8 729	52	434	1 253	1 754	3 114	1 488	497	137
Other offences	5 953	268	878	1 217	1 113	1 574	641	198	64
Offence not known	1 010	71	174	205	161	220	114	50	15
Females									
Total	3 340	103	355	585	671	1 039	435	134	18
Violence against the person	534	27	67	70	86	160	86	33	5
Sexual offences	22	-	1	-	-	11	6	3	1
Burglary	230	9	37	54	50	68	11	1	-
Robbery	310	19	63	84	67	62	12	3	-
Theft, handling, fraud and forgery	584	22	56	99	141	175	67	20	4
Drugs offences	1 333	8	93	212	260	478	214	61	7
Other offences	258	12	32	49	52	70	33	9	1
Offence not known	69	6	6	17	15	15	6	4	-

1 Includes persons committed in default of payment of a fine.

Source: Home Office: 020 7217 5567

11.12 Expenditure on prisons
England and Wales
Operating cost and total capital employed, years ending 31 March

£ thousand

		1996/97	1997/98	1998/99	1999/00	2000/01	2001/02	2002/03
Expenditure								
Staff costs	KWUV	948 700	939 700	995 200	1 044 700	1 094 500	1 138 400	1 213 600
Accommodation costs	KXCO	113 900	116 200	163 400	149 300	153 700	193 100	200 000
Other operating costs	KXCP	373 900	472 600	538 800	584 300	654 200	706 100	802 100
Depreciation	KXCQ	123 600	160 200	146 100	115 700	117 200	128 100	132 600
Cost of capital	KXCR	225 500	231 300	262 500	254 900	259 900	284 900	292 700
Total expenditure	KXCS	1 785 600	1 920 000	2 106 000	2 148 900	2 279 500	2 450 600	2 641 000
Income								
Contributions from industries	KXCT	−6 600	−7 900	−8 300	−10 400	−10 600	−11 600	−10 100
Other operating income	KXCU	−5 300	−8 500	−8 500	−9 600	−10 300	−13 100	−15 500
Income from other Government Departments[1]	GDPM	..	..	..	..	−123 900	−180 600	−210 200
Total income	KXCV	−11 900	−16 400	−16 800	−20 000	−144 800	−205 300	−235 800
Net operating costs	KXCW	1 773 700	1 903 600	2 089 200	2 128 900	2 134 700	2 245 300	2 405 200
Total capital employed	KXCX	3 920 900	4 116 900	4 345 100	4 382 600	4 726 200	4 859 600	4 821 500

1 Income from the Youth Justice Board (a non-departmental public body of the Home Office) for the provision of juvenile custody within the Prison Service and Department for Education and Skills for the provision of education services.

Source: Home Office: 020 7217 5567

11.13 Crimes and offences recorded by the police[1]
Scotland

Thousands

		1992	1993	1994	1995	1996	1997	1998	1999	2000	2001	2002
Non-sexual crimes of violence against the person	BEBC	16.8	14.3	14.5	14.7	14.7	13.2	14.3	15.5	15.2	15.1	16.5
Serious assault, etc	KAFS	7.7	6.5	6.7	6.9	7.0	6.1	6.6	7.2	7.0	7.3	7.6
Handling offensive weapons	KAFT	6.5	5.2	5.3	6.5	6.8	6.0	6.7	7.9	8.2	8.7	9.7
Robbery	KAFU	6.8	5.6	5.3	5.3	5.3	4.5	5.0	5.1	4.4	4.2	4.9
Other	KAFV	2.2	2.1	2.5	2.4	2.5	2.6	2.8	3.3	3.8	3.6	3.9
Crimes involving indecency	BEBD	6.2	6.0	6.0	5.5	5.7	7.1	7.4	6.0	5.8	6.0	6.6
Rape and attempted rape[2]	OXBQ	0.5	0.5	0.6	0.6	0.6	0.7	0.8	0.8	0.7	0.8	0.9
Indecent assault[2]	OXBR	1.1	1.1	1.0	1.0	1.1	1.2	1.4	1.2	1.1	1.2	1.3
Lewd and indecent behaviour	KAFY	2.6	2.7	2.7	2.4	2.5	3.0	3.0	2.4	2.3	2.4	2.7
Other	KAFZ	2.0	1.7	1.7	1.5	1.5	2.2	2.3	1.7	1.6	1.7	1.6
Crimes involving dishonesty	BEBE	415.0	374.9	350.3	321.2	295.4	267.2	275.4	276.2	260.9	239.9	235.7
Housebreaking	KAGB	113.2	97.8	88.4	74.2	64.5	55.5	56.6	53.8	48.7	44.9	43.8
Theft by opening lockfast places	KAGC	92.2	84.8	74.9	66.5	60.5	51.1	51.8	50.2	45.0	39.7	40.0
Theft of a motor vehicle	KAGD	47.4	42.8	42.0	37.5	34.2	28.6	28.4	29.8	26.2	23.2	22.5
Shoplifting	KAGE	29.7	26.7	26.6	28.0	26.9	26.3	29.6	32.0	32.3	31.6	29.5
Other theft	KAGF	98.8	93.3	88.9	87.7	82.6	79.6	80.1	81.1	78.1	74.7	75.0
Fraud	KAGG	22.6	19.1	17.7	17.1	16.1	15.7	18.6	18.6	21.2	17.4	16.6
Other	KAGH	11.1	10.3	12.0	10.2	10.8	10.3	10.2	10.6	9.4	8.4	8.2
Fire-raising, vandalism, etc[3]	BEBF	92.2	84.2	88.5	86.5	89.0	81.0	79.2	79.6	83.2	94.9	95.5
Fire-raising[3]	KAGJ	4.7	4.1	3.6	3.3	3.3	2.8	2.5	2.3	2.4	2.8	3.6
Vandalism, etc[3]	KAGK	87.6	80.1	85.0	83.2	85.7	78.2	76.6	77.2	80.8	92.2	91.8
Other crimes[4]	BEBG	34.7	37.8	40.7	47.7	47.1	52.1	55.2	58.4	58.1	65.2	72.9
Crimes against public justice[4]	KAGM	14.4	14.5	16.0	16.4	16.1	16.6	16.9	18.5	18.4	20.3	22.7
Handling offensive weapons[5]	KAFT	6.5	5.2	5.3	6.5	6.8	6.0	6.7	7.9	8.2	8.7	9.7
Drugs	KAGN	13.6	18.0	19.3	24.8	24.0	29.4	31.5	31.9	31.4	36.2	40.4
Other	KAGO	0.2	0.2	0.2	0.2	0.1	0.1	0.1	0.1	0.1	0.1	0.1
Total crimes[4]	KAGQ	564.9	517.2	500.1	475.7	452.0	420.6	431.6	435.7	423.2	421.0	427.0
Miscellaneous offences	BEBH	127.5	126.6	133.2	134.4	146.1	155.9	153.7	151.0	153.8	162.5	167.5
Petty assault	KAGS	42.5	41.3	45.1	46.6	47.6	50.1	51.0	54.0	54.8	54.9	54.7
Breach of the peace	KAGT	60.0	61.4	65.5	66.1	70.8	73.1	71.7	71.0	70.0	72.6	74.2
Drunkenness	KAGU	10.4	10.1	10.3	9.7	9.6	9.7	8.5	7.8	7.8	7.9	7.1
Other	KAGV	14.6	13.7	12.3	11.9	18.0	23.1	22.6	18.2	21.3	27.1	31.6
Motor vehicle offences	BEBI	306.4	315.1	330.7	317.5	305.9	331.0	362.1	353.4	345.8	362.1	341.3
Dangerous and careless driving	KAGX	22.5	20.0	21.1	18.7	17.3	16.3	15.8	14.0	12.3	12.0	12.7
Drunk driving	KAGY	11.3	10.9	10.8	10.7	11.8	11.2	10.6	10.8	10.7	11.4	11.8
Speeding	KAGZ	93.6	85.4	85.8	85.1	82.4	91.9	115.5	125.3	116.8	123.2	111.8
Unlawful use of a motor vehicle	KAHA	79.9	85.8	88.7	83.4	79.1	79.1	75.5	77.8	85.2	88.1	91.1
Vehicle defect offences	KAHB	47.8	51.4	56.9	56.3	53.5	60.1	63.6	52.9	48.3	47.3	46.3
Other	KAHC	51.5	61.7	67.4	63.2	61.8	72.3	81.2	72.5	72.5	80.1	67.7
Total offences	KAHD	433.9	441.7	463.9	451.9	452.0	486.9	515.8	504.5	499.6	524.6	508.9
Total crimes and offences[4]	BEBB	998.8	959.0	964.0	927.6	903.9	907.5	947.3	940.2	922.8	945.7	935.9

1 See chapter text.

2 The category of "sexual assault" was split into "rape and attempted rape" and "indecent assault with effect from 2001, allowing the police Statutory Performance Indicator of serious violent crime to be readily calculated. The statutory Performance Indicator of serious violent crime includes all "non-sexual crimes", excluding "handling an offensive weapon", and includes "rape and attempted rape".

3 A High Court ruling on crimes of fire raising led to a switch in recording practices. Many cases, which previously would have been recorded as vandalism, are now recorded as fire raising. This explains the large increase in fire raising of 31 percent and the corresponding decrease in other vandalism.

4 Data from 1983 onwards has been revised as a result of a legislative change which came into force on 1 April 1996. From this date "offending while on bail" is no longer regarded as an offence in its own right.

5 "Handling offensive weapons" used to be included in the group "non-sexual crimes of violence".

Source: The Scottish Executive Justice Department: 0131 244 2225

11.14 Persons proceeded against[1]
Scotland

		1991	1992	1993	1994	1995	1996	1997	1998	1999	2000	2001
Non-sexual crimes of violence	KEHC	3 965	4 717	4 948	4 622	4 867	5 682	5 601	5 248	5 467	5 497	6 268
Homicide	KEHD	106	148	150	122	157	159	119	104	110	100	101
Serious assault, etc	KEHE	1 032	1 120	1 212	1 218	1 194	1 355	1 445	1 397	1 503	1 480	1 579
Handling offensive weapons	KEHF	1 504	2 028	2 208	2 001	2 357	2 946	2 882	2 664	2 741	2 900	3 591
Robbery	KEHG	885	949	1 006	990	855	933	852	763	825	758	730
Other violence	KEHH	438	472	372	291	304	289	303	320	288	259	267
Crimes of indecency	KEHI	1 660	1 563	1 683	1 587	1 452	1 154	1 379	1 496	1 083	835	781
Sexual assault	KEHJ	200	203	229	195	182	194	212	207	184	171	162
Lewd and libidinous practices	KEHK	429	363	370	399	350	376	399	400	408	319	362
Other indecency	KEHL	1 031	997	1 084	993	920	584	768	889	491	345	257
Crimes of dishonesty	KEHM	40 037	40 152	37 678	35 719	33 948	32 528	31 073	29 815	27 912	25 166	25 613
Housebreaking	KEHN	7 269	7 115	6 379	6 135	5 457	4 642	4 058	3 709	3 662	3 213	3 291
Theft by opening lockfast places	KEHO	3 895	3 688	3 631	3 556	3 106	2 903	2 661	2 299	2 104	1 964	1 876
Theft of motor vehicle	KEHP	3 476	3 688	3 480	3 494	3 449	3 497	3 259	2 849	2 531	2 299	1 990
Shoplifting	KEHQ	7 921	8 469	8 262	7 260	7 185	7 840	7 959	8 357	8 424	8 255	8 945
Other theft	KEHR	9 944	9 485	8 565	7 532	7 485	7 170	7 113	6 761	6 198	5 314	5 236
Fraud	KEHS	2 710	2 528	2 592	2 884	2 720	2 399	2 344	2 400	2 045	1 836	1 859
Other dishonesty	KEHT	4 822	5 179	4 769	4 858	4 546	4 077	3 679	3 440	2 948	2 285	2 416
Fire-raising, vandalism, etc	KEHU	6 593	6 651	6 029	5 644	5 808	6 198	5 917	5 475	4 893	4 765	4 782
Fire-raising	KEHV	192	213	188	203	177	173	149	150	137	134	152
Vandalism, etc	KEHW	6 401	6 438	5 841	5 441	5 631	6 025	5 768	5 325	4 756	4 631	4 630
Other crime	KEHX	11 990	12 126	13 751	15 108	16 018	17 243	15 515	14 414	13 940	12 985	13 778
Crime against public justice	KFBK	7 537	7 377	8 407	8 892	9 424	9 748	7 248	6 224	6 218	6 508	7 022
Drugs offences	KFBL	4 413	4 713	5 313	6 185	6 556	7 454	8 219	8 153	7 689	6 458	6 716
Other	KFBM	40	36	31	31	38	41	48	37	33	19	40
Total crimes	KEHB	64 245	65 209	64 089	62 680	62 093	62 805	59 485	56 448	53 295	49 248	51 222
Miscellaneous offences	KEHZ	60 081	61 811	55 799	49 978	52 235	53 940	52 727	48 179	40 234	39 056	40 482
Simple assault	KEIA	15 507	15 139	14 831	14 250	14 911	15 636	15 907	15 207	13 832	13 111	13 946
Breach of the peace	KEIB	21 955	21 148	20 353	19 102	20 613	22 377	22 336	20 732	16 589	15 432	16 140
Drunkenness	KEIC	2 376	2 253	1 803	1 483	1 364	1 160	983	783	523	463	406
Other miscellaneous offences	KEID	20 243	23 271	18 812	15 143	15 347	14 767	13 501	11 457	9 290	10 050	9 990
Motor vehicle offences	KEIE	76 566	72 055	64 580	66 009	62 840	58 712	60 344	54 605	53 312	48 722	47 892
Dangerous and careless driving	KEIF	7 840	7 177	5 883	5 162	5 273	5 193	5 150	4 199	3 742	3 131	3 525
Drunk driving	KEIG	8 679	8 314	7 812	7 601	7 798	8 313	8 900	7 527	7 236	7 071	7 133
Speeding[2]	KEIH	22 066	19 768	15 727	16 851	15 308	12 777	12 315	12 613	14 408	11 473	10 101
Unlawful use of vehicle	KEII	21 742	22 033	21 951	22 947	21 528	21 124	22 213	20 062	18 597	19 085	20 004
Vehicle defect offences	KEIJ	4 489	4 111	3 308	3 560	3 683	3 548	3 775	2 960	2 363	1 869	1 521
Other motor vehicle offences	KEIK	11 750	10 652	9 899	9 888	9 250	7 757	7 991	7 244	6 966	6 093	5 608
Total offences	KEHY	136 647	133 866	120 379	115 987	115 075	112 652	113 071	102 784	93 546	87 778	88 374
Total crimes and offences	KEHA	200 892	199 075	184 468	178 667	177 168	175 457	172 556	159 232	146 841	137 026	139 596

1 See chapter text.
2 Includes motorway and clearway offences.

Source: Scottish Executive Justice Department: 0131 244 2229

11.15 Persons proceeded against in court[1]
Scotland

Number of persons

		1991	1992	1993	1994	1995	1996	1997	1998	1999	2000	2001
Court procedure												
High Court[2]	KEIQ	1 227	1 419	1 601	1 228	1 390	1 420	1 356	1 225	1 357	1 196	1 078
Sheriff Court	KEIU	100 028	100 108	96 391	97 579	98 304	100 928	98 867	92 519	89 266	85 481	91 511
District Court	KEIV	87 186	84 705	74 920	68 183	66 039	62 485	61 648	57 182	49 020	44 899	41 075
Stipendiary Magistrate Court	KEIW	11 522	11 732	10 472	10 893	10 649	9 973	9 943	7 794	6 689	5 081	5 644
Total called to court[3]	KEIZ	200 017	198 038	183 674	178 067	176 423	174 844	171 932	158 815	146 474	136 772	139 345

1 See chapter text.
2 Including cases remitted to the High Court from the Sheriff Court.
3 Includes court type not known.

Source: Scottish Executive Justice Department: 0131 244 2229

11.16 Persons with charge proved: by main penalty[1]
Scotland

Number of persons

Main penalty		1991	1992	1993	1994	1995	1996	1997	1998	1999	2000	2001
Restriction of liberty order[2]	ZBRE	..	..	..	..	..	..	..	71	206	215	201
Supervised attendance order[3]	ZBRF	..	..	..	..	..	8	73	68	107	75	48
Drug treatment and testing order[4]	OEWA	..	..	..	..	..	..	..	..	..	80	276
Absolute discharge	KEXA	887	967	989	839	939	1 000	1 064	957	985	967	986
Admonition or caution	KEXB	17 137	17 441	16 976	16 243	15 857	15 859	15 039	13 893	12 914	11 801	11 975
Probation	KEXC	4 877	5 385	5 722	6 145	6 145	6 435	6 814	7 144	7 340	7 360	8 171
Remit to children's hearing	KEXD	81	72	83	124	172	193	219	177	136	106	159
Community service order	KEXE	5 190	5 473	5 079	5 320	5 339	5 711	5 707	5 246	4 888	4 684	4 869
Fine	KEXF	135 479	131 842	116 918	112 748	110 337	105 384	103 861	94 917	83 479	76 237	75 643
Compensation order	KEXG	1 591	1 575	1 578	1 535	1 527	1 415	1 304	1 298	1 154	1 111	1 138
Insanity, hospital, guardianship order	KYAN	148	133	138	133	136	159	162	129	135	108	111
Prison	KEXI	9 222	10 085	10 832	11 583	11 561	12 134	11 621	11 447	11 591	10 936	12 255
Young offenders' institution	KEXJ	4 318	4 488	4 461	4 472	4 646	4 744	4 557	4 459	4 483	4 318	4 228
Detention of child	KEXM	35	22	30	36	48	45	29	20	17	11	16
Total persons with charge proved	KEXO	178 965	177 483	162 806	159 178	156 707	153 087	150 450	139 826	127 435	118 009	120 076

1 See chapter text.
2 A community sentence introduced by Section 5 of the Crime and Punishment (Scotland) Act 1995 and available on a pilot basis to 3 Scottish sheriff courts since August 1998. This sentence was made available to High Court, Sheriff Courts and Stipendiary Magistrates court from 1 May 2002.
3 The pilot scheme under the Criminal Procedure (Scotland) Act 1995, where fines for 16 & 17 year olds were replaced by supervised attendance orders, was discontinued in December 1999. The majority of supervised attendance orders recorded in the year 2000 were disposals relating to breaches of an existing order.

4 Drug treatment and testing orders are new measures made available on a pilot basis to courts in Fife and Glasgow since February 2000.

Source: Scottish Executive Justice Department: 0131 244 2229

11.17 Persons with charge proved[1]: by age and sex
Scotland

Number of persons

		1991	1992	1993	1994	1995	1996	1997	1998	1999	2000	2001
Males	KEWA	150 482	147 693	136 127	136 533	133 330	130 961	129 461	120 482	110 326	101 208	103 599
Under 16	KEWB	189	138	138	171	180	149	137	135	75	54	75
16 to 20	KEWC	38 284	36 494	32 589	30 708	30 113	31 704	31 310	29 311	26 927	24 338	25 160
21 to 30	KEWD	59 532	59 561	56 052	56 519	54 184	52 218	50 684	46 121	41 667	38 523	39 730
Over 30	KEWE	49 802	49 094	45 701	47 788	47 648	45 799	46 281	44 047	40 786	37 548	38 219
Age not known	KEWF	2 675	2 406	1 647	1 347	1 205	1 091	1 049	868	871	745	415
Females	KEWG	26 340	28 051	25 405	21 650	22 412	21 308	20 246	18 667	16 539	16 366	16 125
Under 16	KEWH	18	9	6	8	17	12	11	5	6	9	5
16 to 20	KEWI	3 927	3 885	3 589	2 939	3 098	3 302	3 424	3 361	3 273	3 050	2 918
21 to 30	KEWJ	10 958	11 998	10 557	9 190	9 284	8 461	8 095	7 456	6 494	6 283	6 375
Over 30	KEWK	10 519	11 409	10 611	9 002	9 439	8 894	8 266	7 531	6 494	6 765	6 713
Age not known	KEWL	918	750	642	511	574	639	450	314	272	259	114
Males and Females	KEWM	176 822	175 744	161 532	158 183	155 742	152 269	149 707	139 149	126 865	117 574	119 724
Under 16	KEWN	207	147	144	179	197	161	148	140	81	63	80
16 to 20	KEWO	42 211	40 379	36 178	33 647	33 211	35 006	34 734	32 672	30 200	27 388	28 078
21 to 30	KEWP	70 490	71 559	66 609	65 709	63 468	60 679	58 779	53 577	48 161	44 806	46 105
Over 30	KEWQ	60 321	60 503	56 312	56 790	57 087	54 693	54 547	51 578	47 280	44 313	44 932
Age not known	KEWR	3 593	3 156	2 289	1 858	1 779	1 730	1 499	1 182	1 143	1 004	529
Companies	KEWS	2 126	1 717	1 263	991	961	812	737	675	551	399	307
Total persons with charge proved[2]	KEWT	178 965	177 483	162 806	159 178	156 707	153 087	150 450	139 826	127 435	118 009	120 076

1 See chapter text.
2 Includes sex unknown.

Source: Scottish Executive Justice Department: 0131 244 2229

11.18 Penal establishments: average daily population and receptions
Scotland

Numbers

		1992	1993	1994	1995	1996	1997	1998	1999	2000	2001	2002
Average daily population												
Male	KEPB	5 099	5 466	5 408	5 451	5 673	5 900	5 825	5 817	5 666	5 889	6 126
Female	KEPC	158	171	177	175	189	184	193	212	203	249	277
Total	KEPA	5 257	5 637	5 585	5 626	5 862	6 084	6 018	6 029	5 869	6 137	6 404
Analysis by type of custody												
Remand	KEPD	876	948	1 015	998	1 000	947	938	1 012	894	960	1 222
Persons under sentence: total	KEPE	4 375	4 686	4 569	4 624	4 861	5 134	5 077	5 016	4 973	5 176	5 180
Adult prisoners[1]	KEPF	3 552	3 795	3 785	3 823	4 026	4 345	4 362	4 318	4 319	4 526	4 583
Young offenders[1]	KEPI	769	819	720	719	770	789	715	697	654	650	597
Persons recalled from supervision/licence	KEPN	32	40	37	44	46	46	72	93	129	193	244
Others	KEPO	21	32	28	38	18	20	17	28	31	47	6
Persons sentenced by court martial	KEPP	6	2	1	3	–	1	2	1	1	–	–
Civil prisoners	KEPQ	1	1	1	–	1	1	1	1	1	1	2
Receptions to penal establishments												
Remand	KEPR	13 546	13 412	14 922	14 253	14 977	14 826	15 098	15 291	13 945	15 433	18 726
Male	KEPS	12 722	12 478	13 985	13 377	13 976	13 850	13 979	14 090	12 916	14 166	17 092
Female	KEPT	824	934	937	876	1 001	976	1 119	1 201	1 029	1 267	1 634
Persons under sentence: total	KEPU	19 966	22 157	21 111	19 030	22 155	23 202	22 269	20 741	18 916	19 247	19 687
Male	KEPV	18 856	20 741	19 697	17 737	20 869	21 936	20 862	19 465	17 739	18 035	18 440
Female	KEPW	1 110	1 416	1 414	1 293	1 286	1 266	1 407	1 276	1 177	1 212	1 247
Imprisoned: Adults:												
directly	KEPX	8 543	9 444	9 349	8 730	10 040	9 698	9 959	9 484	8 713	9 617	10 408
in default of fine	KEPY	6 603	7 956	7 377	6 299	7 432	8 873	7 866	7 154	6 542	6 088	6 056
in default of compensation order[2]	KEPZ	40	41	26	13	..	..	..	..	..	..	..
Sentenced to young offenders' institution:												
directly	KEQA	3 041	3 052	2 855	2 772	3 111	2 784	2 844	2 687	2 500	2 414	2 205
in default of fine	KEQB	1 736	1 660	1 498	1 210	1 567	1 847	1 593	1 411	1 161	1 128	1 018
in default of compensation order[2]	KEQC	2	4	6	4	..	..	..	..	..	..	..
Persons recalled from supervised release orders	JYYD	1	–	–	2	5	11	7	5	–	–	–
Persons sentenced by court martial	KEQH	2	7	5	4	4	4	5	3	2	1	3
Civil prisoners[3]	KEQI	34	37	27	25	32	23	10	14	12	9	12

1 Figures for 1998 have been revised to reflect improved treatment of missing data.
2 From 1996 compensation orders are included in the figures for default of fine.
3 For 1995 and 1996 data are estimated.

Source: The Scottish Executive Justice Department: 0131 244 2225

11.19 Expenditure on penal establishments[1]
Scotland
Years ended 31 March

£ thousands

		1992/93	1993/94	1994/95	1995/96	1996/97	1997/98	1998/99	1999/00	2000/01	2001/02	2002/03
Departmental Expenditure												
Manpower and Associated Services	KPHC	129 597	135 301	140 009	135 941	143 107	137 890	144 660	170 347	160 242	172 490	168 593
Prisoner and Associated Costs	KPHD	10 274	10 795	11 679	12 373	13 377	16 313	18 891	22 930	23 501	24 652	23 363
Capital Expenditure	KPHE	13 681	11 845	15 636	15 377	22 577	22 136	23 697	28 918	24 283	24 955	36 519
Gross Expenditure	KPHF	153 552	157 941	167 324	163 691	179 061	176 339	187 248	222 195	208 026	222 097	228 475
Less Receipts	KPHG	3 542	3 598	3 042	2 800	2 600	2 810	8 160	6 668	8 380	8 194	3 485
Net Departmental Expenditure	KPHH	150 010	154 343	164 282	160 891	176 461	173 529	179 088	215 527	199 646	213 903	224 990
Plus Annually Managed Expenditure Capital Charges	DSJI	..	..	..	..	..	..	..	..	..	31 341	40 432
Total Net Expenditure	DSNX	150 010	154 343	164 282	160 891	176 461	173 529	179 088	215 527	199 646	245 244	265 422

1 See chapter text.

Source: The Scottish Executive Justice Department: 0131 244 2225

11.20 Recorded crime statistics[1]
Northern Ireland

Thousands

		Old counting rules							New counting rules				
		1993	1994	1995	1996	1997	1998 /99		1998 /99	1999 /00	2000 /01	2001 /02	2002 /03
Violence against the person	RVCP	4.6	4.8	5.2	5.6	5.2	6.6	RVCQ	18.5	21.4	21.4	26.1	28.5
Sexual offences	RVCR	1.2	1.3	1.7	1.7	1.4	1.5	RVCS	1.6	1.3	1.2	1.4	1.5
Burglary	RVCT	15.7	16.9	16.5	16.1	14.3	15.5	RVCU	15.5	16.1	15.8	17.1	18.7
Robbery	RVCV	1.7	1.6	1.5	1.7	1.7	1.4	RVCW	1.4	1.4	1.8	2.2	2.5
Theft	RVCX	33.2	33.2	33.5	32.8	29.5	34.6	RVCY	35.4	37.0	36.9	41.7	41.9
Fraud and forgery	RVCZ	5.6	5.1	4.9	4.1	3.8	5.3	RVDA	6.8	7.9	8.0	8.6	8.8
Criminal damage	RVDB	2.9	3.1	3.8	4.8	4.7	9.8	RVDC	27.7	31.2	32.3	40.0	36.6
Offences against the state	RVDD	0.4	0.4	0.3	0.4	0.5	0.5	RVDE	0.6	0.7	0.8	1.2	1.8
Other notifiable offences	RVDF	1.0	1.4	1.5	1.2	1.1	1.5	RVDG	1.7	2.1	1.7	1.4	2.4
of which drug offences	RVDH	0.8	1.3	1.4	1.1	1.0	1.4	RVDI	1.4	1.7	1.5	1.1	1.9
Total	RVDR	66.2	67.9	68.8	68.5	62.2	76.6	RVDS	109.1	119.1	119.9	139.8	142.5

1 See chapter text.

Source: The Police Service of Northern Ireland

11.21 Persons found guilty at all courts by offence group[1]
Northern Ireland

Numbers

		1990	1991	1992	1993	1994	1995	1996	1997	1998	1999	2000
Violence against the person	KYCT	1 750	1 634	1 558	1 674	1 498	1 685	1 597	1 594	1 596	1 699	1 858
Sexual offences	KEVG	275	193	184	126	148	182	184	130	128	90	130
Burglary	KYBW	1 362	1 208	1 149	1 114	979	951	801	715	647	703	703
Robbery	KYBX	220	162	202	159	168	195	161	166	134	129	122
Theft	KYBY	3 399	3 429	3 158	3 254	3 044	3 128	2 765	2 596	2 342	1 995	2 111
Fraud and forgery	KYBZ	699	648	683	633	568	533	467	491	426	476	403
Criminal damage	KYCA	1 054	1 019	967	1 145	1 134	1 008	1 076	1 163	1 043	931	1 060
Offences against the state	KYCB	233	195	187	184	137	166	147	165	198	178	174
Other indictable	KYCC	287	368	448	606	669	863	899	739	936	943	1 012
Total indictable[2]	KYCD	9 279	8 856	8 536	8 895	8 345	8 711	8 097	7 759	7 450	7 144	7 573
Summary	KYCE	4 293	4 278	4 115	4 307	4 369	4 137	4 402	4 435	4 062	3 598	3 967
Motoring[3]	KYCF	27 248	20 169	20 808	21 882	21 502	20 124	18 177	18 770	15 369	15 782	15 078
All offences	KYCG	40 820	33 303	33 459	35 084	34 216	32 972	30 676	30 964	26 881	26 524	26 618

1 See chapter text.
2 Excludes indictable motoring offences
3 Includes indictable motoring offences

Source: Northern Ireland Office: 028 9052 7534

11.22 Juveniles found guilty at all courts by offence group[1,2]
Northern Ireland

Numbers

		1990	1991	1992	1993	1994	1995	1996	1997	1998	1999	2000
Violence against the person	KYCH	44	38	46	43	49	51	75	49	97	73	77
Sexual offences	KAHF	17	8	11	7	8	7	4	8	12	12	4
Burglary	KYCI	232	194	165	155	180	170	137	124	108	117	125
Robbery	KYCJ	10	7	8	4	9	22	13	18	4	7	15
Theft	KYCK	329	328	247	280	283	345	338	334	304	227	254
Fraud and forgery	KYCL	10	10	16	14	14	21	14	11	4	10	2
Criminal damage	KYCM	90	92	82	94	117	116	121	136	139	102	143
Offences against the state	KYCN	6	5	6	1	8	9	6	10	11	12	8
Other indictable	KYCO	10	11	8	2	6	14	24	10	20	17	21
Total indictable[3]	KYCP	748	693	589	600	674	755	732	700	699	577	649
Summary	KYCQ	138	111	113	125	131	180	182	198	187	163	180
Motoring[4]	KYCR	92	71	40	44	74	74	58	57	98	97	71
All offences	KYCS	978	875	742	769	879	1 009	972	955	984	837	900

1 See chapter text.
2 Juveniles are aged 10 - 16 years inclusive.
3 Excludes indictable motoring offences.
4 Includes indictable motoring offences.

Source: Northern Ireland Office: 028 9052 7534

11.23 Disposals given to those convicted by court
Northern Ireland

Numbers

		1990	1991	1992	1993	1994	1995	1996	1997	1998	1999	2000
Magistrates court - all offences												
Prison[1]	KYAO	1 009	960	830	1 027	945	1 046	1 003	989	996	1 278	1 356
Young offenders centre	KYAP	370	502	588	575	499	483	443	430	326	243	191
Training school[2]	KYAQ	153	177	120	125	193	169	147	148	136	13	–
Juvenile Justice Centre order[2]	OEUX	–	–	–	–	–	–	–	–	–	22	78
Total immediate custody	KYAR	1 532	1 639	1 538	1 727	1 637	1 698	1 593	1 567	1 458	1 556	1 625
Prison suspended	KYAS	1 513	1 379	1 420	1 529	1 558	1 674	1 722	1 506	1 025	1 080	1 247
YOC suspended	KYAT	310	432	507	447	447	385	444	461	139	104	93
Attendance centre	KYAU	118	90	66	94	89	101	91	66	55	14	20
Probations/supervision	KYAV	854	742	849	881	1 017	1 137	1 134	1 155	1 473	1 246	1 096
Community supervision order	KYAW	575	547	464	536	551	547	591	561	622	678	726
Combination order	OEUZ	–	–	–	–	–	–	–	–	38	7	48
Fine[3]	KYAX	26 644	19 569	23 418	25 166	24 390	22 726	20 612	21 313	17 955	18 076	17 716
Recognizance	KYAY	399	514	713	858	961	1 001	1 203	1 267	1 134	1 089	1 357
Conditional discharge	KYAZ	1 982	2 102	1 965	2 021	1 830	1 928	1 679	1 597	1 538	1 439	1 286
Absolute discharge	KYBA	1 274	845	732	690	661	608	509	424	303	223	242
Penalty points[3]	OEVA	–	–	–	–	–	–	–	–	44	105	1
Fine plus Disqualification[4]	KYBB	4 335	4 211	640	6	6	2	5	2	57	97	9
Other	KYBC	28	24	12	7	11	8	10	6	23	19	47
Total	KYBD	39 564	32 094	32 324	33 962	33 158	31 815	29 593	29 925	25 864	25 733	25 513
Crown court - all offences												
Prison[1]	KYBE	493	493	447	555	471	533	469	475	520	386	521
Young offenders centre	KYBF	106	125	119	130	87	76	106	111	63	67	32
Training school[2]	KYBG	4	13	5	2	5	6	–	4	2	–	–
Juvenile Justice Centre order[2]	VQEV	–	–	–	–	–	–	–	–	–	–	–
Total immediate custody	KYBH	603	631	571	687	563	615	575	590	585	453	553
Prison suspended	KYBI	295	238	249	211	277	265	253	220	199	185	313
YOC suspended	KYBJ	78	46	63	37	43	63	71	60	49	41	48
Combination order	ZAEP	..	..	..	..	..	..	..	..	13	6	7
Attendance centre	KYBK	–	–	–	–	1	–	–	–	–	–	–
Probation/supervision	KYBL	85	103	95	73	58	60	49	47	70	43	68
Community supervision order	KYBM	105	89	79	48	59	60	54	37	33	24	29
Fine[3]	KYBN	33	23	17	33	23	27	39	40	25	20	40
Recognizance	KYBO	8	7	9	5	16	–	7	10	7	–	4
Conditional discharge	KYBR	37	53	36	19	15	64	30	31	23	17	38
Absolute discharge	KYBS	2	5	8	3	2	1	–	1	6	–	3
Fine plus Disqualification[4]	KYBT	10	6	2	–	–	–	–	–	1	–	1
Other	KYBU	–	8	6	6	1	2	3	3	6	2	1
Total	KYBV	1 256	1 209	1 135	1 122	1 058	1 157	1 081	1 039	1 017	791	1 105

1 Figures include all custody probation orders.
2 The Juvenile Justice Centre order replaced the training school order from 31st January 1999.
3 For 2000, fine incorporates 'fine plus disqualification' and 'fine plus penalty points'.
4 For 2000, figures relate to disqualification only.

Source: Northern Ireland Office: 028 9052 7534

11.24 Prisons and Young Offenders Centres
Northern Ireland
Receptions and average population

Numbers

		1992	1993	1994	1995	1996	1997	1998	1999	2000	2001	2002
Receptions:												
Reception of untried prisoners	KEOA	1 987	2 045	2 043	2 003	2 292	2 188	2 284	2 497	2 197	1 922	2 337
Reception of sentenced prisoners:												
Imprisonment under sentence of immediate custody[1]	KEOB	941	1 135	1 029	1 070	1 070	1 062	· 949	963	1 001	791	916
Imprisonment in default of payment of a fine	KEOC	1 352	1 221	1 190	1 248	1 374	1 513	1 530	1 423	1 261	1 090	990
Total	KEOD	2 293	2 356	2 219	2 318	2 444	2 575	2 479	2 386	2 262	1 881	1 906
Reception into Young Offender Centres:												
Detention under sentence of immediate custody	KEOE	371	416	346	371	362	331	347	346	282	252	315
Detention in default of payment of a fine	KEOF	364	353	276	351	373	366	385	417	389	303	250
Total	KEOG	735	769	622	722	735	697	732	763	671	555	565
Other receptions:												
Civil committals	KEOI	10	21	13	45	27	42	70	38	56	58	57
Total	KEOL	10	21	13	45	27	42	70	38	56	58	57
Daily average population:												
Total	KEOM	1 810	1 934	1 899	1 762	1 639	1 632	1 507	1 244	1 068	910	1 026
Unconvicted[2]	KEON	414	427	440	322	337	376	383	377	317	272	347
Convicted[3]	KEOP	1 396	1 507	1 459	1 440	1 302	1 256	1 124	867	751	638	679

1 Includes those detained under Section 73 of the Children and Young Persons (NI) Act 1968.
2 Prisoners on remand or awaiting trial and prisoners committed by civil process.
3 Includes those sentenced to immediate custody and fine defaulters.

Source: Northern Ireland Office: 028 9052 7534

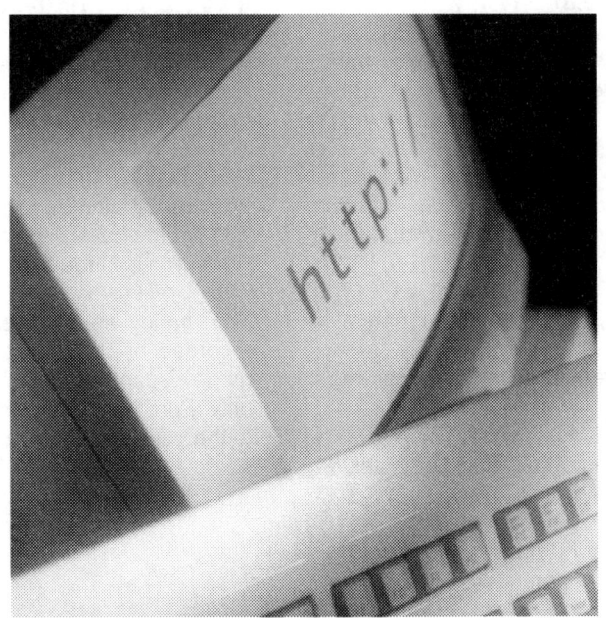

12 Lifestyles

Lifestyles

Expenditure by the Department for Culture, Media and Sport *(Table 12.1)*

The figures in this table are taken from the Department's Annual Report and are outturn figures for each of the headings shown (later figures are the estimated outturn). The Department's planned expenditure for future years is also shown.

Cinema statistics *(Table 12.3)*

This table now includes data from CAA/Gallup/Nielsen EDI which replaces the previous ONS Inquiry data which are no longer collected.

Tourist attractions *(Table 12.5)*

The figures in this table are compiled using data from the Visits to Visitor Attraction Survey. The tourist attractions included within the headings shown are as follows: -

Country parks: Country parks and forest parks.

Farms: Farms, rare breeds, shire horse centres and farm animals.

Gardens: Gardens, arboretums and botanical gardens.

Historic properties: Historic houses, palaces, castles, forts, historic monuments, archaeological sites, historic ships and other historic properties.

Leisure and theme parks: Leisure parks and theme parks.

Museums and art galleries: Museums and/or art galleries and science centres.

Steam and heritage railways: Steam railways and heritage railways.

Visitor and heritage centres: Visitor and heritage centres.

Wildlife attractions: Nature reserves, wetlands, wildlife trips, safari parks, zoos, aquariums and aviaries.

Workplaces: Distilleries, vineyards, breweries and industrial or craft premises.

Domestic tourism *(Table 12.6)*

The figures in this table are compiled using data from the United Kingdom Tourism Survey and represent trips of one or more nights away from home.

International tourism and Holidays abroad *(Tables 12.7 and 12.8)*

The figures in these tables are compiled using data from the International Passenger Survey. A holiday abroad is a visit made for holiday purposes. Business trips and visits to friends and relatives are excluded.

Gambling *(Table 12.10)*

The National Lottery figures in this table are the latest expenditure figures at the time of going to press which have been released by OFLOT - the National Lottery regulator, and represent ticket sales for each of the games which comprise the lottery. The figures have been adjusted to real terms using the Retail Prices Index.

The National Lottery commenced on the 19 November 1994, with the first instant ticket being sold in March 1995. Various other games have been started since, the latest shown in the table being the Hot Picks game. The sum of the individual games may not agree exactly with the figures for total sales, and also includes the Easy Play games which commenced in 1998, but were dropped in 1999.

The other gambling figures in this table are obtained from the Gaming Board for Great Britain Annual Report. The figures have been adjusted to real terms using the Retail Prices Index.

The money spent at casinos represents the money recorded as having been exchanged for chips. The money spent at bingo clubs refers to licensed clubs only. Prior to 1994-95 the figures for bingo clubs relate to the year ending August.

12.1 Expenditure by the Department for Culture, Media and Sport[1]

£ millions

	Museums, galleries and libraries[2]	The arts (England)	Sports (UK)	Historic buildings, monuments, and sites (England)	The Royal Parks (UK)	Tourism (UK)	Broadcasting and media (UK)	Administration and research	Other gambling and gaming bodies	Commemorative services (Queen's Golden Jubilee)	European regional development fund	Culture online
	GQIF	KWFP	KWFQ	KWFR	LQYY	KWFS	KWFT	GQIG	SNKA	SNKB	JYXQ	GQII
1993/94	335	235	54	164	23	46	85	22	–	..	..	..
1994/95	372	195	53	164	24	44	93	21	–	..	..	..
1995/96	399	200	54	164	25	45	98	20	–	..	6	..
1996/97	336	195	52	162	23	46	97	21	–	..	16	..
1997/98	321	196	50	156	22	45	43	21	–	..	26	..
1998/99	375	193	46	143	23	44	99	23	–	..	33	..
1999/00	391	230	51	145	30	48	104	28	–	..	28	..
2000/01	425	239	52	145	25	48	104	29	–	..	35	1
2001/02	464	254	67	140	24	66	103	33	1	–	27	1
2002/03[3]	494	297	115	155	27	72	110	39	3	4	6	–
2003/04[4]	531	337	111	155	26	53	115	47	3	..	6	..
2004/05[4]	548	367	120	153	26	54	122	49	3	..	6	..
2005/06[4]	564	412	123	153	26	55	122	51	2	..	6	..

1 See chapter text.
2 Includes museums and galleries (England), libraries (UK) and museums library archives (UK).
3 Data are estimated outturn.
4 Data are plans.

Source: Department for Culture, Media and Sport: 020 7211 6121

12.2 Employment in tourism related industries
Great Britain

At June in each year

Thousands, not seasonally adjusted

	Hotels and other tourist accommodation	Restaurants, cafes etc.	Bars, public houses and nightclubs	Travel agents, tour operators	Libraries, museums and other cultural activities	Sport and other recreation activities	All tourism related industries		
								Of which:	
							All	Employee jobs	Self-employment jobs
	KWFV	KWFW	KWFX	KWFY	KWFZ	KWGA	LQZA	KWGB	KWGC
1992	311.0	303.0	414.2	69.2	74.8	320.8	1 671.0	1 493.0	178.0
1993	317.6	298.0	370.6	69.3	75.6	316.5	1 643.6	1 447.6	196.0
1994	375.3	372.2	399.1	83.7	75.6	355.7	1 663.3	1 455.5	207.8
1995	385.8	386.2	445.1	90.7	77.3	363.5	1 751.6	1 536.6	215.0
1996	399.1	487.9	506.4	104.0	73.9	352.1	1 923.4	1 706.3	217.0
1997	371.0	505.1	553.9	115.8	75.4	359.2	1 980.3	1 762.1	218.2
1998	385.0	520.8	555.3	111.0	74.8	347.1	1 994.0	1 809.0	185.0
1999	409.9	535.1	555.6	123.2	76.2	367.3	2 067.3	1 906.7	160.6
2000	406.2	555.2	576.1	131.4	88.9	385.6	2 143.5	1 971.6	171.9
2001	410.2	550.8	533.0	141.7	80.0	406.7	2 122.5	1 962.5	160.0
2002	418.0	545.4	535.9	133.6	81.4	412.9	2 127.2	1 964.0	163.2

Source: Department for Culture, Media and Sport: 020 7211 6121

12.3 Cinema statistics[1,2]
United Kingdom

	Sites	Screens	Total number of admissions[3]	Gross box office takings	Revenue per admission[3]	Revenue per screen
	number	£ million	£ million	£ million	£	£ million
	JMHX	JMHY	JMHZ	JMIA	JMIB	JMIC
1994	696	1 919	123.5	355.8	2.88	185.4
1995	728	2 003	114.6	354.2	3.09	176.8
1996	742	2 166	123.5	407.2	3.30	188.0
1997	747	2 383	138.9	486.2	3.50	204.0
1998	761	2 638	135.2	504.9	3.73	191.4
1999	751	2 825	139.1	549.7	3.95	194.6
2000	754	3 017	142.5	572.8	4.02	189.9
2001	766	3 248	155.9	645.0	4.14	198.6
2002	775	3 402	175.9	755.3	4.29	222.0

1 See chapter text.
2 Includes Isle of Man and the Channel Islands.
3 Admissions are based on all cinemas taking advertising.

Source: CAA/Gallup/Nielsen EDI

12.4 Films
United Kingdom

	Production of UK films		Expenditure on feature films (Current prices)				
	Films produced in the UK	Production costs (1998 prices)	UK box office	Video rental	Video retail	Subscriptions to movie channels	Box office, video, subscription channels
	Number	£ million	£ million	£ million	£ million	£ million	£ million
	KWGD	KWGE	KWHU	KWHV	KWHW	KWHX	KWHY
1992	47	208.6	291	389	506	283	1 469
1993	67	214.0	319	350	643	350	1 662
1994	84	436.0	364	339	698	540	1 941
1995	78	421.0	385	351	789	721	2 246
1996	128	726.0	426	382	803	1 319	2 930
1997	116	558.0	506	369	858	..	1 733
1998	88	487.0	515	437	940	..	1 892
1999	100	570.0	606	408	882	..	1 896
2000	98	792.5	628	444	1 104	..	2 176
2001	96	..	692	465	1 490	..	..
2002	90	..	668	..	..	..	..

Source: Department for Culture, Media and Sport: 020 7211 6121

12.5 Visits to tourist attractions[1]
United Kingdom

Index 1989 = 100

	Country Parks	Farms	Gardens	Historic properties	Leisure and theme parks	Museums and art galleries	Steam and heritage railways	Visitor and heritage centres	Wildlife attractions and zoos	Workplaces	All attractions
	MKDZ	MKEA	LQZC	LQZB	MKEB	LQZD	MKEC	MKED	LQZE	MKEE	LQZG
1989	100	100	100	100	100	100	100	100	100	100	100
1990	105	117	102	102	102	106	101	103	101	102	103
1991	108	123	106	98	100	107	99	100	95	101	102
1992	106	127	105	98	99	110	95	103	87	101	102
1993	107	141	111	100	103	109	98	106	89	106	104
1994	110	148	116	99	106	110	98	108	87	108	105
1995	118	153	122	103	106	108	100	112	86	106	107
1996	118	160	125	106	106	111	107	117	90	112	110
1997	122	165	127	108	106	111	108	117	92	115	112
1998	117	165	118	107	103	112	108	116	92	113	110
1999	120	176	122	106	106	111	112	115	94	113	111
2000	119	162	120	101	105	108	115	114	92	108	109
2001	112	122	124	94	110	110	112	109	88	105	107
2002	125	178	138	99	110	118	119	119	99	108	115

1 See chapter text.

Source: The National Tourist Boards: 020 8563 3011

12.6 Domestic tourism[1]
United Kingdom

	Number of trips	Number of nights spent	Expenditure at current prices	Average nights spent	Average expenditure per trip
	Millions	Millions	£ million	Numbers	£
	GQGY	GQGZ	GQHA	GQHB	GQHC
1995	147.8	526.0	20 072	3.6	135.8
1996	154.2	532.8	22 041	3.5	142.9
1997	162.2	555.3	24 137	3.4	148.8
1998	148.8	515.9	22 814	3.5	153.3
1999	173.1	568.6	25 635	3.3	148.1
2000	175.4	576.4	26 133	3.3	150.0
2001	163.1	529.6	26 094	3.2	160.0
2002	167.3	531.9	26 699	3.2	159.6

1 See chapter text.

Source: The National Tourist Boards: 020 8563 3011

12.7 International tourism[1]

	Visits to the UK by overseas residents	Spending in the UK by overseas residents		Visits overseas by UK residents	Spending overseas by UK residents	
		Current prices	Constant 1995 prices		Current prices	Constant 1995 prices
	Thousands	£ million	£ million	Thousand	£ million	£ million
	GMAA	GMAK	CQPR	GMAF	GMAM	CQPS
1992	18 533	7 892	8 784	33 832	11 243	12 678
1993	19 863	9 487	10 188	36 720	12 972	13 184
1994	20 794	9 786	10 050	39 630	14 365	14 852
1995	23 537	11 763	11 763	41 345	15 386	15 386
1996	25 163	12 290	11 954	42 050	16 223	15 897
1997	25 515	12 244	11 542	45 957	16 931	18 652
1998	25 745	12 671	11 573	50 872	19 489	21 847
1999	25 394	12 498	11 133	53 881	22 020	24 676
2000	25 209	12 805	11 102	56 837	24 251	27 281
2001	22 835	11 306	9 528	58 281	25 332	27 710
2002	24 180	11 737	9 641	59 377	26 962	29 311

1 See chapter text.

Sources: International Passenger Survey, Office for National Statistics;
020 7533 5765

12.8 Holidays abroad by destination

Percentages

		1971	1981	1991	1996	1997	1998	1999	2000	2001	2002
Spain	JTKC	34.3	21.7	21.3	25.5	26.3	27.5	27.2	27.8	27.9	28.5
France	JTKD	15.9	27.2	25.8	23.4	23.1	20.2	19.7	18.3	18.3	19.0
United States	JTKE	1.0	5.5	6.8	7.4	6.7	7.0	7.5	7.3	6.3	5.4
Greece	JTKF	4.5	6.7	7.6	4.9	4.7	5.3	6.5	6.8	7.8	7.0
Italy	JTKG	9.2	5.8	3.5	3.8	4.2	4.0	4.1	4.2	4.3	4.6
Portugal	JTKH	2.6	2.8	4.8	3.6	4.0	3.6	3.7	3.9	3.6	4.0
Irish Republic	JTKI	..	3.6	3.0	3.4	3.6	3.5	5.5	4.6	4.1	4.1
Turkey	JTKJ	..	0.1	0.7	3.5	3.1	3.0	2.1	1.8	2.0	2.2
Netherlands	JTKK	3.6	2.4	3.5	2.5	2.8	2.7	2.4	2.2	2.6	2.8
Cyprus	JTKL	1.0	0.7	2.4	2.3	2.2	2.6	2.4	3.3	3.5	3.0
Belgium	JTKM	..	2.1	2.1	2.3	2.2	2.3	1.9	1.8	2.1	2.0
Germany	JTKN	3.4	2.6	2.7	1.6	1.7	1.8	1.6	1.7	1.4	1.5
Malta	JTKO	..	2.6	1.7	1.4	1.2	1.3	1.0	1.1	1.0	1.0
Austria	JTKP	5.5	2.5	2.4	1.1	1.1	1.3	1.0	1.0	1.1	1.4
Other countries	JTKQ	19.0	13.7	11.8	13.3	13.2	13.9	13.3	14.1	13.8	13.6

1 See chapter text.
2 Excludes the Canary Islands prior to 1981.

Sources: International Passenger Survey, Office for National Statistics;
020 7533 5765

12.9 Attendance at leisure and cultural activities[1]
Great Britain

Percentages

		1992 /93	1993 /94	1994 /95	1995 /96	1996 /97	1997 /98	1998 /99	1999 /00	2000 /01	2001 /02	2002 /03
Attendance by men at:												
Cinema	JSPR	46	50	53	53	55	55	57	58	57	58	62
Plays	JSPS	21	22	22	21	21	20	20	21	20	21	22
Art galleries and exhibitions	JSPT	20	21	22	22	22	20	20	21	21	22	23
Classical music	JSPU	11	12	12	12	12	11	10	11	12	12	12
Ballet	JSPV	4	5	5	4	4	4	4	4	4	4	5
Opera	JSPW	6	6	6	6	6	6	5	6	6	6	6
Contemporary dance	JSPX	3	3	3	3	3	4	3	3	3	3	4
Sporting events	JSPY	90	89	89	88	87	87	86	85	85	78	76
Concerts	JSPZ	7	7	8	7	7	6	6	7	7	7	7
Attendance by women at:												
Cinema	JSQA	44	49	51	50	52	54	57	54	54	57	60
Plays	JSQB	24	26	26	25	26	25	23	25	25	26	27
Art galleries and exhibitions	JSQC	21	22	21	22	23	22	22	22	22	23	25
Classical music	JSQD	12	13	12	13	12	13	12	12	12	13	13
Ballet	JSQE	8	9	9	9	9	8	8	9	8	8	9
Opera	JSQF	7	8	7	7	7	7	7	7	7	7	8
Contemporary dance	JSQG	4	4	4	5	5	5	5	5	5	6	6
Sporting events	JSQH	73	73	72	72	69	67	66	65	65	56	58
Concerts	JSQI	5	6	5	6	5	5	5	5	5	6	6
Attendance by all persons at:												
Cinema	JSQJ	45	50	52	51	54	55	57	56	55	57	61
Plays	JSQK	23	24	24	23	24	22	22	23	23	24	24
Art galleries and exhibitions	JSQL	20	22	21	22	22	21	21	22	21	22	24
Classical music	JSQM	12	12	12	12	12	12	11	12	12	12	13
Ballet	JSQN	6	7	7	7	7	6	6	6	6	6	7
Opera	JSQO	6	7	7	6	7	6	6	6	6	6	7
Contemporary dance	JSQP	3	3	4	4	4	5	4	4	4	5	5
Sporting events	JSQQ	80	80	80	80	78	78	76	75	75	67	68
Concerts	JSQR	6	6	6	6	6	6	6	6	6	6	6

1 Percentage of resident population aged 15 and over attending 'these days'.

Sources: Target Group Index;
Cinema Advertising Association;
BMRB International: 020 8433 4125

12.10 Gambling[1]
United Kingdom

£ millions at 2002/03 prices[2]

		1992 /93	1993 /94	1994 /95	1995 /96	1996 /97	1997 /98	1998 /99	1999 /00	2000 /01	2001 /02	2002 /03
Money spent on gambling												
National Lottery - Total[3]	JSOI	..	..	1 379	6 226	5 476	6 153	5 695	5 334	5 091	4 914	4 548
On-line	JSOW	..	..	1 367	4 405	4 474	5 266	4 955	4 518	4 239	3 954	3 385
Instants	JSOX	..	..	12	1 821	1 003	887	731	604	546	585	574
Thunderball	JSOY	..	..	..	..	..	..	..	210	257	247	280
Lottery Extra	JSOZ	..	..	..	..	..	..	..	..	50	128	90
Hot Picks	JSPA	..	..	..	..	..	..	..	..	..	..	218
Lotteries (excluding the National Lottery)[4,5]	JSPB	60	54	47	94	133	140	174	110	111	111	130
Casinos[5]	JSPC	2 630	2 797	3 004	3 013	3 001	3 040	2 892	3 316	3 436	3 656	3 797
Bingo clubs[5]	JSPD	1 004	1 017	1 030	1 071	1 117	1 139	1 128	1 148	1 158	1 188	1 222

1 See chapter text.
2 Adjusted to real terms using the Retail Prices Index.
3 Includes Easy Play tickets which are not shown separately.
4 From 2002-03 includes Hotspot lotteries.
5 Great Britain only.

Sources: Department for Culture, Media and Sport: 020 7211 6121;
Gaming Board for Great Britain: 020 7306 6253

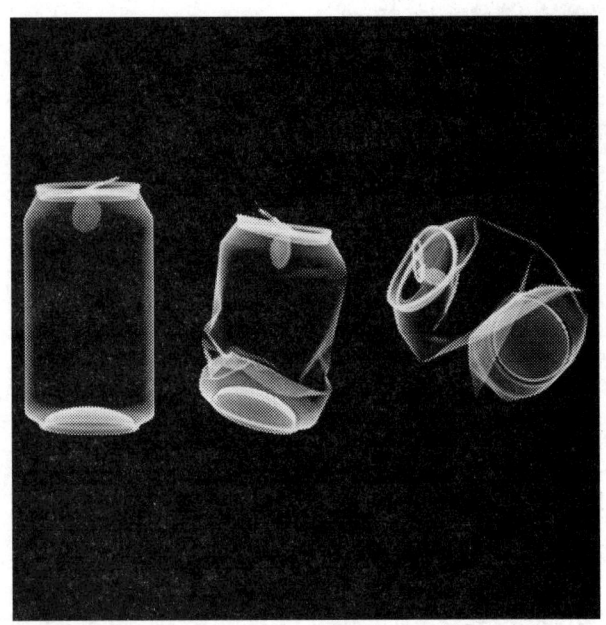

13 Environment

Environment

Air emissions *(Table 13.1 to 13.7)*

Emissions of air pollutants arise from a wide variety of sources. The National Atmospheric Emissions Inventory (NAEI) is prepared annually for the Government and the devolved administrations by the National Environmental Technology Centre (NETCEN), with the work being co-ordinated by Defra. Information is available for a range of point sources, including the most significant polluters. However, a different approach has to be taken for diffuse sources such as transport and domestic emissions where this type of information is not available and estimates for these are derived from statistical information and from research on emission factors for stationary and mobile sources. Although for any given year considerable uncertainties surround the emission estimates for each pollutant, trends over time are likely to be more reliable.

UK national emission estimates are updated annually and any developments in methodology are applied retrospectively to earlier years. Adjustments in the methodology are made to accommodate new technical information and to improve international comparability.

Three different classification systems are used in the tables presented here: a National Accounts basis (Table 13.1); the format required by the Inter-governmental Panel on Climate Change (IPCC) (Table 13.2); and the EMEP format used by the United Nations Economic Commission for Europe (UNECE) (Tables 13.3-13.7).

The EMEP source categories are detailed below, together with details of the main sources of these emissions.

Power stations: Public power plants, including power generation from waste incineration.

Refineries: Petroleum refineries combustion.

Combustion in fuel extraction and transformation: Combustion in smokeless fuel plant, collieries, oil and gas plant, offshore industry (not flaring).

Domestic combustion: Combustion in residential plant, including domestic boilers and fires.

Commercial, public and agricultural combustion: Commercial and institutional plants; plants in agriculture, forestry and aquaculture.

Power generation within industry: Boilers, gas turbines and other stationary engines for power generation within industry, including iron and steel industry.

Other iron and steel combustion: Iron and steel reheating furnaces, sinter plant, foundries.

Other industrial combustion: Industrial combustion plants, furnaces, industrial production.

Production processes: Processes in petroleum, iron and steel, non-ferrous metal, chemical, wood, food, drink and other industries.

Extraction and distribution of fossil fuels: Extraction of solid, liquid and gaseous fossil fuels, including off-shore activities (apart from gas flaring); liquid fuel, gasoline and gas distribution.

Solvent use: Paint application; degreasing; chemical products manufacturing or processing; other use of solvents.

Road transport: Passenger cars, light and heavy duty vehicles, mopeds, motorcycles; gasoline evaporation from vehicles, tyre and brake wear.

Military: Military aircraft and naval vessels, military machinery (military road vehicles are included in road transport).

Railways: Railway locomotives.

Shipping: Inland waterways boats; domestic navigation, fishing vessels.

Civil aircraft: Domestic and international ground movement and take off and landing cycles up to 1 km from the airport.

Other mobile sources: Agricultural machinery; gardening, construction and aircraft support equipment; mobile industrial equipment powered by diesel or petrol engines.

Waste treatment and disposal: Treatment of domestic, industrial and other waste, including landfill, but excluding incineration with energy recovery; off-shore gas flaring.

Agriculture: Culture with and without fertilisers; stubble straw burning; enteric fermentation and manure management of animals; managed forests.

Forests: Volatile organic compounds emissions from managed and unmanaged forests only.

In tables 13.3 and 13.5, the figures on emissions from individual large combustion plants (LCPs) for 1991 onwards are totals of those reported by the Environment Agency to Defra. For 1970-1990, estimates are made assuming all power station emissions from coal, fuel oil and orimulsion stations are included, plus 79 per cent of refineries' emissions, 12 per cent of iron and steel emissions and 38 per cent of other (Table 13.3), and 88 per cent of refineries' emissions, 11 per cent of iron and steel emissions and 40 per cent of other industrial combustions in fuel extraction and transformation (Table 13.5). It is not possible to calculate LCP figures from the categories presented in these tables as refineries and other industrial combustion are both included in more than one category.

Estimated atmospheric emissions on a National Accounts basis *(Table 13.1)*

The National Accounts figures in Table 13.1 differ from those on an IPCC basis in that they include estimated emissions from fuels purchased by UK residents either at home or abroad, including emissions from UK international shipping and aircraft operators and exclude emissions in the UK resulting from the activities of non-residents.

Greenhouse gases include carbon dioxide, methane, nitrous oxide, hydro-fluorocarbons, perfluorocarbons and sulphur hexafluoride which are expressed in thousand tonnes of carbon dioxide equivalent.

Acid rain precursors include sulphur dioxide, nitrogen oxides and ammonia which are expressed as thousand tonnes of sulphur dioxide equivalent.

PM[10] are carbon particles in the air arising from incomplete combustion.

Estimated total emissions of greenhouse gases on a IPCC basis *(Table 13.2)*
The IPCC classification is used to report greenhouse gas emissions under the Framework Convention on Climate Change and includes land use change and all emissions from domestic aviation and shipping, but excludes international marine and aviation bunker fuels. Estimates of the relative contribution to global warming of the main greenhouse gases, or classes of gases, is presented weighted by their global warming potential.

Emissions of PM[10] *(Table 13.4)*
Emissions of PM[10] includes particles which pass through a size selective inlet with a 50 per cent efficiency cut-off at 10μm aerodynamics diameter.

Emissions of nitrogen oxides *(Table 13.5)*
Most of the figures in this table are based on a single NO_x emission factor for each fuel which is held constant over time. Emissions are expressed as nitrogen dioxide equivalent.

Emissions of carbon monoxide *(Table 13.6)*
Most of the figures in this table are based on a single carbon monoxide emission factor for each fuel held constant over time.

Emissions of volatile organic compounds *(Table 13.7)*
Most of the figures in this table are based on a single volatile organic compound emission factor for each source held constant over time.

Biological and chemical quality of rivers and canals *(Table 13.9)*
The chemical quality of river and canal waters is monitored in a series of separate national surveys in England and Wales and Northern Ireland. The General Quality Assessment (GQA) Scheme used in the surveys provides a rigorous and objective method for assessing the basic chemical quality of rivers and canals based on three determinants – dissolved oxygen, biochemical oxygen demand (BOD), and ammoniacal nitrogen. The GQA grades river stretches into six categories (A-F) of chemical quality and these in turn have been grouped into four broader groups – good (classes A and B), fair (C and D), poor (E) and bad (F).

To provide a more comprehensive picture of the health of rivers and canals, biological testing has also been carried out. The biological grading is based on the

monitoring of tiny animals (invertebrates) which live in or on the bed of the river. Research has shown that there is a relationship between species composition and water quality. Using a procedure known as the River Invertebrate Prediction and Classification System (RIVPACS), species groups recorded at a site were compared with those which would be expected to be present in the absence of pollution, allowing for the different environmental characteristics in different parts of the country. Two different summary statistics (known as ecological quality indices (EQI)) were calculated and then the biological quality was assigned to one of six bands based on a combination of these two statistics.

River length stretches were allocated to Government Office Regions using a 1995 digitised map. This provides consistently smaller total river lengths for local areas than the equivalent Environment Agency figures. This is because of differences between stretch lengths used by the Environment Agency and those calculated using the map, and because it was not possible to link all stretch codes to the map, so some stretches were excluded. It should be noted that the monitoring network only covers stretches the Environment Agency are required to monitor, that is rivers and streams with a flow greater than 1m³ / second. On this basis 40,000km of river network are monitored in England and Wales out of an estimated total river length of 150,000km. No canals are classified in Northern Ireland. The figures in table 13.9 are rounded to the nearest 10km and may not sum to totals.

Water quality of rivers and canals *(Table 13.10)*
In Scotland, river and canal water quality is based upon the Scottish River Classification Scheme of 20 June 1997 which combines chemical, biological, nutrient and aesthetic quality using the following classes: excellent (A1), good (A2), fair (B), poor (C) and seriously polluted (D). The figures in the table are also rounded to the nearest 10km and may not sum to totals.

During 2000 a new digitised river network (DRN) was developed, based on 1:50,000 ordnance survey data digitised by the Institute of Hydrology. The new network ensures consistency between all SEPA areas and includes the Scottish Islands which were not previously covered. Data based on this network are published for the first time in the 2004 edition of Annual Abstract and are not consistent with data which have previously been published. The DRN includes:

all mainland and islands rivers with a catchment area of 10 km² or more. This is known as the "baseline network".

mainland and islands stream stretches with a catchment of less than 10 km² which are classified as fair, poor or seriously polluted and have been monitored. These are added to the baseline network to give a "classification network".

It is intended that future emphasis will be placed on the classification network, which is likely to be reportable for the purposes of the EC Water Framework Directive. Efforts to improve the quality of the downgraded smaller

Environment

streams will continue, but once this has been sustainably achieved, their monitoring may be reduced. Many of these streams are the subject of current attention because of their influence on the quality of larger classification network rivers.

Using the DRN scheme, data for every routine sampling point are automatically applied to an identified river stretch of predetermined length. The loss in total river length in moving to the DRN (i.e. despite the first time inclusion of islands rivers) arises mainly from the exclusion from classification of thousands of small remote headwater streams which were never monitored, but assumed to be of excellent quality. The smaller reduction in length of downgraded waters arises mainly from using 1:50,000 maps for the DRN; in the former system lengths were hand measured from 1:10,000 maps, so more minor channel bends were included.

Water industry expenditure *(Table 13.12)*
The table is informed by the annual and regulatory accounts of water and sewerage companies and water companies of England and Wales. Figures are given based on current cost rather than historical cost accounting principles. The elements which make up operating expenditure are as follows: manpower costs, other costs of employment, power, agencies, associated companies, Environment Agency charges, bulk supply imports, general and support, customer services, scientific services, other business activities, local authority rates, water charges, local authority sewerage agencies, materials and consumables, hired and contracted services, charge for bad and doubtful debts, depreciation, infrastructure renewals expenditure, infrastructure renewals accrual, exceptional items and other operating costs. Capital expenditure figures are the addition to tangible fixed assets including management and general expenditure but excluding infrastructure renewals expenditure. Adopted assets at nil cost are also included.

Water pollution incidents *(Table 13.13)*
The Environment Agency responds to complaints and reported incidents of pollution in England and Wales. Each incident is then logged and categorised according to its severity. The category describes the impact of each incident on our water, land and air. The impact of an incident on each medium is considered and reported separately. If no impact has occurred for a particular medium, the incident is reported as a Category 4. Before 1999, the reporting system was used only for water pollution incidents, thus the total number of substantiated incidents was lower as it did not include incidents not relating to the water environment.

Bathing waters *(Table 13.14)*
Under the EC Bathing Water Directive 76/160/EEC, eleven physical, chemical and microbiological parameters are measured including total and faecal coliforms which are generally considered to be the most important indicators of the extent to which water is contaminated by sewage. The mandatory value for total coliforms is 10,000 per 100 ml, and for faecal coliforms 2,000 per 100 ml. For a bathing water to comply with the coliform standards, the Directive requires that at least 95 per cent of samples taken for each of these parameters over the bathing season are less than or equal to the mandatory values. In the UK a minimum of 20 samples are normally taken at each site. In practice this means that where 20 samples are taken, a maximum of only one sample may exceed the mandatory value for the bathing water to comply, and where less than 20 samples are taken none may exceed the mandatory value for the bathing water to comply.

The bathing water season is from mid-May to end-September in England and Wales, but shorter in Scotland and Northern Ireland. Bathing waters which are closed for the season are excluded for that year.

The table shows Environment Agency (EA) regions for England and Wales. The boundaries of which are based on river catchment areas and not county borders. In particular, the figures shown for Wales are the EA Welsh Region, the boundary of which does not coincide with the boundary of Wales.

Surface and groundwater abstractions *(Table 13.15)*
From 1991 data were collected on a different basis. Figures are therefore not strictly comparable with those in previous years. Some regions report licensed and actual abstracts for financial rather than calendar years. As figures represent an average for the whole year expressed as daily amounts, differences between amounts reported for financial and calendar years are small.

The following changes have occurred in the classification of individual sources:-

Public water supply: The 1991 figures include some private water supply.

Spray irrigation: This category includes small amounts of non-agricultural spray irrigation.

Mineral washing: From 1999 was not reported as a separate category, licences for mineral washing are now contained in 'Other industry'.

Private water supply: was shown as separate category from 1992 and includes private abstractions for domestic use and individual households.

Fish farming, cress growing, amenity ponds: Includes amenity ponds, but excludes miscellaneous from 1991.

Other: The figure for 1991 included some private domestic water supply wells and boreholes, public water supply transfer licences and frost protection use.

Radioactive wastes *(Table 13.16)*
Solid radioactive wastes are not discharged to the environment but stored and conditioned by processes such as supercompaction, cementation or turning into glass. Such wastes cover a wide range of materials and can be classified, according to the nature and

quantity of radioactivity associated with them, as high level wastes (HLW), intermediate level wastes (ILW) or low level wastes (LLW). HLW result from the reprocessing of irradiated nuclear fuel and are intensely radioactive. They contain over 95 per cent of all the radioactivity in wastes from nuclear establishments. HLWs are of relatively small in volume, but have a high heat output as a result of the energy from radioactive decay. ILW include the irradiated metal cladding for nuclear reactor fuel, reactor components, and chemical process residues and filters. They have a lower radioactivity and heat output than HLW but their radioactivity content exceeds the upper limits for LLW. LLW includes concrete, rubble and soil from building demolition, discarded protective clothing and worn out or damaged plant and equipment. LLW do not normally require shielding against radiation emissions during handling and transport. LLW volumes are reported, in most cases, as the volumes before supercompaction and grouting before disposal.

The table shows recent trends in the volume of radioactive waste stocks for particular groups of nuclear sites. Data are presented in two physical states – as stored and conditioned. "As stored" is the form in which the waste is currently stored. For the majority of LLW, storage is short term prior to disposal. "Conditioned" is the form of waste suitable for long-term storage (ie, vitrified) in the case of HLW or ultimate disposal to deep underground repositories in the case of ILW. There is no simple relationship between as-stored and conditioned volumes of waste, since the effects of conditioning can vary with different wastes. Conditioning of HLW has yet to start at Dounreay. Volume indicates predicted final conditioned volume. Estimates of conditioned wastes are indicative only and should be interpreted with care.

The table excludes waste from defence establishments prior to 1991. Such ILW and LLW will add no more than 20 per cent to the volumes of radioactive waste from civil sources before 1991.

Annual waste arisings *(Table 13.17)*
Agriculture: The estimate is derived from a survey of agricultural waste commissioned by Defra and relates to Great Britain. It includes all waste streams, eg excreta from all livestock (both housed and grazing animals) and other wastes including straw, plastics and packaging, animal carcasses and slurries.

Mining and quarrying: The minerals waste estimate is based on ratios of waste to product.

Sewage sludge: The estimate of sewage sludge arisings has been made on the basis of dry weight (wet weight can be estimated on the basis of 4 per cent solid content on average - giving a total of 26,450,000 tonnes).

Dredged material: The data for dredged material are for all UK waters.

Municipal waste: The UK estimate for municipal waste is based on returns made by Waste Disposal Authorities in England and Wales to a Defra/National Assembly for Wales survey.

Commercial and industrial: UK totals estimated from figures for England and Wales, based on survey by EA.

Demolition and construction: UK total estimated from figures for England and Wales, based on survey by the Office of the Deputy Prime Minister (ODPM).

Designated areas *(Table 13.18)*
National Parks, Areas of Outstanding Natural Beauty (AONB's) in England, Wales and Northern Ireland and National Scenic Areas in Scotland are the major areas which have been designated to protect their landscape importance. National Scenic Areas in Scotland are the equivalent of AONB's in England, Wales and Northern Ireland.

Some areas may be in more than one category. All areas shown in the table are at March 2003, except for Green Belt land which relates to 1 January 1997.

The area for Green Belt land is based on a new methodology in which the extent of Green Belt land is captured in digital form. This approach provides much more reliable figures than those previously published in earlier years.

Noise complaints *(Table 13.19)*
The table shows trends in the number of complaints received by local authority Environmental Health Officers (EHOs). The figures are from those authorities making returns and are calculated per million people based on the population of the authorities making returns.

Most complaints about traffic noise are usually addressed to highways authorities or Department for Transport (DfT) Regional Directors, and will not necessarily be included in the figures. Similarly, complaints about noise from civil aircraft are generally received by aircraft operators, the airport companies, the DfT or Civil Aviation Authority. Complaints about military flying are dealt with either by Station Commanding Officers or by Ministry of Defence headquarters. It is also true that railway noise will be reported elsewhere. Thus the figures in this table will not necessarily include these complaints and are likely to be considerably understated. Therefore the information reported to the EHOs is considered to give, at best, only a very approximate indication of the trend in noise complaints from these sources.

Over time some of the categories shown in this table have changed. These have included:- Up until 1996/97 Section 62 of the Control of Pollution Act 1974 covered noise in the streets - it primarily included the chimes of ice-cream vendors and the use of loudspeakers other than for strictly defined purposes. From 1997/98 all complaints about noise in the street are included with 'vehicles machinery and equipment in streets'. From 1997/98 complaints about road works are included with 'vehicles machinery and equipment in streets'. The use of the category "Other" was discontinued in England and Wales from 1997/98. It included some complaints not covered by the other speciified sources, but also those where the source was not certain or was due to more than one source. From 1997/98 in England and Wales more vigourous procedures have allocated complaints to the most appropriate source.

Environment

Material flows *(Table 13.20)*
Economy-wide material flow accounts record the total mass of natural resources and products that are used by the UK economy, either directly in the production and distribution of products and services, or indirectly through the movement of materials which are displaced in order for production to take place.

The direct movement of materials into the economy derives primarily from domestic extraction, that is from biomass (agricultural harvest, timber, fish and animal grazing), fossil fuel extraction (such as coal, crude oil and natural gas) and mineral extraction (metal ores, industrial minerals such as pottery clay, and construction material such as crushed rock, sand and gravel). This domestic extraction is supplemented by the imports of products, which may be of raw materials such as unprocessed agricultural products, but can also be semi-manufactured or finished products. In a similar way the UK produces exports of raw materials, semi-manufactured and finished goods which can be viewed as inputs to the production and consumption of overseas economies.

Indirect flows of natural resources consist of the unused material resulting from domestic extraction such as mining and quarrying overburden and the soil removed during construction and dredging activities. They also include the movement of used and unused material overseas which is associated with the production and delivery of imports. Water – except for that included directly in products – is excluded from the accounts.

There are three main indicators used to measure inputs. The **Direct Material Input (DMI)** measures the input of used materials into the economy, that is all materials which are of economic value and are used in production and consumption activities (including the production of exports). **Domestic material consumption (DMC)** measures the total amount of material directly used in the economy, ie it includes imports but excludes exports. The **Total Material Requirement (TMR)** measures the total material basis of the economy, that is the total primary resource requirements of all the production and consumption activities. It includes not only the direct use of resources for producing exports, but also indirect flows from the production of imports and the indirect flows associated with domestic extraction. Although TMR is widely favoured as a resource use indicator, the estimates of indirect flows are less reliable than those for materials directly used by the economy, and the indicator therefore needs to be considered alongside other indicators.

Further details regarding tables 13.2 to 13.7, 13.9 and 13.13 to 13.18 can be found in Defra's *e-Digest of Environmental Statistics* (on the Defra website at: *www.defra.gov.uk/environment/statistics/index.htm*). If you would like to discuss the tables, Adrian Redfern can be contacted at Defra on 020 7082 8608.

13.1 Estimated atmospheric emissions 2001 on National Accounts basis[1]
United Kingdom

Thousand tonnes

| | Greenhouse gases[2] | Acid rain precursors[3] | Emissions affecting air quality | | | | | | | |
			PM$_{10}$	Carbon monoxide	Volatile organic compounds[4]	Benzene	Butadiene	Lead (Tonnes)	Cadmium (Tonnes)	Mercury (Tonnes)
Agriculture	51 300	520	19.1	50.3	145.6	0.1	0.1	0.4	0.01	-
Mining and quarrying	31 500	70	23.0	50.8	207.4	0.4	-	0.4	0.02	0.01
Manufacturing	135 100	510	42.9	954.8	411.4	3.2	0.8	135.9	3.30	4.30
Electricity, gas and water supply	175 500	1 000	18.0	86.3	75.0	0.8	-	15.4	0.60	1.64
Construction	3 800	10	5.5	45.7	58.6	0.1	0.1	0.2	0.07	-
Wholesale and retail trade	18 200	50	4.3	124.2	81.7	0.6	0.2	1.2	0.03	0.01
Transport and communication	94 600	730	25.2	356.6	137.0	3.9	2.7	4.4	0.29	0.03
Financial intermediation	9 600	20	2.1	100.4	12.1	0.2	0.1	0.9	0.02	-
Public administration	10 900	60	1.7	21.6	3.6	0.3	-	0.9	0.01	0.06
Education, health and social work	10 800	20	1.4	11.7	2.5	0.1	-	1.5	0.02	0.10
Other services	16 500	40	5.2	35.6	13.8	0.9	-	3.7	0.38	2.10
Domestic	156 000	370	42.8	2 128.4	416.5	8.4	2.0	31.9	0.50	0.59
Total	**713 800**	**3 400**	**191.1**	**3 966.5**	**1 565.2**	**19.1**	**6.2**	**196.8**	**5.25**	**8.85**
Of which, emissions from road transport	126 100	600	36.0	2 339.3	301.8	5.6	3.6	20.8	0.39	-

1 See chapter text.
2 Thousand tonnes of carbon dioxide equivalent.
3 Thousand tonnes of sulphur dioxide equivalent.
4 Excluding methane, but including benzene and 1,3-butadiene.

Sources: National Environmental Technology Centre;
Office for National Statistics: 020 7533 5904

13.2 Estimated total emissions[1] of greenhouse gases on IPCC basis[2]
United Kingdom

Million tonnes (Carbon dioxide equivalent[3])

		1990	1991	1992	1993	1994	1995	1996	1997	1998	1999	2000	2001
Carbon dioxide	JZCK	604.4	608.1	593.3	578.0	573.7	564.8	585.1	560.6	563.6	555.1	559.4	572.5
Methane	GXDO	76.9	75.9	74.3	71.3	64.9	64.3	62.7	59.6	56.4	52.6	48.8	46.1
Nitrous oxide	GXDP	67.9	65.9	59.1	55.4	59.8	57.1	59.1	60.8	58.0	44.9	44.7	42.4
Hydrofluorocarbons	JZCN	11.37	11.86	12.35	12.90	13.81	15.21	16.38	18.38	19.96	8.19	8.86	8.68
Perfluorocarbons	JZCO	2.28	1.79	0.96	0.81	0.98	1.09	1.02	0.71	0.63	0.66	0.74	0.71
Sulphur hexafluoride	JZCP	0.72	0.78	0.83	0.89	1.06	1.13	1.27	1.26	1.48	1.50	1.64	1.76
Total	GXDQ	763	764	741	719	714	704	726	701	700	663	664	672
1990 Baseline[4]	GXJK	767	..	..	..	..	..	..	..	..	..	..	..
Percentage change from 1990 baseline	GXDR	..	−0.3	−3.4	−6.2	−6.8	−8.2	−5.3	−8.5	−8.7	−13.5	−13.4	−12.3

1 Weighted by global warming potential. Emissions inventories based on the the methodology developed by the Intergovernmental Panel on Climate Change (IPCC) are used to report UK emissions to the Climate Change Convention.
2 See chapter text.
3 12 tonnes of carbon is equivalent to 44 tonnes of carbon dioxide.

4 The 1990 baseline, used for comparison with the Kyoto target, is the sum of 1990 totals for carbon dioxide, methane and nitrous oxide and 1995 totals for hydrofluorocarbons, perfluorocarbons and sulphur hexafluoride.

Sources: National Environmental Technology Centre;
for Department for Environment, Food and Rural Affairs 020 7082 8608

13.3 Estimated emissions of sulphur dioxide (SO$_2$) by source[1]
United Kingdom

Thousand tonnes

By source category (UNECE/EMEP)		Percentage of total in 2001	1970	1980	1990	1991	1992	1993	1994	1995	1996	1997	1998	1999	2000	2001
Power stations	JZCR	66	2 913	3 007	2 723	2 535	2 434	2 083	1 762	1 591	1 320	1 025	1 072	776	821	743
Refineries	GPKK	6	242	262	153	161	146	148	135	142	144	134	98	93	72	72
Combustion in fuel extraction and transformation	JZCT	1	231	25	8	8	6	5	4	3	3	6	7	9	10	8
Domestic	JZCU	4	522	226	108	115	103	113	92	67	71	63	53	52	45	49
Commercial, public and agricultural combustion	JZCV	1	451	218	93	88	90	95	81	60	57	47	34	27	17	16
Power generation within industry	ESYA	10	1 697	815	353	374	433	433	360	269	217	195	158	113	92	108
Other iron and steel combustion	ESYB	1	35	10	18	17	18	18	16	17	17	17	15	15	11	12
Other industrial combustion	ESYC	4	102	83	62	51	47	45	49	55	54	54	49	45	40	40
Production processes	GPLN	4	120	95	71	67	62	59	57	57	56	51	52	46	38	42
Extraction and distribution of fossil fuels	GPKD	-	5	5	16	6	7	5	6	6	7	6	6	1	1	1
Road transport	JZCZ	-	44	42	63	58	62	59	63	51	38	28	23	14	6	3
Military	GPKX	1	9	9	9	10	9	8	8	8	8	8	6	6	6	6
Railways	GPUX	-	14	7	3	3	3	2	2	2	2	1	1	1	1	1
Shipping	GPUY	1	35	25	27	30	29	30	29	29	30	27	25	22	20	16
Civil Aircraft	GPUZ	-	–	–	–	–	–	–	–	–	–	–	–	–	–	–
Other mobile sources	GPLD	-	35	19	8	8	8	8	7	5	5	5	5	5	4	4
Waste treatment and disposal	GPVA	-	5	6	5	5	5	4	3	3	2	2	2	5	3	3
Total	JZDC	100	6 460	4 854	3 719	3 535	3 461	3 115	2 675	2 365	2 029	1 670	1 608	1 229	1 188	1 125

Emissions from large combustion plants

			1970	1980	1990	1991	1992	1993	1994	1995	1996	1997	1998	1999	2000	2001
Large plants	ZBZK		3 565	3 405	2 919	2 747	2 674	2 329	1 969	1 756	1 468	1 107	1 207	894	899	822
Index (1980=100)	ZBZL		105	100	86	81	79	68	58	52	43	33	35	26	26	24

1 See chapter text.

Sources: National Environmental Technology Centre; Environment Agency; for Department for Environment, Food and Rural Affairs 020 7082 8608

13.4 Estimated emissions of PM$_{10}$ by source[1]
United Kingdom

Thousand tonnes

By source category (UNECE/EMEP)		Percentage of total in 2001	1970	1980	1990	1991	1992	1993	1994	1995	1996	1997	1998	1999	2000	2001
Power stations	JZDN	10	67	76	70	70	66	55	49	38	35	24	25	20	21	18
Refineries	GQOZ	1	5	5	3	4	4	4	4	4	4	4	4	3	3	2
Combustion in fuel extraction and transformation	GQPA	-	16	2	–	–	–	–	–	–	–	–	–	–	–	–
Domestic	GQPB	18	222	102	52	55	51	53	43	33	35	33	33	34	28	33
Commercial, public & agricultural combustion	JZDP	3	22	11	8	8	8	7	7	6	6	7	6	5	5	5
Power generation within industry	EUID	7	66	27	20	22	24	23	21	19	16	15	14	13	10	13
Other iron and steel combustion	EVNZ	2	17	8	8	7	7	7	7	7	6	6	5	4	4	3
Other industrial combustion	EVPN	4	13	11	11	10	9	9	10	10	11	10	10	9	8	7
Production processes in industry	GQPE	7	16	14	16	15	15	15	16	15	15	15	15	14	13	12
Construction, mining and quarrying	GQPF	15	31	25	35	31	29	30	32	30	28	28	28	26	26	26
Road transport	JZDS	19	40	48	57	56	55	53	53	50	49	45	42	40	35	35
Other transport and mobile sources	GQPG	5	15	13	13	13	12	12	12	11	12	11	11	10	10	9
Waste treatment and disposal	GQPH	1	2	4	3	3	3	3	3	2	2	2	2	2	2	2
Agriculture	GQPI	8	11	12	12	13	12	12	12	12	13	13	14	14	14	14
Total	JZGA	100	542	358	309	307	296	284	269	239	233	213	207	196	178	178

1 See chapter text.

Sources: National Environmental Technology Centre; for Department for Environment, Food and Rural Affairs 020 7082 8608

13.5 Estimated emissions of nitrogen oxides (NOx) by source[1]
United Kingdom

Thousand tonnes

By source category (UNECE/EMEP)		Percentage of total in 2001	1970	1980	1990	1991	1992	1993	1994	1995	1996	1997	1998	1999	2000	2001
Power stations	JZGB	23	812	861	781	683	671	567	527	495	449	372	365	338	365	379
Refineries	JZGC	2	43	42	40	41	40	37	36	35	35	33	39	31	28	28
Combustion in fuel extraction and transformation	JZGD	3	56	42	61	62	63	65	75	47	47	47	50	53	53	53
Domestic	JZGE	4	62	64	64	71	69	72	69	66	75	69	71	71	72	75
Commercial, public and agricultural combustion	JZGF	2	74	46	38	41	40	38	38	38	39	36	34	34	32	32
Power generation within industry	GWDV	7	292	182	127	131	131	128	129	120	118	116	112	109	104	110
Other iron and steel combustion	GWDW	1	20	6	10	10	10	10	13	13	13	14	13	14	13	13
Other industrial combustion	GWEL	3	108	96	99	84	77	78	84	86	104	93	80	60	44	48
Production processes	JZGI	-	13	14	11	9	8	8	7	4	4	4	4	4	4	3
Extraction and distribution of fossil fuels	GQRZ	-	–	–	1	1	1	–	1	1	1	1	1	1	1	1
Road transport	JZGJ	46	764	981	1 290	1 260	1 211	1 144	1 114	1 067	1 067	1 024	958	915	848	781
Military	GQSB	1	32	32	35	34	31	29	28	28	28	28	22	23	22	22
Railways	GQSC	1	25	15	21	21	19	18	14	15	14	12	12	11	11	10
Shipping	GQSD	3	62	66	72	75	72	71	66	64	69	66	62	56	55	44
Civil aircraft	GQSE	-	1	2	3	3	3	3	3	3	3	3	4	4	4	4
Other mobile sources	GQSA	4	120	104	89	92	92	90	88	85	89	87	88	81	78	73
Waste treatment and disposal	JZGL	-	6	12	9	9	9	7	8	8	7	5	5	4	4	4
Agriculture	JZGM	-	10	15	9	8	6	–	–	–	–	–	–	–	–	–
Total	**JZGO**	**100**	2 501	2 581	2 759	2 633	2 553	2 367	2 301	2 174	2 164	2 012	1 918	1 810	1 737	1 680

Emissions from large combustion plants

			1970	1980	1990	1991	1992	1993	1994	1995	1996	1997	1998	1999	2000	2001
Large plants	ZBZM		932	952	849	749	742	636	572	524	471	371	369	333	341	348
Index (1980=100)	ZBZN		98	100	89	79	78	67	60	55	49	39	39	35	36	37

1 See chapter text.

Sources: National Environmental Technology Centre; Environment Agency; for Department for Environment, Food and Rural Affairs 020 7082 8608

13.6 Estimated emissions of carbon monoxide (CO) by source[1]
United Kingdom

Thousand tonnes

By source category (UNECE/EMEP)		Percentage of total in 2001	1970	1980	1990	1991	1992	1993	1994	1995	1996	1997	1998	1999	2000	2001
Power stations	JZGP	2	117	121	114	113	110	99	106	104	102	71	73	61	70	72
Refineries	GPVW	-	8	8	7	7	7	8	7	8	8	8	8	7	6	4
Combustion in fuel extraction and transformation	JZGQ	1	45	24	22	22	20	20	20	22	23	23	26	27	28	27
Domestic	JZGR	6	1 237	608	345	369	347	369	324	260	268	246	239	244	215	238
Commercial, public and agricultural combustion	JZGS	-	46	26	23	23	21	21	20	19	19	19	18	18	18	18
Power generation within industry	HFLY	1	103	40	36	38	42	39	39	37	33	33	30	28	22	26
Other iron and steel combustion	HFLZ	8	757	215	385	364	377	378	342	348	347	353	339	343	241	281
Other industrial combustion	HFMA	3	137	101	97	89	83	86	87	91	92	89	78	113	114	117
Production processes	GPVZ	6	217	182	238	228	217	218	226	231	235	239	216	199	213	211
Extraction and distribution of fossil fuels	GPWA	-	2	2	7	3	3	2	3	3	3	3	3	1	1	1
Road transport	GPWB	62	5 267	5 304	5 411	5 226	4 989	4 644	4 381	4 112	4 075	3 740	3 417	3 101	2 651	2 303
Military	GPWD	-	11	11	13	11	10	10	10	10	10	9	8	8	7	8
Railways	GPWE	-	9	6	6	6	6	5	4	4	4	3	3	3	3	3
Shipping	GPWF	-	8	9	9	10	9	9	9	8	9	9	8	7	7	6
Civil aircraft	GPWG	-	1	2	3	3	3	3	3	3	4	4	4	4	4	4
Other transport and mobile sources	GPWC	11	584	512	428	445	453	439	428	407	408	407	407	406	405	403
Waste treatment and disposal	GPWH	-	6	48	34	31	31	30	38	28	28	23	24	20	19	16
Agriculture	JZGY	-	288	449	266	228	165	4	–	–	–	–	–	–	–	–
Total	**JZHA**	**100**	8 843	7 669	7 445	7 214	6 895	6 384	6 048	5 695	5 666	5 280	4 902	4 591	4 025	3 737

1 See chapter text.

Sources: National Environmental Technology Centre; Environment Agency; for Department for Environment, Food and Rural Affairs 020 7082 8608

13.7 Estimated emissions of volatile organic compounds[1] by source[2]
United Kingdom

Thousand tonnes

By source category (UNECE/EMEP)		Percentage of total in 2001	1970	1980	1990	1991	1992	1993	1994	1995	1996	1997	1998	1999	2000	2001
Power stations	JZHB	1	7	8	7	7	7	7	8	8	9	8	6	8	8	9
Refineries	GQJF	-	1	1	1	1	1	1	1	1	1	1	1	1	1	1
Combustion in fuel extraction and transformation	GQJG	-	2	2	2	2	3	3	3	1	1	1	1	1	1	1
Domestic	JZHC	3	292	128	63	66	61	61	48	37	40	37	38	41	32	38
Commercial, public and agricultural combustion	GQJH	-	4	3	3	4	4	4	4	4	4	4	4	4	4	4
Power generation within industry	GWEO	-	6	5	4	4	4	4	5	5	5	5	5	5	5	5
Other iron and steel combustion	GWEP	-	1	–	–	–	–	–	1	1	1	1	1	1	–	–
Other industrial combustion	GWEQ	-	12	9	5	4	3	3	4	3	3	3	3	2	3	3
Production processes	GQJL	12	291	308	340	331	330	321	314	321	307	283	263	215	207	184
Extraction and distribution of fossil fuels	GQJM	19	64	208	298	301	292	290	315	306	312	344	313	282	284	284
Solvent use	GQJN	28	596	582	674	636	602	590	584	543	531	517	505	471	443	425
Road transport[3]	JZHG	20	593	718	879	860	825	762	706	641	590	529	460	409	346	299
Military	GQJP	-	2	2	2	2	2	2	2	2	2	2	1	1	1	1
Railways	GQJQ	-	4	3	3	3	3	3	3	2	2	2	2	2	1	1
Shipping	GQJR	-	2	2	3	3	3	3	2	2	3	2	2	2	2	2
Civil aircraft	GQJJ	-	–	–	1	1	1	1	1	1	1	1	1	1	1	1
Other transport and mobile sources	GQJO	4	70	64	58	59	59	58	58	56	57	56	57	56	55	55
Waste treatment and disposal	JZHI	1	12	58	45	42	41	40	48	39	38	33	31	26	22	22
Agriculture	JZHJ	-	37	58	35	30	22	–	–	–	–	–	–	–	–	–
Forests[4]	JZHK	12	178	178	178	178	178	178	178	178	178	178	178	178	178	178
Total	JZHM	100	2 172	2 338	2 603	2 534	2 440	2 331	2 281	2 149	2 082	2 007	1 871	1 704	1 596	1 514

1 Excluding methane.
2 See chapter text.
3 Includes evaporative emissions from the petrol tank and carburettor of petrol-engined vehicles.

4 An order of magnitude estimate of natural emissions from managed and un-managed forests.

Sources: National Environmental Technology Centre; Environment Agency; for Department for Environment, Food and Rural Affairs 020 7082 8608

13.8 Average annual rainfall[1]
United Kingdom

		1961 - 1990 rainfall average (= 100%) millimetres	Annual rainfall as a percentage of the 1961-1990 rainfall average										
National Rivers Authority Regions			1992	1993	1994	1995	1996	1997	1998	1999	2000	2001[2]	2002[2]
United Kingdom	JSJB	1 080	113	107	113	98	87	98	121	117	123	95	115
North West	JSJC	1 201	103	97	113	85	80	92	119	108	131	90	119
Northumbria	JSJD	853	99	113	103	96	85	98	122	109	125	95	117
Severn Trent	JSJE	754	112	111	114	90	82	98	117	120	130	102	116
Yorkshire	JSJF	821	102	109	108	84	85	94	116	107	131	96	120
Anglian	JSJG	596	118	122	108	91	79	97	120	112	128	123	121
Thames	JSLK	688	116	112	108	100	78	91	118	110	136	113	128
Southern	JSLL	778	103	117	122	98	83	101	112	104	143	111	126
Wessex	JSLM	839	101	115	123	111	93	105	120	114	134	98	127
South West	JSLN	1 173	96	118	126	100	96	102	122	104	119	86	116
England	JSLO	823	106	111	113	93	83	96	117	111	131	103	120
Wales	JSLP	1 355	107	105	121	92	88	97	120	116	133	97	118
Scotland	JSLQ	1 436	121	104	112	104	88	99	121	116	111	88	108
Northern Ireland	JSLR	1 059	109	109	110	101	102	99	120	115	114	83	127

1 See chapter text.
2 Provisional.

Sources: Met Office; Centre for Ecology and Hydrology, Wallingford: 01491 838800

13.9 Biological[1] and chemical[2] quality of rivers and canals[3]
England, Wales and Northern Ireland

| | | Length surveyed (kms) | | | | | | | Percentage of total | |
| | | Good | | Fair | | | | | | |
	Years	A	B	C	D	Poor E	Bad F	Total	Good or fair	Poor or bad
Biological quality										
North East	1990	590	770	300	160	140	30	1 990	91	9
	2002	860	780	230	150	30	10	2 050	98	2
North West	1990	450	1 210	630	340	710	460	3 790	69	31
	2002	870	1 400	1 090	680	570	90	4 710	86	14
Yorkshire and the Humber	1990	790	500	340	250	210	220	2 330	81	19
	2002	1 180	920	740	360	290	60	3 560	90	10
East Midlands	1990	340	800	1 160	320	160	40	2 830	93	7
	2002	830	1 030	1 050	230	90	30	3 260	96	4
West Midlands	1990	480	610	560	360	120	80	2 200	91	9
	2002	920	900	890	370	200	70	3 350	92	8
East	1990	620	1 140	930	240	100	20	3 050	96	4
	2002	1 510	1 270	500	100	50	-	3 430	99	1
London	1990	-	30	80	80	80	20	290	65	35
	2002	20	90	80	110	60	-	360	82	18
South East	1990	1 020	1 210	700	240	130	30	3 330	95	5
	2002	1 850	1 440	760	200	40	-	4 290	99	1
South West	1990	2 380	2 300	720	220	120	60	5 800	97	3
	2002	3 640	1 870	510	210	70	10	6 320	99	1
England[4]	1990	6 980	9 010	5 640	2 300	1 850	990	26 770	89	11
	2002	12 390	10 400	6 280	2 610	1 540	280	33 500	95	5
Wales	1990	1 240	1 380	480	180	50	10	3 330	98	2
	2002	1 430	2 020	810	90	30	10	4 380	99	1
Northern Ireland	1991	710	950	410	100	10	-	2 190	100	-
	2002	1 100	1 850	1 490	550	150	-	5 140	97	3
Chemical quality										
North East	1990	540	840	320	130	130	60	2 030	90	10
	2002	970	790	250	40	40	20	2 120	97	3
North West	1990	800	1 100	820	600	870	580	4 770	70	30
	2002	2 100	1 190	1 080	580	450	40	5 430	91	9
Yorkshire and the Humber	1990	670	1 130	470	420	660	180	3 530	76	24
	2002	1 080	1 330	810	460	360	40	4 070	90	10
East Midlands	1990	70	630	1 220	780	610	90	3 410	79	21
	2002	600	1 490	1 020	320	120	-	3 550	97	3
West Midlands	1990	200	1 170	900	660	560	100	3 590	82	18
	2002	790	1 870	680	350	220	20	3 940	94	6
East	1990	50	690	1 350	790	580	70	3 530	82	18
	2002	480	1 480	910	430	280	-	3 580	92	8
London	1990	-	50	120	110	110	10	390	71	29
	2002	-	120	120	110	50	-	420	87	13
South East	1990	330	1 410	1 350	590	630	60	4 370	84	16
	2002	820	1 730	1 210	400	270	-	4 440	94	6
South West	1990	1 620	2 350	1 320	730	380	60	6 460	93	7
	2002	2 760	2 630	790	210	180	10	6 570	97	3
England[4]	1990	4 200	9 160	7 670	4 640	4 300	770	30 740	84	16
	2002	10 290	13 420	7 240	3 000	2 110	140	36 190	94	6
Wales	1990	1 830	1 210	270	130	60	30	3 520	98	2
	2002	3 020	1 190	210	70	70	10	4 570	98	2
Northern Ireland	1991	100	640	680	170	60	20	1 680	95	5
	2002	250	2 030	1 220	510	120	-	4 130	97	3

1 Based on the River Invertebrate Prediction and Classification System (RIVPACS).
2 Based on the General Quality Assessment (GQA) chemical classification system.
3 See chapter text.

4 Figures for the English regions will not add to the national figure for England because a small amount of river lengths which are located along the border between England and Wales are counted in both the national figures figures for England and Wales.

Sources: Environment Agency;
Environment and Heritage Service

13.10 Water quality of rivers and canals[1]
Scotland

| | Year | Length surveyed (kms) | | | | | | | Percentage of total | |
		Excellent A1	Good A2	Unclassified assumed good	Fair B	Poor C	Seriously polluted D	Total	Good or fair[2]	Poor or seriously polluted
Scottish Environment Protection Agency Regions										
Higlands, Islands and Grampian	1999	..	..	..	480	150	30	11 400	..	2
	2000	960	1 650	8 260	390	140	10	11 400	99	1
	2001	1 420	1 560	7 950	380	90	20	11 420	99	1
	2002	2 020	3 480	5 140	660	90	10	11 400	99	1
South East Scotland	1999	1 120	1 890	2 700	900	450	20	7 090	93	7
	2000	1 430	2 270	2 120	920	390	20	7 160	94	6
	2001	1 520	2 450	1 670	1 000	520	20	7 170	93	7
	2002	2 260	2 800	610	980	510	10	7 160	93	7
South West Scotland	1999	580	2 260	2 340	1 200	470	40	6 890	93	7
	2000	780	2 170	2 440	1 150	320	30	6 900	95	5
	2001	930	2 320	2 340	960	320	40	6 920	95	5
	2002	1 000	2 370	2 230	930	310	40	6 880	95	5
Scotland	1999	..	..	..	2 580	1 080	90	25 380	..	5
	2000	3 170	6 090	12 820	2 450	850	70	25 450	96	4
	2001	3 870	6 320	11 960	2 340	930	80	25 510	96	4
	2002	5 280	8 660	7 990	2 560	900	60	25 440	96	4

1 See chapter text.
2 Classes A1, A2, B and unclassified.

Source: Scottish Environmental Protection Agency: 01786 457700

13.11 Water reservoir stocks[1] by month
England and Wales

Percentages

		1992	1993	1994	1995	1996	1997	1998	1999	2000	2001	2002
January	JTAS	84.5	90.5	94.9	95.1	61.2	79.1	90.5	95.8	95.8	94.8	86.5
February	JTAT	84.1	95.8	96.6	97.9	71.3	75.6	93.1	97.0	95.9	94.4	93.7
March	JTAU	87.6	89.8	95.5	98.3	81.8	91.6	92.3	96.5	97.4	95.0	95.5
April	JTAV	91.8	85.0	97.3	97.3	84.9	92.3	96.9	96.9	95.2	95.5	94.5
May	JTAW	94.5	92.3	95.8	92.7	86.2	87.1	97.0	97.0	97.0	96.7	91.9
June	JTAX	90.7	94.6	91.5	87.6	88.1	87.7	93.9	95.4	95.7	91.9	97.0
July	JTAY	83.1	90.2	86.6	79.5	82.2	87.8	95.1	92.0	93.8	85.1	94.9
August	JTAZ	75.6	87.2	76.2	69.1	73.4	81.3	93.5	82.6	88.5	80.7	91.1
September	JTBA	80.2	82.5	68.8	52.8	63.0	73.8	88.3	76.9	83.2	77.9	85.9
October	JTBB	84.2	81.3	71.7	47.3	54.6	70.6	86.6	79.7	88.0	77.0	77.3
November	JTBC	85.4	81.4	74.7	51.6	63.3	69.1	93.3	81.7	95.2	85.5	82.9
December	JTBD	89.1	79.9	85.6	56.5	77.3	76.4	93.1	84.9	96.7	87.9	91.8

1 Reservoir content are based on a representative selection of reservoirs.
Percentage of live capacity at the start of the month.

Sources: Water PLCs;
Environment Agency;
Centre for Ecology and Hydrology, Wallingford: 01491 838800

13.12 Water industry expenditure[1]
England and Wales

£ millions

		1992 /93	1993 /94	1994 /95	1995 /96	1996 /97	1997 /98	1998 /99	1999 /00	2000 /01	2001 /02	2002 /03
Operating expenditure												
Water supply	KQQX	2 037.7	2 113.5	2 215.0	2 319.6	2 314.9	2 339.3	2 386.1	2 448.1	2 391.0	2 426.9	2 544.2
Sewerage services	KQQY	1 635.6	1 757.0	1 764.0	1 738.4	1 780.7	1 854.6	1 971.3	2 069.8	2 087.1	2 167.6	2 265.2
Capital expenditure												
Water supply	KQSX	1 358.2	1 386.7	1 081.0	1 074.5	1 314.3	1 467.2	1 294.1	1 290.0	935.0	1 132.5	1 347.1
Sewerage	KQSY	455.3	410.7	381.0	375.6	479.9	455.2	507.5	488.5	352.0	362.4	507.2
Sewage treatment and disposal	KQSZ	906.0	735.3	763.0	773.0	959.4	1 296.3	1 374.5	1 440.8	1 040.9	996.0	1 066.2

1 See chapter text.

Source: Office of Water Services: 0121 625 1312

13.13 Water pollution incidents[1]
United Kingdom

		1992	1993	1994	1995	1996	1997	1998		1999[2]	2000[2]	2001[2]	2002[2]
Categories 1 to 3													
Environment Agency Regions													
North West	JZIA	3 270	3 656	3 532	3 717	2 818	2 160	2 201	MKDB	1 668	1 757	1 734	1 805
North East	JZIB	3 059	3 642	3 243	2 576	2 143	2 404	1 993	MKDC	1 828	1 822	1 952	1 789
Midlands	JZKR	4 420	4 876	4 895	4 259	4 305	4 411	4 061	MKDD	2 804	3 106	2 862	2 843
Anglian	JZKS	2 462	2 625	2 819	2 156	2 417	2 411	2 163	MKDE	1 726	1 369	1 606	1 716
Thames	JZKT	1 955	2 071	2 006	1 972	1 959	1 917	1 819	MKDF	1 208	1 379	1 510	1 630
Southern	JZKU	1 089	1 355	1 316	1 235	1 189	1 174	1 138	MKDG	1 317	1 540	1 585	1 511
South West	JZKV	4 278	4 129	4 340	4 558	3 042	2 847	2 603	MKDH	2 463	2 294	2 292	1 929
Welsh	JZKW	2 798	2 945	3 264	2 990	2 285	2 247	1 885	MKDI	1 360	1 395	1 475	1 287
England and Wales	JZKX	23 331	25 299	25 415	23 463	20 158	19 571	17 863	MKDJ	14 374	14 662	15 016	14 510
Scotland[3]	JZKY	3 020	3 081	3 170	2 752	2 878	3 356	2 329	MKDK	2 306	2 345	1 829	1 409
Northern Ireland	JZKZ	..	..	..	..	2 087	1 826	1 644	MKDL	1 507	1 705	1 546	1 510
By category in England and Wales													
Category 1	MKCW	388	331	229	199	156	194	128	MKDM	90	77	118	82
Category 2	MKCX	..	6 768	6 567	2 194	1 510	1 354	1 238	MKDN	863	758	860	784
Category 3	MKCY	..	18 200	18 619	21 070	18 492	18 023	16 497	MKDO	13 421	13 827	14 038	13 644
Category 4[2,4]	MKCZ	..	..	..	..	..	..	..	MKDP	16 548	21 744	18 706	15 370
Total substantiated incidents[4]	MKDA	23 331	25 299	25 415	23 463	20 158	19 571	17 863	MKDQ	30 922	36 406	33 722	29 880

1 See chapter text. Substantiated incidents to water, unless otherwise specified.
2 From 1999, categories 1-3 do not include all substantiated incidents to water. An additional category (Category 4) was introduced which includes all
incidents which were substantiated, but which had no impact on the water
environment. Therefore, data are not comparable to previous years

3 Data for all years refer to financial years.
4 Category 4 and Total substantiated incidents include incidents to other media
(air, land), which did not involve the water environment.

Sources: Environment Agency;
Scottish Environment Protection Agency;
Environment and Heritage Service

13.14 Bathing water surveys[1]
United Kingdom

		Compliance with EC Bathing Water Directive coliform standards during the bathing season												*Percentage complying*
		Identified bathing waters						Numbers complying						
		1999	2000	2001	2002	2003		1999	2000	2001	2002	2003		2003
Coastal bathing waters														
Environment Agency Regions														
United Kingdom	GPKA	535	545	546	547	554	GPKN	497	515	520	536	545	GPLA	98
North East	GPKB	55	56	55	56	55	GPKO	52	51	55	55	53	GPLB	96
North West	GPKC	34	34	34	34	34	GPKP	23	28	30	33	33	GPLC	97
Anglian	GPKE	36	37	37	38	38	GPKR	34	37	36	38	38	GPLE	100
Thames	GPKF	3	3	5	5	8	GPKS	3	3	5	5	8	GPLF	100
Southern	GPKG	79	79	79	79	79	GPKT	74	77	78	78	79	GPLG	100
South West	GPKH	184	187	187	186	188	GPKU	167	179	184	183	186	GPLH	99
England	GPKI	391	396	397	398	402	GPKV	361	375	388	393	397	GPLI	99
Wales	GPKJ	70	75	75	75	78	GPKW	69	74	70	75	77	GPLJ	99
Scotland	GPKL	58	58	58	58	58	GPKY	51	49	49	53	55	GPLL	95
Northern Ireland	GPKM	16	16	16	16	16	GPKZ	16	16	13	15	16	GPLM	100
Inland bathing waters														
United Kingdom	JTIG	11	11	11	11	11	JTIH	10	9	11	11	11	JTII	100

1 See chapter text.

Sources: Environment Agency;
Scottish Environment Protection Agency;
Environment and Heritage Service, Northern Ireland

13.15 Estimated abstractions from all surface and groundwater sources by purpose[1]
England and Wales

Megalitres per day

		1991	1992	1993	1994	1995	1996	1997	1998	1999	2000	2001
Public water supply	JZLA	17 562	17 953	16 651	16 735	17 346	17 453	16 820	16 765	16 255	16 990	16 231
Spray irrigation	JZLB	366	269	164	283	352	369	292	282	325	291	259
Agriculture (excl spray irrigation)[2,3]	JZLC	131	129	139	115	103	136	108	111	142	152	108
Electricity supply industry[2,3]	JZLD	30 359	37 693	26 581	27 732	29 510	31 294	33 307	34 587	26 515	31 546	32 263
Other industry	JZLE	5 469	5 326	6 017	4 292	3 808	4 960	4 352	4 964	5 428	5 433	4 772
Mineral washing	JZLF	173	213	198	222	262	250	297	223	..	..	..
Fish farming, cress growing, amenity ponds	JYXG	3 882	4 479	3 818	3 985	4 268	4 338	4 211	5 495	4 867	4 709	4 657
Private water supply	JZLG	..	53	81	82	98	171	162	175	91	102	92
Other	JZLH	1 254	1 794	93	194	223	531	408	289	526	559	108
Total	JZLI	59 196	67 909	53 742	53 640	55 970	59 503	59 957	62 891	54 148	59 782	58 489

1 See chapter text.
2 In South West region in 1991 and 1992, Hydroelectric licences were classified as "Other", in 1993 they were classified as "Other industry" and from 1994 they were classified correctly as "Electricity supply".

3 A new power station was commissioned in the Thames region in 1994 and began abstracting from tidal waters in 1995. In the Southern region a power station was demolished and rebuilt in 1998-1999.

Source: Environment Agency: 01225 487635

13.16 Radioactive waste stocks and arisings[1,2,3]
Great Britain

Stocks in cubic metres

		1986	1987	1988	1989	1991	1994	1998	2001
High level waste									
As stored	JTCG	1 351	1 430	1 463	1 575	1 686	1 639	1 804	1 961
Sellafield	JTBE	1 200	1 250	1 250	1 320	1 415	1 476	1 577	1 766
Dounreay[4]	JTBF	151	180	213	255	271	163	227	195
Conditioned	JTCH	436	517	594	674	681	653	717	765
Sellafield	JTBG	430	445	509	572	573	640	701	740
Dounreay[4]	JTBH	6	72	85	102	108	13	16	25
Intermediate level waste									
As stored	JTCI	41 887	43 602	47 783	45 313	51 558	61 494	70 948	75 415
Sellafield	JTBI	28 200	29 000	32 900	30 500	33 100	40 000	47 620	51 913
Dounreay	JTBJ	1 620	1 740	1 810	1 900	2 278	3 316	3 636	3 558
Other BNFL sites[5]	JTBK	78	78	73	74	92	61	55	61
Other UKAEA[6]	JTBL	2 340	2 620	2 680	2 630	3 000	3 117	3 370	2 808
Power stations[7]	JTBM	9 520	9 780	9 920	9 820	10 762	11 938	12 580	12 624
Amersham plc	JTBN	129	384	400	389	380	290	293	358
URENCO[8]	JTBO	–	–	–	–	–	27	1	1
Ministry of Defence	JTBP	..	..	..	..	1 946	2 745	3 393	4 092
Conditioned	JTCJ	56 211	59 479	66 020	81 762	78 512	66 102	74 131	74 466
Sellafield	JTBQ	43 600	44 500	51 600	64 100	57 084	37 360	43 942	47 874
Dounreay	JTBR	3 230	3 050	3 100	3 330	3 606	7 092	6 052	5 679
Other BNFL sites[5]	JTBS	99	85	84	81	92	100	121	130
Other UKAEA[6]	JTBT	2 680	2 800	2 800	5 460	5 655	5 808	6 058	3 020
Power stations[7]	JTBU	6 220	8 520	7 870	8 210	9 494	12 606	14 959	14 531
Amersham plc	JTBV	382	524	566	581	605	597	293	345
URENCO[8]	JTBW	–	–	–	–	–	54	1	1
Ministry of Defence	JTBX	..	..	..	..	1 976	2 485	2 705	2 886
Low level waste									
As stored	JTCK	2 429	2 343	1 002	13 752	6 252	7 882	7 983	14 584
Sellafield	JTBY	120	540	523	601	423	1 633	1 913	1 580
Dounreay	JTBZ	–	–	–	12 000	2 686	–	1 086	5 639
Other BNFL sites[5]	JTCA	827	669	151	259	1 042	2 833	2 046	3 474
Other UKAEA[6]	JTCB	810	831	91	229	393	555	226	489
Power stations[7]	JTCC	672	303	237	663	454	780	937	1 682
Amersham plc	JTCD	–	–	–	–	55	5	–	–
URENCO[8]	JTCE	–	–	–	–	–	–	79	70
Ministry of Defence	JTCF	..	..	..	..	1 199	2 076	1 696	1 650

1 See chapter text.
2 Up to 1991 as at 1st January and from 1994 as at 1st April.
3 Excludes waste from defence establishments before 1991.
4 The fall between 1991 and 1994 is due to increased evaporation of liquid waste and its planned vitrification.
5 Includes Calder Hall, Chapelcross, Capenhurst and Springfields.

6 UKAEA (United Kingdom Atomic Energy Authority) includes wastes from minor producers. Some of this is stored at Harwell, while low level waste suitable for disposal goes to Drigg.
7 Includes all BNFL Magnox stations (except Calder Hall and Chapelcross), British Energy power stations and Berkeley Centre.
8 In 1993, BNFL's enrichment business at Capenhurst was transferred to the newly formed Urenco (Capenhurst) Ltd.

Source: Electrowatt Ekono (UK) Ltd: 020 7082 8608

13.17 Estimated total annual waste arisings by sector[1]
United Kingdom

Million tonnes

Sector		Annual arisings						Percentage of total arisings
		1997	1998	1999	2000	2001		2001[2]
Non controlled waste[3]								
Agriculture[4]	JSNA	..	..	87	..	..	JSNP	20
Minerals (Mining and quarrying)								
Colliery	JSNB	15	12	10	9	..	JSNU	2
Coal	JSNC	9	8	8	7	..	JSNV	2
China clay	JSND	26	22	21	22	..	JSNW	5
Clay	JSNE	14	14	14	14	..	JSNX	3
Slate	JSNF	7	9	7	7	..	JSNY	2
Quarrying	JSNG	47	36	47	34	..	JSNZ	8
Controlled waste[5]								
Sewage sludge	JSNH	1	1	..	..	..	JSOA	–
Dredged material	JSNI	22	17	33	..	..	JSOB	8
Municipal waste	JSNJ	31	32	33	34	35	JSOC	8
of which household	JSNK	28	28	30	30	31	JSOD	7
Commercial	JSNL	..	28	..	..	..	JSOE	6
Industrial	JSNM	..	55	..	..	..	JSOF	13
Demolition and construction	JSNN	..	..	80	..	102	JSOG	24
Total (latest available year)	JSNO	..	..	..	..	434	JSOH	100

1 See chapter text.
2 Or latest available year.
3 Not classed as a controlled waste under the terms of the Environmental
Protection Act (Controlled Waste Regulations) 1992.

4 Great Britain only.
5 Classed as controlled wastes under the terms of the Environmental Protection
Act (Controlled Waste Regulations) 1992.

Sources: Department for Environment, Food and Rural Affairs 020 7082 8608;
Environment Agency;
Water UK

13.18 Designated areas[1]

	National Parks		Areas of Outstanding Natural Beauty[2]		Green Belt Land		Defined Heritage Coasts length (km)
	Area (thousand hectares)	Percentage of total area in region	Area (thousand hectares)	Percentage of total area in region	Area (thousand hectares)	Percentage of total area in region	
United Kingdom	1 974	8	3 410	14	2 032	8	1 553
North East	111	13	147	17	53	6	138
North West	261	18	157	11	252	18	6
Yorkshire and the Humber	315	21	92	6	264	17	80
East Midlands	92	6	52	3	80	5	-
West Midlands	20	2	127	10	267	21	..
East	30	2	112	6	237	12	121
London	-	-	..	..	36	22	..
South East	-	-	641	31	356	19	74
South West	165	7	712	30	106	4	638
England	994	7	2 040	16	1 650	13	1 057
Wales	413	20	83	4	..	..	496
Scotland	567	6	1 002	13	155	2	..
Northern Ireland	-	-	285	20	227	16	..

1 See chapter text.
2 The South East includes London.

Source: Department for Environment, Food and Rural Affairs 020 7082 8608

13.19 Noise complaints received by Environmental Health Officers[1]

Number per million people

England and Wales

		1991/92	1992/93	1993/94	1994/95	1995/96	1996/97		1997/98	1998/99	1999/00	2000/01	2001/02
Not controlled by the Environmental Protection Act 1990:													
Road traffic	JZLJ	65	59	59	60	66	62	JZLJ	52	39	38	44	37
Aircraft	JZLK	72	73	64	111	48	58	JZLK	92	109	121	26	101
Railway								JTHH	19	14	17	16	12
Other[2]	JZLL	99	105	84	91	90	74						
Total	JZLM	236	237	207	262	204	194	JUZR	163[2]	162	176	86	150
Controlled by the Environmental Protection Act 1990:													
Industrial/commercial premises	JZLN	1 037	1 108	1 120	1 320	1 466	1 455	JZLN	1 647	1 280	1 368	1 381	1 273
Road works, construction and demolition	JZLO	148	191	168	300	229	242	SNLE	285	248	292	325	347
Domestic premises	JZLP	2 627	3 137	3 468	3 949	4 895	5 051	JZLP	5 050	4 330	5 149	5 001	5 540
Vehicles, machinery and equipment in streets[3]	JZLQ	..	..	..	249	225	206	JZLQ	300	252	269	365	372
Total	JZLR	3 812	4 436	4 756	5 818	6 815	6 954	JZLR	7 282	6 110	7 078	7 072	7 532
Controlled by Section 62 of the Control and Pollution Act 1974:													
Noise in streets	JZLS	100	76	92	89	109	111						
Total complaints received	JZLT	4 148	4 749	5 055	6 169	7 128	7 259	JUZS	7 445[2]	6 272	7 254	7 158	7 682

		1991	1992[4] /93	1993 /94	1994 /95	1995 /96	1996 /97	1997 /98		1998 /99	1999 /00	2000 /01	2001 /02
Scotland[5]													
Not controlled by the Environmental Protection Act 1990:													
Road traffic	JZLU	51	35	..	..	..	24	21	SNMB	16	..	14	..
Aircraft	JZLV	8	14	..	..	..	14	7	SNMC	5	..	8	..
Other	JZLW	128	172	..	..	..	304	229	SNMD	4	..	6	..
Total	JZLX	187	221	..	..	..	342	257	SNME	25	..	28	..
Controlled by the Environmental Protection Act 1990:													
Industrial/commercial premises	JZLY	519	560	..	..	..	845	504	SNMF	424	..	451	..
Road works, construction and demolition	JZLZ	177	89	..	..	..	206	177	SNMG	114	..	154	..
Domestic premises	JYWN	302	431	..	..	..	754	787	SNMH	660	..	769	..
Vehicles, machinery and equipment in streets[3]	JYXH	..	..	..	..	..	12	41	SNMI	19	..	20	..
Total	JYWO	998	1 080	..	..	..	1 817	1 509	SNMJ	1 218	..	1 394	..
Controlled by Section 62 of the Control and Pollution Act 1974:													
Noise in streets	JYXI	61	33	..	..	..	27	22					
Total complaints received	JYWP	1 246	1 334	..	..	..	2 186	1 788	SNMK	1 244	..	1 422	..

1 See chapter text.
2 In addition, in 1997/98 there were 210 complaints in the "Other" category which have not been included in this table.
3 Noise & Statutory Nuisance Act 1993 applies.

4 1992/93 figures cover a period of 15 months from January 1992 to March 1993 due to the change from calendar year to financial year in order to come into line with England and Wales.
5 The method of collection changed from 1998/99. Data have been slightly reallocated to correspond as closely as possible to the existing categories.

Sources: The Chartered Institute of Environmental Health;
The Royal Environmental Health Institute of Scotland

13.20 Material flows[1]
United Kingdom

Million tonnes

		1970	1975	1980	1985	1990	1995	1997	1998	1999	2000	2001
Domestic extraction												
Biomass												
Agricultural harvest	JKUN	42	38	47	47	46	47	53	51	52	51	45
Timber	JKUO	3	3	4	5	6	8	7	7	7	7	7
Animal grazing	JKUP	49	49	49	48	46	44	45	44	43	43	43
Fish	JKUQ	1	1	1	1	1	1	1	1	1	1	1
Total biomass	JKUR	96	92	101	100	100	100	107	103	104	103	97
Minerals												
Ores	JKUS	12	5	1	1	–	–	–	–	–	–	–
Clay	JKUT	38	33	25	23	21	18	15	16	15	15	14
Other industrial minerals	JKUU	14	12	11	11	11	10	10	8	8	8	9
Sand and gravel	JKUV	122	131	110	112	128	106	103	103	105	106	109
Crushed stone	JKUW	156	169	150	160	212	200	182	181	179	176	173
Total minerals	JKUX	342	350	298	307	373	334	310	309	308	305	304
Fossil fuels												
Coal	JKUY	149	129	130	94	94	53	48	41	37	31	32
Natural gas	JKUZ	11	37	39	37	43	71	86	90	99	109	106
Crude oil	JKVA	–	2	80	128	92	130	128	132	137	126	117
Total fossil fuels	JKVB	161	168	249	259	229	254	263	264	273	266	255
Total domestic extraction	JKVC	598	609	648	666	701	688	679	676	685	674	656
Imports												
Biomass	JKVD	38	33	30	31	38	40	41	42	42	42	46
Minerals	JKVE	30	32	24	34	41	51	51	54	50	49	52
Fossil fuels	JKVF	123	111	74	76	89	73	79	76	70	83	99
Other products	JKVG	5	6	13	14	19	23	28	31	29	34	34
Total imports	JKVH	197	183	140	156	187	187	200	203	191	208	230
Exports												
Biomass	JKVI	3	5	8	11	13	15	18	17	16	17	13
Minerals	JKVJ	17	20	26	22	25	39	43	46	45	44	42
Fossil fuels	JKVK	23	19	60	102	67	103	106	103	108	115	118
Other products	JKVL	5	7	8	11	12	17	19	19	19	20	20
Total exports	JKVM	47	51	101	146	117	174	185	185	187	196	193
Indirect flows												
From domestic extraction[2], excluding soil erosion	JKVN	579	597	665	653	720	666	671	633	644	614	622
Of which:												
Unused biomass	JKVO	16	16	22	25	27	27	31	30	29	30	25
Fossil fuels	JKVP	188	228	326	312	355	317	323	285	297	264	276
Minerals and ores	JKVQ	177	158	121	115	135	117	110	112	110	108	112
Soil excavation and dredging	JKVR	198	196	196	200	204	205	207	207	207	208	209
From production of imports	JKVS	394	395	368	423	457	527	541	597	549	614	711
Summary aggregates												
Direct material input												
(Domestic extraction + imports)	JKVT	795	792	788	821	888	875	879	879	876	882	887
Domestic material consumption												
(Domestic extraction + imports - exports)	JKVU	748	741	687	676	771	702	694	695	689	686	694
Total material requirement												
(Direct material input + indirect flows)	JKVV	1 768	1 784	1 821	1 897	2 065	2 068	2 091	2 109	2 069	2 110	2 220

1 See chapter text.
2 Indirect flows from domestic extraction relate to unused material which is moved during extraction, such as overburden from mining and quarrying.

Sources: Wuppertal Institute;
Office for National Statistics: 020 7533 5904

14 Housing

Housing

Permanent dwellings completed *(Table 14.1)*

Local housing authorities include the Commission for the New Towns and New Towns Development Corporations, Communities Scotland and the Northern Ireland Housing Executive. The figures shown for housing associations include dwellings provided by housing associations other than the Communities Scotland and the Northern Ireland Housing Executive and provided or authorised by government departments for the families of police, prison staff, the Armed Forces and certain other services.

Homeless households living in temporary accommodation *(Table 14.9)*

Comprises households in accommodation arranged by local authorities pending enquiries or after being accepted as homeless under the 1996 Act (includes residual cases awaiting re-housing under the 1985 Act). Excludes "homeless at home" cases.

Private sector accommodation: Comprises dwellings operated by Registered Social Landlords or local authorities on lease or under licence from the private sector, or placed directly with a private sector landlord.

14.1 Stock of dwellings[1]

Thousands

		1993	1994	1995	1996	1997	1998	1999	2000	2001	2002	2003
England												
Owner occupied	JUTY	13 434	13 553	13 700	13 865	14 040	14 237	14 432	14 630	14 802	14 963	15 186
Rented	JUUC	6 553	6 586	6 606	6 603	6 582	6 541	6 495	6 445	6 404	6 367	6 278
Local Authority	JUTZ	3 760	3 666	3 565	3 470	3 401	3 309	3 178	3 012	2 812	2 708	2 457
Privately	JUUA	2 079	2 141	2 184	2 191	2 196	2 192	2 171	2 160	2 168	2 192	2 200
Registered Social Landlords	JUUB	714	779	857	942	985	1 040	1 146	1 273	1 424	1 467	1 621
All dwellings	JUUD	19 987	20 139	20 305	20 468	20 622	20 778	20 927	21 075	21 207	21 330	21 464
Wales												
Owner occupied	JUUE	854	862	870	878	885	894	902	911	920	930	..
Rented	JUUI	350	352	354	355	357	357	357	356	354	352	..
Local Authority	JUUF	216	213	210	207	204	201	197	193	188	183	..
Privately	JUUG	99	101	102	104	105	106	108	109	111	112	..
Registered Social Landlords	JUUH	35	38	42	45	48	50	52	54	55	57	..
All dwellings	JUUJ	1 204	1 214	1 224	1 233	1 243	1 251	1 259	1 267	1 274	1 282	..
Scotland												
Owner occupied	JUUK	1 217	1 258	1 293	1 327	1 367	1 402	1 436	1 468	1 506	..	..
Rented	JUUO	976	953	938	921	900	883	870	858	839	..	..
Local Authority	JUUL	755	721	692	668	631	608	584	558	535	..	..
Privately	JUUM	154	155	155	154	154	154	155	155	156	..	..
Registered Social Landlords	JUUN	67	77	91	99	115	121	131	145	148	..	..
All dwellings	JUUP	2 193	2 210	2 230	2 248	2 267	2 285	2 305	2 325	2 345	..	..
Northern Ireland												
Owner occupied	JUUQ	395	411	409	422	434	446	455	471	..	489	504
Rented	JUUU	194	189	188	186	183	180	180	179	..	171	165
Local Authority	JUUR	161	155	152	148	142	137	131	126	..	116	109
Privately	JUUS	21	21	22	23	26	27	32	34	..	34	34
Registered Social Landlords	JUUT	12	13	14	15	15	16	17	19	..	21	22
All dwellings	JUUV	590	600	597	608	618	626	636	649	..	660	669
United Kingdom[2]												
Owner occupied	JUVY	15 848	16 027	16 239	16 445	16 674	16 932	17 182	17 432	17 661	17 888	..
Rented	JUWC	8 098	8 108	8 102	8 085	8 046	7 981	7 915	7 851	7 795	7 729	..
Local Authority	JUVZ	4 923	4 795	4 651	4 521	4 421	4 283	4 120	3 920	3 684	3 542	..
Privately	JUWA	2 353	2 417	2 462	2 472	2 478	2 478	2 460	2 456	2 468	2 494	..
Registered Social Landlords	JUWB	822	896	989	1 092	1 147	1 220	1 335	1 475	1 643	1 693	..
All dwellings	JUWD	23 946	24 135	24 341	24 529	24 720	24 913	25 097	25 283	25 456	25 617	..

1 At 31 March for England and Wales and at 31 December for Scotland. At 31 March for Northern Ireland, but data prior to 2002 are at 31 December.
2 Calculated from data for England, Wales and Northern Ireland for the current year with Scotland data for the previous year, except for 2001 and earlier where Northern Ireland data for the previous year are used.

Sources: Office of the Deputy Prime Minister;
National Assembly for Wales;
Scottish Executive;
Department for Social Development (NI)

14.2 Tenure by type of accommodation, 2001-02
United Kingdom

Percentages

	House or bungalow			Flat or maisonette		
	Detached	Semi-detached	Terraced	Purpose-built	Other[1]	All dwellings[2]
Owner-occupied						
Owned outright	34	34	22	7	2	100
Owned with mortgage	26	35	29	8	2	100
All owner-occupied	29	35	26	8	2	100
Rented from social sector						
Local authority	1	26	30	42	2	100
Housing association	2	18	32	41	6	100
All rented from social sector	1	24	31	41	3	100
Rented privately[3]						
Furnished	7	11	28	26	28	100
Unfurnished[4]	16	24	32	13	14	100
All rented privately	13	20	31	17	18	100
All tenures	21	31	28	16	4	100

1 Includes converted flats, part of a house and rooms.
2 Includes other type of accomodation, such as mobile homes
3 Includes rent free accommodation.
4 Includes partly furnished accommodation.

Sources: General Household Survey, Office for National Statistics;
Continuous Household Survey, Northern Ireland Statistics Research Agency

14.3 Permanent dwellings completed[1]

Numbers

	United Kingdom				England and Wales			
	All dwellings	Local authorities[2]	Private enterprise	Registered Social Landlords[3]	All dwellings	Local authorities[2]	Private enterprise	Registered Social Landlords[3]
	KAAD	KAAE	KAAF	KAAG	KAAH	KAAI	KAAJ	KAAK
1978	288 689	110 165	152 233	26 291	254 068	97 779	134 645	21 644
1979	251 823	86 316	144 121	21 386	220 788	78 125	125 372	17 291
1980	241 999	88 534	131 989	21 476	214 934	78 539	116 179	20 216
1981	206 985	68 554	118 647	19 784	180 147	58 633	104 069	17 445
1982	182 853	40 091	129 022	13 740	159 407	33 544	113 893	11 970
1983	209 018	39 161	153 038	16 819	181 391	31 625	134 901	14 865
1984	220 414	37 573	165 555	17 286	191 112	31 338	145 263	14 511
1985	207 465	30 420	163 395	13 650	178 284	24 359	142 020	11 905
1986	216 544	25 377	178 008	13 159	187 710	20 496	156 056	11 158
1987	226 234	21 833	191 250	13 151	198 732	17 435	169 895	11 402
1988	242 359	21 448	207 423	13 488	214 156	16 921	185 733	11 502
1989	221 463	19 323	187 542	14 598	190 990	15 332	163 344	12 314
1990	203 388	17 862	167 473	18 053	175 099	14 625	144 849	15 625
1991	191 635	11 229	159 536	20 870	165 197	8 544	138 839	17 814
1992	179 362	5 709	147 322	26 331	154 088	3 650	127 020	23 418
1993	186 040	3 371	146 673	35 996	157 592	1 603	123 255	32 734
1994	193 383	2 882	153 334	37 167	165 210	1 321	130 066	33 823
1995	199 716	3 440	157 233	39 043	166 953	974	132 549	33 430
1996	188 942	1 758	154 082	33 102	159 436	576	129 278	29 582
1997	191 074	1 543	161 187	28 344	158 384	291	135 003	23 090
1998	179 721	1 111	154 472	24 138	149 266	289	127 563	21 414
1999	182 128	361	157 334	24 433	148 235	84	129 747	18 404
2000	178 874	379	154 670	23 825	144 403	207	126 180	18 016
2001	175 534	487	152 472	22 575	138 298	390	122 340	15 568
2002	183 112	283	162 471	20 358	145 197	213	130 637	14 347

	Scotland				Northern Ireland			
	All dwellings	Local authorities[2]	Private enterprise	Registered Social Landlords[3]	All dwellings	Local authorities[2]	Private enterprise	Registered Social Landlords[3]
	BLFI	BAEZ	BLFK	BLFO	BLGI	BAFA	BLGK	BLGO
1978	25 778	6 705	14 443	4 630	8 843	5 681	3 145	17
1979	23 782	4 755	15 175	3 852	7 253	3 436	3 574	243
1980	20 611	7 488	12 242	881	6 454	2 507	3 568	379
1981	20 011	7 062	11 021	1 928	6 827	2 859	3 557	411
1982	16 423	3 733	11 523	1 167	7 023	2 814	3 606	603
1983	17 929	3 492	13 166	1 271	9 698	4 044	4 971	683
1984	18 838	2 647	14 115	2 076	10 464	3 588	6 177	699
1985	18 411	2 828	14 435	1 148	10 770	3 233	6 940	597
1986	18 637	2 301	14 870	1 466	10 197	2 580	7 082	535
1987	17 707	2 634	13 904	1 169	9 795	1 764	7 451	580
1988	18 272	2 815	14 179	1 278	9 931	1 712	7 511	708
1989	20 190	2 283	16 287	1 620	10 283	1 708	7 911	664
1990	20 362	1 938	16 461	1 963	7 927	1 299	6 163	465
1991	19 529	1 732	15 533	2 264	6 909	953	5 164	792
1992	17 620	1 010	14 389	2 221	7 654	1 049	5 913	692
1993	21 221	958	17 711	2 552	7 227	810	5 707	710
1994	21 203	661	17 753	2 789	6 970	900	5 515	555
1995	24 325	1 161	18 310	4 854	8 438	1 305	6 374	759
1996	20 950	292	18 092	2 566	8 556	890	6 712	954
1997	22 522	177	17 838	4 507	10 168	1 075	8 346	747
1998	20 378	139	18 328	1 911	10 077	683	8 581	813
1999	24 396	81	19 404	4 911	9 497	196	8 183	1 118
2000	23 059	95	18 070	4 894	11 412	77	10 420	915
2001	23 586	72	18 012	5 502	13 650	25	12 120	1 505
2002	24 068	51	18 897	5 120	13 847	19	12 937	891

1 See chapter text.
2 Including the Commission for the New Towns Development Corporations, Communities Scotland, the Northern Ireland Housing Executive.
3 Dwellings provided by housing associations other than Communities Scotland and the Northern Ireland Housing Trust and provided or authorised by government departments for families of police, prison staff, the armed forces and certain other services.

Sources: Office of the Deputy Prime Minister 0117 372 8055;
Scottish Executive;
National Assembly for Wales;
Department for Social Development, Northern Ireland

14.4 Stock of dwellings: Estimated annual gains and losses
England

Thousands of dwellings

		1992/93	1993/94	1994/95	1995/96	1996/97	1997/98	1998/99	1999/00	2000[2]/01	2001/02	2002/03
Dwelling stock at start of financial year	GRWM	19 836	19 987	20 139	20 305	20 468	20 622	20 778	20 927	21 075	21 207	21 330
Gains to dwelling stock:												
Housebuilding completions	GRWN	142.5	147.7	158.0	154.6	146.2	149.6	138.6	141.8	133.7	130.1	137.9
Conversions (net gain)[1]	GRWO	8.3	7.5	9.9	8.9	8.6	2.8	4.2	3.5	2.8	5.1	3.8
Change of use	GRWP	..	..	..	..	..	11.6	15.9	13.9	9.2	14.8	16.2
Non-permanent dwellings additions	GRWQ	..	..	..	..	..	0.2	0.2	0.3	0.3	0.3	0.7
Losses from dwelling stock:												
Slum clearance (non LA owned dwelling demolished)	GRWR	2.0	3.9	3.0	2.7	2.9	1.3	1.3	1.4	1.7	1.6	1.2
Other demolitions[1]	GRWS	4.3	5.2	5.8	4.8	4.1	12.8	13.2	15.8	18.3	24.7	22.0
Change of use	GRWT	..	..	..	..	..	0.7	1.4	0.8	0.7	0.8	1.2
Non-permanent dwelling losses	GRWU	..	..	..	..	..	0.1	0.2	0.1	0.3	0.3	0.2
New gain in year	GRWV	144.5	146.2	159.0	156.0	147.8	149.3	143.0	141.3	125.0	122.8	134.0
Adjustment[3]	VQDN	6.6	6.6	6.6	6.6	6.6	6.6	6.6	6.6	6.6	–	–
Dwelling stock at end of financial year	GRWW	19 987	20 139	20 305	20 468	20 622	20 778	20 927	21 075	21 207	21 330	21 464

1 Figures prior to 1997/98 include change of use, and zero for net non-permanent dwellings.
2 Figures for 2000/01 conversions, change of use and non permanent dwellings are based on reported figures and do not include estimates for missing returns.

3 Series has been adjusted so that the 2000/01 estimates matches the 2001 Census.

Source: Office of the Deputy Prime Minister: 0117 372 8055

14.5 Housebuilding completions: by number of bedrooms

Percentages

		1992/93	1993/94	1994/95	1995/96	1996/97	1997/98	1998/99	1999/00	2000/01	2001/02	2002/03
England												
1 bedroom	JUWJ	17	14	12	11	8	7	7	7	7	7	6
2 bedrooms	JUWK	33	33	32	32	29	27	27	26	27	25	29
3 bedrooms	JUWL	31	33	34	35	36	38	36	35	34	31	30
4 or more bedrooms	JUWM	19	19	22	23	26	28	30	32	32	37	34
All houses and flats	JUWN	100	100	100	100	100	100	100	100	100	100	100
Wales												
1 bedroom	JUWO	13	10	7	8	5	4	3	5	5	4	6
2 bedrooms	JUWP	30	33	30	30	27	24	21	19	18	19	18
3 bedrooms	JUWQ	42	43	47	44	47	46	46	43	42	39	35
4 or more bedrooms	JUWR	16	15	15	18	21	26	30	34	34	38	41
All houses and flats	JUWS	100	100	100	100	100	100	100	100	100	100	100

Sources: Office of the Deputy Prime Minister; National Assembly for Wales

14.6 Mortgages
United Kingdom

		1992	1993	1994	1995	1996	1997	1998	1999	2000	2001	2002
Mortgages[1] (Thousands)	JUTH	9 922	10 137	10 410	10 521	10 637	10 738	10 821	10 981	11 169	11 243	11 360
Arrears and repossessions[1] (Thousands)												
Loans in arrears at end-period												
By 6-12 months	JUTI	205	165	134	127	101	74	74	57	48	43	34
By over 12 months	JUTJ	147	152	117	85	67	45	35	30	21	20	16
Properties repossessed in period	JUTK	69	59	49	49	43	33	34	30	23	18	12
Type of mortgage for house purchase[2] (Percentages)												
Standard repayment	JUTL	15.4	21.0	25.7	33.7	38.5	39.6	42.7	46.0	60.0	71.9	81.4
Endowment	JUTM	73.3	64.2	61.0	50.6	37.6	35.3	33.1	26.7	17.0	10.4	4.8
Other[3]	JUTN	11.3	14.8	13.3	15.7	23.9	25.1	24.3	27.3	23.0	17.7	13.8

1 Estimates cover only members of the Council of Mortgage Lenders; these account for 98 per cent of all mortgages outstanding.
2 Includes new mortgages advanced by building societies and other major lenders. Includes sitting tenants.
3 Includes interest only, PEP/ISA and pension.

Sources: Council of Mortgage Lenders;
Office of the Deputy Prime Minister

14.7 County Court mortgage possession orders[1]

Thousands

		1991	1996	1997	1998	1999	2000	2001	2002
Actions entered									
England and Wales	JURS	186.6	79.8	67.0	84.8	81.6	73.0	65.0	61.7
North East	JURT	6.0	3.5	3.0	4.3	4.2	4.0	3.4	3.1
North West	JURU	22.3	12.7	10.9	14.2	13.8	12.4	11.7	10.7
Yorkshire and the Humber	JURV	14.1	7.6	6.9	8.2	8.1	7.8	6.9	6.2
East Midlands	JURW	13.5	5.9	4.9	6.4	6.8	5.7	5.4	4.7
West Midlands	JURX	17.7	7.6	6.7	8.1	9.5	9.8	7.6	6.3
East	JURY	18.6	8.3	6.7	8.5	7.3	6.2	5.5	5.4
London	JURZ	35.3	11.4	9.2	11.4	10.0	8.1	7.4	8.7
South East	JUSA	32.2	11.6	9.1	11.2	9.4	8.6	8.2	8.0
South West	JUSB	16.7	6.3	5.7	7.3	7.0	5.2	4.4	4.1
England	JUSC	176.4	74.9	63.1	79.6	77.1	67.7	60.5	57.1
Wales	JUSD	10.2	4.9	3.9	5.4	5.5	5.3	4.5	4.7
Northern Ireland[2]	JUSE	3.1	1.2	1.2	1.6	1.9	1.7	1.6	1.6
Suspended orders									
England and Wales	JUSF	69.1	43.4	34.8	40.8	36.6	31.7	27.9	23.5
North East	JUSG	2.9	2.0	1.6	2.3	2.3	1.9	1.6	1.2
North West	JUSH	8.6	7.7	5.5	6.4	6.0	5.7	5.0	4.5
Yorkshire and the Humber	JUSI	5.1	3.9	3.5	4.3	4.1	3.7	3.2	2.5
East Midlands	JUSJ	4.5	3.0	2.6	3.1	2.8	2.4	2.4	1.8
West Midlands	JUSK	6.5	3.9	3.4	3.8	4.0	3.7	3.5	2.5
East	JUSL	6.0	4.0	3.0	3.9	3.5	2.5	2.2	2.0
London	JUSM	13.1	6.4	4.7	5.3	4.5	3.1	2.7	2.7
South East	JUSN	13.2	6.6	5.4	5.8	4.4	3.9	3.4	2.9
South West	JUSO	5.8	3.3	2.7	3.0	2.8	2.3	1.8	1.7
England	JUSP	65.6	40.7	32.4	37.9	34.9	29.1	25.8	21.7
Wales	JUSQ	3.5	2.7	2.4	2.8	2.2	2.6	2.1	1.9
Northern Ireland[2]	JUSR	..	..	..	0.2	0.3	0.2	0.2	0.2
Orders made									
England and Wales	JUSS	73.9	27.8	22.5	25.3	23.6	20.4	17.8	16.2
North East	JUST	1.9	1.1	1.0	1.2	1.1	1.1	1.1	0.8
North West	JUSU	7.5	4.0	3.3	3.7	3.7	3.7	3.4	3.0
Yorkshire and the Humber	JUSV	5.7	2.6	2.3	3.1	3.0	2.4	2.2	1.7
East Midlands	JUSW	5.2	2.0	1.7	1.7	1.8	1.6	1.4	1.4
West Midlands	JUSX	6.9	2.1	2.0	2.4	2.3	2.3	2.1	1.7
East	JUSY	8.4	3.4	2.5	2.6	2.2	1.6	1.4	1.3
London	JUSZ	14.4	4.8	3.4	3.5	3.4	2.1	1.8	2.3
South East	JUTA	13.2	4.0	3.1	3.4	2.7	2.6	1.9	1.8
South West	JUTB	6.5	2.4	1.9	2.1	2.0	1.3	1.1	1.0
England	JUTC	69.9	26.4	21.2	23.7	22.2	18.7	16.4	15.0
Wales	JUTD	4.0	1.4	1.3	1.7	1.4	1.6	1.4	1.2
Northern Ireland[2]	JUTE	..	..	..	0.5	0.7	0.6	0.7	0.5

1 Local authority and private.
2 Mortgage possession actions are heard in Chancery Division of Northern Ireland High Court.

Sources: The Court Service: 020 7210 1752;
Northern Ireland Court Service: 028 9032 8594

14.8
Sales and transfers of local authority dwellings[1]
Great Britain

Numbers

		1992	1993	1994	1995	1996	1997	1998	1999	2000	2001	2002
Right to buy sales	JUQV	64 258	60 448	65 241	49 599	44 980	58 056	55 972	66 765	71 254	66 545	78 328
Large scale voluntary transfers	JUQW	21 867	27 500	41 019	47 676	29 862	21 116	36 871	88 672	111 443	100 753	102 467
Other sales and transfers	JUQX	6 901	6 021	4 560	3 161	2 962	3 414	2 660	3 349	2 436	1 634	1 407
Total sales and transfers	JUQY	93 026	93 969	110 820	100 436	77 804	82 586	95 503	158 786	185 133	168 932	182 202

1 In Wales, except for 1993, large scale and voluntary transfers are included in other sales and transfers.

Sources: Office of the Deputy Prime Minister;
National Assembly for Wales;
Scottish Executive

14.9
Homeless households living in temporary accommodation[1]
England

As at 31 March of each year

Thousands

		1992	1993	1994	1995	1996	1997	1998	1999	2000	2001	2002
Bed and breakfast hotels[2]	JUWF	7 630	4 900	4 130	4 500	4 160	4 520	7 240	8 000	9 870	11 970	12 620
Hostels/women's refuges	JUWG	10 840	10 210	9 730	9 660	9 640	8 730	9 760	9 660	10 790	10 310	9 710
Private sector accommodation	JXVN	27 910	23 270	15 800	11 530	10 980	14 040	17 400	19 820	25 260	26 040	34 030
Other accommodation[3]	JXVO	16 690	15 200	15 970	18 450	17 410	17 580	19 390	24 700	27 160	30 290	28 560
All accommodation	JUWI	63 070	53 580	45 630	44 140	42 190	44 870	53 790	62 180	73 080	78 610	84 930

1 See chapter text.
2 From 2002 some self-contained accommodation in Annexe-style units, previously recorded under Bed and breakfast hotels, is now more appropriately attributed to private sector accommodation.
3 Includes local authorities' and Registered Social Landlords' own stock.

Source: Office of the Deputy Prime Minister

15 Transport and communications

Transport and communications

Road data *(Tables 15.4, 15.5, 15.6 and 15.7)*
The Department of Transport has undertaken significant development work over the last two years to improve its traffic estimates and measurement of traffic flow on particular stretches of the road network. This work has previously been outlined in a number of publications (Road Traffic Statistics: 2001 SB(02)23, Traffic in Great Britain Q4 2002 Data SB(03)5 and Traffic in Great Britain Q1 2003 SB(03)6).

The main point to note is that figures for 1993 to 2002 have been calculated on a different basis from years prior to 1993. Therefore, figures prior to 1993 are not directly comparable with estimates for later years. Estimates on the new basis for 1993 and subsequent years were first published by the Department on 8th May 2003 in Traffic in Great Britain Q1 2003 SB(03)6.

A summary of the main methodological changes to take place over the last couple of years appears below:

Traffic estimates are now disaggregated for roads in urban and rural areas rather than between built-up and non built-up roads. Built-up roads were defined as those with a speed limit of 40mph or lower. This created difficulties in producing meaningful disaggregated traffic estimates because an increasing number of clearly rural roads were subject to a 40mph speed limit for safety reasons. The urban/rural split of roads is largely determined by whether roads lie within the boundaries of urban areas with a population of 10,000 or more with adjustments in some cases for major roads at the boundary. At the time of publication the urban areas based on the 2001 census had not been finalised, the figures in this bulletin are therefore provisional.

Traffic estimates are based on the results of many 12-hour manual counts in every year which are grossed up to estimates of annual average daily flows using expansion factors based on data from automatic traffic counters on similar roads. These averages are needed so that traffic in off-peak times, at weekends and in the summer and winter months (when only special counts are undertaken) can be taken into account when assessing the traffic at each site. For this purpose roads are now sorted into 22 groupings (previously there were only 7) and this allows a better match of manual count sites with our automatic count sites. These groupings are based on a detailed analyses of the results from all the individual automatic count sites and take into account regional groupings, road category (i.e. both the urban/rural classification of the road and the road class) and traffic flow levels. The groupings range from lightly-trafficked, rural minor roads in holiday areas such as Cornwall and Devon, to major roads in Central London.

With the increasing interest in sub-regional statistics, we have undertaken a detailed study of traffic counts on minor roads carried out in the last ten years. This has been done in conjunction with a Geographic Information System to enable us to establish general patterns of minor road traffic in each local authority. As a result of this, we have been able to produce more reliable estimate of traffic levels in each authority in our base year of 1998. This in turn has enabled us to produce better estimates of traffic levels back to 1993, as well as more reliable estimates for 1999 onwards.

The Department created a database for major roads based on a Geographic Information System and Ordnance Survey data. This was checked by local authorities and discussed with Government Regional Offices and the Highways Agency to ensure that good local knowledge supplemented the available technical data.

Road class *(Tables 15.5 and 15.6)*
Urban roads are defined as being within an urban settlement with a population of more than 10,000 people, and rural roads are outside of these settlements.

New vehicle registrations *(Table 15.9)*
Special concession group
Various revisions to the vehicle taxation system were introduced on 1 July 1995 and on 29 November 1995. Separate taxation classes for farmers' goods vehicles were abolished on 1 July 1995; after this date new vehicles of this type were registered as HGVs. The total includes 5,900 vehicles registered between 1 January and 30 June in the (now abolished) agricultural and special machines group in classes which were not eligible to register in the special concession group. The old agricultural and special machines taxation group was abolished at end June 1995. The group includes agricultural and mowing machines, snow ploughs and gritting vehicles. Electric vehicles are also included in this group and are no longer exempt from VED. Steam propelled vehicles were added to this group from November 1995.

Other licensed vehicles
Includes three wheelers, pedestrian controlled vehicles, general haulage and showmen's tractors and recovery vehicles. Recovery vehicle tax class introduced January 1988.

Special vehicles group
The special vehicles group was created on 1 July 1995 and consists of various vehicle types over 3.5 tonnes gross weight but not required to pay VED as heavy goods vehicles. The group includes mobile cranes, works trucks, digging machines, road rollers and vehicles previously taxed as showman's goods and haulage. Figure shown for 1995 covers period from 1 July to 31 December only.

Full car driving licence holders - National Travel Survey data *(Table 15.11)*
The 2002 National Travel Survey (NTS) is the latest in a series of household surveys designed to provide a databank of personal travel information for Great Britain. The survey is part of a continuous survey that began in July 1988, following ad hoc surveys since the mid-1960s. The survey is designed to pick up long-term trends and is not suitable for monitoring short-term trends.

The drawn sample size for 2002 was nearly trebled compared with previous years following recommendations in a National Statistics Review of the National Travel Survey. This enables key results to be presented on a single year basis for the first time since the survey became continuous.

Changes to the methodology in 2002 mean that there are some inconsistencies with data for earlier years. The 2002 results presented in the table should be regarded as provisional.

During 2002, individuals in over 7,400 households provided details of their personal travel by filling in travel diaries over a period of seven days, compared with nearly 3,500 households in 2001. Previously, data have been shown for a three year time period because of the smaller sample size.

Travel details provided by respondents include trip purpose, method of travel, time of day and trip length. The households also provided personal information, such as their age, sex, working status, and driving licence holding, and details of the cars available for their use.

Because estimates made from a sample survey depend upon the particular sample chosen they generally differ from the true values of the population. This is not usually a problem when considering large samples (such as all car trips in Great Britain), but may give misleading information when considering data from small samples.

The most recent editions of all NTS publications are available on the DfT website at *www.transtat.dft.gov.uk*. Bulletins of key results are published annually. The most recent bulletin is *National Travel Survey: 1999/ 2001 Update*. A more detailed NTS bulletin, including results from new questions introduced in 2002, will be published by DfT in Spring 2004.

Activity at civil aerodromes *(Table 15.28)*
Figures exclude Channel Island airports. 'Other' covers local pleasure flights and non-transport charter flights for reward (for example: aerial survey work, crop dusting and delivery of empty aircraft) and 'Non-commmercial' covers test and training flights, scheduled service positioning flights, private, aeroclub and official flights, and Business Aviation etc.

International passenger movements by air and sea *(Table 15.31)*
Figures shown in the table are for arrivals plus departures.

EC Europe includes Azores, Madeira, Canary and Cape Verde Islands, Austria, Finland and Sweden joined the EC in 1995, but are included in the EC section for all years to show a consistent time series. Other Western Europe includes Iceland and the Faroe Islands.

For Pleasure cruises, passengers are included at both departure and arrival if their journeys begin and end at the United Kingdom seaports.

Postal services and television licences *(Table 15.32)*
Data for letters, postal orders and telegrams sent, is shown upto 31 March of each year and data for television licences is at 31 March each year.

Letters posted category includes printed papers, newspapers, postcards and sample packets, Airmail includes letters without special charge for air transport. Business reply and freepost is now known as Response Services.

15.1 Trips per person per year by main mode[1] and purpose, 1999/2001
Great Britain

Numbers

	Walk	Bicycle	Car/van driver	Car/van passenger	Motor-cycle	Other private	Buses in London
Commuting	18	6	89	18	2	1	3
Business	3	-	25	3	-	-	-
Education	30	1	3	18	-	3	2
Escort education	20	-	20	6	-	-	-
Shopping	60	2	81	49	-	-	4
Other escort	9	-	48	23	-	-	-
Other personal business	27	1	44	24	-	1	1
Visiting friends at home	27	2	50	43	-	-	1
Visiting friends elsewhere	14	-	12	14	-	-	-
Social/entertainment	9	1	25	22	-	1	-
Holidays/day trips	2	2	9	12	-	-	-
Other, including just walk	43	-	1	-	-	-	-
All purposes	**263**	**16**	**407**	**231**	**3**	**8**	**13**

	Other local bus	Non-local bus	LT Under-ground	Surface rail	Taxi/ minicab	Other public	All modes
Commuting	9	-	3	6	2	-	156
Business	-	-	-	1	-	-	35
Education	8	-	-	1	-	-	67
Escort education	-	-	-	-	-	-	47
Shopping	13	-	-	1	2	-	214
Other escort	1	-	-	-	-	-	82
Other personal business	4	-	-	1	1	-	105
Visiting friends at home	4	-	-	1	2	-	133
Visiting friends elsewhere	2	-	-	-	3	-	46
Social/entertainment	2	-	-	-	1	-	62
Holidays/day trips	-	-	-	-	-	-	29
Other, including just walk	-	-	-	-	-	-	44
All purposes	**44**	**2**	**7**	**13**	**12**	**2**	**1 019**

1 Main mode is that used for the longest part of the trip.

Source: Department for Transport 020 7944 3097

15.2 Retail Prices Index: real changes in the cost of transport and disposable income
Great Britain

Constant prices

Index 1974=100

	Petrol/oil	All motoring	Rail	Bus and coach fares	Disposable income
	ZCFV	ZCFW	ZCFX	ZCFY	ZCFZ
1977	92.5	99.9	125.0	114.1	98.4
1978	81.2	99.6	132.0	119.4	105.7
1979	94.1	104.0	128.7	118.3	111.7
1980	102.2	103.8	135.6	127.0	113.4
1981	108.5	103.9	138.5	125.6	112.9
1982	107.4	101.0	146.4	133.2	112.6
1983	109.8	103.3	148.5	134.6	115.3
1984	108.2	100.7	142.0	131.0	119.5
1985	108.5	99.4	142.3	128.9	123.6
1986	91.3	94.7	147.0	135.1	128.7
1987	88.4	96.3	148.3	137.3	133.2
1988	83.4	95.9	151.2	140.1	140.3
1989	82.9	93.9	153.1	140.1	146.8
1990	84.6	90.9	152.1	135.0	151.9
1991	85.9	92.3	158.7	145.5	154.6
1992	85.2	95.0	164.1	150.1	159.3
1993	90.5	97.6	172.9	154.3	164.3
1994	92.4	98.5	176.3	154.5	167.0
1995	93.9	97.0	178.0	154.9	171.3
1996	96.3	97.5	180.3	156.9	175.4
1997	102.7	99.6	178.9	157.5	183.0
1998	104.2	99.3	180.0	157.5	182.7
1999	111.3	100.2	183.8	160.6	189.7
2000	122.4	101.0	181.6	162.3	198.5
2001	114.0	98.7	185.3	166.1	212.0
2002	108.7	96.3	186.5	168.5	216.8

Source: Office for National Statistics: 020 7533 5874

15.3 Domestic freight transport: by mode
Great Britain

		1992[1]	1993	1994	1995	1996	1997	1998	1999	2000	2001	2002
Goods moved (Billion tonnes kilometres)												
Petroleum products												
Road[2]	ZBZP	4.5	5.0	5.1	5.7	6.1	5.8	5.1	4.9	6.3	5.8	5.2
Rail	ZBZQ	2.0	1.9	1.8	1.8	..	..	1.6[4]	1.5	1.4	1.2	1.1
Water[3]	ZBZR	42.7	41.7	43.0	42.5	45.9	38.3	45.2	48.6	54.8	..	..
of which: coastwise	ZBZS	29.4	28.9	28.9	31.4	38.7	33.8	36.4	33.3	27.6	..	..
Pipeline	ZBZT	11.0	11.6	12.0	11.1	11.6	11.2	11.7	11.6	11.4	11.5	10.9
All modes	ZBZU	60.2	60.2	61.9	61.1	63.6[5]	55.3[5]	63.6	66.6	73.9	..	..
Coal and coke												
Road[2]	ZBZV	3.5	3.1	2.9	2.7	2.5	2.7	2.0	2.2	1.5	2.1	1.5
Rail	ZBZW	5.4	3.9	3.3	3.6	3.9	4.4	4.5[4]	4.8	4.8	6.2	5.7
Water[3]	ZBZX	1.8	1.5	1.4	2.3	0.6	0.6	0.5	0.5	0.2	..	..
All modes	ZBZY	10.7	8.5	7.6	8.6	6.9	7.7	7.0	7.5	6.5	..	..
Other traffic												
Road[2]	ZBZZ	118.5	126.4	135.7	141.2	145.3	148.6	152.4	149.6	150.2	149.0	150.6
Rail	ZCAA	8.1	7.9	7.9	7.9	11.2	12.5	11.2[4]	11.9	11.9	12.3	11.9
Water[3]	ZCAB	10.4	8.0	7.8	8.3	8.7	9.2	11.2	9.6	12.4	..	..
All modes	ZCAC	137.0	142.3	151.4	157.4	165.3	170.3	174.8	171.1	174.5	..	..
All traffic												
Road[2]	KCTA	126.5	134.5	143.7	149.6	153.9	157.1	159.5	156.7	158.0	156.9	157.3
Rail	KCTB	15.5	13.8	13.0	13.3	15.1	16.9	17.3[4]	18.2	18.1	19.7	18.7
Water[3]	ZCAD	54.9	51.2	52.2	53.1	55.3	48.1	56.9	58.7	67.4	..	..
Pipeline	KCTE	11.0	11.6	12.0	11.1	11.6	11.2	11.7	11.6	11.4	11.5	10.9
All modes	KCTF	207.9	211.1	220.9	227.1	235.9	233.3	245.4	245.2	254.9	..	..
Percentage of all traffic												
Road[2]	ZCAE	61	64	65	66	65	67	65	64	62	..	..
Rail	ZCAF	7	7	6	6	6	7	7[4]	7	7	..	..
Water[3]	ZCAG	26	24	24	23	23	21	23	24	26	..	..
Pipeline	ZCAH	5	5	5	5	5	5	5	5	4	..	..
All modes	ZCAI	100	100	100	100	100	100	100	100	100	..	..
Goods lifted (Million tonnes)												
Petroleum products												
Road[2]	ZCAJ	63	67	68	71	75	73	61	61	74	74	59
Rail	ZCAK	10	9	8	6	..	..	..	..	..	..	..
Water[3]	ZCAL	66	64	70	72	71	69	76	72	68	..	..
of which: coastwise	ZCAM	43	42	43	47	54	52	55	52	43	..	..
Pipeline	ZCAN	106	125	161	168	157	148	153	155	151	151	146
All modes	ZCAO	245	265	307	317	303[5]	290[5]	290[5]	288[5]	293	..	..
Coal and coke												
Road[2]	ZCAP	55	48	42	34	32	37	22	28	22	21	17
Rail	ZCAQ	68	49	43	45	52	50	45	44[6]	46	46	41
Water[3]	ZCAR	6	5	4	4	3	4	3	3	3	..	..
All modes	ZCAS	129	102	89	83	87	91	70	75	71	..	..
Other traffic												
Road[2]	ZCAT	1 437	1 500	1 579	1 596	1 623	1 630	1 646	1 572	1 593	1 565	1 632
Rail	ZCAU	45	45	47	50	50	55	57	48[6]	50	48	46
Water[3]	ZCAV	68	65	66	67	67	69	70	70	66	..	..
All modes	ZCAW	1 550	1 610	1 692	1 713	1 740	1 754	1 773	1 690	1 709	..	..
All traffic												
Road[2]	KCTG	1 555	1 615	1 689	1 701	1 730	1 740	1 727	1 661	1 689	1 660	1 708
Rail	KCTH	122	103	97	101	102	105	102	92[6]	95	94	87
Water[3]	ZCAX	140	134	140	143	142	142	149	144	137	..	..
Pipeline	KCTK	106	125	161	168	157	148	153	155	151	151	146
All modes	KCTL	1 923	1 977	2 087	2 113	2 131	2 135	2 131	2 052	2 072	..	..
Percentage of all traffic												
Road[2]	ZCAY	81	82	81	80	81	81	81	81	82	..	..
Rail	ZCAZ	6	5	5	5	5	5	5	4[6]	5	..	..
Water[3]	ZCBA	7	7	7	7	7	7	7	7	7	..	..
Pipeline	ZCBB	6	6	8	8	7	7	7	8	7	..	..
All modes	ZCBC	100	100	100	100	100	100	100	100	100	..	..

1 Figures for rail are for financial years.
2 All goods vehicles, including those under 3.5 tonnes gross vehicle weight. These estimates were revised following a survey in 1993.
3 Figures for water are for UK traffic.

4 Figures for goods moved by rail is a new series from 1998.
5 Excludes rail.
6 Figures for goods lifted by rail have been revised from 1999.

Source: Department for Transport

15.4 Passenger transport[1]: by mode
Great Britain

		1993	1994	1995	1996	1997	1998	1999	2000	2001	2002
Billion passenger kilometres											
Road											
Buses and coaches[2]	GRXK	44	44	44	43	44	45	45	45	46	46
Cars, vans and taxis	GRXG	583	590	592	602	605	611	611	614	622	634
Motor cycles	GRXH	4	4	4	4	4	4	5	5	5	5
Pedal cycles	GRXI	4	4	4	4	4	4	4	4	4	4
All road	GRXJ	635	641	644	653	658	665	666	669	678	690
Rail[3]	KCTN	37	35	37	39	42	44	46	47	47	48
Air	KCTM	5.1	5.5	5.9	6.3	6.8	7.0	7.3	7.6	7.7	8.5
All modes[4]	GRXM	676	682	687	698	706	715	719	723	733	746
Percentages											
Road											
Buses and coaches[2]	GRXN	6	6	6	6	6	6	6	6	6	6
Cars, vans and taxis	GRXO	86	86	86	86	86	85	85	85	85	85
Motor cycles	GRXP	1	1	1	1	1	1	1	1	1	1
Pedal cycles	GRXQ	1	1	1	1	1	1	1	1	1	1
All road	GRXR	94	94	94	94	93	93	93	93	92	92
Rail[3]	ZCBJ	5	5	5	6	6	6	6	6	6	6
Air	ZCBK	0.8	0.8	0.9	0.9	1.0	1.0	1.0	1.1	1.1	1.1
All modes[4]	GRXU	100	100	100	100	100	100	100	100	100	100

1 Because of changes in methodology figures based on road traffic data (car/van/taxi, motorcycle, and pedal cycle), have been revised for all years since 1993, and are not directly comparable with data for earlier years. See chapter text.
2 Data for 2002 are provisional.

3 Financial years. Former British Rail companies and Urban Rail systems.
4 Excluding travel by water within the United Kingdom (including the Channel Islands), estimated at 0.7 billion passenger kilometres in 2000.

Source: Department for Transport

15.5 Motor vehicle traffic: by road class[1]
Great Britain

Billion vehicle kilometres

		1993	1994	1995	1996	1997	1998	1999	2000	2001	2002
Motorways	JSZV	68.2	70.7	73.9	78.5	82.1	86.3	87.7	88.2	90.7	92.4
Rural major roads											
Trunk	JSZW	55.0	56.5	57.9	60.6	62.5	63.4	64.6	64.1	66.2	68.0
Principal	JSZX	58.4	60.1	61.6	63.3	64.2	65.7	66.1	65.8	67.0	68.5
All	JSZY	113.3	116.5	119.5	123.8	126.7	129.1	130.7	129.9	133.2	136.5
Urban major roads											
Trunk	JSZZ	13.7	13.9	13.8	14.0	13.8	13.9	14.0	14.1	14.4	14.3
Principal	JTAA	63.6	64.7	66.2	67.2	67.1	67.6	67.6	67.3	67.2	67.5
All	JTAB	77.3	78.5	80.1	81.2	80.9	81.4	81.5	81.3	81.5	81.8
Minor roads											
Minor rural roads	JTAC	56.1	57.6	57.8	58.9	60.0	60.4	61.3	61.5	61.6	64.5
Minor urban roads	JTAD	97.4	98.1	98.5	99.6	100.7	102.4	105.3	105.5	106.9	110.8
All	JTAE	153.5	155.7	156.2	158.5	160.7	162.8	166.6	167.0	168.5	175.3
All roads	JTAF	412.4	421.6	429.7	442.0	450.3	459.6	466.5	466.5	473.9	486.0

1 See chapter text.

Source: Department for Transport: 020 7944 3095

15.6 Public road length[1]: by road type
Great Britain

Kilometres

		1993	1994	1995	1996	1997	1998	1999	2000	2001	2002
Trunk motorway	JSZD	3 178	3 209	3 236	3 302	3 374	3 419	3 405	3 422	3 432	3 432
Principal motorway	JSZE	72	72	72	45	45	45	45	45	45	45
Rural major roads:											
Trunk	JSZF	10 608	10 586	10 597	10 715	10 779	10 661	10 611	10 594	10 601	10 601
Principal	JSZG	24 716	24 766	24 916	24 816	24 791	24 941	24 859	24 898	24 920	24 924
Total	JSZH	35 324	35 353	35 513	35 531	35 570	35 602	35 470	35 492	35 521	35 525
Urban major roads:											
Trunk	JSZI	1 181	1 168	1 155	1 142	1 129	1 116	1 086	1 085	1 091	1 091
Principal	JSZJ	10 038	10 048	10 058	10 068	10 078	10 088	10 013	10 031	10 043	10 049
Total	JSZK	11 219	11 216	11 213	11 210	11 207	11 204	11 100	11 116	11 133	11 140
Rural minor roads:											
B roads	JSZL	24 625	24 618	24 610	24 602	24 594	24 586	24 578	24 570	24 562	24 555
C roads	JSZM	72 937	73 031	73 124	73 218	73 311	73 405	73 499	73 593	73 687	73 782
Unclassified	JSZN	110 049	110 265	110 481	110 698	110 915	111 132	111 350	111 568	111 787	112 006
All	JSZO	207 612	207 913	208 215	208 517	208 820	209 123	209 427	209 732	210 037	210 342
Urban minor roads:											
B roads	JSZP	5 603	5 607	5 611	5 615	5 619	5 622	5 626	5 630	5 634	5 638
C roads	JSZQ	10 878	10 900	10 921	10 943	10 965	10 987	11 009	11 031	11 053	11 075
Unclassified	JSZR	111 412	111 746	112 081	112 417	112 755	113 093	113 432	113 772	114 114	114 456
All	JSZS	127 893	128 252	128 613	128 975	129 338	129 702	130 067	130 433	130 801	131 169
All minor roads	JSZT	335 505	336 166	336 828	337 492	338 158	338 825	339 494	340 165	340 837	341 511
All roads	JSZU	385 297	386 015	386 862	387 579	388 354	389 095	389 513	390 239	390 968	391 653

1 See chapter text.

Source: Department for Transport 020 7944 3095

15.7 Road traffic[1]: by type of vehicle
Great Britain

Billion vehicle kilometres

		1993	1994	1995	1996	1997	1998	1999	2000	2001	2002
Cars and taxis	JTAH	338.1	345.0	351.1	360.5	365.8	371.4	377.0	376.3	382.3	392.4
Motor cycles etc.	JTAI	3.8	3.8	3.8	3.8	4.0	4.1	4.5	4.6	4.8	5.1
Larger buses and coaches	JTAJ	4.6	4.6	4.9	5.0	5.2	5.2	5.3	5.2	5.2	5.2
Light vans[2]	JTAK	41.6	43.4	44.5	46.3	48.6	50.9	51.6	52.3	53.6	55.0
Goods vehicles:											
2 axles rigid	JTAL	10.7	10.8	10.7	10.9	11.0	11.2	11.6	11.7	11.5	11.6
3 axles rigid	JTAM	1.4	1.4	1.6	1.7	1.6	1.9	1.7	1.7	1.8	1.8
4 or more axles rigid	JTAN	1.5	1.5	1.5	1.5	1.5	1.6	1.5	1.5	1.4	1.5
3 and 4 axles artic.	JTAO	3.6	3.6	3.3	3.3	3.2	3.0	2.9	2.7	2.5	2.3
5 axles artic.	JTAP	5.7	5.7	6.4	6.6	7.1	7.4	7.2	6.6	6.4	6.4
6 or more axles artic.	JTAQ	1.5	1.8	2.0	2.3	2.5	2.9	3.3	4.1	4.5	4.8
All	JTAR	24.3	24.8	25.4	26.3	26.9	27.9	28.1	28.2	28.0	28.3
All motor vehicles	JURA	412.4	421.6	429.7	442.0	450.4	459.6	466.5	466.5	473.9	486.0
Pedal cycles	JURB	4.0	4.0	4.1	4.1	4.1	3.9	4.1	4.1	4.2	4.4

1 See chapter text.
2 Not exceeding 3,500 kgs gross vehicle weight.

Source: Department for Transport 020 7944 3095

Transport and communications

15.8 Motor vehicles currently licensed at end of year
Great Britain

Thousands

	Private and light goods										Body type cars	
	Body type cars	Other vehicles	Motor cycles, scooters and mopeds	Public transport vehicles[1]	Goods vehicles	Special machines/ special concessionary	Other vehicles	Crown and exempt vehicles	Special vehicles group	All vehicles	All	Percentage of company cars
	BMBJ	BMBK	BMBB	BMBE	BMBD	KSBY	BMBF	BMBL	KSBZ	BMBI	ZCGR	ZCGS
1992	19 870	2 198	684	107	432	324	59	903	..	24 577	20 444	11.1
1993	20 102	2 187	650	107	428	318	55	979	..	24 826	20 755	10.7
1994	20 479	2 192	630	107	434	309	50	1 030	..	25 231	21 199	10.4
1995[2]	20 505	2 217	594	74	421	274	44	1 169	28	25 369[3]	21 394	10.4
1996	21 172	2 267	609	77	413	254	40	1 424	48	26 302	22 238	10.3
1997	21 681	2 317	626	79	414	249	38	1 522	48	26 974	22 832	10.5
1998	22 115	2 362	684	80	412	243	37	1 558	47	27 538	23 293	10.4
1999	22 785	2 427	760	84	415	241	36	1 573	47	28 368	23 975	10.0
2000	23 196	2 469	825	86	418	233	34	1 590	46	28 898	24 406	10.3
2001	23 899	2 544	882	89	422	233	33	1 602	45	29 747	25 126	9.7
2002	24 543	2 622	941	92	425	243	32	1 611	46	30 557	25 782	9.0

1 Includes taxis for years up to 1994. Taxation group now restricted to only vehicles with 9 or more seats.
2 The vehicle taxation system was subject to substantial revision from 1 July 1995.
3 Contains 44,000 vehicles still taxed in classes abolished from 1 July 1995.

Source: Department for Transport 020 7944 6386

15.9 New vehicle registrations by taxation class
Great Britain

Thousands

		1992	1993	1994	1995	1996	1997	1998	1999	2000	2001	2002
Total	BBKD	1 901.8	2 073.9	2 249.0	2 306.5	2 410.1	2 597.7	2 740.3	2 765.8	2 870.9	3 137.7	3 229.4
Private and light goods												
Private cars	BMAA	1 528.0	1 694.6	1 809.1	1 828.3	1 888.4	2 015.9	2 123.5	2 100.4	2 174.9	2 431.8	2 528.8
Other vehicles	BMAE	166.4	158.8	182.6	195.7	205.0	228.4	244.5	241.6	254.9	277.9	286.8
Total	BMAK	1 694.4	1 853.4	1 991.7	2 024.0	2 093.4	2 244.3	2 368.0	2 342.0	2 429.8	2 709.7	2 815.6
Motor cycles, etc:												
Up to 50 c.c.	KCUH	9.1	6.5	6.9	6.3	8.9	14.2	22.6	36.2	49.4	45.6	35.6
Other	KCUI	56.5	51.9	57.7	62.6	80.7	107.1	120.7	132.2	133.5	131.5	126.6
Total	BMAL	65.6	58.4	64.6	68.9	89.6	121.3	143.3	168.4	182.9	177.1	162.2
Public road passenger vehicles												
Buses, coaches, taxis, etc												
Not over 8 seats[1]	KCUJ	2.0	1.8	2.5	1.3	..	..	..	..	..	..	..
Over 8 seats	KCUK	3.1	3.6	4.2	5.2	6.5	6.6	7.4	8.0	7.5	6.8	7.8
Total	BBJZ	5.1	5.4	6.7	6.5	6.5	6.6	7.4	8.0	7.5	6.8	7.8
Heavy general goods and farmers[2]												
Goods vehicles: by weight	BBJY	28.7	32.8	41.1	48.0	45.5	41.8	49.1	48.3	50.4	48.6	44.9
Special concession group	BBKA	..	..	..	33.3	25.7	21.7	15.2	17.3	16.9	19.8	23.1
Other licensed vehicles	KCUM	1.6	1.4	1.3	1.0	1.0	1.5	1.5	1.5	1.2	1.2	1.2
Special vehicles group	DMNR	..	..	..	3.3	8.1	8.6	7.6	7.6	6.5	7.0	7.2
Exempt from license duty												
Crown vehicles	KCUN	3.7	3.1	4.1	3.3	1.2	0.7	1.1	1.1	1.0	1.0	1.4
All other exempt vehicles[3]	KCUO	78.7	89.4	104.3	118.1	139.1	150.7	146.6	170.4	173.9	166.5	166.1
Total	KCUP	82.3	92.4	108.4	121.4	140.3	151.4	147.7	171.6	174.9	167.5	167.5

1 From 1 July 1995 separate taxation of public transport vehicles with 8 or fewer seats was abolished. After this date new vehicles of this type were registered as PLG.
2 Until June 1995 included Agricultural vans and Lorries and Showman's goods vehicles licensed to draw trailers. From 1st July 1995 separate taxation group for Farmers and Showman were abolished.

3 Between 1980 and 30 June 1995 electric vehicles were exempt from duty. From 1 July 1995 electric vehicles pay VED as part of the special concession group.

Source: Department for Transport: 020 7944 3077

15.10 Driving test pass rates: by sex and type of vehicle licence
Great Britain

Percentages

		1989 /90	1991 /92	1996 /97	1997 /98	1998 /99	1999 /00	2000 /01	2001 /02	2002 /03
Males										
Motorcycle	JTRB	72	69	69	70	69	67	68	67	66
Car	JTRC	58	57	50	52	51	48	48	47	47
Bus	JTTG	..	..	50	48	48	49	47	46	44
Lorry	JTTH	..	..	49	53	52	53	53	50	50
All males	JTTI	..	..	..	..	..	51	51	50	49
Females										
Motorcycle	JTTJ	68	63	58	65	63	55	56	55	54
Car	JTTK	47	46	40	43	42	40	40	40	40
Bus	JTTL	..	..	40	49	47	46	45	40	40
Lorry	JTTM	..	..	37	53	50	49	53	47	46
All females	JTTN	..	..	..	..	..	40	41	41	40
All										
Motorcycle	JTTO	..	..	68	69	68	66	66	66	65
Car	JTTP	..	..	45	47	46	44	44	43	43
Bus	JTTQ	..	..	49	45	48	49	47	45	44
Lorry	JTTR	..	..	47	53	52	53	52	50	49
All persons	JTTS	..	..	..	..	..	46	46	46	45

Source: Driving Standards Agency 0115 901 2873

15.11 Private motoring: full car driving licence holders by age and sex
Great Britain

Percentages

	Age							Estimated number of licence holders (millions)
	17-20	21-29	30-39	40-49	50-59	60-69	70 or over	
All adults								
1975/76	28	59	67	60	50	35	15	19.4
1985/86	33	63	74	71	60	47	27	24.3
1991/93	49	75	81	78	70	57	34	29.1
1996/98	43	73	82	82	76	64	38	30.4
1999/01	36	73	83	84	78	71	44	31.7
2002[1]	32	67	82	84	81	70	45	32.1
Males								
1975/76	36	78	85	83	75	58	32	13.4
1985/86	37	73	86	87	81	72	51	15.1
1991/93	58	84	90	88	87	80	59	17.1
1996/98	48	79	89	90	88	82	64	17.2
1999/01	41	81	89	91	88	86	69	17.6
2002[1]	34	74	88	91	89	85	68	17.7
Females								
1975/76	20	43	48	37	24	15	4	6.0
1985/86	29	54	62	56	41	24	11	9.2
1991/93	40	68	73	68	54	37	17	12.1
1996/98	38	68	75	73	63	48	20	13.2
1999/01	31	66	77	77	69	57	25	14.0
2002[1]	31	60	77	79	74	56	28	14.4

1 See chapter text. Data are provisional.

Source: Department for Transport: 020 7944 3097

15.12 Private motoring: households with regular use of cars[1]
Great Britain

Percentages

	No car	One car	Two cars	Three or more cars	Total (millions)
	ZCGA	ZCGB	ZCGC	ZCGD	ZCGE
1991	32	45	19	4	22.4
1992	32	45	20	4	22.6
1993	31	45	20	4	22.9
1994	32	45	20	4	23.1
1995	30	45	21	4	23.3
1996	30	45	21	4	23.5
1997	30	45	21	5	23.7
1998	28	44	23	5	23.9
1999	28	44	22	5	24.1
2000	27	45	23	5	24.4
2001	27	46	23	5	..

	No car	One car	Two or more cars	Total
Government Office Regions, 2001				
Great Britain	27	46	28	100
North East	35	43	22	100
North West	29	46	25	100
Yorkshire and the Humber	32	45	23	100
East Midlands	23	47	30	100
West Midlands	25	46	29	100
East	20	46	34	100
London	34	46	20	100
South East	18	45	37	100
South West	19	47	35	100
England	26	46	29	100
Wales	26	47	27	100
Scotland	35	45	20	100

	No car	One car	Two or more cars	Total
Area type, 1999/01				
London	37	45	18	100
Metropolitan areas	38	42	20	100
Other urban areas with population:				
Over 250,000	32	47	21	100
25,000 - 250,000	27	48	25	100
10,000 - 25,000	23	48	29	100
3,000 - 10,000	21	49	30	100
Rural areas	15	47	38	100
Great Britain	28	47	25	100

1 Includes cars and light vans normally available to the household.

Sources: Office for National Statistics;
Department for Transport 020 7944 3097

15.13 Vehicles with current licences[1]
Northern Ireland

Numbers

		1992	1993	1994	1995	1996[2]	1997	1998	1999	2000	2001[3]	2002
Private cars, etc	KNKA	516 194	515 185	514 760	521 610	540 083	575 923	584 706	608 316	615 180	644 968	666 731
Cycles and tricycles	KNKB	9 023	8 634	8 775	9 142	10 026	10 932	11 663	13 087	14 116	15 205	17 598
Public road passenger vehicles:												
Taxis up to 4 seats	KNKD	494	462	623	739	..	..	..	..	..	..	..
Buses, coaches, over 4 seats	KNKE	2 250	2 217	2 455	1 353	2 090	2 144	2 175	2 204	2 266	2 315	2 322
Total	KNKC	2 744	2 679	3 078	2 092	2 090	2 144	2 175	2 204	2 266	2 315	2 322
General (HGV) goods vehicles:	KNKF	14 286	14 576	14 810	16 338	17 401	18 172	18 312	17 075	17 864	19 415	20 244
Farmers' goods vehicles[4]	KNKJ	5 315	5 498	5 904	..	..	..	..	..	..	..	..
Agricultural tractors and engines, etc[4]	KNKM	6 892	7 201	7 317	9 074	5 911	6 378	5 906	5 505	5 048	4 901	5 731
Other	KNKN	343	329	354	1 257	1 019	1 188	1 193	1 446	1 287	1 366	1 347
Vehicles exempt from duty:												
Government owned	KNKP	5 004	4 828	4 818	3 872	3 753	3 705	3 785	4 032	3 822	6 427	6 383
Other:												
Ambulances	KNKQ	97	101	104	250	371	389	425	417	452	318	299
Fire engines	KNKR	251	205	194	301	292	291	285	286	290	181	174
Other exempt[5]	KNKS	18 163	27 089	35 837	47 626	58 340	64 447	66 981	68 277	70 405	72 209	73 648
Total	KNKO	23 515	32 223	40 953	52 049	62 756	68 832	71 476	73 012	74 969	79 135	80 504
Total	KNKT	578 312	586 325	595 951	611 562	639 286	683 569	695 431	720 645	730 730	767 305	794 477

1 Licences current at any time during the quarter ended December.
2 Due to a revision of taxation classes, 1996 data are not directly comparable with previous years.
3 Taxation classes have been revised from 2001.
4 Owned by a farmer and available for hauling produce and requisites for his farm. From 1 July 1995 farmers goods taxation classes have been abolished

5 Changes in the Mobility Allowance (DSS) have contributed to the increase in Other exempt.

Source: Driver and Vehicle Licensing, Northern Ireland: 028 7034 1461

15.14 New vehicles registrations
Northern Ireland

Numbers

		1992	1993	1994	1995	1996	1997	1998	1999	2000	2001	2002
Private cars, etc	KNLA	62 777	65 360	70 765	73 718	77 817	83 968	91 141	89 078	84 973	88 592	83 402
Cycles and tricycles	KNLB	1 993	1 885	1 943	2 362	2 803	3 376	4 307	5 310	6 010	5 591	5 596
Public road passenger vehicles	KNLC	551	466	1 143	622	724	714	486	568	565	451	439
Goods vehicles:												
General haulage vehicles[1]:												
Under 3.5 tonnes	KNLH	6 236	6 468	6 908	7 357	7 232	8 468	10 107	11 054	12 617	13 274	12 007
3.5 tonnes and over	KNLJ	2 471	2 593	2 668	2 935	3 492	3 521	3 572	3 697	3 502	4 534	3 669
Agricultural tractors[2]	KNLM	1 184	1 658	1 558	1 619	1 292	1 364	971	987	1 313	301	1
Vehicles exempt from duty	KNLR	2 463	4 550	6 423	8 333	10 520	10 885	10 718	11 083	10 789	12 126	12 515
General haulage and special types	JTAG	..	..	..	..	..	..	..	..	..	..	15
Total	KNLS	77 675	82 980	91 408	96 946	103 880	112 296	121 302	121 777	119 769	124 869	117 644

1 Unladen weight.
2 Agricultural tractors driven on public roads. From April 2001 tractors are exempt.

Source: Driver and Vehicle Licensing, Northern Ireland: 028 7034 1461

15.15 Local bus services: passenger journeys by area

Millions

		1991 /92	1992 /93	1993 /94	1994 /95	1995 /96	1996 /97	1997 /98	1998 /99	1999 /00	2000 /01	2001 /02
Great Britain	ZCET	4 665	4 480	4 385	4 420	4 383	4 350	4 330	4 248	4 281	4 309	4 347
London	KILS	1 149	1 129	1 117	1 167	1 205	1 242	1 294	1 279	1 307	1 359	1 434
English Metropolitan Counties	KILT	1 478	1 383	1 337	1 331	1 292	1 246	1 232	1 195	1 162	1 165	1 150
English Shire Counties	KILU	1 333	1 307	1 274	1 277	1 265	1 265	1 247	1 246	1 263	1 236	1 219
All outside London	ZCES	3 516	3 351	3 268	3 253	3 178	3 108	3 036	2 970	2 973	2 949	2 913
England	ZCER	3 961	3 819	3 727	3 775	3 762	3 753	3 773	3 719	3 732	3 760	3 802
Scotland	KILV	571	532	525	513	494	467	438	413	434	435	441
Wales	KILW	133	129	133	132	127	130	120	116	114	113	104

Source: Department for Transport 020 7944 3076

15.16 Local bus services: fare indices by area
Current prices

Index 1995=100

		1992 /93	1993 /94	1994 /95	1995 /96	1996 /97	1997 /98	1998 /99	1999 /00	2000 /01	2001 /02	2002 /03
Great Britain	KNEU	88.4	92.4	96.7	101.2	106.3	112.0	117.1	122.0	126.4	130.6	134.5
London	KNEP	84.2	90.9	96.2	101.1	105.4	109.3	113.7	117.2	117.2	115.5	114.8
English Metropolitan Counties	KILD	88.6	92.9	96.4	101.5	106.9	113.3	118.7	124.6	129.9	137.4	142.7
English Shire Counties	KILE	90.4	93.1	97.0	101.1	106.0	111.5	116.7	122.0	128.6	135.1	141.6
All outside London	ZCEQ	89.4	92.8	96.8	101.2	106.6	112.8	118.2	123.4	129.2	135.3	140.7
England	ZCEP	88.3	92.5	96.7	101.2	106.1	111.4	116.5	121.5	125.9	130.3	134.2
Scotland	KILF	88.2	91.3	96.9	100.8	108.0	116.5	121.8	125.3	129.9	131.8	134.5
Wales	KILG	90.4	93.8	97.4	100.7	104.4	110.1	116.3	122.2	127.5	133.5	139.5
Retail Prices Index (1995=100)	KNEV	93.3	94.9	97.5	100.7	103.1	106.5	109.9	111.6	114.9	116.6	119.1

Source: Department for Transport 020 7944 3076

15.17 Road accident casualties : by road user type and severity
Great Britain

Numbers

		1992	1993	1994	1995	1996	1997	1998	1999	2000	2001	2002
Child pedestrians:												
Killed	ZCDH	180	165	160	132	131	138	103	107	107	107	79
Killed or seriously injured	KIJS	4 901	4 231	4 610	4 400	4 132	3 954	3 737	3 457	3 226	3 144	2 828
All severities	ZCDI	20 124	18 250	19 263	18 590	18 510	18 407	17 971	16 876	16 184	15 819	14 231
Adult pedestrians:												
Killed	ZCDJ	1 163	1 072	953	897	858	835	803	760	750	719	696
Killed or seriously injured	KIJT	9 125	8 260	8 114	7 716	7 300	6 925	6 592	6 221	6 112	5 920	5 803
All severities	ZCDK	30 354	28 750	28 129	27 178	26 827	26 223	25 827	24 806	24 481	24 758	24 553
Child pedal cyclists:												
Killed	ZCDL	48	37	42	48	54	33	32	36	27	25	22
Killed or seriously injured	KIJU	1 195	1 146	1 234	1 249	1 231	1 016	915	950	758	674	594
All severities	ZCDM	7 725	7 386	8 075	8 133	8 217	7 899	6 930	7 920	6 260	5 451	4 809
Adult pedal cyclists:												
Killed	ZCDN	156	148	129	164	148	150	126	135	98	113	108
Killed or seriously injured	KIJV	2 752	2 598	2 710	2 673	2 517	2 542	2 345	2 172	1 954	2 004	1 856
All severities	ZCDO	16 488	16 115	16 097	16 140	15 778	16 181	15 326	14 834	13 630	13 663	12 298
Motorcyclists[1] and passengers:												
Killed	ZCDP	469	427	444	445	440	509	498	547	605	569	609
Killed or seriously injured	ZCDQ	7 338	6 882	6 666	6 615	6 208	6 446	6 442	6 908	7 374	6 595	7 500
All severities	BMDH	26 891	25 094	24 354	23 524	23 133	24 492	24 610	26 192	28 212	24 164	28 353
Car drivers and passengers:												
Killed	ZCDS	1 978	1 760	1 764	1 749	1 806	1 795	1 696	1 687	1 665	1 749	1 747
Killed or seriously injured	ZCDT	25 124	22 833	23 892	23 461	24 048	23 191	21 676	20 368	19 719	19 424	18 728
All severities	ZCDU	185 662	187 479	195 154	194 027	205 336	211 448	210 474	205 735	206 799	202 802	197 425
Bus/coach drivers and passengers:												
Killed	ZCDV	19	35	21	35	11	14	18	11	15	14	19
Killed or seriously injured	KCUZ	655	725	815	836	695	601	631	611	578	562	551
All severities	ZCDW	9 103	9 307	10 090	9 278	9 345	9 439	9 839	10 252	10 088	9 884	9 005
LGV drivers and passengers:												
Killed	ZCDX	117	91	64	69	61	64	67	65	66	64	70
Killed or seriously injured	ZCDY	1 308	1 082	1 101	1 106	989	928	949	867	813	811	780
All severities	ZCDZ	8 129	7 420	7 558	7 200	7 215	7 476	7 672	7 124	7 007	7 304	7 007
HGV drivers and passengers:												
Killed	ZCEA	70	59	41	57	63	45	60	52	55	54	63
Killed or seriously injured	ZCEB	659	635	571	635	555	573	560	540	571	500	524
All severities	ZCEC	3 326	3 333	3 370	3 331	3 245	3 302	3 444	3 484	3 597	3 388	3 178
All road users:[2]												
Killed	BMDC	4 229	3 814	3 650	3 621	3 598	3 599	3 421	3 423	3 409	3 450	3 431
Killed or seriously injured	ZCEE	53 485	48 834	50 190	49 154	48 097	46 583	44 255	42 545	41 564	40 560	39 407
All severities	BMDA	310 753	306 135	315 359	310 687	320 578	327 803	325 212	320 310	320 283	313 309	302 605

1 Includes mopeds and scooters.
2 Includes other motor or non-motor vehicle users, and unknown road user
  type and casualty age.

Source: Department for Transport 020 7944 3078

15.18 Freight transport by road: goods moved by goods vehicles over 3.5 tonnes[1]
Great Britain

Billion tonne kilometres

		1992	1993	1994	1995	1996	1997	1998	1999	2000	2001	2002
By mode of working												
Mainly public haulage	KNND	86.4	93.2	100.8	106.5	109.1	112.2	114.3	110.9	113.0	114.7	110.6
Mainly own account	KNNC	34.9	35.4	37.0	37.2	37.7	37.4	37.6	38.3	37.5	34.7	39.2
All modes	KNNB	121.3	128.6	137.8	143.7	146.8	149.6	151.9	149.2	150.5	149.4	149.8
By gross weight of vehicle												
Rigid vehicles:												
3.5-17 tonnes	ZCIL	19.0	18.7	19.9	18.7	19.5	19.2	17.8	17.9	15.8	13.1	11.9
17-25 tonnes	ZCIM	6.5	6.6	6.1	5.6	5.3	4.7	4.2	4.3	4.8	5.7	6.3
25 tonnes and over	ZCIN	10.7	11.3	12.4	13.3	13.5	14.3	14.7	15.3	15.4	15.6	17.3
All rigids	ZCIO	36.2	36.5	38.4	37.5	38.3	38.1	36.6	37.5	36.0	34.5	35.6
Articulated vehicles:												
3.5-33 tonnes	ZCIP	16.7	16.5	16.9	15.9	15.9	14.3	14.4	14.0	14.0	12.8	9.9
33 tonnes and over	ZCIQ	68.4	75.6	82.5	90.2	92.6	97.1	100.9	97.7	100.4	102.1	104.4
All articulated vehicles	ZCIR	85.0	92.1	99.4	106.1	108.5	111.4	115.3	111.7	114.4	114.9	114.3
All vehicles												
3.5-25 tonnes	ZCIS	26.3	25.9	26.6	24.7	25.3	24.3	22.5	22.7	21.3	19.3	18.7
25 tonnes and over	KNNG	95.0	102.7	111.2	119.0	121.5	125.2	129.4	126.5	129.2	130.1	131.1
All weights	ZCIT	121.3	128.6	137.8	143.7	146.8	149.6	151.9	149.2	150.5	149.4	149.8
By commodity												
Food, drink and tobacco	ZCIU	33.2	35.9	36.5	37.5	39.3	40.8	42.5	41.5	44.3	41.4	43.1
Wood, timber and cork	ZCIV	2.6	3.1	3.3	3.2	3.8	3.5	3.6	3.8	3.7	3.9	3.8
Fertiliser	ZCIW	1.4	1.5	1.3	1.4	1.5	1.3	1.2	1.4	1.2	1.2	1.2
Crude minerals	ZCIX	12.7	12.6	14.1	13.5	13.5	13.6	13.3	12.7	12.4	13.0	13.9
Ores	ZCIY	1.2	1.6	1.4	1.5	1.3	1.7	1.1	1.3	1.2	1.2	1.1
Crude materials	ZCIZ	2.0	1.7	2.0	1.9	2.1	2.1	2.6	2.6	2.6	2.3	2.7
Coal and coke	ZCJA	3.5	3.1	2.9	2.7	2.5	2.7	2.0	2.2	1.5	2.1	1.5
Petrol and petroleum products	ZCJB	4.5	5.0	5.1	5.7	6.1	5.8	5.2	5.0	6.4	5.8	5.2
Chemicals	ZCJC	6.8	7.2	8.1	7.4	7.7	8.2	7.9	7.4	6.8	7.2	6.5
Building materials	ZCJD	8.0	9.3	10.0	10.7	9.6	11.1	10.7	10.6	10.6	11.7	10.9
Iron and steel products	ZCJE	6.5	6.4	6.7	7.8	7.2	7.9	7.7	6.8	6.8	5.7	5.3
Other metal products[2]	ZCJF	2.0	1.9	2.0	1.7	1.7	1.5	1.7	1.7	1.7	1.4	1.5
Machinery and transport equipment	ZCJG	6.0	5.7	6.8	7.4	7.7	8.4	9.1	8.7	9.1	8.9	8.5
Miscellaneous manufactures[2]	ZCJH	12.0	12.4	13.4	13.3	14.2	14.2	15.9	15.7	15.1	15.4	16.2
Miscellaneous transactions[3]	ZCJI	19.0	21.3	24.3	27.8	28.4	26.8	27.5	27.9	27.1	28.2	28.4
All commodities	ZCJJ	121.3	128.6	137.8	143.7	146.8	149.6	151.9	149.2	150.5	149.4	149.8

1 Rigid vehicles or articulated vehicles (tractive unit and trailer) with gross
  vehicle weight over 3.5 tonnes.
2 Includes not elsewhere specified.
3 Includes not elsewhere specified and commodity not known.

Source: Department for Transport 020 7944 3093

15.19 Freight transport by road: goods lifted by goods vehicles over 3.5 tonnes[1]
Great Britain

Million tonnes

		1992	1993	1994	1995	1996	1997	1998	1999	2000	2001	2002
By mode of working												
Mainly public haulage	ZCJK	843	911	980	987	1 011	1 044	1 041	991	1 038	1 052	1 019
Mainly own account	ZCJL	620	612	618	622	618	599	589	576	556	529	608
All modes	ZCJM	1 463	1 523	1 597	1 609	1 628	1 643	1 630	1 567	1 593	1 581	1 627
By gross weight of vehicle												
Rigid vehicles:												
3.5-17 tonnes	ZCJN	315	322	317	298	306	294	268	254	229	203	188
17-25 tonnes	ZCJO	219	211	202	162	133	120	106	86	87	86	90
25 tonnes and over	ZCJP	282	307	332	373	371	380	401	408	424	443	491
All rigids	ZCJQ	817	840	852	833	811	793	776	748	741	733	768
Articulated vehicles:												
3.5-33 tonnes	ZCJR	142	144	142	139	138	124	125	113	107	97	81
33 tonnes and over	ZCJS	505	540	604	637	679	726	729	706	746	751	778
All articulated vehicles	ZCJT	646	683	746	776	817	850	854	819	852	848	859
All vehicles												
3.5-25 tonnes	ZCJU	544	541	527	467	447	419	382	346	325	294	283
25 tonnes and over	ZCJV	919	982	1 070	1 142	1 181	1 224	1 248	1 221	1 268	1 287	1 343
All weights	ZCJW	1 463	1 523	1 597	1 609	1 628	1 643	1 630	1 567	1 593	1 581	1 627
By commodity												
Food, drink and tobacco	ZCJX	290	300	302	308	326	342	346	333	346	321	339
Wood, timber and cork	ZCJY	20	25	24	24	27	26	27	28	26	28	28
Fertiliser	ZCJZ	13	12	10	11	13	10	9	11	10	9	11
Crude minerals	ZCKA	327	310	355	319	320	329	327	297	308	298	333
Ores	ZCKB	15	21	18	18	18	25	18	20	16	16	17
Crude materials	ZCKC	17	14	16	16	18	17	20	20	18	20	21
Coal and coke	ZCKD	55	48	42	34	32	37	26	28	22	21	17
Petrol and petroleum products	ZCKE	63	67	68	71	75	73	61	61	75	74	59
Chemicals	ZCKF	42	47	51	50	51	53	53	47	49	50	41
Building materials	ZCKG	136	153	156	161	142	156	161	159	165	165	167
Iron and steel products	ZCKH	46	45	47	54	52	55	54	48	49	44	39
Other metal products[2]	ZCKI	18	20	17	17	15	16	18	17	16	14	14
Machinery and transport equipment	ZCKJ	47	46	57	61	59	71	73	67	69	70	68
Miscellaneous manufactures[2]	ZCKK	75	81	84	85	88	90	96	91	97	97	105
Miscellaneous transactions[3]	ZCKL	300	332	351	379	393	343	342	340	328	353	367
All commodities	ZCKM	1 463	1 523	1 597	1 609	1 628	1 643	1 630	1 567	1 593	1 581	1 627

1 Rigid vehicles or articulated vehicles (tractive unit and trailer) with gross vehicle weight over 3.5 tonnes.
2 Includes not elsewhere specified.
3 Includes not elsewhere specified and commodity not known.

Source: Department for Transport 020 7944 3093

15.20 Rail systems summary

		1992 /93	1993 /94	1994 /95	1995 /96	1996 /97	1997 /98	1998 /99	1999[1] /00	2000[1] /01	2001[1] /02	2002 /03
Passenger journeys (Millions)												
National Rail network[2]	ZCKN	770	740	735	761	801	846	892	931	957	960	976
London Underground	KNOE	728	735	764	784	772	832	866	927	970	953	942
Docklands Light Railway	ZCKO	7	8	12	14	17	21	28	31	38	41	46
Glasgow Underground	ZCKP	14	14	15	14	14	14	15	15	14	14	13
Tyne and Wear Metro	ZCKQ	39	39	37	36	35	35	34	33	33	33	37
West Midlands Metro[3]	ZCKR	..	..	..	..	..	..	..	5	5	5	5
Croydon Tramlink[4]	GEOE	..	..	..	..	..	..	..	..	15	18	19
Manchester Metrolink[5]	ZCKS	8	11	12	13	13	14	13	14	17	18	19
Stagecoach Supertram (Sheffield)	ZCKT	..	..	2	5	8	9	10	11	11	11	12
All rail	ZCKU	1 566	1 547	1 577	1 627	1 660	1 771	1 858	1 967	2 061	2 054	2 068
of which: light rail[6]	GENZ	54	58	63	68	73	79	85	94	120	127	136
Passenger receipts (£ million at current prices)												
National Rail network[2]	KNDL	2 154	2 193	2 171	2 379	2 573	2 821	3 089	3 368	3 413	3 548	3 663
London Underground	KNOA	589	637	718	765	797	899	977	1 058	1 129	1 151	1 138
Docklands Light Railway	ZCKV	3	5	6	9	12	14	20	22	29	32	36
Glasgow Underground	ZCKW	6	7	7	8	8	9	9	10	11	10	10
Tyne and Wear Metro	ZCKX	19	19	19	20	21	22	23	24	24	25	29
West Midlands Metro[3]	ZCKY	..	..	..	..	..	..	..	..	3	4	5
Croydon Tramlink[4]	GEOF	..	..	..	..	..	..	..	..	12	13	15
Manchester Metrolink[5]	ZCKZ	7	10	10	11	13	14	..	..	18	20	21
Stagecoach Supertram (Sheffield)	ZCLA	..	..	2	4	5	6	6	7	7	8	10
All rail	ZCLB	2 778	2 871	2 933	3 196	3 429	3 785	..	..	4 646	4 810	4 926
of which: light rail[6]	GEOA	29	34	37	44	51	56	..	..	93	102	115
Passenger kilometres (Millions)												
National Rail network[2]	KNDZ	31 700	30 400	28 700	30 000	32 100	34 700	36 300	38 454	38 218	39 104	39 700
London Underground	KNOI	5 758	5 814	6 051	6 337	6 153	6 479	6 716	7 171	7 470	7 451	7 367
Docklands Light Railway	ZCLC	33	39	55	70	86	103	144	172	200	207	232
Glasgow Underground	ZCLD	39	41	43	41	40	45	47	47	46	44	43
Tyne and Wear Metro	ZCLE	271	273	271	261	254	249	238	230	229	238	275
West Midlands Metro[3]	ZCLF	..	..	..	..	..	..	..	50	56	50	50
Croydon Tramlink[4]	GEOG	..	..	..	..	..	..	..	..	96	99	100
Manchester Metrolink[5]	ZCLG	53	73	79	81	86	88	117	126	152	161	167
Stagecoach Supertram (Sheffield)	ZCLH	..	..	8	20	29	34	35	37	38	39	40
All rail	ZCLI	37 854	36 640	35 206	36 810	38 748	41 698	43 597	46 287	46 505	47 394	47 974
of which: light rail[6]	GEOB	357	385	412	432	455	474	534	615	771	795	864
Route kilometres open for passenger traffic (Numbers)												
National Rail network[2]	ZCLJ	14 317	14 357	14 359	15 002	15 034	15 024	15 038	15 038	15 042	15 042	15 042
London Underground	ZCLK	394	394	392	392	392	392	392	408	408	408	408
Docklands Light Railway	ZCLM	14	14	22	22	22	22	22	27	27	27	27
Glasgow Underground	ZCLN	11	11	11	11	11	11	11	11	11	11	11
Tyne and Wear Metro	ZCLO	59	59	59	59	59	59	59	59	59	77	78
West Midlands Metro[3]	ZCLP	..	..	..	..	..	..	..	21	20	20	20
Croydon Tramlink[4]	GEOH	..	..	..	..	..	..	..	..	28	28	28
Manchester Metrolink[5]	ZCLQ	31	31	31	31	31	31	31	39	39	39	39
Stagecoach Supertram (Sheffield)	ZCLR	..	7	22	29	29	29	29	29	29	29	29
All rail	ZCLS	14 826	14 873	14 896	15 546	15 578	15 568	15 582	15 632	15 663	15 682	15 682
of which: light rail[6]	GEOC	104	111	134	141	141	141	141	175	202	221	221
Stations served (Numbers)												
National Rail network[2]	ZCLT	2 468	2 493	2 489	2 497	2 498	2 495	2 499	2 503	2 508	2 508	2 508
London Underground	KNOO	246	245	245	245	245	245	246	253	253	253	253
Docklands Light Railway	ZCLU	16	27	27	28	28	29	29	34	34	34	34
Glasgow Underground	ZCLV	15	15	15	15	15	15	15	15	15	15	15
Tyne and Wear Metro	ZCLW	46	46	46	46	46	46	46	46	46	58	58
West Midlands Metro[3]	ZCLX	..	..	..	..	..	..	..	23	23	23	23
Croydon Tramlink[4]	GEOI	..	..	..	..	..	..	..	..	38	38	38
Manchester Metrolink[5]	ZCLY	26	26	26	26	26	26	26	36	36	36	37
Stagecoach Supertram (Sheffield)	ZCLZ	..	9	37	45	45	46	47	47	47	48	48
All rail	ZCLL	2 817	2 861	2 885	2 902	2 903	2 902	2 908	2 957	3 000	3 013	3 014
of which: light rail[6]	GSOC	88	108	136	145	145	147	148	186	224	237	238

1 National Rail passenger journeys and passenger kilometres revised by the Strategic Rail Authority.
2 Franchised train operating companies from February 1996 following rail privatisation.
3 West Midlands Metro opened in 1999.
4 Croydon tramlink opened in 2000.
5 Transfer of 20 stations from the national rail network to Manchester Metrolink.
6 Light rail excludes London Underground and Glasgow Underground.

Sources: Railtrack; Strategic Rail Authority; Transport for London; Passenger Transport Executives and operators

15.21 National railways freight[1]
Great Britain

Billion tonne kilometres

		1992/93	1993/94	1994/95	1995/96	1996/97	1997/98	1998/99	1999/00	2000/01	2001/02	2002/03
Freight moved by commodity												
Coal	ZCGG	5.4	3.9	3.3	3.6	3.9	4.4	4.5	4.8	4.8	6.2	5.7
Metals	ZCGH	2.3	2.1	1.7	1.7	..	..	2.1	2.2	2.1	2.4	2.7
Construction	ZCGI	2.5	2.3	2.5	2.3	..	..	2.1	2.0	2.4	2.8	2.6
Oil and petroleum	ZCGJ	2.0	1.9	1.8	1.8	..	..	1.6	1.5	1.4	1.2	1.1
Other traffic	ZCGK	3.3	3.5	3.8	3.9	11.3	12.5	7.1	7.6	7.4	7.0	6.5
All traffic	VOXD	15.5	13.8	13.0	13.3	15.1	16.9	17.3	18.2	18.1	19.4	18.7
Freight lifted by commodity												
Coal	ZCGL	67.9	48.9	42.5	45.2	52.2	50.3	45.3	44.3	45.7	46.1	40.7
Metals	ZCGM	15.9	15.8	16.9	15.1	..	..	..	..	..	..	..
Construction	ZCGN	15.8	16.1	16.8	11.5	..	..	..	..	..	..	..
Oil and petroleum	ZCGO	9.5	9.0	8.1	6.3	..	..	..	..	..	..	..
Other traffic	ZCGP	13.2	13.4	13.0	22.6	49.6	55.1	56.8	47.6	49.7	48.3	46.4
All traffic	VOXE	122.4	103.2	97.3	100.7	101.8	105.4	102.1	91.9	95.4	94.4	87.0

1 Because of changes in the way freight traffic has been estimated following privatisation, figures since 1996/97 are not strictly comparable with those or previous years. The series calculation was revised again from 1998/99 and from 1999/00 due to revisions from freight operators.

Source: Department for Transport: 020 7944 3094

15.22 Railways: permanent way and rolling stock
Northern Ireland
At end of year

Numbers

		1992	1993	1994	1995	1996	1997	1998	1999	2000	2001	2002
Length of road open for traffic[1] (km)	KNRA	332	330	331	333	335	335	335	335	356	334	334
Length of track open for traffic (km)												
Total	KNRB	553	504	503	506	506	505	526	526	547	480	480
Running lines	KNRC	500	463	462	464	464	464	484	484	505	464	464
Sidings (as single track)	KNRD	53	41	41	42	42	42	42	42	42	16	16
Locomotives												
Diesel-electrics	KNRE	9	9	11	11	8	6	5	6	6	6	6
Passenger carrying vehicles												
Total	KNRF	114	112	112	112	112	112	120	108	108	106	106
Rail motor vehicles:												
Diesel-electric, etc	KNRG	30	30	30	30	30	30	28	30	30	29	28
Trailer carriages:												
Total locomotive hauled	KNRH	28	28	28	28	28	28	38	21	21	25	22
Ordinary coaches	KNRI	26	26	26	26	26	26	36	19	19	23	20
Restaurant cars	KNRJ	2	2	2	2	2	2	2	2	2	2	2
Rail car trailers	KNRK	56	54	54	54	54	54	54	54	54	52	50
Rolling stock for maintenance and repair	KNRT	36	42	41	41	41	41	26	18	18	18	18

1 The total length of railroad open for traffic irrespective of the number of tracks comprising the road.

Source: Translink: 028 9089 9400

15.23 Operating statistics of railways
Northern Ireland

		Unit	1992	1993	1994	1995	1996	1997	1998	1999	2000	2001	2002
Maintenance of way and works													
Material used:													
Ballast	KNSA	Thousand m^2	30.2	16.0	33.2	22.5	27.0	51.3	38.5	40.0	47.0	80.0	40.0
Rails	KNSB	Thousand tonnes	2.26	2.00	1.80	1.76	2.12	0.37	2.50	3.00	3.50	2.50	1.00
Sleepers	KNSC	Thousands	31.23	14.60	22.40	22.90	27.50	5.10	32.00	30.00	40.00	50.00	5.00
Track renewed	KNSD	Km	14.00	16.00	12.00	16.00	20.00	2.40	22.50	7.00	29.00	15.00	5.00
New Track laid	KPGD	Km	..	..	3.2	2.5	–	–	–	–	21.0	–	–
Engine kilometres													
Total[1]	KNSE	Thousand Km	3 540	3 640	3 640	4 000	4 100	4 100	4 100	4 100	4 100	4 056	4 056
Train kilometres:													
Total	KNSF	"	3 210	3 210	3 210	3 570	3 670	3 670	3 670	3 670	3 670	3 626	3 626
Coaching	KNSG	"	3 206	3 206	3 206	3 566	3 666	3 666	3 666	3 666	3 666	3 622	3 622
Freight	KNSH	"	4	4	4	4	4	4	4	4	4	4	4

1 Including shunting, assisting, light, departmental, maintenance and repair.

Source: Translink: 028 9089 9400

15.24 Main output[1] of United Kingdom airlines

		1992	1993	1994	1995	1996	1997	1998	1999	2000	2001	2002
All services: total	KNTA	23 145	25 144	27 714	29 904	32 210	35 538	40 021	42 002	43 379	42 370	40 550
Percentage growth on previous year	KNTB	14.8	8.5	10.2	7.4	7.7	10.3	12.5	5.0	3.6	−2.4	−4.3
Scheduled services: total	KNTC	17 065	18 605	20 360	22 016	23 793	26 504	29 756	31 815	32 938	31 866	30 433
Percentage growth on previous year	KNTD	12.4	9.0	9.4	8.1	8.1	11.4	12.3	6.9	3.5	−3.3	−4.5
Non-scheduled services: total	KNTE	6 079	6 510	7 265	7 695	8 044	9 034	10 265	10 186	10 440	10 505	10 117
Percentage growth on previous year	KNTF	22.0	7.1	13.0	5.9	4.5	7.3	13.3	−0.7	4.1	0.6	−3.7

1 Available tonne kilometres (millions).

Source: Civil Aviation Authority: 020 7453 6246

15.25 Air traffic between the United Kingdom and abroad[1]

Thousands

		1992	1993	1994[2]	1995	1996	1997	1998	1999	2000	2001	2002
Flights												
United Kingdom airlines												
Scheduled services	KNUA	283.0	290.8	325.8	342.1	373.0	410.3	443.7	480.9	520.3	536.7	531.3
Non-scheduled services	KNUB	236.2	215.2	195.0	204.8	198.0	208.2	218.7	212.6	216.2	208.5	218.6
Overseas airlines[3]												
Scheduled services	KNUC	328.0	336.2	351.3	363.3	390.0	399.6	426.4	467.6	467.6	496.8	487.5
Non-scheduled services	KNUD	33.9	38.0	35.1	31.5	31.3	32.5	34.8	31.7	31.7	26.0	36.7
Total	KNUE	881.1	880.2	907.2	941.7	992.3	1 050.6	1 123.6	1 192.8	1 235.8	1 268.0	1 274.1
Passengers carried												
United Kingdom airlines												
Scheduled services	KNUF	27 138.8	29 798.2	32 578.0	34 934.7	37 902.2	41 854.7	46 747.7	50 148.5	54 522.8	53 591.7	54 360.0
Non-scheduled services	KNUG	23 347.6	24 777.1	19 501.0	20 484.5	26 304.4	28 699.5	31 616.6	32 603.8	33 185.9	34 009.1	33 935.7
Overseas airlines[3]												
Scheduled services	KNUH	29 240.9	31 163.4	35 134.5	34 568.5	36 992.1	39 900.7	42 554.5	46 628.0	46 627.9	51 107.8	51 317.6
Non-scheduled services	KNUI	3 222.6	3 638.0	3 509.5	4 244.2	4 416.3	4 413.0	4 569.7	4 156.5	4 156.5	3 966.1	3 956.3
Total	KNUJ	82 949.9	89 376.7	90 723.0	94 231.9	105 615.0	114 867.9	125 488.5	133 536.8	138 493.1	142 674.7	143 569.6

1 Excludes travel to and from the Channel Islands.
2 Due to the introduction of European licencing, off shore helicopter movements are no longer included in this figure.

3 Includes airlines of overseas UK Territories.

Source: Civil Aviation Authority: 020 7453 6246

15.26 Operations and traffic on scheduled services: revenue traffic
United Kingdom airlines[1]

		Unit	1992	1993	1994	1995	1996	1997	1998	1999	2000	2001	2002
All services													
Aircraft stage flights:													
Number	KNFA	Numbers	601 500	601 620	621 272	658 958	702 492	749 806	797 682	835 031	878 582	921 556	911 518
Average length	KNFB	Kilometres	916	971	1 023	1 032	1 047	1 079	1 111	1 134	1 156	1 138	1 149
Aircraft-kilometres flown	KNFC	Millions	551.2	584.3	663.2	679.9	735.3	809.2	886.3	946.9	1 016.3	1 048.6	1 047.1
Passengers uplifted	KNFD	"	38.2	40.1	43.9	47.5	51.1	56.3	61.7	65.4	70.3	69.7	72.2
Seat-kilometres used	KNFE	"	86 731.4	94 670.1	104 294.5	115 347.1	124 846.5	136 388.2	151 969.1	160 336.4	170 469.0	158 650.7	156 493.9
Cargo uplifted:[2]													
Total	KNFF	Tonnes	507 356	541 986	618 067	643 181	690 806	782 855	831 436	860 291	897 184	742 705	768 736
Tonne-kilometres used:		Millions											
Passenger	KNFH	"	8 135.2	8 905.3	9 789.2	11 171.5	12 189.6	13 287.2	14 754.9	15 517.7	16 507.0	15 258.0	15 035.1
Freight	KNFI	"	2 644.1	2 919.6	3 378.1	3 567.3	3 831.9	4 454.0	4 663.3	4 924.9	5 159.9	4 548.3	4 940.5
Mail	KNFJ	"	161.1	141.5	147.3	151.1	176.0	172.2	177.7	153.0	179.2	101.9	56.6
Total	KNFG	"	10 940.5	11 966.4	13 314.6	14 889.9	16 197.5	17 913.4	19 595.9	20 595.6	21 846.1	19 908.2	20 032.2
Domestic services													
Aircraft stage flights:													
Number	KNFK	Numbers	299 893	300 416	301 652	318 884	331 109	336 218	352 936	354 864	353 525	365 881	359 400
Average length	KNFL	Kilometres	305.7	311.3	314.8	317.0	320.0	330.0	333.1	337.0	343.5	350.3	350.0
Aircraft-kilometres flown	KNFM	Millions	91.6	93.5	94.9	101.1	105.8	111.0	117.6	119.6	121.4	128.2	126.0
Passengers uplifted	KNFN	"	11.6	12.1	13.0	14.0	15.0	15.9	16.6	17.1	18.0	18.2	19.8
Seat-kilometres used	KNFO	"	4 728.2	4 933.8	5 334.0	5 753.6	6 204.3	6 645.7	6 947.5	7 183.9	7 541.8	7 644.5	8 321.9
Cargo uplifted:[2]													
Total	KNFP	Tonnes	35 420	30 660	32 670	33 659	35 432	30 679	31 879	25 964	24 644	19 498	16 755
Tonne-kilometres used:		Millions											
Passenger	KNFR	"	387.4	405.2	417.3	485.0	527.8	568.9	592.6	609.9	640.2	648.5	702.8
Freight	KNFS	"	6.6	5.6	6.3	6.9	7.4	6.1	6.0	6.0	5.8	4.1	3.6
Mail	KNFT	"	7.0	6.5	6.7	6.6	6.4	6.0	6.0	4.0	3.7	3.5	2.8
Total	KNFQ	"	401.1	417.3	430.3	498.5	541.6	581.0	604.7	619.9	649.7	656.1	709.2
International services													
Aircraft stage flights:													
Number	KNFU	Numbers	301 607	301 204	319 620	339 714	371 400	413 588	444 746	480 167	525 057	555 675	552 118
Average length	KNFV	Kilometres	1 523	1 629	1 693	1 703	1 695	1 688	1 729	1 723	1 704	1 656	1 670
Aircraft-kilometres flown	KNFW	Millions	459.5	490.8	541.4	578.8	629.5	698.2	768.8	827.3	894.9	920.5	921.1
Passengers uplifted	KNFX	"	26.5	28.0	30.9	33.5	36.1	40.4	45.1	48.2	52.2	51.5	52.4
Seat-kilometres used	KNFY	"	82 003.1	89 736.3	98 960.5	109 593.4	118 642.2	129 742.5	145 021.6	153 152.5	162 927.2	151 005.5	148 172.1
Cargo uplifted:[2]													
Total	KNFZ	Tonnes	471 936	511 326	585 397	609 522	655 374	752 176	799 557	834 327	872 540	723 206	751 975
Tonne-kilometres used:		Millions											
Passenger	KNJX	"	7 747.8	8 500.1	9 352.3	10 686.4	11 661.9	12 718.2	14 162.3	14 908.0	15 867.0	14 609.5	14 331.6
Freight	KNJY	"	2 637.4	2 914.0	3 371.8	3 560.4	3 824.5	4 448.0	4 657.2	4 919.0	5 154.1	4 544.3	4 936.9
Mail	KNJZ	"	154.0	135.0	140.5	144.4	169.5	166.3	171.7	149.0	175.5	98.3	53.8
Total	KNJW	"	10 539.3	11 549.1	12 864.6	14 391.2	15 655.9	17 332.5	18 991.2	19 976.0	21 196.6	19 252.1	19 322.3

1 Includes services of British Airways and other UK private companies.
2 Cargo has been re-defined as freight and mail.

Source: Civil Aviation Authority: 020 7453 6246

15.27 Accidents on scheduled fixed wing passenger-carrying services[1,2]
United Kingdom airlines

	Number of fatal accidents	Passenger casualties		Crew casualties		Thousand aircraft stage flights per fatal accident	Million aircraft-kms. flown per fatal accident	Thousand passengers carried per passenger killed	Million passenger kms. flown per passenger killed	Fatal accidents		Passengers killed per hundred million passenger-kms.
		Killed	Seriously injured	Killed	Seriously injured					per 100 000 aircraft stage flights	per hundred million aircraft-kms.	
1950-54	7	194	9	28	4	107.4	61.8	46.1	50.1	0.93	1.62	2.00
1955-59	7	123	28	29	8	158.3	92.1	155.2	158.5	0.63	1.09	0.63
1960-64	5	104	35	21	6	303.7	182.2	373.4	390.6	0.33	0.55	0.26
1965-69	6	273	2	32	2	282.7	194.9	222.2	255.2	0.35	0.51	0.39
1970-74	2	167	5	14	2	889.5	737.1	464.3	657.7	0.11	0.14	0.15
1975-79	1	54	6	9	-	1 773.0	1 523.5	1 688.2	3 239.9	0.06	0.07	0.03
1980-84	-	-	4	-	1	-	-	-	-	-	-	-
1985-89	2	47	79	1	8	1 220.0	1 014.5	3031.0	6 262.9	0.08	0.10	0.02
1990-94	-	-	1	-	9	-	-	-	-	-	-	-
1995-99	1	9	1	3	3	3 699.9	4 026.0	31 265.6	76 539.4	0.03	0.02	0.001
	KCVN	KCVO	KCVP	KCVQ	KCVR							
2000	-	-	1	-	-	-	-	-	-	-	-	-
2001	-	-	-	-	-	-	-	-	-	-	-	-
2002	-	-	-	-	3	-	-	-	-	-	-	-

1 Excluding accidents involving the deaths of third parties only.
2 Following a review of historical data for this table, some revisions have been made to earlier years.

Source: Civil Aviation Authority: 01293 573346

15.28 Activity at civil aerodromes
United Kingdom[1]

		1992	1993	1994	1995	1996	1997	1998	1999	2000	2001	2002
Movement of civil aircraft (Thousands)												
Commercial Transport	KNQC	1 448	1 487	1 552	1 615	1 686	1 764	1 871	1 959	2 045	2 095	2 094
Other	KNQD	112	109	112	124	128	143	162	159	159	150	120
Total	KNQB	1 561	1 596	1 664	1 739	1 814	1 907	2 033	2 118	2 204	2 245	2 214
Non-commercial	KNQE	1 321	1 523	1 684	1 809	1 281	1 330	1 343	1 263	1 186	1 207	1 100
Total	KNQA	2 881	3 119	3 348	3 548	3 095	3 237	3 376	3 381	3 390	3 452	3 314
Passengers handled												
Terminal	KNQG	106 123	112 277	122 159	129 369	135 810	146 657	158 856	168 363	179 885	181 231	188 761
Transit	KNQH	1 681	1 620	1 565	1 490	1 486	1 405	1 226	1 156	1 167	1 087	1 054
Total	KNQF	107 804	113 897	123 724	130 859	137 296	148 062	160 082	169 519	181 052	182 318	189 815
Commercial freight handled[2] (Tonnes)												
Set down	KNQJ	658 185	696 056	788 995	849 226	886 507	981 861	1 072 127	1 135 065	1 174 635	1 093 142	1 124 026
Picked up	KNQK	580 213	680 256	799 793	854 267	885 080	960 859	1 008 358	1 053 902	1 139 292	1 052 379	1 071 407
Total	KNQI	1 238 398	1 376 312	1 588 788	1 703 493	1 771 587	1 942 720	2 080 485	2 188 967	2 313 927	2 145 521	2 195 433
Mail handled												
Set down	KNQM	78 411	85 806	70 776	72 376	80 937	88 366	88 766	92 974	101 743	98 690	90 738
Picked up	KNQN	95 468	101 097	89 780	93 700	105 964	115 066	113 993	114 752	123 352	117 389	99 747
Total	KNQL	173 879	186 903	160 556	166 076	186 901	203 432	202 759	207 726	225 095	216 079	190 485

1 See chapter text.
2 With effect from 2001, passengers, freight and mail handled; excludes traffic carried on air taxi operations.

Source: Civil Aviation Authority: 020 7453 6258

15.29 United Kingdom ports: foreign, coastwise and one-port traffic

Thousand tonnes

		1991	1992	1993	1994	1995	1996	1997	1998	1999	2000	2001
Inwards:												
Foreign												
Liquid bulk	JURC	64 144	64 640	68 824	63 512	58 512	59 309	61 060	61 346	56 528	70 534	74 495
Other traffic	JURD	117 969	117 946	120 633	126 575	131 789	133 393	144 634	147 933	147 053	150 147	163 869
All traffic	HHEL	182 112	182 586	189 457	190 087	190 302	192 702	205 694	209 279	203 581	220 681	238 364
Coastwise												
Liquid bulk	JURE	43 713	40 134	41 893	44 178	48 393	52 354	49 981	51 514	48 164	36 999	37 008
Other traffic	JURF	17 980	18 060	17 540	19 102	19 504	17 563	17 526	19 222	18 811	20 803	20 268
All traffic	HHEO	61 693	58 194	59 433	63 279	67 898	69 917	67 508	70 736	66 975	57 801	57 276
One-port												
Liquid bulk	JURG	13 446	14 107	10 063	13 725	10 848	10 861	6 871	10 587	20 220	24 965	18 245
Other traffic	JURH	16 397	14 871	13 739	14 851	15 878	14 244	14 974	15 498	16 187	12 896	15 005
All traffic	HHER	29 843	28 978	23 802	28 577	26 726	25 105	21 844	26 085	36 407	37 862	33 250
Total inwards												
Liquid bulk	JURI	121 302	118 881	120 780	121 415	117 754	122 524	117 912	123 446	124 913	132 498	129 748
Other traffic	JURJ	152 346	150 876	151 912	160 528	167 171	165 200	177 134	182 654	182 050	183 846	199 142
All traffic	HHEU	273 648	269 758	272 692	281 943	284 926	287 724	295 046	306 100	306 963	316 344	328 890
Outwards:												
Foreign												
Liquid bulk	JURK	85 668	90 947	96 616	113 936	111 651	106 169	104 654	106 041	110 591	118 074	110 321
Other traffic	JURL	57 494	59 249	60 874	65 052	67 150	69 620	74 644	75 620	73 776	74 599	70 062
All traffic	HHEX	143 162	150 196	157 490	178 988	178 801	175 790	179 298	181 661	184 367	192 673	180 383
Coastwise												
Liquid bulk	JURM	44 225	42 696	44 557	46 135	51 459	57 146	53 753	52 622	51 966	42 488	36 049
Other traffic	JURN	18 528	18 093	17 469	18 664	20 676	18 169	18 251	19 324	19 132	19 812	18 877
All traffic	HHFA	62 753	60 789	62 027	64 799	72 134	75 316	72 004	71 946	71 098	62 300	54 926
One-port												
Liquid bulk	JURO	9 287	9 472	9 137	8 850	8 882	8 847	8 560	4 365	126	488	647
Other traffic	JURP	5 781	5 437	4 878	3 550	3 487	3 566	3 621	4 430	3 059	1 244	1 520
All traffic	HHFD	15 068	14 908	14 015	12 400	12 369	12 413	12 181	8 794	3 186	1 732	2 167
Total outwards												
Liquid bulk	JURQ	139 179	143 114	150 311	168 921	171 992	172 163	166 967	163 028	162 684	161 050	147 017
Other traffic	JURR	81 804	82 779	83 222	87 266	91 312	91 356	96 516	99 374	95 967	95 656	90 460
All traffic	HHFH	220 983	225 893	233 532	256 187	263 304	263 519	263 484	262 402	258 651	256 706	237 477
Total goods handled	HHFI	494 631	495 651	506 224	538 130	548 230	551 243	558 530	568 502	565 614	573 050	566 366

Source: Department for Transport; 020 7944 3087

15.30 Roll-on/roll-off ferry and Channel Tunnel traffic; road goods vehicles outward to mainland Europe: by country of registration

Thousands

		1992	1993	1994	1995	1996	1997	1998	1999	2000	2001	2002
Powered vehicles:												
United Kingdom	ZCGT	373.7	398.0	453.1	486.0	531.1	543.2	544.3	562.7	544.8	514.6	493.3
Austria	ZCGU	..	..	..	9.7	8.6	5.4	10.2	14.9	17.0	42.0	45.8
Belgium/Luxembourg	ZCGV	37.2	29.4	37.1	45.7	41.0	53.6	74.5	96.7	114.1	119.3	121.4
Denmark	ZCGW	6.9	4.9	5.0	4.5	4.6	5.5	7.3	8.7	9.5	12.0	16.9
Finland	ZCGX	..	..	..	0.3	0.2	0.8	0.6	0.7	0.9	3.1	2.0
Germany	ZCGY	30.8	27.7	28.1	28.0	30.4	39.3	52.4	73.1	111.5	132.0	148.2
France	ZCGZ	141.2	144.0	163.2	154.9	181.7	234.2	272.4	319.1	338.8	352.4	363.1
Greece	ZCHA	2.2	1.5	1.3	1.8	2.1	2.6	1.9	2.6	2.9	2.6	2.8
Irish Republic	ZCHB	24.7	35.6	32.4	31.0	30.1	32.3	38.8	44.7	48.5	46.6	44.6
Italy	ZCHC	13.5	13.0	22.7	29.3	28.8	30.4	35.3	45.8	67.8	91.1	127.8
Netherlands	ZCHD	71.9	73.3	76.3	84.6	87.2	107.0	125.4	153.3	185.1	187.5	186.3
Spain	ZCHE	32.4	29.5	35.2	38.4	39.4	45.1	56.3	67.7	81.8	93.9	102.2
Sweden	ZCHF	..	..	..	0.7	0.9	8.9	10.3	1.0	1.4	1.8	1.8
Portugal	ZCHG	3.4	3.3	3.7	3.4	3.1	5.1	6.7	9.2	10.7	10.2	11.0
European Union (excluding UK)	ZCHH	364.2	362.2	405.2	432.2	458.1	569.5	692.1	837.3	990.0	1 094.5	1 174.0
Non-European Union	ZCHI	29.8	30.2	34.2	29.0	26.3	28.0	33.6	47.4	52.9	82.3	116.2
Unknown	ZCHJ	2.1	5.8	4.0	4.0	2.2	5.7	4.5	6.3	17.7	20.5	18.1
All countries	ZCHK	769.8	796.2	896.5	950.2	1 017.7	1 146.4	1 274.5	1 453.7	1 605.4	1 711.9	1 801.5
Unaccompanied trailers	ZCHL	629.3	593.4	701.6	677.4	626.4	740.0	737.5	737.8	712.9	686.4	726.0
Powered vehicles and unaccompanied trailers	ZCHM	1 399.1	1 389.6	1 598.1	1 627.6	1 644.1	1 886.4	2 012.3	2 191.4	2 318.3	2 398.3	2 527.5

Source: Department for Transport; 0117 987 8484

15.31 United Kingdom international passenger movements by air and sea[1]

Thousands

		1992	1993	1994	1995	1996	1997	1998	1999	2000	2001	2002
By air												
EC Europe	ZCDD	48 640	51 506	58 042	59 987	60 949	66 089	73 360	79 003	84 930	87 534	91 419
Other Western Europe	ZCDE	8 103	8 507	8 797	9 364	9 473	10 385	11 089	11 246	11 897	12 062	12 053
Rest of the world	ZCDF	25 455	27 335	28 915	31 542	34 499	37 594	40 263	42 619	45 293	42 591	42 611
All air passenger movements	KMUP	82 198	87 348	95 754	100 893	104 921	114 068	124 712	132 868	142 120	142 187	146 082
By sea												
Irish Republic, European continent and Mediterranean Sea area	ZCDG	32 882	34 685	36 733	34 321	34 543	36 258	33 226	31 381	28 516	27 754	28 726
Rest of the world	BMMF	27	37	34	33	24	29	23	26	26	27	32
Pleasure cruises[2]	KMRQ	138	193	236	207	233	..	..	445	461	469	537
All sea passenger movements[2]	KMUO	33 046	34 915	37 002	34 562	34 792	36 288	33 249	31 852	29 003	28 249	29 295

1 See chapter text.
2 Figure for 2002 is provisional.

Sources: Civil Aviation Authority;
Department for Transport: 020 7944 3088

15.32 Postal services and television licences[1]
United Kingdom

		1993	1994	1995	1996	1997	1998	1999	2000	2001	2002	2003
Letters, etc posted(millions)	KMRA	16 364	16 651	17 468	18 322	18 101	18 350	18 878	19 711	20 076	20 648	21 979
of which:												
Registered and insured	KMRB	21.5	21.8	21.5	23.5	25.6	28.7	31.6	30.2	32.3	36.1	38.5
Airmail (Commonwealth and foreign)	KMRC	534.4	545.0	567.1	655.1	684.5	658.4	693.2	672.3	659.2	600.7	541.6
Business reply and freepost items	KMRD	481.3	482.9	477.6	493.1	505.8	524.7	503.6	475.3	487.4	486.2	434.4
Postal orders												
Total issued (thousands)[2]	KMRH	38 401	39 089	37 901	35 542	33 404	31 907	30 289	30 153	30 931	29 150	28 666
Television licences (thousands)												
in force on 31 March	KMQL	20 067	20 413	20 732	21 105	21 305	21 723	22 240	22 625	22 839	23 157	23 486
of which:												
Colour	KMQM	19 031	19 524	19 957	20 505	20 849	21 344	21 944	22 413	22 684	23 040	23 392

1 See chapter text.
2 Excluding those issued on HM ships, in many British possessions and in other places abroad. For 1992 to 1998 includes Postal Orders issued Overseas and by Ministry of Defence.

*Sources: Royal Mail: 01246 547012;
Capita Business Services Limited: 0117 3021003;
Post Office Counters Limited: 020 7921 9384*

16 National accounts

National accounts

National accounts *(Tables 16.1 to 16.22)*
The tables which follow are based on those in the *Blue Book 2002 Edition*. Some of the figures are provisional and may be revised later; this applies particularly to the figures for 2000 and 2001.

The accounts are based on the European System of Accounts 1995 (ESA95). The *Blue Book* contains an introduction to the system of the UK accounts outlining some of the main concepts and principles of measurement used. It explains how key economic indicators are derived from the sequence of accounts and how the figures describing the whole economy are broken down by sector and by industry. A detailed description of the structure for the accounts is provided in a separate ONS publication *United Kingdom National Accounts: Concepts, Sources and Methods* (TSO 1998). Further information on the financial accounts is given in the *Financial Statistics Explanatory Handbook.*

In the tables in this chapter on national income, analyses by industry are based, as far as possible, on the Standard Industrial Classification Revised 1992. The principal aggregate measured in these tables is the **Gross domestic product** (GDP). This is a concept of the value of the total economic activity taking place in UK territory. It can be viewed as incomes earned, as expenditures incurred, or as production. Adding all primary incomes received from the rest of the world and deducting all primary incomes payable to non-residents produces **Gross national income** (previously known as gross national product). This is a concept of the value of all incomes earned by UK residents.

ESA95, the internationally compatible accounting framework, provides a systematic and detailed description of the UK economy. It includes the sector accounts which provide, by institutional sector, a description of the different stages of the economic process from production through income generation, distribution and use of income to capital accumulation and financing; and the input-output framework, which describes the production process in more detail. It contains all the elements required to compile such aggregate measures as GDP, gross national income (GNI) and saving.

Gross domestic product and national income *(Tables 16.1, 16.2, 16.3)*
Table 16.1 shows the main national accounts aggregates, at current prices and at chained volume measures (reference year 2000).

Table 16.2 shows the various money flows which generate the gross domestic product and gross national income. The output approach to GDP shows the total output of goods and services, the use of goods and services in the production process (intermediate consumption) and taxes and subsidies on products. The expenditure approach to GDP shows consumption expenditure by households and government, gross capital formation and expenditure on UK exports by overseas purchasers. The sum of these items overstates the amount of income generated in the United Kingdom by the value of imports of goods and

services; this item is therefore subtracted to produce gross domestic product at market prices. The income approach to GDP shows gross operating surplus, mixed income and compensation of employees (previously known as income from employment). Taxes are added and subsidies are deducted to produce the total of the income-based components at market prices.

Table 16.2 also shows the primary incomes received from the rest of the world, which are added to GDP and primary incomes payable to non-residents, which are deducted from GDP, to arrive at **Gross national income.** Primary income comprises compensation of employees, taxes *less* subsidies on production and property and entrepreneurial income.

Table 16.3 shows the expenditure approach to GDP at chained volumed measures (reference year 2000). When looking at the change in the economy over time the main concern is usually whether more goods and services are actually being produced now than at some time in the past. Over time changes in current price GDP show changes in the monetary value of the components of GDP and, as these changes in value can reflect changes in both price and volume, it is difficult to establish how much of an increase in the series is due either to increased activity in the economy or to an increase in the price level. As a result, when looking at the real growth in the economy over time it is useful to look at volume (or constant price) estimates of GDP. In constant price series, for all years the transactions are re-valued to a constant price level using the average prices of a selected year, known as the base year, presently 2000.

Industrial analysis *(Tables 16.4, 16.5)*
The analysis of gross value added by industry at current prices shown in Table 16.4 reflects the estimates based on the Standard Industrial Classification, Revised 1992 (SIC92). The table is based on current price data reconciled through the input-output process for 1992 to 2000. The estimates are valued at basic prices, that is, the only taxes included in the price will be taxes paid as part of the production process, such as business rates, and not any taxes specifically levied on the production of a unit of output, for example VAT.

Table 16.5 shows constant price estimates of gross value added at basic prices by industry. Constant price gross value added (output approach) provides the lead indicator of economic change in the short term. The output analysis of gross value added is estimated in terms of change and expressed in index number form. It is therefore inappropriate to show as a statistical adjustment any divergence of an output measure of GDP derived from it from other measures of GDP. Such an adjustment does, however, exist implicitly.

Sector analysis - Distribution of income accounts and capital account *(Tables 16.6-16.13)*
The new national accounts accounting framework includes the sector accounts which provide, by institutional sector, a description of the different stages of the economic process from production through income generation, distribution and use of income to capital accumulation and financing.

Tables 16.6-16.12 show the allocation of primary income account and the secondary distribution of income account for the non-financial corporations, financial corporations, government and households sectors. Additionally, Table 16.12 shows the use of income account for the households sector and Table 16.13 provides a summary of the capital account. The full sequence of accounts is shown in the *Blue Book.*

The allocation of primary income account shows the resident units and institutional sectors as recipients rather than producers of primary income. It demonstrates the extent to which operating surpluses are distributed to the owners of the enterprises. The resources side of the allocation of primary income accounts includes the components of the income approach to measurement of GDP. The balance of this account is the gross balance of primary income (B.5g) for each sector, and if the gross balance is aggregated across all sectors of the economy the result is **gross national income.**

The secondary distribution of income account describes how the balance of income for each sector is allocated by redistribution; through transfers such as taxes on income, social contributions and benefits and other current transfers. The balancing item of this account is gross disposable income (B.6g). For the households sector, gross disposable income at constant prices is shown as real household disposable income.

Table 16.12 shows, for the households sector, the use of disposable income where the balancing item is saving (B.8g). For the non-financial corporations sector the balancing item of the secondary distribution of income account, gross disposable income (B.6g) is equal to saving (B.8g).

The summary capital account *(Table 16.13)* brings together the saving and investment of the several sectors of the economy. It shows saving, capital transfers, gross capital formation and net acquisition of non-financial assets for each of the four sectors.

Household and non-profit institutions serving households (NPISH) consumption expenditure at current and constant prices *(Tables 16.14-16.17)*
Household and NPISH consumption expenditure is a major component of the expenditure measure of gross domestic product at current prices *(Table 16.2)* and at constant prices *(Table 16.3).*

Household final consumption expenditure includes the value of income-in-kind and imputed rent of owner-occupied dwellings but excludes business expenditure allowed as deductions in computing income for tax purposes. It includes expenditure on durable goods, for instance motor cars, which from the point of view of the individual might more appropriately be treated as capital expenditure. The only exceptions are the purchase of land and dwellings and costs incurred in connection with the transfer of their ownership and expenditure on major improvements by occupiers, which are treated as personal capital expenditure.

The estimates of household consumption expenditure include purchases of second-hand as well as new goods, *less* the proceeds of sales of used goods.

The most detailed figures are published quarterly in *Consumer Trends* (available as a web-only publication on the National Statistics website: *www.statistics.gov.uk*).

Change in inventories (previously known as value of physical increase in stocks and work in progress) *(Table 16.18)*
This table gives a broad analysis by industry, and, for manufacturing industry, by asset, of the value of entries *less* withdrawals and losses of inventories (stocks).

Gross fixed capital formation *(Tables 16.19-16.22)*
Gross fixed capital formation comprises expenditure on the replacement of, and additions to, fixed capital assets located in the United Kingdom, including all ships and aircraft of UK ownership.

16.1 UK national and domestic product[1]
Main aggregates: index numbers and values
At current prices and chained volume measures (Reference year 2000)

		1994	1995	1996	1997	1998	1999	2000	2001	2002
INDICES (2000=100)										
VALUES AT CURRENT PRICES										
Gross domestic product at current market prices ("money GDP")	YBEU	71.6	75.6	80.2	85.2	90.3	95.0	100.0	104.5	109.7
Gross value added at current basic prices	YBEX	72.5	76.3	81.1	85.8	90.8	95.1	100.0	105.0	110.3
CHAINED VOLUME MEASURES										
Gross domestic product at market prices	YBEZ	83.3	85.7	88.0	90.9	93.7	96.4	100.0	102.1	103.9
Gross national disposable income at market prices	YBFP	82.8	84.1	86.6	90.5	94.5	96.2	100.0	102.9	105.9
Gross value added at basic prices	CGCE	83.3	85.5	87.9	90.7	93.9	96.3	100.0	101.9	103.3
PRICES										
Implied deflator of GDP at market prices	YBGB	85.9	88.2	91.2	93.8	96.4	98.6	100.0	102.3	105.6

VALUES AT CURRENT PRICES (£ million)

Gross measures (before deduction of fixed capital consumption) at current market prices

		1994	1995	1996	1997	1998	1999	2000	2001	2002
Gross Domestic Product ("money GDP")	YBHA	681 327	719 176	763 290	810 944	859 436	903 865	951 265	994 037	1 043 945
Employment, property and entrepreneurial income from the rest of the world (receipts *less* payments)	YBGG	3 348	2 101	1 204	3 905	12 906	2 422	9 763	16 188	21 119
Subsidies (receipts) *less* taxes (payments) on products from/to the rest of the world	-QZOZ	-3 349	-5 220	-3 116	-2 919	-3 651	-3 288	-3 838	-3 772	-2 493
Other subsidies on production from/to the rest of the world	-IBJL	286	293	261	208	241	338	335	582	519
Gross National Income (GNI)	ABMX	681 612	716 350	761 639	812 138	868 932	903 337	957 525	1 007 035	1 063 090
Current transfers from the rest of the world (receipts *less* payments)	-YBGF	-2 309	-2 649	-1 902	-3 209	-4 966	-4 435	-6 253	-3 421	-6 822
Gross National Disposable Income	NQCO	679 303	713 701	759 737	808 929	863 966	898 902	951 272	1 003 614	1 056 268

Adjustment to current basic prices

		1994	1995	1996	1997	1998	1999	2000	2001	2002
Gross Domestic Product (at current market prices)	YBHA	681 327	719 176	763 290	810 944	859 436	903 865	951 265	994 037	1 043 945
Adjustment to current basic prices (*less* taxes *plus* subsidies on products)	-NQBU	-72 587	-79 268	-83 084	-90 573	-97 077	-106 051	-112 071	-113 133	-118 361
Gross Value Added (at current basic prices)	ABML	608 740	639 908	680 206	720 371	762 359	797 814	839 194	880 904	925 584

Net measures (after deduction of fixed capital consumption) at current market prices

		1994	1995	1996	1997	1998	1999	2000	2001	2002
	-NQAE	-79 908	-83 135	-86 866	-88 715	-92 695	-99 076	-104 358	-109 319	-115 786
Net domestic product	NHRK	601 419	636 041	676 424	722 229	766 741	804 789	846 907	884 718	928 159
Net national income	NSRX	601 704	633 215	674 773	723 423	776 237	804 261	853 167	897 716	947 304
Net national disposable income	NQCP	599 395	630 566	672 871	720 214	771 271	799 826	846 914	894 295	940 482

CHAINED VOLUME MEASURES (Reference year 2000, £ million)

Gross measures (before deduction of fixed capital consumption) at market prices

		1994	1995	1996	1997	1998	1999	2000	2001	2002
Gross Domestic Product	ABMI	792 717	815 234	837 158	864 710	891 684	916 639	951 265	971 565	988 338
Terms of trade effect ("Trading gain or loss")	YBGJ	-6 176	-11 491	-10 129	-3 882	752	2 206	–	-1 999	7 101
Real gross domestic income	YBGL	786 541	803 743	827 029	860 828	892 436	918 845	951 265	969 566	995 439
Real employment, property and entrepreneurial income from the rest of the world (receipts *less* payments)	YBGI	3 847	2 335	1 300	4 139	13 399	2 463	9 763	15 800	20 179
Subsidies (receipts) *less* taxes (payments) on production from/to the rest of the world	-QZPB	-3 439	-6 700	-5 972	-1 948	-2 764	-2 722	-3 838	-3 499	-2 542
Other subsidies on production from/to the rest of the world	-IBJN	287	293	256	200	236	328	335	647	595
Gross National Income (GNI)	YBGM	789 844	802 880	825 690	864 083	903 789	919 343	957 525	982 512	1 013 670
Real current transfers from the rest of the world (receipts *less* payments)	-YBGP	-2 653	-2 944	-2 053	-3 401	-5 156	-4 510	-6 253	-3 339	-6 518
Gross National Disposable Income	YBGO	787 191	799 936	823 637	860 682	898 633	914 833	951 272	979 173	1 007 152

Adjustment to basic prices

		1994	1995	1996	1997	1998	1999	2000	2001	2002
Gross Domestic Product (at market prices)	ABMI	792 717	815 234	837 158	864 710	891 684	916 639	951 265	971 565	988 338
Adjustment to basic prices (*less* taxes *plus* subsidies on products)	-NTAQ	-93 929	-97 511	-99 712	-103 483	-103 395	-108 487	-112 071	-116 648	-121 651
Gross Value Added (at basic prices)	ABMM	698 849	717 888	737 579	761 412	788 231	808 156	839 194	854 917	866 687

Net measures (after deduction of fixed capital consumption) at market prices

		1994	1995	1996	1997	1998	1999	2000	2001	2002
	-CIHA	-91 077	-90 438	-92 815	-94 959	-97 841	-101 860	-104 358	-106 464	-111 553
Net national income at market prices	YBET	694 941	707 538	730 116	768 494	805 261	816 465	853 167	876 048	902 117
Net national disposable income at market prices	YBEY	692 289	704 593	728 068	765 095	800 103	811 953	846 914	872 709	895 599

1 See chapter text.

Source: Office for National Statistics: 020 7533 6031

16.2 UK gross domestic product and national income[1]
Current prices

£ million

		1994	1995	1996	1997	1998	1999	2000	2001	2002
GROSS DOMESTIC PRODUCT										
Gross domestic product: Output										
Gross value added, at basic prices										
Output of goods and services	NQAF	1 281 635	1 373 303	1 470 378	1 553 537	1 646 278	1 731 678	1 836 349	1 915 208	1 959 103
less intermediate consumption	-NQAJ	-672 895	-733 395	-790 172	-833 166	-883 919	-933 864	-997 155	-1 034 304	-1 033 519
Total Gross Value Added	ABML	**608 740**	**639 908**	**680 206**	**720 371**	**762 359**	**797 814**	**839 194**	**880 904**	**925 584**
Value added taxes (VAT) on products	QYRC	46 117	48 424	51 389	55 454	57 055	62 124	64 917	68 082	72 202
Other taxes on products	NSUI	33 450	37 995	39 724	43 003	46 933	50 512	54 086	52 303	53 046
less subsidies on products	-NZHC	-6 980	-7 151	-8 029	-7 884	-6 911	-6 585	-6 932	-7 252	-6 887
Gross Domestic Product at market prices	YBHA	**681 327**	**719 176**	**763 290**	**810 944**	**859 436**	**903 865**	**951 265**	**994 037**	**1 043 945**
Gross domestic product: Expenditure										
Final consumption expenditure										
Actual individual consumption										
Household final consumption expenditure	ABPB	422 397	443 367	474 311	503 813	536 933	570 440	603 349	635 704	666 877
Final consumption expenditure of NPISH	ABNV	15 287	16 481	18 338	19 509	21 053	22 069	23 188	24 676	26 009
Individual government final consumption expenditure	NNAQ	77 545	81 093	84 771	87 243	91 666	99 303	106 263	115 973	129 043
Total actual individual consumption	NQEO	515 229	540 941	577 420	610 565	649 652	691 812	732 800	776 353	821 929
Collective government final consumption expenditure	NQEP	58 710	59 938	61 418	60 933	62 293	67 034	71 531	75 222	79 953
Total final consumption expenditure	ABKW	573 939	600 879	638 838	671 498	711 945	758 846	804 331	851 575	901 882
Households and NPISH	NSSG	437 684	459 848	492 649	523 322	557 986	592 509	626 537	660 380	692 886
Central government	NMBJ	84 385	86 791	89 935	91 429	94 559	100 220	106 620	115 174	127 252
Local government	NMMT	51 870	54 240	56 254	56 747	59 400	66 117	71 174	76 021	81 744
Gross capital formation										
Gross fixed capital formation	NPQX	108 314	117 448	126 291	133 776	150 540	154 647	161 210	166 691	169 972
Changes in inventories	ABMP	3 708	4 512	1 771	4 621	5 026	6 060	5 271	2 995	1 584
Acquisitions less disposals of valuables	NPJO	113	-121	-160	-27	429	229	3	396	213
Total gross capital formation	NQFM	112 135	121 839	127 902	138 370	155 995	160 936	166 484	170 082	171 769
Exports of goods and services	KTMW	180 508	203 509	223 969	233 027	230 334	238 794	267 007	271 708	272 727
less imports of goods and services	-KTMX	-185 255	-207 051	-227 419	-231 951	-238 838	-254 711	-286 557	-299 328	-304 016
External balance of goods and services	KTMY	-4 747	-3 542	-3 450	1 076	-8 504	-15 917	-19 550	-27 620	-31 289
Statistical discrepancy between expenditure components and GDP	RVFD	–	–	–	–	–	–	–	–	1 583
Gross Domestic Product at market prices	YBHA	**681 327**	**719 176**	**763 290**	**810 944**	**859 436**	**903 865**	**951 265**	**994 037**	**1 043 945**
Gross domestic product: Income										
Operating surplus, gross										
Non-financial corporations										
Public non-financial corporations	NRJT	9 111	10 987	10 856	9 758	10 216	9 477	9 248	9 779	9 347
Private non-financial corporations	NRJK	133 037	142 165	157 745	168 871	174 261	177 452	183 805	184 711	188 962
Financial corporations	NQNV	20 708	17 838	17 135	14 806	18 436	15 785	15 559	16 469	30 289
Adjustment for financial services	-NSRV	-23 119	-23 215	-22 580	-22 396	-27 998	-30 121	-37 949	-40 242	-44 211
General government	NMXV	5 991	6 447	7 482	7 665	7 926	8 399	8 566	8 902	9 302
Households and non-profit institutions serving households	QWLS	35 354	38 165	40 113	43 054	47 959	51 580	54 390	59 682	62 558
Total operating surplus, gross	ABNF	181 082	192 387	210 751	221 758	230 800	232 572	233 619	239 301	256 247
Mixed income	QWLT	44 319	46 647	49 564	51 040	50 876	54 181	56 967	60 773	63 957
Compensation of employees	HAEA	369 645	386 718	405 835	433 306	465 854	495 596	532 518	564 067	587 488
Taxes on production and imports	NZGX	94 288	101 633	106 158	113 643	119 803	129 118	136 050	138 786	145 380
less subsidies	-AAXJ	-8 007	-8 209	-9 018	-8 803	-7 897	-7 602	-7 889	-8 890	-8 980
Statistical discrepancy between income components and GDP	RVFC	–	–	–	–	–	–	–	–	-147
Gross Domestic Product at market prices	YBHA	**681 327**	**719 176**	**763 290**	**810 944**	**859 436**	**903 865**	**951 265**	**994 037**	**1 043 945**

16.2 UK gross domestic product and national income[1]
continued
Current prices

GROSS NATIONAL INCOME at market prices		1994	1995	1996	1997	1998	1999	2000	2001	2002
Gross Domestic Product at market prices	YBHA	681 327	719 176	763 290	810 944	859 436	903 865	951 265	994 037	1 043 945
Compensation of employees										
receipts from the rest of the world	KTMN	681	887	911	1 007	840	960	1 032	1 087	1 121
less payments to the rest of the world	-KTMO	−851	−1 183	−818	−924	−850	−759	−882	−1 021	−1 054
Total	KTMP	−170	−296	93	83	−10	201	150	66	67
less Taxes on products paid to the rest of the world										
plus Subsidies received from the rest of the world	-QZOZ	−3 349	−5 220	−3 116	−2 919	−3 651	−3 288	−3 838	−3 772	−2 493
Other subsidies on production	-IBJL	286	293	261	208	241	338	335	582	519
Property and entrepreneurial income										
receipts from the rest of the world	HMBN	73 702	87 132	91 621	95 337	103 667	99 729	134 436	141 438	121 954
less payments to the rest of the world	-HMBO	−70 184	−84 735	−90 510	−91 515	−90 751	−97 508	−124 823	−125 316	−100 902
Total	HMBM	3 518	2 397	1 111	3 822	12 916	2 221	9 613	16 122	21 052
Gross National Income at market prices	ABMX	681 612	716 350	761 639	812 138	868 932	903 337	957 525	1 007 035	1 063 090

1 See chapter text.

Source: Office for National Statistics: 020 7533 6031

16.3 UK gross domestic product[1]
Chained volume measures (Reference year 2000)

£ million

GROSS DOMESTIC PRODUCT		1994	1995	1996	1997	1998	1999	2000	2001	2002
Gross domestic product: expenditure approach										
Final consumption expenditure										
Actual individual consumption										
Household final consumption expenditure	ABPF	486 600	494 324	512 918	531 882	552 186	577 665	603 349	622 136	644 441
Final consumption expenditure of non-profit institutions serving households	ABNU	19 161	19 796	19 850	20 290	21 713	21 543	23 188	23 845	24 553
Individual government final consumption expenditure	NSZK	95 686	98 279	100 364	102 062	103 687	105 270	106 263	107 345	109 485
Total actual individual consumption	YBIO	600 858	611 660	632 432	653 656	677 197	704 310	732 800	753 326	778 479
Collective government final consumption expenditure	NSZL	68 016	67 732	66 923	64 910	65 539	69 202	71 531	73 530	75 699
Total final consumption expenditure	ABKX	668 913	679 422	699 384	718 576	742 739	773 506	804 331	826 856	854 178
Gross capital formation										
Gross fixed capital formation	NPQR	116 814	120 389	127 238	135 876	153 148	155 576	161 210	167 032	170 002
Changes in inventories	ABMQ	4 882	4 540	1 851	4 016	4 913	6 426	5 271	2 938	1 496
Acquisitions less disposals of valuables	NPJP	30	−28	−43	−3	57	28	3	362	193
Total gross capital formation	NPQU	120 657	124 875	129 203	140 253	158 246	161 851	166 484	170 332	171 691
Gross domestic final expenditure	YBIK	788 414	803 281	827 597	858 325	901 069	935 377	970 815	997 187	1 025 869
Exports of goods and services	KTMZ	176 971	193 364	210 032	227 702	233 982	243 985	267 007	273 724	271 186
Gross final expenditure	ABME	961 621	994 532	1 036 858	1 086 372	1 135 080	1 179 410	1 237 822	1 270 911	1 297 055
less imports of goods and services	-KTNB	−175 287	−185 038	−202 982	−222 787	−243 400	−262 601	−286 557	−299 347	−310 214
Statistical discrepancy between expenditure components and GDP	GIXS	–	–	–	–	–	–	–	–	1 497
Gross Domestic Product at market prices	ABMI	792 717	815 234	837 158	864 710	891 684	916 639	951 265	971 565	988 338
of which External balance of goods and services	KTNC	1 684	8 326	7 050	4 915	−9 418	−18 616	−19 550	−25 623	−39 028

1 See chapter text.

Source: Office for National Statistics: 020 7533 6031

16.4 Gross value added at current basic prices: by industry[1,2]

£ million

		1994	1995	1996	1997	1998	1999	2000	2001	2002
Agriculture, hunting, forestry and fishing	EWSH	10 617	11 766	12 058	10 239	9 546	9 359	8 915	8 634	9 035
Production										
Mining and quarrying										
Mining and quarrying of energy producing materials										
Mining of coal	QTOQ	1 048	1 223	1 045	988	817	643	611	564	539
Extraction of mineral oil and natural gas	QTOR	12 494	13 703	17 125	15 435	13 204	15 044	22 833	21 608	22 743
Other mining and quarrying	QTOS	1 247	1 442	1 599	1 695	1 645	1 717	1 795	1 855	2 251
Total mining and quarrying	EWSL	14 788	16 369	19 768	18 118	15 666	17 403	25 240	24 027	25 531
Manufacturing										
Food; beverages and tobacco	QTOU	18 231	18 261	19 891	20 329	20 013	20 226	20 300	20 935	21 743
Textiles and textile products	QTOV	6 452	6 821	7 264	7 734	6 988	6 450	6 003	5 633	5 596
Leather and leather products	QTOW	1 018	946	892	845	823	808	750	709	699
Wood and wood products	QTOX	1 746	1 918	2 026	2 237	2 328	2 248	2 335	2 429	2 422
Pulp, paper and paper products; publishing and printing	QTOY	16 214	17 582	18 154	18 405	18 995	19 880	20 556	20 477	20 481
Coke, petroleum products and nuclear fuel	QTOZ	2 688	2 924	2 530	2 381	2 576	2 664	2 513	2 611	2 984
Chemicals, chemical products and man-made fibres	QTPA	13 908	15 311	15 724	15 338	15 083	15 337	15 183	15 423	15 614
Rubber and plastic products	QTPB	6 321	6 789	7 222	8 015	8 237	7 944	7 842	7 858	7 864
Other non-metal mineral products	QTPC	4 697	5 158	5 188	5 196	5 017	4 952	5 014	5 031	5 305
Basic metals and fabricated metal products	QTPD	14 242	16 124	16 410	17 120	17 632	16 674	16 024	15 816	15 890
Machinery and equipment not elsewhere classified	QTPE	11 052	12 273	12 467	13 402	13 592	12 731	12 341	12 067	12 012
Electrical and optical equipment	QTPF	16 523	17 758	18 592	20 020	20 176	20 792	20 839	19 344	19 222
Transport equipment	QTPG	13 257	13 066	14 318	15 611	16 089	15 944	15 886	16 509	17 195
Manufacturing not elsewhere classified	QTPH	4 417	4 857	5 394	6 028	6 297	6 422	6 556	6 711	7 028
Total manufacturing	EWSP	130 767	139 789	146 071	152 658	153 844	153 073	152 147	151 553	154 051
Electricity, gas and water supply	EWST	16 158	15 586	16 280	16 141	16 087	15 968	16 112	16 234	15 181
Total production	QTPK	161 713	171 744	182 119	186 917	185 597	186 444	193 499	191 815	194 764
Construction	EWSX	31 216	33 005	34 643	36 933	39 001	41 721	45 474	50 218	57 555
Service industries										
Wholesale and retail trade (including motor trade); repair of motor vehicles, personal and household goods	QTPM	71 537	74 612	79 319	86 002	92 901	99 170	103 592	110 035	116 293
Hotels and restaurants	QTPN	16 854	18 254	20 276	22 439	24 434	26 224	27 914	29 492	31 554
Transport, storage and communication										
Transport and storage	QTPO	31 391	33 044	34 973	37 309	39 773	40 850	42 860	43 603	44 368
Communication	QTPP	18 180	18 296	18 731	20 115	22 588	24 146	27 194	28 939	31 293
Total	EWTF	49 572	51 340	53 705	57 424	62 361	64 996	70 055	72 543	75 661
Financial intermediation	QTPR	42 358	40 089	40 852	40 512	45 211	43 404	45 952	48 487	48 868
Adjustment for financial services (FISIM)	–NSRV	–23 119	–23 215	–22 580	–22 396	–27 998	–30 121	–37 949	–40 242	–44 211
Real estate, renting and business activities										
Letting of dwellings including imputed rent of owner occupiers	QTPS	42 366	45 083	46 717	50 272	55 714	59 588	62 710	68 479	71 567
Other real estate, renting and business activities	QTPT	68 131	73 970	82 406	93 170	108 041	118 548	129 447	140 425	147 098
Total	QTPU	110 496	119 052	129 122	143 444	163 756	178 137	192 157	208 905	218 663
Public administration and defence (PAD)[3]	EWTN	39 597	39 756	40 673	40 721	40 692	42 155	44 061	45 768	48 554
Education[3]	QTPW	32 770	34 208	37 005	39 247	41 663	44 980	48 080	51 891	56 035
Health and social work	QTPX	39 495	42 051	43 005	45 136	47 890	51 137	54 925	58 235	64 515
Other social and personal services, private households with employees and extra-territorial organisations	EWTV	25 634	27 247	30 008	33 754	37 305	40 207	42 520	45 125	48 304
Total service industries	QTPZ	405 194	423 394	451 386	486 282	528 215	560 290	591 306	630 239	664 229
All industries	ABML	608 740	639 908	680 206	720 371	762 359	797 814	839 194	880 904	925 584

1 See chapter text. Components may not sum to totals as a result of rounding.
2 Because of differences in the annual and monthly production inquiries, estimates of current price output and value added by industry derived from the current price input-output supply-use balances are not consistent with the equivalent measures of constant price growth given in Table 15.5. These differences do not affect GDP totals. For further information see "Experimental Constant Price Input-Output Supply-Use Balances: An approach to improving the quality of the national accounts" Nadim Ahmad, *Economic Trends*, July 1999 (No. 548).

3 Central government expenditure on education is included in PAD in 1994 and 1995. For 1996 onwards it is included in Education.

Source: Office for National Statistics: 020 7533 6031

16.5 Gross value added at basic prices: by industry[1,2,3,4]
Chained volume indices

Indices 2000=100

	Weight per 1000[1]		1994	1995	1996	1997	1998	1999	2000	2001	2002
	2000										
Agriculture, hunting, forestry and fishing	10.6	GDQA	95.9	94.7	92.6	94.7	97.4	100.6	100.0	89.9	99.7
Production											
Mining and quarrying											
Mining and quarrying of energy producing materials											
Mining of coal	0.7	CKZP	163.2	172.6	164.8	155.9	132.1	117.1	100.0	99.5	93.5
Extraction of mineral oil and natural gas	27.2	CKZO	88.5	92.0	97.1	96.4	98.9	103.6	100.0	94.4	93.3
Other mining and quarrying	2.1	CKZQ	101.0	96.7	84.8	83.6	89.5	96.3	100.0	93.8	107.8
Total mining and quarrying	30.1	CKYX	92.0	95.1	98.1	97.1	99.1	103.3	100.0	94.5	94.3
Manufacturing											
Food; beverages and tobacco	24.2	CKZA	100.3	98.5	100.1	102.1	100.8	100.7	100.0	100.8	101.6
Textiles and textile products	7.2	CKZB	128.4	123.5	121.3	118.6	110.3	102.4	100.0	87.5	81.3
Leather and leather products	0.9	CKZC	132.1	133.4	131.4	137.9	120.0	113.4	100.0	102.9	90.1
Wood and wood products	2.8	CKZD	116.6	107.9	106.2	103.1	101.8	97.4	100.0	100.4	101.5
Pulp, paper and paper products; publishing and printing	24.5	CKZE	98.2	99.8	97.8	98.6	99.4	99.6	100.0	100.4	100.1
Coke, petroleum products and nuclear fuel	3.0	CKZF	106.9	118.6	109.4	112.7	105.4	95.0	100.0	94.2	96.3
Chemicals, chemical products and man-made fibres	18.1	CKZG	83.3	87.5	88.1	90.7	91.6	94.9	100.0	106.1	106.0
Rubber and plastic products	9.3	CKZH	96.0	98.1	96.9	97.3	100.4	100.0	100.0	96.4	92.1
Other non-metallic mineral products	6.0	CKZI	103.2	100.7	96.9	99.8	97.3	97.0	100.0	100.7	98.4
Basic metals and fabricated metal products	19.1	CKZJ	96.0	98.4	98.9	101.1	100.3	98.0	100.0	97.9	93.4
Machinery and equipment not elsewhere classified	14.7	CKZK	109.2	109.7	107.5	106.7	106.4	100.1	100.0	102.0	96.3
Electrical and optical equipment	24.8	CKZL	64.7	69.2	72.7	74.7	78.6	87.0	100.0	92.5	78.9
Transport equipment	18.9	CKZM	86.2	86.0	92.0	96.1	100.7	103.3	100.0	97.7	95.0
Manufacturing not elsewhere classified	7.8	CKZN	95.6	94.0	95.6	97.4	98.9	101.4	100.0	99.0	100.5
Total manufacturing	181.3	CKYY	92.4	93.8	94.6	96.3	96.9	97.6	100.0	98.7	95.2
Electricity, gas and water supply	19.2	CKYZ	85.7	87.7	92.0	92.3	95.3	97.9	100.0	102.4	103.7
Total production	230.6	CKYW	91.8	93.4	94.7	96.0	97.0	98.1	100.0	98.4	95.8
Construction	54.2	GDQB	92.3	92.3	94.8	97.3	98.4	98.7	100.0	103.4	111.2
Service industries											
Wholesale and retail trade (including motor trade); repair of motor vehicles, personal and household goods	123.4	GDQC	82.0	84.2	88.2	90.8	94.3	96.9	100.0	102.3	107.3
Hotels and restaurants	33.3	GDQD	87.8	86.8	87.5	91.0	94.9	98.7	100.0	100.2	101.9
Transport, storage and communication											
Transport and storage	51.1	GDQF	78.4	81.6	82.2	86.8	93.2	93.8	100.0	101.6	102.8
Communication	32.4	GDQG	48.5	53.5	60.4	68.5	74.6	87.1	100.0	107.9	109.4
Total	83.5	GDQH	65.4	69.7	73.3	79.4	85.6	91.2	100.0	104.0	105.4
Financial intermediation	54.8	GDQI	78.8	81.5	84.0	87.5	91.8	95.0	100.0	105.2	106.5
Adjustment for financial services (FISIM)	−45.2	GDQJ	70.7	76.5	81.7	85.2	90.7	92.9	100.0	104.8	109.2
Real estate, renting and business activities											
Letting of dwellings, including imputed rent of owner occupiers	74.7	GDQL	89.7	92.1	92.8	94.7	97.7	100.6	100.0	102.3	104.3
Other real estate, renting and business activities	154.3	GDQK	66.0	71.1	75.3	81.9	89.4	92.9	100.0	104.5	107.3
Total	229.0	GDQM	73.5	77.8	80.8	86.0	92.0	95.3	100.0	103.8	106.3
Public administration and defence (PAD)[4]	55.6	GDQO	100.2	99.8	98.5	97.5	97.6	97.7	100.0	100.5	102.0
Education[4]	57.3	GDQP	91.2	92.4	93.3	93.8	95.1	98.4	100.0	99.5	99.8
Health and social work[4]	62.3	GDQQ	82.7	86.2	89.2	91.2	93.9	96.1	100.0	103.3	107.8
Other social and personal services, private households with employees and extra-territorial organisations	50.7	GDQR	78.7	81.8	85.7	87.7	93.9	96.3	100.0	102.0	102.4
Total service industries	704.6	GDQS	79.8	82.5	85.1	88.5	92.8	95.9	100.0	102.6	105.0
All industries	1 000.0	CGCE	83.3	85.5	87.9	90.7	93.9	96.3	100.0	101.9	103.3

1 See chapter text. The weights are in proportion to total gross value added (GVA) in 2000. and are used to combine the industry output indices to calculate the totals for 2001 and 2002. For 2000 and earlier, totals are calculated using the equivalent weight for the previous year (eg totals for 2000 use 1999 weights).

2 As GVA is expressed in index number form, it is inappropriate to show as a statistical adjustment any divergence from the other measures of GDP. Such an adjustment does, however, exist implicitly.

3 See footnote 2 to Table 15.4.

4 The GVA for PAD, education and Health and social work in this table follows SIC(92) and differs from that used in Table 2.3, which is based on Input-Output groups. The administration costs of the NHS are included in PAD in this table but are included in Health and social work in Table 2.3. Central government expenditure on teachers is included in this table but, for 1994 and 1995 only, are included in PAD in Table 2.3.

Source: Office for National Statistics: 020 7533 6031

16.6 Non-financial corporations[1]
ESA95 sector S.11

£ million

		1994	1995	1996	1997	1998	1999	2000	2001	2002
ALLOCATION OF PRIMARY INCOME ACCOUNT										
before deduction of fixed capital consumption										
Resources										
Operating surplus, gross	NQBE	142 148	153 152	168 601	178 629	184 477	186 929	193 053	194 490	198 309
Property income, received										
Interest	EABC	7 566	9 361	9 660	9 874	13 939	10 840	14 408	13 728	9 620
Distributed income of corporations	EABD	16 446	22 367	22 919	26 548	25 086	21 493	26 518	39 915	32 210
Reinvested earnings on direct foreign investment	HDVR	12 138	11 376	13 417	11 747	10 979	16 214	20 118	20 501	23 123
Attributed property income of insurance policy-holders	FAOF	338	395	423	386	463	338	290	258	302
Rent	FAOG	108	110	114	118	118	117	117	117	118
Total	FAKY	36 596	43 609	46 533	48 673	50 585	49 002	61 451	74 519	65 373
Total resources	FBXJ	178 744	196 761	215 134	227 302	235 062	235 931	254 504	269 009	263 682
Uses										
Property income, paid										
Interest	EABG	23 243	26 513	26 047	27 738	32 972	33 317	39 473	41 792	37 655
Distributed income of corporations	NVCS	60 304	71 532	76 116	80 830	78 248	86 945	84 881	105 252	91 868
Reinvested earnings on direct foreign investment	HDVB	4 310	4 662	6 117	5 187	3 117	2 776	7 348	4 434	6 505
Rent	FBXO	693	719	815	756	584	564	1 319	1 898	1 853
Total	FBXK	88 550	103 426	109 095	114 511	114 921	123 602	133 021	153 376	137 881
Balance of primary incomes, gross	NQBG	**90 194**	**93 335**	**106 039**	**112 791**	**120 141**	**112 329**	**121 483**	**115 633**	**125 801**
Total uses	FBXJ	178 744	196 761	215 134	227 302	235 062	235 931	254 504	269 009	263 682
After deduction of fixed capital consumption	−DBGF	−51 379	−53 703	−54 597	−54 554	−56 494	−59 203	−61 813	−64 051	−66 608
Balance of primary incomes, net	FBXQ	38 815	39 632	51 442	58 237	63 647	53 126	59 670	51 582	59 193

1 See chapter text.

Source: Office for National Statistics: 020 7533 6031

16.7 Non-financial corporations[1]
ESA95 sector S.11

£ million

		1994	1995	1996	1997	1998	1999	2000	2001	2002
SECONDARY DISTRIBUTION OF INCOME ACCOUNT										
Resources										
Balance of primary incomes, gross	NQBG	**90 194**	**93 335**	**106 039**	**112 791**	**120 141**	**112 329**	**121 483**	**115 633**	**125 801**
Social contributions										
Imputed social contributions	NSTJ	2 884	3 329	3 200	3 173	3 801	3 983	4 312	4 650	5 342
Current transfers other than taxes,										
social contributions and benefits										
Non-life insurance claims	FCBP	4 031	4 716	5 508	4 190	4 849	4 151	5 923	5 839	7 789
Miscellaneous transfers	NRJY	420	494	537	557	595	611	622	619	616
Total	NRJB	4 451	5 210	6 045	4 747	5 444	4 762	6 545	6 458	8 405
Total resources	FCBR	97 529	101 874	115 284	120 711	129 386	121 074	132 340	126 741	139 548
Uses										
Current taxes on income, wealth etc.										
Taxes on income	FCBS	15 259	19 252	23 348	28 932	27 256	22 948	26 406	25 457	23 813
Social benefits other than social transfers in kind	NSTJ	2 884	3 329	3 200	3 173	3 801	3 983	4 312	4 650	5 342
Current transfers other than taxes,										
social contributions and benefits										
Net non-life insurance premiums	FCBY	4 031	4 716	5 508	4 190	4 849	4 151	5 923	5 839	7 789
Miscellaneous current transfers	FDBI	364	400	1 518	479	444	569	413	411	422
Total, other current transfers	FCBX	4 395	5 116	7 026	4 669	5 293	4 720	6 336	6 250	8 211
Gross Disposable Income	NRJD	**74 991**	**74 177**	**81 710**	**83 937**	**93 036**	**89 423**	**95 286**	**90 384**	**102 182**
Total uses	FCBR	97 529	101 874	115 284	120 711	129 386	121 074	132 340	126 741	139 548
After deduction of fixed capital consumption	−DBGF	−51 379	−53 703	−54 597	−54 554	−56 494	−59 203	−61 813	−64 051	−66 608
Disposable income, net	FCCF	23 612	20 474	27 113	29 383	36 542	30 220	33 473	26 333	35 574

1 See chapter text.

Source: Office for National Statistics: 020 7533 6031

16.8 General government[1]
ESA95 sector S.13 Unconsolidated

£ million

		1994	1995	1996	1997	1998	1999	2000	2001	2002
ALLOCATION OF PRIMARY INCOME ACCOUNT										
Resources										
Operating surplus, gross	NMXV	5 991	6 447	7 482	7 665	7 926	8 399	8 566	8 902	9 302
Taxes on production and imports, received										
Taxes on products										
Value added tax (VAT)	NZGF	42 996	43 579	46 918	52 057	52 827	58 313	60 713	64 507	69 394
Taxes and duties on imports excluding VAT										
Import duties	NMXZ	–	–	–	–	–	–	–	–	–
Taxes on imports excluding VAT and import duties	NMBT	–	–	–	–	–	–	–	–	–
Taxes on products excluding VAT and import duties	NMYB	31 218	35 482	37 380	40 621	44 815	48 442	51 956	50 203	51 102
Total taxes on products	NVCC	74 214	79 061	84 298	92 678	97 642	106 755	112 669	114 710	120 496
Other taxes on production	NMYD	14 721	15 214	15 045	15 186	15 815	16 482	17 047	18 401	20 132
Total taxes on production and imports, received	NMYE	88 935	94 275	99 343	107 864	113 457	123 237	129 716	133 111	140 628
less Subsidies, paid										
Subsidies on products	-NMYF	–4 976	–5 013	–4 330	–5 024	–4 216	–3 992	–4 436	–5 349	–4 628
Other subsidies on production	-LIUF	–741	–765	–728	–711	–745	–679	–622	–1 056	–1 574
Total	-NMRL	–5 717	–5 778	–5 058	–5 735	–4 961	–4 671	–5 058	–6 405	–6 202
Property income, received										
Total Interest	NMYL	8 385	8 553	9 031	8 575	9 250	9 148	9 157	8 963	8 159
Distributed income of corporations	NMYM	6 754	6 915	6 882	6 527	7 456	7 102	7 203	7 589	7 094
Property income attributed to insurance policy holders	NMYO	30	32	28	33	48	33	54	24	30
Rent										
from sectors other than general government	NMYR	658	684	780	721	547	528	1 283	1 862	1 816
Total	NMYU	15 827	16 184	16 721	15 856	17 301	16 811	17 697	18 438	17 099
Total resources	NMYV	105 036	111 128	118 488	125 650	133 723	143 776	150 921	154 046	160 827
Uses										
Property income, paid										
Total interest	NRKB	26 804	30 076	31 905	33 809	34 874	30 649	30 619	28 004	25 440
Total	NMYY	26 804	30 076	31 905	33 809	34 874	30 649	30 619	28 004	25 440
Balance of primary incomes, gross	NMZH	**78 232**	**81 052**	**86 583**	**91 841**	**98 849**	**113 127**	**120 302**	**126 042**	**135 387**
Total uses	NMYV	105 036	111 128	118 488	125 650	133 723	143 776	150 921	154 046	160 827
After deduction of fixed capital consumption	-NMXO	–5 991	–6 447	–7 482	–7 665	–7 926	–8 399	–8 566	–8 902	–9 302
Balance of primary incomes,net	NMZI	72 241	74 605	79 101	84 176	90 923	104 728	111 736	117 140	126 085

1 See chapter text.

Source: Office for National Statistics: 020 7533 6031

16.9 General government[1]
ESA95 sector S.13 Unconsolidated

£ million

		1994	1995	1996	1997	1998	1999	2000	2001	2002
SECONDARY DISTRIBUTION OF INCOME ACCOUNT										
Resources										
Balance of primary incomes, gross	NMZH	78 232	81 052	86 583	91 841	98 849	113 127	120 302	126 042	135 387
Current taxes on income, wealth etc.										
Taxes on income	NMZJ	85 316	95 014	99 267	107 717	124 104	129 485	140 306	147 611	142 505
Other current taxes	NVCM	11 140	11 937	13 510	14 778	15 953	17 191	18 223	19 168	20 286
Total	NMZL	96 456	106 951	112 777	122 495	140 057	146 676	158 529	166 779	162 791
Social contributions										
Actual social contributions										
Employers' actual social contributions	NMZM	24 913	25 917	27 344	29 038	30 593	32 805	36 292	38 233	38 728
Employees' social contributions	NMZN	19 649	21 091	21 700	24 121	25 234	26 645	27 506	28 786	29 379
Social contributions by self- and non-employed persons	NMZO	1 469	1 541	1 771	1 848	1 729	1 784	1 973	2 112	2 146
Total	NMZP	46 031	48 549	50 815	55 007	57 556	61 234	65 771	69 131	70 253
Imputed social contributions	NMZQ	5 419	5 279	5 299	5 356	5 880	5 823	6 157	6 499	6 848
Total	NMZR	51 450	53 828	56 114	60 363	63 436	67 057	71 928	75 630	77 101
Other current transfers										
Non-life insurance claims	NMZS	363	377	371	349	499	410	403	295	395
Current transfers within general government	NMZT	57 736	58 587	59 464	59 513	60 455	64 820	66 462	71 970	77 091
Current international cooperation	NMZU	1 752	1 233	2 424	1 739	1 384	3 176	2 084	4 568	3 112
Miscellaneous current transfers										
from sectors other than general government	NMZX	405	455	411	459	433	308	225	398	285
Other current transfers	NNAA	60 256	60 652	62 670	62 060	62 771	68 714	69 174	77 231	80 883
Total resources	NNAB	286 394	302 483	318 144	336 759	365 113	395 574	419 933	445 682	456 162
Uses										
Social benefits other than social transfers in kind	NNAD	106 263	110 381	113 081	117 004	117 593	121 161	126 630	136 317	140 867
Other current transfers										
Net non-life insurance premiums	NNAE	363	377	371	349	499	410	403	295	395
Current transfers within general government	NNAF	57 736	58 587	59 464	59 513	60 455	64 820	66 462	71 970	77 091
Current international cooperation	NNAG	2 007	2 224	1 814	1 700	1 705	1 667	2 418	2 434	2 573
Miscellaneous current transfers										
to sectors other than general government	NNAI	10 440	10 614	12 564	13 933	15 820	17 305	18 638	18 899	22 849
Of which: GNP based fourth own resource	NMFH	2 071	1 826	2 454	2 458	3 920	4 632	4 379	3 858	5 335
Other current transfers	NNAN	70 546	71 802	74 213	75 495	78 479	84 202	87 921	93 598	102 908
Gross Disposable Income	NNAO	**109 585**	**120 300**	**130 247**	**143 459**	**168 211**	**189 350**	**204 522**	**214 847**	**211 447**
Total uses	NNAB	286 394	302 483	318 144	336 759	365 113	395 574	419 933	445 682	456 162
After deduction of fixed capital consumption	-NMXO	–5 991	–6 447	–7 482	–7 665	–7 926	–8 399	–8 566	–8 902	–9 302
Disposable income, net	NNAP	103 594	113 853	122 765	135 794	160 285	180 951	195 956	205 945	202 145

1 See chapter text.

Source: Office for National Statistics: 020 7533 6031

16.10 Households and non-profit institutions serving households[1]
ESA95 sectors S.14 and S.15

£ million

		1994	1995	1996	1997	1998	1999	2000	2001	2002
ALLOCATION OF PRIMARY INCOME ACCOUNT before deduction of fixed capital consumption										
Resources										
Operating surplus, gross	QWLS	35 354	38 165	40 113	43 054	47 959	51 580	54 390	59 682	62 558
Mixed income, gross	QWLT	44 319	46 647	49 564	51 040	50 876	54 181	56 967	60 773	63 957
Compensation of employees										
Wages and salaries	QWLW	322 179	336 973	352 651	377 272	404 715	428 073	457 473	484 906	502 958
Employers' social contributions	QWLX	47 296	49 449	53 277	56 117	61 129	67 724	75 195	79 227	84 597
Total	QWLY	369 475	386 422	405 928	433 389	465 844	495 797	532 668	564 133	587 555
Property income										
Interest	QWLZ	22 240	26 468	23 826	26 585	30 076	24 132	28 192	26 873	20 597
Distributed income of corporations	QWMA	28 582	32 279	33 757	37 186	37 440	39 221	43 308	50 283	44 809
Attributed property income of insurance policy holders	QWMC	37 301	42 358	47 807	52 144	55 587	55 590	56 538	56 976	56 496
Rent	QWMD	97	99	103	105	105	105	105	105	105
Total	QWME	88 220	101 204	105 493	116 020	123 208	119 048	128 143	134 237	122 007
Total resources	QWMF	537 368	572 438	601 098	643 503	687 887	720 606	772 168	818 825	836 077
Uses										
Property income										
Interest	QWMG	36 965	40 288	38 442	42 042	51 445	47 682	53 205	53 718	51 884
Rent	QWMH	198	202	210	216	216	215	215	215	216
Total	QWMI	37 163	40 490	38 652	42 258	51 661	47 897	53 420	53 933	52 100
Balance of primary incomes, gross	QWMJ	**500 205**	**531 948**	**562 446**	**601 245**	**636 226**	**672 709**	**718 748**	**764 892**	**783 977**
Total uses	QWMF	537 368	572 438	601 098	643 503	687 887	720 606	772 168	818 825	836 077
After deduction of										
fixed capital consumption	-QWLL	−18 049	−18 922	−21 100	−22 967	−24 561	−27 506	−30 064	−32 441	−35 361
Balance of primary incomes, net	QWMK	482 156	513 026	541 346	578 278	611 665	645 203	688 684	732 451	748 616

1 See chapter text.

Source: Office for National Statistics: 020 7533 6031

16.11 Households and non-profit institutions serving households[1]
ESA95 sectors S.14 and S.15

£ million

		1994	1995	1996	1997	1998	1999	2000	2001	2002
SECONDARY DISTRIBUTION OF INCOME ACCOUNT										
Resources										
Balance of primary incomes, gross	QWMJ	500 205	531 948	562 446	601 245	636 226	672 709	718 748	764 892	783 977
Imputed social contributions	RVFH	425	455	429	410	478	450	476	502	571
Social benefits other than social transfers in kind	QWML	142 197	149 123	156 560	165 765	170 975	181 607	198 453	208 026	211 143
Other current transfers										
Non-life insurance claims	QWMM	13 272	14 123	19 360	14 004	15 224	13 762	16 150	12 661	16 920
Miscellaneous current transfers	QWMN	17 119	17 833	20 358	20 868	21 577	22 620	24 623	25 229	27 923
Total	QWMO	30 391	31 956	39 718	34 872	36 801	36 382	40 773	37 890	44 843
Total resources	QWMP	673 218	713 482	759 153	802 292	844 480	891 148	958 450	1 011 310	1 040 534
Uses										
Current taxes on income, wealth etc										
Taxes on income	QWMQ	69 473	74 315	74 163	75 242	89 697	96 460	105 604	112 283	112 217
Other current taxes	NVCO	11 140	11 937	12 907	13 977	15 123	16 330	17 363	18 248	19 346
Total	QWMS	80 613	86 252	87 070	89 219	104 820	112 790	122 967	130 531	131 563
Social contributions										
Actual social contributions										
Employers' actual social contributions	QWMT	38 146	39 934	43 925	46 773	50 499	57 020	63 760	67 092	71 274
Employees' social contributions	QWMU	49 615	53 747	59 900	66 890	70 726	74 764	75 925	74 245	73 012
Social contributions by self and non-employed	QWMV	1 469	1 541	1 771	1 848	1 729	1 784	1 973	2 112	2 146
Total	QWMW	89 230	95 222	105 596	115 511	122 954	133 568	141 658	143 449	146 432
Imputed social contributions	QWMX	9 150	9 515	9 352	9 344	10 630	10 704	11 435	12 135	13 323
Total	QWMY	98 380	104 737	114 948	124 855	133 584	144 272	153 093	155 584	159 755
Social benefits other than social transfers in kind	QWMZ	880	925	899	880	950	922	948	977	1 047
Other current transfers										
Net non-life insurance premiums	QWNA	13 272	14 123	19 360	14 004	15 224	13 762	16 150	12 661	16 920
Miscellaneous current transfers	QWNB	8 152	8 327	8 434	9 346	9 677	10 033	10 643	11 019	11 239
Total	QWNC	21 424	22 450	27 794	23 350	24 901	23 795	26 793	23 680	28 159
Gross Disposable Income	QWND	**471 921**	**499 118**	**528 442**	**563 988**	**580 225**	**609 369**	**654 649**	**700 538**	**720 010**
Total uses	QWMP	673 218	713 482	759 153	802 292	844 480	891 148	958 450	1 011 310	1 040 534
After deduction of fixed capital consumption	-QWLL	−18 049	−18 922	−21 100	−22 967	−24 561	−27 506	−30 064	−32 441	−35 361
Disposable income, net	QWNE	453 872	480 196	507 342	541 021	555 664	581 863	624 585	668 097	684 649

1 See chapter text.

Source: Office for National Statistics: 020 7533 6031

16.12 Households and non-profit institutions serving households[1]
ESA95 sectors S.14 and S.15

£ million

		1994	1995	1996	1997	1998	1999	2000	2001	2002
USE OF DISPOSABLE INCOME ACCOUNT										
Resources										
Disposable income, gross	QWND	471 921	499 118	528 442	563 988	580 225	609 369	654 649	700 538	720 010
Adjustment for the change in net equity of households in pension funds	NSSE	10 577	11 690	14 824	15 131	16 105	16 087	8 620	7 453	11 499
Total resources	NSSF	482 498	510 808	543 266	579 119	596 330	625 456	663 269	707 991	731 509
Uses										
Final consumption expenditure										
Individual consumption expenditure	NSSG	437 684	459 848	492 649	523 322	557 986	592 509	626 537	660 380	692 886
Saving, gross	NSSH	44 814	50 960	50 617	55 797	38 344	32 947	36 732	47 611	38 623
Total uses	NSSF	482 498	510 808	543 266	579 119	596 330	625 456	663 269	707 991	731 509
Saving ratio (per cent)	RVGL	9.3	10.0	9.3	9.6	6.4	5.3	5.5	6.7	5.3

1 See chapter text.

Source: Office for National Statistics: 020 7533 6031

16.13 The sector accounts: Key economic indicators[1]

£ million

		1994	1995	1996	1997	1998	1999	2000	2001	2002
Net lending/borrowing by:										
Non-financial corporations	EABO	12 863	4 058	5 574	−3 549	−4 789	−13 492	−10 375	−15 164	3 277
Financial corporations	NHCQ	4 473	2 978	−1 843	−3 019	−4 666	−13 361	−22 503	−16 883	4 205
General government	NNBK	−45 844	−41 443	−31 726	−17 829	637	10 020	15 016	8 117	−14 942
Households and NPISH's	NSSZ	21 773	25 925	22 254	24 442	5 362	−3 272	−150	7 303	−8 730
Rest of the world	NHRB	6 735	8 482	5 741	−45	3 456	20 105	18 012	16 627	17 920
Private non-financial corporations										
Gross trading profits										
Continental shelf profits	CAGJ	10 776	12 124	15 702	13 978	11 696	13 864	21 333	19 822	18 742
Others	CAED	117 450	125 151	133 508	145 693	150 975	153 954	153 142	153 445	160 050
Rental of buildings	FCBW	8 641	9 379	9 493	9 561	10 837	11 435	12 271	12 999	13 284
less Holding gains of inventories	−DLQZ	−3 830	−4 489	−958	−361	753	−1 801	−2 941	−1 555	−3 114
Gross operating surplus	NRJK	133 037	142 165	157 745	168 871	174 261	177 452	183 805	184 711	188 962
Households and NPISH										
Household gross disposable income	QWND	471 921	499 118	528 442	563 988	580 225	609 369	654 649	700 538	720 010
Implied deflator of household and NPISH individual consumption expenditure index 2000=100[2]	YBFS	86.5	89.5	92.5	94.8	97.2	98.9	100.0	102.2	103.6
Real household disposable income:										
£ million at 2000 prices	RVGK	545 269	557 940	571 440	595 043	596 745	616 235	654 649	685 263	695 183
Index 2000=100	OSXR	83.3	85.2	87.3	90.9	91.2	94.2	100.0	104.7	106.2
Gross saving	NSSH	44 814	50 960	50 617	55 797	38 344	32 947	36 732	47 611	38 623
Households total resources	NSSJ	560 043	591 901	628 037	666 362	687 996	724 759	769 532	823 964	860 552
Saving ratio, per cent	RVGL	9.3	10.0	9.3	9.6	6.4	5.3	5.5	6.7	5.3

1 See chapter text.
2 Rounded to one decimal place

Source: Office for National Statistics: 020 7533 6031

16.14
Household final consumption expenditure: classified by purpose[1]
At current market prices

£ million

		1994	1995	1996	1997	1998	1999	2000	2001	2002
FINAL CONSUMPTION EXPENDITURE OF HOUSEHOLDS										
Durable goods										
Furnishings, household equipment and routine maintenance of the house	LLIJ	12 776	13 508	14 321	15 250	15 873	16 566	17 798	20 104	22 868
Health	LLIK	1 432	1 401	1 453	1 549	1 717	1 881	1 997	2 163	2 439
Transport	LLIL	22 657	23 588	26 469	29 444	30 851	31 854	33 171	36 457	38 307
Communication	LLIM	291	244	276	282	440	512	601	707	784
Recreation and culture	LLIN	8 332	9 388	10 592	11 920	12 853	14 262	14 778	16 157	16 155
Miscellaneous goods and services	LLIO	2 787	2 963	3 094	3 295	3 320	3 398	3 403	3 525	3 573
Total durable goods	UTIA	48 275	51 092	56 205	61 740	65 054	68 473	71 748	79 113	84 126
Semi-durable goods										
Clothing and footwear	LLJL	26 314	27 426	28 865	30 270	31 540	32 561	34 759	35 655	37 067
Furnishings, household equipment and routine maintenance of the house	LLJM	7 758	7 990	8 429	9 091	9 751	10 577	11 877	12 509	14 021
Transport	LLJN	2 022	2 165	2 293	2 529	2 925	3 018	2 772	2 749	3 152
Recreation and culture	LLJO	10 909	11 770	12 887	14 724	17 292	19 049	20 405	21 041	21 151
Miscellaneous goods and services	LLJP	1 406	1 497	1 581	1 700	1 816	1 926	2 018	2 189	2 587
Total semi-durable goods	UTIQ	48 409	50 848	54 055	58 314	63 324	67 131	71 831	74 143	77 978
Non-durable goods										
Food & drink	ABZV	47 855	49 790	53 025	53 832	55 192	57 025	58 563	59 938	60 843
Alcohol & tobacco	ADFL	18 359	18 776	20 439	21 553	22 459	24 458	24 617	25 329	26 308
Housing, water, electricity, gas and other fuels	LLIX	20 876	21 357	22 757	22 656	22 094	21 800	22 265	23 212	23 778
Furnishings, household equipment and routine maintenance of the house	LLIY	2 387	2 374	2 433	2 495	2 505	2 657	2 786	2 941	3 151
Health	LLIZ	2 362	2 518	2 746	2 828	2 975	3 111	3 268	3 609	3 621
Transport	LLJA	11 968	11 986	12 767	13 818	14 396	15 200	16 711	15 676	14 459
Recreation and culture	LLJB	9 920	10 408	11 192	11 788	12 136	12 665	12 959	13 076	13 906
Miscellaneous goods and services	LLJC	6 464	7 257	8 014	8 383	8 727	9 121	9 463	9 850	10 174
Total non-durable goods	UTII	120 191	124 466	133 373	137 353	140 484	146 037	150 632	153 631	156 240
Total goods	UTIE	216 875	226 406	243 633	257 407	268 862	281 641	294 211	306 887	318 344
Services										
Clothing and footwear	LLJD	547	604	620	631	698	714	720	746	744
Housing, water, electricity, gas and other fuels	LLJE	56 502	60 055	63 173	67 558	74 103	79 411	83 389	90 425	94 617
Furnishings, household equipment and routine maintenance of the house	LLJF	2 258	2 415	2 545	2 686	2 873	3 046	3 206	3 315	3 237
Health	LLJG	2 874	2 916	3 048	3 189	3 389	3 537	3 722	3 730	4 060
Transport	LLJH	23 323	24 994	26 929	29 667	32 115	34 121	37 002	39 257	42 368
Communication	LLJI	8 352	8 823	9 083	9 732	10 607	11 493	12 755	13 440	14 233
Recreation and culture	LLJJ	16 391	19 509	20 737	21 539	22 967	23 756	24 075	25 123	28 301
Education	ADIE	5 487	6 197	6 405	7 440	7 814	8 943	9 634	9 119	8 417
Restaurants and hotels	ADIF	48 394	50 383	54 848	57 266	61 759	64 413	68 424	71 607	76 579
Miscellaneous goods and services	LLJK	39 496	40 612	42 951	45 793	49 377	53 987	59 270	62 506	65 684
Total services	UTIM	203 624	216 508	230 339	245 501	265 702	283 421	302 197	319 268	338 240
Final consumption expenditure in the UK by resident and non-resident households (domestic concept)	ABQI	420 499	442 914	473 972	502 908	534 564	565 062	596 408	626 155	656 584
Final consumption expenditure outside the UK by UK resident households	ABTA	13 058	13 721	14 377	14 942	16 913	19 690	21 654	22 932	24 565
Less Final consumption expenditure in the UK by households resident in the rest of the world	CDFD	−11 160	−13 268	−14 038	−14 037	−14 544	−14 312	−14 713	−13 383	−14 272
Final consumption expenditure by UK resident households in the UK and abroad (national concept)	ABPB	422 397	443 367	474 311	503 813	536 933	570 440	603 349	635 704	666 877

1 See chapter text. Additional detail is published in *Consumer Trends* and table A7 of *UK Economic Accounts*, available from the ONS website (http//:www. statistics.gov.uk/products/p242.asp).

Source: Office for National Statistics: 020 7533 6031

16.15 Household final consumption expenditure: classified by purpose[1]
Chained volume measures (Reference year 2000)

£ million at 2000 prices

		1994	1995	1996	1997	1998	1999	2000	2001	2002
FINAL CONSUMPTION EXPENDITURE OF HOUSEHOLDS										
Durable goods										
Furnishings, household equipment and routine maintenance of the house	LLME	13 920	14 182	14 501	15 244	15 737	16 373	17 798	19 901	22 424
Health	LLMF	3 026	2 614	2 452	2 344	2 236	2 102	1 997	1 949	1 992
Transport	LLMG	23 640	24 033	26 161	27 895	29 404	30 926	33 171	37 556	39 743
Communication	LLMH	190	164	188	214	359	478	601	728	878
Recreation and culture	LLMI	5 521	6 402	7 264	8 343	10 041	12 782	14 778	17 905	19 655
Miscellaneous goods and services	LLMJ	3 044	3 178	3 277	3 464	3 420	3 441	3 403	3 479	3 485
Total durable goods	UTIC	47 121	48 912	52 452	56 381	60 573	65 984	71 748	81 518	88 177
Semi-durable goods										
Clothing and footwear	LLNG	24 430	25 436	26 939	28 026	29 419	31 241	34 759	37 382	40 913
Furnishings, household equipment and routine maintenance of the house	LLNH	7 848	7 967	8 289	8 877	9 483	10 351	11 877	12 545	14 112
Transport	LLNI	2 311	2 447	2 480	2 648	2 999	3 045	2 772	2 762	3 119
Recreation and culture	LLNJ	10 545	11 341	12 197	13 811	16 140	18 362	20 405	21 101	21 692
Miscellaneous goods and services	LLNK	1 335	1 447	1 549	1 670	1 782	1 902	2 018	2 161	2 570
Total semi-durable goods	UTIS	46 445	48 613	51 449	55 016	59 788	64 880	71 831	75 951	82 406
Non-durable goods										
Food & drink	ADIP	51 589	51 601	53 271	54 228	54 966	56 670	58 563	57 919	58 356
Alcohol & tobacco	ADIS	24 269	23 651	24 685	25 001	24 736	25 458	24 617	24 588	25 197
Housing, water, electricity, gas and other fuels	LLMS	21 113	20 916	21 962	22 106	21 985	21 695	22 265	23 138	23 257
Furnishings, household equipment and routine maintenance of the house	LLMT	2 440	2 403	2 440	2 539	2 506	2 603	2 786	2 969	3 216
Health	LLMU	2 876	2 938	3 074	3 047	3 119	3 189	3 268	3 538	3 542
Transport	LLMV	18 465	17 688	17 992	17 832	17 674	17 193	16 711	16 519	15 752
Recreation and culture	LLMW	11 800	11 883	12 184	12 590	12 722	13 014	12 959	12 808	13 466
Miscellaneous goods and services	LLMX	7 718	8 214	8 705	8 768	8 666	8 885	9 463	9 789	10 290
Total non-durable goods	UTIK	139 557	138 797	143 877	145 773	146 110	148 550	150 632	151 268	153 076
Total goods	UTIG	230 742	234 402	246 019	255 830	265 733	279 126	294 211	308 737	323 659
Services										
Clothing and footwear	LLMY	684	724	721	709	744	733	720	721	694
Housing, water, electricity, gas and other fuels	LLMZ	77 621	78 102	79 012	80 159	81 840	82 842	83 389	84 082	85 418
Furnishings, household equipment and routine maintenance of the house	LLNA	2 997	3 097	3 126	3 160	3 219	3 255	3 206	3 109	2 861
Health	LLNB	3 901	3 839	3 783	3 765	3 757	3 690	3 722	3 474	3 639
Transport	LLNC	28 828	29 934	30 972	32 305	33 537	35 501	37 002	35 954	37 419
Communication	LLND	7 153	7 809	8 211	9 003	9 935	11 046	12 755	14 467	15 055
Recreation and culture	LLNE	19 306	22 051	22 643	22 875	23 686	23 951	24 075	25 021	25 633
Education	ADMJ	7 445	8 013	7 950	8 782	8 738	9 455	9 634	8 607	7 517
Restaurants and hotels	ADMK	60 612	60 757	63 751	64 156	66 291	66 694	68 424	68 694	70 500
Miscellaneous goods and services	LLNF	51 313	51 226	51 943	52 940	53 879	56 743	59 270	59 953	61 718
Total services	UTIO	258 561	264 745	271 502	277 407	285 401	293 814	302 197	304 082	310 454
Final consumption expenditure in the UK by resident and non-resident households (domestic concept)	ABQJ	488 181	497 829	516 652	532 703	550 751	572 782	596 408	612 819	634 113
Final consumption expenditure outside the UK by UK resident households	ABTC	12 102	12 329	12 546	14 622	16 819	19 603	21 654	22 313	23 840
Less Final consumption expenditure in the UK by households resident in the rest of the world	CCHX	–13 211	–15 402	–15 762	–15 277	–15 333	–14 708	–14 713	–12 996	–13 512
Final consumption expenditure by UK resident households in the UK and abroad (national concept)	ABPF	486 600	494 324	512 918	531 882	552 186	577 665	603 349	622 136	644 441

1 See chapter text. Additional detail is published in *Consumer Trends*
  and table A7 of *UK Economic Accounts*, available from the ONS website
  (http//:www.statistics.gov.uk/products/p242.asp).

Source: Office for National Statistics: 020 7533 6031

16.16 Individual consumption expenditure at current market prices by households, non-profit institutions serving households and general government[1]

Classified by function (COICOP/COPNI/COFOG)[2]

£ million

		1994	1995	1996	1997	1998	1999	2000	2001	2002
FINAL CONSUMPTION EXPENDITURE OF HOUSEHOLDS										
Food and non-alcoholic beverages	ABZV	47 855	49 790	53 025	53 832	55 192	57 025	58 563	59 938	60 843
Food	ABZW	42 665	44 324	47 323	47 996	49 134	50 670	51 840	52 820	53 503
Non-alcoholic beverages	ADFK	5 190	5 466	5 702	5 836	6 058	6 355	6 723	7 118	7 340
Alcoholic beverages and tobacco	ADFL	18 359	18 776	20 439	21 553	22 459	24 458	24 617	25 329	26 308
Alcoholic beverages	ADFM	7 426	7 257	8 174	8 905	9 096	10 166	10 395	10 750	11 377
Tobacco	ADFN	10 933	11 519	12 265	12 648	13 363	14 292	14 222	14 579	14 931
Clothing and footwear	ADFP	26 861	28 030	29 485	30 901	32 238	33 275	35 479	36 401	37 811
Clothing	ADFQ	22 587	23 711	25 158	26 500	27 799	28 932	31 048	31 820	33 016
Footwear	ADFR	4 274	4 319	4 327	4 401	4 439	4 343	4 431	4 581	4 795
Housing, water, electricity, gas and other fuels	ADFS	77 378	81 412	85 930	90 214	96 197	101 211	105 654	113 637	118 395
Actual rentals for housing	ADFT	17 379	17 906	18 784	19 821	21 155	22 584	23 595	25 284	25 808
Imputed rentals for housing	ADFU	34 591	37 479	39 548	42 426	47 336	51 003	53 732	58 933	61 941
Maintenance and repair of the dwelling	ADFV	6 458	6 526	6 943	7 920	8 396	8 650	8 762	9 707	10 894
Water supply and miscellaneous dwelling services	ADFW	4 051	4 290	4 558	4 772	4 961	5 201	5 033	5 061	5 238
Electricity, gas and other fuels	ADFX	14 899	15 211	16 097	15 275	14 349	13 773	14 532	14 652	14 514
Furnishings, household equipment and routine maintenance of the house	ADFY	25 179	26 287	27 728	29 522	31 002	32 846	35 667	38 869	43 277
Furniture, furnishings, carpets and other floor coverings	ADFZ	9 287	9 843	10 471	11 072	11 667	12 437	13 758	14 934	17 897
Household textiles	ADGG	2 843	3 020	3 227	3 404	3 676	3 972	4 465	4 677	5 317
Household appliances	ADGL	4 195	4 405	4 609	4 997	5 080	5 038	4 948	6 054	5 859
Glassware, tableware and household utensils	ADGM	2 751	2 767	2 887	3 159	3 410	3 722	4 431	4 657	5 226
Tools and equipment for house and garden	ADGN	1 889	1 911	1 998	2 179	2 332	2 586	2 722	2 960	3 154
Goods and services for routine household maintenance	ADGO	4 214	4 341	4 536	4 711	4 837	5 091	5 343	5 587	5 824
Health	ADGP	6 668	6 835	7 247	7 566	8 081	8 529	8 987	9 502	10 120
Medical products, appliances and equipment	ADGQ	3 794	3 919	4 199	4 377	4 692	4 992	5 265	5 772	6 060
Out-patient services	ADGR	1 754	1 781	1 825	1 893	2 005	2 092	2 178	2 200	2 364
Hospital services	ADGS	1 120	1 135	1 223	1 296	1 384	1 445	1 544	1 530	1 696
Transport	ADGT	59 970	62 733	68 458	75 458	80 287	84 193	89 656	94 139	98 286
Purchase of vehicles	ADGU	22 657	23 588	26 469	29 444	30 851	31 854	33 171	36 457	38 307
Operation of personal transport equipment	ADGV	22 977	23 861	25 556	28 044	29 826	31 440	33 783	34 123	35 295
Transport services	ADGW	14 336	15 284	16 433	17 970	19 610	20 899	22 702	23 559	24 684
Communication	ADGX	8 643	9 067	9 359	10 014	11 047	12 005	13 356	14 147	15 017
Postal services	CDEF	961	967	960	951	1 064	899	873	800	880
Telephone & telefax equipment	ADWO	291	244	276	282	440	512	601	707	784
Telephone & telefax services	ADWP	7 391	7 856	8 123	8 781	9 543	10 594	11 882	12 640	13 353
Recreation and culture	ADGY	45 552	51 075	55 408	59 971	65 248	69 732	72 217	75 397	79 513
Audio-visual, photographic and information processing equipment	ADGZ	9 620	10 862	11 974	13 501	15 032	16 312	16 934	17 871	17 096
Other major durables for recreation and culture	ADHL	1 818	2 133	2 548	2 854	3 089	3 582	3 944	4 310	4 564
Other recreational items and equipment; flowers, garden and pets	ADHZ	10 646	11 284	12 758	14 488	16 237	17 655	18 636	19 373	20 365
Recreational and cultural services	ADIA	15 251	18 241	19 246	20 005	21 357	22 127	22 435	23 426	26 500
Newspapers, books and stationery	ADIC	8 217	8 555	8 882	9 123	9 533	10 056	10 268	10 417	10 988
Package holidays[3]	ADID	–	–	–	–	–	–	–	–	–
Education										
Education services	ADIE	5 487	6 197	6 405	7 440	7 814	8 943	9 634	9 119	8 417
Restaurants and hotels	ADIF	48 394	50 383	54 848	57 266	61 759	64 413	68 424	71 607	76 579
Catering services	ADIG	41 040	42 182	46 219	48 332	52 623	55 190	58 886	62 339	66 661
Accommodation services	ADIH	7 354	8 201	8 629	8 934	9 136	9 223	9 538	9 268	9 918
Miscellaneous goods and services	ADII	50 153	52 329	55 640	59 171	63 240	68 432	74 154	78 070	82 018
Personal care	ADIJ	9 353	10 378	11 361	11 887	12 574	13 229	13 883	14 552	15 215
Personal effects not elsewhere classified	ADIK	3 657	3 898	4 083	4 351	4 490	4 673	4 748	4 980	5 151
Social protection	ADIL	8 413	8 187	8 220	8 241	8 332	8 446	8 643	8 938	9 483
Insurance	ADIM	16 408	16 306	16 520	17 841	19 513	21 789	23 807	25 934	26 977
Financial services not elsewhere classified	ADIN	5 705	5 853	6 966	7 935	8 582	9 856	11 819	11 504	11 840
Other services not elsewhere classified	ADIO	6 617	7 707	8 490	8 916	9 749	10 439	11 254	12 162	13 352
Final consumption expenditure in the UK by resident and non-resident households (domestic concept)	ABQI	420 499	442 914	473 972	502 908	534 564	565 062	596 408	626 155	656 584
Final consumption expenditure outside the UK by UK resident households	ABTA	13 058	13 721	14 377	14 942	16 913	19 690	21 654	22 932	24 565
less Final consumption expenditure in the UK by households resident in the rest of the world	CDFD	–11 160	–13 268	–14 038	–14 037	–14 544	–14 312	–14 713	–13 383	–14 272
Final consumption expenditure by UK resident households in the UK and abroad (national concept)	ABPB	422 397	443 367	474 311	503 813	536 933	570 440	603 349	635 704	666 877

16.16
continued

Individual consumption expenditure at current market prices by households, non-profit institutions serving households and general government[1]

Classified by function (COICOP/COPNI/COFOG)[2]

£ million

		1994	1995	1996	1997	1998	1999	2000	2001	2002
CONSUMPTION EXPENDITURE OF UK RESIDENT HOUSEHOLDS										
Final consumption expenditure of UK resident households in the UK and abroad	ABPB	422 397	443 367	474 311	503 813	536 933	570 440	603 349	635 704	666 877
FINAL INDIVIDUAL CONSUMPTION EXPENDITURE OF NPISH										
Final individual consumption expenditure of NPISH	ABNV	15 287	16 481	18 338	19 509	21 053	22 069	23 188	24 676	26 009
FINAL INDIVIDUAL CONSUMPTION EXPENDITURE OF OF GENERAL GOVERNMENT										
Health	QYOT	37 272	38 981	41 568	42 741	45 480	50 172	53 923	59 610	64 847
Recreation and culture	QYSU	3 246	3 172	3 384	3 476	3 488	3 735	3 967	3 996	4 732
Education	QYSE	24 202	25 291	25 506	26 147	27 281	28 593	30 446	33 791	36 917
Social protection	QYSP	12 825	13 649	14 313	14 879	15 417	16 803	17 927	18 576	22 547
Housing	QYXO	–	–	–	–	–	–	–	–	–
Final individual consumption expenditure of general government	NNAQ	77 545	81 093	84 771	87 243	91 666	99 303	106 263	115 973	129 043
Total, individual consumption expenditure/ actual individual consumption	NQEO	515 229	540 941	577 420	610 565	649 652	691 812	732 800	776 353	821 929

1 See chapter text.

2 "Purpose" or "function" classifications are designed to indicate the "socio-economic objectives" that institutional units aim to achieve through various kinds of outlays. COICOP is the Classification of Individual Consumption by Purpose and applies to households. COPNI is the Classification of the Purposes of Non-profit Institutions Serving Households and COFOG the Classification of the Functions of Government. The introduction of ESA95 coincides with the redefinition of these classifications and data will be available on a consistent basis for all European Union member states.

3 Package holidays data are dispersed between components (transport etc).

Source: Office for National Statistics: 020 7533 6031

16.17 Individual consumption expenditure at market prices by households, non-profit institutions serving households and general government

Classified by function (COICOP/COPNI/COFOG)[2]

£ million at 2000 prices

		1994	1995	1996	1997	1998	1999	2000	2001	2002
FINAL CONSUMPTION EXPENDITURE OF HOUSEHOLDS										
Food and non-alcoholic beverages	ADIP	51 589	51 601	53 271	54 228	54 966	56 670	58 563	57 919	58 356
Food	ADIQ	45 631	45 657	47 346	48 320	49 031	50 417	51 840	50 802	51 030
Non-alcoholic beverages	ADIR	5 981	5 965	5 935	5 914	5 940	6 255	6 723	7 117	7 326
Alcoholic beverages and tobacco	ADIS	24 269	23 651	24 685	25 001	24 736	25 458	24 617	24 588	25 197
Alcoholic beverages	ADIT	7 997	7 649	8 512	9 172	9 221	10 226	10 395	10 797	11 455
Tobacco	ADIU	16 727	16 505	16 507	16 007	15 657	15 265	14 222	13 791	13 742
Clothing and footwear	ADIW	25 091	26 133	27 642	28 724	30 152	31 968	35 479	38 103	41 607
Clothing	ADIX	21 169	22 191	23 622	24 528	25 840	27 680	31 048	33 503	36 713
Footwear	ADIY	3 939	3 961	4 044	4 220	4 335	4 299	4 431	4 600	4 894
Housing, water, electricity, gas and other fuels	ADIZ	98 786	98 984	101 133	102 389	103 855	104 521	105 654	107 220	108 675
Actual rentals for housing	ADJA	23 987	23 134	23 334	23 501	23 581	23 609	23 595	23 784	23 598
Imputed rentals for housing	ADJB	47 585	48 988	49 798	50 620	52 272	53 363	53 732	54 332	55 552
Maintenance and repair of the dwelling	ADJC	7 974	7 830	7 980	8 647	8 823	8 916	8 762	9 394	10 240
Water supply and miscellaneous dwelling services	ADJD	4 900	4 903	4 948	4 953	4 879	4 888	5 033	5 028	5 080
Electricity, gas and other fuels	ADJE	14 149	14 023	14 789	14 508	14 271	13 779	14 532	14 682	14 205
Furnishings, household equipment and routine maintenance of the house	ADJF	27 122	27 550	28 269	29 755	30 896	32 554	35 667	38 524	42 613
Furniture, furnishings, carpets and other floor coverings	ADJG	10 895	10 972	11 092	11 415	11 806	12 438	13 758	14 647	17 295
Household textiles	ADJH	2 864	3 001	3 137	3 297	3 532	3 835	4 465	4 687	5 402
Household appliances	ADJI	3 887	4 067	4 271	4 695	4 826	4 862	4 948	6 111	5 985
Glassware, tableware and household utensils	ADJJ	2 890	2 824	2 882	3 123	3 355	3 669	4 431	4 664	5 190
Tools and equipment for house and garden	ADJK	1 853	1 877	1 955	2 111	2 277	2 556	2 722	2 982	3 191
Goods and services for routine household maintenance	ADJL	4 871	4 915	5 011	5 154	5 115	5 200	5 343	5 433	5 550
Health	ADJM	9 513	9 243	9 225	9 095	9 082	8 973	8 987	8 961	9 173
Medical products, appliances and equipment	ADJN	5 616	5 403	5 443	5 330	5 324	5 283	5 265	5 487	5 534
Out-patient services	ADJO	2 479	2 411	2 334	2 313	2 273	2 204	2 178	2 057	2 147
Hospital services	ADJP	1 434	1 438	1 455	1 457	1 487	1 487	1 544	1 417	1 492
Transport	ADJQ	72 047	73 112	76 830	80 147	83 266	86 512	89 656	92 791	96 033
Purchase of vehicles	ADJR	23 640	24 033	26 161	27 895	29 404	30 926	33 171	37 556	39 743
Operation of personal transport equipment	ADJS	32 151	32 232	33 012	33 821	34 339	34 132	33 783	33 983	34 507
Transport services	ADJT	17 117	17 657	18 263	18 901	19 863	21 598	22 702	21 252	21 783
Communication	ADJU	7 322	7 938	8 367	9 184	10 283	11 523	13 356	15 195	15 933
Postal services	CCGZ	1 030	1 033	1 000	973	1 081	915	873	791	864
Telephone & telefax equipment	ADQF	190	164	188	214	359	478	601	728	878
Telephone & telefax services	ADQG	6 190	6 830	7 252	8 056	8 884	10 141	11 882	13 676	14 191
Recreation and culture	ADJV	45 306	49 836	52 704	56 379	61 828	67 916	72 217	76 835	80 446
Audio-visual, photographic and information processing equipment	ADJW	6 428	7 500	8 344	9 605	11 730	14 638	16 934	19 585	20 677
Other major durables for recreation and culture	ADJX	2 143	2 392	2 717	2 951	3 143	3 580	3 944	4 284	4 409
Other recreational items and equipment; flowers, gardens and pets	ADJY	10 653	11 181	12 403	13 929	15 621	17 302	18 636	19 437	20 911
Recreational and cultural services	ADJZ	17 860	20 487	20 883	21 132	21 933	22 244	22 435	23 400	23 989
Newspapers, books and stationery	ADKM	10 169	10 129	9 943	9 982	10 096	10 328	10 268	10 129	10 460
Package holidays[3]	ADMI	–	–	–	–	–	–	–	–	–
Education										
Education services	ADMJ	7 445	8 013	7 950	8 782	8 738	9 455	9 634	8 607	7 517
Restaurants and Hotels	ADMK	60 612	60 757	63 751	64 156	66 291	66 694	68 424	68 694	70 500
Catering services	ADML	51 603	50 874	53 566	53 987	56 310	56 953	58 886	59 965	61 487
Accommodation services	ADMM	9 055	9 911	10 215	10 197	9 999	9 752	9 538	8 729	9 013
Miscellaneous goods and services	ADMN	63 269	64 012	65 480	66 872	67 761	70 963	74 154	75 382	78 063
Personal care	ADMO	11 443	12 103	12 743	12 817	12 863	13 163	13 883	14 280	14 908
Personal effects not elsewhere classified	ADMP	3 874	4 090	4 241	4 500	4 578	4 705	4 748	4 943	5 093
Social protection	ADMQ	11 344	10 529	10 107	9 644	9 327	8 992	8 643	8 373	8 377
Insurance	ADMR	20 742	20 420	20 166	20 798	21 434	22 941	23 807	24 537	24 847
Financial services not elsewhere classified	ADMS	7 242	7 372	8 125	8 898	8 855	10 183	11 819	12 082	13 380
Other services not elsewhere classified	ADMT	8 845	9 649	10 201	10 277	10 774	11 010	11 254	11 167	11 458
Final consumption expenditure in the UK by resident and non-resident households (domestic concept)	ABQJ	488 181	497 829	516 652	532 703	550 751	572 782	596 408	612 819	634 113
Final consumption expenditure outside the UK by UK resident households	ABTC	12 102	12 329	12 546	14 622	16 819	19 603	21 654	22 313	23 840
less Final consumption expenditure in the UK by households resident in the rest of the world	CCHX	–13 211	–15 402	–15 762	–15 277	–15 333	–14 708	–14 713	–12 996	–13 512
Final consumption expenditure by UK resident households in the UK and abroad (national concept)	ABPF	486 600	494 324	512 918	531 882	552 186	577 665	603 349	622 136	644 441

16.17
continued

Individual consumption expenditure at market prices by households, non-profit institutions serving households and general government
Classified by function (COICOP/COPNI/COFOG)[2]

£ million at 2000 prices

		1994	1995	1996	1997	1998	1999	2000	2001	2002
CONSUMPTION EXPENDITURE OF UK RESIDENT HOUSEHOLDS										
Final consumption expenditure of UK resident households in the UK and abroad	ABPF	486 600	494 324	512 918	531 882	552 186	577 665	603 349	622 136	644 441
FINAL INDIVIDUAL CONSUMPTION EXPENDITURE OF NPISH										
Final individual consumption expenditure of NPISH	ABNU	19 161	19 796	19 850	20 290	21 713	21 543	23 188	23 845	24 553
FINAL INDIVIDUAL CONSUMPTION EXPENDITURE OF GENERAL GOVERNMENT										
Health	EMOA	46 723	48 597	49 878	51 010	52 345	53 424	53 923	54 961	56 364
Recreation and culture	QYXK	3 527	3 357	3 610	3 666	3 623	3 843	3 967	3 921	4 526
Education	EMOB	28 796	29 149	29 467	29 749	29 996	30 246	30 446	30 530	30 569
Social protection	QYXM	16 560	17 157	17 386	17 622	17 733	17 760	17 927	17 933	18 026
Housing	QYXN	–	–	–	–	–	–	–	–	–
Final individual consumption expenditure of general government	NSZK	95 686	98 279	100 364	102 062	103 687	105 270	106 263	107 345	109 485
Total, individual consumption expenditure/ actual individual consumption	YBIO	600 858	611 660	632 432	653 656	677 197	704 310	732 800	753 326	778 479

Source: Office for National Statistics: 020 7533 6031

1 See chapter text.
2 "Purpose" or "function" classifications are designed to indicate the "socio-economic objectives" that institutional units aim to achieve through various kinds of outlays. COICOP is the Classification of Individual Consumption by Purpose and applies to households. COPNI is the Classification of the Purposes of Non-profit Institutions Serving Households and COFOG the Classification of the Functions of Government. The introduction of ESA95 coincides with the redefinition of these classifications and data will be available on a consistent basis for all European Union member states.
3 Package holidays data are dispersed between components (transport etc).

16.18
Change in inventories at constant prices[1,2]

£ million

	Mining and quarrying	Manufacturing industries				Electricity, gas and water supply	Distributive trades		Other industries[4]	Change in inventories
		Materials and fuel	Work in progress	Finished goods	Total		Wholesale[3]	Retail[3]		
	FADO	FBID	FBIE	FBIF	DHBH	FADP	FAJM	FBYH	DLWV	ABMQ
1993	−40	–	−1 118	−372	−1 489	−306	769	371	–	363
1994	−405	133	227	342	703	−649	491	1 041	–	4 882
1995	−126	518	1 124	980	2 625	−210	572	820	819	4 540
1996	−47	−105	−214	6	−314	15	654	646	906	1 851
1997	56	406	−1 309	334	−582	105	1 649	809	1 999	4 016
1998	261	726	−577	359	509	−158	528	999	2 799	4 913
1999	−219	688	−118	−466	112	−162	1 692	1 492	3 516	6 426
2000	−177	732	520	470	1 722	285	1 903	1 269	269	5 271
2001	21	−604	−303	411	−496	−81	479	514	2 501	2 938
2002	−9	−657	−582	−728	−1 967	−38	−203	1 858	1 855	1 496

1 See chapter text. Estimates are given to the nearest £ million but cannot be regarded as accurate to this degree.
2 Components may not sum to totals due to rounding.
3 Wholesaling and retailing estimates exclude the motor trades.
4 Quarterly alignment adjustment included in this series.

Source: Office for National Statistics 020 7533 6031

16.19 Gross fixed capital formation at current purchasers' prices
Analysis by broad sector and type of asset[1,2]

Total economy

£ million

		1994	1995	1996	1997	1998	1999	2000	2001	2002
Private sector										
New dwellings, excluding land	DFDF	18 285	18 860	20 205	22 017	23 317	23 921	25 604	27 184	33 401
Other buildings and structures	EQBU	16 430	18 023	20 763	25 228	28 403	31 017	32 041	32 615	31 844
Transport equipment	EQBV	10 112	10 224	11 325	12 107	15 279	14 303	12 726	14 420	15 011
Other machinery and equipment and cultivated assets	EQBW	35 586	42 157	47 586	49 376	57 469	57 335	60 504	58 458	52 012
Intangible fixed assets	EQBX	2 982	3 179	3 278	3 395	3 555	3 624	4 048	4 285	4 628
Costs associated with the transfer of ownership of non-produced assets	EQBY	5 208	5 173	6 726	7 647	7 453	9 859	11 206	12 590	15 123
Total	EQBZ	88 603	97 616	109 883	119 770	135 476	140 059	146 129	149 552	152 019
Public non-financial corporations										
New dwellings, excluding land	DEER	139	162	163	123	49	8	–	–	–
Other buildings and structures	DEES	3 492	3 781	3 369	2 671	2 466	2 720	3 058	3 450	3 254
Transport equipment	DEEP	512	354	225	190	171	154	168	156	131
Other machinery and equipment and cultivated assets	DEEQ	761	857	759	705	760	964	886	1 543	928
Intangible fixed assets	DLXJ	374	496	585	595	605	625	551	397	556
Costs associated with the transfer of ownership of non-produced assets	DLXQ	349	126	101	267	352	−8	6	−62	−6
Total	FCCJ	5 627	5 776	5 202	4 551	4 403	4 463	4 669	5 484	4 863
General government										
New dwellings, excluding land	DFHW	2 809	2 642	2 148	1 788	1 856	1 771	1 790	2 129	2 196
Other buildings and structures	EQCH	10 118	10 039	8 693	7 556	8 172	7 943	8 779	9 703	11 298
Transport equipment	EQCI	771	717	672	675	693	610	550	592	683
Other machinery and equipment and cultivated assets	EQCJ	1 879	1 998	1 852	1 452	1 283	1 467	1 308	1 458	1 684
Intangible fixed assets	EQCK	257	264	273	259	387	396	367	334	358
Costs associated with the transfer of ownership of non-produced assets	EQCL	−1 750	−1 604	−2 432	−2 275	−1 730	−2 062	−2 382	−2 561	−3 129
Total	NNBF	14 084	14 056	11 206	9 455	10 661	10 125	10 412	11 655	13 090
Total gross fixed capital formation	NPQX	108 314	117 448	126 291	133 776	150 540	154 647	161 210	166 691	169 972

1 See chapter text.
2 Components may not sum to totals due to rounding.

Source: Office for National Statistics: 020 7533 6031

16.20 Gross fixed capital formation at current purchasers' prices
Analysis by type of asset[1,2]

Total economy

£ million

		1994	1995	1996	1997	1998	1999	2000	2001	2002
Tangible fixed assets										
New dwellings, excluding land	DFDK	21 233	21 664	22 516	23 928	25 222	25 700	27 394	29 311	35 597
Other buildings and structures	DLWS	30 040	31 843	32 825	35 455	39 041	41 680	43 878	45 768	46 396
Transport equipment	DLWZ	11 395	11 295	12 222	12 972	16 143	15 067	13 444	15 168	15 825
Other machinery and equipment and cultivated assets	DLXI	38 226	45 012	50 197	51 533	59 512	59 766	62 698	61 461	54 624
Total	EQCQ	100 894	109 814	117 760	123 888	139 918	142 213	147 414	151 708	152 442
Intangible fixed assets	DLXP	3 613	3 939	4 136	4 249	4 547	4 645	4 966	5 016	5 542
Costs associated with the transfer of ownership of non-produced assets	DFBH	3 807	3 695	4 395	5 639	6 075	7 789	8 830	9 967	11 988
Total gross fixed capital formation	NPQX	108 314	117 448	126 291	133 776	150 540	154 647	161 210	166 691	169 972

1 See chapter text.
2 Components may not sum to totals due to rounding.

Source: Office for National Statistics: 020 7533 6031

16.21 Gross fixed capital formation[1,2,3]
Chained volume measures (Reference year 2000)
Total economy: Analysis by broad sector and type of asset

£ million at 2000 prices

		1994	1995	1996	1997	1998	1999	2000	2001	2002
Private sector										
New dwellings, excluding land	DFDP	23 962	23 691	24 629	26 079	26 377	25 508	25 604	25 937	30 914
Other buildings and structures	EQCU	18 734	19 974	22 982	27 914	31 043	31 825	32 041	31 904	30 882
Transport equipment	EQCV	11 034	10 679	11 414	12 505	15 591	14 373	12 726	14 537	15 287
Other machinery and equipment and cultivated assets	EQCW	29 819	34 594	38 970	42 006	51 779	54 586	60 504	62 085	58 497
Intangible fixed assets	EQCX	3 486	3 690	3 653	3 800	3 740	3 712	4 048	4 206	4 456
Costs associated with the transfer of ownership of non-produced assets	EQCY	11 477	10 407	12 260	12 482	10 510	11 485	11 206	11 207	12 226
Total	EQCZ	95 196	100 319	111 135	121 945	138 534	141 125	146 129	149 876	152 262
Public non-financial corporations										
New dwellings, excluding land	DEEW	194	209	190	141	55	9	–	–	–
Other buildings and structures	DEEX	4 529	4 460	3 776	2 949	2 612	2 785	3 058	3 340	3 067
Transport equipment	DEEU	533	386	242	199	174	154	168	155	129
Other machinery and equipment and cultivated assets	DEEV	741	671	596	570	685	916	886	1 582	1 009
Intangible fixed assets	EQDE	441	567	652	643	632	643	551	390	536
Costs associated with the transfer of ownership of non-produced assets	EQDF	−221	−78	−94	−239	−278	4	6	−55	−14
Total	EQDG	6 600	6 321	5 490	4 746	4 506	4 519	4 669	5 412	4 727
General government										
New dwellings, excluding land	DFID	3 630	3 154	2 507	2 051	2 055	1 854	1 790	2 062	2 059
Other buildings and structures	EQDI	13 178	11 721	9 721	8 512	8 611	8 168	8 779	9 346	10 502
Transport equipment	EQDJ	851	759	694	728	690	602	550	603	637
Other machinery and equipment and cultivated assets	EQDK	1 288	1 386	1 282	1 037	1 044	1 341	1 308	1 624	1 955
Intangible fixed assets	EQDL	287	307	297	304	410	404	367	327	354
Costs associated with the transfer of ownership of non-produced assets	EQDM	−4 347	−3 599	−4 965	−4 198	−2 748	−2 475	−2 382	−2 218	−2 494
Total	EQDN	14 402	13 231	10 493	9 172	10 086	9 935	10 412	11 744	13 013
Total gross fixed capital formation	NPQR	116 814	120 389	127 238	135 876	153 148	155 576	161 210	167 032	170 002

1 See chapter text.
2 For the years before 2000, the total differs from the sum of their components.
3 Components may not sum to totals due to rounding.

Source: Office for National Statistics: 020 7533 6031

16.22 Gross fixed capital formation[1,2,3]
Chained volume measures (Reference year 2000)
Total economy: Analysis by type of asset

£ million at 2000 prices

		1994	1995	1996	1997	1998	1999	2000	2001	2002
Tangible fixed assets										
New dwellings, excluding land	DFDV	27 857	27 103	27 358	28 278	28 490	27 372	27 394	27 999	32 973
Other buildings and structures	EQDP	37 865	35 978	36 454	39 382	42 281	42 778	43 878	44 590	44 451
Transport equipment	DLWJ	12 511	11 778	12 339	13 424	16 455	15 128	13 444	15 296	16 053
Other machinery and equipment and cultivated assets	DLWM	31 950	37 074	40 928	43 635	53 491	56 849	62 698	65 290	61 461
Total	EQDS	105 372	108 913	115 144	122 761	139 960	141 863	147 414	153 175	154 938
Intangible fixed assets	EQDT	4 019	4 360	4 607	4 752	4 782	4 758	4 966	4 923	5 346
Costs associated with the transfer of ownership of non-produced assets	DFDW	7 894	7 073	7 773	8 928	8 329	9 023	8 830	8 934	9 718
Total gross fixed capital formation	NPQR	116 814	120 389	127 238	135 876	153 148	155 576	161 210	167 032	170 002

1 See chapter text.
2 For the years before 2000, the total differs from the sum of their components.
3 Components may not sum to totals due to rounding.

Source: Office for National Statistics: 020 7533 6031

17 Prices

Prices

Producer price index numbers *(Tables 17.1 and 17.2)*
The producer price indices were published for the first time in August 1983, replacing the former wholesale price indices. Full details of the differences between the two indices were given in an article published in *British Business*, 15 April 1983. The producer price indices are calculated using the same general methodology as that used by the wholesale price indices.

The high level index numbers in Tables 17.1 and 17.2 are constructed on a net sector basis. That is to say, they are intended to measure only transactions between the sector concerned and other sectors. Within sector transactions are excluded. Index numbers for the whole of manufacturing are thus not weighted averages of sector index numbers.

The index numbers for selected industries in Tables 17.1 and 17.2 are constructed on a gross sector basis i.e. all transactions are included in deriving the weighting patterns, including sales within the same industry.

All the index numbers are compiled exclusive of value-added tax. Excise duties on cigarettes, manufactured tobacco and alcoholic liquor are included, as is the duty on hydrocarbon oils.

The indices relate to the average prices for a year. The movement in these prices are weighted to reflect the relative importance of the composite products in a chosen year (known as the base year), currently 2000.

Since July 1995, PPIs have been published fully reclassified to the 1992 version of the Standard Industrial Classification (SIC). From 1998, high level PPIs on the 1980 SIC will also be shown in Tables 17.1 and 17.2.

Further details are available from the National Statistics website: *www.statistics.gov.uk/ppi.*

Purchasing power of the pound *(Table 17.3)*
Changes in the internal purchasing power of a currency may be defined as the 'inverse' of changes in the levels of prices; when prices go up, the amount which can be purchased with a given sum of money goes down. Movements in the internal purchasing power of the pound are based on the consumers' expenditure deflator (CED) prior to 1962 and on the General index of retail prices (RPI) from January 1962 onwards. The CED shows the movement in prices implied by the national accounts estimates of consumers' expenditure valued at current and at constant prices, whilst the RPI is constructed directly by weighting together monthly movements in prices according to a given pattern of household expenditure derived from the Expenditure and Food Survey. If the purchasing power of the pound is taken to be 100p in a particular month (quarter, year), the comparable purchasing power in a subsequent month (quarter, year) is:

$$100 \quad \times \quad \frac{\text{earlier period price index}}{\text{later period price index}}$$

where the price index used is the CED for years 1946-1961 and the RPI for periods after 1961.

Consumer prices index *(Table 17.4)*
The consumer prices index (CPI) is the main United Kingdom domestic measure of inflation for macro-economic purposes. Like the RPI (see below) it measures the average change from month to month in the prices of consumer goods and services purchased in the UK, but there are differences in coverage and methodology. A detailed description of these differences is given in the paper entitled "*The New Inflation Target: the Statistical Perspective*". This paper is available on the National Statistics website: *www.statistics.gov.uk/StatBase/Product.asp?vlnk=10913.*

Since 10 December 2003, the Government inflation target for the UK has been defined in terms of the CPI measure of inflation. Prior to that the CPI had been published in the UK as the harmonised index of consumer prices (HICP); the two shall remain one and the same index.

The HICPs are calculated in each Member State of the European Union (EU), according to rules specified in a series of European Regulations developed by the EU statistical office in conjunction with the EU Member States. The HICPs are used to compare inflation rate across the EU. Since January 1999 it has also been used by the European Central Bank (ECB) as the measure of price stability across the euro area. Additional information on HICPs is available from the National Statistics website: *www.statistics.gov.uk/hicp*

CPI inflation rates prior to 1997 and index levels prior to 1996 are estimated. See article on National Statistics website: *www.statistics.gov.uk/cci/article.asp?ID=31* Also the coverage of CPI categories for health, education and miscellaneous goods and services have been extended between 2000 and 2002. Details are given in articles available on the website: *www.statistics.gov.uk/cci/searchres2.asp?ct=6&term=HICP*

Further details on the CPI are available from the National Statistics website: *www.statistics.gov.uk/cpi*

Retail prices index *(Table 17.5)*
The retail prices index (RPI) is the most familiar general purpose measure of inflation in the UK, measuring the percentage changes month by month in the average level of prices of the goods and services purchased by the great majority of households in the United Kingdom. The uses of the RPI include indexation of pensions, state benefits and index-linked gilts. The expenditure pattern on which the index is based is revised each year using information from the Expenditure and Food Survey. The expenditure of certain higher income households and households of retired people dependent mainly on social security benefits is excluded.

The index covers a large and representative selection of more than 650 separate goods and services, for which price movements are regularly measured in around 150 locations throughout the country. Around 120,000 separate price quotations are used in compiling the index.

Further details are available from the National Statistics website: *www.statistics.gov.uk/rpi*

Tax and price index (TPI) *(Table 17.6)*

The purpose and methodology of the TPI were described in an article in the August 1979 issue (No 310) of *Economic Trends* (The Stationery Office). The TPI measures the change in *gross* taxable income needed for taxpayers to maintain their purchasing power, allowing for changes in retail prices. The TPI thus takes account of the changes to direct taxes (and employees' National Insurance contributions) facing representative cross-section of taxpayers as well as changes in the retail prices index (RPI).

When direct taxation or employees' National Insurance contributions change, the TPI will rise by less than or more than the RPI according to the type of changes made. Between Budgets, the monthly increase in the TPI is normally slightly larger than that in the RPI, since all the extra income needed to offset any rise in retail prices is fully taxed.

Index numbers of agricultural prices
(Tables 17.7 and 17.8)

The Indices of producer prices of agricultural products are currently based on the calendar year 1995. They are designed to provide short-term and medium-term indications of movements in these prices. All annual series are base-weighted Laspeyres type, using value weights derived from the Economic Accounts for Agriculture prepared for the Statistical Office of the European Union. Prices are measured exclusive of VAT. For table 17.6 it has generally been necessary to measure the prices of materials (inputs) ex-supplier. For table 17.7, it has generally been necessary to measure the prices received by producers (outputs) at the first marketing stage. The construction of the indices enables them to be combined with similar indices for other member countries of the European Union to provide an overall indication of trends within the Union which appears in the Union's Eurostat series of publications.

Index numbers at a more detailed level and for earlier based series are available from the Department for Environment and Rural Affairs, Stats C&S SSP, Room 145 Foss House, Kingspool 1-2 Peasholme Green, York, YO1 7PX Tel 10904 455253

17.1 Producer price index numbers of materials and fuels purchased
United Kingdom
All manufacturing and selected industries SIC(92)[1]

2000 = 100

			Annual averages							
			1995	1996	1997	1998	1999	2000	2001	2002
Net sector										
Materials and fuel purchased by manufacturing industry[2]	RNNK	6292000050	114.4	113.0	103.7	94.3	93.1	100.0	98.8	94.4
Materials	PLKX	6292000010	114.9	114.6	104.5	93.6	92.3	100.0	98.1	93.7
Fuels[2]	RNNL	6292000060	113.2	103.8	99.9	103.8	103.6	100.0	107.1	103.4
Materials and fuels purchased by manufacturing industry-seasonally adjusted[2]	RNPE	6292008950	114.4	112.9	103.6	94.3	93.1	100.0	98.8	94.4
Materials and fuels purchased by manufacturing industry other than food, beverages, petroleum and tobacco[2]	RNNQ	6292990050	117.0	112.0	104.9	100.0	96.4	100.0	98.7	94.0
Materials purchased by manufacturing industry other than food, drink and tobacco	RWCJ	6292990010	118.4	114.4	106.5	99.7	95.8	100.0	98.1	93.2
Fuel purchased by manufacturing industry other than food and beverages[2]	RNNS	6292990060	117.6	107.8	103.7	103.9	103.7	100.0	106.8	103.1
Materials and fuels purchased by manufacturing industries other than food, beverages, petroleum and tobacco-seasonally adjusted[2]	RNPF	6292998950	117.0	112.0	104.8	100.0	96.4	100.0	98.7	94.0
Gross sector[3]										
All manufacturing	RBBO	6192000000	106.3	106.5	103.0	98.3	96.3	100.0	99.5	97.4
Other mining and quarrying products	RABE	6112140000	86.7	88.3	89.2	87.5	90.2	100.0	96.9	92.3
Manufacture of food products	RBBQ	6192151600	114.5	114.2	107.8	104.0	102.3	100.0	103.4	102.5
Food products and beverages	RABF	6112150000	110.2	111.3	106.5	104.0	102.3	100.0	103.4	102.5
Tobacco products	RABG	6112160000	111.9	112.9	107.1	102.3	100.8	100.0	100.1	101.3
Manufacture of textiles	RBBR	6192171800	110.5	109.6	106.3	102.8	98.7	100.0	100.7	98.7
Textiles	RABH	6112170000	111.3	110.3	106.7	102.7	98.7	100.0	100.8	99.0
Wearing apparel	RABI	6112180000	109.2	108.7	105.8	103.1	98.5	100.0	100.5	97.9
Manufacture of leather	RBBS	6192190000	106.1	107.1	104.2	99.8	97.9	100.0	102.0	100.2
Manufacture of wood and wood products	RBBT	6192200000	114.8	113.7	112.6	105.6	100.2	100.0	99.4	96.8
Manufacture of pulp, paper, publishing and printing	RBBU	6192212200	108.6	107.7	101.1	98.5	97.0	100.0	101.0	99.4
Pulp and paper products	RABL	6112210000	109.6	108.6	102.1	98.7	96.0	100.0	101.1	97.9
Printed matter and recording material	RABM	6112220000	108.2	107.4	100.7	98.4	97.4	100.0	101.0	100.1
Manufacture of coke	RBBV	61922300000	64.8	76.5	69.6	51.1	65.4	100.0	92.1	89.3
Manufacture of chemical products	RBBW	6192240000	107.5	106.0	103.1	99.6	96.1	100.0	101.4	99.8
Manufacture of rubber products	RBBX	6192250000	116.9	110.7	105.4	99.3	96.6	100.0	99.4	98.0
Manufacture of other non-metallic mineral products	RBBY	6192260000	97.7	98.3	98.0	97.6	97.4	100.0	101.1	100.5
Manufacture of basic metals	RBBZ	6192272800	106.5	105.8	103.6	100.2	94.8	100.0	98.9	97.1
Basic metals	RABV	6112270000	107.4	106.1	103.4	98.9	93.4	100.0	99.0	97.4
Fabricated metal products	RABW	6112280000	105.4	105.3	103.8	101.3	96.1	100.0	98.7	96.8
Manufacture of machinery and equipment not elsewhere classified	RBCA	6192290000	102.3	103.1	102.8	100.9	97.8	100.0	99.0	97.3

17.1

continued

Producer price index numbers of materials and fuels purchased
United Kingdom
All manufacturing and selected industries SIC(92)[1]

2000 = 100

			Annual averages							
			1995	1996	1997	1998	1999	2000	2001	2002
Manufacture of electrical and optical equipment	RBCB	6192303300	120.1	117.1	111.5	104.6	99.8	100.0	97.3	92.6
Office machinery and computers	RABY	6112300000	136.5	128.9	116.6	104.7	99.5	100.0	95.5	87.5
Electrical machinery and apparatus not elsewhere classified	RACB	6112310000	108.3	107.6	105.7	101.6	98.1	100.0	98.7	96.0
Radio, television and communication equipment	RACC	6112320000	115.2	113.3	109.5	103.8	99.0	100.0	98.2	94.7
Medical, precision, optical instruments and clocks	RACD	6112330000	113.2	111.8	108.5	103.2	99.0	100.0	98.3	95.4
Manufacture of transport equipment	RBCC	6192343500	101.3	103.1	103.3	102.1	99.6	100.0	99.2	97.4
Motor vehicles, trailers and semi-trailers	RACE	6112340000	102.5	104.4	104.4	103.1	100.3	100.0	99.4	98.2
Other transport equipment	RACF	6112350000	98.1	100.0	100.4	99.8	97.8	100.0	98.9	95.6
Manufacturing not elsewhere classified	RBCD	6192363700	105.9	105.8	104.6	101.4	97.8	100.0	99.2	98.0
Electricity incl.CCL	RNOD	4010990050	118.7	114.7	107.7	107.5	107.5	100.0	96.2	92.5
Gas incl.CCL	RNOH	4020990050	111.0	84.8	87.8	92.4	91.9	100.0	140.7	136.5
Collected and purified water	PQNB	4100000000	84.3	88.5	92.5	97.7	102.4	100.0	101.6	103.4
Construction materials	ROGG	6101451800	100.0	100.5	102.1	102.9	101.6	103.8	105.7	..
House building materials	ROGH	6101452800	100.0	100.7	102.2	103.0	102.1	104.1	106.2	..

SIC (80) Net sector

Materials and fuels purchased by manufacturing industry	DZBR	6200000000	100.0	96.4	89.0	84.1	82.0	83.9	85.2	82.6

1 See chapter text.
2 These indices include the Climate Change Levy which was introduced in April
3 The Climate Change Levy is excluded from the detailed industry input index.

Source: Office for National Statistics: 01633 812106

17.2 Producer price index numbers of output
United Kingdom
All manufacturing and selected industries SIC(92)

2000 = 100

			Annual averages							
			1995	1996	1997	1998	1999	2000	2001	2002
Net sector										
Output of manufactured products	PLLU	7209200000	94.8	97.2	98.1	98.1	98.5	100.0	99.7	99.8
All manufacturing excluding duty	PVNP	7209200010	98.1	100.3	100.4	99.4	99.0	100.0	99.7	99.7
All manufacturing excluding duty - seasonally adjusted	PVNQ	7209200890	98.0	100.3	100.4	99.4	99.0	100.0	99.7	99.8
Products of manufacturing industries other than the food, beverages, petroleum and tobacco manufacturing industries -unadjusted	PLLV	7209299000	100.2	102.1	102.3	101.3	100.2	100.0	99.4	99.3
All manufacturing excluding food, beverages, tobacco and petroleum - seasonally adjusted	PLLW	7209299890	100.2	102.1	102.3	101.3	100.2	100.0	99.4	99.3
Gross sector										
Manufactured product	POKE	7109200000	99.3	101.3	100.6	98.3	97.8	100.0	99.4	99.1
Manufactured products excluding food, drink, tobacco and petroleum	POKF	7109299000	102.3	103.7	102.9	101.5	100.1	100.0	99.4	99.3
Other mining and quarrying products[1]	ROFV	711214800	84.3	88.5	91.1	94.8	96.2	100.0	104.4	120.3
Food products, beverages and tobacco excluding duty	POKH	7111151600	97.5	100.5	100.5	100.3	100.5	100.0	101.9	103.3
Food products, beverages and tobacco including duty	RBGA	7111151680	93.3	96.3	96.9	97.8	99.1	100.0	102.0	103.3
Food products and beverages including duty	RPUN	7112150080	98.5	101.2	100.7	100.4	100.4	100.0	101.5	102.6
Food products excluding beverages	RBGD	7112159900	99.9	103.0	102.0	101.1	100.9	100.0	101.7	102.7
Alcoholic beverages including duty	RPUX	7113159080	93.0	92.7	94.2	97.3	98.7	100.0	101.6	103.1
Tobacco products including duty	RPUS	7112160080	65.0	70.0	75.3	81.8	91.6	100.0	105.0	107.8
Textiles and textile products	POKI	7111171800	94.8	97.3	99.2	100.3	99.9	100.0	99.2	98.8
Textiles	POKZ	7112170000	96.2	98.5	100.2	101.0	100.2	100.0	99.4	99.2
Wearing apparel: Furs	POLA	7112180000	91.6	94.6	97.3	98.8	99.2	100.0	99.0	97.9
Leather and leather products	POKJ	7111190000	97.7	100.3	101.0	100.4	99.2	100.0	102.5	102.7
Wood and wood products	POKK	7111200000	106.4	105.1	106.7	104.9	101.5	100.0	99.9	100.0
Pulp, paper and paper products, recorded media and printing services	POKL	7111212200	96.3	99.6	98.3	98.4	98.2	100.0	101.5	102.1
Pulp, paper and paper products	POLD	7112210000	102.6	104.3	99.5	98.2	96.8	100.0	101.0	100.3
Printed matter and recorded media	POLE	7112220000	93.3	97.4	97.8	98.5	98.8	100.0	101.7	102.7
Chemicals, chemical, products and manmade fibres	POKN	7111240000	105.3	104.1	102.5	98.5	97.2	100.0	100.2	100.5
Rubber and plastic products	POKO	7111250000	103.7	105.2	104.6	102.2	100.4	100.0	100.3	100.4
Other non-metallic mineral products	POKP	7111260000	91.7	92.7	94.9	97.6	99.3	100.0	101.9	105.0
Base metals and fabricated metal products	POKQ	7111272800	102.4	103.8	103.0	102.5	98.7	100.0	99.9	99.5
Base metals	POLJ	712270000	111.4	110.1	106.9	103.1	94.7	100.0	98.4	96.1
Fabricated metal products, except machinery and equipment	POLK	7112280000	97.3	100.3	101.2	102.2	100.6	100.0	100.6	101.1
Machinery and equipment not elsewhere classified	POKR	7111290000	92.2	94.9	97.4	98.3	99.1	100.0	100.9	101.8

17.2
continued

Producer price index numbers of output
United Kingdom
All manufacturing and selected industries SIC(92)

			Annual averages							
			1995	1996	1997	1998	1999	2000	2001	2002
Gross sector continued										
Electrical and optical equipment	POKS	7111343500	134.9	131.2	122.6	112.2	106.2	100.0	94.7	90.0
Office machinery and computers	POLM	7112300000	259.8	236.2	193.5	146.6	124.1	100.0	75.2	64.6
Electrical machinery and apparatus not elsewhere classified	POLN	7112310000	100.4	102.0	102.5	102.3	101.3	100.0	99.9	100.4
Radio, television and communication equipment and apparatus	POLO	7112320000	129.5	124.1	116.7	109.4	104.2	100.0	97.3	88.0
Medical precision and optical instruments, watches and clocks	POLP	7112330000	93.2	97.1	97.8	98.7	99.2	100.0	101.1	102.4
Transport equipment	POKT	7111343500	93.0	95.7	97.1	99.0	100.9	100.0	98.4	98.8
Motor vehicles, trailers and semi-trailers	POLQ	7112340000	96.1	98.9	100.2	101.9	102.3	100.0	96.6	96.3
Other transport	POLR	7112350000	85.6	88.1	89.8	92.9	98.0	100.0	102.3	103.8
Furniture: other manufactured goods not elsewhere classified	POLS	7112360000	95.7	99.2	100.6	101.7	100.9	100.0	100.3	100.9

1 These indices include the Aggregates Levy which was introduced in April 2002. These indices do not feed into Net Sector output (PLLV).

Source: Office for National Statistics: 01633 812106

17.3

Internal purchasing power of the pound (based on RPI)[1,2,3]
United Kingdom

Pence

	Year in which purchasing power was 100p																		
	1984	1985	1986	1987	1988	1989	1990	1991	1992	1993	1994	1995	1996	1997	1998	1999	2000	2001	2002
	BAMQ	BAMR	BAMS	BAMT	BAMU	BAMV	BAMW	BASX	CZVM	CBXX	DOFX	DOHR	DOLM	DTUL	CDQG	JKZZ	ZMHO	IKHI	FAUI
1984	100	106	110	114	120	129	141	150	155	158	162	167	171	177	183	185	191	194	198
1985	94	100	103	108	113	122	133	141	146	149	152	158	161	166	172	175	180	183	186
1986	91	97	100	104	109	118	129	136	142	144	147	152	156	161	167	169	174	177	180
1987	88	93	96	100	105	113	124	131	136	138	141	146	150	155	160	162	167	170	173
1988	83	88	92	95	100	108	118	125	130	132	135	139	143	147	152	155	159	162	165
1989	77	82	85	88	93	100	109	116	120	122	125	129	133	137	141	144	148	150	153
1990	71	75	78	81	85	91	100	106	110	112	114	118	121	125	129	131	135	137	140
1991	67	71	73	76	80	86	94	100	104	105	108	112	114	118	122	124	128	130	132
1992	64	68	71	74	77	83	91	96	100	102	104	108	110	114	118	119	123	125	127
1993	63	67	70	72	76	82	90	95	98	100	102	106	109	112	116	118	121	123	125
1994	62	66	68	71	74	80	88	93	96	98	100	103	106	109	113	115	118	120	122
1995	60	63	66	68	72	77	85	90	93	94	97	100	102	106	109	111	114	116	118
1996	58	62	64	67	70	75	83	87	91	92	94	98	100	103	107	108	112	113	115
1997	57	60	62	65	68	73	80	85	88	89	92	95	97	100	103	105	108	110	112
1998	55	58	60	63	66	71	77	82	85	86	88	92	94	97	100	102	105	106	108
1999	54	57	59	62	65	70	76	81	84	85	87	90	92	95	98	100	103	105	107
2000	52	56	57	60	63	68	74	78	81	83	85	88	90	92	96	97	100	102	103
2001	51	55	56	59	62	66	73	77	80	81	83	86	88	91	94	95	98	100	102
2002	51	54	56	58	61	65	72	76	79	80	82	85	87	89	92	94	97	98	100

1 See chapter text.
2 To find the purchasing power of the pound in 1995, given that it was 100 pence in 1990, select the column headed 1990 and look at the 1995 row. The result is 85 pence.

3 These figures are calculated by taking the inverse ratio of the respective annual averages of the Retail Prices Index.

Source: Office for National Statistics: 020 7533 5874

17.4 Consumer Prices Index[1]: Detailed figures by division

Index level (1996=100)

	Food and non-alcoholic beverages	Alcoholic beverages and tobacco	Clothing and footwear	Housing, water, electric-ity, gas & other fuels	Furniture, household equipment & routine mainte-nance	Health	Transport	Commun-ication	Recreation and culture	Education	Restaur-ants and hotels	Miscell-aneous goods and services	CPI (overall index)
COICOP Division	01	02	03	04	05	06	07	08	09	10	11	12	
Weights 2003	108	47	62	104	68	23	144	25	163	20	135	101	1000
	CHVK	CHVL	CHVM	CHVN	CHVO	CHVP	CHVQ	CHVR	CHVS	CHVT	CHVU	CHVV	CHVJ
2001 Nov	104.5	126.9	76.2	109.7	99.4	117.4	110.0	84.4	104.4	136.0	121.1	115.7	107.2
Dec	105.1	126.2	75.9	109.8	100.9	117.5	110.3	84.4	104.6	136.0	121.3	116.1	107.5
2002 Jan	106.1	127.2	71.4	110.5	97.5	118.3	110.4	84.1	104.4	136.0	121.5	116.5	107.1
Feb	106.0	127.4	71.3	110.6	98.4	118.1	110.6	84.3	104.6	136.0	121.7	116.5	107.3
Mar	106.2	127.4	72.0	110.6	99.8	118.6	111.4	83.8	104.9	136.0	122.1	116.6	107.7
Apr	106.0	127.6	71.7	111.9	98.5	119.6	113.0	83.9	105.4	136.0	122.7	117.6	108.1
May	105.6	128.7	72.0	112.1	99.3	120.0	113.5	83.7	105.2	136.0	123.1	117.9	108.4
Jun	104.9	128.5	71.3	112.2	98.5	120.5	114.1	83.9	105.5	136.0	123.6	117.6	108.4
Jul	104.8	129.4	67.0	112.2	97.2	120.3	115.6	83.8	105.3	136.0	123.9	117.3	108.1
Aug	104.6	129.0	67.7	112.3	97.6	121.0	115.9	84.0	106.0	136.0	124.3	117.6	108.4
Sep	104.8	129.6	71.1	112.3	98.8	121.1	113.7	84.1	106.2	139.2	124.6	117.8	108.7
Oct	105.0	129.4	70.7	112.5	97.9	121.4	113.5	84.4	106.4	147.6	124.9	119.2	108.9
Nov	104.9	129.0	71.7	112.5	98.7	121.5	112.2	84.5	106.5	147.6	125.1	119.1	108.9
Dec	104.9	128.4	70.3	112.7	100.1	121.4	115.1	84.4	106.3	147.6	125.4	119.6	109.3
2003 Jan	104.9	129.3	67.4	112.8	96.8	122.2	114.4	84.5	105.8	147.6	125.6	118.6	108.6
Feb	105.6	129.4	68.2	113.0	97.4	122.6	115.0	84.5	106.0	147.6	125.8	118.8	109.0
Mar	105.9	129.4	68.7	113.0	98.9	122.7	116.0	84.6	105.8	147.6	126.2	119.0	109.4
Apr	106.3	130.8	68.6	113.7	97.5	123.3	117.8	84.5	105.7	147.6	126.7	119.1	109.7
May	106.9	131.2	68.7	113.7	98.8	123.7	116.8	84.6	105.2	147.6	127.1	119.2	109.7
Jun	106.3	131.3	68.1	113.8	98.2	123.9	116.7	83.9	104.8	147.6	127.5	119.4	109.6
Jul	106.3	131.4	65.5	114.2	97.1	125.0	118.1	84.6	104.2	147.6	127.8	120.1	109.5
Aug	106.3	132.1	66.9	114.3	97.3	125.1	118.7	84.6	104.4	147.6	128.0	120.6	109.9
Sep	107.1	132.0	68.7	114.6	98.5	125.4	117.4	85.0	104.4	151.3	128.3	121.0	110.2
Oct	107.3	132.2	68.4	114.9	97.6	125.8	117.2	84.7	104.3	154.5	128.5	122.5	110.4
Nov	107.6	131.1	68.6	115.0	98.4	125.9	116.4	84.2	104.1	154.5	128.9	122.5	110.3

Percentage change on a year earlier

	CJYS	CJYT	CJYU	CJYV	CJYW	CJYX	CJYY	CJYZ	CJZA	CJZB	CJZC	CJZD	CJYR
2001 Nov	3.0	2.5	−7.7	2.1	0.4	4.4	−2.6	−4.0	1.5	4.9	3.6	2.9	0.8
Dec	3.3	2.4	−7.4	2.2	0.4	4.1	−1.9	−2.9	1.7	4.9	3.6	3.1	1.0
2002 Jan	4.1	2.6	−6.2	3.1	0.8	4.2	−1.3	−0.2	1.8	4.9	3.6	3.1	1.6
Feb	3.8	2.0	−7.5	3.0	0.8	3.9	−0.8	1.1	1.6	4.9	3.6	2.7	1.5
Mar	2.7	1.2	−8.0	3.1	0.9	3.6	0.5	2.1	1.8	4.9	3.6	2.6	1.5
Apr	2.2	1.0	−7.4	2.4	0.1	3.7	0.4	2.3	1.9	4.9	3.5	2.9	1.3
May	−0.9	2.1	−7.2	2.3	0.3	3.4	−0.4	1.7	1.4	4.9	3.3	2.6	0.8
Jun	−2.1	1.7	−8.0	2.3	−0.3	4.5	−0.3	2.2	1.6	4.9	3.4	2.0	0.6
Jul	−0.2	2.5	−6.8	2.5	0.3	3.7	0.6	1.1	1.3	4.9	3.3	2.2	1.1
Aug	−0.1	2.0	−8.5	2.4	−0.1	4.0	0.7	−0.2	1.7	4.9	3.4	2.2	1.0
Sep	0.2	2.0	−6.8	2.0	−0.3	3.9	0.4	−0.1	1.7	2.9	3.4	1.8	1.0
Oct	0.2	1.6	−6.7	2.5	−0.2	4.0	1.0	−0.4	1.9	8.5	3.3	3.0	1.4
Nov	0.4	1.7	−5.9	2.6	−0.7	3.5	2.0	0.1	2.0	8.5	3.3	2.9	1.6
Dec	−0.2	1.7	−7.4	2.6	−0.8	3.3	4.4	−	1.6	8.5	3.4	3.0	1.7
2003 Jan	−1.1	1.7	−5.6	2.1	−0.7	3.3	3.6	0.5	1.3	8.5	3.4	1.8	1.4
Feb	−0.4	1.6	−4.3	2.2	−1.0	3.8	4.0	0.2	1.3	8.5	3.4	2.0	1.6
Mar	−0.3	1.6	−4.6	2.2	−0.9	3.5	4.1	1.0	0.9	8.5	3.4	2.1	1.6
Apr	0.3	2.5	−4.3	1.6	−1.0	3.1	4.2	0.7	0.3	8.5	3.3	1.3	1.5
May	1.2	1.9	−4.6	1.4	−0.5	3.1	2.9	1.1	−	8.5	3.2	1.1	1.2
Jun	1.3	2.2	−4.5	1.4	−0.3	2.8	2.3	−	−0.7	8.5	3.2	1.5	1.1
Jul	1.4	1.5	−2.2	1.8	−0.1	3.9	2.2	1.0	−1.0	8.5	3.1	2.4	1.3
Aug	1.6	2.4	−1.2	1.8	−0.3	3.4	2.4	0.7	−1.5	8.5	3.0	2.6	1.4
Sep	2.2	1.9	−3.4	2.0	−0.3	3.6	3.3	1.1	−1.7	8.7	3.0	2.7	1.4
Oct	2.2	2.2	−3.3	2.1	−0.3	3.6	3.3	0.4	−2.0	4.7	2.9	2.8	1.4
Nov	2.6	1.6	−4.3	2.2	−0.3	3.6	3.7	−0.4	−2.3	4.7	3.0	2.9	1.3

1 See chapter text. Prior to 10 December 2003, the consumer prices index (CPI) was published in the UK as the harmonised index of consumer prices (HICP).

Source: Office for National Statistics: 020 7533 5874

17.5 Retail Prices Index[1]
United Kingdom

13 January 1987=100

| | ALL ITEMS (RPI) | All items excluding | | | | | Food and catering | Alcohol and tobacco | Housing and household expenditure | Personal expenditure | Travel and leisure | Consumer durables | All items excluding mortgage interest payments & indirect taxes (RPIY)[4] |
		mortgage interest payments (RPIX)	mortgage interest payments and depreciation[2]	housing	food	seasonal food[3]							
Weights													
	CZGU	CZGY	DOGZ	CZGX	CZGV	CZGW	CBVV	CBVW	CBVX	CBVY	CBVZ	CBWA	
1995	1 000	958	928	813	861	978	184	111	356	93	256	123	
1996	1 000	958	929	810	857	978	191	113	353	92	251	116	
1997	1 000	961	932	814	864	981	185	114	351	96	254	122	
1998	1 000	955	923	803	870	982	178	105	359	95	263	121	
1999	1 000	958	928	807	872	980	179	100	358	95	268	127	
2000	1 000	960	924	805	882	982	170	95	355	101	279	126	
2001	1 000	954	914	795	884	982	169	97	362	96	276	125	
2002	1 000	964	924	801	886	980	166	99	363	94	278	126	
2003	1 000	961	919	797	891	983	160	98	365	92	285	126	
Annual averages													
	CHAW	CHMK	CHON	CHAZ	CHAY	CHAX	CHBS	CHBT	CHBU	CHBV	CHBW	CHBY	CBZW
1994	144.1	143.8	143.8	141.6	146.5	144.8	138.5	161.4	144.4	131.9	145.7	115.5	141.3
1995	149.1	147.9	148.0	145.4	151.4	149.6	143.9	169.0	150.8	133.6	148.4	116.2	144.5
1996	152.7	152.3	152.3	149.3	154.9	153.4	148.9	175.9	153.0	135.1	152.8	117.1	148.2
1997	157.5	156.5	156.4	152.9	160.5	158.5	150.4	183.2	158.4	137.7	159.0	117.3	151.5
1998	162.9	160.6	160.3	156.2	166.5	163.8	153.4	192.3	166.2	139.9	162.8	115.9	154.5
1999	165.4	164.3	163.6	158.9	169.4	166.5	155.4	202.6	167.7	139.6	165.6	112.3	157.1
2000	170.3	167.7	166.4	161.3	175.1	171.4	156.7	210.3	176.2	137.2	170.3	108.0	159.9
2001	173.3	171.3	169.5	163.7	178.0	174.3	162.2	216.9	180.0	135.7	172.0	105.0	163.7
2002	176.2	175.1	172.5	166.0	181.1	177.2	164.8	222.3	184.6	133.2	174.2	101.9	167.5
Monthly figures													
2000 Nov	172.1	169.2	167.7	162.5	177.1	173.2	158.1	212.8	179.0	138.4	171.2	108.2	161.2
Dec	172.2	169.3	167.7	162.5	177.1	173.2	158.4	212.3	179.8	137.7	170.8	108.6	161.3
2001 Jan	171.1	168.1	166.5	161.1	175.8	172.1	158.8	213.3	178.5	132.9	170.3	102.8	160.2
Feb	172.0	169.0	167.3	162.0	176.9	173.0	159.0	214.1	179.2	135.5	170.9	104.9	161.1
Mar	172.2	169.6	168.0	162.7	176.9	173.2	160.4	215.4	178.7	137.1	170.5	106.7	162.1
Apr	173.1	170.8	169.1	163.2	177.9	174.1	160.9	216.6	180.2	136.7	171.5	105.7	162.9
May	174.2	172.1	170.4	164.7	178.6	174.8	163.9	216.9	180.3	137.1	173.0	106.4	164.4
Jun	174.4	172.5	170.8	165.1	178.7	174.9	164.7	217.3	179.8	137.2	173.6	106.3	164.9
Jul	173.3	171.4	169.5	163.6	177.9	174.2	162.9	217.4	179.6	132.3	173.3	102.4	163.9
Aug	174.0	172.0	170.0	164.1	178.7	175.0	162.8	217.7	180.7	134.2	173.3	103.8	164.6
Sep	174.6	172.8	170.7	164.9	179.4	175.6	162.8	218.3	181.7	136.6	173.3	105.6	165.4
Oct	174.3	172.6	170.5	164.7	179.0	175.2	163.2	219.0	180.9	136.2	172.6	104.6	165.2
Nov	173.6	172.2	170.2	164.3	178.3	174.6	163.1	218.8	180.5	136.4	171.0	105.2	164.8
Dec	173.4	172.5	170.5	164.5	177.9	174.3	163.8	218.2	180.0	136.1	170.6	106.1	165.0
2002 Jan	173.3	172.4	170.3	164.2	177.6	174.0	164.9	219.2	179.5	132.3	171.7	101.1	165.0
Feb	173.8	172.8	170.7	164.7	178.1	174.6	164.9	219.6	179.9	133.0	172.2	102.0	165.4
Mar	174.5	173.5	171.4	165.5	178.9	175.2	165.3	220.2	180.8	134.1	172.7	103.7	166.1
Apr	175.7	174.7	172.7	166.1	180.4	176.6	165.1	220.9	182.7	134.2	174.8	102.7	166.9
May	176.2	175.2	173.0	166.4	181.0	177.2	165.0	222.3	183.6	134.4	174.8	103.1	167.3
Jun	176.2	175.1	172.7	166.1	181.2	177.3	164.4	222.6	184.2	133.6	174.7	102.2	167.2
Jul	175.9	174.8	172.1	165.4	180.9	177.0	164.3	223.6	184.8	129.5	174.6	99.5	167.0
Aug	176.4	175.3	172.4	165.7	181.5	177.6	164.4	223.5	185.6	130.7	174.8	100.1	167.6
Sep	177.6	176.4	173.4	166.8	182.8	178.7	164.7	224.0	187.2	134.1	175.1	102.3	168.7
Oct	177.9	176.6	173.5	166.9	183.1	179.0	165.0	224.2	188.0	133.8	175.1	101.5	169.1
Nov	178.2	177.0	173.7	167.1	183.5	179.3	165.1	224.0	188.7	134.7	175.1	102.2	169.6
Dec	178.5	177.2	173.8	167.2	183.9	179.6	165.1	223.7	190.2	133.6	174.8	102.6	169.8
2003 Jan	178.4	177.1	173.5	166.8	183.8	179.5	165.3	224.6	189.7	130.6	176.1	98.4	169.8
Feb	179.3	177.9	174.4	167.8	184.6	180.4	166.1	224.9	190.3	132.9	176.7	99.9	170.6
Mar	179.9	178.7	175.2	168.7	185.3	181.0	166.6	225.6	190.8	133.8	177.5	101.4	171.4
Apr	181.2	180.0	176.5	169.0	186.7	182.3	167.2	227.4	193.1	133.9	178.4	100.3	171.8
May	181.5	180.2	176.6	169.1	186.8	182.4	168.2	228.3	193.9	133.8	177.4	100.8	171.9
Jun	181.3	180.0	176.4	168.8	186.8	182.4	167.8	228.7	194.2	133.0	177.2	99.9	171.7
Jul	181.3	179.9	176.1	168.5	186.7	182.4	168.0	229.0	194.7	130.6	177.1	97.8	171.6
Aug	181.6	180.4	176.5	168.9	187.1	182.7	168.1	229.6	194.8	132.5	177.2	98.7	172.2
Sep	182.5	181.3	177.2	169.7	188.0	183.5	168.9	229.7	196.3	134.6	177.0	100.4	173.2
Oct	182.6	181.3	177.2	169.6	188.0	183.6	169.2	230.0	196.7	134.3	176.7	99.7	173.1
Nov	182.7	181.4	177.2	169.6	188.1	183.7	169.4	229.4	197.4	134.5	176.2	100.0	173.1

1 See chapter text.
2 This series has been constructed using the index for all items excluding mortgage interest payments prior to February 1995.
3 Seasonal food is defined as items of food the prices of which show significant seasonal variations. These are fresh fruit and vegetables, fresh fish, eggs and home-killed lamb.
4 There are no weights available for RPIY.

Source: Office for National Statistics: 020 7533 5874

17.6 Tax and Price Index[1]

Tax and Price Index: January 1987 = 100

DQAB

	1989	1990	1991	1992	1993	1994	1995	1996	1997	1998	1999	2000	2001	2002	2003
January	107.1	113.9	123.6	128.1	128.7	132.1	137.2	141.6	143.6	147.1	150.5	152.7	156.7	156.5	161.4
February	108.0	114.7	124.3	128.8	129.6	132.9	138.2	142.3	144.2	147.9	150.8	153.7	157.6	157.0	162.3
March	108.5	115.9	124.9	129.3	130.2	133.4	138.8	143.0	144.6	148.4	151.2	154.6	157.8	157.7	163.0
April	109.8	118.2	125.4	129.6	131.3	135.3	140.3	141.7	143.8	149.7	151.2	155.7	156.3	158.6	164.9
May	110.5	119.4	125.8	130.2	131.8	135.8	141.0	142.0	144.4	150.6	151.7	156.3	157.4	159.1	165.2
June	110.9	119.9	126.5	130.2	131.7	135.8	141.2	142.1	145.0	150.5	151.7	156.7	157.6	159.1	165.0
July	111.1	120.0	126.2	129.6	131.4	135.1	140.4	141.5	145.0	150.1	151.1	156.1	156.5	158.8	165.0
August	111.4	121.4	126.5	129.7	132.1	135.8	141.3	142.2	146.0	150.8	151.5	156.1	157.2	159.3	165.4
September	112.2	122.7	127.0	130.3	132.7	136.1	142.0	143.0	146.9	151.5	152.3	157.3	157.8	160.6	166.3
October	111.7	123.8	127.5	130.8	132.6	136.4	141.2	143.0	147.1	151.6	152.6	157.2	157.5	160.9	166.4
November	112.8	123.4	128.1	130.6	132.4	136.5	141.2	143.1	147.2	151.5	152.8	157.7	156.8	161.2	166.5
December	113.1	123.3	128.2	130.1	132.7	137.2	142.1	143.6	147.6	151.5	153.4	157.8	156.6	161.5	..

Retail Prices Index: January 1987 = 100

CHAW

	1989	1990	1991	1992	1993	1994	1995	1996	1997	1998	1999	2000	2001	2002	2003
January	111.0	119.5	130.2	135.6	137.9	141.3	146.0	150.2	154.4	159.5	163.4	166.6	171.1	173.3	178.4
February	111.8	120.2	130.9	136.3	138.8	142.1	146.9	150.9	155.0	160.3	163.7	167.5	172.0	173.8	179.3
March	112.3	121.4	131.4	136.7	139.3	142.5	147.5	151.5	155.4	160.8	164.1	168.4	172.2	174.5	179.9
April	114.3	125.1	133.1	138.8	140.6	144.2	149.0	152.6	156.3	162.6	165.2	170.1	173.1	175.7	181.2
May	115.0	126.2	133.5	139.3	141.1	144.7	149.6	152.9	156.9	163.5	165.6	170.7	174.2	176.2	181.5
June	115.4	126.7	134.1	139.3	141.0	144.7	149.8	153.0	157.5	163.4	165.6	171.1	174.4	176.2	181.3
July	115.5	126.8	133.8	138.8	140.7	144.0	149.1	152.4	157.5	163.0	165.1	170.5	173.3	175.9	181.3
August	115.8	128.1	134.1	138.9	141.3	144.7	149.9	153.1	158.5	163.7	165.5	170.5	174.0	176.4	181.6
September	116.6	129.3	134.6	139.4	141.9	145.0	150.6	153.8	159.3	164.4	166.2	171.7	174.6	177.6	182.5
October	117.5	130.3	135.1	139.9	141.8	145.2	149.8	153.8	159.5	164.5	166.5	171.6	174.3	177.9	182.6
November	118.5	130.0	135.6	139.7	141.6	145.3	149.8	153.9	159.6	164.4	166.7	172.1	173.6	178.2	182.7
December	118.8	129.9	135.7	139.2	141.9	146.0	150.7	154.4	160.0	164.4	167.3	172.2	173.4	178.5	..

Percentage changes on one year earlier[1]

	1990	1991	1992	1993	1994	1995	1996	1997	1998	1999	2000	2001	2002	2003
Tax and Price Index[1]														
January	6.3	8.5	3.6	0.5	2.6	3.9	3.2	1.4	2.4	2.3	1.5	2.6	−0.1	3.1
February	6.2	8.4	3.6	0.6	2.5	4.0	3.0	1.3	2.6	2.0	1.9	2.5	−0.4	3.4
March	6.8	7.8	3.5	0.7	2.5	4.0	3.0	1.1	2.6	1.9	2.2	2.1	−0.1	3.4
April	7.7	6.1	3.3	1.3	3.0	3.7	1.0	1.5	4.1	1.0	3.0	0.4	1.5	4.0
May	8.1	5.4	3.5	1.2	3.0	3.8	0.7	1.7	4.3	0.7	3.0	0.7	1.1	3.8
June	8.1	5.5	2.9	1.2	3.1	4.0	0.6	2.0	3.8	0.8	3.3	0.6	1.0	3.7
July	8.0	5.2	2.7	1.4	2.8	3.9	0.8	2.5	3.5	0.7	3.3	0.3	1.5	3.9
August	9.0	4.2	2.5	1.9	2.8	4.1	0.6	2.7	3.3	0.5	3.0	0.7	1.3	3.8
September	9.4	3.5	2.6	1.8	2.6	4.3	0.7	2.7	3.1	0.5	3.3	0.3	1.8	3.5
October	10.8	3.0	2.6	1.4	2.9	3.5	1.3	2.9	3.1	0.7	3.0	0.2	2.2	3.4
November	9.4	3.8	2.0	1.4	3.1	3.4	1.3	2.9	2.9	0.9	3.2	−0.6	2.8	3.3
December	9.0	4.0	1.5	2.0	3.4	3.6	1.1	2.8	2.6	1.3	2.9	−0.8	3.1	..
Retail Prices Index														
January	7.7	9.0	4.1	1.7	2.5	3.3	2.9	2.8	3.3	2.4	2.0	2.7	1.3	2.9
February	7.5	8.9	4.1	1.8	2.4	3.4	2.7	2.7	3.4	2.1	2.3	2.7	1.0	3.2
March	8.1	8.2	4.0	1.9	2.3	3.5	2.7	2.6	3.5	2.1	2.6	2.3	1.3	3.1
April	9.4	6.4	4.3	1.3	2.6	3.3	2.4	2.4	4.0	1.6	3.0	1.8	1.5	3.1
May	9.7	5.8	4.3	1.3	2.6	3.4	2.2	2.6	4.2	1.3	3.1	2.1	1.1	3.0
June	9.8	5.8	3.9	1.2	2.6	3.5	2.1	2.9	3.7	1.3	3.3	1.9	1.0	2.9
July	9.8	5.5	3.7	1.4	2.3	3.5	2.2	3.3	3.5	1.3	3.3	1.6	1.5	3.1
August	10.6	4.7	3.6	1.7	2.4	3.6	2.1	3.5	3.3	1.1	3.0	2.1	1.4	2.9
September	10.9	4.1	3.6	1.8	2.2	3.9	2.1	3.6	3.2	1.1	3.3	1.7	1.7	2.8
October	10.9	3.7	3.6	1.4	2.4	3.2	2.7	3.7	3.1	1.2	3.1	1.6	2.1	2.6
November	9.7	4.3	3.0	1.4	2.6	3.1	2.7	3.7	3.0	1.4	3.2	0.9	2.6	2.5
December	9.3	4.5	2.6	1.9	2.9	3.2	2.5	3.6	2.8	1.8	2.9	0.7	2.9	..

1 See chapter text.

Source: Office for National Statistics: 020 7533 5874

17.7 Index of purchase prices of the means of agricultural production[1]
United Kingdom
Annual averages

1995 = 100

		Weights	1992	1993	1994	1995	1996	1997	1998	1999	2000	2001	2002
Goods and services currently consumed	BYEA	100	91.6	96.1	96.5	100.0	104.5	99.8	94.8	93.5	95.4	100.5	100.2
Seeds	BYEB	4.0	100.5	83.5	85.2	100.0	100.7	89.4	91.7	83.2	76.3	82.4	81.1
Energy, lubricants	BYED	6.0	97.2	100.6	101.6	100.0	103.4	103.4	94.6	102.5	127.1	122.4	116.5
Fuels for heating	KVBA	0.7	97.4	105.8	96.5	100.0	120.4	111.7	90.4	100.4	150.4	143.3	130.6
Motor fuel	KVBB	3.3	91.2	97.6	101.9	100.0	102.3	105.8	96.7	109.4	144.6	139.0	131.3
Electricity	KVBC	1.9	108.1	104.3	103.2	100.0	99.5	96.1	91.8	90.2	87.7	85.0	84.4
Lubricants	KVBD	0.1	96.9	97.4	99.4	100.0	99.3	101.1	103.4	113.5	117.2	118.4	123.5
Fertilisers and soil improvers	BYEE	9.7	86.6	81.7	88.7	100.0	107.2	97.3	86.2	83.4	88.0	102.1	98.5
Straight nitrogen	EDOZ	3.9	89.7	81.7	88.7	100.0	110.7	95.1	79.2	75.6	91.1	117.6	109.5
Compound fertilisers	KVBF	5.3	84.3	80.9	88.0	100.0	104.7	98.2	89.2	86.8	83.5	90.1	89.0
Other fertiliser (mainly lime and chalk)	KVBG	0.4	90.8	93.8	98.4	100.0	107.9	109.7	112.5	113.5	117.3	118.0	122.0
Plant protection products	BYEF	6.2	95.9	97.2	100.6	100.0	106.0	105.7	98.0	96.4	90.0	87.7	86.2
Animal feedstuffs	BYEG	32.0	97.3	103.4	97.7	100.0	107.9	97.1	83.0	77.1	77.5	83.0	80.7
Feed wheat	KVBI	2.6	105.1	106.4	93.0	100.0	101.4	80.3	68.4	66.6	60.2	66.7	58.6
Whole barley	KVBJ	2.9	103.2	107.9	96.4	100.0	99.6	77.6	67.1	69.2	62.4	63.9	55.1
Whole oats	KVBL	0.2	117.8	134.6	108.8	100.0	108.3	85.1	68.5	73.8	69.3	69.1	62.5
Maize glutten feed	ZBUW	0.4	96.2	97.2	96.6	100.0	111.4	81.7	66.0	69.4	69.3	76.2	71.3
Oilcake	KVBM	2.0	96.7	110.6	101.7	100.0	129.7	124.8	86.2	77.4	94.0	102.8	94.4
White fish meal	KVBN	0.6	94.6	88.7	86.9	100.0	127.9	120.4	132.6	89.6	96.2	110.7	129.5
Other straight feedstuffs	ZBUX	3.4	91.1	95.2	93.4	100.4	107.1	93.6	77.3	70.3	77.3	86.3	86.7
All straight feedstuffs	KVBH	12.3	99.3	104.3	95.2	100.1	108.4	92.6	76.7	71.2	72.7	79.3	75.0
Feedstuffs non-concentrates	EDPA	0.6	98.8	103.6	95.0	99.8	108.4	92.5	76.3	71.1	72.9	79.8	74.9
Compound feedstuffs	KVBP	19.1	96.0	102.9	99.4	100.0	107.6	100.2	87.3	81.1	80.7	85.5	84.6
for:													
Cattle and calves	ZBUY	7.7	96.8	105.4	100.8	100.0	107.9	100.9	87.0	82.7	82.8	88.0	87.7
Pigs	KVBS	4.9	95.6	102.6	98.2	100.0	106.6	98.0	85.2	77.0	75.5	79.8	77.6
Poultry	KVBT	5.3	97.1	101.4	99.1	100.0	108.1	99.8	89.0	82.4	81.9	87.1	85.7
Sheep	KVBU	1.2	86.8	94.3	97.7	100.0	108.2	106.0	90.7	82.1	83.9	85.7	89.1
Maintenance and repair of plant	BYEI	7.5	90.5	95.7	97.7	100.0	104.9	109.3	112.5	116.6	120.9	126.2	132.5
Maintenance and repair of buildings	BYEJ	3.9	87.7	90.3	94.5	100.0	100.9	102.6	103.8	102.8	104.9	107.0	110.0
Veterinary services	BYEK	3.0	98.9	99.4	99.5	100.0	100.9	102.3	103.5	103.8	102.8	101.6	101.0
General expenses	BYEL	18.0	85.4	95.9	98.7	100.0	98.7	99.9	105.5	109.4	112.4	118.7	120.0
Goods and services contributing to investment in agriculture	BYEM	100	93.0	95.9	97.7	100.0	103.9	107.0	109.0	109.7	109.7	108.6	109.8
Machinery and other equipment	BYEN	74.0	94.1	97.2	98.5	100.0	104.8	107.6	109.0	109.4	107.8	104.9	104.6
Machinery and plant for cultivation	KVBV	8.4	92.7	95.3	97.1	100.0	110.0	114.5	119.8	121.5	122.7	122.1	120.9
Machinery and plant for harvesting	KVBW	15.2	94.1	96.9	96.9	100.0	103.0	106.2	108.0	109.7	109.7	101.3	97.5
Farm machinery and installations	KVBX	6.4	94.3	95.6	98.0	100.0	101.3	103.2	106.6	108.3	111.3	118.6	120.7
Tractors	KVBY	30.2	93.9	99.1	100.1	100.0	105.7	108.4	109.0	109.8	107.3	103.8	105.6
Other vehicles	KVBZ	13.7	95.4	95.5	97.7	100.0	103.2	105.5	104.7	101.0	96.1	94.5	92.9
Buildings	BYEO	26.0	90.0	92.2	95.4	100.0	101.2	105.1	109.0	110.8	115.1	118.9	124.5
Farm buildings	KVCA	17.8	89.1	91.5	95.2	100.0	102.0	105.9	109.1	110.9	115.1	119.3	124.8
Engineering and soil improvement operations	KVCB	8.2	91.8	93.8	95.8	100.0	99.4	103.3	108.9	110.8	115.2	118.0	123.8

Note: The sum of the Percentages of categories included in "Goods and Services currently consumed" does not add up to 100% due to the exclusion of some minor categories.

1 See chapter text.

Source: Department for Environment, Food and Rural Affairs: 01904 455253

17.8 Index of producer prices of agricultural products[1]
United Kingdom
Annual averages

1995 = 100

		Weights	1992	1993	1994	1995	1996	1997	1998	1999	2000	2001	2002
All products	BYEP	100	86.0	92.0	92.5	100.0	98.0	85.7	78.6	76.3	74.6	80.5	78.0
All crop products	BYEQ	37.6	84.3	87.0	88.9	100.0	90.0	76.3	77.2	75.5	70.8	79.4	74.7
Cereals	BYER	13.7	103.6	105.3	93.7	100.0	99.7	79.3	68.3	66.5	59.9	64.5	57.1
Wheat for:													
breadmaking	KVDA	1.6	110.3	113.4	96.2	100.0	103.0	87.3	76.8	70.7	62.6	68.6	63.5
other milling	KVDB	0.9	108.9	106.5	93.1	100.0	101.3	82.1	71.2	68.1	61.4	66.0	57.1
feeding	KVDC	6.4	104.3	106.8	92.9	100.0	100.2	81.2	68.3	66.2	59.9	66.2	57.8
Barley for:													
feeding	KVDD	2.5	103.7	108.7	96.4	100.0	97.9	76.9	67.9	70.1	62.1	63.7	55.3
malting	KVDE	1.9	90.3	84.5	88.7	100.0	95.7	67.7	60.5	57.9	52.7	55.2	51.3
Oats for:													
milling	KVDF	0.2	115.3	123.3	103.2	100.0	101.7	81.3	66.2	69.3	63.1	69.3	56.4
feeding	KVDG	0.2	116.2	127.0	102.2	100.0	105.4	74.8	63.3	71.7	66.1	65.9	58.7
Root crops	BYES	7.9	48.6	45.8	67.7	100.0	59.4	39.0	56.3	57.9	44.1	55.7	45.2
Potatoes:													
early	KVDH	0.4	61.0	61.7	115.2	100.0	70.8	50.3	70.8	63.5	69.0	104.1	80.7
main crop	KVDI	5.5	31.7	25.5	54.9	100.0	42.6	21.5	48.6	52.1	33.9	46.3	30.9
Sugar beet	KVDJ	2.0	91.0	96.5	92.8	100.0	101.6	83.2	74.2	72.4	66.6	71.5	76.5
Fresh vegetables	BYET	6.2	83.2	90.9	93.4	100.0	96.6	90.9	96.8	90.6	93.0	105.5	104.5
Cauliflowers	KVDK	0.4	94.7	97.3	103.1	100.0	96.8	85.8	95.2	89.3	108.4	112.6	127.5
Lettuce	KVDL	0.8	100.4	107.1	105.1	100.2	84.1	101.7	85.7	91.4	85.8	113.7	111.9
Tomatoes	KVDM	0.4	105.6	103.9	94.1	100.0	117.0	90.8	94.5	91.1	105.1	95.4	110.4
Carrots	KVDN	0.6	50.6	64.0	77.1	100.0	92.0	61.9	88.1	83.8	70.3	117.0	105.7
Cabbage	KVDO	0.4	84.4	91.4	80.0	100.0	99.2	83.7	95.5	94.5	101.8	121.1	109.4
Beans	KVDP	0.1	88.3	110.0	124.2	100.0	100.8	103.4	132.3	101.1	120.8	143.3	133.7
Onions	KVDQ	0.5	68.8	98.2	118.9	100.0	73.0	83.4	109.4	72.2	70.0	88.6	85.9
Mushrooms	KVDR	0.9	83.2	91.5	90.1	100.0	102.7	92.0	91.9	91.1	92.9	84.6	89.0
Fresh fruit	BYEU	1.5	90.6	90.9	91.4	99.9	102.0	105.6	99.6	93.8	101.6	98.5	110.6
Dessert apples	KVDS	0.3	93.9	77.5	83.9	99.9	108.8	103.7	89.5	83.3	82.1	90.8	92.4
Dessert pears	KVDT	0.1	100.9	88.2	90.5	100.0	101.0	97.3	90.9	89.5	82.3	105.9	102.8
Cooking apples	KVDU	0.2	84.2	83.7	96.8	100.0	116.8	125.7	127.9	95.8	95.1	100.4	104.0
Strawberries	KVDV	0.4	122.8	114.4	112.8	100.0	102.3	106.6	93.4	102.1	99.7	94.3	121.3
Raspberries	KVDW	0.2	53.8	78.0	71.3	100.0	90.2	100.4	82.2	88.7	97.2	100.0	125.3
Seeds	BYEV	0.5	98.5	76.7	81.6	100.0	93.5	78.9	77.4	67.2	56.5	64.6	63.4
Flowers and plants	BYEW	3.7	93.8	93.6	99.1	100.0	100.8	103.9	104.0	107.4	103.6	107.6	109.0
Other crop products	BYEX	4.0	77.2	93.7	98.7	100.0	92.1	80.7	85.4	82.5	86.8	106.1	105.1
Animals and animal products	BYEY	56.4	87.6	95.4	94.6	100.0	102.8	90.5	77.0	74.0	74.3	78.5	76.4
Animals for slaughter	BYEZ	33.1	91.2	99.5	97.1	100.0	103.7	91.3	76.2	74.2	78.2	79.1	80.7
Calves	KVDX	0.5	90.2	118.8	115.3	100.0	90.9	74.5	62.0	47.8	41.5	39.2	50.0
Clean cattle	KVDY	9.7	89.2	103.8	99.4	100.0	85.3	77.9	69.1	74.0	72.7	73.3	75.5
Cows and bulls	KVDZ	2.4	93.7	111.4	99.4	100.0	92.9	71.8	68.0	58.6	58.6	58.6	58.6
Clean pigs	KVEA	6.6	96.6	86.8	83.7	100.0	115.4	92.9	67.7	65.9	79.0	81.9	78.0
Sows and boars	KVEB	0.3	101.0	76.1	78.9	100.0	109.1	85.3	44.0	44.0	54.3	58.3	50.9
Sheep	KVEC	4.4	76.4	89.9	97.6	100.0	118.5	108.7	80.4	74.9	83.0	84.1	98.4
Ewe and ram	KVED	0.4	88.3	106.2	101.3	100.0	138.4	144.9	84.8	59.3	73.0	111.3	109.2
Poultry	KVEE	7.9	96.1	104.7	103.5	100.0	111.1	101.9	93.5	90.0	91.7	90.1	88.7
Chickens	KVEF	5.5	99.3	109.4	105.9	100.0	112.1	104.2	91.1	87.1	85.9	86.1	85.6
Turkeys	KVEG	2.1	88.2	93.8	98.4	100.0	109.0	95.0	97.1	95.7	106.2	100.3	95.7
Cows' milk	BYFA	20.0	81.6	88.0	89.0	100.0	100.3	88.7	77.7	73.6	67.9	77.2	68.6
Eggs	BYFB	2.2	90.7	106.7	108.4	100.0	113.1	94.6	83.3	74.1	76.0	80.8	87.7
Other animal products:													
Wool (clip)	BYFC	0.3	85.2	66.3	101.5	100.0	91.8	79.4	52.1	49.4	52.9	46.0	51.0

Note: The sum of the Percentages of categories included in "All products" does not add up to 100% due to the exclusion of some minor categories.

1 See chapter text.

Source: Department for Environment, Food and Rural Affairs: 01904 455253

17.9 Commodity price trends[1]
United Kingdom

			1992	1993	1994	1995	1996	1997	1998	1999	2000	2001	2002
Wheat £ per tonne	KVAA	Average ex-farm price[2,3]	120.5	124.2	106.4	115.6	112.5	91.8	77.8	75.4	67.9	76.6	65.5
Barley £ per tonne	KVAB	Average ex-farm price[2,3]	113.9	113.6	105.4	107.6	103.7	86.3	79.2	74.2	69.9	72.0	64.8
Oats £ per tonne	KVAC	Average ex-farm price[2,3]	115.1	128.8	108.4	101.4	107.4	82.3	66.4	71.1	64.1	67.2	58.1
Rye £ per tonne	KVAD	Average ex-farm price[2]	115.20	113.40	112.80	107.90	113.90	..	..	..	..	..	..
Hops £ per tonne	KVAE	Average farm-gate price	3 208	3 357	4 005	3 595	3 360	3 550	3 676	4 033	3 861	3 532	2 774
Potatoes £ per tonne	KVAF	Average farm-gate price[4]	75.20	64.10	125.80	187.70	100.50	66.00	121.54	119.12	83.32	111.33	80.90
Sugar beet £ per tonne	KVAG	Producer price[5]	38.00	36.50	34.70	38.30	37.70	32.90	29.84	26.42	27.77	30.76	29.64
Oilseed rape	KVAH	Average market price[6]	133.00	153.00	185.40	177.70	186.90	160.20	167.47	112.86	120.40	148.35	148.15
Apples £ per tonne	KPUE	Dessert average farm-gate price[7]	355.0	315.1	344.9	418.6	528.0	525.7	480.3	436.8	357.8	352.2	385.2
	KVAI	Dessert average market price	414.0	370.0	447.4	465.7	474.7	538.1	..	..	..	311.6	..
	KVAJ	Culinary average market price	312.0	327.0	446.4	405.9	462.8	558.4	..	..	..	389.8	..
	KPUJ	Culinary average farm-gate price	152.9	210.9	241.5	243.1	279.1	322.0	341.4	248.9	215.3	175.7	284.7
Pears £ per tonne	KPUG	Average farm-gate price	522.3	498.8	486.8	385.7	412.6	453.0	445.7	441.9	405.1	426.4	283.3
	KVAK	Average market price	461.0	380.0	408.3	447.5	441.7	433.1	394.2	..	..	397.3	..
Tomatoes £ per tonne	LQMH	Average farm-gate price[7]	522.2	590.3	685.0	585.1	742.4	546.9	594.6	576.5	751.6	725.3	789.3
	KVAL	Average market price[7]	494.0	552.8	675.2	624.0	700.1	655.6	..	..	..	542.8	..
Cauliflowers £ per tonne	KPUI	Average farm-gate price[7]	205.3	226.2	234.4	247.8	270.9	236.8	216.3	211.3	270.0	276.9	324.3
	KVAM	Average market price[7]	253.0	296.9	323.5	394.9	442.6	372.0	..	..	..	347.4	..
Cattle (rearing)	KVAN	1st quality Hereford/cross bull calves[8,9]	145.44	185.95	182.06	166.32	131.81	146.95	107.86	88.24	79.52	..	84.90
£ per head	KVAO	1st quality beef/ cross yearling steers[9]	419.49	478.00	471.00	475.00	445.00	427.00	369.00	382.00	400.05	..	403.85
Cattle (fat) p per kg liveweight	KVAP	Clean cattle[10]	109.58	128.04	121.71	123.15	105.52	96.89	86.10	92.12	89.85	87.53	91.38

17.9 Commodity price trends[1]
United Kingdom
continued

			1992	1993	1994	1995	1996	1997	1998	1999	2000	2001	2002
Sheep (store) £ per head	KVAQ	1st quality lambs, hoggets and tegs[8]	37.90	35.56	40.02	44.46	46.83	53.42	31.28	28.62	34.50	..	47.88
Sheep (fat) p per kg estimated dressed carcase weight	KVAR KVAS	Great Britain[11] Northern Ireland[12]	182.12 172.37	218.96 199.50	236.88 221.95	236.40 214.41	283.13 260.46	239.02 228.23	192.46 179.06	180.27 165.71	196.44 182.67	.. ..	.. ..
Pigs £ per kg deadweight	KVAT	Average price clean pigs	115.12	103.02	99.57	118.84	137.73	110.83	80.65	78.56	94.36	97.77	93.32
Broilers p per kg carcass weight	KVAU	Average producer price	129.6	128.9	87.1	84.0	90.9	86.1	76.7	72.1	70.7	70.4	68.5
Milk p per litre	KVAV	Average net return to producers[13]	20.94	22.68	23.19	24.96	25.01	22.31	19.44	18.55	17.34	20.14	17.39
Eggs p per dozen	KVAW	Average producer price[14]	36.78	41.90	42.31	38.23	45.70	39.33	36.23	34.12	36.67	37.59	39.53
Wool p per kg	KHWQ	Average producer price for clip paid to producers by the British Wool Marketing Board	80.90	62.00	98.90	95.00	86.90	74.90	48.00	46.60	51.30	47.00	50.00

1 This table gives indications of the movement in commodity prices at the first point of sale. The series do not always show total receipts by farmers; for some commodities additional premiums or deficiency payments are made to achieve support price levels.
2 Weighted average ex-farm prices of United Kingdom cereals.
3 Data from 1997 onwards have been revised and are not directly comparable with earlier years.
4 Weighted average price paid to growers for early and main crop potatoes in the United Kingdom (includes all potatoes and a value for sacks).
5 Returns to growers figures since 1986 prices per 'adjusted' tonne at 16% sugar content.
6 Typical contract price adjusted to delivered basis and 40 per cent oil content.
7 Weighted average wholesale prices for England and Wales. Average farm-gate price for England and Wales, crop year (June-May).
8 Average prices at representative markets in England and Wales.

9 Category change 1988: formerly 1st quality yearling steers beef/dairy cross, now consists of Hereford/cross, Charolais/cross, Limousin/cross, Simmental/cross, Belgian/cross, other continental cross, other beef/dairy cross, other beef/beef cross.
10 Based on Meat and Livestock Commission all clean cattle prices.
11 Average of Great Britain weekly market prices as used to determine the level of ewe premium.
12 Average of Northern Ireland weekly market prices used to determine the level of ewe premium.
13 Derived by dividing total value of output by the total quantity of output available for human consumption.
14 Average price of all Class A eggs weighted according to quantity in each grade.

Source: Department for Environment, Food and Rural Affairs: 01904 455332

18 Government finance

Government finance

Public sector *(Tables 18.1 to 18.3 and 18.5)*
In Table 18.1 the term public sector describes the consolidation of central government, local government and public corporations. General government is the consolidated total of central government and local government. The table shows details of the key public sector finances' indicators, consistent with the European System of Accounts 1995 (ESA95), by sub sector.

The concepts in Table 18.1 are consistent with the format for public finances in the *Economic and Fiscal Strategy Report (EFSR),* published by HM Treasury 11 June 1998, and The Budget. The public sector surplus on current budget is equivalent to net saving in national accounts plus capital tax receipts. Net investment is gross capital formation, plus payments less receipts of investment grants, less depreciation. Net borrowing is net investment less surplus on current budget. Net borrowing differs from the net cash requirement (see below) in that it is measured on an accruals basis whereas the net cash requirement is mainly a cash measure which includes some financial transactions.

Table 18.2 shows the Public sector key fiscal balances. The table shows the component detail of the public sector key fiscal balance by economic category. The tables are consistent with table C22 published in *Budget 2002.*

Table 18.3 shows public sector net debt. Public sector net debt consists of the public sector's financial liabilities at face value minus its liquid assets - mainly foreign currency exchange reserves and bank deposits. General government gross debt (consolidated) in table 18.3 is consistent with the definition of general government gross debt reported to the European Commission under the requirements of the Maastricht Treaty.

More information on the concepts in table 18.1, 18.2 and 18.3 can be found in a guide to monthly public sector finance statistics, *GSS Methodology Series No 12,* the ONS First Releases *Public Sector Finances* and *Public Sector Accounts* and *Financial Statistics Explanatory Handbook.*

Table 18.5 shows the taxes and national insurance contributions paid to central government, local government, and to the institutions of the European Union. The table is the same as table 11.1 of the Blue Book. More information on the data and concepts in the table can be found in Chapter 11 of the Blue Book.

Consolidated Fund and National Loans Fund *(Tables 18.4, 18.6 and 18.7)*
The central government embraces all bodies for whose activities a Minister of the Crown, or other responsible person, is accountable to Parliament. It includes, in addition to the ordinary government departments, a number of bodies administering public policy but without the substantial degree of financial independence which characterises the public corporations; it also includes certain extra-budgetary funds and accounts controlled by departments.

The government's financial transactions are handled through a number of statutory funds, or accounts. The most important of these is the Consolidated Fund which is the government's main account with the Bank of England. Up to 31 March 1968 the Consolidated Fund was virtually synonymous with the term 'Exchequer' which was then the government's central cash account. From 1 April 1968 the National Loans Fund, with a separate account at the Bank of England, was set up by the National Loans Act, 1968. The general effect of this Act was to remove from the Consolidated Fund most of the government's domestic lending and the whole of the government's borrowing transactions and to provide for them to be brought to account in the National Loans Fund.

Revenue from taxation and miscellaneous receipts, including interest and dividends on loans made from Votes, continue to be paid into the Consolidated Fund. After meeting the ordinary expenditure on Supply Services and the Consolidated Fund Standing Services, the surplus or deficit of the Consolidated Fund (Table 18.4), is payable into or met by the National Loans Fund.

Table 18.4 also provides a summary of the transactions of the National Loans Fund. The service of the National Debt, previously borne by the Consolidated Fund, is now met from the National Loans Fund which receives (a) interest payable on loans to the nationalised industries, local authorities and other bodies, whether the loans were made before or after 1 April 1968 and (b) the profits of the Issue Department of the Bank of England, mainly derived from interest on government securities, which were formerly paid into the Exchange Equalisation Account. The net cost of servicing the National Debt after applying these interest receipts and similar items is a charge on the Consolidated Fund as part of the standing services. Details of National Loans Fund loans outstanding are shown in Table 18.7.

Details of borrowing and repayments of debt, other than loans from the National Loans Fund, are shown in Table 18.6.

Income tax *(Table 18.10)*
Following the introduction of Independent Taxation from 1990-91 the married couple's allowance was introduced. It is payable in addition to the personal allowance and between 1990-91 and 1992-93 went to the husband unless the transfer condition was met. The condition was that the husband was unable to make full use of the allowance himself and in that case he could transfer only part or all of the married couple's allowance to his wife. In 1993-94 all or half of the allowance could be transferred to the wife if the couple had agreed beforehand. The wife has the right to claim half the allowance. The married couple's allowance, and allowances linked to it, were restricted to 20 per cent in 1994-95 and to 15 per cent from 1995-96.

The age allowance replaces the single allowance, provided the taxpayer's income is below the limits shown in the table. From 1989-90, for incomes in excess of the limits, the allowance is reduced by £1 for each additional £2 of income until the ordinary limit is reached (before it was £2 for each £3 of additional income). The relief is due where the taxpayer is aged 65 or over in the year of assessment.

The additional personal allowance could be claimed by a single parent (or by a married man if his wife was totally incapacitated) who maintained a resident child at his or her own expense. Widow's bereavement allowance was due to a widow in the year of her husband's death and in the following year provided the widow had not remarried before the beginning of that year. Both the additional personal allowance and the widow's bereavement allowance were abolished from April 2000.

The blind person's allowance may be claimed by blind persons (in England and Wales, registered as blind by a local authority) and surplus blind person's allowance may be transferred to a husband or wife. Relief on life assurance premiums is given by deduction from the premium payable. From 1984-85, it is confined to policies made before 14 March 1984.

Rateable values *(Table 18.12)*
Major changes to local government finance in England and Wales took effect from 1 April 1990. These included the abolition of domestic rating - replaced by the community charge (replaced in 1993 by the council tax), the revaluation of all non-domestic properties, and the introduction of the Uniform Business Rate. Also in 1990, a new classification scheme was introduced which has resulted in differences in coverage. Further differences are caused by legislative changes which have changed the treatment of certain types of property.

There was little change in the total rateable value of non-domestic properties when all these properties were revalued in April 1995. Rateable values for offices fell and there was a rise for all other property types shown in the table.

With effect from 1 April 2000 all non-domestic properties were revalued. Overall there was an increase in rateable values of over 25% compared to the end of the 1995 list. The largest proportionate increase was for offices and cinemas, with all property types given in the table showing rises.

18.1 Sectoral analysis of key fiscal balances[1]
United Kingdom
Not seasonally adjusted

£ millions[2]

		1992 /93	1993 /94	1994 /95	1995 /96	1996 /97	1997 /98	1998 /99	1999 /00	2000 /01	2001 /02	2002 /03
Surplus on current budget[3]												
Central Government	ANLV	−32 276	−39 181	−30 573	−23 184	−20 891	4	11 077	23 303	23 885	11 988	−8 231
Local government	NMMX	2 627	2 768	2 016	446	−112	−457	−352	−2 605	−2 263	−1 976	−1 521
General Government	ANLW	−29 649	−36 413	−28 557	−22 738	−21 003	−453	10 725	20 698	21 622	10 012	−9 752
Public corporations	FDDP	−4 682	−4 225	−4 261	−1 667	−569	−553	−763	−1 373	−1 235	−1 163	−2 051
Public sector	ANMU	−34 331	−40 638	−32 818	−24 405	−21 572	−1 006	9 962	19 325	20 387	8 849	−11 803
Net investment[4]												
Central government	−ANNS	19 253	13 100	14 165	13 717	9 286	7 698	7 511	7 341	8 269	11 795	15 524
Local government	−ANNT	−3 044	1 208	2 157	−220	−961	−552	−259	−1 662	−2 556	−1 440	−3 580
General Government	−ANNV	16 209	14 308	16 322	13 497	8 325	7 146	7 252	5 679	5 713	10 355	11 944
Public corporations	−ANNU	−3 853	−3 950	−5 931	−3 161	−2 452	−1 577	−842	−1 531	−719	−806	−1 223
Public sector	−ANNW	12 356	10 358	10 391	10 336	5 873	5 569	6 410	4 148	4 994	9 549	10 721
Net borrowing[5]												
Central government	−NMFJ	51 529	52 281	44 738	36 901	30 177	7 694	−3 566	−15 962	−15 616	−193	23 755
Local government	−NMOE	−5 671	−1 560	141	−666	−849	−95	93	943	−293	536	−2 059
General Government	−NNBK	45 858	50 721	44 879	36 235	29 328	7 599	−3 473	−15 019	−15 909	343	21 696
Public corporations	−CPCM	829	275	−1 670	−1 494	−1 883	−1 024	−79	−158	516	357	828
Public sector	−ANNX	46 687	50 996	43 209	34 741	27 445	6 575	−3 552	−15 177	−15 393	700	22 524
Net cash requirement												
Central government[6]	RUUX	42 312	48 850	39 057	35 628	24 995	2 650	−6 190	−10 551	−37 161	3 829	24 169
Local government	ABEG	−5 735	−2 780	−961	−1 139	−843	−820	−404	979	−611	−392	−2 685
General Government	RUUS	36 577	46 070	38 096	34 489	24 152	1 830	−6 594	−9 572	−37 772	3 437	21 484
Public corporations	ABEM	−317	61	−1 408	−3 004	−1 424	−718	−385	1 031	523	−119	878
Public sector	RURQ	36 260	46 131	36 688	31 485	22 728	1 112	−6 979	−8 541	−37 249	3 318	22 362
Public sector debt												
Public sector net debt (£ billion)	RUTN	202.3	249.4	289.3	321.3	348.4	352.0	348.5	340.9	306.9	311.3	332.8
Public sector net debt as % GDP	RUTO	32.0	37.2	40.7	42.7	43.7	41.5	39.1	36.2	31.2	30.2	30.8

1 National accounts entities as defined under the European System of Accounts 1995 (ESA95) consistent with the latest national accounts. See chapter text.
2 Unless otherwise stated
3 Net saving, plus capital taxes.
4 Gross capital formation, plus payments less receipts, of investment grants less depreciation.

5 Net borrowing = net investment minus surplus on current budget. A version of General government net borrowing is reported to the European Commision under the requirements of the Maastricht Treaty.
6 Central government net cash requirement (own account).

Source: Office for National Statistics: 020 7533 5984

18.2 Public sector transactions and fiscal balances[1]
United Kingdom

£ millions

		1992 /93	1993 /94	1994 /95	1995 /96	1996 /97	1997 /98	1998 /99	1999 /00	2000 /01	2001 /02	2002 /03
Current receipts												
Taxes on income and wealth	ANSO	78 226	78 592	87 804	96 422	102 261	114 933	123 886	133 710	144 156	145 022	143 190
Taxes on production	NMYE	79 891	83 091	90 389	96 304	99 830	109 726	115 719	125 706	129 905	134 700	142 175
Other current taxes[2]	MJBC	10 688	10 535	11 312	12 130	13 162	14 214	15 468	16 541	17 635	18 414	19 671
Taxes on capital	NMGI	1 211	1 335	1 409	1 518	1 558	1 684	1 805	2 054	2 236	2 383	2 376
Social contributions	ANBO	36 972	40 136	42 832	45 007	47 165	51 692	54 746	57 163	62 068	63 156	63 495
Gross operating surplus	ANBP	12 504	14 440	15 392	18 271	17 992	17 790	18 200	17 836	17 909	18 862	18 523
Interest and dividends from private sector and RoW	ANBQ	5 030	4 275	4 133	4 435	4 363	4 472	4 986	4 256	6 041	4 716	4 483
Interest and dividends (net) from public sector												
Rent and other current transfers[3]	ANBS	873	1 249	1 571	1 629	1 869	1 612	1 431	1 543	2 499	2 778	2 627
Total current receipts	ANBT	225 395	233 653	254 842	275 716	288 200	316 123	336 241	358 809	382 449	390 031	396 540
Current expenditure												
Current expenditure on goods and services[4]	GZSN	130 500	131 829	138 140	142 687	146 010	148 372	156 990	168 646	181 225	196 539	214 382
Subsidies	NMRL	5 768	4 712	5 537	5 744	5 944	5 741	4 629	4 638	5 185	6 220	6 787
Social benefits	ANLY	87 721	95 266	97 715	100 660	104 894	106 830	107 645	111 310	116 827	124 505	128 751
Net current grants abroad[5]	GZSI	112	−371	553	458	−751	102	−847	−253	−146	−1 861	−626
Current grants (net) within general government												
Other current grants	NNAI	4 675	10 108	9 739	10 907	13 591	14 458	16 180	16 984	19 353	19 472	23 369
Interest and dividends paid to private sector and RoW	ANLO	19 045	20 764	23 488	26 765	28 118	29 717	29 340	25 283	26 406	22 524	21 328
Total current expenditure	ANLT	247 821	262 308	275 172	287 221	297 806	305 220	313 937	326 608	348 850	367 399	393 991
Saving, gross plus capital taxes	ANSP	−22 426	−28 655	−20 330	−11 505	−9 606	10 903	22 304	32 201	33 599	22 632	2 549
Depreciation	−ANNZ	−11 905	−11 983	−12 488	−12 900	−11 966	−11 909	−12 342	−12 876	−13 212	−13 783	−14 352
Surplus on current budget	ANMU	−34 331	−40 638	−32 818	−24 405	−21 572	−1 006	9 962	19 325	20 387	8 849	−11 803
Net investment												
Gross fixed capital formation[6]	ANSQ	19 347	17 905	19 114	19 136	14 255	13 467	13 968	13 155	14 855	17 000	17 948
Less depreciation	−ANNZ	−11 905	−11 983	−12 488	−12 900	−11 966	−11 909	−12 342	−12 876	−13 212	−13 783	−14 352
Increase in inventories and valuables	ANSR	−165	−224	−662	21	34	139	231	−472	−170	−	−90
Capital grants (net) within public sector												
Capital grants to private sector and RoW	ANSS	5 418	5 153	4 854	4 432	4 032	4 388	4 920	4 768	4 277	7 271	8 106
Capital grants from private sector and RoW	−ANST	−339	−493	−427	−353	−482	−516	−367	−427	−756	−939	−891
Total net investment	−ANNW	12 356	10 358	10 391	10 336	5 873	5 569	6 410	4 148	4 994	9 549	10 721
Net borrowing[7]	−ANNX	46 687	50 996	43 209	34 741	27 445	6 575	−3 552	−15 177	−15 393	700	22 524
Financial transactions determining net cash requirement												
Net lending to private sector and RoW	ANSU	−	133	−1 167	−1 749	−655	−224	267	2 036	2 687	1 870	2 275
Net acquisition of UK company securities	ANSV	−7 909	−5 194	−6 374	−2 344	−3 992	−1 642	423	−504	835	−652	99
Accounts receivable/payable	ANSW	−1 665	917	75	3 139	−275	−686	−65	5 309	−22 394	2 360	−410
Adjustment for interest on gilts	ANSX	−1 255	−791	−1 036	−1 895	−382	−2 349	−2 446	−1 295	−2 630	−376	−1 521
Other financial transcations[8]	ANSY	402	70	1 981	−407	587	−562	−1 606	1 090	−354	−584	−605
Public sector net cash requirement	RURQ	36 260	46 131	36 688	31 485	22 728	1 112	−6 979	−8 541	−37 249	3 318	22 362

1 See chapter text.
2 Includes domestic rates, council tax, community charge, motor vehicle duty paid by household, and some licence fees.
3 ESA95 transactions D44, D45, D74, D75 and D72-D71: includes rent of land, oil royalties, other property income, and fines.
4 Includes non-trading capital consumption.

5 Net of current grants received from abroad.
6 Including net acquisition of land.
7 Net borrowing equals net investment minus surplus on current budget.
8 Includes statistical discrepancy, finance leasing and similar borrowing, insurance technical reserves and some other minor adjustments.

Source: Office for National Statistics: 020 7533 5984

18.3 Public sector net debt[1]
United Kingdom

£ millions

		1994/95	1995/96	1996/97	1997/98	1998/99	1999/00	2000/01	2001/02	2002/03
Central government sterling gross debt:										
British government stock										
Conventional gilts	BKPK	186 666	208 943	231 869	232 292	223 105	218 687	204 285	200 833	206 119
Index linked gilts	BKPL	39 207	46 133	51 535	58 729	62 289	65 740	70 316	70 417	75 966
Total	BKPM	225 872	255 075	283 404	291 021	285 394	284 427	274 601	271 250	282 085
Sterling Treasury bills	BKPJ	8 051	10 781	4 996	2 106	4 721	4 453	3 521	9 700	15 000
National savings	ACUA	51 843	56 965	61 754	63 271	64 346	63 331	62 611	62 275	63 032
Tax instruments	ACRV	1 612	1 222	853	706	574	535	491	478	376
Other sterling debt[2]	BKSK	25 773	26 758	26 578	25 340	26 249	26 771	28 240	26 293	30 164
Central government sterling gross debt total	BKSL	313 151	350 801	377 585	382 444	381 284	379 517	369 464	369 996	390 657
Central government foreign currency gross debt:										
US$ bonds	BKPG	4 241	4 524	4 294	4 180	4 338	4 388	4 924	2 107	–
DM bonds[3]	EYST	2 245	2 219	1 828	–	–	–	–	–	–
ECU bonds	EYSJ	2 045	2 059	1 777	1 606	1 672	1 500	–	–	–
ECU/euro Treasury notes	EYSV	4 499	4 118	3 199	2 891	3 010	2 701	2 486	1 225	–
ECU/euro Treasury bills	EYSN	2 863	2 883	2 488	2 249	2 341	–	–	–	–
Other foreign currency debt	BKPH	1 018	982	752	537	456	364	291	243	172
Central government foreign currency gross debt total	BKPI	16 912	16 785	14 338	11 463	11 816	8 954	7 701	3 575	172
Central government gross debt total	BKPW	330 063	367 586	391 923	393 907	393 100	388 471	377 165	373 571	390 829
Local government gross debt total	EYKP	50 229	50 552	49 856	50 193	51 039	51 702	52 517	52 561	51 324
less										
Central government holdings of local government debt	-EYKZ	–40 707	–41 266	–42 348	–43 172	–45 045	–46 563	–47 789	–47 530	–44 836
Local government holdings of central government debt	-EYLA	–149	–153	–155	–170	–273	–77	–31	–29	–153
General government gross debt (consolidated)	BKPX	339 436	376 719	399 276	400 758	398 821	393 533	381 862	378 573	397 164
Public corporations gross debt	EYYD	26 916	26 595	26 158	26 044	26 775	26 813	27 740	26 669	26 606
less:										
Central government holdings of public corporations debt	-EYXY	–26 279	–25 980	–25 664	–25 668	–26 440	–26 453	–27 181	–26 335	–26 193
Local government holdings of public corporations debt	-EYXZ	–3	–	–1	–	–4	–123	–124	–122	–121
Public corporations holdings of central government debt	-BKPZ	–3 503	–5 723	–7 187	–7 530	–6 604	–6 297	–6 359	–5 092	–4 661
Public corporations holdings of local government debt	-EYXV	–1 586	–890	–134	–139	–108	–141	–106	–60	–50
Public sector gross debt (consolidated)	BKQA	334 981	370 721	392 448	393 465	392 440	387 332	375 832	373 633	392 745
Public sector liquid assets:										
Official reserves	AIPD	28 330	30 463	25 547	21 293	22 147	21 498	30 423	28 055	26 348
Central government deposits[4]	BKSM	1 816	1 808	2 083	2 293	1 762	1 879	2 797	2 802	2 900
Other central government	BKSN	–	–	–	–	–	4 756	15 663	10 734	9 403
Local government deposits[4]	BKSO	9 335	10 229	11 313	11 828	12 301	10 221	11 522	11 723	12 730
Other local government short term assets	BKQG	2 621	2 826	3 256	3 693	4 335	5 468	5 719	5 990	6 061
Public corporations deposits[4]	BKSP	2 622	3 089	2 040	1 721	2 050	1 455	1 633	1 801	1 371
Other public corporations short term assets	BKSQ	943	1 054	686	668	1 300	1 128	1 212	1 180	1 132
Public sector liquid assets total	BKQJ	45 667	49 469	44 925	41 496	43 895	46 405	68 969	62 285	59 945
Public sector net debt	BKQK	289 314	321 253	347 523	351 969	348 545	340 927	306 863	311 348	332 800
as percentage of GDP[5]	RUTO	40.7	42.7	43.7	41.5	39.1	36.2	31.2	30.2	30.8

1 See chapter text.
2 Including overdraft with Bank of England.
3 Matured on 28 October 1997.
4 Bank and building society deposits.
5 Gross domestic product at market prices from 12 months centred on the end of the month.

Source: Office for National Statistics: 020 7533 5984

18.4 Consolidated Fund and National Loans Fund[1]: revenue and expenditure; receipts and payments

United Kingdom   Years ending 31 March

£ millions

		1993 /94	1994 /95	1995 /96	1996 /97	1997 /98	1998 /99	1999 /00	2000 /01	2001 /02	2002 /03
Consolidated Fund											
Revenue											
Inland Revenue	KCWZ	77 270.6	87 230.4	97 100.9	103 892.4	117 632.8	128 249.8	139 384.0	149 084.8	149 112.4	145 898.0
Customs and Excise	KCXA	66 885.5	72 485.6	76 668.6	82 351.6	89 839.6	94 018.3	97 291.5	102 168.0	104 854.8	108 719.8
Motor vehicle duties	KCXB	3 752.3	3 805.9	4 043.6	4 217.5	4 543.0	4 666.3	4 893.0	4 642.1	4 402.3	4 399.4
National Non-Domestic Rates	KPOI	..	11 469.8	13 373.4	14 269.3	14 036.9	15 878.3	13 403.8	15 482.0	16 009.3	17 592.9
Miscellaneous receipts	KCXE	22 150.2	16 280.3	10 289.3	12 634.6	14 176.6	10 737.1	8 799.0	29 329.4	7 796.6	9 425.0
Total revenue	KCXF	170 058.6	191 272.0	201 475.8	217 365.4	240 228.9	253 549.8	263 771.3	300 706.3	282 175.4	286 035.1
Expenditure											
Supply services	KCXG	204 376.1	207 465.8	211 403.3	214 226.0	209 440.8	213 439.2	226 989.6	241 685.1	271 998.6	290 183.0
Debt interest[2]	KCXH	13 459.6	16 039.8	18 423.2	20 702.3	21 605.7	21 320.8	18 535.3	16 629.2	15 325.6	14 680.9
Payments to Northern Ireland	KCXI	3 090.3	4 052.6	3 903.5	3 685.2	4 581.5	4 709.3	3 104.4	–	–	–
Payments to the European Communities, etc	KCXJ	6 079.5	5 258.2	7 650.7	6 875.3	7 039.9	8 060.7	7 001.8	8 417.1	4 785.8	6 504.0
Other expenditure[3]	KCXL	−453.3	271.6	−14.0	876.2	−53.8	−62.1	223.7	170.1	257.9	−72.4
Total expenditure	KCXM	226 552.2	233 088.0	241 366.5	246 365.0	242 614.1	247 467.9	255 854.8	266 901.5	292 367.9	311 295.5
Deficit met from the National Loans Fund	KCXN	56 493.6	41 816.0	39 890.7	28 999.6	2 385.2	−6 081.9	−7 916.5	−33 804.8	−10 192.5	−25 260.4
National Loans Fund											
Receipts											
Profits of the Issue Department of the Bank of England - income[4]	KZAW	996.6	955.2	1 275.5	1 200.9	1 604.8	1 600.9	1 327.3	1 603.0	1 362.9	1 240.2
Other miscellaneous receipts	KZAX	106.6	4.8	4.4	3.6	5.0	5.0	4.4	6.0	7.3	10.6
Interest on loans	KCXO	4 695.2	4 564.5	4 598.7	4 393.5	5 103.6	4 409.7	4 533.3	6 215.4	5 901.2	5 791.5
Service of the National Debt - balance met from the Consolidated Fund	KCXP	13 459.6	16 039.8	18 423.2	20 702.3	21 605.7	21 320.8	18 535.3	16 629.2	15 325.6	14 680.9
Gilt Edged Official Operations Account Net Income	KJDO	2.0	–	–	–	–	–	127.5	–	–	–
Total	KCXQ	19 260.0	21 564.3	24 301.8	26 300.3	28 319.1	27 336.4	24 527.8	24 453.6	22 597.0	21 723.2
Exchange Equalisation Account- sterling capital	KCXR	400.0	1 250.0	2 750.0	2 150.0	3 650.0	1 880.0	975.0	−5 205.0	4 849.0	4 620.0
Net borrowing[5]	KCXS	58 939.5	39 848.1	37 688.8	27 547.9	–	–	4 997.3	–	4 884.8	11 004.4
International Monetary Fund- maintenance of sterling holdings	KCXT	–	–	–	82.1	707.0	181.2	–	–	–	98.2
Profits of the Issue Department of the Bank of England: capital appreciation	KZAY	..	..	..	18.8	21.2	19.3	1.7	2.5	6.4	9.0
Reduction of National Debt Commissioners' Liability in respect of the National Savings Bank Investment Account	KCXU	–	–	–	–	–	–	–	–	–	–
Change in balances and other items	KCXV	–	–	–	–	–	–	–	–	–	–
NILO Gilt-Edged operations A/C	KJDL	2 500.0	2 500.0	2 500.0	2 000.0	2 500.0	2 500.0	5 000.0	–	–	–
Debt Management Account	GPJW	–	–	–	–	–	–	–	20 000.0	–	7 000.0
Total	KCXW	81 099.5	65 162.4	67 240.6	58 099.1	35 197.3	31 916.9	35 501.8	39 251.1	32 337.2	44 454.8
Payments											
Service of the National Debt: Interest	KJDM	19 107.0	21 334.7	24 004.0	25 942.5	27 877.8	26 792.1	24 073.7	23 855.8	22 041.2	21 297.2
Management and expenses	KCXY	153.0	229.6	297.8	357.8	441.3	544.3	454.1	597.8	555.8	426.0
Total	KCXZ	19 260.0	21 564.3	24 301.8	26 300.3	28 319.1	27 336.4	24 527.8	24 453.6	22 597.0	21 723.2
Consolidated Fund deficit met from the National Loans Fund	KCYA	56 493.6	41 816.0	39 890.7	28 999.6	2 385.2	6 081.9	7 916.5	33 804.8	10 192.6	25 260.4
Net repayment[5]	KCYB	–	–	–	–	2 482.1	3 558.2	–	7 083.4	–	–
Net lending[6]	KCYC	−286.6	−974.8	334.1	280.6	−4.2	1 766.3	1 255.9	1 496.5	−786.2	−2 532.4
International Monetary Fund- maintenance of value of sterling holding	KCYD	632.5	226.2	202.1	–	–	–	126.1	21.2	315.2	–
International Monetary Fund- additional subscription	KCYE	–	–	–	–	–	2 826.5	–	–	–	–
NILO Gilt-Edged Operations A/C	KJDN	5 000.0	2 500.0	2 500.0	2 500.0	2 000.0	2 500.0	2 500.0	–	–	–
Discharge of Treasury Liability to the Bank of England Issue Department	KPUK	–	30.7	11.9	18.6	15.1	11.4	8.5	1.2	18.6	3.6
Debt Management Account	ZAFB	..	..	..	..	..	..	..	15 000.0	40 000.0	–
Total	KCYF	81 099.5	65 162.4	67 240.6	58 099.1	35 197.3	31 916.9	35 501.8	39 251.1	32 337.2	44 454.8

1 See chapter text.
2 Payment to National Loans Fund representing its payments for the service of the National Debt *less* its receipts of interest on loans outstanding, etc.
3 Includes net issues to Contingencies Fund.
4 Prior to 1996-97, receipts from the Bank of England for appreciation of the assets of the Issue Department were included in the total ammount for the profits of the Issue Department.

5 See Table 17.6.
6 Minus sign indicates a net issue repayment.

Source: HM Treasury: 020 7270 4761

18.5 Taxes paid by UK residents to general government and the European Union[1]

Total economy sector S.1

£ million

		1993/94	1994/95	1995/96	1996/97	1997/98	1998/99	1999/00	2000/01	2001/02	2002/03
GENERATION OF INCOME											
Uses											
Taxes on production and imports											
Taxes on products and imports											
Value added tax (VAT)											
Paid to central government	NZGF	39 389	43 686	44 598	46 995	52 454	54 281	59 309	61 529	65 754	70 258
Paid to the European Union	FJKM	4 276	3 220	4 942	4 661	3 531	4 105	3 451	4 172	3 592	2 518
Total	QYRC	43 665	46 906	49 540	51 656	55 985	58 386	62 760	65 701	69 346	72 776
Taxes and duties on imports excluding VAT											
Paid to CG: import duties[2]	NMBS	–	–	–	–	–	–	–	–	–	–
Paid to EU: import duties	FJWE	2 169	2 185	2 468	2 290	2 261	2 042	2 049	2 103	2 024	1 893
Total	QYRB	2 169	2 185	2 468	2 290	2 261	2 042	2 049	2 103	2 024	1 893
Taxes on products excluding VAT and import duties											
Paid to central government											
Customs & excise revenue											
Beer	GTAM	2 481	2 527	2 637	2 631	2 699	2 733	2 848	2 798	2 907	2 952
Wines, cider, perry & spirits	GTAN	2 893	3 017	2 983	2 999	3 057	3 301	3 652	3 814	4 067	4 433
Tobacco	GTAO	6 385	6 952	7 405	7 701	7 622	7 551	7 796	7 638	7 639	8 039
Hydrocarbon oils	GTAP	12 736	14 251	15 679	17 171	19 451	21 553	22 510	22 630	21 916	22 147
Car tax	GTAT	–2	–	–	–	–	–	–	–	–	–
Betting, gaming & lottery	CJQY	1 106	1 233	1 591	1 460	1 539	1 527	1 500	1 517	1 437	1 292
Air passenger duty	CWAA	–	89	354	359	522	845	882	956	803	803
Insurance premium tax	CWAD	–	259	648	685	1 179	1 248	1 511	1 751	1 921	2 187
Landfill tax	BKOF	–	–	–	113	364	322	456	475	504	532
Other	ACDN	–	–	–	–	–	–	–	–	–	–
Fossil fuel levy	CIQY	1 327	1 379	1 272	880	256	164	84	52	92	117
Gas levy	GTAZ	149	211	171	199	188	–44	–	–	–	–
Stamp duties	GTBC	1 736	1 799	2 018	2 414	3 456	4 623	6 898	8 165	6 983	7 556
Levies on exports (Third country trade)	CUDF	–	–	–	–	–	–	–	–	–	–
Camelot payments to National Lottery Distribution Fund	LIYH	–	319	1 527	1 263	1 572	1 665	1 593	1 542	1 520	1 382
Purchase Tax	EBDB	–	–	–	–	–	–	–	–	–	–
Hydro-benefit	LITN	23	24	28	31	32	32	38	44	44	44
Other taxes and levies	GCSP	–	–	–	–	–	–	–	–	–	–
Total paid to central government	NMBV	28 834	32 060	36 313	37 906	41 937	45 520	49 768	51 382	49 833	51 484
Paid to the European Union											
Sugar levy	GTBA	61	116	36	37	72	44	46	43	27	25
European Coal & Steel Community levy	GTBB	1	–	–	–	–	–	–	–	–	–
Total paid to the European Union	FJWG	62	116	36	37	72	44	46	43	27	25
Total taxes on products excluding VAT & import duties	QYRA	28 896	32 176	36 349	37 943	42 009	45 564	49 814	51 425	49 860	51 509
Total taxes on products and imports	NZGW	74 730	81 267	88 357	91 889	100 255	105 992	114 623	119 229	121 230	126 178
Production taxes other than on products											
Paid to central government											
Consumer Credit Act fees	CUDB	160	153	166	113	168	158	140	150	143	146
National non-domestic rates	CUKY	13 090	12 785	13 481	13 010	13 283	13 764	14 353	15 168	16 236	16 728
Old style non-domestic rates	NSEZ	110	124	124	126	136	130	123	132	131	123
Levies paid to CG levy-funded bodies	LITK	131	130	134	147	162	171	241	207	175	144
Selective employment tax	CSAH	–	–	–	–	–	–	–	–	–	–
National insurance surcharge	GTAY	–	–	–	–	–	–	–	–	–	–
London regional transport levy	GTBE	–	–	–	–	–	–	–	–	–	–
IBA levy	GTAL	–	–	–	–	–	–	–	–	–	–
Motor vehicle duties paid by businesses	EKED	1 218	1 290	1 331	1 365	1 405	1 503	1 559	1 115	1 383	1 972
Regulator fees	GCSQ	71	69	57	54	57	61	69	72	62	60
Climate change levy	LSNT	–	–	–	–	–	–	–	–	822	825
Aggregates Levy	MDUQ	–	–	–	–	–	–	–	–	–	291
Total	NMBX	14 780	14 551	15 293	14 815	15 211	15 787	16 485	16 844	18 952	20 289
Paid to local government											
Old style non-domestic rates	NMYH	88	92	100	114	124	131	144	150	161	144
Total production taxes other than on products	NMYD	14 868	14 643	15 393	14 929	15 335	15 918	16 629	16 994	19 113	20 433
Total taxes on production and imports, paid											
Paid to central government	NMBY	83 003	90 297	96 204	99 716	109 602	115 588	125 562	129 755	134 539	142 031
Paid to local government	NMYH	88	92	100	114	124	131	144	150	161	144
Paid to the European Union	FJWB	6 507	5 521	7 446	6 988	5 864	6 191	5 546	6 318	5 643	4 436
Total	NZGX	89 598	95 910	103 750	106 818	115 590	121 910	131 252	136 223	140 343	146 611

18.5

continued

Taxes paid by UK residents
to general government and the European Union[1]

Total economy sector S.1

£ million

		1993 /94	1994 /95	1995 /96	1996 /97	1997 /98	1998 /99	1999 /00	2000 /01	2001 /02	2002 /03
SECONDARY DISTRIBUTION OF INCOME											
Uses											
Current taxes on income, wealth etc											
Taxes on income											
Paid to central government											
Household income taxes	DRWH	65 806	70 361	74 974	75 191	81 895	89 739	96 967	106 866	108 542	110 774
Petroleum revenue tax	DBHA	359	711	968	1 729	963	502	853	1 518	1 310	958
Windfall tax	EYNK	–	–	–	–	2 610	2 614	–	–	–	–
Other corporate taxes	BMNX	12 601	17 031	20 748	25 715	29 844	31 263	36 164	35 878	35 227	31 520
Total	NMCU	78 766	88 103	96 690	102 635	115 312	124 118	133 984	144 262	145 079	143 252
Other current taxes											
Paid to central government											
Motor vehicle duty paid by households	CDDZ	2 409	2 557	2 686	2 802	3 045	3 116	3 296	3 155	2 831	2 624
Old style domestic rates	NSFA	73	80	79	104	115	114	117	108	109	117
Licences	NSNP	7	9	11	10	11	8	8	2	–	–
National non-domestic rates paid by non-market sectors	BMNY	–	–	–	930	929	971	1 002	997	1 087	1 094
Total	NMCV	2 490	2 645	2 776	3 846	4 100	4 209	4 423	4 262	4 027	3 835
Paid to local government											
Old style domestic rates	NMHK	57	56	60	61	64	62	68	76	80	72
Community charge	NMHL	–	–	–	–	–	–	–	–	–	–
Council tax	NMHM	7 988	8 611	9 294	10 059	10 850	12 037	12 918	14 155	15 247	16 704
Total	NMIS	8 045	8 667	9 354	10 120	10 914	12 099	12 986	14 231	15 327	16 776
Total	NVCM	10 535	11 312	12 130	13 966	15 014	16 308	17 409	18 493	19 354	20 611
Total current taxes on income, wealth etc											
Paid to central government	NMCP	81 256	90 748	99 466	106 481	119 412	128 327	138 407	148 524	149 106	147 087
Paid to local government	NMIS	8 045	8 667	9 354	10 120	10 914	12 099	12 986	14 231	15 327	16 776
Total	NMZL	89 301	99 415	108 820	116 601	130 326	140 426	151 393	162 755	164 433	163 863
Social contributions											
Actual social contributions											
Paid to central government											
(National Insurance Contributions)											
Employers' compulsory contributions	CEAN	23 478	23 334	24 533	25 950	27 761	29 779	31 717	35 087	35 685	35 420
Employees' compulsory contributions	GCSE	15 183	17 974	18 889	19 557	22 073	23 255	23 623	24 973	25 344	25 903
Self- and non-employed persons' compulsory contributions	NMDE	1 475	1 524	1 585	1 658	1 858	1 712	1 823	2 008	2 127	2 172
Total	AIIH	40 136	42 832	45 007	47 165	51 692	54 746	57 163	62 068	63 156	63 495
CAPITAL ACCOUNT											
Changes in liabilities and net worth											
Other capital taxes											
Paid to central government											
Inheritance tax	GILF	1 307	1 383	1 484	1 517	1 649	1 764	2 016	2 181	2 346	2 322
Tax on other capital transfers	GILG	28	26	34	41	35	41	38	55	37	54
Development land tax and other	GCSV	–	–	–	–	–	–	–	–	–	–
Total	NMGI	1 335	1 409	1 518	1 558	1 684	1 805	2 054	2 236	2 383	2 376
TOTAL TAXES AND COMPULSORY SOCIAL CONTRIBUTIONS											
Paid to central government	GCSS	205 730	225 286	242 195	254 920	282 390	300 466	323 186	342 583	349 184	354 989
Paid to local government	GCST	8 133	8 759	9 454	10 234	11 038	12 230	13 130	14 381	15 488	16 920
Paid to the European Union	FJWB	6 507	5 521	7 446	6 988	5 864	6 191	5 546	6 318	5 643	4 436
Total	GCSU	220 370	239 566	259 095	272 142	299 292	318 887	341 862	363 282	370 315	376 345
Total taxes and social contributions as percentage of GDP	GDWM	33.8	34.7	35.5	35.0	36.4	36.6	37.2	37.8	36.8	35.6

1 See chapter text.
2 These taxes existed before the UK's entry into the EEC in 1973

Sources: HM Treasury;
Office for National Statistics: 020 7533 5991

18.6 Borrowing and repayment of debt[1]
United Kingdom
Years ending 31 March

£ millions

		1993/94	1994/95	1995/96	1996/97	1997/98	1998/99	1999/00	2000/01	2001/02	2002/03
Borrowing											
Government securities: new issues	KQGA	55 959.2	32 137.5	34 150.3	40 800.8	28 484.4	12 048.0	26 426.5	25 789.8	43 433.4	54 068.9
National savings securities:											
National savings certificates	KQGB	3 381.5	2 187.9	3 425.9	3 695.5	4 435.2	3 028.7	1 962.7	3 086.2	2 580.7	2 434.3
Capital bonds	KQGC	556.2	521.5	504.8	450.8	619.0	469.6	35.4	29.0	40.9	107.3
Income bonds	KQGD	1 940.8	1 255.7	780.7	1 272.7	1 043.4	1 371.7	653.4	760.5	625.6	484.8
Deposit bonds	KQGE	–	–	–	–	..	–	–	–	–	–
British savings bonds	KQGF	–	–	–	–	–	–	–	–	–	–
Premium savings bonds	KQGG	931.5	1 837.2	2 040.6	2 552.5	3 158.8	3 652.8	3 449.4	3 296.0	3 859.6	4 604.5
Save As You Earn	KQGH	76.4	66.5	50.8	34.1	20.7	11.4	5.0	0.3	–	–
Yearly plan	KQGI	112.4	116.5	94.1	–	–	5.2	–	–	–	–
National savings stamps and gift tokens	KQGJ	–	–	–	–	–	–	–	–	–	–
National Savings Bank Investments	KQGK	1 370.5	1 368.1	1 312.1	1 478.7	1 282.3	1 085.0	901.6	955.3	864.9	1 012.4
Children's Bonus Bonds	KGVO	91.2	118.9	144.9	352.4	255.3	205.0	58.5	53.4	45.0	54.0
First Option Bonds	KIAR	1 026.0	812.0	826.4	1 139.8	1 152.9	1 001.8	34.3	–	–	–
Pensioners Guaranteed Income Bond	KJDW	786.1	1 190.3	2 104.2	2 863.8	1 126.9	201.0	590.7	687.2	603.5	662.9
Treasurer's account	KWNF	..	..	..	21.1	39.9	17.1	13.6	12.5	15.2	19.4
Individual Savings Account	ZAFC	..	..	..	..	..	–	257.8	265.9	397.8	405.6
Fixed Rate Savings Bonds	ZAFD	..	..	..	..	..	–	175.9	284.7	192.7	193.0
Guaranteed Equity Bonds	ECPU	..	..	..	..	..	..	..	..	27.2	274.8
Certificate of tax deposit	KQGL	470.6	91.2	76.2	109.4	84.1	66.4	121.4	76.5	77.6	59.6
Nationalised industries', etc temporary deposits	KQGM	28 700.9	29 294.0	36 870.6	53 198.2	46 375.9	39 962.4	40 343.3	56 106.6	62 150.0	55 395.1
British Gas corporation deposits	KQGN										
Sterling Treasury bills (net receipt)	KQGO	–	5 196.1	2 606.1	–	–	3 546.2	–	–	–	–
ECU Treasury bills (net receipt)	KQGP										
ECU Treasury notes (net receipt)	KDZZ	2 073.2	429.8	–	–	–	–	721.1	–	–	–
Ways and means (net receipt)	KQGQ	9 007.0	8 891.7	1 162.3	511.1	–	183.6	5 599.0	12 126.0	12 095.3	3 899.9
Other debt : payable in sterling : Interest free notes	KQGR	796.6	382.6	247.4	99.2	32.4	2 130.9	373.5	972.7	1 427.2	754.0
Other debt : payable in external currencies	KHCY	9 243.9	–	–	2 565.2						
Total receipts	KHCZ	116 524.0	85 897.5	86 397.4	111 145.3	88 111.2	68 986.8	81 723.1	104 502.6	128 436.6	124 430.5
Repayment of debt											
Government securities: redemptions	KQGS	7 390.5	9 333.3	4 652.7	14 488.4	20 678.9	18 575.5	19 815.8	33 722.2	43 642.3	42 109.9
Statutory sinking funds	KQGT	2.4	2.3	2.2	2.2	2.1	2.0	2.0	2.0	1.9	1.9
Terminable annuities:											
National Debt Commissioners	KQGU	–	–	–	–	–	–	–	–	–	–
National savings securities:											
National savings certificates	KQGV	2 208.0	1 612.6	2 258.4	3 263.7	4 058.5	3 449.0	2 405.2	4 546.8	4 177.7	4 146.7
Capital bonds	KQGW	398.0	647.7	509.0	698.3	1 160.5	888.3	324.2	375.0	175.9	155.9
Income bonds	KQGX	1 000.7	1 181.8	1 256.9	1 394.0	1 148.9	880.8	1 686.3	857.0	933.8	1 144.2
Deposit bonds	KQGY	71.8	72.3	72.5	64.8	72.6	84.2	70.2	71.1	45.4	369.9
Yearly Plan	KQGZ	88.9	77.0	101.9	96.3	113.2	120.0	141.8	18.4	4.5	3.0
British savings bonds	KQHA										
Premium savings bonds	KQHB	181.0	333.0	590.1	869.3	1 203.1	1 398.4	1 923.8	1 872.6	1 942.9	2 343.3
Save As You Earn	KQHC	96.3	92.3	98.7	70.1	68.2	37.1	34.5	22.9	8.0	3.2
National savings stamps and gift tokens	KQHD	0.7									
National Savings Bank Investments (repayments)	KQHE	1 646.3	1 745.3	1 755.8	1 837.0	2 175.7	2 027.0	1 886.3	1 654.1	1 415.8	1 350.1
Children's Bonus Bonds	KGVQ	1.2	4.3	0.1	257.8	187.9	183.2	69.3	95.0	114.5	92.6
First Option Bonds	KIAS	1 085.1	969.9	732.7	833.9	1 283.0	1 055.5	298.1	225.2	111.6	77.4
Pensioners Guaranteed Income Bond	KPOB	–	57.0	104.5	185.0	318.8	897.8	935.3	2 003.8	1 640.4	703.9
Treasurer's account	KWNG	..	..	..	1.2	11.8	13.7	16.4	13.9	16.5	16.9
Individual Savings Account	ZAFE	..	..	..	..	..	..	12.3	39.9	70.3	105.9
Fixed Rate Savings Bonds	ZAFF	..	..	..	..	..	..	2.8	62.1	110.1	133.6
Guaranteed Equity Bonds	JUWE	..	..	..	..	..	..	..	..	..	3.9
Certificates of tax deposit	KQHF	722.6	612.1	466.0	478.9	229.0	199.9	159.9	120.1	91.4	161.5
Tax reserve certificates	KQHG	–	–	–	–	–	–	–	–	–	–
Nationalised industries', etc temporary deposits	KQHH	28 098.5	28 557.8	35 263.1	51 979.3	46 835.7	41 776.9	41 089.4	56 004.0	63 127.9	55 695.6
Debt to the Bank of England	KPOC	–	11.0	–	–	–	–	–	–	–	–
British Gas Corporation (Repayment of Deposits)	KQHI	–	–	–	–	–	–	–	–	–	–
Sterling Treasury bills (net repayment)	KQHJ	1 547.5	–	–	4 009.6	1 928.5	–	3 014.8	6 194.2	–	–
ECU Treasury bills (net repayment)	KJEG	73.3	–	–	–	–	–	2 492.9	–	–	–
ECU Treasury notes (net repayment)	KSPA	..	..	439.1	318.3	3.3	13.2	–	1 391.9	1 359.6	1 453.1
Ways and means (net repayment)	KQHK	–	–	–	–	5 815.4	–	–	–	–	–
Other debt : payable in sterling : Interest free notes	KQHL	101.3	225.2	301.3	87.6	1 215.5	850.5	246.4	458.2	1 723.3	1 393.3
Other	KQHM	–	–	–	–	–	–	–	–	–	–
Other debt : payable in external currencies	KQHN	12 870.4	514.5	103.6	2 661.7	2 082.7	92.0	98.1	1 835.6	2 838.1	1 960.3
Total payments	KQHO	57 584.5	46 049.4	48 708.6	83 597.4	90 593.3	72 545.0	76 725.8	111 586.0	123 551.9	113 426.1
Net borrowing	KQHP	58 939.5	39 848.1	37 688.8	27 547.9	–	–	4 997.3	–	4 884.7	11 004.4
Net repayment	KHDD	–	–	–	–	2 482.1	3 558.2	–	7 083.4	–	–

1 See chapter text.

Source: HM Treasury: 020 7270 4761

18.7 Consolidated Fund and National Loans Fund: assets and liabilities[1]
United Kingdom
At 31 March in each year

£ millions

		1993	1994	1995	1996	1997	1998	1999	2000	2001	2002
CONSOLIDATED FUND											
Total estimated assets	KQIA	18 872.0	26 914.5	33 992.4	33 809.0	36 177.4	36 061.0	36 148.0	33 932.1	35 967.9	37 458.5
Subscriptions and contributions to international financial organisations	KQIB	5 009.2	5 438.2	5 898.1	6 470.8	6 528.9	6 660.8	7 059.7	6 903.6	7 298.4	7 564.4
International Bank for Reconstruction and Development	KQIC	259.8	274.5	265.2	271.6	265.0	262.5	266.0	267.1	279.2	279.0
International Finance Corporation	KQID	53.1	60.9	62.0	73.1	74.9	72.9	75.6	76.5	85.8	85.7
International Development Association	KQIE	2 576.0	2 785.4	3 005.5	3 205.8	3 372.7	3 562.2	3 733.3	3 900.0	4 134.0	4 347.8
African Development Bank	KQIF	108.1	127.9	141.2	148.3	162.9	180.0	199.1	215.7	229.8	259.8
Asian Development Bank	KQIG	180.9	188.9	201.5	214.6	240.4	272.5	304.6	339.3	365.5	393.3
Caribbean Development Bank	KQIH	29.4	31.2	32.6	34.2	34.1	34.6	36.8	40.7	41.9	44.0
European Investment Bank	KQII	1 588.9	1 713.7	1 876.4	2 166.6	2 036.5	1 840.7	2 083.1	1 706.6	1 767.3	1 742.1
European Bank for Reconstruction and Development	KPOD	61.3	99.4	146.3	189.4	175.6	164.2	179.2	170.0	187.4	197.6
Inter-American Development Bank	KQIJ	109.8	112.5	107.2	119.6	117.5	219.3	127.8	130.6	145.7	147.3
International Fund for Agricultural Development	KQIK	38.5	40.2	42.7	44.2	46.1	48.8	51.0	53.7	56.4	59.1
Multilateral Investment Guarantee Agency	KQIL	3.5	3.5	3.2	3.4	3.2	3.1	3.2	3.3	5.4	8.7
Amounts due from overseas governments	KQIM	–	–	–	–	–	–	–	–	–	–
War of 1939-45	KQIN	–	–	–	–	–	–	–	–	–	–
Other	KQIO	–	–	–	–	–	–	–	–	–	–
Loans from Votes	KQIP	6 709.2	11 057.4	13 599.7	12 967.0	13 684.7	14 050.0	11 546.3	3 970.3	7 015.3	9 006.1
Issues of public dividend capital:	KQIQ	4 920.0	7 979.2	11 467.0	12 161.1	12 424.8	13 157.1	16 238.5	21 338.3	20 083.6	19 546.2
British Airways Board	KQIR	–	–	–	–	–	–	–	–	–	–
British Steel Corporation	KQIS	–	–	–	–	–	–	–	–	–	–
Royal Ordnance Factories	KQIT	–	–	–	–	–	–	–	–	–	–
National Enterprise Board	KQIU	–	–	–	–	–	–	–	–	–	–
Royal Mint	KQIV	7.0	7.0	7.0	7.0	7.0	7.0	7.0	7.0	7.0	5.5
Post Office	KQIW	–	–	–	–	–	–	–	–	–	–
Scottish Development Agency	KQIX	–	–	–	–	–	–	–	–	–	–
Welsh Development Agency	KQIY	12.6	11.6	10.9	9.8	8.9	8.8	8.6	9.1	9.1	11.0
British Aerospace	KQIZ	–	–	–	–	–	–	–	–	–	–
British Shipbuilders	KQJA	1 598.3	1 598.3	1 598.3	1 598.3	1 598.5	1 598.3	50.0	21.0	21.0	21.0
Patent Office	KIAT	6.3	6.3	6.3	6.3	6.3	6.3	6.3	6.3	6.3	6.3
NHS Trusts	KIAU	3 279.6	6 336.2	9 603.1	10 173.8	10 349.7	11 078.0	14 158.7	19 216.6	19 539.2	19 184.1
Companies House	KIAV	15.9	15.9	15.9	15.9	15.9	15.9	15.9	15.9	15.9	15.9
Central Office of Information	KIAW	0.3	0.3	0.3	0.3	0.3	0.3	0.3	0.3	0.3	0.3
Chessington Computer Centre	KPOE	–	3.5	3.5	3.5	–	–	–	–	–	–
OGC Buying Solutions[2]	KWNH	..	..	0.1	0.4	0.4	0.4	0.4	0.4	0.4	0.4
Defence Aviation Repair Agency	JRVU	–	–	–	–	–	–	–	–	–	50.4
Defence Evaluation and Research Agency	KWNI	..	..	128.8	253.0	274.5	274.5	275.4	275.4	275.4	–
Defence Scientific Technology Laboratory	JRVV	–	–	–	–	–	–	–	–	–	42.3
Fire Service College	KWNJ	..	..	16.7	16.7	16.7	16.7	16.7	16.7	16.7	16.7
Forensic Science Service	GPVB	..	..	..	..	..	..	–	18.0	18.0	18.0
Hydrographic Office	GPVC	..	..	..	..	..	..	..	13.3	13.3	13.3
Land Registry	KWNK	..	..	55.4	55.4	61.5	61.5	61.5	61.5	61.5	61.5
Medicines Control Agency	KWNL	..	..	1.6	1.6	1.6	1.6	1.6	1.6	1.6	1.6
Meteorological Office	KZAZ	..	..	..	..	58.9	58.9	58.9	58.9	58.9	58.9
NHS Estates	GPVD	..	..	..	..	..	..	..	0.4	0.4	0.4
Registers of Scotland	KZBA	..	..	..	..	4.3	4.3	4.3	–	–	–
Vehicle Inspectorate	KWNM	..	..	19.1	19.1	20.3	20.3	20.3	20.3	20.3	20.3
Driving Standards Agency	LQMI	..	..	..	..	..	3.5	3.5	3.5	3.5	3.5
Ordnance Survey	GPVE	..	..	..	..	..	..	..	14.0	14.0	14.0
Queen Elizabeth II Conference Centre	LQMJ	..	..	..	..	..	0.8	0.8	0.8	0.8	0.8
Contingencies Fund - capital	KQJB	947.0	347.0	447.0	297.0	977.0	577.0	277.0	277.0	277.0	277.0
Balance on revenue accounts	KQJC	477.6	358.7	1 433.6	1 096.1	954.9	1 546.0	1 026.5	1 442.9	1 293.6	1 064.8
Privatisation receipts	KIAX	809.0	1 734.0	1 147.0	817.0	1 607.1	70.1	–	–	–	–
Total liabilities	KQJD	–	–	– 333 927.9	364 803.0	364 950.8	363 625.5	354 807.7	327 180.6	341 162.2	
Liability to balance National Loans Fund	KQJE	182 102.2	240 351.0	286 055.9	331 164.9	362 506.5	362 582.5	361 065.3	351 626.3	324 336.7	338 550.1
Payment from Votes:	KQJF	66.1	65.2	64.3	63.4	62.4	61.3	60.2	59.0	57.7	56.4
Married quarters for Armed Forces	KQJG	66.1	65.2	64.3	63.4	62.4	61.3	60.2	59.0	57.7	56.4
Liability to Post Office Superannuation Fund	KQJH	–	–	–	–	–	–	–	–	–	–
Post-war credits outstanding and interest due - estimated	KQJI	46.0	46.0	46.0	45.9	45.9	45.9	45.9	45.8	45.8	45.8
Revenue paid over in advance of collection	KQJJ	–	83.7	37.0	–	28.2	13.8	177.9	259.7	301.7	662.9
Inland Revenue	KQJK	–	–	–	–	–	–	177.9	259.7	301.7	662.9
Customs and Excise	KQJL	–	–	–	–	28.2	–	–	–	–	–
Broadcast receiving licences	KQJM	–	–	–	–	–	–	–	–	–	–
Vehicle Excise Duty	KQJN	–	83.7	37.0	–	–	13.8	–	–	–	–

18.7 Consolidated Fund and National Loans Fund: assets and liabilities[1]
United Kingdom
continued At 31 March in each year

£ millions

		1993	1994	1995	1996	1997	1998	1999	2000	2001	2002
CONSOLIDATED FUND (*continued*)											
Promissory notes issued by Minister of Overseas Development	KQJQ	979.5	1 002.6	996.7	1 005.8	1 021.9	822.1	963.1	783.1	939.9	891.9
International Development Association	KQJR	673.1	670.5	656.5	663.2	673.6	484.0	612.3	445.6	553.1	509.7
African Development Fund	KQJS	100.7	106.6	93.2	86.2	95.3	95.2	105.6	89.1	141.6	145.5
Asian Development Bank	KQJT	–	–	–	–	–	–	–	1.9	2.5	2.4
Asian Development Fund	KQJU	108.7	131.8	140.5	127.6	136.0	120.5	105.4	87.8	78.6	73.2
Caribbean Development Bank	KQJV	0.1	1.2	1.3	1.4	1.3	1.3	1.3	1.3	1.5	1.5
Special Development Fund	KQKC	6.9	8.0	9.5	10.6	13.2	15.8	16.4	16.9	15.9	13.8
European Community/International Development Association Special Action Account	KQJW	–	–	–	–	–	–	–	–	–	–
European Investment Bank	KQJX	–	–	–	–	–	–	–	–	–	–
Inter-American Development Bank	KQJY	2.6	2.2	1.3	2.0	1.8	1.9	1.0	2.0	1.4	0.7
Fund for special operations	KQJZ	15.4	16.4	13.1	11.3	8.8	6.3	2.6	2.1	1.1	–
International Fund for Agricultural Development	KQKA	16.1	18.2	15.8	14.2	12.3	14.2	16.5	18.4	15.6	12.9
International Bank for Reconstruction and Development	KQKB	30.2	24.2	39.2	60.7	71.7	81.9	94.3	105.9	112.5	114.6
European Bank for Reconstruction and Development	KIAY	20.4	19.9	20.9	21.0	6.1	–	7.7	12.1	16.1	17.6
United Nations Environment Programme	KJEH	5.3	3.6	5.4	7.6	1.8	1.0	–	–	–	–
Other contributions and instalments due in respect of international subscriptions, etc	KQYX	1 520.7	2 165.8	1 499.6	1 647.9	1 138.1	1 425.2	1 313.1	1 669.2	1 174.0	955.1
NATIONAL LOANS FUND											
Total assets	KQKD	248 643.5	306 872.6	349 159.5	390 681.8	419 548.9	418 444.7	421 635.7	426 239.2	425 955.6	434 544.6
Total National Loans Fund loans outstanding	KQKE	48 705.9	48 470.8	47 496.1	46 600.9	46 746.8	46 742.6	48 513.6	49 788.8	51 037.6	50 251.4
Loans to Public Corporations:											
Consignia PLC (previously Post Office)	KQKF	–	–	–	–	–	–	–	–	500.0	500.0
British Coal	KQKG	180.0	–	–	–	–	–	–	–	–	–
Electricity Council	KQKH	–	–	–	–	–	–	–	–	–	–
North of Scotland Hydro-Electric Board	KQKI	–	–	–	–	–	–	–	–	–	–
Scottish Hydro-Electric	KQKJ	–	–	–	–	–	–	–	–	–	–
South of Scotland Electricity Board	KQKK	–	–	–	–	–	–	–	–	–	–
Scottish Power	KQKL	–	–	–	–	–	–	–	–	–	–
Scottish Nuclear Ltd	KQKM	199.2	196.8	194.1	96.1	–	–	–	–	–	–
British Gas Corporation	KQKN	–	–	–	–	–	–	–	–	–	–
British Steel Corporation	KQKO	–	–	–	–	–	–	–	–	–	–
British Airways Board	KQKP	–	–	–	–	–	–	–	–	–	–
Railtrack	KTCR	..	..	1 287.7	–	–	–	–	–	–	–
European Passenger Services	KTCS	..	..	99.0	761.2	–	–	–	–	–	–
Civil Aviation Authority	KQKQ	311.9	403.7	453.3	476.1	447.5	420.9	365.7	342.5	92.5	9.8
British Airports Authority	KQKR	–	–	–	–	–	–	–	–	–	–
British Railways Board	KQKS	1 923.9	2 445.6	749.2	718.3	601.2	573.7	546.2	518.7	481.3	–
British Transport Docks Board	KQKT	–	–	–	–	–	–	–	–	–	–
British Waterways Board	KQKU	19.2	18.6	18.3	18.2	18.2	18.2	18.2	18.2	16.7	16.3
National Freight Corporation	KQKV	–	–	–	–	–	–	–	–	–	–
National Bus Company	KQKW	–	–	–	–	–	–	–	–	–	–
Scottish Transport Group	KQKX	–	–	–	–	–	–	–	–	–	–
British National Oil Corporation	KQKY	–	–	–	–	–	–	–	–	–	–
British Aerospace	KQKZ	–	–	–	–	–	–	–	–	–	–
British Shipbuilders	KQLA	–	–	–	–	–	–	–	–	–	–
British Telecommunications	KQLB	–	–	–	–	–	–	–	–	–	–
Regional Water Authorities	KQLC	–	–	–	–	–	–	–	–	–	–
New Towns - Development Corporations and Commission	KQLD	1 303.9	1 130.1	1 008.8	314.3	122.2	36.2	8.0	8.0	8.0	8.0
Scottish Special Housing Association	KQLE	–	–	–	–	–	–	–	–	–	–
Scottish Homes	KQLF	401.2	399.4	397.3	395.0	392.5	259.8	190.9	179.0	161.6	149.7
Housing Corporation (Scotland)	KQLG	–	–	–	–	–	–	–	–	–	–
Housing Corporation (England)	KQLH	986.0	899.0	869.9	926.3	848.7	4.0	4.0	3.0	3.0	2.0
Housing for Wales	KQLI	86.7	86.4	69.2	59.0	–	–	–	–	–	–
Covent Garden Market Authority	KQLJ	–	–	–	–	–	–	–	–	–	–
National Enterprise Board	KQLK	–	–	–	–	–	–	–	–	–	–
Land Authority for Wales	KQLL	10.3	6.2	3.2	3.2	1.3	1.3	–	–	–	–
Scottish Enterprise	KQLM	2.7	1.9	1.3	0.6	0.5	0.1	–	–	–	–
Welsh Development Agency	KQLN	1.5	1.2	0.9	1.1	1.2	1.2	0.9	0.6	0.3	0.2
Land Registry Trading Fund	KPOF	–	54.9	–	–	–	–	–	–	–	–
Development Board for Rural Wales	KQLO	8.8	8.8	8.8	7.9	4.1	4.0	4.0	4.0	4.0	4.0
Royal Mint	KQLP	–	–	–	–	–	–	–	2.0	5.0	14.8
Royal Ordnance Factories	KQLQ	–	–	–	–	–	–	–	–	–	–
The Crown Suppliers	KQLR	–	–	–	–	–	–	–	–	–	–
Crown Agents	KQLS	2.3	2.1	2.0	1.9	–	–	–	–	–	–
Her Majesty's Stationery Office	KQLT	6.7	3.3	–	7.0	–	–	–	–	–	–
Urban Development Corporations	KQLU	0.7	1.0	–	–	–	–	–	–	–	–
Harbour Authorities	KQLV	7.1	1.5	0.8	0.7	0.6	0.5	0.4	0.2	0.1	0.1
Commonwealth Development Corporation	KQLW	–	–	–	–	–	–	–	–	–	–
UK Atomic Energy Authority	KQLX	149.8	125.0	147.3	141.0	–	–	–	–	–	–
Ordnance Survey	GPVF	..	..	..	..	..	..	..	15.5	13.9	12.3

18.7 Consolidated Fund and National Loans Fund: assets and liabilities[1]
United Kingdom
continued
At 31 March in each year

£ millions

		1993	1994	1995	1996	1997	1998	1999	2000	2001	2002
Loans to public corporations: (*continued*)											
Central Office of Information	KJEI	1.0	0.8	0.5	0.3	–	–	–	–	–	–
Registers of Scotland	KZBB	..	..	..	..	6.4	5.6	5.1	4.5	4.0	3.7
East of Scotland Water Authority	KZBC	..	..	..	..	163.0	229.0	288.0	283.0	268.0	258.0
North of Scotland Water Authority	KZBD	..	..	..	..	155.0	189.2	242.0	236.5	236.5	236.5
West of Scotland Water Authority	KZBE	..	..	..	..	185.0	304.9	425.6	412.4	412.4	412.4
Loans to local authorities	KQLY	41 464.6	40 979.2	40 440.7	40 969.2	42 134.0	42 951.1	44 742.7	46 099.2	47 239.1	47 093.4
Loans to private sector:											
Shipbuilding Industry Board	KQLZ	–	–	–	–	–	–	–	–	–	–
Shipowners (Ship credit scheme)	KGVR	–	–	–	–	–	–	–	–	–	–
Housing associations	KGVS	14.1	13.8	13.2	12.7	0.5	0.5	0.5	0.5	0.5	–
Building societies	KGVT	–	–	–	–	–	–	–	–	–	–
British Nuclear Fuels Ltd	KGVU	–	–	–	–	–	–	–	–	–	–
British Aerospace plc	KGVV	–	–	–	–	–	–	–	–	–	–
Loans within central government:											
Northern Ireland Exchequer	KGVW	1 558.3	1 626.2	1 666.3	1 627.4	1 602.5	1 681.1	1 611.2	1 602.0	1 533.1	1 473.9
Married quarters for Armed Forces	KGVX	66.1	65.2	64.3	63.4	62.4	61.3	60.2	59.0	57.7	56.4
Redundancy Fund	KGVY	–	–	–	–	–	–	–	–	–	–
Other assets:											
Exchange Equalisation Account - capital	KGVZ	7 200.0	6 800.0	5 550.0	2 800.0	650.0	..	..	475.0	5 680.0	831.0
Subscriptions and contributions to international financial organisations:											
International Monetary Fund	KGXE	6 893.0	7 066.4	7 172.2	7 102.6	6 241.2	5 895.6	9 048.1	9 067.4	9 496.6	9 494.5
Gilt-Edged Official Operations Account -advances outstanding	KPUF	–	2 500.0	2 500.0	2 500.0	3 000.0	2 500.0	2 500.0	–	–	–
-surplus not paid to the National Loans Fund	KPUH	–	2.0	–	–	–	141.6	190.8	–	–	–
Borrowing included in national debt but not brought to account by 31 March	KGXF	3 742.5	1 682.4	385.2	513.4	404.7	568.6	317.9	281.6	405.9	417.5
Debt Management Account -advances outstanding	GPVG	..	..	..	..	..	..	..	15 000.0	35 000.0	35 000.0
National Debt Commissioners' liability in respect of the National Savings Bank's Investment Fund	KCYG	–	–	–	–	–	–	–	–	–	–
Other	KCYH	–	–	–	–	–	–	–	–	–	–
Consolidated Fund liability	KCYI	182 102.2	240 351.0	286 055.9	331 164.9	362 506.2	362 596.4	361 065.3	351 626.3	324 335.5	338 550.2
Total liabilities											
National Loans Fund - national debt outstanding	KCYJ	248 643.5	306 872.6	349 159.5	390 681.8	419 548.9	418 444.7	421 635.7	426 239.2	425 955.6	434 544.6

Source: HM Treasury: 020 7270 4761

1 See chapter text.
2 Formerly The Buying Agency.

18.8 British government and government guaranteed marketable securities[1]
Nominal values of official and market holdings by maturity[2,3]
At 31 March in each year

£ millions

		1993	1994	1995	1996	1997	1998	1999	2000	2001	2002	2003
Total holdings	KQMO	162 642	209 507	232 486	262 262	290 259	297 366	291 788	290 629	285 915	278 808	292 787
Up to 5 years	KQMP	46 019	58 437	69 011	81 122	90 357	86 094	95 112	95 131	92 090	92 780	106 084
Over 5 and up to 15 years	KQMQ	72 612	94 308	101 960	111 510	125 401	131 758	124 603	116 910	120 101	106 044	101 466
Over 15 years (including undated)	KQMR	44 010	56 762	61 515	69 630	74 501	79 515	72 074	78 587	73 724	79 984	85 237
Official holdings:[3]												
Total	HHAW	4 138	6 239	6 614	7 186	6 858	6 345	6 394	6 204	8 210	7 558	10 651
Up to 5 years	HHAY	1 434	1 685	2 007	2 345	2 850	2 499	2 600	2 849	4 652	3 928	4 797
Over 5 and up to 15 years	HHAZ	1 826	3 194	3 700	3 774	3 041	2 726	2 989	2 567	3 009	2 844	4 115
Over 15 years (including undated)	HHBA	879	1 359	907	1 068	967	1 120	805	788	549	786	1 738
Market holdings:												
Total	HHBB	158 503	203 268	225 872	255 075	283 402	291 021	285 394	284 425	277 705	271 250	282 136
Up to 5 years	HHBD	44 585	56 751	67 004	78 777	87 508	83 595	92 512	92 282	87 438	88 852	101 286
Over 5 and up to 15 years	HHBE	70 786	91 115	98 260	107 736	122 360	129 032	121 614	114 343	117 092	103 200	97 350
Over 15 years (including undated)	HHBF	43 131	55 403	60 608	68 562	73 536	78 395	71 269	77 800	73 175	79 198	83 500

1 The government guaranteed securities of nationalised industries only. A relatively small amount of other government guaranteed securities is excluded.
2 Securities with optional redemption dates are classified according to the final redemption date. The nominal value of index-linked British Government Stock has been raised by the amount of accrued capital uplift.

3 Official holdings were changed following the introduction of the central bank sector in the UK national accounts. These holdings now principally include those of the Debt Management Office and other government departments. The Issue and Banking Departments of the Bank of England are classified within the central bank sector and are therefore part of market holdings.

Source: Bank of England: 020 7601 3598

18.9 Income tax: allowances and reliefs[1]
United Kingdom

£

		1993 /94	1994 /95	1995 /96	1996 /97	1997 /98	1998 /99	1999 /00	2000 /01	2001 /02	2002 /03	2003 /04
Personal allowances												
Personal allowance	KDZP	3 445	3 445	3 525	3 765	4 045	4 195	4 335	4 385	4 535	4 615	4 615
Married couples allowance	KDZR	1 720	1 720	1 720	1 790	1 830	1 900	1 970	..	..	..	..
Age allowance:												
Personal (aged 65-74)	KSOH	4 200	4 200	4 630	4 910	5 220	5 410	5 720	5 790	5 990	6 100	6 610
Personal (aged 75 or over)	KSOI	4 370	4 370	4 800	5 090	5 400	5 600	5 980	6 050	6 260	6 370	6 720
Married couple's (either partner between 65-74 but neither partner 75 or over)[2]	KEDI	2 465	2 665	2 995	3 115	3 185	3 305	5 125	5 185	5 365	5 465	5 565
Married couples (either partner 75 or over)	KEIY	2 505	2 705	3 035	3 155	3 225	3 345	5 195	5 255	5 435	5 535	5 635
Income limit	KEOO	14 200	14 200	14 600	15 200	15 600	16 200	16 800	17 000	17 600	17 900	18 300
Marginal fraction		1/2	1/2	1/2	1/2	1/2	1/2	1/2	1/2	1/2	1/2	1/2
Additional personal allowance	KEPG	1 720	1 720	1 720	1 790	1 830	1 900	1 970	..	..	..	..
Widow's bereavement allowance	KEPH	1 720	1 720	1 720	1 790	1 830	1 900	1 970	..	..	..	..
Blind person's allowance												
Single or married (one spouse blind)	KSOJ	1 080	1 200	1 200	1 250	1 280	1 330	1 380	1 400	1 450	1 480	1 510
Married (both spouses blind)	KSOK	2 160	2 400	2 400	2 500	2 560	2 660	2 760	2 800	2 900	2 960	3 020
Life Assurance Relief												
Percentage of gross premium	KFDR	*12.5 or Nil*	*12.5 or Nil*	*12.5 or Nil*	*12.5 or Nil*	*12.5 or Nil*	*12.5 or Nil*	*12.5 or Nil*	*12.5 or Nil*	*12.5 or Nil*	*12.5 or Nil*	*12.5 or Nil*

1 See chapter text.
2 At least one of the partners must be aged 65 before April 2000 to be entitled to the MCA. This means that only people born before 6 April 1935 are entitled to MCA

Source: Board of Inland Revenue: 020 7438 4335

18.10 Rates of Income tax
United Kingdom

	1994/95		1995/96		1996/97		1997/98		1998/99	
	Bands of taxable income (£)[1]	Rate of tax - Percentages	Bands of taxable income (£)[1]	Rate of tax - Percentages	Bands of taxable income (£)[1]	Rate of tax - Percentages	Bands of taxable income (£)[1]	Rate of tax - Percentages	Bands of taxable income (£)[1]	Rate of tax - Percentages
Lower rate	1 - 3 000	*20*	1 - 3 200	*20*	1 - 3 900	*20*	1 - 4 100	*20*	1 - 4 300	*20*
Basic rate	3 001 - 23 700	*25[2]*	3 201 - 24 300	*25[2]*	3 901 - 25 500	*24[3]*	4 101 - 26 100	*23[3]*	4 301 - 27 100	*23[3]*
Higher rate	over 23 700	*40*	over 24 300	*40*	over 25 500	*40*	over 26 100	*40*	over 27 100	*40*

	1999/00		2000/01		2001/02		2002/03		2003/04	
	Bands of taxable income (£)[1]	Rate of tax - Percentages	Bands of taxable income (£)[1]	Rate of tax - Percentages	Bands of taxable income (£)[1]	Rate of tax - Percentages	Bands of taxable income (£)[1]	Rate of tax - Percentages	Bands of taxable income (£)[1]	Rate of tax - Percentages
Lower rate	1 - 1 500	*10[4]*	1 - 1 520	*10[4]*	1 - 1 880	*10[4]*	1 - 1 920	*10[4]*	1 - 1 960	*10[4]*
Basic rate	1 501 - 28 000	*23[5]*	1 520 - 28 400	*22[5]*	1 880 - 29 400	*22[5]*	1 920 - 29 900	*22[5]*	1 960 - 30 500	*22[5]*
Higher rate	over 28 000	*40[6]*	over 28 400	*40[6]*	over 29 400	*40[6]*	over 29 900	*40[6]*	over 30 500	*40[6]*

1 Taxable income is defined as gross income for income tax purposes less any allowances and reliefs available at the taxpayer's marginal rate.
2 The basic rate of tax on dividend income is 20%.
3 The basic rate of tax on dividends and savings income is 20%.
4 The starting rate also applies to savings.
5 The basic rate of tax on dividends is 10% and savings income is 20%
6 The higher rate of tax on dividends is 32.5%.

Source: Board of Inland Revenue: 020 7438 4335

18.11 Rateable values[1]
England and Wales
At 1 April in each year

			1993	1994	1995	1996	1997	1998	1999	2000	2001	2002	2003
Number of properties		Thousands											
Total - all classes	KMIH	"	1 737	1 734	1 723	1 726	1 725	1 719	1 720	1 729	1 740	1 745	1 749
Commercial: total	KMIN	"	1 230	1 227	1 223	1 228	1 225	1 223	1 219	1 223	1 230	1 234	1 236
Shops and cafes	KMIO	"	567	565	562	497	491	488	484	478	476	473	469
Offices	KMIP	"	248	251	252	255	255	257	258	261	269	273	279
Other	KMIQ	"	415	411	409	476	479	478	477	484	485	487	488
On-licensed premises: total	KMIR	"	55	55	60	59	59	59	60	61	61	60	60
Entertainment and recreational: total	KMIS	"	93	92	87	87	87	81	80	79	79	80	80
Cinemas	KMIT	"	1	1	1	1	1	1	1	1	1	1	1
Theatres and music-halls	KMIU	"	1	1	1	1	1	1	1	1	1	1	1
Other	KMIV	"	92	91	86	85	86	80	79	76	76	77	77
Public utility: total	KMIW	"	15	15	9	8	8	9	9	8	8	8	8
Educational and cultural: total	KMIX	"	42	41	41	41	41	41	41	41	42	42	42
Miscellaneous: total	KMIY	"	58	58	56	55	55	56	61	67	70	70	72
Industrial: total	KMIZ	"	244	247	248	249	249	250	250	250	251	250	250
Value of assessments		£ million											
Total - all classes	KMHA	"	35 263	34 129	33 912	34 245	34 299	33 909	33 649	42 985	43 626	44 136	44 053
Commercial: total	KMHG	"	21 336	20 662	19 626	19 822	19 859	19 733	19 652	26 320	27 255	27 622	27 713
Shops and cafes	KMHH	"	7 335	7 068	7 780	6 094	5 959	5 860	5 840	6 801	6 972	6 953	6 863
Offices	KMHI	"	8 239	8 027	5 587	5 630	5 641	5 624	5 575	8 625	9 191	9 388	9 555
Other	KMHJ	"	5 762	5 568	6 260	8 098	8 259	8 249	8 237	10 894	11 092	11 281	11 295
On-licensed premises: total	KMHK	"	679	642	968	969	970	980	997	1 311	1 347	1 345	1 334
Entertainment and recreational: total	KMHL	"	1 022	988	1 009	1 018	1 033	1 040	1 045	1 310	1 369	1 430	1 416
Cinemas	KMHM	"	25	24	32	32	36	39	45	79	92	104	106
Theatres and music-halls	KMHN	"	21	19	21	21	21	21	20	24	25	26	26
Other	KMHO	"	975	946	956	965	975	979	980	1 207	1 252	1 300	1 284
Public utility: total	KMHP	"	3 505	3 424	3 455	3 469	3 488	3 380	3 361	3 828	3 411	3 460	3 444
Educational and cultural: total	KMHQ	"	1 883	1 813	1 873	1 883	1 894	1 773	1 672	1 829	1 872	1 902	1 895
Miscellaneous: total	KMHR	"	1 367	1 319	1 429	1 500	1 494	1 464	1 439	2 142	2 172	2 220	2 218
Industrial: total	KMHS	"	5 470	5 280	5 550	5 584	5 561	5 540	5 463	6 249	6 202	6 157	6 034

1 See chapter text.

Source: Board of Inland Revenue: 020 7438 6314

18.12 Local authorities: gross loan debt outstanding[1]
At 31 March in each year

£ millions

		1993	1994	1995	1996	1997	1998	1999	2000	2001	2002	2003
United Kingdom												
Total debt	KQBR	55 943	55 869	..	..	..	..	..	..	..	..	..
Public Works Loan Board	KQBS	41 447	40 803	40 388	40 445	41 683	42 901	44 701	46 044	47 073	46 867	44 589
Northern Ireland Consolidated Fund	KQBT	109	126	138	157	175	220	..	..	..	..	..
Other debt	KQBU	..	..	..	..	..	..	..	..	..	..	..
England and Wales												
Total debt	KQBV	47 357	46 695	..	..	..	..	..	..	..	..	..
of which Public Works Loan Board	KQBW	*34 082*	*33 132*	*32 448*	*32 617*	*33 660*	*34 606*	*36 049*	*37 172*	*38 013*	*37 627*	*36 673*
Scotland												
Total debt[2]	KQBX	8 429	8 999	9 984	10 850	..	..	..	..	..	..	..
of which Public Works Loan Board	KQBY	*7 365*	*7 671*	*7 940*	*7 828*	*8 023*	*8 295*	*8 652*	*8 872*	*9 060*	*9 241*	*7 902*
Northern Ireland												
Total debt	KQBZ	157	175	186	183	211	225	250	..	..	..	..

1 The sums shown exclude inter-authority loans and debt transfers, and temporary loans and overdrafts obtained for the purpose of providing for current expenses. No deduction has been made in respect of sums held in sinking funds for the repayment of debt.

2 Data for 1996 are before transfer of responsibility for Water & Sewerage and the Scottish Childrens Reporters Administration.

Sources: Office of the Deputy Prime Minister: 020 7944 4163;
Public Works Loan Board: 020 7862 6610;
Department of the Environment for Northern Ireland: 028 9054 0707;
Chartered Institute of Public Finance and Accountancy

18.13 Revenue expenditure of local authorities

	2000/01 outturn £m	2001/02 outturn £m	2002/03 budget[1] £m	2003/04 budget £m
England				
Education	23 747	26 121	27 502	30 186
Personal social services	10 750	11 504	12 677	14 083
Police	7 282	7 912	8 257	9 140
Fire	1 524	1 608	1 709	1 852
Highway maintenance	1 783	1 969	2 011	2 341
EPC services	16 180	17 318	18 520	20 648
Comprising:				
Central services	2 081	2 495	2 639	2 973
Court services	363	398	374	391
Cultural	1 737	1 840	2 496	2 680
Environmental	3 238	3 480	3 113	3 457
Non-HRA housing	795	780	852	1 318
Housing benefit	5 335	5 744	5 987	6 399
Planning	959	1 107	1 236	1 428
Parking and public transport	847	1 083	1 162	1 397
Other	824	391	662	604
Net current expenditure	61 265	66 430	70 676	78 250
Capital charges	1 904	1 861	2 058	2 317
CERA[2]	623	672	673	661
Interest receipts	-1 058	-917	-697	-657
Other non-current[3]	2 515	2 348	2 466	2 701
Gross revenue expenditure[4]	65 249	70 395	75 176	83 272
Specific grants outside AEF	-7 920	-8 443	-9 924	-10 799
Revenue expenditure	57 329	61 952	65 252	72 473
Specific and special grants inside AEF	-4 671	-6 552	-7 618	-9 187
Net revenue expenditure	52 658	55 400	57 634	63 286
Other adjustments	-36	-49	-55	-23
Use of reserves	201	-8	-435	-246
Budget requirement	52 823	55 343	57 144	63 016
SSA reduction grant	-18	-2	-	-
Police grant	-3 627	-3 798	-3 808	-4 079
Revenue support grant	-19 437	-21 093	-19 889	-24 215
Central Support Protection Grant	-34	-1	-	-
Council Tax Benefit Subsid Limitation Scheme	54	83	-	-
Non-domestic rates	-15 400	-15 137	-16 626	-15 611
Greater London Authority Grant	-22	-23	-28	-130
Other items	-139	-126	-145	-130
Precepts/demand on collection fund	14 200	15 246	16 648	18 946
Scotland				
Net revenue expenditure on general fund	7 271	7 714	..	..

18.13 Revenue expenditure of local authorities
continued

£ millions

	2000/01 outturn	2001/02 outturn	2002/03 budget	2003/04 budget
Wales[5]				
Education	1 516.7	1 650.9	1 964.5	1 892.8
Personal social services	681.1	746.5	836.4	938.5
Council fund housing, including housing benefit[6]	274.0	287.0	290.9	332.9
Local environmental services[7]	228.6	241.5	255.1	284.5
Roads and transport	176.6	188.4	228.3	247.7
Libraries, culture, heritage, sport and recreation	112.4	137.3	140.6	148.5
Planning, economic development, community development and tourism	62.1	73.3	72.0	92.0
Magistrates', coroners' and other courts	52.9	24.6	26.9	28.9
Council tax benefit and administration[8]	14.9	16.6	16.7	19.3
Local tax collection	15.4	17.0	14.9	16.4
Debt financing costs: counties	239.9	247.3	259.6	260.6
Central administrative and other revenue expenditure: counties[9,10]	125.0	169.9	206.1	245.6
Total county and county borough council expenditure	3 499.8	3 800.3	4 042.0	4 507.7
Police operational expenditure	395.2	419.2	439.9	487.2
Other police expenditure[9,11]	6.2	15.8	13.7	16.3
Total police expenditure	401.3	435.1	453.6	503.5
Fire operational expenditure	97.8	100.6	107.7	112.7
Other fire expenditure[9,11]	1.3	3.2	2.7	3.0
Total fire expenditure	99.1	103.8	110.4	115.7
National park operational expenditure	9.6	11.1	10.8	12.0
Other national park expenditure[9,11]	0.1	0.1	2.1	2.4
Total national park expenditure	9.8	11.2	12.9	14.4
Gross revenue expenditure	4 010.0	4 350.4	4 618.9	5 141.2
Less specific and special government grants (except council tax benefit grant)	-498.8	-601.1	-644.4	-846.8
Net revenue expenditure	3 511.2	3 749.2	3 974.5	4 294.4
Putting to (-)/drawing from (+) reserves	29.0	7.8	-16.9	-33.0
Buget requirement	3 540.2	3 747.0	3 957.6	4 261.4
Plus discretionary non-domestic rate relief	1.9	1.7	1.9	2.2
Less revenue support grant	-2 030.9	-2 146.8	-2 339.9	-2 533.4
Less police grant	-186.0	-194.6	-196.2	-209.2
Less re-distributed non-domestic rates income	-638.0	-697.0	-643.0	-660.0
Less transitional grant	-17.0	-4.0	-4.8	..
Council tax requirement	670.1	716.4	775.6	861.0
of which:				
Paid by council tax benefit grant from the Department for work and pensions	108.2	110.1	113.7	128.8
Paid directly by council tax payers	561.9	606.3	661.9	732.2
Northern Ireland				
Total expenditure[12]				
Capital	..	..	..	..
Other	404.5	..	..	..
Total income	404.5	..	..	..

1 For Scotland figure for 2000/2001 is a provisional outurn figure not a budget figure.

2 Capital Expenditure charged to the Revenue Account

3 Includes:
(i) Gross expenditure on council tax benefit.
(ii) Expenditure on council tax reduction scheme.
(iii) Discretionary (non-domestic) rate relief.
(iv) Flood defence payments to the National Rivers Authority (now Environment Agency).
(v) Payments in respect of grant maintained schools (1998/99 only).
(vi) Bad debt provision.

4 This measure of expenditure is referred to as 'Gross Revenue Expenditure' on local authority returns, but is actually net of expenditure met by sales, fees, charges and interest receipts, and excludes most expenditure on the housing revenue account and on trading services.

5 Service expenditure is shown excluding that financed by sales, fees and charges, but including that financed by specific and special government grants. For definitions of the below please e-mail: LGFS.Transfer@Wales.gsi.gov.uk

6 Includes housing benefit, and private sector housing costs such as provision for the homeless. Excludes council owned housing.

7 Includes cemeteries and crematoria, community safety, environmental health, food safety, open spaces and waste collection / disposal.

8 Expenditure on council tax benefit expenditure funded by the specific grant from the Department for Work and Pensions is excluded. This amount is part of the financing of the council tax requirement, and would be double counted within gross revenue expenditure if it was also recorded within the line for council tax benefit expendture. As such, this line records only that council tax benefit expenditure funded directly by the local authorities.

9 Includes central administrative costs of corporate management, democratic representation and certain costs, such as those relating to back-year or additional pension contributions which should not be allocated to individual services.

10 Includes agricultural services, central services to the public such as birth registration and elections, coastal and flood defence, community councils, consumer protection and licensing. Also includes capital expenditure charged to the revenue account and are net of any interest expected to accrue on balances.

11 Includes debt financing costs, capital expenditure charged to the revenue account and are net of any interest expected to accrue on balances. The figures cannot be reliably split out from the police, fire and national park total expenditure figures.

12 'Capital' and 'Other' figures cannot be added to give 'Total' figure because of double counting of loan charges, which is recorded as both 'Capital' and 'Other' expenditure.

Sources: Office of the Deputy Prime Minister: 020 7944 4158;;
Scottish Executive, Economic Advice & Statistics: 0131 244 7033;
National Assembly for Wales: 029 2082 5355;
Department of the Environment for Northern Ireland: 028 9054 0707

18.14 Funding of revenue expenditure
Years ending 31 March

£ millions

		Community charge system			Council tax system									
		1991[1] /92	1992 /93	1993 /94	1994 /95	1995 /96	1996 /97	1997 /98	1998 /99	1999 /00	2000 /01	2001 /02	2002[2] /03	2003[2] /04
England														
Revenue expenditure[3]														
2003/04 prices £m[4]	KRTM	53 984	55 668	53 660	55 633	55 611	55 952	55 121	56 977	59 468	62 136	65 530	67 007	72 473
Cash £m	KRTN	39 472	42 020	41 506	43 602	44 827	46 532	47 256	50 189	53 651	57 329	61 952	65 252	72 473
Government grants[5]														
Cash £m	KRTO	18 620	20 968	21 685	23 679	23 335	23 003	23 840	25 291	26 421	27 809	31 469	31 343	37 517
Per cent	KRTP	47	50	52	54	52	49	50	50	49	49	51	48	52
Non- domestic rates[6]														
Cash £m	KRTQ	12 408	12 306	11 584	10 692	11 361	12 743	12 034	12 531	13 619	15 407	15 144	16 633	15 618
Per cent	KRTR	32	29	28	25	25	27	25	25	25	27	24	25	22
Community charges and council taxes[7]														
Cash £m	KRTS	8 533	9 521	8 912	9 239	9 777	10 461	11 241	12 332	13 278	14 200	15 246	16 648	18 946
Per cent	KRTT	22	23	21	21	22	22	24	25	25	25	25	26	26
Wales[8]														
Revenue expenditure	ZBXH	2 473	2 644	2 624	2 755	2 932	2 990	3 121	3 246	3 424	3 605	3 860	4 093	4 488
General government grants[1,9]	ZBXI	1 660	1 753	1 807	1 881	1 873	2 001	1 957	2 009	2 093	2 234	2 345	2 541	2 743
Specific government grants[1,10]	ZBXG	64	69	70	73	70	73	75	84	80	94	111	118	193
Share of redistributed non- domestic rates	ZBXJ	525	536	470	464	520	459	584	612	656	638	697	643	660
Community charge/council tax income[11]	ZBXK	231	299	323	354	394	449	483	542	596	670	716	776	861
Other[12]	ZBXL	−7	−12	−46	−17	75	9	22	–	−1	−31	−10	15	31

1 In 1991-92, a grant of £140 per taxpayer was given to local authorities in Wales to reduce community charge bills. Although identified separately from general government grants in 1991-92 it has been included under that heading as it was added into revenue support grant in subsequent years.

2 Budget figures

3 'Revenue expenditure to compare with TSS' ie. expenditure financed from revenue support grants, specific grants within Aggregate External Finance, special grants, non domestic rates, community charges/council taxes and balances. Also include spending met by community charge grant (1991-92), and additional grant for teacher pay (1992-93), SSA reduction grant (1994/95 onwards), police grant (1995/96 onwards), Central Support Reduction Grant (1999/00 onwards) and Greater London Local Authority Grant (2000/01 onwards). This series is not the total of the others. The difference is due to funding by balances and other adjustments.

4 Revenue expenditure at 2003/04 prices have been calculated using the GDP deflator. Major function changes include:
(i) Increased responsibilities as a result of care in the community since 1 April 1993.
(ii) Funding for colleges of further education and sixth form colleges transferred to the Further Education Funding Council (FEFC) on 1 April 1993.

5 Revenue support grants, specific and special grants within AEF, community charge grant (1991/92), teachers' pay award additional grant (1995/96 onward) and Greater London Authority Grant (2000/01 onwards).

6 1990/91 onwards: distributables amount from non-domestic rate pool. 1993/94 onwards: includes City Offset.

7 1990/91 to 1992/93: gross of community charge benefit community charge transitional relief/community charge reduction scheme grant. 1993/94 onwards: gross of council tax benefit. 1993/94 to 1995/96: council tax transitional reduction scheme.

8 Revenue expenditure is gross revenue expenditure excluding that funded by specific grants outside AEF. This excludes expenditure on services, which are mainly administered by the local authorities on behalf of local government, for example mandatory students awards, so that the measure is a better reflection of total local authority expenditure. Revenue expenditure is often referred to as expenditure on a total standard spending basis (total assumed spending for 2003/04).

9 Includes all hypothecated grants, namely revenue support grant, police grant, council tax reduction scheme grant and the adjustment to reverse the transfer out of nursery voucher monies in 1997-98.

10 Comprises specific and supplementary grants within aggregate external finance, excluding police grant.

11 This includes community council precepts, and income covered by community charge/council tax benefit grant, but excludes council tax reduction scheme grant.

12 This includes use of, or contributions to, local authority reserves and other minor adjustments.

Sources: Office of the Deputy Prime Minister: 020 7944 4158;;
National Assembly for Wales: 029 2082 5355

18.15 Local authority capital expenditure and receipts[1]
England
Years ending 31 March

£ millions

		1997	1998	1999	2000	2001	2002
		1996/97 final outturn	1998/99 final outturn	1999/00 final outturn	2000/01 final outturn	2001/02 final outturn[2]	2002/03 provisional outturn[2]
Expenditure[3]							
Education	KRUD	857	995	1 139	1 533	2 064	2 172
Personal Social Services	KRUE	150	140	134	156	158	189
Transport	KRUC	1 114	1 053	1 086	1 410	1 877	2 410
Housing	KRUB	2 346	2 513	2 406	2 779	3 110	3 676
Arts and libraries	GEKZ	130	150	195	194	213	175
Agriculture and fisheries	GELA	55	57	48	45	38	13
Sport and recreation	KRUH	205	235	241	291	314	293
Other[4]	GELB	1 121	1 140	1 299	1 341	1 513	1 720
Fire and civil defence	GELC	50	49	50	46	62	70
Police and probation	GELD	253	263	286	291	359	393
Magistrates courts	GELE	19	33	28	22	33	33
Total	KRUR	6 298	6 630	6 912	8 109	9 741	11 146
Receipts							
Education	KRUT	133	82	102	119	146	203
Personal social services	KRUV	43	52	51	63	71	64
Transport	KRUU	34	64	105	98	138	115
Housing	KRUS	1 438	1 630	2 249	2 441	2 245	3 331
Arts and libraries	GELF	2	6	2	19	19	20
Agriculture and fisheries	GELG	64	51	48	44	42	39
Sport and recreation	KRUX	13	10	8	12	12	22
Other[4]	GELH	544	687	960	600	801	960
Fire and civil defence	GELI	9	3	5	8	7	10
Police and probation	GELJ	70	76	118	104	86	66
Magistrates court	GELK	1	–	2	4	12	6
Total	KRVB	2 349	2 662	3 651	3 512	3 579	4 836

1 'Total capital expenditure' in this table includes acquisition of share or loan capital. Similarly 'Total capital receipts' in this table include the disposal of share or loan capital and disposal of other investments.

2 The figures shown here have been adjusted based on historical differences between provisional and final outturn

3 Expenditure funded by Regeneration (including SRB) resources is included in gross expenditure.

4 'Other' covers other environmental services, consumer protection and employment services.

Source: Office of the Deputy Prime Minister: 020 7944 4076

18.16 Capital expenditure and income

£ millions

	Expenditure			Income				
	Expenditure on land works, etc	Capital assigned to repayment of debt	All expenditure	Loans	Government grants	Miscellaneous	All income	Gross debt at end of year
Financial year	KRVC	KRVD	KRVE	KRVF	KRVG	KRVH	KRVI	KRVJ
1971/72	1 938	170	2 109	1 605	116	421	2 143	14 450
1972/73	2 418	213	2 631	2 030	122	531	2 682	16 105
1973/74	3 286	225	3 511	2 781	143	619	3 544	18 300
1974/75[1]	3 712	127	3 839	3 209	128	498	3 835	18 884
1975/76	3 917	198	4 115	3 285	177	647	4 109	21 930
1976/77	3 783	312	4 095	3 097	249	803	4 149	24 534
1977/78	3 487	352	3 839	2 677	255	981	3 913	26 282
1978/79	3 621	390	4 011	2 627	351	1 139	4 117	27 103
1979/80	4 249	331	4 580	2 992	385	1 367	4 745	30 187
1980/81	4 476	413	4 889	2 900	492	1 864	5 256	32 076
1981/82	4 061	563	4 623	2 527	470	2 177	5 174	34 069
1982/83	5 090	634	5 724	3 358	416	3 100	6 874	36 231
1983/84	5 890	562	6 452	3 538	379	3 294	7 211	38 698
1984/85	6 352	515	6 867	3 381	327	3 283	6 991	40 554
1985/86	5 748	348	6 096	3 008	360	3 239	6 607	40 138
1986/87	5 899	328	6 227	2 814	388	3 878	7 081	43 033
1987/88	6 091	486	6 577	2 953	297	4 286	7 536	44 904
1988/89	7 166	658	7 824	2 985	270	6 122	9 376	47 295
1989/90	9 590	474	10 064	2 919	440	6 110	9 469	48 695

			Income				Capital receipts set aside[2]	Credit ceiling[3]	Provision for credit liabilities[3]
	Gross capital expenditure	Credit approvals used	Government grants	Capital receipts	Other income	Total income			
Financial year									
At 1 April 1990	-	-	-	-	-	-	4 241	42 167	4 241
	KRVK	KRVL	KRVM	KRVN	KRVO	KRVP	KRVQ	KRVR	KRVS
1990/91	6 869	2 786	907	3 165	542	7 400	2 022	41 125	5 677
1991/92	6 572	3 140	1 041	2 251	674	7 106	1 353	41 234	6 502
1992/93	6 567	3 229	1 210	2 110	619	7 168	908	37 051	6 282
1993/94	7 124	2 948	1 279	3 310	651	8 188	356	37 941	6 041
1994/95	6 950	2 722	1 176	2 458	724	7 080	1 409	37 673	6 921
1995/96	6 910	2 264	1 484	1 966	1 278	6 992	1 160	37 103	7 677
1996/97	6 419	2 120	1 388	2 183	1 132	6 823	1 039	37 261	8 172
1997/98	6 298	2 099	1 262	2 349	1 129	6 839	1 186	36 711	7 540
1998/99	6 630	2 334	1 160	2 662	1 413	7 569	1 130	36 782	7 108
1999/00	6 912	2 301	1 161	3 651	1 487	8 600	1 483	36 364	7 201
2000/01	8 109	3 216	1 298	3 512	2 219	10 245	1 642	36 628	7 231
2001/02	9 741	2 551	2 027	3 579	2 994	11 151	1 403	36 688	7 081

1 Reorganisation of local government in April 1974 transferred responsibility for various services to regional health and water authorities.
2 Excluding Social Housing Grant and European Regional Development Fund (ERDF) grants.
3 At end of year.

Source: Office of the Deputy Prime Minister: 020 7944 4076

18.17 Expenditure of local authorities
Scotland
Year ending 31 March

£ thousand

		1992/93	1993/94	1994/95	1995/96	1996/97	1997/98	1998/99	1999/00	2000/01	2001/02
Out of revenue:[1] Total	KQTA	8 560 071	8 713 471	9 111 751	9 690 424	9 196 125	9 566 936	10 033 985	10 439 999	10 924 634	11 553 927
General Fund Services:	KQTB	6 542 916	6 589 420	6 904 228	7 324 381	7 151 759	6 679 396	7 021 038	7 429 626	7 884 168	8 428 217
Education	KQTC	2 757 058	2 537 582	2 563 049	2 654 158	2 629 961	2 512 725	2 649 170	2 855 945	3 037 780	3 283 827
Libraries, museums and galleries	KQTD	117 243	125 791	132 055	149 427	138 483	121 387	124 648	131 696	134 174	138 318
Social work	KQTE	806 613	914 436	1 045 638	1 222 693	1 289 928	1 315 387	1 394 142	1 519 191	1 632 843	1 793 732
Law, order and protective services	KQTF	763 917	804 616	828 480	866 567	816 315	931 795	952 940	1 006 000	1 047 034	1 088 791
Roads[2]	KQTG	633 874	650 555	684 452	676 116	716 570	440 712	546 945	527 018	564 738	506 326
Environmental services	KQTH	305 645	322 534	330 039	351 689	329 674	343 565	349 413	373 050	393 333	414 975
Planning	KQTI	188 753	202 027	211 346	226 073	210 827	163 380	179 078	198 285	194 771	223 414
Leisure and recreation	KQTJ	383 081	396 874	405 083	451 952	426 422	364 853	368 023	375 579	387 115	401 904
Other services	KQTL	456 198	516 842	580 561	591 766	562 462	456 219	430 790	435 155	465 612	572 136
Other general fund expenditure[3]	KQTM	130 534	118 163	123 525	133 940	31 117	29 373	25 889	7 707	26 768	4 794
Housing	KQTN	1 672 566	1 738 427	1 806 022	1 924 930	2 000 684	1 658 935	1 754 686	1 821 380	1 886 189	1 954 444
Trading services:	KQTO	475 123	503 787	525 026	575 053	74 799	75 976	79 644	87 321	80 355	61 899
Water supply	KQTP	218 864	239 291	255 081	274 773	..	..	..	..	..	..
Sewerage	KQTQ	194 576	200 036	209 323	233 525	..	..	..	..	..	..
Passenger transport	KQTR	859	681	685	794	2 849	1 524	121	336	162	343
Ferries	KQTS	8 336	7 203	7 574	7 744	6 831	7 512	8 930	9 709	10 005	9 650
Harbours, docks and piers	KQTT	27 811	16 215	16 804	15 301	13 482	12 884	15 697	15 923	13 604	10 912
Road bridges	KQTV	9 508	10 948	7 579	11 755	12 759	16 064	16 408	8 231	8 606	6 914
Slaughterhouses	KQTW	1 282	985	976	1 000	794	850	228	4	..	..
Markets	KQTX	8 145	8 462	8 615	10 336	14 278	13 479	13 161	14 106	23 844	16 657
Other trading services	KQTY	5 742	19 966	18 389	19 825	23 806	23 663	25 099	39 012	24 134	17 423
Loan charges:[4] Total	KQTZ	1 343 768	1 346 433	1 383 167	1 451 179	1 121 448	1 126 637	1 152 728	1 109 379	1 100 690	1 114 161
Allocated to :											
General Fund services	KMHV	631 479	649 212	677 377	710 801	639 380	651 982	710 371	701 515	708 822	739 351
Housing	KMHW	528 488	505 407	499 904	504 162	475 507	471 274	438 556	402 936	386 512	369 943
Trading services	KMHX	183 801	191 814	205 886	236 216	6 561	3 381	3 801	4 928	5 356	4 867
On capital works:[5] Total	KQUA	1 344 250	1 428 545	1 518 362	1 528 167	889 572	813 900	815 981	816 473	802 672	929 631
General Fund Services:	KQUB	650 779	699 250	760 564	767 795	540 127	540 096	541 769	557 119	538 843	610 485
Education	KQUC	92 584	85 619	113 121	114 128	101 898	112 753	125 341	136 508	127 781	143 268
Libraries, museums and galleries	KQUD	15 319	11 077	12 822	16 757	11 602	9 974	13 231	10 261	5 834	8 683
Social work	KQUE	32 940	29 040	29 067	30 298	20 658	19 660	22 554	22 097	21 539	31 359
Law, order and protective services	KQUF	28 230	32 951	33 635	35 847	41 326	37 701	37 727	37 132	35 761	39 901
Roads and Transport	KQUG	179 275	189 525	198 178	187 988	116 881	108 227	113 954	108 500	117 485	147 975
Environmental services	KQUH	13 239	18 905	16 595	14 580	10 226	21 193	18 397	14 936	17 944	16 396
Planning	KQUI	69 065	76 477	102 152	103 221	51 182	69 648	50 854	52 045	47 684	33 312
Leisure and recreation	KQUJ	44 774	74 563	65 411	57 243	36 232	29 692	40 926	52 365	44 516	39 240
Administrative buildings and equipment	KQUK	24 980	17 888	23 994	14 693	40 014	45 374	35 107	35 824	34 633	53 189
Other services	KQUL	150 373	163 205	165 589	193 040	110 108	85 814	83 678	87 451	85 666	97 162
Housing	KQUM	460 140	467 811	497 997	517 593	345 713	270 005	268 135	255 019	255 189	300 054
Trading Services:	KQUN	233 331	261 484	259 801	242 779	3 732	3 799	6 077	4 335	8 640	19 092
Water supply	KQUO	109 655	128 081	123 564	107 064	..	..	..	..	..	..
Sewerage	KQUP	113 998	127 047	130 634	131 684	..	..	..	..	..	..
Ferries	KQUR	18	..	376	355	521	770	268	1 030	23	467
Harbours, docks and piers	KQUS	5 020	2 300	1 982	1 218	934	1 175	1 626	1 389	6 192	15 898
Airports	KQUT	2	184	173	763	1 149	439	..	..	607	663
Road bridges	KQUU	694	799	830	805	277	973	2 791	600	964	882
Slaughterhouses	KQUV	87	1 068	139	63	112	69	54	12	..	40
Other trading services	KMHY	3 857	2 005	2 103	827	739	373	1 338	1 304	854	1 142

1 Gross expenditure less inter-authority and inter-account transfers.
2 Including general fund support for transport (LA and NON-LA).
3 General fund contributions to Housing and Trading services (excluding transport), are also included in the expenditure figures for these services. From 1996/97 water and sewerage are excluded from other general fund expenditure.

4 From 1997/98 loan charges are not included within individual service totals.
5 Expenditure out of loans, government grants and other capital receipts.

Source: Scottish Executive, Local Government Finance Statistics: 0131 244 7033

18.18 Income of local authorities: classified according to source
Scotland
Year ending 31 March

£ thousand

		1991 /92	1992 /93	1993 /94	1994 /95	1995 /96	1996 /97	1997 /98	1998 /99	1999 /00	2000 /01	2001 /02
Revenue account												
Rates[1]	KQXA	1 414 346	1 336 395	1 258 863	1 198 575	1 310 721	1 313 531	1 326 129	1 437 646	1 440 522	1 662 691	1 553 926
Community charges	KQXB	802 005	932 994	–	–	–	–	–	–	–	–	–
Council tax	KPUC	–	–	822 830	918 502	976 465	9 681 531	70 405	1 146 366	1 193 693	1 273 316	1 363 399
Government grants												
RSG:	KQXC	2 706 629	3 546 958	3 582 127	3 741 567	3 716 567	3 649 694	3 520 461	3 483 815	3 537 043	3 440 842	3 935 328
Rate rebate grant	KQXG	37 304	33 741	41 772	39 860	4 456	496	–	–	–	–	–
Community charge grant[2]	KIMJ	437 105	15 512	–	–	–	–	–	–	–	–	–
Community charge rebate grants	KQXH	112 904	153 231	–	–	–	–	–	–	–	–	–
Council tax rebate grants	KPUD	–	–	166 015	186 219	193 937	226 132	260 424	274 940	275 789	279 459	285 131
Other grants and subsidies	KQXI	951 871	1 049 899	1 118 978	1 179 327	1 236 160	1 347 706	1 480 890	1 642 045	1 778 216	1 891 839	2 061 297
Sales	KQXJ	45 134	54 399	61 970	59 182	64 284	59 059	46 874	39 595	43 660	49 826	..
Fees and charges[3]	KQXK	1 410 355	1 435 951	1 421 565	1 471 320	1 528 270	1 539 611	1 625 952	1 668 223	1 682 385	1 776 455	1 789 428
Other income[4]	KQXL	161 791	184 581	194 151	209 819	207 005	238 985	290 427	324 932	398 894	453 458	490 574
Capital account												
Sale of fixed assets	KQXM	415 475	413 083	441 600	529 528	500 838	499 143	327 569	335 037	303 582	149 504	165 016
Revenue contributions to capital	KQXP	73 896	111 710	163 228	134 156	197 606	119 641	149 423	204 982	213 564	210 912	147 760
Transfer from special funds	KMHZ	1 218	1 751	7 902	10 679	9 035	2 652	36 929	26 959	125 365	27 317	37 087
Other receipts[5]	KMGV	23 110	42 631	32 554	38 736	29 571	45 067	32 118	45 028	39 014	45 351	90 360

1 Excluding government grants towards rate rebates and domestic element of revenue support grant (RSG). Including domestic water rate receipts.
2 Payment to local authorities in respect of the £140 reduction in community charge awarded.
3 From 2001-02 onwards, fees & charges incorporates sales.
4 From 1996-97 Other Income includes income from Health Boards and Trusts, Other Public Bodies and Interest on Revenue Balances.
5 2001-02 figure includes £41,238K public sector contributions

Source: Scottish Executive, Local Government Finance Statistics: 0131 244 7033

18.19 Income of local authorities from government grants[1]
Scotland
Year ending 31 March

£ thousand

		1991 /92	1992 /93	1993 /94	1994 /95	1995 /96	1996 /97	1997 /98	1998 /99	1999 /00	2000 /01	2001 /02
General fund services	KQYA	368 717	403 437	428 927	450 056	468 660	487 734	557 536	690 569	818 537	935 452	1 032 591
Education	KQYB	17 699	20 439	21 791	17 452	17 186	18 324	61 960	92 368	225 668	324 340	380 726
Libraries, museums and galleries	KQYC	106	154	108	247	123	137	326	627	507	634	1 137
Social work	KQYD	24 817	32 626	36 734	48 091	50 230	57 576	59 892	62 167	71 611	78 611	86 533
Law, order and protective services	KQYE	253 548	274 149	288 835	295 600	312 812	330 767	359 811	366 961	382 246	401 485	423 636
Roads and Transport[2]	KQYF	3 325	3 540	1 993	4 315	4 788	403	237	97 649	68 429	57 702	49 900
Environmental services	KQYG	56	50	84	82	42	119	159	89	71	301	2 272
Planning and Economic Development	KQYH	947	785	1 310	867	3 030	3 337	4 885	2 695	4 311	4 375	20 351
Leisure and recreation	KQYI	1 503	1 396	1 476	1 609	1 830	1 509	1 856	1 509	1 491	2 377	3 322
Central administration[3]	KQYJ	..	..	..	..	..	..	..	..	..	..	..
Other services	KQYK	66 716	70 298	76 596	81 793	78 619	75 562	68 410	66 504	64 203	65 627	64 714
Housing	KQYL	577 321	640 127	684 519	723 604	762 172	856 435	920 700	948 232	959 276	956 239	1 028 529
Trading services including:	KQYM	4 739	5 405	4 954	4 009	4 557	..	..	..		403	148	177
Water supply	KQYN	4 139	4 255	4 823	4 009	4 459	..	..	..	..	..	..
Ferries	KQYO	1	46	47	..	..	..	..	..	..	..	..
Other trading services	KQYP	599	1 104	84	..	98	..	..	..	403	148	177
Grants not allocated to specific services[4]	KMGY	3 293 942	3 749 442	3 789 914	3 781 426	3 721 023	3 650 190	3 520 461	3 483 815	3 537 043	3 440 842	3 935 328
Total	KMGZ	4 244 719	4 798 411	4 908 314	4 959 095	4 956 412	4 994 362	4 998 697	5 122 616	5 315 259	5 332 681	5 996 625

1 Including grants for capital works.
2 The significant increase in 1998/99 is due to the different reporting of a grant in aid of expenditure on rail passenger services in the Strathclyde Passenger Transport area.
3 From 1990/91 Central Administration income is included in the relevant service income.
4 Revenue support grant, community charge grant and community charge rebate grants.

Source: Scottish Executive, Local Government Finance Statistics: 0131 244 7033

18.20 Expenditure of local authorities
Northern Ireland
Years ending 31 March

£ thousand

		Out of revenue and special funds										
		1990 /91	1991 /92	1992 /93	1993 /94	1994 /95	1995 /96	1996 /97	1997 /98	1998 /99	1999 /00	2000 /01
Total	KQVA	193 450	203 650	214 107	230 666	251 737	252 794	294 563	304 305	413 698	388 419	409 930
Libraries, museums and art galleries	KQVB	3 881	4 030	4 644	5 647	7 214	8 481	10 956	13 928	14 571	19 900	23 097
Environmental health services:												
Refuse collection and disposal	KQVC	29 363	32 131	33 582	39 952	42 109	41 284	52 267	56 246	56 360	62 226	65 289
Public baths	KQVD	1 571	1 808	1 505	1 562	1 648	1 703	1 838	2 585	2 634	1 750	1 724
Parks, recreation grounds, etc	KQVE	68 593	74 439	80 601	91 258	101 319	100 418	111 884	115 302	118 396	158 304	170 999
Other sanitary services	KQVF	24 237	26 251	27 593	32 074	34 582	35 706	39 545	39 682	42 923	44 214	45 552
Housing (grants and small dwellings acquisition)[1]	KQVG	1 130	860	792	873	553	472	489	545	358	37	28
Trading services:												
Gas supply	KQVH	3 472	–	–	–	–	–	..	..	..	..	..
Cemeteries	KQVI	4 492	4 908	5 044	5 352	5 984	5 489	5 120	5 626	5 887	5 973	6 151
Other trading services (including markets, fairs and harbours)	KQVJ	7 340	7 778	7 335	7 123	6 587	4 254	8 672	7 016	10 779	9 366	7 209
Miscellaneous	KQVK	49 371	51 445	53 011	46 825	51 741	54 987	63 792	63 375	161 790	86 649	89 881
Total loan charges	KQVL	19 430	20 226	21 693	19 194	20 797	21 122	24 363	34 823	26 413	..	..
Loan charges included in terms of expenditure above:												
Allocated to rate fund services	KQVM	15 155	16 777	18 785	..	..	..	..	..	..	..	..
Allocated to trading services	KQVN	3 904	3 102	2 689	..	..	..	..	..	..	..	..
Not allocated	KQVO	371	347	219	..	..	..	..	..	..	..	..

1 Expenditure met out of loans, government grants for capital works, sales of property and other capital receipts.

Source: Department of the Environment for Northern Ireland: 028 9054 0707

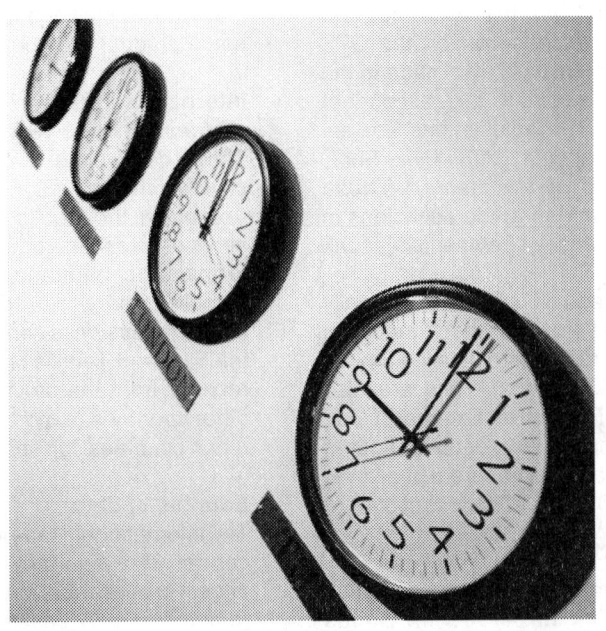

19 External trade and investment

External trade and investment

External trade *(Table 19.1 and 19.3 to 19.6)*
The statistics in Table 19.1 are on a Balance of Payments (BoP) basis; all other statistics in this section are on an Overseas Trade Statistics (OTS) basis, compiled from information provided to HM Customs and Excise by importers and exporters, which values exports 'f.o.b.' (free on board) and imports 'c.i.f.' (including insurance and freight). In addition to deducting these freight costs and insurance premiums from the OTS figures, coverage adjustments are made to convert the OTS data to a BoP basis. Adjustments are also made to the level of all exports and EU imports to take account of estimated under-recording. The adjustments are set out and described in the annual ONS *'Pink Book' (United Kingdom Balance of Payments)*. These adjustments are made to conform to the definitions in the 5th edition of the IMF Balance of Payments Manual.

Aggregate estimates of trade in goods, seasonally adjusted and on a BoP basis are published monthly in the ONS First Release UK Trade. More detailed figures are available from the ONS Databank and are also published in the Monthly Review of External Trade Statistics (Business Monitor MM24). Detailed figures for EU and non-EU trade on an OTS basis are published by The Stationery Office in Overseas Trade Statistics of the United Kingdom.

A fuller description of how trade statistics are compiled can be found in Statistics on Trade in Goods (Government Statistical Service Methodological Series).

Overseas Trade Statistics
HM Customs and Excise provide accurate and up to date information via the website www.uktradeinfo.com They also produce publications 'Overseas Trade Statistics'.

Import penetration and export sales ratios *(Table 19.2)*
The ratios were first introduced in the August 1977 edition of *Economic Trends* in an article 'The Home and Export Performance of United Kingdom Industries'. The article described the conceptual and methodological problems involved in measuring such variables as import penetration.

The industries are grouped according to the 1992 Standard Industrial Classification. The four different ratios are defined as follows:

Ratio 1: percentage ratio of imports to home demand
Ratio 2: percentage ratio of imports to (home demand plus exports)
Ratio 3: percentage ratio of exports to total manufacturers' sales
Ratio 4: percentage ratio of exports to (total manufacturers' sales plus imports)

Home demand is defined as total manufacturers' sales plus imports minus exports. **This is only an approximate estimate as different sources are used for the total manufacturers' sales and the import and export data. Total manufacturers' sales are determined by the ProdCom inquiry and import and export data are provided by Customs & Excise.**

Ratio 1 is commonly used to describe the import penetration of the home market. Allowance is made for the extent of a domestic industry's involvement in export markets by using Ratio 2; this reduces as exports increase.

Similarly Ratio 3 is the measure normally used to relate exports to total sales by UK producers and Ratio 4 makes an allowance for the extent that imports of the same product are coming into the UK.

International trade in services *(Tables 19.7 and 19.8)*
These data relate to overseas trade in services and cover both production and non-production industries (excluding the Public Sector). In terms of types of services traded this equates to trade in royalties, various forms of consultancy, computing and telecommunications services, advertising and market research and other business services. A separate inquiry covers the Film and Television industries. The surveys cover receipts from the provision of services to residents of other countries (exports) and payments to residents of other countries for services rendered (imports).

Sources of data
The International Trade in Services (ITIS) surveys (which consist of a quarterly component addressed to the largest businesses and an annual component for the remainder) are based on a sample of companies derived from the Inter-departmental Business register. The companies are asked to show the amounts for their imports and exports against the geographical area to which they were paid or from which they were received - irrespective of where they were first earned.

The purpose of the ITIS survey is to record international transactions which impact on the UK's Balance of Payments, hence companies are asked to exclude from their earnings trade expenses such as the cost of services purchased abroad. Exports and imports of Services are excluded where they are included within an invoice for the import or export of goods; in this case they will already be counted in the estimate for Trade in Goods. However, earnings from third country trade, i.e. from arranging the sale of goods between two countries other than the UK and where the goods never physically enter the UK (known as merchanting), are included. Earnings from commodity trading are also included. Together these two comprise "Trade Related Services".

"Royalties" are the largest part of the total trade in services collected in the ITIS survey: these cover transactions for items such as printed matter, sound recordings, performing rights, patents, licences, trademarks, designs, copyrights, manufacturing rights, the use of technical "know-how" and technical assistance.

Balance of payments *(Tables 19.9 to 19.12)*
Tables 19.9 to 19.12 are derived from *United Kingdom Balance of Payments 2001 edition* - the ONS Pink Book. The following general notes to the tables provide brief definitions and explanations of the figures and terms used. Further notes are included in the Pink Book.

Summary of Balance of Payments

The Balance of Payments consists of the current account, the capital account, the financial account and the International Investment Position. The **current account** consists of trade in goods and services, income and current transfers. **Income** consists of investment income and compensation of employees. The **capital account** mainly consists of capital transfers and the **financial account** covers financial transactions. The **International Investment Position** covers balance sheet levels of UK external assets and liabilities. Every credit entry in the balance of payments accounts should, in theory, be matched by a corresponding debit entry so that total current, capital and financial account credits should be equal to, and therefore offset by, total debits. In practice there is a discrepancy termed **net errors and omissions**.

The Current Account

Trade in goods

The goods account covers exports and imports of goods. Imports of motor cars from Japan, for example, are recorded as debits in the trade in goods account whereas exports of vehicles manufactured in the UK are recorded as credits. Trade in goods forms a component of the expenditure measure of Gross Domestic Product (GDP).

Trade in services

The services account covers exports and imports of services (e.g, civil aviation). Passenger tickets for travel on UK aircraft sold abroad, for example, are recorded as credits in the services account whereas the purchases of airline tickets from foreign airlines by UK passengers are recorded as debits. Trade in services, along with trade in goods, forms a component of the expenditure measure of Gross Domestic Product (GDP).

Income

The income account consists of compensation of employees and investment income and is dominated by the latter. Compensation of employees covers employment income from cross-border and seasonal workers which is less significant in the UK than in other countries. Investment income covers earnings (e.g, profits, dividends and interest payments and receipts) arising from cross-border investment in financial assets and liabilities. For example, earnings on foreign bonds and shares held by financial institutions based in the UK are recorded as credits in the investment income account, whereas earnings on UK company securities held abroad are recorded as investment income debits. Investment income forms a component of Gross National Income (GNI) but not Gross Domestic Product (GDP).

Current transfers

Current transfers are composed of central government transfers (e.g, taxes and payments to, and receipts from, the European Union) and other transfers (e.g, gifts in cash or kind received by private individuals from abroad or receipts from the EU, where the UK government acts as an agent for the ultimate beneficiary of the transfer). Current transfers do not form a component either of Gross Domestic Product (GDP) or of Gross National Income (GNI). For example payments to the UK farming industry under the EU Agricultural Guarantee Fund are recorded as credits in the current transfers account while payments of EU agricultural levies by the UK farming industry are recorded as debits in the current transfers account.

Capital Account

Capital account transactions involve transfers of ownership of fixed assets, transfers of funds associated with acquisition or disposal of fixed assets and cancellation of liabilities by creditors without any counterparts being received in return. The main components are migrants transfers, EU transfers relating to fixed capital formation (regional development fund and agricultural guidance fund) and debt forgiveness. Funds brought into the UK by new immigrants would, for example, be recorded as credits in the capital account, while funds sent abroad by UK residents emigrating to other countries would be recorded as debits in the capital account. The size of capital account transactions are quite minor compared with the current and financial accounts.

Financial Account

While investment income covers earnings arising from cross-border investments in financial assets and liabilities, the financial account of the balance of payments covers the flows of such investments. Earnings on foreign bonds and shares held by financial institutions based in the UK are, for example, recorded as credits in the investment income account, but the acquisition of such foreign securities by UK based financial institutions are recorded as net debits in the financial account or portfolio investment abroad. Similarly the acquisitions of UK company securities held by foreign residents are recorded in the financial account as net credits or portfolio investment in the UK.

International Investment Position

While the financial account covers the flows of foreign investments and financial assets and liabilities, the International Investment Position records the levels of external assets and liabilities. While the acquisition of foreign securities by UK based financial institutions are recorded in the financial account, as net debits, the total holdings of foreign securities by UK based financial institutions are recorded as levels of UK external assets. Similarly the holdings of UK company securities held by foreign residents are recorded as levels of UK liabilities.

Foreign direct investment
(Tables 19.13 to 19.18)

Direct investment refers to investment that adds to, deducts from or acquires a lasting interest in an enterprise operating in an economy other than that of the investor, the investor's purpose being to have an effective voice in the management of the enterprise. (For the purposes of the statistical inquiry, an effective voice is taken as equivalent to a holding of 10 per cent or more in the foreign enterprise.) Other investments in which the investor does not have an effective voice in the

External trade and investment

management of the enterprise are mainly portfolio investments and these are not covered here. Cross-border investment by public corporations or in property (which is regarded as direct investment in the national accounts) is not covered here, but is shown in the balance of payments. Similarly foreign direct investment earnings data are shown net of tax in Tables 19.15 and 19.18 but are gross of tax in the balance of payments.

Direct investment is a financial concept and is not the same as capital expenditure on fixed assets. It covers only the money invested in a related concern by the parent company and the concern will then decide how to use the money. A related concern may also raise money locally without reference to the parent company.

The investment figures are published on a net basis, that is, they consist of investments net of disinvestments by a company into its foreign subsidiaries, associate companies and branches.

Definitional changes from 1997
The new European System of Accounts (ESA(95)) definitions were introduced from the 1997 estimates. The changes were as follows:

i)   Previously for the measurement of direct investment, an effective voice in the management of an enterprise was taken as the equivalent of a 20 per cent shareholding. This is now 10 per cent.

ii)   The Channel Islands (Jersey, Guernsey etc.) and the Isle of Man have been excluded from the definition of the economic territory of the UK. Prior to 1987 these islands were considered to be part of the United Kingdom.

iii) Interest received or paid was replaced by interest accrued in the figures on earnings from direct investment. There is deemed to be little or no impact arising from this definitional change on the estimates.

New register sources available from 1998 have led to revisions for the figures from that year onwards. These sources gave an improved estimate of the population satisfying the criteria for foreign direct investment.

The definitional changes have been introduced from 1997 and the register changes from 1998. The data prior to these years have not been reworked in Tables 19.13 to 19.18. For clarity, the Offshore Islands are identified separately on the tables. The breaks in the series for the other definitional changes are not quantified but are relatively small. More detailed information on the effect of these changes appears in the business monitor, MA4 – Foreign Direct Investment 2000, which was published in February 2002 and is available on the ONS website.

Sources of data
The figures in Tables 19.13 to 19.18 are based on annual inquiries into foreign direct investment for 2000. These were sample surveys which involved sending around 1050 forms to UK businesses investing abroad and 2250 forms to UK businesses in which foreign parents and associates had invested. The tables also contain some revisions to 1998 and 1999 as a result of new information coming to light in the course of the latest inquiries. Further details from the latest annual inquiries, including analyses by industry and by components of direct investment, are available in business monitor MA4. Initial figures were published on the ONS website in a first release, "Foreign Direct Investment 2000", in December 2001. Data for 2001 will be published in a first release in December 2002, followed by the full business monitor MA4 in February 2003.

Country allocation
The analysis of inward investment is based on the country of ownership of the immediate parent company. Thus, inward investment in a UK company may be attributed to the country of the intervening overseas subsidiary, rather than the country of the ultimate parent. Similarly, the country analysis of outward investment is based on the country of ownership of the immediate subsidiary. As an example, to the extent that overseas investment in the UK is channelled through holding companies in the Netherlands, the underlying flow of investment from this country is overstated and the inflow from originating countries is understated.

Further information
More detailed statistics on foreign direct investment are available on request from Simon Harrington, Office for National Statistics, Financial & Accounting Surveys Division, Room D.245, Government Buildings, Cardiff Road, Newport, South Wales, United Kingdom, NP10 8XG. Telephone: 01633 813314, Fax: 01633 812855, e-mail *simon.harrington@ons.gov.uk*.

19.1 Trade in goods United Kingdom
On a balance of payments basis[1]

		1992	1993	1994	1995	1996	1997	1998	1999	2000	2001	2002
Value(£ millions)												
Exports of goods	BOKG	107 863	122 229	135 143	153 577	167 196	171 923	164 056	166 166	187 936	190 050	186 257
Imports of goods	BOKH	120 913	135 295	146 269	165 600	180 918	184 265	185 869	195 217	220 912	230 670	232 712
Balance on trade in goods	BOKI	−13 050	−13 066	−11 126	−12 023	−13 722	−12 342	−21 813	−29 051	−32 976	−40 620	−46 455
Price index numbers 2000 = 100												
Exports of goods	BQKR	93.8	105.4	107.5	111.3	112.0	106.2	101.0	98.9	100.0	98.3	98.9
Imports of goods	BQKS	91.8	101.0	104.4	111.1	110.9	103.5	97.3	96.8	100.0	99.1	96.4
Terms of trade[2]	BQKT	102.2	104.4	103.0	100.2	101.0	102.6	103.8	102.2	100.0	99.2	102.6
Volume index numbers 2000 = 100												
Exports of goods	BQKU	58.5	60.7	66.7	73.3	78.9	85.4	86.4	89.2	100.0	102.7	100.8
Imports of goods	BQKV	57.1	59.3	61.9	65.7	71.9	79.0	85.7	91.5	100.0	105.4	109.5

1 See chapter text. Statistics of trade in goods on a balance of payments basis are obtained by making certain adjustments in respect of valuation and coverage to the statistics recorded in the *Overseas Trade Statistics*. These adjustments are described in detail in *The Pink Book 2003*.

2 Export price index as a percentage of the import price index.

Source: Office for National Statistics: 020 7533 6064

19.2 Import penetration and export sales ratios for products of manufacturing industry [1,2]
United Kingdom: SIC 92

			1999	2000	2001
Ratio 1 Imports/Home Demand					
Description		*SIC Division*			
Total of divisions below	BAZY		39	54	58
Mining of Metal Ores[3]	BAZZ	13	..	..	..
Other Mining and Quarrying	BBAM	14	132	165	155
Food products and beverages	BBAN	15	22	22	23
Tobacco products	BBAO	16	8	8	15
Textiles	BAZJ	17	..	60	65
Wearing Apparel: Dressing and dyeing of fur	BAZK	18	..	86	91
Tanning and dressing of leather:luggage, handbags, saddlery, harness and footwear	BBAP	19	89	93	92
Wood products of wood and cork (except furniture) articles of straw and plaiting materials	BBAQ	20	37	35	35
Pulp, paper and paper products	BBAR	21	38	39	40
Publishing, printing and reproduction of recorded media	BBAS	22	10	8	10
Chemicals and chemical products	BAZL	24	..	65	74
Rubber and plastic products	BBAT	25	28	30	30
Other non metallic mineral products	BBAU	26	20	21	21
Basic metals	BBAV	27	62	74	76
Fabricated metal products (except machinery and equipment)	BBAW	28	20	47	73
Machinery and equipment not elsewhere classified	BBAX	29	51	60	62
Office machinery and computers	BBAY	30	87	109	122
Electrical machinery not elsewhere classified	BBAZ	31	56	64	65
Radio, television and communication equipment and apparatus	BBBA	32	94	112	148
Medical, precision and optical instruments, watches and clocks	BBBB	33	71	80	84
Motor vehicles, trailers and semi-trailers	BBBC	34	59	65	65
Other transport equipment	BBBD	35	58	74	89
Furniture and manufacturing not elsewhere classified	BBBE	36	51	53	56
Ratio 2 Imports/Home Demand plus Exports					
Description		*SIC Division*			
Total of divisions below	BBBF		30	38	39
Mining of Metal Ores[3]	BBBG	13	..	..	..
Other Mining and Quarrying	BBBH	14	62	65	61
Food products and beverages	BBBI	15	20	19	20
Tobacco products	BBBJ	16	5	5	8
Textiles	BAZN	17	..	45	49
Wearing Apparel: Dressing and dyeing of fur	BAZO	18	..	68	73
Tanning and dressing of leather:luggage, handbags, saddlery, harness and footwear	BBBK	19	69	72	73
Wood products of wood and cork (except furniture) articles of straw and plaiting materials	BBBL	20	35	34	33
Pulp, paper and paper products	BBBM	21	32	33	35
Publishing, printing and reproduction of recorded media	BBBN	22	9	7	9
Chemicals and chemical products	BAZP	24	..	38	40
Rubber and plastic products	BBBO	25	23	24	24
Other non metallic mineral products	BBBP	26	17	18	18
Basic metals[2]	BBBQ	27	43	46	48
Fabricated metal products (except machinery and equipment)	BBBR	28	17	31	42
Machinery and equipment not elsewhere classified	BBBS	29	33	37	38
Office machinery and computers	BBBT	30	56	60	61
Electrical machinery not elsewhere classified	BBBU	31	37	41	40
Radio, television and communication equipment and apparatus	BBBV	32	50	56	56
Medical, precision and optical instruments, watches and clocks	BBBW	33	41	45	46
Motor vehicles, trailers and semi-trailers	BBBX	34	43	44	47
Other transport equipment	BBBY	35	35	40	44
Furniture and manufacturing not elsewhere classified	BBBZ	36	40	42	44

19.2
continued

Import penetration and export sales ratios for products of manufacturing industry [1,2]
United Kingdom: SIC 92

			1999	2000	2001
Ratio 3 Exports/Sales					
Description		*SIC Division*			
Total of divisions below	BBCK			34	49	53
Mining of Metal Ores[3]	BBCL	13	..	..	..
Other Mining and Quarrying	BBCM	14	139	172	156
Food products and beverages	BBCN	15	15	14	14
Tobacco products	BBCO	16	41	44	51
Textiles	BAZR	17	..	45	49
Wearing Apparel:Dressing and dyeing of fur	BAZS	18	..	66	73
Tanning and dressing of leather:luggage, handbags, saddlery, harness and footwear	BBCP	19	73	82	77
Wood products of wood and cork (except furniture) articles of straw and plaiting materials	BBCQ	20	8	6	6
Pulp, paper and paper products	BBCR	21	20	20	20
Publishing, printing and reproduction of recorded media	BBCS	22	14	11	13
Chemicals and chemical products	BAZT	24	..	68	76
Rubber and plastic products	BBCT	25	24	25	24
Other non metallic mineral products	BBCU	26	18	18	18
Basic metals	BBCV	27	54	70	71
Fabricated metal products (except machinery and equipment)	BBCW	28	18	48	74
Machinery and equipment not elsewhere classified	BBCX	29	52	60	62
Office machinery and computers	BBCY	30	82	112	128
Electrical machinery not elsewhere classified	BBDK	31	54	62	63
Radio, television and communication equipment and apparatus	BBDL	32	93	114	142
Medical, precision and optical instruments, watches and clocks	BBDM	33	72	79	83
Motor vehicles, trailers and semi-trailers	BBDN	34	49	56	51
Other transport equipment	BBDO	35	62	77	90
Furniture and manufacturing not elsewhere classified	BBDP	36	36	34	38
Ratio 4 Exports/Sales plus Imports					
Description		*SIC Division*			
Total of divisions below	BBDQ			24	31	32
Mining of Metal Ores[3]	BBDR	13	..	..	..
Other Mining and Quarrying	BBDS	14	53	61	60
Food products and beverages	BBDT	15	12	12	11
Tobacco products	BBDU	16	39	42	47
Textiles	BAZV	17	..	25	25
Wearing Apparel: Dressing and dyeing of fur	BAZW	18	..	21	20
Tanning and dressing of leather: luggage, handbags, saddlery, harness and footwear	BBDV	19	23	23	21
Wood products of wood and cork (except furniture) articles and straw and plaiting materials	BBDW	20	5	4	4
Pulp, paper and paper products	BBDX	21	13	13	13
Publishing, printing and reproduction of recorded media	BBDY	22	13	10	12
Chemicals and chemical products	BAZX	24	..	42	46
Rubber and plastic products	BBDZ	25	19	19	18
Other non-metallic mineral products	BBEA	26	15	15	15
Basic metals	BBEB	27	31	38	37
Fabricated metal products (except machinery and equipment)	BBEC	28	15	33	43
Machinery and equipment not elsewhere classified	BBED	29	35	38	38
Office machinery and computers	BBEE	30	36	44	50
Electrical machinery not elsewhere classified	BBEF	31	34	37	38
Radio, television and communication equipment and apparatus	BBEG	32	46	50	62
Medical, precision and optical instruments, watches and clocks	BBEH	33	43	43	45
Motor vehicles, trailers and semi-trailers	BBEI	34	28	31	27
Other transport equipment	BBEJ	35	40	46	50
Furniture and manufacturing not elsewhere classified	BBEK	36	22	20	21

1 See chapter text.
2 Division 23 (coke, refined petroleum products and nuclear fuel) and SIC 24610 (manufacture of explosives) are excluded from the analysis. SIC 27100 (basic iron and steel and ferro-alloys) is not incorporated in PRODCOM and therefore also does not form part of the analysis.
3 Division 13 (mining of metal ores) has not been published since 1995.

Source: Office for National Statistics: 01633 813065

19.3 United Kingdom exports, by commodity[1]

£ million BOP-consistent basis seasonally adjusted

		1993	1994	1995	1996	1997	1998	1999	2000	2001	2002
0. Food and live animals	BOGG	5 869	6 305	7 079	6 997	6 581	6 286	5 925	5 827	5 499	5 685
Of which:											
01. Meat and meat preparations	BOGS	997	1 229	1 466	1 081	925	746	657	642	428	516
02. Dairy products and eggs	BQMS	658	692	820	732	745	745	689	660	621	628
04 & 08. Cereals and animal feeding stuffs	BQMT	1 600	1 523	1 702	2 008	1 800	1 714	1 568	1 604	1 392	1 448
05. Vegetables and fruit	BQMU	315	398	456	470	455	408	437	403	405	435
1. Beverages and tobacco	BQMZ	3 304	3 734	4 113	4 331	4 522	3 930	4 022	4 081	4 151	4 292
11. Beverages	BQNB	2 656	2 865	2 986	3 138	3 305	2 875	3 004	3 065	3 225	3 312
12. Tobacco	BQOW	648	869	1 127	1 193	1 217	1 055	1 018	1 016	926	980
2. Crude materials	BQOX	2 158	2 397	2 725	2 583	2 489	2 267	2 087	2 447	2 429	2 640
Of which:											
24. Wood, lumber and cork	BQOY	22	45	46	52	52	55	66	72	72	82
25. Pulp and waste paper	BQOZ	22	50	66	57	64	47	54	78	80	106
26. Textile fibres	BQPA	508	571	636	611	568	493	447	496	446	477
28. Metal ores	BQPB	628	663	771	657	642	560	518	759	819	929
3. Fuels	BOPN	9 075	9 492	9 942	11 578	11 016	7 513	9 929	17 057	16 379	16 001
33. Petroleum and petroleum products	ELBL	8 624	9 079	9 384	10 928	10 239	7 018	9 123	15 584	14 809	14 325
32, 34 & 35. Coal, gas and electricity	BOQI	451	413	558	650	777	495	806	1 473	1 570	1 676
4. Animal and vegetable oils and fats	BQPI	118	171	221	207	264	245	197	156	150	211
5. Chemicals	ENDG	17 742	18 806	20 999	22 166	21 901	22 102	23 071	24 992	27 607	28 370
Of which:											
51. Organic chemicals	BQPJ	4 484	4 731	4 923	5 152	4 974	4 914	5 494	5 718	6 108	5 695
52. Inorganic chemicals	BQPK	1 249	1 120	1 236	1 190	1 183	1 153	1 137	1 491	1 643	1 370
53. Colouring materials	CSCE	1 455	1 479	1 618	1 641	1 578	1 542	1 534	1 555	1 528	1 581
54. Medicinal products	BQPL	3 784	4 010	4 926	5 333	5 416	5 850	6 279	7 217	9 100	10 106
55. Toilet preparations	CSCF	1 702	2 012	2 124	2 409	2 569	2 446	2 462	2 597	2 718	2 819
57 & 58. Plastics	BQQA	2 530	2 800	3 276	3 294	3 166	3 194	3 144	3 366	3 422	3 519
6. Manufactures classified chiefly by material	BQQB	17 760	19 574	22 459	23 142	22 675	21 243	20 302	22 673	22 837	21 815
Of which:											
63. Wood and cork manufactures	BQQC	133	170	189	228	250	253	278	255	262	272
64. Paper and paperboard manufactures	BQQD	1 882	2 049	2 350	2 343	2 309	2 197	2 020	2 096	2 088	2 013
65. Textile manufactures	BQQE	2 661	2 950	3 282	3 471	3 421	3 259	3 020	3 051	3 026	2 850
67. Iron and steel	BQQF	3 220	3 660	4 345	4 059	3 637	3 321	2 576	2 848	2 885	2 913
68. Non-ferrous metals	BQQG	1 955	2 233	2 864	2 680	2 774	2 433	2 130	3 171	3 044	2 546
69. Metal manufactures	BQQH	2 319	2 648	3 086	3 346	3 368	3 591	3 553	3 595	3 864	3 647
7. Machinery and transport equipment[2]	BQQI	49 443	55 852	65 353	73 366	79 002	78 011	78 875	87 812	87 801	84 241
71 - 716, 72, 73 & 74. Mechanical machinery	BQQK	15 179	16 272	18 337	20 481	22 329	22 695	21 888	22 140	24 488	22 680
716, 75, 76 & 77. Electrical machinery	BQQL	21 110	24 900	30 652	32 939	34 252	34 464	36 012	42 681	42 230	38 617
78. Road vehicles	BQQM	8 520	9 654	11 644	14 278	14 811	14 550	15 077	15 604	13 929	16 304
79. Other transport equipment	BQQN	4 634	5 026	4 720	5 668	7 610	6 302	5 898	7 387	7 154	6 640
8. Miscellaneous manufactures[2]	BQQO	15 101	17 315	18 859	20 873	21 530	20 563	20 263	21 206	22 158	21 929
Of which:											
84. Clothing	CSCN	2 377	2 717	3 056	3 356	3 259	2 976	2 804	2 722	2 592	2 487
85. Footwear	CSCP	417	479	519	595	605	535	532	514	494	451
87 & 88. Scientific and photographic	BQQQ	4 824	5 357	5 900	6 594	6 974	6 705	6 732	7 333	7 856	7 208
9. Other commodities and transactions	BOQL	1 659	1 497	1 827	1 953	1 943	1 896	1 495	1 685	1 039	1 073
TOTAL UK EXPORTS	BOKG	122 229	135 143	153 577	167 196	171 923	164 056	166 166	187 936	190 050	186 257

1 See chapter text. The numbers on the left hand side of the table refer to the code numbers of the *Standard International Trade Classification*, Revision 3, which was introduced in January 1988.

2 Sections 7 and 8 are shown by broad economic category in table G2 of the *Monthly Review of External Trade Statistics*.

Source: Office for National Statistics: 020 7533 6064

19.4 United Kingdom imports, by commodity[1]

£ million BOP-consistent basis seasonally adjusted

		1993	1994	1995	1996	1997	1998	1999	2000	2001	2002
0. Food and live animals	BQQR	11 219	11 660	12 923	14 030	13 318	13 223	13 336	13 310	14 287	14 856
Of which:											
01. Meat and meat preparations	BQQS	1 913	1 884	2 237	2 540	2 231	2 006	2 144	2 366	2 692	2 792
02. Dairy products and eggs	BQQT	1 007	1 092	1 077	1 194	1 101	1 112	1 167	1 165	1 243	1 285
04 & 08. Cereals and animal feeding stuffs	BQQU	1 768	1 682	1 781	1 915	1 991	1 806	1 719	1 762	1 964	1 982
05. Vegetables and fruit	BQQV	3 033	3 285	3 820	4 173	3 898	4 017	4 040	3 894	4 103	4 369
1. Beverages and tobacco	BQQW	2 081	2 228	2 638	3 392	3 593	4 027	4 451	4 350	4 230	4 468
11. Beverages	EGAT	1 667	1 829	2 065	2 479	2 610	2 881	3 064	2 910	2 860	3 021
12. Tobacco	EMAI	414	399	573	913	983	1 146	1 387	1 440	1 370	1 447
2. Crude materials	ENVB	4 620	5 041	5 893	5 859	5 670	5 076	4 861	5 816	5 934	5 413
Of which:											
24. Wood, lumber and cork	ENVC	1 053	1 300	1 142	1 202	1 239	1 100	1 088	1 193	1 160	1 209
25. Pulp and waste paper	EQAH	505	578	979	656	572	477	510	763	612	490
26. Textile fibres	EQAP	454	576	636	639	590	452	413	412	398	360
28. Metal ores	EHAA	1 053	1 028	1 358	1 474	1 460	1 314	1 308	1 811	2 008	1 455
3. Fuels	BQAT	7 473	6 342	6 161	7 284	6 824	4 892	5 428	10 016	10 502	9 843
33. Petroleum and petroleum products	ENXO	6 012	5 142	5 061	6 118	5 679	3 976	4 675	9 048	9 232	8 838
32, 34 & 35. Coal, gas and electricity	BPBI	1 461	1 200	1 100	1 166	1 145	916	753	968	1 270	1 005
4. Animal and vegetable oils and fats	EHAB	457	498	561	686	603	555	568	491	520	537
5. Chemicals	ENGA	12 980	14 156	17 481	18 095	17 405	17 379	18 619	20 633	22 836	23 881
Of which:											
51. Organic chemicals	EHAC	3 109	3 421	4 670	4 719	4 462	4 508	4 788	5 374	5 548	5 666
52. Inorganic chemicals	EHAE	983	1 063	1 086	1 233	1 107	1 015	1 056	1 046	1 179	1 069
53. Colouring materials	CSCR	870	788	930	1 000	975	1 003	956	1 002	982	949
54. Medicinal products	EHAF	2 021	2 254	2 785	3 061	3 100	3 305	4 124	4 714	6 182	7 216
55. Toilet preparations	CSCS	1 014	1 193	1 364	1 477	1 506	1 617	1 774	2 005	2 267	2 490
57 & 58. Plastics	EHAG	3 311	3 672	4 597	4 338	4 168	3 903	3 819	4 144	4 103	4 051
6. Manufactures classified chiefly by material	EHAH	21 697	23 844	27 760	28 700	28 007	27 695	26 930	29 232	30 225	28 691
Of which:											
63. Wood and cork manufactures	EHAI	872	997	1 037	1 078	1 083	1 089	1 145	1 245	1 347	1 440
64. Paper and paperboard manufactures	EHAJ	3 763	4 180	5 200	4 961	4 550	4 504	4 321	4 407	4 867	4 578
65. Textile manufactures	EHAK	3 974	4 401	4 806	5 075	5 003	4 862	4 380	4 365	4 316	4 148
67. Iron and steel	EHAL	2 574	2 905	3 620	3 604	3 337	3 205	2 473	2 731	3 055	3 037
68. Non-ferrous metals	EHAM	2 848	2 915	3 753	3 720	3 625	3 709	2 942	3 711	3 792	3 220
69. Metal manufactures	EHAN	2 546	2 812	3 239	3 492	3 561	3 721	3 789	4 065	4 337	4 481
7. Machinery and transport equipment[2]	EHAO	53 353	59 993	68 044	76 120	80 518	83 300	90 183	102 420	105 636	106 738
71 - 716, 72, 73 & 74. Mechanical machinery	EHAQ	11 802	13 095	15 148	16 540	17 037	17 156	17 313	17 867	18 767	18 893
716, 75, 76 & 77. Electrical machinery	EHAR	23 559	26 146	31 487	35 299	35 792	36 900	42 423	53 631	51 195	49 503
78. Road vehicles	EHAS	14 463	15 893	17 831	20 238	21 704	22 472	24 000	23 117	26 365	28 394
79. Other transport equipment	EHAT	3 529	4 859	3 578	4 043	5 985	6 772	6 447	7 805	9 309	9 948
8. Miscellaneous manufactures[2]	EHAU	19 989	21 325	22 522	24 987	26 568	27 917	29 042	32 798	35 220	36 833
Of which:											
84. Clothing	CSDR	4 699	4 779	5 178	6 059	6 630	7 023	7 483	8 495	9 160	9 792
85. Footwear	CSDS	1 233	1 427	1 514	1 770	1 912	1 859	2 041	2 001	2 244	2 363
87 & 88. Scientific and photographic	EHAW	4 620	4 837	5 382	6 001	6 067	6 102	6 170	7 273	7 691	7 039
9. Other commodities and transactions	BQAW	1 426	1 182	1 617	1 765	1 759	1 805	1 799	1 846	1 280	1 452
TOTAL UK IMPORTS	BOKH	135 295	146 269	165 600	180 918	184 265	185 869	195 217	220 912	230 670	232 712

1 See chapter text. The numbers on the left hand side of the table refer to the code numbers of the *Standard International Trade Classification*, Revision 3, which was introduced in January 1988.

2 Sections 7 and 8 are shown by broad economic category in table G2 of the *Monthly Review of External Trade Statistics*.

Source: Office for National Statistics: 020 7533 6064

19.5 United Kingdom exports, by area[1]

£ million BOP-consistent basis seasonally adjusted

		1993	1994	1995	1996	1997	1998	1999	2000	2001	2002
European Union:	ENOF	69 402	76 876	89 536	95 758	96 048	95 690	97 860	107 990	109 710	109 611
EMU members:	QAKW	64 884	71 644	83 271	89 124	89 504	89 241	91 771	101 464	103 493	103 020
Germany	ENYO	16 097	17 339	20 242	20 715	20 685	20 590	20 464	22 789	23 647	22 020
Greece	CHNT	929	933	1 038	1 147	1 047	1 045	1 153	1 229	1 112	1 193
France	ENYL	12 215	13 655	15 265	17 093	16 601	16 449	16 907	18 577	19 243	18 720
Italy	CHNO	6 094	6 836	7 883	8 027	8 214	8 608	7 831	8 429	8 400	8 493
Netherlands	CHNP	8 121	9 593	12 346	13 484	13 923	12 983	13 632	15 167	14 596	13 984
Belgium and Luxembourg	CHNQ	7 150	7 367	8 298	8 522	8 451	8 445	9 241	10 322	9 893	10 534
Irish Republic	CHNS	6 369	7 163	7 794	8 661	9 357	9 604	10 783	12 372	13 829	15 385
Portugal	CHNU	1 376	1 259	1 469	1 677	1 752	1 722	1 712	1 660	1 578	1 516
Spain	CHNV	4 494	5 131	6 098	6 725	6 745	7 171	7 526	8 302	8 361	8 473
Finland	CHMZ	1 121	1 316	1 716	1 810	1 570	1 434	1 354	1 471	1 610	1 439
Austria	CHMY	918	1 052	1 122	1 263	1 159	1 190	1 168	1 146	1 224	1 263
Non-EMU members	QAKZ	4 518	5 232	6 265	6 634	6 544	6 449	6 089	6 526	6 217	6 591
Sweden	CHNA	2 900	3 411	4 157	4 420	4 451	4 392	4 035	4 211	3 950	3 867
Denmark	CHNR	1 618	1 821	2 108	2 214	2 093	2 057	2 054	2 315	2 267	2 724
Other Western Europe:	HCJD	5 317	5 772	6 417	7 279	7 851	7 579	6 433	7 431	7 167	6 535
Of which:											
Norway	EPLX	1 505	2 047	2 002	2 039	2 609	2 658	1 999	2 018	1 862	1 691
Switzerland	EPLV	2 282	2 480	2 729	3 166	2 955	2 892	2 768	3 061	3 578	3 074
Turkey	EOBA	1 047	821	1 149	1 545	1 734	1 562	1 198	1 800	1 179	1 286
Iceland	EPLW	148	110	138	152	157	158	159	193	154	131
North America:	HBZQ	17 779	19 722	20 450	22 341	23 817	24 091	27 582	33 714	33 772	32 256
Of which:											
USA	EOBB	15 403	17 081	17 901	19 753	20 853	21 082	24 040	29 276	29 561	28 192
Canada	EOBC	1 848	1 935	1 804	1 963	2 146	2 147	2 532	3 487	3 239	3 106
Mexico	EPJX	336	393	277	316	428	516	577	675	689	704
Other OECD countries:	HCII	6 677	7 843	9 467	11 116	10 900	8 786	9 245	11 039	10 910	10 767
Of which:											
Japan	EOBD	2 673	3 047	3 814	4 296	4 180	3 127	3 300	3 672	3 743	3 588
Australia	EPMA	1 611	1 957	2 140	2 492	2 454	2 188	2 155	2 699	2 344	2 119
South Korea	ERDM	805	987	1 162	1 314	1 222	666	949	1 350	1 284	1 462
Poland	ERDR	732	716	953	1 358	1 354	1 178	1 177	1 304	1 310	1 313
New Zealand	EPMB	335	422	440	474	409	336	324	305	314	310
Czech Republic	FKML	290	383	571	719	709	698	738	934	1 088	1 029
Hungary	QALC	209	263	296	351	435	486	490	616	621	747
Oil exporting countries:	HDII	6 589	5 811	6 296	7 906	9 426	7 289	5 524	6 031	6 472	6 227
Of which:											
Dubai	QALI	681	624	701	746	866	830	790	966	1 011	938
Saudi Arabia	ERDI	1 844	1 534	1 621	2 425	3 656	2 605	1 481	1 557	1 523	1 387
Indonesia[2]	FKMR	333	371	518	809	674	369	385	404	313	324
Kuwait	QATB	313	319	548	565	481	325	293	338	358	308
Nigeria	QATE	641	467	430	426	410	454	447	524	686	711
Rest of the World	HCHW	16 461	19 122	21 413	22 796	23 881	20 621	19 522	21 731	22 019	20 861
Of which:											
Brazil	FKMO	422	539	679	853	1 030	899	739	775	819	880
China	ERDN	755	868	832	741	922	860	1 211	1 468	1 735	1 493
Egypt	QALL	347	378	385	434	501	505	539	498	458	461
Hong Kong	ERDG	2 177	2 356	2 664	2 943	3 215	2 671	2 312	2 673	2 717	2 410
India	ERDJ	1 155	1 340	1 689	1 718	1 576	1 242	1 450	2 058	1 797	1 754
Israel	ERDL	895	1 060	1 113	1 277	1 178	1 079	1 295	1 516	1 376	1 428
Malaysia	ERDK	985	1 346	1 192	1 169	1 206	677	934	907	1 045	876
Pakistan	FKMU	336	362	342	347	271	228	221	207	234	240
Philippines	FKMX	313	364	436	398	601	301	239	273	397	352
Russia	ERDQ	561	728	871	1 018	1 233	929	532	668	903	980
Singapore	ERDH	1 459	1 811	2 072	2 158	2 047	1 598	1 597	1 625	1 613	1 443
South Africa	EPME	1 149	1 452	1 837	1 894	1 646	1 520	1 281	1 413	1 558	1 597
Taiwan	ERDP	681	752	965	945	1 036	867	865	1 015	890	847
Thailand	ERDO	677	769	838	981	863	386	463	582	601	529

1 See chapter text.
2 Includes East Timor.

Source: Office for National Statistics: 020 7533 6064

19.6 United Kingdom imports, by area[1]

£ million BOP-consistent basis seasonally adjusted

		1993	1994	1995	1996	1997	1998	1999	2000	2001	2002
European Union:	ENOS	74 434	82 448	94 059	100 628	100 516	101 983	106 249	113 259	121 385	129 858
EMU members	QAKX	68 735	76 082	87 323	93 395	93 507	95 466	99 258	105 678	113 799	121 977
Germany	ENYS	19 891	21 860	26 234	27 597	25 632	25 095	26 817	28 461	29 882	32 262
Greece	CHOB	315	348	429	401	396	363	399	443	482	586
France	ENYP	13 430	15 037	16 457	16 873	18 020	17 956	18 415	18 642	20 114	20 329
Italy	CHNW	6 660	7 496	8 264	8 900	9 548	9 744	9 385	9 516	9 852	10 642
Netherlands	CHNX	8 973	10 064	11 516	12 596	12 328	13 408	13 772	15 379	15 384	16 043
Belgium and Luxembourg	CHNY	6 678	7 121	8 130	9 026	9 390	9 831	10 156	10 927	12 131	13 099
Irish Republic	CHOA	5 449	5 897	7 045	7 342	7 391	7 802	8 708	10 261	12 135	13 008
Portugal	CHOC	1 235	1 283	1 467	1 686	1 763	1 790	1 822	1 734	1 623	1 751
Spain	CHOD	3 266	3 678	4 356	5 120	5 102	5 738	5 967	6 140	7 347	9 097
Finland	CHNC	1 880	2 271	2 500	2 682	2 544	2 328	2 364	2 765	2 961	2 780
Austria	CHNB	958	1 027	925	1 172	1 393	1 411	1 453	1 410	1 888	2 380
Non-EMU members:	QALA	5 699	6 366	6 736	7 233	7 009	6 517	6 991	7 581	7 586	7 881
Sweden	CHND	3 566	4 196	4 537	4 840	4 693	4 361	4 649	4 950	4 665	4 314
Denmark	CHNZ	2 133	2 170	2 199	2 393	2 316	2 156	2 342	2 631	2 921	3 567
Other Western Europe:	HBTS	9 489	9 374	10 341	11 315	10 755	9 783	10 678	13 164	12 549	12 571
Of which:											
Norway	EPMX	4 027	3 711	4 175	4 751	4 666	3 440	3 546	5 563	5 596	5 175
Switzerland	EPMV	4 590	4 677	4 981	5 183	4 636	4 755	5 341	5 485	4 604	4 576
Turkey	EOBU	515	610	768	892	990	1 103	1 204	1 450	1 692	2 152
Iceland	EPMW	242	233	244	255	229	251	282	365	286	287
North America:	HCRB	17 960	19 379	22 293	25 130	27 277	27 815	28 035	33 460	34 903	29 602
Of which:											
USA	EOBV	15 886	17 233	19 615	22 287	24 329	24 785	24 360	28 416	29 588	24 973
Canada	EOBW	1 805	1 827	2 300	2 409	2 480	2 519	3 026	4 009	3 693	3 537
Mexico	EPJY	160	233	288	326	371	366	395	613	686	502
Other OECD countries:	HDJQ	11 421	12 312	13 762	13 699	14 636	15 019	15 795	18 241	17 402	16 843
Of which:											
Japan	EOBX	8 140	8 584	9 276	8 545	9 031	9 124	9 118	10 214	9 146	8 248
Australia	EPNA	954	1 035	1 068	1 230	1 320	1 363	1 338	1 543	1 791	1 727
South Korea	ERDY	1 029	1 068	1 505	1 935	2 147	2 201	2 784	3 416	2 776	2 789
Poland	ERED	429	533	616	570	597	653	662	905	1 164	1 255
New Zealand	EPNB	474	527	555	602	555	517	565	544	549	533
Czech Republic	FKMM	234	271	312	353	450	555	571	800	1 094	1 240
Hungary	QALD	145	232	358	402	465	535	656	683	706	843
Oil exporting countries:	HCPC	3 600	3 049	2 930	3 266	3 351	3 201	3 228	4 258	3 971	3 759
Of which:											
Dubai	QALJ	123	123	169	208	286	337	433	401	398	497
Saudi Arabia	ERDU	1 208	757	649	654	841	791	783	977	931	671
Indonesia[2]	FKMS	665	728	814	852	862	854	931	1 081	1 128	1 001
Kuwait	QATC	204	223	133	158	168	164	121	314	297	270
Nigeria	QATF	110	117	163	254	100	121	112	89	65	90
Rest of the World	HCIF	18 391	19 704	22 215	26 880	27 730	28 068	31 232	38 530	40 460	40 079
Of which:											
Brazil	FKMP	872	891	936	942	911	883	910	1 114	1 283	1 357
China	ERDZ	1 279	1 592	1 843	2 110	2 379	2 816	3 384	4 826	5 773	6 695
Egypt	QALM	180	245	235	271	256	277	255	411	408	414
Hong Kong	ERDS	2 894	2 988	3 364	3 904	4 146	4 391	4 909	5 917	5 787	5 533
India	ERDV	1 050	1 249	1 363	1 542	1 546	1 382	1 426	1 651	1 824	1 795
Israel	ERDX	530	555	659	796	839	875	996	1 025	947	873
Malaysia	ERDW	1 350	1 166	1 414	2 280	1 931	1 892	1 961	2 288	1 950	1 724
Pakistan	FKMV	312	348	344	375	362	340	318	363	426	469
Philippines	FKMY	266	237	335	858	726	855	983	1 155	1 163	939
Russia	EREC	792	781	916	1 222	1 418	1 406	1 324	1 496	2 061	1 940
Singapore	ERDT	1 558	1 836	2 101	2 465	2 585	2 343	2 348	2 395	2 079	1 948
South Africa	EPNE	964	941	1 058	1 170	1 323	1 351	1 636	2 553	2 861	2 673
Taiwan	EREB	1 561	1 535	1 640	2 001	2 230	2 217	2 626	3 561	2 801	2 375
Thailand	EREA	746	884	987	1 140	1 166	1 264	1 291	1 602	1 617	1 545

1 See chapter text.
2 Includes East Timor.

Source: Office for National Statistics: 020 7533 6064

19.7 Services supplied (exports) and purchased (imports)[1,2]: 2001

£ millions

	Exports	Imports	Net
Business services			
Legal	1 702	381	1321
Accounting	641	228	414
Management consulting	1 050	536	514
Advertising	1 294	666	628
Market research	328	174	154
Research and development	2 910	661	2249
Insurance: premiums	..	146	..
claims	24	-	24
Insurance broking	869	18	851
Financial Services	2 147	403	1 744
Property	16	32	-16
Other business services	3 672	1 447	2 225
Telecommunications services			
Communications	1 256	1 434	-178
Computer	2 525	859	1 666
Information	527	316	211
Technical services			
Architectural	152	35	118
Engineering (consulting, process etc.)	3 239	1 074	2 165
Surveying	65	31	34
Construction	173	107	67
Agriculture	11	2	9
Other technical	1 248	572	677
Miscellaneous services			
Operational leasing	237	212	25
Cultural services			
TV and radio services	153	38	115
Music services (excluding royalties)	19	9	10
Other cultural	247	167	80
Royalties	4 867	3 590	1 277
Trade related services			
Own account earning	484	54	429
Commission	1 493	575	918
Commodity trading	297	378	-82
Management services to affiliated companies	1 482	1 069	413
All other services	1 377	497	880
WORLD TOTAL	34 507	15 712	18 795

1 See chapter text.
2 Due to rounding, the sum of constituent items may not always equal the total shown. Data excludes the following industries: Financial, Film and TV, Travel and Transport, Public Sector (including Education) and Law Society members.

Source: Office for National Statistics

19.8 International trade in services[1,2] by country: 2002

£ millions

	Exports	Imports	Net
European Union			
Austria	141	86	55
Belgium/Luxembourg	1 121	606	515
Denmark	393	123	270
Finland	354	67	287
France	1 617	1 186	431
Germany	2 659	1 401	1 258
Greece	138	57	81
Irish Republic	1 996	610	1 386
Italy	784	550	233
Netherlands	2 095	1 007	1 088
Spain	485	267	219
Sweden	593	256	337
Portugal and EU Institutions	124	56	68
EFTA			
Iceland	21	2	19
Liechtenstein	12	5	7
Norway	394	264	130
Switzerland	1 678	498	1 180
Other European countries			
Czech Republic	65	25	40
Poland	99	34	65
Russia	104	68	36
Channel Islands	205	56	149
Isle of Man	18	7	11
Turkey	92	19	73
Rest of Europe	340	221	119
Europe Unallocated	904	206	698
Africa			
South Africa	256	79	177
Rest of Africa	710	209	501
Africa Unallocated	145	16	129
America			
Brazil	114	72	42
Canada	584	332	252
Mexico	88	86	2
USA	8 841	4 350	4 491
Rest of America	713	358	355
America Unallocated	239	51	187
Asia			
China	163	62	101
Hong Kong	228	120	108
India	151	222	-70
Indonesia	67	20	48
Israel	154	186	-32
Japan	1 269	620	648
Malaysia	133	25	108
Pakistan	48	24	23
Phillippines	60	17	44
Singapore	818	97	721
South Korea	107	41	66
Taiwan	63	23	40
Thailand	54	41	13
Rest of Asia	2 134	567	1 563
Asia Unallocated	298	117	181
Australia and Oceania			
Australia	392	142	250
New Zealand	38	24	14
Rest of Australia and Oceania	38	4	34
Oceania Unallocated	16	7	9
Rest of World Unallocated			
International Orgainisations	147	119	28
WORLD TOTAL	34 507	15 712	18 789
Economic Zones			
OCED	25 449	12 635	12 814
NAFTA	9 003	4 768	4 235
Central and Eastern Europe	363	135	228
OPEC	2 035	490	1 545
ASEAN	1 163	204	959
CIS	272	157	115
NICs1	1 215	281	935
Offshore Financial centres	1 697	555	1 142
ACP	563	270	292

1 See chapter text
2 Due to rounding, the sum of constituent items may not always equal the total shown. Data excludes the following industries: Financial, Film and TV, Travel and Transport, Public Sector (including Education) and Law Society members.

Source: Office for National Statistics

19.9 Summary of balance of payments[1] in 2002
United Kingdom

£ millions

	Credits	Debits
1. Current account		
A. Goods and services	272 727	304 016
1. Goods	186 257	232 712
2. Services	86 470	71 304
2.1. Transportation	12 019	16 739
2.2. Travel	13 995	27 847
2.3. Communications	1 943	2 025
2.4. Construction	176	111
2.5. Insurance	6 922	756
2.6. Financial	13 585	3 086
2.7. Computer and information	2 978	1 110
2.8. Royalties and licence fees	5 776	4 440
2.9. Other business	25 904	12 493
2.10. Personal, cultural and recreational	1 594	800
2.11. Government	1 578	1 897
B. Income	123 075	101 956
1. Compensation of employees	1 121	1 054
2. Investment income	121 954	100 902
2.1 Direct investment	49 881	19 892
2.2 Portfolio investment	31 949	31 420
2.3 Other investment (including earnings on reserve assets)	40 124	49 590
C. Current transfers	11 703	20 498
1. Central government	3 544	9 296
2. Other sectors	8 159	11 202
Total current account	**407 505**	**426 470**
2. Capital and financial accounts		
A. Capital account	2 311	1 266
1. Capital transfers	2 130	968
2. Acquisition/disposal of non-produced, non-financial assets	181	298
B. Financial account	128 620	125 084
1. Direct investment	18 474	27 812
Abroad		27 812
1.1. Equity capital		17 868
1.2. Reinvested earnings		28 561
1.3. Other capital[2]		−18 617
In United Kingdom	18 474	
1.1. Equity capital	11 812	
1.2. Reinvested earnings	8 583	
1.3. Other capital[3]	−1 921	
2. Portfolio investment	50 817	609
Assets		609
2.1. Equity securities		−2 451
2.2. Debt securities		3 060
Liabilities	50 817	
2.1. Equity securities	1 931	
2.2. Debt securities	48 886	
3. Financial derivatives (net)		−1 001
4. Other investment	59 329	98 123
Assets		98 123
4.1 Trade credits		559
4.2 Loans		15 976
4.3 Currency and deposits		81 336
4.4 Other assets		252
Liabilities	59 329	
4.1. Trade credits	−	
4.2. Loans	−30 047	
4.3. Currency and deposits	89 674	
4.4. Other liabilities	−298	
5. Reserve assets		−459
5.1. Monetary gold		−266
5.2. Special drawing rights		26
5.3. Reserve position in the IMF		469
5.4. Foreign exchange		−530
Total capital and financial accounts	**130 931**	**126 350**
Total current, capital and financial accounts	**538 436**	**552 820**
Net errors and omissions	14 384	

1 See chapter text.
2 Other capital transaction on direct investment abroad represents claims on affiliated enterprises less liabilities to affiliated enterprises

3 Other capital transactions on direct investment in the United Kingdom represents liabilities to direct investors less claims on direct investors

Source: Office for National Statistics

19.10 Summary of balance of payments[1]
Balances (credits less debits)
United Kingdom

£ millions

			Current account								
	Trade in goods	Trade in services	**Total goods and services**	Compensation of employees	Investment income	**Total income**	**Current transfers**	**Current balance**	Capital account	Financial account	Net errors & omissions
	LQCT	KTMS	KTMY	KTMP	HMBM	HMBP	KTNF	HBOG	FKMJ	HBNT	HHDH
1948	−152	−64	−216	−20	223	203	96	83	−17	−58	−8
1949	−137	−43	−180	−20	206	186	29	35	−12	−103	80
1950	−54	−4	−58	−21	378	357	39	338	−10	−447	119
1951	−692	32	−660	−21	322	301	29	−330	−15	426	−81
1952	−272	123	−149	−22	231	209	169	229	−15	−229	15
1953	−244	123	−121	−25	207	182	143	204	−13	−177	−14
1954	−210	115	−95	−27	227	200	55	160	−13	−174	27
1955	−315	42	−273	−27	149	122	43	−108	−15	34	89
1956	50	26	76	−30	203	173	2	251	−13	−250	12
1957	−29	121	92	−32	223	191	−5	278	−13	−313	48
1958	34	119	153	−34	261	227	4	384	−10	−411	37
1959	−116	118	2	−37	233	196	–	198	−5	−68	−125
1960	−404	39	−365	−35	201	166	−6	−205	−6	−7	218
1961	−144	51	−93	−35	223	188	−9	86	−12	23	−97
1962	−104	50	−54	−37	301	264	−14	196	−12	−195	11
1963	−123	4	−119	−38	364	326	−37	170	−16	−30	−124
1964	−551	−34	−585	−33	365	332	−74	−327	−17	392	−48
1965	−263	−66	−329	−34	405	371	−75	−33	−18	49	2
1966	−111	44	−67	−39	358	319	−91	161	−19	22	−164
1967	−601	157	−444	−39	354	315	−118	−247	−25	179	93
1968	−708	341	−367	−48	303	255	−119	−231	−26	688	−431
1969	−214	392	178	−47	468	421	−109	490	−23	−794	327
1970	−18	455	437	−56	527	471	−89	819	−22	−818	21
1971	205	590	795	−63	481	418	−90	1 123	−23	−1 330	230
1972	−736	665	−71	−52	407	355	−142	142	−35	477	−584
1973	−2 573	803	−1 770	−68	1 074	1 006	−336	−1 100	−39	1 031	108
1974	−5 241	1 118	−4 123	−92	1 184	1 092	−302	−3 333	−34	3 185	182
1975	−3 245	1 447	−1 798	−102	518	416	−313	−1 695	−36	1 569	162
1976	−3 930	2 532	−1 398	−140	1 100	960	−534	−972	−12	507	477
1977	−2 271	3 306	1 035	−152	−280	−432	−889	−286	11	−3 286	3 561
1978	−1 534	3 777	2 243	−140	138	−2	−1 420	821	−79	−2 655	1 913
1979	−3 326	4 076	750	−130	155	25	−1 777	−1 002	−103	864	241
1980	1 329	3 829	5 158	−82	−1 683	−1 765	−1 653	1 740	−4	−2 157	421
1981	3 238	3 951	7 189	−66	−1 058	−1 124	−1 219	4 846	−79	−5 312	545
1982	1 879	3 198	5 077	−95	−1 273	−1 368	−1 476	2 233	6	−1 233	−1 006
1983	−1 618	4 076	2 458	−89	280	191	−1 391	1 258	75	−3 287	1 954
1984	−5 409	4 491	−918	−94	1 284	1 190	−1 566	−1 294	107	−7 130	8 317
1985	−3 416	6 767	3 351	−120	−877	−997	−2 924	−570	185	−1 657	2 042
1986	−9 617	6 403	−3 214	−156	1 850	1 694	−2 094	−3 614	135	−122	3 601
1987	−11 698	6 813	−4 885	−174	1 091	917	−3 570	−7 538	333	10 764	−3 559
1988	−21 553	4 450	−17 103	−64	817	753	−3 500	−19 850	235	17 201	2 414
1989	−24 724	3 643	−21 081	−138	−654	−792	−4 448	−26 321	270	18 001	8 050
1990	−18 707	4 337	−14 370	−110	−2 869	−2 979	−4 932	−22 281	497	15 083	6 701
1991	−10 223	4 102	−6 121	−63	−3 244	−3 307	−1 231	−10 659	290	5 269	5 100
1992	−13 050	5 482	−7 568	−49	177	128	−5 534	−12 974	421	5 089	7 464
1993	−13 066	6 581	−6 485	35	−226	−191	−5 243	−11 919	309	11 330	280
1994	−11 126	6 379	−4 747	−170	3 518	3 348	−5 369	−6 768	33	2 126	4 609
1995	−12 023	8 481	−3 542	−296	2 397	2 101	−7 574	−9 015	533	5 005	3 477
1996	−13 722	10 272	−3 450	93	1 111	1 204	−4 755	−7 001	1 260	3 959	1 782
1997	−12 342	13 418	1 076	83	3 822	3 905	−5 918	−937	982	−5 136	5 091
1998	−21 813	13 309	−8 504	−10	12 916	12 906	−8 198	−3 796	516	2 219	1 061
1999	−29 051	13 134	−15 917	201	2 221	2 422	−7 383	−20 878	773	20 944	−839
2000	−32 976	13 426	−19 550	150	9 613	9 763	−9 752	−19 539	1 527	24 944	−6 932
2001	−40 620	13 000	−27 620	66	16 122	16 188	−6 606	−18 038	1 411	22 180	−5 553
2002	−46 455	15 166	−31 289	67	21 052	21 119	−8 795	−18 965	1 045	3 536	14 384

1 See chapter text.

Source: Office for National Statistics

19.11 Balance of Payments[1]: current account
United Kingdom

£ millions

		1992	1993	1994	1995	1996	1997	1998	1999	2000	2001	2002
Credits												
Exports of goods and services												
Exports of goods	LQAD	107 863	122 229	135 143	153 577	167 196	171 923	164 056	166 166	187 936	190 050	186 257
Exports of services	KTMQ	36 228	41 411	45 365	49 932	56 773	61 104	66 278	72 628	79 071	81 658	86 470
Total exports of goods and services	KTMW	144 091	163 640	180 508	203 509	223 969	233 027	230 334	238 794	267 007	271 708	272 727
Income												
Compensation of employees	KTMN	551	595	681	887	911	1 007	840	960	1 032	1 087	1 121
Investment income	HMBN	66 153	72 333	73 702	87 132	91 621	95 337	103 667	99 729	134 436	141 438	121 954
Total income	HMBQ	66 704	72 928	74 383	88 019	92 532	96 344	104 507	100 689	135 468	142 525	123 075
Current transfers												
Central government	FJUM	2 180	2 826	2 138	1 730	2 828	2 173	1 943	3 542	2 465	4 991	3 544
Other sectors	FJUN	10 295	9 565	9 454	10 751	17 121	10 823	10 527	9 768	8 305	9 153	8 159
Total current transfers	KTND	12 475	12 391	11 592	12 481	19 949	12 996	12 470	13 310	10 770	14 144	11 703
Total	HBOE	**223 270**	**248 959**	**266 483**	**304 009**	**336 450**	**342 367**	**347 311**	**352 793**	**413 245**	**428 377**	**407 505**
Debits												
Imports of goods and services												
Imports of goods	LQBL	120 913	135 295	146 269	165 600	180 918	184 265	185 869	195 217	220 912	230 670	232 712
Imports of services	KTMR	30 746	34 830	38 986	41 451	46 501	47 686	52 969	59 494	65 645	68 658	71 304
Total imports of goods and services	KTMX	151 659	170 125	185 255	207 051	227 419	231 951	238 838	254 711	286 557	299 328	304 016
Income												
Compensation of employees	KTMO	600	560	851	1 183	818	924	850	759	882	1 021	1 054
Investment income	HMBO	65 976	72 559	70 184	84 735	90 510	91 515	90 751	97 508	124 823	125 316	100 902
Total income	HMBR	66 576	73 119	71 035	85 918	91 328	92 439	91 601	98 267	125 705	126 337	101 956
Current transfers												
Central government	FJUO	3 812	4 343	4 977	5 022	5 297	5 260	6 787	7 482	8 015	7 584	9 296
Other sectors	FJUP	14 197	13 291	11 984	15 033	19 407	13 654	13 881	13 211	12 507	13 166	11 202
Total current transfers	KTNE	18 009	17 634	16 961	20 055	24 704	18 914	20 668	20 693	20 522	20 750	20 498
Total	HBOF	**236 244**	**260 878**	**273 251**	**313 024**	**343 451**	**343 304**	**351 107**	**373 671**	**432 784**	**446 415**	**426 470**
Balances												
Trade in goods and services												
Trade in goods	LQCT	−13 050	−13 066	−11 126	−12 023	−13 722	−12 342	−21 813	−29 051	−32 976	−40 620	−46 455
Trade in services	KTMS	5 482	6 581	6 379	8 481	10 272	13 418	13 309	13 134	13 426	13 000	15 166
Total trade in goods and services	KTMY	−7 568	−6 485	−4 747	−3 542	−3 450	1 076	−8 504	−15 917	−19 550	−27 620	−31 289
Income												
Compensation of employees	KTMP	−49	35	−170	−296	93	83	−10	201	150	66	67
Investment income	HMBM	177	−226	3 518	2 397	1 111	3 822	12 916	2 221	9 613	16 122	21 052
Total income	HMBP	128	−191	3 348	2 101	1 204	3 905	12 906	2 422	9 763	16 188	21 119
Current transfers												
Central government	FJUQ	−1 632	−1 517	−2 839	−3 292	−2 469	−3 087	−4 844	−3 940	−5 550	−2 593	−5 752
Other sectors	FJUR	−3 902	−3 726	−2 530	−4 282	−2 286	−2 831	−3 354	−3 443	−4 202	−4 013	−3 043
Total current transfers	KTNF	−5 534	−5 243	−5 369	−7 574	−4 755	−5 918	−8 198	−7 383	−9 752	−6 606	−8 795
Total (Current balance)	HBOG	**−12 974**	**−11 919**	**−6 768**	**−9 015**	**−7 001**	**−937**	**−3 796**	**−20 878**	**−19 539**	**−18 038**	**−18 965**

1 See chapter text.

Source: Office for National Statistics

19.12 Balance of payments[1]: summary of international investment position, financial account and investment income

United Kingdom   £ billions

		1992	1993	1994	1995	1996	1997	1998	1999	2000	2001	2002
Investment abroad												
International investment position												
Direct investment	HBWD	151.8	172.6	176.1	203.7	201.6	223.3	299.6	428.1	607.4	625.0	644.8
Portfolio investment	HHZZ	327.2	469.8	429.8	499.3	548.2	651.0	703.8	838.3	906.1	942.5	865.3
Other investment	HLXV	639.7	684.4	708.6	808.1	852.6	1 068.2	1 105.5	1 130.4	1 435.0	1 613.1	1 676.5
Reserve assets	LTEB	28.3	29.7	30.7	31.8	27.3	22.8	23.3	22.2	28.8	25.6	25.4
Total	HBQA	**1 146.9**	**1 356.5**	**1 345.2**	**1 542.9**	**1 629.7**	**1 965.3**	**2 132.2**	**2 418.9**	**2 977.3**	**3 206.2**	**3 212.1**
Financial account transactions												
Direct investment	-HJYP	11.3	18.2	22.7	28.7	22.3	38.2	73.3	125.0	155.0	43.2	27.8
Portfolio investment	-HHZC	28.6	89.6	−21.8	39.3	59.6	52.0	32.1	21.3	65.5	86.5	0.6
Other investment	-XBMM	31.7	45.3	27.8	47.5	138.7	168.3	19.0	56.8	269.9	173.8	98.1
Reserve assets	-AIPA	−1.4	0.7	1.0	−0.2	−0.5	−2.4	−0.2	−0.6	7.3	−2.3	−2.3
Total	-HBNR	**68.9**	**153.5**	**27.3**	**113.6**	**219.1**	**255.0**	**127.3**	**199.8**	**492.8**	**292.0**	**125.1**
Investment income												
Direct investment	HJYW	13.8	17.4	21.9	24.8	28.5	29.4	29.8	33.1	44.9	46.6	49.9
Portfolio investment	HLYX	12.6	16.7	16.4	19.7	20.2	23.8	29.3	25.7	33.0	34.9	31.9
Other investment	AIOP	38.4	36.8	33.8	41.0	41.3	40.7	43.4	39.8	55.5	59.0	39.3
Reserve assets	HHCB	1.5	1.5	1.6	1.7	1.6	1.4	1.1	1.2	1.0	1.0	0.8
Total	HMBN	**66.2**	**72.3**	**73.7**	**87.1**	**91.6**	**95.3**	**103.7**	**99.7**	**134.4**	**141.4**	**122.0**
Investment in the UK												
International investment position												
Direct investment	HBWI	130.8	135.9	129.9	146.2	152.6	173.7	213.6	250.3	310.4	380.6	397.5
Portfolio investment	HLXW	247.1	306.9	320.0	406.3	480.0	583.3	692.8	828.9	998.2	954.4	892.6
Other investment	HLYD	756.3	882.3	877.4	1 013.0	1 064.9	1 282.1	1 359.0	1 410.4	1 704.8	1 900.9	1 931.1
Total	HBQB	**1 134.2**	**1 325.1**	**1 327.3**	**1 565.5**	**1 697.5**	**2 039.1**	**2 265.5**	**2 489.5**	**3 013.4**	**3 236.0**	**3 221.3**
Financial account transactions												
Direct investment	HJYU	9.4	10.9	7.1	13.8	17.6	22.8	45.1	55.2	80.6	42.7	18.5
Portfolio investment	HHZF	9.6	28.8	30.7	37.3	43.0	26.7	20.9	114.1	164.5	43.9	50.8
Other investment	XBMN	55.0	125.2	−8.3	67.5	162.5	200.4	63.6	51.5	272.6	227.6	59.3
Total	HBNS	**74.0**	**164.9**	**29.5**	**118.6**	**223.1**	**249.9**	**129.6**	**220.8**	**517.7**	**314.2**	**128.6**
Investment income												
Direct investment	HJYX	5.6	11.1	10.6	13.8	16.6	14.9	8.6	17.0	27.4	22.8	19.9
Portfolio investment	HLZC	13.3	14.2	17.2	20.6	23.7	26.6	29.1	31.2	30.7	34.3	31.4
Other investment	HLZN	47.1	47.2	42.5	50.3	50.1	50.0	53.0	49.3	66.7	68.2	49.6
Total	HMBO	**66.0**	**72.6**	**70.2**	**84.7**	**90.5**	**91.5**	**90.8**	**97.5**	**124.8**	**125.3**	**100.9**
Net investment												
International investment position												
Direct investment	HBWQ	20.9	36.7	46.2	57.5	49.0	49.5	85.9	177.8	297.1	244.4	247.3
Portfolio investment	CGNH	80.1	162.9	109.8	93.0	68.2	67.7	11.0	9.4	−92.2	−11.9	−27.3
Other investment	CGNG	−116.6	−197.9	−168.8	−204.9	−212.3	−213.9	−253.6	−280.0	−269.8	−287.9	−254.6
Reserve assets	LTEB	28.3	29.7	30.7	31.8	27.3	22.8	23.3	22.2	28.8	25.6	25.4
Net investment position	HBQC	**12.8**	**31.4**	**17.9**	**−22.6**	**−67.8**	**−73.8**	**−133.2**	**−70.6**	**−36.1**	**−29.8**	**−9.2**
Financial account transactions												
Direct investment	HJYV	−1.8	−7.2	−15.6	−14.9	−4.7	−15.4	−28.3	−69.8	−74.4	−0.5	−9.3
Portfolio investment	HHZD	−19.1	−60.8	52.5	−2.0	−16.6	−25.3	−11.2	92.8	99.0	−42.6	50.2
Other investment	HHYR	23.3	79.8	−36.1	20.0	23.8	32.0	44.6	−5.3	2.7	53.8	−38.8
Reserve assets	AIPA	1.4	−0.7	−1.0	0.2	0.5	2.4	0.2	0.6	−7.3	2.3	2.3
Net transactions	HBNT	**5.1**	**11.3**	**2.1**	**5.0**	**4.0**	**−5.1**	**2.2**	**20.9**	**24.9**	**22.2**	**3.5**
Investment income												
Direct investment	HJYE	8.2	6.2	11.4	10.9	11.9	14.5	21.3	16.1	17.6	23.8	30.0
Portfolio investment	HLZX	−0.7	2.5	−0.8	−0.9	−3.5	−2.8	0.2	−5.5	2.3	0.6	0.5
Other investment	CGNA	−8.7	−10.4	−8.7	−9.4	−8.8	−9.3	−9.6	−9.5	−11.2	−9.3	−10.3
Reserve assets	HHCB	1.5	1.5	1.6	1.7	1.6	1.4	1.1	1.2	1.0	1.0	0.8
Net earnings	HMBM	**0.2**	**−0.2**	**3.5**	**2.4**	**1.1**	**3.8**	**12.9**	**2.2**	**9.6**	**16.1**	**21.1**

1 See chapter text.

Source: Office for National Statistics

19.13 Net outward foreign direct investment by UK companies[1] analysed by area and main country [2,3]

£ millions

		1991	1992	1993	1994	1995	1996	1997	1998	1999	2000	2001
Europe	GQBX	3 978	4 911	6 171	9 241	9 184	13 321	19 964	23 286	44 140	127 448	15 996
EU	CAUU	3 919	4 613	6 146	8 278	9 457	13 432	17 368	11 777	38 821	124 564	12 202
Austria	CBJD	45	16	13	102	90	102	16	26	−18	240	1 622
Belgium and Luxembourg	CAUV	316	−191	160	132	438	991	1 536	−118	151	147	966
Denmark	CAUW	66	47	237	64	416	−176	47	−105	111	−67	−182
Finland	CBJE	−1	7	10	26	112	28	−5	80	217	−196	62
France	CAUX	486	628	471	423	1 515	2 375	2 380	−46	2 171	6 398	3 079
Germany	CAUY	155	536	1 333	1 261	1 478	1 184	1 078	1 463	1 308	113 762	488
Greece	CAUZ	37	167	44	84	163	106	302	221	−52	624	178
Irish Republic	CAVA	388	895	1 082	100	776	755	450	1 165	..	4 679	2 047
Italy	CAVB	258	222	282	298	406	421	447	554	190	327	547
Netherlands	CAVC	985	1 585	2 436	4 615	2 953	6 577	9 804	7 772	6 781	−4 335	6 598
Portugal	CAVD	61	237	25	169	159	56	112	6	180	105	120
Spain	CAVE	982	217	−31	460	431	735	864	232	617	1 574	−1 561
Sweden	CBJG	141	249	84	546	522	277	335	529	..	1 309	−1 758
EFTA	CAVG	−42	163	−84	645	−594	−12	2 195	8 806	3 251	408	−1 217
of which												
Norway	CBJF	35	156	92	662	−255	96	1 997	782	226	−75	487
Switzerland	CBJH	−74	−1	−177	−16	−338	−110	197	8 015	3 024	483	−1 705
Other European Countries	GQBY	100	135	110	317	322	−97	402	2 703	2 068	2 476	5 013
of which												
Russia[4]	GLAA	−2	..	11	115	39	132	448	−171	231	246	417
UK offshore islands	GLAC	−	−	−	−	−	−	−933	2 476	1 296	1 952	2 215
America	GQBZ	2 628	2 657	8 673	8 464	13 460	3 277	13 953	48 972	73 891	29 558	27 123
of which												
Bermuda	CBKZ	−438	506	586	349	291	142	−43	469	−91	−270	794
Brazil	CBLA	89	121	38	291	473	692	337	323	855	596	180
Canada	CAVK	318	−106	5	−4	244	−159	823	406	849	2 566	3 452
Chile	GQCA	80	−22	101	76	220	89	168	169	−693	295	259
Colombia	GQCB	−264	..	−245	204	123	100	241	346	340	58	56
Mexico	GLAD	39	114	44	42	79	110	760	152	106	195	−190
Panama	GLAE	100	211	−100	94	75	103	..	311	153	19	−14
USA	CAVJ	2 235	1 321	7 975	6 549	11 840	1 837	10 509	46 116	70 006	24 249	19 617
Asia	GQCI	853	959	1 596	2 049	1 657	2 823	2 251	1 718	4 572	−3 568	−12
Near and Middle East Countries	CBKF	489	44	−239	253	154	28	350	1 674	−914	43	1 139
of which												
Gulf Arabian countries[5]	GQCC	476	27	−236	250	116	30	260	1 620	−677	−13	1 066
Other Asian Countries	GQCD	364	915	1 834	1 796	1 503	2 794	1 901	45	5 486	−3 611	−1 151
of which												
Hong Kong	CAVN	−245	−18	456	128	734	730	−359	1 554	312	−3 309	448
India	GLAF	2	−27	139	87	61	110	171	209	148	287	188
Indonesia	GLAG	74	−59	69	92	−28	155	170	97	−31	122	−16
Japan	CAVM	−4	13	−49	245	169	378	383	14	1 929	1 390	−4 225
Malaysia	CBKN	140	272	363	286	28	184	731	619	227	−250	−296
Singapore	CBKQ	232	569	528	590	−48	535	352	−2 473	1 373	−3 387	851
South Korea	GLAH	20	37	44	27	47	32	−26	281	172	−30	−9
Thailand	GLAI	24	51	103	177	245	194	103	88	28	257	179
Australasia and Oceania	GQCE	1 239	1 280	658	959	2 596	1 843	827	208	730	−595	1 852
of which												
Australia	CBJO	1 089	989	655	625	2 258	1 472	737	221	715	−482	1 459
New Zealand	CBJP	66	110	71	264	67	244	255	−111	78	−53	399
Africa	GQCF	606	300	262	327	707	561	623	−25	1 175	1 401	972
of which												
Kenya	GLAJ	22	23	33	9	67	24	73	39	51	137	47
Nigeria	CBJY	227	138	347	−197	−271	−94	234	−145	160	57	74
South Africa	CAVO	151	72	314	170	466	−25	401	−197	386	629	151
Zimbabwe	CBKD	72	59	36	28	16	25	1	36	74	38	38
World Total	CDQD	9 304	10 107	17 358	21 040	27 604	21 823	37 619	74 159	124 508	154 242	45 929
OECD	GQCG	7 673	7 343	14 864	16 880	23 686	17 545	33 212	68 175	115 813	153 389	33 489
Central and Eastern Europe[6]	GQCH	18	37	41	168	194	201	214	465	111	263	1 533

1 See chapter text.
2 Net investment includes unremitted profits.
3 Minus sign indicates net disinvestment overseas.
4 Prior to 1995 Russia covers other former USSR countries, the Baltic States and Albania.

5 Includes Abu Dhabi, Bahrain, Dubai, Iraq, Kuwait, Oman, Other Gulf States, Qatar, Saudi Arabia and Yemen.
6 Includes Albania, Bulgaria, Croatia, Czech Republic, Estonia, Hungary, Latvia, Lithuania, Poland, Romania, Serbia and Montenegro, Slovakia, Bosnia and Herzegovina, Macedonia FYR and Slovenia.

Sources: ONS Foreign Direct Investment Inquiries: 01633 813314;
Bank of England

19.14 UK outward foreign direct international investment[1] position - book value of net assets analysed by area and main country at year end

£ millions

		1991	1992	1993	1994	1995	1996	1997	1998	1999	2000	2001
Europe	GQCJ	37 272	44 213	57 853	66 705	76 434	87 582	99 263	117 181	170 905	384 204	373 427
EU	CDLN	34 312	40 620	53 914	61 674	72 808	83 902	92 072	96 817	149 804	355 725	335 772
Austria	CDLZ	384	371	379	454	734	578	461	506	731	1 054	2 432
Belgium and Luxembourg	CDLO	2 505	3 804	2 687	3 189	3 172	5 326	5 701	5 560	11 062	59 798	70 147
Denmark	CDLP	739	863	1 301	1 538	2 803	2 273	2 123	2 295	3 048	2 143	2 507
Finland	CDMA	80	122	104	117	271	215	217	254	390	597	599
France	CDLQ	7 290	8 043	8 619	10 357	12 913	13 128	11 368	10 217	12 774	21 845	25 356
Germany	CDLR	3 998	3 804	5 974	8 442	9 215	8 943	8 328	10 319	10 892	23 354	15 933
Greece	CDLS	156	288	294	203	500	465	366	508	393	1 001	1 192
Irish Republic	CDLT	2 743	3 333	4 169	4 436	4 587	6 282	6 182	7 792	27 000	33 305	23 550
Italy	CDLU	2 400	2 427	2 287	2 475	2 698	3 196	3 064	3 149	3 035	3 643	4 519
Netherlands	CDLV	8 369	11 980	23 190	25 228	29 906	37 676	48 240	50 175	69 257	182 944	170 095
Portugal	CDLW	1 032	1 171	1 195	932	1 210	1 190	1 023	1 067	1 074	1 069	905
Spain	CDLX	3 796	3 471	2 820	3 157	3 399	3 477	3 748	3 299	3 674	5 907	7 777
Sweden	CDMD	821	942	894	1 146	1 401	1 154	1 250	1 675	6 475	19 064	10 760
EFTA of which	CDLY	2 545	2 968	3 303	4 113	2 522	2 161	1 533	10 547	9 298	10 708	16 652
Norway	CDMC	542	736	803	1 513	1 244	1 171	1 116	470	3 874	4 236	4 317
Switzerland	CDME	2 003	2 232	2 500	2 594	1 279	988	415	10 072	5 421	6 466	12 328
Other European Countries of which	GQCK	415	626	636	918	1 103	1 520	5 658	9 818	11 803	17 771	21 004
Russia[2]	GQAA	10	20	7	26	120	238	401	201	247	283	844
UK offshore islands	GQAB	–	–	–	–	–	–	2 690	6 937	9 057	14 930	14 618
America of which	GQCU	62 939	74 868	77 003	75 390	83 275	67 592	80 324	139 031	208 078	173 409	193 751
Bermuda	CDOA	4 628	5 382	4 869	5 403	5 504	5 295	4 942	4 689	5 075	6 054	6 729
Brazil	CDOB	1 345	1 880	1 963	2 059	2 323	2 421	2 214	1 607	2 374	3 281	2 743
Canada	CDML	6 253	6 766	7 162	4 919	5 395	4 563	5 748	4 952	5 627	10 142	11 843
Chile	GQCT	363	416	481	439	666	670	970	1 101	1 080	1 506	1 793
Colombia	GQCS	594	1 109	839	1 071	1 207	1 274	1 197	559	986	1 691	1 269
Mexico	GQAC	428	504	419	334	350	553	1 327	801	1 036	1 018	1 389
Panama	GQAD	232	630	435	507	467	744	..	..	750	226	211
USA	CDMM	45 367	54 688	57 380	55 174	62 159	49 170	59 083	121 408	186 410	141 355	159 724
Asia	GQCL	9 633	12 230	14 118	16 095	18 038	19 916	19 389	20 957	24 148	24 616	29 342
Near and Middle East Countries of which	CDNH	749	748	698	754	788	676	917	2 675	1 030	1 760	2 707
Gulf Arabian countries[3]	GQCM	657	592	617	660	704	586	658	2 374	626	704	1 864
Other Asian Countries of which	GQCR	8 884	11 482	13 419	15 341	17 250	19 239	18 472	18 283	23 118	22 856	26 635
Hong Kong	CDNN	1 895	2 753	3 569	3 373	4 033	4 636	4 406	5 330	5 533	4 745	6 454
India	GQAE	302	245	490	601	498	532	703	705	869	1 204	1 266
Indonesia	GQAF	316	222	272	295	418	391	801	641	421	611	1 593
Japan	CDMP	1 674	1 998	1 936	2 613	2 397	2 437	1 605	1 855	3 628	4 613	1 781
Malaysia	CDNQ	845	1 285	1 750	2 119	1 813	2 164	2 411	1 908	2 088	2 423	2 488
Singapore	CDNT	2 691	3 516	3 706	4 445	5 287	5 822	5 186	5 632	6 072	3 286	5 301
South Korea	GQAG	69	114	155	183	250	238	154	219	603	443	391
Thailand	GQAH	253	359	404	511	920	1 053	1 009	630	375	682	907
Australasia and Oceania of which	GQCN	10 210	11 222	12 287	13 517	13 985	14 636	13 312	12 179	11 652	10 080	13 806
Australia	CDMO	9 057	9 605	10 299	11 153	11 365	12 213	10 598	9 071	9 475	8 101	11 850
New Zealand	CDMQ	700	930	1 443	1 689	1 670	1 640	1 663	1 625	1 855	1 701	1 434
Africa of which	GQCQ	4 039	4 080	4 570	5 409	4 955	4 876	5 873	4 232	9 876	9 383	9 614
Kenya	GQAI	233	249	165	673	276	237	361	415	389	373	332
Nigeria	CDNA	419	490	754	681	335	321	1 060	463	508	906	999
South Africa	CDMR	2 239	2 311	2 622	2 202	2 827	2 429	2 527	1 698	6 620	3 747	4 854
Zimbabwe	CDNF	324	411	248	331	262	200	192	114	171	130	151
World Total	CDOO	124 093	146 613	165 831	177 116	196 687	194 601	218 162	293 581	424 660	601 692	619 940
OECD	GQCO	100 517	118 430	136 247	142 332	159 476	157 652	175 434	249 340	368 986	536 232	545 819
Central & Eastern Europe[4]	GQCP	36	123	106	460	427	622	1 782	2 178	1 313	2 032	4 303

1 See chapter text.
2 Prior to 1995 Russia covers other former USSR countries, the Baltic States and Albania.
3 Includes Abu Dhabi, Bahrain, Dubai, Iraq, Kuwait, Oman, Other Gulf States, Qatar, Saudi Arabia and Yemen.

4 Includes Albania, Bulgaria, Croatia, Czech Republic, Estonia, Hungary, Latvia, Lithuania, Poland, Romania, Serbia and Montenegro, Slovakia, Bosnia and Herzegovina, Macedonia FYR and Slovenia.

Sources: ONS Foreign Direct Investment Inquiries: 01633 813314;
Bank of England

19.15 Net earnings from foreign direct investment overseas[1] by UK companies analysed by area and main country [2,3]

£ millions

		1991	1992	1993	1994	1995	1996	1997	1998	1999	2000	2001
Europe	GQCV	4 182	3 315	5 182	7 033	8 289	9 700	10 440	11 349	14 355	21 760	24 890
EU	CAWG	3 721	2 499	4 450	6 138	7 251	8 557	8 994	9 822	11 244	17 399	21 633
Austria	CBLQ	43	54	35	52	73	82	65	49	45	77	64
Belgium and Luxembourg	CAWH	259	404	412	387	308	358	297	632	401	2 151	2 623
Denmark	CAWI	71	115	207	115	286	208	191	215	220	248	231
Finland	CBLR	–	24	22	30	43	–	36	58	95	95	72
France	CAWJ	598	279	50	607	619	999	1 036	994	1 222	1 693	1 556
Germany	CAWK	617	260	381	834	1 032	951	844	828	1 241	946	766
Greece	CAWL	12	50	58	−202	−106	172	122	77	162	72	110
Irish Republic	CAWM	414	393	669	516	639	847	1 112	1 245	1 367	1 638	2 208
Italy	CAWN	175	75	113	219	272	327	268	327	403	539	592
Netherlands	CAWO	1 141	758	2 459	2 986	3 248	3 748	4 143	4 481	5 246	8 348	11 577
Portugal	CAWP	93	83	53	162	188	184	96	162	152	174	182
Spain	CAWQ	197	−5	39	234	338	493	561	464	389	749	704
Sweden	CBLT	103	12	−48	200	310	188	224	288	300	668	948
EFTA of which	CAWS	433	740	639	792	899	963	991	848	1 618	2 393	1 013
Norway	CBLS	214	281	119	267	224	311	242	134	248	409	449
Switzerland	CBLU	219	459	520	524	675	652	747	705	1 369	1 983	563
Other European Countries of which	GQCW	28	75	95	103	139	180	454	680	1 494	1 968	2 244
Russia[4]	GQAJ	..	..	2	3	12	24	−30	−214	–	62	256
UK offshore islands	GQAK	–	–	–	–	–	–	225	685	1 081	1 172	909
America of which	GQCX	4 624	5 530	6 126	8 007	10 254	10 698	11 867	11 976	12 841	14 886	12 892
Bermuda	CBNK	449	562	428	446	509	506	70	440	466	344	−90
Brazil	CBNL	87	182	193	348	432	650	380	322	113	256	184
Canada	CAWW	189	175	283	357	374	571	913	844	868	1 140	898
Chile	GQCY	88	118	139	195	263	265	236	147	143	236	143
Colombia	GQCZ	21	−40	16	−22	28	23	53	2	78	293	190
Mexico	GQAL	−2	41	43	48	52	74	145	95	186	105	−85
Panama	GQAM	17	−27	69	51	45	67	..	180	..	46	48
USA	CAWV	3 255	4 065	4 621	5 894	7 803	8 034	9 339	9 672	9 681	11 142	10 283
Asia	GQDA	2 355	2 636	2 792	3 449	2 501	3 776	3 249	4 137	2 768	4 434	4 583
Near and Middle East Countries of which	CBMS	303	342	283	297	262	241	475	921	485	908	781
Gulf Arabian countries[5]	GQDB	300	317	273	293	260	212	424	878	443	721	608
Other Asian Countries of which	GQDC	2 053	2 293	2 509	3 152	2 239	3 536	2 774	3 215	2 283	3 527	3 802
Hong Kong	CAYB	440	846	972	1 427	1 362	1 463	623	959	881	708	329
India	GQAN	77	−2	−190	121	100	81	124	194	188	311	353
Indonesia	GQAO	71	18	60	48	71	87	143	114	54	81	155
Japan	CAWY	115	182	142	199	212	281	313	167	545	505	386
Malaysia	CBNA	197	229	248	221	248	332	360	247	352	400	296
Singapore	CBND	1 010	839	977	781	−144	883	795	1 291	28	902	1 269
South Korea	GQAP	10	5	8	29	40	34	17	34	13	37	96
Thailand	GQAQ	17	28	78	84	75	101	95	16	130	90	181
Australasia and Oceania of which	GQDD	541	960	1 233	2 131	2 044	2 269	1 950	1 532	1 434	1 591	1 680
Australia	CBMB	535	809	991	1 776	1 587	1 747	1 503	1 092	1 139	1 393	1 403
New Zealand	CBMC	5	73	213	302	322	319	278	147	263	171	276
Africa of which	GQDE	986	844	1 465	737	807	1 055	965	658	1 097	1 567	1 877
Kenya	GQAR	36	41	34	41	46	35	94	78	67	71	76
Nigeria	CBML	273	280	498	−27	−35	61	46	49	65	88	92
South Africa	CAWZ	425	280	488	366	438	503	521	399	656	734	1 021
Zimbabwe	CBMQ	81	77	54	58	58	50	58	53	73	60	60
World Total	GLAB	12 688	13 285	16 796	21 355	23 894	27 498	28 470	29 652	32 496	44 237	45 922
OECD	GQDF	8 279	8 624	11 454	15 578	18 567	20 621	22 601	22 810	25 812	34 824	36 600
Central & Eastern Europe[6]	GQDG	1	7	11	−24	16	15	118	75	252	465	783

1 See chapter text.
2 A minus sign indicates net losses.
3 Net earnings equal profits of overseas branches plus UK companies' receipts of interest and their share of profits of overseas subsidiaries and associates. Earnings are after deducting provisions for depreciation and overseas tax on profits, dividends and interest.
4 Prior to 1995 Russia covers other former USSR countries, the Baltic States and Albania.

5 Includes Abu Dhabi, Bahrain, Dubai, Iraq, Kuwait, Oman, Other Gulf States, Qatar, Saudi Arabia and Yemen.
6 Includes Includes Albania, Bulgaria, Croatia, Czech Republic, Estonia, Hungary, Latvia, Lithuania, Poland, Romania, Serbia and Montenegro, Slovaki Slovakia, Bosnia and Herzegovina, Macedonia FYR and Slovenia.

Sources: ONS Foreign Direct Investment Inquiries: 01633 813314; Bank of England

19.16 Net inward Foreign direct investment[1] in the UK analysed by area and main country [2,3]

£ millions

		1991	1992	1993	1994	1995	1996	1997	1998	1999	2000	2001
Europe	GQDH	4 910	4 044	2 202	3 065	4 626	6 931	8 394	22 892	39 398	53 839	30 164
EU	CAYO	4 578	3 433	1 589	3 367	3 555	4 673	6 905	12 654	39 676	52 394	30 770
Austria	CBOB	11	−45	13	60	21	20	18	154	−13	175	−148
Belgium and Luxembourg	CAYP	201	65	−427	357	520	6	174	1 068	551	825	179
Denmark	CAYQ	122	91	97	76	68	151	228	227	398	481	173
Finland	CBOC	8	54	−42	32	−36	2	193	129	228	87	57
France	CAYR	1 333	802	−37	310	1 004	1 321	2 647	778	3 217	31 722	10 031
Germany	CAYS	396	1 261	656	71	2 090	835	1 123	484	26 278	10 564	1 613
Greece	CAYT	..	..	..	..	..	..	..	1	3	..	4
Irish Republic	CAYU	137	−32	49	224	−35	221	1 127	724	78	384	723
Italy	CAYV	45	−37	80	177	328	−184	−32	99	23	469	2 873
Netherlands	CAYW	2 335	1 135	1 244	1 915	−633	2 610	1 180	9 019	7 860	4 629	14 780
Portugal	CAYX	..	..	..	21	..	..	..	5	11	−6	7
Spain	CAYY	−11	3	14	21	17	66	71	99	119	..	236
Sweden	CBOE	5	129	−56	119	184	−379	147	−132	924	657	246
EFTA of which	CAZB	327	674	550	−176	1 036	2 211	1 512	9 859	−660	740	−1 255
Norway	CBOD	−71	−34	49	−131	124	1 060	182	−116	−502	−392	−224
Switzerland	CBOF	399	710	501	−44	912	1 151	1 320	9 967	−165	1 119	−1 090
Other European Countries of which	GQDI	5	−62	64	−125	36	47	−21	379	382	704	650
Russia[4]	GQAS	−11	..	49	−	19	61	19	..	..	..	19
UK offshore islands	GQAT	−	−	−	−	−	−	−74	426	325	646	613
America of which	GQDJ	1 898	3 720	5 993	2 344	8 750	7 210	10 615	18 770	17 159	15 032	10 720
Canada	CAZF	265	−45	33	−246	−438	444	374	58	519	1 882	127
USA	CAZE	1 879	3 748	5 142	2 138	9 293	6 742	10 045	18 596	15 953	12 741	9 193
Asia	GQDK	255	630	570	186	−189	412	402	1 421	−2 189	7 725	854
Near and Middle East Countries	GQAU	137	251	115	78	58	64	103	81	137	88	90
Other Asian Countries of which	GQAV	118	380	456	110	−248	348	299	1 340	−2 326	7 637	764
Hong Kong	GQAW	53	280	106	45	−124	10	15	60	17	921	66
Japan	CAZH	48	−21	277	4	−379	209	288	968	−2 646	5 765	505
Singapore	GQAX	7	9	14	2	40	1	41	15	329	800	67
South Korea	GQAY	..	..	43	2	85	−8	−78	187	−112	−18	1
Australasia and Oceania of which	GQDL	1 328	323	995	387	−647	992	714	986	−133	1 483	170
Australia	CBOJ	937	340	995	260	−708	1 096	721	1 093	..	1 440	148
New Zealand	CBOK	391	−17	−	127	60	−104	−6	−107	..	40	22
Africa of which	GQAZ	27	99	111	63	117	118	170	808	143	416	63
South Africa	CAZJ	30	85	58	50	125	109	149	585	130	378	51
World Total	CBDH	8 418	8 816	9 871	6 046	12 654	15 662	20 296	44 877	54 376	78 495	41 972
OECD	GQBA	8 428	8 221	8 636	5 346	12 511	15 235	19 758	43 306	52 590	74 995	39 512
Central & Eastern Europe[5]	GGBB	−	−7	−	−141	15	−19	14	−16	2	8	10

1 See chapter text.
2 Net investment includes unremitted profits.
3 A minus sign indicates net disinvestment in the UK.
4 Prior to 1995 Russia covers other former USSR countries, the Baltic States and Albania.

5 Includes Albania, Bulgaria, Croatia, Czech Republic, Estonia, Hungary, Latvia, Lithuania, Poland, Romania, Serbia and Montenegro, Slovakia, Bosnia and Herzegovina, Macedonia FYR and Slovenia.

Sources: ONS Foreign Direct Investment Inquiries: 01633 813314; Bank of England

19.17 UK inward foreign direct international investment[1] position - book value of net liabilities analysed by area and main country at year end

£ millions

		1991	1992	1993	1994	1995	1996	1997	1998	1999	2000	2001
Europe	GQDM	45 205	46 928	47 770	47 281	52 144	55 856	58 037	81 385	118 793	150 203	190 211
EU	CDOT	38 036	39 547	40 266	39 998	43 493	43 774	44 927	69 248	107 249	136 686	176 345
Austria	CDPF	103	−30	93	428	412	280	79	334	253	565	303
Belgium and Luxembourg	CDOU	1 812	1 817	1 801	2 221	2 170	1 233	1 856	2 810	4 143	4 055	4 360
Denmark	CDOV	701	877	1 339	1 072	1 127	850	927	1 560	1 971	2 758	3 971
Finland	CDPG	364	437	300	356	352	334	444	729	921	1 042	1 115
France	CDOW	9 000	8 749	7 880	7 728	8 289	9 147	13 880	16 265	19 797	48 947	56 941
Germany	CDOX	4 597	5 627	5 921	5 589	8 854	9 508	10 078	11 573	36 250	26 140	32 896
Greece	CDOY	..	..	..	..	..	..	..	..	47	..	92
Irish Republic	CDOZ	840	865	681	956	686	703	1 837	2 807	3 098	3 474	3 830
Italy	CDPA	649	845	875	839	1 223	988	824	1 406	1 540	2 415	6 523
Netherlands	CDPB	16 547	16 715	18 477	18 511	17 173	18 692	12 131	28 227	33 891	41 565	62 106
Portugal	CDPC	..	..	..	..	..	..	..	..	179	..	129
Spain	CDPD	329	356	346	178	164	78	247	463	1 015	475	617
Sweden	CDPI	3 058	3 274	2 542	2 105	2 908	1 871	2 521	2 910	4 144	3 929	3 464
EFTA of which	CDPE	7 040	7 308	7 225	7 111	8 188	11 735	12 379	9 103	9 203	10 103	8 796
Norway	CDPH	661	647	701	506	665	1 571	1 866	1 559	560	854	912
Switzerland	CDPJ	6 375	6 657	6 519	6 605	7 523	10 164	10 422	7 444	8 516	9 091	7 596
Other European Countries of which	GQDN	129	73	280	172	463	348	731	3 035	2 341	3 414	5 070
Russia[2]	GQBC	18	−51	43	24	80	212	..	258	192	..	..
UK offshore islands	GQBD	−	−	−	−	−	−	341	2 465	1 780	2 774	4 364
America of which	GQDU	49 682	50 910	55 209	55 918	59 420	62 253	77 408	101 645	104 331	113 882	144 274
Canada	CDPM	4 427	4 065	4 101	4 593	2 652	3 517	4 129	4 090	7 070	9 307	9 018
USA	CDPN	44 434	46 001	49 537	49 829	55 129	55 956	70 270	93 419	93 469	101 245	129 865
Asia	GQDO	7 378	6 935	7 655	7 782	7 934	8 072	9 166	10 308	7 050	17 890	19 443
Near and Middle East Countries	GQBE	1 372	1 099	1 427	2 027	1 324	1 274	1 450	1 380	1 026	1 370	1 843
Other Asian Countries of which	GQBF	6 006	5 836	6 228	5 755	6 609	6 797	7 715	8 928	6 024	16 520	17 600
Hong Kong	GQBG	200	422	262	233	19	31	56	331	445	..	3 544
Japan	CDPQ	5 346	4 929	5 427	5 105	5 542	5 888	6 562	7 387	4 174	10 545	10 927
Singapore	GQBH	..	..	415	421	500	503	757	447	834	1 656	1 674
South Korea	GQBI	−43	−28	−3	−203	12	−206	−305	−66	−202	−245	108
Australasia and Oceania of which	GQDP	8 715	9 135	9 560	9 644	8 527	7 707	7 354	7 839	7 147	10 661	11 671
Australia	CDPP	7 655	8 083	8 598	7 968	7 021	6 169	6 003	5 938	5 450	9 875	10 930
New Zealand	CDPR	832	824	844	1 676	1 506	1 538	1 351	1 554	1 055	780	721
Africa of which	GQBJ	393	501	811	712	861	766	991	1 641	953	1 312	917
South Africa	CDPS	342	438	618	549	665	578	743	1 228	767	969	757
World Total	CDPZ	111 373	114 409	121 005	121 336	128 885	134 654	152 956	202 817	238 274	293 949	366 515
OECD	GQBK	107 814	110 816	116 082	116 171	123 761	128 475	145 336	190 717	227 529	278 358	346 729
Central & Eastern Europe[3]	GQBL	29	24	21	10	258	14	24	63	103	110	84

1 See chapter text.
2 Prior to 1995 Russia covers other former USSR countries, the Baltic States and Albania.

3 Includes Albania, Bulgaria, Croatia, Czech Republic, Estonia, Hungary, Latvia, Lithuania, Poland, Romania, Serbia and Montenegro, Slovakia, Bosnia and Herzegovina, Macedonia FYR and Slovenia.

Sources: ONS Foreign Direct Investment Inquiries: 01633 813314;
Bank of England

19.18

Net earnings from foreign direct investment in the UK[1] analysed by area and main country [2,3]

£ millions

		1991	1992	1993	1994	1995	1996	1997	1998	1999	2000	2001
Europe	GQDQ	1 243	2 482	4 833	3 661	5 432	6 401	5 746	1 485	6 643	15 304	11 566
EU	CBDJ	1 025	1 932	3 556	3 659	4 657	5 631	5 231	2 908	6 232	13 798	10 456
Austria	CBOR	..	..	−5	94	30	55	13	12	15	79	93
Belgium and Luxembourg	CBDK	−53	−1	224	272	249	209	139	408	349	136	157
Denmark	CBDL	42	−17	92	18	152	137	171	269	208	373	258
Finland	CBOS	−71	−36	−52	2	88	74	80	70	106	207	197
France	CBDM	377	340	633	227	836	705	1 239	648	1 871	2 186	1 624
Germany	CBDN	22	221	576	507	700	706	563	−185	−171	2 233	−120
Greece	CBDO	..	..	..	..	..	..	..	23	28	21	45
Irish Republic	CBDP	−27	−12	74	92	155	141	222	397	251	422	429
Italy	CBDQ	−55	−24	97	246	196	318	430	249	189	155	398
Netherlands	CBDR	927	1 731	1 820	2 076	2 070	3 053	2 034	640	2 947	7 611	6 823
Portugal	CBDS	..	..	..	..	..	..	..	−5	2	9	6
Spain	CBDT	−29	−5	55	17	42	69	106	85	127	88	202
Sweden	CBOU	−56	−177	46	107	127	146	219	300	309	280	346
EFTA of which	CBDW	146	846	1 188	−33	685	709	408	−1 411	311	1 451	741
Norway	CBOT	−14	−35	27	12	11	−58	121	−171	−212	120	60
Switzerland	CBOV	338	885	1 161	−45	675	768	277	−1 248	518	1 323	673
Other European Countries of which	GQDR	−104	−296	88	36	89	60	108	−9	100	55	368
Russia[4]	GQBM	..	..	55	1	15	31	..	..	12	..	..
UK offshore islands	GQBN	−	−	−	−	−	−	33	42	47	−34	313
America of which	GQDV	2 948	2 391	4 917	4 992	5 824	7 589	6 775	6 365	7 857	8 482	7 633
Canada	CBEA	199	47	234	506	228	281	65	198	368	774	54
USA	CBDZ	2 951	2 284	4 441	4 372	5 606	6 986	6 512	5 848	7 586	7 789	7 516
Asia	GQDS	193	107	106	172	459	300	−332	−597	137	1 227	982
Near and Middle East Countries	GQBO	−89	−31	16	−8	112	89	96	46	137	68	159
Other Asian Countries of which	GQBP	283	139	90	181	347	211	−428	−643	−	1 159	823
Hong Kong	GQBQ	47	207	52	4	−2	28	21	−185	26	36	11
Japan	CBEC	246	−41	45	171	334	151	−502	−391	−61	925	585
Singapore	GQBS	3	−2	4	1	5	−	41	−79	88	235	91
South Korea	GQBT	..	..	7	15	−6	−6	−11	−20	−60	−85	3
Australasia and Oceania of which	GQDT	74	211	418	327	472	594	860	629	508	222	232
Australia	CBOZ	92	222	410	330	479	566	830	602	..	195	147
New Zealand	CBPA	−18	..	8	−1	−6	28	..	85	..	21	33
Africa of which	GQBU	3	..	19	25	49	44	55	7	127	180	210
South Africa	CBED	−1	6	9	21	38	35	46	−23	114	167	175
World Total	CBEV	4 461	5 197	10 293	9 176	12 235	14 928	13 103	7 889	15 272	25 415	20 623
OECD	GQBV	4 878	5 371	9 998	9 118	12 081	14 388	12 583	7 838	14 905	24 907	19 571
Central & Eastern Europe[5]	GQBW	−	2	1	24	60	13	18	−12	11	5	5

1 See chapter text.
2 A minus sign indicates net losses.
3 Net earnings equal profits of UK branches plus overseas investors' receipts of interest and their share of the profits of UK subsidiaries and associates. Earnings are after deducting provisions for depreciation and UK tax on profits and interest.

4 Prior to 1995 Russia covers other former USSR countries, the Baltic States and Albania.
5 Includes Albania, Bulgaria, Croatia, Czech Republic, Estonia, Hungary, Latvia, Lithuania, Poland, Romania, Serbia and Montenegro, Slovakia, Bosnia and Herzegovina, Macedonia FYR and Slovenia.

Sources: ONS Foreign Direct Investment Inquiries: 01633 813314;
Bank of England

20 Research and development

Research and development

Research and experimental development (R&D) is defined for statistical purposes as 'creative work undertaken on a systematic basis in order to increase the stock of knowledge, including knowledge of man, culture and society, and the use of this stock of knowledge to devise new applications'.

R&D is financed and carried out mainly by businesses, the Government, and institutions of higher education. A small amount is performed by non-profit-making bodies. Gross Expenditure on R&D (GERD) is an indicator of the total amount of R&D performed within the UK: it has been approximately 2 per cent of GDP in recent years. Detailed figures are reported each year in a First Release published in March and the August edition of the ONS's *Economic Trends*. Table 20.1 shows the main components of GERD.

The ONS conducts an annual survey of expenditure and employment on R&D performed by Government, and of Government funding of R&D. The survey collects data on outturn and planning years. Until 1993 the detailed results were reported in the *Annual Review of Government Funded R&D* produced by the Office of Science and Technology (OST). From 1997 the results have appeared in OST's *Science, Engineering and Technology Statistics* publication. Table 20.2 gives some broad totals for gross expenditure by Government (expenditure before deducting funds received by Government for R&D). Table 20.3 gives a breakdown of net expenditure (receipts are deducted).

The ONS conducts an annual survey of R&D in business. Tables 20.4 and 20.5 give a summary of the main trends up to 2002. The latest set of results from the survey will be available in a First Release dated 28 November 2003 and a Business Monitor (MA14) to be published in January 2003.

Statistics on expenditure and employment on R&D in Higher Education Institutions (HEIs) are based on information collected by Higher Education Funding Councils and HESA (Higher Education Statistics Agency). In 1994 a new methodology was introduced to estimate expenditure on R&D in HEIs. This is based on the allocation of various Funding Council Grants. Full details of the new methodology are contained in SET Statistics available on the Office of Science and Technology Web Site at *www.ost.gov.uk/setstats/*.

The most comprehensive international comparisons of resources devoted to R&D appear in Main Science and Technology Indicators published by the organisation for Economic Co-operation and Development (OECD). The Statistical Office of the European Union and the United Nations also compile R&D statistics based on figures supplied by member states.

To make international comparisons more reliable the OECD have published a series of manuals giving guidance on how to measure various components of R&D inputs and outputs. The most important of these is the Frascati Manual, which defines R&D and recommends how resources for R&D should be measured. The UK follows the Frascati Manual as far as possible.

For information on available aggregated data on Research and Development please contact Jane Morgan on 01633 813109 (e-mail *jane.morgan@ons.gov.uk*).

20.1 Cost of research and development: analysis by sector[1]
United Kingdom

	1995		1996		1997		1998		1999		2000		2001	
	£m	%	£m	%	£m	%	£m	%	£m	%	£m	%	£m	%
Sector carrying out the work (£m cash terms)														
Government	1 462	10	1 495	10	1 427	10	1 487	10	1 450	9	1 489	8	1 160	6
Research Councils	581	4	575	4	590	4	591	4	622	4	646	4	670	4
Business enterprise	9 116	65	9 297	65	9 556	65	10 133	66	11 302	67	11 510	66	12 336	67
Higher education	2 696	19	2 792	19	2 893	20	3 040	20	3 324	20	3 648	21	4 034	21
Private non-profit	177	1	177	1	190	1	203	1	231	1	255	1	269	1
Total	14 034	100	14 336	100	14 657	100	15 454	100	16 929	100	17 547	100	18 469	100
Sector providing the funds (£m cash terms)														
Government	2 514	18	2 402	17	2 332	16	2 535	16	2 601	15	2 547	15	2 842	15
Research Councils	1 078	8	1 092	8	1 135	8	1 117	7	1 185	7	1 250	7	1 358	7
Higher Education Funding Councils	1 018	7	1 027	7	1 033	7	1 085	7	1 157	7	1 276	7	1 474	8
Higher education	119	1	120	1	123	1	130	1	142	1	158	1	177	1
Business enterprise[2]	6 765	48	6 817	48	7 321	50	7 356	48	8 213	49	8 648	49	8 741	46
Private non-profit	511	4	545	4	578	4	621	4	701	4	815	5	888	5
Abroad	2 029	14	2 331	16	2 136	15	2 610	17	2 929	17	2 854	16	3 385	18
Total	14 034	100	14 336	100	14 657	100	15 454	100	16 929	100	17 547	100	18 866	100

1 See chapter text.
2 Including research associations and public corporations.

Source: Office for National Statistics: 01633 813109

20.2 Gross Central Government expenditure on research and development[1]
United Kingdom

£ millions

	1996/97		1997/98		1998/99		1999/00		2000/01		2001/02	
	Intra-mural	Extra-mural[2]	Intra-mural	Extra-mural[2]	Intra-mural	Extra-mural[2]	Intra-mural	Extra-mural[2]	Intra-mural	Extra-mural[2]	Intra-mural	Extra-mural[2]
Defence	804	1 429	774	1 639	818	1 436	784	1 716	828	1 718	419	1 685
Research councils	593	851	608	852	608	865	644	894	667	1 024	695	1 244
Higher Education Institutes	-	1 027	-	1 033	-	1 085	-	1 157	-	1 276	-	1 474
Other programmes	290	628	253	681	266	714	274	810	283	841	282	982
Total (excluding NHS)	1 686	3 936	1 635	4 205	1 692	4 100	1 703	4 577	1 778	4 859	1 396	5 385

1 See chapter text.
2 Including work performed overseas and excluding monies spent with other government departments.

Source: Office for National Statistics: 01633 813109

20.3 Net central government expenditure on research and development[1], using European Union objectives for research and development expenditure

United Kingdom

£ millions

		1991 /92	1992 /93	1993 /94	1994 /95	1995 /96	1996 /97	1997 /98	1998 /99	1999 /00	2000 /01	2001 /02
Exploration and exploitation of the earth	KDVP	143.9	120.5	98.8	106.8	105.2	95.4	81.3	78.5	79.5	85.5	106.0
Infrastructure and general planning of land-use	KDVQ	64.2	85.6	96.7	98.1	94.1	98.8	98.9	103.5	104.4	102.4	100.3
Control of environmental pollution	KDVR	71.9	69.5	108.7	117.2	131.8	128.7	136.2	142.8	147.0	151.1	129.1
Protection and promotion of human health (ex NHS)	KDVS	298.4	341.5	383.1	397.2	416.0	427.4	444.8	450.1	519.5	530.6	571.6
Production, distribution and rational utilisation of energy	KDVT	133.0	120.0	96.8	55.5	52.3	43.2	41.0	28.0	29.0	31.9	36.8
Agricultural production and technology	KDVU	216.2	261.1	284.6	263.4	281.9	257.0	268.9	255.5	260.6	266.6	265.2
Industrial production and technology	KDVV	399.0	394.1	458.7	184.4	165.8	144.6	116.9	61.6	56.5	109.2	237.0
Social structures and relationships	KDVW	115.5	141.9	149.1	141.9	137.1	120.7	113.8	154.7	217.6	270.2	268.8
Exploration and exploitation of space	KDVX	134.2	149.1	187.4	161.5	153.0	164.1	164.4	142.5	142.7	146.3	139.8
Research financed from General University Funds	KDVY	919.1	963.3	968.4	1 017.9	1 018.6	1 027.5	1 033.3	1 085.1	1 157.1	1 276.1	1 473.5
Non-oriented research	KDVZ	287.6	337.1	267.3	612.5	653.5	680.5	671.0	677.0	700.5	789.3	918.2
Other civil research	KDWA	35.5	23.8	34.0	22.2	24.7	20.5	21.6	25.8	20.6	22.3	19.7
Defence	KDWB	2 208.8	2 071.1	2 268.6	2 021.9	2 098.9	2 143.5	2 312.1	2 099.5	2 347.3	2 384.1	2 063.0
Total (excluding NHS)	KDWC	5 027.4	5 078.6	5 402.3	5 200.4	5 332.9	5 351.8	5 504.2	5 304.5	5 782.1	6 165.6	6 329.0

1 See chapter text.

Source: Office for National Statistics: 01633 813109

20.4 Intramural expenditure on business enterprise research and development[1]

United Kingdom

At Current Prices and Constant Prices

£ millions

		Total				Civil				Defence		
		1999	2000	2001		1999	2000	2001		1999	2000	2001
Current Prices												
Total	KDWD	11 302	11 510	12 336	KDWN	9 626	9 838	10 513	KDWX	1 675	1 671	1 824
Manufacturing Total	KDWE	8 995	9 231	9 788	KDWO	7 376	7 582	8 089	KDWY	1 619	1 649	1 699
Chemicals	KDWF	3 253	3 528	3 562	KDWP	3 252	3 527	3 562	KDWZ	1	–	–
Mechanical engineering	KDWG	712	776	907	KDWQ	434	463	470	KDXA	279	314	437
Electrical machinery	KJRT	1 335	1 558	1 599	KJTC	1 013	1 163	1 200	KJUL	322	395	399
Aerospace	KDWJ	1 235	1 094	1 189	KDWT	1 159	1 023	1 106	KDXD	77	71	82
Transport equipment	KDWK	1 237	1 091	1 260	KDWU	535	457	621	KDXE	701	634	639
Other manufacturing	KDWL	1 222	1 183	1 271	KDWV	983	948	1 130	KDXF	239	235	141
Services	KDWM	1 972	1 905	2 280	KDWW	1 915	1 883	2 155	KDXG	57	22	125
Other: Total	HFRU	335	374	268	HFRZ	335	374	268	MKFB	–	–	–
Agriculture, hunting and forestry; Fishing	HFRV	115	135	96	HFSA	115	135	96	MKFC	–	–	–
Extractive industries	HFRW	42	46	43	HFSB	42	46	43	MKFD	–	–	–
Electricity, gas and water supply	HFRX	137	160	99	HFSC	137	160	99	MKFE	–	–	–
Construction	HFRY	41	34	30	HFSE	41	34	30	MKFF	–	–	–
2001 Prices												
Total	HFWY	11 801	11 757	12 336	HFXH	10 051	10 050	10 513	HFYM	1 749	1 707	1 824
Manufacturing Total	HFWZ	9 392	9 429	9 788	HFXI	7 702	7 745	8 089	HFYN	1 690	1 684	1 699
Chemicals	HFXA	3 397	3 604	3 562	HFXJ	3 396	3 603	3 562	HFYO	1	–	–
Mechanical engineering	HFXB	743	793	907	HFXK	453	473	470	HFYP	291	321	437
Electrical machinery	HFXC	1 394	1 592	1 599	HFYH	1 058	1 188	1 200	HFYQ	336	403	399
Aerospace	HFXD	1 290	1 118	1 189	HFYI	1 210	1 045	1 106	HFYR	80	73	82
Transport equipment	HFXE	1 292	1 114	1 260	HFYJ	559	467	621	HFYS	732	648	639
Other manufacturing	HFXF	1 276	1 208	1 271	HFYK	1 026	968	1 130	HFYT	250	240	141
Services	HFXG	2 059	1 946	2 280	HFYL	2 000	1 923	2 155	HFYU	60	22	125
Other: Total	HFSF	350	382	268	HFSK	350	382	268	MKFG	–	–	–
Agriculture, hunting and forestry: Fishing	HFSG	120	138	96	HFSL	120	138	96	MKFH	–	–	–
Extractive industries	HFSH	44	47	43	HFSM	44	47	43	MKFI	–	–	–
Electricity, gas and water supply	HFSI	143	163	99	HFSN	143	163	99	MKFJ	–	–	–
Construction	HFSJ	43	35	30	HFSO	43	35	30	MKFK	–	–	–

1 See chapter text.

Source: Office for National Statistics: 01633 813109

20.5 Sources of funds for research and development within Business Enterprises[1]
United Kingdom

		Total				Civil				Defence		
		1999	2000	2001		1999	2000	2001		1999	2000	2001
Funds for Business Enterprise R&D												
£m cash terms												
Total	KDYL	11 302	11 510	12 336	KDYT	9 626	9 838	10 513	KDZB	1 675	1 671	1 824
Government funds	KDYM	1 157	1 013	1 101	KDYU	316	228	191	KDZC	841	785	911
Overseas funds	KDYN	2 570	2 470	3 012	KDYV	2 092	2 003	2 585	KDZD	478	467	427
Mainly own funds	KDYO	7 575	8 026	8 223	KDYW	7 219	7 607	7 738	KDZE	356	418	485
Funds for Business Enterprise R&D												
Percentage												
Total	KDYP	100	100	100	KDYX	100	100	100	KDZF	100	100	100
Government funds	KDYQ	10	9	9	KDYY	3	2	2	KDZG	50	47	50
Overseas funds	KDYR	23	21	24	KDYZ	22	20	25	KDZH	29	28	23
Mainly own funds	KDYS	67	70	67	KDZA	75	77	74	KDZI	21	25	27

1 See chapter text.

Source: Office for National Statistics: 01633 813109

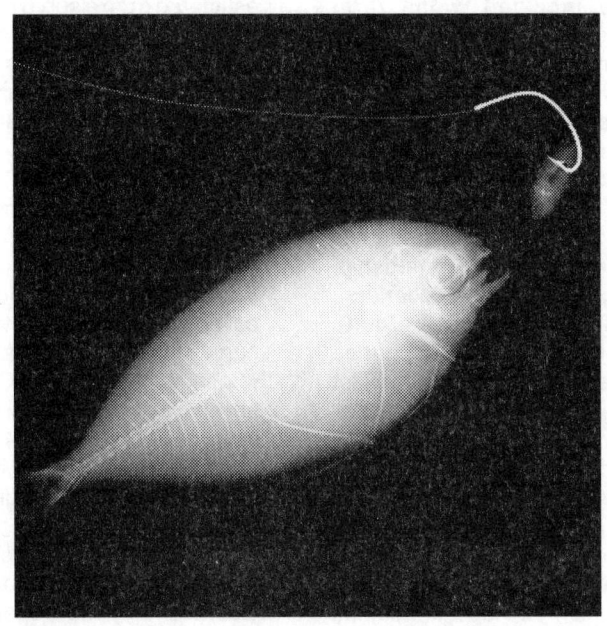

21 Agriculture, fisheries and food

Agriculture, fisheries and food

Output and input *(Tables 21.1 and 21.2)*
For both tables, output is a net of VAT collected on the sale of non-edible products. Figures for total output include subsidies on products, but not other subsidies.

Unspecified crops include turf, other minor crops and arable area payments for fodder maize. Eggs include the value of duck eggs and exports of eggs for hatching. Landlords' expenses are included within farm maintenance, miscellaneous expenditure and depreciation of buildings and works. Also included within "other farming costs" are livestock and crop costs, water costs, insurance premia, bank charges, professional fees, rates, and other farming costs.

Other subsidies
Agri-Environment schemes include Environmentally and Nitrate Sensitive Areas, Countryside Stewardship, Countryside Premium, Tir Cymen, Tir Gofal, Moorland, Habitat, Farm Woodland and Organic Farming Schemes. Included in "other" subsidies are guidance premium for beef and sheep meat production, Pilot Beef and Sheep Extensification Scheme, non-agricultural horse grazing and farm accounts grant as well as historic data for fertiliser and lime grant and payments to small scale cereal producers.

Compensation of employees and interest charges
Total compensation of employees excludes the value of work done by farm labour on own account capital formation in buildings and work. "Interest" relates to interest charges on loans for current farming purposes and buildings and less interest on money held on short-term deposit.

Rent
Rent paid (after deductions) is the rent paid on all tenanted land including "conacre" land in Northern Ireland, less landlords' expenses and the benefit value of dwellings on that land. Rent received (after deductions) is the rent received by farming landowners from renting of land to other farmers, less landlords' expenses and the benefit value of dwellings on that land. Total net rent is the net rent flowing out of the agricultural sector paid to non-farming landowners, including that part of tenanted land in Northern Ireland. (Although there has been some updating of the technical procedures for calculating this figure, it corresponds with the previous net rent variable.)

Agricultural censuses and surveys
(Tables 21.3, 21.5 and 21.13)
The coverage for holdings includes all main and minor holdings for each country. Northern Ireland data are now based on all active farm business.

Estimated quantity of crops and grass harvested *(Table 21.4)*
The estimated yields of sugar beet and hops are obtained from production figures supplied by British Sugar plc, and the main hop producers in England and Wales. In Great Britain potato yields are estimated in consultation with the British Potato Council.

Forestry *(Table 21.6)*
Statistics for state forestry are from the Annual Reports and Accounts of Forest Enterprise in Great Britain and the Forest Service in Northern Ireland.

For private forestry in Great Britain, statistics on new planting and restocking are based on records of the Woodland Grant Scheme, and timber removals are estimated from a survey of the largest timber harvesting companies. Woodland area figures are based on data obtained from censuses of woodlands and adjusted to reflect subsequent changes. Figures are based on results from the 1995-1999 National Inventory of Woodlands and Trees.

Average weekly earnings and hours of agricultural and horticultural workers *(Tables 21.11 and 21.12)*
Since 1998, data on the Earnings and Hours of Agricultural and Horticultural workers have been collected via an annual telephone survey. This annual survey collects information for a snapshot in time, relating to the month of September. The survey covers seven main categories of workers and in 2001 data were collected on 1,274 workers. Prior to 1998, data were collected from a monthly postal survey, which mainly covered male full-time workers.

The survey provides data which are used by the Agricultural Wages Board when considering wage claims and by the Department for Environment, Food and Rural Affairs (DEFRA) in considering the cost of labour in agriculture and horticulture.

Data on earnings represents the total earnings of regular full-time male workers, aged 20 and over. Figures include all payments-in-kind, valued where applicable in accordance with the Agricultural Wages Order. The earnings and hours of hire farm managers are excluded. Part-time workers are defined as those working less than 39 basic hours per week. Casual workers are those employed on a temporary basis.

The survey was reviewed in 2002 and it was concluded that the frequency of the survey should be increased to four times per year to enable the production of more representative annual estimates. The annual sample size has been retained and has been split between four quarterly surveys. Results for other quarters can be found on the DEFRA website.

Fisheries *(Tables 21.14 and 21.15)*
Data relating to the weight and value of landings of fish in the United Kingdom (Table 21.14) is generally obtained from sales notes completed at fish market auctions.

Fishing fleet information (Table 21.15) is obtained from vessel registers maintained by the Department for Environment, Food and Rural Affairs in England and Wales and the Scottish Executive Agriculture and Fisheries Department.

Estimated average household food consumption - 'Family Food' Expenditure & Food Survey *(Table 21.16)*

The Expenditure & Food Survey replaced both the National Food Survey and the Family Expenditure Survey in April 2001. The new survey is a voluntary sample survey of private households throughout the United Kingdom and the results are produced for the financial year ending 31st March each year. This represents a break in the continuity of the data as results from the National Food Survey were produced for Great Britain and for the calendar year ended 31st December.

The basic unit of the survey is the household which is defined as a group of persons living at the same address and sharing common catering arrangements. Each individual aged 16 or over in the household visited is asked to keep diary records, for a two-week period, of daily expenditure on and weight/volume of food and drink brought into the home and expenditure on food and drink eaten out. Children aged between 7 and 15 are asked to keep simplified diaries.

For the year 2001/02 the sample size includes nearly 7,500 households and over 18,000 persons.

21.1 Production and income account at current prices[1]
United Kingdom

£ millions

		1992	1993	1994	1995	1996	1997	1998	1999	2000	2001	2002[2]
Output[3]												
1. Total cereals:												
wheat	KFKA	1 682.5	1 782.5	1 723.4	2 078.7	2 315.1	1 851.0	1 652.3	1 524.9	1 577.6	1 226.2	1 490.0
rye	VQBG	2.8	3.4	4.3	5.1	5.6	5.4	5.0	3.5	3.1	2.5	2.8
barley	KFKB	855.1	844.5	846.8	1 108.5	1 183.4	976.8	781.3	734.7	686.1	725.0	623.2
oats and summer cereal mixtures	KFKC	58.0	71.7	81.7	89.0	85.6	70.6	60.5	58.2	65.2	64.8	71.1
other cereals	VQBH	1.1	2.3	2.5	3.7	3.3	3.1	3.2	4.2	4.8	4.1	4.8
2. Total industrial crops	VQBI	920.4	1 204.5	1 055.6	1 150.6	1 107.0	1 007.6	1 011.5	1 012.4	790.8	816.7	884.1
oilseeds	VQBJ	384.7	594.2	415.9	427.9	473.7	457.5	485.1	502.6	283.1	291.0	299.5
oilseed rape	KFKG	300.9	410.3	376.9	387.3	434.3	406.0	417.2	370.6	248.9	275.1	293.8
other oil seeds	KIBT	83.8	183.9	39.0	40.6	39.4	51.5	67.9	132.1	34.3	15.8	5.7
sugar beet	KFKH	386.3	352.9	342.7	354.9	358.2	329.1	298.5	279.6	252.1	256.4	272.1
other industrial crops	VQBK	149.4	257.4	297.0	367.8	275.1	221.0	227.9	230.2	255.5	269.4	312.5
fibre plants	VQBL	–	1.6	13.3	14.2	17.0	15.2	12.8	11.4	8.3	3.7	1.8
hops	KFKI	17.8	20.8	20.2	16.7	19.5	19.6	14.1	13.3	11.5	9.8	10.7
others[4]	VQBM	131.5	235.0	263.5	336.9	238.5	186.2	201.0	205.5	235.7	255.9	300.0
3. Total forage plants	VQBO	147.6	219.3	182.7	171.5	170.8	159.4	141.2	143.5	138.2	170.1	164.4
4. Total vegetables and horticultural products	VQBP	1 463.0	1 481.4	1 602.9	1 696.8	1 758.1	1 630.0	1 636.3	1 676.7	1 558.9	1 711.6	1 673.9
5. Total potatoes (including seeds)	KFKO	533.4	390.1	710.2	1 095.1	636.3	389.9	630.0	750.0	453.7	636.6	463.0
6. Total fruit	KFKQ	281.5	272.5	246.6	257.6	292.0	198.7	258.8	256.8	228.6	235.1	257.4
7. Other crop products including seeds	VQBQ	40.5	41.9	41.5	41.0	42.7	46.9	43.0	45.1	39.7	37.4	26.0
8. Total crop output (1+2+3+4+5+6+7)	VQBR	5 985.9	6 314.0	6 498.3	7 697.5	7 599.8	6 339.4	6 223.1	6 210.2	5 546.7	5 630.2	5 660.5
9. Total livestock production	VQBS	6 236.4	6 916.3	7 044.5	7 247.9	7 448.1	7 016.4	6 086.7	5 630.8	5 582.6	5 232.3	5 665.9
primarily for meat	KFLA	5 546.6	6 036.8	6 206.4	6 554.8	6 861.5	6 298.5	5 495.9	5 236.8	5 196.1	4 632.6	4 940.1
cattle	KFKU	1 999.1	2 371.9	2 467.8	2 579.8	2 546.1	2 276.3	1 981.7	2 047.1	1 993.9	1 771.7	2 024.4
pigs	KFKW	1 149.2	1 042.5	1 036.8	1 177.4	1 372.5	1 202.6	886.7	784.7	793.9	748.9	686.7
sheep	VQBT	1 145.3	1 226.5	1 218.0	1 317.6	1 273.9	1 176.8	1 112.1	984.4	952.5	625.0	839.6
poultry	KFXX	1 128.1	1 267.4	1 353.9	1 345.7	1 526.2	1 493.6	1 366.6	1 271.6	1 303.2	1 332.1	1 226.1
other animals	KFKY	124.9	128.5	130.0	134.3	142.8	149.1	148.8	148.9	152.6	154.9	163.3
Gross fixed capital formation	KFLI	689.9	879.5	838.1	693.1	586.6	718.0	590.8	394.1	386.4	599.7	725.7
cattle	KUJZ	419.0	616.8	565.0	407.9	289.4	378.3	297.1	207.1	188.5	345.9	422.9
pigs	LUKB	18.4	14.0	13.9	15.4	19.1	15.2	5.6	6.8	5.6	5.2	7.8
sheep	LUKA	138.7	133.3	150.6	149.7	150.0	196.1	154.0	55.9	62.2	122.2	167.8
poultry	LUKC	113.8	115.4	108.5	120.0	128.2	128.3	134.2	124.3	130.2	126.3	127.3
10. Total livestock products	KFLF	3 380.2	3 658.6	3 790.7	3 950.9	4 011.3	3 629.0	3 135.0	3 044.6	2 809.3	3 266.7	3 006.5
milk	KFLB	2 925.0	3 187.4	3 310.4	3 497.7	3 494.7	3 153.6	2 709.0	2 653.4	2 393.0	2 822.2	2 489.3
eggs	KFLC	390.7	417.4	412.0	383.0	453.0	415.0	381.0	344.0	371.0	406.0	475.6
raw wool	KFLD	41.2	29.8	46.2	45.9	39.9	35.1	23.9	21.4	22.7	17.3	18.6
other animal products	KFLE	23.4	24.0	22.1	24.4	23.7	25.3	21.0	25.7	22.6	21.3	23.0
11. Total livestock output (9+10)	VQBV	9 616.6	10 575.0	10 835.1	11 198.8	11 459.4	10 645.4	9 221.7	8 675.4	8 391.9	8 499.0	8 672.4
12. Total other agricultural activities	LUOS	478.6	580.2	634.8	696.7	782.6	699.5	679.3	715.9	634.0	628.2	656.9
agricultural services	LUKD	437.1	471.1	501.8	552.9	608.0	575.0	570.2	609.5	583.1	604.2	625.8
leasing out quota	VQBW	41.5	109.1	133.0	143.8	174.6	124.5	109.1	106.4	50.9	24.0	31.1
13. Total inseparable non-agricultural activities	LUOT	267.9	295.1	322.5	326.6	362.1	371.6	421.1	430.4	436.1	582.9	518.4
14. Gross output at basic prices (8+11+12+13)	KFLT	16 349.1	17 764.2	18 290.8	19 919.6	20 203.9	18 056.0	16 545.1	16 031.9	15 008.6	15 340.3	15 508.2
15. Total subsidies (less taxes) on product	LUOU	804.5	1 763.3	1 686.1	2 106.9	2 782.1	2 587.8	2 436.1	2 373.2	2 187.0	1 912.3	2 060.3
16. Output at market prices (14-15)	LUOV	15 544.6	16 000.9	16 604.7	17 812.7	17 421.8	15 468.2	14 109.0	13 658.7	12 821.6	13 428.0	13 447.8
of which transactions within the agricultural industry	LUNP	..	..	..	..	..	..	..	..	..	..	..
feed wheat	LUNQ	114.4	81.3	74.7	55.4	67.0	77.3	78.8	64.4	39.8	38.5	38.5
feed barley	LUNR	265.3	232.9	200.9	198.9	205.6	192.8	163.6	147.9	136.9	151.5	136.9
feed oats	LUNS	18.8	21.3	21.5	16.5	16.1	11.8	11.5	14.5	12.6	12.4	11.4
seed potatoes	LUNT	23.0	12.7	13.8	41.1	33.7	9.5	12.2	29.6	9.0	12.8	12.6
straw	LUNU	108.7	207.2	235.8	308.0	211.6	160.3	173.0	175.6	205.2	221.9	265.1
contract work	LUNV	437.1	471.1	501.8	552.9	608.0	575.0	570.2	609.5	583.1	604.2	625.8
leasing of quota	LUNW	41.5	109.1	133.0	143.8	174.6	124.5	109.1	106.4	50.9	24.0	31.1
total capital formation in livestock	LUNX	689.9	879.5	838.1	693.1	586.6	718.0	590.8	394.1	386.4	599.7	725.7

21.1

Production and income account at current prices[1]
United Kingdom

continued

£ millions

		1992	1993	1994	1995	1996	1997	1998	1999	2000	2001	2002[2]
Intermediate consumption												
17.Seeds	KFME	315.1	296.5	325.8	383.5	380.0	336.7	330.8	330.8	272.7	292.5	294.6
cereals	KFMC	114.0	113.5	112.3	121.2	123.7	103.5	84.2	93.7	81.1	90.7	85.3
other	KFMD	201.0	182.9	213.4	262.3	256.3	233.3	246.6	237.1	191.6	201.8	209.4
18.Energy	VQDO	571.5	594.0	585.7	590.0	646.4	628.9	597.3	620.8	683.4	684.9	651.1
electricity	VQDQ	244.7	245.7	243.4	237.0	247.6	232.7	231.0	221.7	228.9	242.4	225.7
fuels	VQDV	326.8	348.3	342.3	353.0	398.8	396.1	366.3	399.2	454.5	442.5	425.4
19.Fertilisers	KFMM	815.7	753.0	768.7	926.0	1 043.3	1 006.9	831.7	756.0	737.8	760.6	754.3
20.Pesticides	KFMN	530.6	547.5	557.3	590.0	646.9	674.6	654.8	621.7	580.5	533.5	527.5
21.Veterinary expenses	KCPC	231.2	253.2	274.3	289.2	297.7	307.8	288.0	270.0	255.7	245.3	241.0
22.Animal feed	KFMB	2 864.8	2 934.1	2 874.5	3 040.2	3 185.4	2 804.0	2 444.4	2 260.9	2 116.8	2 323.1	2 175.5
compounds[5]	LUNY	1 670.8	1 764.2	1 689.1	1 806.2	1 959.5	1 772.2	1 523.5	1 402.4	1 285.0	1 401.3	1 365.4
straights[5]	LUNZ	795.5	834.4	888.3	963.3	937.3	749.9	667.0	631.7	642.5	719.4	623.3
feed purchased from other farms	LUOA	398.5	335.5	297.1	270.8	288.6	281.9	253.9	226.8	189.3	202.4	186.8
23.Total Maintenance[6]	VQDW	893.9	949.8	977.3	1 089.9	1 111.2	1 092.0	1 025.2	1 016.8	942.7	988.2	1 022.0
materials	KFMO	600.7	637.6	631.3	721.9	746.2	721.7	699.8	698.9	651.2	663.3	689.5
buildings	KCPB	293.2	312.2	346.1	368.1	365.0	370.3	325.4	317.9	291.5	324.8	332.5
24.Agricultural services	LUOE	437.1	471.1	501.8	552.9	608.0	575.0	570.2	609.5	583.1	604.2	625.8
25.Other goods and services[6,7]	VQDX	1 743.8	1 962.3	2 066.4	2 170.4	2 268.8	2 291.7	2 241.0	2 257.5	2 086.9	2 057.5	2 099.6
26.Total intermediate consumption (17+18+19+20+21+22+23+24+25)	KCPM	8 403.6	8 761.3	8 931.7	9 632.3	10 187.8	9 717.6	8 983.4	8 743.9	8 259.6	8 489.9	8 391.3
27.Gross value added at basic prices (14-26)	LUOG	7 945.4	9 002.9	9 359.0	10 287.3	10 016.2	8 338.4	7 561.8	7 288.0	6 749.0	6 850.4	7 116.9
28.Total consumption of Fixed Capital	KCPS	2 259.8	2 540.2	2 548.5	2 590.6	2 618.3	2 669.7	2 587.4	2 423.7	2 491.5	2 587.7	2 638.1
equipment	KCPR	1 109.5	1 141.5	1 179.7	1 230.2	1 294.0	1 321.7	1 325.0	1 311.1	1 275.9	1 280.3	1 270.9
buildings[6,8]	LUOH	567.9	568.2	581.5	640.0	681.2	671.2	682.7	700.0	689.8	688.5	686.8
livestock	VQEA	582.4	830.5	787.3	720.4	643.1	676.8	579.7	412.5	525.8	618.9	680.5
cattle	LUOI	329.8	577.3	529.2	415.8	313.5	391.3	314.1	207.4	278.1	323.6	406.0
pigs	LUOK	17.7	14.0	14.7	16.7	17.4	14.6	8.4	7.6	7.9	6.2	7.9
sheep	LUOJ	120.2	137.4	141.5	174.0	189.4	155.1	117.6	68.7	118.5	168.9	142.7
poultry	LUOL	114.7	101.8	101.9	113.7	122.9	115.7	139.6	128.8	121.3	120.3	123.9
29.Net value added at basic prices (27-28)	KCPT	5 685.7	6 462.7	6 810.5	7 696.8	7 397.9	5 668.7	4 974.4	4 864.3	4 257.5	4 262.7	4 478.7
30.Compensation of employees[9]	LUOR	1 783.6	1 786.6	1 827.5	1 836.3	1 880.9	1 929.8	1 976.9	2 030.2	1 903.4	1 909.5	1 906.8
31.Other taxes on production	VQEB	−53.7	−63.6	−68.1	−73.1	−81.4	−84.6	−88.6	−90.4	−91.1	−84.1	−75.5
32.Other subsidies on production	VQEC	37.4	197.9	268.1	274.7	252.3	199.3	231.5	329.2	325.7	573.7	587.1
animal disease compensation	LUOM	6.0	10.4	6.8	6.9	5.4	15.3	24.2	27.9	40.8	27.7	37.3
set-aside	LUON	–	142.0	206.3	198.4	159.5	90.2	87.7	170.0	127.3	179.7	152.0
agri-environment schemes[10]	ZBXC	31.4	45.5	55.1	69.4	87.2	93.7	119.6	131.4	157.7	198.1	240.6
other inlcuding Less Favoured Areas schemes[11]	VQED	–	–	–	–	–	–	–	–	–	168.1	157.2
33.Net value added at factor cost (29+31+32)	LUOQ	5 669.3	6 596.9	7 010.5	7 898.3	7 568.8	5 783.4	5 117.3	5 103.1	4 492.2	4 752.3	4 990.3
34.Rent	KCPV	175.2	178.5	181.6	175.5	228.7	255.8	250.1	238.4	222.3	250.3	247.6
rent paid[12]	ZBXE	175.2	178.5	181.6	175.5	302.8	335.8	330.6	320.7	301.2	328.7	346.8
rent received[13]	ZBXF	–	–	–	–	−74.1	−80.1	−80.5	−82.4	−78.9	−78.4	−99.1
35.Interest[14]	KCPU	714.7	524.0	536.2	587.3	553.3	621.2	680.6	594.5	623.9	551.5	479.5
Total income from farming (33-30-34-35)	KCQB	2 996.0	4 107.8	4 465.2	5 299.3	4 905.9	2 976.6	2 209.7	2 240.1	1 742.5	2 041.0	2 356.4

1 See chapter text.
2 Provisional.
3 Output is net of VAT collected on the sale of non-edible products. Figures for total output include subsidies on products, but not other subsidies.
4 Includes straw and minor crops.
5 For years prior to 1992 the split between compounds and straights has been estimated based on the split present in later years.
6 Landlords' expenses are included within total maintenance, other goods and services and Consumption of Fixed Capital of buildings.
7 Includes livestock and crop costs, water costs, insurance premiums, bank charges, professional fees, rates and other farming costs.
8 A more empirically based methodology for calculating landlords' consumption of fixed capital was introduced in 2000. The new series has been linked with the old one using a smoothing procedure for the transition year of 1996.
9 Excludes the value of work done by farm labour on own account capital formation in buildings and works.

10 Includes Environmentally and Nitrate Sensitive Areas, Countryside Stewardship and other management schemes, and Moorland, Habitat, Farm Woodland and Organic Farming Schemes.
11 Land area based schemes which replaced the Hill Livestock Compensatory Allowance Scheme in 2001. These are Tir Mynydd in Wales, Less Favoured Area Compensatory Scheme in Northern Ireland, Less Favoured Areas Support Scheme in Scotland and Hill Farm AI.
12 Rent paid on all tenanted land (including 'conacre' land in Northern Ireland) less landlords' expenses, landlords' consumption of fixed capital and the benefit value of dwellings on that land.
13 Rent received by farming landowners from renting of land to other farmers less landlords' expenses. This series starts in 1996 following a revision to the methodology of calculating net rent.
14 Interest charges on loans for current farming purposes and buildings and works less interest on money held on short term deposit.

Source: Department for Environment, Food and Rural Affairs: 01904 455080

21.2 Output and input volume indices[1]
United Kingdom

1995=100

		1992	1993	1994	1995	1996	1997	1998	1999	2000	2001	2002
Outputs[2]												
1. Total cereals:	VQAN	101.0	89.1	91.3	100.0	111.6	106.6	103.2	100.1	108.4	86.6	104.9
wheat	LUKH	98.9	90.1	93.2	100.0	112.2	104.1	107.5	103.4	116.3	81.1	112.0
rye	VQAO	85.7	82.1	92.9	100.0	103.6	103.6	82.1	82.1	78.6	82.1	82.1
barley	LUKI	107.8	88.4	87.4	100.0	112.0	112.7	95.7	94.8	93.8	96.1	89.6
oats and summer cereal mixtures	LUKJ	81.6	77.9	97.4	100.0	95.6	93.6	95.0	87.0	103.4	99.2	118.3
other cereals	VQAP	100.2	93.6	89.1	100.0	87.9	85.2	98.5	146.0	176.2	121.5	139.4
2. Total industrial crops:	VQAQ	108.3	101.4	96.1	100.0	110.3	115.5	113.2	120.5	86.0	82.9	91.3
oil seeds	VQAR	131.2	112.1	103.1	100.0	116.5	131.1	139.8	161.6	81.8	83.7	99.4
oilseed rape	VQAS	112.2	95.8	101.8	100.0	117.5	131.0	134.9	134.7	93.0	96.2	118.0
other oil seeds	LUKN	279.4	239.0	116.0	100.0	107.3	131.7	177.6	374.9	52.9	47.7	22.6
other industrial crops	VQAU	66.9	75.8	81.4	100.0	89.7	80.4	74.3	66.6	67.9	64.3	63.9
fibre plants	VQAV	0.9	12.8	96.7	100.0	131.2	132.4	109.0	106.8	69.5	48.0	24.5
hops	LUKP	116.0	127.8	108.3	100.0	126.2	119.6	81.9	69.8	62.8	56.8	59.8
others[3]	VQAW	67.1	75.6	79.3	100.0	86.0	75.9	72.6	65.0	68.1	65.1	64.9
3. Total forage plants	VQAX	115.1	151.5	124.5	100.0	103.2	116.3	110.2	116.8	123.1	144.8	146.2
4. Total vegetables and horticultural products:	VQAY	108.5	105.3	103.7	100.0	101.2	99.7	97.2	99.2	97.0	91.5	95.1
fresh vegetables	LUKX	113.1	107.1	106.1	100.0	105.4	100.4	98.4	99.3	92.8	86.7	91.2
plants and flowers	LUKZ	101.2	102.3	99.9	100.0	94.7	98.0	95.0	98.5	102.2	97.7	100.0
5. Total potatoes (including seeds)	LUKW	120.8	105.1	98.3	100.0	107.7	102.3	90.4	107.2	94.6	96.3	93.5
6. Total fruit	LUKY	128.8	121.7	106.1	100.0	104.7	70.2	89.4	92.8	84.3	88.2	85.9
7. Other crop products including seeds	VQAZ	102.4	111.9	109.4	100.0	90.7	99.2	91.5	101.4	98.5	96.6	67.3
8. Total crop output (sum 1-7)	VQBA	107.0	99.1	97.1	100.0	108.0	104.5	101.8	104.5	100.1	90.4	99.0
9. Total livestock production	VQBB	97.1	96.6	100.6	100.0	90.5	95.4	97.9	96.0	91.0	84.2	87.5
mainly for meat processing	LULH	96.6	96.2	100.2	100.0	89.3	94.0	97.0	95.3	91.2	82.4	86.2
cattle	LULC	98.0	93.6	100.4	100.0	74.7	81.0	83.6	84.6	82.1	72.9	81.7
pigs	LULE	101.0	102.5	105.7	100.0	101.0	110.2	112.2	102.4	86.3	79.2	76.3
sheep	LULD	103.2	102.0	99.4	100.0	94.2	93.7	99.7	98.8	94.6	67.6	74.9
poultry	LULF	85.5	90.7	96.3	100.0	103.8	106.2	108.6	106.0	106.4	110.9	106.8
other animals	LULG	98.9	100.7	100.1	100.0	101.8	102.3	102.3	101.7	101.7	101.4	101.8
gross fixed capital formation	LULR	101.4	99.5	104.7	100.0	104.3	111.6	107.9	103.9	88.0	102.4	101.9
cattle	LULN	99.0	100.5	100.6	100.0	99.9	98.5	96.0	96.6	84.4	97.8	95.5
pigs	LULP	119.0	113.6	115.6	100.0	109.9	115.5	87.1	97.4	66.5	54.9	88.8
sheep	LULO	111.4	98.1	125.4	100.0	90.8	117.9	122.7	92.4	60.9	97.2	104.1
poultry	LULQ	93.3	89.5	96.0	100.0	138.1	141.0	123.7	130.2	119.6	114.8	108.8
10. Total livestock products	LULM	100.6	101.0	102.2	100.0	99.5	100.8	99.6	101.3	99.2	101.4	103.6
milk	LULI	100.0	100.8	102.4	100.0	99.6	100.5	99.0	101.4	98.6	99.9	101.2
eggs	LULJ	104.1	102.2	101.7	100.0	100.1	103.7	105.5	101.8	105.5	116.6	124.8
raw wool	LULK	105.4	99.7	96.7	100.0	95.1	97.0	103.3	95.3	91.7	76.2	79.5
other animal products	LULL	112.1	111.2	92.6	100.0	85.1	90.7	80.7	95.7	80.4	71.3	75.8
11. Total livestock output (9+10)	VQBC	98.3	98.1	101.2	100.0	93.6	97.3	98.5	97.9	93.8	89.9	92.9
12. Total other agricultural activities	VQBD	87.6	93.0	97.1	100.0	106.4	109.2	116.2	123.9	116.8	122.4	124.3
agricultural services	VQBE	92.8	96.9	98.8	100.0	107.8	109.4	115.2	123.2	115.5	119.7	124.0
leasing out quota	VQBF	66.6	79.0	90.6	100.0	101.5	108.7	121.8	127.8	125.5	156.9	105.0
13. Total inseparable non-agricultural activities	LULX	90.7	97.6	103.1	100.0	108.5	107.5	118.1	118.9	116.2	150.7	130.2

21.2

Output and input volume indices[1]
United Kingdom

continued

1995=100

		1992	1993	1994	1995	1996	1997	1998	1999	2000	2001	2002
14.Gross output(at basic prices) (8+11+12+13)	LULY	100.8	98.2	99.5	100.0	99.5	100.7	100.9	101.8	97.6	92.8	97.2
15.Total subsidies (less taxes) on product	VQEE	107.2	101.5	98.7	100.0	98.4	104.1	105.6	106.7	98.8	84.7	96.2
16.Output at market prices (14-15)	VQEG	100.2	97.8	99.6	100.0	99.7	100.1	100.1	101.0	97.3	94.0	97.4
of which transactions within the agricultural industry												
feed wheat	LULZ	190.4	141.2	145.7	100.0	121.5	176.0	209.9	175.0	120.1	103.0	124.1
feed barley	LUMA	124.3	107.3	105.0	100.0	105.2	125.8	123.5	113.6	112.2	121.1	123.2
feed oats	LUMB	93.7	94.9	119.4	100.0	89.2	81.6	100.1	118.2	108.8	105.5	108.2
seed potatoes	LUMC	132.0	121.4	87.8	100.0	119.1	86.4	79.3	84.4	76.2	60.0	67.5
straw	LUMD	63.6	72.9	77.6	100.0	84.5	73.3	69.5	61.0	64.4	61.2	60.9
contract work	LUME	92.8	96.9	98.8	100.0	107.8	109.4	115.2	123.2	115.5	119.7	124.0
leasing of quota	LUMF	66.6	79.0	90.6	100.0	101.5	108.7	121.8	127.8	125.5	156.9	105.0
total capital formation in livestock	LUMG	101.4	99.5	104.7	100.0	104.5	111.8	108.2	104.2	88.3	102.7	102.2
Intermediate Consumption												
17.Seeds	LUMO	99.5	96.7	98.0	100.0	102.3	99.1	94.8	95.7	93.2	98.1	95.5
cereals	LUMM	92.7	95.9	95.0	100.0	104.5	95.1	83.1	93.0	83.2	91.0	89.5
other	LUMN	103.4	96.9	99.5	100.0	101.3	100.9	100.1	97.2	98.1	101.6	98.4
18.Energy	VQEH	99.9	100.1	97.6	100.0	106.2	103.1	108.0	102.8	90.2	93.8	94.2
electricity	VQEI	98.2	99.0	101.3	100.0	99.6	98.0	106.9	100.3	91.8	100.8	99.2
fuels	VQEJ	101.3	101.0	95.2	100.0	110.7	106.6	108.9	104.7	89.7	90.7	92.2
19.Ferilisers	VQEK	102.7	100.6	93.3	100.0	105.2	115.2	107.9	101.0	88.4	82.4	88.2
20.Pesticides	LUMQ	94.5	96.2	93.3	100.0	103.1	107.0	111.3	108.6	106.9	101.6	105.7
21.Veterinary expenses	LUMW	80.9	88.1	95.3	100.0	102.1	104.1	96.3	90.2	86.4	84.1	83.8
22.Animal feed	LUML	95.6	95.5	100.2	100.0	97.8	94.5	94.7	95.4	91.1	93.5	90.0
compounds[4]	LUMH	95.6	98.4	100.4	100.0	101.3	97.3	94.9	97.5	89.8	92.6	90.7
straights[4]	LUMI	83.7	85.2	96.0	100.0	88.7	79.6	83.6	84.0	88.2	89.8	81.2
feed purchased from other farms	LUMJ	135.2	113.1	114.1	100.0	107.5	133.2	139.8	126.5	113.8	116.5	122.6
23.Total maintenance[5]	VQEL	91.6	93.5	93.5	100.0	97.5	94.6	88.8	87.1	79.1	80.9	81.0
materials	LUMU	93.3	94.4	90.7	100.0	97.7	93.8	91.2	89.1	81.2	80.4	79.9
buildings	LUMT	88.2	91.7	99.0	100.0	97.1	96.3	84.0	83.1	75.1	82.2	83.4
24.Agricultural services	VQEM	92.8	96.9	98.8	100.0	107.8	109.4	115.2	123.2	115.5	119.7	124.0
25.Other goods and services[5,6]	VQEO	94.2	96.1	97.9	100.0	103.1	104.9	99.6	96.8	88.5	86.4	84.9
26.Total intermediate consumption (sum 17-25)	LUNE	95.1	96.0	97.4	100.0	101.4	101.4	99.4	97.8	90.7	90.7	90.4
27.Gross value added at basic prices (14-26)	LUNF	106.7	100.2	101.6	100.0	97.8	100.1	103.0	107.1	106.8	95.3	106.2
28.Total consumption of Fixed Capital	LUNN	94.9	96.5	97.7	100.0	101.9	100.2	99.7	98.0	96.9	95.1	90.5
equipment	LUNI	99.9	98.9	99.2	100.0	101.3	101.2	99.5	97.5	95.0	92.2	89.9
buildings[5,7]	LUNG	100.0	100.1	100.3	100.0	101.4	101.3	100.3	98.7	94.9	96.9	95.2
livestock	VQES	84.1	90.5	93.5	100.0	103.5	97.2	99.6	98.2	105.8	101.4	88.9
cattle	LUNJ	79.7	88.2	88.9	100.0	105.6	93.2	92.3	94.0	106.7	91.9	88.1
pigs	LUNL	104.8	102.2	110.4	100.0	92.7	101.0	108.2	97.5	82.6	56.8	83.2
sheep	LUNK	84.3	88.0	102.6	100.0	96.7	80.6	82.7	92.5	95.8	117.0	76.9
poultry	LUNM	98.4	99.4	99.0	100.0	109.5	142.9	159.5	137.0	139.4	134.2	126.4
29.Net value added at basic prices (27-28)	LUNO	111.6	101.6	103.1	100.0	96.4	100.3	105.1	112.4	112.5	94.8	116.4

1 See chapter text.
2 Output is net of VAT collected on the sale of non-edible products. Figures for total output include subsidies on products, but not other subsidies.
3 Includes straw and minor crops.
4 For years prior to 1992 the split between compounds and straights has been estimated based on the split present in later years.
5 Landlords' expenses are included within farm maintenance, miscellaneous expenditure and depreciation of buildings and works.
6 Includes livestock and crop costs, water costs, insurance premiums, bank charges, professional fees, rates, and other farming costs.
7 A more empirically based methodology for calculating landlords' depreciation was introduced in 2000. The new series has been linked with the old one using a smoothing procedure for the transition year of 1996.

Source: Department for Environment, Food and Rural Affairs: 01904 455080

21.3 Agriculture land-use
United Kingdom
Area at the June census[1]

Thousand hectares

		1992	1993	1994	1995	1996	1997	1998	1999	2000	2001	2002
Total Agricultural area	BFAH	18 849	18 890	18 850	18 746	18 750	18 653	18 604	18 579	18 311	18 555	18 388
Crops	BFAA	4 982	4 520	4 470	4 544	4 722	4 990	4 971	4 709	4 665	4 454	4 573
Bare fallow	BFAB	53	50	46	43	37	29	34	33	37	43	33
Total tillage	KIJR	5 035	4 569	4 516	4 586	4 759	5 020	5 005	4 742	4 702	4 497	4 605
All grass under 5 years old	KFEM	1 584	1 582	1 456	1 407	1 395	1 405	1 301	1 226	1 226	1 205	1 230
Total arable land	KFEN	6 618	6 152	5 972	5 993	6 154	6 425	6 306	5 968	5 928	5 702	5 835
All grasses 5 years old and over	KFEO	5 279	5 274	5 388	5 375	5 354	5 282	5 364	5 449	5 364	5 584	5 422
Total tillage and grass	KFEP	11 897	11 426	11 360	11 368	11 507	11 706	11 671	11 417	11 292	11 286	11 257
Sole right rough grazing	BFAD	4 943	4 879	4 825	4 785	4 760	4 657	4 621	4 575	4 445	4 435	4 484
Set aside[2]	DMNF	160	677	728	633	509	306	313	572	567	800	611
All other land on agricultural holdings including woodland	BFAE	618	680	712	734	751	763	773	789	780	801	802
Total land on agricultural holdings	BFAF	17 619	17 661	17 626	17 520	17 527	17 432	17 377	17 352	17 083	17 323	17 154
Common rough grazing (estimated)	BFAG	1 230	1 229	1 224	1 226	1 223	1 221	1 227	1 227	1 228	1 232	1 234
Crops	BFAA	4 982	4 520	4 470	4 544	4 722	4 990	4 971	4 709	4 665	4 454	4 573
Cereals	BFAJ	3 489	3 033	3 043	3 182	3 359	3 514	3 418	3 141	3 348	3 014	3 245
Wheat	BFAK	2 067	1 759	1 811	1 859	1 976	2 036	2 045	1 847	2 086	1 635	1 996
Barley	BFAL	1 299	1 166	1 108	1 193	1 269	1 359	1 253	1 179	1 128	1 245	1 101
Oats	BFAM	100	92	109	112	96	100	98	92	109	112	126
Mixed corn	BFAN	4	3	3	3	3	2	2	2	2	3	4
Rye[3]	BFAO	8	6	7	8	8	9	10	8	7	5	5
Triticale[4]	DMNH	11	7	6	7	7	8	11	13	16	14	14
Other arable crops (excluding potatoes)	DMNI	1 115	1 128	1 073	993	937	1 125	1 210	1 211	979	1 103	993
Oilseed rape	BFAP	421	377	404	354	356	445	507	417	332	404	357
Sugar beet not for stock feeding[3]	BFAQ	197	197	195	196	199	196	189	183	173	177	169
Hops[5]	DMNJ	4	3	3	3	3	3	3	3	2	1	2
Peas for harvesting dry and field beans	DMNK	208	244	228	195	178	197	213	202	208	276	249
Linseed[2]	DMNL	144	150	58	54	49	73	100	209	71	31	12
Other crops	DMNM	141	157	185	195	204	210	200	197	192	214	204
Potatoes	BFAR	181	171	164	172	178	166	164	178	166	165	158
Horticultural	BFAV	198	188	189	187	189	184	180	179	172	173	176
Vegetables grown in the open	DMNN	135	126	127	130	132	126	125	126	119	120	124
Orchard fruit	BFBG	33	32	32	28	28	30	30	28	28	28	26
Soft fruit	DMNO	14	13	13	12	12	11	10	9	10	9	9
Ornamentals[6]	DMNP	14	14	14	15	14	14	14	13	14	14	15
Glasshouse crops	DMNQ	2	2	2	2	2	2	2	2	2	2	2

1 Includes estimates for minor holdings for all countries. See chapter text.
2 Figures are for Great Britain only in 1992.
3 Figures are for England and Wales only.
4 Figures are for Great Britain only.

5 Figures are for England only.
6 Includes non-commercial orchards.

Source: Agricultural Departments: 01904 455332

21.4 Estimated quantity of crops and grass harvested[1,2]
United Kingdom

Thousand tonnes

		1992	1993	1994	1995	1996	1997	1998	1999	2000	2001	2002
Cereals												
Wheat	KFQA	14 095	12 890	13 320	14 310	16 100	15 020	15 450	14 870	16 700	11 580	15 973
Barley	KFQB	7 368	6 050	5 950	6 840	7 790	7 830	6 620	6 580	6 490	6 660	6 128
Oats	KFQC	503	480	600	615	590	575	585	540	640	621	753
Mixed corn for threshing	KFQD	16	14	13	16	12	11	7	11	13	10	18
Rye for threshing	KFQE	37	30	43	43	51	53	55	43	44	23	29
Maize for threshing	KFQF	1 975	2 730	..	..	..	..	..	..	..	..	..
Potatoes												
Early crop	KFQG	411	426	337	373	325	386	336	341	276	172	235
Main crop	KFQH	7 402	6 647	6 203	6 033	6 900	6 739	6 081	6 759	6 359	6 477	6 732
Fodder crops												
Beans for stockfeeding	KFQI	445	612	454	319	318	377	378	397	450	606	632
Turnips, swedes	KFQJ	760	620	..	..	..	..	..	..	..	..	..
Fodder beet and mangolds	KFQK	710	655	..	..	..	..	..	..	..	..	..
Maize for threshing or stock-feeding	KFQL	..	..	..	..	..	..	..	..	..	..	..
Kale, cabbage, savoys and kohl rabi	KFQN	515	485	..	..	..	..	..	..	..	..	..
Peas harvested dry for stock-feeding	KFQP	209	266	246	229	239	297	259	286	253	285	254
Other crops												
Sugar beet[3,4]	KFQQ	10 148	9 666	8 720	8 431	10 420	11 084	10 002	10 584	9 335	8 335	9 557
Rape grown for oilseed	KFQR	1 166	1 100	1 243	1 224	1 415	1 527	1 566	1 737	1 129	1 157	1 468
Hops[4]	KFQS	5	6	5	4	5	5	4	4	3	3	3
Horticultural crops												
Vegetables grown in the open												
Brussels sprouts	KFQW	115	98	105	78	80	78	72	78	65	55	43
Cabbage (including savoys and spring greens)	KFQX	402	381	401	342	360	310	284	269	254	282	244
Cauliflowers	KFQY	341	310	289	243	237	195	192	172	156	107	116
Carrots	KFQZ	608	591	633	512	624	623	618	673	726	725	755
Parsnips	KFRA	60	64	70	63	75	96	91	97	85	92	101
Turnips and swedes	KFRB	158	141	139	125	139	116	117	123	126	129	119
Beetroot	KFRC	74	93	87	73	72	74	70	63	67	69	56
Onions, Dry bulb	KFRD	235	274	274	225	284	336	342	391	393	375	283
Onions, Salad	KFRE	28	24	25	24	28	26	25	26	19	13	11
Leeks	KFRF	72	60	61	62	54	46	52	51	44	44	38
Broad beans	KFRG	17	11	12	11	10	10	13	12	13	11	12
Runner beans including French	KFRH	39	46	36	30	35	35	30	24	22	19	19
Peas, Green for market	KFRI	6	6	6	8	7	8	7	7	7	6	7
Peas, Green for processing	KFRJ	211	208	181	198	216	168	152	143	177	162	170
Celery	KFRK	44	41	42	39	38	39	35	40	36	43	32
Lettuce	KFRL	206	145	178	192	187	158	152	155	136	123	110
Rhubarb	KFRM	20	20	21	20	20	20	21	23	19	19	19
Protected crops												
Tomatoes	KFRN	122	110	109	113	115	114	108	117	113	109	101
Cucumbers	KFRO	90	104	83	88	86	82	84	84	80	71	74
Lettuce	KFRP	44	37	33	30	27	24	21	20	19	21	23
Fruit crops												
Total Dessert Apples	KFRQ	165.0	167.0	176.0	138.0	105.0	96.0	98.0	134.0	101.0	104.0	84.0
Total Culinary Apples	KFRR	203.0	159.0	130.0	135.0	118.0	91.0	86.0	112.0	107.0	107.0	93.0
Pears	KFRS	31.0	31.0	33.0	30.0	36.0	33.0	26.0	23.0	27.0	39.0	34.0
Plums	KFRT	21.0	12.0	11.0	14.0	20.0	12.0	6.0	9.0	5.0	15.0	12.0
Cherries	KFRU	4.0	2.0	1.0	3.0	4.0	1.0	1.0	1.0	–	1.0	1.0
Soft fruit	KFRV	94.0	93.0	77.0	76.0	81.0	59.0	60.0	65.0	63.0	64.0	63.0

1 For Horticultural crops the output marketed refers to calender year data.
2 Except for sugar beet and hops, the production area for England and Wales is the area returned at the June census together with estimates for very small holdings (known as minor holdings). In Scotland and Northern Ireland the area returned at June is also the production area, except that estimates for minor holdings are included in Scotland for potatoes and in Northern Ireland Ireland for barley, oats and potatoes.

3 Figures are adjusted to constant 16% sugar content.
4 See chapter text.

Source: Agricultural Departments: 01904 455332

21.5 Cattle, sheep, pigs and poultry on agricultural holdings[1]
United Kingdom
At June each year

Thousands

		1992	1993	1994	1995	1996	1997	1998	1999	2000	2001	2002
Total cattle and calves	BFCG	11 924	11 851	11 954	11 857	12 040	11 637	11 519	11 423	11 135	10 602	10 345
of which:												
dairy cows	BFCH	2 683	2 668	2 716	2 603	2 587	2 478	2 439	2 440	2 336	2 251	2 227
beef cows	BFCI	1 731	1 784	1 809	1 840	1 864	1 862	1 947	1 924	1 842	1 708	1 657
heifers in calf	BFCJ	768	803	775	775	818	848	787	763	718	701	728
Total sheep and lambs	BFCM	44 540	44 436	43 813	43 304	42 086	42 823	44 471	44 656	42 264	36 716	35 834
of which:												
ewes and shearlings	CKUQ	20 732	20 881	20 861	20 830	20 550	20 696	21 260	21 458	20 449	17 921	17 630
lambs under one year old	BFCP	22 607	22 394	21 758	21 350	20 443	21 032	22 138	22 092	20 857	17 769	17 310
Total pigs	BFCQ	7 707	7 853	7 892	7 627	7 590	8 072	8 146	7 284	6 482	5 845	5 588
of which:												
sows in pig and other sows for breeding	CKUU	683	698	691	654	649	683	675	603	537	527	483
gilts in pig	CKUR	110	117	106	101	107	116	103	85	73	71	74
Total fowls	KPSV	124 842	131 093	126 653	127 035	..	..	..	..	..	..	..
of which:												
table fowls including broilers	CKUT	73 748	79 940	75 696	77 177	..	..	98 244	101 625	105 689	112 531	105 137
laying fowls[2]	CKUV	33 348	32 965	32 682	31 837	..	34 286	29 483	29 258	28 687	29 895	28 778
growing pullets	CKUW	10 849	10 750	10 388	10 210	..	11 510	9 860	9 583	9 461	9 367	9 784

1 Includes estimates for minor holdings for all countries. See chapter text.
2 Excludes fowls laying eggs for hatching.

Sources: Department for Environment, Food and Rural Affairs;
Farming Statistics: 01904 455332

21.6 Forestry[1]
United Kingdom

Woodland area[2] - (Thousand hectares)	1980	1990	1999	2000	2001	2002	2003
United Kingdom	2 175	2 400	2 775	2 793	2 790	2 800	2 807
England[3]	948	958	1 097	1 103	1 100[4]	1 104	1 110
Scotland[3]	920	1 120	1 308	1 318	1 317[4]	1 324	1 327
Wales[3]	241	248	288	289	289	288	285
Northern Ireland	67	74	82	83	83	84	85
Forestry Commission / Forest Service	946	956	891	886	861[4]	855	848
Other[5]	1 230	1 443	1 884	1 907	1 929	1 945	1 960
Conifer	1 372	1 576	1 656	1 663	1 660	1 658	1 652
Broadleaved[6]	804	824	1 120	1 131	1 130	1 143	1 155

	1992/93	1993/94	1994/95	1995/96	1996/97	1997/98	1998/99	1999/00	2000/01	2001/02	2002/03
New Planting[7] - (Thousand hectares)											
United Kingdom	19.0	18.6	19.9	16.4	17.2	16.7	16.7	17.4	18.3	13.9	13.0
England	5.1	6.2	5.1	4.4	4.4	4.1	4.9	5.5	5.5	4.9	5.3
Scotland	12.1	10.5	13.4	10.6	11.7	11.4	10.5	10.4	11.7	8.0	6.7
Wales	0.4	0.6	0.6	0.4	0.4	0.5	0.6	0.7	0.4	0.3	0.3
Northern Ireland	1.3	1.3	0.9	1.0	0.8	0.6	0.7	0.8	0.7	0.7	0.6
Forestry Commission / Forest Service	2.8	1.8	1.2	0.6	0.6	0.2	0.2	0.3	0.3	0.8	0.9
Other[8]	16.2	16.8	18.7	15.8	16.6	16.4	16.5	17.2	18.0	13.1	12.1
Conifer	10.1	7.4	9.4	7.4	7.7	7.0	6.6	6.5	5.2	3.9	4.0
Broadleaved	8.9	11.2	10.5	8.9	9.5	9.7	10.1	10.9	13.2	10.0	8.9
Restocking[7] - (Thousand hectares)											
United Kingdom	17.0	16.8	14.6	13.9	15.0	14.1	14.0	15.1	15.2	13.7	14.3
England	6.7	6.4	4.9	4.2	4.3	4.3	4.0	3.8	3.8	3.3	3.2
Scotland	7.5	7.6	6.6	6.8	7.2	6.3	6.3	8.0	8.0	7.8	8.5
Wales	2.4	2.4	2.6	2.3	3.0	2.7	3.0	2.6	2.2	1.9	1.9
Northern Ireland	0.5	0.5	0.6	0.6	0.6	0.7	0.6	0.6	1.1	0.8	0.7
Forestry Commission / Forest Service	8.9	8.4	8.4	8.4	8.4	8.5	8.5	8.8	8.9	9.1	9.1
Other[8]	8.1	8.5	6.2	6.6	6.6	5.6	5.6	6.3	6.2	4.6	5.2
Conifer	11.5	11.5	11.0	10.9	11.4	11.2	11.3	11.9	12.2	11.4	12.0
Broadleaved	5.5	5.3	3.6	3.0	3.4	2.9	2.8	3.2	2.9	2.3	2.3

	1995	1996	1997	1998	1999	2000	2001	2002
Wood Production (volume - Thousand m³ overbark standing)								
United Kingdom	8 830	8 730	9 150	9 070	9 580	9730	9 730	9 940
Great Britain								
Softwood	7 610	7 610	7 990	8 000	8 510	8 630	8 630	8 840
Forestry Commission	4 130	4 290	4 570	4 830	5 440	5 530	5 140	5 210
Private Woodland	3 480	3 320	3 420	3 170	3 070	3 100	3 490	3 630
Hardwood[9]	970	870	890	790	750	720	710	690
Northern Ireland[10]	250	250	260	290	320	380	400	410

1 See chapter text.
2 Areas as at 31 March.
3 For England, Scotland and Wales, 1980 woodland area figures are the published results from the 1979-1982 Census of Woodlands and Trees and figures for 1990 are adjusted to reflect subsequent changes. From 1998 onwards they are based on results from the 1995-1999 National Inventory of Woodlands and Trees, adjusted to reflect subsequent changes.
4 The apparent fall in woodland cover in 2001 is due to the reclassification of Forestry Commission open land within the forest.
5 "Other" is private woodland and non-Forestry Commission / Forest Service public woodland.

6 Broadleaved includes coppice. For data based on 1979-82 Census, all scrub and other non-plantation woodland have been assumed to be broadleaved.
7 Figures shown are for the areas of new planting and restocking in the year to 31 March.
8 "Other" figures are for grant aided planting on non-Forestry Commission/ Forest Service woodland. They exclude areas planted without the aid of grants.
9 Hardwood is timber from broadleaved species. Most hardwood production comes from private woodlands; the figures are estimates based on reported deliveries to wood processing industries.
10 Most Northern Ireland production is from the Forest Service. The figures shown include Forest Service estimates of private sector production.

Sources: Forest Service Agency;
Department of Agriculture and Rural Development (Northern Ireland);
Forestry Commission: 0131 334 0303

21.7 Sales for food of agricultural produce and livestock
United Kingdom

			1992	1993	1994	1995	1996	1997	1998	1999	2000	2001	2002
Cereals:		Thousand											
Wheat[1]	KCQK	tonnes	4 212	3 865	4 234	4 668	4 842	4 737	4 676	4 826	4 707	4 885	4 768
Barley	KCQL	"	3 599	2 762	3 190	3 776	3 692	3 411	3 483	3 412	3 750	2 611	2 927
Oats[2]	KCQM	"	222	208	215	216	235	259	273	270	263	283	311
Potatoes[3]	KCQN	"	6 008	6 382	6 519	5 961	6 146	6 279	5 997	6 210	6 675	6 606	6 874
Milk[4]:													
Milk utilised for liquid consumption	KCQO	Million litres	6 966	7 026	6 926	6 922	6 838	6 748	6 739	6 853	6 768	6 761	..
Milk utilised for manufacture	KCQP	Million litres	6 876	6 880	7 134	6 918	6 934	7 059	6 821	6 988	6 550	6 715	..
Total milk available for domestic use[5]	KCQQ	Million litres	14 189	14 228	14 420	14 255	14 194	14 258	13 973	14 234	13 737	13 942	..
Hen eggs in shell	KCQR	Million dozens	806	791	787	774	775	794	792	743	747	806	854
Animals slaughtered:													
Cattle and calves:													
Cattle	KCQS	Thousands	3 383	2 944	3 089	3 266	2 291	2 264	2 297	2 217	2 275	2 072	2 184
Calves	KCQT	"	33	19	22	26	24	20	32	75	152	92	98
Total	KCQU	"	3 416	2 963	3 111	3 292	2 315	2 284	2 329	2 292	2 427	2 164	2 282
Sheep and lambs	KCQV	"	19 428	18 864	18 962	19 311	18 049	16 660	18 688	19 116	18 442	12 964	14 993
Pigs:													
Clean pigs	MBGD	"	14 143	14 265	14 681	14 021	13 897	15 132	15 470	14 293	12 370	10 446	10 260
Sows and boars	KCQZ	"	373	356	389	355	324	363	415	379	321	180	314
Total	KCRA	"	14 515	14 620	15 069	14 376	14 221	15 496	15 885	14 671	12 692	10 626	10 575
Poultry:[6] slaughtered	KCRB	Millions	696	721	761	783	823	850	856	848	843	866	851

Note: The figures for cereals and for animals slaughtered relate to periods of 52 weeks

1 Flour millers' receipts of home-grown wheat.
2 Oatmeal millers' receipts of home-grown oats.
3 Total sales for human consumption in the UK.
4 Data to 1994 sourced from the Milk Marketing Boards. Data from 1995 sourced from surveys run by the agricultural departments. 1994 includes two months of data sourced from the surveys run by the agricultural departments.

5 The totals of liquid consumption and milk used for manufacture may not add up to the total available for domestic use because of adjustments for dairy wastage, stock changes and other uses, such as farmhouse consumption, milk fed to stock and on farm waste.
6 Total fowls, ducks, geese and turkeys.

Source: Department for Environment, Food and Rural Affairs: 01904 455332

21.8 Stocks of food and feedingstuffs[1]
United Kingdom

At end-December in each year

Thousand tonnes

		1992	1993	1994	1995	1996	1997	1998	1999	2000	2001	2002
Wheat and flour (as wheat)	KCRC	1 839	1 255	1 236	1 074	1 031	992	1 000	869	826	719	823
Barley (GB only)	KCRD	2 028	1 401	1 375	1 542	1 502	1 441	1 296	1 373	1 340	1 278	1 231
Maize	KCRE	109	23	32	33	25	45	67	43	37	36	66
Oilcake and meal[2]	KCRF	107	92	108	103	89	79	69	72	..	..	..
Oilseeds and nuts (crude oil equivalent)	KCRG	11	17	28	34	25	18	12	18	..	..	..
Vegetable oil (as crude oil)	KCRI	94	90	109	96	100	99	98	97	82	..	..
Marine oil (as crude oil)	KCRJ	8	8	18	17	10	4	–	–	–	..	..
Butter[3]	KCRK	63	34	19	11	14	7	11	22	17	18	..
Meat and offal[4]	KCRL	218	199	103	77	129	162	157	84	54	57	49
Raw coffee[5]	KCRM	10	12	13	11	8	7	8	7	8	13	9
Tea[6]	KCRN	40	44	43	38	39	37	38	38	28	31	29
Sugar	KCRO	888	1 069	1 016	766	807	1 003	928	..	..	..	..

1 Recorded stocks, including stocks in bond or held by the main processors.
2 Excluding castor meal, cocoa cake and meal.
3 In addition to stocks in public cold stores surveyed by DEFRA, closing stocks include all intervention stocks in private cold stores.

4 Stocks of imported and home-produced meat and offal held in public cold stores, excluding poultrymeat, bacon and ham.
5 Including manufacturers' stocks and additional public warehouses.
6 Covering stocks held by primary wholesalers and held in public/private warehouses.

Source: Department for Environment, Food and Rural Affairs: 01904 455332

21.9 Processed food and animal feedingstuffs: production
United Kingdom

Thousand tonnes

		1992	1993	1994	1995	1996	1997	1998	1999	2000	2001	2002
Flour milling:												
Wheat milling: total	KFTA	5 022	5 236	5 290	5 338	5 501	5 535	5 707	5 668	5 617	5 667	5 616
Home produced	KFTB	4 192	3 781	4 106	4 598	4 772	4 667	4 582	4 701	4 609	4 790	4 648
Imported	KFTC	830	1 455	1 184	740	729	868	1 125	966	1 008	877	968
Flour produced	KFTD	3 975	4 120	4 232	4 294	4 454	4 439	4 526	4 497	4 486	4 487	4 413
Offals produced	KFTE	1 045	1 123	1 078	1 079	1 111	1 111	1 221	1 181	1 148	1 169	1 179
Oat milling:												
Oats milled by oatmeal millers	KFTF	225	207	209	217	250	259	272	266	261	287	312
Products of oat milling	KFTG	124	105	102	110	123	129	154	157	155	171	186
Seed crushing:												
Oilseeds and nuts processed	KFTH	1 807	1 903	2 035	2 122	2 466	2 587	2 683	2 398	2 380	2 252	2 332
Crude oil produced, including production of maize oil	KFTI	636	658	739	779	862	909	915	832	820	786	805
Oilcake and meal produced, excluding castor meal, cocoa cake and meal	KFTJ	1 125	1 187	1 242	1 305	1 541	1 614	1 687	1 484	1 475	1 396	1 451
Production of home-killed meat: total including												
meat subsequently canned	KFTK	2 391	2 260	2 380	2 383	2 084	2 157	2 273	2 139	2 064	1 767	1 881
Beef	KFTL	970	858	915	973	701	695	704	675	703	649	690
Veal	KFTM	1	1	1	1	1	1	1	2	4	2	3
Mutton and lamb	KFTN	362	349	352	364	345	321	356	361	361	259	300
Pork	KFTO	786	783	807	752	769	871	934	826	727	606	632
Offal[1]	KFTP	272	268	305	293	268	269	278	275	269	249	256
Production of poultry meat[2]	KFTQ	1 226	1 289	1 344	1 397	1 461	1 502	..	..	..	..	..
Production of bacon and ham, including meat subsequently canned	KFTR	189	216	233	247	243	242	240	237	214	203	200
Production of milk products:												
Butter[3]	KFTS	127	141	148	133	130	139	137	141	132	126	..
Cheese (including farmhouse)	KFTT	332	338	341	362	377	377	366	368	340	395	..
Condensed milk: includes skim concentrate and condensed milk used in manufacture of chocolate crumb	KFTU	206	191	196	181	206	214	192	177	162	161	..
Milk powder: excluding buttermilk and whey powder												
Full cream	KFTV	84	71	83	90	83	96	97	102	105	83	..
Skimmed	KFTW	106	132	142	117	108	109	107	102	83	71	..
Cream, fresh and sterilised; including farm cream[3]	KFTX	240	255	274	281	281	268	266	275	270	263	..
Sugar: production from home-grown sugar-beet (as refined sugar)	KFTY	1 472	1 433	1 263	1 469	1 324	1 524	1 439	1 548	1 325	1 222	1 430
Production of compound fats:												
Margarine and other table spreads	KFTZ	477	493	487	490	491	461	448	421	388	409	410
Solid cooking fats	KFUA	116	129	109	110	123	109	131	125	135	121	116
Production of other processed foods:												
Syrup and treacle[4]	KFUC	49	52	50	48	..	..	..	..	..	..	..
Chocolate confectionery	KSJS	532	563	573	592	608	569	567	553	544	559	584
Sugar confectionery	KSJT	300	302	322	322	351	345	337	317	307	322	338
Cocoa beans excluding re-exports	KFVX	159	171	163	160	189	174	172	168	..	..	..
Breakfast cereals, other than oatmeal and oatmeal flakes	KFUJ	303	302	325	335	343	359	349	354	334	344	343
Glucose	KFUM	568	580	593	607	642	637	644	630	657	701	727
Compound feedingstuffs: total	KFUP	10 514	11 141	11 402	11 609	11 801	11 304	11 206	11 404	10 612	..	..
Cattle food	KFUQ	4 098	4 271	4 347	4 476	4 430	3 926	3 844	4 264	4 039	..	..
Calf food	KFUR	242	261	286	307	277	227	198	187	190	..	..
Pig food	KFUS	2 489	2 561	2 547	2 453	2 566	2 659	2 740	2 435	2 089	..	..
Poultry food	KFUT	2 737	3 123	3 179	3 243	3 280	3 324	3 213	3 139	3 063	..	..
Other compounds	KFUU	948	925	1 043	1 130	1 249	1 168	1 210	1 378	1 231	..	..

Note: The figures relate to periods of 52 weeks (53 weeks in 1992 and 1998) with the following exceptions which are on a calendar year basis: butter, cheese, cream, canned meat, soft drinks, condensed milk and milk powder, canned vegetables, canned and bottled fruit, jam and marmalade, and soups.

1 Including poultry offal.
2 Total of fowl, ducks, geese and turkeys (carcase weight).
3 Includes cream from the residual elements of low fat milk production.
4 This survey ceased at the end of 1995.

Source: Department for Environment, Food and Rural Affairs: 01904 455332

21.10 Food and animal feedingstuffs: disposals

Thousand tonnes

		1992	1993	1994	1995	1996	1997	1998	1999	2000	2001	2002
Flour	KFPU	3 932	4 076	4 200	4 293	4 457	4 434	4 529	4 487	4 489	4 481	4 408
Sugar (as refined sugar): total disposals	KFPV	2 319	2 154	2 196	2 177	2 200	2 040	2 143	..	..	..	..
For food in the United Kingdom[1]	KFPW	2 292	2 123	2 165	2 157	2 180	2 007	2 106	..	..	..	..
Syrup and treacle[2]	KFPX	49	52	50	48	..	..	..	..	..	..	..
Meat and fish:												
Fresh and frozen meat and offal, including usage for canning:												
Beef and veal	KFPY	1 145	1 094	1 228	1 206	804	865	872	942	921	907	995
Mutton and lamb	KFPZ	497	470	474	504	501	468	496	497	496	373	423
Pork	KFVA	877	895	922	917	954	1 035	1 113	1 059	997	861	940
Offal[3]	KFVB	335	316	351	354	312	320	316	324	328	305	316
Poultry-meat[4,5]	KFVC	1 328	1 361	1 459	1 500	1 581	1 560	1 649	1 696	1 707	1 714	1 696
Bacon and ham, including usage for canning	KFVD	428	453	457	476	505	481	472	466	483	483	493
Dairy products:												
Butter	KFVI	258	279	284	255	240	256	238	244	255	241	..
Cheese	KFVJ	560	523	559	577	617	614	632	645	595	663	..
Condensed milk[6]	KFVK	218	202	208	195	217	229	205	190	177	172	..
Milk powder, excluding buttermilk and whey powder:												
Full cream	KFVM	91	75	91	97	94	105	107	112	117	88	..
Skimmed	KFVN	136	144	149	138	95	103	91	127	162	86	..
Hen eggs in shell[7]	KFVO	831	821	837	818	833	838	819	795	822	912	982
Oils (as crude oil):												
Vegetable oil	KFVP	1 488	1 492	1 567	1 905	1 960	2 010	1 780	2 449	2 452	2 052	..
Marine oil for the manufacture of margarine and compound fat	KFVQ	114	95	91	105	100	52	31	8	8	2	2
Potatoes	KFVR	7 876	8 288	7 835	7 055	7 661	7 938	7 626	7 584	8 297	7 793	8 402
Other foods:												
Chocolate confectionery	KFVT	640	667	696	674	698	672	697	670	672	666	668
Sugar confectionery, excluding medicated	KFVU	367	366	382	380	410	420	415	393	393	400	387
Tea excluding re-exports	KFVV	147	157	149	141	148	152	145	133	144	133	136
Raw coffee	KFVW	108	116	119	105	116	118	122	115	109	105	116
Barley:												
For brewing and distilling and for food	KFVY	3 436	2 682	3 092	3 574	3 579	3 439	3 502	3 324	3 646	..	..
Maize (including maize meal): total disposals	KFVZ	1 451	1 437	1 367	1 411	1 389	1 439	1 448	1 256	1 183	1 219	1 057
Animal feed	KCRT	166	175	158	156	174	184	197	216	230	235	96
Oilcake and meal	KCRQ	3 646	3 891	4 152	4 462	4 429	4 041	3 677	4 035	..	..	..
Wheat milling offals	KCRR	1 086	1 170	1 121	1 131	1 157	1 158	1 273	1 209	1 176	1 205	1 220
Fish and poultry meal for animal feed,[8] figures relate to sales	KCRS	430	382	385	378	257	233	216	194	193	..	..

Note: The figures relate to periods of 52 weeks with the following exceptions which are on a calendar year basis: fish and potatoes; condensed milk; milk powder; butter and sugar.

1 Including sugar used in the manufacture of other foods subsequently exported. Excluding sugar in imported manufactured foods.
2 This survey ceased at the end of 1995.
3 Including poultry offal.
4 Carcase weight.
5 Total of fowls, ducks, geese and turkeys.
6 Includes skim concentrate and condensed milk used in the manufacture of chocolate crumb.
7 Million dozen eggs
8 Before a ban on 29 March 1996 this included poultry meat as well as mammalian meat and bonemeal.

Source: Department for Environment, Food and Rural Affairs: 01904 455332

21.11 Average weekly earnings and hours of male agricultural workers[1,2,3,4]
England and Wales
At September in each year

		1998	1999	2000	2001	2002	2003
Average weekly earnings (£)	LQML	301.24	301.22	298.24	332.66	366.82	352.88
95% confidence interval		(+/-£12.69)	(+/-£11.88)	(+/-£13.84)	(+/-£15.08)	(+/-£18.88)	(+/-£30.30)
Average weekly hours worked	LQMM	50.7	50.9	49.0	51.9	54.1	51.1
95% confidence interval		(+/-1.5)	(+/-1.4)	(+/-1.4)	(+/-1.7)	(+/-2.1)	(+/-3.0)
Average earnings/hours (£)	LQMN	5.94	5.92	6.09	6.42	6.78	6.91
95% confidence interval		(+/-£0.18)	(+/-£0.15)	(+/-£0.18)	(+/-£0.20)	(+/-£0.19)	(+/-£0.31)
Number of workers in the sample		274	292	234	251	204	72

1 See chapter text.

Source: Department for Environment, Food and Rural Affairs: 01904 455332

21.12 Average weekly earnings and hours of different types of agricultural workers[1]
England and Wales
At September 2003

	Full-time		Part-time[3]		Casual[4]		Managers
	Male	Female	Male	Female	Male	Female	
Average weekly earnings (£)	352.88	267.51	121.66	117.30	236.02	120.22	471.76
95% confidence interval	(+/-£30.30)	(+/-£23.84)	(+/-£20.43)	(+/-£15.27)	(+/-£37.00)	(+/-£39.78)	(+/-£45.36)
Average weekly hours worked	51.1	41.6	20.3	21.5	37.8	22.6	..
95% confidence interval	(+/-3.0)	(+/-1.4)	(+/-3.2)	(+/-2.5)	(+/-5.3)	(+/-7.2)	
Average earnings/hour (£)	6.91	6.43	5.99	5.47	6.24	5.33	..
95% confidence interval	(+/-£0.31)	(+/-£0.51)	(+/-£0.41)	(+/-£0.38)	(+/-£0.32)	(+/-£0.41)	
Number of workers in the sample	72	43	43	35	52	21	50

1 See chapter text.

Source: Department for Environment, Food and Rural Affairs: 01904 455332

21.13 Number of workers employed in agriculture [1,2]
United Kingdom
At June

Thousands

	Regular workers					Seasonal or casual workers			All workers			Salaried managers[3]
		Whole - time		Part - time								
	Total	Male	Female	Male	Female	Total	Male	Female	Total	Male	Female	
	BANC	BAMY	BAMZ	BANA	BANB	BANF	BAND	BANE	BANI	BANG	BANH	KAYG
1992	169.9	99.9	14.8	29.1	26.1	86.2	54.4	31.9	256.2	183.3	72.8	7.8
1993	165.3	96.5	13.7	29.8	25.3	85.4	55.0	30.4	250.7	181.3	69.4	7.6
1994	161.0	93.6	13.2	30.0	24.2	82.2	53.9	28.4	243.2	177.5	65.7	7.8
1995	157.4	90.4	13.0	30.0	24.1	83.7	56.5	27.2	241.2	176.8	64.3	7.7
1996	156.4	89.2	12.6	31.2	23.4	81.5	55.6	25.8	237.9	176.0	61.9	7.8
1997	154.4	87.5	12.6	31.2	23.1	80.9	55.3	25.5	235.2	174.0	61.2	7.8
1998[4,5]	155.6	88.0	13.1	29.7	24.7	79.5	55.6	23.8	235.0	172.8	62.2	12.1
1999	144.7	82.7	11.9	27.5	22.6	73.0	51.8	21.2	217.7	162.0	55.6	13.8
2000	128.9	73.4	10.3	24.6	20.6	64.4	45.9	18.5	193.3	143.9	49.4	11.1
2001[6]	120.8	69.0	10.9	22.0	18.9	63.2	44.6	18.6	184.0	135.6	48.5	13.4
	123.4	70.3	11.2	22.5	19.4	64.1	45.4	18.8	187.6	138.2	49.4	14.1
2002	116.3	64.7	11.5	21.7	18.4	64.2	46.2	18.0	193.9	132.6	47.9	13.4

1 Includes estimates for minor holdings for all countries.
2 Figures exclude school children, farmers, partners, directors and their spouses and most trainees.
3 Great Britain only.
4 Results from 1998 onwards are not comparable with previous years, due to changes in the labour questions on the June Agricultural and Horticultural Census in England, Wales and Scotland.

5 From 1998, all farmers managing holdings for limited companies or other institutions in England and Wales were asked to classify themselves as salaried managers.
6 Due to an English register improvement only the top figure for 2001 is directly comparable with June 2000, while the bottom figure for 2001 is only comparable with June 2002.

Sources: Department for Environment, Food and Rural Affairs; Farming Statistics: 01904 455332

21.14 Landings of fish by United Kingdom vessels: live weight and value[1] into United Kingdom

		Quantity (thousand tonnes)							Value (£ thousand)					
		1997	1998	1999	2000	2001	2002		1997	1998	1999	2000	2001	2002
Total all species	KSJU	593.3	552.5	506.5	464.7	458.3	465.6	KSLN	467 694	484 005	464 131	422 063	423 687	414 689
Total wet fish	KSJV	467.2	428.3	389.8	337.6	332.1	334.9	KSLO	314 712	323 297	297 831	268 816	256 364	250 845
Brill	KSJX	0.5	0.4	0.3	0.4	0.4	0.4	KSLP	2 244	1 674	1 405	1 839	2 032	1 785
Catfish	KSJY	1.0	0.8	0.7	0.8	0.7	0.5	KSLQ	1 152	1 070	1 006	1 081	896	738
Cod	KSJZ	71.0	72.7	46.8	37.0	28.1	25.7	KSLR	67 641	79 450	62 587	50 635	37 368	35 009
Dogfish	KSKA	8.6	7.4	6.9	7.3	7.0	5.8	KSLS	5 586	5 535	5 295	5 862	6 280	5 433
Haddock	KSKB	82.6	82.8	71.3	50.3	42.3	51.9	KSLT	44 778	57 131	59 286	51 181	36 295	34 631
Hake	KSKC	2.7	2.5	3.9	3.5	2.2	2.1	KSLU	6 375	5 117	7 839	6 941	5 303	5 646
Lemon Soles	KSKD	5.2	4.7	4.5	4.0	3.6	2.3	KSLV	11 786	10 620	10 374	9 934	9 937	7 313
Ling	KSKE	9.4	10.0	8.8	7.6	6.9	7.2	KSLW	6 568	8 291	8 502	7 571	7 384	7 654
Megrims	KSKF	6.0	5.3	5.0	5.0	4.3	4.0	KSLX	9 467	8 573	9 326	8 914	7 035	7 991
Monks or Anglers	KSKG	25.6	18.5	15.5	14.7	15.1	13.1	KSLY	45 947	38 540	35 591	33 609	33 789	27 927
Plaice	KSKH	12.9	11.5	9.5	8.6	7.7	5.9	KSLZ	15 484	13 185	12 549	9 869	9 011	6 645
Pollack (Lythe)	KSKI	3.0	2.6	2.3	2.5	2.6	2.5	KSMA	2 491	2 423	2 734	3 197	3 300	3 026
Saithe	KSKJ	12.3	10.1	10.4	10.2	9.7	9.9	KSMB	4 894	4 971	4 878	4 089	4 258	4 130
Sand Eels	KSKK	14.5	11.6	6.8	9.7	1.3	1.2	KSMC	815	742	283	400	..	55
Skates and Rays	KSKL	7.2	6.8	5.6	5.5	5.5	5.3	KSMD	6 215	6 403	5 380	5 677	5 679	5 299
Soles	KSKM	2.3	2.0	2.0	1.9	2.1	2.1	KSME	14 800	13 960	13 829	11 295	13 223	12 751
Turbot	KSKN	0.7	0.6	0.5	0.5	0.5	0.6	KSMF	4 263	3 614	2 918	2 859	3 277	4 192
Whiting	KSKO	34.5	26.7	25.4	23.3	15.1	11.4	KSMG	15 939	13 380	14 010	14 317	9 913	6 603
Whiting, Blue	KSKP	12.4	27.8	38.4	17.7	20.0	8.6	KSMH	693	2 003	1 476	743	936	561
Witches	KSKQ	2.3	1.9	2.2	2.4	2.7	2.2	KSMI	2 263	1 587	2 202	2 352	2 678	2 478
Other Demersal[2]	KSKR	13.2	12.7	15.7	14.6	17.7	15.1	KSMJ	16 000	15 612	18 559	16 025	19 765	18 513
Total Demersal[3]	KSKS	327.9	319.3	282.6	227.3	195.5	178.1	KSMK	285 402	293 882	280 028	248 392	218 414	198 381
Herring[4]	KSKT	57.4	39.5	45.3	39.5	43.8	42.5	KSML	6 430	4 897	5 057	4 073	10 447	6 873
Horse Mackerel	KSKU	5.5	5.1	2.1	2.7	3.5	1.8	KSMM	878	783	304	440	587	367
Mackerel[4]	KSKV	63.2	54.4	41.3	54.6	63.9	96.6	KSMN	19 822	21 754	9 544	13 848	23 877	42 694
Pilchards	KSKW	4.7	4.7	3.5	2.9	6.8	5.8	KSMO	696	765	550	602	1 665	1 005
Sprats	KSKX	8.3	5.0	14.3	8.3	5.1	5.7	KSMP	1 386	1 112	2 053	1 040	607	677
Tuna	KSKY	..	..	0.1	..	..	-	KSMQ	46	44	111	20	..	-
Other Pelagic	KSKZ	0.1	0.2	0.6	2.3	3.6	4.4	KSMR	52	60	184	401	762	848
Total Pelagic	KSLA	139.3	108.9	107.2	110.3	126.7	156.8	KSMS	29 309	29 416	17 803	20 424	37 949	52 464
Cockles	KSLB	19.5	12.1	14.2	20.3	19.0	14.3	KSMT	3 632	4 162	2 526	2 953	3 832	4 170
Crabs	KSLC	22.5	27.2	23.0	25.7	25.0	23.3	KSMU	24 264	32 290	26 983	28 036	27 830	26 014
Lobsters	KSLD	1.5	1.6	1.8	1.2	1.1	1.2	KSMV	13 060	14 489	14 928	12 458	11 436	11 680
Mussels	KSLE	9.6	12.7	8.4	7.5	14.9	17.2	KSMW	3 102	3 502	2 107	1 442	4 835	4 515
Nephrops	KSLF	31.1	28.6	31.1	28.3	28.4	28.4	KSMX	63 480	56 810	74 327	60 778	68 433	68 754
Periwinkles	KSLG	2.9	2.0	1.2	1.1	0.8	0.2	KSMY	2 735	1 892	1 165	1 089	791	221
Queens	KSLH	5.6	8.1	5.9	5.3	8.7	10.8	KSMZ	1 954	2 887	2 563	2 292	3 667	4 156
Scallops	KSLI	18.5	20.1	19.1	19.7	19.5	18.8	KSNA	27 576	30 156	29 145	30 741	29 853	27 963
Shrimps/Prawns	KSLJ	1.0	2.2	2.0	1.6	2.6	1.5	KSNB	960	2 594	2 931	2 062	3 566	2 574
Squid	KSLK	1.6	2.2	2.1	1.4	1.4	2.1	KSNC	4 044	4 362	4 190	2 716	3 903	4 908
Other shellfish	KSLL	12.2	7.6	8.0	14.8	14.9	13.1	KSND	8 176	7 564	5 434	8 680	9 177	8 889
Total shellfish	KSLM	126.1	124.2	116.7	127.0	136.2	130.7	KSNE	152 983	160 708	166 299	153 247	167 323	163 844

1 See chapter text.
2 Includes roes and livers.
3 Includes fish roes.

4 Includes transshipments, i.e. caught by UK boats but not actually landing at UK ports. These quantities are transshipped to foreign vessels in coastal waters and are later recorded as exports.

Source: Department for Environment, Food and Rural Affairs: 01904 455332

21.15 United Kingdom fishing fleet[1]
At 31 December each year

Numbers

		1992	1993	1994	1995	1996	1997	1998	1999	2000	2001	2002
By size												
10m and under	KSNF	7 376	7 666	7 195	6 320	5 606	5 474	5 487	5 409	5 273	5 227	5 287
10.01 - 12.19m	KSNG	1 450	1 361	1 167	1 016	800	732	628	577	547	536	514
12.20 - 17.00m	KSNH	787	751	680	622	540	523	491	468	467	442	409
17.01 - 18.29m	KSNI	232	220	193	187	164	162	154	154	131	143	129
18.30 - 24.38m	KSNJ	697	657	610	574	509	471	443	414	406	405	322
24.39 - 30.48m	KSNK	200	210	211	212	223	227	226	224	219	218	185
30.49 - 36.58m	KSNL	120	124	126	127	114	104	89	80	77	75	65
over 36.58m	KSNM	117	119	116	117	117	119	121	122	122	123	122
Total over 10m	KSNN	3 603	3 442	3 103	2 855	2 467	2 338	2 152	2 039	1 969	1 942	1 746
Total UK fleet (excluding Islands)	KSNO	10 979	11 108	10 297	9 174	8 073	7 812	7 639	7 448	7 242	7 169	7 033
By segment												
Pelagic gears	KSNP	76	69	68	67	58	49	50	46	44	47	45
Beam trawl	KSNQ	227	240	212	220	215	153	123	114	111	116	113
Demersal trawls and seines	KXET	..	..	..	..	1 040	..	..	..	..	..	..
Demersal trawls	KSIX	1 039	988	854	856	..	..	..	..	..	..	..
Nephrop trawls	KSIY	566	560	593	528	411	..	..	..	..	..	..
Seines	KSIZ	255	203	197	165	..	..	..	..	..	..	..
Demersal, Seines and Nephrops	JZCI	..	..	..	..	..	1 428	1 318	1 235	1 208	1 158	969
Lines and Nets	KSNR	339	329	300	267	224	214	187	172	165	146	136
Shellfish: mobile	KSNS	214	181	206	194	265	227	241	243	211	229	228
Shellfish: fixed	KSNT	306	312	305	283	339	352	311	301	297	301	304
Distant water	KSNU	16	14	13	12	15	13	14	12	13	11	10
Under 10m	KSNV	7 831	8 128	7 607	6 757	6 091	6 022	6 027	5 916	5 769	5 713	5 773
Non-active/non-TAC	KSNW	692	668	472	371	–	–	–	–	–	–	–
Other: Mussel Dredgers	JZCJ	..	..	..	..	..	3	2	2	2	7	15
Total UK fleet[2]	KSNX	11 561	11 692	10 827	9 720	8 658	8 461	8 273	8 041	7 820	7 728	7 593

1 See chapter text.
2 The UK figures here include Channel Islands and Isle of Man.

Source: Department for Environment, Food and Rural Affairs: 01904 455332

21.16 Estimated household food consumption by all households[1]

Grammes per person per week

		Great Britain											United Kingdom
		1991	1992	1993	1994	1995	1996	1997	1998	1999	2000		2001 /02
Liquid wholemilk[2] (ml)	KPQM	1 104	995	898	870	812	776	712	693	634	664	VQEW	599
Fully skimmed (ml)	KZBH	198	213	217	207	204	137	158	164	167	164	VQEX	160
Semi skimmed (ml)	KZBI	579	752	814	863	899	935	978	945	958	975	VQEZ	931
Other milk and cream (ml)	KZBJ	247	262	249	252	255	259	248	243	248	278	VQFA	333
Cheese	KPQO	117	114	109	106	108	111	109	104	104	110	VQFB	112
Butter	KPQP	44	41	40	39	36	39	38	39	37	39	VQFC	42
Margarine	KPQQ	89	79	70	43	41	36	26	26	20	21	VQFD	13
Low and reduced fat spreads	KZBK	47	51	52	74	72	79	77	69	71	68	VQFE	72
All other oils and fats (ml for oils)	KPQR	60	74	69	70	69	71	62	62	58	58	VQFF	70
Eggs (number)	KPQS	2	2	2	2	2	2	2	2	2	2	VQFG	2
Preserves and honey	KPQT	51	45	42	43	39	41	41	38	33	33	VQFH	35
Sugar	KPQU	167	156	151	144	136	144	128	119	107	105	VQFI	112
Beef and veal	KPQV	152	141	133	131	121	101	110	109	110	124	VQFJ	118
Mutton and lamb	KPQW	86	71	66	54	54	66	56	59	57	55	VQFK	51
Pork	KPQX	82	72	80	77	71	73	75	76	69	68	VQFL	61
Bacon and ham, uncooked	KPQY	85	77	77	77	76	77	72	76	68	71	VQFM	68
Bacon and ham, cooked (including canned)	KPQZ	33	33	35	38	39	33	41	40	39	41	VQFN	45
Poultry uncooked	JZCH	202	216	222	209	215	233	221	218	201	214	VQFO	206
Cooked poultry (not purchased in cans)	KYBP	14	15	16	20	22	23	33	33	35	39	VQFQ	43
Other cooked and canned meats	KPRB	60	68	60	63	63	62	52	49	48	51	VQFR	54
Offals	KPRC	13	12	11	9	9	7	7	5	5	5	VQFS	6
Sausages, uncooked	KPRD	62	61	60	61	63	63	63	60	58	60	VQFT	66
Other meat products	KPRE	173	183	194	203	211	207	209	216	221	239	VQFU	313
Fish, fresh and processed (including shellfish)	KPRF	65	67	71	71	68	72	70	70	70	67	VQFV	..
Canned fish	KPRG	30	32	30	30	29	31	31	29	31	32	VQFW	..
Fish and fish products, frozen	KPRH	43	43	44	44	46	50	46	46	42	44	VQFX	..
Fish, fresh chilled or frozen	VQAB	..	..	..	..	..	..	..	..	..	..	VQAI	51
Other fish and fish products	VQAC	..	..	..	..	..	..	..	..	..	..	VQAJ	105
Potatoes (excluding processed)	KPRI	959	901	875	812	803	805	745	715	673	707	VQFY	647
Fresh green vegetables	KPRJ	259	250	240	245	225	233	251	246	245	240	VQFZ	..
Other fresh vegetables	KPRK	461	475	477	464	470	489	497	486	500	492	VQGB	..
Frozen potato products	KYBQ	82	92	98	103	99	113	106	111	113	120	VQGC	..
Other frozen vegetables	KPRL	117	106	105	107	101	94	94	88	87	80	VQGG	..
Potato products not frozen	JZCF	59	75	80	82	89	92	90	89	86	82	VQGH	..
Canned beans	KPRM	123	120	112	111	117	125	122	118	112	114	VQGI	..
Other canned vegetables (excl. potatoes)	KPRN	120	124	114	103	110	113	104	99	92	97	VQGL	..
Other processed vegetables (excl. potatoes)	LQZH	43	50	52	55	48	55	52	54	59	54	VQGM	..
Fresh green vegetables	VQAD	..	..	..	..	..	..	..	..	..	..	VQAK	229
Other fresh vegetables	VQAF	..	..	..	..	..	..	..	..	..	..	VQAL	502
All processed vegetables	VQAG	..	..	..	..	..	..	..	..	..	..	VQAM	620
Apples	KPRO	190	187	179	180	183	175	179	181	169	180	VQGN	175
Bananas	KPRP	129	144	151	162	176	185	195	198	202	206	VQGO	203
Oranges	KPRQ	76	72	62	65	66	63	62	63	50	54	VQGP	55
All other fresh fruit	KPRR	216	216	224	238	247	263	276	274	290	304	VQGS	318
Canned fruit	KPRS	52	51	48	46	45	43	44	37	38	38	VQGT	40
Dried fruit, nuts and fruit and nut products	KPRT	39	38	39	36	34	36	35	34	30	35	VQGU	39
Fruit juices (ml)	KPRU	250	222	236	240	244	258	277	304	284	303	VQGX	327
Flour	KPRV	81	81	82	62	57	70	54	55	56	67	VQGY	55
Bread	KPRW	752	755	757	758	756	752	746	742	717	720	VQGZ	769
Buns, scones and teacakes	KPRX	39	40	39	38	36	47	43	41	40	43	VQHA	37
Cakes and pastries	KPRY	79	76	79	85	85	87	93	88	87	89	VQHB	139
Biscuits	KPRZ	147	148	142	138	135	150	138	137	132	141	VQHC	166
Breakfast cereals	KPSA	134	132	129	134	135	140	135	136	134	143	VQHE	133
Oatmeal and oat products	KPSB	19	15	14	11	11	13	16	11	13	15	VQHF	12
Other cereals and cereal products	JZCG	204	217	218	218	251	304	293	270	284	291	VQHG	345
Tea	KPSC	42	39	36	38	39	38	36	35	32	34	VQHK	34
Instant coffee	KPSD	15	14	13	13	12	13	11	12	11	11	VQHL	13
Canned soups	KPSE	69	70	66	68	64	72	70	71	67	71	VQHM	79
Pickles and sauces	KPSF	69	72	77	77	80	84	92	96	91	107	VQHN	121

1 See chapter text.
2 Including also school and welfare milk.

Sources: Expenditure and Food Survey, Department for Environment,; Food and Rural Affairs: 01904 455077

22 Production

Production

Annual Business Inquiry *(Table 22.1)*

The Annual Business Inquiry (ABI) estimates cover all UK businesses registered for Value Added Tax (VAT) and/ or Pay As You Earn (PAYE), classified to the 1992 Standard Industrial Classification (SIC(92)) headings listed in the tables. The ABI obtains details on these businesses from the ONS Inter-Departmental Business Register (IDBR).

As with all its statistical inquiries, the ONS is concerned to minimise the form-filling burden of individual contributors and as such the ABI is a sample inquiry. The sample was designed as a stratified random sample of about 69,600 businesses, the inquiry population is stratified by SIC(92) and employment using the information from the register.

The inquiry results are grossed up to the total population, so that they relate to all active UK businesses on the IDBR for the sectors covered.

The results meet a wide range of needs for government, economic analysts and the business community at large. In official statistics the inquiry is an important source for the national accounts and input-output tables, but also provides weights for the indices of production and producer prices. Inquiry results also enable the United Kingdom to meet statistical requirements of the European Union.

Data from 1995 and 1996 were calculated on a different basis from those for 1997 and later years. In order to provide a link between the two data series, the 1995 and 1996 data were subsequently reworked to provide estimates on a consistent basis.

Revised Annual Business Inquiry results down to SIC(92) 4 digit class level for 1995-2001, giving both analysis and tabular detail, are now available free of charge from the ONS Website at *www.statistics.gov.uk/abi/*, with further extracts and bespoke analyses available on request. This service replaces existing publications.

Manufacturers' sales by industry *(Table 22.2)*

This table shows the total manufacturers' sales for products classified to the 1992 Standard Industrial Classification and collected under the PRODCOM (Products of the European Community) Inquiry since its introduction in 1993. Some data are not available for confidentiality reasons or where data have not been published for a given period. Detailed product sales data together with exports and imports data are available in the Product Sales and Trade quarterly and annual reports (PRQ and PRA series).

Number of local units in manufacturing industries in 2003 *(Table 22.3)*

This table shows the number of local units (sites) in manufacturing by employment sizebands. The classification breakdown is at division level (2 digit) as classified to the 2003 Standard Industrial Classification held on the Inter-Departmental Business Register (IDBR). This register became fully operational in 1995 and combines information on VAT traders and PAYE employers in a statistical register comprising 2 million enterprises (businesses), representing nearly 99 per cent of economic activity. Business Monitor PA1003 – Size Analysis of United Kingdom Businesses 2003 provides further details and contains detailed information on enterprises in the UK including size, classification and location. Additionally, this information is available for manufacturing local units.

For further information on the IDBR see the National Statistics website at *www.statistics.gov.uk/idbr*.

Production of primary fuels *(Table 22.4)*

This table shows indigenous production of primary fuels. It includes the extraction or capture of primary commodities and the generation or manufacture of secondary commodities. Production is always gross; that is, it includes the quantities used during the extraction or manufacturing process. Primary fuels are coal, natural gas (including colliery methane), oil, primary electricity (i.e. electricity generated by hydro, nuclear wind and tide stations and also electricity imported from France through the interconnector) and renewables (includes solid renewables such as wood, straw and waste and gaseous renewables such as landfill gas and sewage gas). The figures are presented on a common basis, expressed in million tonnes of oil equivalent. Estimates of the gross calorific values used for converting the statistics for the various fuels to these are given in the Digest of UK Energy Statistics (published by The Stationery Office and available on the Internet at *www.dti.gov.uk/energy/inform/dukes/*). Chapter 1 of the Digest of UK Energy Statistics gives more information on these figures.

Total inland energy consumption *(Table 22.5)*

This table shows energy consumption by fuel and final energy consumption by fuel and class of consumer. Primary energy consumption covers consumption of all primary fuels (defined above) for energy purposes. This measure of energy consumption includes energy that is lost by converting primary fuels into secondary fuels, i.e. the energy lost burning coal to generate electricity or the energy used by refineries to separate crude oil into fractions, in addition to losses in distribution. The other common way of measuring energy consumption is to measure the energy content of the fuels supplied to consumers. This is called final energy consumption. It is net of fuel used by the energy industries, conversion, transmission and distribution losses. The figures are presented on a common basis, measured as energy supplied and expressed in million tonnes of oil equivalent. Estimates of the gross calorific values used for converting the statistics for the various fuels to these are given in the *Digest of UK Energy Statistics* (published by The Stationery Office and available on the Internet at *www.dti.gov.uk/energy/inform/dukes/*). So far as practicable the user categories have been grouped on the basis of the SIC(2003) although the methods used by each of the supply industries to identify end users are slightly different. Chapter 1 of the *Digest of UK Energy Statistics* gives more information on these figures.

Coal *(Table 22.6)*

Since 1995, aggregate data on coal production have been obtained from the Coal Authority. In addition, main coal producers provide data in response to an annual DTI inquiry which covers production (deepmined and opencast), trade, stocks and disposals. HM Customs and Excise also provide trade data for solid fuels. The DTI collects information on the use of coal from UK Iron and Steel Statistics Bureau, and consumption of coal for electricity generation is covered by data provided by the electricity generators.

Gas *(Table 22.7)*
Production figures, covering the production of gas from the UKCS offshore and onshore gas fields and gas obtained during the production of oil, are obtained from returns made under the DTI's Petroleum Production Reporting System. Additional information is used on imports and exports of gas and details from the operators of gas terminals in the UK to complete the picture.

It is no longer possible to present information on fuels input into the gas industry and gas output and sales in the same format as in previous editions of this table. As such, users are directed to Chapter 4 of the 2002 edition of the *Digest of UK Energy Statistics*, where more detailed information on gas production and consumption in the UK is available.

DTI carry out an annual survey of gas suppliers to obtain details of gas sales to the various categories of consumer. Estimates are included for the suppliers with the smallest market share since the DTI inquiry covers only the largest suppliers (i.e. those more than about 0.5 per cent share of the UK market up to 1997 and those known to supply more than 1,750 GWh per year from 1998 onwards).

Electricity *(Tables 22.8 - 22.10)*
The electricity Tables 22.8 to 22.10 cover all generators and suppliers of electricity in the United Kingdom.

The relationship between generation, supply, availability and consumption is as follows:

Electricity generated
- *less* electricity used on works
- *equals* electricity supplied (gross)

- *less* electricity used in pumping at pumped storage stations
- *equals* electricity supplied (net)

- *plus* imports (net of exports) of electricity
- *equals* electricity available

- *less* losses and statistical differences
- *equals* electricity consumed.

In table 22.8 'major power producers' are those generating companies corresponding to the old public sector supply system, i.e. AES Electric Ltd., American Electric Power., Anglian Power Generation., Baglan Generation Ltd., Barking Power Ltd., BNFL Magnox, British Energy plc., Coolkeeragh Power Ltd., Corby Power Ltd., Coryton Energy Company Ltd., Deeside Power, Derwent Cogeneration Ltd., EDF Energy Plc, Edison Mission Energy Ltd., Enfield Energy Centre Ltd., Entergy Power Group Ltd., Fellside Heat and Power Ltd., Fibrogen Ltd., Fibropower Ltd., Fibrothetford Ltd., Fife Power Ltd., Great Yarmouth Power Ltd., Humber Power Ltd., Innogy plc., International Power plc.,

Killingholme Power Ltd., Lakeland Power Ltd., Medway Power Ltd., National Grid Company (Kielder), NIGEN, Peterborough Power Ltd., PowerGen plc. (including former TXU Europe Power Ltd stations), Premier Power Ltd., Regional Power Generators Ltd., Rocksavage Power Company Ltd., Saltend Co-generation Company Ltd., Sita Tyre Recycling Ltd., Scottish Power plc., Scottish and Southern Energy plc., Seabank Power Ltd., SELCHP Ltd. (South East London Combined Heat & Power Ltd.), South Coast Power Ltd., South Western Electricity, Sutton Bridge Power Ltd., Teesside Power Ltd.

In Table 22.10 all fuels are converted to the common unit of million tonnes of oil equivalent, i.e. the amounts of oil which would be needed to produce the output of electricity generated from those fuels.

More detailed statistics on energy are given in the *Digest of United Kingdom Energy Statistics 2003*. Readers may wish to note that the production and consumption of fuels are presented using commodity balances. A commodity balance shows the flows of an individual fuel through from production to final consumption, showing its use in transformation and energy industry own use.

Oil and oil products *(Tables 22.11 - 22.13)*
The data on the production of crude oil, condensates and natural gases given in Table 22.11 are collected by the DTI direct from the operators of production facilities and terminals situated on UK territory, either onshore or offshore, ie on the UK Continental Shelf. Data are also collected from the companies on their trade in oil and oil products. These data are used in preference to the foreign trade as recorded by HM Customs & Excise in the Overseas Trade Statistics.

Data on the internal UK oil industry (i.e. on the supply, refining and distribution of oil and oil products in the UK) are collected by the UK Petroleum Industry Association. These data, reported by individual refining companies and wholesalers, and supplemented where necessary by data from other sources, provide the contents of Tables 22.12 and 22.13. The data are presented in terms of deliveries to the inland UK market. This is regarded as an acceptable proxy for actual consumption of products. The main shortcoming is that, whist changes in stocks held by companies in central storage areas are taken into account, changes in the levels of stocks further down the retail ladder (such as stocks held on petrol station forecourts) are not. This is not thought to result in a significant degree of difference in the data.

Iron and steel *(Tables 22.14 - 22.16)*

Iron and steel industry
The general definition of the UK iron and steel industry is based on groups 271 "ECSC iron and steel", 272 "Tubes", and 273 "Primary Transformation" of the UK Standard Industrial Classification (1992), except those parts of groups 272 and 273 which cover cast iron pipes, drawn wire, cold formed sections and Ferro alloys.

The definition excludes certain products which may be made by works within the industry, such as refined iron,

Production

finished steel castings, steel tyres, wheels, axles and rolled rings, open and closed die forgings, colliery arches and springs. Iron foundries and steel stockholders are also considered to be outside of the industry.

Statistics

The statistics for the UK iron and steel industry are compiled by ISSB Ltd. from data collected from UK steel producing companies with the exception of trade data which is based on HM Customs data.

Crude steel is the total of usable ingots, usable continuously cast semi-finished products and liquid steel for castings.

Production of finished products is the total production at the mill of that product after deduction of any material which is immediately scrapped.

Deliveries are based on invoiced tonnages and will include deliveries made to steel stockholders and service centres by the UK steel industry.

For more detailed information on definitions etc please contact ISSB Ltd. on 020 7343 3900.

Minerals (Table 22.19)

Table 22.19 gives, separately for Great Britain and Northern Ireland, the production of minerals extracted from the ground. The figures for chemicals and metals are estimated from the quality of the ore which is extracted. The data come from an annual census of the quarrying industry which, for Great Britain, is conducted by the Office for National Statistics for the Office of the Deputy Prime Minister and the Department of Trade and Industry.

Building Materials (Table 22.20)

Table 22.20 gives the production of a number of building materials which are closely associated with material extracted from the ground. The data come from surveys conducted by the Office for National Statistics on behalf of the Department of Trade and Industry

Construction (Tables 22.21 - 22.22)

Table 22.21 shows the value of contractors' output in the construction industry in Great Britain. Contractors' output is defined as the amount chargeable to customers for building and civil engineering work done in the relevant period. The data come from surveys run by the Department of Trade and Industry (DTI). As well as being an important input to the National Accounts, it is used by the government and the construction industry in their efforts to fully understand the industry, and also by Eurostat.

Table 22.22 shows the value of new orders in the construction industry; this is also collected by DTI. This information relates to contracts for new construction work awarded to main contractors by clients in both the public and private sectors; it also includes speculative work, undertaken on the initiative of the firm, where no contract is awarded. New orders are used as a good indicator of future output.

Motor vehicle production (Table 22.25)

The figures represent the output of United Kingdom based manufacturers classified to Class 34.10 (motor vehicles) of the Standard Industrial Classification 2003. They are derived from the Motor Vehicle Production Inquiry (MVPI).

These figures include vehicles produced in the form of kits for assembly. The value of the kit must be 50% or more of the value of a corresponding complete vehicle.

Drink and tobacco (Tables 22.26 and 22.27)

Data for these tables are derived by Customs and Excise from the systems for collecting excise duties. Alcoholic drinks and tobacco products become liable to duty when released for consumption in the UK. Figures for releases include both home-produced products and commercial imports. Production figures are also available for potable spirits distilled and beer brewed in the UK.

Alcoholic drink (Table 22.26)

The figures for Imported and other spirits released for home consumption include gin and other UK produced spirits, for which a breakdown is not available.

Since June 1993 beer duty has been charged when the beer leaves the brewery or other registered premises. Previously duty was chargeable at an earlier stage (the worts stage) in the brewing process, and an allowance was made for wastage. Figures for years prior to 1994 include adjustments to bring them into line with current data. The change in June 1993 also led to the availability of data on the strength; a series in hectolitres of pure alcohol is shown from 1994.

Made wine with alcoholic strength from 1.2 per cent to 5.5 per cent is termed 'coolers'. Included in coolers are alcoholic lemonade and similar products of appropriate strength.

Tobacco Products (Table 22.27)

Releases of cigarettes and other tobacco products tend to be higher in the period before a Budget. Products may then be stocked, duty paid, before being sold.

22.1
Production and construction[1]: summary table
United Kingdom

	Estimates for all firms (£ million)					
			Stocks and work in progress		Capital expenditure *less* disposals	Total employment costs
	Total turnover	Gross value added	At end of year	Change during year		

Standard Industrial Classification: Revised 1992

Production and construction
Sections C-F

	Total turnover	Gross value added	At end of year	Change during year	Capital expenditure *less* disposals	Total employment costs
	ZIYQ	KSCD	KSCE	KSCF	KSCG	AWKC
1997	636 664	215 435	72 099	−149	32 090	108 042
1998	631 265	212 933	70 062	365	34 097	112 326
1999	644 749	220 338	66 400	1 539	30 007	114 584
2000	675 149	228 161	66 571	3 962	27 478	115 943
2001	678 207	230 327	65 927	750	28 569	118 012

Production industries (Revised definitions)
Sections C-E

	ZIYR	KSCL	KSCM	KSCN	KSCO	AWKH
1997	539 940	181 805	58 492	−1 161	30 215	89 332
1998	528 819	178 459	55 354	−601	32 275	93 692
1999	533 384	181 189	54 867	204	28 139	93 774
2000	553 601	185 886	54 945	3 200	25 261	94 209
2001	547 075	182 358	52 762	−827	26 145	94 303

Mining and quarrying
Section C

	ZIYS	KSCT	KSCU	KSCV	KSCW	AWKI
1997	26 791	16 530	1 214	17	4 799	2 577
1998	23 953	13 120	1 138	55	6 303	2 542
1999	26 270	15 245	1 138	−5	4 058	2 469
2000	36 513	22 289	957	−2	2 810	2 669
2001	37 467	22 428	958	64	4 271	2 684

Mining and quarrying of energy producing materials
Subsection CA

	ZIYT	KSDB	KSDC	KSDD	KSDE	KSDF
1997	22 961	14 759	926	−9	4 537	1 929
1998	19 866	11 512	732	23	5 985	1 862
1999	21 975	13 615	850	−19	3 738	1 765
2000	31 704	20 489	657	−24	2 572	1 905
2001	32 647	20 629	658	33	4 006	1 936

Mining and quarrying except energy producing materials
Subsection CB

	ZIYU	KSDJ	KSDK	KSDL	KSDM	KSDN
1997	3 830	1 771	288	26	262	647
1998	4 087	1 609	406	32	318	680
1999	4 295	1 630	289	14	320	704
2000	4 809	1 800	300	21	237	765
2001	4 820	1 798	300	31	264	749

Manufacturing (Revised definition)
Section D

	ZIYV	KSDR	KSDS	KSDT	KSDU	AWKL
1997	469 787	148 927	55 822	−1 154	20 314	82 903
1998	460 677	149 892	52 675	−643	20 386	87 079
1999	461 771	150 449	52 005	309	18 125	87 334
2000	469 146	148 793	52 167	3 150	17 004	87 456
2001	461 899	145 179	50 077	−806	16 347	87 753

22.1
continued

Production and construction[1]: summary table
United Kingdom

	Total turnover	Gross value added	Stocks and work in progress		Capital expenditure *less* disposals	Total employment costs
			At end of year	Change during year		

Estimates for all firms (£ million)

Standard Industrial Classification: Revised 1992

Manufacture of food; beverages and tobacco
 Subsection DA

	ZIYW	KSDZ	KSEA	KSEB	KSEC	AWKM
1997	77 320	20 041	7 616	259	2 665	9 243
1998	73 482	19 351	8 023	−221	2 763	9 333
1999	73 655	19 977	7 958	−62	2 725	9 885
2000	73 872	20 184	7 605	−88	2 271	9 929
2001	74 804	20 370	7 598	37	2 643	10 062

Manufacture of textile and textile products
 Subsection DB

	ZIYX	KSEH	KSEI	KSEJ	KSEK	AWKN
1997	18 874	7 664	3 046	29	506	4 607
1998	17 365	6 699	2 906	−140	552	4 476
1999	16 137	5 930	2 610	−67	460	4 035
2000	14 358	5 506	2 285	−19	275	3 541
2001	13 345	5 147	2 045	32	255	3 152

Manufacture of leather and leather products
 Subsection DC

	ZIYY	KSEP	KSEQ	KSER	KSES	AWKO
1997	2 152	787	409	45	49	478
1998	2 005	689	301	−11	42	461
1999	1 819	673	243	−2	38	360
2000	1 728	676	230	−18	9	330
2001	1 766	673	266	7	23	323

Manufacture of wood and wood products
 Subsection DD

	ZIYZ	KSEX	KSEY	KSEZ	KSFA	AWKP
1997	6 145	2 218	667	15	237	1 267
1998	5 797	2 270	593	6	255	1 360
1999	5 838	2 101	508	−14	238	1 246
2000	6 186	2 303	610	30	227	1 292
2001	6 604	2 345	589	−16	220	1 370

Manufacture of pulp, paper and paper products; publishing and printing
 Subsection DE

	ZIZA	KSFF	KSFG	KSFH	KSFI	AWKQ
1997	42 166	17 717	3 035	−44	2 087	9 762
1998	42 734	18 309	2 660	−28	1 957	10 277
1999	43 387	19 280	2 608	71	1 719	10 260
2000	45 291	19 492	2 544	125	1 813	10 857
2001	44 903	19 444	2 629	8	1 612	10 877

Manufacture of coke, refined petroleum products and nuclear fuel
 Subsection DF

	ZIZB	KSFN	KSFO	KSFP	KSFQ	AWKR
1997	25 593	2 024	1 171	−175	704	787
1998	23 322	2 289	885	−196	730	923
1999	25 310	3 087	1 333	449	766	912
2000	27 855	2 302	1 199	114	623	920
2001	26 217	2 968	1 021	−204	730	965

22.1
continued

Production and construction[1]: summary table
United Kingdom

			Estimates for all firms (£ million)			
	Total turnover	Gross value added	Stocks and work in progress		Capital expenditure *less* disposals	Total employment costs
			At end of year	Change during year		

Standard Industrial Classification: Revised 1992

Manufacture of chemicals, chemical products and man-made fibres
Subsection DG

	ZIZC	KSFV	KSFW	KSFX	KSFY	AWKS
1997	47 984	14 818	5 716	−55	2 984	6 861
1998	44 825	14 341	5 659	114	3 161	7 374
1999	46 282	14 939	5 911	75	2 830	7 710
2000	47 544	15 069	6 249	481	2 729	7 549
2001	47 575	14 850	6 175	−18	2 454	7 863

Manufacture of rubber and plastic products
Subsection DH

	ZIZD	KSGD	KSGE	KSGF	KSGG	AWKT
1997	20 323	7 834	1 908	34	1 072	4 631
1998	20 420	8 062	2 021	54	1 102	4 855
1999	19 520	7 554	1 898	24	1 088	4 940
2000	19 743	7 644	1 824	59	961	4 767
2001	19 902	7 632	1 844	−	731	4 854

Manufacture of other non-metallic mineral products
Subsection DI

	ZIZE	KSGL	KSGM	KSGN	KSGO	AWKU
1997	11 866	5 092	1 527	17	571	2 798
1998	11 346	4 904	1 420	29	656	2 771
1999	11 710	4 865	1 364	−106	747	2 759
2000	12 014	5 154	1 460	94	621	2 821
2001	11 532	4 852	1 316	−8	488	2 835

Manufacture of basic iron and of ferro-alloys
Subsection DJ

	ZIZF	KSGT	KSGU	KSGV	KSGW	AWKV
1997	43 401	16 335	4 289	−23	1 744	9 988
1998	44 399	17 030	4 255	−203	2 024	10 713
1999	40 879	15 941	4 047	99	1 464	10 450
2000	41 028	15 912	4 063	192	1 334	10 340
2001	40 765	15 269	3 930	−35	1 120	10 147

Manufacture of machinery and equipment not elsewhere specified
Subsection DK

	ZIZG	KSHB	KSHC	KSHD	KSHE	AWKW
1997	36 045	13 373	5 483	96	1 109	8 345
1998	35 580	13 414	5 084	46	982	8 637
1999	33 306	12 254	5 044	−230	954	8 356
2000	33 821	12 286	4 826	−40	872	8 437
2001	32 949	11 696	4 464	−100	807	8 356

Manufacture of electrical and optical equipment
Subsection DL

	ZIZH	KSHJ	KSHK	KSHL	KSHM	AWKX
1997	61 008	18 964	7 337	16	2 792	10 766
1998	61 037	19 202	6 832	−10	2 688	11 568
1999	64 891	19 587	7 014	119	1 861	11 881
2000	69 110	20 504	8 521	1 700	2 331	12 587
2001	63 660	16 070	7 241	−1 065	1 955	12 683

22.1
continued

Production and construction[1]: summary table
United Kingdom

| | Estimates for all firms (£ million) | | | | | |
| | Total turnover | Gross value added | Stocks and work in progress | | Capital expenditure *less* disposals | Wages and salaries |
			At end of year	Change during year		
Standard Industrial Classification: Revised 1992						
Manufacture of transport equipment Subsection DM						
	ZIZI	KSHR	KSHS	KSHT	KSHU	AWKY
1997	61 465	16 204	11 729	−1 427	3 237	9 876
1998	63 009	17 179	10 463	−193	2 948	10 840
1999	63 239	17 955	9 648	−128	2 749	10 866
2000	60 440	15 553	9 048	454	2 444	10 520
2001	61 018	17 411	9 253	479	2 729	10 559
Manufacture not elsewhere classified Subsection DN						
	ZIZJ	KSHZ	KSIA	KSIB	KSIC	AWKZ
1997	15 443	5 856	1 890	62	557	3 494
1998	15 356	6 153	1 574	110	528	3 493
1999	15 798	6 306	1 820	82	485	3 674
2000	16 156	6 208	1 703	67	496	3 565
2001	16 860	6 452	1 708	78	580	3 708
Electricity, gas and water supply Section E						
	ZIZK	KSIH	KSII	KSIJ	KSIK	AWLA
1997	43 361	16 348	1 456	−25	5 102	3 852
1998	44 189	15 446	1 542	−14	5 586	4 071
1999	45 342	15 496	1 723	−100	5 955	3 970
2000	47 942	14 804	1 821	52	5 448	4 084
2001	47 710	14 751	1 726	−84	5 527	3 866
Construction Section F						
	ZIZL	KSIP	KSIQ	KSIR	KSIS	AWLB
1997	96 724	33 630	13 607	1 012	1 875	18 711
1998	102 446	34 474	14 708	966	1 822	18 634
1999	111 365	39 150	11 533	1 335	1 869	20 810
2000	121 549	42 275	11 626	762	2 216	21 734
2001	131 132	47 969	13 166	1 577	2 423	23 708

1 See chapter text.

Source: Office for National Statistics: 01633 812435

22.2 Manufacturers' sales by industry[1]
United Kingdom

£ millions

Industry	SIC (92)	1998	1999	2000	2001
Other mining and quarrying					
Quarrying of stone for construction	KSPF	14110	31	37	37	44
Quarrying of limestone, gypsum and chalk	KSPG	14120	..	222	209	237
Quarrying of slate	KSPH	14130	3	3	3	4
Operation of gravel and sand pits	KSPJ	14210	1 605	1 615	..	..
Mining of clays and kaolin	KSPK	14220	..	..	306	..
Mining of chemical and fertilizer minerals	KSPL	14300	59	59	62	79
Production of salt	KSPM	14400	..	..	158	159
Other mining and quarrying not elsewhere classified	KSPN	14500	71	71	67	67
Manufacture of food products and beverages					
Production and preserving of meat	KSPO	15110	3 143	3 196	3 211	3 082
Production and preserving of poultry meat	KSPP	15120	1 577	1 695	1 884	1 966
Bacon and ham production	KSPQ	15131	..	1 132	1 094	1 101
Other meat and poultry meat processing	KSPR	15139	3 656	3 770	4 011	3 971
Processing and preserving of fish and fish products	KSPS	15200	1 347	1 542	1 534	1 673
Processing and preserving of potatoes	KSPT	15310	..	..	..	..
Fruit and vegetable juice	KSPU	15320	..	543	546	547
Processing and preserving of fruit and vegetables not elsewhere classified	KSPV	15330	1 970	1 961	2 182	2 383
Crude oils and fats	KSPW	15410	635	508	425	531
Refined oils and fats	KSPX	15420	492	466	486	468
Margarine and similar edible fats	KSPY	15430	462	471	..	..
Operation of dairies	KTEH	15510	5 752	5 630	5 545	5 726
Ice cream	KSPZ	15520	530	553	498	..
Grain mill products	KSQA	15610	2 700	2 684	2 639	2 478
Starches and starch products	KSQB	15620	375	379	377	403
Prepared feeds for farm animals	KSPI	15710	2 099	1 912	1 983	1 947
Prepared pet foods	KSQC	15720	1 300	1 144	1 162	1 118
Bread; fresh pastry goods and cakes	KSQD	15810	4 190	4 007	4 035	3 916
Rusks and biscuits; preserved pastry goods and cakes	KSQE	15820	2 974	..	..	3 107
Sugar	KSQF	15830	1 204	1 127	1 047	1 140
Cocoa; chocolate and sugar confectionery	KSQG	15840	3 323	..	3 414	3 356
Macaroni, noodles, couscous and similar farinaceous products	KSQH	15850	..	..	476	555
Processing of tea and coffee	KSQI	15860	1 484	..	..	..
Condiments and seasonings	KSQJ	15870	..	..	..	1 235
Homogenised food preparations and dietetic foods	KSQK	15880	184	196	158	133
Manufacture of other food products not elsewhere classified	KSQL	15890	1 824	1 867	2 010	1 964
Distilled potable alcoholic beverages	KSQM	15910	2 126	2 176	1 987	1 898
Production of ethyl alcohol from fermented materials	KSQN	15920	103	101	..	..
Wines	KSQO	15930	130	..	63	61
Cider and other fruit wines	KSQP	15940	466	565	475	505
Other non-distilled fermented beverages	KSQQ	15950	–	–	–	–
Beer	KSQR	15960	4 722	4 660	3 685	3 627
Malt	KSQS	15970	295	264	234	250
Mineral waters and soft drinks	KSQT	15980	2 807	2 794	2 682	2 973
Manufacture of tobacco products					
Tobacco products	KSQU	16000	2 482	2 443	2 282	1 796
Manufacture of textiles					
Preparation and spinning of textile fibres	KSQV	17100	1 000	891	798	668
Textile weaving	KSQW	17200	1 073	972	902	831
Finishing of textiles	KSQX	17300	715	629	575	509
Soft furnishings	KSQY	17401	492	444	458	525
Canvas goods, sacks etc	KSQZ	17402	123	161	137	137
Household textiles	KSRA	17403	896	942	987	893
Carpets and rugs	KSRB	17510	1 083	1 029	973	898
Cordage, rope, twine and netting	KSRC	17520	82	80	79	98

22.2
Manufacturers' sales by industry[1]
United Kingdom

continued

£ millions

Industry		SIC (92)	1998	1999	2000	2001
Manufacture of textiles continued						
Nonwovens and articles made from nonwovens, except apparel	KSRD	17530	145	158	..	167
Lace	KSRE	17541	62	39	34	28
Narrow fabrics	KSRF	17542	233	223	210	189
Other textiles not elsewhere classified	KSRG	17549	519	498	516	488
Knitted and crocheted fabrics	KSRH	17600	..	..	374	..
Knitted and crocheted hosiery	KSRI	17710	452	363	..	306
Knitted and crocheted pullovers, cardigans and similar	KSRJ	17720	759	664	582	413
Manufacture of wearing apparel; dressing and dyeing of fur						
Leather clothes	KSRK	18100	17	14	16	25
Workwear	KSRL	18210	290	279	261	253
Men's outerwear	KSRM	18221	763	613	421	340
Other women's outerwear	KSRN	18222	1 297	1 001	915	790
Men's underwear	KSRO	18231	553	437	294	..
Women's underwear	KSRP	18232	911	779	737	626
Hats	KSRQ	18241	70	63	..	54
Other wearing apparel and accessories	KSRR	18249	652	604	568	481
Dressing/dyeing of fur; articles of fur	KSRS	18300	7	6	5	3
Tanning and dressing of leather; manufacture of luggage, handbags, saddlery, harness and footwear						
Tanning and dressing of leather	KSRT	19100	362	304	309	310
Luggage, handbags and the like, saddlery and harness	KSRU	19200	221	234	226	215
Footwear	KSRV	19300	905	760	610	624
Manufacture of wood and of products of wood and cork, except furniture; manufacture of articles of straw and plaiting materials						
Sawmilling and planing of wood, impregnation of wood	KSRW	20100	624	699	642	627
Veneer sheets	KSRX	20200	686	722	719	710
Builders' carpentry and joinery	KSRY	20300	2 030	1 797	2 673	2 817
Wooden containers	KSRZ	20400	499	454	423	409
Other products of wood	KSSA	20510	387	392	328	583
Articles of cork, straw and plaiting materials	KSSB	20520	14	15	15	13
Manufacture of pulp, paper and paper products						
Paper and paperboard	KSSC	21120	3 501	3 294	3 347	3 140
Corrugated paper and paperboard, sacks and bags	KSSD	21211	..	561	593	550
Cartons, boxes, cases and other containers	KSSE	21219	3 463	3 340	3 254	3 399
Household and sanitary goods and toilet requisites	KSSF	21220	..	1 484	1 544	1 611
Paper stationery	KSSG	21230	683	669	693	697
Wallpaper	KSSH	21240	302	268	..	..
Other articles of paper and paperboard not elsewhere classified	KSSI	21250	798	743	822	798
Publishing, printing and reproduction of recorded media						
Publishing of books	KSSJ	22110	2 913	3 067	3 240	3 362
Publishing of newspapers	KSSK	22120	3 577	3 659	3 929	3 951
Publishing of journals and periodicals	KSSL	22130	6 172	6 666	6 948	7 028
Publishing of sound recordings	KSSM	22140	..	238	256	174
Other publishing	KSSN	22150	477	525	455	508
Printing of newspapers	KSSO	22210	..	..	181	..
Printing not elsewhere classified	KSSP	22220	9 268	9 433	9 684	9 204
Bookbinding and finishing	KSSQ	22230	422	433	492	461
Composition and plate-making	KSSR	22240	538	543	614	..
Other activities related to printing	KSSS	22250	655	732	700	637
Reproduction of sound recording	KSST	22310	336	..	555	366
Reproduction of video recording	KSSU	22320	193	..	173	184
Reproduction of computer media	KSSV	22330	119	..	..	89
Manufacture of chemicals and chemical products						
Industrial gases	KSSW	24110	625	530	..	539
Dyes and pigments	KSSX	24120	1 017	1 049	1 095	1 067
Other inorganic basic chemicals	KSSY	24130	1 369	1 251	1 155	1 159
Other organic basic chemicals	KSSZ	24140	4 013	4 151	5 412	5 740
Fertilizers and nitrogen compounds	KSTA	24150	617	737	714	596

22.2
Manufacturers' sales by industry[1]
United Kingdom

continued

£ millions

Industry	SIC (92)	1998	1999	2000	2001
Manufacture of chemicals and chemical products continued					
Plastics in primary forms	KSTB	24160	3 305	3 500	3 775	3 642
Synthetic rubber in primary forms	KSTC	24170	346	..	351	323
Pesticides and other agro-chemical products	KSTD	24200	..	725	1 049	1 129
Paints, varnishes and similar coatings, printing ink and mastic	KSTE	24300	2 468	2 627	2 600	2 512
Basic pharmaceutical products	KSTF	24410	508	521	666	705
Pharmaceutical preparations	KSTG	24420	6 030	7 298	7 264	7 986
Soap and detergents, cleaning and polishing preparations	KSTH	24510	1 827	1 922	1 917	1 941
Perfumes and toilet preparations	KSTI	24520	2 465	2 529	2 656	2 584
Explosives	KSTJ	24610	123	107	109	..
Glues and gelatines	KSTK	24620	380	353	318	342
Essential oils	KSTL	24630	461	526		612
Photographic chemical material	KSTM	24640	1 204	..	605	361
Prepared unrecorded media	KSTN	24650	134	141	131	..
Other chemical products not elsewhere classified	KSTO	24660	2 206	2 315	2 382	2 097
Man-made fibres	KSTP	24700	754	673	739	659
Manufacture of rubber and plastic products					
Rubber tyres and tubes	KSTQ	25110	1 014	970	859	811
Retreading and rebuilding of rubber tyres	KSTR	25120	..	120	..	..
Other rubber products	KSTS	25130	1 834	1 746	1 680	1 681
Plastic plates, sheets, tubes and profiles	KSTT	25210	3 170	3 095	3 177	3 082
Plastic packing goods	KSTU	25220	2 695	2 694	2 622	2 613
Builders' ware of plastic	KSTV	25230	3 211	3 141	3 550	3 993
Other plastic products	KSTW	25240	3 891	4 245	4 297	3 693
Manufacture of other non-metallic mineral products					
Flat glass	KSTX	26110	159	187	231	..
Shaping and processing of flat glass	KSTY	26120	832	766	773	816
Hollow glass	KSTZ	26130	720	711	677	688
Glass fibres	KSUA	26140	282	276	265	257
Manufacturing and processing of other glass including technical glassware	KSUB	26150	317	283	333	297
Ceramic household and ornamental articles	KSUC	26210	655	563	563	515
Ceramic sanitary fixtures	KSUD	26220	..	213	222	200
Ceramic insulators and insulating fittings	KSUE	26230	..	29	28	34
Other technical ceramic products	KSUF	26240	..	27	28	26
Other ceramic products	KSUG	26250	22	..	16	..
Refractory ceramic products	KSUH	26260	479	453	416	411
Ceramic tiles and flags	KSUI	26300	103	97	87	100
Bricks, tiles and construction products in baked clay	KSUJ	26400	592	627	618	632
Cement	KSUK	26510	..	..	..	..
Lime	KSUL	26520	..	..	70	..
Plaster	KSUM	26530	..	105	..	113
Concrete products for construction purposes	KSUN	26610	1 611	..	1 799	1 777
Plaster products for construction purposes	KSUO	26620	267	..	321	..
Ready mixed concrete	KSUP	26630	1 134	1 224	1 216	1 301
Mortars	KSUQ	26640	..	92	104	..
Fibre cement	KSUR	26650	91	88	..	..
Other articles of concrete, plaster and cement	KSUS	26660	..	96	97	103
Cutting, shaping and finishing of stone	KSUT	26700	238	280	328	346
Abrasive products	KSUU	26810	230	218	208	194
Other non-metallic mineral products not elsewhere classified	KSUV	26820	758	721	675	682
Manufacture of basic metals					
Cast iron tubes	KSUW	27210	244	..	207	..
Steel tubes	KSUX	27220	1 304	1 015	1 028	1 081
Cold drawing	KSUY	27310	157	128	137	146

22.2
Manufacturers' sales by industry[1]
United Kingdom
continued

£ millions

Industry	SIC (92)	1998	1999	2000	2001
Manufacture of basic metals continued					
Cold rolling of narrow strip	KSUZ 27320	126	104	106	97
Cold forming or folding	KSVA 27330	149	..	..	122
Wire drawing	KSVB 27340	334	289	271	225
Other first processing of iron and steel not elsewhere classified	KSVC 27350	83	78	83	87
Precious metals production	KSVD 27410	228	259	277	326
Aluminium production	KSVE 27420	2 147	2 019	2 214	2 199
Lead, zinc and tin production	KSVF 27430	389	368	351	372
Copper production	KSVG 27440	873	757	785	718
Other non-ferrous metal production	KSVH 27450	604	521	583	594
Casting of iron	KSVI 27510	651	572	578	519
Casting of steel	KSVJ 27520	186	152	160	160
Casting of light metals	KSVK 27530	316	283	290	289
Casting of other non-ferrous metals	KSVL 27540	462	399	405	424
Manufacture of fabricated metal products, except machinery and equipment					
Metal structures and parts of structures	KSVM 28110	4 750	5 267	4 791	5 140
Builders' carpentry and joinery of metal	KSVN 28120	803	860	854	964
Tanks, reservoirs and containers of metal	KSVO 28210	..	..	..	370
Central heating radiators and boilers	KSVP 28220	631	624	595	545
Steam generators, except central heating hot water boilers	KSVQ 28300	533	569	574	457
Forging, pressing, stamping and roll forming of metal	KSVR 28400	2 305	2 187	2 097	1 962
Treatment and coating of metals	KSVS 28510	1 143	1 109	1 055	1 116
General mechanical engineering	KSVT 28520	2 837	2 942	2 777	2 862
Cutlery	KSVU 28610	218	..	..	..
Tools	KSVV 28620	1 040	952	1 008	995
Locks and hinges	KSVW 28630	673	633	621	595
Steel drums and similar containers	KSVX 28710	165	141	..	138
Light metal packaging	KSVY 28720	1 258	..	..	..
Wire products	KSVZ 28730	571	557	523	492
Fasteners, screw machine products, chain and spring	KSWA 28740	787	701	689	626
Other fabricated metal products not elsewhere classified	KSWB 28750	1 725	1 618	1 552	1 615
Manufacture of machinery and equipment not elsewhere classified					
Engines and turbines, except aircraft, vehicles and cycle engines	KSWC 29110	1 710	1 687	1 712	1 933
Pumps	KSWD 29121	1 013	1 025	1 031	977
Compressors	KSWE 29122	1 210	1 224	1 352	1 251
Taps and valves	KSWF 29130	1 349	1 171	1 193	1 143
Bearings, gears, gearing and driving elements	KSWG 29140	1 109	1 015	1 032	1 005
Furnaces and furnace burners	KSWH 29210	424	336	299	290
Lifting and handling equipment	KSWI 29220	2 936	2 794	2 777	2 771
Non-domestic cooling and ventilation equipment	KSWJ 29230	2 665	2 544	..	3 280
Other general purpose machinery not elsewhere classified	KSWK 29240	2 132	2 060	2 106	2 106
Agricultural tractors	KSWL 29310	1 060	919	..	..
Other agricultural and forestry machinery	KSWM 29320	603	532	539	401
Machine tools	KSWN 29400	2 026	1 924	1 792	1 593
Machinery for metallurgy	KSWO 29510	91	77	85	..
Machinery for mining	KSWP 29521	466	385	385	442
Earth-moving equipment	KSWQ 29522	996	..	..	983
Equipment for concrete crushing and screening and roadworks	KSWR 29523	503	..	..	..
Machinery for food, beverage and tobacco processing	KSWS 29530	664	642	592	584
Machinery for textile, apparel and leather production	KSWT 29540	303	245	220	159
Machinery for paper and paperboard production	KSWU 29550	329	242	208	198
Other special purpose machinery not elsewhere classified	KSWV 29560	2 167	2 002	2 064	2 098
Weapons and ammunition	KSWW 29600	1 870	1 671	1 523	1 389

22.2
continued

Manufacturers' sales by industry[1]
United Kingdom

£ millions

Industry	SIC (92)	1998	1999	2000	2001
Manufacture of machinery and equipment not elsewhere classified continued					
Electric domestic appliances	KSYR 29710	1 902	1 781	1 870	1 858
Non-electric domestic appliances	KSWX 29720	..	531	499	..
Manufacture of office machinery and computers					
Office machinery	KSWY 30010	1 155	1 173	1 172	1 032
Computers and other information processing equipment	KSWZ 30020	9 927	9 903	11 599	9 391
Manufacture of electrical machinery and apparatus not elsewhere classified					
Electric motors, generators and transformers	KSXA 31100	2 294	2 223	2 400	2 517
Electricity, distribution and control apparatus	KSXB 31200	2 813	2 765	2 753	2 674
Insulated wire and cable	KSXC 31300	1 412	1 294	1 395	1 432
Accumulators, primary cells and batteries	KSXD 31400	489	500	558	405
Lighting equipment and electric lamps	KSXE 31500	1 301	1 273	1 215	1 125
Electrical equipment for engines and vehicles not elsewhere classified	KSXF 31610	1 146	1 110	..	..
Other electrical equipment not elsewhere classified	KSXG 31620	1 686	1 653	1 888	2 045
Manufacture of radio, television and communication equipment and apparatus					
Electronic valves and tubes and other electronic components	KSXH 32100	4 233	3 645	4 492	3 647
Telegraph and telephone apparatus and equipment	KSXI 32201	3 952	4 887	5 467	4 231
Radio and electronic capital goods	KSXJ 32202	2 700	3 002	3 600	..
Television and radio receivers, sound or video recording etc	KSXK 32300	3 272	3 070	3 267	3 087
Manufacture of medical, precision and optical instruments, watches and clocks					
Medical and surgical equipment and orthopaedic appliances	KSXL 33100	1 627	1 673	1 667	1 876
Instruments and appliances for measuring, checking, testing etc	KSXM 33200	4 943	5 003	5 195	5 722
Industrial process control equipment	KSXN 33300	866	779	686	683
Optical instruments and photographic equipment	KSXO 33400	946	1 012	964	1 001
Watches and clocks	KSXP 33500	86	91	72	59
Manufacture of motor vehicles, trailers and semi-trailers					
Motor vehicles	KSXQ 34100	21 102	22 353	19 689	20 040
Bodies (coachwork) for motor vehicles (excluding caravans)	KSXR 34201	876	797	838	853
Trailers and semi-trailers	KSXS 34202	998	910	863	929
Caravans	KSXT 34203	340	380	412	391
Parts and accessories for motor vehicles and their engines	KSXU 34300	8 957	8 778	8 486	8 358
Manufacture of other transport equipment					
Building and repairing of ships	KSXV 35110	1 602	2 449	1 567	1 613
Building and repairing of pleasure and sporting boats	KSXW 35120	453	459	501	585
Railway and tramway locomotives and rolling stock	KSXX 35200	1 114	932	1 245	1 269
Aircraft and spacecraft	KSXY 35300	..	13 988	12 790	11 738
Motorcycles	KSXZ 35410	..	..	..	..
Bicycles	KSYA 35420	115	112	114	103
Invalid carriages	KSYB 35430	..	123	116	120
Other transport equipment not elsewhere classified.	KSYC 35500	..	89	81	85
Manufacture of furniture; manufacturing not elsewhere classified					
Chairs and seats	KSYD 36110	2 458	2 458	2 532	2 678
Other office and shop furniture	KSYE 36120	1 259	1 278	1 432	1 333
Other kitchen furniture	KSYF 36130	908	1 065	975	927
Other furniture	KSYG 36140	1 967	2 170	2 072	2 107
Mattresses	KSYH 36150	501	524	542	566
Striking of coins and medals	KSYI 36210	..	..	..	..
Jewellery and related articles not elsewhere classified	KSYJ 36220	540	565	599	490
Musical instruments	KSYK 36300	60	51	52	42
Sports goods	KSYL 36400	269	252	257	275
Games and toys	KSYM 36500	465	460	426	454
Imitation jewellery	KSYN 36610	31	32	29	28
Brooms and brushes	KSYO 36620	168	164	169	165
Miscellaneous stationers' goods	KSYP 36631	270	245	216	..
Other manufacturing not elsewhere classified	KSYQ 36639	515	535	486	462

1 See chapter text. ProdCom data is published on the ONS website in the PRA and PRQ series of reports. Data not yet available for 2002 may eventually become available on the website.

Source: Office for National Statistics: 01633 813065

22.3 Number of local units in manufacturing industries in 2003[1]
United Kingdom
Standard Industrial Classification 2003 Division by Employment Sizeband

		Employment size								Total
		0 - 4	5 - 9	10 - 19	20 - 49	50 - 99	100 - 249	250 - 499	500 - 999	1,000+	

Number of local units

Division

		0 - 4	5 - 9	10 - 19	20 - 49	50 - 99	100 - 249	250 - 499	500 - 999	1,000+	Total
15/16	Food products; beverages and tobacco	3 355	2 220	1 545	1 180	610	605	270	130	35	9 950
17	Textiles and textile products	2 440	930	665	585	305	220	50	10	-	5 210
18	Wearing apparel; dressing and dyeing of fur	2 590	905	630	485	130	75	20	5	-	4 840
19	Leather and leather products	395	185	105	75	45	30	10	-	-	845
20	Wood and wood products	4 825	1 630	990	615	165	70	20	-	-	8 315
21	Pulp, paper and paper products	970	365	315	405	235	215	40	10	-	2 560
22	Publishing, printing and reproduction of recorded media	19 250	4 690	2 820	1 800	650	375	115	40	15	29 755
23	Coke, refined petroleum products and nuclear fuel	90	40	35	35	20	15	10	5	5	250
24	Chemicals, chemical products and man-made fibres	1 565	655	550	580	360	290	140	60	20	4 215
25	Rubber and plastic products	2 620	1 435	1 235	1 210	585	360	100	20	5	7 570
26	Other non-metallic mineral products	3 620	1 170	750	585	305	195	50	10	-	6 685
27	Basic metals	935	400	310	350	200	150	50	15	5	2 415
28	Fabricated metal products, except machinery and equipment	14 795	5 510	3 935	2 810	905	360	55	20	-	28 390
29	Machinery and equipment not elsewhere classified	5 840	2 400	1 935	1 680	710	410	145	35	15	13 165
30	Office machinery and computers	595	170	95	100	60	55	15	5	10	1 100
31	Electrical machinery and apparatus not elsewhere classified	2 470	840	735	690	335	235	90	30	-	5 435
32	Radio, television and communication equipment and apparatus	1 255	350	265	310	140	115	45	25	10	2 520
33	Medical, precision and optical instruments, watches and clocks	2 065	825	670	605	275	180	50	20	5	4 700
34	Motor vehicles, trailers and semi-trailers	1 020	465	375	400	220	190	105	40	30	2 845
35	Other transport equipment	1 175	415	255	215	130	125	45	35	30	2 420
36/37	Manufacturing not elsewhere classified	12 415	3 410	1 775	1 075	410	235	60	25	-	19 400
Total manufacturing (15/37)		84 285	29 010	19 990	15 790	6 795	4 505	1 485	540	185	162 585

1 See chapter text. The count of units refers to local units, i.e. individual sites, rather than whole businesses. All counts have been rounded to avoid disclosure.

Source: Office for National Statistics: 01633 812293

22.4 Production of primary fuels[1]
United Kingdom

Million tonnes of oil equivalent

		1992	1993	1994	1995	1996	1997	1998	1999	2000	2001	2002
Coal	HFZQ	51.5	41.6	29.7	32.8	31.1	30.3	25.8	23.2	19.6	20.0	18.8
Petroleum[2]	HGCY	103.7	109.6	138.9	142.7	142.1	140.4	145.3	150.2	138.3	127.8	127.0
Natural Gas[3]	HGDB	51.5	60.5	64.6	70.8	84.2	85.9	90.2	99.1	108.4	105.8	103.6
Primary electricity[4]	HGDN	18.9	22.0	21.7	21.7	22.4	23.5	24.0	22.9	20.2	21.2	20.7
Renewables and waste[5]	HGDO	0.8	1.2	1.6	1.7	1.8	1.9	2.1	2.2	2.3	2.5	2.7
Total Production	HGDP	226.5	234.9	256.6	269.7	281.6	282.1	287.2	297.7	288.7	277.4	272.8

1 See chapter text.
2 Crude oil plus all condensates and petroleum gases extracted at gas separation plants.
3 Includes colliery methane.

4 Includes nuclear, hydro and other non-thermal renewables (wind, tide etc).
5 Includes biofuels and waste, solar heating and photovoltaics, and geothermal aquifers.

Source: Depatment of Trade and Industry: 020 7215 2710

22.5 Total inland energy consumption
United Kingdom
Heat supplied basis

Million tonnes of oil equivalent

		1992	1993	1994	1995	1996	1997	1998	1999	2000	2001	2002
Inland energy consumption of primary fuels and equivalents[1]	KLWA	216.7	220.7	217.5	218.4	230.1	226.8	230.8	230.4	233.5	236.4	229.6
Coal[2]	KLWB	63.1	54.9	51.3	48.9	45.7	40.8	40.9	36.7	38.1	41.2	37.8
Petroleum[3]	KLWC	77.5	78.1	76.7	75.4	77.8	75.5	76.1	76.0	76.1	75.3	73.1
Primary electricity	KLWD	20.4	23.4	23.1	23.1	23.8	25.0	25.0	24.2	21.4	22.1	21.4
Natural gas	KLWE	55.1	62.9	64.9	69.2	81.0	83.5	86.9	91.4	95.6	95.3	94.7
Renewables and waste	GYUY	0.8	1.2	1.6	1.7	1.8	1.9	2.1	2.2	2.3	2.5	2.7
less Energy used by fuel producers and losses in conversion and distribution	KLWF	65.7	68.0	64.9	68.0	73.0	72.9	75.0	74.2	74.4	75.2	72.3
Total consumption by final users[1]	KLWG	151.1	152.7	152.5	150.4	157.0	153.9	155.8	157.1	158.9	161.2	157.2
Final energy consumption by type of fuel												
Coal (direct use)	KLWH	8.1	7.6	6.9	5.3	4.4	4.3	3.7	3.5	2.0	3.0	2.3
Coke and breeze	KLWI	3.9	3.8	3.9	3.9	1.0	0.8	0.9	1.0	1.0	0.8	0.9
Other solid fuel[4]	KLWJ	0.7	0.8	0.8	0.7	0.8	0.7	0.7	0.5	0.5	0.5	0.3
Coke oven gas	KLWK	0.5	0.6	0.6	0.6	0.4	0.5	0.4	0.2	0.2	0.2	0.1
Natural gas (direct use)	KLWL	48.4	49.3	49.9	50.1	56.5	54.2	55.9	55.1	57.1	58.0	56.3
Electricity	KLWM	24.2	24.6	24.4	25.3	26.5	26.8	27.1	27.8	28.3	28.6	28.6
Petroleum (direct use)[5]	KLWN	64.6	65.4	65.2	63.7	66.1	65.4	66.0	65.7	66.7	66.9	66.0
Renewables	GYVA	0.7	0.7	0.9	1.0	1.0	0.9	0.9	0.7	0.6	0.6	0.6
Final energy consumption by class of consumer												
Agriculture	KLWP	1.4	1.4	1.4	1.3	1.4	1.3	1.4	1.3	1.2	1.3	1.1
Iron and steel industry	KLWQ	6.5	7.0	6.9	6.9	4.2	4.2	4.0	3.8	3.8	3.6	3.2
Other industries	KLWR	30.2	29.5	30.8	29.4	30.3	30.4	30.5	30.9	30.9	32.0	31.6
Railways[6]	KLWS	1.2	1.3	1.3	1.3	1.3	1.2	1.3	1.2	1.2	1.2	1.1
Road transport	KLWT	39.4	39.5	39.7	39.3	40.8	41.3	41.0	41.4	41.6	41.5	41.5
Water transport	KLWU	1.4	1.3	1.2	1.2	1.3	1.3	1.2	1.1	1.0	0.8	0.7
Air transport	KLWV	7.4	7.9	8.1	8.5	8.9	9.3	10.2	11.0	12.0	11.4	11.3
Domestic	KLWW	44.1	45.5	43.9	42.7	48.1	44.8	46.1	46.1	46.9	48.5	47.9
Public administration	KLWX	8.7	8.1	8.3	8.5	8.8	8.4	8.1	8.4	8.1	7.9	7.2
Commercial and other services	KLWY	10.9	11.2	11.0	11.3	11.9	11.7	12.0	11.9	12.2	12.9	11.6

1 Includes heat sold from 1999.
2 Includes net trade and stock change in other solid fuels.
3 Refinery throughput of crude oil, *plus* net foreign trade and stock change in petroleum products. Petroleum products not used as fuels (chemical feedstock, industrial and white spirits, lubricants, bitumen and wax) are excluded.

4 Includes briquettes, ovoids, Phurnacite, Coalite, etc, and wood, waste etc, used for heat generation.
5 Includes manufactured liquid fuels from 1994.
6 Includes fuel used at transport premises.

Source: Department of Trade and Industry: 020 7215 5187

22.6 Coal: supply and demand[1]
United Kingdom

Million tonnes

			1992	1993	1994	1995	1996	1997	1998	1999	2000	2001	2002
Supply													
Production of deep-mined coal	KLXA		65.8	50.5	31.9	35.2	32.2	30.3	25.7	20.9	17.2	17.3	16.4
Production of opencast coal	KLXB		18.2	17.0	16.8	16.4	16.3	16.7	14.3	15.3	13.4	14.2	13.1
Total	KLXC		84.0	67.5	48.7	51.5	48.5	47.0	40.0	36.2	30.6	31.5	29.5
Recovered slurry, fines, etc	KLXD		0.5	0.7	0.1	1.5	1.7	1.5	1.1	0.9	0.6	0.4	0.5
Imports	KLXE		20.3	18.4	15.1	15.9	17.8	19.8	21.2	20.3	23.4	35.5	28.7
Total	KLXF		104.8	86.6	64.9	68.9	68.0	68.3	62.4	57.4	54.6	67.5	58.7
Change in colliery stocks	KLXG	KSOL	2.2	1.8	−4.2	−4.2	−3.0	0.7	−0.2	0.6	−3.5	−0.1	0.9
Change in stocks at opencast sites	KLXH		0.6	0.5	−0.5								
Total supply	KLXI		102.0	84.5	69.6	73.1	70.9	67.6	62.7	56.8	58.2	67.5	57.8
Home consumption													
Total home consumption	KLXW		100.6	86.6	81.7	76.9	71.4	63.1	63.2	55.7	58.9	64.2	58.6
Overseas shipments and bunkers	KLXX		1.0	1.1	1.2	0.9	1.0	1.1	1.0	0.8	0.7	0.5	0.5
Total consumption and shipments	KLXY		101.6	87.7	82.9	77.8	72.4	64.2	64.1	56.5	59.5	64.8	59.2
Change in distributed stocks[2]	KLXZ		1.2	−3.6	−13.9	−4.4	−0.9	3.0	−1.2	0.6	−1.2	2.9	−1.2
Balance[3]	KLYA		−0.8	0.4	0.6	−0.3	−0.5	0.3	−0.3	−0.3	−0.2	−0.2	−0.2
Stocks at end of year													
Distributed[2]	KLYB		33.5	29.9	16.0	11.6	10.8	13.8	12.6	13.2	12.0	15.0	13.7
At collieries	KLYC	KSOM	10.9	12.7	8.5	7.1	4.2	4.8	4.6	5.2	1.6	1.6	2.5
At opencast sites	KLYD		2.8	3.3	2.8								
Total stocks	KLYE		47.2	45.9	27.3	18.7	14.9	18.6	17.2	18.3	13.7	16.5	16.2

1 See chapter text. Figures relate to periods of 52 weeks. For 1998, figures relate to 52 weeks estimate for period ended 26 December 1998.
2 Excludes distributed stocks held in merchant yards etc, mainly for the domestic market, and stocks held by the industrial sector.

3 This is the balance between supply and consumption, shipments and changes in known distributed stocks.

Source: Department of Trade and Industry: 020 7215 2717

22.7 Fuel input and gas output: gas sales[1]
United Kingdom

Public supply

Giga-watt hours

		1992	1993	1994	1995	1996	1997	1998	1999	2000	2001	2002
Analysis of gas sales												
Fuel producers												
Power stations[2]	KIKK	17 894	81 778	114 575	145 790	201 929	251 787	267 703	315 400	324 413	309 732	326 220
Coal extraction and manufacture of solid fuels	KIKL	1 042	415	266	368	344	193	67	14	6	4	–
Coke ovens	KIKM	108	191	1	1	–	–	–	–	–	–	–
Petroleum refineries	KIKN	1 940	2 449	1 933	2 922	2 907	3 002	3 753	4 155	3 641	4 192	3 240
Nuclear fuel production	KIKO	508	565	550	467	874	923	989	1 021	472	1 210	402
Production and distribution of other energy	KIKP	447	178	114	352	437	487	549	629	619	451	709
Total final producers	KIKQ	21 939	85 576	117 439	149 900	206 491	256 392	273 061	321 219	329 151	315 589	330 571
Final users:												
Iron and steel industry	KIKR	13 908	15 577	20 327	19 988	20 940	20 577	20 105	21 622	22 551	20 969	19 533
Other industries	KIKS	132 936	132 719	143 979	150 697	12 646	13 429	14 415	13 905	15 153	16 585	16 433
Domestic	KIKT	330 100	340 162	329 710	326 010	375 841	345 532	355 895	358 066	369 909	379 163	376 327
Public administration	KIKU	43 817	38 725	41 119	46 308	51 411	52 315	51 976	43 253	44 552	46 121	43 715
Agriculture	KIKV	1 286	1 277	1 227	1 210	1 417	1 440	953	1 155	1 522	1 623	1 509
Miscellaneous	KIKW	54 769	58 917	58 790	61 502	65 080	59 022	64 695	62 079	64 382	65 046	56 080
Total final users	KIKX	576 816	587 377	595 152	605 715	527 335	492 315	508 039	500 080	518 069	529 507	513 597
Total sales	KIKY	598 755	672 952	712 592	755 615	733 826	748 707	781 100	821 299	847 220	845 096	844 168

1 See chapter text. The breakdown of consumption by industrial users is made according to the 1980 Standard Industrial Classification.
2 Includes auto-production of electricity.

Source: Department of Trade and Industry: 020 7215 2717

22.8 Electricity: generation, supply and consumption[1]
United Kingdom

Gigawatt-hours

		1992	1993	1994	1995	1996	1997	1998	1999	2000	2001	2002
Electricity generated												
Major power producers: total	KLUA	300 177	305 434	306 726	313 958	326 235	324 133	333 764	336 608	341 784	352 770	354 208
Conventional thermal and other[2]	AWLC	..	..	175 187	170 056	160 791	133 591	134 009	118 762	131 063	138 626	134 933
Combined cycle gas turbine stations	KJCS	2 991	22 811	36 971	48 720	65 880	86 974	93 832	114 620	117 935	117 966	123 893
Nuclear stations	KLUC	76 807	89 353	88 282	88 964	94 671	98 146	99 486	95 133	85 063	89 870	88 043
Hydro-electric stations:												
Natural flow	KLUE	4 591	3 522	4 317	4 096	2 801	3 337	4 237	4 431	4 331	3 215	3 925
Pumped storage	KLUF	1 697	1 437	1 463	1 552	1 556	1 486	1 624	2 902	2 694	2 356	2 652
Renewables other than hydro	KLUG	45	165	506	570	536	599	576	760	698	737	762
Other generators: total	KLUH	20 864	17 669	18 252	20 084	24 632	26 534	28 938	31 544	35 285	31 913	32 934
Conventional thermal and other[2]	AWLD	..	..	14 263	15 387	18 334	18 629	19 091	19 434	19 095	16 811	15 752
Combined cycle gas turbine stations	KJCT	409	607	1 505	2 126	3 535	4 412	5 428	7 127	10 859	8 979	10 521
Hydro-electric stations (natural flow)	KLUK	840	780	777	742	592	832	881	905	755	840	860
Renewables other than hydro	KILA	1 028	1 417	1 707	1 829	2 171	2 661	3 538	4 078	4 577	5 283	5 800
All generating companies: total	KLUL	321 043	323 102	324 978	334 042	350 867	350 667	362 702	368 152	377 069	384 683	387 142
Conventional thermal and other[2]	AWYH	..	..	189 451	185 443	179 125	152 220	153 100	138 196	150 158	155 437	150 685
Combined cycle gas turbine stations	KJCU	3 400	23 418	38 475	50 846	69 415	91 386	99 260	121 747	128 794	126 945	134 414
Nuclear stations	KLUN	76 807	89 353	88 282	88 964	94 671	98 146	99 486	95 133	85 063	89 870	88 043
Hydro-electric stations:												
Natural flow	KLUP	5 431	4 302	5 094	4 838	3 393	4 169	5 118	5 336	5 086	4 055	4 785
Pumped storage	KLUQ	1 697	1 437	1 463	1 552	1 556	1 486	1 624	2 902	2 694	2 356	2 652
Renewables other than hydro	KLUR	1 073	1 582	2 213	2 399	2 707	3 260	4 114	4 838	5 275	6 020	6 562
Electricity used on works: Total	KLUS	20 237	19 287	17 491	17 411	16 078	16 560	17 408	16 707	16 304	17 114	17 360
Major generating companies	KLUT	18 485	17 391	16 696	16 510	14 967	15 411	16 140	15 462	14 952	15 779	15 960
Other generators	KLUU	1 752	1 896	795	901	1 111	1 149	1 268	1 245	1 352	1 335	1 400
Electricity supplied (gross)												
Major power producers: total	KLUV	281 692	287 264	290 780	299 000	311 268	308 722	317 624	321 146	326 832	336 991	338 248
Conventional thermal and other[2]	AWYI	..	..	167 866	163 818	155 086	127 419	127 788	112 919	124 829	131 885	128 105
Combined cycle gas turbine stations	KJCV	2 964	22 611	36 815	48 525	65 604	86 682	93 005	112 768	116 110	115 894	121 886
Nuclear stations	KLUX	69 135	80 979	79 962	80 598	85 820	89 341	90 590	87 672	78 334	82 985	81 090
Hydro-electric stations:												
Natural flow	KLUZ	4 579	3 513	4 265	4 051	2 763	3 299	4 225	4 409	4 316	3 204	3 914
Pumped storage	KLVA	1 635	1 388	1 417	1 502	1 507	1 439	1 569	2 804	2 603	2 340	2 562
Renewables other than hydro	KLVB	37	136	455	506	488	542	447	574	640	683	691
Other generators: total	KLVC	19 112	16 522	18 207	20 909	23 521	25 385	27 670	30 299	33 933	30 578	31 534
Conventional thermal and other[2]	AWYJ	..	..	14 333	16 338	17 492	17 815	18 250	18 655	18 499	16 181	15 141
Combined cycle gas turbine stations	KJCW	394	584	1 466	2 100	3 358	4 192	5 157	6 771	10 318	8 531	9 996
Hydro-electric stations (natural flow)	KLVF	832	772	769	733	584	822	869	894	743	829	849
Renewables other than hydro	KIKZ	987	1 360	1 639	1 738	2 085	2 555	3 393	3 978	4 374	5 037	5 548
All generating companies: total	KLVG	300 804	303 815	308 987	319 909	334 789	334 107	345 294	351 445	360 765	367 569	369 782
Conventional thermal and other[2]	AWYK	..	..	182 199	180 156	172 578	145 234	146 038	131 574	143 328	148 066	143 246
Combined cycle gas turbine stations	KJCX	3 358	23 195	38 281	50 625	68 962	90 874	98 162	119 539	126 428	124 425	131 882
Nuclear stations	KLVI	69 135	80 979	79 962	80 598	85 820	89 341	90 590	87 672	78 334	82 985	81 090
Hydro-electric stations:												
Natural flow	KLVK	5 411	4 285	5 034	4 784	3 347	4 121	5 094	5 303	5 059	4 033	4 763
Pumped storage	KLVL	1 635	1 388	1 417	1 502	1 507	1 439	1 569	2 804	2 603	2 340	2 562
Renewables other than hydro	KLVM	1 024	1 496	2 094	2 244	2 573	3 097	3 840	4 552	5 014	5 720	6 239
Electricity used in pumping												
Major power producers	KLVN	2 257	1 948	2 051	2 282	2 430	2 477	2 594	3 774	3 499	3 210	3 463
Electricity supplied (net): Total	KLVO	298 547	301 868	306 936	317 627	332 359	331 630	342 700	347 671	357 267	364 359	366 318
Major power producers	KLVP	279 435	285 316	288 729	296 718	308 838	306 245	315 030	317 372	323 333	333 781	334 785
Other generators	KLVQ	19 112	16 552	18 207	20 909	23 521	25 385	27 670	30 299	33 933	30 578	31 534
Net imports	KGEZ	16 694	16 716	16 887	16 313	16 755	16 574	12 468	14 244	14 174	10 399	8 414
Electricity available	KGIZ	315 241	318 584	323 830	333 940	349 114	348 203	355 168	361 915	371 440	374 758	374 733
Losses in transmission etc	KGKW	23 788	22 838	31 000	30 020	29 335	27 138	29 818	29 862	31 143	31 980	30 902
Electricity consumption: Total	KGKX	291 453	295 746	292 830	303 920	319 779	321 065	325 350	332 053	340 297	342 778	343 831
Fuel industries	KGKY	9 984	9 615	7 518	8 070	9 211	8 624	8 406	8 037	9 704	8 625	9 977
Final users: total	KGKZ	281 468	286 130	285 310	295 849	310 567	312 441	316 944	324 016	330 593	334 153	333 854
Industrial sector	KGLZ	95 277	96 842	96 120	101 780	107 631	108 102	108 443	112 250	115 286	112 867	112 823
Domestic sector	KGMZ	99 482	100 456	101 407	102 210	107 513	104 455	109 410	110 308	111 842	115 336	114 535
Other sectors	KGNZ	86 711	88 833	87 790	91 860	95 423	99 884	99 091	101 458	103 465	105 950	106 496

1 See chapter text.
2 Includes electricity supplied by gas turbines and oil engines and plants producing electricity from renewable resources other than hydro.

Source: Department of Trade and Industry: 020 7215 5190

22.9 Electricity: plant capacity and demand
United Kingdom

Megawatts

		At end of March				At end of December[1]						
		1994	1995	1996		1996	1997	1998	1999	2000	2001	2002
Major power producers[2]:												
Total declared net capability	KGON	64 901	64 923	66 100	GUFY	69 090	68 288	68 390	70 058	72 030	73 219	70 439
Conventional steam stations	KGOO	41 143	38 453	38 242	GUFZ	38 230	37 395	35 081	35 427	34 640	34 640	32 032
Combined cycle gas turbine stations	KJCZ	5 463	8 364	9 034	GUGA	12 052	12 252	14 638	16 110	19 349	20 517	20 249
Nuclear stations[3,4]	KGOP	11 894	12 037	12 762	GUGB	12 916	12 946	12 956	12 956	12 486	12 486	12 486
Gas turbines and oil engines	KGOQ	2 248	1 895	1 890	GUGC	1 721	1 526	1 492	1 333	1 323	1 323	1 463
Hydro-electric stations:												
Natural flow	KGOR	1 314	1 314	1 314	GUGD	1 313	1 311	1 327	1 327	1 327	1 348	1 304
Pumped storage	KGOS	2 787	2 788	2 788	GUGE	2 788	2 788	2 788	2 788	2 788	2 788	2 788
Renewables other than hydro	KGOT	52	72	71	GUGF	70	70	108	117	117	117	117
Other generators:												
Total capacity of own generating plant[5]	KGOU	3 622	3 818	4 025	GUGG	4 181	4 625	4 990	5 388	6 258	6 269	6 149
Conventional steam stations[6]	KGOV	3 096	3 257	3 234	GUGH	3 192	3 240	3 248	3 315	3 544	3 437	3 132
Combined cycle gas turbine stations	KJDA	150	153	343	GUGI	410	757	1 005	1 243	1 709	1 777	1 840
Hydro-electric stations (natural flow)	KGOX	111	111	118	GUGJ	142	145	148	150	158	160	162
Renewables other than hydro	KILB	265	297	330	GUGK	437	483	589	680	847	895	1 015
All generating companies: Total capacity[5]	KGOY	68 523	68 741	70 126	GUGL	73 271	72 913	73 380	75 446	78 288	79 488	76 588
Conventional steam stations[6]	KGOZ	44 239	41 710	41 476	GUGM	41 422	40 635	38 329	38 742	38 184	38 077	35 164
Combined cycle gas turbine stations	KJDC	5 613	8 517	9 377	GUGN	12 462	13 009	15 643	17 353	21 058	22 294	22 089
Nuclear stations[3]	KGPM	11 894	12 037	12 762	GUGO	12 916	12 946	12 956	12 956	12 486	12 486	12 486
Gas turbines and oil engines	KGPN	2 248	1 895	1 890	GUGP	1 721	1 526	1 492	1 333	1 323	1 323	1 463
Hydro-electric stations:												
Natural flow	KGPO	1 425	1 425	1 432	GUGQ	1 455	1 456	1 475	1 477	1 485	1 508	1 466
Pumped storage	KGPP	2 787	2 788	2 788	GUGR	2 788	2 788	2 788	2 788	2 788	2 788	2 788
Renewables other than hydro	KGPQ	317	369	401	GUGS	507	553	697	797	964	1 012	1 132
Major power producers[2]:												
Simultaneous maximum load met[7]	KGPR	54 848	52 362	55 611	GUGT	56 815	56 965	56 312	57 849	58 452	58 589	61 717
System load factor[8] (percentage)	KGQY	63.8	67.3	65.4	GUGU	66.3	66.2	67.5	66.7	67.4	68.7	64.6

1 From 1996 data are on a calendar year basis.
2 See chapter text.
3 The 1995 figure includes 300 MW of the 1,188 MW capacity of Sizewell B which began to produce electricity in March 1995.
4 Nuclear generators are now included under "major power producers" only.
5 Capacity figures for other generators are as at end-December of the previous year.

6 For other generators, conventional steam stations cover all types of stations not separately listed.
7 Maximum load in year to end of March.
8 The average hourly quantity of electricity available during the year ended March expressed as a percentage of the maximum demand.

Source: Department of Trade and Industry: 020 7215 5190

22.10 Electricity: fuel used in generation
United Kingdom

Million tonnes of oil equivalent

		1992	1993	1994	1995	1996	1997	1998	1999	2000	2001	2002
Major power producers[1]: total all fuels	KGPS	71.3	72.3	71.7	72.7	74.6	71.5	74.9	73.6	74.4	77.3	76.0
Coal	FTAJ	46.0	38.3	35.9	35.0	32.4	27.1	28.7	24.5	27.8	30.6	28.6
Oil[2]	FTAK	5.0	4.4	3.6	3.1	3.0	1.2	0.8	0.8	0.8	0.8	0.7
Gas[3]	KGPT	1.0	6.3	9.1	11.4	15.2	19.3	20.3	24.2	24.4	23.8	25.0
Nuclear[4]	FTAL	18.5	21.6	21.2	21.3	22.2	22.0	23.4	22.2	19.6	20.7	20.3
Hydro (natural flow)	FTAM	0.4	0.3	0.4	0.4	0.2	0.3	0.4	0.4	0.4	0.3	0.3
Other fuels used by UK companies[3]	KGPU	–	0.1	0.1	0.1	0.1	0.2	0.2	0.2	0.2	0.3	0.3
Net imports	KGPV	1.4	1.4	1.5	1.4	1.4	1.4	1.1	1.2	1.2	0.9	0.7
Other generators: total all fuels	KGPW	6.7	4.5	3.5	5.8	6.0	6.7	7.1	7.3	8.0	7.2	7.6
Transport undertakings												
Gas	KGPX	0.2	0.2	0.2	0.2	0.2	0.2	0.2	0.2	0.2	0.2	0.2
Undertakings in industrial sector												
Coal	KGPY	1.0	1.3	1.2	1.3	1.2	1.2	1.2	1.0	0.9	1.0	0.9
Oil	KGPZ	3.1	1.4	0.5	1.0	1.0	0.8	0.7	0.7	0.8	0.6	0.6
Gas	KGQM	0.3	0.8	0.6	1.6	1.8	2.2	2.5	2.7	3.3	2.6	2.9
Hydro (natural flow)	KGQO	0.1	0.1	0.1	0.1	0.1	0.1	0.1	0.1	0.1	0.1	0.1
Other fuels	KGQP	1.1	1.0	1.0	1.7	1.8	2.2	2.4	2.6	2.8	2.7	2.9
All generating companies: total fuels	KGQQ	78.0	76.8	75.2	78.6	80.6	78.2	82.0	80.9	82.4	84.5	83.6
Coal	KGQR	46.9	39.6	37.1	36.3	33.6	28.3	29.9	25.5	28.7	31.6	29.6
Oil	KGQS	8.1	5.8	4.1	4.1	4.0	2.0	1.5	1.5	1.5	1.4	1.3
Gas[3]	KGQT	1.5	7.0	9.9	13.3	17.2	21.7	23.0	27.1	27.9	26.6	28.1
Nuclear[4]	KGQU	18.5	21.6	21.2	21.3	22.2	22.0	23.4	22.2	19.6	20.7	20.3
Hydro (natural flow)	KGQV	0.5	0.4	0.4	0.4	0.3	0.4	0.4	0.5	0.4	0.3	0.4
Other fuels used by UK companies[3,5]	KGQW	1.1	1.0	1.1	1.8	1.9	2.4	2.6	2.9	3.0	2.9	3.2
Net imports	KGQX	1.4	1.4	1.5	1.4	1.4	1.4	1.1	1.2	1.2	0.9	0.7

1 See chapter text.
2 Includes oil used in gas turbine and diesel plant for lighting up coal fired boilers and Orimulsion.
3 For 1991 gas used by major power producers was included with other fuels for reasons of confidentiality.

4 Nuclear generators are now included under "major power producers" only.
5 Main fuels included are coke oven gas, blast furnace gas, waste products from chemical processes and sludge gas.

Source: Department of Trade and Industry: 020 7215 5190

22.11 Indigenous production, refinery receipts, imports and exports of oil[1]

Thousand tonnes

		1992	1993	1994	1995	1996	1997	1998	1999	2000	2001	2002
Total indigenous petroleum production[2]	KMBA	94 251	100 188	126 812	129 894	129 742	128 234	132 363	137 099	126 245	116 678	115 944
Crude petroleum[3]:												
Refinery receipts total	KMBB	92 789	97 400	93 771	93 572	96 660	97 023	93 797	88 286	88 014	83 343	85 389
Foreign trade[4]												
Imports	KMBF	57 683	61 701	53 096	48 749	50 099	49 994	47 958	44 869	54 387	53 551	56 690
Exports	AXRB	57 627	64 415	83 205	84 578	81 563	79 400	84 610	91 797	92 918	86 918	86 812
Net imports	AXRC	56	–2 714	–30 109	–35 829	–31 464	–29 406	–36 652	–46 928	–38 531	–33 367	–30 122
Petroleum products												
Foreign trade[4]												
Imports[4]	BHMI	10 567	10 064	10 441	9 878	9 315	8 705	11 327	13 896	14 212	16 978	13 696
Exports[4]	AXRD	20 250	23 060	22 157	21 614	23 681	26 755	24 375	21 730	20 677	19 088	22 827
Net imports[4]	AXRE	–9 683	–12 996	–11 716	–11 736	–14 366	–18 049	–12 957	–7 834	–6 465	–2 110	–9 131
International marine bunkers	BHMK	2 546	2 478	2 313	2 465	2 664	2 961	3 080	2 329	2 079	2 274	2 466

1 See chapter text. The term 'indigenous' is used in this table to cover oil produced on the UK Continental Shelf. This includes small amounts produced onshore.
2 Crude oil *plus* condensates and petroleum gases derived at onshore treatment plants.

3 Includes process (partly refined) oils.
4 Foreign trade as recorded by the petroleum industry and may differ from figures published in *Overseas Trade Statistics*.

Source: Department of Trade and Industry: 020 7215 5184

22.12 Throughput of crude and process oils and output of refined products from refineries[1]

United Kingdom

Thousand tonnes

		1992	1993	1994	1995	1996	1997	1998	1999	2000	2001	2002
Throughput of crude and process oils	KMAU	92 334	96 274	93 162	92 743	96 661	97 024	93 797	88 285	88 014	83 343	85 389
less: Refinery fuel:	KMAA	6 080	6 383	6 256	6 481	6 623	6 572	6 468	5 969	5 245	5 162	4 873
Losses	KMAB	471	308	261	129	152	86	1 005	1 554	1 672	1 250	845
Total output of refined products	KMAC	85 783	89 583	86 645	86 133	89 885	90 366	86 615	81 195	81 582	77 239	79 750
Gases:												
Butane and propane	KMAE	1 583	1 575	1 605	1 815	1 828	1 950	1 961	1 975	1 981	1 764	2 157
Other petroleum	KMAF	172	162	132	133	144	139	394	361	287	295	582
Naphtha and other feedstock	KMAG	3 040	2 696	2 794	2 711	2 824	2 854	2 316	2 430	3 081	3 405	3 090
Aviation spirit	KMAH	–	–	–	–	–	–	–	16	30	101	28
Motor spirit	KMAJ	27 980	28 394	27 562	27 254	28 046	28 260	27 166	25 230	23 445	21 455	23 178
Industrial and white spirit	KMAK	150	159	143	143	136	128	135	129	122	122	121
Kerosene:												
Aviation turbine fuel	KMAL	7 681	8 341	7 697	7 837	8 305	8 342	7 876	7 249	6 484	5 910	5 603
Burning oil	KMAM	2 450	2 707	2 967	2 924	3 510	3 336	3 442	3 553	3 078	3 088	3 344
Gas/diesel oil	KMAN	25 650	27 361	27 137	27 169	28 903	28 778	27 532	25 750	28 219	26 746	28 383
Fuel oil	KMAO	12 388	13 183	11 378	10 969	11 479	11 747	11 125	10 446	10 390	10 119	8 621
Lubricating oil	KMAP	1 163	1 264	1 296	1 261	1 111	1 231	1 125	907	702	656	516
Bitumen	KMAQ	2 336	2 450	2 569	2 459	2 189	2 258	2 172	1 644	1 438	1 707	1 909
Petroleum wax	KMAR	62	59	64	46	41	65	59	261	437	416	447
Petroleum coke	KMAS	535	621	679	759	714	598	678	648	820	765	890
Other products	KMAT	593	613	623	653	655	680	634	596	1 068	690	881

1 See chapter text. Crude and process oils comprise all feedstocks, other than distillation benzines, for treatment at refinery plants. Refinery production does not cover further treatment of finished products for special grades such as in distillation plant for the preparation of industrial spirits.

Source: Department of Trade and Industry: 020 7215 5184

22.13 Deliveries of petroleum products for inland consumption[1]
United Kingdom

Thousand tonnes

		1992	1993	1994	1995	1996	1997	1998	1999	2000	2001	2002
Total (including refinery fuel)	KMCA	81 550	82 173	81 213	80 175	82 013	79 073	78 437	77 985	76 678	76 077	75 254
Total (excluding refinery fuel)	KMCB	75 470	75 970	74 957	73 694	75 390	72 501	71 969	72 009	71 433	70 915	70 402
Butane and propane	ECAQ	1 890	1 992	2 486	2 481	2 439	2 426	2 368	2 249	2 070	2 155	2 543
Other Petroleum Gases (includes Ethane)	ECAR	1 201	1 261	1 459	1 489	1 482	1 561	1 534	1 829	1 707	1 873	1 953
Naphtha	ECAS	3 281	3 117	2 866	2 885	3 010	2 640	2 882	3 100	2 344	1 594	1 592
Aviation spirit	KMCI	27	27	29	29	32	37	36	45	52	59	52
Motor spirit:												
Retail deliveries:												
Leaded Premium / Lead Replacement Petrol	KMCK	12 481	11 046	9 503	7 993	7 043	6 138	4 595	2 629	1 462	837	394
Super Premium Unleaded	KMCL	1 401	1 439	1 323	925	698	506	409	473	403	420	687
Premium Unleaded	KMCM	9 541	10 754	11 536	12 603	14 228	15 188	16 432	18 307	19 208	19 095	18 135
Total Retail Deliveries	ECAT	23 423	23 239	22 362	21 521	21 969	21 832	21 436	21 409	21 073	20 352	19 217
Commercial consumers:												
Leaded Premium / Lead Replacement Petrol	KMCO	294	217	178	149	135	112	91	61	44	34	19
Super Premium Unleaded	KMCP	22	25	26	17	11	9	4	6	6	9	17
Premium Unleaded	KMCQ	304	286	277	285	294	298	318	311	480	538	499
Total Commercial Consumers	ECAU	620	528	481	451	440	419	413	378	530	581	535
Total Motor spirit	BHOD	24 043	23 767	22 843	21 972	22 409	22 251	21 849	21 787	21 603	20 933	19 752
Industrial and white spirits	KMCS	159	164	170	178	184	195	179	174	170	150	165
Kerosene:												
Aviation turbine fuel	BHOE	6 666	7 106	7 284	7 660	8 049	8 411	9 241	9 939	10 806	10 297	10 148
Burning oil	KMCT	2 472	2 625	2 655	2 774	3 336	3 343	3 575	3 633	3 838	4 244	3 851
Gas/diesel oil:												
Derv fuel:												
Retail Deliveries	ECAV	3 449	3 765	4 345	4 814	5 537	6 127	6 602	7 137	7 713	8 198	8 599
Commercial Consumers	ECAW	7 683	8 041	8 569	8 643	8 828	8 849	8 541	8 371	8 168	8 220	9 055
Total Derv fuel	BHOI	11 132	11 806	12 914	13 457	14 365	14 976	15 143	15 508	15 881	16 418	17 654
Other gas/diesel oil (includes Mdf)	ECAX	8 616	8 516	8 167	7 879	8 349	8 053	8 005	7 196	7 036	7 008	6 334
Fuel oil	BHOK	11 481	10 770	9 275	7 975	6 854	3 936	2 935	2 415	1 833	2 202	2 121
Lubricating oils	BHOL	786	806	795	895	864	872	813	790	804	796	850
Bitumen	BHOM	2 555	2 523	2 595	2 420	2 146	2 015	1 967	1 928	1 975	1 923	1 983
Petroleum wax	KMCU	47	48	47	44	44	44	18	37	32	32	48
Petroleum coke	KMCV	682	778	911	1 008	1 210	1 095	887	660	776	760	893
Miscellaneous products	KMCW	431	661	461	548	617	646	537	719	463	472	464

1 See chapter text.

Source: Department of Trade and Industry: 020 7215 5184

22.14 Iron and steel[1]: Summary of steel supplies, deliveries and stocks
United Kingdom

		1992	1993	1994	1995	1996	1997	1998	1999	2000	2001	2002
Supply, disposal and consumption - (Finished product weight - Thousand tonnes)												
UK producers' home deliveries	KLTA	7 315	7 567	7 827	8 257	8 383	8 626	8 260	7 652	7 255	6 762	6 507
Imports excluding steelworks receipts	KLTB	4 418	4 132	5 012	5 384	5 147	5 894	6 466	6 014	6 387	6 978	6 796
Total deliveries to home market (a)	KLTC	11 733	11 698	12 839	13 641	13 530	14 520	14 726	13 666	13 642	13 740	13 303
Total exports (producers, consumers, merchants)	KLTD	7 718	7 621	8 120	8 228	8 917	9 060	8 008	7 623	7 446	6 512	6 318
Exports by UK producers	KLTE	7 587	7 536	7 873	7 828	8 305	8 534	7 876	7 416	7 163	6 182	5 614
Derived consumers' and merchants' exports (b)	KLTF	131	85	247	400	612	526	132	207	283	330	704
Net home disposals (a)-(b)	KLTG	11 602	11 614	12 592	13 241	12 918	13 994	14 594	13 460	13 359	13 410	12 599
Consumers' and merchants' stock change	KLTH	60	60	390	..	..	..	..	..	..	..	..
Estimated home consumption	KLTI	11 542	11 554	12 202	13 241	12 918	13 994	14 594	13 460	13 359	13 410	12 599
Stocks - (Finished product weight - Thousand tonnes)												
Producers												
- ingots & semis	KLTJ	933	1 005	946	1 068	767	946	717	747	727	705	690
- finished steel	KLTK	1 573	1 425	1 389	1 274	1 515	1 358	1 495	1 318	1 039	981	932
Consumers	KLTL	1 410	1 300	1 470	..	..	..	..	..	..	..	..
Merchants	KLTM	890	1 060	1 280	..	..	..	..	..	..	..	..
Estimated home consumption - (Crude steel equivalent - Million tonnes)												
Crude steel production[2]	KLTN	16.21	16.62	17.28	17.60	17.99	18.50	17.32	16.28	15.15	13.54	11.67
Producers' stock change	KLTO	−0.30	−0.09	−0.12	0.01	−0.07	0.03	−0.11	−0.19	−0.33	−0.14	−0.08
Re-usable material	KLTP	0.06	0.08	0.09	0.08	0.07	0.06	0.02	..	..	..	..
Total supply from home sources	KLTQ	16.57	16.79	17.49	17.67	18.13	18.53	17.45	16.47	15.48	13.68	11.75
Total imports[3]	KLTR	5.99	5.44	6.58	7.05	7.01	7.49	8.38	7.81	8.43	9.11	9.86
Total exports[3]	KLTS	9.07	8.95	9.55	9.63	10.26	10.43	9.25	8.70	8.61	7.53	7.39
Net home disposals	KLTT	13.49	13.28	14.52	15.09	14.88	15.59	16.58	15.58	15.30	15.26	14.22
Consumers' and merchants' stock change	KLTU	0.07	0.07	0.48	..	..	..	..	..	..	..	..
Estimated home consumption	KLTV	13.42	13.21	14.04	15.09	14.88	15.59	16.58	15.58	15.30	15.26	14.22

1 See chapter text. The figures relate to periods of 52 weeks (53 weeks in 1992).
2 Includes liquid steel for castings.
3 Based on HM Customs Statistics, reflecting total trade rather than producers' trade.

Source: Iron and Steel Statistics Bureau: 020 8686 9050 ext 126

Production

22.15 Iron and steel[1]: Iron ore, manganese ore, pig iron and iron and steel scrap
United Kingdom

		1992	1993	1994	1995	1996	1997	1998	1999	2000	2001	2002
Iron ore												
Jurassic	KLOA	29	–	–	–	–	–	–	–	–	–	–
Hematite	KLOB	–	–	–	–	–	–	–	–	–	–	–
Production: total	KLOC	29	–	–	–	–	–	–	–	–	–	–
Home produced	KLOD	29	–	–	–	–	–	–	–	–	–	–
Imported	KLOE	17 235	17 507	18 161	18 670	19 720	20 820	19 532	18 739	16 955	15 108	13 181
Consumption: total	KLOF	17 264	17 507	18 161	18 670	19 720	20 820	19 532	18 739	16 928	15 113	13 185
Manganese ore												
Consumption	KLOG	308	152	64	32	48	37	22	14	36	4	4
Pig iron (and blast furnace ferro-alloys)												
Average number of furnaces in blast during period	KLOH	*8*	*8*	*8*	*8*	*9*	*9*	*9*	*9*	*8*	*7*	*5*
Production												
Steelmaking iron	KLOI	11 469	11 534	11 943	12 236	12 830	13 054	12 746	12 139	10 890	9 870	8 561
Foundry iron	KLOJ	73	–	–	–	–	–	–	–	–	–	–
Speigeleisen and ferro-manganese	KLOK	137	45	–	–	–	–	–	–	–	–	–
In blast furnaces: total	KLOL	11 679	11 579	11 943	12 236	12 830	13 054	12 746	12 139	10 890	9 870	8 561
In steel works and steel foundries	KLOM	11 463	11 554	11 889	12 121	12 753	13 044	12 746	12 139	10 890	9 870	8 561
In iron foundries	KLON	214	–	–	–	–	–	–	–	–	–	–
Consumption of pig iron: total	KLOO	11 677	11 554	11 889	12 121	12 753	13 044	12 746	12 139	10 890	9 870	8 561
Iron and steel scrap												
Steelworks and steel foundries												
Circulating scrap	KLOQ	2 449	2 303	2 326	2 390	2 639	2 459	2 380	2 488	2 287	2 019	1 882
Purchased receipts	KLOR	3 739	4 149	4 533	4 688	4 130	5 418	4 045	3 433	3 327	3 001	2 271
Consumption	KLOS	6 190	6 550	6 874	7 012	6 828	7 207	6 408	5 884	5 675	5 006	4 216
Stocks (end of period)	KLOT	365	267	253	319	260	236	253	290	229	224	161
Iron foundries												
Arisings	KLOU	587	–	–	–	–	–	–	–	–	–	–
Consumption	KLOV	1 556	–	–	–	–	–	–	–	–	–	–

1 See chapter text. The figures relate to periods of 52 weeks (53 weeks in 1992).

Source: Iron and Steel Statistics Bureau: 020 8686 9050 ext 126

22.16 Iron and steel[1]: Number of furnaces and production of steel
United Kingdom

		1992	1993	1994	1995	1996	1997	1998	1999	2000	2001	2002
Steel furnaces - (Number in existence at end of period)[2]												
Total	KLPA	206	202	202	192	192	192	190	181	181	181	173
Oxygen converters	KLPC	11	11	11	11	11	11	11	11	11	11	8
Electric	KLPD	195	191	191	181	181	181	179	170	170	170	165
Production of crude steel (thousand tonnes)												
Total	KLPF	16 212	16 625	17 286	17 604	17 992	18 499	17 315	16 284	15 155	13 543	11 667
by process												
Oxygen converters	KLPH	12 092	12 330	12 909	13 082	13 758	13 986	13 426	12 634	11 551	10 271	8 956
Electric	KLPI	4 120	4 295	4 377	4 522	4 234	4 513	3 889	3 650	3 604	3 272	2 711
by cast method												
Cast to ingot	KLPK	2 083	2 140	2 033	2 174	1 892	1 660	784	534	539	369	339
Continuously cast	KLPL	13 958	14 319	15 079	15 250	15 912	16 653	16 346	15 637	14 470	13 024	11 182
Steel for castings	KLPM	171	166	174	180	188	186	185	127	146	150	146
by quality												
Non alloy steel	KLPN	15 195	15 558	16 062	16 243	16 708	17 193	16 145	15 263	14 004	12 482	10 657
Stainless and other alloy steel	KLPO	1 017	1 067	1 224	1 361	1 284	1 306	1 170	1 035	1 151	1 061	1 010
Production of finished steel products (All quantities)[3](thousand tonnes)												
Rods and bars for reinforcement (in coil and lengths)	KLPP	1 130	1 229	1 269	1 154	1 182	1 118	1 133	893	812	755	487
Wire rods and other rods and bars in coil	KLPQ	1 327	1 427	1 524	1 642	1 536	1 565	1 492	1 407	1 408	1 389	1 394
Hot rolled bars in lengths	KLPR	1 178	1 140	1 275	1 311	1 499	1 716	1 791	1 542	1 545	1 449	1 267
Bright steel bars[4]	KLPS	281	295	363	424	357	385	336	311	337	296	271
Light sections other than rails	KLPT	349	294	306	286	298	302	318	264	183	201	188
Heavy sections	KGQZ	2 361	2 408	2 412	2 549	2 557	2 397	2 346	2 303	1 915	1 931	1 873
Hot rolled plates, sheets and strip in coil and lengths	KLPW	7 145	7 230	7 715	8 077	8 512	8 956	8 454	7 893	7 278	5 821	5 708
Cold rolled plates and sheets in coil and lengths	KLPX	3 532	3 635	3 835	4 100	4 221	4 437	4 288	3 914	3 612	2 944	2 854
Cold rolled strip[4]	KLPZ	222	229	243	267	246	255	259	233	218	201	179
Tinplate	KLQW	805	829	767	791	739	754	772	736	753	602	562
Other coated sheet	KLQX	1 795	1 865	2 021	2 306	2 366	2 534	2 610	2 475	2 471	1 773	1 786
Tubes and pipes[4]	KLQY	1 187	1 155	1 136	1 183	1 317	1 310	1 276	1 100	1 061	1 096	1 071
Forged bars[4]	KLQZ	4	2	2	3	3	3	3	2	1	1	–

1 See chapter text. The figures relate to periods of 52 weeks (53 weeks in 1992).
2 Includes steel furnaces at steel foundries.
3 Includes material for conversion into other products listed in the table.
4 Based on producers' deliveries.

Source: Iron and Steel Statistics Bureau: 020 8686 9050 ext 126

22.17 Non-ferrous metals
United Kingdom

Thousand tonnes

		1991	1992	1993	1994	1995	1996	1997	1998	1999	2000	2001
Copper												
Production of refined copper:												
Primary	KLAA	16.6	10.4	10.7	11.1	12.0	13.0	9.1	6.4	1.7	–	–
Secondary	KLAB	53.5	31.7	35.9	35.6	43.0	43.6	51.3	47.4	48.6	–	–
Home consumption:												
Refined	KLAC	269.4	308.3	325.0	377.3	397.9	396.0	408.3	374.1	305.3	322.7	285.9
Scrap (metal content)	KLAD	118.5	83.2	77.9	88.0	81.0	81.0	69.0	64.6	112.5	132.4	127.0
Stocks (end of period)[1,2]	KLAE	9.3	9.7	9.3	8.1	7.5	6.6	12.8	7.5	7.3	10.4	7.3
Analysis of home consumption												
(refined and scrap):[3] total	KLAF	387.9	391.5	403.0	468.0	493.2	477.3	477.4	438.7	417.7	455.2	412.9
Wire[4]	KLAG	191.9	247.0	253.9	306.2	321.4	309.4	312.5	287.2	276.1	310.2	..
Rods, bars and sections	KLAH	52.7	51.5	53.2	54.9	59.0	58.3	58.3	53.6	46.9	43.6	..
Sheet, strip and plate	KLAI	37.1	31.0	30.7	33.0	37.1	34.0	36.5	30.5	27.7	32.3	..
Tubes	KLAJ	65.5	62.0	65.2	73.9	75.7	75.6	70.1	67.4	67.1	69.4	..
Castings and miscellaneous	KLAK	40.7	..	..	..	..	..	..	..	..	..	..
Zinc												
Slab zinc:												
Production	KLAL	100.7	96.8	102.4	101.3	106.0	96.9	107.7	99.6	132.8	99.6	99.6
Home consumption	KLAM	183.7	190.1	195.9	196.5	198.4	195.7	194.8	187.9	198.9	206.5	197.1
Stocks (end of period)	KLAN	11.2	11.4	11.4	10.5	9.8	10.5	10.1	10.6	10.9	10.9	9.5
Other zinc (metal content):												
Consumption	KLAO	49.5	46.7	45.4	45.0	46.8	41.3	41.5	37.3	41.6	46.3	48.2
Analysis of home consumption												
(slab and scrap): total	KLAP	233.2	236.8	241.3	241.5	245.2	237.1	236.3	226.2	236.7	242.5	231.2
Brass	KLAQ	47.2	40.9	41.6	42.6	45.2	39.1	41.6	36.6	33.6	34.4	32.2
Galvanized products	KLAR	96.6	103.4	105.1	107.4	110.7	110.3	108.4	103.8	116.6	120.9	111.8
Zinc sheet and strip	KLAS	3.6	4.1	4.0	4.6	3.0	3.0	3.3	3.3	3.3	3.3	3.3
Zinc alloy die castings	KLAT	45.4	45.2	46.5	46.5	46.5	46.5	46.5	46.5	46.5	46.5	46.5
Zinc oxide	KLAU	20.3	22.5	20.7	21.6	21.6	20.7	20.6	20.4	21.1	21.8	21.8
Other products	KLAV	20.2	20.8	23.4	18.8	18.2	17.5	16.1	11.0	11.0	11.0	11.0
Refined lead												
Production[5,6]	KLAW	311.0	346.8	363.8	352.5	320.7	351.4	384.1	349.7	347.3	327.9	366.3
Home consumption[6,7]												
Refined lead	KLAX	263.8	263.6	263.6	267.6	285.4	272.8	270.4	275.5	283.3	294.0	298.3
Scrap and remelted lead[6]	KLAY	33.6	38.7	35.2	38.5	41.6	43.4	39.1	38.4	32.2	40.9	40.7
Stocks (end of period)[8]												
Lead bullion	KLAZ	22.8	36.3	20.7	10.2	9.5	32.9	15.5	20.9	17.1	10.0	17.2
Refined soft lead at consumers	KLBA	21.8	24.5	25.0	23.5	24.9	28.8	29.1	27.4	25.7	25.8	26.1
In LME Warehouses (UK)	KLBB	8.0	9.0	9.5	6.1	0.4	3.0	2.4	–	0.1	–	–
Analysis of home consumption												
(refined and scrap): total	KLBC	297.4	302.3	298.8	306.1	327.0	316.2	309.5	313.9	315.5	333.5	338.9
Cables	KLBD	8.6	9.3	8.9	9.3	9.8	9.8	9.7	9.7	9.7	9.6	9.6
Batteries (excluding oxides)	KLBE	51.9	53.4	48.7	52.5	52.7	52.3	54.7	51.6	47.4	50.5	48.2
Oxides and compounds:												
Batteries	KLBF	54.2	53.1	53.9	55.2	56.2	54.9	56.1	54.4	53.1	55.9	54.7
Other uses	KLBG	55.0	55.6	56.3	53.9	53.8	56.1	54.5	56.4	57.0	56.8	53.8
Sheets and pipes	KLBH	79.8	82.8	82.7	84.6	101.2	94.1	91.1	96.1	94.9	102.3	102.3
Solder	KLBJ	7.7	7.4	7.4	7.4	7.4	7.4	7.4	7.4	7.4	7.4	7.4
Alloys	KLBK	12.2	14.7	14.1	15.3	15.9	12.1	9.4	9.4	11.9	15.2	24.3
Other uses	KLBL	28.0	26.2	26.8	27.9	30.0	29.5	26.6	28.9	34.1	35.8	38.6

22.17

Non-ferrous metals
United Kingdom

continued

		1992	1993	1994	1995	1996	1997	1998	1999	2000	2001	2002
Tin												
Tin ore (metal content):												
Production	KLBM	2.0	2.2	1.9	2.0	2.1	2.3	0.4	–	..	..	..
Tin metal[9]:												
Production[10]	KLBO	–	–	–	–	–	–	..	..	..	..	..
Home consumption[10]	VQIX	10.4	10.5	10.6	10.5	10.5	10.4	10.6	9.6	10.0	10.3	9.9
Exports and re-exports[11]	KLBQ	0.2	0.3	1.2	2.7	0.6	0.3	3.4	0.1	0.1	0.4	0.3
Stocks (end of period):												
Consumers	KLBR	1.0	1.0	1.0	1.0	1.0	1.0	1.0	1.0	1.0	1.0	1.0
Analysis of home consumption												
(excluding scrap): total	KLBT	10.4	10.4	10.4	10.5	10.5	9.8	9.6	10.0	9.6	9.6	9.6
Tinplate	KLBU	3.6	3.6	3.6	3.6	3.6	2.8	2.6	3.0	3.0	3.0	3.0
Alloys	KLBV	3.4	3.4	3.3	3.4	3.5	3.6	3.6	3.6	3.6	3.6	3.6
Solder	KLBW	1.1	1.1	1.1	1.1	1.1	1.1	1.1	1.1	1.1	1.1	1.1
Other uses	KLBX	2.3	2.3	2.4	2.4	2.3	2.3	2.3	2.3	1.9	1.9	1.9
Primary aluminium[12]												
Production	KLBY	244.2	239.1	231.2	237.9	240.0	247.7	258.4	269.7	305.1	340.8	..
Despatches to consumers	KLBZ	587.2	815.3	610.6	459.4	593.7	456.4	648.5	480.1	234.4	450.7	..
Secondary aluminium												
Production	KLCA	197.3	236.2	224.3	229.7	261.0	242.7	274.8	258.3	241.3	248.6	..
Exports	KLCC	83.5	98.3	124.8	145.8	152.2	153.3	156.6	143.1	84.2	59.9	..
Fabricated aluminium												
Total despatches[13]	KLCD	598.2	592.0	643.1	648.3	633.5	663.2	668.5	668.7	738.7	690.5	..
Rolled products[14]	KLCE	328.9	309.3	346.4	359.2	327.9	350.4	352.5	349.7	419.1	384.8	..
Extrusions and tubes[15]	KLCF	132.8	136.2	142.7	142.1	149.6	160.8	168.0	181.7	184.7	167.5	..
Castings	KLCH	116.3	133.0	143.4	147.0	156.0	152.0	148.0	137.3	134.9	138.2	..
Refined nickel												
Production (including ferro-nickel)	KLCM	28.0	28.0	28.4	35.1	38.6	36.1	39.1	39.5	38.0	33.8	33.8

1 Unwrought copper (electrolytic, fire refined and blister).
2 Reported stocks of refined copper held by consumers and those held in London Metal Exchange (LME) warehouses in the United Kingdom.
3 Copper content.
4 Consumption for high-conductivity copper and cadmium copper wire represented by consumption of wire rods, production of which for export is also included.
5 Lead reclaimed from secondary and scrap material and lead refined from bullion and domestic ores.
6 Figures for production and consumption of refined lead include antimonial lead, and for scrap and remelted lead, exclude secondary antimonial lead.
7 Including toll transactions involving fabrication.
8 Excluding goverment stocks.

9 Including production from imported scrap and residues refined on toll.
10 Primary and secondary metal.
11 Including re-exports on toll transactions.
12 Including primary alloys. Despatches to consumers are calculated as the despatches by UK industry plus imports, minus exports but deliveries to LME warehouses are not included.
13 Includes wrought, cast products, and excludes foil products.
14 Includes foil stock and excludes foil products.
15 Excluding forging bars, wirebars, and almost two-thirds of despatches of hot rolled rod.

Sources: World Bureau of Metal Statistics: 01920 461274;
Aluminium Federation: 0121 456 1103

22.18 Fertilisers[1]
Years ending 30 June

Thousand tonnes

		1992	1993	1994	1995	1996	1997	1998	1999	2000	2001	2002
Nutrient Content												
N (nitrogen):												
Straight	KGRM	587	537	553	602	685	615	664	618	637	479	521
Compounds	KGRN	378	377	413	449	444	420	406	430	398	400	419
P_2O_5 (phosphate)	KGRO	227	218	236	272	284	287	296	291	253	228	235
K_2O (potash)	KGRP	287	284	299	343	353	356	360	357	309	269	289
Compounds - total product	KGRQ	2 254	2 216	2 378	2 656	2 688	2 664	2 620	2 727	2 523	2 228	2 329

1 Deliveries to UK agriculture by Members of the Agricultural Industries Confederation - Fertiliser Sector.

Source: Agricultural Industries Confederation: 01780 781360

22.19 Minerals: production[1]

Thousand tonnes

		1992	1993	1994	1995	1996	1997	1998	1999	2000	2001	2002
Great Britain												
Limestone	KLEA	86 000	90 069	102 844	90 933	82 442	84 252	85 382	82 714	80 810	83 492	88 013
Sandstone	KLEB	11 586	12 100	13 494	15 017	12 581	12 457	13 545	11 870	12 056	11 897	11 788
Igneous rock	KLEC	48 630	49 209	50 014	49 641	43 731	42 370	39 838	45 294	44 633	45 053	44 544
Clay/shale	KLED	12 155	10 891	12 464	13 930	11 804	11 322	12 230	11 355	10 838	10 426	10 306
Industrial sand	KLEE	3 615	3 587	4 038	4 344	4 861	4 704	4 662	4 092	4 095	3 848	3 833
Chalk	KLEF	9 171	9 076	10 236	9 949	9 239	9 550	9 934	9 667	9 213	8 205	8 587
Fireclay	KLEG	572	479	679	708	536	338	577	545	595	459	491
Barium sulphate	KLEH	77	33	34	74	93	57	64	59	54	70	56
Calcium fluoride	KLEI	76	70	50	46	..	58	52	46	21	46	22
Copper	KLEJ	–	–	–	–	–	–	–	–	–	–	–
Lead	KLEK	..	..	2	..	..	..	1	1	..	1	..
Tin	KLEL	2.0	2.2	1.9	2.0	2.1	2.0	–	–	–	–	–
Zinc	KLEM	..	..	..	..	..	–	–	–	–	–	–
Iron ore: crude	KLEN	4	..	2	2	1	2	2	1	1	1	1
Iron ore: iron content	KLEO	2	1	1	1	1	1	1	1	1	..	..
Calcspar	KLEP	4	3	..	..	..	13	15	..	..	12	..
China clay	KLEQ / KILC	2 732	2 852	2 977	3 076	2 654	2 798	2 866	2 841	2 779	2 804	2 467
Ball clay	KIMS	..	..	913	..	..	..	..	..	..	..	..
Chert and flint	KLER	..	..	..	..	..	..	..	6	..	2	2
Fuller's earth	KLES	203	153	193	150	183	162	111	83	103	..	33
Lignite	KLET	3	3	2	–	..	–	–	–	–	–	–
Rock salt	KLEU	..	..	..	..	..	..	..	..	..	..	..
Salt from brine	KLEV	..	..	..	..	..	..	..	..	..	..	..
Salt in brine	KLEW	3 401	4 076	4 009	3 548	3 512	3 561	..	..	..	..	..
Anhydrite	KLEX	..	..	..	..	–	..	–	–	–	–	–
Dolomite	KLEY	18 539	17 985	17 616	17 966	16 555	17 282	15 632	13 698	13 069	14 314	12 946
Gypsum	KLEZ	..	..	..	..	..	..	..	..	..	..	..
Slate[2]	KLFA	326	462	402	275	408	347	425	361	479	551	742
Soapstone and talc	KLFB	5	5	5	4	5	5	5	6	5	5	6
Sand and gravel (land-won)	KLFC	78 341	79 380	86 341	78 031	70 489	74 362	73 016	74 785	74 877	74 599	69 889
Sand and gravel (marine dredged)	KLFD	10 557	10 090	11 331	11 625	11 508	12 004	12 952	13 424	14 356	13 611	12 832
Northern Ireland												
Sand and gravel	KLFG	3 697	4 318	5 109	5 262	7 684	5 138	5 300	5 517	5 073	6 194	5 512
Basalt and igneous rock (other than granite)	KLFH	9 024	8 557	6 480	7 564	6 974	6 286	6 107	7 861	9 480	6 448	6 681
Limestone	KLFI	3 398	3 236	..	3 703	4 122	3 500	3 892	4 219	3 538	4 746	4 514
Sandstone[3]	KLFJ	3 304	3 959	5 480	4 779	4 941	6 042	6 584	3 615	2 844	8 070	6 574
Granite	KLFL	..	..	..	..	–	–	–	–	–	–	–
Others[4]	KLFN	..	647	896	812	1 392	625	473	1 579	3 098	753	242

1 See chapter text.
2 Includes waste used for constructional fill, and powder and granules used in manufacturing.

3 Prior to 1993 the 'Sandstone' heading was called 'Grit and conglomerate'. The new heading is all encompassing and was confirmed as correct with the Geological Survey in Northern Ireland.
4 Rock salt, Chalk, Diatomite and Fireclay.

Source: Office for National Statistics: 01633 812082

22.20 Building materials and components: production[1]
Great Britain

		Unit	1992	1993	1994	1995	1996	1997	1998	1999	2000	2001	2002
Building bricks[2]	KLGA	Millions	3 000	2 639	3 114	3 256	3 046	2 997	3 000	2 939	2 864	2 754	2 070
Common bricks	GRTD	"	497	436	464	480	401	422	385	367	342	320	250
Facing bricks	GRTE	"	2 266	1 978	2 421	2 546	2 430	2 386	2 411	2 369	2 287	2 211	1 666
Engineering bricks	GRTF	"	237	225	229	230	216	190	204	204	235	223	153
Clay bricks (including sand-lime)	GRTG	"	2 819	2 447	2 900	3 065	2 880	2 828	2 830	2 759	2 694	2 595	1 955
Concrete bricks	GRTH	"	181	192	214	191	166	169	171	180	170	159	114
Cement (grey Portland)[3]	KLGB	Thousand tonnes	11 006	11 039	12 307	11 805	12 214	12 638	12 409	12 697	12 452	11 090	11 089
Sand and gravel	GRTI	"	88 898	89 470	97 672	89 656	81 997	86 366	85 968	88 209	89 234	88 210	82 721
Building sand[4]	KLGC	"	16 769	17 406	18 534	17 389	14 655	15 337	13 810	13 941	14 219	13 772	13 221
Concreting sand	KLGD	"	28 573	28 021	30 977	29 390	28 659	30 130	30 244	31 730	31 167	31 656	31 224
Gravel[5]	KLGE	"	43 557	44 043	48 162	42 877	38 683	40 899	41 914	42 538	43 847	42 782	38 276
Crushed rock	GRTJ	"	143 967	149 576	161 757	150 838	132 894	133 787	131 716	132 598	130 307	133 759	126 568
Coated roadstone	KLGF	"	26 647	27 238	28 512	28 972	26 270	23 906	23 131	22 260	21 785	23 340	23 281
Uncoated roadstone	KLGG	"	53 471	54 412	51 121	49 307	40 893	40 186	36 816	38 114	36 509	34 638	27 323
Fill and ballast	KLGH	"	48 919	52 141	65 779	56 140	50 982	51 396	51 623	52 144	53 417	47 225	49 622
Concrete aggregate	KLGI	"	14 929	15 786	16 345	16 419	14 748	18 300	20 146	20 080	18 595	28 556	26 342
Ready mixed concrete[6]	GRXA	Thousand m³	20 776	20 771	22 931	21 676	20 892	22 327	22 983	23 550	23 043	23 008	22 597
Concrete building blocks	GRTK	Thousand m²	68 194	74 287	87 548	78 287	75 866	82 537	84 662	87 767	90 219	87 922	91 476
Dense aggregate	KLGN	"	29 732	30 116	36 997	36 933	34 996	37 250	39 439	38 439	37 629	36 598	35 744
Lightweight aggregate	KLGO	"	17 479	19 235	22 048	18 147	16 316	17 783	19 110	20 830	22 991	22 684	23 480
Aerated concrete	KLGP	"	20 984	24 936	28 503	23 207	24 554	27 505	26 113	28 497	29 599	28 639	32 252
Concrete roofing tiles	KLGM	"	21 490	24 574	28 149	26 118	24 651	24 958	24 981	25 972	26 765	24 825	25 023
Roofing & architectural slates	GRXB	Tonnes	41 615	37 321	44 910	42 030	48 474	44 578	46 159	46 998	41 214	45 604	50 530
Fibre cement products	KLGK	Thousand tonnes	121.1	128.7	154.1	160.5	146.2	163.5	160.9	156.2	..	..	..

1 See chapter text.
2 Excluding refractory and glazed bricks.
3 United Kingdom up until 2000. Great Britain for 2001 and 2002.
4 Includes sand and gravel used for coating.
5 Includes hoggin.
6 United Kingdom.

Source: Department of Trade & Industry: 020 7215 1555

22.21 Construction: Value of output in Great Britain[1]

£ millions

		1992	1993	1994	1995	1996	1997	1998	1999	2000	2001	2002
All work: total	FGAY	47 472	46 323	49 439	52 643	55 243	58 352	62 060	65 704	69 676	74 690	83 593
New work: total	BLAB	24 814	23 556	25 086	26 672	27 926	29 928	32 491	35 587	37 660	39 970	45 370
New housing: total	KLQA	6 084	6 628	7 417	7 135	7 013	7 983	8 430	8 418	9 985	10 233	12 072
For public sector	BLAC	1 243	1 415	1 671	1 660	1 421	1 232	1 069	1 012	1 319	1 437	1 714
For private sector	BLAD	4 841	5 213	5 746	5 475	5 592	6 751	7 361	7 406	8 666	8 796	10 358
Infrastructure: total	KIAM	5 716	5 544	5 149	5 660	6 338	6 311	6 182	6 200	6 453	7 146	8 085
Other new work: total (excluding infrastructure)	KLQB	13 015	11 384	12 521	13 877	14 575	15 635	17 879	20 969	21 222	22 591	25 213
For public sector	BLAE	4 181	4 045	4 384	4 661	4 441	3 756	4 151	4 919	4 854	5 330	6 870
For private sector	KLQC	8 834	7 339	8 137	9 217	10 134	11 879	13 728	16 049	16 369	17 262	18 343
Private Industrial	BLAF	2 234	2 208	2 489	3 008	3 119	3 491	3 810	3 973	3 716	3 701	3 374
Private Commercial	BLAG	6 600	5 131	5 648	6 209	7 015	8 388	9 917	12 076	12 653	13 560	14 969
Repair and maintenance: total	BLAH	22 658	22 767	24 353	25 971	27 317	28 423	29 569	30 117	32 016	34 720	38 223
Housing: total	KLQD	12 586	12 809	13 767	14 595	15 035	15 754	16 202	16 370	16 907	17 620	19 170
For public sector	BLBK	4 991	5 439	5 963	6 465	6 637	6 629	6 506	6 485	6 552	6 630	6 412
For private sector	BLBL	7 595	7 370	7 804	8 130	8 398	9 126	9 696	9 885	10 354	10 990	12 758
Public other work	BLAJ	5 087	4 916	5 211	5 398	5 252	5 079	5 220	5 371	5 685	6 110	6 712
Private other work	BLAK	4 985	5 042	5 375	5 978	7 030	7 590	8 147	8 376	9 424	10 991	12 340

1 See chapter text. Output by contractors, including unrecorded estimates by small firms and self-employed workers, and output by public sector direct labour departments - classified to construction in the *1992 Standard Industrial Classification*.

Source: Department of Trade and Industry: 020 7215 1953

22.22 Construction: Value of new orders obtained by contractors[1]
Great Britain

£ millions

		1992	1993	1994	1995	1996	1997	1998	1999	2000	2001	2002
New work: total	FHAA	17 493	19 965	21 285	22 065	22 834	24 806	27 477	26 079	28 120	29 643	33 411
Public housing	BLBC	1 246	1 668	1 386	1 182	1 073	995	933	969	910	1 084	1 129
Private housing[2]	BLBD	4 016	4 874	5 721	4 905	5 416	6 253	5 997	5 901	6 085	6 525	8 088
New housing: total	FGAU	5 263	6 542	7 106	6 087	6 487	7 248	6 930	6 869	6 995	7 610	9 217
Infrastructure:												
Water	KIBV	669	421	412	500	640	733	957	760	1 084	531	936
Sewerage	KIBW	469	447	389	394	481	656	737	789	380	540	524
Electricity	KIBX	281	211	170	218	294	382	359	254	244	279	294
Roads	KIBY	1 322	1 435	1 356	1 531	1 710	928	821	957	1 445	1 572	1 999
Gas, communications, air	KIBZ	554	642	494	904	745	693	745	713	1 085	584	485
Railways	KIDP	200	623	412	351	524	416	573	471	539	1 271	1 052
Harbours	KIDQ	252	220	218	273	270	182	287	250	215	377	264
Total	BAWT	3 746	3 998	3 451	4 170	4 664	3 991	4 479	4 195	4 992	5 154	5 555
of which												
- Public	KIDS	1 690	2 472	2 211	2 327	1 671	1 352	1 505	1 495	1 430	2 085	2 491
- Private	KIDT	2 056	1 525	1 240	1 843	2 993	2 639	2 974	2 700	3 562	3 068	3 064
Other public non-housing:												
Factories	KIDU	128	111	111	94	91	72	84	72	64	30	65
Warehouses	KIDV	54	23	38	29	14	27	20	24	12	10	11
Oil, steel, coal	KIDW	47	30	12	13	4	4	2	5	1	8	1
Schools and colleges	KIDX	584	655	658	710	707	749	770	791	986	1 498	1 397
Universities	KIDY	203	353	376	373	355	273	405	345	329	378	667
Health	KIDZ	644	697	752	717	681	491	769	635	685	813	1 065
Offices	KIFP	499	684	469	393	379	391	292	390	291	395	854
Entertainment	KIFQ	189	281	308	285	259	342	432	435	359	392	400
Garages	KIFR	28	42	49	51	28	34	19	36	44	30	53
Shops	KIFS	23	26	14	21	12	35	35	29	34	38	53
Agriculture	KIFT	14	44	22	12	8	33	17	9	12	46	16
Miscellaneous	KIFU	351	450	844	508	418	441	660	503	999	479	1 328
Total	BAWU	2 763	3 397	3 654	3 206	2 956	2 894	3 504	3 273	3 815	4 117	5 910
Private industrial:[2]												
Factories	KIFW	1 006	1 221	1 451	2 055	1 603	2 184	1 878	1 698	1 444	1 588	1 341
Warehouses	KIFX	426	429	498	594	663	901	1 014	821	1 110	911	866
Oil, steel, coal	KIFY	72	27	51	76	71	64	79	38	34	43	40
Total	BAWV	1 503	1 677	1 999	2 725	2 337	3 149	2 971	2 558	2 589	2 542	2 247
Private commercial:[2]												
Schools, universities	KIHP	121	134	115	105	156	189	351	393	577	702	850
Health	KIHQ	193	179	255	288	277	356	651	411	455	349	575
Offices	KIHR	1 691	1 471	1 777	2 123	2 169	2 506	3 472	3 566	4 384	4 748	3 947
Entertainment	KIHS	747	751	928	940	1 407	1 847	2 244	2 224	1 873	1 674	1 861
Garages	KIHT	234	308	300	301	265	344	315	266	169	190	199
Shops	KIHU	1 034	1 278	1 453	1 871	1 795	1 937	2 154	1 901	1 889	2 212	2 570
Agriculture	KIBN	94	108	120	124	123	148	146	100	77	105	107
Miscellaneous	KIBO	103	122	127	126	198	198	259	321	305	242	374
Total	BAWW	4 218	4 351	5 075	5 877	6 390	7 525	9 593	9 184	9 729	10 221	10 482

1 See chapter text. Classified to construction in the *1992 Standard Industrial Classification*.

2 Figures for private sector include work to be carried out by contractors on their own initiative for sale.

Source: Department of Trade and Industry: 020 7215 1953

22.23

**Total engineering
Total turnover of UK based manufacturers[1]**
Standard Industrial Classification 2003.

£ millions

Activity heading Product group		1997	1998	1999	2000	2001	2002
Class 29: Manufacture of machinery and equipment not elsewhere classified							
2911 Manufacture of engines and turbines except aircraft, vehicle and cycle engines	MXVO	1 419.1	1 494.4	1 359.4	1 445.3	1 911.8	1 823.9
2912 Manufacture of pumps and compressors	MXXO	2 323.4	2 494.9	2 393.0	2 481.5	2 337.4	2 535.5
2913 Manufacture of taps and valves	MXZH	1 401.8	1 504.4	1 218.5	1 346.2	1 358.2	1 323.9
2914 Manufacture of bearings, gears, gearing and driving elements	MYCT	1 484.2	1 477.7	1 344.9	1 282.8	1 227.0	1 004.9
2922 Manufacture of lifting and handling equipment	MYLS	3 686.9	3 752.8	3 881.5	3 687.8	3 348.7	3 080.7
2923 Manufacture of non-domestic cooling and ventilation equipment	MYPT	3 277.5	3 359.7	3 082.0	3 160.0	3 411.9	3 298.7
2924 Manufacture of other general purpose machinery not elsewhere classified	MYRM	2 504.5	2 494.7	2 715.0	2 693.3	2 947.6	2 573.4
2941/3 Manufacture of other machine tools	MYYP	957.2	868.6	839.5	777.3	834.3	745.8
2942 Manufacture of metalworking machine tools	MYWY	950.2	1 002.0	866.9	937.0	912.6	738.6
2952 Manufacture of machinery for mining, quarrying and construction	MZCE	2 374.7	2 449.4	2 339.0	2 434.8	2 392.4	2 215.9
2953 Manufacture of machinery for food, beverage and tobacco processing	MZFS	729.3	648.6	576.0	593.8	629.1	710.8
2954 Manufacture of machinery for textile, apparel and leather production	MZJP	327.5	298.8	203.1	207.6	194.7	158.0
2956 Manufacture of other special purpose machinery not elsewhere classified	MZQF	2 632.2	2 515.1	2 360.8	2 153.9	2 148.8	2 187.1
2971 Manufacture of electric domestic appliances	MZTZ	2 086.3	2 098.1	2 008.9	2 046.7	2 230.9	2 196.4
Class 30 : Manufacture of electrical and optical equipment							
3001 Manufacture of office machinery	MZXQ	1 244.7	1 318.1	1 409.3	1 528.6	1 481.1	1 129.8
3002 Manufacture of computers and other information processing equipment	VBCE	13 260.8	13 483.6	13 452.6	12 410.7	12 086.4	8 687.6
Class 31 : Manufacture of electrical machinery and apparatus not elsewhere classified							
3110 Manufacture of electric motors, generators and transformers	VBEB	2 931.4	2 892.8	3 150.0	3 302.5	3 287.6	2 732.3
3120 Manufacture of electricity distribution and control apparatus	VBFU	3 656.5	3 560.7	3 813.9	4 213.0	4 090.5	3 661.5
3130 Manufacture of insulated wire and cable	VBHW	2 189.7	1 905.6	1 739.2	1 753.7	1 414.7	1 271.6
3140 Manufacture of accumulators, primary cells and primary batteries	VBJW	684.9	632.0	587.5	606.2	493.7	444.6
3150 Manufacture of lighting equipment and electric lamps	VBLP	1 994.5	1 880.5	1 913.2	1 865.8	1 712.1	1 485.2
3161 Manufacture of other electrical equipment for engines and vehicles not otherwise classified	VBNI	1 363.7	1 265.8	1 068.5	1 030.6	1 034.2	1 042.5
3162 Manufacture of other electrical equipment not elsewhere classified	VBPK	3 084.3	3 422.2	3 438.5	2 756.5	2 728.1	2 480.9
Class 32 : Manufacture of radio, television and communication equipment and apparatus							
3210 Manufacture of electronic valves and tubes and other electronic components	VBRI	5 545.7	5 551.7	4 652.9	6 695.8	4 460.0	4 063.0
3220 Manufacture of television and radio transmitters and apparatus for line telephony and line telegraphy	VBTF	7 077.7	7 840.7	11 881.6	15 349.1	10 527.5	7 127.1
3230 Manufacture of television and radio receivers, sound or video recording or reproducing apparatus and associated goods	VBVJ	4 196.7	3 945.1	3 826.5	4 044.2	4 038.0	3 195.0
Class 33 : Manufacture of medical, precision and optical instruments, watches and clocks							
3310 Manufacture of medical and surgical equipment and orthopaedic appliances	VBXH	2 407.7	2 331.9	2 597.0	2 691.2	2 967.5	3 167.7
3320 Manufacture of instruments and appliances for measuring, checking, testing, navigating and other purposes, except industrial process control equipment	VBZF	6 844.2	6 533.1	6 261.8	6 541.0	7 104.8	6 330.6
3340 Manufacture of optical instruments and photographic equipment	VCCV	1 004.9	1 061.7	935.1	998.4	999.6	1 030.0

1 The figures shown represent the output of UK based manufacturers classified to Subsections DK and DL of the Standard Industrial Classification 2003. The figures shown are derived from the monthly production inquiry (MPI) and include estimates for non-responders and for establishments which are not sampled. Orders on hand figures are given for the end of the period to which they relate.

Source: Office for National Statistics: 01633 812786

22.24
Volume index numbers of turnover and orders for the engineering industries
United Kingdom

	Total			Home			Export		
	Orders on hand end of period (2000 average = 100)	2000 average monthly sales = 100		Orders on hand end of period (2000 average = 100)	2000 average monthly sales = 100		Orders on hand end of period (2000 average = 100)	2000 average monthly sales = 100	
		New orders[1]	Turnover		New orders[1]	Turnover		New orders[1]	Turnover
Total Engineering industries SIC 1992 Class 29, 30, 31, 32 and 33									
	JIQI	JIQH	JIQJ	JIQC	JIQB	JIQD	JIQF	JIQE	JIQG
1996	82.6	..	84.8	83.7	..	88.1	80.6	..	80.5
1997	84.5	83.0	85.3	86.5	85.1	87.7	81.3	80.2	82.1
1998	81.9	84.2	87.8	79.1	82.5	88.3	86.7	86.4	87.3
1999	92.0	91.8	91.9	92.8	94.2	93.5	90.8	88.6	89.9
2000	103.4	100.0	100.0	104.9	100.0	100.0	100.8	100.0	100.0
2001	94.4	89.5	95.3	104.6	94.5	98.4	77.2	82.9	91.2
2002	91.5	80.4	84.0	103.9	87.1	90.9	70.5	71.3	75.0
Manufacture of Machinery and Equipment SIC 1992 Class 29									
	JINX	JINW	JINY	JINR	JINQ	JINS	JINU	JINT	JINV
1996	103.7	..	107.9	103.7	..	109.9	103.6	..	104.3
1997	109.4	106.5	106.3	111.4	110.9	108.8	105.0	98.9	101.8
1998	92.6	97.9	106.0	91.0	97.7	106.8	96.1	98.3	104.6
1999	95.1	99.5	100.4	96.9	105.1	103.6	91.2	89.9	94.6
2000	99.9	100.0	100.0	99.1	100.0	100.0	101.7	100.0	100.0
2001	95.0	97.2	100.8	95.1	100.8	103.3	94.9	91.0	96.4
2002	98.9	95.5	95.8	100.3	98.8	97.6	96.0	89.9	92.6
Manufacture of Electrical and Optical Equipment SIC 1992 Class 30, 31, 32 and 33									
	JIPQ	JIPP	JIPR	JIPK	JIPJ	JIPL	JIPN	JIPM	JIPO
1996	69.0	..	74.3	68.9	..	76.2	69.3	..	72.1
1997	68.6	72.6	75.7	67.9	71.8	76.2	69.6	73.5	75.2
1998	75.1	78.0	79.5	70.3	74.7	78.2	82.1	82.2	81.1
1999	90.0	88.4	88.1	89.7	88.6	88.0	90.5	88.1	88.2
2000	105.7	100.0	100.0	109.3	100.0	100.0	100.4	100.0	100.0
2001	94.0	86.1	92.8	111.7	91.2	95.8	68.4	80.0	89.4
2002	86.8	73.7	78.7	106.6	81.1	87.3	58.0	64.7	68.7

1 Net of cancellations.

Source: Office for National Statistics: 01633 812786

22.25 Motor vehicle production[1]
United Kingdom

Numbers

Motor vehicles		1992	1993	1994	1995	1996	1997	1998	1999	2000	2001	2002
SIC 1992, Class 34-10												
Passenger cars: total	JCYM	1 291 880	1 375 524	1 466 823	1 532 084	1 686 134	1 698 001	1 748 258	1 786 623	1 641 452	1 492 365	1 629 744
1 000 c.c. and under	GKAB	22 037	98 034	98 178	95 198	108 645	119 894	112 044	113 204	96 043	93 695	79 545
Over 1 000 c.c. but not over 1 600 c.c.	GKAD	793 307	709 615	729 397	814 873	845 084	829 079	814 595	776 111	676 438	632 747	711 553
Over 1 600 c.c. but not over 2 800 c.c.	GKAF	437 951	515 487	573 357	528 444	635 861	653 147	720 556	758 478	723 294	634 573	720 067
Over 2 800 c.c.	GKAH	38 585	52 388	65 891	93 569	96 544	95 881	101 063	138 830	145 677	131 350	118 579
Commercial vehicles: total	JCYG	248 453	193 467	227 815	233 001	238 314	237 706	227 379	185 905	172 442	192 873	191 267
Of which:												
Light commercial vehicles	GKDH	216 477	171 141	197 285	199 346	205 372	210 942	203 629	162 176	145 655	169 705	168 311
Trucks:												
Under 7.5 tonnes	GKDJ	9 558	4 755	8 154	9 523	8 913	6 254	5 006	4 107	5 160	5 000	4 600
Over 7.5 tonnes	GKDL	11 113	8 269	10 016	11 727	10 128	7 932	7 002	6 443	6 849	7 359	7 357
Motive units for articulated vehicles	GKCV	2 788	2 283	2 794	3 476	2 631	2 574	2 492	2 739	2 673	2 539	1 795
Buses, coaches and mini buses	GKDN	8 517	7 019	9 566	8 939	11 270	10 004	9 250	10 440	12 105	8 270	9 204

1 See chapter text. Figures for motor vehicles relate to periods of 52 weeks (53 weeks in 1993).

Source: Office for National Statistics: 01633 812963

22.26 Alcoholic drink[1]
United Kingdom

			1992	1993	1994	1995	1996	1997	1998	1999	2000	2001	2002
Spirits[2]		Thousand hectolitres of alcohol											
Production	KMEA	"	4 219	3 974	4 106	4 507	4 868	5 297	5 145	4 705	4 210	4 368	4 508
Released for home consumption													
Home produced whisky	KMEE	"	356	374	383	310	321	312	289	323	314	321	321
Spirit-based Ready-to-drink[3]	SNET	"	..	..	..	..	..	..	..	..	..	..	57
Imported and other	KMEG	"	505	504	531	481	495	533	505	596	615	647	737
Total	KMEH	"	861	878	914	791	815	845	794	919	929	968	1 115
Beer[4]		Thousand hectolitres											
Production	BFNK	"	57 616	56 746	58 333	56 800	58 072	59 139	56 652	57 854	55 279	56 802	56 672
Released for home consumption	BAYL	"	60 973	59 177	60 575	59 129	59 894	61 114	58 835	58 917	57 007	58 234	59 384
Production	JYXJ	Thousand hectolitres of pure alcohol	..	..	2 345	2 298	2 360	2 406	2 333	2 364	2 299	2 358	2 352
Released for home consumption	JYXK	"	..	..	2 453	2 410	2 448	2 504	2 439	2 428	2 382	2 429	2 473
Wine of fresh grapes													
Released for home consumption		Thousand hectolitres											
Fortified	KMEM	"	345	335	329	330	331	323	370	316	289	287	325
Still table	KMEN	"	6 166	6 471	6 759	6 576	6 995	7 653	7 979	8 391	8 864	9 534	10 319
Sparkling	KMEO	"	292	296	297	315	358	382	416	576	543	515	578
Total	KMEP	"	6 803	7 102	7 385	7 221	7 684	8 358	8 765	9 284	9 696	10 336	11 222
Made-wine													
Released for home consumption													
Other than coolers	KMEQ	"	439	505	470	516	513	485	406	416	431	364	367
Coolers[3]	KJDD	"	433	485	549	903	1 781	1 153	1 244	1 802	2 800	3 712	1 606
Cider and perry													
Released for home consumption	KMER	"	4 398	4 496	4 811	5 575	5 656	5 513	5 548	6 022	6 006	5 911	5 939

1 See chapter text.
2 Potable spirits distilled.
3 Made wine with alcoholic strength 1.2% to 5.5%. Includes alcoholic lemonade of appropriate strength and similar products. From 28 April 2002, duty on spirit-based "coolers" is charged at the same rate as spirits per litre of alcohol. Coolers for calendar year 2002 includes only wine based "coolers".

4 A new system was introduced for beer duty in June 1993. The figures in this table include adjustments to data prior to this date to bring them into line with current data.

Source: HM Customs and Excise: 020 7865 5323

22.27 Tobacco products: released for home consumption[1]
United Kingdom

			1992	1993[2]	1994	1995	1996	1997	1998	1999	2000	2001	2002
Cigarettes:		Thousand million											
Home produced	KMFA	"	76.4	85.8	82.4	70.8	73.8	71.1	67.8	28.2	49.3	47.7	49.6
Imported	KMFB	"	9.3	9.5	10.2	9.5	9.5	9.9	7.5	6.0	7.3	6.8	6.5
Total	KMFC	"	85.7	95.2	92.6	80.3	83.3	81.0	75.3	34.2	56.6	54.5	56.1
Cigars:		Million kg											
Home produced	KMFD	"	1.8	1.7	1.6	1.5	1.4	1.3	1.2	0.9	1.0	0.9	0.9
Imported	KMFE	"	0.1	0.1	0.1	0.1	0.1	0.1	0.1	0.1	0.1	0.1	0.1
Total	KMFF	"	1.9	1.8	1.7	1.6	1.5	1.4	1.3	1.0	1.1	1.0	1.0
Hand-rolling tobacco:													
Home produced	KMFG	"	3.7	3.5	3.0	2.4	2.1	1.8	1.7	2.0	2.1	2.8	2.8
Imported	KMFH	"	0.1	0.1	0.1	0.1	0.1	0.1	0.1	–	–	–	–
Total	KMFI	"	3.8	3.6	3.2	2.6	2.3	1.9	1.8	2.0	2.2	2.8	2.8
Other smoking and chewing tobacco:													
Home produced	KMFJ	"	1.8	1.8	1.5	1.3	1.2	1.1	1.0	0.6	0.7	0.7	0.6
Imported	KMFK	"	0.2	0.1	0.1	0.1	0.1	0.1	0.1	0.1	0.1	0.1	0.1
Total	KMFL	"	2.0	1.9	1.6	1.4	1.3	1.2	1.1	0.7	0.8	0.8	0.7

1 See chapter text.
2 1993 contained two Budgets, in March and November.

Source: HM Customs and Excise: 020 7865 5323

23 Banking, insurance etc

Banking, insurance etc

Other banks' balance sheet *(Table 23.3)*

The implementation of the review of banking statistics at end-September 1997 has resulted in several changes to this table:

(a)   The table now includes the business of all monthly and quarterly reporting banks in the UK; it formerly covered only the business of monthly reporting institutions.

(b)   The Channel Islands and Isle of Man are no longer treated as part of the UK for statistical purposes. Banking institutions in the Channel Islands and Isle of Man no longer have the option of being within the UK banking sector and their business, along with the business of offshore island branches of UK mainland banks, is now excluded from the figures within this table. Additionally, the business of the UK banking sector with offshore island residents and entities has been reclassified from UK residents to non-residents.

(c)   The table now contains more comprehensive detail of business with building societies. This business was previously included indistinguishably within the UK private sector elements of the table.

(d)   The aggregate balance sheet of the banking sector has been inflated because it is now reported on an accrual basis rather than a cash basis (accrued amounts payable/ receivable are shown under liabilities and assets respectively). Additionally, acceptances have been brought onto the balance sheet and are shown under both liabilities and assets.

With effect from 1998, the balance sheet of the Banking Department of the Bank of England is excluded from this table, and other banks' business with the Issue Department is reclassified from "UK public sector" to "UK banks".

Data for 1999 reflect the acquisition of Birmingham Midshires Building Society by Halifax during that year. Data for end-2000 reflect the entry of Bradford and Bingley plc to the banking sector during the year. Data for end-2000 also reflect the new reporting during the year of agency business as a result of collateral management via repos and reverse repos.

Bank lending to, and bank deposits from, UK residents *(Tables 23.4 and 23.5)*

These are series of statistics based on the Standard Industrial Classification 1992.

Table 22.4 comprises loans, advances (including under reverse repos), finance leasing, acceptances, facilities and holdings of sterling and euro commercial paper. It includes lending under the Department of Trade and Industry special scheme for domestic shipbuilding. Holdings of investments and bills and adjustments for transit items are not included.

Table 22.5 includes borrowing under sale and repurchase agreements (repro). Adjustments for transit items are not included.

Figures for both tables are supplied by monthly reporting banks and grossed to cover quarterly reporters. They exclude lending to building societies and to residents of the Channel Islands and Isle of Man.

Capital issues and redemptions *(Table 23.14)*

The estimates in this table relate to new money raised on the stock market by issues of ordinary, preference and loan capital (public issues, offers for sale, issues by tender, placings and issues to shareholders and employees) by non-resident borrowers split between central government, state and local governments and companies.

The estimates include UK local government negotiable bonds (of not less than one year) issue to or through the agency of banks, discount houses, issuing houses or brokers. Mortgages, bank advances and any other loans redeemable in less than twelve months are excluded; so also are loans from UK government funds (including the former Industrial Reorganisation Corporation and the National Enterprise Board) but not government subscriptions to company issues made *pari passu* with the market. Issues to shareholders are included only if the sole or principal share register is maintained in the United Kingdom.

Estimates of issues are based on the prices at which securities are offered to the market. Subscriptions are recorded under the periods in which they are due to be paid. Redemptions exclude share buy-backs where the shares are cancelled. They relate to fixed interest securities of the kinds included as issues; conversion issues in lieu of cash repayment are included in the gross figures of both issues and redemptions. These figures include issues of debentures and loan stock carrying the right of conversion into, or subscription to, equity capital.

The division between the United Kingdom and non-resident company borrowers is determined by the location of the registered office. The industrial classification of companies is according to the primary occupation of the borrowing company or group. Until 1982 it is based on the Standard Industrial Classification (SIC) 1968, from 1983 to 1995 on SIC 1983 and subsequently on SIC 92.

The estimates exclude issues on the unlisted securities market which was launched by the Stock Exchange in November 1980. These issues are mainly of ordinary shares by private non-financial corporations.

Building societies *(Table 23.15)*

Building society figures are sourced from societies' annual returns and for each year relate to accounting years ending on dates between 1 February and 31 January of the following year. Figures are society-only as opposed to group consolidated.

Consumer credit *(Table 23.16)*

Figures for net lending refer to changes in amounts outstanding adjusted to remove distortions caused by revaluations of debt outstanding, such as write-offs. Lending by retailers refers to self-financed credit advanced by food retailers, clothing retailers, household goods retailers, mixed business retailers (other than co-operative societies) and general mail order houses. Class 3 loans are advanced under the terms of the Building Societies' Act 1986. Loans on personal accounts exclude loans for house purchase and bridging finance.

Data relating to the narrower coverage cover finance houses and other specialist credit grantors, bank credit cards (operated under the VISA and Mastercard systems), and secured loans by building societies. A high proportion of credit advanced in certain types of agreement, notably on credit cards, is repaid within a month. This reflects use of such agreements as a method of payment rather than a way of obtaining credit.

23.1 Bank of England

£ millions

		December										
		1992	1993	1994	1995	1996	1997	1998	1999	2000	2001	2002
Issue Department												
Liabilities:												
Notes in circulation	AEFA	17 542	18 218	20 055	21 262	22 407	23 715	24 573	27 232	29 412	32 226	33 639
Notes in Banking Department	AEFB	8	12	5	7	12	5	7	8	8	4	1
Assets:												
Government securities[1]	AEFC	7 808	6 816	11 468	14 552	16 524	16 416	15 826	17 264	13 498	13 996	13 841
Other securities[2]	AEFD	9 742	11 414	8 592	6 717	5 896	7 304	8 754	9 976	15 921	18 234	19 799
Banking Department												
Liabilities:												
Total[3]	AEFE	5 623	11 095	6 192	7 114	6 229	7 221	6 802	52 072	10 397	12 639	14 366
Public deposits[4]	AEFF	97	6 205	938	1 159	1 001	1 192	237	195	391	437	414
Bankers' deposits[5]	AEFH	1 553	1 700	1 855	2 001	2 021	2 800	1 388	1 357	1 520	2 354	1 722
Reserves and other accounts[6]	AEFI	3 959	3 175	3 385	3 941	3 193	3 214	5 163	50 506	8 471	9 834	12 215
Assets:												
Total	KCYT	5 623	11 095	6 192	7 114	6 229	7 221	6 802	52 071	10 397	12 640	14 366
Government securities	AEFJ	1 237	1 174	1 050	1 090	1 232	1 373	1 352	1 444	1 504	1 795	1 510
Advances and other accounts	AEFK	3 935	9 411	4 696	5 499	2 339	5 388	3 302	46 895	6 533	6 413	6 938
Premises, equipment and other securities[6]	AEFL	443	498	441	518	2 646	455	2 141	3 724	2 352	4 428	5 917
Notes and coin	AEFM	8	12	5	7	12	5	7	8	8	4	1

1 Including the historic liability of the Treasury of £11 million until 1993 (repaid on 27 July 1994).
2 Including gilt and Treasury bill repurchase agreements from 1994 (previously in "Government securities").
3 The only liability not shown separately is the Bank's capital (held by the Treasury) which has been constant at £14.6 million.
4 Excluding local government and public corporations' deposits which are included under Reserves and other accounts.

5 These consist of operational deposits held mainly by the clearing banks and non-operational cash ratio deposits for which institutions authorised under the Financial Services and Markets Act, deposit - taking UK branches of "European Authorised Institutions" and (from 1998) building societies are liable.
6 Large increases from 1999 arise from the Bank of England's role in TARGET, as a result of which other European central banks may hold substantial credit balances or overdrafts with the Bank.

Source: Bank of England: 020 7601 3236

23.2 Value of inter-bank clearings[1]

£ billions

		1992	1993	1994	1995	1996	1997	1998	1999	2000	2001	2002
Bulk paper clearings												
Cheque (formerly general)	KCYY	1 052	1 065	1 075	1 097	1 161	1 200	1 214	1 226	1 214	1 210	1 178
Credit (formerly credit clearing)	KCYZ	101	97	93	92	94	94	92	88	82	80	75
High-value clearings												
Town	KCZA	1 387	1 069	681	59	–	–	–	–	–	–	–
CHAPS Sterling only	KCZB	20 928	23 545	25 053	26 719	28 881	36 032	41 501	44 704	49 146	52 913	51 896
Electronic clearing (BACS)	KCZC	803	836	941	1 055	1 250	1 432	1 602	1 761	1 922	2 166	2 382

1 Excludes inter-branch clearings and clearings in Scotland and Northern Ireland.

Source: Association for Payment Clearing Services (APACS): 020 7711 6323

23.3 Other banks' balance sheet[1]

£ millions

		1993	1994	1995	1996	1997	1998	1999	2000	2001[2]	2002[3]
Sterling liabilities											
Notes outstanding & cash loaded cards	TBFA	2 186	2 456	2 576	2 717	2 832	2 929	3 311	3 359	3 866	3 957
Sight deposits											
UK banks	TBFB	14 768	16 222	16 983	20 138	44 573	37 839	33 463	40 054	59 573	101 905
UK building societies	TBFC	..	..	..	..	950	1 277	841	1 168	1 466	2 403
UK public sector	TBFD	3 335	3 301	3 824	3 641	3 781	3 003	3 450	3 403	4 283	3 997
Other UK residents	TBFE	161 907	164 451	192 297	211 179	271 233	295 068	325 392	372 725	415 180	457 077
Non-residents	TBFF	15 075	16 425	18 690	17 707	37 730	43 528	44 581	55 489	55 837	57 218
Time deposits											
UK banks	TBFG	68 531	75 629	90 044	95 798	99 782	111 970	112 530	110 955	125 261	141 401
UK building societies	TBFH	–	–	–	–	5 682	4 361	4 253	4 688	4 856	4 487
UK public sector	TBFI	4 223	4 908	7 896	6 087	9 059	9 748	8 064	8 241	8 306	8 936
Other UK residents	TBFJ	162 053	166 505	190 707	210 045	284 629	295 924	282 789	301 007	302 715	306 453
of which TESSAs	TBFK	5 896	7 517	10 314	9 389	20 394	21 568	22 868	24 265	9 752	5 235
of which SAYE	TBFL	–	–	–	–	2 254	2 604	2 840	2 726	2 439	2 367
of which cash ISAs	TFDG	..	..	..	..	..	..	5 210	13 684	31 298	42 269
Non-residents	TBFM	58 583	62 905	68 274	63 995	91 040	97 953	116 967	134 844	150 964	151 306
Acceptances granted	TBFN	–	–	–	–	19 952	16 658	12 854	10 012	10 627	9 954
Liabilities under sale and repurchase agreements											
of which British govt. securities	TBFU	–	–	–	22 668	47 297	55 561	56 145	83 819	83 330	78 155
UK banks[4]	TBFP	–	–	–	13 718	29 089	43 314	48 213	56 408	60 551	52 079
UK building societies	TBFQ	..	..	..	..	20	32	200	36	–	107
UK public sector[4]	TBFR	–	–	–	2 279	6 044	–	–	14 351	5 127	1 402
Other UK residents	TBFS	–	–	–	7 703	18 114	20 918	17 165	22 974	25 732	19 759
Non-residents	TBFT	–	–	–	–	5 664	5 469	5 542	9 849	8 643	19 072
CDs and other short-term paper issued	TBFV	52 783	63 880	70 277	96 390	119 266	138 248	158 826	151 153	153 768	157 354
Total sterling deposits	TBFW	541 260	574 224	658 993	749 364	1 046 609	1 125 311	1 175 130	1 297 356	1 392 890	1 494 910
Sterling items in suspense and transmission	TBFX	11 011	8 412	10 423	12 120	16 054	15 714	17 307	15 261	16 702	13 318
Net derivatives	TBFY	..	..	..	..	8 186	8 342	8 324	10 992	4 029	2 491
Accrued amounts payable	TBFZ	..	..	..	..	20 713	24 632	22 122	23 726	22 836	21 541
Sterling capital and other internal funds	TBGA	71 833	78 775	82 160	90 464	103 462	103 868	100 575	133 436	148 294	173 318
Total sterling liabilities	TBGB	626 290	663 868	754 152	854 666	1 197 856	1 280 796	1 326 769	1 484 130	1 588 618	1 709 535
Foreign currency liabilities											
Sight and time deposits											
UK banks	TBGC	95 921	105 813	104 769	91 314	90 858	77 128	77 684	99 447	106 368	111 536
UK building societies	TBGD	..	..	..	..	1 027	639	681	233	279	373
UK public sector	TBGE	..	..	..	..	226	149	126	1 808	926	833
Other UK residents	TBGF	..	..	..	..	64 188	60 513	65 203	79 627	95 666	81 590
Non-residents	TBGG	580 951	618 769	696 380	605 439	716 573	766 934	736 792	914 888	1 001 321	997 398
Acceptances granted	TBGH	..	..	..	..	743	729	619	689	638	754
Sale and repurchase agreements											
UK banks	TBGJ	–	–	–	17 114	21 311	30 669	25 170	38 901	54 499	90 407
UK building societies	TBGK	..	..	..	..	–	–	–	–	–	–
UK public sector	TBGL	..	..	..	..	22	–	–	468	1	71
Other UK residents	TBGM	..	..	..	..	25 716	26 742	21 997	35 145	52 438	54 463
Non-residents	TBGN	–	–	–	61 307	100 936	118 909	115 357	139 656	154 976	211 276
CDs and other short-term paper issued	TBGO	61 017	67 869	89 032	101 005	131 620	124 151	151 009	199 510	224 225	234 731
Total foreign currency deposits	TBGP	790 361	851 856	972 832	975 619	1 153 220	1 206 562	1 194 637	1 510 373	1 691 336	1 783 432
Items in suspense and transmission	TBGQ	20 714	14 779	13 881	21 272	35 713	25 026	30 548	46 678	47 363	38 355
Net derivatives	TBGR	..	..	..	..	8 654	2 656	3 704	–4 472	–3 854	5 816
Accrued amounts payable	TBGS	..	..	..	..	21 996	25 184	18 080	18 568	17 756	16 312
Capital and other internal funds	TBGT	21 581	21 081	26 430	25 535	31 676	46 952	69 798	89 359	85 489	87 047
Total foreign currency liabilities	TBGU	832 656	887 716	1 013 143	1 022 426	1 251 258	1 306 380	1 316 767	1 660 506	1 838 090	1 930 961
Total liabilities	TBGV	1 458 946	1 551 584	1 767 295	1 877 092	2 449 114	2 587 177	2 643 536	3 144 636	3 426 708	3 640 497

23.3 Other banks' balance sheet[1]

continued

£ millions

		1993	1994	1995	1996	1997	1998	1999	2000	2001[2]	2002[3]
Sterling assets											
Notes and coins	TBGW	4 711	4 983	5 357	4 812	5 225	6 699	9 047	8 007	6 566	6 621
With UK central bank											
Cash ratio deposits	TBGX	1 415	1 490	1 682	1 888	2 566	1 068	1 141	1 275	1 386	1 495
Other	TBGY	183	103	113	533	216	383	676	117	143	249
Market loans											
UK banks	TBGZ	79 281	88 582	103 006	109 500	139 996	148 138	144 537	149 174	181 350	237 771
UK bank CDs	TBHB	19 028	23 632	26 767	36 922	62 584	65 510	75 071	65 156	68 868	68 728
UK bank commercial paper	TBHC	..	..	..	..	29	130	208	8	52	62
UK building societies CDs etc and deposits	TBHD	5 360	5 358	4 387	4 891	4 242	4 505	5 093	4 748	3 933	4 293
Non-residents	TBHE	43 571	44 582	47 470	50 585	79 368	84 162	74 403	94 381	102 404	89 848
Acceptances granted											
UK building societies	TBHF	..	..	..	..	–	–	–	–	–	–
UK public sector	TBHG	..	..	..	..	–	–	–	–	–	–
Other UK residents	TBHH	..	..	..	..	18 573	15 394	11 933	9 496	9 992	9 111
Non-residents	TBHI	..	..	..	..	1 379	1 264	920	516	635	842
Bills											
Treasury bills	TBHJ	1 561	4 166	10 404	1 652	554	779	2 749	1 612	8 474	18 752
UK bank bills	TBHA	..	..	..	..	18 221	14 110	11 426	7 011	8 098	8 491
UK building societies	TBHK	..	..	..	..	–	–	–	–	–	–
Other UK	TBHL	..	..	..	..	1 116	1 221	818	1 202	1 601	485
Non-residents	TBHM	..	..	..	..	309	207	206	287	744	979
Claims under sale and repurchase agreements											
of which British govt. securities	TBHT	–	–	–	26 030	47 158	56 639	64 943	86 362	84 068	77 460
UK banks	TBHO	–	–	–	16 853	27 611	41 969	39 667	46 088	46 585	37 197
UK building societies	TBHP	..	..	..	..	345	134	91	116	327	86
UK public sector	TBHQ	..	..	..	..	–	–	–	9 067	4 692	5 159
Other UK residents	TBHR	..	..	..	..	21 283	23 803	30 338	35 058	36 222	31 363
Non-residents	TBHS	..	..	..	..	6 873	5 907	6 310	7 266	7 010	14 271
Advances											
UK public sector	TBHU	3 309	3 526	3 549	2 912	3 872	3 403	2 567	2 746	2 442	3 783
Other UK residents[5]	TBHV	371 086	380 615	426 936	460 107	636 162	672 812	732 649	823 787	891 790	986 835
Non-residents	TBHW	12 268	12 163	13 403	16 759	21 102	21 039	23 364	24 494	29 483	31 380
Banking dept. lending to central govt. (net)	TBNU	–5 407	–947	–1 801	948	–2 741	–	–	..	..	..
Investments											
British government stocks	TBHX	13 753	14 366	17 135	19 910	23 078	14 714	9 243	2 867	499	–3 545
Other public sector	TBHY	204	303	409	303	283	215	124	88	116	158
UK banks[6]	TBHZ	..	..	..	..	11 922	13 415	13 584	22 935	23 965	23 542
UK building societies	TBIA	5 492	4 769	4 639	4 898	2 875	2 223	2 506	2 251	2 099	1 835
Other UK residents[7]	TBIB	..	..	..	..	45 134	48 781	57 391	77 647	82 013	76 773
Non-residents	TBIC	..	..	..	..	9 343	11 834	13 775	20 572	23 462	22 821
Items in suspense and collection	TBID	17 135	16 477	17 613	19 830	23 526	23 888	23 441	21 982	24 024	19 577
Accrued amounts receivable	TBIE	..	..	..	..	15 003	17 352	15 173	15 919	13 528	15 486
Other assets	TBIF	11 146	10 242	10 525	10 267	12 218	12 593	13 036	12 654	12 876	12 685
Total sterling assets	TBIG	630 527	668 960	755 937	852 075	1 192 264	1 257 652	1 321 486	1 468 527	1 595 380	1 727 136

23.3 Other banks' balance sheet[1]

continued

£ millions

		1993	1994	1995	1996	1997	1998	1999	2000	2001[2]	2002[3]
Foreign currency assets											
Market loans and advances											
UK banks	TBIH	96 129	99 885	98 305	83 920	90 367	72 263	74 250	93 269	104 107	114 809
UK banks' CDs etc	TBII	8 642	7 226	9 345	7 793	13 633	11 065	14 364	13 171	13 298	10 128
UK building societies CDs etc. and deposits	TBIJ	..	..	..	..	83	259	451	173	354	357
UK public sector	TBIK	3 421	28	38	36	25	45	20	30	13	83
Other UK residents	TBIL	71 326	76 538	102 061	72 213	76 356	83 968	88 847	107 707	118 106	117 669
Non-residents	TBIM	489 439	534 589	604 783	505 953	598 541	616 832	599 146	743 781	783 057	783 168
Claims under sale and repurchase agreement											
UK banks	TBIO	–	–	–	21 189	24 184	31 900	28 008	41 801	61 188	91 488
UK building societies	TBIP	..	..	..	..	–	–	–	–	–	–
UK public sector	TBIQ	..	..	..	..	22	–	–	737	23	486
Other UK residents	TBIR	..	..	..	..	55 945	39 764	33 027	57 876	73 237	86 866
Non-residents	TBIS	–	–	–	75 376	121 101	147 562	146 756	199 990	219 449	256 663
Acceptances granted	TBIT	..	..	..	..	743	729	619	689	638	754
Bills	TBIU	15 398	10 490	14 429	9 660	12 728	15 239	19 508	21 878	25 399	20 803
Investments											
British government stocks	TBIV	..	..	..	..	3 453	4 755	4 473	3 518	890	226
Other public sector	TBIW	..	..	..	..	–	–	–	–	4	18
UK banks[8]	TBIX	..	..	..	..	2 850	4 310	8 607	11 706	10 633	10 298
UK building societies	TBIY	889	997	728	701	414	526	631	939	850	1 170
Other UK residents	TBIZ	..	..	..	..	4 055	4 584	5 679	12 298	18 129	20 130
Non-residents	TBJA	114 904	128 507	154 398	161 045	186 288	234 563	243 147	297 404	324 073	326 035
Items in suspense and collection	TBJB	19 371	15 572	17 598	21 664	40 175	30 229	29 706	44 885	55 026	44 037
Accrued amounts receivable	TBJC	..	..	..	..	23 673	27 821	20 163	21 279	18 969	19 434
Other assets	TBJD	2 791	1 868	1 817	1 809	2 215	3 111	4 648	2 978	3 880	8 735
Total foreign currency assets	TBJE	828 419	882 624	1 011 358	1 025 017	1 256 850	1 329 525	1 322 050	1 676 109	1 831 322	1 913 355
Total assets	TBJF	1 458 946	1 551 584	1 767 295	1 877 092	2 449 114	2 587 177	2 643 536	3 144 636	3 426 702	3 640 491
Holdings of own sterling acceptances	TBJG	21 814	18 274	18 721	21 521	1 823	2 137	1 725	1 231	916	1 220
Holdings of own FC acceptances	TBJH	914	640	1 153	1 031	291	170	150	171	118	58
Eligible banks' total sterling acceptances	TBJI	21 726	18 168	18 476	21 220	21 366	18 722	14 523	10 597	11 320	10 805
Eligible liabilities	TBJJ	425 353	440 032	507 279	564 648	766 683	807 803	849 289	952 062	1 012 194	1 087 879

1 See chapter text.

2 During 2001 sterling advances to other UK residents were reduced by £4.1 bn as a result of securitisations and other loan transfers.

3 During 2002 sterling advances to other UK residents were reduced by £16.2 bn as a result of securitisations and other loan transfers.

4 There is a break in this series in 1998 as a result of the reclassification of the Issue Department of the Bank of England from UK public sector to UK banks. From 2000 the UK public sector reflects assumption by the Debt Management Office (an Executive Agency of HM Treasury) of responsibility for government cash management.

5 During 2000, sterling advances to other UK residents were reduced by £10.3 bn as a result of securitisations and other loan transfers to non-banks.

6 Investments in UK banks in 2000 were boosted by Barclay's £5.8 bn investment in Woolwich.

7 Investments in other UK residents in 2000 were boosted by Lloyds TSB's £5.8 bn investment in Scottish Widows Group.

8 Includes investments in Bank of England Euro Notes from January 2001.

Source: Bank of England: 020 7601 3236

23.4 Industrial analysis of bank lending to UK residents[1]
Not seasonally adjusted

£ millions

	UK residents					Manufacturing			
	Total to	of which sterling	Agriculture, hunting and forestry	Fishing	Mining & quarrying	Total	Food, beverages & tobacco	Textiles & leather	Pulp, paper, publishing & printing
Amounts outstanding (sterling & other currencies)									
Loans & advances (including under repo & sterling commercial paper)									
	TBOA	TBOB	TBOC	TBOD	TBOE	TBOF	TBOG	TBOH	TBOI
2001	1 126 933	935 369	7 493	463	3 911	56 996	9 697	1 749	7 008
2002	1 232 712	1 027 315	7 838	441	3 391	50 599	10 378	1 883	5 832
Acceptances									
	TBQA	TBQB	TBQC	TBQD	TBQE	TBQF	TBQG	TBQH	TBQI
2001	5 553	5 265	23	–	151	1 472	480	85	72
2002	4 737	4 459	9	–	91	1 109	397	59	18
Total									
	TBSA		TBSC	TBSD	TBSE	TBSF	TBSG	TBSH	TBSI
2001	1 132 486		7 516	463	4 061	58 469	10 178	1 834	7 079
2002	1 237 449		7 847	441	3 482	51 708	10 775	1 942	5 850
of which in sterling									
	TBUA		TBUC	TBUD	TBUE	TBUF	TBUG	TBUH	TBUI
2001	940 635		7 434	425	2 527	37 169	7 752	1 394	4 870
2002	1 031 774		7 760	414	1 701	34 231	7 479	1 507	4 324
Facilities granted									
	TCAA		TCAC	TCAD	TCAE	TCAF	TCAG	TCAH	TCAI
2001	1 403 404		9 609	544	12 031	107 144	23 492	2 832	12 627
2002	1 507 605		9 996	519	10 798	96 946	23 071	2 846	11 553
of which in sterling									
	TCCA		TCCC	TCCD	TCCE	TCCF	TCCG	TCCH	TCCI
2001	1 125 620		9 501	496	3 987	62 290	13 585	2 271	7 694
2002	1 230 620		9 886	485	2 900	57 848	12 105	2 298	7 367

	Manufacturing					Electricity, gas and water supply		
	Chemicals, man-made fibres, rubber & plastics	Non-metallic mineral products & metals	Machinery, equipment & transport equipment	Electrical, medical & optical equipment	Other manufacturing	Electricity, gas & heated water	Cold water purification & supply	Construction
Amounts outstanding (sterling & other currencies)								
Loans & advances (including under repo & sterling commercial paper)								
	TBOJ	TBOK	TBOL	TBOM	TBON	TBOO	TBOP	TBOQ
2001	6 328	7 319	10 309	8 239	6 347	7 135	1 266	13 471
2002	6 007	6 446	7 811	6 674	5 568	6 384	1 696	14 701
Acceptances								
	TBQJ	TBQK	TBQL	TBQM	TBQN	TBQO	TBQP	TBQQ
2001	237	116	225	169	88	350	10	105
2002	104	98	239	106	87	315	10	128
Total								
	TBSJ	TBSK	TBSL	TBSM	TBSN	TBSO	TBSP	TBSQ
2001	6 565	7 435	10 534	8 409	6 434	7 485	1 276	13 576
2002	6 112	6 544	8 050	6 780	5 656	6 699	1 706	14 829
of which in sterling								
	TBUJ	TBUK	TBUL	TBUM	TBUN	TBUO	TBUP	TBUQ
2001	4 282	4 636	6 019	4 012	4 203	6 178	1 029	12 726
2002	4 057	4 230	4 720	3 682	4 233	5 733	1 582	14 287
Facilities granted								
	TCAJ	TCAK	TCAL	TCAM	TCAN	TCAO	TCAP	TCAQ
2001	14 321	11 811	18 505	13 402	10 152	18 807	3 707	21 299
2002	13 090	11 094	15 201	11 065	9 025	14 308	5 325	22 821
of which in sterling								
	TCCJ	TCCK	TCCL	TCCM	TCCN	TCCO	TCCP	TCCQ
2001	7 695	7 436	10 891	6 292	6 426	11 453	2 534	19 533
2002	7 508	7 000	9 062	6 261	6 246	10 146	4 630	21 302

23.4

Industrial analysis of bank lending to UK residents[1]
Not seasonally adjusted

continued

£ millions

	Wholesale and retail trade					Real estate, renting, computer and other business activities		
Total	Sale & repair of motor vehicles & fuel	Other wholesale trade	Other retail trade & repair	Hotels and restaurants	Transport, storage & communication	Total	Development, buying, selling, renting of real estate	Renting of machinery & equipment
Amounts outstanding (sterling & other currencies)								
Loans & advances (including under repo & sterling commercial paper)								
TBOR	TBOS	TBOT	TBOU	TBOV	TBOW	TBOX	TBOY	TBPA
2001 34 967	8 896	13 490	12 581	17 810	23 260	99 596	71 025	7 243
2002 36 306	9 018	11 906	15 382	17 839	30 572	115 622	86 380	7 175
Acceptances								
TBQR	TBQS	TBQT	TBQU	TBQV	TBQW	TBQX	TBQY	TBRA
2001 957	133	620	204	5	80	454	258	14
2002 900	16	646	238	18	42	518	373	35
Total								
TBSR	TBSS	TBST	TBSU	TBSV	TBSW	TBSX	TBSY	TBTA
2001 35 924	9 028	14 110	12 785	17 815	23 340	100 050	71 283	7 257
2002 37 207	9 035	12 552	15 620	17 857	30 614	116 140	86 754	7 209
of which in sterling								
TBUR	TBUS	TBUT	TBUU	TBUV	TBUW	TBUX	TBUY	TBVA
2001 28 478	8 502	8 531	11 445	15 366	18 539	95 227	70 330	6 376
2002 30 541	8 693	8 440	13 408	16 078	25 644	111 296	85 627	6 190
Facilities granted								
TCAR	TCAS	TCAT	TCAU	TCAV	TCAW	TCAX	TCAY	TCBA
2001 56 965	11 989	21 614	23 361	21 762	50 343	131 233	89 706	8 261
2002 59 236	12 424	19 873	26 939	22 804	52 215	151 747	109 960	8 298
of which in sterling								
TCCR	TCCS	TCCT	TCCU	TCCV	TCCW	TCCX	TCCY	TCDA
2001 43 996	10 993	14 083	18 920	18 055	29 751	121 838	87 541	7 032
2002 46 880	11 259	13 963	21 658	20 037	35 961	143 159	107 905	7 024

Real estate, renting, computer and other business activities					Recreational, personal & community service activities		Financial intermediation (excl. insurance & pension funds)	
Computer & related activities	Legal, accountancy, consultancy & other business activities	Public administration & defence	Education	Health & social work	Recreational, cultural & sporting activities	Personal & community services activities	Total	Financial leasing corporations
Amounts outstanding (sterling & other currencies)								
Loans & advances (including under repo & sterling commercial paper)								
TBPB	TBPC	TBPD	TBPE	TBPF	TBPH	TBPG	TBPI	TBPJ
2001 3 453	17 876	7 253	3 545	7 350	8 280	3 966	273 579	36 315
2002 3 632	18 435	9 179	4 083	8 020	8 420	4 472	290 269	37 887
Acceptances								
TBRB	TBRC	TBRD	TBRE	TBRF	TBRH	TBRG	TBRI	TBRJ
2001 7	175	–	–	–	72	3	1 655	152
2002 32	78	–	–	–	71	6	1 340	124
Total								
TBTB	TBTC	TBTD	TBTE	TBTF	TBTH	TBTG	TBTI	TBTJ
2001 3 460	18 051	7 253	3 545	7 350	8 352	3 969	275 234	36 467
2002 3 664	18 513	9 179	4 083	8 021	8 490	4 477	291 608	38 011
of which in sterling								
TBVB	TBVC	TBVD	TBVE	TBVF	TBVH	TBVG	TBVI	TBVJ
2001 2 810	15 711	7 225	3 517	7 245	7 611	3 672	148 272	34 871
2002 3 092	16 388	8 634	4 054	7 914	7 668	4 120	149 872	35 508
Facilities granted								
TCBB	TCBC	TCBD	TCBE	TCBF	TCBH	TCBG	TCBI	TCBJ
2001 5 681	27 586	8 978	4 612	8 986	12 418	5 142	311 029	38 997
2002 5 047	28 442	10 941	5 213	9 446	13 159	5 769	323 384	41 936
of which in sterling								
TCDB	TCDC	TCDD	TCDE	TCDF	TCDH	TCDG	TCDI	TCDJ
2001 4 359	22 907	8 576	4 552	8 786	10 623	4 655	170 105	37 046
2002 4 059	24 171	10 190	5 158	9 308	11 226	5 240	171 127	39 131

23.4 Industrial analysis of bank lending to UK residents[1]
Not seasonally adjusted
continued

£ millions

	Financial intermediation (excl. insurance & pension funds)							
	Non-bank credit grantors, excl. credit unions	Credit unions	Factoring corporations	Mortgage & housing credit corporations	Investment & unit trusts excl. money market mutual funds	Money market mutual funds	Bank holding companies	Securities dealers (f)	Other financial intermediaries

Amounts outstanding (sterling & other currencies)

Loans & advances (including under repo & sterling commercial paper)

	TBPK	TBPL	TBPM	TBPN	TBPO	TBPP	TBPQ	TBPR	TBPS
2001	10 468	3	2 790	17 558	8 552	182	16 290	124 505	56 917
2002	11 761	1	2 935	24 458	8 941	311	18 453	117 733	67 788

Acceptances

	TBRK	TBRL	TBRM	TBRN	TBRO	TBRP	TBRQ	TBRR	TBRS
2001	591	–	153	14	8	–	36	52	649
2002	507	15	149	5	–	–	32	42	464

Total

	TBTK	TBTL	TBTM	TBTN	TBTO	TBTP	TBTQ	TBTR	TBTS
2001	11 059	3	2 942	17 572	8 560	182	16 326	124 557	57 566
2002	12 269	17	3 085	24 463	8 941	311	18 485	117 775	68 252

of which in sterling

	TBVK	TBVL	TBVM	TBVN	TBVO	TBVP	TBVQ	TBVR	TBVS
2001	9 431	3	2 691	17 512	5 027	158	13 107	33 478	31 993
2002	10 487	17	2 696	24 408	5 255	173	14 993	22 238	34 097

Facilities granted

	TCBK	TCBL	TCBM	TCBN	TCBO	TCBP	TCBQ	TCBR	TCBS
2001	12 483	18	3 074	19 190	20 741	187	17 066	132 997	66 276
2002	13 513	30	3 289	26 257	20 423	338	18 738	122 169	76 691

of which in sterling

	TCDK	TCDL	TCDM	TCDN	TCDO	TCDP	TCDQ	TCDR	TCDS
2001	10 533	6	2 808	19 056	14 260	158	13 429	35 542	37 267
2002	11 452	20	2 866	26 199	14 883	190	15 084	22 880	38 423

	Activities auxiliary to financial intermediation			Individuals & individual trusts		
	Insurance companies & pension funds	Fund management activities	Other	Total	Lending secured on dwellings inc. bridging finance	Other loans & advances

Amounts outstanding (sterling & other currencies)

Loans & advances (including under repo & sterling commercial paper)

	TBPT	TBPU	TBPV	TBPW	TBPX	TBPY
2001	16 116	6 777	18 495	515 204	407 406	107 798
2002	13 714	6 558	26 293	576 315	455 101	121 213

Acceptances

	TBRT	TBRU	TBRV			
2001	202	–	14			
2002	172	–	7			

Total

	TBTT	TBTU	TBTV	TBTW	TBTX	TBTY
2001	16 318	6 777	18 509	515 204	407 406	107 798
2002	13 886	6 558	26 300	576 315	455 101	121 213

of which in sterling

	TBVT	TBVU	TBVV	TBVW	TBVX	TBVY
2001	14 792	4 287	4 111	514 802	407 365	107 437
2002	12 728	4 087	7 610	575 819	455 055	120 764

Facilities granted

	TCBT	TCBU	TCBV	TCBW	TCBX	TCBY
2001	27 481	8 704	19 636	562 977	432 258	130 719
2002	24 660	8 653	27 787	631 881	489 062	142 819

of which in sterling

	TCDT	TCDU	TCDV	TCDW	TCDX	TCDY
2001	22 281	5 338	4 827	562 441	432 164	130 277
2002	20 497	4 759	8 705	631 178	488 965	142 214

1 See chapter text.

Source: Bank of England: 020 7601 3236

23.5 Industrial analysis of bank deposits from UK residents[1]

£ millions

	Total from UK residents	Agriculture, hunting and forestry	Fishing	Mining & quarrying	Manufacturing			
					Total	Food, beverages & tobacco	Textiles & leather	Pulp, paper, publishing & printing

Amounts outstanding (sterling & other currencies)

Deposit liabilities (including under repos)

	TDAA	TDAB	TDAC	TDAD	TDAE	TDAF	TDAG	TDAH
2001	910 267	3 667	113	3 730	33 673	3 599	1 126	4 111
2002	934 618	3 403	134	2 869	32 330	3 075	1 126	3 721

of which in sterling

	TDCA	TDCB	TDCC	TDCD	TDCE	TDCF	TDCG	TDCH
2001	761 236	3 554	100	1 844	24 752	2 868	961	3 455
2002	797 661	3 296	111	1 682	23 216	2 580	966	3 087

	Manufacturing				Electricity, gas and water supply		
	Chemicals, man-made fibres, rubber & plastics	Non-metallic mineral products & metals	Machinery, equipment & transport equipment	Electrical, medical & optical equipment	Other manufacturing	Electricity, gas & heated water	Cold water purification & supply	Construction

Amounts outstanding (sterling & other currencies)

Deposit liabilities (including under repos)

	TDAI	TDAJ	TDAK	TDAL	TDAM	TDAN	TDAO	TDAP
2001	4 329	3 577	6 855	6 695	3 381	5 095	1 558	9 915
2002	4 603	3 215	6 228	6 680	3 681	4 406	1 250	11 132

of which in sterling

	TDCI	TDCJ	TDCK	TDCL	TDCM	TDCN	TDCO	TDCP
2001	2 700	2 857	5 097	3 984	2 829	3 968	1 261	9 701
2002	2 665	2 596	4 700	3 829	2 793	3 904	1 223	10 867

	Wholesale and retail trade					Real estate, renting, computer and other business activities		
	Total	Sale & repair of motor vehicles & fuel	Other wholesale trade	Other retail trade & repair	Hotels and restaurants	Transport, storage & communication	Total	Development, buying, selling, renting of real estate	Renting of machinery & equipment

Amounts outstanding (sterling & other currencies)

Deposit liabilities (including under repos)

		TDAR	TDAS	TDAT	TDAU	TDAV	TDAW	TDAX	TDAY
	TDAQ								
2001	24 972	2 819	10 987	11 166	3 658	17 836	63 558	17 484	1 089
2002	25 622	2 945	11 367	11 310	4 157	18 807	70 989	20 258	1 252

of which in sterling

	TDCQ	TDCR	TDCS	TDCT	TDCU	TDCV	TDCW	TDCX	TDCY
2001	21 834	2 729	8 748	10 357	3 558	14 709	59 038	17 239	1 037
2002	22 035	2 849	8 470	10 716	4 071	15 646	66 115	19 914	1 185

23.5 Industrial analysis of bank deposits from UK residents[1]

continued

£ millions

	Real estate, renting, computer and other business activities					Recreational, personal & community service activities		Financial intermediation (excl. insurance & pension funds)	
	Computer & related activities	Legal, accountancy, consultancy & other business activities	Public administration & defence	Education	Health & social work	Recreational, cultural & sporting activities	Personal & community services activities	Total	Financial leasing corporations

Amounts outstanding (sterling & other currencies)

Deposit liabilities (including under repos)

	TDAZ	TDBA	TDBB	TDBC	TDBD	TDBF	TDBE	TDBG	TDBH
2001	7 012	37 973	16 875	4 829	6 809	7 074	10 494	173 380	3 130
2002	6 559	42 920	13 829	5 294	7 672	8 272	10 847	159 081	3 570

of which in sterling

	TDCZ	TDDA	TDDB	TDDC	TDDD	TDDF	TDDE	TDDG	TDDH
2001	5 836	34 925	15 992	4 705	6 687	6 596	10 008	87 321	2 458
2002	5 595	39 421	12 980	5 159	7 567	7 648	10 552	83 586	2 687

	Financial intermediation (excl. insurance & pension funds)							
	Non-bank credit grantors, excl. credit unions	Credit unions	Factoring corporations	Mortgage & housing credit corporations	Investment & unit trusts excl. money market mutual funds	Money market mutual funds	Bank holding companies	Securities dealers	Other financial intermediaries

Amounts outstanding (sterling & other currencies)

Deposit liabilities (including under repos)

	TDBI	TDBJ	TDBK	TDBL	TDBM	TDBN	TDBO	TDBP	TDBQ
2001	3 410	169	279	2 247	17 626	528	9 589	78 036	58 364
2002	3 699	195	327	3 711	17 855	190	10 231	68 632	50 662

of which in sterling

	TDDI	TDDJ	TDDK	TDDL	TDDM	TDDN	TDDO	TDDP	TDDQ
2001	2 747	169	216	2 247	13 757	505	7 991	28 119	29 114
2002	3 146	195	228	3 513	13 351	142	9 043	18 177	33 103

	Insurance companies & pension funds	Activities auxiliary to financial intermediation		
		Placed by fund managers	Other	Individuals & individual trusts

Amounts outstanding (sterling & other currencies)

Deposit liabilities (including under repos)

	TDBR	TDBS	TDBT	TDBU
2001	56 199	34 096	28 009	404 727
2002	55 897	33 045	30 377	435 204

of which in sterling

	TDDR	TDDS	TDDT	TDDU
2001	49 089	24 927	8 596	402 998
2002	49 744	24 357	10 415	433 489

1 See chapter text.

Source: Bank of England: 020 7601 3236

23.6 Public sector net cash requirement and other counterparts to changes in money stock during the year

Not seasonally adjusted

£ millions

		1992	1993	1994	1995	1996	1997	1998	1999	2000	2001	2002
Public sector net cash requirement (surplus-)	ABEN	28 411	43 316	39 376	35 430	24 699	11 833	−6 431	−1 791	−37 338	−2 808	17 131
Sales(-) of public sector debt to M4 private sector	KHGZ	−20 111	−30 748	−23 333	−21 627	−18 976	−15 979	1 508	−1 263	13 588	−11 905	−8 074
M4 lending[1]	AVBS	25 537	22 680	31 604	57 744	59 120	68 208	63 955	78 087	111 230	82 446	107 654
External and foreign currency finance of the public sector	KHJP	−12 647	−10 782	623	−3 640	−10 884	−2 453	−4 717	6 198	3 616	23 556	2 486
Other external and foreign currency flows[2]	AVBW	8 830	14 273	−8 173	−3 443	18 020	24 566	13 975	−44 743	7 072	−21 636	−25 050
Net non-deposit liabilities (increase-)	AVBX	−11 480	−14 680	−14 540	−8 578	−12 652	−7 032	−8 165	−3 103	−30 948	−10 786	−25 290
Money stock (M4)	AUZI	17 843	23 877	25 557	55 885	59 337	80 362	60 125	33 386	67 220	58 868	67 858

1 Bank and building society lending, plus holdings of commercial bills by the Issue Department of the Bank of England.
2 Including sterling lending to non-residents sector.

Source: Bank of England: 020 7601 5468

23.7 Money stock and liquidity

£ millions

		1992	1993	1994	1995	1996	1997	1998	1999	2000	2001	2002
Amounts outstanding at end-year												
Notes and coin in circulation with the M4 private sector[1]	VQKT	16 698	17 716	18 661	19 847	20 642	22 242	23 705	26 269	28 174	30 450	31 898
UK private sector sterling non-interest bearing sight deposits[2,3]	AUYA	28 667	34 521	33 502	35 450	38 447	38 937	37 262	43 011	46 604	50 205	46 144
Money stock (M2)[3,4]	VQXV	373 179	394 438	410 396	436 957	460 108	484 593	515 005	559 214	598 260	649 636	704 479
Money stock M4[3]	AUYM	517 883	544 055	567 157	623 385	682 786	721 977	783 240	816 545	884 839	942 433	1 008 707
Changes during the year[5]												
Notes and coin in circulation with the M4 private sector[1]	VQLU	1 066	1 023	956	1 177	797	1 611	1 501	2 582	1 957	2 284	1 501
UK private sector sterling non-interest bearing sight deposits[2,3]	AUZA	−327	4 203	1 092	1 782	3 530	5 349	−624	5 759	3 364	3 830	−5 761
Money stock (M2)[3,4]	AUZE	17 125	18 851	17 624	26 491	24 323	35 963	30 976	42 397	38 953	51 730	54 707
Money stock M4[3]	AUZI	17 843	23 877	25 557	55 885	59 337	80 362	60 125	33 386	67 220	58 868	67 858

1 The estimates of levels of coin in circulation include allowance for wastage, hoarding, etc.
2 Non-interest bearing deposits are confined to those with institutions included in the United Kingdom banks sector (See Table 23.3).
3 Revised rules on netting of customers' credit balances against their borrowing increased the UK private sector's outstanding balances of deposits and borrowing by £2.5bn at end-December 1993. Within retail deposit, £1.7bn of the increase was in NIB bank deposits. Re-netting during 1994 amounted to £1.7bn. Changes data have been adjusted to exclude these effects. Building societies' data from 1992 onwards are affected by the revised treatment of building society transit items within M4.

4 With effect from the flow for December 1992, M2 comprises the UK non-monetary financial institutions and non-public sector, i.e. M4 private sector's holdings of notes and coin together with its sterling denominated retail deposits with UK monetary financial institutions.
5 As far as possible the changes exclude the effect of changes in the number of contributors to the series, and also of the introduction of new statistical returns. Changes are not seasonally adjusted.

Source: Bank of England: 020 7601 5468

23.8 Selected retail banks' base rate[1]
Percentage rates operative between dates shown

Rates

Date of change	New rate	Date of change	New rate	Date of change	New rate
1986 Jan 9	12.50	Jul 19	10.50	Mar 8	6.00
Mar 19	11.50	Aug 8	10.50-11.00	Jun 6	5.75
Apr 8	11.00-11.50	Aug 9	11.00	Oct 30	5.75-6.00
Apr 9	11.00	Aug 25	11.00-12.00	Oct 31	6.00
Apr 21	10.50	Aug 26	12.00		
May 23	10.00-10.50	Nov 25	13.00	1997 May 6	6.25
May 27	10.00			Jun 6	6.25-6.50
Oct 14	10.00-11.00	1989 May 24	14.00	Jun 9	6.50
Oct 15	11.00	Oct 5	15.00	Jul 10	6.75
				Aug 7	7.00
1987 Mar 10	10.50	1990 Oct 8	14.00	Nov 6	7.25
Mar 18	10.00-10.50				
Mar 19	10.00	1991 Feb 13	13.50	1998 Jun 4	7.50
Apr 28	9.50-10.00	Feb 27	13.00	Oct 8	7.25
Apr 29	9.50	Mar 22	12.50	Nov 5	6.75
May 11	9.00	Apr 12	12.00	Dec 10	6.25
Aug 6	9.00-10.00	May 24	11.50		
Aug 7	10.00	Jul 12	11.00	1999 Jan 7	6.00
Oct 23	9.50-10.00	Sep 4	10.50	Feb 4	5.50
Oct 29	9.50			Apr 8	5.25
Nov 4	9.00-9.50	1992 May 5	10.00	Jun 10	5.00
Nov 5	9.00	Sep 16[1]	12.00	Sep 8	5.00-5.25
Dec 4	8.50	Sep 17[1]	10.00-12.00	Sep 10	5.25
		Sep 18	10.00	Nov 4	5.50
1988 Feb 2	9.00	Sep 22	9.00		
Mar 17	8.50-9.00	Oct 16	8.00-9.00	2000 Jan 13	5.75
Mar 18	8.50	Oct 19	8.00	Feb 10	6.00
Apr 11	8.00	Nov 13	7.00		
May 17	7.50-8.00			2001 Feb 8	5.75
May 18	7.50	1993 Jan 26	6.00	Apr 5	5.50
Jun 2	7.50-8.00	Nov 23	5.50	May 10	5.25
Jun 3	8.00			Aug 2	5.00
Jun 6	8.00-8.50	1994 Feb 8	5.25	Sep 18	4.75
Jun 7	8.50	Sep 12	5.75	Oct 4	4.50
Jun 22	8.50-9.00	Dec 7	6.25	Nov 8	4.00
Jun 23	9.00				
Jun 28	9.00-9.50	1995 Feb 2[1]	6.25-6.75	2003 Feb 6	3.75
Jun 29	9.50	Feb 3	6.75	Jul 10	3.50
Jul 4	9.50-10.00	Dec 13	6.50	Nov 6	3.75
Jul 5	10.00				
Jul 18	10.00-10.50	1996 Jan 18	6.25		

1 Data obtained from Barclays Bank, Lloyds/TSB Bank, HSBC Bank and National Westminster Bank whose rates are used to compile this series. Where all the rates did not change on the same day a spread is shown.

Source: Bank of England: 020 7601 4342

23.9 Average three month sterling money market rates[1]

Rate per cent

	1993	1994	1995	1996	1997	1998	1999	2000	2001	2002	2003
Treasury bills:[2] KDMM											
January	5.79	4.88	5.93	6.08	6.01	6.80	5.28	5.72	5.49	3.83	3.80
February	5.38	4.76	6.16	5.94	5.81	6.88	5.04	5.83	5.46	3.87	3.50
March	5.37	4.85	6.09	5.79	5.92	6.95	4.92	5.86	5.23	3.97	3.47
April	5.32	4.87	6.30	5.80	6.09	7.00	4.90	5.92	5.12	3.97	3.45
May	5.28	4.81	6.20	5.82	6.15	7.01	4.93	5.95	4.98	3.95	3.44
June	5.17	4.89	6.37	5.58	6.37	7.29	4.76	5.85	4.99	3.98	3.47
July	5.12	5.12	6.62	5.49	6.63	7.22	4.76	5.83	5.01	3.84	3.31
August	5.08	5.34	6.58	5.54	6.83	7.19	4.85	5.81	4.72	3.77	3.40
September	5.18	5.39	6.51	5.54	6.88	6.94	5.12	5.78	4.43	3.79	3.52
October	5.09	5.44	6.57	5.61	6.94	6.54	5.23	5.75	4.16	3.75	3.65
November	4.90	5.63	6.40	6.05	7.09	6.31	5.20	5.68	3.78	3.80	3.81
December	4.88	5.87	6.20	6.05	7.07	5.72	5.46	5.62	3.83	3.84	..
Eligible bill: KDMY											
January	6.43	5.07	6.41	6.18	6.15	7.28	5.63	5.90	5.64	3.91	3.87
February	5.59	4.95	6.54	6.00	5.99	7.24	5.28	6.01	5.56	3.92	3.65
March	5.62	4.90	6.40	5.87	6.01	7.25	5.11	5.98	5.37	3.99	3.54
April	5.66	4.93	6.44	5.83	6.26	7.24	5.02	6.05	5.21	4.04	3.52
May	5.67	4.92	6.54	5.85	6.31	7.20	5.08	6.09	5.06	4.01	3.52
June	5.62	4.94	6.44	5.66	6.50	7.42	4.94	6.03	5.08	4.04	3.45
July	5.63	5.01	6.66	5.57	6.80	7.49	4.89	5.97	5.07	3.94	3.39
August	5.59	5.44	6.64	5.60	6.95	7.40	4.94	5.97	4.82	3.86	3.42
September	5.58	5.54	6.55	5.63	7.02	7.20	5.16	5.95	4.57	3.86	3.59
October	5.50	5.74	6.58	5.76	7.10	6.91	5.42	5.92	4.26	3.82	3.69
November	5.31	5.89	6.49	6.10	7.27	6.52	5.43	5.88	3.85	3.84	3.88
December	5.04	6.12	6.29	6.18	7.31	6.05	5.59	5.78	3.88	3.71	..
Interbank rate: AMIJ											
January	6.94	5.39	6.56	6.36	6.32	7.48	5.80	6.06	5.76	3.98	3.91
February	6.16	5.22	6.75	6.16	6.19	7.46	5.43	6.15	5.69	3.98	3.69
March	5.98	5.16	6.66	6.05	6.20	7.48	5.30	6.15	5.47	4.06	3.58
April	5.98	5.21	6.67	6.00	6.38	7.44	5.23	6.21	5.33	4.11	3.58
May	5.97	5.17	6.72	6.02	6.45	7.41	5.25	6.23	5.17	4.08	3.57
June	5.89	5.13	6.64	5.85	6.66	7.63	5.12	6.14	5.19	4.11	3.57
July	5.95	5.20	6.80	5.73	6.96	7.71	5.07	6.11	5.19	3.99	3.42
August	5.84	5.53	6.79	5.75	7.15	7.66	5.18	6.14	4.93	3.92	3.45
September	5.91	5.67	6.72	5.77	7.21	7.38	5.32	6.12	4.65	3.93	3.63
October	5.76	5.91	6.73	5.94	7.26	7.14	5.94	6.08	4.36	3.90	3.73
November	5.57	6.06	6.64	6.30	7.54	6.89	5.78	6.00	3.93	3.91	3.91
December	5.33	6.37	6.49	6.35	7.62	6.38	5.97	5.89	3.99	3.95	..
Certificate of deposits: KOSA											
January	6.82	5.29	6.48	6.31	6.27	7.44	5.74	6.02	5.73	3.96	3.90
February	6.00	5.14	6.67	6.11	6.14	7.42	5.38	6.10	5.66	3.96	3.68
March	5.87	5.09	6.59	6.01	6.15	7.43	5.26	6.09	5.44	4.04	3.57
April	5.84	5.12	6.62	5.96	6.33	7.40	5.19	6.17	5.30	4.08	3.57
May	5.86	5.10	6.66	5.98	6.39	7.37	5.22	6.19	5.15	4.06	3.56
June	5.77	5.06	6.56	5.79	6.62	7.59	5.09	6.10	5.16	4.09	3.56
July	5.81	5.11	6.72	5.69	6.92	7.66	5.03	6.08	5.17	3.97	3.41
August	5.71	5.45	6.73	5.71	7.12	7.61	5.14	6.09	4.90	3.90	3.44
September	5.79	5.58	6.66	5.74	7.17	7.34	5.28	6.08	4.62	3.91	3.62
October	5.65	5.81	6.68	5.89	7.22	7.09	5.86	6.05	4.33	3.88	3.72
November	5.46	5.97	6.58	6.25	7.50	6.82	5.72	5.98	3.91	3.89	3.90
December	5.23	6.25	6.44	6.29	7.57	6.32	5.89	5.85	3.96	3.93	..
Local authority deposits: KDPX											
January	6.84	5.30	6.52	6.31	6.27	7.43	5.76	6.03	5.73	3.85	3.87
February	6.09	5.12	6.69	6.13	6.15	7.40	5.38	6.09	5.62	3.88	3.61
March	5.93	5.08	6.59	6.02	6.14	7.40	5.27	6.08	5.39	4.01	3.55
April	5.95	5.14	6.60	5.98	6.33	7.38	5.17	6.12	5.26	4.05	3.54
May	5.94	5.12	6.68	6.00	6.38	7.34	5.19	6.14	5.13	4.06	3.54
June	5.86	5.08	6.58	5.80	6.57	7.56	5.07	6.09	5.10	4.05	3.57
July	5.90	5.18	6.76	5.69	6.90	7.64	5.01	6.04	5.12	3.95	3.39
August	5.80	5.44	6.74	5.71	7.11	7.55	5.11	6.06	4.86	3.87	..
September	5.85	5.62	6.65	5.72	7.19	7.35	5.19	6.05	4.58	3.88	..
October	5.70	5.84	6.68	5.86	7.21	7.08	5.83	6.03	4.29	3.86	..
November	5.51	5.99	6.60	6.24	7.49	6.85	5.64	5.96	3.82	3.87	..
December	5.26	6.32	6.43	6.30	7.56	6.35	5.88	5.80	3.87	3.93	..

1 A full definition of these series is given in Section 7 of the ONS Financial
  Statistics Explanatory Handbook.
2 Average rate of discount at weekly (Friday) tender.

Source: Bank of England: 020 7601 3644

23.10 Average foreign exchange rates[1]

	1993	1994	1995	1996	1997	1998	1999	2000	2001	2002	2003
Sterling exchange rate index (1990 = 100) AGBG											
January	88.8	92.0	88.5	83.2	95.9	104.7	99.6	108.5	104.4	106.9	104.0
February	84.7	90.4	87.4	83.8	97.4	104.7	100.8	108.4	104.1	107.4	102.4
March	86.4	89.8	85.6	83.5	97.4	106.8	102.8	108.4	105.0	106.5	100.6
April	88.9	89.2	84.5	83.8	99.5	107.1	103.4	110.1	105.8	107.1	99.8
May	89.0	88.9	84.3	84.6	99.0	103.4	104.2	108.5	106.6	105.3	97.9
June	88.3	89.1	84.1	86.0	100.4	105.4	104.7	104.6	106.8	103.6	99.6
July	90.5	87.9	83.6	85.7	104.5	105.3	103.5	105.6	107.2	105.3	99.4
August	90.3	87.8	84.4	84.7	102.5	104.6	103.3	107.4	105.1	105.4	99.0
September	89.8	88.1	84.8	86.1	100.4	103.3	104.7	106.2	106.1	106.5	99.2
October	89.4	89.1	84.3	88.4	101.1	100.7	105.4	109.2	105.8	106.7	99.8
November	90.2	89.1	83.3	92.0	103.8	100.6	105.7	107.3	106.1	105.9	100.4
December	91.0	89.1	82.9	93.8	104.4	100.4	106.7	106.4	106.5	105.5	..
Sterling/US Dollar AUSS											
January	1.5325	1.4939	1.5747	1.5306	1.6587	1.6353	1.6509	1.6402	1.4769	1.4323	1.6169
February	1.4386	1.4799	1.5720	1.5364	1.6246	1.6407	1.6276	1.5998	1.4529	1.4231	1.6046
March	1.4625	1.4917	1.6005	1.5271	1.6063	1.6620	1.6220	1.5802	1.4454	1.4225	1.5836
April	1.5472	1.4837	1.6074	1.5145	1.6295	1.6733	1.6105	1.5837	1.4350	1.4434	1.5747
May	1.5481	1.5029	1.5868	1.5152	1.6334	1.6366	1.6154	1.5075	1.4259	1.4593	1.6230
June	1.5099	1.5252	1.5949	1.5418	1.6446	1.6507	1.5950	1.5089	1.4014	1.4863	1.6606
July	1.4963	1.5463	1.5953	1.5539	1.6702	1.6437	1.5747	1.5088	1.4139	1.5546	1.5980
August	1.4911	1.5427	1.5681	1.5502	1.6034	1.6320	1.6073	1.4910	1.4365	1.5377	1.5950
September	1.5261	1.5651	1.5584	1.5597	1.6015	1.6822	1.6243	1.4355	1.4635	1.5561	1.6131
October	1.5037	1.5651	1.5779	1.5862	1.6329	1.6952	1.6572	1.4511	1.4517	1.5574	1.6787
November	1.4806	1.5886	1.5623	1.6626	1.6890	1.6620	1.6214	1.4256	1.4358	1.5723	1.6901
December	1.4904	1.5595	1.5398	1.6647	1.6597	1.6705	1.6132	1.4625	1.4409	1.5863	..
Sterling/Euro THAP											
January	1.2383	1.3295	1.2525	1.1631	1.3559	1.5166	1.4236	1.6201	1.5753	1.6222	1.5222
February	1.1884	1.3082	1.2331	1.1707	1.3906	1.5196	1.4534	1.6266	1.5786	1.6348	1.4893
March	1.2164	1.2915	1.2038	1.1692	1.3944	1.5507	1.4902	1.6377	1.5901	1.6224	1.4649
April	1.2453	1.2840	1.1890	1.1763	1.4243	1.5490	1.5051	1.6730	1.6084	1.6282	1.4505
May	1.2493	1.2719	1.1893	1.1923	1.4217	1.4834	1.5185	1.6655	1.6304	1.5914	1.4030
June	1.2522	1.2709	1.1828	1.2094	1.4499	1.5110	1.5374	1.5882	1.6434	1.5515	1.4234
July	1.2969	1.2455	1.1693	1.2007	1.5247	1.5091	1.5204	1.6052	1.6433	1.5665	1.4277
August	1.2977	1.2420	1.1836	1.1845	1.5043	1.4912	1.5146	1.6478	1.5955	1.5723	1.4286
September	1.2735	1.2469	1.1903	1.2066	1.4591	1.4617	1.5458	1.6471	1.6060	1.5861	1.4338
October	1.2727	1.2563	1.1759	1.2407	1.4623	1.4200	1.5491	1.6994	1.6024	1.5868	1.4334
November	1.2958	1.2613	1.1612	1.2873	1.4914	1.4290	1.5706	1.6664	1.6166	1.5694	1.4426
December	1.3076	1.2672	1.1589	1.3192	1.5053	1.4254	1.5953	1.6302	1.6151	1.5566	..

1 Working day average. A full definition of these series is given in Section 7 of the ONS Explanatory Handbook.

Source: Bank of England: 020 7601 3644

23.11 Average Zero Coupon Yields[1]

	1993	1994	1995	1996	1997	1998	1999	2000	2001	2002	2003
Nominal Five Year Yield ZBRG											
January	7.46	5.89	8.63	6.85	7.15	6.18	4.30	6.28	5.07	4.90	4.15
February	7.06	6.23	8.53	7.12	6.82	6.10	4.46	6.13	5.04	4.94	3.88
March	6.94	6.96	8.45	7.45	7.07	6.09	4.69	5.89	4.86	5.22	3.94
April	7.23	7.58	8.25	7.52	7.28	5.93	4.66	5.80	4.96	5.21	4.10
May	7.47	7.97	7.95	7.53	6.94	5.95	4.95	5.82	5.14	5.22	3.85
June	7.34	8.45	7.77	7.46	6.96	6.04	5.28	5.61	5.25	5.05	3.72
July	7.02	8.27	7.89	7.30	7.01	6.12	5.49	5.58	5.26	4.88	3.96
August	6.62	8.47	7.70	7.19	6.97	5.80	5.75	5.65	5.03	4.54	..
September	6.59	8.71	7.47	7.18	6.72	5.32	6.00	5.65	4.90	4.31	..
October	6.43	8.64	7.56	6.97	6.51	4.94	6.25	5.46	4.74	4.36	..
November	6.35	8.49	7.21	7.18	6.69	4.92	5.86	5.33	4.55	4.38	..
December	5.89	8.49	6.88	7.20	6.46	4.51	5.90	5.14	4.88	4.34	..
Nominal Ten Year Yield ZBRH											
January	8.51	6.39	8.57	7.46	7.52	5.96	4.24	5.62	4.75	4.85	4.39
February	8.25	6.78	8.50	7.80	7.15	5.91	4.39	5.44	4.90	4.90	4.25
March	7.95	7.43	8.45	8.08	7.41	5.85	4.60	5.18	4.64	5.18	4.35
April	8.06	7.79	8.31	8.06	7.58	5.69	4.53	5.14	4.90	5.19	4.49
May	8.32	8.24	8.07	8.10	7.08	5.73	4.83	5.23	5.05	5.22	4.24
June	8.11	8.65	8.04	8.09	7.04	5.60	5.07	5.05	5.11	5.05	4.13
July	7.74	8.47	8.20	7.96	6.92	5.65	5.24	5.09	5.10	4.95	4.42
August	7.23	8.54	8.07	7.86	6.97	5.41	5.25	5.18	4.88	4.68	..
September	7.09	8.77	7.93	7.86	6.70	5.03	5.51	5.25	4.91	4.47	..
October	7.00	8.64	8.09	7.56	6.37	4.93	5.68	5.09	4.77	4.60	..
November	6.97	8.51	7.78	7.56	6.46	4.83	5.11	4.98	4.58	4.62	..
December	6.45	8.43	7.52	7.52	6.22	4.44	5.19	4.80	4.83	4.55	..
Nominal Twenty Year Yield ZBRI											
January	9.19	6.57	8.23	7.89	7.74	5.94	4.36	4.45	4.33	4.69	4.46
February	8.97	6.88	8.16	8.19	7.39	5.88	4.44	4.38	4.42	4.72	4.40
March	8.67	7.45	8.15	8.37	7.59	5.78	4.60	4.25	4.45	4.99	4.56
April	8.63	7.69	8.09	8.30	7.73	5.61	4.53	4.35	4.76	5.02	4.69
May	8.74	7.98	7.92	8.38	7.16	5.67	4.75	4.40	4.87	5.08	4.49
June	8.51	8.18	7.98	8.41	7.08	5.42	4.77	4.37	4.98	4.93	4.44
July	8.12	8.08	8.24	8.34	6.80	5.45	4.67	4.38	4.90	4.82	4.70
August	7.56	8.15	8.14	8.26	6.86	5.30	4.53	4.49	4.69	4.57	..
September	7.37	8.29	8.05	8.27	6.64	4.91	4.62	4.63	4.88	4.40	..
October	7.27	8.23	8.30	7.98	6.36	4.87	4.56	4.61	4.92	4.54	..
November	7.20	8.18	7.98	7.81	6.37	4.73	4.07	4.39	4.53	4.60	..
December	6.63	8.08	7.80	7.67	6.17	4.47	4.20	4.30	4.65	4.59	..
Real Ten Year Yield ZBRJ											
January	3.56	2.73	3.87	3.42	3.45	3.10	2.00	2.10	2.22	2.52	2.00
February	3.19	2.86	3.86	3.54	3.27	3.06	1.91	2.17	2.27	2.50	1.74
March	3.01	3.09	3.87	3.67	3.43	3.00	1.85	2.05	2.33	2.53	1.79
April	3.07	3.25	3.79	3.63	3.56	2.91	1.70	2.08	2.56	2.43	1.96
May	3.23	3.48	3.57	3.72	3.57	2.92	1.91	2.14	2.58	2.43	1.81
June	3.25	3.76	3.56	3.77	3.66	2.85	1.89	2.12	2.54	2.33	1.67
July	3.19	3.84	3.58	3.70	3.62	2.77	1.90	2.14	2.56	2.42	1.85
August	3.15	3.78	3.48	3.58	3.60	2.65	2.19	2.25	2.42	2.33	..
September	3.09	3.81	3.45	3.57	3.52	2.59	2.31	2.28	2.51	2.20	..
October	3.02	3.82	3.63	3.41	3.23	2.67	2.26	2.33	2.53	2.36	..
November	2.95	3.81	3.52	3.43	3.25	2.40	2.05	2.34	2.39	2.33	..
December	2.79	3.83	3.43	3.42	3.11	2.11	1.98	2.23	2.58	2.24	..
Real Twenty Year Yield ZBRK											
January	3.84	3.07	3.89	..	3.67	3.06	2.07	2.01	1.88	2.26	2.07
February	3.68	3.23	3.89	3.79	3.49	3.05	1.99	1.95	1.88	2.30	1.96
March	3.53	3.45	3.88	3.81	3.59	2.98	1.93	1.78	1.99	2.32	2.05
April	3.54	3.51	3.80	3.75	3.68	2.85	1.81	1.84	2.25	2.25	2.13
May	3.63	3.68	3.64	3.82	3.66	2.83	1.99	1.91	2.32	2.25	2.04
June	3.59	3.91	3.69	3.86	3.69	2.63	1.97	1.87	2.27	2.17	1.99
July	3.52	3.93	3.71	3.81	3.57	2.58	2.00	1.90	2.24	2.24	2.15
August	3.35	3.84	3.62	3.75	3.57	2.53	2.14	1.96	2.16	2.15	..
September	3.25	3.88	3.61	3.76	3.48	2.49	2.26	1.96	2.31	2.06	..
October	3.19	3.87	3.73	3.61	3.22	2.59	2.22	1.99	2.32	2.22	..
November	3.21	3.85	3.61	3.62	3.18	2.36	1.92	1.94	2.12	2.25	..
December	3.08	3.87	3.56	3.62	3.06	2.14	1.87	1.87	2.24	2.21	..

1 Working day average. Calculated using the Variable Roughness Penalty (VRP) model.

Source: Bank of England: 020 7601 3644

23.12 Average rates on representative British Government Stocks[1]

	1993	1994	1995	1996	1997	1998	1999	2000	2001	2002	2003
5 Year Conventional Rate KORP											
January	6.88	5.76	8.61	6.78	7.19	6.33	4.25	6.36	5.17	4.94	4.15
February	6.72	6.05	8.52	7.02	6.86	6.24	4.41	6.23	5.13	4.96	3.88
March	6.62	6.72	8.44	7.56	7.08	6.26	4.65	6.01	4.94	5.23	3.93
April	6.91	7.33	8.26	7.43	7.30	6.11	4.66	5.95	4.97	5.26	4.08
May	7.10	7.74	7.96	7.61	6.98	6.14	4.93	5.97	5.15	5.48	3.83
June	7.01	8.22	7.79	7.52	7.01	6.31	5.27	5.78	5.32	5.10	3.68
July	6.70	8.06	7.90	7.35	7.09	6.14	5.49	5.75	5.34	4.92	3.72
August	6.35	8.31	7.69	7.21	7.02	5.84	5.80	5.81	5.09	4.57	4.30
September	6.34	8.61	7.45	7.20	6.78	5.34	6.04	5.81	4.94	4.25	4.42
October	6.17	8.57	7.54	7.01	6.59	4.88	6.24	5.66	4.78	4.38	4.70
November	6.09	8.44	7.16	7.22	6.79	4.86	5.89	5.50	4.59	4.40	4.88
December	5.66	8.49	6.83	7.26	6.60	4.45	5.91	5.27	4.88	4.34	..
10 year Conventional Rate KORQ											
January	8.22	6.23	8.66	7.42	7.53	6.07	4.16	5.75	4.86	4.84	4.37
February	7.91	6.61	8.59	7.75	7.17	6.02	4.32	5.56	4.88	4.91	4.25
March	7.66	7.29	8.53	8.05	7.41	5.97	4.54	5.29	4.75	5.15	4.51
April	7.82	7.68	8.39	8.05	7.60	5.81	4.48	5.25	4.95	5.23	4.64
May	8.06	8.13	8.12	8.08	7.13	5.85	4.77	5.35	5.13	5.51	4.26
June	7.87	8.54	8.08	8.04	7.10	5.77	5.02	5.15	5.09	5.06	4.38
July	7.49	8.37	8.23	7.91	7.01	5.67	5.20	5.18	5.16	4.94	4.23
August	6.98	8.52	8.10	7.81	7.05	5.56	5.24	5.27	4.92	4.66	4.59
September	6.90	8.80	7.92	7.80	6.77	5.10	5.52	5.32	4.92	4.46	4.69
October	6.81	8.70	8.08	7.51	6.47	4.93	5.70	5.15	4.76	4.57	4.89
November	6.77	8.57	7.75	7.56	6.59	4.87	5.16	5.06	4.58	4.59	5.04
December	6.29	8.53	7.45	7.54	6.34	4.49	5.24	4.88	4.88	4.52	..
20 Year Conventional Rate KORR											
January	8.74	6.53	8.45	7.73	7.71	6.04	4.36	4.91	4.52	4.81	4.46
February	8.44	6.88	8.43	8.04	7.35	5.98	4.47	4.80	4.58	4.83	4.37
March	8.19	7.49	8.40	8.28	7.58	5.90	4.64	4.64	4.56	5.12	4.51
April	8.42	7.81	8.30	8.26	7.74	5.73	4.58	4.71	4.84	5.14	4.64
May	8.58	8.18	8.09	8.31	7.21	5.79	4.83	4.77	4.98	5.45	4.44
June	8.36	8.48	8.08	8.31	7.15	5.59	4.92	4.68	5.10	5.03	4.38
July	7.98	8.35	8.30	8.21	6.93	5.63	4.88	4.70	5.05	4.92	4.59
August	7.46	8.46	8.19	8.12	6.98	5.43	4.82	4.79	4.83	4.65	4.67
September	7.31	8.65	8.06	8.11	6.74	5.02	4.97	4.90	4.94	4.46	4.74
October	7.18	8.56	8.26	7.84	6.45	4.92	4.97	4.84	4.80	4.59	4.85
November	7.12	8.46	7.93	7.77	6.50	4.79	4.46	4.64	4.55	4.65	4.93
December	6.57	8.39	7.70	7.67	6.32	4.49	4.56	4.51	4.75	4.61	..
10 Year Index-Linked Rate KORS											
January	3.60	2.70	3.89	3.42	3.44	3.01	2.00	2.11	2.21	2.61	2.07
February	3.23	2.81	3.87	3.57	3.23	2.94	1.94	2.16	2.30	2.53	1.81
March	3.07	3.07	3.86	3.70	3.41	2.89	1.90	2.06	2.34	2.55	1.88
April	3.11	3.25	3.79	3.66	3.55	2.80	1.74	2.08	2.55	2.45	1.90
May	3.30	3.51	3.58	3.74	3.52	2.83	1.96	2.15	2.61	2.58	1.74
June	3.31	3.78	3.58	3.80	3.62	2.81	1.93	2.13	2.56	2.35	1.59
July	3.22	3.85	3.61	3.82	3.68	2.67	1.93	2.14	2.57	2.46	1.67
August	3.16	3.82	3.52	3.59	3.59	2.55	2.20	2.25	2.45	2.37	1.89
September	3.09	3.85	3.46	3.57	3.47	2.59	2.32	2.29	2.56	2.24	1.99
October	3.03	3.84	3.65	3.41	3.17	2.66	2.26	2.33	2.55	2.42	2.08
November	2.96	3.84	3.54	3.42	3.23	2.39	2.03	2.32	2.42	2.39	2.16
December	2.75	3.85	3.45	3.41	3.01	2.11	1.99	2.20	2.65	2.30	..
20 Year Index-Linked rate KORT											
January	3.84	2.96	3.91	3.58	3.62	3.01	2.06	2.01	1.96	2.35	2.10
February	3.64	3.11	3.89	3.70	3.43	3.01	1.97	1.98	1.99	2.36	1.99
March	3.50	3.35	3.89	3.82	3.55	2.92	1.93	1.83	2.09	2.39	2.07
April	3.51	3.45	3.81	3.77	3.65	2.80	1.81	1.90	2.35	2.32	2.10
May	3.62	3.64	3.64	3.84	3.61	2.79	1.99	1.97	2.41	2.43	2.00
June	3.57	3.88	3.67	3.88	3.65	2.61	1.97	1.94	2.38	2.23	1.93
July	3.48	3.90	3.71	3.72	3.68	2.56	1.97	1.96	2.36	2.30	2.05
August	3.32	3.83	3.62	3.75	3.54	2.51	2.12	2.03	2.25	2.21	2.09
September	3.22	3.87	3.60	3.74	3.43	2.51	2.23	2.04	2.39	2.12	2.13
October	3.15	3.86	3.74	3.60	3.17	2.58	2.18	2.08	2.38	2.29	2.17
November	3.14	3.85	3.62	3.59	3.16	2.35	1.91	2.02	2.19	2.31	2.16
December	2.98	3.86	3.55	3.58	3.02	2.12	1.88	1.94	2.33	2.26	..

1 Working day average.

Source: Bank of England: 020 7601 3644

23.13 Capital issues and redemptions[1]

£ millions

		1992	1993	1994	1995	1996	1997	1998	1999	2000	2001	2002
Total issues and redemptions												
Gross issues	KDSF	20 649	40 615	37 110	25 929	38 354	38 217	33 000	54 989	75 891	73 612	67 681
Gross redemptions	KDSG	7 011	11 399	11 866	10 367	14 123	14 579	11 607	12 661	10 472	11 281	14 622
Issues *less* redemptions: total	KDSH	13 638	29 216	25 244	15 562	24 231	23 638	21 393	42 328	65 419	62 331	53 059
Loan capital	KDSI	12 744	22 560	24 640	20 788	29 493	29 960	28 624	37 639	55 409	50 461	53 881
Preference shares	DEDO	589	1 700	603	2 875	710	−881	−330	−438	275	1 816	628
Ordinary shares	DEDF	6 224	16 671	14 620	9 777	10 273	8 614	4 637	10 127	19 517	18 734	16 391
UK borrowers: total	DEDX	13 638	29 216	25 244	15 562	24 231	23 638	21 393	42 328	65 419	62 331	53 059
Local government	DEEA	1	−1	–	–	–	–	–	–	–	–	–
Listed public companies	KDSN	13 637	29 217	25 244	15 562	24 231	23 638	21 393	42 328	65 419	62 331	53 059
Non-resident borrowers: total	KDSO	1 829	9 237	3 285	2 153	9 452	10 790	3 935	3 356	7 390	71	−2 353
Government[2]	KIMI	2 001	5 525	749	652	1 929	2 724	2 889	2 080	5 766	3 336	−1 032
Companies[3]	KHDR	−172	3 712	2 536	1 501	7 523	8 066	1 046	1 276	1 624	−3 265	−1 321
UK listed public companies												
All companies: total	KDSN	13 637	29 217	25 244	15 562	24 231	23 638	21 393	42 328	65 419	62 331	53 059
Loan capital	KDSS	6 824	10 846	10 021	2 910	13 248	15 905	17 086	32 639	45 627	41 781	36 040
Preference shares	KDST	589	1 700	603	2 875	710	−881	−330	−438	275	1 816	628
Ordinary shares	KDSU	6 224	16 671	14 620	9 777	10 273	8 614	4 637	10 127	19 517	18 734	16 391
Financial corporations: total	DEEC	5 427	12 523	11 774	−341	11 030	6 711	6 830	16 104	26 120	28 549	32 632
Loan capital	KDSW	3 898	7 455	6 972	−4 005	7 508	4 142	6 190	13 191	22 267	22 970	27 940
Preference shares	KDSX	459	1 221	138	1 538	868	−536	175	−438	292	1 773	628
Ordinary shares	DELC	1 070	3 847	4 664	2 126	2 654	3 105	465	3 351	3 561	3 806	4 064
Other companies: total	DEEB	8 210	16 694	13 470	15 903	13 201	16 927	14 563	26 224	39 299	33 782	20 427
Loan capital	KDTA	2 926	3 391	3 049	6 915	5 740	11 763	10 896	19 448	23 360	18 811	8 100
Preference shares	KDTB	130	479	465	1 337	−158	−345	−505	–	−17	43	–
Ordinary shares	DEEY	5 154	12 824	9 956	7 651	7 619	5 509	4 172	6 776	15 956	14 928	12 327
UK listed public companies												
Financial companies: total	KDTD	5 426	12 519	11 774	−342	11 032	8 172	6 828	16 106	26 119	28 549	32 628
Monetary financial institutions	KDTE	1 972	4 764	3 763	−648	9 618	22	2 161	2 312	14 231	14 911	15 070
Insurance corporations	DELR	394	1 694	501	578	1 007	1 805	617	1 843	85	2 591	2 354
Investment trust companies	DELS	709	3 027	4 118	1 415	1 537	927	427	231	2 396	1 723	271
Other[4]	KDTH	2 351	3 034	3 392	−1 687	−1 130	5 418	3 623	11 720	9 407	9 324	14 933
Other companies: total	DEEB	8 210	16 694	13 470	15 903	13 201	16 927	14 563	26 224	39 299	33 782	20 427
Manufacturing industries: total	KDTJ	4 460	7 133	4 814	9 536	1 888	1 849	−413	3 637	6 129	3 566	4 351
Minerals and metal manufacture	DEKN	1 116	447	76	534	−947	−549	−325	637	822	−3	198
Chemicals and allied industries	DEKO	51	2 043	283	1 759	1 124	854	−295	393	−419	1 142	818
Metal goods, engineering and vehicles	DEKP	1 197	1 441	1 535	1 097	365	676	94	987	498	338	638
Electrical and electronic engines	DEKQ	339	119	376	868	447	451	145	167	4 086	342	−128
Food, drink and tobacco	DEKR	561	1 136	1 242	3 730	−112	−279	−474	876	−396	295	1 610
Other manufacturing	DEKS	1 196	1 947	1 302	1 548	1 011	696	442	577	1 538	1 452	1 215
Energy	DEKT	539	1 413	1 173	948	1 821	1 781	1 829	3 255	1 409	3 456	2 651
Water	DEKU	168	212	251	648	354	509	1 025	1 642	210	643	−95
Construction	DEKV	238	662	1 284	53	623	703	54	258	203	23	940
Distribution, hotels and repairs	DEKW	1 064	2 191	1 137	901	854	1 481	1 242	1 291	2 603	1 603	3 458
Transport and communications	DEKX	418	872	912	1 134	3 744	4 769	6 946	10 220	16 381	15 124	−190
Property companies	DEKY	212	2 007	1 873	1 370	1 907	2 798	1 196	1 605	1 704	4 853	2 540
Services	DEKZ	1 118	2 207	2 025	1 310	2 011	3 039	2 689	4 322	10 660	4 519	6 780

1 See chapter text. Components of aggregated series may not always sum to the total due to rounding discrepancies.

2 The main issuers within the non-resident central/ local government sectors appear to have been raising finance from programme bond issues. Therefore, there have been few stand alone bond issues. Conversely, the bonds they have previously issued are now beginning to mature. Hence the reason for the low figures for 2001.

3 Non-resident companies including public corporations.

4 'Other' includes special finance agencies (listed public companies engaged in the provision of medium and long-term finance to industry, eg ICFC) and those finance houses and other consumer credit grantors not included under banks and building societies.

Source: Bank of England: 020 7601 5949

23.14 Building societies[1,2]
United Kingdom

		1993	1994	1995[3]	1996[3]	1997[3]	1998[3]	1999[3]	2000[4]	2001	2002
Number and balance sheets											
Societies on register (number)	KRNA	101	96	94	88	82	78	72	68	65	65
Share investors (thousands)	KRNB	37 809	38 150	38 998	37 768	19 234	21 195	21 774	22 237	20 311	20 724
Depositors (thousands)	KRNC	3 686	5 369	6 143	6 718	882	820	642	660	501	440
Borrowers (thousands)	KRND	7 140	7 222	6 906	6 586	2 703	2 934	2 868	2 925	2 579	2 520
Assets and liabilities (£ million)											
Liabilities:											
Shares	KRNE	194 975.1	201 812.2	200 682.0	196 546.4	90 092.8	103 289.8	109 137.7	119 298.5	119 815.2	132 372.9
Deposits and loans	KRNF	62 301.2	69 925.2	67 513.8	73 919.1	31 033.7	33 311.2	34 746.6	44 262.4	37 358.9	37 933.0
Taxation and other	KRNG	2 565.7	2 939.2	3 306.2	3 727.4	1 338.8	1 586.4	1 665.4	1 664.0	1 244.9	1 088.4
General reserves	KRNH	14 269.5	16 312.3	17 218.3	17 940.3	7 331.2	7 926.4	8 301.5	8 987.1	8 511.2	9 043.4
Other Capital	KRNI	3 900.9	4 125.7	3 498.0	4 762.3	1 643.9	1 550.7	1 529.2	1 861.0	1 416.1	1 709.2
Assets: total	KRNJ	278 012.4	295 114.6	292 218.3	296 895.5	131 440.4	147 664.5	155 380.4	176 073.0	168 346.2	182 146.8
Mortgages	KRNK	221 237.6	240 297.2	236 841.0	241 472.9	107 531.5	118 288.4	123 183.4	137 072.3	130 229.6	140 839.7
Investments and cash	KHVZ	47 174.2	50 786.7	50 894.1	51 016.7	21 869.8	27 102.0	29 917.8	36 574.2	35 925.9	38 952.7
Other	KRNN	9 600.6	4 030.7	4 483.2	4 405.9	2 039.1	2 274.1	2 279.2	2 426.6	2 190.7	2 354.4
Current transactions (£ million)											
Mortgage advances	KRNU	32 259.0	34 829.0	34 673.0	38 488.0	28 771.7	21 988.3	23 997.9	28 233.6	29 320.0	33 077.0
Management expenses	KRNX	2 952.5	3 136.7	3 352.6	3 555.3	2 270.5	1 501.7	1 573.8	1 640.7	1 528.0	1 623.6

1 See chapter text.
2 The figures for each year relate to accounting years ending on dates between 1 February of that year and 31 January of the following year.
3 The societies which have converted to the banking sector, namely Cheltenham & Gloucester (August 1995), National & Provincial (August 1996), Alliance & Leicester (April 1997), Halifax (June 1997), Woolwich (July 1997), Bristol & West (July 1997), Northern Rock (October 1997), and Birmingham Midshires (April 1999) have been included in flow figures (using flows up to the date of conversion), but have been excluded from the end of year balances.

4 Bradford & Bingley, which converted to the banking sector in December 2000, is included within flow figures and the end of year balances.

Source: Financial Services Authority: 020 7066 1000

23.15 Consumer credit[1]

£ millions

		1992	1993	1994	1995	1996	1997	1998	1999	2000	2001	2002
Total amount outstanding	AILA	52 609	52 330	..	..	..	..	..	..	..	..	..
	VZRD	53 486	53 301	58 056	68 203	77 481	88 081	102 222	116 155	128 041	141 719	157 755
Total net lending	-AIKL	284	2 423	..	..	..	..	..	..	..	..	..
	VZQC	484	2 653	5 743	8 234	11 215	12 013	14 511	14 857	14 235	17 722	21 064
Retailers	AAPP	25	69	83	-133	75	208	7	103	-285	-27	59
Building societies' class 3 loans	ALPY	-69	46	89	238	383	120	–	11	111	68	187
Banks	AIKN	792	843	3 704	5 606	7 682	9 027	11 709	10 999	13 195	16 181	17 352
of which												
Credit cards	VTFY	126	700	..	..	..	..	..	..	..	..	..
	VZQS	141	719	1 483	2 103	3 029	3 507	4 858	5 676	6 686	6 229	7 579
Loans on personal accounts	VTGA	615	156	..	..	..	..	..	..	..	..	..
Other	VZQT	346	1 934	4 260	6 132	8 186	8 507	9 656	9 181	7 550	11 495	13 487
Insurance companies	-AIKQ	29	165	..	..	..	..	..	..	..	..	..
	RSBK	29	170	-178	39	-81	4	-16	223	-265	-18	-86
Non-bank credit companies	-AGSJ	-483	1 332	1 856	2 222	2 805	2 287	2 409	2 928	676	980	2 865
Other specialist lenders	VZQQ	-297	1 525	2 045	2 485	3 156	2 654	2 810	3 521	1 478	1 518	3 553
Total gross lending	VZQG	11 913	54 094	75 039	89 114	103 215	116 079	133 710	147 014	158 711	175 056	193 877
Narrower coverage[2]												
Total amount outstanding	RLWE	30 120	32 204	37 027	..	..	..	..	..	..	..	..
Total net lending	RLWF	367	3 042	5 515	..	..	..	..	..	..	..	..
Total new credit advanced	RLBY	48 865	54 859	62 050	..	..	..	..	..	..	..	..

1 See chapter text.
2 Data no longer available from 1995.

Source: Office for National Statistics: 01633 812789

23.16 End-year assets and liabilities of investment trust companies, unit trusts[1] and property unit trusts[2]

£ millions

		1992	1993	1994	1995	1996	1997	1998	1999	2000	2001	2002
Investment trust companies												
Short-term assets and liabilities (net):	CBPL	390	623	273	627	1 076	1 157	2 263	71	423	161	–
Cash and UK bank deposits	AHAG	820	992	1 006	1 660	1 424	1 577	2 647	1 227	2 202	2 513	1 821
Other short-term assets	CBPN	645	1 030	772	738	794	1 445	1 734	1 097	1 082	656	805
Short-term liabilities	−CBPS	−595	−794	−942	−1 120	−805	−1 865	−2 118	−2 253	−2 861	−3 008	−2 626
Medium and long-term liabilities and capital:	−CBPO	−28 895	−36 140	−40 180	−43 882	−50 911	−54 117	−49 985	−57 616	−60 412	−54 630	−38 054
Issued share and loan capital	−CBPQ	−4 827	−8 286	−10 978	−13 250	−8 330	−8 625	−8 837	−8 565	−8 934	−8 796	−8 711
Foreign currency borrowing	−CBPR	−407	−473	−354	−1 061	−638	−658	−607	−880	−994	−933	−780
Other borrowing	−CBQA	−802	−849	−1 354	−622	−823	−1 296	−1 723	−1 716	−2 503	−3 251	−2 246
Reserves and provisions, etc	−AHBC	−22 859	−26 532	−27 494	−28 949	−41 120	−43 538	−38 818	−46 455	−47 981	−41 650	−26 317
Investments:	CBPM	28 586	35 300	39 586	43 410	50 034	53 076	46 313	56 491	59 948	54 822	37 748
British government securities	AHBF	996	1 013	2 490	1 194	1 422	1 052	815	1 217	821	645	471
UK company securities:												
Loan capital and preference shares	CBGZ	814	854	1 000	846	832	1 320	1 351	1 425	1 654	1 516	946
Ordinary and deferred shares	CBGY	12 825	14 892	15 926	19 384	25 046	29 082	24 729	28 010	33 456	30 338	19 475
Overseas company securities:												
Loan capital and preference shares	CBHA	514	533	896	740	279	1 165	768	979	963	1 143	677
Ordinary and deferred shares	AHCC	11 943	16 886	17 873	19 485	21 047	17 747	17 741	23 330	21 355	19 476	14 453
Other investments	CBPT	1 494	1 122	1 401	1 761	1 408	2 868	1 051	1 530	1 699	1 704	1 945
Unit trusts												
Short-term assets and liabilities:	CBPU	2 099	2 673	3 266	3 116	3 822	5 048	6 883	5 894	8 340	7 979	8 041
Cash and UK bank deposits	AGYE	1 793	2 579	3 102	3 326	3 895	4 731	6 020	4 797	6 969	5 748	5 321
Other short-term assets	CBPW	920	1 013	1 364	986	1 201	869	1 343	1 545	2 319	2 763	3 072
Short-term liabilities	−CBPX	−614	−919	−1 200	−1 196	−1 274	−552	−480	−448	−948	−532	−352
Foreign currency borrowing	−AGYK	−8	−39	−21	−1	–	–	–	–	–	–	–
Investments:	CBPZ	58 785	88 479	83 495	104 069	125 841	144 038	162 929	213 553	222 844	204 899	210 002
British government securities	CBHT	664	959	1 414	1 774	2 716	3 087	3 771	3 627	4 693	4 690	7 077
UK company securities:												
Loan capital and preference shares	CBHU	1 664	2 906	2 970	3 298	5 029	6 494	9 290	13 322	14 654	16 318	21 152
Ordinary and deferred shares	RLIB	33 356	49 657	43 335	59 122	67 509	85 742	93 291	119 496	116 808	103 704	82 851
Overseas company securities:												
Loan capital and preference shares	CBHV	570	864	1 001	2 145	1 288	1 834	1 801	3 032	3 212	4 113	5 916
Ordinary and deferred shares	RLIC	21 862	32 904	33 473	36 062	47 346	42 898	51 119	70 256	79 601	71 329	63 152
Other assets	CBQE	669	1 189	1 302	1 668	1 953	2 518	3 657	3 820	3 876	4 800	9 997
Property unit trusts												
Short-term assets and liabilities (net)	AGVC	103	237	119	280	255	328	254	205	285	247	242
Property	CBQG	1 373	1 492	2 197	1 807	2 582	3 895	2 740	2 722	3 488	2 078	4 026
Other assets	AGVL	34	60	11	11	11	168	197	436	380	151	677
Long-term borrowing	−AGVM	−42	−42	–	−131	−45	−247	−106	−75	−391	−90	−75

Note: Assets are shown as positive: liabilities as negative.
1 Including open ended investment companies (OEICs).
2 Investments are at market value.

Source: Office for National Statistics: 01633 812789

23.17 Self-administered pension funds: market value of assets
United Kingdom

End year

£ millions

		1991	1992	1993	1994	1995	1996	1997	1998	1999	2000	2001
Total pension funds[1]												
Total net assets	AHVA	343 634	381 997	480 547	443 467	508 581	543 879	656 874	699 191	812 228	765 199	711 572
Short-term assets	RYIQ	16 881	18 492	20 279	22 617	26 114	31 521	35 368	39 005	32 703	36 638	31 337
British government securities	AHVK	24 041	25 188	34 279	41 854	52 659	57 783	80 533	91 084	98 882	92 458	83 754
UK local authority long-term debt	AHVO	15	34	81	250	83	89	156	183	133	177	125
Overseas government securities	AHVT	9 162	10 529	11 044	11 092	11 721	11 800	13 079	15 493	16 684	19 206	20 383
UK company securities												
Ordinary shares	AHVP	173 592	202 311	251 099	219 189	256 625	276 001	339 687	334 648	357 230	299 318	260 696
Other	AHVQ	8 843	5 905	5 758	3 935	7 064	6 180	5 618	8 168	9 258	16 978	22 301
Overseas company securities												
Ordinary shares	AHVR	60 476	63 276	84 118	74 813	82 164	84 163	104 187	108 884	148 335	135 514	127 893
Other	AHVS	1 720	1 787	2 103	3 045	1 184	4 909	3 851	3 842	5 099	12 736	11 781
UK loans and mortgages	RLDQ	302	232	260	44	34	83	160	22	14	7	3
UK land, property and ground rent	AHWA	24 527	19 914	21 932	24 353	21 317	21 637	24 176	24 355	31 107	32 945	30 617
Authorised unit trust units	AHVU	5 331	8 569	13 188	13 345	15 212	21 767	21 979	30 596	33 731	34 587	38 083
Property unit trusts	AHVW	993	1 745	1 905	2 463	2 485	2 666	3 219	3 211	5 498	4 835	5 280
Other assets	RKPL	20 881	28 794	38 761	31 318	36 352	30 628	32 978	47 136	82 273	90 841	90 139
Total liabilities	GQFX	3 131	4 781	4 261	4 852	4 412	5 347	8 118	7 436	8 719	11 041	10 819

1 These figures cover funded schemes only and therefore exclude the main superannuation arrangements in the central government sector.

Source: Office for National Statistics: 01633 812726

23.18

Insurance companies: balance sheet
Market values
End year

£ millions

		1992	1993	1994	1995	1996	1997	1998	1999	2000	2001
Long-term insurance companies											
Assets											
Total current assets (gross)	RYEW	18 101	16 925	16 690	24 171	31 699	42 795	46 165	56 360	62 937	63 855
Agents' and reinsurance balances (net)	AHNY	799	457	−209	−157	−232	155	1 383	508	384	620
Other debtors[1]	RKPN	4 198	4 368	4 562	7 565	12 982	15 708	18 210	18 613	21 045	27 285
British government securities	AHNJ	50 970	72 575	64 921	80 268	90 996	107 847	127 903	126 223	116 734	119 513
UK local authority securities etc	AHNN	667	772	815	1 322	1 088	914	1 722	1 456	1 170	1 407
UK company securities[2]	RKPO	172 204	237 020	217 034	272 554	304 587	386 734	438 666	539 834	557 293	505 691
Overseas company securities	RKPP	32 101	49 087	48 195	59 950	62 378	73 428	82 122	120 665	107 439	127 259
Overseas government securities	AHNS	8 793	8 874	6 871	8 793	7 554	8 471	17 515	18 494	18 004	21 285
Loans and mortgages	RKPQ	8 345	7 885	6 833	7 305	6 653	8 271	11 027	10 914	9 687	10 048
UK land, property and ground rent	AHNX	30 074	33 939	35 914	35 596	36 209	42 275	45 903	50 387	49 705	53 726
Overseas land, property and ground rent	RGCP	124	144	151	118	114	98	252	206	1 975	498
Other investments	RKPR	2 663	3 096	4 644	2 162	3 886	3 416	5 654	8 334	8 385	7 420
Total	RFXN	329 039	435 142	406 421	499 647	557 914	690 112	796 522	951 994	954 760	938 609
Net value of direct investment in:											
Non-insurance subsidiaries and associate companies in the United Kingdom	RYET	2 569	2 288	2 547	2 773	3 033	3 426	3 035	3 045	6 133	4 486
UK associate and subsidiary insurance companies and insurance holding companies	RYEU	639	1 186	504	701	575	−239	148	2 245	3 586	4 206
Overseas subsidiaries and associates	RYEV	773	1 016	1 034	987	986	1 104	1 087	3 638	4 002	5 581
Total assets	RKBI	333 020	439 632	410 506	504 108	562 508	694 403	800 792	960 922	968 481	952 882
Liabilities											
Borrowing:											
Borrowing from UK banks	RGDF	1 162	1 234	1 570	1 907	2 234	3 027	3 252	6 064	8 272	8 790
Other UK borrowing	RGDE	1 007	553	982	796	1 349	786	1 040	3 070	2 823	5 350
Borrowing from overseas	RGDD	603	381	176	79	90	104	148	159	38	81
Long-term business:											
Funds	RKDC	280 276	354 711	357 263	424 866	470 893	581 009	669 301	800 184	838 485	831 051
Claims admitted but not paid	RKBM	951	1 035	1 085	1 419	1 441	1 436	1 712	2 032	2 249	2 547
Provision for taxation net of amounts receivable:											
UK authorities	RYPI	−1 119	−141	−470	502	2 568	4 207	5 443	6 344	5 381	3 951
Overseas authorities	RYPJ	−14	−20	29	−11	9	25	67	314	67	45
Provision for recommended dividends	RYPK	46	83	76	195	276	368	359	201	183	87
Other creditors and liabilities	RYPL	3 763	4 020	4 399	5 979	6 303	8 083	12 509	17 042	19 031	18 468
Excess of assets over above liabilities:											
Excess of value of assets over liabilities in respect of long-term funds	RKBR	43 511	74 160	42 608	63 255	71 817	89 790	96 456	116 951	79 173	63 337
Minority interests in UK subsidiary companies	RKTI	30	30	–	3	–	2	–	25	–	–
Shareholders' capital and reserves in respect of general business	RKBS	1 952	890	1 143	2 050	2 576	3 862	6 299	6 139	10 287	17 044
Other reserves including profit and loss account balances	RKBT	852	2 696	1 645	3 068	2 952	1 704	4 206	2 396	2 492	2 130
Total liabilities	RKBI	333 020	439 632	410 506	504 108	562 508	694 403	800 792	960 922	968 481	952 882

23.18
continued

Insurance companies: balance sheet
Market values
End year

£ millions

		1992	1993	1994	1995	1996	1997	1998	1999	2000	2001
Other than long-term insurance companies											
Assets											
Total current assets (gross)	RYME	6 523	6 467	7 426	8 318	11 559	12 628	8 524	10 468	8 772	12 264
Agents' and reinsurance balances (net)	AHMX	6 380	5 887	6 123	7 494	11 569	9 405	10 528	12 177	8 362	7 941
Other debtors[1]	RKPS	1 765	1 847	2 118	3 403	6 097	5 998	6 277	7 059	7 179	9 056
British government securities	AHMJ	8 378	11 474	12 320	14 363	16 893	15 666	16 409	15 938	14 561	15 064
UK local authority securities etc	AHMN	49	59	50	56	42	16	14	10	8	6
UK company securities[2]	RKPT	10 480	14 533	14 312	17 425	17 825	18 845	18 440	18 800	18 585	17 101
Overseas company securities	RKPU	3 747	4 163	3 578	4 422	5 072	6 594	8 676	6 284	8 190	6 402
Overseas government securities	AHMS	4 660	5 324	5 064	6 511	9 546	8 215	10 459	7 980	6 849	7 134
Loans and mortgages	RKPV	1 147	1 234	1 321	1 337	1 593	1 385	1 335	1 070	1 429	1 348
UK land, property and ground rent	AHMW	2 398	2 375	2 121	2 100	2 077	2 842	1 146	1 085	1 069	860
Overseas land, property and ground rent	RYNK	185	80	89	128	120	149	107	83	45	4
Other investments	RKPW	633	418	536	665	716	2 465	2 366	2 638	2 294	1 608
Total	RKAL	46 345	53 861	55 058	66 222	83 106	84 208	84 281	84 027	77 343	78 789
Net value of direct investment in:											
Non-insurance subsidiaries and associate companies in the United Kingdom	RYNR	2 617	2 214	2 474	2 449	3 195	6 950	5 553	7 074	7 038	10 456
UK associate and subsidiary insurance companies and insurance holding companies	RYNS	1 087	1 835	1 738	1 642	7 170	4 204	6 424	5 617	5 400	8 837
Overseas subsidiaries and associates	RYNT	9 908	12 275	11 854	15 485	14 859	16 402	14 239	17 775	15 993	14 260
Total assets	RKBY	59 957	70 185	71 124	85 798	108 330	111 764	110 497	114 493	105 774	112 342
Liabilities											
Borrowing:											
Borrowing from UK banks	RYMB	434	721	1 382	1 584	1 524	3 029	1 825	1 392	783	481
Other UK borrowing	RYMC	1 677	1 989	2 354	2 370	2 536	2 996	1 551	3 186	4 239	10 621
Borrowing from overseas	RYMD	1 296	1 103	1 626	1 876	1 976	1 202	1 600	3 045	1 867	1 964
General business technical reserves	RKCT	38 005	39 746	42 374	47 493	58 618	59 527	60 775	59 455	60 236	60 995
Long-term business:											
Funds	RKTF	–	–	–	–	–	–	–	–	–	–
Claims admitted but not paid	RKTK	–	–	–	–	–	–	–	–	–	–
Provision for taxation net of amounts receivable:											
UK authorities	RYPO	−295	235	397	841	807	1 253	1 197	939	874	594
Overseas authorities	RYPP	24	14	22	16	22	7	11	11	11	7
Provision for recommended dividends	RYPQ	650	794	874	1 098	1 407	2 048	1 318	1 817	2 682	1 957
Other creditors and liabilities	RYPR	1 921	1 987	2 551	2 955	3 886	3 873	3 793	4 981	6 293	6 410
Excess of assets over above liabilities:											
Excess of value of assets over liabilities in respect of long-term funds	RKCG	–	–	–	–	–	–	–	–	–	–
Minority interests in UK subsidiary companies	RKCH	33	80	52	22	24	60	68	29	33	276
Shareholders' capital and reserves in respect of general business	RKCI	14 552	21 355	17 628	25 545	35 069	35 172	34 397	35 372	24 699	26 190
Other reserves including profit and loss account balances	RKCJ	1 660	2 161	1 864	1 998	2 461	2 597	4 215	4 265	4 056	2 847
Total liabilities	RKBY	59 957	70 185	71 124	85 798	108 330	111 764	110 497	114 493	105 774	112 342

1 Including outstanding interest, dividends and rents (net).
2 Including authorised unit trust units.

Source: Office for National Statistics: 01633 812726

23.19 Individual insolvencies

Numbers

		1992	1993	1994	1995	1996	1997	1998	1999	2000	2001	2002
England and Wales												
Bankruptcies[1]	AIHW	32 106	31 016	25 634	21 933	21 803	19 892	19 647	21 611	21 550	23 447	24 292
Individual voluntary arrangements[2,3]	AIHI	4 688	5 687	5 105	4 386	4 468	4 549	4 902	7 195	7 978	6 298	6 295
Total	AIHK	36 794	36 703	30 739	26 319	26 271	24 441	24 549	28 806	29 528	29 775	30 587
Scotland												
Sequestrations[4]	KRHA	10 845	6 828	2 182	2 188	2 503	2 502	3 016	3 195	2 965	3 048	3 215
Northern Ireland												
Bankruptcies[5]	KRHB	406	474	438	399	415	393	394	401	347	292	334
Individual voluntary arrangements[3,6]	KJRK	42	67	84	64	101	84	122	173	260	177	206
Total	KRHD	448	541	522	463	516	477	516	574	607	469	540

1 Comprises receiving and administration orders under the Bankruptcy Act 1914 and bankruptcy orders under the Insolvency Act 1986. Orders later consolidated or rescinded are included in these figures.
2 Introduced under the Insolvency Act 1986.
3 For statistical purposes deeds of arrangement are now included with individual voluntary arrangements.
4 Sequestrations awarded but not brought into operation are included in these figures.

5 Comprises bankruptcy adjudication orders, arrangement protection orders and orders for the administration of estates of deceased insolvents. Orders later set aside or dismissed are included in these figures.
6 Introduced under the Insolvency Northern Ireland order 1989.

Source: Department of Trade and Industry: 020 7215 3291/3305

23.20 Company insolvencies

Numbers

		1992	1993	1994	1995	1996	1997	1998	1999	2000	2001	2002
England and Wales												
Compulsory liquidations	AIHR	9 734	8 244	6 597	5 519	5 080	4 735	5 216	5 209	4 925	4 675	6 230
Creditors' voluntary liquidations	AIHS	14 691	12 464	10 131	9 017	8 381	7 875	7 987	9 071	9 392	10 297	10 075
Total	AIHQ	24 425	20 708	16 728	14 536	13 461	12 610	13 203	14 280	14 317	14 972	16 305
Scotland												
Compulsory liquidations	KRGA	310	286	242	252	266	254	338	364	344	378	556
Creditors' voluntary liquidations	KRGB	360	265	202	189	175	223	228	208	239	224	232
Total	KRGC	670	551	444	441	441	477	566	572	583	602	788
Northern Ireland												
Compulsory liquidations	KRGD	79	73	69	72	68	60	53	58	83	60	49
Creditors' voluntary liquidations	KRGE	77	85	52	37	54	53	46	45	53	40	53
Total	KRGF	156	158	121	109	122	113	99	103	136	100	102

Source: Department of Trade and Industry: 020 7215 3291/3305

23.21 Industry analysis: bankruptcies[1]
England and Wales

Numbers

		1992	1993	1994	1995	1996	1997	1998	1999	2000	2001	2002
Industry												
Self-employed												
Agriculture and horticulture	KRFY	313	277	231	218	168	155	157	183	173	183	132
Manufacturing:												
Food, drink and tobacco	KRFZ	56	34	33	30	31	18	21	17	18	10	19
Chemicals	KRLA	9	7	23	8	5	5	7	4	2	2	6
Metals and engineering	KRLB	634	612	523	396	411	413	378	385	306	339	257
Textiles and clothing	KRLC	174	160	95	114	91	76	81	87	81	75	33
Timber and furniture	KRLD	317	207	176	158	118	98	96	94	90	88	59
Paper, printing and publishing	KRLE	205	161	142	142	117	104	101	112	80	75	70
Other	KRLF	125	169	133	146	117	116	110	111	84	79	111
Total	KRLG	1 520	1 350	1 125	994	890	830	794	810	661	668	555
Construction and transport:												
Construction	KRLH	4 692	4 361	3 362	2 783	2 713	2 182	1 919	1 911	1 741	1 783	1 637
Transport and communication	KRLI	2 038	1 754	1 402	1 138	1 227	1 162	1 060	1 187	1 120	1 134	1 095
Total	KHGP	6 730	6 115	4 764	3 921	3 940	3 344	2 979	3 098	2 861	2 917	2 732
Wholesaling:												
Food, drink and tobacco	KRLJ	114	114	94	103	77	62	53	45	49	40	48
Motor vehicles	KRLK	48	21	28	33	36	28	20	22	29	20	14
Other	KRLL	220	191	160	122	101	78	92	83	83	61	44
Total	KHGQ	382	326	282	258	214	168	165	150	161	121	106
Retailing:												
Food, drink and tobacco	KRLM	1 001	1 107	981	782	662	546	514	438	424	347	311
Motor vehicles and filling stations	KRLN	399	412	343	316	327	276	238	241	237	199	138
Other	KRLO	2 159	2 087	1 615	1 566	1 268	1 048	971	1 032	801	792	680
Total	KHGR	3 559	3 606	2 939	2 664	2 257	1 870	1 723	1 711	1 462	1 338	1 129
Services:												
Financial institutions	KRLP	266	292	241	185	125	105	79	54	45	39	31
Business services	KRLQ	1 859	1 843	1 537	1 354	1 176	1 117	1 057	1 162	1 127	1 107	1 057
Hotels and catering	KRLR	2 366	2 437	2 102	1 956	1 736	1 603	1 309	1 376	1 263	1 187	1 041
Total	KHGS	4 491	4 572	3 880	3 495	3 037	2 825	2 445	2 592	2 435	2 333	2 129
Other	KHGT	2 530	2 315	1 893	1 732	2 161	2 077	2 157	2 179	2 199	2 279	2 071
Total: self-employed	KRLT	19 525	18 561	15 114	13 282	12 667	11 269	10 420	10 723	9 952	9 839	8 854
Other individuals												
Employees	KRLU	2 588	2 507	2 279	1 981	2 471	2 625	3 141	4 357	4 601	5 525	5 900
No occupation and unemployed	KRLV	4 325	4 816	3 696	2 859	3 294	3 051	3 384	4 457	4 856	5 848	6 965
Directors and promoters of companies	KRLW	965	862	628	484	368	310	272	330	296	328	323
Occupation unknown	KRLX	4 703	4 270	3 917	3 327	3 003	2 637	2 430	1 744	1 845	1 937	2 250
Total: other individuals	KRLY	12 581	12 455	10 520	8 651	9 136	8 623	9 227	10 888	11 598	13 638	15 438
Total bankruptcies	KRLZ	32 106	31 016	25 634	21 933	21 803	19 892	19 647	21 611	21 550	23 477	24 292

1 From January 1991 Industrial Analysis excludes Deeds of Arrangement.

Source: Department of Trade and Industry: 020 7215 3291/3305

23.22

Industry analysis: company insolvencies[1]
England and Wales

Numbers

Industry		1992	1993	1994	1995	1996	1997	1998	1999	2000	2001	2002
Agriculture and horticulture	KRMA	191	157	166	99	89	51	65	75	67	90	76
Manufacturing:												
Food, drink and tobacco	KRMB	215	213	142	130	163	93	89	67	104	71	61
Chemicals	KRMC	141	91	108	69	65	31	57	35	61	37	46
Metals and engineering	KRMD	1 621	1 381	932	681	658	591	594	698	683	704	739
Textiles and clothing	KRME	1 120	917	736	567	568	596	526	419	423	320	304
Timber and furniture	KRMF	508	333	252	267	249	181	149	190	187	199	179
Paper, printing and publishing	KRMG	830	777	579	452	438	364	426	387	386	484	545
Other	KRMH	1 014	878	859	681	599	613	652	780	678	717	768
Total	KRMI	5 449	4 590	3 608	2 847	2 740	2 469	2 493	2 576	2 522	2 532	2 642
Construction and transport:												
Construction	KRMJ	3 830	3 189	2 401	1 844	1 610	1 419	1 325	1 529	1 474	1 509	1 840
Transport and communication	KRMK	1 261	1 082	774	706	682	540	504	443	526	481	652
Total	KHGU	5 091	4 271	3 175	2 550	2 292	1 959	1 829	1 972	2 000	1 990	2 492
Wholesaling:												
Food, drink and tobacco	KRML	388	231	244	205	183	158	139	187	150	125	142
Motor vehicles	KRMM	186	142	112	83	95	41	60	38	29	24	64
Other	KRMN	672	639	638	678	429	340	364	394	391	363	512
Total	KHGV	1 246	1 012	994	966	707	539	563	619	570	512	718
Retailing:												
Food, drink and tobacco	KRMO	406	388	299	246	236	219	186	193	200	114	132
Motor vehicles and filling stations	KRMP	339	229	226	195	227	132	120	142	141	172	174
Other	KRMQ	1 732	1 388	1 186	1 127	956	891	847	919	853	833	902
Total	KHGW	2 477	2 005	1 711	1 568	1 419	1 242	1 153	1 254	1 194	1 119	1 208
Services:												
Financial institutions	KRMR	563	421	259	198	222	111	101	118	57	28	35
Business services	KRMS	2 788	2 415	1 807	1 525	1 500	1 528	1 617	1 831	1 605	1 618	3 215
Hotels and catering	KRMT	1 010	912	777	692	708	609	626	562	530	538	740
Total	KJRS	4 361	3 748	2 843	2 415	2 430	2 248	2 344	2 511	2 192	2 184	3 990
Other	KHGX	5 610	4 925	4 231	4 091	3 784	4 102	4 756	5 273	5 772	6 545	5 179
Total company insolvencies	KHGY	24 425	20 708	16 728	14 536	13 461	12 610	13 203	14 280	14 317	14 972	16 305

1 Including partnerships.

Source: Department of Trade and Industry: 020 7215 3291/3305

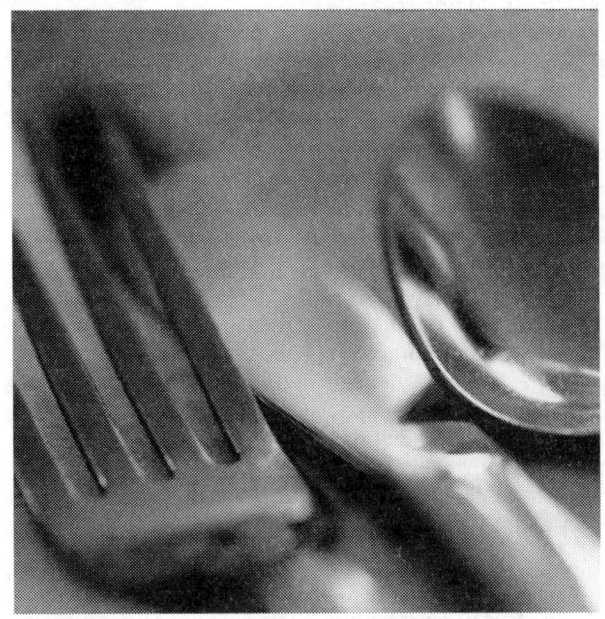

24 Service industry

Service industry

Annual Business Inquiry *(Tables 24.1, 24.3 and 24.4)*
For details of the Annual Business Inquiry, see the text accompanying table **22.1**.

Retail trade: index numbers of value and volume *(Table 24.2)*

The main purpose of the Retail Sales Inquiry (RSI) is to provide up to date information on short period movements in the level of retail sales. In principle, the RSI covers the retail activity of every business classified in the retail sector (Division 52 of the 1992 Standard Industrial Classification) in Great Britain. A business will be classified to the retail sector if its main activity is one of the individual 4 digit SIC categories within Division 52. The retail activity of a business is then defined by its retail turnover i.e. the sale of all retail goods (note that petrol, for example, is not a retail good).

The RSI is compiled from the information returned to the statutory monthly retail trades inquiry. The inquiry is addressed to a stratified sample of 5000 businesses classified to the retail sector, the stratification being by 'type of store' (the individual 4 digit SIC categories within Division 52) and by size. The sample structure is designed to ensure that the inquiry estimates are as accurate as possible. In terms of the selection, this means that:

-   each of the individual 4 digit SIC categories are represented, their coverage depending upon the relative size of the category and the variability of the data.

-   within each 4 digit SIC category, the larger retailers tend to be fully enumerated with decreasing proportions of medium and smaller retailers.

The structure of the inquiry is updated periodically, by reference to the more comprehensive results of the Annual Business Inquiry (ABI). The monthly inquiry also incorporates a rotation element for the smallest retailers. This helps to spread the burden more fairly, as well as improving the representativeness between successive benchmarks.

During 2003, the retail sales index was rebased using detailed information from the 2000 annual business inquiry. The reference year is now set at 2000=100. Details of the work, together with revised figures, were published by the ONS on 30 September 2003 and are available via the National Statistics Website: *www.statistics.gov.uk/statbase/Product.asp?vlnk=10729*

The latest summary statistics are published each month by *First Release*. More disaggregated value indices (not seasonally adjusted) are published each month in *Business Monitor SDM28*, via the National Statistics Website: *www.statistics.gov.uk/rsi*.

24.1

Retail businesses[1]
United Kingdom

£ million

		1998	1999	2000	2001
Number of businesses	ZABE	216 000	216 826	214 876	210 691
Total turnover[2]	ZABL	221 204	230 822	241 418	251 331
Value added tax in total turnover	ZABM	21 778	22 494	23 695	25 245
Retail turnover[2]	ZABN	202 538	209 962	218 013	227 184
Non-retail turnover[2]	ZABO	18 666	20 860	23 406	24 147
Other income					
Value of commercial insurance claims received	ZABP	117	85	88	89
Subsidies received from UK government sources and the EC	ZAEN	12	19	7	24
Employment costs[3]	ZABQ	22 958	25 072	26 475	28 074
Gross wages and salaries	ZABR	20 552	22 430	23 857	25 356
Redundancy and severance payments	ZABS	145	329	144	130
Employers' National Insurance contributions	ZABT	1 514	1 547	1 650	1 734
Contributions to pension funds[4]	ZABU	747	767	824	854
Stocks					
Increase during year	ZABV	1 204	1 271	735	923
Value at end of year	ZABW	19 849	21 095	21 150	21 572
Total turnover[3] divided by end-year stocks (Quotient)	ZABX	10.0	9.9	10.3	10.5
Purchases of goods, materials and services[3]	ZABY	157 694	161 841	168 520	175 435
Goods bought for resale without processing	ZABZ	134 241	135 830	141 330	147 310
Energy and water products for own consumption[5]	ZACA	1 832	1 826	1 921	2 029
Goods and materials[5]	ZACB	3 035	3 484	3 413	3 506
Hiring, leasing or renting of plant, machinery and vehicles	ZACC	662	761	828	788
Commercial insurance premiums	ZACD	554	582	616	687
Road transport services	ZACE	1 847	1 627	1 784	1 962
Telecommunication services	ZACF	474	506	558	602
Computer and related services	ZACG	534	636	661	587
Advertising and marketing services	ZACH	2 429	2 771	2 772	2 877
Other services	ZACI	12 085	13 818	14 638	15 086
Taxes, duties and levies	ZACJ	3 823	3 987	4 132	4 387
National non-domestic (business) rates	ZACK	3 116	3 253	3 353	3 625
Other amounts paid for taxes, duties and levies	ZACL	707	734	779	762
Capital expenditure					
Cost of acquisitions	ZACM	8 264	8 215	8 312	8 446
Proceeds from disposals	ZACN	1 141	2 270	1 683	1 605
Net capital expenditure	ZACO	7 123	5 945	6 629	6 842
Amount included in acquisitions for assets under finance leasing arrangements	ZACP	284	498	531	473
Work of a capital nature carried out by own staff (included in acquisitions)	ZACQ	80	78	79	144
Gross margin					
Amount	ZACR	65 774	72 655	75 929	78 884
As a percentage of adjusted turnover[6]	ZACS	*33.0*	*34.9*	*34.9*	*34.9*
Approximate gross value added at basic prices	ZACT	42 438	47 287	49 415	51 148

24.1
continued

Retail businesses[1]
United Kingdom

£ million

		1998	1999	2000	2001
Total turnover	ZABL	221 204	230 822	241 418	251 331
Retail turnover	ZABN	202 538	209 962	218 013	227 184
1 Fruit (including fresh, chilled, dried, frozen, canned and processed)	DSSX	3 851	3 960	3 999	4 106
2 Vegetables (including fresh, chilled, dried, frozen, canned and processed)	DSSY	5 423	5 403	5 802	6 648
3 Meat (including fresh, chilled, smoked, frozen, canned and processed)	DSSZ	11 665	11 334	10 729	11 121
4 Fish, crustaceans and molluscs (including fresh, chilled, frozen, canned and processed)	DSTA	2 083	2 092	2 180	2 169
5 Bakery products and cereals (including rice and pasta products)	DSTC	8 379	8 510	9 067	9 427
6 Sugar, jam, honey, chocolate and confectionery (including ice-cream)	DSTD	5 825	6 009	6 040	5 977
7 Alcoholic drink	DSTE	9 116	9 947	10 579	10 624
8 Non-alcoholic beverages (including tea, coffee, fruit drinks and vegetable drinks)	DSTF	5 351	5 546	5 587	5 761
9 Tobacco (excluding smokers requisites, eg pipes, lighters, etc)	DSTG	8 734	8 845	8 293	8 600
10 Milk, cheese and eggs (including yoghurts and cream)	DSTH	6 748	6 866	6 933	7 002
11 Oils and fats (including butter and margarine)	DSTI	1 158	1 113	1 245	1 313
12 Food products not elsewhere classified (including sauces, herbs, spices and soups)	DSTJ	10 227	10 121	9 998	9 983
13 Pharmaceutical products	DSTK	1 791	1 930	2 432	2 730
14 National Health Receipts	DSTL	5 588	5 799	6 412	6 938
15 Other medical products and therapeutic appliances and equipment	DSTN	2 006	2 267	2 690	2 730
16 Other appliances, articles and products for personal care	DSTO	6 894	7 506	8 099	8 587
17 Other articles of clothing, accessories for making clothing	DSTP	1 220	1 356	1 520	1 247
18 Garments	DSTQ	24 506	26 092	25 542	26 690
19 Footwear (excluding sports shoes)	DSTR	4 391	4 213	4 380	4 650
20 Travel goods and other personal effects not elsewhere classified	DSTT	699	644	683	858
21 Household textiles (including furnishing fabrics, curtains, etc)	DSTV	3 230	3 478	3 369	3 578
22 Household and personal appliances whether electric or not	DSUA	5 126	5 088	5 477	6 709
23 Glassware, tableware and household utensils (including non-electric)	DSUB	2 636	2 815	2 651	2 744
24 Furniture and furnishings	DSUC	9 846	10 353	10 630	11 071
25 Audio and visual equipment (including radios, televisions and video recorders)	DSUE	3 655	3 770	4 064	4 500
26 Recording material for pictures and sound (including audio and video tapes, blank and pre-recorded records, etc)	DSUG	2 848	3 080	3 436	3 304
27 Information processing equipment (including printers, software, calculators and typewriters)	DSUL	2 827	2 953	3 205	3 222
28 Decorating and DIY supplies	DSUM	4 633	5 019	5 488	6 276
29 Tools and equipment for house and garden	DSUN	2 061	2 165	2 451	2 616
30 Books	DSUP	2 214	2 226	2 252	2 364
31 Newspapers and periodicals	DSUQ	3 416	3 503	3 541	3 652
32 Stationery and drawing materials and miscellaneous printed matter	DSUW	3 398	3 648	3 768	3 598
33 Carpets and other floor coverings (excluding bathroom mats, rush and door mats)	DSUX	2 803	2 944	3 123	3 182
34 Photographic and cinematographic equipment and optical instruments	DSUZ	863	968	1 062	1 058
35 Telephone and telefax equipment (including mobile phones)	DSVA	1 203	1 503	2 264	2 500
36 Jewellery, silverware and plate; watches and clocks	DSVB	2 763	2 806	3 448	3 809
37 Works of art and antiques (including furniture, floor coverings and jewellery)	DSVF	1 640	1 666	1 585	1 883
38 Equipment and accessories for sport, camping, recreation and musical instruments	DSVH	3 482	3 520	3 725	3 851
39 Spare part and accessories for all types of vehicle and sales of bicycles	DSVI	745	558	652	750
40 Games, toys, hobbies (including video game software, video game computers that plug into the tv, video-games cassettes and CD-ROMs)	DSVM	3 642	3 744	4 204	4 542
41 Other goods not elsewhere classified (including sale of new postage stamps and sales of liquid and solid fuels)	DSVN	4 675	5 029	5 420	3 823
42 Non-durable household goods (including household cleaning, maintenance products) and paper products and other non-durable household goods	DSVO	3 454	3 609	4 043	4 322
43 Natural or artificial plants and flowers	DSVQ	2 492	2 456	2 653	3 026
44 Pets and related products (including pet food)	DSVR	2 271	2 241	2 348	2 719
45 Repair of household and personal items	DSVS	963	1 266	944	921

1 See chapter text.
2 Inclusive of VAT.
3 Exclusive of VAT.
4 Previously combined with employers' National Insurance contributions for 1997.

5 Previously combined with purchases of energy, water and materials for 1997.
6 Turnover is adjusted to take out VAT.

Source: Office for National Statistics: 01633 812435

24.2 Retail trade: Index numbers of value and volume of sales[1]
Great Britain

Weekly average 2000 = 100, not seasonally adjusted

		Sales in 2000 £ million	1992	1993	1994	1995	1996	1997	1998	1999	2000	2001	2002
Value													
All retailing: total	EAFY	207 149	70.1	73.8	77.3	80.2	84.6	89.9	93.4	96.5	100.0	105.9	111.2
All retailing: large	EAFZ	153 022	63	67	71	76	81	87	92	96	100	106	113
All retailing: small	EAGA	54 128	94	96	96	94	97	97	99	98	100	104	106
Predominantly food stores	EAFS	89 041	68.8	72.4	75.8	80.3	84.6	88.9	93.4	96.6	100.0	106.1	110.4
Predominantly non-food stores	EAFT	106 359	69.6	73.7	77.4	79.8	84.4	90.6	93.2	96.3	100.0	106.0	112.2
Non specialised predominantly non-food stores	EAGE	18 781	69.8	74.0	76.4	79.2	85.7	91.5	92.6	95.2	100.0	105.0	107.5
Textiles, clothing, footwear and leather	EAFU	27 880	72.8	76.1	80.8	83.5	87.0	93.4	93.8	96.0	100.0	105.8	112.2
Household goods stores	EAFV	27 699	63.8	68.2	71.2	73.4	79.2	86.8	91.6	95.7	100.0	108.6	116.0
Other specialised non-food stores	EAFW	31 999	70.7	75.1	79.0	81.2	84.5	89.3	93.1	96.8	100.0	104.5	111.7
Other retail sale (non-store) and repair	EAFX	11 749	84.7	87.0	88.9	85.3	87.6	91.8	97.1	98.8	100.0	103.2	106.8
Volume													
All retailing	EAHC	207 149	76.6	78.9	81.8	82.8	85.4	89.9	92.5	95.7	100.0	106.1	112.7
Predominantly food stores	EAGW	89 041	81.6	83.3	86.0	87.7	89.3	92.9	95.5	97.2	100.0	104.1	108.2
Predominantly non-food stores	EAGX	106 359	71.0	74.0	77.3	78.6	82.1	87.4	89.9	94.3	100.0	107.7	116.4
Non specialised predominantly non-food stores	EAHI	18 781	76.7	79.6	81.2	82.0	86.9	91.5	91.5	94.0	100.0	105.9	110.4
Textiles,clothing, footwear and leather	EAGY	27 880	70.6	73.2	77.3	79.3	82.7	88.1	88.8	92.9	100.0	109.4	120.9
Household goods stores	EAGZ	27 699	59.3	63.2	66.7	68.5	73.2	80.3	85.8	92.6	100.0	110.9	120.9
Other specialised non-food stores	EAHA	31 999	80.5	82.9	85.8	85.8	86.9	90.7	93.6	97.1	100.0	104.6	112.2
Other retail sale (non-store) and repair	EAHB	11 749	86.6	87.6	88.6	83.5	84.6	88.2	93.2	96.2	100.0	106.1	113.4

1 See chapter text.

Source: Office for National Statistics: 01633 812609

403

24.3 Motor trades[1]
United Kingdom

	Number of businesses	Total turnover	Motor trades turnover	Retail sales of		Sales to other dealers of		Gross sales of used motor vehicles and motorcycles	Turnover from sales of petrol, diesel, oil and other petroleum products	Other motor trades sales and receipts (including parts and accessories, workshop receipts)	Non-motor trades turnover
				New cars	Other new motor vehicles and motorcycles	New cars	Other new motor vehicles and motorcycles				
	Number	£ million	£ million	£ million	£ million	£ million	£ million	£ million	£ million	£ million	£ million

Sale, maintenance and repair of motor vehicles and motorcycles; retail sale of automotive fuel (SIC 92 50.00)

	MKEQ	CMRH	CMRI	CMRJ	CMRK	CMRL	CMRM	CMRN	CMRO	CMRP	CMRQ
1997	72 527	119 069	115 445	23 119	3 311	15 762	2 395	28 328	12 871	29 656	3 624
1998	72 105	123 130	119 817	24 492	3 626	16 922	2 547	27 327	13 445	31 457	3 314
1999	72 298	128 956	125 752	25 992	3 598	16 780	2 936	28 233	15 448	32 765	3 204
2000	71 413	129 675	126 357	24 377	3 543	16 241	3 101	30 126	17 090	31 881	3 318
2001	70 942	135 461	130 898	29 030	3 483	15 905	3 121	30 891	16 364	32 104	4 563

Sale of motor vehicles (SIC 92 50.10)

	MKER	EWRI	FDFZ	FDGA	FDGB	FDGC	FDGD	FDGE	FDGF	FDGG	FDHJ
1997	34 664	84 394	83 548	22 554	2 890	15 737	2 255	26 910	1 182	12 020	846
1998	31 196	87 035	86 122	23 897	3 125	16 896	2 435	26 124	1 379	12 266	913
1999	29 761	88 644	87 918	25 073	2 977	16 752	2 622	26 063	1 335	13 095	726
2000	27 948	86 755	86 160	23 185	2 476	16 228	2 741	28 254	1 112	12 164	594
2001	26 801	91 269	90 049	27 809	2 500	15 879	2 682	28 200	1 083	11 896	1 220

Maintenance and repair of motor vehicles (SIC 92 50.20)

	MKES	FDHK	FDHL	FDHM	FDHN	FDHO	FDHP	FDHQ	FDHR	FDHS	FDHT
1997	22 027	8 011	7 832	417	78	20	5	662	286	6 361	179
1998	24 680	8 975	8 862	297	54	17	–	312	343	7 839	114
1999	26 089	11 118	10 951	724	61	22	8	1 416	656	8 063	167
2000	27 202	11 218	10 992	977	567	12	32	1 169	387	7 847	226
2001	27 862	11 904	11 571	1 023	502	7	43	1 594	368	8 033	332

Sale of motor vehicle parts and accessories (SIC 92 50.30)

	MKET	FDIW	FDIX	FDIY	FDIZ	FDJA	FDJB	FDJC	FDJD	FDJE	FDJF
1997	6 583	10 741	10 567	9	21	–	–	70	79	10 388	175
1998	7 187	10 962	10 808	8	5	–	–	89	111	10 595	154
1999	7 630	11 128	11 085	46	34	1	–	112	73	10 819	44
2000	7 757	11 094	11 014	–	83	–	–	82	60	10 789	81
2001	7 800	11 882	11 688	22	46	19	–	173	200	11 228	194

Sale, maintenance and repair of motorcycles and related parts and accessories (SIC 92 50.40)

	MKEU	FDKI	FDKJ	FDKK	FDKL	FDKM	FDKN	FDKO	FDKP	FDKQ	FDKR
1997	1 522	1 248	1 225	–	322	–	135	344	2	422	23
1998	1 782	1 274	1 196	–	441	–	112	281	1	361	78
1999	2 077	1 665	1 626	17	526	–	306	342	3	432	40
2000	2 277	1 827	1 819	22	416	–	328	386	1	667	8
2001	2 402	1 722	1 707	–	433	–	395	329	1	549	15

Retail sale of automotive fuel (SIC 92 50.50)

	MKEV	FDLV	FDLW	FDLX	FDLY	FDLZ	FDMA	FDMB	FDMC	FDMD	FDME
1997	7 701	14 674	12 273	139	–	5	–	342	11 322	465	2 400
1998	7 260	14 884	12 829	290	1	9	–	521	11 611	396	2 056
1999	6 741	16 401	14 173	130	–	5	1	300	13 382	356	2 228
2000	6 229	18 781	16 372	192	1	–	–	234	15 530	414	2 409
2001	6 077	18 684	15 883	175	3	–	1	594	14 712	398	2 801

24.3
Motor trades[1]
United Kingdom

continued

	Total purchases	Energy, water and materials	Used motor vehicles and motorcycles	Parts used solely in repair and servicing activities	Other goods for resale	Hiring, leasing and renting of plant, machinery and vehicles	Commercial insurance premiums	Road transport services	Telecommun-ication services	Computer and related services	Advertising and marketing services	Other services
	£ million	£ million	£ million	£ million	£ million	£ million	£ million	£ million	£ million	£ million	£ million	£ million

Purchases of goods, materials and services

Sale, maintenance and repair of motor vehicles and motorcycles; retail sale of automotive fuel (SIC 92 50.00)

	CMNR	CMRS	COBU	CMRT	CMRU	CMRV	CMRW	CMRX	CMRY	CMRZ	CMSA	CMSB
1997	102 470	643	25 327	5 615	64 809	245	361	327	245	130	1 190	3 579
1998	106 434	1 638	24 673	6 237	67 545	228	343	326	250	185	1 464	3 545
1999	111 324	1 280	25 223	6 249	71 895	247	360	356	282	232	1 713	3 488
2000	112 157	1 354	26 931	5 181	71 589	282	398	402	280	229	1 630	3 881
2001	115 699	1 410	27 220	5 321	74 425	252	406	444	270	263	1 683	4 005

Sale of motor vehicles (SIC 92 50.10)

	FDGH	FDGI	FDGJ	FDGK	FDGL	FDGM	FDGN	FDGO	FDGP	FDGQ	FDGR	FDGS
1997	74 662	298	24 065	2 803	43 307	106	179	191	133	88	998	2 495
1998	77 395	975	23 604	2 592	46 218	90	156	205	126	99	1 233	2 097
1999	78 607	632	23 444	2 720	47 629	74	177	196	151	142	1 462	1 979
2000	76 980	629	25 367	2 050	44 428	64	163	240	137	140	1 373	2 388
2001	79 973	625	25 070	2 280	47 358	62	179	271	128	161	1 459	2 379

Maintenance and repair of motor vehicles (SIC 92 50.20)

	FDHU	FDHV	FDHW	FDHX	FDHY	FDHZ	FDIA	FDIB	FDIC	FDID	FDIE	FDIF
1997	5 103	176	604	2 291	1 235	97	102	37	49	18	70	423
1998	5 667	292	300	3 171	846	86	112	23	54	21	74	688
1999	7 236	298	1 150	3 080	1 590	115	116	33	66	35	92	661
2000	7 375	366	965	2 606	2 313	138	147	21	71	42	90	615
2001	7 874	346	1 338	2 532	2 489	114	131	33	61	43	94	693

Sale of motor vehicle parts and accessories (SIC 92 50.30)

	FDJG	FDJH	FDJI	FDJJ	FDJK	FDJL	FDJM	FDJN	FDJO	FDJP	FDJQ	FDJR
1997	8 336	74	68	328	7 186	31	46	89	46	21	92	355
1998	8 625	169	144	346	7 089	43	50	88	53	42	111	489
1999	8 825	257	103	290	7 359	49	36	76	46	39	118	452
2000	8 903	260	71	293	7 424	57	52	92	49	31	89	484
2001	9 529	295	145	321	7 796	62	63	90	59	46	73	581

Sale, maintenance and repair of motorcycles and related parts and accessories (SIC 92 50.40)

	FDKT	FDKU	FDKV	FDKW	FDKX	FDKY	FDKZ	FDLA	FDLB	FDLC	FDLD	FDLE
1997	1 059	17	293	43	629	1	8	4	4	1	11	49
1998	1 089	46	226	29	731	1	4	3	2	1	21	24
1999	1 423	10	314	55	958	1	7	6	4	3	22	44
2000	1 488	26	330	124	889	1	9	6	6	3	24	68
2001	1 367	33	228	75	918	4	11	4	6	3	24	62

Retail sale of automotive fuel (SIC 92 50.50)

	FDMF	FDMG	FDMH	FDMI	FDMJ	FDMK	FDML	COBV	COBW	COBX	COBY	COBZ
1997	13 311	78	297	149	12 452	10	26	6	13	2	19	258
1998	13 657	154	399	98	12 661	8	21	7	14	23	25	247
1999	15 232	82	213	105	14 357	8	24	46	15	13	18	351
2000	17 411	71	197	109	16 534	22	27	42	17	12	53	326
2001	16 957	112	439	113	15 865	11	22	46	16	10	34	289

24.3 Motor trades[1]
United Kingdom

continued

	Taxes, duties and levies			Capital Expenditure			
	Total taxes and levies	National (non-domestic business) rates	Other amounts paid for taxes, duties and levies	Cost of acquisitions	Cost of disposals	Net capital expenditure	Work of a capital nature carried out by own staff (included in acquisitions)
	£ million	£ million	£ million	£ million	£ million	£ million	£ million

Sale, maintenance and repair of motor vehicles and motorcycles; retail sale of automotive fuel (SIC 92 50.00)

	CMSC	CMSD	CMSE	CMSF	CMSG	CMSH	CMSI
1997	691	499	192	1 550	569	981	14
1998	951	497	454	2 035	836	1 198	39
1999	904	535	369	1 964	685	1 280	21
2000	873	538	335	1 938	658	1 280	9
2001	934	585	349	2 085	759	1 325	14

Sale of motor vehicles (SIC 92 50.10)

	FDGT	FDGU	FDGV	FDGW	FDGX	FDGY	FDGZ
1997	373	277	96	934	398	535	7
1998	610	240	370	1 232	655	577	27
1999	543	246	297	1 211	461	749	13
2000	482	225	257	1 112	463	649	6
2001	530	263	267	1 288	544	744	9

Maintenance and repair of motor vehicles (SIC 92 50.20)

	FDIG	FDIH	FDII	FDIJ	FDIK	FDIL	FDIM
1997	141	84	58	266	38	228	4
1998	141	114	28	437	97	340	2
1999	172	132	39	389	86	303	7
2000	183	141	42	358	75	283	2
2001	193	145	49	389	87	302	3

Sale of motor vehicle parts and accessories (SIC 92 50.30)

	FDJS	FDJT	FDJU	FDJV	FDJW	FDJX	FDJY
1997	105	80	25	239	81	158	3
1998	100	73	27	181	43	138	6
1999	97	85	13	193	67	126	1
2000	104	87	18	212	50	162	1
2001	103	78	25	205	63	142	2

Sale, maintenance and repair of motorcycles and related parts and accessories (SIC 92 50.40)

	FDLF	FDLG	FDLH	FDLI	FDLJ	FDLK	FDLL
1997	12	11	1	24	6	18	–
1998	17	10	6	26	10	16	4
1999	18	7	11	23	3	20	1
2000	22	12	11	29	11	18	–
2001	20	15	5	26	20	6	–

Retail sale of automotive fuel (SIC 92 50.50)

	COCA	COCB	COCC	COCD	COCE	COCF	COCG
1997	60	48	12	88	47	41	–
1998	83	59	24	158	31	128	–
1999	73	65	9	149	67	82	–
2000	81	74	8	227	59	168	–
2001	87	84	3	176	45	131	–

24.3 Motor trades[1]
United Kingdom
continued

	Stocks			Employment costs			Gross margin		Approximate gross value added at basic prices
	Increase during year	Value at end of year	Total turnover divided by end-year stocks	Total employment costs	Gross wages and salaries paid	National insurance and pension contributions	Amount	As a percentage of adjusted turnover	
	£ million	£ million	Quotient	£ million	£ million	£ million	£ million	Percentage	£ million

Sale, maintenance and repair of motor vehicles and motorcycles; retail sale of automotive fuel (SIC 92 50.00)

	CMSJ	CMSK	CMSL	CMSM	COBP	COBQ	COBR	COBS	COBT
1997	1 388	12 079	9.9	6 982	6 229	753	24 703	21.6	17 809
1998	1 133	12 861	9.6	7 660	6 801	859	25 809	21.7	17 463
1999	1 042	13 738	9.4	8 179	7 295	884	26 398	21.5	18 726
2000	616	13 364	9.7	8 261	7 376	885	26 279	20.3	18 214
2001	1 557	14 817	9.1	9 109	8 164	945	29 842	22.0	21 261

Sale of motor vehicles (SIC 92 50.10)

	FDHA	FDHB	FDHC	FDHD	FDHE	FDHF	FDHG	FDHH	FDHI
1997	1 213	9 494	8.9	3 765	3 349	417	15 433	18.8	10 856
1998	948	10 233	8.5	4 048	3 594	454	15 569	18.0	10 273
1999	995	10 797	8.2	4 285	3 815	469	15 676	18.2	11 064
2000	561	10 405	8.3	4 341	3 859	483	15 255	17.6	10 335
2001	1 429	11 698	7.8	4 746	4 228	517	17 852	19.6	12 692

Maintenance and repair of motor vehicles (SIC 92 50.20)

	FDIN	FDIO	FDIP	FDIQ	FDIR	FDIS	FDIT	FDIU	FDIV
1997	46	544	14.7	1 436	1 273	162	3 924	67.7	2 901
1998	28	515	17.4	1 718	1 517	201	4 687	80.4	3 318
1999	3	747	14.9	1 930	1 725	205	5 283	65.7	3 898
2000	43	670	16.7	1 919	1 715	204	5 236	46.7	3 883
2001	63	793	15.0	2 183	1 967	216	5 566	46.8	4 076

Sale of motor vehicle parts and accessories (SIC 92 50.30)

	FDJZ	FDKA	FDKB	FDKC	FDKD	FDKE	FDKF	FDKG	FDKH
1997	66	1 329	8.1	1 231	1 104	127	3 225	30.8	2 450
1998	53	1 332	8.2	1 291	1 141	149	3 436	32.2	2 374
1999	31	1 403	7.9	1 295	1 151	144	3 401	31.4	2 332
2000	35	1 440	7.7	1 353	1 210	144	3 328	30.0	2 219
2001	63	1 511	7.9	1 464	1 314	150	3 664	30.8	2 400

Sale, maintenance and repair of motorcycles and related parts and accessories (SIC 92 50.40)

	FDLM	FDLN	FDLO	FDLP	FDLQ	FDLR	FDLS	FDLT	FDLU
1997	25	263	4.7	93	83	10	309	25.6	214
1998	77	333	3.8	102	90	11	365	29.1	259
1999	24	291	5.7	128	115	13	313	19.5	218
2000	27	361	5.1	90	81	9	501	27.4	370
2001	11	378	4.6	132	120	13	488	28.3	346

Retail sale of automotive fuel (SIC 92 50.50)

	COCH	COCI	COCJ	COCK	COCL	COCM	COCN	CMQN	CMQO
1997	37	449	32.7	456	420	36	1 812	12.4	1 388
1998	27	449	33.1	501	458	43	1 752	11.7	1 240
1999	43	502	32.7	541	488	53	1 725	10.6	1 215
2000	36	488	38.5	557	512	46	1 960	10.4	1 407
2001	12	437	42.8	584	535	49	2 271	12.2	1 747

1 See chapter text. Figures are exclusive of VAT.

Source: Office for National Statistics: 01633 812435

24.4 Catering and allied trades[1]
United Kingdom

	Number of businesses	Total turnover[3]	Taxes and levies[2]			Capital expenditure[2]			Work of a capital nature carried out by your own staff (included in acquisitions)
			Total taxes and levies	National (non-domestic business) rates	Other amounts paid for taxes duties and levies	Capital acquisitions	Capital disposals	Net capital expenditure	
	Number	£ million	£ million	£ million	£ million	£ million	£ million	£ million	£ million
Total catering and allied trades (SIC 92 55.00)									
	MKEK	CMKX	CMLM	CMLJ	CMLL	CMLP	CMLQ	CMLK	CMLR
1997	110 245	45 844	1 082	899	183	3 909	465	3 444	14
1998	111 815	48 680	1 215	1 053	162	4 453	519	3 934	30
1999	114 353	51 315	1 295	1 156	139	4 793	649	4 144	49
2000	116 568	55 058	1 343	1 251	92	4 945	484	4 461	35
2001	118 988	58 003	1 548	1 401	146	5 014	551	4 463	27
Hotels and motels (SIC 92 55.11 and 55.12)									
	MKEL	CMLW	CMML	CMMI	CMMK	CMMO	CMMP	CMMJ	CMMQ
1997	11 555	9 589	255	228	28	1 116	99	1 018	8
1998	11 374	10 333	259	254	5	1 221	105	1 116	3
1999	11 381	10 970	269	260	9	1 333	203	1 130	8
2000	11 188	11 595	300	292	8	1 402	106	1 296	10
2001	10 890	12 098	370	350	21	1 297	97	1 200	6
Camping sites and other provision of short-stay accommodation (SIC 92 55.21 to 55.23)									
	MKEM	CMMV	CMNK	CMNH	CMNJ	CMNN	CMNO	CMNI	CMNP
1997	3 289	1 945	59	50	9	253	36	216	2
1998	3 435	2 071	67	62	6	261	37	224	2
1999	3 688	1 932	61	53	8	274	38	236	7
2000	3 851	2 152	69	63	6	228	46	182	5
2001	3 928	2 231	76	73	3	286	21	265	6
Restaurants or cafes, take-away food shops (SIC 92 55.30)									
	MKEN	CMNU	CMOJ	CMOG	CMOI	CMOM	CMON	CMOH	CMOO
1997	46 984	12 660	272	250	22	720	62	657	2
1998	48 362	13 710	305	290	15	971	122	849	1
1999	49 955	14 618	386	360	26	1 048	137	911	7
2000	51 395	16 934	405	383	23	1 305	128	1 176	2
2001	52 633	18 266	509	454	55	1 351	128	1 222	5
Licensed clubs with entertainment, independent, tenanted, managed public houses or wine bars (SIC 92 55.40)[4]									
	MKEO	CMOT	CMPI	CMPF	CMPH	CMPL	CMPM	CMPG	CMPN
1997	44 198	16 792	451	336	115	1 734	265	1 470	2
1998	44 283	17 820	559	429	130	1 910	251	1 658	12
1999	44 647	18 423	551	460	92	2 032	263	1 769	25
2000	45 139	18 578	538	484	54	1 861	196	1 665	18
2001	46 320	19 160	560	497	62	1 906	291	1 615	11
Canteen operator, catering contractor (SIC 92 55.51 and 55.52)									
	MKEP	CMPS	CMQH	CMQE	CMQG	CMQK	CMQL	CMQF	CMQM
1997	4 219	4 858	44	35	9	86	3	83	..
1998	4 361	4 748	24	19	5	91	5	87	12
1999	4 682	5 372	28	23	5	106	8	99	2
2000	4 995	5 799	31	30	1	148	7	141	–
2001	5 217	6 247	33	28	5	174	14	160	–

24.4 Catering and allied trades[1]
continued United Kingdom

	Stocks[2]		Purchases of goods and services[2]									
	Increase during year	Value at end of year	Total purchases	Energy, water and materials	Goods for resale	Hiring, leasing of plant, machinery etc.	Commercial insurance premiums	Road transport services	Telecommun-ication services	Computer and related services	Advertising and marketing services	Other services
	£ million	£ million	£ million	£ million	£ million	£ million	£ million	£ million	£ million	£ million	£ million	£ million
Total catering and allied trades (SIC 92 55.00)												
	CMLN	CMLO	CMLI	CMKZ	CMLA	CMLB	CMLC	CMLD	CMLE	CMLF	CMLG	CMLH
1997	48	840	21 371	8 053	7 338	234	285	89	187	50	546	4 589
1998	43	969	22 702	9 335	7 094	273	271	51	189	62	581	4 846
1999	60	1 067	23 856	8 848	8 028	306	272	100	213	105	608	5 377
2000	36	1 077	25 130	10 136	7 757	344	370	101	232	115	628	5 446
2001	67	1 247	26 267	11 093	7 395	278	373	98	238	133	595	6 063
Hotels and motels (SIC 92 55.11 and 55.12)												
	CMMM	CMMN	CMMH	CMLY	CMLZ	CMMA	CMMB	CMMC	CMMD	CMME	CMMF	CMMG
1997	−1	137	3 532	1 487	506	68	73	27	60	17	162	1 132
1998	1	157	3 702	1 633	512	54	72	11	58	17	169	1 178
1999	−5	208	3 817	1 667	450	65	67	25	60	36	167	1 280
2000	−3	181	3 947	1 793	383	64	71	28	56	29	182	1 340
2001	−1	206	4 124	1 743	465	49	81	18	62	31	174	1 499
Camping sites and other provision of short-stay accommodation (SIC 92 55.21 to 55.23)												
	CMNL	CMNM	CMNG	CMMX	CMMY	CMMZ	CMNA	CMNB	CMNC	CMND	CMNE	CMNF
1997	8	87	887	172	278	11	23	5	10	5	55	327
1998	−1	91	932	212	265	11	22	3	15	6	76	321
1999	3	85	852	184	220	5	28	10	12	6	66	321
2000	−4	84	887	201	243	9	35	10	14	9	57	308
2001	49	139	1 052	233	269	6	31	4	15	20	77	396
Restaurants or cafes, take-away food shops (SIC 92 55.30)												
	CMOK	CMOL	CMOF	CMNW	CMNX	CMNY	CMNZ	CMOA	CMOB	CMOC	CMOD	CMOE
1997	14	206	6 175	2 926	1 538	27	78	22	41	7	159	1 376
1998	16	231	6 683	3 197	1 611	49	66	10	43	11	159	1 537
1999	26	291	7 079	3 183	1 934	53	70	29	61	19	200	1 530
2000	12	274	7 962	3 791	2 120	45	92	36	64	29	232	1 555
2001	9	293	8 529	4 198	2 161	42	95	33	62	35	203	1 701
Licensed clubs with entertainment, independent, tenanted, managed public houses or wine bars (SIC 92 55.40)[4]												
	CMPJ	CMPK	CMPE	CMOV	CMOW	CMOX	CMOY	CMOZ	CMPA	CMPB	CMPC	CMPD
1997	15	340	8 665	2 042	4 800	95	96	17	64	13	158	1 379
1998	21	408	9 147	2 796	4 389	96	96	15	62	17	160	1 517
1999	24	392	9 386	2 028	4 924	147	91	15	67	28	161	1 925
2000	32	432	9 486	2 366	4 525	193	152	15	80	34	137	1 982
2001	−10	487	9 466	2 811	4 055	146	139	16	80	26	114	2 080
Canteen operator, catering contractor (SIC 92 55.51 and 55.52)												
	CMQI	CMQJ	CMQD	CMPU	CMPV	CMPW	CMPX	CMPY	CMPZ	CMQA	CMQB	CMQC
1997	12	71	2 111	1 427	216	32	14	18	11	9	11	374
1998	7	82	2 237	1 497	317	63	16	12	11	10	18	293
1999	12	92	2 721	1 785	500	35	17	21	14	15	14	321
2000	−1	104	2 848	1 986	486	32	20	13	18	14	20	261
2001	20	121	3 096	2 108	446	35	27	27	19	20	26	387

24.4 Catering and allied trades[1]
United Kingdom
continued

	Employment costs[2]			Gross margin[5]			Accommodation	
	Total employment costs	Gross wages and salaries paid	National insurance and pension contributions	Amount	As a percentage of turnover	Value added at basic prices[5]	Number of establishments	Letting bedplaces
	£ million	£ million	£ million	£ million	Percentage	£ million	Number	Number

Total catering and allied trades (SIC 92 55.00)

	CMKY	CMKV	CMKW	CMQP	CMQQ	CMQR	CMLS	CMLT
1997	9 200	8 493	707	32 088	81.1	18 055	23 207	1 591 979
1998	10 261	9 461	799	34 870	82.9	19 333	23 038	1 481 204
1999	11 012	10 169	844	36 159	81.5	20 568	23 667	1 731 601
2000	11 668	10 777	891	39 528	83.4	22 326	25 589	1 788 115
2001	13 038	12 003	1 035	42 315	84.8	23 661	22 834	1 806 492

Hotels and motels (SIC 92 55.11 and 55.12)

	CMLX	CMLU	CMLV	CMQS	CMQT	CMQU	CMMR	CMMS
1997	2 257	2 071	186	7 663	93.6	4 636	13 505	727 016
1998	2 460	2 251	209	8 284	94.2	5 101	12 907	701 488
1999	2 605	2 392	213	8 922	95.0	5 595	12 583	757 491
2000	2 775	2 539	236	9 542	95.9	6 012	13 803	780 158
2001	3 058	2 804	254	9 924	95.2	6 297	11 978	825 731

Camping sites and other provision of short-stay accommodation (SIC 92 55.21 to 55.23)

	CMMW	CMMT	CMMU	CMQV	CMQW	CMQX	CMNQ	CMRR
1997	312	293	19	1 456	84.0	846	4 598	770 397
1998	350	326	24	1 574	85.4	913	4 396	669 423
1999	355	325	30	1 460	85.3	865	4 913	844 311
2000	405	370	35	1 615	85.4	1 003	4 827	860 261
2001	433	396	37	1 681	86.3	947	4 289	836 310

Restaurants or cafes, take-away food shops (SIC 92 55.30)

	CMNV	CMNS	CMNT	CMQY	CMQZ	CMRA	CMOP	CMOQ
1997	2 404	2 231	174	9 352	85.8	4 715	655	29 815
1998	2 787	2 590	196	10 258	86.5	5 223	692	31 680
1999	2 985	2 762	223	10 665	84.5	5 592	1 033	45 449
2000	3 318	3 071	247	12 375	85.2	6 564	1 053	60 329
2001	3 780	3 499	281	13 485	86.0	7 139	1 117	55 537

Licensed clubs with entertainment, independent, tenanted, managed public houses or wine bars (SIC 92 55.40)[4]

	CMOU	CMOR	CMOS	CMRB	CMRC	CMRD	CMPO	CMPP
1997	2 657	2 451	205	9 494	66.0	5 629	4 449	64 751
1998	2 982	2 752	230	10 793	70.6	6 052	5 044	78 614
1999	3 206	2 975	231	10 762	68.1	6 383	5 137	84 351
2000	3 170	2 954	216	11 343	71.3	6 432	5 906	87 366
2001	3 670	3 376	294	12 167	74.4	6 858	5 449	88 915

Canteen operator, catering contractor (SIC 92 55.51 and 55.52)

	CMPT	CMPQ	CMPR	CMRE	CMRF	CMRG		
1997	1 569	1 447	122	4 123	95.1	2 228		
1998	1 681	1 541	140	3 962	93.0	2 044		
1999	1 861	1 715	146	4 349	89.9	2 133		
2000	1 999	1 842	157	4 653	90.3	2 315		
2001	2 096	1 928	169	5 058	92.0	2 419		

1 See chapter text.
2 Exclusive of VAT.
3 Inclusive of VAT.

4 Includes figures for managed public houses owned by breweries.
5 The total turnover figure used to calculate these data excludes VAT.

Source: Office for National Statistics: 01633 812435

SOURCES

This index of sources gives the titles of official publications or other sources containing statistics allied to those in the tables of this *Annual Abstract*. These publications provide more detailed analyses than are shown in the *Annual Abstract*. This index includes publications to which reference should be made for short-term (monthly or quarterly) series. No entry is made in this index for items where the data have been obtained from departmental records. Further advice on published statistical sources is available from the National Statistics Public Enquiry Service on the numbers provided on page ii.

Subject	Table number in *Abstract*	Government department or other organisation	Official publication or other source
1. Area			
	1.1	Ordnance Survey Ordnance Survey of Northern Ireland Office for National Statistics	 Regional Trends (annual, The Stationery Office (TSO))
2. Parliamentary elections			
Elections	2.1	University of Plymouth for the Electoral Commission	British Electoral Facts 1832-1999 (Ashgate) Dod's Parliamentary Companion (annual)
By-elections	2.2	University of Plymouth for the Electoral Commission	Vachers Parliamentary Companion (quarterly) Social Trends (annual, TSO)
3. International development			
	3.1, 3.2	Department for International Development	Statistics on International Development (annual)
4. Defence			
	4.1 - 4.11	Ministry of Defence/ DASA	UK Defence Statistics 2003 (TSO)
5. Population and vital statistics			
Population	5.1 - 5.3, 5.5, 5.6	Office for National Statistics	*England and Wales*: Census reports 1911, 1921, 1931, 1951, 1961, 1971, 1981 and 1991 Census 1991, Key Population and Vital Statistics; Great Britain Digest of Welsh Statistics (annual, National Assembly for Wales)
		General Register Office (Scotland)	*Scotland*: Census reports 1951, 1961, 1971, 1981 and 1991 Census 1991, Key statistics for urban areas: Scotland
		Northern Ireland Statistics and Research Agency	*Northern Ireland*: Census of population 1951, 1961, 1966 and 1971, 1981 and 1991
		Office for National Statistics	*England and Wales*: Series FM (Family statistics), DH (Deaths), MB (Morbidity), PP (Population estimates and projections), MN (Migration) and VS (Key population and vital statistics) Series PP1, Population estimates: The Registrar General's estimates of the population of regions and local government areas of England and Wales Population Trends (quarterly TSO) Health Statistics Quarterly (TSO)
		General Register Office (Scotland)	*Scotland*: Annual report of the Registrar General for Scotland Annual estimate of the population of Scotland
		Northern Ireland Statistics and Research Agency	*Northern Ireland*: Annual report of the Registrar General
Projections	5.1 - 5.3	Government Actuary's Department Office for National Statistics	 Series PP2, Population projections - national figures
Migration	5.7 5.8, 5.9	Office for National Statistics	International Migration - first release of 2002 estimates Series MN (International migration) Population Trends (quarterly, TSO)
	5.10, 5.11	Home Office	Control of immigration statistics United Kingdom (annual)
Vital statistics	5.4, 5.12 - 5.22	Office for National Statistics	*England and Wales*: Series FM (Births, marriages and divorce statistics), DH (Deaths), MB (Morbidity), PP (Population estimates and projections), MN (International migration) and VS (Key population and vital statistics) Population Trends (quarterly, TSO)

SOURCES

Subject	Table number in *Abstract*	Government department or other organisation	Official publication or other source
	5.4, 5.12 - 5.21	General Register Office (Scotland)	*Scotland*: Annual report of the Registrar General for Scotland Quarterly return of births, deaths and marriages
		Northern Ireland Statistics and Research Agency	*Northern Ireland*: Annual report of the Registrar General Quarterly return of births, deaths and marriages
	5.14	Northern Ireland Court Service	Northern Ireland Judicial Statistics (annual)
	5.18	Scottish Executive	
	5.22	Government Actuary's Department	*England and Wales*: Interim Life Table *Scotland*: Interim Life Table *Northern Ireland*: Annual Report of the Registrar General
	5.23	Office for National Statistics General Register Office (Scotland) Northern Ireland Statistics and Research Agency	

6. Education

	6.1 - 6.11	Department for Education and Skills	Education and Training Statistics for the United Kingdom (annual,TSO)
		National Assembly for Wales	Digest of Welsh Statistics (annual) Statistics of education and training in Wales (annual and ad-hoc, NAfW)
		Scottish Executive	Scottish educational statistics (annual and ad-hoc, SE) Scottish Social Statistics (annual)
		Northern Ireland Department of Education	Annual Abstract of Statistics, Northern Ireland (annual,DENI) Northern Ireland education statistics (annual and ad-hoc, DENI)
		Northern Ireland Department for Employment and Learning	Northern Ireland further and higher education statistics (annual and ad-hoc, DELNI)

7. Labour market

Subject	Table	Government department	Official publication or other source
Labour Force Survey	7.1 - 7.3, 7.6, 7.9, 7.10, 7.12, 7.15 - 7.17	Office for National Statistics	Labour Market Trends (monthly, TSO)
	7.4, 7.5	Office for National Statistics	
	7.7	Cabinet Office	Civil Service Statistics (annual) Monthly Digest of Statistics (TSO)
	7.8	Office for National Statistics Home Office Scottish Executive	Labour Market Trends (monthly, TSO)
Claimant count	7.11, 7.13 7.14, 7.27	Office for National Statistics	Labour Market Trends (monthly, TSO)
	7.18	Office for National Statistics	Labour Market Trends (monthly TSO) Monthly Digest of Statistics (TSO)
New Earnings Survey	7.19, 7.20, 7.23, 7.25	Office for National Statistics	New Earnings Survey (annual, ONS)
Average Earnings Index	7.21, 7.22	Office for National Statistics	Labour Market Trends (monthly, TSO) Monthly Digest of Statistics (TSO)
	7.24	Department of Enterprise, Trade and Investment (Northern Ireland)	New Earnings Survey Northern Ireland (annual) (some details in Northern Ireland Annual Abstract of Statistics)
	7.26	Department of Trade and Industry	Labour Market Trends (monthly, TSO)

8. Personal income, expenditure and wealth

	8.1	Office for National Statistics	Economic Trends, May (monthly, TSO)
	8.2	Board of Inland Revenue	Inland Revenue Statistics (annual, TSO) Economic Trends (monthly, TSO)

Subject	Table number in *Abstract*	Government department or other organisation	Official publication or other source
	8.3 - 8.5	Office for National Statistics	Expenditure and Food Survey, (annual) (1990 onwards edition-FamilySpending) (annual, TSO)

9. Health

Subject	Table	Department	Source
National health service	9.1	Department of Health	Appropriation Accounts (annual) Health and Personal Social Services Statistics for England (annual)
		National Assembly for Wales	Health Statistics Wales (annual)
	9.2	The Scottish Executive, Common Services Agency	
	9.3	Department of Health, Social Services and Public Safety (Northern Ireland)	Summary of Health and Personal Social Services (Northern Ireland) Accounts (annual) Hospital Statistics (annual)
	9.4	Department of Health Scottish Health Service, Common Services Agency National Assembly for Wales	Health and Personal Social Services Statistics for England (annual) Department of Health, Medical and Dental Workforce Census
Public health	9.5	Office for National Statistics	
		General Register Office (Scotland)	
		Northern Ireland Statistics and Research Agency	
	9.6	HPA Communicable Disease Surveillance Centre	Communicable Disease Statistics Series MB2 (annual) Annual Review of Communicable Diseases
		NHS in Scotland Common Services Agency	Scottish Health Statistics (annual)
		Northern Ireland Statistics and Research Agency	Annual report of the Registrar General Northern Ireland Quarterly return of births, deaths and marriages
	9.7 - 9.9	Health and Safety Executive	Health and Safety Statistics (annual)

10. Social protection

Subject	Table	Department	Source
Social security pensions, benefits and allowances	10.1, 10.2,	Department for Work and Pensions Board of Inland Revenue Department of Health, Social Services and Public Safety (Northern Ireland)	National Insurance Fund Account (annual)
	10.2	Board of Inland Revenue	
	10.4	Board of Inland Revenue	
	10.3, 10.5, 10.6 - 10.17	Department for Work and Pensions, Information and Analysis Directorate	
Working Family Tax Credit	10.13	Board of Inland Revenue	Quarterly Enquiry United Kingdom (quarterly)
Social services	10.18 - 10.22	Office for National Statistics Department for Education and Skills	Appropriation Accounts (annual) Northern Ireland Annual Abstract of Statistics
	10.18	HM Treasury	HM Treasury Exependiture Statistical Analyses
Housing	10.23	Office for National Statistics	

11. Crime and justice

Subject	Table	Department	Source
	11.1	Home Office	Police Service Strength England and Wales 2002/03 Home Office Statistical Bulletin 11/03

SOURCES

Subject	Table number in *Abstract*	Government department or other organisation	Official publication or other source
	11.2	Home Office	Crime in Englan and Wales 2002/03 Home Office Statistical Bulletin 7/03
		Scottish Executive Justice Department The Police Service of Northern Ireland	*Scotland:* Report of Her Majesty's Chief Inspector of Constabulary for Scotland (annual) The Chief Constable's Annual Report
	11.3 - 11.11	Home Office	Criminal Statistics, England and Wales (annual) (TSO) Prison statistics, England and Wales (annual) Digest of Welsh Statistics (annual, Welsh Office)
	11.12	Home Office	HM Prison Service Annual Report and Accounts April 2001 - March 2002
	11.13	Scottish Executive Justice Department	Recorded Crime in Scotland, 2002
	11.14- - 11.17	Scottish Executive Justice Department	Criminal Proceedings in Scottish Courts, 2001
	11.18, 11.19	Scottish Executive Justice Department	Prison Statistics Scotland, 2002 Scottish Prison Service Annual Report and Accounts 2001-02
	11.21 - 11.24	Northern Ireland Office	

12. Lifestyles

Subject	Table number in *Abstract*	Government department or other organisation	Official publication or other source
	12.1	Department for Culture, Media and Sport	Department for Culture, Media and Sport Annual Report 2002
	12.2	Department for Culture, Media and Sport	Table B17 – Labour Market Trends
	12.3	Cinema Advertising Association	
	12.4	Department for Culture, Media and Sport	British Film Institute Film and Television Handbook
	12.5	Office for National Statistics	Travel Trends (annual, TSO) Overseas Travel and Tourism First Release Monthly Digest of Statistics (TSO)
		VisitBritain	The UK Tourist: Statistics (annual) Sightseeing in the UK (annual) www.staruk.org.uk The national tourism statistics website
		Wales Tourist Board/ VisitScotland/Northern Ireland Tourist Board	
	12.6	VisitBritain/	Sightseeing in the UK (annual) Wales Tourist Board/ VisitScotland/Northern Ireland Tourist Board
	12.7	Department for Culture, Media and Sport Gaming Board for Great Britain	Camelot - National Lottery Press Releases The Gaming Board for Great Britain Annual Report www.gbgb.org.uk The Gaming Board website
	12.8	Office for National Statistics	International Passenger Survey MQ6 Overseas Travel and Tourism
	12.9	Cinema Advertisting Association Target Group Index BMRB International	
	12.10	Department for Culture, Media and Sport Gaming Board for Great Britain	

13. Environment

Subject	Table number in *Abstract*	Government department or other organisation	Official publication or other source
Environment	13.1, 13.19	Office for National Statistics	Environmental Accounts 2003 Autumn edition (biennial) (www.nationalstatistics.gov.uk/statbase/Product.asp?vink=3698)
	13.2 - 13.7 13.9 -13.17	Department for Environment, Food and Rural Affairs	Digest of Environmental Statistics (annual, www.defra.gov.uk/environment/statistics/des) The Environment in your Pocket (annual)

Subject	Table number in *Abstract*	Government department or other organisation	Official publication or other source
Water	13.8	Office of Water Services (OFWAT)	Companies 2003 June Return to OFWAT (annual)
	13.10	Scottish Environmental Protection Agency	
	13.19	Centre for Ecology and Hydrology Met Office	www.ceh-nerc.ac.uk/data/NWA.htm www.met-office.gov.uk
	13.20	Centre for Ecology and Hydrology Environment Agency	www.ceh-nerc.ac.uk/data/NWA.htm www.environment-agency.gov.uk/water plcs

14. Housing

	14.1	Office of the Deputy Prime Minister National Assembly for Wales Scottish Executive Department for Social Development, Northern Ireland	
	14.2	Office for National Statistics Northern Ireland Statistics and Research Agency	General Household Survey Continuous Household Survey
	14.3	Office of the Deputy Prime Minister National Assembly for Wales Scottish Executive Department for Social Development, Northern Ireland	www.housing.odpm.gov.uk/statistics Live Tables 241-247 Welsh Housing Statistics (annual, NAfW) Statistical Bulletins on Housing (SE) Northern Ireland Housing Statistics (annual)
	14.4	Office of the Deputy Prime Minister	www.housing.odpm.gov.uk/statistics Live Table 111
	14.5	Office of the Deputy Prime Minister National Assemby for Wales	
	14.6	Council of Mortgage Lenders Office of the Deputy Prime Minister	
	14.7	The Court Service Northern Ireland Court Service	
	14.8	Office of the Deputy Prime Minister National Assembly for Wales Scottish Executive	
	14.9	Office for the Deputy Prime Minister	Homelessness Statistical Release (quarterly) www.housing.gov.uk/HousingStatistics/LiveTables623

15. Transport and communications

Subject	Table number in *Abstract*	Government department or other organisation	Official publication or other source
General	15.1, 15.2, 15.4	Department for Transport	
	15.3	Office for National Statistics	
Road transport	15.5 - 15.12	Department for Transport	Transport Statistics Great Britain (annual, TSO) Vehicle Licensing Statistics (annual, TSO) Monthly Digest of Statistics (TSO) Road accidents in Great Britain (annual, TSO) Road accidents Wales (annual, National Assembly for Wales)
	15.11		Driving Standards Agency
	15.13, 15.14	Department of Regional Development, Northern Ireland	Transport Statistics NI
Rail transport	15.20, 15.21	Department for Transport	Transport Statistics Great Britain (annual, TSO) Health and Safety Executive: Industry and Services (annual) Bulletin of Rail Statistics (quarterly)

Subject	Table number in *Abstract*	Government department or other organisation	Official publication or other source
	15.22, 15.23	Department of Regional Development, Northern Ireland	
Air transport	15.24 - 15.28	Civil Aviation Authority	Monthly Digest of Statistics (TSO) Civil Aviation Authority; Annual Statements of Movements, Passengers and Cargo Civil Aviation Authority; Monthly Statements of Movements, Passengers and Cargo Accidents to aircraft on the British Register (annual)
Sea transport	15.29, 15.30	Department for Transport	Maritime Statistics (annual, TSO) Monthly Digest of Statistics (TSO)
Passenger movement	15.31	Department for Transport Civil Aviation Authority	Monthly Digest of Statistics (TSO)
Communications	15.32	Royal Mail Parcel Force Capita Business Services Ltd. Post Office Counters Ltd	Monthly Digest of Statistics (TSO) Post Office report and accounts (annual)

16. National accounts

	16.1 - 16.22	Office for National Statistics	United Kingdom National Accounts (annual, TSO) Monthly Digest of Statistics (TSO)

17. Prices

Subject	Table	Organisation	Source
Producer prices	17.1, 17.2	Office for National Statistics	Producer Price Index Press Notice (monthly) Business Monitor MM22, Producer Price Indices (monthly, TSO) Monthly Digest of Statistics (TSO)
Consumer prices	17.3 - 17.5	Office for National Statistics	Monthly Digest of Statistics (TSO) Labour Market Trends (monthly, TSO) Focus on Consumer Price Indices (monthly, National Statistics website)
	17.6, 17.7	Department for Environment, Food and Rural Affairs	Agriculture in the UK (annual) Agricultural Price Indices (Monthly Statistical Notice) Monthly Digest of Statistics (TSO)
	17.8	Department for Environment, Food and Rural Affairs	Agriculture in the UK (annual) Economic Trends (monthly, TSO) UK Economic Accounts (quarterly, TSO)

18. Government finance

Subject	Table	Organisation	Source
Central government	18.1 - 18.3	Office for National Statistics	Financial Statistics (monthly, TSO)
	18.4	Office for National Statistics	Financial Statistics (monthly, TSO)
	18.5	Office for National Statistics	Blue Book (annual)
	18.6 - 18.7	HM Treasury Office for National Statistics	Consolidated Fund and National Loans Fund Accounts Financial Statistics (monthly, TSO)
	18.8	Bank of England	
Central government	18.9, 18.10	Board of Inland Revenue	Inland Revenue website
Rateable values Local authorities	18.11	Board of Inland Revenue	Inland Revenue website
	18.12, 18.13	Office of the Deputy Prime Minister	Local government financial statistics (England) (annual)
		National Assembly for Wales	Welsh local government financial statistics (annual)
		Public Works Loan Board	Annual report of the Public Works Loan Board
		Scottish Executive, Economic Advice and Statistics	Local financial returns (Scotland) (annual)
		Department of the Environment for Northern Ireland	
		Chartered Institute of Public Finance and Accountancy	

SOURCES

Subject	Table number in *Abstract*	Government department or other organisation	Official publication or other source
	18.14, 18.15	Office of the Deputy Prime Minister National Assembly for Wales	Local government financial statistics (England) (annual) Welsh local government financial statistics (annual)
	18.16	Office of the Deputy Prime Minister	Local government financial statistics (England) (annual)
	18.17 - 18.19	Scottish Executive, Economic Advice and Statistics	Local financial returns (Scotland) (annual)
	18.20	Department of the Environment for Northern Ireland	District Council - Summary of Statement of Accounts (annual)

19. External trade and investment

Subject	Table number in *Abstract*	Government department or other organisation	Official publication or other source
	19.1 - 19.8	HM Customs and Excise	OTS1 Overseas Trade Statistics, (formerly MM20), monthly publication Extra EC OTS2 Overseas Trade Statistics, (formerly MM20A), monthly publication Intra EC and World OTSQ Overseas Trade Statistics, (formerly MQ20), quarterly publication Intra EC OTSA Overseas Trade Statistics, (formerly MA20), annual publication Extra and Intra EC
		Office for National Statistics	Business Monitor MM24, Monthly Review of External Trade Statistics (monthly, TSO) Overseas Trade Analysed in Terms of Industries MQ10 (quarterly, TSO) Monthly Digest of Statistics (monthly, TSO)
	19.9 - 19.18	Office for National Statistics Bank of England	United Kingdom Balance of Payments (annual, TSO) Quarterly figures: UK Economic Accounts Financial Statistics (monthly, TSO) Foreign Direct Investment MA4 (annual, National Statistics website)

20. Research and development

Subject	Table number in *Abstract*	Government department or other organisation	Official publication or other source
	20.1 - 20.5	Office for National Statistics	Business Monitor MA14, Research and Development in UK Business (annual, ONS)

21. Agriculture, fisheries and food

Subject	Table number in *Abstract*	Government department or other organisation	Official publication or other source
Agriculture	21.1, 21.2	Department for Environment, Food and Rural Affairs	Agriculture in the United Kingdom (annual)
	21.3 - 21.5	Department for Environment, Food and Rural Affairs	Agricultural Statistics; United Kingdom (annual) Scottish Agricultural Economics (annual) Welsh Agricultural Statistics (annual, National Assembly for Wales)
	21.6	Forestry Commission	Great Britain: Annual Report and Accounts of the Forestry Commission
		Department of Agriculture and Rural Development (Northern Ireland)	Northern Ireland Annual Abstract of Statistics
	21.7, 21.8	Department for Environment, Food and Rural Affairs	DEFRA Statistical Notice
Food	21.9 - 21.12	Department for Environment, Food and Rural Affairs	Monthly Digest of Statistics (TSO)
	21.13	Department for Environment, Food and Rural Affairs	Agricultural Statistics, United Kingdom (annual) As for notes 20.3 - 20.5
Fisheries	21.14, 21.15	Department of Environment, Food and Rural Affairs; Scottish Executive Agricultural Departments	*England and Wales*: Sea fisheries statistical tables (annual) *Scotland*: Fisheries of Scotland report (annual) Scottish Sea fisheries statistics (annual, TSO)
Family Food	21.16	Department for Environment, Food and Rural Affairs	Expenditure and Food Survey

Subject	Table number in *Abstract*	Government department or other organisation	Official publication or other source
22. Production			
Production and construction	22.1	Office for National Statistics	Annual Business Inquiry (www.statistics.gov.uk/abi/)
Manufacturers sales	22.2	Office for National Statistics	ProdCom Product Sales and Trade PRA and PRQ series of reports
	22.3	Office for National Statistics	Size analysis of United Kingdom Businesses (Business Monitor PA1003) (annual, ONS)
Energy	22.4 - 22.13	Department of Trade and Industry (Energy Market Units)	Digest of United Kingdom Energy Statistics (annual) Energy Trends (monthly and quarterly) Annual Business Inquiry (www.statistics.gov.uk/abi/)
Iron and steel	22.14 - 22.16	Iron and Steel Statistics Bureau	Iron and steel industry: annual statistics published by the Iron and Steel Statistics Bureau Corporation Regional Trends (annual, TSO)
Industrial materials	22.17	World Bureau of Metal Statistics	World Metal Statistics (monthly) Annual Business Inquiry (www.statistics.gov.uk/abi/) Aluminium Federation
	22.18	Fertiliser Manufacturers' Association	Monthly Digest of Statistics (TSO) Annual Business Inquiry (www.statistics.gov.uk/abi/)
Minerals	22.19	Office of the Deputy Prime Minister Department of Trade and Industry Department of Economic Development (Northern Ireland)	Minerals (Business Monitor PA 1007) (annual, ONS) Natural Environment Research Council: United Kingdom Minerals Yearbook Northern Ireland Annual Abstract of Statistics
Building Materials	22.20	Department of Trade and Industry	Mionthly Statistics of Building Materials and Components (DTI) Monthly Digest of Statistics (TSO)
Construction (output)	22.21	Department of Trade and Industry	Construction Statistics Annual (DTI)
Construction (new orders)	22.22	Department of Trade and Industry	Construction Statistics Annual (DTI)
Engineering	22.23, 22.24	Office for National Statistics	Annual Business Inquiry (www.statistics.gov.uk/abi/) Business Monitor PA1003 - Size Analysis of United Kingdom Businesses 2002
Motor vehicle production	22.25	Office for National Statistics	Business Monitor PM 34.10, (monthly, ONS) Annual Business Inquiry (www.statistics.gov.uk/abi/) Sector Review- Motor Trades (formerly Business Monitor SDA27) (annual, TSO)
Drink and tobacco	22.26, 22.27	HM Customs and Excise	Annual report of the Commissioners of HM Customs
		Office for National Statistics	Monthly Digest of Statistics (TSO)
23. Banking, insurance, etc			
Banking	23.1	Bank of England	Bank of England Annual Report and Accounts
	23.2	Association for Payment Clearing Services	Yearbook of Payment Statistics 2003
	23.3 - 22.5	Bank of England	Bank of England, Statistical Interactive Database
	23.6	Bank of England	Bank of England, Statistical Interactive Database
	23.7	Bank of England	Bank of England, Statistical Interactive Database
	23.8	Bank of England	Bank of England Quarterly Bulletin
	23.9 - 23.12	Bank of England	Monthly Digest of Statistics (TSO) Financial Statistics (monthly, TSO)
	23.13	Bank of England	Financial Statistics (monthly, TSO), tables E2.1 to E2.10
Other financial institutions	23.14	Financial Services Authority	Building Societies: Statistical Tables www.fsa.gov.uk/pubs/annual/report_mutuals.pdf
	23.15	Office for National Statistics	Business Monitor SDQ7, Assets and Liabilities of Finance Houses and Other Credit Companies (quarterly, ONS)

Subject	Table number in *Abstract*	Government department or other organisation	Official publication or other source
	23.16	Office for National Statistics	Financial Statistics (monthly, TSO) Monthly Digest of Statistics (TSO) Business Monitor MQ5, Insurance Companies; Pension Funds and Trusts Investments (quarterly, ONS) First Release
	23.17, 23.18	Office for National Statistics	Financial Statistics (monthly, TSO) Business Monitor MQ5, Insurance Companies; Pension Funds and Insolvency Trusts Investments (quarterly, ONS)
	23.19 - 23.22	Department of Trade and Industry	Insolvency Annual Report (DTI) Companies (DTI) Financial Statistics (monthly, TSO)

24. Service industry

Subject	Table number in *Abstract*	Government department or other organisation	Official publication or other source
Retail trades	24.1	Office for National Statistics	Annual Business Inquiry (www.statistics.gov.uk/abi/)
	24.2	Office for National Statistics	Business Monitor SDM 28, via National Statistics Website: www.statistics.gov.uk
Motor trades	24.3	Office for National Statistics	Annual Business Inquiry (www.statistics.gov.uk/abi/)
Catering	24.4	Office for National Statistics	Annual Business Inquiry (www.statistics.gov.uk/abi/)

INDEX

INDEX

Figures indicate table numbers

INDEX

INDEX

Figures indicate table numbers

Gravel and sand:
production, 22.19
Greengrocers:
retail trade, 24.1, 24.2
Greenhouse gases:
emissions, 13.1, 13.2
Grocery and provision dealers:
retail trade, 24.1, 24.2
Gross domestic product, 16.1-16.3
Gross national product, 16.1,
Guardians' allowances, 10.1, 10.3, 10.5
Gypsum:
production, 22.19

H

Hay:
harvest, 21.4
Health, 9.1-9.9. *see also* National health
service
central government expenditure,
10.18, 10.20 - 10.22
grants to local authorities, 18.15,
18.19
local authority expenditure, 10.18,
10.20, 18.13, 18.15, 18.17, 18.20
Heart disease:
deaths from: 9.5
Heavy goods, registration, 14.9
Higher education: 6.8-6.10
courses taken, 6.9
degrees and diplomas obtained, 6.10
expenditure on Research and
Development, 20.1, 20.2
government expenditure, 10.19
National Diplomas/Certificates, 6.10
students, 6.8-6.9
Hire purchase, *see* Consumer credit
HM Forces, *see* Armed Forces
Holiday camps, 24.4
Holidays, 12.6-12.8
Homeless households, 14.9
Home population, 5.1, 5.3, 5.5
Hops:
agricultural output, 21.1, 21.2
area,21.3
harvested, 21.4
prices, 17.9
Horticultural crops, land use, 21.3
Hospitals:
services, 9.1-9.4, 10.20
Hotels, 24.4
Hours worked, 7.6, 7.20
Housebreaking offences, 11.13
Housebuilding completions, 14.5
Household goods:
consumer prices index, 17.4
household expenditure, 16.15
retail prices index, 17.5
retail trade, 24.1, 24.2
Households:
average incomes, 8.2
expenditure, 8.5, 16.14 - 16.17
food consumption, 21.16
source of income, 8.3
Housing:
central government expenditure,
10.18, 10.23
consumer prices index, 17.4
dwellings completed, 14.3
homeless households, 14.9
household expenditure, 16.16
grants to local authorities, 18.19,

local authority expenditure, 10.18,
10.23, 18.13, 18.15, 18.17, 18.20
mortgages, 14.6
output by contractors, 22.24
benefit, 10.5
retail prices index, 17.4
stock of dwellings, 14.1
tenure, 14.2
Hypertensive disease,
deaths from, 9.5

I

Igneous rock:
production, 22.19
IMF, official financing, 19.9
Immigration, 5.8, 5.9
acceptances for settlement by
nationality, 5.10
Imports:
analysis by source, 19.6
balance of payments, 19.1, 19.9,
19.10
by commodity, 19.4
food, beverages and tobacco, 19.4
manufactured goods, 19.4
mineral fuels and lubricants, 19.4
penetration and export sales, 19.2
Imprisonments,11.7, 11.8
Improvement grants, *see* Renovation
grants
Incapacity benefit, 10.1, 10.2, 10.7,
10.8, 10.22
Income:
before and after tax, 8.1
GDP, income based, 16.2
local authorities, 18.13-18.16, 18.18,
18.19
national, 16.2
of households, 8.2, 8.3
personal, 16.2
Income support, 10.3, 10.5, 10.6, 10.15,
10.16, 10.17, 10.22
Income tax:
allowances, 18.9
personal incomes before and after,
8.2
rates, 18.10
Index number of:
agricultural prices, 17.7, 17.8
average earnings, 7.22
consumer prices index, 17.4
gross domestic product, 16.1
gross national product, 16.1
industrial share prices, 23.11
producer prices, 17.1-17.7
retail prices, 17.5
retail trade, 24.2
tax and price, 17.6
Indictable offences:
juveniles found guilty, 11.22
offenders cautioned, 11.4, 11.6
offenders found guilty, 11.3, 11.5
sentence or order, 11.7
Individual voluntary arrangement, 23.20
Industrial:
deaths from accidents, 9.9
disablement pensions, 10.3, 10.5
diseases, 9.7
injuries benefit, 10.3, 10.5, 10.22
premises:
noise from, 13.19
production, index of 22.1

spirit:
deliveries, 22.12
output, 22.13
stoppages, 7.18
waste arisings, 13.17
Infant mortality, 5.20
Infectious diseases:
deaths from, 9.5
notifications, 9.6
Influenza:
deaths from, 9.5
Insolvencies:
individual, 23.19
company, 23.20, 23.22
Instrument engineering:
sales, 22.24
size of establishments, 22.3
Insulation board etc:
production, 22.20
Insurance, *see also* National Insurance,
23.18
Insurance companies balance sheet,
23.18
Interest profits and dividends:
balance of payments, 19.9, 19.10
International tourism, 12.7
Intoxication offences, 11.3, 11.4, 11.13,
11.23
Invalidity benefits, 10.1, 10.3, 10.5,
10.7-10.8, 10.22
Investment overseas, 19.13-19.18
Investment trusts, 23.16
Iron and steel:
exports, 22.17
furnaces, 22.16
imports, 22.15
production, 22.15, 22.16
scrap, 22.17
supplies, deliveries and stocks, 22.17
Iron and steel industry:
employment, 7.5
fuel consumption, 22.5

J

Jam and marmalade:
production, 21.12
Jobcentre vacancies, 7.27
Jobseeker's Allowance, 10.1, 10.3,
10.5, 10.6, 10.22
Juveniles found guilty, 11.5, 11.17, 11.22

K

Kerosene:
deliveries, 22.13
output, 22.12

L

Labour disputes, 7.18
Labour force, 7.1
Lamps, electric, sales, 22.23
Land:
area, 1.1
held by Ministry of Defence, 4.7
Law enforcement, 11.1-11.24
Lead:
production, consumption and stocks,
22.17
Leather and leather goods:
census of production, 22.1
employment, 7.5

INDEX

Figures indicate table numbers

INDEX

Figures indicate table numbers

INDEX